THOMAS HARDY

A TO Z

The Essential Reference to His Life and Work

SARAH BIRD WRIGHT

Facts On File, Inc.

Thomas Hardy A to Z: The Essential Reference to His Life and Work

Copyright © 2002 by Sarah Bird Wright

Facts On File, Inc.
132 West 31st Street
New York NY 10001

Library of Congress Cataloging-in-Publication Data

Wright, Sarah Bird
    Thomas Hardy A to Z : the essential reference to his life and work / Sarah Bird Wright.
        p. cm.
    Includes index.
    ISBN 0-8160-4289-6 (alk. paper)
      1. Hardy, Thomas, 1840–1928—Encyclopedias. 2. Authors, English—19th
    century—Biography—Encyclopedias. 3. Authors, English—20th
    century—Biography—Encyclopedias. 4. Wessex (England)—In literature—Encyclopedias.
    I. Title.

PR4752.W75 2002
823'.8—dc21   2002021481

Facts On File books are available at special discounts when purchased in bulk quantities for businesses, associations, institutions, or sales promotions. Please call our Special Sales Department in New York at (212) 967-8800 or (800) 322-8755.

You can find Facts On File on the World Wide Web at http://www.factsonfile.com

Jacket design by Cathy Rincon

Printed in the United States of America

VB Hermitage 10 9 8 7 6 5 4 3 2 1

This book is printed on acid-free paper.

Contents

LIST of ILLUSTRATIONS

FOREWORD

The first Thomas Hardy *Dictionary*, by F. Outwin Saxelby, appeared early in the 20th century (1911)—a period piece unique to Hardy's own time and clime but clearly not comprehensive, for, of course, Hardy was still alive and in his prime. The Wessex editions of the novels had yet to appear together with *A Changed Man* (1913), *The Famous Tragedy of the Queen of Cornwall* (1923), and five out of a total of eight volumes of verse: *Satires of Circumstance* (1914), *Moments of Vision* (1917), *Late Lyrics and Earlier* (1922), *Human Shows* (1925), and *Winter Words* (1928). Latterly, a comprehensive *Hardy Dictionary* has never, in fact, materialized, although Frank Pinion's *Dictionary* of 1989, if taken in tandem with his *A Hardy Companion* of 1968, has certainly helped to fill the gap.

Strictly speaking, a dictionary deals with words (or classes of words)—their orthography, pronunciation, and signification. By extension, any book that offers information, references, or knowledge in which the items are arranged in alphabetical order is also a dictionary, but in the case of *Thomas Hardy A to Z*, I feel that *encyclopedia* is more apt. Nothing less than "encyclopedic" could describe the scope and range of Sarah Bird Wright's extensive undertaking in this book, not to mention the capaciousness of her own intellectual resources. Consider, for example, that 51 world-class scholars were required for the making of the recently published *Oxford Reader's Companion to Hardy*—contributors supplying chapters and sections according to their area of specialization. Note also that in the *Companion*, all commentary on Hardy's poetry is restricted, with a few exceptions, to an overview of each individual collection (for example, *Wessex Poems*) and that these entries are made by half a dozen scholars. By contrast, *Thomas Hardy A to Z* offers a gloss on 216 poems and each is the work of one scholar, Sarah Bird Wright. This is clearly preferable in a work of reference in which each part of the whole has significance. Moreover, Hardy himself confesses that any given poetry collection of his—to which he only ever found it an intense struggle to offer an introductory overview—is, systemically speaking, incoherent, shapeless, and indeterminate. Aside from these contingencies, to have the solo runner undertake the marathon in place of the relay runners is to avoid covering some of the same ground—that slight overlap of introductory, contextual, or background material that occurs when half a dozen contributors write, in a general way, on Hardy's poetry collections.

However, the challenge of providing a gloss on so many poems in such a limited space would daunt the best of us, and Wright is no exception: she feared the comments would be inadequate, reductive, inexpert, simplistic. This "fear" is not misplaced in a scholar of Wright's caliber. It is worth remembering, however, that no one is looking to *Thomas Hardy A to Z* for in-depth textual analysis. On the contrary, what the Greeks would have described as "encyclical education" and what they valued as paramount on the road to wisdom takes precedence here: extensive range is the aim; the circle of learning is the process. To begin at a small, single, precise point on the circumference of the ever-expanding circle is what *Thomas Hardy A to Z* encourages. Or, as Wright herself subsequently reflected, the gloss she provides is but a stepping-stone for the student, a signpost for the aficionado, and a reference point for the scholar.

Reflecting in 1922 on *Late Lyrics*, Hardy speaks of the problems in striking the right note in the arrangement of "miscellanies of verse"—an "arrangement" he refers to as "the juxtaposition of unrelated, even discordant, effusions." Sensitive to reader expectations, he feels that "the difficulties of arranging the themes in a graduated kinship of moods would have been so great that irrelation was almost inevitable with efforts so diverse." He fears a reader may still be chuckling when turning to face, say, an elegy. This is not, of course, a contingency to be feared in the case of *Thomas Hardy A to Z*, reader expectations being already tuned to an "irrelation" of "effusions." But the same principle of emotional and intellectual readiness applies. Hardy wished to avoid "misfires": *Thomas Hardy A to Z*, would, in similar vein, seek to "trust for right note-catching to those finely-touched spirits who can divine without half a whisper, whose intuitiveness is proof against all the accidents of inconsequence" ("Apology," *Late Lyrics and Earlier*, 1922).

Guided by her own methodical diligence, Wright sought to minimize the "accidents of inconsequence," or certainly the accidents of error, by consulting every world-class Hardyan available, even tracking down and writing (for permissions) to Christine O'Connor, the granddaughter of Gertrude Bugler—famously the "Tess" of Hardy's dramatization and of his enchanted heart. These consultations are, in themselves, a remarkable feat. On my own count, I can vouch for more than a hundred letters that have passed between us both this past year, and I know personally of Wright's struggle to attain comprehensiveness and authentication of documentation by, in a far smaller way, looking up, on her behalf, my own scholar-contacts in China, Japan, Korea, and other distant shores. Indefatigably, Wright even trekked the Wessex region, that enchanted land immortalized by Hardy, checking out the topography, seeking and finding for herself the places, names, and people and, not least, taking photographs. These are exceptionally fine, artistic photographs having the exquisite quality of engravings—as the beneficiaries, the readers of this book, will discover for themselves.

The following anecdote will illustrate the kind of difficulty the non-Hardy-specialist (as Wright regarded herself before embarking on the *A to Z*) can encounter and the degree to which she can overcome almost any hazard en route, if intent on applying the talents of the explorer who is determined, at all costs, to become the discoverer. On looking over Wright's beautiful photographs in the earlier days of the making of this book, I noticed that her image of Egdon Heath did not represent the heath as Hardy knew it, described it, and reinvented it. The reason for the dissimilarity is that the heath has since been heavily planted with conifers by the Forestry Commission.[1] Thickly planted! There was no way that Wright could have known this. But because it

barely resembles its earlier character, Wright's image would have been something of a puzzle to readers: how could Eustacia have signaled to Wildeve with her "Promethean" fires when the dense growth of trees would have obscured those fires? How would the "observer," with tall trees blocking the horizon, have been able to picture Eustacia on Rainbarrow silhouetted against the night sky as the "perfect, delicate, and necessary finish" to the "dark pile of hills"? (*RN*, Ch. II). Why would Clym's mother have suffered the heat exhaustion caused by overexposure to the naked heath's scorching sun if she could have escaped to the shady forest that beckoned at every point? And beyond *The Return of the Native*, in ancient days, it was the practice to light barrow fires on the highest peak as a warning signal of invasion (long before Eustacia adopted the practice); such alarms, sighted for miles and miles around, operated as an effective warning system but would have been ineffectual if the fires had been submerged beneath canopies of forest trees (as they would be today). As it was, the beacons, fired in succession from the coastal barrows to the higher points of the Weald, transmitted signals from coastguards to the Admiralty in London within the hour. Traditional practices such as these would have been familiar to Hardy, who embues the fires of the heathfolk on Egdon with a multifaceted symbolism. First there are the Fawkes fires, still celebrated today on November 5th, which commemorate the overthrow of the Gunpowder Plot and the seizure of latter-day terrorists as they were about to blow up the Houses of Parliament in London. Not every celebrant of this ancient feast of fires necessarily sides with the government overthrow: there are elements of anarchy in this annual ritual, not least in the toting of images of Guy Fawkes around town, mostly in the south of England and mostly by children, intoning "A Penny for the Guy"! Second, in *The Return of the Native*, Eustacia represents more persuasively the pagan and anarchic aspects of human nature and the world of nature, respectively, and her "Promethean" lighting of fires partakes of both worlds—she, like the fires she keeps, remains an elemental force from first to last. And the Egdon she roams has, of necessity, to be primeval, as are the ancient heathlands themselves, and definitely not a man-made region of forests.

I have dwelled on this at some length to illustrate the kind of reverberations we can encounter in the evocation of a single image, in this instance of Egdon Heath, and the importance of paying scrupulous attention to such details, as does Wright. Inconvenient as it may have been to jettison her own image in favor of an alternative, she did not hesitate. She turned to the best alternative available—albeit not comparable to her own fine photographs in terms of artistry, clarity, and resolution. These, for authenticity, had to be the work of Hardy's contemporary, namely the inimitable Hermann Lea.

---

[1] In justice to the powers-that-be I have to mention that tree-planting will cease and the heath will be allowed to return to its original form and habitats. The heathlands, with their heather, gorse, and bracken, defy farming and have been considered unproductive in the past due to a thin, acid, sandy layer of soil covering what is known as an "iron pan," which is resistant to plowing. Hardy's Egdon is a composite construct and incorporates three Bronze Age barrows in the form of one, central Rainbarrow.

Hardy, an intensely reticent man, who rigorously fended off biographers and intensely disliked those he couldn't forfend, would have felt more comfortable with this *A to Z* than with most literary attempts to put his life and work into order. One of the first of the biographers to incur his wrath was Ernest Brennecke, who insinuated himself into the Max Gate household under the guise of a being a visiting enthusiast from the United States. Shortly after his visit, he furnished Hardy with a manuscript for a book to be called *Thomas Hardy's Universe*. This met with Hardy's terse approval, but when subsequently Brennecke tried his hand at *The Life of Thomas Hardy*, he met with outright hostility. The innocuous *Universe* had been replaced with something altogether different, falling as it did into suppositions and events conjured from yet more suppositions, and Hardy was enraged. He wrote to the London publishers to have the book banned from importation.

On the other hand, the photographer and author Hermann Lea, who developed a close friendship with Hardy as they roamed the highways and byways of Wessex together, was trusted, respected, and confided in by Hardy at all times. It is significant perhaps that Lea did not ever attempt to publish a biography, nor indeed any of the many confidences placed in his keeping, but instead a guide to the settings of Hardy's work entitled *Thomas Hardy's Wessex* (1913), together with a few biographical fragments later published in *Thomas Hardy Through the Camera's Eye* (1964). Similarly, the author of *A Thomas Hardy Dictionary*, F. Outwin Saxelby, retained Hardy's trust and respect, if not altogether the intimate friendship Lea enjoyed, and he, too, in not overstepping the boundaries of reticence, appears to have survived the hazards of the Hardy Privacy Rules.

Hence, in this respect, *Thomas Hardy A to Z* follows a tradition of which Hardy would have soundly approved, although I hasten to say that I am not contemplating the notion that we might see "his ghostly arms revolving"—beyond, that is, the confines of his poetic lines. To these, and to his great oeuvre in general, Sarah Bird Wright's magisterial work will testify—and, in the way of all good testimony, with the utmost brevity.

—Rosemarie Morgan, Yale University
President, The Thomas Hardy Association

ACKNOWLEDGMENTS

When I first began research for this book, immersing myself in Thomas Hardy's life and works, I was reminded of Henry James's cautionary words in *What Maisie Knew:* "The effort really to see and really to represent is no idle business in face of the *constant* force that makes for muddlement." I was clearly subject to muddlement: What to include? All the novels, yes, and the short stories, but which poems, people, events, places, artists, honors, beliefs, organizations, interests, characters, essays, residences, journeys? I had read only a fraction of Hardy's work—several of his novels and some of his poetry, at that point. As I pondered and discussed the project with friends and relatives, and as I began reading, the horizon of his life and works slowly seemed to assume a faintly manageable shape and scope.

I was, almost immediately, offered books as well as wise counsel. Professor Elsa Nettels of the College of William and Mary sent several critical works along with her article on Hardy and William Dean Howells; Professor Jean Frantz Blackall, Emerita of Cornell University but now living in Williamsburg, offered her small red leather volumes of *The Dynasts,* and my Montana cousins Wally and Rose King sent Wally's prized copy of Ruth Firor's *Folkways in Thomas Hardy.* Professor Welford Taylor of the University of Richmond brought over Carl Weber's *Hardy in America.* He had known Professor Marguerite Roberts, as had my friend Rosemary Dietrick. Their memories of her enthusiasm for Hardy and his works have greatly enriched this volume, just as her early investigations into Hardy and the theater, during the lifetime of Florence Hardy, had resulted in extensive Hardy accessions for Boatwright Library at the University of Richmond. Such wealth engendered discipline: I soon plunged into reading and research.

My family and friends have seen me through this project with unwavering support and encouragement. My husband, Lewis Wright, tracked down Hardy books, both on-line and in bookstores, with the zest of an antiquarian and the energy of a neurosurgeon and author of medical and historical books and papers. I am grateful to my son, Alexander Wright, and to Jennifer Kilian, who never made me feel dumb, but, rather, untutored, as they applied their technical expertise to a variety of software and hardware problems and illuminated the intricacies of the Web. My brother and sister-in-law, Oscar and Jane Grant, provided havens for reflection: their porch at Wrightsville Beach, N.C., and their Ketch, *Sea Fever.* Both retreats instilled confidence and intensified my energy. My niece, Louise Grant, generously assisted with recommendations based on her teaching of secondary school students. I am grateful to my nephew, Rick Grant, and his wife, Kathy, for their dedicated support and interest. I counted on feedback for portions of the text from my nephews Ashley Martin Grant and Charlie d'Arcy Grant, members of the student population for whom this volume is intended. My cousins Elise Williams, Laura and Bill Satterwhite, Rose King, Ashley Coats, Blair Norris, and Susan Bradford were keen observers of my labors throughout the Martin family reunion at Wrightsville Beach in July 2000 and have followed its progress since that time, letter by letter.

Mary Ann Caws's electrifying enthusiasm determined the direction of my resolve and expanded its scope; Peg Rorison was, as always, the most attentive of listeners and an astute critic. Shirley Uber, of North Kingstown, Rhode Island, generously sent me a photograph taken at Max Gate by her late husband, Tom Uber, and Dori Rockefeller kindly took several photographs of Salisbury Cathedral and the Hardy memorial tablet on the cathedral grounds. The Rev. Dr. Reginald Fuller and his wife, Ilse, have shed much light on Hardy from the perspective of their lives in Britain before moving to America. Vicky and Lynn Fischer of

Monterey, California, have been a source of unwavering support, always keen to know about progress on the book. Rita Holt has shared many memories of her native England that have brought the world of Hardy to life. Martha Edmonds assisted in countless ways, offering encouragement and inviting me to teach in the School of Continuing Studies at the University of Richmond, a position with the invaluable corollaries of computer support and access to Boatwright Library. Elizabeth Scott arranged for me to present my experiences in research and writing before her humanities class in the School of Continuing Studies. Janet and Phil Schwarz, long-time friends, have both made invaluable suggestions about research and gathering illustrations. Professor Beverly Peterson of Pennsylvania State University, Uniontown, and Dr. Nancy Parrish, my close friends in the doctoral program in American Studies, College of William and Mary, have been very helpful in suggesting principles of selection and interpretation appropriate for college and high school students.

My research was immeasurably aided from the beginning by my acquisition of Professor Michael Millgate's *Thomas Hardy: A Biography,* which provided an invaluable overview of Hardy's life, friends, writings, and family. The seven-volume edition of Hardy's letters, scrupulously edited by Professor Millgate and Richard L. Purdy, has been my constant companion and resource during the entire time I have worked on the book. In June 2000 I was able to spend a few days in Dorset; there I found a copy of Richard L. Purdy's *Thomas Hardy: A Bibliographical Study,* an impeccable archive of information about places of first publication and varying editions of Hardy's works. Professor Millgate, with whom I have corresponded a number of times on-line, has sorted out many vexing genealogical problems; his exemplary scholarship has been an inspiration even while setting a standard virtually impossible to attain.

I was materially aided in every aspect of this book by Professor Rosemarie Morgan of Yale University, president of The Thomas Hardy Association and editor of *The Hardy Review,* who for several years has moderated the worldwide Hardy on-line list. With scrupulous care, she has read the entire manuscript, catching countless innumerable errors of fact and interpretation. Very early on I visited the welcoming website of The Thomas Hardy Association and discovered a worldwide community of lovers of Hardy. William Morgan of Illinois State University, who leads the on-line Poem of the Month discussions, reviewed my provisional list of poems and suggested dozens more. I am much indebted to him for his explication of poems and his patience with neophytes, including the present writer. The Hardy list, supervised by Betty and John Cortus, has been a constant source of enlightenment. Alas, it has not been possible to include references to the innumerable dis-

cussion threads that have been carried on regarding Hardy's individual works, his philosophy, his relationships, and his preoccupations—some have been archived but others may have passed on into cyberspace. Any Hardy devotee would be well advised to subscribe to the Hardy list (URL: http://www.yale.edu/hardysoc/Welcome/welcomet.htm), which will lead to many absorbing and informative discussions.

I am greatly indebted to Prof. Robert C. Schweik of the State University of New York at Fredonia for much information he has contributed to the Hardy on-line forum, and for off-line discussions of the Hardy tour pamphlets; to Professor Phillip Mallett of the University of St. Andrews, for inviting me to take part in the 2002 Thomas Hardy conference in Dorchester; to Professor Birgit Plietzsch of the University of St. Andrews for helping me sort out the illustrations for *A Pair of Blue Eyes;* to Professor Philip Allingham of Lakehead University, Ontario, Canada, for enlightenment about the original illustrations for *The Return of the Native;* to Professor Suleiman Ahmad of the University of Damascus, Syria, for bibliographic information about the tour pamphlet for *The Hand of Ethelberta;* and to Professor Pamela Dalziell of the University of British Columbia, Vancouver, B.C., who generously offered advice about procuring copies of the illustrations for the serialized versions of Hardy's novels. Professor Martin Ray of the University of Aberdeen took the time to clarify textual questions related to Hardy's poem "Your Last Drive," and Professor Suguru Fukasawa of Chuo University, president of the Thomas Hardy Society of Japan and a vice president of the Thomas Hardy Society (United Kingdom), generously reviewed my list of Japanese translations of Hardy's works, corrected errors, and added several of which I had been unaware. I was also greatly helped by the Japanese scholar Professor Kiyoko Tsuda and her daughter, Kaori Tsuda, a lecturer at Kansai University, who provided extensive information about Japanese translations of Hardy's works. To them and to Professor Fukasawa I would like to say *Arigatou Gozaimasu!* Dong-Uk Kim, a doctoral student at Sheffield University in England, contributed comprehensive, very welcome details about the many Korean translations of the prose and poetry of Hardy.

Betty and James Gibson of the Thomas Hardy Society in England answered many questions, sent me a photocopy of Tour Pamphlet No. 11 in the series published by the Society, and gave me permission to reproduce the map of Egdon Heath. Alistair Chisholm, Dorset Town Crier, gave me a memorable tour of the town and nearby Hardy sites I could not have reached on my own.

I have been materially aided by many curators and librarians: the staff at Boatwright Library, the University of Richmond, Richmond, Virginia, especially Suzanne McGinnis, who made several photographs from early periodicals; Alfred Mueller of the Beinecke Library, Yale University; and Christine Reynolds, Assistant Keeper of the Muniments, Westminster Abbey. Lilian Swindall of the Dorset County Museum in Dorchester not only provided generous assistance with photographic research but also tracked down biographical information about the sculptor Maggie Richardson. Others who have helped were Ivor Kerslake of the British Museum, who made the photograph of the Elgin Marbles, and Glenda LaCoste of the Perkins Library at Duke University, who arranged for photographs of many illustrations from the serialized versions of Hardy's novels in their vast collection of periodicals. I am also indebted to Eileen Doyle of Art Resource, who assisted in finding illustrations relevant to *The Dynasts* and *The Well-Beloved*. Prof. Keith G. Wilson of the University of Ottawa generously allowed me to make use of his extensive research about media adaptations of Hardy's works (Appendix II).

John Gould of Phillips Academy, Andover, Massachusetts, offered several photographs he had taken in the course of his research on Hardy, including the Maumbury Ring. Sally and Chris Searle of the Old Rectory, St. Juliot, Cornwall, provided interior and exterior photographs of the church and the rectory.

Many people in tourism offices have helped make visible places Hardy visited or locales in his works. The Zermatt Tourist Office sent a selection of early photographs of the Matterhorn and the intrepid climbers who made the first ascent, including the Englishman Edward Whymper, subject of Hardy's sonnet "Zermatt: To the Matterhorn." Regina Stephenson of West Wiltshire Tourist Information, Claire Mawson and Mary Pocock of Salisbury Tourist Information, and Rachel Ackerman of the West Dorset District Council all assisted with photographs of Salisbury Cathedral and of Stonehenge. Sylviane Pittet of the Musée Historique, Lausanne, Switzerland, provided a lithograph of the Hotel Gibbon, where Thomas Hardy and his wife, Emma, had stayed in 1897.

Finally, I am thankful for the patience and excellent judgment of my editor, Anne Savarese, and for the labor of Lauren Goldberg, who wrestled gamely with the Hardy and Hand family trees. I am also grateful to Michael G. Laraque of Facts On File, who has unparalleled skill at detecting errors overlooked by others, and to Laurie Likoff, who first saw the need for such a book. My agent, Jeanne Fredericks, deserves enormous praise for her meticulous attention to detail and for her support.

INTRODUCTION

To Virginia Woolf, Thomas Hardy had the power of a "true novelist" to make his readers believe that his characters were "fellow-beings driven by their own passions and idiosyncrasies, while they have … something symbolical about them which is common to us all."[1] His novels and poetry endure today because they deal with such universal experiences as birth, death, love, struggle, heartache, and guilt. They often begin with what appear to be provincial scenes, but then expand to achieve a profound exploration of human nature and society as a whole.

Hardy was born on June 2, 1840, in Higher Bockhampton, near the town of Dorchester in Dorset. His parents, of yeoman stock, were Jemima Hand Hardy and Thomas Hardy, who was a building contractor and master mason. Hardy had only eight years of formal schooling, but he read widely in English and began studying Latin at 12 and French at 15. It is thought that the death of Hardy's paternal grandmother in 1857, when he was 17, first prompted him to begin writing poetry. His interests were wide-ranging: literature, philosophy, and theology. He experienced a crisis of faith as a young man and abandoned conventional Christianity, although he had an intimate knowledge of the Bible and developed a lifelong interest in church architecture.

In 1856, at the age of 16, Hardy was apprenticed to John Hicks, a Dorchester architect, his employer for the next six years. It was at this time that he came to know the Dorchester schoolmaster and distinguished dialect poet William Barnes, who remained a close and influential friend until Barnes's death in 1886. Barnes encouraged Hardy to write poetry. In 1862 Hardy went to London, where he became an assistant architect in the office of Sir Arthur William Blomfield. He developed a lifelong devotion to the city, absorbing its culture, architecture, and historic sites. While there he read at the British Museum, attended plays and concerts, visited the National Gallery, and wrote poetry he was unable to sell. He realized that, given the realities of the marketplace, successful authorship was contingent on his writing fiction, particularly novels.

Hardy's health declined in London, forcing him, in 1867, to return to Dorchester, where he again worked for John Hicks. In 1869 he returned to London. Hicks died that year, however, and his successor, G. R. Crickmay, asked Hardy to assist him in his Weymouth office. Hardy accepted the post, although he was becoming increasingly dissatisfied with the profession of architecture. In 1870 Hardy was sent on an architectural assignment to investigate the restoration of St. Juliot Church, Cornwall. There he met Emma Gifford; they married in 1874, after he began selling his fiction. They lived for two decades in various leased houses until Max Gate, their home near Dorchester, was completed. Hardy spent the remainder of his life at Max Gate, although he and Emma often rented furnished apartments in London for the stylish "season" (April through July). After Emma Hardy died in 1912, Hardy married Florence Dugdale, who had been his research assistant.

Hardy's career as a novelist began after he met Emma Hardy. He wrote a novel, *The Poor Man and the Lady,* for which he failed to find a publisher. In 1871 his novel *Desperate Remedies* was published anonymously. *Under the Greenwood Tree,* Hardy's second novel, was also published anonymously (1872). Sir Leslie Stephen (the father of Virginia Woolf) read it and asked for a novel for the magazine he edited, the *Cornhill.* Hardy's first successful novel was *A Pair of Blue Eyes* (1873); Stephen then published, anonymously, *Far from the Madding Crowd* in serial installments in the *Cornhill* (1874). These four novels were followed by 10 others over the ensuing 24 years.

Hardy's fiction is marked by a tragic intensity, his characters defeated by their own flaws and inability to counteract the strictures of society. Among his best-known novels are *The Return of the Native* (1878), *Tess of the d'Urbervilles* (1891), and *Jude the Obscure* (1895). *Tess of the d'Urbervilles,* possibly the most admired of Hardy's novels, outsold, on publication, all of his previous works. *Jude the Obscure,* his last novel, depicted the conflict between spiritual and carnal life and was widely attacked as immoral. The reception of *Jude* caused Hardy to abandon novel writing and return to writing poetry.

Hardy constructed, in his fiction, an imaginary region he called Wessex. The name originally designated the southwestern region of Britain ruled by the West Saxons in the Middle Ages. As Simon Gatrell observes, however, the term has now come to mean not only the region populated with imaginary characters but "the whole culture—predominantly rural and pre-industrial—found in Hardy's novels and poems."[2] J. I. M. Stewart comments that Hardy is both the "natural" and "social" historian of Wessex, spreading his "powers of observation and humor and memory over a field very reasonably full of a diversity of folk." Stewart further suggests that Hardy's poetry is also deeply rooted in Wessex, transforming our knowledge of it into a "country of the mind."[3]

Wessex has become as real to readers as the Narnia of C. S. Lewis or Jonathan Swift's Houyhnhnmland. Desmond Hawkins describes it as "an unofficial English province more closely and elaborately defined than any comparable example."[4] Hardy's own map of the region has been widely reprinted, and is reproduced in this book. The Thomas Hardy Society of England publishes guides to the Wessex terrain of each novel, with detailed maps showing farms and footpaths. The map showing Egdon Heath, which figures not only in *The Return of the Native* but also in other works, has been reproduced in this volume.

Hardy's fiction is universal in its depiction of the human condition. His battalion of characters rise in his readers' memories long after they have read of Tess Durbeyfield, Angel Clare, Bathsheba Everdene, Gabriel Oak, Fanny Robin, Eustacia Vye, Diggory Venn, Clym Yeobright, Thomasin Yeobright Wildeve, Michael Henchard, Sue Bridehead, Jude Fawley, Jocelyn Pierston, Paula Power, George Somerset, Giles Winterbourne, Grace Melbury Fitzpiers, William Boldwood, Picotee Chickerel, Ethelberta Petherwin, Miller Loveday, Anne Garland, Lady Viviette Constantine. Even such unsavory characters as Francis Troy, Alec d'Urberville, Arabella Fawley Donn, Felice Charmond, Alfred Neigh, Festus Derriman, and William Dare are all lodged firmly in our minds once encountered, speaking to us over the years with authority, evoking delight, envy, dread, sympathy, and astonished recognition.

Hardy's life bridged two worlds—that of the 19th century, when he was born, and that of the 20th, when he died. His work, based on what Jean Brooks has called his "backbone of certainties about fundamental human values,"[5] has come to have a worldwide appeal to readers. His novels and short stories have been translated into Japanese, French, German, Russian, Italian, Spanish, Portuguese, Chinese, Panjabi, Persian, Finnish, Korean, Romanian, Scottish Gaelic, Basque, Czech, Croatian, Polish, and other languages.

Hardy's poetry, although seldom translated, presents a haunting natural world at least as complex and unforgettable as Wessex. In "At Rushy-Pond," the pond reflects the Moon as perceived by a young lover at the end of a romance, "corkscrewed" like a "wriggling worm." "The Souls of the Slain" depicts the whirring "night-moths" depositing a train of "sprites without mold" on Portland Bill, the outer tip of the Isle of Portland. This spot stands approximately on a line drawn from South Africa to the middle of the United Kingdom, and the "sprites" are the souls of soldiers slain in South Africa during the Boer War. The "forms of old time talking," visible on the walls and trees by moonlight in "The House of Hospitalities," evoke the festive Christmases Hardy once knew. "Voices from Things Growing in a Churchyard" presents a cacophonous interchange among the discordant and uneasy souls of deceased villagers, from "little Fanny Hurd," who once flitted about but now waves "in daisy shapes," to Thomas Voss, who has "burrowed away from the moss" that covers the sod of his grave and entered a yew tree; he now has merged into "berries of juice and gloss." In "Friends Beyond" Hardy imagines a dialogue among the dead in Stinsford Churchyard. Here he evokes the camaraderie of "William Dewy, Tranter Reuben, Farmer Ledlow late at plough.../And the Squire, and Lady Susan," who are all "gone for good" and "lie in Melstock churchyard." He envisions them disposing of their goods, incurious now about external events. He "visits" them in his imagination and hears them "murmur" to him.

Matthew Arnold said of Sophocles, "he saw life steadily and saw it whole"; the same could be said of Hardy. He felt tragedy keenly, from the loss of the *Titanic,* the subject of "The Convergence of the Twain" (Lines on the Loss of the "Titanic"), to the young British soldier buried in the South African veldt in "Drummer Hodge" to the forlorn cat caught in a snowstorm in "Snow in the Suburbs" to the blind giant being led by a dwarf about the fair in "At a Country Fair." He was well aware of comic and ironic situations also, as in the story of "The Ruined Maid," when Melia taunts her poorly dressed but virtuous friend, and "The Sergeant's Song," anticipating the time when "Boney" (Napoleon Bonaparte) comes "pouncing down." This was published in *The Trumpet-Major.*

Many of Hardy's poems deal with the human panorama. An example is "At Casterbridge Fair," which contains a vignette called "A Wife Waits." The poet depicts a faithful wife shivering outside a building late at night waiting to "steady" her husband home. The husband is down in the clubroom, "where the tall liquor-cups foam," dancing with another woman, although he had promised always to be faithful to his wife when they married. Hardy's vision of the universe is sometimes benign, but more often ironic or tragic. His perceptions often seem more extraordinary when narrowed and distilled within his poetry than when amplified on a larger fictional canvas. Hardy told Lillah McCarthy, after he ceased writing fiction, "'I now tell the story of a novel in verse of twenty lines'" (*Myself and My Friends*, 101–103). He was entirely accurate in making this assertion.

Entries in this book are arranged alphabetically with cross-references to other entries indicated in small capitals. References to articles and books for further reading follow many entries; full bibliographical details are given in Appendix VII. I have provided a list of abbreviations used for the most frequently cited of Hardy's works and for the principal biographical and critical sources on which I have relied.

Conceptually the entries fall into 17 categories. (These categories and the entries within each are listed in Appendix I.) These groupings do not always allow a precise delineation. In the first category, for instance, which includes Hardy's family, friends, acquaintances, teachers, and employers, I included Edward Clodd, who wrote a volume of memories of Hardy but whose primary relationship to him seemed to be as a close friend whose home in Aldeburgh, in Suffolk, was a hospitable retreat for Hardy. The members of the Moule family are all in this grouping, although some of them were also writers.

The second category, novels, is self-explanatory, except for *The Poor Man and the Lady*. This was Hardy's first novel, never published and now lost. However, the novelist George Meredith, then a manuscript reader for Chapman and Hall, advised him to "attempt a novel with a purely artistic purpose, giving it a more complicated 'plot.'" Hardy destroyed most of the manuscript and followed this advice in writing *Desperate Remedies*, his first published novel. He incorporated sections of it in later novels.

The third category, short fiction, includes short stories as well as some longer works such as Hardy's juvenile novel, *Our Exploits at West Poley*. The complication in this group is that there are sketches within longer stories: "A Few Crusted Characters" contains linked sketches of such people as Netty Sargent and Andrey Satchel and was published as a subcategory in another volume, *Life's Little Ironies*, which includes eight other stories. The framework is somewhat similar to Geoffrey Chaucer's *Canterbury Tales*, as the tales are narrated in the course of a journey by various travelers. The 10 stories collected in *A Group of Noble Dames* are also linked, in that they concern clever titled women attempting, not always successfully, to outwit men. The epigraph, from Milton's "L'Allegro," is "… Store of ladies, whose bright eyes/Rain influence." The situations in Hardy's short stories, though perhaps less well known than those in his novels, are equally poignant. One example is "The Son's Veto," concerning the widowed Sophy Twycott, prevented from marrying Sam Hobson, her faithful first love, by her cold and snobbish son Randolph Twycott.

The category involving the most painful choices was, without question, the fourth, poetry. There are 947 poems in *The Complete Poems of Thomas Hardy*, the New Wessex Edition, ably edited by James Gibson. I have included more than two hundred, but space prohibited my being comprehensive. Here I am much indebted to Rosemarie Morgan for surveying the first list and recommending that I add an essential 35 others.

The web site of The Thomas Hardy Association contains an active online poetry discussion forum, managed by Professor William Morgan of the University of Illinois. Many poems have been discussed here, and the discussions, once removed from the web site, will be preserved online also. At the outset Professor Morgan recommended a number of essential poems for inclusion.

The fifth category, dramatic works and dramatizations, contains Hardy's verse dramas *The Dynasts* and *The Famous Tragedy of the Queen of Cornwall* as well as *The Mellstock Quire*, a play by A. H. Evans based on Hardy's novel *Under the Greenwood Tree*. "The Play of St. George" is also in this category; it was acted by the Hardy Players at Max Gate in 1920, a performance which, Hardy declared, was just as he had seen it given in his childhood. "The Three Wayfarers," Hardy's adaptation of a short story, "The Three Strangers," was performed in Dorchester, London, and Oxford. The dramatization titled "Wessex Scenes from *The Dynasts*" was given by the Hardy Players in Dorchester. Appendix II contains a listing of theatrical, film, and musical adaptations of Hardy's works.

The sixth category consists of a listing of the principal characters in Hardy's novels, most of which have separate entries. It was, again, difficult to make choices here. They were sometimes all but overshadowed by minor characters, each an unforgettable sketch: Amos Fry, the rustic laborer and philosopher in *Two on a Tower*; Gertrude Jethway of *A Pair of Blue Eyes*, who haunts Elfride Swancourt throughout the novel; Matilda Johnson in *The Trumpet-Major*, trying artfully to conceal her theatrical past; Jane Day in *Under the Greenwood Tree*, changing the table linens in the middle of a meal lest her stepdaughter and guests question her housekeeping; Abel Whittle in *The Mayor of Casterbridge*, loyally attending Michael Henchard until the end of his life.

Hardy's wide-ranging interests and concerns are evident in the entries assigned to the seventh category, comprising his miscellaneous writings, from his *Architectural Notebook* to his moving essay on "The Dorsetshire Laborer."

In the eighth group are entries on writers and poets whom Hardy knew personally, as well as on those whose works were important to him. This listing is, of course, incomplete, as his works are saturated with literary and biblical allusions. I drew mainly on his autobiography (*The Early Life of Thomas Hardy, 1840–1891* and *The Later Years of Thomas Hardy, 1892–1928,* edited by Florence Hardy; now recognized as Hardy's own work), on the biography of Hardy by Michael Millgate, and on his letters, ably edited by R. L. Purdy and Michael Millgate, in considering which persons to include. Six of these eminent writers served as Hardy's pallbearers: John Galsworthy, A. E. Housman, Sir Edmund Gosse, George Bernard Shaw, Sir James Barrie, and Rudyard Kipling. Hardy welcomed many others to Max Gate—among them Virginia Woolf, Siegfried Sassoon, and H. G. Wells. He made a point of calling on Algernon Charles Swinburne, who was ill, at Putney, and corresponded with him. The Honourable Florence Henniker is in this category, since she and Hardy collaborated on a short story, "The Spectre of the Real." Lady Agnes Grove is also included here; she dedicated her volume of essays, *The Social Fetich,* to Hardy, "In grateful recognition of timely aid and counsel, and in memory of old and enduring friendship."

The ninth category, on fine arts, is something of a melting pot, including not only the sculptors and artists who made likenesses of Hardy, but also the exhibitions he is known to have attended, along with dramatists, actors, actresses, theaters and theater groups, and music. Harley Granville-Barker, who produced scenes from *The Dynasts* in London, is included here, as is Hermann Lea, who photographed much of the topography in Hardy's novels and who wrote two guidebooks to the Dorset evoked in his works.

The 10th group, emphasizing Hardy's special interests and concerns, was constructed on the basis of his writings and, particularly, his letters. His love of animals is clear throughout his fiction. The death and burial of Prince, a horse in *Tess of the d'Urbervilles,* are among Hardy's most memorable scenes, and Edred Fitzpiers's mistreatment of Grace Melbury's horse Darling, given her by Giles Winterbourne in *The Woodlanders,* is a clear key to his character. Hardy left money in his will to alleviate animals' suffering as they were transported to market, and he was devoted to the Max Gate cats and dogs, ordering a headstone for his dog Wessex. Hardy had many other interests: music, bicycling, genealogy, and, of course, the natural world, a subject that permeates his writings.

Category 11 deals with specific places important in Hardy's life, including such residences as his birthplace, Higher Bockhampton, and his longtime Dorchester home, Max Gate. This group also includes regions with special meaning, such as Cornwall, where he met Emma, and foreign countries he visited, including France, Belgium, Italy, and Switzerland. In 1876 he and Emma visited the field of Waterloo, site of the Battle of Waterloo. This visit served him well when he wrote about the campaign in *The Dynasts* three decades later.

The 12th category includes entries in the field of publishing: editors, critics, illustrators, translators, publishers, and periodicals, as well as writers Hardy knew. The literary figures here range from his French translator, Madeleine Rolland, who visited Max Gate, to his publishers, such as William Tinsley and Sir Frederick Macmillan. Hardy had more dealings with the house of Macmillan than with any other; he and Sir Frederick corresponded about various matters for more than 40 years, from 1885 to 1925. The periodical editors who purchased his work, such as Arthur Locker of *The Graphic* and Sir Leslie Stephen of the *Cornhill Magazine,* fall into this category, as well as his illustrators: Helen Paterson, John Collier, Arthur Hopkins, and others. This grouping also includes the periodicals in which Hardy's work appeared, such as *Harper's New Monthly Magazine* and *Longman's Magazine.*

Group 13 brings together institutions and organizations that enabled Hardy to maintain friendships and make contacts that greatly enriched his life. Perhaps foremost among them are his prestigious clubs, the Savile and the Athenaeum, both of which gave him a London pied-à-terre where he could work, write letters, and offer and receive hospitality. Michael Millgate calls the Savile, on Piccadilly, the "leading literary club of the day." The Athenaeum, on Pall Mall, is housed in a magnificent classical building. In May 1910 Hardy saw the funeral procession of King Edward VII from the balcony, an experience that inspired his poem "A King's Soliloquy." Hardy always took a keen interest in Dorset history, and was an active member of the Dorset Natural History and Antiquarian Field Club. On May 13, 1884, he read a paper before the members titled "Some Romano-British Relics Found at Max Gate, Dorchester."

The 14th category of the book encompasses religious architecture, churches, traditions, holidays, and celebrations, all of which meant a good deal to Hardy. As an architect, he was concerned that churches, such as Fordington St. George, not be ruined by overzealous restoration. Candlemas, originally a religious feast, falls into this category; Hardy was always concerned with the plight of laborers hired each year at a fair held on a nearby day.

Category 15 is devoted to more secular places, traditions, and celebrations, many of which figure in his writings. The Maumbury Ring, a legacy of the Roman occupation of Britain, is in this category, along with club-walking, a traditional pastime mentioned in *Tess of the d'Urbervilles.* Folklore and mythology belong to this division; Ruth Firor's study, *Folkways in the Works of Thomas Hardy,* was a seminal investigation of his use of ancient traditions.

The 16th grouping is devoted to historic events and personages. Hardy was never reclusive, but was always keenly interested in significant events. He was greatly disturbed by both the Boer War and World War I, which he treated in his poetry and fiction. King George III figures in *The Dynasts, The Trumpet-Major,* and other works.

The 17th and final category includes the honors and prizes conferred on Hardy. King Edward VII awarded him the Order of Merit in 1910, on his 70th birthday; Hardy received honorary degrees from Cambridge University, Oxford University, and the University of Aberdeen. He was made an honorary fellow of Magdalene College, Cambridge University, and was awarded a gold medal by the Royal Society of Literature. He was much moved by the "Poets' Tribute," given him soon after his 79th birthday, a beautifully bound volume of holograph poems from 43 living poets.

Hardy has never been outside the canon of English literature, and his work has never ceased being taught at the secondary school, undergraduate, and graduate levels. Because he wrote so perceptively about women he has come to be of considerable interest to feminist critics, and his social criticism and humanitarian concerns have attracted extensive political analysis. Literary critics have found his works ceaselessly interesting and provocative. In his 1940 compilation *The First Hundred Years of Thomas Hardy, 1840–1940: A Centenary Bibliography of Hardiana,* Carl Weber apologized because the "voluminous literature" had made it impossible for him to append a "detailed bibliography" to his *Hardy of Wessex.* Now, more than 60 years later, studies of Hardy's life and works have multiplied geometrically. I have had, of necessity, to be selective in compiling the bibliography, but have included those I believed would be of particular interest to students and to the general reader.

From the beginning of the project it seemed to me that photographs and other illustrations were essential in order to make the text more visible and comprehensible to students. Soon after I began writing, I went to the Perkins Library at Duke University, where hard copies of hundreds of 19th-century periodicals are stored in two subbasements. I was able to obtain many photographs of illustrations from the serialized versions of the novels; the prints were made by the medical photography laboratory at Duke Hospital and are, I believe, of exceptional quality. I visited London and Dorset, photographing places where Hardy had lived and institutions important to him, such as the Athenaeum Club, Hyde Park Mansions, his birthplace at Higher Bockhampton, Stinsford Church, St. Peter's Church, his statue in Dorchester, Corfe Castle, and Avice's cottage, which figures in *The Well-Beloved* and is now part of the Portland Museum on the Isle of Portland. With the generous assistance of Lillian Swindall at the Dorset County Museum, I was able to look through the many photographs and maps in their collection and order copies of some of them. I found others in the Richard L. Purdy Collection at the Beinecke Library, Yale University. Other images were supplied by the British Museum; Chris and Sally Searle of the Old Rectory, St. Juliot, Cornwall; John Gould, Phillips Academy, Andover, Massachusetts; Westminster Abbey; Art Resource of New York; the tourism offices of Lausanne and Zermatt, Switzerland, and by the Salisbury District Council and the West Dorset District Council.

1. Virginia Woolf, "The Novels of Thomas Hardy," in *The Common Reader,* second series.
2. Simon Gatrell, "Wessex," in *The Cambridge Companion to Thomas Hardy,* ed. Dale Kramer (Cambridge, U.K.: Cambridge University Press, 1999).
3. J. I. M. Stewart, *Thomas Hardy: A Critical Biography* (New York: Dodd, Mead and Co., 1971), 219.
4. Desmond Hawkins, "Wessex," *Oxford Reader's Companion to Hardy,* ed. Norman Page (New York: Oxford University Press, 2000), 462.
5. Jean Brooks, *Thomas Hardy: The Poetic Structure* (Ithaca, N.Y.: Cornell University Press, 1971), 302.

ABBREVIATIONS

AL	*A Laodicean*
Bailey	J. O. Bailey, *The Poetry of Thomas Hardy: A Handbook and Commentary*
CM	*A Changed Man and Other Tales*
D	*The Dynasts*
DR	*Desperate Remedies*
FFMC	*Far from the Madding Crowd*
GND	*A Group of Noble Dames*
HE	*The Hand of Ethelberta*
HS	*Human Shows, Far Phantasies, Songs, and Trifles*
JO	*Jude the Obscure*
Letters	*The Collected Letters of Thomas Hardy*
Life	*The Life of Thomas Hardy 1840–1928* [purportedly by Florence Emily Hardy, but actually Thomas Hardy's dictated autobiography]
LLE	*Late Lyrics and Earlier*
LLI	*Life's Little Ironies*
LN	*Literary Notebooks*
MC	*The Mayor of Casterbridge*
MV	*Moments of Vision and Miscellaneous Verses*
PBE	*A Pair of Blue Eyes*
Pinion	F. B. Pinion, *A Hardy Companion. A Guide to the Works of Thomas Hardy and Their Background*
PML	*The Poor Man and the Lady*
PPP	*Poems of the Past and Present*
Purdy	Richard Little Purdy, *Thomas Hardy: A Bibliographical Study*
RN	*The Return of the Native*
SC	*Satires of Circumstance*
TD	*Tess of the d'Urbervilles*
TL	*Time's Laughingstocks and Other Verses*
TM	*The Trumpet-Major*
TT	*Two on a Tower*
UGT	*Under the Greenwood Tree*
W	*The Woodlanders*
WB	*The Well-Beloved*
WP	*Wessex Poems and Other Verses*
WT	*Wessex Tales: Strange, Lively and Commonplace*
WW	*Winter Words in Various Moods and Metres*

Abbey, Edwin Austin (1852–1911) American-born painter, illustrator, and mural decorator. His *King Lear* is at the Metropolitan Museum, New York, and he was noted for his 1901 illustrations for *HARPER'S MONTHLY MAGAZINE* of Shakespeare's works. Abbey and Hardy were friends and dined together from time to time, but Abbey did not illustrate any of Hardy's works. In June 1886, while Thomas and Emma Hardy were living temporarily at 28 Upper Bedford Place, London, Hardy invited him to visit them one afternoon (*Letters* II, 304; I, 148).

"The Abbey Mason" *Inventor of the "Perpendicular" Style of Gothic Architecture (With Memories of John Hicks, Architect)* Poem published in *HARPER'S MONTHLY MAGAZINE* in December 1912 with five drawings by Harvey Emrich. The reference to John HICKS was added to the original poem when it was included in *SATIRES OF CIRCUMSTANCE* (1914). Hardy takes a romantic view of the history of English Gothic church architecture, considering the perpendicular style of the 15th century "the only Gothic style of architecture that can be called especially and exclusively English." In 1911 he traveled to Gloucester cathedral to ascertain the exact origin of the style there. He was struck by the anonymity of the inventor of the style and composed the poem from the point of view of a mason laboring to replicate the style of the 14th century. Hardy imagines the mason's suddenly coming to view that style as boring and passé. He suddenly sees icy rain drops streaming "in small white threads/ From the upper segments to the heads/ Of arcs below, uniting them/ Each by a stalactitic stem." Using his experience as an architect, Hardy goes on to single out and commend each feature of the new perpendicular style. He observes that the mason is modest about his accomplishment. Having convinced people he did not deserve credit, the mason was not recognized in his lifetime for his achievement and he remained anonymous after his death. The perpendicular style, however, "flew" to other locations and was adapted not only for cathedrals but also for other buildings.

"Absent-mindedness in a Parish Choir" *See* "FEW CRUSTED CHARACTERS, A."

"The Absolute Explains" Poem first published in *HUMAN SHOWS, FAR PHANTASIES, SONGS, AND TRIFLES* (1925). Dated, at the end, "New Year's Eve, 1922," it was written a little more than a decade after Hardy's first wife, Emma Gifford HARDY, died (on November 27, 1912).

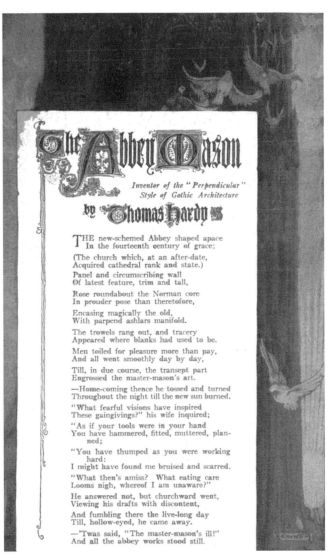

"The Abbey Mason" (first page), Harper's Monthly Magazine *CXXVI (December 1912)* (Boatwright Library, University of Richmond)

Hardy had read Albert Einstein's theories of relativity, which suggest that time be considered a "fourth dimension" containing both past and future in the present (Pinion, *A Commentary on the Poems of Thomas Hardy*, 214.) The speaker of the poem, "It" (or The Absolute), argues that Emma Hardy's "lifedoings" are intact, living on, "unalloyed," because all things are shaped to exist eternally. What we think of as "Now" is only a "gleam," whereas the "Past" and the "Future" exist outside our perception. It is as though we are on a dark highway, seeing only what our lantern reveals, although the highway stretches behind us and before us. Time is a "mock," according to Hardy; Emma has "not passed out / Of continuity, / But is in me." Thus "Being" itself transcends "Time's ancient regal claim / To see all lengths begin and end." Both past and present coexist in "The Fourth Dimension." Time is "toothless" and essentially meaningless, because the present is "phasmal" (a phantom, an apparition). In Hardy's view, he and Emma belong to the past, the future being unknown.

"According to the Mighty Working" First published in *LATE LYRICS AND EARLIER* (1922), this poem was written in 1917, during *WORLD WAR I*. The title is taken from the Church of England burial service. The poem says that although a period of time may seem peaceful, it is important to realize that the "spinner's wheel" is always creating change beyond what we can perceive. The universe has many cause-and-effect relationships, all ultimately the consequence of a First Cause.

"After a Journey" Poem written after Hardy's March 1913 visit to Pentargan Bay, Cornwall, and published in *SATIRES OF CIRCUMSTANCE* (1914). It is a poignant evocation of Emma HARDY as she was during his visits to Cornwall in 1870. He encounters her "voiceless ghost" everywhere as he recalls her "nut-coloured hair, / And gray eyes, and rose-flush coming and going." He acknowledges that their years together had begun in the "sweets" of summer but were succeeded by the "division" of autumn. Here, however, she is leading him back to the time when they "haunted here together" beneath the waterfall and she was "all aglow."

The preening birds and flopping seals are oblivious of his pain. He will soon leave the site but hopes her ghost will bring him there again. He finds consolation in recalling his early courtship.

In *SOME RECOLLECTIONS*, dated 1911 but written over several years, Emma describes riding her mare Fanny as Hardy walked beside her. She showed him "the cliffs . . . sometimes gazing down at the solemn small shores below, where the seals lived, coming out of great deep caverns very occasionally" (*Life*, 71).

Hardy describes the scene in *A PAIR OF BLUE EYES*, when Elfride goes to Pentargan and searches for Stephen KNIGHT's ship (chapter 21).

"After a Romantic Day" Poem published in *LATE LYRICS AND EARLIER* (1922). A young man is traveling on a train away from a city, through an "earthen cutting." Instead of being depressed at the mutilation of the countryside, he projects his mental visions on its "weathered face." By moonlight it is "enough/For poetry of place."

In *A LAODICEAN* Hardy admires the "massive archivault" of the railway tunnel built by the father of Paula POWER. The tunnel is now "weather-stained, lichened, and mossed over in harmonious rusty-browns, pearly greys, and neutral greens," contradicting the "popular commonplace that science, steam, and travel must always be unromantic and hideous" (chapter 12).

Purdy notes that, in the manuscript, Hardy adds, "Your young men shall see visions," a quotation from Acts 2:17 (Purdy, 222). It is possible that the poem was written after a visit to Emma Gifford, whom he later married (*see* HARDY, EMMA) in CORNWALL.

"Afternoon Service at Mellstock" *(Circa 1850)* Poem published in *MOMENTS OF VISION* (1917), recalling Hardy's boyhood experience singing in the parish church at STINSFORD ("Mellstock" is Hardy's fictional name for Stinsford). The date "1850" indicates that he would have been about 10 years of age. The choir sings a psalm as they gaze outside at the elms and rooks, "swaying like trees." Hardy reflects that the outpourings of the psalms were "mindless" and have been replaced by "subtle thought," but doubts that he has gained by his rationalist rejection of the faith he once had.

Hardy enjoyed church services at that time; if rain prevented him from attending, he and a cousin would hold services at home, Hardy reading morning prayer wrapped in a tablecloth with one of his cousins playing the choir (Bailey, *The Poetry of Thomas Hardy*, 342–43).

"After the Last Breath" *(J. H. 1813–1904)* Poem dated 1904, but first published in *TIME'S LAUGHING-STOCKS* (1909). The title refers to the death of Thomas Hardy's mother, Jemima Hand HARDY, who died on Easter Sunday, 1904. Hardy evokes the scene just after his mother's death when he and his brother and sisters gather at her bedside. They gaze "blankly," and are "free to go or stay." Her medicines are mere "silly" palliatives now. And yet they feel a "numb relief" in knowing that she is no longer a "prisoner in the cell/Of Time." Through her death, she has escaped the "Wrongers"—possibly infirmities, such as deafness—that had plagued her (Bailey, *The Poetry of Thomas Hardy*, 243). She looked younger and more serene in a photograph taken after her death than she had before.

"After the Visit" *(To F.E.D.)* Poem first published in the *SPECTATOR* on August 13, 1910. Hardy added the dedication when the poem was collected in *SATIRES OF CIRCUMSTANCE* (1914). By then, Florence Emily Dugdale (HARDY) had become Hardy's second wife. Miss Dugdale had assisted Hardy with research and had visited MAX GATE during the lifetime of Hardy's first wife, Emma HARDY; J. O. Bailey suggests that it may have been in June 1907 (Bailey, *The Poetry of Thomas Hardy*, 267). The first three stanzas recall her appearance, with feet as "light on the green as a thistledown ball." The three final stanzas focus on her spiritual qualities, her "large luminous living eyes" seeming to pose the questions with which the poet himself was preoccupied: "The eternal question of what Life was,/And why we were there, and by whose strange laws/That which mattered most could not be."

"Afterwards" First published in *MOMENTS OF VISION* (1917), when Hardy was 77, this poem anticipates his own death and suggests that he believes he will not live long enough to write another volume of poetry. Hardy actually lived 11 years after the publication of *Moments of Vision*. He hopes that his poetic legacy will include his observations of nature and his concern for all creatures, and envisions the times of day at which he might die. If it should be dusk, when the hawk alights on the "wind-warped upland thorn," an onlooker might recall that the sight would have been familiar to him. Should it be during the night, when the hedgehog "travels furtively over the lawn," an observer might say "He strove that such innocent creatures should come to no harm." If friends and neighbors, hearing of Hardy's death, come to his door during the winter "full-starred heavens," perhaps they will think of him as having had "an eye for such mysteries." He envisions the tolling of the church bell after his death, perhaps interrupted by a "crossing breeze," and hopes mourners will remember that he "used to notice such things."

The poem touches on all the seasons; it begins in May, continues on to dusk of a summer evening, to the "nocturnal blackness" of autumn, and then encompasses winter's starry skies.

"The Ageing House" This poem, published in *MOMENTS OF VISION* (1917), after the death of Emma HARDY, is a commentary on the threefold parallel ageing of MAX GATE, Hardy's first wife, and the sycamore tree planted soon after the house was built. In the first stanza, the brick walls of the house are now "mouldy green." He recalls the "fresh fair head" that would lean "From the "sunny casement / And scan the scene" while the wind would speak "blithely" to the small sycamore tree. Hardy had planted hundreds of trees around the house after it was built in 1884–85.

The second stanza reflects the changes wrought by many years. It mentions that there have been storms about the walls, and suggests that there have also been storms within. Emma has aged, and his affection for her has lessened: "trust grows doubt." The wind "fiercely" girds the sycamore tree, now "long-limbed."

"Ah, Are You Digging on My Grave?" Poem first published in the *SATURDAY REVIEW* on September 27, 1913; it was later included in *SATIRES OF CIRCUMSTANCE* (1914). It takes the form of a dialogue between a deceased woman and her little dog. The woman hopes the sound of the digging above her grave is her loved one "planting rue," but the dog replies that her loved one has gone to wed another. Is it her kin planting flowers? No, they find it useless. Is it her enemy? No, for her enemy finds her not worth hating now. She learns with relief that her little dog is "the one true heart" remaining above ground. Nothing, she cries, can equal a dog's fidelity. The dog replies that it has merely come to bury a bone in case of future hunger; "I quite forgot / It was your resting place." There is a pattern of assumption and disavowal; the "unquiet grave" convention, in which the lover will not let his loved one sleep, is given an ironic twist.

In June 1899 Hardy met the poet A.E. HOUSMAN; they bicycled together in August. In November 1913 they met again in Cambridge, just before this poem was published. In 1933 Housman wrote a friend that Hardy's favorite among his poems had been "Is My Team Ploughing?" in *A Shropshire Lad* (1896). In Housman's poem it is revealed at the end that the speaker is dead, and that his beloved has married his best friend. Hardy's poem begins with the revelation that a dead woman's lover has married another woman. Critics have speculated that Housman's poem was a direct influence on, or inspiration for, Hardy's own poem, since Housman's ending serves as a departure point for the ironic disappointments revealed, one after another, to the dead woman by her dog (Bailey, *The Poetry of Thomas Hardy*, 288).

"The Alarm" Poem published in *WESSEX POEMS AND OTHER VERSES* (1898), with the epigraph "In Memory of one of the Writer's Family who was a Volunteer during the War with Napoleon." It is based on the experience of Hardy's paternal grandmother, Mary HARDY, who in 1803, at the time of the conflict with Napoleon, was on the point of giving birth to a son, John. Believing some of the lurid practices put out in propaganda literature, she feared for the child's life if Napoleon invaded England. The poem recounts the hurried visit of the child's father, a volunteer with the British forces. Before rushing down to the coast, he tries to reassure his wife that "Buonaparte" is "not like to land!" En route, he sees the Barrow-Beacon burning—a signal "to expect the foe." The beacon was on the hill Hardy called Rainbarrow; it was lit to warn of Napoleon's possible plan to invade England by bringing his fleet to the WEYMOUTH harbor. (There was no actual physical feature officially named "Rainbarrow," although there are several prehistoric burial mounds on the heath; this is a name invented by Hardy). He is tempted to return home to his wife when he rescues a small bird tangled "among the crowfoot tufts" of the river. Released, the bird flies south toward the coast. The husband takes this as an omen and continues south, where the shoreline is "planted with Foot and Horse for miles." Napoleon has miscalculated and his fleet has paused, missing the optimal time for invasion. The husband returns home "in modest bliss" and sings a hymn of praise with his wife and friends.

Aldbrickham Fictional name for the town of Reading in JUDE THE OBSCURE. Jude FAWLEY and Sue BRIDEHEAD lived together on Spring Street, which has been tentatively located in the district near Southampton and Whitley Streets; they see a wedding at St. Giles Church, which still exists today. Sam Hobson, a character in the short story "The SON'S VETO," buys a greengrocery business in Aldbrickham. (Denys Kay-Robinson, *The Landscape of Thomas Hardy*, 160–61).

Aldclyffe, Captain Gerald Fellcourt Character in DESPERATE REMEDIES. Formerly Captain Bradleigh, a naval officer and father of Cytherea (Bradleigh) ALDCLYFFE, he must change his name in order to inherit Knapwater House and its surrounding estate from his wife's family. He is at odds with his daughter and dies the first evening Cytherea GRAYE spends as Miss Aldclyffe's companion.

Aldclyffe, Cytherea Character in DESPERATE REMEDIES. Born Cytherea Bradleigh, she was seduced by a cousin, a handsome soldier, at 17, and gave birth to a son, Aeneas MANSTON. An architect, Ambrose GRAYE, falls in love with her, not knowing her past, but she abruptly rejects him and disappears with her parents. Her father, Captain Gerald Fellcourt ALDCLYFFE, who must change his name as a condition of inheritance from his wife's family, inherits Knapwater House in DORSET. After his death, Cytherea Aldclyffe becomes the autocratic owner of the estate. She reigns in a queenly, manipulative way, trying to control the lives of those around her. She has secretly followed the life of the unscrupulous Aeneas.

Meanwhile, Ambrose Graye has married and has two children. His daughter, named Cytherea GRAYE, finds a post as Miss Aldclyffe's companion and suffers greatly from the older woman's bizarre attachment and consequent scheme to marry her namesake to Aeneas. Aeneas, having murdered his first wife, commits suicide in jail. Miss Aldclyffe dies of a brain hemorrhage, begging Cytherea Graye's forgiveness.

Aldritch, Dr. In FAR FROM THE MADDING CROWD, the Casterbridge surgeon who examines Sergeant Francis TROY after he has been fatally shot by William BOLDWOOD.

Alfredston The fictional name for Wantage in JUDE THE OBSCURE, this town is the setting for many events in the novel. It is near Oxford; today the Bear Hotel still stands. For the history of the "little car" that Sue BRIDEHEAD takes from the hotel to return to Jude FAWLEY, see Denys Kay-Robinson, *The Landscape of Thomas Hardy*, 169.

"Alicia's Diary" Short story published in A CHANGED MAN AND OTHER TALES (1913). On March 12, 1887, Hardy wrote TILLOTSON & SON, a newspaper syndicate, that he had just finished The WOODLANDERS and was unsure when he could deliver the "promised story."

The story takes the form of diary entries written by Alicia, the spinster daughter of an English clergyman. Alicia's younger sister, Caroline, has gone abroad with their mother to visit old friends near Versailles, an economical way to introduce Caroline to Paris. Alicia stays behind to make a home for their father, and writes spiteful comments in her diary. Caroline makes a rapid transition from a dreamy girl devoted to her pony to an attractive young woman. Her letters reveal that a friend of the Marletts, Charles de la Feste, a French painter who has lived much in England, is becoming increasingly interested in her. They become engaged, but the marriage is postponed. The mother becomes ill and dies, and the father goes to Paris to assess Charles. He approves of the artist, and in time Charles comes to England. Alicia does her best to attract him, appealing to his intellect and discussing John Ruskin's *Modern Painters* with him, then disingenuously concludes that, although she has "done nothing to encourage him to be faithless" to her sister, Charles has fallen in love with her and regards Caroline as a "sister only."

Charles leaves, feeling guilty about his attachment to Alicia, but Caroline falls into a decline. Convincing herself that Caroline will soon die and that she can then marry Charles herself, Alicia eventually arranges a counterfeit marriage between Charles and her sister. Theophilus Higham, a young Scripture reader, assists with the ceremony by impersonating a clergyman. Charles leaves for Venice immediately afterward. Caroline recovers and follows Charles; Alicia and her father pursue them. When Caroline learns the truth, she is horrified; under pressure from Alicia, Charles agrees to go through a legitimate ceremony, although he loves Alicia and not Caroline. He warns Alicia, however, that he "will not answer for the consequences."

They all return to England, where Caroline and Charles marry simply in the village church, but a few hours later Charles is found drowned in the water-meadows nearby. In time, Theophilus Higham becomes enamored of Caroline. Alicia believes she and Theophilus have both atoned for their sins in deceiving Caroline. Alicia is then left to care for her father, with no prospect of marriage herself.

Throughout the story, Caroline is naive and too eager to please, yet consistently high-principled. Alicia is high-strung, nervous, and devious, plotting to undermine Caroline even as she pretends to be helping her. Charles is pliable, and his stature as an artist is not altogether established. His capacity for extreme emotion, however, contrasts with Alicia's cool strategies, which end as blunders.

The story offers an authentic depiction of the Venice many of Hardy's readers might have known, with its gondoliers, hotels, small pensions, and churches, such as the Church of the Frari with its notable Bellini altarpiece. The Hardys went to ITALY in March 1887 and spent time in Venice, which was, of all Italian cities, Hardy's favorite.

The diary framework seems, at times, cumbersome, since the reader must deduce the sequence of events and their significance entirely from Alicia's entries. At the same time, the structure intensifies Alicia's jealous and vindictive attitude toward her more attractive younger sister. Desmond Hawkins observes that Hardy had a low opinion of many of the stories in *A CHANGED MAN AND OTHER TALES*, describing the contents, in a prefatory note, as "a dozen minor novels" reprinted "for what they may be worth" (Hawkins, "Introduction," *Thomas Hardy: Collected Short Stories*, xiv).

Allhusen, Dorothy Stanley (1877–1965) Younger daughter of Hardy's friend Mary JEUNE by her first husband, John Constantine Stanley. Hardy attended her wedding to Henry Allhusen in 1896. During her childhood Dorothy had known Hardy as "Uncle Tom." Once, while staying with the Jeunes, Hardy escorted Dorothy and her sister Madeleine to the theater in London. He was much amused when Dorothy said to him, "I do hope it will be something very *risqué . . .* So as to make our hair curl!" Throughout the play the girls then asked Hardy whether a scene was risqué, "not knowing of their own judgment" (Millgate, *Thomas Hardy: A Biography*, 357–58). Hardy continued to be fond of Dorothy throughout his life. In 1902 he sent her a volume of short stories with a letter saying he had put the inscription on a leaf which could be removed if she repented of her "kind wish to possess the stories" (*Letters* III, 1).

In 1908 she sent Hardy a rare plant, the *Mimosa pudica* or *Mimosa sensitiva*, which he had admired while visiting her family at Stoke Poges. He wrote that it had arrived "uninjured in spite of all its sensitiveness," though it had arrived looking "frightened" (*Letters* III, 328). One of his last letters to her was in November 1927, to thank her for flowers she had sent him. (He died in January 1928.)

Allingham, Helen Paterson (Mrs. William) *See* PATERSON, HELEN.

"Amabel" An early poem dated 1865 and published in *WESSEX POEMS AND OTHER VERSES* (1898). The poet has loved a woman in his youth and enshrined his idealized conception of her in his heart. On seeing her in later life he tries to reconcile her altered mien with the girl of his memory. Her attire, her demeanor, her gait, and her laugh have all changed. Every man, he reflects, has an "Amabel," a youthful vision. But nature ensures that the race goes on; men idealize women even when their beauty fades.

Hardy illustrated the poem with an hourglass and two butterflies; F. B. Pinion states that they represent "the flight of time and the imminent departure of the soul, which had known companionship on earth." The poem might refer to Julia Augusta MARTIN, of Kingston Maurward House, whom Hardy had adored when he attended a school she had established. Encountering her again when he was in his early 20s, he was shocked to see how she had aged. The poem was not published until after Mrs. Martin's death (Bailey, *The Poetry of Thomas Hardy*, 49–50).

The sentiment may be compared with Swithin ST. CLEEVE's encounter with Lady CONSTANTINE several years after their parting in the novel *TWO ON A TOWER*: her cheeks have lost their "firm contour" and her masses of once dark hair are tinged with gray.

For further reading: Hardy, "Some Unpublished Poems by Thomas Hardy," 36–37.

ancestry and Thomas Hardy The matter of genealogy was of interest to Thomas Hardy from both a personal and a literary point of view. In 1906 Hardy responded to a letter from James Rose, an unidentified correspondent, who had written to ask for information about Hardy's ancestors because he was working on a volume about "Dorsetshire Worthies." Hardy replied that he could not give any "documentary information" linking his own family to other branches of Hardys, but told Rose that "we have all been for centuries settled in Dorset." He then listed some of the villages associated with the various Dorset Hardys and remarked, "All are believed to have a common ancestor in John le Hardy, who came from Jersey & settled in Weymouth in the 15th century" (*Letters* III, 235). Further details about the Jersey Hardys are given in the *Life*, in which he confesses that he was tempted to call himself "Thomas le Hardy," but never did so. He points out that by the time of his birth the "family had declined . . . from whatever importance it once might have been able to claim," but is pleased to note that an "ancestral Thomas Hardy, living in Dorchester in 1724, was a subscriber to "Thirty Select Anthems in Score" by the organist of the Chapel Royal and Westminster Abbey.

In 1905 Hardy was invited by Reginald Smith to contribute a poem to the CORNHILL MAGAZINE to mark the 100th anniversary of the October 1805 Battle of Trafalgar. Admiral Lord Nelson's flag captain at Trafalgar had been Sir Thomas Masterman Hardy, a baronet. Hardy answered that he was unable to send such a poem, as he had exhausted the theme of Trafalgar in The DYNASTS. In any case, Sir Thomas would have pronounced him "out of kin . . . the divergence of my line from his having been so long ago" (Letters III, 170). He was undoubtedly proud of being distantly related to Sir Thomas Hardy, however, and depicted him in The Dynasts. In Part I, Act 3, Scene 1, William Pitt tries to convince King George III that he should be suspicious of Napoleon, but the king says he has conferred with Lord Nelson's Captain (Captain Thomas Hardy), and that the navy is in "thick night" about Napoleon's future plans. Captain Hardy figures heroically at the Battle of Trafalgar, at which Lord Nelson is killed. For Nelson's funeral at St. Paul's, Captain Hardy is chosen to carry a velvet pincushion covered with Nelson's stars and garters. At a scene in Weymouth, the local citizens discuss him, observing that he has aged a great deal since transporting Nelson's body home in a cask of "sperrits," but the men had "drink him dry" in order to survive the long journey home. They sing a ballad, "The Night of Trafalgar."

Hardy was descended, on his maternal side, from the Anglo-Saxon Chiles (or Childs), Hand, and Swetman families. He notes with pride that his grandmother, Elizabeth ("Betty") Childs Hand, was extremely well versed in literature and "knew the writings of Addison, Steele, and others of the Spectator group almost by heart," as well as the works of Samuel Richardson, Henry Fielding, John Milton, and John Bunyan. Hardy's grandfather died young, leaving Elizabeth with a large and impoverished young family, including his mother, Jemima HARDY. The latter dealt with her "stressful experiences" by "reading every book she could lay her hands on." In 1839 she married Thomas Hardy's father (Life, 5–8).

Several of Hardy's finest novels, including TESS OF THE D'URBERVILLES and TWO ON A TOWER, turn on the question of lineage: its transmission, corruption, status, and power. One of his earliest novels, The HAND OF ETHELBERTA, is a satire about the frivolities of social class in Victorian England, but many critics believe it would have been more successful if written later, after Hardy had developed a more intimate acquaintance with the aristocracy. His short story collection A GROUP OF NOBLE DAMES deals with the lives of 10 titled women, but the tellers of the tales do not belong to the nobility. By the time this book was published Hardy had become very well known, and he remarks in the preface to the 1896 edition that several "Noble Dames yet in the flesh" had offered anecdotes from their own families that he might use as the basis for further tales, an offer he declined.

Hardy came to have a number of friends with hereditary titles, including the earl and countess of PORTSMOUTH and their daughters, Lady Eveline Camilla WALLOP and Lady Margaret WALLOP; Lady Portsmouth's brother-in-law and sister, Lord and Lady CARNARVON; Lady Burghclere (Lady Winifred HERBERT); Lady Agnes GROVE; and the noted London hostess Mary JEUNE (later Lady St. Helier).

For further reading: Millgate, *Thomas Hardy: A Biography;* Southerington, *The Early Hardys.*

"Ancient to Ancients, An"   Poem first published in the CENTURY MAGAZINE (New York) in May 1922 and that year collected in LATE LYRICS AND EARLIER (1922). When it appeared in the *Century Magazine*, it was illustrated with a two-page headpiece by the American artist Rockwell KENT, who had written Hardy that he would be most interested in illustrating some of Hardy's works (*Letters* V, 319).

The poem takes the form of a genial address an older man might have given at a club dinner to juniors waiting to take his place. He reminds the younger audience of "Gentlemen" that he and his contemporaries once had youthful revels, when they escorted young damsels, danced the polka and the quadrille, and attended fashionable operas. But contemporary paintings do not hold the interest that the works of William Etty, William Mulready, and Daniel Maclise once did. In his youth Hardy and his friends embraced the authors "Bulwer, Scott, Dumas, and Sand" (Edward Bulwer-Lytton, Sir Walter Scott, Alexandre Dumas, and George Sand), along with Alfred, Lord Tennyson, as did his deceased first wife, Emma Gifford HARDY: "Even she who voiced those rhymes is dust." Hardy's reference to his having read Tennyson with his wife in a bower might have taken place at ST. JULIOT, a church Hardy was restoring in CORNWALL, during their courtship days. The reference has a double meaning: first, that scientific philosophy undermined Tennyson's religious views and, second, that the trellised summer house has long since decayed (Pinion, *A Commentary on the Poems of Thomas Hardy,* 199–200). The speaker and his contemporaries observe that they leave the younger audience much "lore" that is "worth the knowing." In fact, many writers, such as Socrates, Thycydides, Herodotus, and Homer "Burnt brightlier towards their setting-day." Bailey (*The Poetry of Thomas Hardy,* 499) observes that the final stanza amounts to a defense of Hardy's writing poetry when he was 82.

An Ancient to Ancients

By THOMAS HARDY
Drawing by ROCKWELL KENT

Where once we danced, where once we sang,
    Gentlemen,
The floors are sunken, cobwebs hang,
And cracks creep; worms have fed upon
The doors. Yea, brighter times were then
Than now, with harps and tabrets gone,
    Gentlemen.

Where once we rowed, where once we sailed,
    Gentlemen,
And damsels took the tiller, veiled
Against too strong a stare (God wot
Their fancy . . . then or any when!),
Upon that shore we are clean forgot,
    Gentlemen.

We have lost somewhat afar and near,
    Gentlemen,
The thinning of our ranks each year
Affords a hint we are nigh undone,
That we shall not be ever again
The marked of many, loved of one,
    Gentlemen.

In dance the polka met our wish,
    Gentlemen,
The paced quadrille, the spry schottische,
"Sir Roger"; and in opera spheres
The "Girl," the famed "Bohemian,"
And "Trovatore," held the ears,
    Gentlemen.

This season's paintings do not please,
    Gentlemen,
Like Etty, Mulready, Maclise;
Throbbing romance has waned and wanned;
No wizard wields the witching pen
Of Bulwer, Scott, Dumas, and Sand,
    Gentlemen.

Headpiece illustration by Rockwell Kent for "An Ancient to Ancients" in The Century Magazine *(New York), May 1922* (Perkins Library, Duke University)

"Andrey Satchel and the Parson and Clerk"   *See* "FEW CRUSTED CHARACTERS, A."

"And There Was a Great Calm" *(On the Signing of the Armistice, 11 Nov. 1918)*   The poem was written in November 1920 at the request of the *Times* (London) and initially published in a special Armistice Day section of the newspaper on November 11, 1920 (Purdy, 211). The title is from Matthew 8:26, a reference to Jesus' calming the tempest in the Sea of Galilee near Capernaum: "he arose, and rebuked the winds and the sea; and there was a great calm." The poem was collected in *LATE LYRICS AND EARLIER* (1922).

Hardy uses some of the Spirits he had created in his verse drama *The DYNASTS*—the Spirit of Irony, the Sinister Spirit, and the Spirit of Pity—to provide outside commentary on the turmoil of WORLD WAR I. The spirits cannot intervene in men's affairs or answer philosophical questions, however. The poem recalls the "Despair" and "Anger" of the war years "heaving high," while the "pensive Spirit of Pity" whispered, "Why?" There was no answer. The "feeble folk" in England had become accustomed to "dug-outs," "snipers," and "Huns." Each morning they had waked to "wish existence timeless, null."

In the remaining stanzas, Hardy makes the point that the very fact of the war, showing man's capacity for evil, has tainted the Armistice. Because the unthinkable happened, peace is tenuous.

After the armistice, soldiers hold their fire, yet there is unrest. The Spirit of Irony jeers at them: "What? / Spoil peradventures woven of Rage and Wrong?" The poem suggests that soldiers on both sides had taken a certain satisfaction in venting their anger by killing the perceived enemy.

Finally, it seems that the war is over. The "worn horses" realize they are no longer whipped, and "weft-winged engines" have ceased flying from Germany to England, blurring the "moon's thin horn." It is calm, and clemency has descended from heaven. There is "peace on earth, and silence in the sky." Even so, many people cannot "shake off misery." Why did the war happen? they seem to be asking. Hardy's cynical commentator, the "Sinister Spirit," sneers, "'It had to be!'" The poem ends on a note of bewilderment. The Spirit of Pity whispers again the unanswerable question which opens the poem: "'Why?'"

Anglebury Fictional name of the town of Wareham in *The HAND OF ETHELBERTA*, in which some of the scenes are set at the Red Lion, a hotel that still exists today. Denys Kaye-Robinson states that the town, not being a coastal resort, has been spared development and remains "Georgian, substantial, and dignified" (*The Landscape of Thomas Hardy*, 68). Portions of Hardy's short story "The WITHERED ARM" are also set in Anglebury.

animals, Hardy's love of Hardy had a lifelong devotion to animals, particularly to his dogs. In December 1890 his dog Moss, who had been much cherished by Hardy and his wife Emma, died. Hardy wrote Edmund GOSSE of her death and burial under the trees on the lawn at MAX GATE. WESSEX (Wessie), who lived for nearly 13 years, was also buried at Max Gate with a headstone designed by Hardy:

THE
FAMOUS DOG
WESSEX
August 1913–27 Dec. 1926
Faithful. Unflinching.

Hardy wrote a poem, "Dead 'Wessex,' the Dog to the Household," in which Wessex asks whether he is missed.

Hardy was distressed by all inhumane treatment of animals, especially during slaughter, and left money in his will to two different societies to lessen their suffering in city slaughterhouses. When *JUDE THE OBSCURE* was published, Hardy was surprised at the attacks on the pig-killing scene but offered it without charge to the editor of the *ANIMALS' FRIEND* magazine, published by the Society for the Protection of Animals. In April 1901 he wrote both Sir George DOUGLAS and Florence HENNIKER that a gloom had been cast over the household because the mail train had run over a favorite cat: "The violent death of dumb creature [*sic*] always makes me revile the contingencies of a world in which animals are in the best of cases pitiable for their limitations." He blamed himself for having let the cat out "after taking the trouble to shut him up myself every night all this winter." The Hardys had several cats; two of them were called Markie and Snowdove (*Letters* II, 283; *Letters* III, 82). Snowdove was later killed by another train on the railway line near Max Gate, and in 1904 Hardy wrote the sculptor Hamo Thornycroft to ask where he could get a sharp chisel to cut the cat's name on a stone in their "Pets' Cemetery"; the stone is still legible in the shrubbery at Max Gate (*Letters* III, 137). In 1908 another cat, Kitsie, was about to have kittens, an event Hardy wrote his wife Emma about in copious detail; Emma was staying at Dover to escape the confusion caused by the enlargement of Max Gate. The same year a cat thought to be more than 20 years old, Comfy, died and was buried in the Pets' Cemetery.

In April 1910 Hardy wrote a letter to the secretary of the Humanitarian League which was published in the *Humanitarian* magazine in May, attracting considerable criticism. He argued that if one accepted Darwin's theory of the common origin of all species, the logical outcome would be "to enlarge 'The Golden Rule' beyond the area of mere mankind to that of the whole animal kingdom . . . though I myself do not at present see how the principle of equal justice all round is to be carried out in its entirety, I recognize that the League is grappling with the question."

There are several instances of Hardy's rescuing animals in distress. In 1911 he discovered an exhausted cow in a field who had been driven while in an unfit condition. He called the police and gave evidence against two men accused and convicted of the crime. He wrote his friend Edith Taylor, "I fear I am supposed to have done much more for that poor cow than I really did. Much could be done in that way if people would only give their time & attention, & show a little courage" (*Letters* IV, 174).

His fictional portrayals of animals are particularly moving. They play an essential role in the daily operation of the farms and dairies in Hardy's fiction, and are a vital means of transport. Treatment of animals is an index to the basic sensitivity and probity of many of Hardy's characters. In *FAR FROM THE MADDING CROWD* Sergeant TROY, for instance, is given to jerking the bit on horses he drives, which is very painful for Bathsheba EVERDENE's horses. Among the noted animals in Hardy's fiction are Blossom (Miller Loveday's horse in *The TRUMPET MAJOR*), Crumplet (Miller Loveday's cow in *The Trumpet-Major*), Dainty and Poppet (Bathsheba's horses in *Far from the Madding Crowd*), Daisy, Whitefoot, Bonny-lass, Jolly-o, Spot, and Twinkle-eye (some of the dairy cows in Bathsheba's herd in *Far from the Madding Crowd*), Darling (horse bought by Giles Winterborne for Grace Melbury in *The WOODLANDERS*), Dumpling, Fancy, Lofty Mist, Old Pretty, Young Pretty, Tidy, and Loud (cows to be milked by Tess in *TESS OF THE D'URBERVILLES*), Strut (one of Mrs. D'URBERVILLE's pet cockerels in *Tess of the d'Urbervilles*), George (Gabriel

OAK's sensitive sheepdog in *Far from the Madding Crowd*), Pansy (Eldride Swancourt's horse in A PAIR OF BLUE EYES), Smart and Smiler (horses belonging to Reuben Dewy in UNDER THE GREENWOOD TREE), Prince (the Durbeyfields' horse, killed by a mail cart, in *Tess of the d'Urbervilles*), and Pleasant (the old horse chosen to pull Fanny ROBIN's coffin in *Far from the Madding Crowd*). Even when they are not named, Hardy renders animals in an engaging way. The flocks of sheep arriving at the Greenhill agricultural fair (Chapter 50) in *Far from the Madding Crowd*, for example, have a particular charm. The Wessex horned breeds, including those belonging to Bathsheba Everdene, have "vermiculated horns lopping gracefully on each side of their cheeks in geometrically perfect spirals, a small pink and white ear nestling under each horn." The Oxfordshire breed has wool that is "beginning to curl like a child's flaxen hair." Their curls, however, are surpassed by the effeminate ones of the Leicesters. The Exmoors have "pied faces and legs, dark and heavy horns, tresses of wool hanging round their swarthy foreheads." Still others are "perfect leopards as to the full rich substance of their coats, and only lacking the spots."

The portraits of animals in Hardy's fiction are of intrinsic interest to readers. Moreover, the attitude of his characters toward animals is an index of their compassion toward other people. Not only the mistreatment of animals, but also indifference to their plight, are predictors of character. Tess DURBEYFIELD, for example, is stricken by the death of the family horse, Prince, and also establishes close relationships with some of the cows at Talbothays. Arabella Fawley's treatment of the family pigs mimics her entrapment of Jude into marriage. Characters who are cruel to animals, such as Francis TROY in *Far from the Madding Crowd*, are equally indifferent to others. Alma Evers gives an excellent overview of the symbolism of Hardy's fictional animals and his hatred of cruelty to all animals in the *Oxford Reader's Companion to Hardy* (8–10).

For further reading: Asker, "'The Birds Shall Have Some Dinner': Animals in Hardy's Fiction"; Campbell, "Thomas Hardy's Attitude toward Animals"; Evers, "Animals"; Evers, "Animals, cruelty to."

Animals' Friend Magazine published by the Society for the Protection of Animals. In November 1895 Hardy wrote the editor, offering him publication rights to the pig-killing scene in JUDE THE OBSCURE (Part First, chapter 10), explaining that he hoped it "might be useful in teaching mercy in the Slaughtering of Animals for the meat-market—the cruelties involved in the business having been a great grief to me for years" (*Letters* II, 97).

"Anna, Lady Baxby" Short story; *see GROUP OF NOBLE DAMES, A.*

Anny A friend of Arbella DONN in JUDE THE OBSCURE; she and another girl are present at Arabella's first meeting with Jude FAWLEY and advise her on how to trap him into marriage. Anny meets Arabella again at the Great Wessex Agricultural Show at Stoke-Barehills; she has been jilted by her young man. The two women share a house in ALFREDSTON during Arabella's widowhood and become interested in religion. It is Anny who learns that Sue BRIDEHEAD and Richard PHILLOTSON are remarried; she tells Arabella, who tells Jude.

"Apostrophe to an Old Psalm Tune" Poem dated Sunday, August 13, 1916, and collected in MOMENTS OF VISION (1917). Hardy addresses the tune to which Psalm 69 was sung and traces his memories of the many times he has sung it, or heard it sung. This was the appropriate evening psalm for the 13th of the month. It begins, "Save me, O God, for the waters are come in, even unto my soul" (Bailey, *The Poetry of Thomas Hardy*, 345).

Hardy recalls singing it to the original tune as a chorister, "full of wonder, and innocent," at STINSFORD CHURCH. He heard it again years later, presumably with Emma Gifford HARDY. Bailey suggests that this was in ST. JULIOT CHURCH, in CORNWALL. The tune had been rewritten and stripped of its "old vesture" by William Henry Monk, the musical editor of *Hymns Ancient and Modern* (1861). Emma had evoked the psalm often. After her death Hardy had assumed the psalm tune had passed on also; he could not bear the memories it brought back as he sat "among strange people/Under their steeple."

Florence HARDY, however, a "new stirrer of tones," enters his life and awakes his memories of the tune. He discerns its "mien in the old attire," and takes comfort from it in the "turmoiled years of belligerent fire" (that is, WORLD WAR I).

"Appeal to America on Behalf of the Belgian Destitute, An" Poem dated December 14, 1914, soon after the outbreak of WORLD WAR I. It was first published in the *New York Times* on January 4, 1915, and later reprinted in MOMENTS OF VISION (1917). Hardy is horrified at the ravages of the war throughout Belgium, where "Seven millions stand/Emaciate." England, however, is "full-charged with our own maimed and dead/And coiled in throbbing conflicts slow and sore," and can do little to assist the Belgian people. He issues a fervent appeal, therefore, to the "great country" of America to lend prompt assistance, hoping the people of the United States will send both food and money for Belgian war relief.

The poem was prefaced by this introduction: "This poem, written as an appeal to the American people on behalf of the destitute people of Belgium by Thomas Hardy, the English writer, was given out by the American Commission for Relief in Belgium yesterday."

"Aquae Sulis"   Poem, possibly written at Bath during Hardy's March 1911 visit, and published in SATIRES OF CIRCUMSTANCE (1914). Bath was built above hot springs, where there was an ancient temple to the British Sul, the goddess of waters (who antedated the Roman invasion of Britain). The Romans conflated the worship of Sul with the worship of their goddess Minerva, who became Sul-Minerva; they erected an altar to her and built elaborate baths. The baths collapsed after the Romans departed from Britain. In 1727 a gilded bronze head of Sul-Minerva was discovered. Excavations in 1755 revealed the Roman baths, temple, and altars; in 1878 further excavations exposed Roman houses. The earlier structures also included a Saxon monastery that preceded Bath Abbey, both eclipsing the pagan Roman temple (Bailey, *The Poetry of Thomas Hardy,* 315).

In Hardy's poem, Minerva-Sul, a "filmy shape," rises from the bubbling waters and recalls that she once had a shrine "stately and shining"; she resents the Gothic arches and pews of the church that have been superimposed on her own temple, as well as the priests that have shamelessly "trampled" its dusty remains. She has pleaded that the church erected above them be removed. The defender of the Christian church retorts that they both hang by a "frail thread" and that both represent images "twitched by people's desires." The ghost of the goddess asks if the ghost of the Christian church, "a Jumping-jack," can be friends with herself, a "poor Jumping-jill," but there is no answer. The "olden dark" hides "the cavities late laid bare" and the only sound is the "gossamery noise" and the "boiling voice of the waters' medicinal pour." Lionel Stevenson summarizes the theme of the poem as the "equality of all religions . . . the anthropomorphic tendency in general" (*Darwin among the Poets*, 248).

Archer, William (1856–1924)   A dramatist and critic, Archer thanked Hardy for sending a copy of TESS OF THE D'URBERVILLES in October 1892. Hardy replied that he had "been so often drawn to yr writings by their accord with my views" but had hesitated to send the book for fear Archer might already have received a copy for review (*Letters*, I, 287).

In 1894 Archer attacked Hardy's LIFE'S LITTLE IRONIES in the *Daily Chronicle.* He noted that George Moore's novel *Esther Waters* had been boycotted, but urged that those who believed that "morality consists in the discouragement of sexual impulse, or even of its unlicensed manifestations" should in fact "clamour for" Moore's novel and "demand the suppression" of Hardy's collection of stories. (*Esther Waters* deals with the effort of an English servant girl to raise her illegitimate son. Eventually the child's father marries Esther, although her happy marriage does not offset her largely melancholy existence. Archer may have been

suggesting that, since Esther succeeds in marrying her son's father, the story has a higher moral message than those in LIFE'S LITTLE IRONIES, in which early love and courtship repeatedly fail to result in a fulfilling marriage.) Mary JEUNE, at Hardy's request, wrote a letter defending *Life's Little Ironies,* stating that she could not recall a single story that "can offend the most sensitive morality" (*Letters* II, 56). Hardy wrote Archer a few days later stating that he realized he was "perfectly conscientious" in his remarks, although he might disagree with them. Archer had written a more "generous" review also, published anonymously in the *Westminster Gazette* (*Letters* II, 57).

Hardy invited Archer to come to MAX GATE for several days in September 1895. Archer reviewed JUDE THE OBSCURE in January 1896, selecting it as "the book of the year." Hardy wrote a letter thanking him and stating, "You see the aim of the story—poor as it is in execution—with an unprejudiced & calm insight which is a contrast indeed to the vision of some reviewers" (*Letters* II, 104). Other reviewers were far less understanding, and when, in 1898, Archer urged Hardy to write another novel, Hardy answered that he did not "incline" to doing so, for lack of an "enlightened literary opinion sufficiently audible to tempt an author, who knows that in the nature of things he must always come short of real excellence." He sent Archer a copy of WESSEX POEMS.

In February 1901 Archer interviewed Hardy for an article in a series called "Real Conversations." It was published in the *Pall Mall Magazine* in April 1901. Archer sent him a copy of the article before publication, and Hardy asked that he omit mention of his poetry. He explained, "I have a horror of spreading myself before the public" (*Letters* II, 279). The interview was collected in Archer's *Real Conversations* (London, 1904).

Architectural Notebook of Thomas Hardy   Edited by C. J. P. Beatty, with a foreword by Sir John Summerson, Hardy's notebook was published in Dorchester by the Dorset Natural History and Archaeological Society in 1966. It contains drawings, sketches, and plans believed by Beatty to have been rendered largely between 1866 and 1871. Among them are sections of timber construction, notes about color and materials, and plans for the ST. JULIOT CHURCH rectory in CORNWALL.

For further reading: Betjeman, "Hardy and Architecture."

architecture   Hardy began his architectural training in the DORCHESTER office of John HICKS in 1856. One of the projects he worked on that year was the restoration of St. Peter's Church in Dorchester. Hardy's plan of the restored church, which he made at age 16, is exhibited in the south-aisle chapel. In 1862, having decided, as he says in the *Life,* "to pursue the art and science of architecture on more advanced lines," (*Life,* 35), Hardy went to LONDON. A friend of Mr. Hicks, the architect John NORTON, of Old Bond Street, invited him to come and make drawings in his office while he looked for further work. Just as he arrived to begin, Norton told him that a friend he had met at the Institute of British Architects asked if he knew of "a young Gothic draughtsman who could restore and design churches and rectory-houses." He had recommended Hardy, and sent him to call on Sir Arthur William BLOMFIELD.

Betjeman observes that Blomfield was a son of the bishop of London, a connection that might have led to Hardy's having many commissions for church work. Hardy's ARCHITECTURAL NOTEBOOK shows his interest in Gothic molding and details of joinery and ironwork. Hardy also, however, received a wide training in architecture from Blomfield, who designed the church of St. Barnabas, Oxford, in the Byzantine style. In 1865, he published an article in CHAMBERS'S JOURNAL, "HOW I BUILT MYSELF A HOUSE," which he states in his autobiography was "written to amuse the pupils of Blomfield." He did not, however, begin writing prose until two or three years later; he had found himself, he recalls, "perilously near coming to the ground between the two stools of architecture and literature." (*Life,* 48).

By 1867, Hardy's health had been weakened by his constant reading and work for Blomfield, in addition to his lack of exercise. Blomfield suggested that Hardy go down to Dorset for a time to regain his strength, but return to London in the fall. He stayed at home for a few weeks, walking into Dorchester every day to work again for John Hicks. This regimen restored his health. At this time he also began his first novel (never published), *The POOR MAN AND THE LADY,* which has an architect for a hero. He completed it in 1868, but was unable to find a publisher. In January 1869, he returned to London. He did not work again for Blomfield, but visited museums and rewrote the novel. Hicks died during the winter, and, in April, his successor, G. R. CRICKMAY, asked Hardy to finish some of the church restoration projects the firm had taken on. After Hardy worked several weeks in the Dorchester office, Crickmay offered him three months' employment in Weymouth. There he directed the rebuilding of Turnworth church, west of Blandford Forum. He also supervised the restoration of several other churches. In August or September a new assistant came to Crickmay's office; he became the model for Edward SPRINGROVE, the young hero/architect in DESPERATE REMEDIES, the novel on which Hardy was working in Weymouth. The character Ambrose GRAYE, who had once loved Miss ALDCLYFFE, is an architect, as is his son, Owen. Knapwater House (actually KINGSTON MAURWARD, near DORCHESTER), is described in detail, as are Aeneas MANSTON's dwelling and the temporary farmhouse housing

Cytherea and Owen after her unconsummated marriage to Manson. The Three Tranters Inn, an early structure, and the bleak London row houses where Edward Springrove tracks down the property of Eunice Manston, are all carefully portrayed in detail.

In February 1870, Crickmay asked Hardy to go to CORNWALL and "take a plan of particulars of a church" he was about to rebuild there. This was ST. JULIOT CHURCH, near Boscastle, of which the rector was the Rev. Caddell HOLDER. His wife's sister, Emma Gifford, (*see* HARDY, Emma Gifford) Hardy's future wife, was staying with them at the time.

Hardy's experience as an architect is represented throughout his 1881 novel *A LAODICEAN,* from the first depiction of the young architect George SOMERSET's visit to Castle de Stancy to his European tour toward the end of the book. Somerset is the epitome of a knowledgeable, conservative, yet imaginative architect. When first visiting the castle, owned by Paula POWER, he tactfully keeps his sketchbook closed, although he

During his architectural training, Hardy worked on the restoration of St. Peter's Church in Dorchester. (Sarah Bird Wright)

longs to jot down notes and sketches from the frames of paintings, ornate furniture, tapestry hangings, and armor he sees. When he goes abroad, he follows Paula and her party to Heidelberg, where he transfers "the fine Renaissance details of the Otto-Heinrichs-Bau" to his sketchbook.

The novel also depicts a less scrupulous and less competent architect, James HAVILL, a local Toneborough man who has a large family to support. Havill expects to restore the castle, but Paula Power becomes suspicious when she realizes from Somerset's questioning that Havill is ignorant of authentic old styles. She decides to mount an architectural competition between Somerset and Havill. The two architects employ draughtsmen and other helpers, perhaps reflecting Hardy's experience in the offices of John Hicks and Sir Arthur Blomfield. It is, perhaps, in this novel that Hardy's architectural expertise is given its fullest fictional expression.

Hardy's 1873 novel A PAIR OF BLUE EYES also has a hero who is an architect, Stephen SMITH. He is a London architect's assistant who, staying in Parson SWANCOURT's Wessex house, falls in love with the parson's daughter, Elfride SWANCOURT, although he is never able to marry her. In his preface to the novel Hardy notes that it was written "at a time when church-restoration had just reached the remotest nooks of western England, where the wild and tragic features of the coast had long combined in perfect harmony with the crude Gothic Art of the ecclesiastical buildings scattered along it."

Hardy also saw an intimate connection between poetry and architecture. He states in his autobiography that he had discovered very early that "regularity" could be "bad art," an opinion strengthened by the analogy between poetry and architecture. In architecture, he reflected, "cunning irregularity is of enormous worth." Gothic architecture embodied the quality of spontaneity in moldings, tracery, and other details. He sought the "unforeseen" in his "metres and stanzas, that of stress rather than of syllable, poetic texture, rather than poetic veneer." In other words, regular rhythms were less effective. He had been taught to avoid "veneer" or "constructed ornament," which was absent from the best Gothic architecture. For instance, "the carved leafage of some capital or spandrel" might stray "freakishly out of its bounds over the moulding," or there might be a sudden blank in a wall where a window was to be expected" (Life, 301).

Hardy designed his home, MAX GATE, completed in 1885, and he retained a lifelong interest in the architecture of historic buildings. In 1901, at the request of the Rev. Sydney BOULTER, he reviewed an appeal for funds for the restoration of the FORDINGTON ST. GEORGE CHURCH, Dorchester. He later decided the architect's modifications had impaired the outline of the church tower.

One of Hardy's last excursions, in the late summer of 1927, was an automobile trip to the small town of Ilminster. He had wanted to see the church and the tomb of the founder of Wadham College. He and his wife Florence also drove past the quarries that were noted for Ham Hill stone. In September they lunched with Mr. and Mrs. H. J. Weld at Lulworth Castle and saw the adjoining church. Later that month they lunched at Charborough Park, which he had written about in TWO ON A TOWER but had never entered.

For further reading: The Architectural Notebook of Thomas Hardy; Beatty, "Hardy the Architect"; Betjeman, "Hardy and Architecture"; Cox, "The Poet and the Architect"; Moore, "The Poet within the Architect's Ring: Desperate Remedies, Hardy's Hybrid Detective-Gothic Narrative."

Arnold, Matthew (1822–1888) English critic and poet. The son of Thomas Arnold (headmaster of the Rugby public school), Arnold was the author of "Thyrsis" (1866), an elegy written on the death of his friend Arthur Hugh Clough and "Dover Beach," perhaps his most famous poem, which expresses his pessimistic concern about the ebbing "sea of faith." He also wrote Culture and Anarchy (1869), an influential collection of essays, and Literature and Dogma (1873), in which he argued for educational emphasis on literature.

In Culture and Anarchy he argued for the education of the masses in England, which he felt were too oriented toward the spirit of "Hebraism" with its focus on Hebrew learning and its teachings of strict conscience. They were less attuned to the more spontaneous spirit of Greek "Hellenism."

Thomas Hardy met Arnold in early 1880 at a dinner at the Continental Hotel in London given by G. Murray Smith, the publisher. The writers Henry JAMES and Richard Jefferies were fellow guests. Hardy wrote that Arnold "had a manner of having made up his mind upon everything years ago, so that it was a pleasing futility for his interlocutor to begin thinking new ideas, different from his own, at that time of day." He liked Arnold better when he met him again at a second dinner given by Mrs. Smith in June 1884 (Life, 134). Hardy noted Arnold's death (April 1888) in his autobiography.

Michael Millgate states that Hardy found Arnold's "idealism somewhat remote and rarefied," but agreed with his ethical approach to the intellectual problems of the day, especially Arnold's analysis of the "modern spirit." He suggests that Arnold's ideas are reflected in The RETURN OF THE NATIVE, A LAODICEAN, and JUDE THE OBSCURE, and that Hardy's later works embody what Arnold considered the most admirable characteristic of Wordsworth's own writing: "the noble & profound application of ideas to life" (Millgate, A Biography, 246).

Asquith, Herbert Henry (1852–1928)   Prime minister of Britain from 1908 to 1916, Asquith offered Thomas Hardy a knighthood in November 1908. Hardy thanked him for thinking of conferring such an honor, but asked that the proposal be deferred. Asquith did not renew the offer, although Hardy received the ORDER OF MERIT in 1910 (*Letters* III, 353.) When Hardy's verse drama *The DYNASTS* was presented at the Kingsway Theatre by Harley GRANVILLE-BARKER in 1914, Hardy wrote A. E. Drinkwater, the theater's general manager, and suggested that he send tickets to the prime minister and Mrs. Asquith. Asquith saw the play on an afternoon in December; Hardy wrote his friend Florence HENNIKER that he "liked it much" (*Letters* IV, 51, 71).

"At a Bridal"   Subtitled *"Nature's Indifference,"* the poem is dated 1866 and was collected in *WESSEX POEMS* (1898). The speaker addresses a young woman about to give birth. He mourns that this child, and perhaps other children, would not be his. He grieves that "lives so matched should miscompose," but finally ascribes the cause to the indifference of the "Great Dame whence incarnation flows."

Constance Oliver speculates that the subject was Mary Waight of Dorchester, who rejected Hardy in favor of George Stroud Oliver, who came from a socially superior family (*Thomas Hardy Proposes to Mary Waight* [Beaminster, Dorset: Toucan Press, 1964], cited by Bailey, *The Poetry of Thomas Hardy*, 53–54).

"At a Country Fair"   A poem collected in MOMENTS OF VISION (1917) in which Hardy recalls the heartrending experience of seeing, at a long-ago West Country fair, a dwarf leading a giant about, tethered with "a red string like a long thin scarf." He realizes that the giant is blind, but is also withered in spirit, with "no independent mind": he trots "meekly" wherever the dwarf wishes him to go.

"At a Lunar Eclipse"   This sonnet was published in *POEMS OF THE PAST AND THE PRESENT* (1902) and probably refers to the lunar eclipse of July 18, 1860. The poet addresses troubled Earth, whose shadow is creeping across the "imperturbable serenity" of the surface of the moon during the eclipse. He asks if this is the gauge of the significance of Earth, whose inhabitants take pride in the intellectual accomplishments of "brains that teem,/Heroes, and women fairer than the skies?" Taken in their entirety, they cast but a small shadow against the moon. Hardy argues that earth is relatively insignificant within the larger universe; achievements, events, and troubles that seem momentous to men are entirely miniscule when measured by the "stellar gauge" of its tiny "shade." The poem expresses a theme that is apparent in much of Hardy's

work: the contrast between "vast imperturbable serenities" and warring nations "on a planet unimportant to the Will of the universe, yet important to man."

"At a Seaside Town in 1869" *(Young Lover's Reverie)*   A poem published in *MOMENTS OF VISION* (1917), it is set in the coastal resort town of WEYMOUTH during the time Hardy was employed by the architect George Rackstrow CRICKMAY. Hardy was then working on the novel *DESPERATE REMEDIES*. The poet depicts himself as a young man torn between his inner vision of an ideal young woman and the outer world. Although he tries to interest himself in the passing ships, the crowds on the esplanade, the band, the "Morgenbläter Waltz," and the "sunlit cliffs," his thoughts are preoccupied by memories of her image. He vows to abandon the struggle and "seek the pure/Thought-world, and bask in her allure," but finds it impossible to turn completely inward; her soul has not thrown a single "beam" upon his own; ". . . she is gone, is gone."

After his interview with Crickmay, when he was offered a position for three months, Hardy had wandered down to the Esplanade and heard the town band play a set of waltzes by Johann Strauss, which he discovered was the "Morgenblätter" (Morning Papers). He became a resident of Weymouth and enjoyed swimming and rowing. He was supposedly engaged to Tryphena SPARKS at the time, but it seems he was not entirely committed to her and she might in fact be a symbol for Hardy's deep yearning to return to writing his novel (Bailey, *The Poetry of Thomas Hardy*, 397). In February Hardy gave up his lodgings at Weymouth and returned home to complete his novel.

"At Castle Boterel"   Poem dated March 1913 and published in *SATIRES OF CIRCUMSTANCE* (1914). He revisits, on a rainy day, Castle Boterel on the Cornish coast, where he had met and courted Emma Gifford (later HARDY). This is his name for the small town of Boscastle. He is reminded of a dry day when he and Emma alighted from a chaise pulled by a "sturdy pony" in order to ease its load. They had climbed a steep lane to the crest of the hill. Hardy does not describe their conversation, but recalls it as "A time of such quality," though it "filled but a minute," that it has never been duplicated in the history of the hill, since their climb or before. The "Primaeval rocks" bordering the road only record that "we two passed."

Bailey notes that Bottreaux Castle had once occupied the site. He identifies the day from Hardy's journal as March 9, 1870, when he, Emma, and Emma's sister, Helen HOLDER, made the excursion together. It is likely that Helen drove the pony while they climbed, and, while they were out of her sight, the particular moment of exhilaration that "filled but a moment" took place (Bailey, *The Poetry of Thomas Hardy*, 303).

Hardy continues to look back on Emma's "phantom figure . . . shrinking, shrinking," and believes it is the last time he will "traverse old love's domain," because his own "sand is sinking."

"At Casterbridge Fair" A seven-part poem dated 1902 and published in TIME'S LAUGHINGSTOCKS (1909). The seven sections are vignettes of scenes at the fair, depicting the heartbreak, painful memories, and hopes (both futile and realized) of various people attending the festivities.

Part I, "The Ballad-Singer," presents a young man who addresses a singer of ballads. He entreats the singer to "start a country song" and sing "from your little book" to make him forget his loved one, who has broken his heart: "Make me forget those heart-breaks, achings, fears; / make me forget her name, her sweet sweet look— / Make me forget her tears."

Part II, "Former Beauties," expresses a man's astonishment that the middle-aged market women were once "pink young things" with whom he and his friends had danced "by the Froom" (the River Frome) and at "Budmouth shore."

Part III, "After the Club-Dance," is a lament by a young woman who regrets her intimacy with "that young man o'mine." Leaving the fair, she believes that the birds perched on roadside elms eye her with shame. She asks why they should judge her: "They, too, have done the same!"

Part IV, "The Market-Girl," depicts a girl attempting in vain to sell honey, apples, and bunches of herbs by the roadside. A young man notes her "sunburnt grace" and sympathizes with her lack of customers. Their conversation begins; he realizes "what the end of it all must be" and finds that, "though no others had bid, a prize had been won by me."

Part V, "The Inquiry," depicts a woman, Patty Beech, seeking a man called John Waywood, who once lived in Hermitage Road. She longs to know whether he is still there and, if so, whether he has ever asked where she might be, or how "she bears life's fag and fret/After so long a day?" They had once been engaged, and were to marry when he became successful, but waiting caused him to lose interest. Time "dooms man's love to die," even as it "Preserves a maid's alive."

Part VI, "A Wife Waits," portrays a patient wife waiting on the pavement while her husband, Will, is at a dance downstairs in the club room "Where the tall liquor-cups foam." She must "steady him home." Will is actually with a partner, a woman; "loving companions they be." He had told his wife, before they were married, that he loved only her. Nevertheless, he is dancing with another while the wife waits for him, "shivering."

Part VII, "After the Fair," depicts the empty market place when the fair is over. The streets no longer ring with the singers' voices, and people roam across Grey's Bridge into byways. The maiden who was shy all day "rattles and talks," but the one who was the "most swaggering there" is now sad. The High Street is peopled only by ghosts of its "buried burghees," going back to the "old Roman hosts/Who loved, laughed, and fought, hailed their friends, drank their toasts/At their meeting-times here, just as these!"

These fairs, which Hardy much enjoyed, were occasions for the hiring of agricultural workers. Originally held at CANDLEMAS, February 2, the fair was eventually moved to a day on or near February 14 and called St. Valentine's Fair. Although the day was festive, the hiring system resulted in insecurity and pain for many laborers, which Hardy describes in detail in "THE DORSETSHIRE LABORER." He praises the laborer, however: Even "if he is not hired, he maintains a "self-repressing mannerliness hardly to be found among any other class" when he talks with his more fortunate friends. Workers hired in February would move to their new posts on "Lady Day," or the Feast of the Annunciation, held in some parts of England, including Dorset, on April 6. There were booths set up for entertainment and food, sideshows, fortune-tellers, and livestock sales. A musical setting of the poem is in the collection of the DORSET COUNTY MUSEUM.

When the critic and poet Edward Thomas was compiling *This England: An Anthology from Her Writers* in 1915, he asked Hardy if he might use "The Sergeant's Song" (from WESSEX POEMS) and "The Spring Call." Hardy responded by asking him to choose the one he thought best for his purpose, for he was unclear about Thomas's primary aim. If Thomas were hoping to "represent a *mood* throughout—that mood being a buoyant one," Hardy said those two poems would be suitable, but if Thomas intended to "illustrate the idiosyncrasy of each writer," he suggested "WHEN I SET OUT FOR LYONNESSE," "TO MEET OR OTHERWISE," or "The Ballad-Singer" (*Letters* V, 87–88).

For further reading: Andrew David Cunningham, "Three Faces of 'Hodge': The Agricultural Labourer in Hardy's Work." *Dissertation Abstracts International*, 51.3 (Sept. 1990), 860A.

Athenaeum English periodical in which some of Thomas Hardy's poetry first appeared. The editor at the time was John Middleton Murry, who wrote Hardy in March 1919 that the young writers associated with the magazine "desire to sail under your flag" (*Letters* V, 298). Two stanzas of "ACCORDING TO THE MIGHTY WORKING" appeared in the issue of April 4, 1919. The poem "AT THE ENTERING OF THE NEW YEAR" was published there on December 31, 1920, and a third poem, "The MAID OF KEINTON-MANDEVILLE," appeared in the issue of April 30, 1920. Hardy also wrote several obituaries for the magazine.

The Athenaeum Club, Pall Mall, London   (Sarah Bird Wright)

Athenaeum Club   One of Thomas Hardy's LONDON clubs. He was elected to membership in April 1891. In 1884 Hardy had been introduced to Lady PORTSMOUTH, who was the sister-in-law of Lady CARNARVON (the countess of Carnarvon). As a result of this friendship, Lord CARNARVON sponsored him for the Athenaeum Club beginning in 1888, although it took three years for him to be elected. He was invited to join as a person of "distinguished merit" in the field of literature, and, from then on, frequently used the club as a highly respectable address for correspondence when in London (Millgate, *Thomas Hardy: A Biography*, 242, 266, 314).

Atlantic Monthly   This magazine, founded in Boston in 1857, has published a number of America's most outstanding writers since its inception. Thomas Bailey Aldrich, James Russell Lowell, James T. Fields, William Dean HOWELLS, Bliss Perry, and Ellery Sedgwick were among the noted editors during the late 19th and early 20th centuries.

In the fall of 1881 the editor of the *Atlantic Monthly*, Thomas Bailey Aldrich, requested a serial for the following year, and Hardy arranged for the magazine to begin serialization of *TWO ON A TOWER* in May 1882. This was a new novel he was beginning; he noted in the *Life* that the title was one he "afterwards disliked, though it was much imitated" *(Life,* 151). After serialization it was published in three volumes in 1882.

"At Lulworth Cove a Century Back"   Written in September 1920, this poem was collected in *LATE LYRICS AND EARLIER* (1922). It evokes the poet John Keats's September 1820 landing on the Dorset coast; Keats had set off for Rome in the hope of curing his consumption (tuberculosis). At that time Keats composed the sonnet "Bright Star! would I were steadfast as thou art."

Hardy imagines being present near Lulworth Cove and seeing Keats. Perceiving him as a "commonplace youth," he has a dialogue with Time, who asks insistently, *"You see that man?"* He responds with a description of Keats's physical appearance, but Time realizes that the significance of the poet is not apparent to the speaker; Keats's work will not be known in his lifetime. Time prophesies that Keats will go on to Rome, where he will experience despair and death. A century later the world "will follow him there,/And bend with reverence where his ashes lie."

The speaker "Time" represents Joseph Severn, Keats's friend, who accompanied him on his visit to Lulworth Cove aboard the ship *Maria Crowther*. It was that night, on the ship, that Keats wrote the sonnet "Bright star, would I were stedfast as thou art." Hardy made a drawing of the Cove in 1868, and his wife Emma Hardy did a watercolor painting of it in 1881 (Bailey, *The Poetry of Thomas Hardy*, 454–55). Hardy's concept of Keats as a "commonplace" youth, an "idling town-sort," may be based on the description given by his friend Mrs. Anne Benson PROCTER, who had met the poet in her youth (*Life*, 136).

"At Mayfair Lodgings" Poem published in *MOMENTS OF VISION* (1917) and inspired by a visit Hardy made to London in December 1894. He was staying in a room near the SAVILE CLUB, and, during a sleepless night, noticed a lighted window adjacent to his where someone was "in pain reclining." The next morning he discovered it had been a woman who had died during the night, "unpardoned, unadieu'd." She had grown up in a neighboring village and he had loved her "as a lass." He feels that if they had married the tragedy of her dying alone might have been averted. Critics have been unable to discover the identity of the girl.

"At Middle-Field Gate in February" Published in *MOMENTS OF VISION* (1917), this poem describes the appearance of a gate and field along Bockhampton Lane in a wintery fog, with damp droplets "like silver buttons" ranged along the gate bars; they "fall at the feeblest jog," while the plowed furrows of the field are in "raw rolls, clammy and clogging." He contrasts this scene with that on a day long past, when field women were working "in curtained bonnets and light array"; once engaged in "amorous play," they now lie underground. When asked who they were, Hardy identified them as Unity Sargent, Susan Chamberlain, Esther Oliver, Emma Shipton, Anna Barrett, Ann West, Elizabeth Hurden, Eliza Trevis, and others—all were young women when he was a child. The gate was probably one near the old Roman road near Hardy's birthplace (Bailey, *The Poetry of Thomas Hardy*, 380–81).

"At Rushy-Pond" Collected in *HUMAN SHOWS, FAR PHANTASIES, SONGS, AND TRIFLES* (1925), this is one of the most haunting of Hardy's poems. The speaker stands in the moonlight by Rushy-Pond, which is on Puddletown Heath, near Hardy's boyhood home at HIGHER BOCKHAMPTON. The pond is "frigid" and the wind blows with a "husky croon" from the north. The pond reflects the moon, but not in a benign, romantic way; It has "stretched it to oval form" and then "corkscrewed it like a wriggling worm."

The speaker is preoccupied by a relationship with a woman in a "secret year" to whom he had called across the pond. He had courted her ardently until the last "weak love-words" were said and "ended was her time." The "bloomage of her prime" has been blurred; she is now only a "troubled orb in the pond's sad shine." She has withdrawn from him, and her days have "dropped out of mine."

Critics have speculated that the woman is Tryphena SPARKS, whom Hardy courted as a young man, although she was 11 years younger than he. Two scholars, Lois Deacon and Terry Coleman, in their book *Providence and Mr. Hardy*, argued that Hardy and Tryphena had been engaged. (Tryphena married Charles Frederick Gale and had four children.) Another scholar, F. R. Southerington, was convinced Hardy and Tryphena had had an illegitimate son. Those who subscribe to these theories find support for them in this poem, since the phrase "ended was her time" might be construed as referring to her pregnancy, and much in the poem suggests that the poet was disconsolate over the relationship.

"At the Entering of the New Year" This poem is dated "31 December. During the War" (WORLD WAR I), but it was not published until December 31, 1920, in the *ATHENAEUM*; it was later included in *LATE LYRICS AND EARLIER* (1922). John Middleton Murry, editor of the *Athenaeum*, requested a poem; Hardy felt that in some ways the world was still threatened by the war (Bailey, *The Poetry of Thomas Hardy*, 470).

The poem is divided into two parts, I ("Old Style") and II ("New Style"). The first section depicts Hardy's experience during his carefree country youth, during peacetime, as he and his friends dance "allemands" (German dances), "heys" (country dances), and "poussettings" (circling around with linked hands). They sing together to welcome the New Year, a "Youth of Promise," their "rhythmic throbbings" floating out through the casement windows.

In the second section, war has ravaged the populace; they hear the "muffled peal" of church bells and think of "bereaved Humanity." This time the New Year will not bring joy but suffering, and it is better not to know what will happen: "Must we avow what we would close confine?" the speaker asks.

"At the Piano" Poem published in *MOMENTS OF VISION* (1917). A young woman is playing the piano by candlelight as a man looks on. He is entranced by the "mould of her face," and her hair, on which the rays of the two candles fall. He is unaware of the "Apparition" that comes "pushing between" them, which causes the lights to "burn pale." She sees no "bale" and he has no "monition" [premonition] of a dark time in the future as the "Phantom," or apparition, hides nearby and Time, personified, laughs "awry."

The poem is thought by critics to have two possible associations. The first is Hardy's recollection of Emma's playing the piano in the rectory at ST. JULIOT CHURCH when he first met her. The "Apparition," of which he had no inkling at the time, is her mental illness, which is also the subject of a poem called "The Interloper." The second is "THE LAST PERFORMANCE," in which the "Apparition" is her approaching death, of which she had no foreknowledge (Bailey, *The Poetry of Thomas Hardy*, 411–12).

"At the Railway Station, Upway"   Poem published in *LATE LYRICS AND EARLIER* (1922). It is set outside the railway station in the village of Upway (Hardy's name for a village north of the coastal town of WEYMOUTH). A man in handcuffs and his companion, a constable, are waiting for the train. A small boy with a violin says he has no money to give the prisoner, but can play his fiddle to him. The prisoner responds by singing "This life so free/Is the thing for me!"

The prisoner would have been on his way to the county jail at DORCHESTER (Pinion, *A Commentary on the Poems of Thomas Hardy*, 175).

"At the Word 'Farewell'"   Poem published in *MOMENTS OF VISION* (1916). Hardy was in CORNWALL in March 1870 and had met his future wife, Emma Gifford (*see* HARDY, Emma Gifford). She was the sister-in-law of the rector of ST. JULIOT CHURCH, which he was restoring. The poem was written on his journey home either after this visit or after the one following.

The morning of his departure, Emma had arranged for Hardy to have breakfast. He observed her from his window out on the lawn, looking "like a bird from a cloud/On the clammy lawn," before a house with "candles alight in the room/For my parting meal." He had no sense at the time that they would later marry. He stepped outside to say goodbye, followed her on "By an alley bare boughs overspread," and kissed her. He reflects, on his way home, that he might not have fallen in love with her except that "one cheek of hers burned When we came in together."

"August Midnight, An"   Poem dated 1899 and published in *POEMS OF THE PAST AND THE PRESENT* (1902). It was written at MAX GATE, Thomas Hardy's home in DORSET. The poet is attempting to write at night by a window, only to find his work interrupted by insects. They "besmear" his newly written line or fly into the lamp and fall, stunned. The poet feels superior to "God's humblest," but then realizes such creatures

know "Earth-secrets" that he does not; their perceptions of the world are distinct and separate.

Austin, Sir Alfred (1835–1913)   English poet (poet laureate 1896–1913) and author of 20 volumes of verse, including *Sacred and Profane Love* (1908). On Austin's death Hardy was one of the poets considered to succeed him, along with Rudyard KIPLING and Robert Bridges: the latter became the new poet laureate. Hardy did not like writing to order and might well have refused the post, which required the writing of commemorative poems.

Austin was editor, with W. J. Courthope, of the literary periodical *National Review;* the first issue appeared in March 1883. In December 1882 he had asked Hardy for a contribution, but Hardy replied that he had nothing ready at present "beyond what has been arranged for" (*Letters* I, 111). After publication of Austin's *Lyrical Poems* (1891), Hardy wrote a congratulatory letter, calling him a "master of expression" (*Letters* I, 238). In February 1892 he wrote Austin to thank him for sending a review of *TESS OF THE D'URBERVILLES* that had been published in the *National Review;* he felt the author had shown a "generous feeling" (*Letters* I, 258).

Authors' Club of London   London club for distinguished writers, possibly located at 40 Dover St. Hardy was a member. In 1893 he wrote the author Oswald Crawfurd that he hoped to come in "after dinner" on Monday, May 8, although he had nothing he could offer to read or be read. Dinners were given in honor of distinguished writers. On September 28, 1923, Emile ZOLA was honored with a dinner, which Hardy apparently planned to attend, but he did not go. In 1899 the club held a dinner in honor of Mark Twain, who gave a witty speech.

Authors' Club of New York   This New York literary society was founded in 1882 by Brander Matthews, Edward Eggleston, E.C. Stedman, R.W. Gilder, and other members of the "Genteel Circle" of literary writers and editors. In 1908 club members elected Thomas Hardy to honorary membership. On December 31, 1908, Hardy wrote the historian Duffield Osborne a letter thanking him for the "interesting" club yearbook (*Letters* III, 364).

autobiography and Hardy   Hardy used the Victorian convention of the pseudonymous biography in writing his own autobiography, which is referred to as the *Life*. It was first published in two volumes: *The Early Life of Thomas Hardy, 1840–1891* and *The Later Years of Thomas Hardy, 1892–1928*. The two volumes were combined in a single edition in 1962 as *The Life of Thomas Hardy* by Florence Emily HARDY (his second wife). Florence Hardy only wrote the final chapter, Chapter 38, "The Last Scene," covering 1926 through January 1928, when Hardy died. All page numbers to the *Life* are to this edition, in which both volumes are combined.

As Rosemarie Morgan points out, Hardy was well aware of structural and textual requirements for autobiography, with all experience filtered through the mode of a first-person narrator. He chose to write from the more objective point of view of a disinterested observer, even though it was, to some extent, contrived. Morgan states that Victorians were shocked by the "first mass privacy invasion by the press," and the pseudonymous biography was a popular resource for resisting such an invasion. It permits a certain degree of camouflaging of emotions and "reported speech." Hardy detested the "biographer" who claimed "close knowledge" of his life and person (Morgan, personal communication with the author).

In her "Prefatory Note" to the *Life*, Florence Hardy states that once Hardy agreed that he should record his experiences and the facts of his career, he began writing down chapter headings and memories of his early days. He also communicated his memories verbally, which she wrote down. She states that "in the book generally Mr. Hardy's own reminiscent phrases have been used or approximated to whenever they could be remembered or were written down at the time of their expression *viva voce*." She points out that many "trivial" experiences were included, because they "embody customs and manners of old West-of-England life that have now entirely passed away."

The fiction that virtually all of the *Life* was recorded by Florence Hardy was exposed by the bibliographer Richard L. PURDY. In a lecture at the Grolier Club, New York, on April 25, 1940, he reported that it was Hardy's work, even though Florence Hardy's name was on the title page and it was written in the third person, as though she were her husband's biographer.

Ball, Cain Character in *FAR FROM THE MADDING CROWD*. Cain, or "Cainy," Ball is a farm boy whose confused mother thought Abel killed Cain in the biblical story. Although "the parson put it right," it was too late to change her son's name within the parish. After Bathsheba EVERDENE goes to Bath, Cain, whose thumb has had a "felon" (joint inflammation) rendering him unable to work, also goes there. He returns to tell Gabriel OAK and the other harvesters that he has seen Bathsheba and a soldier walking along together, then sitting in a park.

Balliol Players (Oxford) An undergraduate theater group at OXFORD UNIVERSITY. In July 1924, when Thomas Hardy was 84, the players visited MAX GATE and performed an English version of Aeschylus' trilogy *Oresteia*, titled *The Curse of the House of Atreus*, on the lawn. The audience consisted of Thomas and Florence HARDY and Harley and Helen GRANVILLE-BARKER. Since it was daytime, the players carried spikes of a giant flowering spiraea instead of lighted torches. Hardy notes in the *Life* that the players had arrived on bicycles, but sent their theatrical properties in "a lorry that sometimes broke down" (*Life*, 426). On June 29, 1926, they gave another performance at Max Gate, *Hippolytus* of Euripides, and, on July 6, 1927, *Iphigenia in Aulis* (Roberts, *Hardy's Poetic Drama*, 6–7).

The Balliol Players, Oxford, performing Aeschylus' trilogy The Oresteia *at Max Gate in July 1924* (Beinecke Rare Book and Manuscript Library, Yale University)

In an unpublished account of the productions at Max Gate, Helen Granville-Barker wrote that the high hedges substituted for "wings, woodwork, and background" and the lawn, trees, and sky were in lieu of a painted canvas backdrop. There were some incongruities, such as the actor with a "hairy chest" and "deep bass voice" playing the role of Phèdre. Hardy sat apart with a translation of Euripedes' text, following the speeches. In one production of *Oresteia*, Anthony "Puffin" Asquith, who later became a film director and actor, played the roles of Clytemnestra, Orestes' old nurse, and the leading Fury.

For further reading: Roberts, *Hardy's Poetic Drama.*

"Barbara of the House of Grebe" Short story. *See GROUP OF NOBLE DAMES, A.*

Barnes, Robert Graphic artist who was on the staff of the *GRAPHIC* and illustrated *The MAYOR OF CASTERBRIDGE*. Jackson remarks that Barnes "delineated character with considerable skill, and he was also able to come to grips with the dramatic situation" (Jackson, *Illustration and the Novels of Thomas Hardy*, 55). Unfortunately, his artistic ability was never fully recognized in his day.

Barnes, Rev. William (1801–1886) Dorset poet and philologist. He was a friend of Thomas Hardy's from the time of Hardy's youth until Barnes's death. Barnes kept school next door to the architectural offices of John HICKS in DORCHESTER, where in 1856 Hardy began studying as an apprentice. Henry BASTOW was already working there, and would become one of Hardy's closest friends. Bastow and Hardy began reading Latin and Greek together, and Hardy would often consult Barnes on points of grammar.

In 1864 Barnes gave up his school and became rector of Winterborne-Came-cum-Whitcombe (near the site where Hardy would later build their home, MAX GATE). Barnes published several collections of dialect verse, in 1844, 1859, and 1862, as well as a single volume of poems, *Poems of Rural Life in the Dorset Dialect* (Kegan Paul) in 1879 (*Letters* III, 292–93). In 1908 Hardy made a selection from these poems for publication by the Clarendon Press, Oxford, at the request of the critic and essayist Walter Alexander Raleigh, a consultant for the press. Barnes's son, the Rev. W. Miles

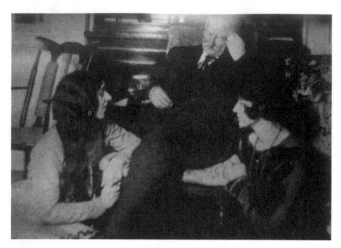

*Gwen Ffrangçon-Davies with Thomas Hardy and an
unidentified cast member of the Hardy Players at Max Gate*
(Mrs. Thomas Uber, North Kingston, Rhode Island and the Dorset
County Museum, Dorchester)

Barnes (1840–1916), first verbally granted, then later
withheld, permission for one poem Hardy wished to
include. Hardy wrote Charles Cannan of the press that
Miles had withdrawn his "original cheerful permission"
and was imposing conditions which, though "of a trifling kind . . . have become unexpectedly troublesome"
(*Letters* III, 337–8). The anthology (*Selected Poems of
William Barnes*, 1908) was published with a poem Hardy
chose as a substitute.

Barnes died in October 1886, and as Hardy walked
along the path from Max Gate to attend his funeral an
incident occurred to which he later alluded in the
poem "The LAST SIGNAL." He wrote an obituary notice
for Barnes for the *ATHENAEUM*, which later became the
source for Barnes's entry in the *Dictionary of National
Biography* (*Life*, 183). In 1886 Hardy corresponded with
W. Miles Barnes about a memorial to his father, which
took the form of a statue that stands today outside St.
Peter's Church, Dorchester (*Letters* I, 155).

For further reading: W. J. Keith, "Thomas Hardy's Edition of William Barnes."

Barnes Theatre   On September 7, 1925, a dramatization of *TESS OF THE D'URBERVILLES* opened at the Barnes
Theatre, near London, south of the Thames between
Mortlake and Putney, produced by Philip RIDGEWAY.
Gwen Ffrangçon-Davies played Tess. Hardy remarks in
the *Life* that he "had not sufficient strength" to attend
the performance. After a run of two months, it moved
to the Garrick Theatre, London, where the 100th performance took place (*Life*, 428; *see* Appendix II, Media
Adaptations of the Works of Thomas Hardy).

On September 8, 1926, the Barnes Theatre mounted
a production of *The MAYOR OF CASTERBRIDGE*, dramatized
by John Drinkwater.

Barrie, Sir James Matthew (1860–1937)   Scottish novelist and dramatist best known for the play *Peter Pan.*
He became a close friend of Thomas Hardy's and especially of Hardy's second wife, Florence HARDY. In April
1893 Barrie suggested that Hardy make a one-act play
from his story "The THREE STRANGERS." Hardy had
thought of doing so, and went to work; on June 3, 1893,
his play "The THREE WAYFARERS" was produced by
Charles Charrington at Terry's Theatre, LONDON, as
one of three. In June 1893 Hardy and his first wife,
Emma, attended Barrie's play *Walker, London,* and in
October 1916 Barrie came to Dorchester to see a performance of *Wessex Scenes,* an extract from *The DYNASTS.*
Hardy stayed with the Barries in February 1919 in London and attended, with Barrie, the annual dinner of
the ROYAL ACADEMY OF ARTS.

On January 10, 1928, as Hardy lay critically ill at
MAX GATE, Barrie came to the house to try to lend any
assistance he could, although he did not speak with
Hardy before he died the next evening. Barrie and Sir
Sydney COCKERELL, Hardy's literary executor, arranged
that Hardy be cremated and his ashes interred at Westminster Abbey (Hardy had planned to be buried at
STINSFORD CHURCH). Hardy's heart was removed
before cremation and buried at Stinsford Church in
the grave of his first wife, Emma Gifford HARDY. Barrie
was one of six pallbearers representing Literature (the
others were John GALSWORTHY, Sir Edmund GOSSE,
A. E. HOUSMAN, Rudyard KIPLING, and George Bernard
SHAW) on Monday, January 16, when Hardy's ashes
were buried in Poets' Corner, Westminster Abbey, London; the service here was one of three held simultaneously. The other two were at STINSFORD CHURCH and
ST. PETER'S CHURCH, DORCHESTER.

Barron, Louis (1847–1914)   French journalist to
whom, in 1893, Hardy had assigned the right to translate *TESS OF THE D'URBERVILLES.* Barron was to publish
his translation in a daily paper or review beginning
not later than December 6, 1894, and to pay Hardy
£10 when it began running. On June 11, 1897, Hardy
wrote the French translator Madeleine ROLLAND that
these conditions had not been met. He gave Rolland
permission to translate the novel and to publish her
translation, which appeared in the *Débats* (*Letters* II,
164–65).

"Barthélémon at Vauxhall"   A poem first published in
the London *Times* on July 23, 1921, and collected in
LATE LYRICS AND EARLIER (1922). According to a note
supplied by Hardy at the beginning, it is based on a
hymn melody written about 1780 by François Hippolite
Barthélémon, who was first-fiddler at Vauxhall Gardens, London (these were opened in Lambeth, London, about 1661, and were the site of fireworks, music,
suppers, and other entertainments). Hardy is dramatiz-

ing a scene he visualized when Barthélémon was composing a "strain to Ken"—that is, Bishop Ken, who wrote the words. Hardy imagined the musician in London returning from an evening of performing in a popular music hall in Vauxhall, pausing on Westminster Bridge to see the sun rise, and then being inspired to write a lofty hymn. Hardy states that it was "probably the most popular morning hymn-tune ever written"; it had been one of his boyhood favorites, although it was sung less often in his later years. Hardy had misgivings about the poem itself. On July 6, 1921, he wrote his friend Walter de la Mare that he was correcting the proofs of "a wretchedly bad poem, that nobody wanted me to write nobody wants to read & nobody will remember who reads it" (*Letters* VI, 95).

When Hardy attended St. Peter's Church, Dorchester, the year he died (1928), the first hymn sung was always "Awake My Soul & with the Sun." It was also sung at the June 1940 memorial services for Hardy, held at STINSFORD CHURCH, Dorset (Bailey, *The Poetry of Thomas Hardy*, 434).

Bastow, Henry (unknown) Fellow pupil of Thomas Hardy in the DORCHESTER office of architect John HICKS in the late 1850s. Bastow, was about three years older than Hardy. At the time, he was closest friend; they read Latin and Greek together. Hardy was hoping to obtain entrance to a university (the lack of a degree caused him an enduring sense of "inferiority and resentment," according to Michael Millgate). Raised at Bridport in a Baptist family, Bastow was baptized and admitted to the Dorchester Baptist congregation, but failed to convert Hardy, despite their frequent discussions of religion (Millgate, *Thomas Hardy: A Biography*, 55, 64). These often took place in the enclosure in Kingston Maurward eweleaze, or sheep pasture, now a cricket ground. Bastow left at the end of his four years as a pupil and eventually went to Tasmania to practice as an architect. In November 1926, in failing health, Hardy told his second wife, Florence, that if he were to live his life again he would "prefer to be a small architect in a country town, like Mr. Hicks at Dorchester." He then reminisced about Henry Bastow, who, he reflected, would be nearly 90 if alive; he assumed he was and living in Australia (*Life*, 31, 443).

"Beeny Cliff" (March 1870–March 1913) Poem published in SATIRES OF CIRCUMSTANCE (1914) evoking two visits Hardy made to Beeny Cliff, in Cornwall. The first was in March 1870, with Emma Gifford (see HARDY, Emma Gifford), who rode her mare, Fanny, while Hardy walked beside her. To him she was "The woman whom I loved so, and who loyally loved me." They "laughed light-heartedly aloft"; possibly Hardy had run down between the chasms in the cliff and was looking up at the silhouette of Emma on her pony

against the sky. A shower came, after which "the Atlantic dyed its levels with a dull misfeatured stain," before the sun burst out from the clouds. In 1913, a year after Emma's death, Hardy returned to the scene alone. He recalls his March 1870 visit to Cornwall. Beeny Cliff has its old "chasmal beauty"; he wonders if he and Emma might ultimately return there in some form and say "anew" the "sweet things" they uttered that March.

Yet even if the "wild weird western shore" still looms in an altered world, the woman he had shared the scene with "nor knows nor cares for Beeny, and will laugh there nevermore."

F. B. Pinion points out that each verse is a separate unit: the second contains sounds "with fine onomatopoeic effects," as when the waves "seemed far away . . . engrossed in saying their ceaseless babbling say,/As we laughed light-heartedly aloft." The third is devoted to changes in the scenery of Beeny Cliff. The fourth stanza, with its felicitous choice of the verb "bulks," perfectly captures the monumental presence of Beeny Cliff:"—Still in all its chasmal beauty bulks old Beeny to the sky." The last verse is linked to the fourth: "What if still in chasmal beauty looms that wild weird western shore." Throughout the poem Hardy makes skillful use of alliteration.

In 1897 the editor of the SATURDAY REVIEW asked Hardy what he would consider the best scenery. Hardy listed, among five locations, "The coast from Trebarwith Strand to Beeny Cliff, Cornwall" (*Life*, 295).

Beerbohm, Sir Max (1872–1956) English essayist and caricaturist, a noted figure during the Gay Nineties in London. He and his wife were friends of Thomas Hardy's. In March 1900 Beerbohm was drama critic of the SATURDAY REVIEW, and he sent Hardy information about the dramatization of TESS OF THE D'URBERVILLES by H. A. Kennedy. Hardy had publicly disclaimed any participation in the adaptation, the rights for which had been given to the dramatist Lorimer STODDARD. He told him he had pleasure in reading his remarks on the Wessex novels (*Letters* VI, 133).

In 1904 Beerbohm and Hardy were both guests at a dinner at the home of Edmund GOSSE. Beerbohm reviewed The DYNASTS in 1909. He found that "the scale and mode of presentation had the effect of reducing the individual historical figures to the stature of marionettes"; to him the Wessex peasants were "the only genuinely human figures" (Millgate, *Thomas Hardy: A Biography*, 431). In April 1913 there was an exhibition of Beerbohm's cartoons at the Leicester Gallery, London. Hardy sent his tickets for the opening to his friend Edward CLODD, with a note, "The show will no doubt be amusing" (*Letters* IV, 264). In June 1923, Hardy notes in the *Life*, Mr. and Mrs. Harley GRANVILLE-BARKER brought the Beerbohms to MAX GATE.

For further reading: Wilson, "Aldous Huxley and Max Beerbohm's Hardy."

"Before and After Summer" Poem written in 1910 and first published in the *New Weekly* on April 4, 1914. It was collected in SATIRES OF CIRCUMSTANCE (1914). The first of its two stanzas presents a fleeting preview of the summer to come as glimpsed on a windy February day when sleet and late snows constitute a "half-transparent blind" through which the rays of the sun shine faintly, or, as the second stanza points out, are "fore-discerned."

In the subsequent stanza, the poet sees shadows of an "October pine" reach into "this room of mine," possibly his study. A bird swings from the pine tree, oblivious of the approaching winter. Just as the bird "bills no word," the poet is also "blank." The pleasures of the summer's "happy suns" have disappeared gradually and imperceptibly.

The poem was set to music in *Before and After Summer: Ten Songs for Baritone and Piano* (London: Boosey & Hawkes, 1949). Evidently Hardy did not care for the poem, considering it a "little scrap," and hoped that Scott James would not publish it in the *New Weekly* (Bailey, *The Poetry of Thomas Hardy*, 290).

"Before Life and After" Published in TIME'S LAUGHINGSTOCKS (1909), this poem comments on the benign indifference and self-sufficiency of the earth before human life, when there was no one to suffer "sickness, love, or loss" or to experience "regret, starved hope, or heart-burnings."

Human beings, and their feelings, appear in the poem as malignant forces; when they "germed" the entire universe of "primal rightness" took on the "tinct of wrong." The poet longs for a time before knowledge—a time of "nescience"—and wonders how long it will before such a time can be "reaffirmed."

James O. Bailey states that the theme is based on Eduard Von Hartmann's theory of the Immanent Will as expressed in his *Philosophy of the Unconscious,* which had a strong influence on Hardy. The Immanent Will, when it comes into being, will "amend all injustice or discreate the universe." The idea that "reflective consciousness" is a source of evil may also be found in *The RETURN OF THE NATIVE* and *The DYNASTS.*

The poem was set to music by Benjamin Britten in *Winter Words* (New York: Boosey and Hawkes, 1954 [Bailey, *The Poetry of Thomas Hardy*, 248]).

Belgium In May and June, 1876, Thomas Hardy and his wife Emma Gifford HARDY went to the Low Countries, visiting Rotterdam and several cities along the Rhine, returning to England via Metz, Brussels, and Antwerp. They were not to visit the country again until September 1896, when they made a second journey to Belgium. At Dover a cyclist ran into Emma and injured her shoulder, forcing the Hardys to delay their departure for Belgium. Eventually they crossed to Ostend and stayed in Bruges, "a bygone, melancholy interesting town," as Hardy wrote his friend Florence HENNIKER. The Hardys then went on to Dinant, Liège, and Brussels.

While in Brussels, Hardy answered a correspondent, Bertram WINDLE, who proposed to write a handbook giving a key to Hardy's place names and their corresponding actual places (*see* PLACE NAMES). Hardy compiled a list covering several pages, prefacing it with a warning, underlined twice: "For private reference only—not to be printed in this form." (*Letters* II, 130–31).

Belgravia London periodical, owned by the publishers CHATTO & WINDUS, in which *The RETURN OF THE NATIVE* was serialized from January to December 1878. In August 1877 Hardy wrote the *Belgravia* editor, the novelist Mary Elizabeth Braddon, that he was sending it early in order to allow time for "full proofs," and that he was also sending it to HARPER'S MONTHLY MAGAZINE, which would be publishing it in America. He added, "should the artist be willing to receive a rough sketch of any unusual objects which come into the story, I shall be happy to furnish them" (*Letters* I, 50–51; *see* HOPKINS, Arthur).

Belmaine, Mrs. Society woman in *The HAND OF ETHELBERTA* who is very kind to Ethelberta PETHERWIN. They attend the boat races together, and visit St. Giles Church, Cripplegate, to see the tomb of John MILTON.

Bencomb, Marcia Daughter of Mr. Bencomb in *The WELL-BELOVED,* who owns the Best-Bed Stone Company, a rival of the father of Jocelyn PIERSTON, who also has a prosperous stone-cutting business. She wants to marry Jocelyn, but her father refuses permission. Hardy suggests that their fathers' rivalry casts Jocelyn as the "son of the Montagues" and Marcia as the "daughter of the Capulets." She marries a gentleman from Jersey, a widower whose stepson, Henri LEVERRE, eventually marries the granddaughter of Avice CARO. After she is widowed in later years she marries Jocelyn.

"Benighted Travellers" First title of "The HONOURABLE LAURA"; *see GROUP OF NOBLE DAMES, A.* The story was published as "Benighted Travellers" in the *Bolton Weekly Journal* on December 17, 1881, and, in America, in *Harper's Weekly,* December 10 and 17, 1881 (Purdy, *Thomas Hardy: A Bibliographical Study*, 64).

Benson, A(rthur) C(hristopher) (1862–1925) One of the sons of Edward White Benson, archbishop of Canterbury, and brother of the popular novelist E. F. Benson, Arthur Christopher Benson was an educator and a man of letters. He was a fellow, and later master, of Magdalene College, Cambridge; author of a biography of his father; coeditor of the correspondence of Queen Victoria; and set words to Edward Elgar's first "Pomp and Circumstance" March as "Land of Hope and Glory." Hardy became an honorary fellow of Magdalene College while Benson was master. In July 1892 Hardy wrote to thank him for the gift of his poems and invited him to visit MAX GATE if he were ever in the vicinity. Benson did visit him, in the company of Edmund GOSSE, on September 5, 1912.

In the autumn of 1913, after Emma HARDY's death, Fuller MAITLAND made a sketch-painting of Hardy for Benson, which was hung with the other portraits in the hall of Magdalene College. In February 1914 Hardy married Florence Emily Dugdale (HARDY), and Benson wrote Hardy a letter about the marriage. Hardy replied in March 1914, saying "it touches me much to know that you & my brethren of the College have been interested in my marriage & have shown such good will concerning it" (*Letters* V, 18).

"Bereft" Poem dated 1901 and published in *TIME'S LAUGHINGSTOCKS* (1909). It takes the form of a poignant lament by a widowed farm woman for her late husband and an evocation of their life together. She will miss small gestures and moments that were almost unmarked during his lifetime. No longer will he strike a light at 5 A.M., the time he used to rise, or draw the curtain aside at the dawn of a summer day and announce to her that "the morning is bright." On market day he will not be waiting at Grey's Bridge for her to finish her shopping. When the supper crock is steaming and "the time is the time of his tread" she will sit by the fire "in a silence as of the dead." She will "leave the door unbarred" and the "clock unwound" and make her "lone bed hard," but wishes that bed were "underground."

Bernhardt, Sarah (1844–1923) Noted French actress, born Rosine Bernard. Hardy was invited to meet her in June 1901 at the home of the novelist and poet Maurice Henry Hewlett. Shortly thereafter, on June 25, Hardy sent Bernhardt a copy of *TESS OF THE D'URBERVILLES*. He recalled meeting her, and asked if she might like to read the novel. He suggested that she dramatize the novel in French and that she play the lead character.

Hardy notes in the *Life* that the novel's publication had brought letters from many prominent actresses offering to play the role of Tess, including (in addition to Bernhardt) Ellen TERRY, Mrs. Patrick CAMPBELL, and Eleanora Duse.

Besant, Sir Walter (1836–1901) Novelist and writer concerned with the economics of the publishing profession. In 1879 he founded the RABELAIS CLUB as "a declaration for virility in literature." In 1879, after publication of *The RETURN OF THE NATIVE*, he invited Hardy to join the club as "the author of the most original the most virile and most humorous of all modern novels." Hardy responded that he was pleased to be asked, but remarked that he could not pass an examination on Rabelais.

In December 1879, Hardy attended the inaugural dinner of the club at the Tavistock Hotel, London, which he described at length in the *Life*. He found the setting "cheerless" and "gloomy." Other guests included Besant, Sir Patrick Colquhoun, and the American author Charles Leland. "Altogether," Hardy concluded, "we were as Rabelaisian as it was possible to be in the foggy circumstances, though I succeeded but poorly." He added that Henry JAMES had been rejected as a member because he had failed to produce a "virile work of the imagination" (*Life*, 132). Michael Millgate states that his election to the club put Hardy in touch with "a whole series of second- and third-rate metropolitan littérateurs," but observes that in the 1860s this had been exactly the literary life to which he had aspired, as they were the counterparts of the "earlier worlds" depicted in Thackeray's *Pendennis* and in Horace MOULE's conversations (Millgate, *Thomas Hardy: A Biography*, 196).

Besant also founded the INCORPORATED SOCIETY OF AUTHORS, PLAYWRIGHTS, AND COMPOSERS and was a strong defender of authors' rights. In 1889 he proposed to establish the Authors' Syndicate, a literary agency that would work in tandem with the Incorporated Society of Authors. He described the scheme to Hardy, who replied that he welcomed any scheme "to form a ring to keep up prices" (*Letters* VII, 111).

In June 1891 Hardy spent a weekend at Aldeburgh, on the Suffolk coast, at the home of a new friend, Edward CLODD, a banker and author of works of popular science and anthropology; Walter Besant and J. M. BARRIE were fellow guests (*Life*, 315).

"Beyond the Last Lamp" *(New Tooting Common)* Poem published under the title "Night in a Suburb" in *Harper's New Monthly Magazine* (New York) for December 1911 and later collected in *SATIRES OF CIRCUMSTANCE* (1914). It is based on one of Hardy's memories from the time he and Emma lived at The Larches, No. 1 Arundel Terrace, Trinity Road, Upper Tooting (1878–81). As he walks, one rainy day, across Tooting Common, an area of about 150 acres, he passes a pair of sad "linked loiterers" constrained by "some heavy thought." They "seemed lovers," but were "absorbed/In mental scenes no longer orbed/By love's young rays." Their apparent love is now overshadowed by other cares—possibly related to illness or death. Hardy allows the leader to speculate as he does. Returning at night several hours "beyond the droop of day" he discovers the two people still pacing slowly and sadly. He still wonders about the "mysterious tragic pair" 30 years later. Although the actual lane probably no longer exists, he returns to it in memory and wonders about the pair, "Creeping slowly, creeping sadly . . . brooding on their pain."

James O. Bailey observes that Hardy draws on this memory in creating the scene in TESS OF THE D'URBERVILLES when Tess follows Angel out into the night after he rejects her. One of the cottagers, seeing them walk one behind the other, as in a funeral procession, recalls the scene long afterward (Bailey, *The Poetry of Thomas Hardy,* 272).

Bible, the   As a child, Hardy attended church every Sunday and, at home, wrapped himself in vestments made of a tablecloth, stood on a chair, and read Morning Prayer (a cousin from across the street gave the responses and his grandmother was the congregation). His attendance at church contributed to the two great passions of his life: words and music. Many of the verse forms he used later were based on Isaac Watts's hymns (Gittings, *Young Thomas Hardy,* 26–27). As a young adult Hardy was a devout Anglican and reader of the King James version of the Bible. He and his friend Henry BASTOW, with whom he worked during the late 1850s in the DORCHESTER office of the architect John HICKS, had many religious discussions. Bastow tried, in vain, to convert Hardy to his own Baptist faith. Once Bastow moved to Australia, however, his evangelical influence faded. Throughout his life, especially between 1860 and 1861, Hardy made a habit of annotating both Bibles and prayer books. When he left the office of John Hicks and went to London in April 1862, a significant professional move, he made many notations in his copies of both. In 1864, when in DORSET, he began a notebook, "Studies, Specimens &c.," with many quotations from the Old Testament as well as from Shakespeare, William Wordsworth, Percy Bysshe Shelley, his friend William BARNES, Algernon Charles SWINBURNE, and others (Millgate, 73, 87). Hardy was greatly inspired by the family of the Reverend Henry MOULE, and especially by his friendship with Moule's eldest son, Henry Joseph MOULE (Millgate, *Thomas Hardy: A Biography,* 64–66).

Hardy became engaged to Emma Gifford (HARDY) during the summer of 1870, but in the opinion of many critics, he had considerable doubts about the wisdom of the betrothal. Throughout the fall he reread much of the New Testament, marking passages that suggested his ambivalence about Emma. In 1872 he and Emma went to the ST. JULIOT CHURCH, now restored, in Cornwall, on which Hardy had been working when they met, and he read the lessons for the day, Jeremiah 36 and Romans 9, making notations in both his Bible and his prayer book. He and Emma were married in September 1874 and, on his 59th birthday, in June 1899, Emma gave him a Bible (Millgate, 146, 399).

Hardy had a thorough knowledge of the Bible, reflected in much of his fiction and poetry. He notes, in the *Life,* that the narrative quality of the Bible is remarkable: "in these Bible lives and adventures there is the spherical completeness of perfect art" (*Life, Thomas Hardy,* 171). For further discussion of Hardy's religious views *see* RELIGION.

bicycling   Hardy did not, apparently, take up bicycling until he was in his mid-50s. Before that, he had developed an interest in adult tricycles. In 1889 he wrote Alfred PARSONS: "I wish you would *tri*cycle. We wd then scour the country" (*Letters* I, 151, 186). A few years later he graduated to bicycling, a sport his wife Emma Gifford HARDY had long enjoyed. In a letter provisionally dated February 1896, he wrote Emma: "I have seen the loveliest 'Byke' for myself—wd suit me admirably— 'The Rover Cob.' It is £20! I can't tell if I ought to have it" (*Letters* II, 109). Apparently he did acquire it, because by July of the same year he wrote a friend, "I have almost forgotten there is such a pursuit as literature in the arduous study of—bicycling!—which my wife is making me learn to keep her company, she doing it rather well (*Letters* II, 106).

By 1897 Hardy was traveling about the countryside on his bicycle; he cycled several times to inspect the White Horse Inn, Maiden Newton, in October, and wrote Thackeray TURNER, the secretary of the SOCIETY FOR THE PROTECTION OF ANCIENT BUILDINGS, that he had incurred no expenses in traveling since his visits had been made on a bicycle.

Five years later, in May 1902, he treated himself to "a bran-new [*sic*] free wheel bicycle," though he wrote Edward CLODD that "no respectable person seems to ride one any longer." That fall he cycled to the Vale of Blackmoor, though, already, he complained that automobiles were "rather a nuisance to humble roadsters like me, one never knowing whether the comers are Hooligan-motorists or responsible drivers" (*Letters* III, 20, 33). He was not altogether intimidated, however; two years later he asked Edmund GOSSE, who was coming to MAX GATE for a visit, to bring a bicycle if he had one.

In October 1908 the American writer May Sinclair, who had written Hardy and received an invitation to call at Max Gate, came to stay at Wareham with an American friend, Mary Moss (the author of an article on Hardy). Hardy bicycled with May Sinclair to WEYMOUTH.

Hardy continued his bicycling; the last mention of it in his letters is in May 1920, when he was nearly 80.

For further reading: Moss, "The Novels of Thomas Hardy"; Wike, "Hintock by Bicycle: Wessex as Critical Orientation."

Blackmore, Richard Doddridge (1825–1900) Novelist; author of *Lorna Doone,* which Hardy called his "finest book." In June 1875 Hardy wrote to congratulate Blackmore on its publication, saying that he was sorry he had not read it before, "considering the kind of work" he had attempted in FAR FROM THE MADDING CROWD. Hardy praised him for his delineation of "little phases of nature which I thought nobody had noticed but myself"; he attributed his feeling of kinship with Blackmore to their both having been bred in the West of England. Blackmore replied that it was generous of Hardy to "be pleased with one who works in your own field" (*Letters* I, 38).

In *Thomas Hardy: A Biography,* Michael Millgate states that, after perceiving "the benefits that might flow from the exploitation of a regional setting" such as Sir Walter Scott and Blackmore employed in their fiction, Hardy asked his publishers to use the phrase "Wessex Novels" in advertising his books (249).

Blackwood, John (1818–1879) Publisher of BLACK-WOOD'S EDINBURGH MAGAZINE. In February 1877 Hardy wrote to ask Blackwood to inform him when a vacancy for a serial story was about to occur in the magazine, as he had begun a novel (*The RETURN OF THE NATIVE*) "somewhat of the nature of 'Far from the Madding Crowd.'" He would be obliged, he added, if Blackwood could let him know before he made other arrangements to publish it. Blackwood declined the novel; he died on October 29, 1879. His brother, William Blackwood, succeeded him as editor, and in October 1887 Hardy submitted the manuscript of "The WITHERED ARM," a short story which, he warned, was "of rather a weird nature" (*Letters* I, 168). The story was published in the magazine in January 1888.

Blackwood, William (1836–1912) Scottish publisher who succeeded his brother John BLACKWOOD as editor of *BLACKWOOD'S EDINBURGH MAGAZINE.* Beginning in 1817, the magazine had been published by the family firm and was one of the leading literary periodicals of its day. It ceased publishing in December 1980 after nearly 180 years.

Blackwood's Edinburgh Magazine A prestigious magazine founded in 1817 by the Scottish publisher William Blackwood as the *Edinburgh Monthly Magazine;* it soon became *Blackwood's Edinburgh Magazine.* John BLACK-WOOD, a son of the founder, was editor in April 1877, when Hardy submitted the first 15 chapters of *The RETURN OF THE NATIVE,* which Blackwood declined. John Blackwood died; he was succeeded by his brother William, who published Hardy's story "The WITHERED ARM" in January 1888.

In 1892 the magazine reviewed Hardy's novel *TESS OF THE D'URBERVILLES* in its Old Saloon section, where new

books were reviewed. Hardy wrote William Blackwood to complain about the reviewer's lack of religious and literary grounding. He had written that the three-pronged fork which Tess imagines (chapter 14) "occurs in certain grim passages of the 'Inferno' but in no more popular reading." Hardy added that he would like to tell the reviewer that he, himself, "as a child, brought up according to strict Church principles, devoutly believed in the devil's pitchfork."

Of Old Saloon section of the magazine where books were submitted for review, Hardy remarked that he always fancied he "could see that venerable apartment—tomes in piles: rich crimson hangings, a trifle dingy; suspicions of a ghost after 12. *minuit*" (*Letters* I, 159).

Blanche, Jacques-Émile (1861–1942) A distinguished French portrait painter and man of letters. He had a studio in Knightsbridge, London, and in 1906 painted an oil portrait of Hardy. As the work was underway Hardy wrote his friend Arthur SYMONS to say that he liked the painting. He invited Clement SHORTER to call at the flat he and his wife had taken at 1 Hyde Park Mansions in the summer of 1906 and meet Blanche, assuring him that Blanche was fluent in English. In addition, he invited Dorothy ALLHUSEN (the daughter of Mary JEUNE, later Lady St. Helier) and her husband to meet Blanche. The same month he wrote Florence HENNIKER, rather proudly, that Blanche had painted his portrait at his "own request." He added, "I think he is not quite satisfied with it, though I don't dislike it" (*Letters* III, 215). He asked that his publishers send a complimentary copy of *The WELL-BELOVED* to Blanche at the Hyde Park Hotel and one of *The WOODLANDERS* to Madame Blanche.

In August 1907 Hardy wrote Dorothy Allhusen from MAX GATE informing her that Blanche's portrait was "in the Salon at the present moment: people say it makes me 10 years older than I am, but time will cure that fault" (*Letters* III, 265). The "salon" was the Salon de la Société Nationale, Paris, a prestigious annual exhibition. Thomas and Emma Hardy became close friends of Blanche and his wife.

For further reading: Frederick Lawton, "Jacques Emile Blanche," *Fortnightly Review,* June 1906.

Blomfield, Sir Arthur William (1829–1899) One of Thomas Hardy's first employers, Blomfield was an architect and a well-known church designer and restorer; he was a son of the bishop of London. In April 1862 Hardy set out for LONDON with two letters of introduction— one to the architect Benjamin Ferrey and one to John Norton, also a practicing architect. Through Norton he met Arthur Blomfield, and began work Monday, May 5, as an assistant architect in his drawing-office at 8 St. Martin's Place. Hardy worked in Blomfield's office from

1862 to 1867. Blomfield designed the Church of St. Barnabas and St. Paul in Oxford (1868–69); it is modeled on the cathedral at Torcello, near Venice. The baldachino over the high altar is in gold leaf and was the first since the Reformation to be erected in an Anglican church. The church figures in JUDE THE OBSCURE as St. Silas in Christminster; Sue BRIDEHEAD goes there after she loses her children. In 1888 Hardy wrote Blomfield to congratulate him on his election as an associate of the ROYAL ACADEMY OF ARTS. Blomfield was an influential architect and had much to do with the preservation of various English cathedrals. In 1896 his proposals for rebuilding part of the west front of Peterborough cathedral were opposed by the SOCIETY FOR THE PROTECTION OF ANCIENT BUILDINGS, which recommended renewing the core of the walls. Hardy commented that it was a difficult problem, "whether to preserve the venerable *lines,* or the venerable *substance,* when you cannot do both" (*Letters* II, 141).

Hardy's early sketch "HOW I BUILT MYSELF A HOUSE" was written to amuse his architectural colleagues when he worked for Blomfield (*Letters* IV, 70). By the summer of 1867 Hardy had begun to tire of London, and he decided to accept an invitation from John HICKS in DORCHESTER to assist him with church restoration. Blomfield hoped Hardy would return to London by October at the latest; but Hardy found life in Dorchester, where he was living with his family and walking each day to Hicks's offices, very restorative. He began writing *The POOR MAN AND THE LADY,* his first novel (unpublished), and returned to London only to collect "books and other impedimenta" (*Life,* 56–57).

Boer War, the   The Boer War (1899–1902) was fought by the South African Republic (Transvaal) and Orange Free State against Great Britain. Britain had long been regarded with hostility by the Boers (i.e., Afrikaners, who were of Dutch descent), a situation aggravated by British prospectors who came into the country following the discovery of gold in 1886. They refused to yield what they considered their commercial rights, and troops were sent from England to defend them. After prolonged and bloody conflict, the Boers submitted to Britain, but the war caused bitterness that affected South African politics for many years.

Hardy was torn, according to Michael Millgate, between hating war on principle, yet finding excitement in military activity (Millgate, *Thomas Hardy: A Biography,* 401). Major Arthur Henniker, the husband of Hardy's friend Florence HENNIKER, was sent to South Africa with the Coldstream Guards, which brought the war closer to home for Hardy.

Hardy wrote several poems about the war: "EMBARCATION," "Departure," "The GOING OF THE BATTERY," "DRUMMER HODGE," "The Colonel's Soliloquy," "A Christmas Ghost-Story" (December 1899), "A Wife in

London," and "Song of the Soldiers' Wives and Sweethearts."

Boldwood, William   Character in FAR FROM THE MADDING CROWD. A tenant farmer of Little Weatherbury Farm, he is about 40 years old and thought to be a confirmed bachelor. He is also known to be a "deepnatured" man, and has done good works in the community, such as arranging for school for Fanny ROBIN. On a whim, Bathsheba EVERDENE sends him a valentine. He instantly falls in love and resolves to marry her. She has unwittingly "thrown a seed" on a "hotbed of tragic intensity." He appears to be winning her over until she falls in love with Sergeant Francis TROY and marries him. Boldwood neglects his farm; it is saved only when he appoints Gabriel OAK as bailiff (Gabriel is in love with Bathsheba also, but has given up hope). Sergeant Troy disappears and Bathsheba agrees to marry Boldwood in seven years if her husband has not returned. Boldwood assembles presents for "Bathsheba Boldwood" and waits patiently, until Sergeant Troy suddenly appears at a Christmas party in Boldwood's home. Boldwood shoots him in a rage, but is judged to be insane and is imprisoned.

Boldwood also appears in *The MAYOR OF CASTERBRIDGE* as a "silent, reserved young man" at the bankruptcy hearing of Michael HENCHARD (chapter 31).

Bookman, The   A literary monthly founded in 1891 by the Scottish man of letters William Robertson Nicoll, who also edited the works of Charlotte Brontë in 1902. In October 1891 he published an anonymous article, "Thomas Hardy's Wessex," now thought to be the work of Nicoll, assisted by Hardy. Hardy wrote an unidentified correspondent that he was not the author of the article. He explained that, with respect to *TESS OF THE D'URBERVILLES,* the inquirer would not be "far wrong" if he assumed "Shaston" to be Shaftesbury; "King's Bere" to be Bere Re[gis]; "Sandbourne," Bournemouth; and "Casterbridge," Dorchester. He used the real names of hills, vales, rivers, and lanes. A poor map of WESSEX accompanied the article, which Hardy found indistinct (*Letters* I, 274, 256).

In February 1899 Annie Macdonnell reviewed *WESSEX POEMS* (1898) for *The Bookman;* it was illustrated by a photograph of the portrait by Winifred THOMSON. Hardy then wrote her to apologize for not having first obtained her permission (*Letters* II, 212).

Clive HOLLAND published a three-part article, "Thomas Hardy's Country: Scenes from the Wessex Novels," in *The Bookman;* it ran in June, July, and August 1899. He then sent Hardy copies of the photographs used to illustrate them (*Letters* II, 233).

In 1908 the poet and novelist Walter de la Mare wrote an article about the completion of Hardy's massive work *The DYNASTS.* His article appeared in the June issue. In June 1920 Harold Hannyngton Child published an article, "Thomas Hardy," in *The Bookman*. (His book, *Thomas Hardy*, had appeared in 1916.)

Boughton, Rutland (1878–1960) Composer and founder (in 1914) of the Glastonbury Festival. In June 1924 he came to MAX GATE to discuss setting *The FAMOUS TRAGEDY OF THE QUEEN OF CORNWALL* to music.

Boulter, Rev. Sydney Vicar of FORDINGTON ST. GEORGE CHURCH, DORCHESTER. In 1901 he prepared an appeal for funds for the restoration of the church and submitted it to Hardy, who made minor revisions and remarked that all church renovation was viewed with "suspicion" at the present time and that Boulter should assure recipients that "no mischief to the architecture is intended" (*Letters* II, 301). Hardy revised his opinion later, believing the modifications ordered by the architect had impaired the outline of the church tower.

For further reading: John Betjeman, "Hardy and Architecture."

Bowen, John Eliot (1858–1890) Author and assistant editor of the New York *Independent*, a magazine of which his father, Henry Chandler Bowen, was the publisher. John Bowen wrote Hardy on September 14, 1883, soliciting a short story; as a result, Hardy's "Emmeline, or Passion versus Principle" appeared in the issue of February 7, 1884. In March 1885 Bowen wrote to request another short story from Hardy, but Hardy replied that he was unable to send one because of "previous engagements." John Bowen died in January 1890, but in November 1890 Hardy wrote that he would be able to submit a story of from 5,000 to 8,000 words. His story "The Doctor's Legend" appeared in the *Independent* on March 26, 1891, but it was never collected by Hardy. The author apparently corresponded with Henry Chandler Bowen only after the death of John Eliot Bowen (*Letters* I, 132; 219–20; VII, 98).

Bowker, Richard Rogers (1848–1933) Publisher and bibliographer. Bowker was the London representative of the American publishing firm Harper & Brothers from 1880 to 1882. From 1884 to 1933 he was the editor of *Publisher's Weekly*. In July 1880 Hardy invited him to dine at the SAVILE CLUB, or to call on him at his home in Upper Tooting (Bowker went to Hardy's home). Hardy's novel *A LAODICEAN* was serialized in the European Edition of *HARPER'S MONTHLY MAGAZINE* from December 1880 to December 1881 (*Letters* I, 79).

In November 1882 Hardy's story "A Legend of the Year Eighteen Hundred and Four" was published in *Harper's Christmas*, a Christmas annual billed as "Pictures & Papers done by the Tile Club & its Literary Friends." Hardy subsequently changed the title of the story to "A TRADITION OF THE YEAR EIGHTEEN HUNDRED AND FOUR" when it was collected.

Brennecke, Ernest Brennecke was an American critic and university teacher who preyed on Hardy for several years, writing unauthorized works about him. In 1923 he wrote Hardy, sending him part of a book he had written, *Thomas Hardy's Universe: A Study of a Poet's Mind*. He proposed to visit Hardy for the purpose of discussing it. Florence Hardy replied for her husband that he was not able to read the manuscript or authorize it in any way and there would be no point in his coming for that purpose (*Letters* VI, 207–08). Brennecke then compiled a book called *Life & Art: By Thomas Hardy*, published in New York (Greenberg, 1925), although Hardy had cabled his disapproval. Hardy realized Brennecke would try to market the book in England. He wrote Sir Frederick MACMILLAN on April 4, 1925, sending a scathing analysis of it and warning him that the entire book and all its contents were unauthorized. One chapter, he noted, had been based on notes Brennecke had taken when he came to Hardy's home "under the pretence of being a student of German philosophy." The biographical section, Hardy pointed out, was "mainly guesswork" and "ridiculously incorrect." Brennecke had included some of Hardy's writings, which were reprinted later in other collections, including "THE PROFITABLE READING OF FICTION." Several British publishers rejected the book (*Letters*, VI, 145, 207, 225, 259, 283, 304, 318–19, 322, 325).

Bridehead, Sue (Susanna Florence Mary Bridehead) Heroine of JUDE THE OBSCURE. A slim, dainty, graceful and extremely sensitive girl with "liquid, untranslatable eyes," she is a cousin of Jude FAWLEY. Her parents had lived with her great-aunt, Drusilla FAWLEY, but had quarreled and separated. Sue has a platonic relationship with a young undergraduate; they live together in LONDON. She moves to CHRISTMINSTER [OXFORD] and works as an illuminator of ecclesiastical texts. There she meets her cousin Jude, who, unknown to her, has a wife in Australia. Jude introduces Sue to a schoolmaster, Richard PHILLOTSON, who encourages her to train as a teacher. She marries Phillotson, but is physically repulsed by him and becomes Jude's mistress. Over several years she and Jude take in Jude's son by Arabella, "Father Time," and have two other children. She is pregnant with a third when Father Time hangs their children and himself. She has a miscarriage and becomes "a staid, worn woman," but is also vulnerable and forthright; her principles are continually at odds with convention. Eventually she returns to Phillotson and remarries him, submitting to him sexually but shrinking from him. Jude remarries Arabella but soon dies.

"Bride-Night Fire, The" *(A Wessex Tradition)*   This poem is the first one Hardy ever published. It initially appeared under the title "Fire at Tranter Sweatley's," in the GENTLEMAN'S MAGAZINE, November 1875, and was collected in WESSEX POEMS (1898). At the end there is a notation by Hardy: *Written 1866; printed 1875.*

The ballad is written in Dorset dialect, which lends an authentic tone to the language. It tells the story of Barbree, a young girl who is forced by her uncle to marry Sweatley, an older man who is a "tranter," or carrier of goods, instead of Tim, the young man she loves. On their wedding night Sweatley, who is given to drink, starts a fire with a candle snuffer that destroys his house. Tim, attracted by the light, discovers Barbree wandering about outside in her nightgown. He takes her to his home, lends her clothes, and hides her in his loft. Sweatley's remains are discovered in the charred ruins, and when news of Barbree's "hiding" is "vent," or made known, she and Tim are married. "Laughing lads" cry "'After Sweatley!'" but Barbree declares "'I stand as a maiden today!'"

Hardy's use of dialect has been compared to that of his friend William BARNES. The humor in the poem has sometimes been misunderstood by critics; it is intentional, with farcical representation of the stock characters and the witty reference to country courtship, with "junketings, maypoles, and flings." In the *Life* Hardy wrote that although he had a "born sense of humour . . . his poetry was sometimes placed by editors in the hands of reviewers deficient in that quality." Satiric humor was wasted on many of them. He pointed out that his friend Frederic Harrison "deplored the painful nature of the bridegroom's end in leaving only a bone behind him." Hardy, however, believed he misunderstood the poem, which had actually been written and published when he was "quite a young man" and which he had hesitated to reprint later "because of its too pronounced obviousness as a jest" (Bailey, *The Poetry of Thomas Hardy*, 106–107).

British Museum   Opened in 1759 and officially established by an act of Parliament in 1853, the British Museum is the United Kingdom's national repository for treasures in art, science, and literature. In 1878 SMITH, ELDER & CO. (publishers of *The RETURN OF THE NATIVE, The MAYOR OF CASTERBRIDGE,* and *The TRUMPET-MAJOR*) recommended Hardy for readers' tickets to the reading room at the museum, where he began gathering background material for *The Trumpet-Major.* In 1885 he had lodgings at 56 Great Russell Street, directly opposite the main gate. He wrote Frederick HARRISON that during his stay he sometimes attended lectures at Newton Hall, in Fetter Lane. The lecture hall was managed by the Positivist Society, where Harrison had lectured on positivism (*Letters* I, 59, 133–34). Thirty years later, in 1908, he sent Alexander Meyrick Broadley, who

was an authority on the Napoleonic period, the notes he made at that time; they were published as the "'Trumpet-Major' Notebook" and included in *The Personal Notebooks of Thomas Hardy* (*Letters* III, 289).

Hardy's poems "CHRISTMAS IN THE ELGIN ROOM" and "IN THE BRITISH MUSEUM" were based on visits to see the Elgin Marbles at the museum. He wrote Edmund GOSSE when the first poem was published in *The Times* on December 24, 1927, just before his death on January 11, 1928, that he had gone to the museum about 1905, but had not written the poem until 1926 (*Letters* VII, 89). It was collected in *WINTER WORDS* (1928). The second poem was published in SATIRES OF CIRCUMSTANCE (1914). Hardy often checked details of his books at the Museum; in 1906 he wrote Arthur SYMONS from his flat at 1 Hyde Park Mansions that he was going there "to verify tedious trifles as to time & place for Dynasts III" (*Letters* III, 209).

In 1911 Hardy donated the manuscripts of TESS OF THE D'URBERVILLES and *The DYNASTS* to the museum; Sir George Frederick Warner was then the Keeper of Printed Books.

British School, Dorchester   *See* EDUCATION OF THOMAS HARDY; LAST, ISAAC GLANDFIELD.

"Broken Appointment, A"   Poem published in POEMS OF THE PAST AND PRESENT (1902). It is a lament on the part of an elderly man whose beloved has failed to meet him. He is less disappointed by her failure to come to their meeting place than he is by her lack of the "high compassion" that could "overbear/Reluctance for pure lovingkindness' sake." As a "time-torn man," he still wishes she had taken the time to soothe him, even though she did not love him.

Richard Purdy believes the poem should be associated with Florence HENNIKER, whom Hardy first met in May 1893, and the BRITISH MUSEUM, speculating that Hardy might have arranged a meeting with her there and that she failed to appear. The poem also addresses the universal experience of a failed expectation, whether on the part of a man or a woman. John Middleton Murry considers it one of the best of modern lyrical poems, and particularly admired the line "And marching Time drew on, and wore me numb." Samuel Hynes praises the parallel images "time-torn man" and "marching Time." To Douglas Brown the poem is in the "grand manner" (Bailey, *The Poetry of Thomas Hardy*, 157).

For further reading: Buckler, "Hardy's 'A Broken Appointment.'"

Browning, Robert (1812–1889)   Thomas Hardy and his wife Emma Gifford HARDY met Robert Browning about 1880 through Anne Benson PROCTER, the widow of the poet Bryan Waller Procter (who wrote under the pseudonym Barry Cornwall). Hardy saw Browning there frequently during the ensuing years, until Mrs. Procter's death in 1888. In 1887, while in Florence, the Hardys visited the tomb of Elizabeth Barrett Browning, who had died in 1861. In 1887 the Hardys were in Venice, where they had an introduction to Katherine Colman Bronson, the widow of Arthur Bronson, who had been a close friend of Robert Browning and of Henry JAMES. She showed them around Venice and introduced them to a countess who might have served as the model for the Italian Contessa in A GROUP OF NOBLE DAMES.

Hardy enjoyed reading the poetry of Browning, although he had some reservations about his work. In July 1901 he wrote Florence HENNIKER that he was "excellent to fall back upon in hot weather: how slowly & surely he is overtopping Tennyson. And yet Browning has his weaknesses" (*Letters* II, 293). Hardy apparently regarded Browning with both admiration and envy. In his preface to the WESSEX EDITION of his novels and poems, dated 1911, he states that he had hoped to write more volumes of verse, but "the night cometh." He quotes Browning's poem "The Last Ride Together": "The petty done, the undone vast!" (*Thomas Hardy's Personal Writings*, 50). Privately, however, he found Browning an enigma. In 1899 he wrote his close friend Edmund GOSSE that Browning's character was "*the* literary puzzle of the 19th century." He wondered how "smug christian optimism worthy of a dissenting grocer" could possibly exist within the poet, who at other times was "so vast a seer & feeler." He even suggested that Browning professed "a certain mass of commonplace opinion" to make his work more acceptable to the public (*Letters* II, 216–17). In 1907 Arthur Symons sent him his book about the poet, *An Introduction to the Study of Browning;* Hardy wrote that he had read it "with great interest from the time it arrived last night till 12" (*Letters* III, 252).

Browning died in Venice in December 1889 and was buried in Westminster Abbey. Hardy noted in the *Life,* "What the *Athenaeum* says is true, though not all the truth, that intellectual subtlety is the disturbing element in his art" (*Life,* 223).

Budmouth Fictional name for WEYMOUTH in *FAR FROM THE MADDING CROWD, The MAYOR OF CASTERBRIDGE, The RETURN OF THE NATIVE, The TRUMPET-MAJOR,* and *TWO ON A TOWER,* as well as in *The WOODLANDERS* and a number of short stories and poems.

The town originally consisted of two boroughs: Melcombe Regis, north of the Harbour, and Weymouth, to the south. They were incorporated during the reign of Elizabeth I. The northern part of the town became fashionable when George III began spending summers there (Pinion, *A Hardy Companion,* 252–53). Hardy sometimes uses "Budmouth" as a location, and at other

times "Budmouth-Regis," meaning the northern part of the town (originally the borough of Melcombe Regis in Weymouth).

"Budmouth Dears" *See* "HUSSAR'S SONG: 'BUDMOUTH DEARS.'"

Bugler, Gertrude (1897–1992) A Dorset-born actress and member of the HARDY PLAYERS. Between 1913 and 1924, Gertrude Bugler played the Hardy heroines in stage adaptations of his principal novels. She married Captain E. F. Bugler, M.C. (1888–1956) in 1921. She played Marty SOUTH in the DORCHESTER DEBATING AND DRAMATIC SOCIETY's 1913 production of *The WOODLANDERS* (adapted by A. H. EVANS), and Fancy DAY and Bathsheba EVERDENE in scenes from *UNDER THE GREENWOOD TREE* and *FAR FROM THE MADDING CROWD,* respectively. By 1920, the actors were known as the Hardy Players. Gertrude Bugler played Eustacia VYE in *The RETURN OF THE NATIVE* (adapted by T. H. Tilley), and Tess DURBEYFIELD in the 1924 and 1925 Dorset productions of *TESS OF THE D'URBERVILLES* (adapted by Thomas Hardy). Although Hardy wrote *The FAMOUS TRAGEDY OF THE QUEEN OF CORNWALL* with Gertrude Bugler in mind for the leading role of Iseult, she was unable to take part in the 1923 production because of pregnancy. The baby, Diana (later Diana Toms) was born in March 1924 (*Letters* VI, 290).

Gertrude Bugler's portrayals were so close to Hardy's own conceptions of his characters that after *The Return of the Native* he described her as "the impersonator of Eustacia." Later, he said of her Tess that she was "the very incarnation," and her physical likeness was so striking, that he insisted that a woodcut portrait of her should be published in Macmillan's 1926 illustrated edition of his novels. Beyond her talent, Hardy savored the coincidence that Gertrude Bugler's mother, Augusta Way, was formerly a resident of Bockhampton, Hardy's native village. She worked in her father's dairy there and it was she who had first suggested the image of Tess to Hardy (Millgate, *Thomas Hardy: A Biography,* 293).

On the strength of her performance in *Tess of the d'Urbervilles,* Gertrude Bugler was offered, and signed, a contract to play the title role at the Haymarket, one of London's most prestigious theaters. However, Hardy's wife, Florence HARDY, undermined these arrangements, giving Gertrude Bugler misleading information and subsequently suggesting that the excitement of a London production would imperil the health of the elderly writer. In response to Gertrude Bugler's withdrawal from the scheduled production, Hardy accepted her decision, but wrote that he did not believe "any London actress" would represent Tess "so nearly as I imagined her as you did" (Millgate, *Thomas Hardy: A Biography,* 557).

Mrs. Bugler was the author of *Personal Recollections of Thomas Hardy* (Dorchester, 1964).

For further reading: Wilson, "Gertrude Bugler," *The Oxford Reader's Companion to Thomas Hardy;* Wilson, *Thomas Hardy on Stage.*

"Building a New Street in the Ancient Quarter" *(April 1887)* See "ROME: BUILDING A NEW STREET IN THE ANCIENT QUARTER."

Bunting, Percy (1836–1911) Social reformer and editor of the *Contemporary Review.* In the autumn of 1883 he wrote Hardy to request an article on the problem of the political disenfranchisement of the farm laborer. On October 12, 1883, Hardy replied that there was little to say about farm laborers as voters. He wrote Bunting again on November 5, 1883, stating that the farm laborer had a "dread of being turned out of his house. There is no doubt that what weighs most heavily upon the *farm*labourer's mind is the general insecurity of his position; this oppresses him much more than the question of so many shillings a week." He commented that the farmer would benefit by a system "by which he could have a personal interest in a particular piece of land" (*Letters* I, 121, 123). Hardy never contributed an article to the *Contemporary Review,* but did focus on this source of considerable anxiety to the farm laborer in *The WOODLANDERS.*

For further reading: Cunningham, "Three Faces of 'Hodge': The Agricultural Labourer in Hardy's Work."

"By the Earth's Corpse" Published in *POEMS OF THE PAST AND THE PRESENT* (1902), this poem is based on Genesis 6.6: "And it repented the Lord that he had made man on the earth, and it grieved him at his heart." The poem takes the form of a conversation between Time and the Lord at a future time when the earth and all living creatures have died. The Lord had not designed the death of the planet; it was caused by the operation of intractable scientific processes. He deeply regrets "the wrongs endured/By Earth's poor patient kind" and, now that "flesh/And herb but fossils be" and are extinct, he reproaches himself for their creation.

In his journal, Hardy wrote at the time that he was trying to "reconcile a scientific view of life with the emotional and spiritual." He set forth, as a general principle: "The emotions have no place in a world of defect, and it is a cruel injustice that they should have developed in it. If Law itself had consciousness, how the aspect of its creatures would terrify it, fill it with remorse!" (*Life,* 148–49).

Since Hardy was writing *The DYNASTS* at the same time he was composing the poem, Time may also be equivalent to the Spirit of the Years. He composed *The Dynasts* between 1897 and 1907, so the poem could have been written about 1898 or 1899. Bailey believes he was thinking about it, however, as early as 1881 (Bailey, *The Poetry of Thomas Hardy,* 151).

"By the Runic Stone" *(Two who became a story)* This poem was collected in *MOMENTS OF VISION* (1917). Hardy describes a couple sitting by a stone with runic inscriptions; he is "white-hatted" and she wears brown but is "Pink-faced, breeze-blown." They sit talking, "rapt," heedless of the time, and, as a result, cast their lot together. The "die" thrown so heedlessly, however, will eventually mar their "encompassment" or union in marriage. Their zest might have been tempered had they been able to foresee, "As in a glass, Time toss their history/From zone to zone!"

Critics usually assume the couple to be Hardy and Emma HARDY, who often dressed in brown. The setting is probably a rocky coastal site in CORNWALL (as evoked in the courtship between Stephen SMITH and Eldride SWANCOURT in *A PAIR OF BLUE EYES*). The last two lines refer, in all likelihood, to their unhappiness after their marriage, which they could not have predicted.

The existence of a runic stone is itself doubtful, however. Local inhabitants of the coast of Cornwall near ST. JULIOT CHURCH have never found one. There is, however, a similar stone projecting from a clump of trees near an old Roman road crossing PUDDLETOWN Heath in DORSET. It is possible the poem refers to Hardy's courtship there of Tryphena SPARKS, to whom he was engaged before meeting Emma (Bailey, *The Poetry of Thomas Hardy,* 374).

C

Caine, (Thomas Henry) Hall (1853–1931) English novelist and journalist. Educated on the Isle of Man and at Liverpool, Caine was on the staff of the Liverpool *Mercury;* in his later years he lived on the Isle of Man and was a member of the Manx legislature. Among his best-known novels are *The Manxman* (1894) and *The Prodigal Son* (1904).

In January 1918 Caine sent Hardy a clipping from the London *Observer;* he had disputed the assertion by the lawyer and politician Sir Edward Clarke that the age of 37 represented the highest point in human achievement. Hardy replied that if the best "*literary work*" is done at the mean age of 37 it must be owing to the "conditions of modern life; for we are told that Homer sang when old and blind, while Aeschylus wrote his best tragedies when over sixty, Sophocles some of his best when nearly ninety, and Euripides did not begin to write till forty, and went on to seventy" (*Letters* V, 246). Caine wrote twice to ask that Hardy's letter be published.

In May 1918 Caine sought permission to use a poem by Hardy that might be set to music by a composer; he was producing a film promoting the aims of Britain in WORLD WAR I. Hardy sent copies of two possible choices—"MEN WHO MARCH AWAY" and "THEN & NOW." The film, though completed, was never shown to the public (*Letters* III, 264).

Calais French port where Emma HARDY and her niece Lilian Gifford stayed in November 1903. They had set out for Dover, but then crossed the channel to Calais, an action that alarmed Hardy. He was reading proofs of *The* DYNASTS and could not follow, but he viewed it as an "escapade" he had not sanctioned. He asked Emma to leave a forwarding address at the hotel if she were to go elsewhere, and to "keep near the sea," as she "might get a cold inland, particularly at Paris." He warned her that he could not send funds quickly from England and advised her to leave France before the winter weather set in, to avoid becoming ill "alone, with a foreign doctor" (*Letters* 85–90). He urged her to bring Lilian back to MAX GATE. He also pointed out that the women might well be stopping at the hotel where Percy Bysshe Shelley and Mary Wollstonecraft Godwin stayed in 1814 when they eloped to the Continent, pursued by Mrs. William Godwin.

Emma and Lilian did not return to Max Gate until early December; Emma apparently enjoyed the town and made some sketches of the port. Hardy wrote Florence HENNIKER, apparently to justify his wife's journey: "Em spent a month partly at Dover, partly at Calais, the air there having an invigorating effect upon her, but I did not go on to her as I had intended" (*Letters* III, 95).

"Call to National Service, A" Poem first published simultaneously in the London *Times,* the *Morning Post,* and other newspapers on March 12, 1917. It was later included in MOMENTS OF VISION (1917). It is dated March 1917; by that time, WORLD WAR I had been under way for some two and a half years. The poem was written "in a great hurry at the request of the N. S. Depart[t],"[1] Hardy wrote Sydney COCKERELL on March 31 (Bailey, *The Poetry of Thomas Hardy,* 424–25).

The poem is a sonnet, with two four-line stanzas and two three-line stanzas. The first two stanzas, the octave section, contain an eloquent summons to "all who have a hand/To lift, a back to bend" to assist England. He enjoins women and men of every class and occupation to say "I come" in order to preserve England. The country must stand "scareless, scathless" and not be left "Untended as a wild of weeds and sand."

In the sestet Hardy, who was then 76, deplores the fact that his age prevents him from entering battle. He wishes to "stir as I once stirred" in his youth.

Cambridge University Around the year 1865, soon after his 25th birthday, Hardy decided to pursue "a scheme of a highly visionary character," as he put it in the *Life.* He wrote a friend in Cambridge about the possibility of matriculating at the university and eventually becoming a village curate. He abandoned the plan because of certain "views" he found himself to hold, but he still attended church and practiced "orthodoxy" (*Life,* 50).

About 1866, Horace MOULE sent Hardy the "Students' Guide" to the University of Cambridge. Hardy realized he would not only have to wait three years to enter, but also would have three years' required residence in a college, plus an additional year before the actual degree would be conferred. There would also be many expenses. He decided it seemed "absurd to live on now with such a remote object in view" (*Letters* I, 7).

In June 1913 Hardy was awarded the honorary degree of Litt. D (*Litterarum Doctor* or Doctor of Letters). In Cambridge he stayed with Sydney COCKERELL (who had played an important role in securing the degree for him) and lunched with the vice chancellor, S. A. Donaldson, at Magdalene College. A. C. BENSON, a friend of Hardy's and a Fellow of Magdalene College, described him as looking "very frail & nervous, but undeniably pleased." His sister Mary HARDY wrote him, "Now you have accomplished it all with greater honour than if you had gone along the road you then saw before you." In a ceremony at the Magdalene College Chapel in November 1913, Hardy was admitted to the College, which was founded in 1428, as an Honorary Fellow. The *Cambridge Review* took note of the ceremony, explaining that it consisted of a Latin formula of admission before the altar, and the handing-in of the new Fellow into his stall. (Masters and Fellows of Cambridge colleges are assigned individual stalls, or tall carved seats, in the chapel.) That night Hardy dined "in Hall," the beautiful college dining hall. The article in the *Cambridge Review* continued his account: "the Master proposed the health of him who was no longer a guest, but one of the Society, and the day's proceedings terminated happily" (*The Cambridge Review*, quoted in *Life*, 362–63).

On Hardy's 80th birthday, June 2, 1920, Peter Giles, vice chancellor of Cambridge University and master of Emmanuel College, sent the author birthday wishes, as did A. C. Benson and the Fellows of Magdalene College. Hardy wrote Benson that he had decided it was "worth while to live to be eighty to discover what friends there were about me up & down the world, & my judgment against the desirability of being so long upon earth is therefore for a time at least suspended" (*Letters* VI, 24).

Campbell, Mrs. Patrick (1865–1940) Mrs. Campbell, the famous British actress, was born Beatrice Stella Tanner but used her married name on the stage. In November 1891 *TESS OF THE D'URBERVILLES* was published, setting off a storm of criticism; but by 1895, several writers had expressed interest in dramatizing the novel. Hardy noted in his autobiography that "almost every actress of note in Europe" had asked him for the chance to play Tess, including Mrs. Campbell, Ellen TERRY, Sarah BERNHARDT, and Eleanora Duse (*Life*, 265). In July 1895 Mrs. Campbell wrote Hardy that she hoped she would soon learn his plans for the dramatization of *Tess of the d'Urbervilles*, and that it could not fail to be a success, whoever played Tess. Hardy answered, "You *must* be the Tess now we have got so far. It would be a thousand pities if you were not" (*Letters* II, 81–82).

Hardy finished the dramatization in February 1896, but it was not produced in England. Hardy wrote Mrs. Campbell in August 1896 that, since the play had not been produced the previous season, he had given up plans to have it staged in England. In March 1897 he wrote her again, saying: "I threw up the whole matter (feeling rightly or wrongly that the dramatizing of novels was questionable art)" (*Letters* II, 151). Mrs. Campbell did not give up the idea of playing Tess, and responded with a request for a copy of the play; she hoped it might be produced in May.

Hardy authorized Lorimer STODDARD to dramatize the novel for the New York stage, with Mrs. Minnie Maddern FISKE in the title role. It was not produced in England, however, and she did not play Tess. Mrs. Campbell was extremely upset that there was not to be a production in London, and an unauthorized dramatization of the novel was mounted for a time. Hardy had to arrange for a London copyright "performance" at the time of the opening in America, a necessary formality. He also had to make a "public disavowal" of this play and bring an injunction against it on behalf of Mrs. Fiske (Millgate, *Thomas Hardy: A Biography*, 376). In 1990 Hardy made a "public disavowal" against another unauthorized version of *Tess* that had been mounted in London; he was forced to bring an injunction against it on behalf of Mrs. Fiske (Millgate, 376). Mrs. Campbell, however, had not been responsible for this production.

For further reading: Roberts, *Tess in the Theatre*.

Candlemas The feast of the purification of the Virgin Mary, February 2, when candles used in the Roman Catholic Church are consecrated. In DORCHESTER a fair was held on a nearby day (not on the holy day, by statute), during which agricultural laborers were hired to begin work on Lady Day (March 25). The fair was an important event for DORSET farmers and local people, serving as the setting for scenes in *FAR FROM THE MADDING CROWD*, *The MAYOR OF CASTERBRIDGE*, and other works. Hardy also discusses the misery inflicted by hiring fairs in "The DORSETSHIRE LABOURER."

"Candour in English Fiction" An essay published in the *New Review*, January 1890, the last in a symposium focusing on the effect of prudishness on the contemporary novel. The other two essays were written by Walter BESANT and the novelist Mrs. E. Lynn Linton.

Hardy states that fictional invention is "conditioned by its surroundings like a river-stream." Critics often view modern fiction as insincere, he says, but too few writers produce a "Fiction that expresses truly the views of life prevalent in its time." Many writers understand that literary taste, which is cyclical, "is arriving anew at a point of high tragedy," and they seek to be "original." Originality is insufficient, however; it "makes scores of failures for one final success."

According to Hardy, only "conscientious fiction" can satisfy the serious reader. He says writers would do well to emulate the ancient Greek writers and Shakespeare, who "reflected life, revealed life, criticized life" and who strive to portray honestly "the relations of the sexes" accurately, without falsely coloring catastrophes. He objects to the preference of English society for a "regulation finish" that "they married and were happy ever after."

The magazine and the circulating library introduce new novels to the public as "household reading," assuming that younger members of a household must be protected from the "true views" that adults permit themselves. Therefore, the market does not "foster the growth of the novel which reflects and reveals life" but instead tries to "exterminate it" by withholding public literary space.

He observes that readers themselves become prudish censors. They forbid an author to break the first, third, or seventh commandments, although some of the others may be infringed in a "genteel manner." A more serious problem is that a serialized story first envisioned as acceptable may change directions as it is developed. The author must then "whip and scourge" his characters into acting against their nature or, alternatively, allow them to "act as they will," which might well "ruin his editor, his publisher, and himself."

Many writers arrange an unreal dénouement "dear to the Grundyist and subscriber." But if the "true artist ever weeps," it is probably when he realizes the price he must pay for "writing in the English language." That price is "total extinction, in the mind of every mature and penetrating reader, of sympathetic belief in his personages." He imagines a "brazen young Shakespeare of our time" offering *Othello, Hamlet,* or *Antony and Cleopatra* (assuming they had not yet appeared) to a modern publisher, and the response he would get "for his mad supposition of such fitness from any one of the gentlemen who so correctly conduct that branch of the periodical Press."

Hardy proposes three solutions: first, that books for adults be offered for purchase rather than borrowing; second, they might be published as a *feuilleton,* or serial story, in adult newspapers (as in France); or, third, they might appear in magazines exclusively for adults. He cautions that he is arguing only for frank treatment of "the position of man and woman in nature."

In this essay Hardy was remarkably prescient, since *TESS OF THE D'URBERVILLES* began appearing in the *GRAPHIC* 18 months later, in July 1891. In book form it provoked a storm of criticism, mixed with praise.

Cannister, Martin   In *A PAIR OF BLUE EYES,* the sexton at the church at Endelstow. He marries UNITY, the parlor maid in the household of the Reverend Christopher SWANCOURT, and becomes landlord of an Endelstow inn called the Welcome Home.

Cantle, Christian   Youngest son of Granfer CANTLE in *The RETURN OF THE NATIVE.* He is 31 and a simpleton, a "faltering man, with reedy hair, no shoulders, and a great quantity of wrist and ankle beyond his clothes." He works for Mrs. YEOBRIGHT, running errands for her. Although timid, he gambles away the money she has entrusted to him to deliver to her niece, Thomasin Yeobright WILDEVE, then refuses to admit what he has done. After this he assists Clym YEOBRIGHT with small jobs.

Cantle, Granfer   The grandfather of Christian CANTLE in *The RETURN OF THE NATIVE,* he is a lively though somewhat senile former soldier, 69, who was present at the burning of Napoleon Bonaparte's effigy on Durnover Green.

Carnarvon, Elisabeth Catharine, Countess of (?–1929)   The second wife of Henry Howard Molyneux Herbert, fourth earl of CARNARVON.

The countess Carnarvon invited Thomas and Emma Hardy to a party on Friday, May 15, 1885, in her LONDON town house; Hardy had taken rooms at 29 Montague Street, London. Emma was in DORSET, but planned to come to London the following week. Hardy attended and wrote his wife that he was "very well received." Robert BROWNING was a fellow guest, as was the novelist Margaret Oliphant. (Hardy did not care for Oliphant, writing Emma that she was "propriety & primness incarnate.")

Carnarvon, Henry Howard Molyneux Herbert, fourth earl of (1831–1890)   A man of letters, Carnarvon had published a verse translation of *The Odyssey;* he was also the brother of Thomas Hardy's friend Lady Portsmouth (see PORTSMOUTH, EARL AND COUNTESS OF). Hardy visited the Carnarvons' LONDON home in 1886, where he met their daughters, including Lady Winifred HERBERT. In July 1888 Hardy wrote Carnarvon to request that he propose Hardy for the ATHENAEUM CLUB. Hardy remarked that his chances were "infinitesimal" but if anything could help it would be a recommendation from someone of Carnarvon's prominence (*Letters* VII, 110). Lord Carnarvon did propose Hardy, who was elected in 1891, the year after Carnarvon died.

Caro, Avice   The first love of Jocelyn PIERSTON in *The WELL-BELOVED.* She is also known as Avice I (Mrs. Jim Caro). Avice has grown up next door to the Pierston family on the Isle of Slingers. They become engaged, but before they leave the island together he meets another native daughter, Marcia BENCOMB, and abandons Avice. Avice marries her cousin, Jim Caro.

Avice appears in two other manifestations within the novel. The first is as her daughter, Ann Avice, or Avice II (Mrs. Isaac Pierston). She is a washer-woman who has often fallen in and out of love. Jocelyn keeps her as his servant in London, but learns that she is secretly married and pregnant.

The second manifestation is as Avice III, daughter of Avice II and granddaughter of Avice I (Mrs. Henri LEVERRE). Forty years after he courts her grandmother, Jocelyn returns to the island. He finds that Avice II has fallen ill, but she urges him to marry her daughter (Avice III). Avice III, however, marries Henri Leverre. Jocelyn eventually marries an earlier love, Marcia Bencomb.

The three Avices are technically three different women, but they are all expressions of the ideal woman Jocelyn Pierston visualizes, the "Well-Beloved," who keeps changing shapes; the spirit of the "well-beloved" migrates. They are *not* merely successive related women with the same name; the concept is more mystical than that. Jocelyn leaves Avice I because the "well-beloved spirit" he seeks has moved to Marcia BENCOMB. Avice I sensibly marries someone else. As he pursues the later two Avices, they distance and relocate themselves from him. Avice II is pregnant with Avice III; when Avice III grows up and Jocelyn courts her, she is shocked, as she finds him very elderly. It should be understood as a novel based to some extent on fantasy; it lacks the realism of, say, *The RETURN OF THE NATIVE.*

Hardy noted in his autobiography that he wished to trace "the story of a face which goes through three generations or more."

Carr, J. W. Comyns (1849–1916)   Critic and dramatist. Some time in 1881, Carr wrote Thomas Hardy for permission to dramatize *FAR FROM THE MADDING CROWD.* Hardy had already dramatized the novel as *The Mistress of the Farm—A Pastoral Drama* and submitted it to St. James's Theatre, LONDON, in 1880. It had been put into rehearsal by the theater management but was then rejected. Hardy sent Carr the play as he had written it. Carr, according to Hardy, "modified it in places, to suit modern stage carpentry &c., and offered it to the St, James's." The manager, William Hunter Kendal, rejected the Hardy–Comyns Carr dramatization, but in December 1881 the theater mounted Pinero's similar play *The Squire.* W. Moy Thomas reviewed it in the *Daily News* on December 30, saying that although Pinero was "under obligations" to the novel *Far from the Madding Crowd,* the "dramatic & narrative methods of presenting a story are so widely different that the dramatist might well afford to own his obligation to the novel." Hardy wrote Thomas the same day, explaining that *Far from the Madding Crowd* also existed as a play, and informing him of the sequence of events. He concluded, "I leave you to draw your own inferences" (*Letters* I, 99; 103). The Hardy–Comyns Carr stage version of the novel was not produced in London, but was staged in Liverpool and Manchester (*Letters,* 94–95).

Cartlett, Mr.   Character in JUDE THE OBSCURE. Arabella DONN marries him in Australia, bigamously, since she is already married to Jude FAWLEY. She eventually divorces Jude and marries CARTLETT legally. He is a publican who has kept a pub in Australia. In England he leases a pub in Lambeth, LONDON. He is a "rather bloated man, with a globular stomach and small legs, resembling a top on two pegs."

Casterbridge   Fictional name for DORCHESTER in *The MAYOR OF CASTERBRIDGE* and other works. In July 1902 Hardy was invited by the Town Clerk of Dorchester to write an introduction to the official *Guide to Dorchester.* He replied that he was unable to do so, but continued,

> . . . as I have said a good deal about Dorchester, under the pseudonym of "Casterbridge", in print during the last 20 years, — (all, in fact, that I have to say) I give the Editor of the Guide full permission to quote any passages descriptive of the Town from "The Mayor of Casterbridge", (in which there are a good many). This, I feel sure, will be likely to produce a better effect on readers than anything I could write specifically for the Handbook — which is, in fact, rather outside my province (*Letters,* III, 28).

In 1910 he was presented with the "FREEDOM OF DORCHESTER" by the mayor and town corporation, and, in response, gave one of his few formal speeches. He remarked that in view of the "liberties" he had taken with the town's "ancient walls, streets, and precincts" in his works he felt he had "treated its external features with the hand of freedom indeed." He also noted that he had "coined" the name in an "off-hand moment" without anticipating that it would become "established and localized." He observed that Casterbridge was never intended to be a literal representation of Dorchester, but a "dream-place that never was outside an irresponsible book." He admitted being pleased when someone remarked that "'Casterbridge' is a sort of essence of the town as it used to be, 'a place more Dorchester than Dorchester itself'" (*Life,* 351).

The name *Casterbridge* is derived from *Dwrinwyr,* the early British name for the settlement by the Dwyr, or dark river, and *castra,* the Latin word for "camp" (Pinion, *A Hardy Companion,* 259–61). The principal work in which the town figures is *The Mayor of Casterbridge,* the setting for most of the scenes in the novel. Among the many identifiable sites are the Corn Exchange, the King's Arms, and Barclay's Bank (thought to be the home of Michael Henchard). Other novels in which Casterbridge figures are *DESPERATE REMEDIES, UNDER THE GREENWOOD TREE, FAR FROM THE MADDING CROWD* (the barracks, the Corn Exchange, the White Hart Inn); *The RETURN OF THE NATIVE* (Wildeve plans to move to Casterbridge with Thomasin), and *The TRUMPET-MAJOR* (Matilda Johnson comes to Casterbridge by road-wagon to meet Bob Loveday).

Casterbridge is the setting for several poems, including "The DANCE AT THE PHOENIX," "CIRCUS-RIDER TO RINGMASTER," and "AT CASTERBRIDGE FAIR." It is also mentioned in a number of short stories, including "The FIDDLER OF THE REELS," "The THREE STRANGERS," several tales collected in A GROUP OF NOBLE DAMES, "A CHANGED MAN," and "A FEW CRUSTED CHARACTERS."

Century Magazine, The   One of the small group of leading intellectual periodicals that were the linchpin and showcase of American literary achievement after the end of the Civil War. The *Century* was an outgrowth of SCRIBNER'S MONTHLY, founded in 1870, which separated from the parent publishing house, Charles Scribner's Sons, in 1881. The magazine continued under the name the *Century Illustrated Monthly Magazine.* The poet Richard Watson Gilder was the editor from 1881 to 1909.

In July 1893 the magazine published an article ("Thomas Hardy") by the critic Harriet W. Preston in response to the publication of TESS OF THE D'URBERVILLES Hardy was aware of the impending article and, in June 1893, wrote Florence HENNIKER that "a lady-critic is going to drag me over the coals in next month's *Century* for the way in which I spoilt 'Tess.' She is an unmarried lady, and I shall be much interested to see how she handles the subject" (*Letters* II, 13–14). In May 1922 Hardy's poem "An ANCIENT TO ANCIENTS" was published in the *Century,* illustrated with a drawing by the American artist Rockwell KENT.

Challow   Character in *JUDE THE OBSCURE.* He is a pig killer who arrives too late to help Jude and Arabella, who must slaughter their pig themselves. The pig-killing scene in Chapter X was one of the most criticized in the novel because of its graphic nature and inhumane treatment of the animal. Hardy describes its "cry of despair; long-drawn, slow and hopeless." As they proceed the pig emits his final "shriek of agony" and stares at Arabella as if "recognizing at last the treachery of those who had seemed his only friends."

Chambers's Journal   William Chambers (1800–83) was the proprietor of this Edinburgh magazine when, on March 18, 1865, Hardy's essay "HOW I BUILT MYSELF A HOUSE" was published. From 1859 to 1874 the journal was edited by the novelist James Payne. In 1888 Charles Edward Stuart Chambers (1859–1936), son of William Chambers, became publisher and editor. In February 1909 he wrote Hardy to ask for a contribution. Hardy replied that he was unable to send anything, because "what I write now, though it interests some, does not interest the general reader" (*Letters* IV, 9). In 1924 Chambers wrote Hardy again, asking for something to print in the journal to mark "the Diamond Jubilee of your reign as an author."

In January 1925 the 1865 essay was reprinted in the magazine along with a new poem submitted by Hardy, "A Bird-Scene at a Rural Dwelling."

"Changed Man, A"   A short story first published in the *Sphere,* April 21 and 28, 1900, with a half-page illustration by A. S. Hartrick; it appeared in the American magazine *Cosmopolitan* in May 1900. It was the title story in the collection A CHANGED MAN AND OTHER TALES (1913), many of which had appeared in American magazines but had not been collected in England.

The story takes place in CASTERBRIDGE (DORCHESTER). The Hussars arrive in the town barracks with an excellent band. Each man wears a "*pelisse*" or "sling-jacket," a frilled half-coat hanging from the left shoulder.

The houses at the "Top o' Town" command a view of the long High Street and all the goings-on there. One of the houses has an oriel window, from which a "burgher," an elderly gentleman, watches all day. He is an invalid and uses a wheel chair. A young woman named Laura also lives at the top of the street at her uncle's home and watches the soldiers from her balcony.

Rumors spread through town that the regiment is "haunted." The gentleman meets Captain Jack Maumbry, one of the Hussars, at an afternoon tea, and an elderly lady asks if the rumor is true. He admits that it is, that a "*thing*" caused by a past crime committed by a member follows them from town to town. The "thing" is a phantom 10 feet high with chattering teeth and grating hipbones. Over the winter several townspeople claim to have been frightened by the specter.

During the winter the Hussars meet several young women of the town, including Laura, and form relationships that break their hearts. Once a week they ride in marching order, each wearing his pelisse. A friend tells the gentleman in the oriel window of rumors that Laura is engaged to Captain Maumbry. The old gentleman is doubtful, but Laura is in fact engaged to the captain. She has idealized the romance of military life and knows little of its realities. However, she not only "has the pleasure" of marrying the man she loves, but also has "the joy of feeling herself hated by the mothers of all the marriageable girls of the neighbourhood."

The man in the oriel window goes to the wedding and writes a poem about it, called "At A Hasty Wedding," beginning and ending with a couplet: "If hours be years the twain are blest, /For now they solace swift desire." The couple settle down happily in south Wessex. Both play in an amateur dramatic entertainment for the benefit of charity.

One Sunday a new curate, Mr. Sainway, appears in the local church pulpit and attracts a large following; at the time, the sermon is regarded as more important than the liturgy. Mr. Sainway wants to stop the regimental band from playing Sunday afternoons in the Casterbridge barrack square. Captain Maumbry accepts Sainway's reasoning, and he and Sainway become friends. After a year Sainway leaves for the midlands; his friends in Casterbridge learn that he has died of a lung inflammation.

Captain Maumbry shocks his wife by telling her that he wants to leave the army and take holy orders. Laura has no wish to be a curate's wife. Maumbry goes to Fountall Theological College and, as the Reverend John Maumbry, returns to another church in Casterbridge as curate. His preaching is dull and he does not build up a following. Meanwhile, Laura has become a friend of the man in the oriel window. The Hussars are recalled to a post nearer London and Laura sits with the man in the window, watching them depart, followed by her husband in his clerical dress. She asks the man whether he thinks Maumbry was justified in his change of calling, but the man is noncommittal. Laura feels she is "'doomed to fester in a hole in Durnover Lane.'"

Cholera infects the region, especially the low-lying poor areas; Reverend Maumbry struggles to help his parishioners, but decides to send Laura away, out of danger. She takes lodgings at Creston (a town near WEYMOUTH). She meets Mr. Vannicock, who is in the BUDMOUTH (Weymouth) infantry. She consults her husband in the open air, to avoid infection, and tells him she wants to participate in a dramatic production at Budmouth to raise money for relief of the afflicted. He is distressed at the idea of her acting, but she plays the heroine; Mr. Vannicock is the hero.

Vannicock is transferred to Bristol, and Laura takes lodgings nearby in Bath. She writes a letter to her husband saying that she is running way. Vannicock meets her at the very spot where she and Jack Maumbry met, which she considers an unlucky omen. They begin their journey, but notice a "lurid glare" coming from Durnover. They come close and see that the inhabitants are burning the clothes of the dead in a large copper pot. The Reverend Maumbry is loading them in and pressing them down with what appears to be a rolling pin. Both Laura and Vannicock go to help. The driver who was to take them from Casterbridge to Ivell, where they would take the railway to Bristol, arrives to see whether they are coming. Maumbry is seized with violent pain and becomes ill. Vannicock summons the driver and places Maumbry in the carriage. They take him to his home and Laura goes inside with him while Vannicock goes on to Ivell. Two days later Maumbry dies. Laura buries her letter in the coffin with him. Vannicock returns the satchel she was taking to run away and asks her, in a perfunctory manner, to marry him; Laura weeps, haunted by "the insistent shadow of that unconscious one; the thin figure of him, moving to and fro in front of the ghastly furnace in the gloom of

Durnover Moor." Within two years Vannicock returns to Budmouth, where Laura still lives, but they do not marry; Laura dies a widow.

The character of the Reverend Maumbry is based on the Reverend Henry MOULE, father of eight sons, including Hardy's close friend Henry Joseph MOULE. During the cholera epidemics of 1849 and 1854 he courageously endangered himself by boiling and burning the clothes of the deceased and by visiting the dying in their homes.

Changed Man and Other Tales, A   Short story collection published in 1913. This was one of the last two of the 20 volumes of the WESSEX EDITION, published by Macmillan, that began to appear in April 1912. Millgate states that Hardy named the collection for his story "A CHANGED MAN," which he considered the "best of a rather poor bunch." He adds that Hardy would not have collected the stories at all except that they had been frequently reprinted in inexpensive American editions. The volume contained six stories that had been published before the introduction, in 1891, of the International Copyright Law. Several of these stories had been reprinted without Hardy's permission, compelling him to republish them in book form for his own protection.

The publishers insisted on a frontispiece, and Hardy suggested MAIDEN CASTLE, the Iron Age hill fort near DORCHESTER. At Hardy's request, Hermann LEA, the Dorchester photographer, sent several images of the castle. Hardy chose one but offered suggestions on obtaining a better view (*Letters* IV, 304).

Edmund GOSSE praised the collection, writing that it was "a cluster of asteroids, which take their proper place in the planetary system, and differ from your novels only in the matter of size. They are uniformly and wonderfully worthy of you, and are wholly precious" (Millgate, *Thomas Hardy: A Biography*, 493).

The volume was published in October 1913. Hardy sent presentation copies to Florence HENNIKER, Léonie Gifford, Dorothy ALLHUSEN, and others.

For further reading: David Baron, "Hardy and the Dorchester Pouncys."

"Channel Firing"   Poem written in April 1914, a few months before the outbreak of WORLD WAR I, and published in SATIRES OF CIRCUMSTANCE (1914). It takes the form of a dialogue between God and a group of skeletons in coffins in a church graveyard near the south coast. Hardy imagines them to have been awakened by the sound of guns thundering out in the English Channel. They think it is Judgment Day and sit up; dogs howl and the cow drools. God answers that it is only "gunnery practice out at sea." God observes wryly that it's a "blessed thing" that judgment hour has not arrived, for some of them would "have to scour Hell's floor for so much threatening." The skeletons lie down again; one of them wonders whether the world will ever be saner than it was when they died. The skeleton of Parson Thirdly says he wishes he had "stuck to pipes and beer," since his preaching has had so little effect. The guns roar again, inland as far as "Stourton Tower, And Camelot, and starlit Stonehenge." (Stourton Tower is the Alfred Tower, about three miles north of the town of Stourton and about 30 miles north of Portland harbor. It commemorates the victory of Alfred the Great in 879 over the Danes.) "Camelot," the location of King Arthur's citadel, has sometimes been placed at Glastonbury or at Cadbury, which is approximately 28 miles north and west of Portland harbor. Stonehenge is about 45 miles northeast of Portland harbor. As Bailey puts it, the three represent civilizations elevated by war into dynasties. He describes the tone of the poem as "humorous, but not frivolous" (Bailey, *The Poetry of Thomas Hardy*, 263–64). The fact that the poem was written before the assassination of Archduke Francis Ferdinand of Austria-Hungary at Sarajevo in late June 1914, considered by many historians to be the immediate cause of the war, makes it all the more prescient, haunting, and ironic.

The poem was set to music in *Before and After Summer* (London: Boosey & Hawkes, 1949; *see* Appendix II).

Chant, Mercy A religious young woman who hopes to marry Angel CLARE in TESS OF THE D'URBERVILLES. Intellectually trained by her revered father, Dr. Chant, she gives Bible classes and glories in her Protestantism. Angel, still in love with Tess DURBEYFIELD despite their difficulties, argues in favor of Roman Catholicism. Mercy becomes engaged to Angel's brother Cuthbert CLARE.

Chapman and Hall London publishing firm noted principally for their failure to accept Hardy's first novel, *The POOR MAN AND THE LADY*. The publisher Alexander Macmillan had rejected it but had given Hardy an introduction to Frederick Chapman. He called at their offices on Piccadilly in late 1868, and saw the Scottish historian and essayist Thomas Carlyle in a back room. Chapman and Hall rejected the manuscript on February 8, 1869, telling Hardy that he "had not got an interesting story to work upon and . . . some of your episodic scenes are fatally injured" (Purdy, *Thomas Hardy: A Bibliographical Study*, 275). The firm hinted that they might publish it if Hardy were to subsidize it. Hardy met with the manuscript reader, George MEREDITH, about the manuscript in March 1869; their conversation resulted in Hardy's withdrawing it.

Charley A boy in *The RETURN OF THE NATIVE*, who is a great admirer of Eustacia VYE. He permits her to take his place as the Turkish Knight in the *The Play of Saint George*, given by the CHRISTMAS MUMMERS at the home of Mrs. YEOBRIGHT. This is one of the most noted scenes in the novel. In exchange, Eustacia permits the boy to hold her hand briefly.

For further reading: Cox, *Mumming and the Mummers' Play of St. George;* Squillace, "Hardy's Mummers."

Charmond, Felice In *The WOODLANDERS*, a wealthy young widow who owns the Hintock estate outside the rural village of Little Hintock. A former actress, her machinations have earned her a reputation as one of Hardy's most detestable women. Hoping to preserve her youthful attractions, she forces Marty SOUTH, a poor village girl, to sell her hair to make her a hairpiece. She also induces Dr. Edred FITZPIERS to leave his wife and goes with him to the Continent. She is shot by an "Italianized American" from South Carolina who had once been her suitor.

Chatto & Windus This firm was an outgrowth of Pickering & Chatto Publishers, one of the oldest book publishing businesses in England. It was founded in 1820 by William Pickering, the original publisher of Samuel Taylor Coleridge's works. After the death of Pickering and his son, the company was purchased by Mr. Chatto, a founding partner of Chatto & Windus. They were the publishers of BELGRAVIA, in which *The RETURN OF THE NATIVE* was serialized in 1877. They also published UNDER THE GREENWOOD TREE and owned the copyright to it, obligating Hardy to obtain permission to include the novel in the various collected editions of his works.

Chickerel, Cornelia Character in *The HAND OF ETHELBERTA*. One of Ethelberta PETHERWIN's elder sisters, she helps keep the secret that Ethelberta is taking in lodgers. She and her sister Gwendoline CHICKEREL marry brothers, who are farmers; both couples emigrate to Australia.

Chickerel, Dan Character in *The HAND OF ETHELBERTA*. One of the many Chickerel siblings he is a carpenter and goes into business with his brother Sol CHICKEREL.

Chickerel, Emmeline Character in *The HAND OF ETHELBERTA*. One of Ethelberta PETHERWIN's sisters, she tutors the younger children while they live concealed in the attic of Ethelberta's LONDON townhouse.

Chickerel, Ethelberta *See* PETHERWIN, ETHELBERTA.

Chickerel, Georgina Character in *The HAND OF ETHELBERTA*. She is one of Ethelberta PETHERWIN's younger sisters whose future Ethelberta hopes to assure when she tries to make, or marry, money.

Chickerel, Gwendoline Character in *The HAND OF ETHELBERTA*. One of Ethelberta PETHERWIN's older sisters, she serves as a cook when Ethelberta takes in lodgers in her LONDON house. She and her sister Cornelia CHICKEREL marry farmers who are brothers; they all emigrate to Australia.

Chickerel, Joseph Character in *The HAND OF ETHELBERTA*. One of Ethelberta PETHERWIN's brothers, he serves as page but becomes infatuated with Mrs. Menlove, the lady's maid, and reveals Ethelberta's humble origins. He later learns Latin.

Chickerel, Mr. R. Character in *The HAND OF ETHELBERTA*. The polished father of the Chickerel siblings, he works as a butler and lives apart from them but is very concerned about the well-being of the entire Chickerel family. He is upset when his daughter Ethelberta PETHERWIN becomes engaged to the ruthless Lord Mountclere, and unsuccessfully tries to prevent their marriage.

Chickerel, Mrs. Character in *The HAND OF ETHELBERTA*. The invalid mother of the Chickerel siblings, she tries to dissuade Ethelberta PETHERWIN from her grand schemes for the betterment of the family, but fails. She had been a nurse in a nobleman's household until she married and had 10 children.

Chickerel, Myrtle Character in *The HAND OF ETHELBERTA*. One of the 10 Chickerel siblings, she is one of the trio of youngest girls who are hidden in Ethelberta PETHERWIN's attic, being tutored, while Ethelberta schemes to provide for their future.

Chickerel, Picotee One of the 10 Chickerel siblings in *The HAND OF ETHELBERTA*. Close in age to Ethelberta PETHERWIN, she is the most mature and perceptive of the girls. She carries out Ethelberta's commissions and assists with the younger children, but has doubts about Ethelberta's schemes for her to rise socially while dissociating herself from her lower-class siblings. She manages to make a happy marriage to Christopher JULIAN.

Chickerel, Sol One of the 10 Chickerel siblings in *The HAND OF ETHELBERTA*. Older than Ethelberta PETHERWIN, he is close to his brother Dan. He objects to Ethelberta's marriage to a much older, titled nobleman who is very repressive. He tries to help her escape from him, but fails. He and Dan go into business together.

"Childhood Among the Ferns" Poem published in *WINTER WORDS* (1928). It is written from the point of view of a young man taking shelter from a rainstorm within a bank of ferns. His surroundings slowly take on the aspect of a dwelling. In order to complete the sensation of shelter he ignores drops that "pierced the green rafters . . . / Making pretense I was not rained upon." When the rain ends and the sun bursts forth there is a "sweet breath" as the "limp ferns" dry; he thinks, "I could live on here thus till death." From within his refuge he then questions the value of the burdens and pursuits that make up adult life. Why, he wonders, "should I have to grow to man's estate, / And this afar-noised World perambulate?" The poem is written in five three-lined rhyming stanzas.

The poetry collection *Winter Words*, published posthumously on October 2, 1928, contains poems written after the collection *HUMAN SHOWS, FAR PHANTASIES, SONGS, AND TRIFLES* was published in 1925. Bailey believes that "Childhood Among the Ferns" might have resulted from the diaries Hardy consulted, along with early memories he recalled, in preparing the *Life*, on which he worked between 1925 and 1928 (Bailey, *The Poetry of Thomas Hardy*, 545).

childlessness of Thomas and Emma Hardy Hardy's biographers have often speculated about whether the Hardys wanted children, but there is evidence that they were deeply disappointed at not having them. Thomas and Emma Hardy were married in 1874. On July 13, 1876, when the young couple were living at STURMINSTER NEWTON, Hardy made a note in his diary, "The sudden disappointment of a hope leaves a scar which the ultimate fulfilment of that hope never entirely removes," suggesting, perhaps, that Emma had suffered a miscarriage. A month later, on August 13, he notes: "We hear that Jane, our late servant, is soon to have a baby. Yet never a sign of one is there for us" (*Life*, 116). In 1885, he had finished *The MAYOR OF CASTERBRIDGE* but had not yet found a publisher. His biographer Evelyn Hardy speculates that the novel was "seared with so much bitterness" that publishers feared for its reception. She believes it might even have been "a final, defiant challenge to manhood and virility, the bitter cry of one who saw himself cheated and childless, trapped by Fate into an unfertile, life-long union" (*Thomas Hardy: A Critical Biography*, 202).

In 1895 Hardy wrote the Australian-born novelist Mary Chavelita CLAIRMONTE, whose pseudonym was George Egerton, about her short-story volume *Keynotes*, which had been criticized for its presentation of sexual matter just as JUDE THE OBSCURE had been. He congratulated her on the birth of a son, and added, "My children, alas, are all in octavo" (*Letters* II, 102). In 1904, when Hardy's mother died, his friend Edward CLODD wrote a letter of sympathy. Hardy wrote to thank him, commenting on the gap left by her death, and adding that perhaps "if one had a family of children one would be less sensible of it" (*Letters* III, 119).

Evelyn Hardy notes that when Hardy made his last will and testament in August 1922, when he was 82 years of age, he was "still hoping for an heir." He provided in three separate clauses for "the first child of mine who shall attain to the age of twenty-one years."

"Christmas: 1924"   Poem written in 1924, first published as "Peace upon Earth" in the *Daily Telegraph* on June 18, 1928, and later collected in WINTER WORDS (1928). It is only four lines long, and consists of an ironic reflection on the fact that the Christmas greeting "Peace upon earth!" and the celebration of "two thousand years of mass" have only brought civilization as far as "poison gas." Hardy had been thinking of the poem ever since the BOER WAR, and wrote his friend Florence HENNIKER on February 25, 1900:

> I met a religious man on Friday . . . & I said, We, the civilized world, have given Christianity a fair trial for nearly 2000 years, & it has not yet taught countries the rudimentary virtue of keeping peace: so why not throw it over, & try, say, Buddhism . . . It shocked him for he could only see the unchristianity of Kruger.

Christmas cards designed by Thomas Hardy   Although Hardy questioned much in organized religion, F. B. Pinion considers him a "Christian at heart" and notes that all his life he was "a lover of church services" (*A Hardy Companion,* 167). Christmas celebrations meant a great deal to him, particularly the tradition of CHRISTMAS MUMMERS. In 1902 he drew and hand-lettered several Christmas cards, which he sent to various friends and relatives, including his sisters Mary HARDY and Katharine HARDY and his cousin, the etcher Nathaniel Sparks.

"Christmas Ghost-Story, A"   Poem dated *"Christmas-eve, 1899"* and first printed in the WESTMINSTER GAZETTE on December 23, 1899, and reprinted in *War Against War in South Africa,* edited by William T. Stead, on December 29, 1899 (Stead was later lost aboard the *Titanic,* which contributed to Hardy's wish to write a poem about the disaster, "The CONVERGENCE OF THE TWAIN"). The poem was collected in POEMS OF THE PAST AND THE PRESENT (1902).

Hardy depicts the body of a young soldier, "your countryman," lying inland from Durban, South Africa, during the BOER WAR. His "phantom," or ghost, asks whether national interests justify warfare; by what "Law /Of Peace, brought in by that Man Crucified, /Was ruled to be inept, and set aside?" Some critics thought Hardy had portrayed the soldier's phantom as "unheroic." Hardy defended it in a letter to the *Daily Chronicle* on December 28, 1899. He argued that the soldier might have been heroic while living, but that his "ghost" has views that are "no longer local; nations are all one to him; his country is . . . co-extensive with the globe itself." He insisted that the phan-

tom of a slain soldier might be assumed to regret, especially on or near Christmas Eve, "the battles of life and war in general." Hardy was making the point also that Christian teachings are at variance with the behavior of nations (Bailey, *The Poetry of Thomas Hardy,* 119–20).

"Christmas in the Elgin Room"   Poem begun in 1905, while Hardy was in the BRITISH MUSEUM gathering material for *The DYNASTS,* but not completed until 1926, and published in WINTER WORDS (1928). It was the last of Hardy's writings to be published during his lifetime. He asked his wife to send it to the London *Times,* which she did; the editor wrote a warm reply, and it was published in the *Times* on December 24, 1927 (just before Hardy's death in early 1928).

Set in the British Museum, LONDON, the poem takes the form of a dialogue between the Elgin Marbles and a museum watchman on Christmas Eve. (The Elgin Marbles are sculptures that originally stood on the Acropolis in Athens, in a temple dedicated to the goddess Athena. Lord Elgin acquired them, brought them back to England, and sold them to the nation in 1816. They are still housed in the British Museum and have been the subject of dispute between England and Greece for many years.)

In the poem, the marbles ask the meaning of the bells they hear ringing outside. The watchman replies that they are Christmas bells, celebrating "a day of cheer." The captive marbles respond that they are those whom "Christmas overthrew"; they have been sold for gold "And brought to the gloom / Of this gaunt room." Despite the bells, they would rather be "Radiant as on Athenai's Hill." They had been placed there long before "this Christ was known." The bells that "sang that night . . . shook them to the core."

These themes were not original with Hardy; other poets, such as Byron, KEATS, and SWINBURNE had also reflected on the inequity of Lord Elgin's acquiring one of the major treasures of Greece and shipping them to England.

Christmas mummers   A tradition in which a troupe of actors and singers go from house to house, dancing, singing, and playing long-established roles. The scene in which mummers perform *The Play of Saint George* is one of the most noted in *The RETURN OF THE NATIVE.* On Christmas night, 1920, carol singers and mummers came to MAX GATE and performed this play; Hardy noted in the *Life* that it was just as he had "seen it performed in his childhood" (*Life,* 411).

In 1901 Hardy was interviewed by the critic William ARCHER for the American magazine *The Critic.* Archer asked about his memories of Christmas mummers, and he replied that the tradition had survived in some places until at least 1880. The usual performance was called "The Play of St. George," containing such traditional characters as the Valiant Soldier, the Turkish Knight, St. George, the Saracen, Father Christmas, the Fair Sabra, and others. Only men and boys took part. A village company might have 12 to 15 actors, going from one farmhouse to another between Christmas and Twelfth Night (January. 6), giving as many as four or five performances per night. They would be given ale and money.

Hardy recalled the "odd sort of thrill" of a performance. The actors would carry a long staff in one hand and a wooden sword in the other, and "pace monotonously round, intoning their parts on one note, and punctuating them by nicking the sword against the staff . . . 'Here comes I, the Valiant Soldier (nick), Slasher is my name (nick).'" The performances ended in "mortal combats" with all the characters killed except St. George. They would be brought to life by another character, the Doctor of Physic" (William Archer, "Real conversations: conversation 1: with Mr. Thomas Hardy" [*The Critic*, 1901]; quoted in Chandler, *Thomas Hardy's Christmas*).

For further reading: Chandler, *Thomas Hardy's Christmas;* Cox, *Mumming and the Mummers' Play of St. George;* Squillace, "Hardy's Mummers."

Christminster   Hardy's name for the town of OXFORD. It is mentioned briefly in his story "Dame the Sixth—Squire Petrick's Lady," *(see A GROUP OF NOBLE DAMES),* when Squire Petrick imagines the Marquis of Christminster might be the father of his wife's son. Christminster figures prominently in *JUDE THE OBSCURE*, when it is clearly intended to be the university town of Oxford. Hardy invents some names, however. The Mitre Hotel is thought to be the "Crozier Hotel," and Christ Church College "Cardinal College." Pinion provides a map of the town with possible identifications (Pinion, *A Hardy Companion*, 279).

"Church Romance, A" *(Mellstock circa 1835)*   This poem first appeared in the *SATURDAY REVIEW* for September 8, 1906; it was later collected in *TIME'S LAUGHING-STOCKS* (1909). It is based on the story of the way in which Hardy's parents met. In the early 1830s, the poet's grandfather, also named Thomas Hardy, played the violoncello at STINSFORD CHURCH; Hardy's father, Thomas, and his uncle, James, also played there. In the *Life*, Hardy described his father as handsome, courteous, and "about five feet nine in height, of good figure, with dark Vandyke-brown hair, and a beard which he wore white and regular to nearly the last years of his life, and blue eyes that never faded grey: a quick step, and a habit of bearing his head a little to one side as he walked." Jemima Hand, who was to be his mother, had a "trim and upright figure" and a buoyant walk. She read omnivorously and sang songs popular at the time, such as Haynes Bayly's "Isle of Beauty" and "Gaily the Trouba-

dour." She came to live near Bockhampton about 1835 or 1836 and attended Stinsford Church, where she met the elder Thomas Hardy who she married in 1839 (Bailey, *The Poetry of Thomas Hardy*, 232–33).

In Hardy's poem, a young girl in the MELLSTOCK church turns around in her pew to scan the instrumentalists playing in the gallery. One young man playing a "strenuous viol" seems to propel a message "from his string to her below," claiming her as his "own forthright!" Their "hearts' bond" begins; they are married, and many years later, when "Age had scared Romance" the gallery-scene would "break upon her mind, / With him as minstrel, ardent, young, and trim, / Bowing 'New Sabbath' or 'Mount Ephraim.'"

"Circus-Rider to Ringmaster"   A poem first published in *HARPER'S MONTHLY MAGAZINE*, New York, in June 1925 and Collected in *HUMAN SHOWS, FAR PHANTASIES, SONGS AND TRIFLES* (1925). In the manuscript the notation" (Casterbridge Fair, 188-)" was added (*see* "AT CASTERBRIDGE FAIR"). Hardy, according to the *Life*, had a "craze for circuses" during the early 1880s and attended those that came to Dorchester. During one performance the equestrienne who had been leaping through hoops missed her footing and fell to the ground. Hardy was very concerned, followed her into her tent, and became extremely interested in her recovery. He states that the incident "seems to have some bearing on the verses of many years after entitled 'Circus Rider to Ringmaster'" (*Life*, 166).

The poem is a plea from an aging woman circus rider to the ringmaster, who has also been her lover and was her master outside the ring as well as in. She begs him, "When I am riding round the ring no longer, / Tell a tale of me." She hopes that when she is dead he will not forget her: "Show how I . . . took the high-hoop leap / Into your arms, who coaxed and grew my lover." Although she is now a "fading form," she hopes he will remember the kisses he would blow up to her when their love was "warm," before tears stained her cheeks.

Clairmonte, Mary Chavelita (1859?–1945)   Australian-born novelist who married Reginald Golding Bright, Thomas Hardy's dramatic agent. Her pseudonym, George Egerton, was taken from the first two names of her second husband, George Egerton Clairmonte. In November 1895 she wrote Hardy a letter praising *JUDE THE OBSCURE*, stating that she found Sue BRIDEHEAD to be "a marvellously true psychological study of a temperament less rare than the ordinary male observer supposes" (*Letters* II, 102).

Clare, Angel   Character in *TESS OF THE D'URBERVILLES*. He is the youngest son of the Reverend James CLARE of Emminster. He prepares for a career in agriculture, as he is thought to be too liberal a thinker for the ministry; he cannot accept all of the dogma of the church. He is sensitive and has the potential to become a scholar, but is also rigid in his outlook. He falls in love with Tess DURBEYFIELD, believing she is the idealization of a "pure woman." He courts her ardently, and they marry, after which she tells him that she was once overpowered and seduced by Alec D'URBERVILLE. He cannot accept her past and blames her. After they part, he eventually is able to see her as a good person despite her circumstances, but it is too late.

Angel is inconsistent: he claims to believe that virtue is far more important than heredity, but is nevertheless snobbish enough to be delighted when he comes to believe Tess is a descendant of the illustrious d'Urberville family. He abandons Tess, goes to Brazil, and selfishly worries about his own plight. Only on his return does he belatedly comprehend that Tess has been too proud to ask for money and has been in a pitiable situation. He then looks on her favorably. After she murders Alec, he tries to help her escape from England, but Tess is identified and arrested at STONEHENGE. Angel never understands the depth of Tess's love for him, nor her wish to murder Alec. When she suggests that he marry her sister, 'Liza-Lu DURBEYFIELD, after she is gone, he is shocked.

Hardy modeled Angel in part on Charles Moule, a younger brother of his friend Horace MOULE, who became president of Corpus Christi College, Cambridge. His name, according to Hardy, came from a monument to the Grey family in STINSFORD CHURCH.

Clare, Cuthbert Elder brother of Angel CLARE in *TESS OF THE D'URBERVILLES*. He is a classical scholar and the dean of his Cambridge college, but is uncharitable himself, and does not attend the marriage of Angel and Tess. He becomes engaged to Mercy CHANT, who has tried, but failed, to attract Angel.

Clare, Felix Elder brother of Angel CLARE in *TESS OF THE D'URBERVILLES*. He is a curate in a neighboring town; like his brother Cuthbert CLARE, he is conventional but rigid and uncharitable. Neither he nor Cuthbert attends the marriage of Angel and Tess.

Clare, Mrs. The second wife of the Reverend James CLARE and mother of his sons, Cuthbert, Felix, and Angel. She regretted that Angel had not been sent to a university. Although she would not have chosen a girl of Tess DURBEYFIELD's class for him, she would have treated Tess sympathetically had Angel not rigidly rejected Tess after they were married.

Clare, Rev. James Character in *TESS OF THE D'URBERVILLES*. He is the vicar of Emminster and father of Angel CLARE. He sees no reason to send Angel to

university if he is not going to be ordained. He and his wife are more charitable Christians than their other sons, Felix and Cuthbert, and are sympathetic toward Tess. Had they been at home when she came to Emminster, they would have received her kindly.

Clodd, Edward (1840–1930) Banker, writer, and rationalist; among his works were *The Childhood of the World* (1872), *Jesus of Nazareth* (1880), *Myths and Dreams* (1885), *Animism: or the Seed of Religion* (1906), and *Magic in Names* (1920). It is unclear just when Clodd and Hardy met, but in the *Life* Hardy refers to him in December 1890, when he was staying in London.

In June 1891 Hardy visited Clodd over the Whitsunday weekend at his home in Aldeburgh, Suffolk, where he met Walter BESANT and J. M. BARRIE. Clodd might have influenced Hardy's reading that summer; he perused Arthur Schopenhauer's *Studies in Pessimism*, John Addington Symonds's *Essays Speculative and Suggestive*, and the first volume of James Frazer's *The Golden Bough* (Millgate, *Thomas Hardy: A Biography*, 315). Hardy attended several of Clodd's congenial Aldeburgh gatherings later; they were often held over the Whitsunday holiday weekend. In May 1894, at Clodd's home, Hardy met the mountaineer Edward Whymper, who had been the only Englishman to survive the Matterhorn tragedy in 1865 (*see* "ZERMATT: TO THE MATTERHORN" *JUNE–JULY 1897*).

In his autobiography Hardy records bicycling about Dorset with Clodd and other friends in July 1899. In 1908 Hardy wrote Clodd that he was almost finished with proofs of *The DYNASTS*, adding that it would be "well" for it to be over, "for I have been living in Wellington's campaigns so much lately that, like George IV, I am almost positive that I took part in the battle of Waterloo, and have written of it from memory." He was glad Clodd liked the description of the fauna on the field of Waterloo on the eve of battle, saying he thought it was the most original part of the epic drama (*Life*, 452–53). Both Hardy and Florence Dugdale, who would become Hardy's second wife, were at the home of Clodd in Aldeburgh for four days in May 1912 (Millgate, ed., *Letters of Emma and Florence Hardy*, 74).

In 1916 Clodd published *Memories*, which Hardy had feared would violate some of his confidences, but when the volume arrived, it contained nothing objectionable to Hardy (Millgate, *Thomas Hardy: A Biography*, 508). Clodd wrote his friend J. M. Bulloch on January 14, 1928, that he considered the partition of Hardy's remains "repellent." After Hardy's death, his second wife, Florence HARDY, had been persuaded by Sir Sydney COCKERELL and Sir James BARRIE to permit his heart to be removed and buried in Emma's grave at STINSFORD CHURCH. His ashes were interred at WESTMINSTER ABBEY.

For further reading: Clodd, *Memories*.

Club-walking   A tradition, probably a survival of the May Day dance, also called the "club revel," in which the women members of a village club, dressed in white gowns of varying styles, engage in a ritualistic procession. According to P. N. Furbank, a "club" was a parish "friendly society," a benefit club; the main activity was the yearly "walking" at Whitsuntide; hence the term "club-walking" (Notes, *Tess of the d'Urbervilles,* New Wessex Edition, ed. P. N. Furbank [London: Macmillan, 1974]). In *TESS OF THE D'URBERVILLES* the club of Marlott has, according to Hardy, "walked for hundreds of years, if not as benefit-club, as votive sisterhood of some sort." There is first a processional march of "two and two" around the parish. Each woman and girl carries a peeled willow wand in her right hand and a bunch of white flowers in her left, all chosen with considerable care. When the procession reaches the village green, where there is an enclosure, dancing begins. At first the girls dance with each other, but as they finish work the "masculine inhabitants of the village, together with other idlers and pedestrians," gather and "negotiate for a partner" (chapter 2).

In *TWO ON A TOWER* the villagers discuss the decline of Lady Viviette CONSTANTINE, whose husband is away in Africa, and who is a "walking weariness." They hope she can "see a little life; though there's no fair, club-walking, nor feast, to speak of, till Easter week" (chapter 2).

Cockerell, Sir Sydney Carlyle (1867–1962)   A longtime friend of Hardy's, Cockerell was director of the Fitzwilliam Museum, Cambridge, from 1908 to 1937.

In 1911 Cockerell urged Hardy to distribute his manuscripts to selected libraries in Britain and the United States, which Hardy began to do at that time. Because Hardy had no descendants, he was concerned that his papers be placed in the right hands.

In 1907 Cockerell married the artist and illuminator Florence Kate Kingsford, called Kate. She developed multiple sclerosis and her health declined over the years, but she remained as active as possible. Their son, Christopher (later inventor of the hovercraft), was born in 1910 (*Letters* V, 218).

In 1916 Hardy wrote to offer Kate Cockerell a Bath chair (a type of upholstered wheelchair) "of the very best make and appearance" that he had bought for his late wife, Emma HARDY. Hardy said that Emma had used the chair very little. It had been in storage since her death in 1912, and he hoped Mrs. Cockerell could make use of it (*Letters* V, 157–58). He had the chair shipped to Cambridge, and apparently she did use it. In 1919 she designed the costumes for the Cambridge University Musical Society's production of Henry Purcell's *The Fairy Queen* (*Letters* V, 200–201, 350).

Sir Sydney Cockerell became, in Hardy's later years, something of a sounding board for Florence HARDY's difficulties in dealing with her husband. In January 1925 he arrived at MAX GATE and discovered that she was extremely upset because her husband had forgotten her birthday. It was Cockerell whom Florence Hardy summoned in January 1928 when Hardy's condition became critical. Cockerell was not admitted to Hardy's bedroom, but arranged for a professional nurse to assist Florence and her sister Eva. After Hardy's death, Cockerell helped Eva put Hardy's scarlet doctoral robe on the body.

Cockerell and Sir James BARRIE, who had come to DORCHESTER and was staying in a hotel, began, as Michael Millgate puts it, "to assert their male authority" over what Cockerell called "the housefull [*sic*] of women." The men believed they represented "the claims of the world of letters and of the nation." Florence was exhausted and unable to protest when they contacted WESTMINSTER ABBEY and asked that his ashes be interred there. They were placed in Poets' Corner. Hardy had intended to be buried in the same grave with Emma at STINSFORD CHURCH. Both Emma and Florence are buried in this grave, as is Hardy's heart. After his heart was removed, Barrie and Cockerell went to the crematorium, oversaw the cremation, and delivered his ashes to the Abbey (Millgate, *Thomas Hardy: A Biography,* 573–75).

Cockerell was one of Hardy's literary executors, along with Barrie. To the distress of Hardy's later biographers, he destroyed the author's pocket notebooks, which Hardy apparently had instructed him to do (Millgate, *Thomas Hardy: A Biography,* 518). Cockerell also offered advice to Florence Hardy as she prepared his memoirs, later published as *The Life of Thomas Hardy,* for publication. Later, however, she broke with him and deeply regretted having yielded to pressure to allow the division of Hardy's remains.

For further reading: Meynell, ed., *Friends of a Lifetime: Letters to Sydney Carlyle Cockerell.*

Coggan, Bob   Small son of Jan COGGAN, a laborer on Bathsheba EVERDENE's Weatherbury Farm in *FAR FROM THE MADDING CROWD.*

Coggan, Jan   Master shearer on Bathsheba EVERDENE's Weatherbury farm in *FAR FROM THE MADDING CROWD.* His first wife, now deceased, would never permit swearing. Gabriel OAK lodges at the Coggans for a time. Jan and Gabriel chase Bathsheba when she goes to Bath, believing someone has stolen her horse, Dainty. Jan is perceptive, but tactful, about Gabriel's love for Bathsheba. His second wife is employed by Bathsheba as a housekeeper.

Coggan, Mrs.   Second wife of Jan COGGAN in *FAR FROM THE MADDING CROWD.* She can "toss a pancake or twirl a mop with the accuracy of pure mathematics." She works for Bathsheba EVERDENE at Weatherbury Farm.

"Collector Cleans His Picture, The" *Fili hominis, ecce ego tollo a te desiderabile oculorum tuorum in plaga.— Ezech., XXIV 16* This poem, published in LATE LYRICS AND EARLIER (1922), is written from the point of view of a "rural parson" whose sole hobby, away from the pressures of the parish, is to search in the "backmost slums" of a nearby city for a "worthy canvas, / Panel, or plaque" that, when cleaned, might yield a "precious art-feat." He finds a painting with many layers of varnish, which he sets about cleaning. At first a remarkable image emerges, a fair Venus with "a curve, a nostril, and next a finger, / Tapering, shapely, significantly pointing slantwise." He rubs the painting all night until he discovers that the owner of the finger is a "hag," pointing towards "a bosom / Eaten away of a rot from the lusts of a lifetime. . ." He sits, stunned, until the church steeple begins chiming and calling him to the morning service.

The poem apparently recalls an incident in the life of the Reverend William BARNES of Came Rectory, who was Hardy's friend and neighbor. The Latin motto is translated in the King James Bible as "Son of man, behold, I take away from thee the desire of thine eyes with a stroke" (Bailey, *The Poetry of Thomas Hardy,* 459).

Collier, John (1850–1934) Illustrator of *The* TRUMPET-MAJOR when it was serialized in GOOD WORDS beginning in January 1880. Hardy supplied Collier with sketches, writing on November 22, 1879, that they were "subject entirely" to Collier's revision. He remarked that he could not decide where the trumpet-major ought to be standing and hoped Collier would "stick him in where he looks best" (*Letters* VII, 93). One of the illustrations, that of the miller's kitchen, was based on Hardy's own drawing (Millgate, *Thomas Hardy: A Biography,* 207).

A graduate of Eton and Heidelberg, Collier had studied art in Munich and Paris, and at the Slade Institute in London. He became a member of the ROYAL ACADEMY OF ARTS. He was as dedicated to accuracy as Hardy, and wrote him that he would "spare no pains" to avoid inaccuracy in his depiction of the "costumes and accessories" (Jackson, *Illustration and the Novels of Thomas Hardy,* 46–47). He contributed 32 drawings to the serial text. He also painted a portrait of Hardy now owned by the Rationalist Press Association (*Letters* V, 23).

"Colonel's Soliloquy, The" (*Southampton Docks: October 1899*) Published in POEMS OF THE PAST AND THE PRESENT (1902), this poem is set during the embarkation from Southampton of British troops bound for the BOER WAR. Hardy presents the thoughts of a retired army colonel, recalled to service, as the ship pulls away from the quay. He states that for himself he has "scanty care," proven in "scrimmages" in "Eastern lands and South." He worries, though, about leaving his wife, no

longer a "girl" but a grandmother. If he "goes underground" she will not recover as she might have done when younger. He himself is more cynical about war than he once was. He no longer responds to the "crowd's farewell 'Hurrah'" as he did once, when it would "lift" him "to the moon."

Bailey suggests, as possible models for the Colonel, Colonel Arthur Henniker, the husband of Florence HENNIKER, or Lieutenant-Colonel Cecil Henry Law, the commander of the Dorsetshire Regiment (Bailey, *The Poetry of Thomas Hardy,* 117). This poem may be compared with "The GOING OF THE BATTERY" in its depiction of the anguish of the departure of British troops.

"Comet at Yell'ham, The" This poem, collected in POEMS OF THE PAST AND THE PRESENT (1902), was occasioned by the appearance of Encke's Comet in September-October 1858. A young man is watching it from Yellowham Hill with a companion. He reflects, as the comet's "fiery train" is about to "swim from sight," that when it returns "long years hence" its "strange swift shine," will fall on Yell'ham, but not on his companion's "sweet form." The companion might have been a girl Hardy was interested in at the time, when he was 18, but it also could have been one of his sisters or his mother (Bailey, *The Poetry of Thomas Hardy,* 168).

"Committee-Man of 'the Terror', A" Short story published in the *Illustrated London News,* which also had an American edition, in the Christmas number, November 22, 1896. It was accompanied by two illustrations drawn by H. Burgess. It was later collected in *A* CHANGED MAN AND OTHER TALES (1913).

The story is set in WEYMOUTH, which Hardy calls a "royal watering-place," about September 1802, when England was at peace with France, and King GEORGE III and his court were established at the seaside resort. A Frenchman of about 45 arrives by stagecoach in the midst of a grand celebration on the Esplanade and seeks lodgings. He is spotted by Mademoiselle V——, the "daughter of an old French family," a governess for General Newbold, who shrieks in horror and faints. He rescues her and helps her into a shop; she engages a coach and drives away. He apparently does not know why she shrieked.

He calls on her at the home of General Newbold, and she accuses him of having been a member of the Committee of Public Safety in Paris (the Comité de Salut Public), which guillotined her father, brother, and uncle. He admits to his membership but says it was a "matter of conscience" and he did not profit by it. She is unforgiving. One evening they both attend a performance of Sheridan's *The Rivals* and happened to sit next to each other; she cries silently. They encounter each other in various places; he declares he was the "instrument of a national principle" and not to blame for the deaths.

He eventually summons her to his lodging, saying he is ill and wants her to know his last wishes. He asks her to rip out some monograms from his linen; she asks whether he repents. He does not, but recovers. In May, Napoleon Bonaparte, who has ascended to power, calls for the arrests of innocent English travelers in France. English magistrates are asked to turn in French aliens. The man proposes to Mademoiselle V—— so that they can leave England together, and perhaps go to Quebec. She is horrified and turns him down. The English become more suspicious of French residents, and her friendship attracts attention. Madame Newbold warns her against the acquaintance.

The man realizes he must leave, although he is "no enemy to England." Mademoiselle V—— agrees to go with him, having become attached to the "lonely and severe man." Before the wedding a friend, also a refugee from the troubles in France, writes her and condemns the Comité de Salut Public. Her fiance soothes her, but she sees a vision of the killing of her relatives and decides she cannot marry him but must flee to LONDON. She boards the stagecoach, but at MELCHESTER (Salisbury) she changes her mind, leaves the coach, and returns to Weymouth. She finds a letter from the man on her mantlepiece, setting her free and saying he has gone to London. She realizes she had seen his form as an outside passenger in the coach leaving Melchester for London. Griefstricken, she takes up her old post as governess for General Newbold. At her death, about 20 years later, her last memory is of the coach at Melchester with her fiance's image "outlined against the stars of the morning."

Florence HENNIKER found the story a melancholy one; Hardy wrote her that it had not occurred to him that the story (or "sketch") was sad, since the marriage would have resulted in "unhappiness for certain, don't you think?" (*Letters* II, 139).

"Compassion" *(An Ode / In Celebration of the Centenary of the Royal Society for the Prevention of Cruelty to Animals)* This poem, dated January 22, 1924, was published in the London *Times* on June 16, 1924, and collected in *HUMAN SHOWS, FAR PHANTASIES, SONGS, AND TRIFLES* (1925). On January 5, 1924, Captain Fairholme of the Royal Society for the Prevention of Cruelty to Animals wrote Florence HARDY to ask whether Hardy might write an ode for the centenary of the Society's foundation; it could later be set to music and a well-known singer might sing it at the meeting. She replied on January 18 that he was beginning something. The society was unable to find a composer, but Captain Fairholme arranged for publication of the ode in the *Times*.

Hardy bemoans the plight of the "mild creatures" whose "deep dumb gaze" is "more eloquent / Than

tongues of widest heed." He points out that "helplessness breeds tyranny" and bemoans the way in which animals are slaughtered. He quotes "Ailinon . . . But may the good prevail!" (from Aeschylus' *Agamemnon*) and "Blessed are the merciful!" from the Sermon on the Mount. *See also* ANIMALS, HARDY'S LOVE OF.

"Concerning Agnes" Poem first published in the London *Daily Telegraph* on May 21, 1928, and collected in *WINTER WORDS* (1928). "Agnes" was the writer Lady (Agnes Geraldine) GROVE, the daughter of General and Mrs. Pitt-Rivers. Hardy recalls dancing with her in September 1895 at the Pitt-Rivers home, Rushmore. (At this time he was finishing *JUDE THE OBSCURE*.) There was dancing on the green under many lamps and the full moon in the village of Larmer. The local paper described the festivities as a grand spectacle of "extraordinary picturesqueness and poetry," and said the dances were "led off by the beautiful Mrs. Grove." Hardy states in the *Life* that his dance with her was "the last occasion on which he ever trod a measure" *Life*, 596–97).

Hardy had been shocked to learn of Agnes's death, which had occurred on December 7, 1926. Hardy died on January 11, 1928, as he was planning a volume of poems for publication, probably for his 88th birthday, which would have been June 2, 1928. The executors of his estate, including Florence HARDY and Sir Sydney COCKERELL, sold the serial rights to 50 of the 105 poems he had written to the *Daily Telegraph*. The paper published the poem in May before the October 1928 publication of the volume *WINTER WORDS* (Bailey, *The Poetry of Thomas Hardy*, 474–75).

In the poem Hardy imagines her tomb, which might depict Agnes resting like "some vague goddess," like "Aphrodite sleeping; or bedraped / Like Kalupso; / Or Amphitrite stretched on the Mid-sea swell." These are four Greek mythological figures: Aphrodite, the goddess of love; Kalupso (Calypso), a nymph who entertained Ulysses for seven years; Amphitrite, the wife of Poseidon; and one of the nine muses.

Coney, Christopher Character in *The MAYOR OF CASTERBRIDGE*. He is an associate of Solomon LONGWAYS; he has never been very successful. After the death of Susan HENCHARD the pennies that closed her eyes were buried in the garden. He digs them up and spends them at the Three Mariners Inn. Pinion points out that a "coney-catcher" is a swindler (F. B. Pinion, *A Hardy Companion*, 285).

Constantine, Lady Viviette In *TWO ON A TOWER*, the beautiful young wife of Sir Blount CONSTANTINE; she lives alone at Welland House. Her husband is away in Africa, hunting lions. She falls in love with Swithin ST. CLEEVE, who is studying astronomy on top of Rings-Hill

Speer, on her property. News comes that Sir Blount has been killed. She and Swithin marry, but the marriage is illegal, as her husband is found to have been still alive at the time, although he later dies. When she realizes she is pregnant, she knows that marrying Swithin legally would deprive him of his legacy, which he needs to travel and make astronomical discoveries. She marries the bishop of MELCHESTER, who is the legal father of her son, but she is unhappy. When the bishop dies she returns to Welland House. Swithin comes home, meets his son, and plans to marry Lady Constantine, but she dies of joy in his arms.

Constantine, Sir Blount   In *TWO ON A TOWER* the absent husband of Lady Viviette CONSTANTINE. He goes to Africa to hunt lions, illegally marries a native princess, and commits suicide there.

"Convergence of the Twain, The" (*Lines on the loss of the* **Titanic**)   One of Hardy's best-known poems, this work was first published in the program of the "Dramatic and Operatic Matinée in Aid of the 'Titanic' Disaster Fund," given at the Covent Garden Theater on April 24, 1912. It was collected in *SATIRES OF CIRCUMSTANCE* (1914).

The poem deals with the sinking of the White Star Line flagship *Titanic* early on the morning of April 15, 1912, shortly after strike an iceberg on its maiden voyage across the Atlantic. Of the 2,224 people on board, 1,513 were lost. Because it was thought the ship was unsinkable, there were not enough lifeboats. As the writer for the *Dorset County Chronicle* observed, the ship was "the most luxuriously appointed vessel that had ever left a port," fitted with Turkish baths, a gymnasium, a palm court with real ivy, mahogany paneling, and bandstands. Hardy wrote his friend Florence HENNIKER that he and his wife Emma had lost two acquaintances: one was William T. Stead, editor of the *Review of Reviews* (*see* "A CHRISTMAS GHOST-STORY"); the other was John Jacob Astor (Bailey, *The Poetry of Thomas Hardy*, 264–65).

The thesis is stated in the first five three-line stanzas. In each stanza, the first two lines depict the splendor of the ship and the ornaments of her passengers; the last line exposes the fallacy of vainglorious pride by exposing their condition under the sea. The ship's "steel chambers" have become the "pyres" of "salamandrine fires." Sea-worms now crawl over the mirrors intended to reflect the opulent, and jewels designed "To ravish the sensuous mind" are now "lightless," their "sparkles bleared and black and blind." As fish gaze at the "gilded gear," they ask, "What does this vaingloriousness down here?"

The answer, according to the poem, is that human purpose caused the building of an unsinkable "smart ship" by men whose "Pride of Life" permitted them to

plan such a vessel. But then the Immanent Will that "stirs and urges everything" prepared a "sinister mate" for the ship, a "Shape of Ice." The human effort is juxtaposed against the forces of nature that become the agent of the ship's destruction. Hardy suggests an inevitability in the colliding destinies of the ship, growing in "stature, grace, and hue" even as the iceberg enlarges in "shadowy silent distance." When the paths of the ship and the iceberg converge, "consummation comes, and jars two hemispheres." No "mortal eye" could envision the "intimate welding of their later history."

The ship assumes the aura of an innocent bride going to meet her menacing bridegroom. They are united by the collision, which seals their later history; they become "twin halves of one august event" (Bailey, *The Poetry of Thomas Hardy*, 266).

For further reading: Fain, "Hardy's 'The Convergence of the Twain'"; Graves, "Hardy's 'The Convergence of the Twain'"; Henderson, "Symbolic Meaning in Hardy's 'The Convergence of the Twain'"; Henry, "Hardy's 'The Convergence of the Twain,'"; Lloyd, "Hopkins's 'The Wreck of the Deutschland' and Hardy's 'The Convergence of the Twain'"; Roti, "Hardy's 'The Convergence of the Twain'"; Simpson, "Pomp and Circumstance— Hardy's 'The Convergence of the Twain'"; Thatcher, "Hardy's 'The Convergence of the Twain.'"

Corfe Castle   Castle between Wareham and Swanage, erected on the Purbeck Downs soon after the Norman Conquest. It occupies the site of the hunting-lodge where Edward the Martyr was assassinated in 979, and was a frequent residence of King John. It figures in *The HAND OF ETHELBERTA* as Corvsgate Castle.

Cornhill Magazine   Magazine edited by Sir Leslie STEPHEN from 1871 to 1882. In October 1873 Stephen accepted Hardy's novel *FAR FROM THE MADDING CROWD* for serialization; it ran in the magazine from January to December 1874. Hardy's novel *The HAND OF ETHELBERTA* ran from July 1875 to May 1876. Other writings published in its pages were the poems "The SOULS OF THE SLAIN," "AT CASTERBRIDGE FAIR," "LET ME ENJOY," "The NOBLE LADY'S TALE," and "Spring Call," as well as his paper "MEMORIES OF CHURCH RESTORATION" (a lecture read in absentia at the General Meeting of the Society for the Protection of Ancient Buildings in June 1906). The editor declined "A TRAMPWOMAN'S TRAGEDY" and *The TRUMPET-MAJOR*.

Cornwall   County comprising the western portion of the southwest peninsula of England, west of the Tamar River, with rugged coastlines, many estuaries and caves, and coastal resorts. In March 1870 Thomas Hardy arrived in Cornwall to assist with the restoration of ST. JULIOT CHURCH, an undertaking his former employer, the architect John HICKS, had left unfinished at his death. Hicks's projects were carried forward by G. R. CRICKMAY, who sent Hardy down to look at the church. Hardy eventually married Emma Gifford (*see* HARDY, Emma Gifford), the sister-in-law of the rector, the Reverend Caddell HOLDER.

Emma Hardy left an account of her meeting with Hardy, his subsequent visits several times a year, and of their travels throughout the region to Boscastle, Tintagel (the legendary site of King Arthur's castle), Trebarwith Strand, Strangles beach, Bude, and Bossiney. Hardy states, in the *Life*, that his wooing in the "'Delectable Duchy' ran . . . without a hitch from beginning to end." His poem "BEENY CLIFF," recalling their courtship, is set in Cornwall. They were married in September 1874.

Hardy later set his drama *The FAMOUS TRAGEDY OF THE QUEEN OF CORNWALL* (1916) on the north Cornish coast at Tintagel Castle, illustrating it with his own drawings.

"Could I but Will" *(Song: Verses 1, 3, key major; verse 2, key minor)* Poem collected in *LATE LYRICS AND EARLIER* (1922), in which Hardy speculates on what might happen if he could exercise free will. In the first stanza, he envisions paradise, with "sweethearts" near him who would dance "Ecstatic reels." In the second stanza he would be "head-god" and awaken a girl he once kissed, but who now lies "with linen-banded brow" in her grave. In the final stanza, he imagines himself as "half-god," with the power to revise "sand-swept plains and Arctic glooms" so that they are green and graced with "waving leaves." He and his old friends would "walk with weightless feet" and talk magic on "uncounted" evenings. It is possible that he is thinking of Emma HARDY during their courtship and early marriage, or of Tryphena SPARKS.

Cresscombe In *JUDE THE OBSCURE*, Hardy's name for the village of Letcombe Bassett, home of the parents of Arabella DONN. Her seduction of Jude FAWLEY takes place here.

Crick, Richard Character in *TESS OF THE D'URBERVILLES*. He is the chief dairyman of Talbothays Dairy, a kindly middle-aged man who welcomes Tess. He regularly attends church on Sunday, and has inspired a local rhyme: "Dairyman Dick / All the week:—/ On Sundays Mister Richard Crick." Aided by his wife, Mrs. Crick, he supervises nearly a hundred milkers, men and women.

Crickmay, George Rackstrow (1830–1907) Weymouth architect who, in April 1869, asked Hardy to complete some church restoration jobs the firm had taken on following the death of John HICKS. After Hardy worked several weeks in the firm's DORCHESTER office, Crickmay offered him three months' employ-

ment in WEYMOUTH. Hardy moved to Weymouth, where he directed the rebuilding of Turnworth church, west of Blandford Forum. He also supervised the restoration of several other churches. In February 1870 Crickmay asked him to go to CORNWALL to look at another church, ST. JULIOT, which was the last of the churches Hicks had begun restoring. It was here that Hardy met, and eventually married, Emma Gifford (*see* HARDY, Emma Gifford), sister-in-law of the rector, the Reverend Caddell HOLDER.

Hardy then began work on *DESPERATE REMEDIES*, published in 1871; in March he resumed working for Crickmay in Weymouth, and continued there for another year. In early 1872 he went to LONDON.

Cripplestraw, Anthony Character in *The TRUMPET-MAJOR*. Said by some critics to be among the most vivid characters in the novel, he is a member of the Locals, a group of volunteers who are preparing for the French invasion. He works for Benjamin DERRIMAN at Oxwell Hall. He torments Festus DERRIMAN by imagining his heroism when he is mown down in the front line during the expected invasion.

"Cry of the Homeless" *(After the Prussian Invasion of Belgium)* Hardy contributed this poem, written in August 1915, during WORLD WAR I, to *The Book of the Homeless*, compiled by the American writer Edith WHARTON to benefit war relief efforts. Hardy did not contribute a poem until Henry JAMES asked him to do so. James wrote on July 28, 1915, asking that he "distil the liquor of your poetic genius, in no matter how mild a form, into three or four blest versicles, on Mrs. Wharton's behalf, by August 10." Hardy sent the poem on August 8 (Bailey, *The Poetry of Thomas Hardy*, 422).

The poem, in three stanzas, implores the "instigator of the ruin" to hear the cry from "each city, shore, and lea / Of thy victims: 'Conqueror, all hail to thee!'" Hardy then passionately inverts his plea, asking that when history has comprehended their crimes, the perpetrators of the German atrocities "be slighted, blighted, And forsaken" by "thy victims, / 'And thy children beg their bread!'" Even better, perhaps compassion for their victims may "dew thy pillow / And bedrench thy sense all" before "death darks thee with his pall."

"Curate's Kindness, The" *A Workhouse Irony* Poem published in *TIME'S LAUGHINGSTOCKS* (1909). The speaker is an elderly man who, after 50 years of hard work and churchgoing, is reluctantly bound for the workhouse. He is ashamed to have to go there, but he hopes to regard it as home and to "find there a friend." His chief consolation is that "peace is assured" because men and women occupy separate wings of the workhouse, so he will not have to live with his wife.

Just as his wagon stops, a young parson steps up to the side of the wagon and announces proudly that he has spoken to "The Guardians," or administrators of the workhouse. They have been swayed by his argument that the rule separating men and women is a "harsh order" and have agreed that it is wrong to divide couples married nearly 40 years. From now on married couples will "abide" in "one wing together."

The speaker is heartsick. His misery will be lifelong, because "To get free of her there was the one thing /

Had made the change welcome to me." In the workhouse he had expected to be surrounded by strangers and to be free of his "forty years' chain." He wants only to "jump out o' waggon and go back and drown me / At Pummery or Ten-Hatches Weir."

Cuxsom, Mother   Character in *The MAYOR OF CASTER-BRIDGE*. A lower-class widow who has been beaten by her husband, she describes the death of Susan HENCHARD to the community.

D

Damson, Suke In *The WOODLANDERS*, a village girl who plays a pivotal role in driving a wedge between Grace Melbury FITZPIERS and her husband, Dr. Edred FITZPIERS. She marries young Timothy TANGS, who is jealous of Fitzpiers and sets a trap for him. They emigrate to New Zealand.

"Dance at the Phoenix, The" Published in *WESSEX POEMS* (1898), this ballad recounts the story of Jenny, a girl whose life had "hardly been / A life of modesty." She had had many loves, including "sundry troopers of / The King's-Own Cavalry,"quartered in CASTERBRIDGE. Then a "gentle youth / From inland" meets Jenny and proposes to her. She promises to be faithful; he trusts her, and they have two sons. After they have grown up and left home, Jenny, nearly 60, learns that "her early loves from war" have returned. She is thrilled to know they have returned to Casterbridge, despite her age.

The troops give a ball at the Phoenix Inn; the sounds reach Jenny as she lies in bed beside her husband. She rises, puts "two bows of red" on her cap, and goes to the inn. The sergeant refuses to admit "Gay Granny," although she insists that before he was born she "knew the regiment all." The men do not have enough partners, so she is admitted, and dances through the night. They cheer her on; at four o'clock, on tip-toe, they escort Jenny, "bosom-beating," to her home. There she has a sharp agonizing pain in her heart as she climbs to her husband's side. She looks down at him, "free from guile," and wishes she were a "single-hearted wife." At six o'clock he rises and looks at her, only to find that she has died during the night. He is told that "some too mighty strain / For one so many-yeared / Had burst her bosom's master-vein," but he is certain that Jenny did not leave his side all night. The King's Own Cavalry "said not a word." They were "truly martial men,"and when they departed from Casterbridge "And vanished over Mellstock Ridge, / 'Twas saddest morn to see."

Dare, William The villain of *A LAODICEAN*, Dare is the illegitimate son of Captain William DE STANCY (later, Sir William), whose family once owned the Castle de Stancy but fell on hard times and sold it. Dare could be 16 or 26; he is boyish and chameleon-like, shifting shapes and gliding secretly in and out of the Castle de Stancy. He tries in vain to better himself by arranging a marriage between his father and Paula POWER, the owner of the castle. He is adept at faking photographs and gambling. When he learns that the architect George SOMERSET is interested in Paula, and that she has commissioned him to draw up plans for restoring the castle, he tries to thwart Somerset by promoting James HAVILL, a rival architect. Dare has no respectable family ties to the de Stancys, nor has he any sense of responsibility. He finally sets fire to the Castle de Stancy. A satanic character, his name suggests "dare-devil."

"Dark-Eyed Gentleman, The" Poem, in the form of a ballad, published in *TIME'S LAUGHINGSTOCKS* (1909). The speaker is a girl working on a farm who has tossed her day's "leazings" (bundles of gleaned corn) into "Crimmercrock Lane" and stopped to tie up her garter. A "dark-eyed gentleman" passes by, ties up her garter for her, and seduces her. The final stanza, whose action takes place after an interval of several years, reveals that she has had a son who is her "dearest joy," "comrade, and friend." She has become a strong woman able to defend herself for her violation of social mores. She does not regret her son's existence and, in fact, is thankful that "his daddy once tied up my garter for me!"

The ballad has a more cheerful outcome than most dealing with this theme. Hardy relates the source of the story in the *Life*. In December 1882, a country woman named Mrs. Cross told him the story of a girl in the same situation. The young woman kept the child and struggled to raise it herself, refusing to marry the father, who had come back after a period of time and proposed to her. Hardy states that her "conduct in not caring to be 'made respectable' won the novelist-poet's admiration." He asked her name, but "the old narrator said, 'oh, never mind their names! they be dead and rotted by now.'" Hardy asserts that he "made use of it in succeeding years in more than one case in his fiction and verse" (*Life,* 157).

"Darkling Thrush, The" Poem dated December 31, 1900, and published in *POEMS OF THE PAST AND THE PRESENT* (1902). The speaker leans upon a country gate at the early close of a December day, reflecting on the wintry landscape; frost has already formed. He envisions the past century as a corpse, buried on the land under a cloud canopy. Springtime is now "shrunken hard and dry" and is also buried in the arid terrain. He envisions "every spirit upon earth" as dry and unfeeling. There are images of death throughout the first two stanzas, including tangled branches and broken lyres.

Suddenly he hears the joyful song of a thrush "frail, gaunt, and small," which has chosen to "fling his soul / Upon the growing gloom." The poet has seen so little cause for rejoicing that he concludes a certain "blessed Hope" has "trembled through / His happy good-night air." Hardy gives a religious significance to the experience with the phrase "full-hearted evensong" in the third stanza, which anticipates the idea of faith in the last stanza, "Some blessed Hope, whereof he knew / And I was unaware."

For further reading: Allingham,"The Significance of 'Darkling' in Hardy's 'The Darkling Thrush'"; Burns, "Imagery in Hardy's 'The Darkling Thrush'"; Lock, "'The Darkling Thrush' and the Habit of Singing"; Ownby, "A Reading of Thomas Hardy's 'The Darkling Thrush'"; Pinion, *A Commentary on the Poems of Thomas Hardy,* 53–55; Southworth, *The Poetry of Thomas Hardy,* 191–95; Vance, "Hardy's 'The Darkling Thrush' and G. F. Watts's 'Hope.'"

"Dawn after the Dance, The" *(Weymouth, 1869)* Poem published in *TIME'S LAUGHINGSTOCKS* (1909) and set in WEYMOUTH, the seaside resort where Thomas Hardy was employed by the architect G. R. CRICKMAY in 1869. The speaker is a young man escorting a girl, possibly from a dance hall, home at nearly dawn, after a New Year's Eve dance (probably December 31, 1869), to her parents' house. The parents' "curtained windows" reveal no thought of the young people's late arrival. He perceives that they have settled into "matrimonial commonplace," a prospect the young man dreads. The young couple's courtship has endured a year, in varying weather and seasons, in the course of which their attachment has been "spun to breaking." His love has become "lighter" and hers burns "no brighter." The "blind bleak windows" of her parents' house suggest that "the vows of man and maid are frail as filmy gossamer." James O. Bailey observes that the poem pictures "a final phase" of the "flirtation" and "love-making by adepts of both sexes." He quotes a letter from the Hardy scholar Frank Southerington, who postulates that the couple were actually Hardy and his cousin Tryphena SPARKS, to whom he was presumably engaged; she lived in Puddletown, however. V. H. Collins asked Hardy about the meaning of the somewhat ambiguous "no brighter." He replied that perhaps he originally wrote "the brighter." This would connote her hope of becoming a wife and mother; but "no brighter" also fits, if the girl is facing the prospect of

motherhood without marriage (Bailey, *The Poetry of Thomas Hardy,* 218–19). "The Conformers," a companion poem also published in *Time's Laughingstocks,* suggests the descent of a once passionate couple into a dull marriage. Despite the "stolen trysts" of their courtship, they evolve into what those around them consider a "worthy pair." Actually, however, they live in a state of controlled hostility: "When we abide alone, / No leapings each to each, / But syllables in frigid tone / Of household speech."

For further reading: Cox, "Tryphena Sparks and 'Young Thomas Hardy'"; Bartle, "Some Fresh Information about Tryphena Sparks: Thomas Hardy's Cousin."

Day, Fancy The heroine of *UNDER THE GREENWOOD TREE.* She teaches school in MELLSTOCK, where she lives in the schoolhouse. "Comely" and "slender," she is the "prettily-dressed prize" at the Christmas party given by the parents of Dick DEWY. She loves Dick, but, in obedience to her father's ambitions for her, permits Frederic SHINAR to court her.

Day, Geoffrey Character in *UNDER THE GREENWOOD TREE;* he is the overprotective father of his only child, Fancy DAY. He has ambitions for her and urges her to marry Frederic SHINAR, although she loves Dick DEWY. He is the keeper of Yalbury Great Wood.

Day, Jane The second wife of Geoffrey DAY and the stepmother of Fancy DAY in *UNDER THE GREENWOOD TREE.* She is a fanatical housekeeper, changing tablecloths in the middle of meals so that "they" (any guests present) won't say her linens are ragged. Her husband says it was "her doom to be nobody's wife at all in the wide universe," but she "made up her mind that she would, and did it twice over."

"Dead and the Living One, The" A war ballad written in 1915 and first printed in the *Sphere* on December 25, 1915. (It was reprinted in the *New York World* on January 2, 1916, and was later collected in MOMENTS OF VISION (1917). As a young woman passes by a new grave, covered with white flowers, she speaks to its occupant, another young woman, remarking, "Never your countenance did I see, / But you've been a good good friend to me!" A "plaintive voice" from the grave asks her meaning. She explains that, on the eve of going to war (WORLD WAR I), the soldier to whom she is now engaged had told his friend that he would willingly break his vow in favor of a "lass" he had met (she is the dead woman in the grave). Therefore, she is grateful to the woman for dying, since, after the campaign, the soldier will return to her.

Just then a "martial phantom of gory dye" appears; it is the ghost of the soldier she loves, who has just been stabbed by the enemy and has died. The phantom calls on the young woman beside the grave to remember that "when the night-wind's whine / Calls over this turf where her limbs recline, / That it travels on to lament by mine." There is a cry from the woman beside the grave, followed by "a laugh from underground" and "deeper gloom around."

The poem is ironic in its message that love can endure beyond life, into the grave. The soldier is now connected with the dead "lass" in death, if not in life, and the young woman who had been so confident he would return to her will not have him.

"Dead Quire, The"   Poem written in 1897 and first published in the Christmas issue of the GRAPHIC in 1901. It was later collected in TIME'S LAUGHINGSTOCKS (1909). The sad, elderly speaker is a ghostly incarnation of the MELLSTOCK quire (choir). Hardy had heard tales of him as a boy. The speaker laments the element of irreverence in Christmas merrymaking. The old members of the choir, such as Dewy, Reuben, and Michael (*see* UNDER THE GREENWOOD TREE), who now lie buried in the church yard, knew how to make music and celebrate Christmas with great joy, but within the context of a religious holiday. William Dewy will not, for instance, permit his grandson, Dick Dewy, to tune his violin for dancing until the end of Christmas Day. In the old days, "the hamleteers / Made merry with ancient Mellstock zest,"but now there are no "Christian harmonies" on Christmas Eve. The young people are gathered in a tavern, drinking and toasting "John Barleycorn." The Quick, or living, pursue the Dead, hoping to hear the former music, but the "ancient Birth-night tune" no longer floats in the village.

The "Mead of Memories" is the meadow beside the Frome River, in Lower Bockhampton, and "Moaning Hill" is the hillock northwest of STINSFORD CHURCH and House. The "sad man" may represent Hardy himself; he departs from an inn, goes down Church Lane, and disappears into the Mead of Memories (Bailey, *The Poetry of Thomas Hardy*, 235–36).

Although, in later life, Hardy's attitude toward religion was marked by uncertainty and skepticism, he retained a lifelong attachment to the Christmas celebrations of his youth. Here he mourns the irreverence of contemporary young people, drinking in a tavern on Christmas Eve rather than making the "harmonies" so important in his youth. In departing from the noisy inn on Christmas Eve, the "sad man" (probably Hardy) disappears into his own memories of a time when Christmas was celebrated more reverently.

This poem is best understood in the context of *Under the Greenwood Tree*, particularly the first four chapters. Here the Mellstock choir of instrumentalists and vocalists leave the home of Reuben DEWY just after midnight Christmas Eve, walking in the frosty air to outlying homesteads and hamlets, singing hymns, and reminiscing about Christmases of their youth. It is past two o'clock in the morning when they return to the church porch for metheglin (mead, i.e., a beverage made of fermented honey) and cider. The choir ranges in age from boys to very elderly men; it is by hearing the memories of the latter that the young come to know and value past traditions.

"Dead 'Wessex' the Dog to the Household"   Two stanzas of this poem were published posthumously in the London *Daily Telegraph* on May 10, 1928 (Hardy had died on January 11 of that year). The full four stanzas were later collected in WINTER WORDS (1928), published on October 2, 1928.

The speaker of the soliloquy is the white-haired terrier WESSEX, who had died on December 27, 1926. Hardy imagines him asking the members of the household, "wistful ones," whether they miss him. If they should call he will not turn to view them and will not come.

In the *Life* Hardy writes of the approaching death of Wessex, which had caused a "sadness" to fall on the household. On December 27 the dog died at 6:30 P.M.; he was buried on December 28. Hardy states that Wessex "sleeps outside the house the first time for thirteen years." His grave is in the pet cemetery at MAX GATE, as are those of other Hardy pets.

d'Erlanger, Baron Frédéric (1868–1943)   Composer, born in Paris of a German father and an American mother. About 1889 he moved to London and became a naturalized British citizen. He composed operas, chamber music, and symphonic and choral works. He composed an opera, *Tess*, based on TESS OF THE D'URBERVILLES, which was performed at the San Carlo Theater, Naples, on April 10, 1906. The date coincided with an eruption of Mount Vesuvius. When Hardy learned of this coincidence he wrote Baron d'Erlanger that if the opera had had "any sort of approval in such circumstances, it must have been an unusually strong one, & really one to build high hopes upon." He expressed a wish that it might be brought to London, and added that "the volcano was all of a piece with Tess's catastrophic career!" (*Letters* III, 204). The opera was first performed in London on July 14, 1909, at Covent Garden.

For further reading: Desmond Hawkins, "Tess in the Opera House."

Derriman, Festus   In *The* TRUMPET-MAJOR, he is the nemesis of Anne GARLAND. Crafty and sly, he showers unwanted attentions on Anne and tries to take money belonging to his uncle, Squire Benjamin DERRIMAN of Oxwell Hall, who had inherited it from his wife. He is called a "florid son of Mars," with red hair and a florid complexion. He is in the yeomanry cavalry when King

GEORGE III comes to BUDMOUTH; his unit expects to fend off the invading French. He marries the conniving Matilda JOHNSON, who abets him in his schemes, which ultimately fail.

Derriman, Squire Benjamin Wily widower in *The TRUMPET-MAJOR*, owner of Oxwell Hall, his manor house, which is crumbling from neglect; pigs and poultry inhabit its quadrangle. Although so aged that "the edge of the skull round his eye-sockets was visible through the skin," Squire Benjamin moves rapidly. He is devoted to his young neighbor, Anne GARLAND, who reads him the newspaper and helps with other matters. He has inherited wealth from his wife, but fears it will be stolen by his detested nephew, Festus DERRIMAN, who bullies and torments him. He buries his papers and money in a treasure box, in the presence of Anne, under a cellar flagstone. Anne loses the paper that reveals the location of the box, and it falls into Festus's hands. Squire Benjamin perceives that Festus knows something about the location and takes the box to Anne one evening. On the way home he dies of a heart attack. The treasure box is found to contain his will, leaving Oxwell Hall and all his property to Anne.

Desperate Remedies The second novel written by Thomas Hardy, this work was published anonymously on March 25, 1871. He had completed another novel, *The POOR MAN AND THE LADY*, in 1869 and submitted it to MACMILLAN & CO., which rejected it but suggested it might be suitable for the publishing firm of CHAPMAN & HALL. In 1869 the novelist George MEREDITH, the manuscript reader for Chapman, advised Hardy that although the firm would be willing to publish the work if it were subsidized, he recommended putting the manuscript away because of its orientation toward social criticism. He suggested that Hardy "attempt a novel with a purely artistic purpose, giving it a more complicated 'plot'" (*Life*, 82). Hardy took his advice, abandoned *The Poor Man and the Lady,* and began a new novel.

He wrote most of *Desperate Remedies* in late 1869 while living in WEYMOUTH at 3 Wooperton Street, near the harbor, where he had moved in April in order to work for the architect George Rackstrow CRICKMAY. The seaside setting of some of the scenes, in addition to the experience of the four architects (Owen GRAYE, Edward SPRINGROVE, Ambrose GRAYE, and Mr. GRADFIELD), are based on his experiences at this time, combined with his earlier experiences in the architectural offices of John HICKS and Sir Arthur William BLOMFIELD.

Hardy sent the manuscript, completed except for the final few chapters, to Macmillan and then went from Weymouth to CORNWALL to begin restoration work on ST. JULIOT CHURCH. Macmillan rejected the novel and he then submitted it to TINSLEY BROTHERS

with a précis of the final chapters. This firm accepted it with the proviso that he complete them, which he did. Emma Gifford, Hardy's future wife (*see* HARDY, Emma Gifford), whom he had met in Cornwall, assisted by making the final fair copies.

In his 1889 prefatory note Hardy remarked that "the principles observed in its composition are, no doubt, too exclusively those in which mystery, entanglement, surprise, and moral obliquity are depended on for exciting interest." The novel was undoubtedly influenced by such writers as Wilkie Collins and bears many similarities to Victorian detective thrillers; as Hardy remarks in chapter 1, it is based on a "long and intricately wrought chain of circumstances." Yet this work contains many elements of Hardy's later novels, such as the careful representation of the dialect, wit, and outlook of the local villagers; wide-ranging allusions to poetry, the Bible, and literature; and intimate knowledge of the philosophy, inhibitions, and concerns of the professional classes as well as of the gentry.

The novel is set principally in the imaginary village of Carriford with scenes in Lewborne Bay (WEYMOUTH), the town of Creston (Preston), and Knapwater House (KINGSTON MAURWARD HOUSE), which is near STINSFORD CHURCH. There are also scenes in LONDON.

SYNOPSIS

Chapters 1–6
The heroine, Cytherea GRAYE, and her brother, Owen Graye, a young architect, are impoverished by the death of their father, Ambrose GRAYE, an architect who takes a false step on the scaffolding of a church spire in the Grayes' native town of Hocbridge and falls to his death. Owen secures a temporary position as an architect in the town of Creston, where he and his sister take lodgings. She meets and becomes attracted to Edward Springrove, a young man in Owen's office. Owen's job becomes uncertain, and Cytherea places an advertisement for a post as a lady's maid, as she hopes not to be a burden to him. Miss Cytherea ALDCLYFFE, the heir to a nearby estate, hires her and Cytherea settles in at Knapwater House. She bears up under the tyranny of Miss Aldclyffe, who soon upgrades her to the level of companion. Miss Aldclyffe's father, Captain ALDCLYFFE, dies. She inherits the estate, and it is eventually revealed that she is the Cytherea Bradleigh who had jilted Cytherea's father long ago in London and for whom Cytherea Graye was named. Through the deaths of several relatives and a mandatory name change, Miss Aldclyffe and her father had succeeded to Knapwater House.

Chapters 7–10
One day Cytherea notices a large flock of sheep outside her window with the markings "ES" and discovers that they belong to John Springrove, Edward's father, a prosperous local farmer and owner of the Three Tran-

ters Inn. This "many-gabled, medieval building" is a "handsome specimen of the genuine roadside inn of bygone times." Cytherea is startled to realize that Edward's home is nearby. Miss Aldclyffe becomes aware of the attachment between Cytherea and Edward, but tries to thwart the couple. She has a mysterious agenda, becoming very maternal toward Cytherea, hoping to keep her permanently at Knapwater House. She advertises for and hires Aeneas MANSTON as steward of her estate. There are rumors that she is in love with Manston, though Farmer Springrove points out that she is "old enough to be his mother."

Cytherea meets Adelaide HINTON, Edward's first cousin, and discovers that she and Edward are informally engaged. Manston is attracted to Cytherea, but the postmistress and other villagers suspect Manston of having another woman in his life who has visited him and to whom he has written. Miss Aldclyffe reads his mail and confronts him, discovering that he had married an American actress, Eunice, in Liverpool the previous summer, but has no interest in her now. He summons Eunice to Carriford, but, when she arrives, fails to meet her because of a misunderstanding about the train schedule. She walks to Manston's house, but no one is there and she decides to spend the night at the Three Tranters Inn. It is now November, and Mr. Springrove has cleared some ground at the back of the house and burned the couch-grass. The fire has died down, but, unknown to him, still smolders, dangerously subject to being rekindled by the slightest breeze.

Everyone at the inn retires, but the smoldering fire flares up and consumes the back of the inn and the piggery. The garden engine is far too weak to cope with the flames, and the entire inn and Springrove's cottages all go up in flames. The insurance has expired. At the railway train station, where Manston awaits Eunice, a day laborer tells him that she has died in the fire.

Chapters 11–12
Manston confesses his love for Cytherea to Miss Aldclyffe, on whom he has a mysterious unexplained hold; she agrees to help him win her. Her strategy is to encourage Edward's marriage to Adelaide, in exchange for which she will permit John Springrove to keep the cottage leases. At the official inquiry into the fire and the death of Mrs. Manston, there is some confusion about whether she stayed at the inn and died in the fire, but they conclude that she did.

Miss Aldclyffe, meanwhile, takes steps to convince Edward that Cytherea has fallen in love with Manston. Edward proposes to Adelaide, and the marriage date is set for the following Christmas. Manston continues, as the subdued widower, to woo Cytherea, but in so subtle a way that Cytherea is unaware of it until Miss Aldclyffe announces he is "involuntarily" attracted by her. Manston then directs more systematic advances toward

Cytherea. Owen, meanwhile, is experiencing increasing lameness and is unable to carry out his duties. Miss Aldclyffe sends Cytherea to visit him, but advises her to accept Manston, since she may never have another chance. She visits Owen, after which he sees another specialist and has an operation, but is unable to work for an unpredictable period of time. She refuses Manston, but eventually agrees to marry him in order to avoid sending Owen to the County Hospital. Manston guarantees Owen's medical care. The wedding days is set for Old Christmas, after Christmas.

Chapters 13–15
Meanwhile, Adelaide marries an elderly, dull, rich farmer, Farmer Bollens. The villagers speculate that, since Cytherea has accepted Manston and apparently rejected Edward, Adelaide had decided to marry someone else also. They assume that, once Cytherea knows Edward is free, she will "throw over the steward" and marry him. Cytherea marries Manston in a grim, plain ceremony, with Edward Springrove watching, hidden in the shadows. Cytherea sees Edward and realizes she still loves him. Owen realizes how she feels, but she assures him she will not disgrace him. The afternoon of the wedding, before leaving for their wedding trip, she walks in the garden and sees a man on the footpath along the river. She hides but realizes it is Edward; standing on either side of a fallen tree, they gaze at each other's images in the water. He tells her Adelaide was married the previous day to someone else and she confesses her love for him. Cytherea realizes her position is "irretrievable," but explains that she had been taught to "dread pauperism" and saw no other solution.

Later in the afternoon Owen accompanies his sister and Manston to the train station, where they see a railway porter, Chinney, looking strangely at them, seeming to be ill. Cytherea gives the porter money. After the train leaves, the villagers and laborers begin looking strangely at Edward Springrove and Owen. The porter has told the rector that Manston's wife did not die in the fire but took the train to London that night, after tipping him and asking him not to tell anyone. Therefore, Cytherea is not legally married. Owen and Springrove both rush, separately, to Southampton, where they are to spend the night before embarking for the Continent, in order to rescue Cytherea. Springrove finds her lodging house and tells her the news; Cytherea immediately moves to a single room and bolts the door. She will speak only to Owen and asks the landlady to say that she is ill. Owen reads Chinney's confession to Manston and asks that Cytherea return home while the matter is sorted out. The proprietor of the hotel calls for a lawyer, who insists that Cytherea stay with Owen until her legal position is clarified.

Back at Knapwater, Manston is advised to advertise for his wife. He goes to London to seek her, advertises again, and a woman claiming to be his wife appears. She is made up to look like Eunice, and takes her place as Manston's wife.

Chapters 16–18
Owen Graye recovers from his illness and cares for Cytherea as she convalesces from the shock. Edward proposes to her, but she refuses. Edward begins working in London. He has discovered that Manston had received a letter from Eunice before the advertisements appeared in the papers. He thinks there has been collusion with her. By searching through back copies of the local newspaper, the Casterbridge *Chronicle*, Cytherea finds Eunice's former address in an account of the fire. Owen pursues the matter by writing Edward; Manston sees him mail the letter, then extracts Springrove's London address from his father. Edward, meanwhile, learns from Eunice's former neighbor that Manston has been in London, searching for her former landlord. Eunice was with him, although she did not speak. The neighbor tells Edward that Eunice apparently was not killed in the fire, but that a few items of hers, such as a workbox, had remained behind and eventually been auctioned off. The woman who appeared with Manston had not asked about them. Edward goes off to search for Eunice's property, followed by the cloaked figure of Manston, who has been lurking nearby. Edward acquires the workbox and finds nothing inside except some accounts, a pressed rosebud, and mounted photographs of Manston and Eunice, which he sends to Owen. Manston has seen Edward's actions through the window, follows him to the Charing Cross post office, and guesses that he has mailed the photographs to Owen. Edward, meanwhile, shakes the workbox and finds a love poem written by Manston to Eunice and a sprig of myrtle, which he sends to Owen in a second letter. The next morning Manston goes by train to Mundsbury, the station before Casterbridge, and walks along the country lanes with a flask of brandy. He plies the postman with it and intercepts the letter. He replaces Eunice's photograph with one of his new wife, who knows what he has done.

When Owen receives the poem, he shows the verse to Cytherea; it contains a reference to Eunice's "azure eyes." Cytherea is stunned, because she has learned from Miss Aldclyffe's housekeeper, Mrs. Morris, that the present Mrs. Manston's eyes are black. Cytherea is horrified to think that the first Mrs. Manston died in the fire and that she is actually his present wife. Owen goes to London to discover whether Eunice's former neighbors have noticed that the present Mrs. Manston is a different person, but she has only appeared veiled, and they cannot be sure. He returns to the village and manages a casual encounter with her that convinces

him her eyes are black. He also notices that her hair is false.

The rector comes to see Owen and Cytherea in the farmhouse where they are living while Owen works on a nearby church. The porter, Chinney, has drowned. In London, Edward discovers that the woman posing as Mrs. Manston is not Manston's former wife, but Anne SEAWAY.

Chapters 19–21
Anne Seaway assumes Eunice is still living somewhere, and quizzes Manston. She begins to wonder why, after marrying Cytherea, he asked her to impersonate Eunice, teaching her Eunice's history and forcing her to read guidebooks to Philadelphia. She insists that he tell her his true motive in bringing her to Knapwater. She suspects he has a secret power over Miss Aldclyffe. He warns her that no one must know she is not his wife.

Anne begins dusting Manston's office the next morning and discovers letters from different women, including Eunice, who had written Manston to ask why he had to come to Knapwater calling himself a bachelor. Eunice had finally written Miss Aldclyffe and explained that she was Manston's wife, and had arranged to come to live publicly with him. From the Three Tranters Inn she had written her cousin James, in Philadelphia, telling him the strange story of her marriage.

Edward and the rector, Mr. Raunham, are still puzzled over Manston, and the rector decides to call on Miss Aldclyffe. He confides his suspicion that the present Mrs. Manston is an imposter named Anne Seaway. That night Miss Aldclyffe spies on the rectory and sees him dinning with Edward Springrove and a second, unknown, man.

Meanwhile, Anne Seaway's perplexity at the letters has given way to vexation. She follows Manston to Froominster and sees him withdraw money from the bank. That evening Miss Aldclyffe comes to call, and Manston asks Anne to leave. Pretending to take a walk, she listens to them from outside the window. She realizes Miss Aldclyffe is willing to "scheme body and soul" on behalf of Manston and becomes terrified of him. At the same time she is highly suspicious: "what is keener than the eye of a mistrustful woman? A man's cunning is to it as was the armor of Sisera to the thin tent-nail."

Anne and Manston retire and she pretends to be asleep; Manston dresses and leaves the room. Anne finds opium in the drawer of the dressing table and assumes he has planned to drug her. She follows him downstairs and discovers that he is burning papers. He leaves the house, locking her in. She escapes from a window and follows him to an outbuilding, where she watches him remove a cupboard from the wall. An oven is behind the wall; he takes "a heavy weight of great bulk," a corn sack full of something, and seals up the wall again. While trying to recover the key to return to the house she discovers another man is watching Manston. Manston leaves the outbuilding, carrying something heavy on his back, followed not only by the watching man but also by a mysterious woman. Anne joins the line, and the four figures go through the dark woods to a pit, filled with leaves. Manston excavates a large hole, throws in the sack, and covers it. He turns and discovers the other woman, who is Miss Aldclyffe. She warns him of the man, the "first watcher," and he hits him over the head with a shovel. Manston and Miss Aldclyffe disappear, and Anne assists the man, who turns out to be a detective employed by Mr. Raunham to "sift" the mystery of Manston. He and Anne reexcavate the pit, open the sack, and discover Eunice's body, identified through her hair.

The detective asks his assistant, waiting with a horse, to detain Miss Aldclyffe. He and Anne set out for the rectory but crash into Manston's empty gig, which apparently he had placed on the road before shifting Eunice's body. They are sure Manston is nearby, but he is silent. The detective ties the horse to the back of his cart and drives to Froominster.

Three days later Manston has not been caught; it is market day at Froominster. News comes that Manston has almost certainly been seen at Creston, on his way to the Channel Isles and St. Malo, but he had changed clothes with a laborer and slipped away. Edward, however, sees Manston at the fair, pretending to be a laborer and carrying straw. He surmises that Manston is going to Palchurch to see Cytherea and follows him diagonally across the fields. While Owen is away, trying to filter out the truth about the strange rumors they have heard, Cytherea sits by a window, reading. Manston approaches and she bolts the door but recognizes his face through the window. He breaks into the house and captures her. Edward then enters and begins wrestling Manston; Cytherea summons three laborers who have also been pursuing Manston, and they subdue him. Cytherea last sees him bound, sitting in a cart, being taken to jail.

A week later, after writing an extended confession, Manston hangs himself in jail and is buried in "a very plain box" of rough elm suitable for "the poor soul." In his confession he admits going to his home the night of the fire and finding Eunice walking toward him. Realizing he has lost Cytherea, he felt, at the time, like a "madman." Eunice had "taunted" him with a secret she had discovered about himself and Miss Aldclyffe. In a frenzy, he struck her on the nape of her neck, killing her—unintentionally, he claimed. Realizing that she would be assumed to have died in the fire, he had taken her body into his house and discovered the oven behind the wall. He had taken her keys and watch and gone to the church cemetery, where he collected fragments of leg- and backbones. Standing behind a hedge,

he had thrown the watch, keys, and bones into the smoldering embers.

On marrying Cytherea, he had known himself to be a widower with a legal right to claim her. But, after the wedding, when the matter was unresolved, he had overhead two poachers talking in an inn. One of them had gone to him the night of the fire to tell him of his wife's death, but Manston had refused to tip him. Angered, he had gone to Manston's fowl house to "operate" upon the birds. He believed he overheard "ghostly mouths talking—then a fall—then a groan" (i.e., the argument among Manston and Eunice), and crept home. He had never told anyone because of his culpability in being near the fowl house. He tells the other poacher that he is sure, if Eunice does not "turn up alive," his mind will be "as sure as a Bible upon her murder" and he will expose Manston. This threat inspires Manston to find a substitute wife to impersonate Eunice. He had known Anne Seaway in London; she had been a housekeeper whose mistress had died, and she was in a precarious financial position. He had brought her to his home as his wife and they had lived quietly until the letter from Mr. Raunham impelled him to bury the body of his wife. Miss Aldclyffe had come to warn him that he was suspicious. Manston explains that he had killed Eunice by accident. Miss Aldclyffe, terrified for him if his secret should be exposed, watched the rectory that evening, saw the detective, and followed him to Manston's residence. She saw him burying the sack, but did not know what it contained.

The evening of Manston's death Miss Aldclyffe sends a message by the vicar to Palchurch that she is seriously ill and wants to see Cytherea. She had caught a cold, which turned into "fullness and heat in the chest." When she learned that Manston had killed himself in jail she shrieked, breaking a blood vessel, and then hemorrhaged. When Cytherea sees Miss Aldclyffe, she learns that more than 30 years earlier she had been "decoyed" into a secret marriage with a man she loved. He was supposed to be an officer, but turned out to be an escaped convict who had forged a will. He fled to Canada and was shot.

She did not assume her married name, but gave birth to a child, pinned all her money on its bosom with a note giving the name she wished him to have, and deposited him on the steps of a house in Clapham. She paid the caretaker well and met her and the child frequently in hotels or coffeehouses. The woman who cared for the baby was named Manston and was the widow of a schoolmaster. She said he was the child of a relation she had adopted. On one occasion Mrs. Manston met her without the child and said he was so ill he might not live through the night; Miss Aldclyffe fainted, and the caretaker came to know the truth. She met another man she could have loved (Cytherea's father), but rejected him because of her secret. She dreamed of Cytherea's marrying her son. Cytherea returns to the home she shares with Owen, promising to return to Miss Aldclyffe at eight the next morning and stay through her illness.

At four A.M. she dreams she sees the wan face of Miss Aldclyffe, very distinctly, and asks why she had not let her stay with her all night. She wakes Owen and asks to go to Knapwater House, but Owen thinks it better to wait until eight, as agreed upon. A messenger arrives from Knapwater; Miss Aldclyffe had died just after 4.00 A.M.

The epilogue relates events 15 months later, told by bell ringers who have been ringing the Carriford Church bells for the wedding of "Teddy" Springrove and Cytherea Graye. When Miss Aldclyffe's will was opened, it was discovered that she had left everything to "the wife of Aeneas Manston"—that is, Cytherea. Cytherea waived her rights to the property in favor of Mr. Raunham, who placed Edward in Knapwater House as agent and steward. An agreement is made that their children will inherit Knapwater after Mr. Raunham's death. The novel ends with Edward rowing Cytherea on their lake, just as he had on Creston Bay three years earlier.

CRITICAL RECEPTION AND COMMENTARY

An anonymous review appeared in the ATHENAEUM on April 1, 1871, marked by speculation about the sex and identity of the author. The reviewer theorized that "certain expressions" in the novel made it unlikely that it could have come from "the pen of an English lady." John Hutton reviewed it anonymously for the SPECTATOR in the issue of April 22, 1871, criticizing the author for publishing the novel anonymously but noting that "there is an *unusual, & very happy* facility in catching & fixing phases of peasant life—in producing for us, not the manners & language only but the tone of thought . . . & simple humour of consequential village worthies & gaping village rustics" (*Letters* I, 11). After he submitted his next novel, UNDER THE GREENWOOD TREE, to Macmillan, Hardy sent copies of the reviews of *Desperate Remedies* to Malcolm Macmillan, commenting that his aim in the novel had been "*simply* to construct an intricate puzzle which nobody should guess till the end—& the characters were, to myself, mere puppets or pegs to weave the work upon." The review in the *Spectator* had convinced him, however, "not to dabble in plot again" but to venture on a "pastoral story" (*Letters* I, 12). A more sympathetic review, also anonymous but possibly written by Hardy's friend Horace MOULE, was published in the SATURDAY REVIEW on September 30, 1871, stating that the novel would appeal to "the sincerest lover of melodrama." Many contemporary reviewers assumed that Hardy had fallen under the influence of Wilkie Collins (Ward, 73).

Desperate Remedies received much critical attention in the late 20th century. In "*Desperate Remedies* and the Victorian Thriller," Paul Ward analyzes the novel in the context of contemporary mysteries, especially Collins's *The Moonstone* and *The Woman in White*. He argues that Hardy's novel is very unlike them in its emphasis on the emotional predicaments of the characters. The construction of the book as a thriller, therefore, is flawed, because Hardy's characters are fully developed outside the dictates of the plot. He sees the novel not as imitative of Collins's novels but, rather, as a "living testimony to what may happen when a writer with strong individual concerns attempts to confine himself artificially" to the strictures of a writer whose "concerns are in many important respects different" (Ward, 76).

Pamela Dalziel, in "Exploiting the *Poor Man:* The Genesis of Hardy's *Desperate Remedies*," analyzes the novel as an outgrowth of the lost first novel, *The Poor Man and the Lady*, that Hardy considered, at one time, to have been the "most original thing, for its date, that he had ever written" but which he later destroyed. She examines Edmund GOSSE's diary record for April 25, 1915, which contains "the only extended description of the plot to survive." The plot concerns the love of a young Dorsetshire man of the peasant class for the daughter of the local squire (*see* entry for *The Poor Man and the Lady*). She states that in later life Hardy considered reconstructing the novel, but lacked the energy and inclination to do so.

Dalziel argues that the motif of "poor-man-and-the-lady" embodies a persistent "single, undifferentiated socioliterary agenda" that marked Hardy's earliest and last published novels. She concludes that the earlier novel dealt with social concerns that were "subtly displaced" in *Desperate Remedies* but laid the groundwork for Hardy's later novels of "social purpose" and their fictional treatment of "courtship, seduction, and marriage and the broader interrelationships of gender and class" that were "regularly discomforting to contemporary reviewers" (Dalziel, 220–32).

C. Glen Wickens, in "Hardy's *Desperate Remedies*," examines Hardy's use of classical mythology in the novel, particularly his choice of the name "Cytherea" (an "epithet of Venus or Aphrodite") for Miss Aldcliffe and Miss Graye. He suggests that Hardy relies on the "classical attributes" of Venus as the bringer of spring and goddess of gardens, and constructs a useful typology of gardens, the one cultivated and the other a wilderness, both represented on Miss Aldclyffe's estate. (Knapwater House is surrounded by ordered parkland; Aeneas Manston's decayed house and overgrown garden are untamed.) Manston's emblem is fire; his first wife, Eunice, is thought consumed by the fire at the Three Tranters Inn; he kills her and conceals her body in an oven. His name,

Seafront at Weymouth, where Thomas Hardy worked, and which figures in his fiction and poetry, including Desperate Remedies, The Well-Beloved, The Trumpet-Major, *and "At a Seaside Town in 1869"*   (Sarah Bird Wright)

Wickens suggests, recalls the burning of Troy and the founding of Rome.

The novel ends with "reason triumphing over blind passion"; Edward Springrove (his name suggesting the growth of spring) is able "to cultivate his own and extended nature" and win Cytherea; he can "thus restore order to the pastoral world in the summer" (Wickens, 12–14).

Kevin Z. Moore, in "The Poet within the Architect's Ring: *Desperate Remedies,* Hardy's Hybrid Detective-Gothic Narrative," analyzes the problems encountered by Hardy's narrator. The "rational/detective" narrative is at odds with the "imaginative/Gothic" one, resulting in continual conflicts throughout the novel that preclude the reader's full engagement. He concludes that Hardy "always had difficulty reconciling the spirit of science with that of religion," and argues that the "detective narrative abides precariously with the Gothic." It is, however, this precarious balance that "produces the uniqueness of Hardy's texts" and that deserves further study if readers are to "comprehend the composition and problematics of Hardy's romantic, nonrational novels" (Moore, 31–41).

For further reading: Dalziel, "Exploiting the Poor Man: The Genesis of Hardy's *Desperate Remedies*"; Moore, "The Poet within the Architect's Ring: *Desperate Remedies,* Hardy's Hybrid Detective-Gothic Narrative";

Neale, "*Desperate Remedies:* The Merits and Demerits of Popular Fiction"; Roberts, "Patterns of Relationship in *Desperate Remedies*"; Sasaki, "Viewer and Victim in *Desperate Remedies:* Links between Hardy's Life and His Fiction"; Springer, "Invention and Tradition: Allusions in *Desperate Remedies*"; Ward, "*Desperate Remedies* and the Victorian Thriller"; Wickens, Hardy's *Desperate Remedies*; Wickens, "Romantic Myth and Victorian Nature in *Desperate Remedies*."

de Stancy, Captain William Character in *A LAODICEAN.* He is 39, the son of Sir William DE STANCY, and the father of the illegitimate William DARE. He inherits the baronetcy on his father's death, and has the little of "Sir William." He returns, exhausted, from his army duty in India and is posted at Toneborough Barracks, near the Castle de Stancy. He declares he is going to renounce wine and women, as his health is failing. Dare stalks him, asking for money, and then schemes to introduce him to Paula POWER at Castle de Stancy, so that he can regain the ancient family seat and fortune. Paula is in love with a young architect, George SOMERSET, but Dare contrives to spread false intelligence about Somerset. Captain de Stancy (now Sir William) almost succeeds in marrying Paula, but his sister, Charlotte DE STANCY, discovers that Somerset has been deceived. Even though it means she has no chance of marrying Somerset herself, she valiantly discloses the truth to Paula. To prevent Paula's informing the police and having Dare jailed, de Stancy admits he is Dare's father. Paula rejects him and marries Somerset.

de Stancy, Charlotte   Character in *A LAODICEAN*. She is a descendant of the noble de Stancy family. Her father is Sir William DE STANCY, formerly owner of Castle de Stancy, and her brother is Captain William DE STANCY (later Sir William). Good natured and cheerful, she is the close friend and confidante of Paula POWER, whose father, a railway magnate, had purchased the castle. She had planned to marry John Ravensbury, a school friend of George SOMERSET's, but he died young. She has delicate health, and is ill on the European tour with Paula. She is secretly in love with George Somerset. Through a chance meeting with him she discovers William DARE's evil machinations. She informs Paula, even though it means she has no chance of marrying George. Eventually she decides to "steal from the world" and enter an Anglican sisterhood. "She was genuine, if anybody ever was; and simple as she was true," George reflects.

de Stancy, Sir William   Character in *A LAODICEAN*. The father of Captain William DE STANCY and Charlotte DE STANCY and former owner of Castle de Stancy, he had been extremely extravagant in his youth—keeping, for example, as many as 30 race horses and investing in a worthless silver mine. As a result he lost Castle de Stancy, which was eventually acquired by John Power, a railroad builder and the father of Paula POWER. Sir William was once angry and bitter, but after living abroad for a number of years his feelings have mellowed. He is content to live economically in a house called Myrtle Villa, near the walls of the Castle de Stancy. His eye sockets are cavernous, "reminding the beholder of the vaults in the castle he once had owned." On his death the title goes to his son, Captain William de Stancy.

"Destiny and a Blue Cloak"   A short story written for the *New York Times*, which published it on October 4, 1874. It was not reprinted by Hardy in his lifetime.

The story concerns two girls, Agatha Pollin, the 19-year-old niece of a miller (a widower with several children), and Frances Lovill, a 25-year-old "beauty" from the village of Cloton, near Beaminster. Agatha, who has traveled to WEYMOUTH wearing a blue cloak she has copied from one Frances owns, is greeted on the esplanade by a young man, Oswald Winwood, who believes her to be Frances. She does not correct his mistake, but spends the day with him; they fall in love. Returning to Beaminster that night in the dark carrier's van, she confesses her true identity. Frances,

who is also in the van, overhears her but says nothing and departs.

Oswald leaves to make his mark in the Indian civil service, but first proposes to Agatha. After a few years Frances has become an "old maid" and all but lost her chances of marriage; she accepts the proposal of Agatha's uncle, the miller. Agatha, meanwhile, waits for Oswald, but an elderly man in the village, "unmarried, substantial, and cheery," proposes to her. She turns him down, as he is repugnant to her and she hopes for Oswald's return, but he persists. Finally he offers a financial inducement to the miller, helping him emigrate to Queensland, Australia, if he can persuade Agatha to accept him.

A deadline is set for Oswald's return, after which Agatha must accept her suitor. Oswald writes that he is coming in 10 days. On the eve of her wedding Agatha enlists a deaf boy, John, who works for her uncle, to help her escape. She climbs in the cart the next morning and hides, but then discovers that the driver is the elderly gentleman, wearing a miller's smock-frock. He has collected her in another cart before John's arrival. She goes through with the wedding, but accuses Frances, her aunt, of revealing her plan. Frances admits it, and says she also told Oswald, who had come at seven that morning, that Agatha was being married that day, and sent him away. He had been prevented by illness from sailing on the day he had planned. Agatha holds her head high and tells Frances that her information does not concern her at all: "I am my husband's darling now, you know, and I wouldn't make the dear man jealous for the world."

Deverell, Miss   Guest at the garden party given by Paula POWER in *A LAODICEAN*. She is a sallow and unattractive lady with a gay laugh and twinkling black eyes.

Dewy, Ann   The wife of Reuben DEWY and mother of Dick DEWY in *UNDER THE GREENWOOD TREE*. She has four younger children, is an excellent cook, willingly entertains the MELLSTOCK singers, and is solicitous about her neighbors.

Dewy, Dick   The hero of *UNDER THE GREENWOOD TREE*, Dick is the son of the tranter (irregular carrier) Reuben DEWY, and is the treble player in the MELLSTOCK choir. When Fancy DAY enters the church, he begins to have "rushings of blood" and "impressions" that there is a "tie between her and himself visible to all the congregation." Dick courts Fancy despite her father's belief that she should marry Fred SHINAR or perhaps Parson MAYBOLD. After various obstacles they become engaged and Dick agrees to have their wedding procession formed "Whichever way you and the company likes"; he is "willing to renounce all other rights in the world with the greatest pleasure."

Dewy, Reuben   The father of Dick DEWY in *UNDER THE GREENWOOD TREE*. He offers a "drop o' the right sort," a home made apple cordial, to the MELLSTOCK singers and plays the tenor violin in the choir. The Dewys' house is based on Hardy's birthplace at HIGHER BOCKHAMPTON.

Dewy, William   The father of Reuben DEWY and grandfather of Dick DEWY in *UNDER THE GREENWOOD TREE*. He plays the bass violoncello for the MELLSTOCK singers.

dialect   Hardy had a keen ear for dialect, and was meticulous about using it properly; he also mourned the gradual disappearance of the colorful and expressive dialect he had known in his youth. In 1888 he wrote the critic Edmund GOSSE about an article the critic's late father (Philip Henry Gosse) had written, "A Country Day-School Seventy Years Ago," and sent a list of dialect variants common in DORSET. In *The WOODLANDERS* he replicates certain dialect phrases in Grammer (Grandmother) Oliver's conversation, such as "Ich woll" and "er woll." Hardy remarked that such phrases were dying out, used only by persons over 70 and then in "impulsive moments when they forget themselves" (*Letters* I, 181).

In 1892 a professor of English literature at King's College, LONDON, John Wesley Hales, wrote Hardy to ask about the phrase "good-now," which occurs in *UNDER THE GREENWOOD TREE* and was also used in Shakespeare's *The Tempest*. Hardy explained that those who thought it meant "good man" or "my good-fellow" were "quite in error," the precise meaning being "you may be sure," or "sure enough."

In about 1901 Hardy wrote the critic Richard GARNETT about two other Dorset phrases he had noticed that were on the verge of becoming extinct: "inkledog" for "earthworm" and "ingotten" for "common earth" (*Letters* II, 299).

The local poet and philologist William BARNES, a friend of Hardy's, had published *Poems of Rural Life in the Dorset Dialect* and articles about the Dorset dialect. In 1908, while editing a selection of his poems, Hardy wrote the scholar and publisher R. W. Chapman, who was then at the Clarendon Press, Oxford, that he thought the best method of explaining dialect words was to place the meanings in the margin opposite the words rather than appending a glossary at the end, which he declared "fatally troublesome to the reader" (*Letters* III, 297).

In 1913 Sir James Murray, the principal editor of the *Oxford English Dictionary*, queried Hardy about the use of "tranter" (used in *Under the Greenwood Tree* and other of his works). He wrote to explain that the word was still used in "remote nooks" of Dorset, meaning a "*carrier*—(either a carrier to order, or a carrier of articles for sale not of his own manufacture)." "He do tranty"

was a phrase designating a man whose continual occupation was doing irregular jobs of carrying, not carrying things on a regular basis (*Letters* IV, 312–13).

Hardy scrupulously answered questions from readers, scholars, and editors. In 1919 he wrote the reviewer Harold Child to explain that "griff" (used in a poem, "The Clock of the Years") was intended to mean "a claw" or "a griffin"; he admitted that he had "no idea" he had used it (*Letters* V, 291).

In 1921, when Madeleine ROLLAND was revising her translation of *TESS OF THE D'URBERVILLES* into French, many dialect words puzzled her. She sent a long list of questionable words, and Hardy patiently responded to each one, writing, for example, that he thought "lynchets," which were "flint slopes in ploughed land," should be retained untranslated. He advised her to use her "ingenuity in thinking of a pattern sound" for the syllable "ur" (as in "hurler") (*Letters* VI, 74–75).

Two years before he died, Hardy wrote the publisher Sir Frederick Macmillan to explain that the phrase he had used in *Tess of the D'Urbervilles*, to have "green malt in floor," means to have an unmarried daughter giving birth to a child (*Letters* VII, 8).

Throughout his fiction, poetry, and drama, Hardy was scrupulous about the spelling and precise connotation of phrases and words in dialect, and his observations served in many cases to authenticate the linguistic history and usage of Dorset.

For further reading: Ulla Baugner, *A Study on the Use of Dialects in Thomas Hardy's Novels and Short Stories with Special Reference to Phonology & Vocabulary.*

"Distracted Preacher, The"   Short story published in the *NEW QUARTERLY MAGAZINE* in April 1879 and collected in *WESSEX TALES* (1888), dealing with smuggling along the DORSET coast between WEYMOUTH and St. Aldhelm's Head. The story takes place sometime in the 1830s. Stockdale, a young Wesleyan minister, comes to the coastal Dorset village of Nether-Moynton to fill a temporary vacancy. He lodges at the home of a young widow, Mrs. Lizzy Newberry, who lives with her elderly mother. He takes cold, and Lizzy undertakes to provide some brandy from a small tub stored, with others, in the adjacent church under the tower stairs. She calls them "tubs of spirit that have accidentally floated over in the dark from France," but finally admits they are owned by smugglers who have given her permission to help herself. A young village girl serves his meals, but he gradually becomes aware that Lizzy sleeps much of the day, and he catches glimpses of her going out at night in a great coat that was once her husband's.

Stockdale learns that Lizzy and her cousin Mr. Owlett are the principal partners in a smuggling operation in which virtually all the villagers participate. He tries in vain to persuade her that smuggling is wrong. One night he accompanies her to the beach and watches as 30 or

40 men descend a steep cliff to meet small boats. They put tubs (or "things," as they are called) on their backs and chests and climb back; the "things" are conveyed by cart to the village and hidden. Lizzy insists that all the villagers would be in severe want during the winter if it were not for the smuggling operation.

The concealed tubs are confiscated by customs house officials, but are recovered by disguised villagers, who tie up the "Preventives," or officials. Stockdale releases them and they abandon their onerous exercise. Lizzy refuses to give up her employment and Stockdale leaves the village for a post in his unnamed native county.

Returning two years later, Stockdale finds that the Crown has offered "blood money" for smugglers and Owlett has been wounded. The villagers have given up smuggling. Stockdale marries Lizzy, whose mother has now died, and they return to his home, where, it is said, Lizzy "wrote an excellent tract called *Render unto Caesar; or, The Repentant Villagers.*"

In May 1912 Hardy appended a note to the story saying the "ending was almost *de rigueur* in an English magazine at the time of writing." However, he admits that it was based on a true story in which Lizzy did not marry the minister but instead, "much to her credit in the author's opinion—stuck to Jim the smuggler, and emigrated with him after their marriage, an expatrial step rather forced upon him by his adventurous antecedents. They both died in Wisconsin between 1850 and 1860."

In 1889 Hardy wrote an unidentified correspondent that he had known several persons, then dead, "who shared in the adventurous doings" along the Dorset coast a half century earlier (*Letters* I, 204). The story was adapted for dramatic presentation by A. H. EVANS and performed in 1911; *see* Appendix II, Media Adaptations of the Works of Thomas Hardy.

"Ditty" Poem dedicated to "E.L.G." (Emma Lavinia Gifford), Hardy's first wife (*see* HARDY, Emma Gifford). They had met in CORNWALL in March 1870, and the poem seems to have been written later that year, in LONDON. It was collected in *WESSEX POEMS* (1898). The poem proposes that all people are "bond-servants of Chance." Hardy finds it painful to think he might never have met his wife. He cannot bear to think he might have loved "Otherwhere" nor have missed her "My life through."

Emma is found within "walls of weathered stone"— that is, the rectory of ST. JULIOT CHURCH, where her brother-in-law was the priest. Critics have called the poem derivative of the work of Robert BROWNING or the Dorset poet and clergyman William BARNES, but Hardy denied such influences.

The poem was set to music by Gerald Finzi in *A Young Man's Exhortation* (Oxford University Press, 1933 [Bailey, *The Poetry of Thomas Hardy*, 60]).

Dobson, Henry Austin (1840–1921) English poet and man of letters. He worked as a clerk in the marine department of the Board of Trade, but he also published collections of verse and prose works, including critical essays and biographies.

In May 1875 the Second Annual Shotover Dinner was held at Oxford, an outgrowth of a series of parodies, *The Shotover Papers, or, Echoes of Oxford*, published between February 1874 and February 1875. Francis Stokes, an undergraduate at Merton College, invited Hardy and Austin Dobson to respond to the toast of "Literature" (*Letters* I, 37). Michael Millgate notes that the *Oxford Undergraduate's Journal* of May 13 mentions that the Shotover staff had entertained "several distinguished Metropolitan and Oxford Literati" at the dinner at the Mitre Hotel, and speculates that Hardy might have "encountered a certain amount of social condescension" on the part of undergraduates (Millgate, *Thomas Hardy: A Biography*, 176).

Hardy appears not to have had a close friendship with Dobson, but instead one of mutual respect and appreciation of literary achievement. In 1892 Hardy sent him an inscribed copy of *TESS OF THE D'URBERVILLES*. In 1910 Dobson published "In Memoriam," a poem occasioned by the death of King Edward VII. Hardy wrote him that he was glad to see he had been "inspired to write a few verses." He called them "direct and forcible lines, with no rhetorical shams in them of the kind we have been treated to in such profusion during the late few days" (*Letters* IV, 90).

"Doctor's Legend, The" Short story published in the *Independent* of March 26, 1891. It was not collected by Hardy, but was published posthumously by Florence HARDY. The tale is narrated by the doctor in a village a few miles from the WESSEX coast. The local squire, "one whom anything would petrify but nothing would soften," has delusions of grandeur and jealously guards his domain. He wishes to be called "Your Honour" and "Squire," and is uncharitable toward those around him.

A poor widow lives outside her gate with her small daughter. The little girl happens to run across the squire's lawn one day and he chases her, terrifying her until her hair and teeth fall out. Her mother detests the squire on her account. The squire marries a gentle woman, Lady Cicely, who is charitable and much liked in the village. One day while Lady Cicely is pregnant she is returning to the manor house on foot, past the churchyard. The little girl and her mother are coming along a nearby path. The mother pulls back the child's hood and raises her up so she is looking over the coping of the churchyard wall. She whispers, "Grin at her, my deary!" Lady Cicely is terrorized by the apparition and faints. Her baby is not affected, however, and is born a few months later.

The squire, meanwhile, wants a title and grafts himself illegally on to that of one of William the Conqueror's knights. His wealth increases. He acquires a nearby abbey and begins tearing it down and moving the monks' bones, to his gentle son's horror. The squire causes the entire village to be moved away, including the local church. When the villagers see their "dear bells going off in procession, never to return," they stand in their doorways and weep. The widow and her deformed child die eventually, followed by the squire's wife.

As the demolition of the abbey continues, the skeleton of a mitred abbot is found. The squire orders that the bones be put in "any hole," but the foreman reports that the more bones they move the more they find. The servants are disturbed because "vestiges of the Old Catholicism . . . still lingered in the minds of the simple folk of this remote nook."

The squire's son has married, and his wife is carving a marble tomb for a London church. She chooses a skull from amid the monks' bones as a model; it happens to be that of the abbot. It is taken to their London house. The son and heir, who is in debt for gambling, comes in late at night, having been drinking. He sees a model his wife has constructed of clay, is reminded of the abbot's skull, and is "overpowered with horror." He shoots himself in a tavern, which the villagers take as "retribution on the ambitious lord for his wickedness." The lord himself dies and the false "title" becomes extinct. On Sunday the minister takes as his text a verse from Isaiah 14: 10–23: "Thy pomp is brought down to the grave. . . . How art thou fallen from Heaven, O Lucifer, son of the morning!" The doctor concludes his story, and his hearers gaze thoughtfully into the fire.

F. B. Pinion states that the "narrative setting" of the opening and conclusion suggest that Hardy intended to include the story in *A GROUP OF NOBLE DAMES*, but that he may have been reluctant to "offend a local family." He derived the story from the history of the Damer family. Joseph Damer of Came House, daughter of the duke of Dorset, had purchased Milton Abbey and become the first earl of Dorchester. He built a mansion by the abbey church and demolished the original small village. His son, who married the sculptress Anne Seymour Conway, had committed suicide in 1776. Pinion believes, however, that Hardy's use of the word "Legend" in the title indicates that he was skeptical about the story (*The New Wessex Edition of The Complete Short Stories of Thomas Hardy*, Notes, 930).

"Domicilum" Hardy's earliest poem, written between 1857 and 1860 and first published as a pamphlet by Clement SHORTER in 1916 (Purdy, 177). It was reprinted in the *Life* as a footnote to his description of his birthplace, with an introductory comment: "Some Wordworthian lines . . . give with obvious and naïve fidelity the appearance of the paternal homestead at a date nearly half a century before the birth of the writer," which would have been about 1790. Hardy notes that his great-grandfather had built the first house in the valley, and his grandparents then settled there.

Hardy describes his paternal grandparents' early home, with its richly cultivated grounds, and recalls asking his grandmother, when she took him out to walk as a young child, what the site was like when she first settled there. She described its treeless and uncultivated state at the time, with "bramble bushes, furze and thorn"; in the summer it was surrounded by snakes and bats. Such walks may have laid the foundation of Hardy's keen interest in the cycles of the natural world, its varied manifestations often imperceptible to the human eye.

Doncastle, John In *The HAND OF ETHELBERTA* a fashionable London gentleman, the uncle of Alfred NEIGH (one of the suitors of Ethelberta PETHERWIN). Doncastle does not realize that his butler, CHICKEREL, is the father of Ethelberta, but when he learns the truth he is even more appreciative of Chickerel than he has been.

Doncastle, Margaret Character in *The HAND OF ETHELBERTA*. She is the wife of John DONCASTLE. When she learns that her husband's butler, CHICKEREL, is the father of Ethelberta PETHERWIN, she is shocked, unlike her husband.

Donn, Arabella Character in *JUDE THE OBSCURE*. The daughter of a pig-jobber at CRESSCOMBE (Letcombe Bassett), she had worked as a barmaid in ALFREDSTON before meeting and marrying Jude FAWLEY. She is called "a fine dark-eyed girl, not exactly handsome, but capable of passing as such at a little distance." As Jude is walking home from his job with a stonemason, thinking of how to acquire the works of Livy, Herodotus, and Aeschylus, Arabella and two friends, one of whom is ANNY, are washing pigs' chitterlings in a stream. Arabella tosses a pig's pizzle (penis) at Jude, which has implications for the future relationship. She seduces Jude and tricks him into marriage, then emigrates with her parents to Australia. Jude himself realizes she is "not worth a great deal as a specimen of womankind."

After Jude moves to CHRISTMINSTER he meets and falls in love with his cousin, Sue BRIDEHEAD. She marries the schoolmaster Richard PHILLOTSON, but divorces him and begins living with Jude. Arabella returns to England with a husband, Mr. CARTLETT, whom she has "married" illegally. She remarries Cartlett in England after divorcing Jude, and sends "Father TIME," the son she had without telling Jude, to live with Jude and Sue. Cartlett dies, and Arabella tries to find consolation in religion. After Father Time hangs himself and the two children of Sue and Jude, Sue becomes very religious; she then forces herself to remarry Phillotson. Arabella once more tricks Jude into marriage, this time plying him with drink until he falls into a stupor. He becomes very ill and dies. Arabella is soon seen at a boat regatta with Physician VILBERT's arm about her waist.

Donn, Mr. Father of Arabella DONN in *JUDE THE OBSCURE*. He is a pig breeder in CRESSCOMBE and emigrates to Australia. Later he returns to England and opens a pork shop in CHRISTMINSTER. Arabella convinces him to hold a long drinking party at his house, at which she persuades Jude to remarry her.

Donn, Mrs. Stepmother of Arabella DONN in *JUDE THE OBSCURE*. She is quiet and obeys Arabella when she schemes to trap Jude. She emigrates to Australia with Mr. Donn but dies of dysentery.

"Doom and She" This poem, published in *POEMS OF THE PAST AND THE PRESENT* (1902), takes the form of an overhead dialogue between two statuesque supernatural figures who dwell in the "vague Immense." One is "She," Mother Nature, a female figure, "Mother of all things made." She is a "World-weaver," who makes patterns throughout the world, but who is sightless; that is, she lacks foresight and cannot evaluate the condition, feelings, and future evolution of earth's "clay-made figures." The second is "Doom," or Fate, who is able to see the entire "domain" which "She" has created, but is "vacant of feeling." He cannot recognize either joy or pain and asks, "Why is Weak worse than Strong?" The mother figure hears a "groan" from time to time, and believes she has "schemed a world of strife, / Working by touch alone." She "broods in sad surmise" throughout the world, on "Alpine height" and "Polar peak."

It has been suggested that the "vague Immense" is the Will of Hardy's verse drama *The DYNASTS* (Bailey, *The Poetry of Thomas Hardy*, 145).

Dorchester The DORSET town in which Hardy lived most of his adult life. He was born nearby in HIGHER BOCKHAMPTON, worked during his youth in Dorchester, and returned there with his wife Emma in 1883. It was to be his permanent home for the remainder of his life.

Under the fictional name of Casterbridge, Dorchester figures in many of Hardy's works, including *The MAYOR OF CASTERBRIDGE*, *The RETURN OF THE NATIVE*, and *FAR FROM THE MADDING CROWD*, as well as a number of short stories. Denys Kay-Robinson observes that, although there are minor variations in the designations of certain place-names in the corpus of Hardy's work,

Statue of Thomas Hardy, Dorchester   (Sarah Bird Wright)

"in the main once Hardy had decided on his Wessex nomenclature he kept to it, and we are left to play the pleasant game of identifying the reality beneath each disguise ("Hardy's Wessex," 111).

Dorchester, as "Casterbridge," was treated extensively in *The Mayor of Casterbridge*. In 1902 Hardy was invited by the Recreation Committee of Dorchester to contribute the introduction to the forthcoming *Guide to Dorchester*. He wrote the town clerk that he was unable to accept, but that he had "said a good deal about Dorchester, under the pseudonym of 'Casterbridge,' in print during the last 20 years,—(all, in fact, that I have to say)." He gave full permission to quote descriptive passages from the novel.

In 1856, Hardy, at the instigation of his father, who was concerned that his son have a profession, was apprenticed to the architect and church-restorer John HICKS, who had moved his practice from Bristol to Dorchester. His office was at 39 South Street, Dorchester. During these years Hardy became a friend of Henry BASTOW, Hooper Tolbert, and Horace MOULE.

Hardy eventually took lodgings in Dorchester, going to Bockhampton on weekends.

In 1862 he left Dorchester for LONDON, where he worked for the architect Sir Arthur BLOMFIELD. After a few years his health began to fail from overwork and excessive study at night, and Blomfield advised him to leave London. His former employer Mr. Hicks offered him a post in church restoration, and he returned to Dorchester in July 1867. He had, meanwhile, been writing poetry, and had thought of writing plays in blank verse and even of trying the stage, but nothing came of either venture.

Hardy's health was restored by daily walks from Higher Bockhampton to the Hicks office in Dorchester. Hardy decided to return to London in January 1869 to try his hand at literature instead of architecture. Mr. Hicks died in Dorchester during the winter, and in April Mr. G. R. CRICKMAY, a WEYMOUTH architect who had purchased his practice, asked if Hardy might assist him in carrying out church restorations. He agreed to come for two weeks, as he had been busy attempting to market his first novel, The POOR MAN AND THE LADY (not published). Hardy did not return to Dorchester permanently for nearly a decade, having married and moved first to STURMINSTER NEWTON, Wandsworth Common, and UPPER TOOTING. In June 1883 the Hardys settled in Dorchester. For the next two decades they spent several months of each spring and summer in London, interspersed with trips abroad.

Having searched in vain for a suitable house in Dorchester, Hardy was able to purchase a plot of land from the Duchy of Cornwall in Fordington Field, a mile outside of town. In digging for a well, workmen found Roman remains, which Hardy described in a paper presented to the DORSET NATURAL HISTORY AND ANTIQUARIAN FIELD CLUB. He planted trees on the site on New Year's Eve, 1884, and he and Emma slept in the house for the first time on June 29, 1885. Hardy lived in the house until his death in 1928; his wife Emma had died in 1912, and he married Florence Dugdale (HARDY) in 1914.

In 1910 Hardy was presented with the FREEDOM OF DORCHESTER, an honor which, he noted in the Life, "appealed to his sentiment more perhaps than did many of those recognitions of his literary achievements that had come from the uttermost parts of the earth at a much earlier time." He admitted being pleased when someone remarked that "'Casterbridge' is a sort of essence of the town as it used to be, 'a place more Dorchester than Dorchester itself'" (Life, 351).

For further reading: Pinion, "Hardy's House in Dorchester and Two Important Houses in Casterbridge"; Skilling, "Walk Round Dorchester (Casterbridge) with Hardy."

Dorchester Debating and Dramatic Society A local theatrical group in DORCHESTER that eventually evolved into the HARDY PLAYERS. In April 1908 they presented some scenes from The DYNASTS in Dorchester. Hardy termed the performance "the first attempt to put on the stage a dramatic epic that was not intended for staging at all" (Life, 341). In the autumn of 1909 Hardy attended a rehearsal of a play, dramatized by A. H. EVANS, based on FAR FROM THE MADDING CROWD; it was then performed in the Corn Exchange, a municipal building in Dorchester. Hardy thought it "a neater achievement than the London version of 1882 by Mr. Comyns Carr" (Life, 348).

In the fall of 1910 the group presented an adaptation of UNDER THE GREENWOOD TREE called The Mellstock Quire, which had been the second title of the novel. (MELLSTOCK is Hardy's name for STINSFORD and the Bockhamptons, three hamlets about two miles from Dorchester.) In November 1911, also in Dorchester, they gave a performance of a play Hardy had dramatized from the story called "The THREE STRANGERS," entitled "The THREE WAYFARERS." Florence HENNIKER came from London to see it.

The evening before the death of Emma HARDY, in November 1912, Hardy attended a rehearsal of an adaptation of The TRUMPET-MAJOR by the company. The performance went on as scheduled the next day, because many people had come from a considerable distance to see it; an announcement of Emma's death was made from the stage. The group performed an adaptation of The WOODLANDERS in November 1913, a few months before the marriage of Thomas Hardy and Florence Dugdale (HARDY).

After 1916 the group was called "The Hardy Players" and, under that name, continued to perform until 1924.

Dorchester Grammar School Endowed by an Elizabethan, Thomas Hardye of Frampton, this school survives today, but Hardy did not attend it. The school contains a number of Hardy artifacts, including a portrait of Hardy by Winifred THOMSON (Letters II, 174). In 1909 Hardy was appointed a representative governor of the school, serving on the board as a representative of the magistrates of the county. He wrote Lady Agnes GROVE that he just realized not a single grammar school had been founded for women (Letters IV, 3).

Hardy's first school had been established by Julia MARTIN, who lived with her husband at KINGSTON MAURWARD, in Bockhampton, near the Hardys, and was childless. She built and endowed a small stone school on the edge of the estate. Hardy attended this school in 1848, but before he entered, Julia Martin had become greatly attached to him. She has been called Hardy's "first love." Mrs. Martin was hurt when the Hardys moved her prize pupil and special protégé in 1849 to the Dorchester day school run by Isaac Glandfield LAST. Hardy's parents apparently believed Last's teaching to be superior to that at the Dorchester Grammar School or at William BARNES's school. Hardy was taught Latin by Last. Michael Millgate, who first identified Last, states that he later founded an Academy, one of the old British schools (Millgate, *Thomas Hardy: A Biography*, 35).

Writing about leaving Mrs. Martin's school much later, Hardy confessed he "mourned the loss of his friend the landowner's wife" (Evelyn Hardy, *Thomas Hardy: A Critical Biography*, 29).

In 1927 Hardy made his final public appearance with an address at the Dorchester Grammar School stone laying. Hardy believed the Thomas Hardye who founded the early grammar school and the Dorset Hardys (including the Thomas Masterman Hardy of Portisham, who was Nelson's flag captain at the Battle of TRAFALGAR and figures in *The DYNASTS*) all descended from the le Hardy family of Jersey, in the Channel Islands (Millgate, *Thomas Hardy: A Biography*, 3–4).

Dorchester Lecture Society A local society charged with securing speakers for town hall lectures. In 1883 Hardy was asked by the secretary to invite the American author Francis Bret Harte, then the United States consul in Glasgow, to lecture to the society. Hardy wrote to issue the invitation and to inquire about Harte's fee, saying that, because the society was "not rich," he might follow the example of other "stars of the platform" and lecture in WEYMOUTH and Exeter at the same time. Hardy added that he and his wife could offer the American a bed "if plain accommodation will suffice." Apparently Harte did not accept the invitation (*Letters* I, 122).

Dorset County in southern England closely associated with Hardy and his writing. Hardy was born in HIGHER BOCKHAMPTON, a tiny hamlet near DORCHESTER, Dorset, on June 2, 1840. With the exception of a few years in LONDON as a young man, occasional travels in other parts of England and abroad, and brief periodic rentals of London flats or houses, he spent most of his life in Dorset. The county is roughly equivalent to the southern part of his fictional domain, WESSEX, which also includes the traditional counties of Gloucestershire, Somerset, and Wiltshire. The region Hardy called Wessex in his work eventually expanded to cover over two-thirds of southern England. The name now evokes not only the geographical features of the rural LANDSCAPE but also the fabled legends, occupations, history, and customs of the inhabitants.

In 1904 the photographer Hermann LEA undertook to capture the Wessex countryside as portrayed in the novels of Thomas Hardy. His two guides were issued as a single volume in 1913 and were included in the Wessex edition of Hardy's works. Lea's Dorset views correspond to many features of Hardy's fictional settings, such as Rainbarrow (the center of Egdon Heath in *The RETURN OF THE NATIVE*), Blackmoor Vale (in *TESS OF THE D'URBERVILLES*), a typical Dorset sheep-dipping pool (in *FAR FROM THE MADDING CROWD*), Puddletown Church (Weatherbury church in *Far from the Madding Crowd*), and Sherborne Castle (Sherton Castle in "Anna, Lady Baxby," one of the stories in *A GROUP OF NOBLE DAMES*).

Hardy's fiction and poetry preserve innumerable aspects of the rural Dorset that existed in the 19th century. He represented country cottages and interiors, barns, inns, churches, farm houses, and manor houses. He also incorporated the superstitions and traditions of the county in his work, and made careful use of local DIALECT in the speech of his characters. Within Hardy's novels and short stories there are poachers, smugglers, tranters (carriers), masons, barbers, reddlemen (dealers in "reddle," used to mark sheep), millers, sextons, farmers, cidermakers, woodcutters, and shoemakers. Hardy portrays the fine church choirs and bands of the day, as well as popular forms of recreation, such as CLUB WALKING and performances by CHRISTMAS MUMMERS. The antiquity of the countryside, and the continuity of its traditions, are an integral part of what makes Hardy's work endure.

The "ferny vegetation" of Egdon Heath in *The Return of the Native*, the circular British earthen bank of the North Wessex downs in *JUDE THE OBSCURE*, the Weatherbury band saluting Gabriel OAK and his wife Bathsheba EVERDENE on the eve of their wedding, the "flanks of infinite cows and calves of bygone years" at Talbothays Farm in *Tess of the d'Urbervilles*—such details form an indelible picture of Dorset scenes, traditions, and daily life.

For further reading: Brown, ed., *Figures in a Wessex Landscape: Thomas Hardy's Picture of English Country Life;* Carter and Whetherly, *Thomas Hardy Catalogue: A List of Books by and about Thomas Hardy, O.M. (1840–1928) in Dorset County Library.*

Dorset County Museum Located on High West Street, Dorchester, near St. Peter's Church, this is an independent museum owned and managed by the Dorset Natural History and Archaeological Society, with funding assisted by the Dorset County Council. The museum is devoted to Dorset writers, including Thomas Hardy, as well as to the archaeology, wildlife, fossils, and general history of Dorset. In 1883 Henry Joseph MOULE, the eldest son of the Reverend Henry MOULE and one of Hardy's oldest friends, became curator of the museum.

The museum contains 14 display rooms and an archaeological gallery with displays on geology, wildlife, local history, and Roman remains. There is a re-creation of Hardy's study at MAX GATE with a violin and cello that belonged to Hardy, his father, or his uncle. In addition, the museum has many other Hardy artifacts: the remnant of his personal library, documents connected with his birthplace at HIGHER BOCKHAMPTON, the notebook he used to jot down material for *The TRUMPET-MAJOR,* a number of watercolor paintings of local scenes painted by Hardy when he was 19, and the notebooks in which he recorded his early visits to the BRITISH MUSEUM. The library contains a large collection of manuscripts, photographs, and drawings related to his life and work. In July 1997 the museum opened new galleries devoted to Hardy and other Dorset writers.

Dorset Natural History and Antiquarian Field Club
Hardy was a longtime member of this society, the name of which was sometimes, in Hardy's correspondence, shortened to the "Field Club." On May 13, 1884, he read a paper before the members titled "Some Romano-British Relics Found at Max Gate, Dorchester." MAX GATE was then being built.

In April 1908 Hardy was invited by Nelson RICHARDSON to become an honorary member of this club, and responded that he might not be able to attend all the meetings, as his literary pursuits tended to "enforce a somewhat hermit life, & that more & more as years roll on" (*Letters* III, 311).

"Dorsetshire Labourer, The" Essay published in *LONGMAN'S MAGAZINE,* July 1883. Thomas Hardy exposes the fallacy of imagining the community of farm laborers to be "a uniform collection of concrete Hodges," Hodge being a name connoting an uncouth, stolid, dimwitted, and inarticulate farm worker. Hardy argues that such assumptions would soon be dispelled if a visitor were to see the farm laborer at home. There, the laborer becomes an individual, different from his brothers, uncles, and neighbors, all of whom have varying "characters, capacities, and interests." His language has exact rules of grammatical inflection, though the "printed tongue" his children learn in the "National School" becomes mixed with the "unwritten, dying, Wessex English that they had learnt of their parents." It is the composite language that lacks "rule or harmony." After six months, the visitor comes to see Hodge as one of a community of "men of many minds," who may be happy, depressed, stupid, clever, austere, or wanton. They contemplate each other's "foibles or vices." Dick the carter, Bob the shepherd, and Sam the ploughman are similar in the "narrowness of their means and their general open-air life," but they remain individuals. Moreover, their outdoor life and "pastoral environment" make them healthier than their counterparts in the slums of big cities.

Hardy deplores would-be philanthropists who call at cottages and judge the cleanliness of laborers by whether the farm woman wears a white apron or whether the walls are painted a cheerful color, not by the actual cleanliness of the pots and pans, sheets, and floors. He also cautions that "actual slovenliness" is not necessarily accompanied by unhappiness. It is more likely that unhappiness among laborers arises from uncertainty about the stability of their employment.

Hardy explains that the Dorset laborer suffers most at the annual hiring fair at CANDLEMAS (February 2), when, if he is not hired, he maintains a "self-repressing mannerliness hardly to be found among any other class" when he talks with his more fortunate friends. Younger laborers are in demand, but those more than 60 years of age, who have no children or whose children are "ingrates" or "far away," are often disappointed. On Lady Day (in early April), farmers convey their laborers to their new cottages by horse and wagon. Hardy has a comprehensive knowledge of the upheaval involved in the annual migration among farm workers. He describes the brief time allotted to the cleaning of the cottages between tenants, the provisions taken along, and the roadside inns. The number of workers changing employers had risen greatly within one generation. This continual dislocation causes the villagers, who consider themselves a step above the laborers, to complain, "'there are no nice homely workfolk now as there use to be.'" The widespread nomadic exchange has blurred the individuality of each district, bringing "mental equality." It has also eroded the loyalty of the laborer to a farm where he has had long associations; he no longer ploughs the fields he had known as a boy, and the landlord does not know his workers by sight, as he would have earlier in the century.

Hardy discusses Joseph Arch (1826–1919), who was instrumental in forming the Warwickshire Agricultural Labourers' Union (1872), later known as the National Agricultural Labourers' Union, whose mission was improving the lot of farm workers. He was from Warwickshire, "Shakespeare's Country, where the humours of the peasantry have a marked family relationship with those of Dorset men." Hardy regards Arch as less of an anarchist, however, than a believer in "social evolution." Arch succeeded in raising the pay of farm laborers, but Hardy observes that the makeup of the family had more to do with prosperity than the addition of a few shillings a week. Several strong boys could contribute far more than "delicate girls." Moreover, "Home-living boys" were an asset to the employer, as they did as much work as their father but could be paid less. Farm women were also in demand, though they were paid less for their field work.

Hardy also expresses great sympathy for the lifeholders, cottagers who have built their own cottages but who are not farm laborers. Cottagers once formed the "backbone of village life," but landowners have pulled down the cottages of all who were not employees. This problem is treated extensively in *The WOODLANDERS.* In this novel Giles WINTERBORNE holds the cottage belonging to John SOUTH and his daughter.

Marty SOUTH. On South's death, all his properties revert to the estate of the malicious Felice CHARMOND; he is unable to will or give them to anyone, including his daughter. The same restriction applies to other cottages Winterborne holds. The situation had developed in many locations in England because the properties had become dilapidated in the past. At the time, the only way for the owners (ancestors of the present owners) to repair them was to exchange their old copyholds for life-leases extending for a maximum of three lives. This system, which Hardy abhorred, resulted in considerable hardship for farm laborers.

Harold Orel, editor of *Thomas Hardy's Personal Writings*, a volume containing this essay, observes that "Hardy's regret for a world that was changing in a way that could never be reversed, although quite marked in this essay, deepened as time passed." He points out that the interest of "The Dorsetshire Labourer" is much larger than simply its "consideration of either agricultural or architectural matters."

Douglas, Sir George Brisbane (1856–1935) Scottish baronet, landowner, and author; his estate was Springwood, Kelso, Roxburgh, Scotland. Sir George and Hardy met in 1881 at Wimborne, where the baronet's brother Frank was studying land-agency. In 1887 Sir George invited the Hardys to visit him in Scotland, but Hardy declined owing to the pressure of his literary commitments (*Letters* I, 166). Sir George visited the Hardys at Easter 1890; they went to see the grave of the Reverend William BARNES, and to Portland, where they lunched at the Mermaid (*Life*, 225).

In 1893 Hardy was the Sir George's luncheon guest at the Conservative Club in LONDON and wrote Florence HENNIKER that they each had "two clubs on the line of the wedding procession" (a reference to the marriage of the Duke of York and Princess Mary of Teck on July 6, 1893). Hardy remarked that if he and Sir George saw any of the procession it would be by walking through the crowd, "which is by far the most interesting feature" (*Letters* II, 20). In December 1919 Sir George lectured in Edinburgh on Hardy's poems.

Douglas was the author of *A History of the Border Counties* (1899); a volume of essays, *Diversions of a Country Gentleman* (1902); a biography of Major General Andrew Gilbert Wauchope (who was killed in the BOER WAR); and other works. Hardy introduced Douglas to his friend Mrs. Florence Henniker and her husband, Colonel (later General) Arthur Henniker, who also fought in the Boer War and who offered to provide information about Major General Wauchope (*Letters* III, 66).

Dowden, Olly A middle-aged broom-maker on EGDON HEATH in *The RETURN OF THE NATIVE*. She is "civil to enemies as well as to friends."

dramatic works Hardy wrote two verse dramas, *The DYNASTS* (composed between 1897 and 1907; published in three parts in 1904, 1906, and 1908), and *The FAMOUS TRAGEDY OF THE QUEEN OF CORNWALL* (He also wrote *The THREE WAYFARERS*, a dramatization of his short story "THE THREE STRANGERS," which was first performed in June 1893. All three works have been performed, at least in part. *See* Appendix II, Media Adaptations of the Works of Thomas Hardy.

drawings From boyhood, Hardy took a keen interest in art. His earliest introduction to it may have been the Grey family monument in STINSFORD CHURCH. The nearby manor house, KINGSTOWN MAURWARD, was built in 1591 for a Grey owner; the family owned the home until the eighteenth century (Robinson, *The Landscape of Thomas Hardy*, 33). The Hardy family pew was adjacent to the monument, and Hardy not only memorized the inscription but also was fascinated by the carving of a skull. His biographer Evelyn Hardy describes it as having "bat-like wings, hollow eye-sockets, grinning teeth, and hideous nose." Hardy's sister Mary told a friend the skull had "haunted his mind as a boy" (Evelyn Hardy, *Thomas Hardy: A Critical Biography*, 22).

As a young man Hardy had a love of painting as well as poetry. While working for the architect Sir Arthur BLOMFIELD in LONDON (1862–67), he went to the National Gallery on the days it was open for 20 minutes after lunch. In the *Life* he states that he would confine his attention "to a single master on each visit, and forbidding his eyes to stray to any other." He recommended this plan to young people, saying that this method of study was more instructive than any book about art could be (*Life*, 52).

While writing *The TRUMPET-MAJOR*, Hardy visited the BRITISH MUSEUM and made sketches of illustrations in old newspapers of the period, such as a woman's cap, a Cockney sportsman's hat, an iron grate, and a silver cream jug and teapot of 1792. Many of these drawings are on display at the DORSET COUNTY MUSEUM.

Hardy had the eye, if not the skill, of a painter. He often made sketches, but even more important, his notes contain frequent references to painting and painters. His poetry and novels are marked by observations about changing light and shade. Well into old age, long after he had stopped writing fiction and going into London, he visited friends' country houses to see paintings (Evelyn Hardy, *Thomas Hardy: A Critical Biography*, 62).

In the poem "Drawing Details in an Old Church" (LATE LYRICS AND EARLIER) (1922), Hardy visualizes sitting alone in a church, drawing "What some Gothic brain designed" while the bell above tolls for someone unknown to him. He does not ask who the person might be, anticipating that, one day, "knolls for / One unguessed" will "sound out for me." A stranger, "loitering under In nave or choir" may think, "'Whose, I wonder?' / But not inquire."

In April 1923 Hardy, at the age of 83, finished a rough draft of his verse drama *The FAMOUS TRAGEDY OF THE QUEEN OF CORNWALL*, and in May he made his last drawing, which he called "an imaginary view of Tintagel Castle." He remarked in his autobiography that it was "delicately drawn, an amazing feat for a man in his eighty-third year, and it indicates his architectural tastes and early training" (*Life*, 419). (When the play was published his drawing was used as an illustration.)

A number of Hardy's sketches survive today in the collection of the Dorset County Museum, including one of Emma HARDY, his first wife, searching for the picnic tumbler she dropped in the Valency river. He immortalized this incident in his poem "UNDER THE WATERFALL."

For further reading: Meyers, "An Allusion to Donne in Hardy's 'Drawing Details in an Old Church.'"

"Dream or No, A"   Poem dated February 1913, after the death of Hardy's first wife, Emma Lavinia GIFFORD (HARDY) in November 1912; it was published in *SATIRES OF CIRCUMSTANCE* (1914). The poem evokes Hardy's poignant memories of St. Juliot, the village in CORNWALL where he had first met Emma in 1870. After her death he did not actually go back to St. Juliot until March 1913. The poem is a reprise of his intricate dreams in which Emma and St. Juliot and Cornwall are linked.

He reflects that "much of his life" claims St. Juliot as "its key." He goes on to explain that he had dreamed of "a maiden abiding," and he had found her long ago, "lonely" with "sea-birds around her." The maiden was Emma, staying, at the time, with her sister, Helen HOLDER, and Helen's husband, the Reverend Caddell HOLDER, who was rector of ST. JULIOT CHURCH. Hardy had come to Cornwall to restore the church.

He recalls that, once he met Emma, "quickly she drew me/To take her unto me,/and lodge her long years with me." As the poem progresses, the poet sees "nought of that maid from Saint-Juliot" and wonders, "Can she ever have been here . . . The woman I thought a long housemate with me?" He then asks, "Does there even a place like Saint-Juliot exist?" Is there a "Vallency Valley . . . /Or Beeny [Beeny High Cliff], or Bos [Boscastle] with its flounce flinging mist?"

When Hardy did revisit St. Juliot in March 1913, the church rectory was the focal point of his return.

"Drummer Hodge"   First titled "The Dead Drummer," this poem was published in *Literature* on November 25, 1899. The poem was later collected in *POEMS OF THE PAST AND THE PRESENT* (1901). It was occasioned by Hardy's reading that one of the drummers killed in the BOER WAR was a native of a local village. He describes

the burial of the young Wessex soldier, whom he calls Drummer Hodge. The soldier is tossed in a grave "uncoffined," never having known the landmarks of the terrain in which he is entombed, such as "the broad Karoo," or the "dusty loam" of the "Bush." Yet, the poet reflects, the soldier's remains will, in time, undergo a metamorphosis and be absorbed into the South African landscape: "His homely Northern breast and brain / Grow to some Southern tree, / And strange-eyed constellations reign / His stars eternally." Each verse contains an image of a new and exotic constellation. He uses South African words: *kopje* (small hill), *veldt* (open pasture land), *karoo* (barren tract of land with plateaus), and *bush* (uncleared or untilled land). *Hodge* is a term for a rural laborer (Pinion, *A Commentary on the Poems of Thomas Hardy*, 33).

Hardy was greatly saddened by the Boer War and the deaths it produced. In October 1899 he witnessed the departure of the British troops to war from Southampton and wrote a sonnet about it, published in the *Daily Chronicle*. In November his verses "The GOING OF THE BATTERY" appeared in *Literature*, and in the same month "A CHRISTMAS GHOST-STORY" was published in the *Westminster Gazette*. (*The Life and Work of Thomas Hardy*, by Thomas Hardy, ed. Michael Millgate, 328).

"Duchess of Hamptonshire, The"   Short story; *see GROUP OF NOBLE DAMES, A*.

Dugdale, Florence Emily   *See* HARDY, FLORENCE EMILY DUGDALE.

"Duke's Reappearance, The"   Short story; *see CHANGED MAN AND OTHER TALES, A*.

du Maurier, George (Louis Palmella Busson) (1834–1896)   English illustrator and novelist, author of *Peter Ibbetson, Trilby*, and *The Martian*. He illustrated the work of Henry JAMES, George MEREDITH, and other writers, as well as that of Hardy. He was famous for his caricatures in *Punch*. He contributed the illustrations for *The HAND OF ETHELBERTA* and *A LAODICEAN*.

In April 1880 Hardy wrote the publishers of the American periodical *HARPER'S MONTHLY MAGAZINE* that he was delighted to learn they were planning an English edition. He offered the British and American serial rights to his new novel *A Laodicean* to the editors. In June he wrote HARPER & BROTHERS to urge the selection of du Maurier as the illustrator, since he felt it important "that the English edition should start with every possible advantage in the way of an artist." Du Maurier had already illustrated *The Hand of Ethelberta*, of which the first installment appeared in the July 1875 *CORNHILL*, and had told Hardy he would be most interested in contributing drawings for another work. Moreover, in Hardy's opinion he was "by far the most popular illustrator here," since he had achieved celebrity with his witty sketches in *Punch*. Hardy gave details of du Maurier's special technique of drawing his sketches on paper in a size larger than necessary, having them photographed on the wood, and then cut. (Many artists at that time drew directly on the wood.) It was agreed that he would illustrate Hardy's new novel.

In late October 1880, however, after a few installments, Hardy became ill. His physician said he was hemorrhaging internally: He must either have surgery or lie immobile with his head lower than the rest of his body. Hardy decided on the latter course, and lay from November until May 1881 in that position, dictating the novel to Emma, who was also nursing him.

In late spring 1883 Hardy attended a dinner in London given by Edmund GOSSE at which he met William Dean HOWELLS; Du Maurier was another guest. The Hardys were in London part of June and July, 1884, and saw du Maurier at an evening party. A few years later, in June 1887, Queen Victoria's Jubilee Year, Hardy recorded talking with du Maurier at the "Royal Academy *Soirée*" (*Life*, 167, 201).

For further reading: Jackson, *Illustration and the Novels of Thomas Hardy*.

d'Urberville, Alec The villain of *TESS OF THE D'URBERVILLES*, who has been called a libertine with Satanic tendencies. His father was Mr. Simon Stoke, who adopted the name of "d'Urberville" to give validity to his pretense of descending from an ancient noble family. He had searched in the BRITISH MUSEUM for "extinct" and "ruined" surnames that would serve this purpose. Alec is cruel and ruthless to Tess DURBEYFIELD; other girls besides Tess have suffered at his hands. He lives with his mother, who is blind, at The Slopes near Tantridge. After seducing and abandoning Tess, he comes to the attention of the Rev. James CLARE, the father of Angel CLARE, who, with evangelical fervor, persuades him to become an itinerant preacher. Alec pursues Tess, even after her marriage to Angel (absent in Brazil). When Tess's father dies, she tries to save her family by going as Alec's wife to SANDBOURNE. Here Angel finds Tess, who is living with Alec in a plushly furnished boarding house. She is horrified when she perceives that Alec had lied to her when he assured her Angel would never return. She solves the problem when she murders Alec by stabbing him, then flees into Angel's arms. She thus "kills the situation," a phrase used by Hardy in his autobiography (*Life*, 221).

d'Urberville, Mrs. The blind mother of Alec D'URBERVILLE in *TESS OF THE D'URBERVILLES*, she is the widow of Simon Stoke, a merchant who took the name d'Urberville. (Stoke discovered the name in the BRITISH MUSEUM as he was combing works in search of "extinct, half-extinct, obscured, and ruined families"

whose name he could adopt.) She keeps pet fowls, a pastime fashionable at the time, as well as bullfinches.

Durbeyfield, Abraham The younger brother of Tess DURBEYFIELD in *TESS OF THE D'URBERVILLES*, he goes with Tess to take the beehives to Kingsbere in the middle of the night and is with her when their horse, Prince, is killed on the way. He weeps with Tess and their sister 'Liza-Lu DURBEYFIELD at Prince's burial.

Durbeyfield, Eliza Louise ("Liza-Lu") The younger sister of Tess DURBEYFIELD in *TESS OF THE D'URBERVILLES*. Tess asks Angel CLARE to marry 'Liza-Lu after she is executed.

Durbeyfield, Joan A former dairymaid, she is the mother of Tess DURBEYFIELD in *TESS OF THE D'URBERVILLES*. She believes in folklore and superstition and likes to sing traditional songs and ballads. She loves her brood of seven children, but is barely able to care for them; Tess must assist her. Resigned to events, Joan is apathetic, and accepting of misfortune. She is a poor judge of character and fails to perceive the true nature of Alec D'URBERVILLE. She believes, in fact, that Tess would be fortunate to marry him.

Durbeyfield, John The father of Tess DURBEYFIELD in *TESS OF THE D'URBERVILLES*. He is a "haggler," or local carrier, not fond of working, and addicted to drinking. Just before the night on which he is scheduled to set out on a lucrative delivery job, he begins celebrating the news that he is descended from a historic noble family. Tess goes in his place, but has an accident in which their faithful horse Prince is killed. John refuses to permit the carcass to be sold for cat meat, and instead has it buried. His life tenancy of their house ends with his death, and the family is evicted. "How are the Mighty Fallen" is inscribed on his headstone.

Durbeyfield, Teresa ("Tess") One of Hardy's memorable and cherished heroines, Tess plays the central role in *TESS OF THE D'URBERVILLES*. As indicated in the novel's subtitle, she is "A Pure Woman Faithfully Presented." The eldest of the many Durbeyfield children, she is the most responsible member of the family. When we first meet her, at the May Day CLUB-WALKING at Marlott, she is described as having a quality of freshness; she is a "fine and handsome girl" with a "mobile peony mouth and large innocent eyes . . . a mere vessel of emotion untinctured by experience." When the village girls are dancing, before the young men arrive from work, Angel CLARE and his brothers pass by. He dances with another girl, but remembers Tess later and feels instinctively that she has been "hurt by his oversight."

Tess evolves from a sensitive girl, burdened by her family, into a complex woman. She has been compared with a bird who has been caught in a trap—the trap of trying to assist her parents and of being seduced by Alec D'URBERVILLE. Her father is obsessed with recapturing the glory of his paternal lineage, and her mother only wants her daughter to find a husband of a better class, regardless of his character. Ironically, Tess's heredity is linked with old nobility, unlike Alec d'Urberville, whose father was a Mr. Simon Stoke. After the death of Prince, the family's horse, Tess goes to work at The Slopes, the home of Alec d'Urberville and his mother. Alec seduces her and she gives birth to a baby boy, called Sorrow. She refuses to marry Alec. After the baby's death she works as a milkmaid at Talbothay's Dairy, where she meets Angel Clare, her future husband. She has an unwavering loyalty to Angel and marries him; he then abandons her after she tells him the truth about her past (a confession her mother had advised against). She takes up arduous farm work at Flintcome Ash, where Alec finds her. In the hope of helping her family she agrees to live with him at SAND-BOURNE. Angel returns, but Tess is in such a state that she ceases to "recognize the body before him as hers—allowing it to drift, like a corpse upon the current, in a direction dissociated from its living will." She realizes that Alec has deceived her in telling her that Angel would never return, and she stabs him. Angel helps her flee, and they enjoy a brief period of happiness before she is arrested at STONEHENGE and executed.

"During Wind and Rain"   Poem published in MOMENTS OF VISION (1917) on the theme of inevitable change, or the mutability of all circumstances and lives. Each of the four seven-line stanzas treats a different phase of the girlhood of Emma Lavina Gifford HARDY, Hardy's first wife. In each stanza, six lines serve to build up a picture of harmony and worthwhile pursuits, while the final seventh line shows their destruction and decay.

The first stanza takes place on Sussex Street, Plymouth, where the Giffords lived as Emma and her sister were growing up. The family group is singing while one member plays the piano; Emma later recalled that they knew how to sing in harmony and "our four voices went well together." However, "the sick leaves reel down in throngs," a portent of the eventual dissolution of the family.

The second stanza presents the tranquil, pleasant, cultivated garden. There are elder trees, and a shady seat, but then "white storm-birds wing across!" In the third stanza, also recalling the bucolic garden, family members and guests are breakfasting under the trees, glimpsing the bay, patting pet fowls, when suddenly "the rotten rose is ript from the wall." This passage refers to the construction of a street through the garden.

In the last stanza the entire family moves to a "high new house" (Bedford Terrace, North Road, now Tavistock Road). There is a terrace with a stone parade topped by handsome houses and furniture on the lawn. With the passage of time, however, rains dull their "brightest things," and eventually "down their carved names the rain-drop ploughs" (that is, the names on the tombstones are eroded by the rain).

After Emma's death, Hardy went to Plymouth to visit some of her surviving relatives and may have seen the Gifford tombstones during a rain (Bailey, *The Poetry of Thomas Hardy,* 393–95).

Dynasts, The   A major epic drama dealing with the era of the Napoleonic Wars, composed between 1897 and 1907 and published in three parts (1904, 1906, and 1908). Hardy subtitles it "An Epic-Drama of the War with Napoleon in Three Parts, Nineteen Acts, and One Hundred & Thirty Scenes"; the actual count of scenes is 131, plus the Fore Scene and the After Scene. The action takes place over about 10 years. The epigraph reads: "And I heard sounds of insult, shame, and wrong/And trumpets blown for wars."

Hardy's friend Edmund GOSSE remarked that Hardy chose all of Europe for his field. He found his achievement remarkable in painting, on an immense canvas, "a panorama of the struggle not unworthy of its stupendous issues" (*Public Opinion,* Feb. 5, 1915, 143; quoted in Roberts, *Hardy's Poetic Drama and the Theatre,* 15).

Harold Orel observes that the poem is longer than Hardy's shorter poems put together (there were more than 900). Many of his friends were sorry that extensive labor on this work prevented his writing more novels. Orel states that many faithful readers of Hardy's fiction and poetry are, in fact, unaware of its existence ("The Dynasts," *Oxford Reader's Companion to Hardy,* ed. Norman Page, 104). Hardy, however, regarded it as "the greatest of all his literary achievements" (Orel, 102–103). Because of its epic subject, immense number of characters, and vast canvas of land and sea, Marguerite Roberts terms it a work "without parallel in poetry, at least in the twentieth century" (*Hardy's Poetic Drama and the Theatre,* 14). It has not, however, attracted many readers compared with Hardy's other works, in part because of the historical context and in part because, compared with most of Hardy's poetry, the verse itself is complex and difficult to comprehend, and, as Susan Dean says, is "inaccessible" to readers (Dean, *Hardy's Poetic Vision in The Dynasts: The Diorama of a Dream,* 3).

The drama has three levels of characters. First, there are peasants and ordinary people. Next there are actual historical figures, including members of Parliament, national rulers, and military leaders preoccupied with Napoleon's ambitious attempt to dominate Europe. Napoleon himself is the central human figure. Finally, there is a group of celestial observers. These are "Phantom Intelligences," spirits who scrutinize developments, provide outside commentary on the turmoil of war from a cosmic point of view and express Hardy's philosophy. They cannot intervene in men's affairs or answer philosophical questions. They include the Spirit Ironic, the Spirit Sinister, the Spirit of the Years, Recording Angels, the Spirit of Pity, the Chorus of Rumours, and others. Their role is derived from Shelley's *Prometheus Unbound*. These abstractions have the power to interpret the sublunary events and to "give universality to his panorama" (Roberts, *Hardy's Poetic Drama and the Theatre*, 14).

The action is on a cosmic scale, clarified and interpreted by the Phantom Intelligences. Hardy terms the work a "Spectacle in the likeness of a Drama," concerned with the "Great Historical Calamity, or Clash of Peoples" which was brought about a hundred years earlier (Preface, vii). He chose the subject because he was familiar with the part of England near the "watering-place" (WEYMOUTH) where King GEORGE III had a summer residence during the war with Napoleon I. Also, the district had been "animated by memories and traditions of the desperate military preparations" for Napoleon's expected invasion of England. After publication of his novel *The TRUMPET-MAJOR* (1880), dealing with the spectre of such an invasion, he felt he had "touched the fringe of a vast international tragedy." Yet little attention had been paid to the role of England throughout Napoleon's meteoric rise to power and his defeats in the Battle of TRAFALGAR and the Battle of WATERLOO.

Hardy states that *The Dynasts* was intended only for "mental performance" and not for the stage. Portions of it were, however, dramatized by the noted playwright and producer Harley GRANVILLE-BARKER. His production opened at the Kingsway Theatre, London, on November 25, 1914. The production ran for 72 performances before closing in 1915 (Orel, *Thomas Hardy's Epic-Drama*, 102). On June 22, 1916, "Wessex Scenes from *The Dynasts*," adapted by Hardy himself, were presented in Weymouth, and on December 6 and 7 they were staged in DORCHESTER (information provided by Prof. Keith Wilson of the University of Ottawa).

The work begins in 1805, when Napoleon I proclaimed himself emperor of the French and king of Italy in Milan Cathedral, and ends in 1815, when he recognized that the Battle of Waterloo had ended his ambition of establishing a pan-European dynasty.

Readers are often mystified by the "Phantom Intelligences," which include The Ancient Spirit of the Years, The Spirit of the Pities, Spirits Sinister and Ironic, The Spirit of Rumour, The Shade of the Earth, Spirit-Messengers, and Recording Angels, that provide a commentary on events. Hardy explains in the preface that the function of each group is self-explanatory except for the Spirit of the Pities, which is what August Wilhelm von Schlegel called "'the Universal Sympathy of human nature—the spectator ideal-

ized.'" The Intelligences function as "supernatural spectators of the terrestrial action," intended to provide, in Coleridge's phrase, a "suspension of disbelief." Hardy states that the scheme of Choruses was "shaped with a single view to the modern expression of a modern outlook, and in frank divergence from classical and other dramatic precedent" (ix). He justifies their presence because the "wide prevalence of the Monistic theory of the Universe" (that is, belief in one God) in the 20th century prevented him from importing "Divine personages from any antique Mythology as sources of causation." Susan Dean rightly points out that this statement, referring to the "contemporary belief in scientific materialism," has caused the "disorientation" of the reader who reaches the Fore Scene (Dean, 5). This scene, in the form of a conversation among the Phantom Intelligences, follows the preface and opens the epic-drama; it consists of a conversation among the Phantom Intelligences.

The Spirit of the Years says that human events are governed by the Immanent Will; they are not susceptible to change by man. The Spirit of the Pities believes "Sublunar shocks" may wake and have an effect; it would be better for the world if ". . .this strange man's career" (that is, Napoleon's) were stopped and his ambitions thwarted. The Recording Angel, reciting from a book, depicts the uneasy rulers of Europe eyeing Napoleon, "flushed from his crowning," about to "shake the enisled neighbour nation," or invade the island of Great Britain.

In a prose vision the "nether sky" opens, disclosing an aerial view of Europe as a "prone and emaciated figure," the Alps a backbone. The focus narrows and comes closer, revealing "perturbed countries" and people "writhing, crawling, heaving, and vibrating in their various cities and nationalities." The Spirit of the Years declares that "man's deeds" are "self-done," and the General Chorus of Intelligences remarks, "We may but muse on, never learn." Dean makes the important point that the Intelligences have the power of sight only; they cannot cause changes in events, as the "personages" in "antique Mythology" were able to do (6).

Each part begins with a comprehensive list of characters divided into two sections: (1) Phantom Intelligences and (II) Persons, both Men and Women. In each part there are more than 80 characters, including historical and military personages (Bonaparte, the Archduke Ferdinand, King George III, William Pitt, Admiral Villeneuve, Admiral Nelson, the Empress Josephine, and many others), servants, couriers, heralds, citizens, priests, choristers, townswomen, ship-women, servants, soldiers, spies, surgeons, secretaries, musicians, camp followers, ladies-in-waiting, villagers. Part III also includes "Minor Sovereigns and Princes of Europe."

Part I was published on January 13, 1904. It consists of six acts divided into 35 scenes. The action opens on a ridge in WESSEX in March 1805. There is a "martial mood" in England; people believe that Bonaparte expects to invade England and that he will strike along the south coast. The Spirit of the Pities calls Napoleon's coronation a "vulgar stroke of vauntery." Napoleon's navy fails to decoy the English fleet by coaxing them westward. Lord Nelson, at Gibraltar, sees through Napoleon's strategy and believes he means to strike at Wessex. He has a premonition of his own death.

Napoleon gives up his plan of invading England from the south, because he cannot protect his troops crossing the English Channel. Instead, his forces leave Boulogne and start toward the Rhine and Danube; he hopes to defeat the Austrian and Russian allies. King George, who is at Weymouth, is very distant from the affairs of the country. William Pitt, the English prime minister, fails to persuade Prussia to join the alliance. The Austrians surrender at Ulm to the French general Soult, and Napoleon watches with a "vulpine smile." The French navy is defeated by Nelson at Trafalgar; William Pitt dies.

Part II was published on February 9, 1906. It has six acts divided into 43 scenes. A man calling himself Guillet de la Gevrillière approaches Fox, the foreign secretary, offering to assassinate Napoleon. Fox deports him. Prussia enters the war. At Jena, Napoleon instructs his troops to vanquish the Prussians, since the previous year his men had captured Ulm and can surely vanquish the Prussians. The Prussians, defeated, retreat from Jena. Queen Louisa of Prussia departs to join the king at Cüstrin. Her ladies-in-waiting admire her heroism, which "So schools her sense of her calamities/As out of grief to carve new queenliness,/And turn a mobile mien to statuesque,/Save for a sliding tear." They are horrified when Napoleon sends all the treasured objects in the Sans-Souci Palace in Potsdam, near Berlin, to Paris as gifts to the Hôtel des Invalides. (Built in the 17th century and now called the Hôtel national des Invalides, this is one of the most prestigious and handsome buildings in Paris, housing four museums in addition to the tomb of Napoleon.) In Tilsit, Queen Louisa meets Napoleon, who is much taken with her beauty and gives her a rose. She begs, "Let Magdeburg [a leading inland port] come with it, sire! O yes!" Napoleon responds, "Some force within me . . . Harries me onward, whether I will or no." He says his "star" is "unswervable." He confesses to Talleyrand that Louisa had been within "an ace of getting over me."

At Tilsit, Napoleon makes a treaty with Czar Alexander of Russia and then plans to conquer Spain. He arrives in Madrid with "thirty thousand men, half cavalry." Rumours chant, "*The Spanish people, handled in such sort,/As chattels of a Court,/Dream dreams of England.*" The Spanish king Carlos, his son Fernando, the Spanish queen María Luisa, and her lover, Manuel Godoy,

all seek protection from Napoleon. Viscount Materosa goes to the English court and appeals for help from the Prince of Wales. Napoleon tells the empress Josephine, who is 43, that he has held out against pressure to annul their "sterile marriage" and is not going to wait any longer; he wants to have a son. The "drugs and quackeries" she has been given cause her harm. She tells him that Caesar had no son, nor had Frederick the Great.

English forces come to the aid of Spain, defeating the French at Coruña; they have been "stiffened" by the "satisfaction of standing to the enemy at last." The Austrians are defeated at Wagram. An allied army of English and Spanish forces engages the French army at Talavera de la Reyna. At Brighton, England, the Prince of Wales is host at his birthday banquet in the Royal Pavilion. He announces that General Arthur Wellesley and Lord Castlereagh have been victorious at Talavera. An English expedition to the island of Walcheren is unsuccessful and abandoned. Napoleon tells Josephine he is leaving her. She wishes at least to be his "in name." He states that "The Empire orbs above our happiness,/And 'tis the Empire dictates this divorce." He says she must act as though she divorces him of her "own free will," and, not only that, but she must help him win his new bride, who will be Maria Louisa of Austria. Josephine faints and Napoleon and his chamberlain-in-waiting carry her to her room. Two servants clear away the coffee service and arrange the chairs where Napoleon and Josephine have been sitting. One says he knew "she was to get the sack" when Napoleon returned. They predict he will choose someone young, strong, and "fruitful as the vine." Josephine's adult daughter, Hortense, tells Napoleon she and her other children will be glad to follow and withdraw themselves with her. Napoleon assures her Josephine will still have palaces, wealth, and rank.

In Vienna, the emperor Francis, father of Maria Louisa, and Metternich, the Austrian prime minister, discuss Maria Louisa. Francis leaves, and, when she comes in from the garden, Metternich introduces the idea of her marrying Napoleon. She thinks of him as a wicked old man and is horrified, but finally says she will do what is best for the realm. A small enamel portrait of Marie Antoinette slips on its face. Francis sends a message that he is making a "personal gift of a beloved child" to Napoleon. There are rumors of a division between France and Russia.

Part III was published on February 11, 1908. It has seven acts divided into 53 scenes, with what Hardy designates an After Scene. This part begins with the French crossing the Niemen River, near Kowno. The Treaty of Tilsit is unraveling; Russia is wary of the "hostile hatchings" of Napoleon's brain and mistrustful of him. The English, led by the marquis of Wellington, defeat the French, under the command of Marmont, duke of Ragusa, at Salamanca in Spain. The Russians desert Moscow before the French arrive. Count Rostopchin orders the Kremlin to be set on fire. Napoleon blames the defection of the Russians on England, to the astonishment of his marshals. He marches his troops toward Lithuania. They are weak and ill, without proper clothing and without food. Napoleon deserts his army and returns to Paris, supposedly to raise a replacement army. The deserted soldiers sing the "Mad Soldier's Song" and vow never to return to Napoleon. The Russian field marshal, Kutúzof, en route to Wilna, finds their bodies.

At Paris, Marie Louise is startled when Napoleon appears in shabby, muddy attire. He says he has come incognito. They have had a child, a son; Napoleon goes in to see him. He tells her that the Grand Army is "Gone all to nothing, dear." He plans to gild the dome of the Invalides to give the French, whom he regards as "children," something to discuss in cafés.

Napoleon mounts another campaign in Spain. The English army, along with their Spanish and Portuguese allies, camp on the plain near Vitoria. On the eve of battle, troop officers discuss their plans. The regiment known as the King's Hussars reminisce about Wessex, especially Budmouth-Regis when the king was in residence. Sergeant Young sings a song their bandmaster wrote, "HUSSAR'S SONG: 'BUDMOUTH DEARS,'" which he used to conduct in front of Gloucester Lodge at the king's mess every afternoon. The verses recall the girls who once "distracted and delayed" the troops as they paced up and down Budmouth beach.

Napoleon is defeated at Vitoria. The officers bring the wives of some of the young French officers to Pamplona. Austria, Prussia, and Russia join to defeat the French at Leipzig. The marquis of Wellington approaches the southern border of France, and the allies enter Paris.

A fête is held at Vauxhall Gardens, London, to celebrate the victory at Vitoria, which has led to Wellington's promotion to field marshal. Austria joins Russia and Prussia against France; there are rumors that England has paid a subsidy to Francis of Austria for his face-about. Several young attachés wonder what Napoleon thinks of his father-in-law now. At Leipzig, Napoleon has a suite in a private mansion; his secretaries are unpacking and laying out his private papers and maps. Napoleon is still planning to fight, although he is surrounded by forces numbering 350,000 men; he has only 190,000. The Spirit Ironic calls Napoleon a "Christ of war" at a "sad Last-Supper talk" with his "disciples." Napoleon's army suffers a "ruinous defeat" at Leipzig; the army of the allies is victorious. He has no headquarters and the French army has retreated. A Dumb Show reveals the Russians invading France. The "Dumb Show" recurs at intervals throughout *The Dynasts,* summarizing large-scale dis-

tant action; it is an oblique bulletin or mute pantomime for the reader.

At the Tuileries, in Paris, after mass, the principal officers of the National Guard are assembled in the Salle des Maréchaux. The emperor Napoleon and the empress Maria Louisa enter from a chapel, and, from another door, the king of Rome, a child between two and three, is brought in by his governess. He wears a miniature military uniform. Napoleon endorses the empress as regent, ruling for the child, aided by his brother, Joseph. Maria Louisa and the child go to Rambouillet. Napoleon still doesn't want to abdicate but plans to gather men and begins tracing new campaigns. Then he drinks poison, but is discovered by his servants. They call Ivan, a physician, who revives him. Caulaincourt, Duke of Vicenza, one of his commanders, and members of his staff ask why he should bring such a cloud on them now. Napoleon decides to go into exile with his wife and son. Napoleon and his escort are threatened as they go through France. The former empress Josephine dies, mourned by the French.

At the London opera house, a performance begins to honor the allied sovereigns who are visiting England to celebrate the peace. The prince regent and the emperor of Russia discuss the news that the ex-empress, Marie Louise, has not joined Napoleon in exile but has gone to the Schönbrunn Palace in Austria.

Napoleon escapes from Elba, intent on conquering Europe, and causes the allied conference in Vienna to disintegrate. Marie Louise hears rumors of his disappearance and resolves to tell Metternich that she had nothing to do with it. The small army shipped from Elba accompanies Napoleon to La Mure, near Grenoble. At the Schönbrunn Palace the emperor Francis and Marie Louise learn that the allies have vowed vengeance on Napoleon for trying to reorganize his armies. In the House of Commons there is lengthy discussion of the implications of his escape for England. They decide to ask the Prince Regent to "induce/Strenuous endeavours in the cause of peace."

There is a comic scene in Wessex, near CASTER-BRIDGE, when the soldiers burn "Boney" in effigy. The allies post a proclamation in Belgium condemning Bonaparte and stating that "as an enemy and disturber of the tranquillity of the world he has rendered himself liable to public vengeance."

A famous ball is given in a ballroom in Brussels by the Duke and Duchess of Richmond, attended by the royalty of various countries. (Hardy states in a note that the precise location has not been identified.) General Müffling arrives and consults with Wellington, Richmond, and the duke of Brunswick. Napoleon is threatening an attack. The various generals assemble their troops. Wellington consults a map and decides he must fight Napoleon at Waterloo. Pinion praises Hardy's impeccable research in reconstructing the Battle of

Waterloo. He visited the battlefield in 1876 and 1895. (Pinion, *A Hardy Companion*, 111).

The Duke of Brunswick is killed at Les Quatre-Bras. The wounded are to be brought to the Hôtel de Ville in Brussels. A courier arrives to say that Napoleon has defeated the Prussians at Ligny.

In Scene VIII, the English forces retreat to a new position at Mont Saint-Jean. They make camp with fires and cookstoves. The French stop at La Belle Alliance, but they lie down without supper and without fire. The Chorus of the Years then offers a lyrical description of the ominous effect of the forthcoming battle on the fauna of the field of Waterloo. Hardy wrote Edward CLODD that this was the "most original" verse in the entire drama. It consists of six three-line stanzas deploring the helpless fright of various species: rabbits, moles, larks, and hedgehogs. Hardy commented that, so far as he knew, "in the many treatments of Waterloo in literature, those particular personages who were present have never been alluded to before" (*Life*, 453).

The final act opens on the field of Waterloo. Marshal Ney, a cavalry commander, leads the French forces. Napoleon tells Soult, his chief of staff, that Wellington "is no foe to reckon with/His army, too, is poor." The battle rages throughout the day. Sir Thomas Picton is killed, followed by Sir William Ponsonby. Wellington encourages his leaders to stand fast. At the women's camp, soldiers' wives, mistresses, and children tend the wounded and prepare bandages. There is also a surgeon.

Napoleon has a dream; he sees Lannes, who says, "What—blood again?" and tells him Marshal Ney's assaults are a "blunder"; they have come an hour too early. An aide comes to tell Napoleon they are surrounded by various regiments. Also, Prussian reinforcements under the command of von Ryssel and von Hacké are marching toward them; there are 20,000 men.

Ney sends word that he needs more infantry. The battle continues; the French lose strength and make no headway against the allied forces. Finally they surrender. Napoleon hides within a crowd of fugitives as the

The Battle of Trafalgar, *by John Callow, depicts one of the battles Hardy describes in* The Dynasts.   (Fine Art Photographic Library, London/Art Resource, New York)

French retreat. In one of the final scenes he realizes he will be remembered as a "miss-mark"; this is his "burnt-out hour."

In an After Scene, the Phantom Intelligences reflect on the events of the preceding ten years. Semichorus I of the Pities sings to "Thee whose eye all Nature owns,/Who hurlest Dynasts from their thrones,/and liftest those of low estate." Pinion comments that the conclusion is ambiguous, expressing "a cry from the heart of the human race which lives in hope" (Pinion, *A Hardy Companion*, 115).

Much of the verse in the drama is stiff, with archaic diction. In one scene, for example, the prince of Orange asks the duke of Wellington whether it behooves him "To start at once, Duke, for Genappe, I deem? (Part Third, Act VI, Scene II). Many prose passages, on the other hand, have far more memorable imagery. For instance, Hardy describes the field of Waterloo after the final battle:

> The reds disappear from the sky, and the dusk grows deeper. The action of the battle degenerates to a hunt. . . . When the tramplings and shouts of the combatants have dwindled, the lower sounds are noticeable that come from the wounded: hopeless appeals, cries for water, elaborate blasphemies, and impotent execrations of Heaven and hell. In the vast and dusky shambles black slouching shapes begin to move, the plunderers of the dead and dying.
>
> Part Third, Act VII, Scene VIII

The Dynasts seems to many readers, at first, to be chaotic. We perceive the developing conflagration as though gazing through a *camera lucida*, at first making little sense of the sudden shifts in viewpoint, the incessant flux of ordinary crowds, titled rulers, servants, functionaries, couriers, priests, messengers, princesses, attendants, soldiers, and sailors. The settings shuttle among dockyards, palaces, boudoirs, mountains, valleys, gardens, banquet rooms, camps, and battlefields. Gradually, however, we are tutored by the Phantom Intelligences, who, at first, seem to be an obstruction to understanding. The Recording Angel's recitatives lend historical and national perspective. For example, in Part I, Scene III, the Angel summarizes the theme succinctly: "England stands forth to the sword of Napoleon/Nakedly." The work as a whole has elements of spectacle, tragedy, comedy, and romance. In the first part the Spirit of the Pities speaks of the forthcoming "terrestrial tragedy"; the speaker/commentator is swiftly corrected by the Spirit Ironic, who says, "Nay, comedy —."

Hardy presents the entire conflict from multiple points of view (both geographic and chronological). He sees the conflict as taking place within a microcosm, arguing implicity that battles among earthly nations, while inevitable, are to some extent insignificant. This is not to suggest that he wishes Napoleon had conquered England. He does, however, regret the misery and torment caused by the conflict. He is tortured by the pathos of the unknowing victims, as when, at Waterloo, the hedgehog's household is unsealed and the mole's tunnels crushed by wheels. Such suffering is not mitigated, for him, by the victory at Waterloo. He deplored war, including the BOER WAR and WORLD WAR I.

At the same time, he did see a certain heroic glory in the entire era. As a young boy he had discovered, in a closet at HIGHER BOCKHAMPTON, an illustrated copy of *A History of the Wars*, which dealt with the Napoleonic Wars and led ultimately to his writing *The Dynasts* and *The Trumpet-Major* (*Life*, 13). *The Dynasts* was the culminating expression of his poetic powers and his historic vision. Hardy, however, would probably not have felt his achievements were "rayed with victory," as the Prince of Wales said of England's arms (Part II, Act IV, Scene VII). It it is more likely that he would have taken his cue from the Duke of Wellington, who said to his troops, even as the French troops fled *en masse*, "No cheering yet, my lads; but bear ahead." It remained for the Semichorus I of the Pities to praise those who "hurlest Dynasts from their thrones, And liftest those of low estate" (III, After Scene).

For further reading: Dean, *Hardy's Poetic Vision in "The Dynasts": The Diorama of a Dream*; Maynard, *Thomas Hardy's Tragic Poetry: The Lyrics and "The Dynasts"*; Orel, *The Dynasts*; Orel, "*The Dynasts* on the English Stage, 1908–1919"; Orel, *Thomas Hardy's Epic-Drama: A Study of "The Dynasts;"* Wain, ed., *The Dynasts*; Roberts, *Hardy's Poetic Drama and the Theatre: "The Dynasts" and "The Famous Tragedy of the Queen of Cornwall"*; Wickens, "Hardy's Inconsistent Spirits and the Philosophic Form of *The Dynasts*"; Wickens, *Thomas Hardy, Monism, and the Carnival Tradition: The One and the Many in* The Dynasts; Wilson, "'Flower of Man's Intelligence': World and Overworld in *The Dynasts*"; Wright, *The Shaping of "The Dynasts:" A Study in Thomas Hardy*.

E

Edlin, Mrs. A widow in the village of Marygreen in JUDE THE OBSCURE. She nurses Jude FAWLEY's great-aunt Drusilla FAWLEY and, at her funeral, invites Sue BRIDEHEAD to stay with her. After Miss Fawley's death she becomes close to Jude and Sue. She is invited to ALDBRICKHAM to witness their second attempt at getting married. Both attempts fail because Sue has serious doubts, at the last minute, that legal relationships can bring fulfillment. As wedding presents she brings apples, jam, brass snuffers, a warming pan, and a bag of goose feathers toward a bed.

While Sue sells her "Christminster" cakes and gingerbreads at the Kennetbridge fair Mrs. Edlin babysits Sue and Jude's two children and takes care of Jude, who is not well. Before Sue remarries Richard PHILLOTSON she stays with Mrs. Edlin, who comes to tell Jude they are now man and wife. When Jude dies, Mrs. Edlin stands by his coffin with his former wife, Arabella DONN (who had married, in order, Jude Fawley, Mr. Cartlett, and Jude Fawley again).

education of Hardy Because of his frail health, Hardy did not attend school until he was eight; he then went for a year to Bockhampton School, founded by Julia Augusta MARTIN, the lady of the nearby manor house. Hardy became attached to her, and remained so for many years (see the poem "HE REVISITS HIS FIRST SCHOOL" for a description of his feelings on returning to this school). He was then sent to the British School in DORCHESTER, founded by Isaac Glandfield LAST. Like Jude FAWLEY, Hardy walked there along the narrow rural lanes, attaining an intimacy with the countryside that had a lasting impact on his fiction and poetry. In 1853 Last founded an academy for older students, which Hardy attended from 1853 to 1856, when his formal schooling ended. At the academy he began Latin, French, and advanced mathematics and entered a period of what Millgate terms "rapid intellectual development." At Christmas 1884 Last presented him with a prize for diligence and good behavior, a book called *Scenes & Adventures at Home and Abroad*. Millgate observes that Last apparently did not consider Hardy to be overly "bookish" but to have ordinary interests and activities. He was given a prize for Latin in 1855, Theodore Beza's *Novum Testamentum* (Millgate, *Thomas Hardy: A Biography,* 51–52). Unfortunately he did not attend school after the summer of 1856, when he turned 16. At that time he began working in the office of the Dorchester architect John HICKS, but, with remarkable discipline, rose at four in the morning and immersed himself in the classics.

In 1865 Hardy considered applying to CAMBRIDGE UNIVERSITY with the aim of combining studies in poetry and theology, but gave it up as incompatible with the religious views he was developing at the time.

For further reading: Collins, "Hardy and Education."

Edward VII (Albert Edward, Prince of Wales) (1841–1910) The eldest son of Queen Victoria, the Prince of Wales was married to Princess Alexandra of Denmark on March 10, 1863. At that time Hardy was living in Kilburn, a neighborhood in north LONDON, and working for Sir Arthur William BLOMFIELD. On February 19 Hardy wrote his sister Mary HARDY, in one of his earliest preserved letters, of the preparations for the wedding. On October 27, 1865, Hardy attended the funeral of Lord Palmerston, the prime minister, in WESTMINSTER ABBEY, writing Mary about it and mentioning that the Prince of Wales and the duke of Cambridge had been present (*Letters* I, 3, 6).

In 1881 Hardy wrote Francis Knollys, private secretary to the Prince of Wales, to ask whether His Royal Highness would do him the honor of accepting a copy of The TRUMPET-MAJOR. Hardy believed the subject might be of interest, as there were many incidents connected with the life of King George III at Weymouth in the novel. He phrased his letter very delicately, saying that he believed such incidents might be a reason "for laying before His Royal Highness a book which otherwise, as a mere narrative, might not have much recommendation" (*Letters* I, 98).

Hardy's home in DORCHESTER, MAX GATE, was built on a plot of land he was able to purchase from the Duchy of Cornwall, of which the Prince of Wales was the proprietor. Hardy's application to purchase the land was made to George Herriot, an official in the London office of the duchy, and not directly to the Prince of Wales. Mr. Herriot brought the matter to the attention of the prince, who agreed to entertain the application and ultimately to permit Hardy to purchase the building site (*Letters* II, 67).

King Edward VII ruled from 1901 to 1910. On his death he was succeeded by his second son, George Frederick Ernest Albert (King George V). His first son, Albert Victor, had died in 1892.

Edward VIII (Edward, Prince of Wales) (1894–1972)
Edward VIII (Edward Albert Christian George Andrew
Patrick David), eldest son of King George V, became
king when his father died, in 1936, but abdicated later
that year in order to marry Mrs. Wallis Simpson, a
divorced American woman.

As Prince of Wales he carried out many public
duties. On July 20, 1923, he went to DORCHESTER to
open the new Drill Hall for the Dorset Territorials;
Hardy was invited to meet him there, and to drive back
to MAX GATE, where he was entertaining the prince and
his accompanying party at lunch. Hardy recalled the
day as very hot, and, in the *Life*, wrote that it could have
proved "fatiguing and irksome" to a man of his years
and retiring nature, but "owing to the thoughtfulness
of the Prince and his simple and friendly manner,"
everything had gone well. Others at the luncheon
included Lord Shaftesbury, Admiral Sir Lionel Halsey,
Sir Godfrey Thomas, Mr. Walter Peacock, and the
Duchy stewards, Messrs. Proudfoot and Wilson. After
lunch the prince and Hardy strolled in the garden
before he left to visit "certain Duchy farms in Dorchester" (*Life*, 422).

Egdon Heath Hardy's fictional name for the wild
upland area near his birthplace, HIGHER BOCKHAMP-
TON, in DORSET. The heath is a virtual character in
many of his novels, especially *The RETURN OF THE NATIVE*.
Egdon stretches from Dorchester to the Avon valley. In
1750 it covered 40,000 hectares (400,000 acres), but by
the 1890s it had been reduced to 23,000 (230,000 acres;
information courtesy Rosemarie Morgan, personal
communication).

*Egdon Heath was Hardy's fictional name for the wild upland
area near his birthplace in Dorchester. The heath appears in
many of Hardy's novels, especially* The Return of the Native.
(Hermann Lea)

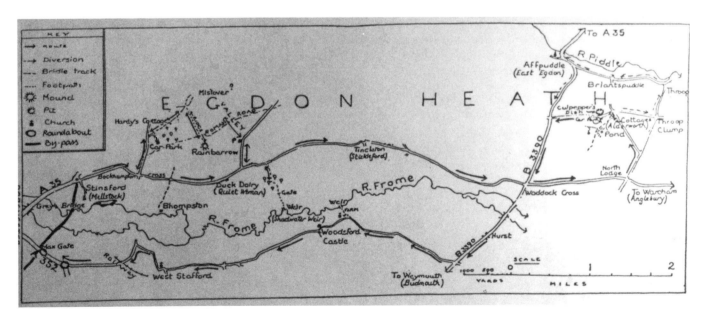

This map of Egdon Heath shows the actual and fictional names of the region depicted in many of Hardy's novels.   (Thomas Hardy
Society, Dorchester, Dorset)

Hardy began *The Return of the Native* in February 1877, when he wrote the publisher John BLACKWOOD about submitting "a story dealing with remote country life" (*Letters* I, 47). It was serialized in BELGRAVIA magazine, published by Chatto & Windus, and published in book form by SMITH, ELDER in 1878. On October 1, 1878, he sent Smith, Elder a sketch of the heathlands near his birthplace. He noted that it was copied from one he had used in writing the story, and hoped it could be used as a frontispiece. The sketch did become the frontispiece of the first edition and the one-volume edition of 1880 (*Letters* I, 61).

Egdon Heath is not only a wild place but also an inhospitable one, as described in Hardy's earliest surviving poem, "DOMICILUM": "Heath and furze/Are everything that seems to grove and thrive/Upon the uneven ground."

Eliot, George (Pseud. of Mary Ann Evans) (1819–1880)

Eminent Victorian novelist whose work is often compared with that of Hardy. Her fiction is didactic, a vehicle for the discussion of moral and social problems prevalent at the time. On New Year's Eve 1873, a chapter from FAR FROM THE MADDING CROWD was published anonymously in the CORNHILL MAGAZINE; one reviewer thought it was the work of Eliot. Hardy recalls in the *Life* how pleased Miss Gifford (Emma Lavinia Gifford HARDY, whom Hardy married in 1874) was to see it; he had kept it from her "to give her a pleasant surprise." Hardy was mystified when a writer from the SPECTATOR thought it might be from "the pen of George Eliot," and stated that if it were not, "then there is a new light among novelists" (Millgate, *Thomas Hardy: A Biography*, 160). Hardy considered Eliot one of the greatest living thinkers and writers, but as far as he could see she "had never touched the life of the fields." Her "country-people" had seemed to him "more like small townsfolk than rustics; and as evidencing a woman's wit cast in country dialogue rather than real country humour, which he regarded as rather of the Shakespeare and Fielding sort" (*Life*, 98). In 1901 Hardy was invited by the publisher William BLACKWOOD to write a volume on George Eliot for the Modern English Writers series his firm was publishing, but he declined and suggested Stephen Gwynn, Arthur SYMONS, and Arthur Waugh as possible writers.

Ellis, Henry Havelock (1859–1939)

English psychologist, essayist, and art critic, best known for his studies in sexual psychology, considered scandalous in his day. Before the end of the Victorian era he had produced a vast study of human sexuality in six volumes, *Studies in the Psychology of Sex*. His most influential work was *Man and Woman* (1894). *The Dance of Life* (1923), his most popular book, argues that the dance symbolizes the vibrant, robust rhythms of the universe.

In April 1883 Ellis published an article highly favorable to Hardy, "Thomas Hardy's Novels," in the *Westminster Review*. Hardy wrote a long letter thanking him for his generosity and expressing interest in reading more of his critical writings (*Letters* I, 117–18). In July 1890 Hardy invited Ellis to lunch at the SAVILE CLUB to discuss an article Ellis was proposing to write about him, stating that he had read his book *The New Spirit*. The article, "The Ancestry of Genius," appeared in the ATLANTIC MONTHLY in March 1893 (*Letters* VII, 113–14). Ellis also analyzed JUDE THE OBSCURE ("Concerning *Jude the Obscure*," *Savoy* 3 (1896), 35–49).

"Embarcation"

Poem written in 1899 at the outset of the BOER WAR and collected in *POEMS OF THE PAST AND THE PRESENT* (1902). The poem is one of three dated October 1899 and occasioned by the departure of troops for the war from the docks at Southampton. Hardy places the exodus in the context of three former conquests of Britain. In A.D. 43–44, during the reign of the emperor Claudius, the Roman legions, commanded by Vespasian, landed on Britain's south coast and made their way to the area now known as Somerset. They thus paved the way for the Roman colonization of Dorset (J. O. Bailey, *The Poetry of Thomas Hardy*, 115). The Romans left Britain in the fifth century, when Cerdic became king of the West Saxons. In 1415 the English, commanded by Henry V, departed from Southampton and invaded France; they "leapt afloat to win/Convincing triumphs over neighbour lands."

Hardy is bitterly cynical about war as a solution to human problems. The soldiers "argue in the selfsame bloody mode/Which this late age of thought, and pact, and code,/Still fails to mend." He observes ironically that the bands of troops tramp toward the "tragical To-be,/None dubious of the cause, none murmuring." Their families are also victims; they wave and smile, "As if they knew not that they weep the while."

The critic Edmund GOSSE, Hardy's friend, wrote on October 25, 1899, that Hardy was "the only poet ... who has said anything worth singing. They [other Poets] all make the blunder of trying to translate our emotion into rhetoric, whereas in this period of suspense rhetoric ... is monstrously out of place" (Bailey, *The Poetry of Thomas Hardy*, 116).

In 1911 Hardy gave permission to Vere Henry Gratz Collins, the Oxford University Press editor in charge of educational books, to include "Embarcation," along with any extracts from *The DYNASTS* he desired, in his anthology of historical poems for use in schools (*Letters* IV, 145).

Endorfield, Elizabeth

Character in UNDER THE GREENWOOD TREE. She is a "shrewd and penetrating" woman who never goes to church and is popularly supposed to be a witch. Highly intuitive and sympathetic, Mrs.

Endorfield imparts a verbal charm (a long list of directions) to Fancy DAY, which Fancy uses to gain permission from her father, Geoffrey DAY, to marry.

"England to Germany in 1914" First published in a pamphlet in February 1917 for Hardy's second wife, Florence (HARDY), this poem was collected in *MOMENTS OF VISION* (1917). It is dated "Autumn 1914," when the horror of WORLD WAR I was beginning to register in England.

It takes the form of a cri de coeur, summarizing all that England has loved about Germany, and asking how Germany could cry, "'O England, may God punish thee!'" This was the slogan by which the war leaders in Germany justified their attack upon England. Hardy points out that the English and Germans are racially brothers. The English have "eaten your bread, you have eaten ours." Traveling to Germany, they have loved "your burgs, your pines' green moan,/Fair Rhine-stream, and its storied towers." The poet argues that England has done nothing to deserve German attacks and holds no malice for Germany. Although a few Englishmen might have scorned Germany, they were "not in their country's key." The German invocation to God, pleading that He punish England, serves only to damage Germany's name and history.

"Enter a Dragoon" Short story written in 1899 and published in *A CHANGED MAN AND OTHER TALES* (1913). The setting is a small hamlet in MELLSTOCK parish ("Mellstock" being Hardy's fictional name for three hamlets near DORCHESTER.) The story concerns Selina Paddock, daughter of a market-gardener, who lives with her small son, Johnny, and her parents in a dilapidated house. Selina had been on the verge of marrying Sergeant Major Clark, a dragoon, when he went to war on the eve of their wedding. She assumes he has been killed in the Battle of the Alma because she has seen "James Clark" on a list nailed to the CASTERBRIDGE town hall door. Thinking "James" was a misprint for "John," she has been too proud to search for him.

She is now engaged to Mr. Miller, who loves her and dotes on Johnny. Suddenly Clark arrives and assumes the provisions he sees have been brought in for his return. Neighbors come in for festive dancing. Clark has no rational explanation for his failure to contact Selina, but she forgives him, puts on what would have been her bridal gown, and dances with him. When he learns Selina has almost married Mr. Miller he becomes pale and weak; he lies down to rest, but dies of heart failure before the doctor arrives. He is buried nearby, with Selina as the only mourner. She resists marrying Mr. Miller and, instead, establishes a small fruit and vegetable shop. Miller once again entreats her to marry him; she refuses, and he marries someone else.

Selina continues to maintain Clark's grave, planting ivy and tending it with loving care. One day she and Johnny find another woman, apparently a widow, accompanied by a small boy, pulling up the ivy she has planted. The woman is Clark's legitimate wife, and her son his heir; they have come from her home in the north of England to see his grave. She speaks condescendingly to Selina, explaining that she and Clark had quarreled, and he had left, vowing to emigrate to New Zealand. She had heard of his death at Mellstock but decided coming to the funeral would be too expensive. She apologizes for pulling up the ivy roots, but has the last word when she tells Selina, "that common sort of ivy is considered a weed in my part of the country."

For further reading: Wanchu, "Thomas Hardy's 'Enter a Dragoon': A Note."

Evans, Alfred Herbert (1862–1946) A DORCHESTER chemist, the father of the Shakespearean actor Maurice Evans (1901–1989). His dramatization of *The TRUMPET-MAJOR* was performed by the DORCHESTER DEBATING AND DRAMATIC SOCIETY in the Dorchester town hall on November 18, 1908. This was the first of a number of theatrical productions based on Hardy's works; the group later became known as the HARDY PLAYERS. Hardy wrote the author and critic Harold Child that the production had its inception when the theater manager asked if he might mount the scene of Miller Loveday's party as part of a miscellaneous local entertainment. To Hardy's surprise, the scene "was received with the wildest enthusiasm," which suggested "making a complete play of it" (*Letters* III, 332). Hardy offered his advice about the structure of the play. Evans later dramatized *FAR FROM THE MADDING CROWD*, *UNDER THE GREENWOOD TREE*, *The MAYOR OF CASTERBRIDGE*, and *The WOODLANDERS* (*see* Appendix II).

"Eve of Waterloo" *(Chorus of Phantoms)* Poem from Hardy's verse drama *The DYNASTS*. Hardy envisions the battlefield on the eve of the "harlequinade" of battle. The spirit choruses protest the coming defilement of the earth by the impending catastrophe: "The green seems opprest, and the Plain afraid." The animals are oblivious of the danger: the mole's "tunnelled chambers" will be crushed by the wheels of the armed forces; the "lark's eggs scattered"; the snail crushed; the butterflies doomed; flower buds destroyed.

The young men, also insensible about the horrors of war, sleep soundly. Older soldiers, however, veterans of other wars, are haunted by their foreknowledge of the havoc and destruction of battle. Hardy envisions each soldier's anticipation of death: "each soul shivers as sinks his head/On the loam he's to lease with the other dead."

Everdene, Bathsheba The heroine of *FAR FROM THE MADDING CROWD*, Bathsheba is a beautiful, dark-haired young woman. She is not without vanity; when Gabriel OAK first sees her, she is riding on top of a wagon and peering into a small mirror when she thinks she is unobserved. Despite her education, she is "too wild" to be a governess. She visits her aunt, Mrs. HURST, at Norcombe Hill, where she first meets Oak, who becomes her first suitor. He proposes, but is rejected; Bathsheba is not, at that time, thinking of marriage.

Her uncle, James EVERDENE, who had been impressed with her proven ability to manage his flocks, dies suddenly, leaving her the lease of Upper Weatherbury Farm. His trustees oppose her inheriting the farm because of her youth, sex, and beauty, but yield to Bathsheba. Owning the farm in her own right, she begins farming. She rises to the challenge with feisty courage, having an "impulsive nature under a deliberative aspect." She hires Oak as shepherd after he saves her hay ricks from burning.

She lightheartedly sends a valentine to her older bachelor neighbor, Farmer William BOLDWOOD, a solemn and antisocial man of about 40. He develops a violent obsession with her, but she then meets Sergeant Frank TROY, an untrustworthy soldier. He performs a stylized, sexually charged "sword exercise" in a grassy pit outside the town of CASTERBRIDGE, and she realizes she has fallen in love with him.

She follows him to Bath and they are married; when he returns to her farm, he threatens to ruin it by careless husbandry. He invites the farm hands to a festive meal celebrating their wedding and plies them with brandy, which they are unused to drinking, and they fall asleep. Gabriel Oak, assisted by Bathsheba, save all the harvested crops from a violent thunderstorm.

Bathsheba discovers that Troy is the father of the child of her former servant, Fanny ROBIN, who dies after he refuses to marry her or help her. Troy disappears after Fanny's funeral and is reported to have drowned; Bathsheba is almost relieved. Boldwood then begins courting her in earnest, making her promise to marry him if Troy has not returned in years, at which time he legally will be presumed dead. Farmer Boldwood gives a party at which he plans to announce their engagement. Troy appears at the party and Boldwood shoots him. Bathsheba is upset when she learns Gabriel might emigrate; he finally proposes, having never stopped loving her. Bathsheba and Gabriel develop a "camaraderie occurring through the similarity of pursuits," which becomes the basis of "the only love which is as strong as death."

Everdene, James   The uncle of Bathsheba EVERDENE in *FAR FROM THE MADDING CROWD*; he leaves her the lease of Upper Weatherbury Farm when he dies, because he believes in her abilities. He also appears in *The MAYOR OF CASTERBRIDGE* as one of Michael HENCHARD's creditors.

"Everything Comes"   Published in *MOMENTS OF VISION* (1917), this poem is a meditation on the growth of the trees Hardy planted at MAX GATE and the simultaneous decline in his wife Emma's health. When the house was finished, Emma HARDY had considered it "bleak and cold/Built so new for me!" and felt exposed to "curious eyes" without "screening trees." Hardy had responded that he was planting trees to shield her "both from winds, and eyes that tease/And peer in for you." The "bower" he had planned would surpass all others known.

Emma had responded, "I will bear it, Love,/And will wait." In time a grove of trees grows, which he proudly points out to her, asking if it is "As you wished, Dear?" She replies, "Yes, I see!/But—I'm dying; and for me/'Tis too late."

Max Gate was finished in 1885, and Emma died 27 years later, in 1912. Hardy lived there until his death in 1928.

"Face at the Casement, The"   Published in *SATIRES OF CIRCUMSTANCE* (1914), this poem explores the prick of conscience in a man who has taken a girl for a drive on a May evening past the house of a man who lies gravely ill. The young woman confesses that the dying man had wanted to marry her. While he is driving away, the man happens to turn and see a white face gazing at them from an upper window. On an impulse, he puts his arm around the girl and the "white face" vanishes "As if blasted, from the casement." The girl smiles at him, but does not guess the reason for his "soft embowment/Of her shoulder at that moment."

Years later, the man wonders what "devil" had made him do it. Although the suffering man has lain in the garth (churchyard) of "sad Saint Cleather" for many years, the speaker still experiences guilt, and believes jealousy to be "Cruel as the grave!"

Kenneth Phelps has made deductions relating the poem to Hardy's courtship of Emma Gifford (later HARDY) in Cornwall. St. Clether (not "Cleather") is a village eight miles east of ST. JULIOT CHURCH, where Emma was living with her sister and brother-in-law at the time Hardy met her. He made a return visit there in May 1871. Phelps suggests that the man was Charles Raymond, a master miller, who may have met Emma between 1860 and 1868 when she was living in Bodmin; she might have been out riding her pony. In 1864 he married Mary Jenkins; they had a daughter, Emma, who died in August 1873, at the age of three months. Raymond died of tuberculosis in December 1873. Phelps suggests that Raymond may have named the baby for Emma Gifford, and links the story of this suitor, of a lower social class than Emma, with the story of Felix JETHWAY and Elfride SWANCOURT in *A PAIR OF BLUE EYES* (*Annotations by Thomas Hardy in his Bibles and Prayer-Book* [St. Peter Port, Guernsey: Toucan Press, 1966], quoted in Bailey, *The Poetry of Thomas Hardy*, 272–73). Hardy first met Emma in March 1870; they were married in 1874.

"Faintheart in Railway Train"   This poem was published in the *London Mercury* for January 1920, under the title "A Glimpse from a Train," and collected in *LATE LYRICS AND EARLIER* (1922). The poem presents a lighthearted look at the thoughts of a young man making a long train journey. Throughout the morning he glimpses ordinary sights from the window: a church, the sea, a town, a forest. At two o'clock he notices a "radiant stranger" on a platform, but she does not see him. He almost yields to an impulse to get out and approach her, but does not dare to do so. The wheels move on; he thinks, "O could it but be/That I had alighted there!"

Fairway, Timothy   A turf-cutter on EGDON HEATH in *The RETURN OF THE NATIVE* who is a hair-cutter on Sunday mornings and a storyteller.

Famous Tragedy of the Queen of Cornwall, The   Drama set at Tintagel Castle, on the Cornish coast, Hardy illustrated it with drawings of TINTAGEL. He began the play in 1916 after he visited CORNWALL with his second wife, Florence DUGDALE HARDY. It was performed locally in 1923 and set to music in 1924.

In September 1916 Hardy and Florence went to CORNWALL and visited Tintagel. He wrote Sydney COCKERELL that he was sorry his hopes for a poem on Iseult were to be disappointed, but that he had visited the place 44 years earlier with "an Iseult of my own," referring to his first wife, Emma (*Letters* V, 179). The play was published seven years later.

In July 1923 Hardy wrote Harley GRANVILLE-BARKER that he had "a little thing" lying about for years (that is, a draft of the play), and had finished it to please the "Dorchester Amateurs, who want something new." He stated that it possessed few virtues except that of "unity of line" (or "time," according to Michael Millgate and Richard Purdy) and place," which were unique in his "rendering" compared with many others. Granville-Barker wrote a 10-page letter with notes about the work, including what Hardy termed "wise counsel on the details of staging" (*Letters* VI, 203–204). The work was produced by the HARDY PLAYERS on November 15, 1923, and published by MACMILLAN on November 23, 1923; it was later set to music by the composer Rutland Boughton (*Letters* VI, 211, 225; 244 *see* Appendix II.) When it was first performed, Alfred NOYES wrote an article about it, one positive on the whole but with some reservations about the quality of the verse. Hardy wrote to thank him (*Letters* VI, 224). An unauthorized version was performed at the Academy of Dramatic Art in April 1924, about which Hardy protested vigorously (*Letters* VI, 245).

Hardy's work is based on the Arthurian legend concerning Tristram and Iseult. King Mark of Cornwall sends his nephew Tristram to Ireland to bring back his bride, Iseult the Fair, an Irish princess. The two drink a magic potion on their way back to Cornwall and fall in love. Iseult and King Mark marry and he banishes Tristram, who goes to Brittany and marries another woman, Iseult the Whitehanded.

Hardy calls the play, in the subtitle, "A New Version of an Old Story, Arranged as a Play for Mummers, in One Act, Requiring No Theatre or Scenery." It is dedicated to four people, "In affectionate remembrance of those with whom I formerly spent many hours at the scene of the tradition, who have now all passed away save one." As identified by Hardy, they are E. L. H. (Emma Lavinia [Gifford] Hardy, his first wife), C. H. (Caddell Holder, M.A., Rector of ST. JULIOT CHURCH, Cornwall, and Emma's brother-in-law), H. C. H. (Helen Catherine Holder, née Gifford, Emma's sister), and F. E. H. (Florence Emily Hardy, his second wife).

The story is closely connected with Hardy's early visits to Cornwall and his courtship of Emma Gifford HARDY. In August 1870, during his second stay at St. Juliot, he, Emma, and the Giffords visited Tintagel and King Arthur's castle. He also recalled the scene in the preface to *A PAIR OF BLUE EYES*: "The place is pre-eminently (for one person at least) the region of dream and mystery."

He sets the play in "any large room," which is assumed to be the interior of the great hall of Tintagel Castle. He suggests strewing the floor with rushes and, as scenery, having an opening at the back with "ramparts" and a view of the Atlantic Ocean. The costumes should be in bright linen colors, "trimmed with ribbon, as in the old mumming shows."

SYNOPSIS

Prologue
The room is darkened; Merlin enters with a white wand. He summarizes the tragic tale of King Mark, Tristram, and Iseult and begs the audience, "Judge them not harshly in a love/Whose hold on them was strong."

Scene I
Men Chanters (Shades of Dead Old Cornish Men) and women Chanters (Shades of Dead Cornish Women) tell of the sojourn of Tristram and Iseult in Gard Castle, after which Sir Tristram goes to Brittany to his "waiting wife" (Iseult the Whitehanded). He thinks of bringing Whitehands (as she is also called) back to Cornwall. King Mark arrives.

Scene II
Dame Brangwain announces Queen Iseult is home again; Chanters state they do not know where she's been, but that she should thank God for "covering up her ways."

Scene III
The king and his retinue gather in the hall; King Mark asks for Queen Iseult. The hound Houdain is there.

Scene IV
Queen Iseult, in a crimson robe, with dark hair and a tiara, greets the king. He asks why Houdain is there. She says she does not know, but King Mark is sure her owner, Sir Tristram, has left her with the Queen. King Mark kicks the dog away. The exchange is evidence of the dispute the King and Queen are having over whether she has been seeing Tristram.

Scene V
Queen Iseult says she hasn't seen Sir Tristram. King Mark says if he "Dallies in Brittany with his good wife" he can't be in Cornwall. However, he has learned of the queen's voyage of "some days." Queen Iseult swears she has not set foot in Brittany; King Mark knows she "sailed off somewhere" but he will not ask the mariners where she went. Queen Iseult denies she has seen Sir Tristram. King Mark says she might well have seen him, "for all the joy/You show in my return" and since she "crept cat-like home." Queen Iseult says Tristram probably died, but King Mark retorts that Sir Tristram has "died too many, many times" for the report of his death to hold. Also, Sir Andret (one of his knights) saw her "dallying" with Sir Tristram.

Scene VI
Queen Iseult sits in dejection. Men Chanters ask why heaven ordained that two such "mismated" people should "bedim" their court with "bleeding loves and discontent." Surely God has favored them "in throne and diadem"; it would seem reasonable that they praise him "throughout their deeds and days." Women Chanters bemoan a queen mourning for Tristram and wonder why Tristram wedded "King Howel's lass of Brittany." Queen Iseult, musing and praying aloud, wonders why the Lord should make King Mark so hated yet let him live, while Sir Tristram may be dead.

Scene VII
Queen Iseult tells Dame Brangwain she did not land in Brittany because Sir Tristram was with Iseult the Whitehanded and was sick with fever. Iseult the Whitehanded had sent for Queen Iseult, hoping she could save Sir Tristram. She had instructed her messenger to raise a white canvas (sail) if he were bringing back Queen Iseult and a black one if he were not. But when the ship reached the quay, Iseult the Whitehanded had come down with news that Sir Tristram had died an hour earlier. Dame Brangwain is skeptical, and asks Queen Iseult whether, she had believed her. Queen Iseult answers that she had, and had fainted at the news. Her crew sailed away with her on board, reached Wales, and nursed her back to health.

Dame Brangwain says Queen Iseult might not have been allowed to see Sir Tristram anyway. The Queen sings sadly to herself. Woman Chanters speculate that Sir Tristram might not have died; men Chanters suggest that he was wounded in Ireland but healed. They agree that Sir Tristram must be living.

Scene VIII

A messenger arrives for Queen Iseult and tells her Sir Tristram is still alive. He reports that Iseult the Whitehanded had falsely declared that Queen Iseult's sail was black, meaning that she was not aboard. She made him pray for death and had church bells toll. When Sir Tristram realized Iseult the Whitehanded had sent Queen Iseult back, he was angered to "hot extremity." The Queen cries that Iseult the Whitehanded is a "Cheat unmatchable!" In the distance Sir Tristram is heard "singing and harping."

Scene IX

An old minstrel comes to Tintagel; it is Sir Tristram, disguised as a harper. Sir Andret is suspicious of him, however, and believes he may be Sir Tristram.

Scene X

Alone with Queen Iseult, Dame Brangwain, and the Chanters, Sir Tristram throws off his cloak and reveals his identity. He tells Queen Iseult that he was duped by Iseult the Whitehanded about the color of the sail. Dame Brangwain goes outside to stand guard.

Scene XI

Queen Iseult greets Sir Tristram as "dear Love" and embraces him. She says Sir Launcelot has told her he calls King Mark "King Fox." She asks why Sir Tristram married Iseult the Whitehanded. He tells her again that King Howell gave him his daughter after he saved the King's lands in battle. Tristram says he was "Arrested by her name—so kin to yours"—and thought that perhaps King Mark had stolen the heart of his beloved Iseult. Queen Iseult replies that a woman's heart has "room for one alone;/A man's for two or three!" He plays the harp and soothes her. A watchman announces a ship is coming.

Scene XII

Dame Brangwain tells Queen Iseult there is a white-robed figure aboard the ship, which comes from Brittany, and she says she thinks it is a woman. King Mark, who has been drinking, summons Queen Iseult. She says she will return soon; he sends Sir Andret to spy on her.

Scene XIII

Sir Tristram looks through the arch and wonders whether Iseult the Whitehanded has followed him. Men Chanters warn him he will not find the peace he came to find; women Chanters tell him one who has the right to "trace thy track" is coming to win him back.

Scene XIV

Iseult the Whitehanded enters, wearing a white robe. She speaks in confusion. She tells Sir Andret she is Iseult of Brittany, wife of Sir Tristram, and believes he is within the castle walls. Sir Andret says "It *was* he, then!" and vows to tell the king.

Scene XV

Iseult the Whitehanded greets Sir Tristram and admits she has "dogged" him "close," but she could not let Queen Iseult land. Sir Tristram calls her an "evil woman." Iseult the Whitehanded begs his forgiveness and says she has never been unfaithful. Queen Iseult and Dame Brangwain listen from the gallery above.

Scene XVI

Queen Iseult asks Dame Brangwain whether she is in fact Iseult the Whitehanded. Dame Brangwain says she can't hear Iseult the Whitehanded and Sir Tristram. He says he will never again be her bedmate; that he was coerced into marriage. Iseult the Whitehanded breaks down; he says he could never bear her "disastrous lying" and advises her to mate with someone else. Iseult the Whitehanded says she wants to be with him and see his face. Sir Tristram says she can't "haunt another woman's house." She offers to be Queen Iseult's "bondwench" and stay at Tintagel. Sir Tristram says "more gently" that she cannot stay. Queen Iseult, above, is frantic because he seems to be softening. She and Dame Brangwain descend from the gallery. Iseult the Whitehanded faints. Dame Brangwain goes to help her and carries her out, Sir Tristram assisting her to the door. The Chanters say Iseult the Whitehanded has "out-tasked her strength."

Scene XVII

Queen Iseult angrily asks Sir Tristram whether she is to share him. He says Iseult the Whitehanded is going back to Brittany, but she should "think kindly of her." Queen Iseult says she and Iseult the Whitehanded are like "oil and water" and can only exist if they live apart. She has sacrificed much for Sir Tristram. She sobs; King Mark and the revellers approach.

Scene XVIII

Tristram, Queen Iseult, Dame Brangwain, and the Chanters are onstage. Dame Brangwain says Iseult the Whitehanded is recovering, so Queen Iseult says she should sleep in her bed; she herself will sleep on the floor. Sir Tristram says Queen Iseult speaks in bitterness; King Mark and Sir Andret enter the gallery.

Scene XIX

King Mark and Sir Andret are above; below are Sir Tristram, Queen Iseult, and the Chanters. Sir Tristram tries to clasp Queen Iseult. A damsel enters with a letter.

Scene XX

The damsel says the letter is from King Mark to King Arthur saying he holds Sir Tristram as his enemy and swearing revenge. King Mark descends from the gallery. In an aside, Queen Iseult tells Sir Tristram she is worried about him and to save himself. Sir Tristram tells the damsel to reseal the letter and send it.

Scene XXI

Sir Tristram says King Mark was drunk when he wrote the letter; Queen Iseult is doubtful. They sing and play. King Mark stabs Sir Tristram with his dagger; Queen Iseult shrieks. Sir Tristram says he had no chance to fight fairly and dies. Queen Iseult fatally stabs King Mark, leaps over the castle parapet, and drowns.

Scene XXII

Brangwain and the Chanters mourn the three deaths. Iseult the Whitehanded enters.

Scene XXIII

Iseult the Whitehanded clasps the body of Sir Tristram. When she learns the sequence of events she declares Sir Tristram had not belonged to Queen Iseult, although she had loved him, "if wickedly."

Scene XXIV

Iseult the Whitehanded regards Mark's body, but decides that, even if she had not come across the water, events would have been the same. She rocks back and forth above the body of Sir Tristram, saying "What a rare beauteous knight has perished here/By this most cruel craft!" The halls of Tintagel are now "hateful" to her; she wants to return to Brittany. Dame Brangwain offers to attend her. She and Iseult, aided by Bower-women, Knights, and Retainers, lift the bodies and carry them out. The Chanters sing a final dirge.

Epilogue

The magician Merlin speaks the Epilogue, reminding the audience that the warriors and "dear women" he has summoned were once "as you are now who muse thereat."

For further reading: Collier, "Thomas Hardy's *The Famous Tragedy of the Queen of Cornwall*: Its Artistry and Relation to His Life, Thought, and Works"; Deane, "The Sources of *The Famous Tragedy of the Queen of Cornwall*"; Gittings, "Note on a Production of *The Famous Tragedy of the Queen of Cornwall*."

Farfrae, Donald A young Scot whose name means "far from home," he stops in CASTERBRIDGE en route to America in *The MAYOR OF CASTERBRIDGE*. He meets Michael HENCHARD, who is impressed by his acumen in the corn business and employs him as manager for his corn business; Henchard is also, at the time, in need of a friend. Eventually Farfrae is so successful that, for many reasons, Henchard becomes jealous and dis-

misses him. Farfrae defeats Henchard in winning the hand of Lucetta LE SUEUR, then takes over his house, and becomes mayor of Casterbridge. As mayor he receives a visiting "Royal Personage." Henchard's and Farfrae's positions are completely reversed, and Henchard's enmity almost results in Farfrae's death, but his better nature prevails. Farfrae lacks compassion and, for most readers, is less appealing than Henchard. Fair, youthful, and fearless, he has been considered David to Henchard's Saul, melancholy and ill-tempered (Pinion, *A Hardy Companion*, 363). After the death of Lucetta he marries Elizabeth-Jane HENCHARD (2), actually the daughter of Richard NEWSON.

Far from the Madding Crowd One of Hardy's major novels, published in 1874. It appeared anonymously as a serial in the *CORNHILL MAGAZINE* (edited by Leslie STEPHEN, the father of Virginia WOOLF) from January to December, 1874. It was enormously successful, and the income it brought Hardy enabled him to marry his first wife, Emma Lavinia Gifford HARDY, whom he had first met in 1870.

Hardy devotes an entire chapter of the *Life* to the novel. In December 1872, after reading UNDER THE GREENWOOD TREE, Stephen wrote Hardy to say it was "long since he had received more pleasure from a new writer," and he believed his readers would welcome another serial story by Hardy. Hardy answered that he had a novel on hand (*A PAIR OF BLUE EYES*) that was spoken for, but if Mr. Stephen could wait, he had in mind another one in which the chief characters would probably be a young woman farmer, a shepherd, and a sergeant of cavalry. Stephen was receptive to the idea and invited Hardy to call and discuss it when he next came to London.

Hardy began writing, and sent part of the manuscript to Stephen in September 1873. It was accepted at once, although, Stephen explained, it was his usual rule not to accept an unfinished novel. Hardy continued to write. At times he found himself without paper and would write, as he recalls in his autobiography, on "dead leaves, white chips left by wood-cutters, or pieces of stone or slate that came to hand" (*Life*, 96).

Stephen asked if he might start serializing the novel in January 1874, another novel he had commissioned having been lost in the mail, according to the author. Hardy agreed and sent Stephen some sketches for illustrations that he had kept in his notebook, including outlines for smockfrocks, sheep crooks, a sheep-washing pool, an old-fashioned malt house, and "some other out-of-the-way things that might have to be shown." Stephen did not reply. To Hardy's surprise, when he opened the latest issue of the *Cornhill* in late December, as he returned from a visit to Emma in CORNWALL, he discovered his story at the beginning of the magazine, without a byline. It had been illustrated by a young woman artist, Helen PATERSON. He writes in his autobiography that it can be imagined "how delighted Miss Gifford was to receive the first number of the story," since he had not told her anything of its nature, and "to find that her desire of a literary course for Hardy was in fair way of being justified." Hardy went to London during the winter and met Helen Paterson as well as Leslie Stephen and his wife and several noted publishers. He continued the novel at Bockhampton, finding it "a great advantage to be actually among the people described at the time of describing them" (*Life*, 99). He submitted the last installment of the manuscript to Stephen in early August 1874. In September Hardy and Emma Lavinia Gifford were married at St. Peter's, Paddington, by her uncle, Dr. Edwin Hamilton GIFFORD, canon of Worcester and later archdeacon of London.

The novel was published in two volumes in November 1874 with illustrations by Helen Paterson, who had married the Irish poet William Allingham during the time the novel was being serialized.

Far from the Madding Crowd is set in the fictional towns of WEATHERBURY (Puddletown, about five miles northeast of DORCHESTER), CASTERBRIDGE (Dorchester), and Greenhill (Woodbury Hill, east of Bere Regis). There was a celebrated annual entertainment and sheep fair in Greenhill in September. In a preface to the 1912 edition, Hardy observes that it was in this novel that he first adopted the word "WESSEX," formerly used in the context of early British history, and gave it a "fictitious significance as the existing name of the district once included in that extinct kingdom." In this preface, written nearly 40 years after the novel was published, Hardy looks back on the "partly real, partly dream-country" he had created. He notes some of the changes since that time in the Dorset of the novel. These include the disappearance of the shearing-supper and the "practice of divination by Bible and key." The root cause of the loss of continuity in old traditions, according to Hardy, was the "supplanting of the class of stationary cottagers" by migratory workers. As Rosemarie Morgan observes, however, Hardy did not envision such changes when he wrote the novel. She suggests that the only "significant social change" in the novel is the advancement of a woman to the position of boss for Weatherbury Farm; the rustics predict that this will lead to the destruction of all (Morgan, private communication with the author).

SYNOPSIS

Chapter 1: "Description of Farmer Oak—An Incident"

Farmer Gabriel OAK, a 28-year-old bachelor, sees, from his fields, a bright yellow wagon drawn by two horses, carrying household goods, with a young, attractive woman on top, wearing a red jacket. The waggoner tells the woman the tailboard of the wagon is gone and goes back to retrieve it. There is a dispute at the tollgate, and Gabriel pays the twopence for them to pass.

Chapter 2: "Night—The Flock—An Interior—Another Interior"

A few days later Gabriel, who farms about a hundred acres, is tending some newborn lambs when he sees the same young woman and an older one in a shed on the hillside with two cows, one of which has just given birth to a calf. The other cow is sick.

Chapter 3: "A Girl on Horseback—Conversation"

The next morning Gabriel returns the young woman's lost hat, which had blown off, and watches her tend the sick cow over the next few days. Gabriel almost suffocates in his hut, owing to poor ventilation, but is saved by the young woman.

Chapter 4: "Gabriel's Resolve—The Visit—The Mistake"

Gabriel finds that the woman's name is Bathsheba EVERDENE; she has come to visit her aunt, Mrs. HURST. Gabriel takes a lamb whose mother has died to Bathsheba, offering to let her raise it. He tells Mrs. Hurst he would like to marry Bathsheba, but she discourages him. As he leaves, Bathsheba runs up and Gabriel repeats his offer, which she declines. She tells Gabriel he should marry a woman with some money who could stock his farm for him.

Chapter 5: "Departure of Bathsheba—A Pastoral Tragedy"

Bathsheba returns home to Weatherbury and Gabriel suffers a tragedy: his younger dog, the son of his faithful and intelligent dog George, drives his flock of sheep over a cliff to their death. Gabriel's farm had been stocked by a dealer; by the time he pays his debts and sells the farm, he is destitute.

Chapter 6: "The Fair—The Journey—The Fire"

Gabriel attends an agricultural fair in Casterbridge to look for work; he decides to become a shepherd and spends his remaining funds on shepherd's garments and a crook. Exhausted, he climbs in the back of a wagon to sleep. He awakes to find the wagon in motion; he overhears the driver discussing Bathsheba, who seems to be the mistress of a nearby estate. Slipping down from the wagon, Gabriel sees a rick of straw on fire that is endangering the stacks of corn nearby. The local men also have seen it but are jumping about helplessly. He calls for a tarpaulin and water and saves the rick, which belongs to Bathsheba. Her uncle has died suddenly and she has come to take over his property, Weatherbury Upper Farm.

Chapter 7: "Recognition—A Timid Girl"

Gabriel Oak offers his services to Bathsheba as a shepherd. He is praised by those who saw him in action saving the ricks of corn. Bathsheba asks him to speak to the bailiff, who hires him, but refers him to Warren's

This illustration by Helen Paterson Allingham for Far from the Madding Crowd, *chapter 3 ("...hands were loosening his neckerchief"), appeared in the* Cornhill Magazine, *January 1874.* (Perkins Library, Duke University)

Malthouse to find lodging. Gabriel is astonished at Bathsheba's transformation into the mistress of the farm, but, as the narrator states, "some women only require an emergency to make them fit for one." On the way to the malthouse Gabriel asks directions of a young, timid girl, who asks him not to tell anyone he has seen her. He gives her a shilling, touching her wrist in the gloom. He notices that her pulse is beating "with a throb of tragic intensity." He feels he is "in the penumbra of a very deep sadness."

Chapter 8: "The Malthouse—The Chat—News"
At Warren's Malthouse, of which the proprietor is Warren SMALLBURY, Gabriel meets the locals. Some of them have known his father and grandfather at Norcombe as well as his grandmother. Gabriel tells them he is thinking of staying in Weatherbury. Warren's son Jacob Smallbury, and his son Billy, "a child of forty," along with Jan COGGAN, Mark Clark, Joseph Poorgrass, Matthew Moon, Laban TALL and others, pass around a large two-handed communal mug of cider, encrusted with baked ashes on the outside but clean on the inside, known as a "God-forgive-me." Gabriel refuses to let them give him a clean mug or wipe it off, to their relief. This proves, as the maltster puts it, "he's his grandfer's own grandson!—his grandfer were just such a nice unparticular man!" They discuss Bathsheba's bailiff, Pennyways, who is rumored to have been fired for theft.

Meanwhile news comes to the malthouse that Bathsheba's youngest servant, Fanny ROBIN, has disappeared. Bathsheba wishes to talk with the men, who go to her garden. Another servant, Maryann, leans from the window to say Fanny has a young man who is a soldier and lives at Casterbridge. Billy Smallbury offers to look for her there the next day. Gabriel Oak spends the night at the home of Jan Coggan and resolves to move his library and other effects from Norcombe to Weatherbury.

Chapter 9: "The Homestead—A Visitor—Half-Confidences"
Bathsheba has settled into Weatherbury Farm, with Mrs. Coggan as housekeeper and Liddy SMALLBURY, the great-granddaughter of Warren, the maltster, as her companion and servant. The next morning the wealthy nearby farmer Mr. William BOLDWOOD, a bachelor of about 40, comes to ask if they know anything about Fanny Robin. She had had no friends as a child, and he had sent her to school and found her the place at Weatherbury Farm under Bathsheba's uncle. Maryann tells Bathsheba all the local girls had tried and failed to marry Boldwood. The farm laborers trail in to see Bathsheba.

Chapter 10: "Mistress and Men"
Bathsheba pays the men their wages and tells them that if they serve her well she will serve them well.

Chapter 11: "Outside the Barracks—Snow—A Meeting"
At the barracks in Casterbridge a "small shape," Fanny Robin, pleads with Sergeant Francis TROY to marry her. He promises to visit her the next day at her lodgings.

Chapter 12: "Farmers—A Rule—An Exception"
Bathsheba, accompanied by Liddy SMALLBURY, her maid, takes her sample bags of corn to the corn exchange in Casterbridge, where all the dealers are men. She sees Farmer Boldwood there but he takes no notice of her.

Chapter 13: "Sortes Sanctorum—The Valentine"
One Sunday, February 13, Bathsheba is bored; she and Liddy try divining their futures from Bible verses. On a whim, Bathsheba sends an anonymous valentine to Farmer Boldwood signed "Marry me."

Chapter 14: "Effect of the Letter—Sunrise"
The reserved Boldwood receives the valentine and has a misty vision of a woman's hand tracing the message. The postman delivers a letter he thinks is for Boldwood, but Boldwood sees that it is addressed to Gabriel Oak and decides to take it to Warren's Malthouse himself.

Chapter 15: "A Morning Meeting—The Letter Again"
At Warren's Malthouse there is a discussion of Bathsheba's situation without a bailiff (Pennyways has been fired.) Gabriel Oak brings in some nearly frozen newborn lambs to warm them up. He stops the men from making jokes about Bathsheba and speculating on her chances of success as a farmer. Boldwood comes in to deliver Gabriel's letter. It is from Fanny Robin; she encloses the shilling Gabriel had given her and says she is going to be married to Sergeant Troy of the 11th Dragoon Guards. Gabriel shows the letter to Boldwood,

who is skeptical about Fanny's plans. He knows Sergeant Troy and thinks him "clever," but foolish for leaving his position as clerk in a lawyer's office in Casterbridge to enlist. He is doubtful that the marriage will take place.

After marking the revived lambs "B. E.," Gabriel starts back to the farm with them. Boldwood shows him the anonymous valentine and asks if he recognizes the handwriting. Gabriel identifies it as Bathsheba's.

Chapter 16: "All Saints' and All Souls"

Sergeant Troy comes to All Saints' Church for his marriage, but Fanny fails to appear—she has gone, by mistake, to All Souls' Church. When she asks him if they can get married the next day instead he laughs and says he won't go through "that experience" again for some time.

Chapter 17: "In the Market-Place"

Boldwood sees Bathsheba in the Casterbridge marketplace and falls in love with her. Bathsheba knows his eyes are following her, and forms an intention to apologize for having sent the valentine. She realizes, however, that such an apology would be awkward, in case he thinks she meant to ridicule him.

Chapter 18: "Boldwood in Meditation—Regret"

Boldwood, as tenant-farmer of Little Weatherbury Farm, is one of the most prominent citizens of the town. Bathsheba has no idea of the depth of his emotions or that she has "thrown a seed" on a "hotbed of tragic intensity." He sees Bathsheba, Gabriel, and his helper Cain BALL in an adjoining meadow and almost goes to speak to them, but passes on. They are trying to make a sheep whose lamb has died "take" to another one by tying the skin of the dead lamb over a live one and penning them together. The process foreshadows Boldwood's vain attempts to make Bathsheba "take" to him, although he is, and will be, an unnatural suitor.

Chapter 19: "The Sheep-Washing—The Offer"

Bathsheba, in a splendid new riding habit, is supervising the sheep-washing ritual. Boldwood comes up and addresses her by name; Bathsheba has an "intuitive conviction" that his appearance is the equivalent of "the reverberation of thunder." He proposes to her, but she responds, with dignity, that her feelings for him would not justify her acceptance. He begs her to say that she can love him at some time. She apologizes for having sent the valentine. He says he will give her everything, including her own pony-chaise; she will have no cares. She is sympathetic to the "deep-natured man," and asks that he be neutral while she thinks about it. He promises to wait.

Chapter 20: "Perplexity—Grinding the Shears—A Quarrel"

As the narrator points out, Boldwood is not being kind to Bathsheba but offering her a "self-indulgent" love.

Bathsheba realizes many women in her position would have been eager to marry him, but is convinced "she couldn't do it to save her life." She helps Gabriel sharpen the shears for the sheep-shearing. He admits that the farm men saw her talking with Farmer Boldwood and believe that their names are "likely to be flung over pulpit together" before the year is out. She tells him it is not true. He chastises her for leading Boldwood on by sending him the valentine. She dismisses Gabriel from the farm and he leaves.

Chapter 21: "Troubles in the Fold—A Message"

The farm workers run to Bathsheba's house on Sunday afternoon to say the sheep have broken the fence and are eating clover, which is disastrous. When they reach the field they find that the sheep are foaming at the mouth and are distended. The only way to save them is by piercing them in the gut to release the gas blockage, called "the bloat." Gabriel is the only person who knows how to do it. They summon him but he refuses to come unless Bathsheba asks him "civilly." She writes a note, *Do not desert me, Gabriel!* and, when it is delivered, he comes. He is able to save 49 sheep from dying of "the bloat." Four others die of the disorder. Bathsheba rehires him.

Chapter 22: "The Great Barn and the Sheep-Shearers"

This chapter and the ensuing one are two of the most celebrated chapters in the novel, depicting the process of sheep-shearing in the vaulted barn with transepts and arches. Morgan observes that here the narrator makes the point that medieval architecture was built along the lines of vaulted arches, even in the case of a humble barn; this building is as sacred as any other, be it lay or ecclesiastical, serving the needs of humanity as well as any church (Rosemarie Morgan, private communication with the author). Gabriel is able to shear a sheep in 23 minutes. All is going well until Farmer Boldwood appears and takes Bathsheba outside. As they talk, Gabriel sees her face redden. He himself is "constrained and sad." Boldwood takes Bathsheba to see his own sheep. The men anticipate "lordly junketing" at night.

Chapter 23: "Eventide—A Second Declaration"

This chapter describes the shearing-supper, which takes place at a long table. Part of it is inside Bathsheba's parlor, where she sits at the head of the table. The remainder is outside on the grass. Gabriel sits beside Bathsheba until he is displaced by Farmer Boldwood. The former bailiff, Pennyways, appears uninvited, which disturbs Bathsheba. Boldwood goes into the house and joins Bathsheba; she sings, accompanied by Gabriel, on his flute, and Boldwood, who has a deep bass voice. Bathsheba tells Boldwood she is seriously thinking of accepting his offer, but is obliged to wait a few weeks before giving her answer.

Chapter 24: "The Same Night—The Fir-Plantation"
As is her custom, Bathsheba walks around the homestead each night before retiring, although, unknown to her, Gabriel has preceded her every night as bailiff. On the night of the shearing-supper, she goes as usual to make sure everything is in order. Her return path takes her through a dark plantation of fir trees. It is also a public footpath. She hears footsteps, and suddenly encounters a man with "warm clothes and buttons." As they pass she is thrown off balance and their clothes become entangled. He takes her lantern, opens it, and in the light she sees he is a military man; his spur has become entangled in her skirt. He pretends to have trouble untangling it, but finally succeeds. He introduces himself as Sergeant Troy and tells her she is beautiful (which Boldwood has never done). She hurries home and asks Liddy who it might be; Liddy confirms that he is Sergeant Troy, home on furlough. She tells Bathsheba he is a doctor's son and a "clever young dand," but that he has wasted his Casterbridge Grammar School education in languages and become a soldier.

Chapter 25: "The New Acquaintance Described"
The narrator describes Troy as living in the present, "moderately truthful towards men," but lying "like a Cretan" to women. He is full of "vegetative" activity. He is well educated for a man of the middle class, and exceptionally well educated for a "common soldier." His fluent speech enables him to "be one thing and seem another." He believes there are only two ways to treat women—by flattering or by cursing and swearing. He voluntarily assists with haymaking on Bathsheba's farm.

Chapter 26: "Scene on the Verge of the Hay-Mead"
Troy addresses Bathsheba as "Queen of the Corn-Market" and says he often assisted her uncle in the fields. He banters with her, flattering her and speaking French (his mother was from Paris). He then tries to give her his father's gold watch, but she insists that he take it back. The workfolk on the farm, meanwhile, watch in astonishment.

Chapter 27: "Having the Bees"
Bathsheba tries to hive the bees—that is, attract them into a hive she has prepared—herself. Troy climbs the tree to assist her; she gives him a veil and gloves. She laughs at him, removing "another stake from the palisade of cold manners" with which she had, up until then, repelled him.

He invites her that night to attend a "sword-exercise"; she has heard of such a thing but never seen one.

Chapter 28: "The Hollow Amid the Ferns"
At eight o'clock, during a golden sunset, Bathsheba goes to a nearby pit, lined with luxurious ferns and with a "thick flossy carpet of moss and grass" on the ground. She watches as Troy begins a stylized series of cuts; there are many sexual overtones to the performance.

He tests her "pluck" by terrifying her with quick thrusts; she thinks he has run the sword through her. Bathsheba is "enclosed in a firmament of light, and of sharp hisses, resembling a sky-full of meteors close at hand." There are "luminous streams" of an "*aurora militaris*" through which she sees the flashing sword. He deftly cuts off a lock of her hair with the sword, and she cries out, horrified. He assures her she had never been in danger, picks up the lock of her hair from the grass with the point of the sword, suddenly kisses her, and departs. She begins to cry.

Chapter 29: "Particulars of a Twilight Walk"
Bathsheba realizes she has fallen in love with Troy "in the way that only self-reliant women love when they abandon their self-reliance." His "deformities" lie too deep for her to see them. One evening Gabriel goes to meet her on her evening walk. He pretends that, since Farmer Boldwood is away, he is taking his place. Bathsheba questions his meaning and he says he assumes there will soon be a wedding between her and Boldwood. She hotly denies any such plans, although she admits Boldwood has proposed to her.

Gabriel then goes on to say he wishes she had never met Sergeant Troy; he may be "well born" and educated, but his course is "down'ard." Gabriel asks her not to trust Troy. She says Troy goes to church; Gabriel replies he has never seen him there. She says he goes in "privately by the old tower door." Gabriel insists this is not true.

She asks him to leave her alone for the moment, and continues her walk. Gabriel sees the figure of Troy appear beside her. On the way home Gabriel passes by the church and sees that ivy has grown from the wall across the old tower door. The door has not been opened "at least since Troy came back to Weatherbury."

Chapter 30: "Hot Cheeks and Tearful Eyes"
Bathsheba returns home; Troy has kissed her again. She writes Boldwood that she cannot marry him. She overhears her woman servants talking about Troy and herself and insists she hates him, but when they call him a "wild scamp" she defends him. Liddy apologizes and then Bathsheba, in private, admits she loves Troy to "distraction." She makes Liddy promise to keep her secret and try to "think him a good man." Liddy tells Bathsheba she frightens her when she storms and would be "a match for any man" when she is in one of her "takings." Bathsheba says she hopes she is not "mannish." Liddy answers that she is "not mannish; but so almighty womanish that 'tis getting on that way sometimes."

Chapter 31: "Blame—Fury"
Liddy has been given a week's holiday to visit her sister. Bathsheba, to avoid Boldwood, decides to accompany her for a day or two. On the way she meets Boldwood, walking in a "stunned and sluggish" way. He looks up, almost paralyzed by pain. He reproaches

her with a silent gaze. He begs her once again to marry him: He would have lived in "cold darkness" had it not been for her valentine. Bathsheba says she pities him deeply.

Boldwood knows, apparently, about Troy, and tells Bathsheba that she has been "dazzled by brass and scarlet." She admits Troy has kissed her, which drives him to new heights of fury; he blames him for stealing Bathsheba with "unfathomable lies." Boldwood warns her to keep Troy away from him, lest he be tempted to kill him. She knows that Troy is in Bath, not back at his barracks, and has another week of his furlough remaining.

Chapter 32: "Night—Horses Tramping"
At Bathsheba's house something wakes Maryann. She looks out the window and sees a moving figure seize the horse grazing the paddock, lead it to a vehicle, harness it, and trot away. She is sure the figure is a thief and calls Jan Coggan, who calls Gabriel Oak. They can tell, by the hoofprints, that the horse is Dainty, who belongs to Bathsheba. They borrow Mr. Boldwood's horses Tidy and Moll, without permission, and ride bareback, chasing Dainty. They catch her at the turnpike, and, to their astonishment, find that Bathsheba is driving the gig. With a cool manner she announces that she is driving to Bath. Gabriel and Jan turn back, agreeing to keep the night's doings quiet.

Chapter 33: "In the Sun—A Harbinger"
Nothing is heard of Bathsheba during the ensuing week. The boy Cain Ball has had a "felon" on his thumb (a painful inflammation of the last joint) and been unable to work; he has gone to Bath and comes home in his best blue coat with brass buttons.

He tells them he has seen Bathsheba and a soldier walking along together, then sitting in a park. Jan Coggan thinks Bathsheba has "too much sense" to become intimate with Troy, but Matthew says Troy is not a "coarse, ignorant man ... 'Twas only wildness that made him a soldier, and maids rather like your man of sin." (Leslie Stephen originally deleted "man of sin" from publication).

Chapter 34: "Home Again—A Trickster"
That evening Gabriel sees a vehicle coming slowly along the lane carrying Bathsheba and Liddy. He is relieved Bathsheba has come home safely. A dark form walks by; it is Boldwood. He goes to Bathsheba's house intending to ask forgiveness for his reproaches; he knows nothing of her trip to Bath. In town he sees Troy arrive in a carrier's van. Boldwood stops Troy and tells him he knows about Fanny Robin and that he should marry her. Troy says he cannot; he is too poor. Boldwood offers to pay him handsomely to marry her, and gives him £50. They hear a light step approaching; it is Bathsheba. Troy agrees that he will give up Bathsheba. She addresses him as "Frank, dearest," to Boldwood's

Illustration by Helen Paterson Allingham for Far from the Madding Crowd, *chapter 34 ("There's not a soul in my house but me to-night"),* Cornhill Magazine, *August 1874* (Perkins Library, Duke University)

horror. Boldwood then offers Troy more money to marry Bathsheba and make an honest woman of her. Troy shows Boldwood a notice in the Bath newspaper of his marriage to Bathsheba. Boldwood calls him a "juggler of Satan" and a "black hound" and vows to punish him. All night Boldwood can be seen walking about the hills of Weatherbury "like an unhappy Shade in the Mournful Fields by Acheron."

Chapter 35: "At an Upper Window"
The next morning Jan and Gabriel see Troy leaning from Bathsheba's window; Gabriel turns white and looks "like a corpse." They manage to greet Troy, who announces plans to redo the classic old house.

Troy asks Coggan whether insanity runs in Boldwood's family. Coggan answers that he knew of an uncle of his that was "queer in the head." Troy tosses them some coins. Coggan warns Oak not to be too disdainful, because Troy will be sure to buy his discharge

and be their master. Boldwood appears, his face without color and his temples throbbing. He rides stiffly
away, his immobility more striking than a collapse
would have been.

Chapter 36: "Wealth in Jeopardy—The Revel"
At the end of August one night, Gabriel senses danger
in the dry, sultry air, the attitude of the sheep, the
behavior of the rooks, and the movements of the
horses. He is sure heavy rain is coming, which will
destroy the unprotected ricks. Sergeant Troy, meanwhile, is giving a harvest supper and dance. Three fiddlers play "The Soldier's Joy." Troy is in high spirits;
even though he has purchased his discharge he will
continue to be a soldier "in spirit and feeling."

Troy announces he and Bathsheba are also celebrating their wedding. He has ordered kettles of brandy
and hot water for all the men. Bathsheba begs him not
to give it to them; they are unused to it, but he doesn't
listen. Soon Bathsheba, the women, and children, leave
the barn; Gabriel leaves a few minutes later.

Gabriel sees ominous signs of an impending storm.
He goes to the barn to search for coverings for the ricks
and sees all the men asleep, the candles either dark or
smoking, and Troy leaning back in his chair. None of
them can help him. From their youth they had had
nothing stronger than cider or mild ale, and cannot be
blamed for succumbing to Troy's brandy.

Gabriel gets the key to the granary and drags tarpau-
lins to cover two wheat ricks. He manages to slope
sheaves over the other three and goes on to try to cover
the barley.

Chapter 37: "The Storm—The Two Together"
Gabriel struggles with the ricks of barley. There are
flashes of lightning; he rigs up a lightning rod in the
form of a tethering chain. One flash reveals Bathsheba
coming out to help. He calls that he is on the rick,
thatching.

She wants to help, so he asks her to bring the reed
sheaves up the ladder, one by one, despite increasingly
dangerous conditions. The lightning splits a tall tree on
the hill. Bathsheba insists on working with him, since he
realizes the men are all asleep in the barn, thanks to Troy.

She insists on explaining that the night she galloped
to Bath she intended to break off her engagement to
Troy. Once there, her horse was lame, and she realized
that staying there with him would be perceived as scandalous. Troy then threatened to leave her for someone
else unless she married him immediately, which she
did, "between jealousy and distraction."

Gabriel sends her home to bed and reflects on the
"contradictoriness" of her heart, which had caused her
to speak more frankly and warmly that night than she
had ever done while unmarried and free.

The weather vane turns, signaling heavy rain.

Chapter 38: "Rain—One Solitary Meets Another"
Gabriel continues to thatch in the rain all night. The
farm workers awake in the barn and straggle out. Going
home, Gabriel sees Boldwood walking slowly ahead of
him. He asks about Boldwood's ricks, and finds he
never bothered to cover them. He realizes Boldwood is
terribly depressed. Boldwood says he no longer has
faith in God, having lost Bathsheba, and that it is better
for him to die than to live. He asks Gabriel not to mention his confidences.

Chapter 39: "Coming Home—A Cry"
Bathsheba and Troy are coming home to Weatherbury,
Troy walking beside the gig. He has been to the horse
races at Budmouth and lost more than £100 in a single
month. She is sure they will have to leave the farm and
says he is cruel to take away her money. He has already
placed bets on the next race. She is agonized; he calls
her "a chicken-hearted creature."

Suddenly a woman appears in very poor clothes.
Troy is standing on the steps of the gig, ready to
remount, and turns to speak to her. He starts visibly
and says he doesn't know. The woman looks up at him,
utters a hysterical cry, and falls down. He insists that
Bathsheba tend to the horse and go ahead to the top of
the hill; he will tend to the woman.

Troy asks the woman, who is Fanny Robin, why she
has not written him. She says she has been afraid to do
so. He gives her every farthing he has, and tells her to
go on to the Casterbridge Union; he will find her a
lodging the next day. He asks her to meet him on Monday, his first free day, at Grey's Bridge, and he will give
her all the money he can "muster."

He rejoins Bathsheba and admits recognizing the
woman, although he pretends he doesn't know her
name. Bathsheba doesn't believe him, but has not recognized Fanny.

Chapter 40: "On Casterbridge Highway"
This chapter is a detailed account of Fanny Robin's
painful and grueling progress toward Casterbridge and
the haven of the Casterbridge Union. She collapses several times on the road and is finally assisted by a faithful
dog, who is stoned away once she is helped into the
building.

Chapter 41: "Suspicion—Fanny is Sent For"
A day or two later, on the eve of the Budmouth races,
Troy asks Bathsheba for £20: she assumes it is for the
races and tries hard to entice him to stay at home. She
finally gives him the money. On leaving, he looks at his
watch and opens the case at the back. Bathsheba is startled to see a small coil of yellow hair there. He admits it
is the hair of a young woman he was about to marry
before he knew Bathsheba. She accuses him of loving
the other woman; he admits it is the hair of the woman
they saw on the road. He leaves. Bathsheba bursts into

sobs; her pride has been "brought low" by her marriage "with a less pure nature than her own." She is represented as Diana, before her marriage, "sufficient unto herself," and wishes she could return to her former state at Norcombe.

The next day, as she goes about her household duties, she is surprised to find herself thinking of Gabriel Oak, for whom she begins to have "the genuine friendship of a sister." She sees Mr. Boldwood coming along the road; he stops to talk a long time with Gabriel Oak, and then they both talk with Joseph Poorgrass. Joseph comes to tell Bathsheba that Fanny Robin has died in the Casterbridge Union. He says Mr. Boldwood will send a wagon to fetch her home and bury her.

Bathsheba says she will take on the duty of fetching Fanny's body, as Fanny had once been her servant. She asks Joseph to use the new spring wagon with the blue body and red wheels and to take evergreens and flowers to put upon her coffin. The horse Pleasant will draw her, as Fanny had known him well.

Bathsheba questions Joseph further and discovers Fanny had been a seamstress in Melchester for several months. She arrived at the Casterbridge Union early Sunday morning and died in the evening. Joseph believes she has died because of "biding in the night wind." Bathsheba realizes it was Fanny she and Troy had met on the Casterbridge road. Liddy confirms that Fanny had golden hair and that her "young man" was in the same regiment as Mr. Troy, who had said there was a "strong likeness between himself and the other young man."

Chapter 42: "Joseph and His Burden—Buck's Head"
Joseph goes to the Casterbridge Union-house and two men lay Fanny's coffin in the wagon. One of them writes on the coffin in chalk, and then covers it with a black cloth. Joseph walks beside the horse for four miles, until he sees the Buck's Head roadside inn. He goes in and finds Jan Coggan and Mark Clark already there; they offer him cider. He prepares to leave, but they ply him with more drink for the journey. They talk until six o'clock, when Gabriel Oak enters the inn and scolds Joseph. He was supposed to have the coffin at the WEATHERBURY CHURCH at 4:45.

The men are in no condition to continue, so Gabriel drives the horse to Bathsheba's home. Parson Thirdly comes out; he has been inquiring about the delay. He asks for the registrar's certificate, which Gabriel realizes is in Joseph's possession, and says it is too late for the burial. Bathsheba is alone; Troy has not returned. She asks that Fanny's body be brought into the house; they place it on benches in a little sitting room next to the hall. Gabriel stares at the coffin and sees the chalk inscription on the lid: *Fanny Robin and child.* He rubs out all but *Fanny Robin.*

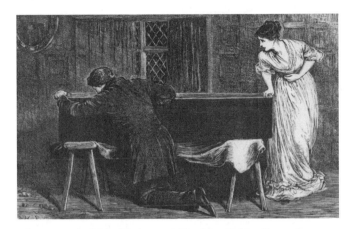

Illustration by Helen Paterson Allingham for Far from the Madding Crowd, *chapter 43 ("Her tears fell fast beside the unconscious pair"),* Cornhill Magazine, *October 1874* (Perkins Library, Duke University)

Chapter 43: "Fanny's Revenge"
Bathsheba questions Liddy about Fanny. Liddy talks with Maryann and then whispers a rumor about Fanny's pregnancy to Bathsheba. They agree it can't be true, as there is only one name on the coffin-cover. Liddy retires, and Bathsheba reflects on what she knows about Fanny. She determines to ask Gabriel Oak about her, and goes to his cottage, but realizes she cannot hint to him how miserable she is. She sees Gabriel close his book, go upstairs, and pray. She goes back home, gazes at the coffin, and wishes she could look in on Fanny and know everything. Then she says to herself, *"And I will."*

She fetches a screwdriver, opens the coffin, and sees a pair of bodies; one is Fanny's baby. Fanny's face is framed by yellow hair matching the hair in Troy's watch case. Bathsheba takes flowers from a vase and lays them around Fanny. Troy returns home and discovers Bathsheba, "pallid as a corpse on end," kneeling beside the coffin.

Troy is horrified by the sight of Fanny. He kneels and kisses her body, telling Bathsheba, "This woman is more to me, dead as she is, than ever you were, or are, or can be."

Chapter 44: "Under a Tree—Reaction"
Bathsheba runs out into the night and sleeps in a thicket of fern. The next morning she realizes the ground slopes to a hollow containing a malignant swamp dotted with fungi. This swampy thicket, now depicted in winter, is the same place where Bathsheba had been figuratively seduced the previous spring by Troy's stylized, terrifying sword exercise (Chapter 28, "The Hollow Amid the Ferns"). A schoolboy comes along the road trying to learn the Collect, repeating, "O Lord, give us, grace that . . ."

Liddy follows the schoolboy, looking for Bathsheba, who has lost her voice during her cold night near the swamp. She brings Bathsheba some bread and hot tea. Bathsheba at first thinks she will never go home, but then decides that a "runaway wife is an encumbrance to everybody," and she must stand her ground. She refuses to tell Liddy what has happened.

Meanwhile, men have removed the coffin. Bathsheba decides to live in the attic; Liddy brings her books and they barricade themselves against Troy. Troy, however, does not return. Liddy reports that a grand carved tombstone has been put up at the church.

Chapter 45: "Troy's Romanticism"

The morning after obtaining £20 from Bathsheba, Troy had risen early to meet Fanny at Grey's Bridge. When she failed to appear he was angry and went to the Budmouth races, but spent little. Reaching home, he saw the coffin. The next morning he rose early, walked to the churchyard, saw the open grave, and went into Casterbridge to a stone and marble mason. He ordered a marble headstone, gave instructions for the lettering, and had it transported to the churchyard. That night he went to see that it was in place, and planted flowers all around the grave. It began to rain and he took shelter on the church porch, falling asleep.

Chapter 46: "The Gurgoyle: Its Doings"

Two of the original eight 14th-century stone gargoyles, which Hardy calls "gurgoyles," on the Weatherbury church tower remain; their purpose is to deflect rain from the walls. One of them, in the shape of a griffin, is so positioned that it spouts water directly on to Fanny Robin's grave, washing away the flowers.

Troy sees the destruction and leaves town; he is seen on the Budmouth road. Bathsheba visits the grave and reads the inscription: *Erected by Francis Troy in Beloved Memory of Fanny Robin.* Gabriel Oak is there also; he fills in the grave and Bathsheba replants the flowers. She asks him to ask the churchwardens to redirect the leadwork of the gargoyle.

Chapter 47: "Adventures by the Shore"

Troy goes on toward Budmouth and decides to swim. He gets dangerously far out and cannot make it back to shore, but he is rescued by the crew of a brig.

Chapter 48: "Doubts Arise—Doubts Linger"

Bathsheba continues as mistress of the farm, and as Troy's wife, indifferent to her fate. She assumes that when Troy returns they will have to give up the tenancy of the Upper Farm, since they will probably not be able to pay the rent.

She manages to go to the Casterbridge fair, where a boy comes to tell her Troy has drowned. She faints but is rescued by Boldwood, who takes her to the King's Arms inn. She revives, declines his offer to drive her home, and drives herself. She refuses to wear mourning and is convinced Troy is alive. (A young doctor from Budmouth, Dr. Barker, saw Sergeant Troy being swept out to sea and assumed he had drowned. The doctor's account is published in the local newspaper.)

Chapter 49: "Oak's Advancement—A Great Hope"

As autumn draws on, Bathsheba installs Gabriel Oak as bailiff or overseer; Boldwood also asks him to act as bailiff for his farm and eventually allows him to receive a share of the receipts. Meanwhile, Boldwood's hopes of winning Bathsheba have "germinated." Bathsheba wears mourning, and Boldwood grills Liddy on whether Bathsheba might marry again. Liddy says it is possible she might after seven years. Boldwood subtracts the year since Troy's disappearance and believes she will remarry after six years.

Chapter 50: "The Sheep Fair—Troy Touches His Wife's Hand"

Bathsheba goes to the Greenhill agricultural fair where various flocks of sheep, of all breeds, are driven from miles away to be sold. The weaker sheep from remote areas ride in pony carts. A performance is announced: The Royal Hippodrome Performance of Turpin's Ride to York and the Death of Black Bess. Boldwood is there, and offers to escort Bathsheba to the performance. He gets her a prominent reserved seat. Troy, playing the part of Dick Turpin (an actual historical figure, a notorious highwayman), sees her through the curtain and tries not to appear, claiming to the manager that he has seen a "blackguard creditor." The manager allows him to go onstage without speaking and Bathsheba does not recognize him. At the evening performance Troy sees Pennyways, the bailiff Bathsheba has discharged, and fears that the man has recognized him. Boldwood, meanwhile, has invited Bathsheba to tea in the refreshment tent. Troy, listening from outside the tent, overhears them talking and hears Pennyways try to speak to her. She refuses to listen to him and he writes her a note: "*Your husband is here. I've seen him. Who's the fool now?*" She refuses to take the folded note, so he drops it in her lap. Troy is sure the note will reveal his identity and manages to snatch it from her hand. He runs away and overhears people talking of a robbery attempt. Troy finds Pennyways and speaks to him.

Chapter 51: "Bathsheba Talks with Her Outrider"

Bathsheba drives herself home from the fair; Boldwood rides on horseback beside her. He presses her again to marry him "someday." She says she cannot give an answer until Christmas.

She confides her problem with Boldwood to Gabriel, saying her only reason for not refusing Boldwood is that he might go out of his mind. Gabriel tells her the real sin is in thinking of marrying a man she does not love "honest and true." Gabriel does not say he hopes she will remain free to marry him, which irks her.

Chapter 52: "Converging Courses"
Boldwood gives a Christmas party. As he dresses he asks Gabriel Oak whether a woman keeps her promises. Gabriel says she may if it is "not inconvenient to her." Boldwood declares that, since it is 15 months since Troy vanished, Bathsheba should be ready to remarry in five years, nine months, and a few days.

Troy, meanwhile, has come to the White Hart tavern at Casterbridge. He is joined by Pennyways, and they discuss Bathsheba and, apparently, a legal separation from her (to Troy's benefit). Troy envies Bathsheba her property and income, while he is living hand to mouth.

Bathsheba dresses for the party, although, as she tells Liddy, she would rather not go. Boldwood takes out a ring for her before descending to welcome his guests. Troy plans to attend the party in disguise. He will walk from Casterbridge to Weatherbury and arrive before nine o'clock.

Chapter 53: "Concurritur—Horae Momento"
Rumors have spread through the small crowd of men outside Boldwood's house that Troy has been seen alive. Tension builds. Bathsheba arrives and is welcomed by Boldwood. Smallbury and the others decide to go to Warren's Malthouse before joining the party. They see Troy outside, looking in and listening to Gabriel Oak and Warren talking. They withdraw and decide one of them must warn Bathsheba. No one wants to be the messenger, so they all decide to attend the party. After an hour Bathsheba prepares to leave. Boldwood discovers her and presses her to give her word to marry him at the end of five years and three-quarters "as a business contract." To keep him from pressing her further, she agrees that if they both live she will marry him in six years. He gives her the ring. She says she cannot wear it, but agrees to do so just for the night.

The men cluster at the party, but no one wants to tell Bathsheba or Boldwood the rumor. Suddenly there is a sharp rapping at the door and Troy enters, wrapped in a greatcoat. Those who have heard the rumor recognize him, as does Bathsheba, who turns pale. Boldwood invites him to drink with them. Troy takes off his coat, faces Boldwood, and begins "to laugh a mechanical laugh." Boldwood recognizes him.

Bathsheba has sunk down and is sitting on the lowest stair, looking distraught. Troy tells her he has come for her. She does not move. Boldwood says, in a strange voice, "Bathsheba, go with your husband." She still does not move. Troy tries to pull her toward him and she shrinks back and screams. Suddenly there is a deafening sound: Boldwood has taken one of the guns mounted on the wall and shot Troy. Boldwood then

tries to shoot himself, but Samway, his servant, stops him. Boldwood kisses Bathsheba's hand, puts on his hat, and goes out into the street.

Chapter 54: "After the Shock"
Boldwood marches along the high road toward Casterbridge to the jail and turns himself in. His deed becomes known in Weatherbury. Gabriel, who has been outside the house, is one of the first on the scene. Bathsheba is holding Troy's body; she asks Gabriel to ride to Casterbridge for a surgeon, even though it is probably useless. Gabriel goes, but realizes he should have sent someone else. He passes Boldwood, walking in the shadows, without seeing him.

Mr. Aldritch, the surgeon, comes, but finds the house dark; Bathsheba has removed Troy to her own house. He, Gabriel Oak, and Parson Thirdly reach the house to find that Bathsheba has undressed the body and laid Troy out in grave-clothes. Mr. Aldritch exclaims the girl "must have the nerve of a stoic!" "The heart of a wife merely," Bathsheba whispers, and faints.

All night Liddy hears Bathsheba berate herself.

Chapter 55: "The March Following—'Bathsheba Boldwood'"
The following March there is a procession of the Western Circuit court to town, ready to sentence and eventually hang Boldwood. That afternoon, however, the villagers discover that Boldwood has a locked closet stocked with dozens of presents for Bathsheba, all packed in paper and labeled *Bathsheba Boldwood* with a date six years ahead. There is a petition that he be treated as insane based on this discovery, plus other evidence, such as the neglect of his corn stacks. Liddy thinks Bathsheba will go out of her mind too if Boldwood is hanged. News comes that he is to be confined, not executed.

Chapter 56: "Beauty in Loneliness—After All"
Bathsheba slowly recovers. She has ordered a monument for Troy, who is buried in the same grave as Fanny and her child, and in August she goes to see it. Gabriel has come to sing at church, and he joins her in looking at the grave. He says he is about to emigrate to California and will have to give up the management of her farm. He will finish the year managing Boldwood's and hers and then leave.

Bathsheba realizes Gabriel has been avoiding her. He sends a formal letter of resignation. She goes to see him in his cottage and tells him she is uneasy at his leaving. He says he has decided not to emigrate but that, instead, he is to take Little Weatherbury Farm. People are saying he is "sniffing about" and waiting for Boldwood's farm and also for Bathsheba. She says for him to think of marrying her is "too absurd … too soon—to think of." He agrees it is absurd. He comes closer and wonders aloud whether she would allow him to love her and win her and marry her.

Bathsheba encourages him to ask, and they become engaged. Their camaraderie has arisen through their knowing the "rougher sides of each other's character," the romance "growing up in the interstices of a mass of hard prosaic reality." This, according to the narrator, is the "only love which is strong as death—that love which many waters cannot quench, nor the floods drown, beside which the passion usually called by the name is evanescent as steam."

Chapter 57: "A Foggy Night and Morning—Conclusion"
Gabriel Oak gets the marriage license and confides their secret to Coggan; because of the circumstances they feel a festive wedding would be unsuitable and do not want the whole parish looking at Bathsheba in church. Laban Tall is now clerk of the parish. They go to his door, but he is away; they leave a message that he must come to the church the next morning in his best clothes to witness Bathsheba's signing "some law-work."

Bathsheba asks Liddy to wake her at six o'clock. She wakes earlier, and finally confides the secret to Liddy. She arranges her hair as she had once worn it at Norcombe, and she and Gabriel go to the church arm-in-arm under the same umbrella. Tall, Liddy, and the parson are waiting, and Gabriel and Bathsheba are married. That evening they are at tea in Bathsheba's parlor when they hear the firing of a cannon followed by trumpets. The original Weatherbury band has come to serenade them. Gabriel and Bathsheba invite the players in to eat and drink, but the players ask, instead, that they send "a drop of som'at down to Warrens." They offer a toast to "neighbour Oak and his comely bride."

Two chapters of the novel were omitted because Leslie Stephen worried about offending the middle-class readership of the *CORNHILL MAGAZINE*. They have survived as Draft-Fragments, which Hardy had bound in 1915 and gave to his second wife, Florence Hardy. One was a chapter called "The Shearing-supper" and the second is called simply "Chapter."

Professor Rosemarie Morgan has edited both fragments and posted them on the Hardy website under "Resources" (http://www.cis.yale.edu/hardysoc.appena. htm). They are included in her edition of the novel published by Penguin World Classics (2000). She observes that Stephen thought he could detect licentious material in the ex-bailiff's story, which refers to Fanny Robin ("Robbin" in this early version of the manuscript) as a successful "fallen" woman. Pennyways, who attends the supper on the pretext of bringing news of Fanny, admits that he has not spoken to her. However, he declares that he has seen her in Melchester (Salisbury) and judged by her dress that she "was too well-off to be anything but a ruined woman."

Morgan points out that, by Victorian standards, Fanny would have been "deemed stained forever—

morally, intellectually, and spiritually." Stephen, moreover, was a strict Puritan who believed in "divine retribution—that is, that disease and destitution should afflict those who flouted the moral law" (Rosemarie Morgan, private communication with the author).

CRITICAL RECEPTION AND COMMENTARY

The initial reception of the novel was favorable, on the whole, except for the puzzling response on the part of the SPECTATOR, of which the coeditor from 1861 to 1897 was the theologian and man of letters Richard Holt Hutton. He suggested the novel had been written by George ELIOT, a response that mystified Hardy. Although Hardy considered Eliot one of the greatest living writers, he believed that she had "never touched the life of the fields." Her country people had seemed, to him, more like "townsfolk" than "rustics" (*Life*, 98).

William Minto, editor of the *Examiner*, a weekly periodical, reviewed it favorably: Hardy wrote to thank him for recognizing the "dramatic aims of the story" (*Letters* 1, 41). The *Echo* praised the scenes of "rustic conversion," and the *Times* (January 25, 1875) suggested that the only fault of the book was that Hardy might be suspected of imitating George Eliot. The *Westminster Review* felt some of the incidents were too sensational, such as "Troy's play with swords, the rick-fire, and the death plunge over the cliff of Gabriel Oak's sheep." The writer for the *ATHENAEUM* found a greater similarity to the work of the novelist Charles Reade than of George Eliot. This critic also found the idiomatic speech of the rustic characters incompatible with their occasional "sophisticated expressions." The *Saturday Review* felt the rustic wit and conversation were "idealized." The "intellectual banter" of the rustic characters was also criticized by Hutton of the *Spectator*. The reviewer for *Scribner's Monthly* termed Hardy "the most original and impressive figure among young English fictionists" (Cox, *Thomas Hardy: The Critical Heritage*, xvii–xix).

The novel was also reviewed in a number of foreign publications. Léon Boucher wrote a long and favorable article about it in the influential *Revue des deux mondes* (Paris, 1875), translating long extracts and praising the presentation of rural life and scenes from nature. The American novelist Henry JAMES, writing for the New York *Nation*, found the book "diffuse" and Bathsheba "artificial," though he commended Hardy for his depiction of nature and the rural atmosphere. He considered the human element "factitious and insubstantial" but declared that Hardy had "gone astray very cleverly" and that the novel was "a really curious imitation of something better."

In 1901 Frederic HARRISON wrote Hardy to say how much he had enjoyed reading the book, and that he ranked it with *Tom Jones* and *Vanity Fair.* Hardy answered that he was very glad to hear it, although he said it was written in monthly installments to fill in a gap in the *Cornhill Magazine* caused by another writer's failing to keep his engagement (*Letters* II, 294).

In 1967 an excellent British film was made of the novel, directed by John Schlesinger and starring Julie Christie as Bathsheba Everdene, Peter Finch as William Boldwood, Alan Bates as Gabriel Oak, and Terence Stamp as Sergeant Frank Troy. A 1998 Masterpiece Theater television adaptation of the novel, made by Granada television and WGBH, Boston, was widely acclaimed; it starred Paloma Baeza as Bathsheba Everdene, Nigel Terry as William Boldwood, Nathaniel Parker as Gabriel Oak, and Jonathan Firth as Sergeant Frank Troy (*see* Appendix II, Media Adaptations of the Works of Thomas Hardy).

For further reading: Adey, "Styles of Love in *Far from the Madding Crowd*"; Babb, "Setting and Theme in *Far from the Madding Crowd*"; Beegel, "Bathsheba's Lovers: Male Sexuality in *Far from the Madding Crowd*"; Carpenter, "Hardy's 'Gurgoyles,'"; Carpenter, "The Mirror and the Sword: Imagery in *Far from the Madding Crowd*"; Cox, *Thomas Hardy: The Critical Heritage;* Dalziel, "'She Matched His Violence with Her Own Wild Passion': Illustrating *Far from the Madding Crowd*"; Gatrell, "*Far from the Madding Crowd* Revisited"; Gatrell, "Hardy the Creator: *Far from the Madding Crowd*"; Guerard, *Thomas Hardy, the Novels and Stories;* Lerner and Holstrom, *Thomas Hardy and His Readers;* Nakano, "Hardy's New Conception of Nature in *Far from the Madding Crowd*"; Sasaki, "On Boldwood's Retina: A 'Moment of Vision' in *Far from the Madding Crowd* and Its Possible Relation to *Middlemarch*"; Schweik, "The Narrative Structure of *Far from the Madding Crowd*"; Shires, "Narrative, Gender, and Power in *Far from the Madding Crowd*"; Wing, *Hardy.*

Fawcett, Millicent Garrett (1847–1929) The wife of Henry Fawcett, she was the leader of the women's suffrage movement and a friend of Hardy's. He and Emma HARDY had met her at the home of Lady PORTSMOUTH (the countess of Portsmouth). In 1892 she had written Hardy praising *TESS OF THE D'URBERVILLES* and asking that he write a short story for working boys and girls that would serve as a warning to them not to treat love too lightly. Hardy replied, declining her idea of a story "showing how the trifling with the physical element in love leads to corruption." He suggested that nothing further on the theme could be done in fiction than had already been done. Moreover, he believed that the British public would not stand for the necessary revelation of precise details about sexual matters. He asked, however, if he might call on her some afternoon (*Letters* I, 264).

In November 1906 she wrote him asking that he express his positive views on women's suffrage for a pamphlet she was compiling. He replied, expressing his support of "woman-suffrage" because he believed the woman's vote would "break up" many conventions related to "manners, customs, religion, illegitimacy … and other matters." Mrs. Fawcett thanked him, but stated that his letter was unpublishable because it would cause too much controversy; "John Bull is not ripe for it at present" (*Letters* III, 238–39). She was the author of several books, including *Women's Suffrage: A Short History of a Great Movement* and a biography of Queen Victoria.

For further reading: Fawcett, *Women's Suffrage: A Short History of a Great Movement* (London and Edinburgh: T. C. and E. C. Jack, 1912); Morgan, *Women and Sexuality in the Novels of Thomas Hardy;* Rubenstein, *A Different World for Women; The Life of Millicent Garrett Fawcett.*

Fawley, Drusilla Aunt of Jude FAWLEY in *JUDE THE OBSCURE.* She lives in Marygreen and takes Jude in after his father dies, warning him, "Jude, my child, don't *you* ever marry. 'Tisn't for the Fawleys to take that step any more." Jude's cousin, Sue BRIDEHEAD, was born in Miss Fawley's house and was "like a child of [her] own" until her parents separated. Miss Fawley is particularly eager that Jude and Sue not even meet, much less marry, because of the ill luck the Fawleys have in marriage and the history of mental illness on both sides.

Miss Fawley has a baking business, and Jude, as a boy, studies Greek and Latin while he delivers her bread. At her funeral Sue and Jude, both married to others, become reconciled.

Fawley, Jude Hero of *JUDE THE OBSCURE,* and one of Hardy's most memorable characters. When we meet him he is 11 and has come to the WESSEX village of Marygreen to live with his aunt, Miss Drusilla FAWLEY. His parents had separated when he was a baby; his mother had drowned herself, and his father has now died. Miss Fawley views him as a "poor useless boy," which is untrue. He helps the schoolmaster, Richard PHILLOTSON, load his moving cart; Phillotson is going to CHRISTMINSTER (Oxford) to work toward a university degree. Jude aspires to emulate him, but is disillusioned when the quack physician VILBERT, whom Jude has assisted, fails to send him the Latin and Greek grammars he has promised. Phillotson, however, supplies them, instead and Jude begins teaching himself in order to prepare himself for application to one of the colleges at Christminster. He assists his aunt in her baking business and apprentices himself to a stonemason to cover his university expenses.

At this point Jude meets Arabella DONN, the earthy daughter of a pig farmer, who traps him into marriage. She observes, "Never such a tender fool as Jude is if a woman seems in trouble." Jude realizes there is "something lacking" in himself. He is beset by self-recrimination when he realizes how coarse and scheming Arabella is, but realizes he is not sufficiently "dignified" for suicide, although he considers taking refuge in liquor. Arabella emigrates to Australia with her parents.

Jude goes to Christminster and meets his high-spirited cousin Sue BRIDEHEAD, with whom he falls in love. To keep her at Christminster, he persuades her to become a teaching assistant to Phillotson, who has not succeeded in being accepted at a college. Sue is not enthusiastic about him, but becomes engaged to him. Jude, being married, cannot propose to Sue, and he goes to Christminster, but is rejected. He begins drinking in a tavern and bitterly recites the Nicene Creed in Latin, demonstrating his classical knowledge. This statement of beliefs is an essential component of the Church of England liturgy.

Sue and Phillotson marry, but Sue leaves him to live with Jude and their marriage is dissolved. Although they have two children, she refuses to marry him, believing such a step would destroy their happiness. Jude's son by Arabella, Father Time, hangs himself and the children. Sue loses a third child owing to the shock, and finally returns to Phillotson. Jude, now ill, fails to win her back and dies.

Jude's noble goals remain unfulfilled, in part because he is an idealist, not ruthless enough toward himself or others, and prone to self-deception. Hardy called Jude "my poor puppet" (*Life,* 272) and wrote that the novel "makes for morality more than any other book I have written" (*Life,* 280). Jude's heredity is a factor; his great-aunt had warned him the Fawleys were unfit for marriage. The novel is also a commentary on the class-based university admission policies in effect at the time, which denied Jude a place at any of the colleges.

"Fellow Townsmen" Short story first published in *HARPER'S WEEKLY* from April 17 through May 15, 1880, and collected in *WESSEX TALES* (1887). A struggling young lawyer in the seaside town of Port-Bredy, Charles Downe, is an old friend of one of the town's wealthier men, George Barnet, who envies him his devoted wife, Emily, and their three small daughters. Barnet's handsome but aloof wife, Xantippe, is preoccupied with building a grand new house, the "Château Ringdale," which Barnet neither needs nor wants. Her unfeeling attitude toward him drives him out of town to visit Miss Lucy Savile, a young woman he had once loved, who has recently lost her father. She is supporting herself by painting flowers. He confesses his regret that he had not proposed at the proper time and leaves in a miserable state of mind.

On the way home he meets the town surgeon, Charlson, who not only owes him money but also makes an ill-bred joke about having seen him emerge from Lucy's house. Barnet is scrupulously careful afterward not to take walks near Lucy's home. After several months he meets Downe, who says Emily would like to try to befriend Mrs. Barnet. Mrs. Barnet takes Emily for a drive toward the harbor in her stylish pony carriage, and Barnet strolls once more past Lucy's home. Lucy is outside, but looks pale and ill. The Port-Bredy harbor becomes windy, but the two women engage a local waterman, John Green, to take them out for a sail. A storm comes up and the boat capsizes. Emily Downe is feared drowned; Downe is hysterical with grief. Xantippe Barnet is taken to her home, but apparently cannot be saved. Barnet stands over her, wondering if it is possible she could be revived. He strolls to the window and wistfully gazes at Lucy Savile's house, but then summons the servants and tries to bring his wife back to life. Another doctor comes, and succeeds.

After a few months, Xantippe Barnet takes her jewels and leaves her husband. By accident he encounters Lucy, who hopes to establish herself as a teacher of "freehand drawing and practical perspective." Downe has been left with four children, and can think of nothing but an ornate tomb for his wife. Barnet gently suggests that he knows the ideal governess for them, Lucy Savile, who could come in daily. Barnet occupies himself by taking an interest in the construction of his house. Lucy begins her work as a governess; one day the Downe children run into the house and begin exploring it. Barnet happens to be there, and welcomes them. As the house nears completion Lucy comes in to thank him warmly for his kindness; she has just learned that it was through his recommendation that she obtained the position.

Barnet receives word that his wife has died in the London suburbs and that Lucy may be going to India to be with her brother. Just as Barnet begins hoping he might win Lucy, Downe sends word that he and Lucy are to be married that very day. Barnet reaches the church just as the ceremony is ending, and composes himself enough to give them his best wishes. He then climbs into a grave the sexton is filling in and, in a state of despair, helps him.

Barnet then withdraws, disposes of his papers and all his effects, and vanishes. His new house is bought by Downe, and his old house is replaced by a Congregational Baptist chapel. After many years Barnet returns to town, aged and unrecognized. He learns that Downe has been dead seven years. He goes to call on Lucy and meets Charlson, the surgeon, who had deliberately given up Mrs. Barnet for dead so that Barnet could marry Lucy. Lucy recognizes him and receives him warmly. Barnet explains that he had left Port-Bredy because he learned she was marrying Downe on the very day he was first free to marry her. He proposes, but she refuses him. He leaves again; she changes her mind, but he never returns, although she waits and waits.

In 1893 Hardy wrote Florence HENNIKER that he had thought the story "rather good," but one "to write *after* you have drawn attention to your work" than one "to draw it with" (*Letters,* 33). In 1896, in a letter to the anthropologist and writer Bertram WINDLE, Hardy provided a list correlating actual Dorset place names with those in many of his works. He identifies Bridport with "Port-Bredy" in *The* MAYOR OF CASTERBRIDGE and in "Fellow Townsmen."

For furthering reading: Herzog, "Hardy's 'Fellow-Townsmen': A Primer for the Novels."

"Few Crusted Characters, A"   Dated March 1891, this group of nine sketches, with an introduction, was included in LIFE'S LITTLE IRONIES, which also contains eight other stories. In a review of *Life's Little Ironies,* the ATHENAEUM called them "delightfully humorous stories, not quiet so ominous as the first part" (Gerber and Davis: *Thomas Hardy: An Annotated Bibliography of Writings about Him,* 65). The sketches bring the escapades of various ingenious and independent village folk to life, but also point up the difficulty of returning to the place of one's birth after an interval of several decades.

Introduction
The structure is perhaps modeled on the *Canterbury Tales,* with various tales, or character sketches, narrated in the course of a journey. The first section sets the sketches on the main street of a market town where a carrier's van, similar to the old French *diligences,* is getting ready to leave for the village of Longpuddle (the actual town of Puddlehinton). Various passengers arrive, such as "Mr. Day, the world-ignored local landscape painter." As it lumbers along the village curate hastens behind, catches it, and then a second passenger overtakes it and climbs aboard. This is John Lackland, a native of the village who, as a child, had emigrated to "foreign parts" more than 35 years earlier with his family. His parents and sister have died, and he is considering moving back to Longpuddle and settling there. He tells the driver that Tony Kytes was the person who had driven the family to CASTERBRIDGE the morning they left.

The carrier's van resumes, and throughout the journey anecdotal accounts of the lives of Longpuddle inhabitants are recounted.

"Tony Kytes, the Arch-Deceiver"
The next section is devoted to Tony Kytes, an unsmiling young man who is much liked by young ladies. He and Milly Richards are thought to be engaged, but Unity Sallet, a former special friend, meets him one day as he is driving his father's wagon and asks for a lift home. She makes her interest in him clear, but suddenly he sees Milly approaching and asks Unity to lie down in the back of the wagon under a tarpaulin. Milly says she has arrived to ride back with him and talk about their future home. On their way they see Hannah Jolliver,

Tony's first serious interest, gazing at them from the upper window of her aunt's house. Tony asks Milly to lie under some sacks in the front of the wagon. Hannah asks to ride home with Tony and climbs into the front seat; Tony is much taken with her and not sure why he had ever liked Milly or Unity. He cries out to Hannah that nothing is settled with Milly, and they hear a "little screaming squeak" come from beneath the sacks. Tony tells Hannah he can throw over Milly and marry her; an "angry, spiteful squeak" and a "long moan" come from beneath the sacks.

Tony drives on until his father sees him with Hannah and summons him into the fields. He tells him it "won't do" to drive about with Hannah if he means to marry Milly, which he recommends. Tony confesses that all three girls are in the wagon. The father realizes that Hannah cannot hold the horse in; the horse is walking on briskly to its stable. Milly, meanwhile, has discovered Unity beneath the tarpaulin. Hannah hears their voices and drops the reins. The wagon turns over and the three girls fall out, unhurt, but begin to quarrel. Hannah's father discovers her in the group, her face bleeding from a bramble scratch, and Hannah angrily refuses Tony as a "false deceiver." Tony then rejects the idea of marrying Milly, since she is his father's choice. He proposes to Unity, who refuses to take Hannah's "leavings." He then proposes again to Milly, and they marry as soon as the banns have been posted. The carrier, who is also the narrator for the section, turns to Mr. Flaxton, the parish clerk, who says he was at the wedding and the party following was "the cause of a very curious change in some other people's affairs; I mean in Steve Hardcome's and his cousin James's."

"The History of the Hardcomes"
The clerk narrates the next section, beginning with Tony's wedding party, "the best wedding-randy that ever I was at." Professor Rosemarie Morgan points out that "randy" is a colloquialism for "rendezvous" (private correspondence with the author). It takes place during the week after Christmas, on a frosty night. Steve and James Hardcome, first cousins, with their intended wives, Emily Darth and Olive Pawle, and friends from nearby settlements all attend and dance. Gradually two of the three fiddlers lay down their instruments; the third keeps up a "faltering tweedle-dee," sitting on a small corner table beneath a hanging cupboard. James and Steve change partners, each dancing more and more with the other's fiancée. Each admits he wouldn't mind having his cousin's girl as his wife. The girls agree, as they are walking home, and each marries "the other's original property."

After two years the couples become less warm to each other. Olive, who loves riding and outdoor activities, is discontented with James, who loves his fireside; Emily, on the other hand, is very domestic, working at samplers. She is ill-matched to Steve, who is "always knocking about hither and thither." They accept the situation, however, until they take a joint holiday at Budmouth-Regis. Olive suggests rowing in the bay after dinner. The parish clerk then turns the narration over to the curate.

Steve's wife, the curate says, hates the sea, as does James. They agree to sit and enjoy the seaside band while the others leave in a hired boat. Emily points out what a handsome couple Steve and Olive are as they row away, out to sea. Olive waves her handkerchief; Emily waves her own in return, not realizing it is a distress signal. James and Emily continue sitting on the esplanade as the bandsmen go home and the Esplanade lamps are lit. Other boats return, but not Steve and Olive. Emily and James search along the shore, but finally take the train back to Casterbridge and drive to Upper Longpuddle. Steve and Olive have not been seen.

Emily and James stay in their respective houses and, the next morning, drive to Casterbridge and take the train back to Budmouth-Regis. It is reported that the couple in the boat have been seen gazing into each other's faces, "as if they were in a dream." That afternoon they learn that two bodies have been found ashore in Lulwind Bay, tightly locked in each other's arms, "his lips upon hers, their features still wrapt in the same calm and dream-like repose which had been observed in their demeanor as they had glided along." The bodies are buried the same day.

James and Emily, "a more thoughtful and far-seeing, though less romantic couple" than Steve and Olive, marry and are very happy, although they have no children; both have died since John Lackland left Longpuddle. William Privett has also died; he had done odd jobs for James and Emily. There was, however, something strange about his death, according to the seedsman's father, who speaks for the first time.

"The Superstitious Man's Story"
A cottager, Betty Privett, who irons for the Hardcomes, hears her husband, William, "a curious, silent man," go out of the house one night on Old Midsummer's Eve. To her astonishment, she finds him sleeping upstairs; he denies having gone out. She meets Nancy Weedle in the village and learns that several people have been to the church porch at midnight where, it is rumored, they can see the faint shapes of people doomed to die within the year as they enter the church. Those who recover from illnesses come out again, but those who die remain inside. They seem to have seen the shape of William. Three days later he dies in the meadow during the noon recess. At the time of his death Philip Hookhorn sees William, "looking very pale and odd," at the spring where his small son had drowned years before. The master thatcher then tells the tale of Andrey Satchel, Jane Vallens, and the Scrimpton parson and clerk.

"Andrey Satchel and the Parson and Clerk"
Andrey Satchel, a man given to drink, and his fiancée, Jane, who is somewhat older and pregnant, plan to marry early one November morning and then drive to Port Bredy (sic) for the day instead of returning to Jane's distant relative, with whom she lived, and "moping about." Andrey, however, has served as godfather at a christening the day before and has been up all night celebrating; he is not altogether sober. The parson, Billy Toogood, detects his condition and refuses to marry the couple. Jane begs the parson to lock them in the church until Billy is sober, and he agrees, saying he will return in two hours. The clerk agrees to lock them in the tower so no one will know what has happened. The parson remembers there is a meeting of the hounds that day; hunting is a sport he loves. The clerk is also eager to go hunting; the parson takes his gray mare and the clerk the cob. They both forget the couple in the church tower.

The parson and clerk hunt all day and come home, never thinking of the couple. The next morning the clerk remembers them, and they see "a little small white face at the belfry-winder and a little small hand waving." Andrey and Jane are married at once; the parson invites them in for a wedding breakfast, and they pretend they have just returned from Port Bredy. Eventually their story is known, but Jane has "saved her name." This tale reminds the schoolmaster, Mr. Profitt, of an experience Andrey's father, known as Old Andrey, once had.

"Old Andrey's Experience as a Musician"
Mr. Profitt, a choirboy at the time, was invited to play and sing at the home of Lord and Lady Baxby, then enjoy a good supper in the servants' hall. Old Andrey, then called Andrew, is eager to join in the meal and borrows a fiddle to pass as a musician. The squire's mother asks why he is not playing with the others. He pretends he has broken his bow on the way to the manor house. She has one brought down from the attic and he simulates playing, but holds his fiddle upside down. Andrew is called an imposter and told to leave the house; the squire orders him turned out of his cottage in two weeks. The squire's wife, however, invites him to come through the back door to the feast in the servants' hall, and nothing more is said about his cottage. Christopher Twink, the master thatcher, tells John Lackland that the old musicians were then replaced by a modern organist, a teetotaller, because they had gotten into "a sort of scrape."

"Absent-mindedness in a Parish Choir"
The six Longpuddle musicians, playing various instruments, are considered very good, ranking near the

MELLSTOCK parish players (in *UNDER THE GREENWOOD TREE* and other works, "Mellstock" is Hardy's name for three hamlets, including HIGHER BOCKHAMPTON, his birthplace). The group is much in demand, particularly during Christmas week. One year they have had no sleep at all, with "one rattling randy after another every night." The Sunday after Christmas is extremely cold, and the gallery lacks heat, so Nicholas Puddingcome, the leader, smuggles in a gallon of hot brandy and beer, wrapping it in Timothy Thomas's bass viol bag. They sip thimblefuls throughout the service, then fall asleep during the protracted sermon. The church becomes almost completely dark as the parson announces the evening hymn. Levi Limpet, a boy in the gallery, nudges the players. Nicholas awakens with a start, believes he is still at the previous night's party, and begins playing "The Devil among the Tailors," shouting out, "'Top couples cross hands! And when I make the fiddle squeak at the end, every man kiss his pardner under the mistletoe!'" The people come out of their pews, horrified. The Squire says not one of the "villainous players" shall ever "sound a note in this church again," since they have insulted him, his family, his visitors, and the parson.

The band members creep down the gallery stairs. The squire orders a barrel organ that will play exactly 22 psalm tunes with a "respectable man" to turn the winch, and the old players play no more.

John Lackland then inquires about Mrs. Winter, and the aged groceress volunteers to explain what used to give her "that hollow-eyed look."

"The Winters and the Palmleys"
The groceress recalls two village women who do not like each other; one tempts away Winter, the other's lover, and marries him. They have a son, Jack. After about 10 years the second woman marries a quiet man named Palmley, and also has a son, rather weak and not too bright. After Palmley dies, Mrs. Winter offers to hire Mrs. Palmley's son as an errand boy. She sends him to the next village with a message on a dark December day. He begs not to go, but she insists. As he returns through Yalbury Wood something frightens him; he becomes a "drivelling idiot" and dies soon afterward.

Mrs. Palmley has nothing to live for, and vows vengeance. Her niece, Harriet Palmley, comes from the city of Exonbury to live with her; she is a "proud and handsome girl." Jack Winter falls in love with her and proposes. She doesn't quite refuse him, but he decides he must obtain a better position to secure her. He goes to Monksbury to superintend a farm and become a farmer himself. His letters are not up to her standard of penmanship, and finally she sends him away as not sufficiently educated for her. Jack returns home to his mother and finds that Harriet is now interested in a road contractor. His handwriting is beautiful, and Jack vows to retrieve his own poorly written letters lest she show them to the other young man. She refuses to return them. Jack leaves, but returns at night and takes the letters.

Jack is arrested by two constables for breaking into the house, and is sent to the Casterbridge jail. He is sentenced to death and executed; this will be Mrs. Palmley's revenge on Mrs. Winter. Harriet marries the road contractor, but her reputation in Longpuddle has been ruined by her treatment of Jack. Mrs. Winter lives on, gaunt and lonely, with a "hollow-eyed look." At the conclusion of the story, John Lackland remarks that Longpuddle has had "sad" experiences as well as "sunny" ones. This prompts the registrar to recall the "shady" character Georgy Crookhill.

"Incident in the Life of Mr. George Crookhill"
Georgy leaves the Melchester fair on a bad horse. He begins talking with a young farmer he envies, who is on a strong, handsome horse, on the way to Casterbridge. They stop at the Woodyates Inn and have drinks together; it begins to rain, so they stop at the village of Trantridge and share a room. Early in the morning Georgy dresses in the farmer's clothes, takes some of his money, pays the bill, saddles the farmer's horse, and departs.

Farmer Jollice, dressed in Georgy's clothes, comes across Georgy as he is being placed under arrest by two constables, who identify him as a deserter from the dragoons. They take Georgy to face an escort of soldiers sent to bring the deserter back. Eventually it is clear that the missing dragoon is the young farmer, who is not a farmer at all, but a man who had met a farmer and coaxed him into changing clothes with him. Farmer Jollice verifies that Georgy is not the deserter, who is never found. He leaves Georgy's horse behind and vanishes.

The group in the wagon, being more concerned with "the remarkable" than "simple chronicles," ask if Lackland remembers Netty Sargent, who had "no harm in her" but was "up to everything." They call on Mr. Day, the "world-ignored old painter," to tell her tale.

"Netty Sargent's Copyhold"
Netty, who lives with her uncle, Mr. Sargent, in a large lonely house, is "a tall spry young woman" with "black hair and dancing eyes." She is courted by Jasper Cliff, a rather selfish young man whose eyes are fixed on Netty but whose mind is fixed on the uncle's house. The house, built by Netty's great-great-grandfather, is "copyhold," granted on successive lives within a family or on a renewal of the copyhold by paying a small fine; otherwise it becomes the property of the squire, who, in this case, is eager to acquire the house. He hates the "tiny copyholds and leaseholds and freeholds, which made islands of independence in the fair, smooth ocean of his estates."

Old Sargent, the uncle, delays renewing the house, as he doesn't care for Jasper Cliff, but finally does prepare the paperwork, as he sees that Netty is serious about Jasper. By this time Old Sargent is so feeble that the agent for the squire promises to come to the house for the transfer of fees and papers. Just two hours before he arrives, Old Sargent loses consciousness and falls from his chair. Netty lifts him back, but he has died and is turning cold.

Netty thinks of an ingenious scheme to secure the copyhold. She wheels the armchair, which is on casters, with the body in it to the table. She places the family Bible open before him, puts his forefinger on the page, opens his eyes, puts on his spectacles, and places a candle on the table. She tells the agent her uncle is not well; he says the uncle must sign the parchment in his presence. Netty declares that the uncle has always been afraid of agents and the law. She offers to have him sign, but without the agent's witnessing the signature. She escorts the agent to the window; from there he can see the end of the room with the old man's head, shoulders, and arm, and the Bible. Netty says he is reading his Bible. She brings the cash fee, wrapped in paper. The agent gives her the parchment paper and permits her to guide her uncle's hand, as she says he is partially paralyzed. Satisfied that the old man has traced his name on the document, the agent leaves.

Netty announces the next morning that her uncle died in bed the night before. She marries Jasper, but within two years, he begins beating her. Netty begins telling people what really happened, and says she has repented of her "pains." The old squire dies, his son inherits the property, and, because Netty is "widerminded" than his father and does not object to little holdings, he takes no action against her.

The carrier's van reaches Longpuddle and begins discharging the passengers. Lackland visits the cemetery, but realizes those he would have known are now there and not among the living. He cannot find his heart "ready-supplied with roots and tendrils," and realizes that, to return, he would have to reestablish himself from the beginning, "precisely as though he had never known the place," because "Time had not condescended to wait his pleasure, nor local life his greeting." After a few days at the inn, he departs, announcing that his original purpose in coming had been "fulfilled by a sight of the place, and by conversation with its inhabitants." His deeper intention, however, of spending the remainder of his life there, would come to naught. Little has now been heard of him for 12 or 15 years.

The sketches point up the ingenuity and perceptiveness of the rural characters.

For further reading: Carpenter, "How to Read 'A Few Crusted Characters.'"

fiction and Hardy   When Hardy first decided to focus less on architecture than on writing, he "felt no consuming interest in prose fiction" and was usually drawn, in his reading, to the work of poets rather than novelists (Page, *Thomas Hardy*, 8). At this time, however, Charles Dickens, George ELIOT, and Anthony Trollope were all writing novels, a far more reliable source of profit than writing poetry. Hardy's first novel, *The POOR MAN AND THE LADY*, was rejected by Macmillan in 1868 and has since vanished. He then began his first published novel, the thriller *DESPERATE REMEDIES*. This genre was completely different from that of his next novel, *UNDER THE GREENWOOD TREE*, an idyllic love story set in a village. Both were published by William TINSLEY; Hardy partially subsidized the first one. He continued, for several years, to combine the practice of architecture and writing. His novels were all serialized in periodicals, a practice profitable to both author and publisher. Serializing novels had succeeded the practice of issuing them in "monthly parts" (small paper-covered installments), which had been standard during the time of Dickens.

In his "General Preface to the Novels and Poems" published in the WESSEX EDITION of his works (I, 1912), Hardy explains his classification of the "fictitious chronicles" contained in the edition. The first group is "Novels of Character and Environment"; the second is "Romances and Fantasies"; the third is "Novels of Ingenuity." The first 20 volumes, which appeared in 1912–13, contain Hardy's final revisions of his novels. The critic F. Manning, in a 1912 article for the *SPECTATOR*, discusses four novels as particularly representative of character and environment—*TESS OF THE D'URBERVILLES, THE RETURN OF THE NATIVE, JUDE THE OBSCURE*, and *THE MAYOR OF CASTERBRIDGE*—and notes that they are all, in varying ways, expressive of his "intuitive sympathy with humanity in all its moods" (Manning, 135). It may be argued that the second category, "romances and fantasies," is represented by *Under the Greenwood Tree* and *Desperate Remedies*, both of which have traditional happy endings. The latter category also contains fanciful and even melodramatic elements such as the night conflagration at the Three Tranters Inn, the murder of Eunice, and the concealment of her body in an oven. Harold Williams, in a 1914 article in the *North American Review*, suggests that *A PAIR OF BLUE EYES, A LAODICEAN*, and *The HAND OF ETHELBERTA* are novels of ingenuity and states that in these works Hardy is almost "toying with his natural aptitude for inventing entanglements and hitches." His characters are "unconvincing" and his plots "improbable" (Williams, 152).

Michael Millgate, Hardy's most eminent biographer, observes that Hardy turned from architecture to writing because, after his years working for John HICKS in DORCHESTER and for Sir Arthur BLOMFIELD in LONDON, he took stock of his progress. He realized that, as an architect, he was doomed to "improving and finishing other men's projects" rather than securing his own commissions. He would not even be as independent as his father, a "jobbing builder," had been throughout his life. Moreover, his "whole being" was directed toward literature (Millgate, *Thomas Hardy: A Biography*, 103).

In 1890 Hardy made a brief contribution to *The Art of Authorship*, a volume compiled and edited by George Bainton. His essay is entitled "Truthfulness to One's Self"; Richard Little Purdy terms it "very slight" (Purdy, Thomas Hardy: *A Bibliographical Study*, 299).

Jude the Obscure, published in 1895, was the last novel Hardy wrote. He had long been writing poetry and nonfiction essays and, after 1895, wrote in these genres and stopped writing fiction. In early 1928 Lillah MCCARTHY called on Hardy, one of the last people to visit him before his death. At that time he told her that, although he had stopped writing novels, "'I now tell the story of a novel in verse of twenty lines'" (Lillah McCarthy, *Myself and My Friends*, 101–3).

For further reading: F. Manning, "Novels of Character and Environment"; Peterson, "'A Good Hand at a Serial': Thomas Hardy and the Art of Fiction"; Williams, "The Wessex Novels of Thomas Hardy."

"Fiddler of the Reels, The" Short story published in *Scribner's Magazine* (New York) in May 1893 and collected in *LIFE'S LITTLE IRONIES* (1894). The story concerns Wat ("Mop") Ollamoor, a dandy and "woman's man," a gifted gypsy violinist, whom men find somewhat repulsive. His origins are mysterious; he first appears as a fiddle player at the Greenhill Fair, and he is known to attract young, unsophisticated women. He almost has the appearance of a satyr, with an olive complexion and dark, oily hair, sometimes supplemented by apparently artificial curls. According to the venerable local musicians, his playing is all "fantastical." He is said to play the fiddle "so as to draw your soul out of your body like a spider's thread."

Car'line Aspent, a village girl from Stickleford, near CASTERBRIDGE, in WESSEX, has encouraged the courtship of Ned Hipcroft, a kindly, retiring mechanic, but is captivated by Mop. She refuses Ned, who makes his slow way to London and obtains construction work on the glass house (the Crystal Palace) for the Great Exhibition of 1851 in Hyde Park. Four years later, Car'line writes to say she will gladly marry him if he will have her and that Mop has been out of her life nearly as long as Ned himself. Ned agrees, and Car'line comes to London on a cold, rainy day. To his astonishment she is accompanied by a small daughter, Carry. He gives them shelter and marries Car'line as soon as the banns are posted, becoming much attached to Carry.

After a year or so Ned's employment comes to an end. The couple decide to return to the countryside and live temporarily with Car'line's father while Ned

searches for work. Car'line is rather proud of herself, "a smiling London wife with a distinct London accent"; she believes her return is "a triumph." The train does not stop at the small station nearest Stickleford but goes on to Casterbridge, where Ned resolves to begin looking for employment while Car'line and Carry begin walking to Stickleford.

At the Quiet Woman inn, on the edge of EGDON HEATH (a noted location in *The RETURN OF THE NATIVE* and, to a lesser degree, in *TESS OF THE D'URBERVILLES* and "The WITHERED ARM"), they stop for refreshment. Suddenly Mop appears, ready to play his fiddle for village dancing. Car'line is wearing a veil, but she trembles as she watches him. The dancing becomes more frenzied, until a five-handed reel is proposed. As people become exhausted and drop out, the dance becomes four-handed, then three-handed, and two-handed. Car'line is finally left dancing alone except for Carry and Mop. The other guests adjourn to the next room for more drink and a change of air. Car'line becomes Mop's frenzied slave, and, "probed" by his "gimlet-like gaze," cannot stop dancing, although Carry begs her to take her home. Instead Car'line falls on the floor. The music stops, Carry bends over her, and Mop rushes over to both of them.

Ned, meanwhile, has followed the same road and stops at the inn for a drink. He discovers that Mop has apparently abducted Carry. He snatches up a hot poker and rushes outside with the other men, but cannot find them. He returns to the inn and sinks down in despair. The other guests taunt him, saying that perhaps he doesn't know Carry is not his child. "'No, I don't think 'tis mine!'" Ned cries, "'But she *is* mine, all the same! Ha'n't I nussed her? Ha'n't I fed her and teached her?'" The others try to comfort him by reporting that at least Car'line has recovered, but Ned replies, "'She's not so particular much to me, especially now she's lost the little maid! But Carry's the whole world to me!'"

Ned searches throughout the district, hearing that Mop and a child dancing on stilts have been seen at a fair near London, but never finds Carry. Car'line seems not to care, saying Mop won't hurt the child. The villagers speculate that Mop has taken Carry to America, having trained her to support him by her earnings as a dancer. The narrator concludes, "There, for that matter, they may be performing in some capacity now, though he must be an old scamp verging on three-score-and-ten, and she a woman of four-and-forty."

"The Fiddler of the Reels" has been one of Hardy's best-liked stories and has attracted much critical attention. Unlike many of his stories, it was written on commission. In October 1892, Charles Scribner's Sons had requested a story for the May Exhibition issue of *SCRIBNER'S MAGAZINE*. Hardy replied on November 20 that he would try. On June 10, 1893, Hardy wrote Florence HENNIKER to ask whether she had liked his "little story in *Scribner*" (*Letters,* II, 13). The story depicts a villain almost as chilling as Aeneas MANSTON or Sergeant Francis TROY.

For further reading: Benazon, "Dark and Fair: Character Contrast in Hardy's 'Fiddler of the Reels,'" *Ariel: A Review of International English Literature* (Calgary, Alberta T2N 1N4, Canada), 9:2 (1978), 75–82; Giordano, "Characterization and Conflict in Hardy's 'The Fiddler of the Reels,'" *Texas Studies in Literature and Language: A Journal of the Humanities,* 17 (1975), 617–33; Potter. "Poetry and the Fiddler's Foot: Meters in Thomas Hardy's Work," *Musical Quarterly,* 65 (1979), 48–71; Sutton, "Hardy's Fiddler and the Bull: A Debt to Baring-Gould?" *English Language Notes,* 32:2 (Dec. 1994), 45–53.

"Figure in the Scene, The" Poem published in MOMENTS OF VISION (1917), inspired by an incident in Hardy's courtship of Emma Gifford HARDY. They were sketching in August 1870 at Beeny Cliff, a scenic site on the Cornish coast not far from ST. JULIOT CHURCH (*see* "BEENY CLIFF"), when it began to rain. Emma wrapped herself in a cloak, while Hardy made a drawing of Emma, huddled beneath her hood. He recalls her "rainy form" as the "Genius," or Soul, of the spot, although she has not returned there. He wrote on it,

Beeny Cliff, in the rain—Aug. 22, 1870. "It never looks like summer." E. L. G. (on Beeny).

Emma is a distant figure, almost indistinguishable from the landscape. The sketch is now in the DORSET COUNTY MUSEUM. Bailey notes that, since Hardy and Emma did not marry until 1874, it is very likely that she did return to Beeny Cliff in the intervening years.

For further reading: Peck, "Hardy and the Figure in the Scene."

film adaptations of works by Hardy *See* Appendix II, Media Adaptations of the Works of Thomas Hardy.

"Fire at Tranter Sweatley's, The" Ballad thought to be one of the earliest written by Hardy. It was published in the GENTLEMAN'S MAGAZINE in November 1875. Before it was collected in WESSEX POEMS (1898) the title was changed to "The BRIDE-NIGHT FIRE" (Purdy, Thomas Hardy: A Bibliographical Study, 103).

"First Countess of Wessex, The" *See* GROUP OF NOBLE DAMES, A.

Fiske, Minnie Maddern (1865–1932) American actress who had the title role in the New York production of the play of TESS OF THE D'URBERVILLES. Mrs.

Patrick CAMPBELL wanted to play Tess in a LONDON production, which she and Hardy discussed, but Hardy was dissatisfied with the terms and decided to arrange, through HARPER & BROTHERS, for the play to be produced in New York. The novel was dramatized by Lorimer STODDARD and opened in New York on March 2, 1897 (*see* Appendix II, Media Adaptations of the Works of Thomas Hardy).

For further reading: Roberts, *Tess in the Theatre.*

Fitzpiers, Edred Brash and incompetent young physician of aristocratic descent in *The* WOODLANDERS. He has studied at Heidelberg but has little experience with patients. He is given to grisly medical experiments. A dilettante and a philanderer, he has an affair with Suke DAMSON, but then courts and marries Grace MELBURY. Grace is naively impressed by his intellectual and scientific interests, but he mistreats her and has an affair with Felice CHARMOND. He goes abroad with Felice, but returns to Grace, who accepts him, although her father, by this time, has taken his measure.

Fitzpiers, Grace Melbury In *The* WOODLANDERS, the daughter of George MELBURY, a prosperous timber merchant. Her mother died soon after her birth, but her father married the nurse who had cared for her as a baby, to whom Grace has become deeply attached. Although not ambitious herself, Grace has been sent away to school by her father. She comes to look down on her village and, to some extent, on her first suitor, Giles WINTERBOURNE. She meets an untrustworthy physician, Edred FITZPIERS, and marries him, in part because her father encourages it. When she discovers Fitzpiers's adultery, however, she turns to Giles, throwing off "the veneer of artificiality which she had acquired at the fashionable schools." They find that it is impossible for her to obtain a divorce. She hides in Giles's hut; he camps outside, becomes ill, and dies. Marty SOUTH, who has long loved Giles, must mourn him alone, as Grace reconciles with her husband and moves to a distant part of England with him. Hardy wrote of Grace in his autobiography, "the heroine is doomed to an unhappy life with an inconstant husband. I could not accentuate this strongly in the book, by reason of the conventions of the libraries, etc." (*Life,* 220).

"Five Students, The" Published in MOMENTS OF VISION (1917), this poem is a commentary on the fleeting lives of four young people, friends of Hardy's youth, in the context of cyclical seasons. The narrator (Hardy himself) and four others—a "dark He, fair He, dark She, fair She—go "beating by," or walking briskly past, rural scenes throughout each year. Hardy correlates representative seasons with the passing of the students (who were not literally students, but his friends), and they did not die within a single year, but over a number of years.

Spring, when all five are present, brings a sparrow taking a bath in a wheel rut; in summer the air is "shaken" and only four are left; "dark He" is "elsewhere." By autumn another has gone, but the remaining three press on through "moors, briar-meshed plantations, clay-pits yellow." "Dark She" is no longer with them. By the time the leaves have dropped, "fair He" has vanished. When winter comes, bringing icicles, the speaker goes on alone, "The rest—anon."

Critics agree that Horace MOULE, who committed suicide at Cambridge in 1873, is "dark He," as authenticated by a letter Hardy wrote to Charles MOULE, Horace's brother (Millgate, *Thomas Hardy: A Biography*, 153–54). Bailey suggests that the others are T. W. Hooper TOLBERT, "fair He," who died in 1883; Hardy's cousin Tryphena SPARKS, "dark She," who died in 1890; and his wife Emma HARDY, "fair She," who followed in 1912. Hardy himself is the narrator. Bailey solves the problem of the sequence (Tryphena Sparks was the third, not the second, to die) by suggesting that Tryphena was "dead" to Hardy after his 1870 marriage to Emma Gifford. Other critics do not accept Tryphena as "dark She," but believe Hardy meant Emma's sister, Helen Gifford HOLDER, who died in 1900, after Tryphena (Bailey, *The Poetry of Thomas Hardy*, 391–92). She was "dark" and Emma "fair," but she was already married at the time Hardy met Emma, which argues against this conjecture. Emma was not a student when Hardy knew her, but she did copy his manuscripts and advocated his devoting himself to literature.

Florence, Italy *See* ITALY.

folklore One of the most compelling aspects of Hardy's fiction and poetry is the blending of the new science and the superstitions of humble country people. From childhood Hardy undoubtedly absorbed knowledge of local customs and beliefs from elder members of his family. Born into the yeoman class, he was unusually cognizant of the past heritage of England and of DORSET in particular—Celtic, Roman, Saxon, medieval, and Georgian. He developed an interest in architecture and painting at an early age and was able, with a painter's eye, to integrate dramatic scenes of country life and legends in such a way as to illuminate the lives and emotions of the characters.

Many of Hardy's short stories have first-person narrators and are told as though they were taken from oral tradition. This is particularly true of those in WESSEX TALES. For Hardy the regional landscape was a document itself. In "The WITHERED ARM," for example, Hardy explores the implications of the hangman, indigenous to every village jail for many years. The chilling short story "The GRAVE BY THE HANDPOST"

shows the taboo against suicide. A man who has committed suicide is buried by a roadside with a "hurdle-saul," or stake from a sheep pen, through his body. He cannot be moved to the consecrated ground of the churchyard, although his son gives money for the purpose. The son eventually commits suicide himself on the site of his father's grave.

Hardy's novels are also marked by the integration of local legends in the plot. In TESS OF THE D'URBERVILLES, for instance, the landmark Cross-in-Hand, the stone pillar on Batcombe Hill, was known as the "site of a miracle, or murder, or both." Hardy tells the story behind the cross in "The LOST PYX," which concerns a monk from Cerne Abbey who dropped the sacrament in the grass one night, on the way to visit a dying man, and discovered it surrounded by kneeling animals, the spot illuminated by a shaft of light from the sky. The poem "THE OXEN" also encapsulates the folklore science dichotomy in the poetry of Hardy. In FAR FROM THE MADDING CROWD, the shepherd Gabriel OAK, with his flute, is in the tradition of such beings as Pan, with his rural reed, or Edmund Spenser's Colin Clout. Rosemarie Morgan points out that Oak actually does not play the flute well, and does not charm trees, birds, or animals. She argues that Hardy is actually presenting a parody of the "idyll" of Pan, just as, in *The* DYNASTS, he parodies the "Edenic garden" ("Introduction," *Far from the Madding Crowd*, ed. Rosemarie Morgan, Penguin World Classics, 2000, and personal communication with the author). Elements of nature in Hardy's works are powerfully symbolic: the malignant swamp, the dry leaves in the ditch that "simmered and boiled," and the "sheet of fathomless shade" between the hill and the horizon. In *The* RETURN OF THE NATIVE Diggory VENN has been called a "tutelary spirit" of EGDON HEATH. On Guy Fawkes night, bonfires cover the heath; in Hardy's words, "Some were large and near, glowing scarlet-red from the shade, like wounds in a black hide. Some were Maenades, with windy faces and blown hair." Ostensibly, the occasion is the annual celebration (still observed today) of the deliverance of England from the Gunpowder Plot. This was a scheme to blow up the English houses of Parliament on Nov. 5, 1605. One of the members of Parliament was warned by a relative not to attend Parliament that day and the plan was exposed. Guy Fawkes, a leading conspirator, was arrested, and is still burned in effigy on November 5 at bonfires all over the country. In reality the dance originated in antiquity. As Hardy's biographer J. I. M. Stewart explains, "when the rustics of Egdon dance round their blaze on Rainbarrow they are doing as their remotest ancestors did as the days shortened and the iron reign of the *Winterkönig* began" (Stewart, 96). Morgan observes that Diggory Venn, who is purposely stained red, rises from the earth "like a demonic spirit" (personal communication with the author).

In such poems as "The PHANTOM HORSEWOMAN" Hardy writes of a "ghost-girl-rider" seen by a man on a beach who gazes out at sea "in a careworn craze," a vision he carries in his brain day and night. There are myriad figures in his verse who traverse the area between the living and the dying, such as the "red-cloaked crone" of "Signs and Tokens," or the "cowled Apparition" who appears to the couple in "AT THE PIANO" or the spinning "spectres" in "REMINISCENCES OF A DANCING MAN."

Perhaps the most valuable study of folklore in the works of Hardy is the 1931 study by Ruth Firor, *Folkways in Thomas Hardy*. Her meticulous examination of Hardy's novels, short stories, poetry, and drama enables her to codify such recurrent elements under the headings "Omens, Premonitions, and Fatality," "Divination," "Ghost and Fairy Lore," "Magic and Witchcraft," "Folk Medicine," "Weather Lore," "Seasonal Festivals and Customs," "Sports and Pastimes, "Folk-Songs, Country-Dances, and Folk-Drama," "Folk Wit and Wisdom," "Prehistory and Survivals of Ancient Religions," and "Medieval Legends and Napoleonana." She observes that Hardy was told of many beliefs and incidents by the "rustics at the village inn" or by family servants. In her study she treats a wide range of native beliefs and practices as they recur in Hardy's works, such as the hallowing of bells, love divinations using bread and cheese, charms against witchcraft, Druidism, ravens as omens of death, betrothal customs, devil masks, fertility dances, premonitions, and midsummer bonfires.

For further reading: Firor, *Folkways in Thomas Hardy;* Lombardi, "Thomas Hardy's Collecting Techniques and Sources for the Folklore in His Wessex Novels"; Steel, *Sexual Tyranny in Wessex: Hardy's Witches and Demons of Folklore;* Taft, "Hardy's Manipulation of Folklore and Literary Imagination: The Case of the Wife Sale in *The Mayor of Casterbridge.*"

Fontover, Miss   An elderly woman with strict principles, she is the CHRISTMINSTER landlady of Sue BRIDEHEAD in *JUDE THE OBSCURE.* She owns an ecclesiastical artwork shop and is the daughter of a clergyman. She discovers Sue's statues of Venus and Apollo, which Sue has told her are of St. Peter and Mary Magdalen, and destroys them. Sue tells Jude they were "not according to her taste," but she does not tell him who the figures had represented.

"For Conscience' Sake"   Short story published in the *FORTNIGHTLY REVIEW* in March 1891 and then collected in *LIFE'S LITTLE IRONIES* (1894). The story concerns a retired middle-aged banker, Mr. Millborne, a bachelor who lives in London as a lodger and goes every day to his club. One day he is slightly unwell, and his friend Dr. Binden comes in to see him. Millborne confesses that he is dissatisfied about an unfulfilled promise he had made 20 years earlier. In an Outer Wessex town called Toneborough he had proposed to a young girl in a music shop, promised to marry her, and, having taken advantage of her, abandoned her because she was "beneath his position." The memory, years later, still destroys his "self-respect."

The young woman, Leonora, who became pregnant, had left Toneborough and gone to Exonbury under another name, settling there as a music teacher. He believes the child was a little girl. The doctor advises him to give them money, but he feels money would not "rectify the past." The doctor then suggests marriage, but Millborne insists he is content as a bachelor and has no love now for the woman. Nevertheless, if he were to hunt her up it would enable him to "recover" his sense of "being a man of honor."

In time the force of his conscience prompts him to search for the woman in the post office directory. She is still living under her assumed name, having gone abroad to bear the child and returned as a young "widow," Mrs. Frankland. She and her daughter, Frances, teach music and dancing. Millborne leaves Paddington for Exonbury, takes rooms opposite their house, and assesses their character. They are excellent citizens, teaching music and dance and helping at charitable bazaars and other civic undertakings. The daughter plays the organ in church. He sends Mrs. Frankland a guarded note proposing to visit her. No answer comes, but he calls anyway and is admitted by the servant. She receives him cheerfully in the large music- and dancing room, not in a private parlor. He offers to fulfill his promise to marry her, but she refuses; it would "complicate matters" and she has a fair income now. Her daughter is now interested in a young curate, the Reverend Percival Cope, and believes her father is dead and buried. Millborne continues to call, but realizes his attentions "pestered her rather than pleased her." Eventually she relents because the family of the young man who is interested in Frances is put off by her mother's music and dancing business. Leonora and Millborne marry and decide to live in London. Cope continues to call on Frances. However, both Leonora and Frances miss the friends and social life of Exonbury.

The Millbornes and Frances go to the Isle of Wight for a week and Cope visits for a few days. They go sailing, and all but the curate become seasick. Returning in the boat, he notices the resemblance between the father and daughter. He begins to lose interest in Frances. She overhears her parents quarreling and her mother crying about Mr. Millborne's intrusion into their lives. She learns the truth, and she and her mother are anguished about the loss of her suitor and the blighting of her life. Millborne proposes that they leave London and return to a manor house he will rent near Ivell, where Cope lives. Millborne sends them down to the manor house, goes to Boulogne, and has his lawyer write that he is settling a large sum on his wife and Frances. He writes that our "evil actions do not remain isolated in the past, waiting only to be reversed: like locomotive plants they spread and re-root, till to destroy the original stem has no material effect in killing them." He then takes up residence in Brussels, and Frances marries Cope. Millborne succumbs to drink and sometimes must be helped to his lodgings, but is "harmless."

Edward Shanks, writing in *The Saturday Review* in April 1928, called the plot "immoderate and pungently odd" (Gerber and Davis, *Thomas Hardy: An Annotated Bibliography of Writings about Him*, I, 316). This story, like "The SON'S VETO," focuses on the pernicious influence adult children can have on their parents' lives, particularly when the happiness of the mother or father is contingent on reestablishing youthful attachments of which their children disapprove or which might injure their own marital prospects.

Fordington DORSET village on the perimeter of DORCHESTER. In Hardy's day it was dilapidated and shabby. In 1854 the Reverend Henry MOULE, the vicar of FORDINGTON ST. GEORGE CHURCH, endangered himself fighting the historic cholera epidemic, boiling and burning clothes of the deceased. Hardy made use of this epidemic in his short story "A CHANGED MAN," published in 1900, in which a clergyman contracts the disease from the infected clothes and steam. Another Fordington neighborhood, which Hardy called Cuckold Row, figures in *The MAYOR OF CASTERBRIDGE*.

Hardy's home, MAX GATE, completed in 1895, was built on part of Fordington Field (a tract of about 3,000 acres), land owned by the Duchy of Cornwall. It is said to have been a source of pride to Hardy that it was the first sale of land by the duchy to a private owner in many years (Evelyn Hardy, *A Critical Biography*, 192).

Fordington St. George Church Historic church in FORDINGTON, DORSET, near DORCHESTER, of which the Reverend Henry MOULE was vicar from 1829 until his death in 1880. His son Horace MOULE was one of Hardy's closest friends. In 1901 Hardy became a member of the Restoration Committee for Fordington St. George Church. In this capacity he drafted an appeal (1901) assuring potential donors that "no mischief to the architecture" was intended. As restoration plans evolved, however, he felt compelled to withdraw from the committee because he felt the architect, Jem Feacey of Dorchester, was in fact violating the lines of the church. He wrote the Reverend Sidney BOULTER in 1903 that he did not agree with the proposed changes. He would, he remarked, have protested had he seen the plans. He considered the church a "venerable mon-

ument," one so admired by Sir Gilbert Scott that he had sent a man "to measure & make an exact drawing of it for preservation" (*Letters* III, 50).

In 1906 he wrote the secretary of the SOCIETY FOR THE PROTECTION OF ANCIENT BUILDINGS to protest plans to destroy the chancel of the church (*Letters* III, 236). In 1911 he refused to donate to the restoration, writing the Reverend Grosvenor Bartelot that he believed the tower would be "ruined by the extension" (*Letters* IV, 146). In June 1914 his second wife, Florence HARDY, was invited to open a bazaar in aid of the restoration fund. She refused, probably because of Hardy's disapproval of the work under way on the church (*Letters* V, 33). *See also* ARCHITECTURE.

Fortnightly Review British periodical in which many of Hardy's short stories and poems were first published. From 1882 to 1886 it was edited by Thomas Hay Sweet Escott, a journalist. Among Hardy's stories first published there were "FOR CONSCIENCE' SAKE" and "The MIDNIGHT BAPTISM." Many of his best-known poems also first appeared in its pages, including "CHANNEL FIRING" and "The CONVERGENCE OF THE TWAIN." In June 1896 the magazine published an attack on *JUDE THE OBSCURE* by R. Y. Tyrell, which Hardy declared "feeble" (*Letters* II, 123).

France Hardy and his first wife, Emma Gifford HARDY, went to Paris on their honeymoon. He wrote his brother Henry on September 18, 1874, a brief letter, postmarked Brighton, in which he announced their marriage the previous day and said they were on the way to Normandy and Paris, where he was to gather materials for his next story (Evelyn Hardy, *A Critical Biography*, 143). The couple visited Rouen, Paris, and several other continental cities. Parts of *The HAND OF ETHELBERTA* are set in Paris and Rouen. In 1875 Hardy first conceived the idea of writing an epic poem on the war with Napoleon, an idea that eventually evolved into *The DYNASTS* (*Life*, 106).

In July 1880 Thomas and Emma Hardy crossed to France and went to several towns in Normandy, including Boulogue, Amiens, Etretat, and Havre, staying at a hotel on the quay that had been recommended by a "stranger on the coach" from Etretat. They found it "old and gloomy" and "sinister," causing them to hide their cash behind one of their beds in a lumber closet. Nothing happened and they "awoke to a bright sunny morning." Etretat later figured in *A LAODICEAN*; Paula POWER and George SOMERSET become engaged there. The Hardys continued to Trouville, where they stayed at the Hotel Bellevue, and on to Honfleur, which Hardy liked, as it was less fashionable than Trouville. They also went to Lisieux and Caen. Some critics speculate that it may have been in France that Hardy was stricken by an infection that manifested itself later that fall, when he developed bleeding in the urinary tract and, to avoid surgery, spent five months in late 1880 and early 1881 lying on a board with his feet elevated (*see* HEALTH AND ILLNESS, HARDY'S CONCERN WITH).

In the autumn of 1882 the Hardys returned to Paris from WEYMOUTH, via Cherbourg, and took a small apartment with two bedrooms and a sitting room on the left bank of the Seine. They stayed for several weeks, visiting Versailles, seeing the pictures at the Louvre and the Luxembourg museum, shopping for groceries, and dining at small restaurants. In 1887, returning from a stay in ITALY, the Hardys passed through Paris and saw an exhibition of the Crown Jewels.

In June 1888 the Hardys went again to Paris for several weeks; they stayed in the Rue du Commandant Rivière and visited the Salon, attended the Grand Prix de Paris at Longchamps, walked to the l'Etoile "in twilight," saw an exhibition of Victor Hugo's manuscripts and letters, and went to the Archives Nationales. He wrote in the *Life* that "mentally, I seemed close to those keys from the Bastille, those letters of the Kings of France, those Edicts, and those corridors of white boxes, each containing one year's shady documents of a past monarchy" (*Life,* 208–209).

Freedom of Dorchester   On November 16, 1910, Hardy was presented with the "Freedom of Dorchester," a signal honor that towns and cities could extend to distinguished citizens. The tribute might include the presentation of a key on a cushion, evoking the medieval days of walled cities.

Hardy was extremely pleased. In the *Life* he recalled the occasion and reproduced the speech itself. He had noted that the honor appealed to his "sentiment" more than many earlier recognitions of his literary achievements. Although he rarely made speeches, he believed that on this occasion he had given what he termed "perhaps the most felicitous and personal" of the few he had given.

He addressed the Mayor and Gentlemen of the Corporation, and expressed his sincere thanks. He remarked that he felt he had already possessed the "freedom" of the Borough of Dorchester because, "to speak plainly," he had taken liberties with its "ancient walls, streets, and precincts through the medium of the printing press." He observed that his "Casterbridge" was not Dorchester—or even the Dorchester of 60 years earlier—but admitted that when someone had said to him "Casterbridge" was a place "more Dorchester than Dorchester itself" he could not contradict him.

He mentioned the sad disappearance of many buildings, but stated that, after all, "our power to preserve is largely an illusion." The shops he knew as a child were gone, as were most of the people. Only the white stones in the town cemetery represented permanence. He believed the town would become more and more resi-

dential, because, while it was situated near the sea, it was far enough away that in the winter it was protected from coastal winds and cold weather. Dorchester's future, he predicted, would not be the same as its past and the town would surely lose its individuality.

Hardy then stated that he would detain his audience no longer from "Mr. Evans's comedy" that was to be played downstairs. After the formal presentation the audience adjourned for a performance by the Dorchester Dramatic Society of an adaptation of UNDER THE GREENWOOD TREE called The MELLSTOCK QUIRE (*Life,* 353).

Frith, William Powell (1819–1909)   A noted painter whose studio Hardy visited in November 1879. While there they met Sir Percy Shelley (the son of the poet Percy Bysshe Shelley) and his wife, Lady Shelley (*Life,* 133).

Frith's works include *Derby Day* and *Charles Dickens, Uncle Toby and the Widow Wadman* (both in the Tate Gallery, LONDON). He praised Hardy in *My Autobiography and Reminiscences,* vol. 3 (London, 1888). Hardy wrote to thank him for the "very handsome way" in which he was mentioned. He recalled that, much earlier, he had gone to the old Academy rooms in Trafalgar Square and noticed a large crowd surrounding *Derby Day* (first exhibited in 1858). A friend accompanying Hardy told him all he could of the "renowned painter of the Derby Day." He little thought he would ever be known to him personally (*Letters,* 183).

Hardy was a friend of Frith's son Walter, a barrister, who was invited to visit MAX GATE when he was in DORSET for the Dorset Assizes (visiting court) in 1891. He also knew his daughters, the novelist Jane Ellen Panton and Isabelle OPPENHEIM.

Fry, Amos ("Haymoss")   One of the laborers at Welland House, the estate of Lady Viviette CONSTANTINE in TWO ON A TOWER. A rustic agricultural worker and philosopher, he tells Lady Constantine that Swithin has "two stations of life in his blood" so he's "good for nothing." He tells Parson TORKINGHAM, "When a feller's young he's too small in the brain to see how soon a constitution can be squandered." Fry had, in his youth, been refused confirmation because he declared "women and wine" to be articles of his belief.

Hardy's next visit to France was with his brother in August 1890, via Southampton and Le Havre. He noted that he went "solely on his brother's account." They stayed in Paris and went to the Moulin Rouge, near the cemetery of Montmartre, where he looked through the back windows, over the heads of the dancing girls, and saw "the last resting-place of so many similar gay Parisians silent under the moonlight..." near the grave of Heinrich Heine.

G

Galsworthy, John (1867–1933) English novelist and playwright, noted for his depiction of the English upper classes in plays and novels. He was trained as a lawyer, but, on a voyage, met the novelist Joseph Conrad and became interested in writing. He is remembered especially for the series of novels making up *The Forsyte Saga* (1922).

Hardy and Galsworthy had a long friendship beginning about 1906, when Galsworthy sent him a copy of *The Man of Property,* the first volume of *The Forsyte Saga.* Galsworthy often wrote to enlist Hardy's support in various causes, such as a protest against the censorship of plays in 1909 (*Letters* IV, 53). In 1911 he sent Hardy the draft of a protest against the use of airplanes in war. Hardy responded that he thought it "an insanity" that anyone in the 20th century could "suppose force to be a moral argument" (*Letters* IV, 161).

In September 1914 Hardy and Galsworthy were among a group of "well-known men of letters" summoned by the chancellor of the Duchy of Lancaster to Wellington House, Buckingham Gate, LONDON, for the purpose of formulating "public statements of the strength of the British case and principles in the war." Hardy recalled the "yellow September sun" as the group sat around a large blue table, "full of misgivings yet unforeseeing in all their completeness the tremendous events that were to follow" (*Life,* 366).

In 1918 Galsworthy refused a knighthood, but he accepted the ORDER OF MERIT in 1929 and the Nobel Prize in 1932. In January 1918 Hardy passed along a friend's remark that Galsworthy had "scored both ways," having had both the honor of being knighted and the honor of refusing (*Letters* V, 241).

Galsworthy was among a deputation from the Society of Authors who called on Hardy on his 80th birthday on June 2, 1920. In the last chapter of the *Life,* written after Hardy's death by Florence HARDY, there is a mention of a visit to MAX GATE by Galsworthy and his wife on September 6, 1927, as they traveled to London. Hardy told them about a murder that had happened 80 years earlier. He recalled that his mother had said, at the time, "The governess hanged him," and that he was unable to understand her meaning. Galsworthy asked whether he had always remembered his early childhood so clearly, or whether it was only recently; Hardy replied that he had always been able to recall it clearly.

Galsworthy was one of the six pallbearers representing Literature at Hardy's funeral in WESTMINSTER ABBEY on Monday, January 16, 1928 (the others were James BARRIE, Edmund GOSSE, A. E. HOUSMAN, Rudyard KIPLING, and George Bernard SHAW).

"Garden Seat, The" Collected in *LATE LYRICS AND EARLIER* (1922), this poem is a meditation on an ageing garden seat. Once green, it is now "blue and thin"; it will soon "break down unaware." The speaker imagines that at night, "when reddest flowers are black," the ghosts of those who once sat there return: "Quite a row of them sitting there." They are "as light as upper air"; the seat does not break down under their weight, nor does "winter freeze them, nor floods drown." In each of the first two stanzas the final line is repeated; in the third it is partly replicated, giving the poem a lilting air.

Hardy identified the setting as MAX GATE (Purdy, *Thomas Hardy: A Bibliographical Study,* 215). According to Bailey, at some unknown date Florence HARDY wrote Lady Grogan that the garden seats at Max Gate were decaying and their legs were sinking into the ground. The poem has been set to music by Michael Head (London: Boosey & Co., 1933 [Bailey, *The Poetry of Thomas Hardy,* 434]).

Garland, Anne The heroine of *The TRUMPET-MAJOR,* Anne lives with her widowed mother, Martha GARLAND, at Overcombe Mill, near BUDMOUTH. The Garlands rent a portion of the mill from Miller LOVEDAY. Anne does good deeds in the village and reads the newspaper to Squire Benjamin DERRIMAN, an elderly local farmer. Miller Loveday's son John LOVEDAY is in love with her, but she favors his brother Robert LOVEDAY until he becomes engaged to Matilda JOHNSON. Anne is also pursued by the uncouth, predatory Festus DERRIMAN. After John is killed in action in Spain, Anne promises to marry Robert if he behaves for six months. She inherits Squire Benjamin's property.

Garland, Martha In *The TRUMPET-MAJOR,* she is the widowed mother of Anne GARLAND; they live in part of Overcombe Mill for economic reasons. Her husband had been a landscape painter. She marries Miller LOVEDAY.

Garnett, Richard (1835–1906) English librarian, critic, biographer, and chief keeper of printed books at the BRITISH MUSEUM from 1890 to 1899. In 1901 Hardy wrote that he understood Garnett and his wife were coming to MAX GATE in the company of the WHITEFRIARS CLUB. As it turned out, the Garnetts did not come at that time, but Hardy urged them to fix another time so that they might spend a night or two (*Letters* II, 291). In September 1901 Garnett sent Hardy his *Idylls and Epigrams, Chiefly from the Greek Anthology*. When Hardy wrote to thank him, he termed it a "real prize" (*Letters* II, 298). In 1904 Garnett sent him another of his works, *Shakespeare, Pedagogue and Poacher;* Hardy noted that it was with "real disappointment" that he neared the end of the book (*Letters* III, 150). Garnett was also the author, with Edmund GOSSE, of a monumental literary history, *English Literature: An Illustrated Record* (1903–04). Hardy wrote Gosse that it would "take years" for the public to apprehend its value (*Letters* III, 98).

Genoa, Italy *See* ITALY.

"Genoa and the Mediterranean" Poem dated March 1887 and included in *POEMS OF THE PAST AND THE PRESENT* (1902). Before visiting Genoa, the poet has dreamed of the city as "multimarbled Genova the Proud," but his first glimpse is of "housebacks pink, green, ochreous." A slit between them shows the blue sea, but the view is marred by laundry hung out to dry. Such "frippery" mocks the vintage nobility and beauty of the city he expected to find. He tells the city, "I grieve, Superba!" He admits that the "orange bowers" of the noted Palazzo Doria "Went far to mend these marrings of thy soul-subliming powers." Nevertheless, addressing the city as "Queen," he begs that "Those dream-endangering eyewounds no more be/Where lovers first behold thy form in pilgrimage to thee."

Hardy and his wife Emma HARDY visited ITALY in 1887, traveling from Turin to Genoa, first seeing the city from the train. He writes in the *Life* that the palaces they toured "nobly redeemed its character" during their stay (*Life*, 187). At that time the train would have crossed the Ligurian Apennines from Turin, going through 11 tunnels. On arriving at the Station Piazza Principe, looking toward the sea, the Hardys would have seen extensive construction having to do with the improvement of the harbor (Bailey, *The Poetry of Thomas Hardy*, 127).

Gentleman's Magazine Periodical in which one of Hardy's earliest poems appeared—the ballad "The FIRE AT TRANTER SWEATLEY'S," published in November 1875. The title was changed to "The BRIDE-NIGHT FIRE" before it was collected in WESSEX POEMS (1898); (Purdy, *Thomas Hardy: A Bibliographical Study*, 103).

George III, King (1738–1820) The first son of Frederick, prince of Wales, and Augusta, George III married Charlotte of Mecklinburg-Strelitz. He is believed to have suffered from a disease called porphyria, which eventually led to mental instability.

In 1760 George succeeded his grandfather, George II. As king he led Britain through various hostilities, including the Seven Years' War with France and the American Revolution, which ended with the American victory at Yorktown in 1781. The French Revolution (1789–99) precipitated the rise of Napoleon Bonaparte, who seized power in France and began his attempt to dominate all of Europe. In 1804, as Napoleon I, he crowned himself emperor of the French. Although Napoleon was defeated at the Battle of TRAFALGAR in 1805, the Napoleonic Wars continued until Napoleon was deposed in 1814 and decisively defeated at the Battle of WATERLOO in 1815. King George III's political power had decreased before that time, and his rule had come to an end in 1811.

King George III figures in several of Hardy's works, including *The DYNASTS, The TRUMPET-MAJOR*, and "A COMMITTEE-MAN OF 'THE TERROR.'" He founded the ROYAL ACADEMY OF ARTS in 1769.

Gifford, Emma *See* HARDY, EMMA GIFFORD.

Gifford, Gordon (unknown) The son of Emma HARDY's brother Walter Gifford. He and his sister Lilian GIFFORD were frequent houseguests at MAX GATE. Gordon was extremely fond of Hardy, but less so of his aunt, who was given to tirades, especially about *JUDE THE OBSCURE*. He became an architect and worked for the London County Council. Hardy contributed to his educational training, as his father, who had been with the post office, left almost nothing (Millgate, *Thomas Hardy: A Biography*, 391, 436).

Gifford, Lilian (unknown) The daughter of Walter Gifford, and a niece of Emma HARDY. Lilian and her brother Gordon visited the Hardys as children, often spending extended periods of time at MAX GATE. In later life she suffered from mental illness, staying in various lodging houses and visiting Max Gate for long periods. She was a "permanent (if irregular) object of Hardy's charity" (Millgate, *Thomas Hardy: A Biography*, 437).

In 1919, seven years after Emma's death, she was admitted to the London County Council asylum at Claybury in Essex as an indigent pauper, although Hardy had provided an annuity for her. He had also given her some excellent securities, which she had disposed of, buying others that were riskier. He considered having her live at Max Gate when she was discharged, but his second wife, Florence HARDY, and his own siblings all objected strongly. Emma Hardy also showed mental instability in later life (Millgate, *Thomas Hardy: A Biography*, 527–28).

Gifford, Rev. Edwin Hamilton (unknown) The Reverend Dr. Gifford was canon of Worcester, later archdeacon of LONDON, and uncle of Emma Lavinia Gifford HARDY. He officiated at the wedding of his niece and Hardy in September 1874 at St. Peter's, Elgin Avenue, Paddington, London. In 1873 Dr. Gifford married Margaret Jeune, the sister of Sir Francis JEUNE. Hardy was a close friend of Mary JEUNE, the wife of Sir Francis.

Gillingham, George An old college friend of Richard PHILLOTSON in *JUDE THE OBSCURE*. Gillingham does not support Phillotson's decision to let his wife, Sue BRIDEHEAD, leave him for Jude FAWLEY and sees that he will be dismissed because of the scandal. He advises Phillotson to resign first. When Sue remarries Phillotson at Marygreen, Gillingham gives her away. He tells Phillotson he has regretted that he was not more forthright in advising him not to let her go earlier and says, "I shan't be content if I don't help you to set the matter right."

Gissing, George (1857–1903) British novelist, critic, and essayist. His best-known novels are *New Grub Street* and *The Nether World*. He and Hardy first met in LONDON in June 1886. Gissing had asked if he might call on Hardy to discuss the writing of novels. Afterward he sent Hardy his novel *The Unclassed* and wrote that he had "constantly found refreshment and onward help" in Hardy's books (*Life*, 182). The next summer Hardy sent him a copy of *The MAYOR OF CASTERBRIDGE* and added, "You are working on, I know. Do not be induced to write too fast" (*Letters* I, 166). Gissing spent the weekend of September 14 to 16, 1895, at MAX GATE (*Letters* II, 86–87), and in 1899 Hardy wrote to congratulate him on an article he had written for the *Review of the Week* (*Letters*, 235).

Glanville, Louis The brother of Lady Viviette CONSTANTINE in *TWO ON A TOWER*. Once in the diplomatic service, he is a manipulative and somewhat sinister character. He enjoys the luxuries afforded by prolonged visits to Welland House and wants his widowed sister to marry well in order to provide for his own future. When she discovers that her marriage to Swithin ST. CLEEVE is invalid and that she is pregnant, he succeeds in bringing about her marriage to Cuthbert HELMSDALE, the bishop of MELCHESTER, and preserving her reputation.

"God-Forgotten" Poem collected in *POEMS OF THE PAST AND THE PRESENT* (1902). There are 12 stanzas, constituting a dialogue between God and Earth. It is in the form of a dream. The speaker begins by saying, "I towered far" (that is, by falling asleep) and concludes by "Homing at dawn" (waking).

The thesis is that God is indifferent to Earth and has forgotten that he made Earth, or the human race; he is unaware of its "sad" lot. God then remembers making Earth, but believes it has already perished. In any case, he has lost interest, because from the beginning Earth failed to fulfill his aims for it and began alienating God as Creator. On being told that Earth still exists, God states that he hears nothing of it. At one time Earth would ask for "gifts of good," but now it is but a "tainted ball" and the Creator is indifferent to her fate.

Pinion calls the poem "a direct attack on the idea of Providence" (Pinion, *A Commentary on the Poems of Thomas Hardy*, 44). Bailey points out that Hardy's notion that the "Prime Cause is unconscious" recurs in his fiction, notebooks, poems, and the verse play *The DYNASTS*. The Prime Cause is here represented as Earth's Creator, or God (Bailey, *The Poetry of Thomas Hardy*, 150).

"God's Education" Published in *TIME'S LAUGHING-STOCKS* (1909), this poem depicts God as an uncaring being who thoughtlessly causes aging and pain. The speaker is a witness as God steals the light from a girl's eyes, then her color, then her "young sprightliness of soul." He asks God why he acts so—is he "hoarding those her sweets" for another day? God replies that they charm him not; he tells Time to throw them "carelessly away." The speaker protests that mortals term such actions "cruelty." God replies that such a thought is new to him: "Forsooth, though I men's master be,/Theirs is the teaching mind!" Men, although created by God, have developed an ability to make moral distinctions that is beyond what He originally envisioned.

Critics note that the "God" of this poem resembles the one in "NEW YEAR'S EVE," in which God listens to man and sinks "to raptness." He also corresponds to the "Immanent Will" of *The DYNASTS* which, speaking as the Chorus of Spirits, cries, "Consciousness the Will informing, till It fashion all things fair!"—that is, as humans have evolved, they have developed an unexpected capacity for compassion and unselfishness.

"God's Funeral" Poem dated 1908–10 (when Hardy began and finished the poem) and first published in the *FORTNIGHTLY REVIEW* in March 1912 with the subtitle "An Allegorical Conception of the present state of Theology." It was later collected in *SATIRES OF CIRCUMSTANCE* (1914).

The poem presents the startling notion that God is dead. The religion that descended from the Old Testament has not brought about human brotherhood. Hardy had long pondered the thesis presented in the poem, having written Edward CLODD as early as 1897 of "the arrest of light and reason by theology for 1600 years." Five years later, on February 27, 1902, he wrote

Clodd that the element of the "supernatural" (that is, superstition) should be removed from religion altogether, leaving churches and cathedrals as "the centres of emotional life that they once were." Hardy visualizes the supernatural as being replaced by a "rationally acceptable religion." Such a religion would include "loving-kindness" that could improve "man's circumstances." Reviewers, however, saw the poem as an attack on religion. In a passage intended for the *Life,* but deleted, Hardy confesses that in one instance he was "denounced as a blaspheming atheist by a 'phrasemongering literary contortionist'" (the Roman Catholic writer G. K. Chesterton). Hardy was disappointed that the poem was not seen as an effort to formulate a new faith for the new century (Bailey, *The Poetry of Thomas Hardy,* 287–89).

The poem, which has 17 four-line stanzas, opens with a grim vision of a long train of figures across a twilit plain. Described as "scoop-eyed and bent and hoar," they are bearing a "strange and mystic form." The sight prompts sorrow in the watcher as though from "latent knowledge." In the third stanza the shape seems to change to "an amorphous cloud of marvellous size,/At times endowed with wings of glorious range," Yet it has a "phantasmal variousness." The watcher silently joins the moving columns.

Thoughts seem to emanate from the columns. The Figure of God is "man-projected"; how did man create a figure that could not be kept alive? Man's need for solace has caused Man to deceive himself. Time, however, has "Mangled the Monarch of our fashioning," and God has ceased to be. Oblivion has enveloped the myth erected by man, causing humans to "creep and grope/Sadlier than those who wept in Babylon."

The poet recalls the days of his youth, and by implication humankind's youth, when it was "sweet" to "start the wheels of day with trustful prayer." He asks what shall take the place of God now, although some people he has seen on the plain say that God still lives to them. The poet seems to see a "pale yet positive gleam" on the horizon, a "small light," but each mourner "shook his head." The crowd of mourners contains some who are "right good" and many who are "the best." The poet follows mechanically, "dazed and puzzled 'twixt the gleam and gloom."

"Going, The"   Poem written in December 1912 and collected in SATIRES OF CIRCUMSTANCE (1914). The poet addresses his deceased wife, Emma HARDY, who had died suddenly the morning of November 27. Because she had been living in a separate part of MAX GATE he had not been aware of the severity of her illness, although she had been unwell for several days. The morning of her death she had seemed better, but then rang the bell violently. Hardy and the maid rushed to her room but found her gasping for breath; she became unconscious and died before the doctor arrived.

In the poem, Hardy records his devastation that Emma had not been able to bid him goodbye or to give him the "softest call." He still imagines he sees her outside "At the end of the alley of bending boughs/Where so often at dusk you used to be." The prospect of "yawning blankness" sickens him. He recalls their courtship in CORNWALL; he wonders why they did not recall those long-ago days and even plan a visit together in the spring. She could not know, nor could he have imagined, "That such swift fleeting/No soul foreseeing—Not even I—would undo me so!"

The initial motto, *Veteris vestigia flammae* ("Relics of the old fire") is from Vergil's *Aeneid,* IV, 1. 23. It summarizes the theme of the 21 poems in the group "Poems of 1912–13" (Bailey, *The Poetry of Thomas Hardy,* 293). This is one of the most anthologized of Hardy's poems, and is regarded as the central one dealing with Hardy's reevaluation of his marriage to Emma after her unexpected death.

"Going of the Battery, The"   This poem, subtitled *"Wives' Lament (2 November 1899),"* was occasioned by the departure of British troops from the south coast of England for the BOER WAR. It was published in the GRAPHIC on November 11, 1899, and collected in *POEMS OF THE PAST AND THE PRESENT* (1902). Written from the point of view of the soldiers' wives, the seven four-line stanzas recall the tragic march of the troops in the rain toward their departure point. As they drew close, "Great guns were gleaming there, living things seeming there,/Cloaked in their tar-cloths, upmouthed to the night." The women lift their pale faces "for one kiss" and tell the men to be careful. The wives believe all they can do is "Wait we, in trust, what Time's fulness shall show."

The young soldiers had been stationed in DORCHESTER. Hardy wrote his friend Florence HENNIKER that the "scene was a pathetic one" as some of the young men had left "at 10 at night, & some at 4 in the morning, amid rain & wind" (*Letters* II, 236).

Goodman, Mrs.   The widowed aunt of Paula POWER in *A LAODICEAN.* She is in reduced circumstances, and acts as Paula's companion, chaperone, and adviser. She lives with Paula, who is extremely wealthy, at Castle de Stancy, and travels abroad with her before her marriage to George SOMERSET. She has doubts about the advisability of her marriage to Captain William DE STANCY and, all along, favors Somerset.

Good Words   English periodical in which *The TRUMPET-MAJOR* was published from January to December 1880. There were 32 illustrations by John COLLIER for the 12 installments, five of which were full-page (Purdy, *Thomas Hardy: A Bibliographical Study,* 32–33).

Good Words, according to Alvar Ellegard, was a "decidedly religious magazine, of some intellectual pretensions." It appealed to the "lower to upper middle classes of fair educational standards" ("The Readership of the Periodical Press in Mid-Victorian Britain," quoted in Jackson, *Illustration and the Novels of Thomas Hardy,* 21).

For further reading: Ellegard, "The Readership of the Periodical Press in Mid-Victorian Britain"; Jackson, *Illustration and the Novels of Thomas Hardy.*

Gosse, Sir Edmund (1849–1928) Poet, man of letters, librarian to the House of Lords, lecturer in English literature at CAMBRIDGE UNIVERSITY, member of the staff at the BRITISH MUSEUM, and author of a number of biographies and volumes of literary criticism. It is uncertain when Gosse and Hardy met, but in December 1882 Hardy sent him a copy of his novel TWO ON A TOWER; in an accompanying letter he wrote that he was sure Gosse would perceive, even if no one else understood, that his attention was "to make science, not the mere padding of a romance, but the actual vehicle of romance" (*Letters* I, 110).

In June 1883 Hardy dined at the SAVILE CLUB with Gosse; they discussed Ralph Waldo Emerson, Henry Wadsworth Longfellow, and Mark Twain. The next month he and Gosse went to Winterborne-Came-cum-Whitcombe church in DORSET to hear the sermon by the clergyman and poet William BARNES, Hardy's long-time friend and mentor. Afterward, Barnes invited them to the rectory to see his collection of engravings and paintings (*Life,* 160). When Barnes died in 1886, Hardy wrote an obituary notice for the ATHENAEUM; Gosse wrote Hardy that he admired it very much, and believed that he ought to have been a biographer rather than a novelist (Evelyn Hardy, *A Critical Biography,* 46).

Gosse and his wife came to MAX GATE for five days in 1890, soon after Hardy and his brother Henry HARDY had returned from their visit to FRANCE. Gosse took some informal photographs of Hardy, which are blurred but provide one of the few remaining images of Hardy and his first wife, Emma Gifford HARDY.

In 1923 Gosse contributed several paragraphs to an 83d birthday tribute the *Sunday Times* was arranging for Hardy; he saluted Hardy as "the first of living men of letters in the world" (*Letters* VI, 197). Gosse became a regular book reviewer for the paper, which Hardy acknowledged, stating that he and Florence HARDY, his second wife, read his articles each week "& cannot think where your energy to write them comes from" (*Letters* VI, 197). Gosse received a knighthood in January 1925.

In January 1928 Gosse served as one of the six pall-bearers representing Literature when Hardy's ashes were buried in Poets' Corner at WESTMINSTER ABBEY (the others were James BARRIE, John GALSWORTHY, A. E. HOUSMAN, Rudyard KIPLING, and George Bernard SHAW). Gosse died later the same year.

For further reading: Harper, "The Literary Influence of Sir Edmund Gosse upon the Victorian Age."

Gradfield, Mr. Character in DESPERATE REMEDIES. He is an architect at Budmouth-Regis (*see* BUDMOUTH).

Owen GRAYE works for him after the death of his father and introduces a fellow architect in the office, Edward SPRINGROVE, to his sister, Cytherea GRAYE.

Granville-Barker, Harley (1877–1946) Critic, dramatist, drama critic, actor, and director. He wrote a number of plays, including *The Voysey Inheritance* and *The Madras House.* He was noted for his innovative staging of Shakespearian plays, and his *Prefaces to Shakespeare,* written from the director's point of view, is still regarded as a classic. Hardy knew both of Granville-Barker's wives, the actress Lillah MCCARTHY Granville-Barker, whom he had married in 1906 (they divorced in 1918 [*Letters* III, 100]) and Helen Granville-Barker. Lillah later became Lady Keeble, the wife of Sir Frederick William Keeble, a civil servant and scientist, and continued to be a friend of Hardy's. Harley and Helen Granville-Barker saw Hardy and his second wife, Florence HARDY, from time to time at MAX GATE.

In 1914 Granville-Barker proposed to produce selected scenes from *The DYNASTS* in LONDON. Hardy made adaptations and arranged the scenes, adding new dialogue, and composing a new prologue and epilogue. The play opened at the Kingsway Theatre on November 25, 1914, and ran for 72 performances, closing January 30, 1915 (Purdy, *Thomas Hardy: A Bibliographical Study,* 135).

***Graphic,* the** Large-format periodical edited by Arthur LOCKER from 1870 to 1891. Hardy's fiction and poetry appeared in the magazine at intervals over a period of nearly 30 years. The first work to appear was a short story, "The ROMANTIC ADVENTURES OF A MILKMAID," in the summer number, 1883. The short story collection *A GROUP OF NOBLE DAMES* appeared in the Christmas number, 1890. Hardy's novel *The MAYOR OF CASTERBRIDGE* was serialized in the periodical from January to May, 1886, and the *Graphic* began serializing TESS OF THE D'URBERVILLES in July 1891. On November 11, 1899, the *Graphic* published "The GOING OF THE BATTERY," about the departure of troops from DORSET for the BOER WAR. Hardy's poem "The DARKLING THRUSH" was also first published in this periodical (December 29, 1900), as was his poem "The Peace Peal (After Years of Silence)," which appeared in the Jubilee Christmas number on November 24, 1919.

For further reading: Allingham, "Robert Barnes' Illustrations for Thomas Hardy's *The Mayor of Casterbridge* as Serialised in *The Graphic*"; Allingham, "Six Original

Illustrations for Hardy's *Tess of the D'Urbervilles* Drawn by Sir Hubert Von Herkomer, R. A., for *The Graphic* (1891)."

"Grave by the Handpost, The" Story published in the British periodical the *St. James's Budget*, Christmas number, 1897, with four illustrations by George M. Patterson. In America it was published with the subtitle "A Christmas Reminiscence" in HARPER'S WEEKLY in December 1897. It was collected in *A CHANGED MAN AND OTHER TALES* (1913), which was published simultaneously in America by HARPER & BROTHERS.

The story takes place at Chalk-Newton (Maiden Newton) and concerns the choir of the large parish church—larger than the Mellstock string band that figures in UNDER THE GREENWOOD TREE, but not as fine a group. One Christmas Eve the choir gathers by the stone stump of the cross in the village near the White Horse inn. According to tradition, no notes may be sounded before midnight and the official arrival of Christmas morning. They decide to begin at outlying cottages, where there are no clocks, and ascend a hill going to the village of Broad Sidlinch.

They notice a light where the road crosses Long Ash Lane, built on the foundation of a Roman road, and discover a new grave into which a corpse has been thrown by four Sidlinch men. The Chalk-Newton choir members ask the identity of the deceased. They discover it is old Sergeant Holway, who, according to the Sidlinch men, had sent his only son, Luke, into the army, although Luke had wanted to be a mechanic. He was sent to India, but became ill. He wrote his father reproaching him for his advice. The father was deeply distressed and began drinking; he then shot himself.

The Sidlinch men fill in the grave, but do not mark it, and there is no funeral service. Members of the Chalk-Newton choir decide to honor him by "lifting up a carrel [carol] over his grave, as 'tis Christmas." Just as they finish singing and are about to depart, a small horse-drawn carriage rapidly appears, and a young private soldier climbs out. It is Luke Holway, who feels agonizing guilt over having caused his father's death. He is grief-stricken to realize his father did not have a proper burial because he committed suicide. He threatens to do away with himself out of grief, but the men try to dissuade him, saying he should be "worthy" of his father. Luke determines he will move his father's body to "a decent Christian churchyard," even if he has to do it himself. He hopes his father can be moved to Chalk-Newton. The parish sexton, Ezra Cattstock, is a member of the choir, and advises Luke to consult the rector, Mr. Oldham, the brother of Lord Wessex.

Mr. Oldham agrees to the removal if it can be carried out at night. Luke must suddenly rejoin his regiment, but he orders a headstone and trusts Ezra Cattstock to arrange for the removal. Ezra and the rec-

tor learn, however, that the corpse was buried with a six-foot stake through it, although the Sidlinch men won't admit it. They fail to move the body, because the stake makes it clear the dead man was a suicide.

The son returns home, now a sergeant-major. He cannot find his father's grave and learns the body is still at the crossroads. He rents a small cottage at Chalk-Newton. One Christmas he hears the choir singing carols, including the one they sang over his father's grave: "He comes the prisoners to release,/In Satan's bondage held." The next morning Luke shoots himself on the site of his father's grave. He leaves instructions that he wishes to be buried with his father, but the paper is lost and he is buried in the churchyard. The poem points up the effect of powerful religious strictures.

For further reading: Haarder, "Fatalism and Symbolism in Hardy: An Analysis of 'The Grave by the Handpost.'"

Graves, Robert (van Ranke) (1895–1986) English poet, critic, and novelist. His early poems deal with WORLD WAR I, in which he served. His historical novels, notably *I, Claudius* and *Claudius the God* (both 1934), are known for their unexpected, mischievous interpretations of historical characters. He devised his own mythology in *The White Goddess* (1948), and also translated and commented ancient legends in *The Greek Myths* (1955). He lived for many years in Majorca, but returned to England in 1961 to become professor of poetry at Oxford University.

Introduced to Hardy by Siegfried SASSOON, Graves spent a weekend at MAX GATE with his wife, Nancy Nicholson, in August 1920. When Hardy asked about his working methods, Graves said that one of his poems was in its sixth draft and he anticipated writing two more drafts, at least. Hardy said that he never wrote more than three or possibly four drafts of a particular poem "for fear of its 'losing its freshness.'" He told Graves that all poets could do is to "write on the old themes in the old styles" but attempt to better the efforts of "those who went before us" (Millgate, *Thomas Hardy: A Biography*, 534).

In 1923, at the request of T. E. LAWRENCE, Graves wrote Hardy a letter of introduction; Lawrence was subsequently invited to tea at Max Gate.

Graye, Ambrose Character in *DESPERATE REMEDIES*. An architect, he is the father of Owen GRAYE and Cytherea GRAYE. In his youth he had fallen in love with Cytherea Bradleigh (later, Cytherea ALDCLYFFE). His life is blighted by his early love; his "gentle and pleasant disposition" deteriorates into a "moody nervousness." He is improvident and takes his son from school at the age of 17 to work in his office and learn the profession of architecture. One day, as he is supervising the completion of a church spire in Hocbridge, he loses his footing and falls to his death. Too trusting, he has made unwise and insecure investments with his wife's property and leaves Owen and Cytherea with very little.

Graye, Cytherea Heroine of *DESPERATE REMEDIES*. Her figure is almost "faultless." Her specialty is "motion"; she has an innate beauty and gracefulness of movement.

She is impoverished by the death of her father, Ambrose GRAYE, as is her brother, Owen GRAYE. Owen finds a position as an architect, and she lives with him while searching for a position. She takes a post as companion to Miss Cytherea ALDCLYFFE of Knapwater House (actually KINGSTON MAURWARD, near Dorchester).

Graye, Owen Character in *DESPERATE REMEDIES*. A young architect, he is the devoted brother of Cytherea GRAYE. After their impecunious architect father, Ambrose GRAYE, dies, Owen begins working in the architectural office of Mr. GRADFIELD in Creston (Preston, north of Weymouth Bay). He introduces Cytherea to Edward SPRINGROVE, a young architect in his office; they fall in love. Owen develops lameness in his leg; Cytherea marries Aeneas MANSTON in order to secure medical assistance from her employer, Miss Cytherea ALDCLYFFE (whose illegitimate son Manston is). Owen eventually settles at Tolchurch (Tolpuddle), where he superintends church restoration projects for Mr. Gradfield.

"Great Things" Poem published in *MOMENTS OF VISION* recounting a bicycle trip Hardy made, as a young man, to WEYMOUTH, a town on the English channel about seven miles from DORCHESTER (often called BUDMOUTH in his fiction and poetry). He stops at Ridgeway en route, probably at the Ship Inn, "thirstily" (Bailey, *The Poetry of Thomas Hardy*, 378). In Weymouth he drinks sweet cyder (cider), dances until dawn by candlelight, and meets many young women. He hopes that "One will call, 'Soul, I have need of thee.'" If this happens, he anticipates having "Joy-jaunts, impassioned flings,/Love, and its ecstasy."

Part of the first line of each stanza is repeated in the next, a device also used in "A TRAMPWOMAN'S TRAGEDY." Sweet cyder, dancing, and love, are all "great things" to him from his youthful perspective. Whether they "will always have been great things" to him later seems conditional on whether he meets his soul-mate.

Great War, The *See* WORLD WAR I.

Green, Charles (1840–1898) Illustrator and painter, who illustrated Thomas Hardy's story "WESSEX FOLK," which appeared in *HARPER'S NEW MONTHLY MAGAZINE* in 1891. Hardy had written James OSGOOD, the American publisher, recommending Green for the Christmas

story. He believed he had special skill at architecture and could provide such essential visual elements as manor houses, woodland scenery, and clothing of the mid-18th century, when the story is set (*Letters* I, 181).

Grein, Jack Thomas (1862–1935) Dramatist, critic, and theatrical director, born in Holland. He collaborated with C. W. JARVIS in founding the Independent Theatre of London in 1891. They wrote Hardy in 1889 asking permission to dramatize *The WOODLANDERS*, which he granted on condition that "a fair share of profits (if any) be awarded me." Writing from the SAVILE CLUB, he observed that the ending of the novel, "hinted rather than stated," was that the heroine was destined to have an unhappy life with a faithless husband. Hardy had, at the time of writing the novel (1887), been unable to emphasize this point because of "the conventions of the libraries." He left it up to the dramatists how they would treat the ending—either stressing it or obscuring it (*Letters* I, 195). They chose to emphasize Hardy's ending, but the play was never performed.

Group of Noble Dames, A A collection of 10 short stories, published in 1891 and republished in 1896, that, like *WESSEX TALES* (1888), is based on the past of Hardy's WESSEX.

The epigraph, from John Milton's "L'Allegro," is "...Store of ladies, whose bright eyes Rain influence." Most of the tales turn on the cleverness of women in using feminine stratagems to outwit men, although occasionally they become their own victims. The tales reveal a whimsical use of history and are set for the most part in the 17th and 18th centuries. Hardy devised an imaginary reconstruction of the period, using as his principal source John Hutchins's *The History and Antiquities of the County of Dorset*. Hardy had been reading Chaucer before he embarked on the tales, which gave him the idea of stringing them together in a loose narrative, a device also used by Boccaccio (Evelyn Hardy, *Thomas Hardy: A Critical Biography*, 224).

In Hardy's structure, various gentlemen have gathered in a local museum; most are staying overnight for the meeting and are housed in local inns and hotels. Four tales are told before dinner and six after dinner. As in Chaucer's *Canterbury Tales*, each narrator is given a descriptive epithet indicating his profession or place. There is little within the tales that tie them to a particular teller, although sometimes the diction differentiates the teller from Hardy as narrator. An example is in "Dame the Ninth: The Duchess of Hamptonshire," when the teller, the "Quiet Gentleman," speaks of the duke of Hamptonshire, who became obsessed with Emmeline. The Crimson Maltster apologizes for his heroine's lack of a title, "it never having been his good fortune to know many of the nobility."

In his preface to the collection, Hardy explains that the pedigrees of the county families, arranged in diagrams, seem dry at first, but a closer look—even the comparison of dates of births, deaths, and marriages—reveals much. The writer then "finds himself unconsciously filling into the framework the motives, passions, and personal qualities" that account for "some extraordinary conjunction in times, events, and personages" that occur in family records.

Hardy seems to take pride in expressing his gratitude to "several bright-eyed Noble Dames yet in the flesh." Since reading the tales in various periodicals, they have offered "interesting comments and conjectures" on narratives they have associated with their own families. They even gave him outlines of events he might use in constructing further tales.

The information about first serial publication, which spanned the 13 years from 1878 to 1891, was compiled by Purdy (*Thomas Hardy: A Bibliographical Study,* 62–64).

Part First: Before Dinner contains the first four tales; *Part Second: After Dinner* contains the remaining six.

"Dame the First—The First Countess of Wessex"
This story was published in HARPER'S NEW MONTHLY MAGAZINE in December 1889, with three illustrations by Alfred PARSONS and four by C. S. REINHART.

Told by the Local Historian, the tale begins early in the 18th century, on a calm winter night, at King's-Hintock Court, a stately country home. Betty, a girl of 12 or

This illustration, "At the Sow-and-Acorn," by C. S. Reinhart, was published with "The First Countess of Wessex" in Harper's New Monthly Magazine, *December 1889.* (Boatwright Library, University of Richmond)

13, is leaning over the window sill of her bedroom, listening to her parents quarrel over her future. She is "beloved ambitiously" by her mother, Susan, and with "uncalculating passionateness" by her father, Squire Thomas Dornell. Her mother, who has inherited King's-Hintock Court, wishes to betroth her to Stephen Reynard, a man of 30, whom Betty has never met. Reynard is willing to wait five or six years, and the mother argues that through the fortune Betty will inherit and the man's brothers' connections at court he may secure a barony. Her father, furious, rides away to his own estate at Falls-Park, 20 miles away.

He later regrets having abandoned Betty and feels that to "protect her from such a repugnant bargain" he should not have ridden away from King's-Hintock Court. He wishes she were only to inherit his "unassuming" little place at Falls-Park. He would like Betty to marry the 15-year-old son of a close deceased friend. He returns to King's-Hintock Court in order to bring Betty to Falls-Park, but learns that his wife has suddenly taken Betty to London.

Suffering from "intolerable heaviness," he invites some men friends to dinner. One of his friends tells him he has heard that "cunning reynard has stolen your little ewe lamb." His wife has brought about a marriage between Betty and Reynard, but they have parted for a period of five or six years. Squire Dornell falls on the floor with an apoplectic stroke. He does not recover for several days, but then learns the details: that Mrs. Dornell and Betty were walking along a street with the footman behind them, when they entered a shop where Reynard was standing. Betty supposedly said to Reynard, "'I want to marry you: will you have me—now or never?'" The squire assumes the mother engineered the speech so that Betty would not appear to have been forced into the marriage. They bought a ring and went to the nearest church, where the marriage took place. Mrs. Dornell pretends she was surprised the contract should have been carried out so soon, but Reynard was becoming a great favorite at court and would soon become a peer. Mrs. Dornell learns of her husband's illness and announces she is coming back to nurse him.

Dornell immediately returns to Falls-Park. He sends a trusted servant, Tupcombe, to Evershead village, near King's-Hintock, to discover what he can. Tupcombe sits in the village pub, the Sow-and-Acorn, and discovers that Reynard has gone to the Continent and Betty has been sent to school. Betty has not understood her position as the child-wife of Reynard. Eventually Mrs. Dornell comes to Falls-Park and finds the squire in bad health, indulging in stimulants that are bad for him.

After several years Mrs. Dornell brings Betty to see her father. She has returned from school, is now 17, and the marriage is almost a dream to her. She had not even realized the meaning of the ceremony. She overhears her parents discussing it, however, and becomes very unhappy. Dornell brings the young man he had chosen before the marriage, Phelipson of Elm-Cranlynch, to see Betty. Betty is love-struck. A few months later Mrs. Darnell and Betty go to Falls-Park, and Betty is dispatched to wander about the grounds while they discuss Reynard's eagerness to claim his bride. Mrs. Darnell sees her outside, talking with young Phelipson, but pretends she has not seen her. Reynard writes that he has landed at Bristol and is coming for Betty.

Betty locks herself in her room, but her mother takes her out for a drive. Betty asks to stop at a cottage where there is a girl ill with smallpox. Distracting her mother, she runs in and kisses the girl. She seems not to be infected. Squire Dornell, meanwhile, learns of Reynard's approach and, in ill health, orders that his horse be saddled, and rides to the inn where Reynard is staying. The squire argues that Betty is too young for Reynard to claim her as a bride, and Reynard insists he is going to King's-Hintock. The squire and Tupcombe slowly make their way back to Falls-Park, but the Squire is too ill to continue. Tupcombe rides to King's-Hintock, arriving to see Charley Phelipson assisting Betty from her room by a ladder; they ride away. Tupcombe delivers the squire's letter to the servants' quarters. Reynard is coming to claim Betty.

Mrs. Dornell discovers Betty's escape, encounters Reynard on his way to Falls-Park, and says he must not call for her yet but may spend the night at King's-Hintock. At Falls-Park she confesses to the squire that Betty has eloped with Phelipson, and he dies happy, saying "'She's her father's own maid! She's game!'" Betty and Phelipson, meanwhile, reach a small inn, where they find that Betty is becoming ill with smallpox. Phelipson takes her back home; he is afraid of being infected. Betty climbs up the ladder and cries in her room. Later she goes down to the dining room and discovers Reynard there. He realizes her condition but kisses her anyway; she goes to bed and Reynard rides for the doctor. The doctor predicts a light case for Betty. Reynard, meanwhile, returns to London and begins courting Betty by mail. He lets her know that he is to receive a barony, and after a few years he will become an earl; she could then be the countess of Wessex. He offers her his heart a third time. Mrs. Dornell says they must wait until Betty is 19, as she is still in mourning for her father. Phelipson is sent to see his parents. Betty assists her mother in arranging for the church of King's-Hintock village to be rebuilt in the squire's memory, and slowly matures. Her mother realizes Betty is pregnant, and Betty confesses she has met her husband at Casterbridge. Mrs. Dornell summons Reynard, who comes as soon as the promised title has been granted and he can address her as "My Lady." They have many children and she becomes, eventually, first countess of Wessex.

This tale has been told by a local historian at a meeting of the South-Wessex Field and Antiquarian Club. Those present agree that the subject of the next tale should be a lady. A member who is a surgeon says he is sure the historian must know many "curious tales of fair dames, of their loves and hates, their joys and their misfortunes, their beauty and their fate." The parson observes that the surgeon himself seemed most likely of all to be "acquainted with such lore." He undertakes to tell the next tale, "Barbara of the House of Grebe."

"Dame the Second—Barbara of the House of Grebe"
This tale was published in the GRAPHIC in December 1890.

Narrated by the Old Surgeon, the tale concerns young Lord Uplandtowers' pursuit of Barbara Grebe, the daughter of Sir John and Lady Grebe, a neighboring couple. At the time, he is 19 and she is 17. He goes to a ball at their home, but Barbara disappears early in the evening. He sees carriage lights disappearing almost as soon as he arrives, but he lingers, to be polite, until midnight, and returns home. The next morning her father comes to ask him where she is. He has no idea, but tells him about the retreating carriage lights. Sir John tells him he suspects Edmond Willowes, son of the widow of a glass painter. Barbara sends a letter confirming the news and declaring her love for Edmond and her fear of being encouraged to marry Lord Uplandtowers. Her indulgent parents agree to send Edmond to the Continent for a year with a tutor, so that his education and polish will be equivalent to hers. He and the tutor depart. He writes from Pisa that he has commissioned a sculptor to make a bust of himself in marble, which is then extended to a full-length statue. Barbara, meanwhile, is busy overseeing the renovation of a small residence nearby her father is providing. While there she sees Lord Uplandtowers riding past.

After 14 months, Edmond is preparing to return home, but he writes that he has been caught in a theater fire in Venice and suffered severe burns. He is disfigured and has lost the sight of one eye. Barbara writes that she accepts her fate and will meet him at the Lornton Inn, where they had met the night of their elopement. He does not appear, and Lord Uplandtowers offers her a ride home. Edmond returns home wearing a flesh-colored mask. When it is removed, she is horrified at his disfigurement. She runs out to the greenhouse before he comes upstairs. When she steels herself to return, she finds he has left for another year. Barbara gives up her little house and moves back to live with her parents. Lord Uplandtowers is a frequent visitor. After a few years they are married. The sculptor writes to say the statue is finished, and she orders it sent to her. Meanwhile, news comes that Edmond has died of an ailment on the Continent. She stands before the statue frequently, but when her husband objects, she has it enclosed in a recess. She continues worshipping the statue in secret until he finds out about it.

Lord Uplandtowers locates Edmond's former tutor and discovers the exact nature of Edmond's injuries in the fire. He then chisels the statue to look the same. Barbara faints. He then has it moved to the foot of their bed and forces her to look at it every night until she is "cured" of her obsession. Over time she has 11 children, only one of which, a girl, survives to maturity. Lord Uplandtowers takes his wife abroad for her health, but she dies there. Later, the sixth earl enlarges the hall and finds fragments of the statue; it "seems to be that of a mutilated Roman satyr" or "an allegorical figure of Death."

The rural dean thanks the surgeon, and says his tale is a "far more striking one" than any he can hope to tell, but he can also offer a story about a lady who has married beneath her.

"Dame the Third—The Marchioness of Stonehenge"

This tale was published in the *Graphic* in December 1890.

Narrated by the "Rural Dean," the story begins with a reference to a classical mansion near MELCHESTER (Salisbury). Lady Caroline lives there, the daughter of an earl, a beautiful young woman who is saturated by the attentions of young noblemen and gentlemen who live in that part of Wessex. She is attracted to the son of the parish clerk, "a plain-looking young man of humble birth and no position." He directs tree-felling and the laying-out of fish ponds. Although he is at first surprised by her interest, he falls in love with her and they secretly marry.

At first they are supremely happy, although they must meet secretly. She realizes, however, that they have little in common socially, and becomes anxious. One night he suddenly dies of heart failure in her room. She almost calls her mother, but realizes she will suffer the "social consequences of her rash act." She manages to drag him down the stairs, outside, and to his father's door, where she leaves him. She returns safely home.

The next morning the news of his demise gets about, and, since his heart condition had been known, his death is accepted. After the funeral, however, it is rumored that a man returning from a horse fair had seen, in the gloom, a woman dragging the body to the door. The marks on the ground are evidence of his being dragged along.

Lady Caroline resolves to continue her cover-up, and she searches for Milly, the young daughter of a woodsman who had loved her husband before they were married. She finds her in mourning. They meet at his grave and she tells Milly of the marriage. Milly has been humiliated in the village for her unrequited love. Lady Caroline says she may have him in death anyway:

she asks Milly to say she was his secret wife, that he had visited her in her cottage the night of his death, and she had dragged him to his house. She is also to say that, using Lady Caroline's name, they were married in Bath. Milly shudders at the idea of becoming a "corpse's bride." Lady Caroline says if she will agree to this, she will always be her friend and her father's friend, but if not, it will be "otherwise."

Milly makes her confession and it is accepted; she becomes "possessed with a spirit of ecstasy at her position. "Lady Caroline gives her the wedding ring as well as funds to buy the "garb of a widow." Milly erects a tombstone and visits the grave every day. Lady Caroline becomes jealous of Milly's position as the widow and asks her to return the ring. She tells Milly she is pregnant and that Milly must recant and tell the truth about the marriage. Milly, however, has now come to regard the young man as her husband and refuses to do so. She loved him and mourns him, she tells Lady Caroline, and is his true widow. Her "character" is worth as much as Lady Caroline's. Lady Caroline sympathizes with Milly, and the two decide that their strength lies in union.

Lady Caroline confides in her mother and the two go away to London. Milly goes to London a little later. The public story is that she has gone to a watering-hole because of her "lonely and defenceless widowhood." In a few months Milly comes home with the baby and a few months later settles in a cottage of her own, courtesy of an allowance from Lady Caroline and her mother.

Lady Caroline marries the marquis of Stonehenge, but has no children. Her son grows up and loves Milly devotedly; he looks much like his father. Lady Caroline does not offer additional help to Milly, who struggles to send him to the grammar school, and at 20 he joins the army and rises in the regiment. Lady Caroline hears of his success. Now that the marquis has died she wishes to see her son again. She drives to the barracks and sees him from a distance. Her motherly emotions are awakened and she berates herself for having given him away. She decides to announce herself to him as her mother and is sure he will be glad to have a peeress instead of a cottager for a mother.

Lady Caroline tells Milly she must give him up. She says she will "avow" her first marriage, and that he is her own "flesh and blood." Milly is contemptuous. The young man is summoned; he has always known there was something mysterious about his birth, so is not as surprised as he might have been otherwise. Lady Caroline offers herself as his mother. He declines, saying "you cared little for me when I was weak and helpless; why should I come to you now I am strong?" He says that Milly tended him from birth, watched over him, nursed him when he was ill, and deprived herself of comforts for his sake. Moreover, since Caroline was once ashamed of his father, who was "a sincere and honest man," he is now ashamed of her.

She asks him to kiss her, which he does, but coldly. His denial of her adds "fuel to the fire of her craving for his love." She dies of a broken heart, having refused the "consolations of religion."

In an afterword, the rural dean draws a moral lesson from the story, saying it is an unfortunate example of the way "honest human affection" can become "shame-faced and mean under the frost of class-division and social prejudices." The "sentimental member" of the group says Lady Caroline's plight deserves some pity but that of her offspring deserves more: There is no pathos like that of an unwanted child. He offers a tale on the same theme, but with a different outcome.

"Dame the Fourth—Lady Mottisfont"

This story was published in the *Graphic* in December 1890.

Told by the "Sentimental Member," the story takes place in Wintoncester (Winchester). This town is described as the most convenient in Wessex "for meditative people to live in," as the cathedral has a long nave and chapels behind which one can saunter. Sir Ashley Mottisfont marries Philippa, his second wife, in the cathedral. When he proposed, he told Philippa that he had a ward, a small girl 15 months old whom he had found "in a patch of wild oats." Philippa promises to do all she can for Dorothy, the child. She is suspicious of her origins, thinking the child must be his, but Dorothy becomes attached to her, and Philippa asks if they may rear her in their own home. He is pleased and assents. She becomes devoted to the child.

One day Sir Ashley receives a letter from a lawyer to whom, years ago, he had mentioned the child. At that time he had asked whether he might know of a lady who was anxious to adopt a child. Philippa is alarmed as she realizes how attached she is to Dorothy. They soon discover that Fernell Hall, the manor house of the adjacent estate, has been leased by an Anglo-Italian countess. Her husband dies, but the countess, her mourning period over, is expected to remarry. Philippa discovers that it was she who wanted to adopt Dorothy. She sees the child and announces that she would still like to adopt her. Philippa protests that she and Sir Ashley can adopt her legally. She calls on the countess, finding that she speaks several languages fluently and is beautiful.

Philippa goes home, frantic, and inspects Dorothy's face. She sees her husband's traits there. Dorothy has become almost her only source of happiness. The Bath season approaches, and Sir Ashley, Lady Philippa, and little Dorothy go there, as does the countess, who is sought by many men. Then the countess snatches Dorothy from danger; while she is out with her nurse, the wall of a house being remodeled begins to collapse. The countess

wants to keep the child. Sir Ashley suggests they should give Dorothy to the countess since she saved her.

Philippa tells Sir Ashley she knows of Dorothy's parentage: she believes she is the child of Sir Ashley and the countess. She asks Dorothy whom she prefers, and Dorothy chooses the countess. Philippa agrees to hand her over, but when they return to the country, she tries to kill herself. Sir Ashley rescues her and takes her to the north of England to recuperate. When they return they find the countess is to be married again and is willing to return Dorothy. By this time Philippa herself is pregnant, and presents a son to Sir Ashley. She no longer pines for Dorothy. Sir Ashley takes Dorothy to the cottager who had raised her as a baby, but she misses the luxury of her other two homes. The countess has other children and Philippa is preoccupied with her son. "Doubly desired and doubly rejected," Dorothy marries a road contractor and finds the "nest which had been denied her by her own flesh and blood of higher degree."

The churchwarden says the tale reminds him of an instance of paternal, rather maternal, affection, which he proceeds to tell after the group has had dinner.

"Dame the Fifth—The Lady Icenway"

This story was published in the *Graphic* in December, 1890.

Told by the churchwarden, the story opens in the reign of GEORGE III. A young lady, Miss Maria Heymere, an orphan, lives with her uncle, Mr. Heymere, between Bristol and the city of Exonbury. One day she goes riding, with a young lad as an attendant, and in a minor mishap slips to the ground. A young gentleman, Mr. Anderling, owner of a plantation in Guiana, is visiting in a nearby house. He comes out to see about her and assists her home.

He becomes fascinated by Maria and prolongs his visit in England. They become engaged and are married. Maria leaves her uncle's home and goes to LONDON with her husband; later, they go to Guiana.

On the voyage he confesses he had had an earlier, unhappy marriage to a woman with a scandalous reputation. He had hoped his wife might have died, but, in London, he has discovered she is alive. He is "wretched and shattered in spirit." Maria insists that he pretend to have died on the voyage and permit her to return to England. He gives her a considerable sum in bonds and jewels. At Paramaribo he says he will turn over all his landed possessions into personal property and wander the earth in remorse for her.

Maria returns to her uncle's house in widow's garments. She tells him the truth, but all others believe Mr. Anderling has died. She eventually has a son. She meets a worthy man, Lord Icenway, and marries him. She moves to his seat beyond Wintoncester, at the other end of Wessex from her home. While Lord Icenway is away, she receives a letter from Anderling saying that his wife has died in Quebec and he is coming to England, where they can be legally married immediately. Lady Icenway sets off to meet him and finds that he has become a man of "strict religious habits, self-denying as a lenten saint," very different from the way he once was.

She informs him she has remarried and tells him about the child. Anderling is shocked that she would remarry so quickly and feels a growing tenderness for the child, whom he has never seen. Lady Icenway returns home and says nothing to her husband. She sees Anderling's features in the face of her child, however. One day Anderling hides in the bushes and throws a note wrapped about a stone at her feet. He has lost all his wealth and longs to speak a word to his son once in his lifetime. She asks him to return another day and takes him in to see the child taking a nap. He kisses the child without waking him. All his emotion is now centered on the child who does not know him and the woman "who had ceased to love him."

Anderling applies himself to tulip horticulture, becomes an expert, and is hired by Lord Icenway's chief gardener. Lady Icenway decides it is wiser not to expose him, and he is given a small cottage by the garden-wall. He gives up Roman Catholicism for Anglicanism and goes to church every Sunday, sitting behind Lady Icenway, her husband, and her son. Anderling then falls ill. She nurses him in his little cottage, and he dies. She erects a stained-glass window in his memory, and has it inscribed *"by his grieving widow."* Lord Icenway, when he sees his stepson, becomes very morose at not having a son. He says it is "a very odd thing, my lady, that you could oblige your first husband, and couldn't oblige me." She murmurs, "Ah! if I had only thought of it sooner!"

Some members of the group find Anderling's fate a hard one, but others disagree. The Bookworm remarks that her husband was very unsuspicious, but then Lady Icenway was very "close-mouthed." Had she been more reckless, her lord might have been suspicious, as in the case of the lady at Stapleford Park in their great-grand-fathers' time. The "crimson man," a retired maltster, tells the tale of the owner of Stapleford Park, who had acquired the mortgage to it and other stately properties by moneylending.

"Dame the Sixth—Squire Petrick's Lady"
This tale was published in the *Graphic* in December 1890.

Told by the "Crimson Maltster," the story concerns Timothy Petrick, who was an attorney skilled at lending money to people guaranteed by their title deeds. As an old man, he has vast estates, including the manor of Stapleford and others. His son is deceased, but he has two grandsons, the elder of whom is married and expecting a child. One grandson, Timothy Petrick, has

a son, but his wife, Annetta, becomes ill and is about to die. She tells Timothy the child's parentage is not what he believes. She dies, and Timothy begs his grandfather to alter his will; he executes another one leaving his estate to Timothy's later male heirs and to the heirs of Edward, the other grandson.

Timothy Petrick plans to marry again immediately, but has become embittered by his wife's infidelity. He has Rupert, the little son his wife left, brought up in the house, but hardly notices him until one day he sees him playing with a snuff-box. He sees his wife's countenance in the child's face. He becomes very fond of Rupert, but then realizes "Rupert" is the name of the young marquis of Christminster, son of the duke of Southwest-erland, and believes the marquis is the boy's father. He loves him even more because of his noble blood. Eventually he lives only for Rupert. Edward, his brother, becomes engaged to the Honourable Harriet Mount-clere, daughter of a viscount, but her title is inferior to Rupert's proper one. He comes to feel that his wife was wise to choose a superior father for the child.

Eventually, however, Timothy fails to see "ducal lineaments" in Rupert. He chances to meet a Budmouth physician who asks whether Timothy had noticed any delusions on the part of Annetta. He tells him about Rupert's paternity, and the doctor says such a story is exactly the "form of delusion" he would have expected from Annetta during a physical crisis. Her mother and grandmother also had hallucinations. Timothy discovers that Annetta's confession could not have had a basis in reality, as the young marquis had gone abroad a year before Timothy's to her marriage. She had an ideal love for the marquis.

With this knowledge, Timothy becomes cold toward Rupert, feeling he lacks the "glory and halo" his brother's children have. He sees the marquis one day and admires his "noble countenance." He asks Rupert why he is only a "commonplace Petrick," when he should be like the marquis. Rupert says he is not related to the marquis, and his father growls he "ought to be."

The group agrees that "such subtle and instructive psychological studies" are highly desirable. The colonel reflects that frequently events causing a lady's action "to set in a particular direction" continue to "enforce the same line of conduct," but she, "like a mangle," suddenly takes a "contrary course" and ends "where she began." The listeners sense a worthwhile story in his words, and the colonel adopts a "good narrative pose" and tells the next tale.

"Dame the Seventh—Anna, Lady Baxby"
This story was published in the *Graphic* in December, 1890.

Told by the Colonel, the story takes place during the Civil War at Sherton Castle, seat of the earls of Severn. The earl and his eldest son, the young Lord Baxby, are away from home raising forces for the king. Lady Baxby, the son's wife, along with friends and servants, remain in the besieged castle, but without a sense of danger.

A nobleman, William, also commands the Parliamentary forces, but he appears sad and depressed. It turns out that Anna, Lady Baxby, is his sister, and he cannot bear to "point his ordnance" at the walls of the castle. He sends a messenger to her requesting that she steal away from the castle by a little gate to the south and make her way to the residence of some friends. Suddenly he sees her coming from the castle on horseback with an attendant. He is greatly alarmed at her risking such an approach when his forces might have inadvertently fired upon her. He clasps her in his tent and she asks why he supports the "disloyal cause." He begs her to come away and save her life. She refuses and prepares to return to the castle, saying if he destroys it he will find the bones of his sister underneath.

He is indecisive and anxious and fails to aim his weapons at the castle. His sister, meanwhile, is feeling sympathetic toward the Parliamentary forces. General Lord Baxby arrives in the evening with reinforcements. William retreats to Ivell (Yeovil), four or five miles away. Anna and her husband quarrel over William's political position, which seems increasingly reasonable to her. Lord Baxby, exhausted, goes to bed and she sits brooding by the window. She thinks of William sleeping outside in the cold. She rises, writes on a slip of paper, *"Blood is thicker than water, dear William—I will come,"* disguises herself in her husband's hat and cloak, and slips down the stairs. A woman stands in the shadows of the outside wall and says "Here I be!," suggesting that Anna's husband is her lover. Anna is furious. She perceives her husband as "wicked," though she had always deemed him "the soul of good faith." She retreats up the staircase and hisses through a loophole, "I am not coming!" She says she hates the woman and all her "wanton tribe." Then she creeps back upstairs, "firmly rooted in Royalist principles." She locks the door, puts the key under her pillow, and ties some of her husband's long hair locks to the bedpost. He wakes in the morning to find himself "strangely tethered" but his "rage" is not great. He had apparently flirted with a young woman at a crossroads and invited her to the castle, but then had forgotten about it.

Subsequently Lord and Lady Baxby get along very well. After several years the castle is besieged, but the women have been safely removed. The surrender of the old place is "a matter of history, and need not be told by me," according to the Colonel.

The Man of Family asks whether the Colonel had heard a well-authenticated, though "less martial," tale of Lady Penelope, who lived in the same century and less than a score of miles from the same place. The Colonel has not heard it, nor have the others.

"Dame the Eighth—The Lady Penelope"

This tale was published in *LONGMAN'S MAGAZINE*, January 1890.

Told by the Man of Family, the story begins in a manor house on the road between CASTERBRIDGE (DORCHESTER) and Ivell (Yeovil). It is the seat of the Drenghards. Near here, in the reign of the first King James, Lady Penelope, a beautiful lady of a noble family, is visiting. Her three leading suitors include Sir George Drenghard, a member of the ancient noble family; Sir John Gale; and Sir William Hervy. They are avid in intercepting her in rides and walks, and their attention sometimes leads to bitter rivalry. A duel is threatened, but she tells them she will not speak to any of the three responsible for breaking the peace. She tells them to have patience and jokes that she will marry them all in turn.

Lady Penelope first chooses the eldest of the knights, Sir George Drenghard. Within three months he dies of his "convivialities." Sir John Gale and Sir William Hervy remain. She thinks of Sir William with more fondness, but Sir John Gale presents himself first. He has been created a baronet. Sir William hesitates to put forth his suit, thinking it would be indelicate. She accepts Sir John and they are married just as Sir William is on his way home from a foreign court to propose to her. Sir John is cruel to her and says she is not worth the trouble he went to in winning her.

Several years later, Sir John is in bed with a slight ailment. From the window Lady Penelope, to her surprise, sees Sir William Hervy approaching. They meet outside; he has heard rumors of her unhappiness. When she goes inside, Sir John wants to know whose voice he heard outside. She admits it was that of Sir William. He is furious, works himself into a state, and dies two weeks later.

Lady Penelope wonders where Sir William is, but she does not hear from him for nearly a year. He returns and proposes; eventually she marries him. He overhears some basketmakers suggest that she poisoned Sir John. He returns home having "aged years," and a "ghastly estrangement" begins. He goes abroad. She gives birth to a stillborn child and begins losing her health. He comes home and she pleads her innocence, then dies. A physician tells Sir William that Sir John died from purely natural causes. Lady Penelope has been killed by "a vile scandal that was wholly unfounded." Sir William survives her by only a few years. People say Lady Penelope had "shown an unseemly wantonness in contracting three marriages in such rapid succession."

The listeners agree that her fate "ought to be quite clearly recognized as a chastisement," and the quiet gentleman sitting nearby declares he knows an instance in point.

"Dame the Ninth—The Duchess of Hamptonshire"
This tale was published under the title of "The Impulsive Lady of Croome Castle" in *Light*, April 6 and 13, 1878.

Told by the Quiet Gentleman, the tale begins with a description of the rather unfeeling duke of Hamptonshire, the fifth to hold the title. He cares little about "ancient chronicles in stone and metal," but much about the "graceless and unedifying pleasures" made possible by his position. His castellated mansion sits on ten thousand acres of fertile land screened by many plantations.

The parish rector, the Honourable and Reverend Mr. Oldbourne, is a widower, stiff and unsympathetic. The curate, Alwyn Hill, is a "handsome young deacon with "curly hair" and "dreamy eyes," who looks about 19, although he is 25. Emmeline Oldbourne, the rector's beautiful daughter, has a "sweet and simple nature" and "a natural inappetency for evil things." The duke sees Emmeline shortly after she turns 17 and falls in love with her. He goes home as though he has seen a "spirit" and decides Emmeline must be his.

Emmeline and the curate, however, have a secret understanding. Her father sends the curate away amid Emmeline's sobs, and she and the duke are married. That night the bell ringers discuss Alwyn, who had been a favorite of theirs. It becomes clear to the duke that Emmeline still loves Alwyn. One night Alwyn returns and meets Emmeline in the shrubbery. He is emigrating from Plymouth. She tells him the duke is torturing her in the hope of making her admit she has been in touch with Alwyn. She wants to escape with him but he says it would be "sin" and refuses.

On his sea journey aboard the *Western Glory* to America Alwyn tries to repress his regrets. He lands in Boston and eventually obtains a position in a college as professor of rhetoric and oratory. After nine years he reads in the newspaper of the death of the duke of Hamptonshire, who has left a widow but no children. By the time Alwyn can leave Boston more than a year has passed, but he returns to England. He finds the duchess giving a ball, but to his astonishment she is not Emmeline. On making inquiries, he finds that Emmeline supposedly left the duke and ran away with the young curate. He finds evidence from an old waterman, who says she boarded the *Western Glory* in Plymouth. He tracks down the sea captain, who says she did sail aboard the ship but was traveling among the poorest class and died five days into the voyage. He then dimly recalls that there had been a death among the steerage class passengers and, because of the fear of disease, the victim was buried at sea. Alwyn had officiated, as there was no chaplain on board.

He realizes that Emmeline must have followed him through the darkness "like a poor pet animal that will not be driven back." He returns to America; but, before

leaving, he tells the story to an old friend. The friend is the grandfather of the narrator of the story.

The Spark announces that, for his part, he prefers a story with an ending in which "such long-separated lovers" are ultimately united.

Most of the listeners are impressed by the Quiet Gentleman's tale, but the Spark walks about and says he prefers something more lively, one in which long-separated lovers are "ultimately united." The members request a specimen, and he obliges.

"Dame the Tenth—The Honourable Laura"
This story was published in the *Bolton Weekly Journal*, September 17, 1881.

The last tale in the group, this story is narrated by the Spark. It begins in the Prospect Hotel, situated on the wild northern coast of Lower Wessex, on a cold, snowy Christmas Eve. A small carriage arrives with two passengers, a very young lady and a foreign-looking man of about 28. They order dinner, but before they finish a second, larger carriage draws up, carrying an elderly gentleman and a younger one. The gentleman is Lord Quantock, in search of his daughter, Laura, and the man with whom she is traveling; the young man is his nephew, Captain James Northbrook. When they are shown into the presence of the first couple, Lord Quantock commands her to come home, but she refuses. Her cousin, James, insists rather strongly, and confesses that he is entitled to order her home because she is his wife. Lord Quantock gives up persuading Laura to return home and leaves. She creeps into another bedroom at the inn.

Signor Smittozzi, Laura's companion, argues with James about her, finally challenging him to a duel. They slip out of the hotel and begin descending along the winding cliff walk toward a chasm one hundred feet below. Smittozzi suddenly pushes James over the cliff, climbs back to the hotel, and escapes with Laura, telling her James has returned home and will have nothing more to do with her. At the tollgate a pedestrian is telling the gatekeeper that two children witnessed the accident and are sure that the man was pushed. Laura realizes the truth and, at the first opportunity, escapes to the Prospect Hotel. James is brought in on a stretcher; he is seriously hurt but she begins nursing him, and, after a few weeks, he seems to be recovering. He takes no interest in her, regarding her only as a nurse.

Lord Quantock dies. James accompanies Laura to the funeral, but refuses to live with her as her husband. "I don't like you," he says, and disappears. Laura rejects all suitors and lives alone in the house she has inherited. Just before Christmas on the 12th year of her solitude, when she is 30, a pedestrian comes to her home in heavy rain. The man asks at the kitchen door if he may dry off, which the cook allows. He learns that

Laura lives in complete loneliness. He then goes to the front door, where a manservant admits him, knowing nothing of his visit to the kitchen. He requests that the servant tell the Honourable Mrs. Northbrook that "the man she nursed many years ago, after a frightful accident, has called to thank her." Laura comes to James, "trembling and pale," and they embrace.

At Christmas, the once "forlorn" home of Laura Northbrook blazes "from basement to attic with light and cheerfulness." Within another 12 months they have a son, a welcome addition to "the dwindled line of the Northbrook family."

The members thank the Spark, who is surprised, for no one had "credited him with a taste for tale-telling." The members of the Field-Club disperse to their lodgings. Their next meeting would not be until summer, months away, and, meanwhile, other interests and preoccupations would supersede the "easy intercourse which now existed between them all." When they have all departed, the museum attendant lowers the fire and the curator locks the room. Soon there is only a "single pirouetting flame" on a single coal to "draw a smile from the varnished skulls of Vespasian's soldiery."

For further reading: Ray, "Hardy's 'The First Countess of Wessex': A Textual Anomaly"; Marroni, "The Negation of Eros in Barbara of the House of Grebe"; Summer, "Hardy Ahead of His Time: 'Barbara of the House of Grebe.'"

Grove, Lady (Agnes Geraldine) (1863–1926) Author and political activist, wife of Sir Walter Grove, Baronet, and daughter of General and the Hon. Mrs. Pitt-Rivers. She and Hardy met in 1895, and he advised her on literary matters.

In September 1895, after he had sent the revised manuscript of *JUDE THE OBSCURE* to his publishers (it had already been serialized), Hardy and his wife, Emma Gifford HARDY, went for a week to Wiltshire, where they stayed at Rushmore, the stately home of General and Mrs. Pitt-Rivers. Hardy recalls in the *Life* that the evening scene "was one of extraordinary picturesqueness and poetry." Hundreds of couples danced on the grounds, which were illuminated by Vauxhall lamps and a full moon. Hardy and Mrs. Grove began the country dancing. Although he had, as he recalled, been "passionately fond of dancing" in his youth, this was "the last occasion on which he ever trod a measure" as he was left "stiff in the knees" for some time (*Life,* 269).

In November 1895, the month *Jude the Obscure* was published, Mrs. Grove asked him to review a response she had written to an article, "Why Women Do Not Want the Ballot," by the bishop of Albany, N.Y., which had appeared in the *North American Review.* He returned it immediately, apologizing for marking it "in a perfectly brutal manner," and stating it was better toward the end than the beginning but might be condensed. He was sure she would not object to his frankness, realizing that in literature the competition is "keen & ruthless" (*Letters* II, 92)

In 1899 Lady Grove sent him her article on objections to woman suffrage, and he responded that it was a "forcible piece of rhetoric. Indeed, I don't know any woman-writer who puts such vigour into her sentences as you do. … [it] makes me proud of you as a pupil." He congratulated her on her "steady advance as a writer & thinker" (*Letters* II, 226).

She continued to write, eventually publishing *The Human Woman, On Fads,* and *The Social Fetich.* The latter work, published in 1907, was dedicated to Hardy.

She wrote Hardy a letter of sympathy when Emma Hardy died in 1912, to which he replied at length, and sent him warm wishes in 1914 on his marriage to Florence Dugdale (HARDY).

For further reading: Hawkins, "Concerning Agnes."

Gruchette, Miss Character in *The HAND OF ETHELBERTA.* She is the mistress of Lord MOUNTCLERE, the husband of Ethelberta PETHERWIN (later, Lady Mountclere). She lives with two servants in an ornamental cottage in his forest, supposedly tending his fowls. She is finally dismissed by Mountclere.

Guide to Dorchester In July 1902, Thomas Hardy was invited by the Dorchester Recreation Committee to write the introduction to the forthcoming *Guide to Dorchester.* He wrote the town clerk declining the invitation, but stating that he had "said a good deal about Dorchester, under the pseudonym of 'Casterbridge,'" over the preceding 20 years and that he could add nothing more. He gave the editor full permission to quote from *The MAYOR OF CASTERBRIDGE,* which would, he believed, produce a "better effect on readers" than anything he would be able to write specifically for the publication (*Letters* III, 28).

H

"Had You Wept" Published in *SATIRES OF CIRCUM-STANCE* (1914), this poem depicts the "deep division" between a man and a woman because she has refused to weep. She would not approach him "Dewy as the face of the dawn, in your large and luminous eye" after certain "tidings" have "slain that day." If she had, she could have smoothed "the things awry." He wonders whether she is unable to cry, or whether she has refused the "gift" of tears. Because of her deep contained feelings, her "torrid sorrow" has been given no "balm." As a result they both have "dark undying pain."

Hardy's biographers agree that the poem is personal in nature, but are uncertain who the woman might be or what the tidings were. Evelyn Hardy suggests that the woman is Florence HARDY. Lois Deacon takes the subject to be Tryphena SPARKS, who had been courted by Horace MOULE; he was unaware of her relationship with Hardy. Carl Weber believes she might be Emma HARDY, who was jealous of other women. James O. Bailey suggests that Hardy himself was "stubborn" when resisted, but "quick to yield" when conscious of causing pain (Bailey, *The Poetry of Thomas Hardy,* 317–18).

A fourth explanation could be related to Emma's deception of Hardy before they were married. According to Michael Millgate, Florence Hardy believed that Emma had trapped Hardy into marriage, probably by telling him she was pregnant (Millgate, *Thomas Hardy: A Biography,* 130). Emma's sister, Helen HOLDER, had been a party to the scheme. In this case, a possible explanation for the "tidings" might be her confession that she was not.

Hand of Ethelberta, The Novel first published serially in *CORNHILL MAGAZINE* (July 1875–May 1876) and then published in 1876. It is a social satire that in recent years has received more serious critical attention than it did in the early 20th century, although it is still regarded as rather frivolous.

The novel concerns the attempts of a woman, Ethelberta PETHERWIN, to climb into high society, a society Hardy sees as basically corrupt. She is the strongest of a family of 10 children, whose mother is an invalid and whose father is a butler. She is dominated by her concern for her family, who are actually doing very well in the country, with good jobs; she moves them to LONDON. Hardy describes her as having a gift "for demure-

ness under difficulties without the cold-bloodedness which renders such a bearing natural and easy, a face and hand reigning unmoved outside a heart by nature turbulent as a wave."

Compared to his depiction of rural England, which Hardy knew first hand, his scenes set in London have been thought by some critics to lack authenticity. F. B. Pinion suggests that, by writing social satire, Hardy was answering critics who had compared *FAR FROM THE MADDING CROWD* with the work of George ELIOT. *The Hand of Ethelberta* apparently came as a disappointment to the *Cornhill's* publishers. However, Hardy had not yet been able to gauge public reaction to *Far from the Madding Crowd,* which he had completed just before marrying and going on a brief wedding trip to FRANCE. He was committed to writing novels, but at the time was unsure where his strength lay. Pinion argues that Hardy's knowledge of the upper classes was too limited at this time for him to undertake the genre of "artificial comedy" with any success, although Oscar Wilde or George Bernard SHAW might have handled the theme well (*A Hardy Companion,* 8, 16, 28–29). As Hardy expressed it in the *Life,* he "constitutionally shrank from the business of social advancement, caring for life as an emotion rather than for life as a science of climbing" (*Life,* 53).

The epigraph on the title page, "*Vitae post-scenia celant*" ("They hide the back-stage activities of life") is from Lucretius's *De Rerum Natura,* book four, and refers to women who, in R. E. Latham's translation, "are at pains to hide all the back-stage activities of life from those whom they wish to keep fast bound in the bonds of love" (*The Hand of Ethelberta,* ed. Toru Sasaki [London: J. M. Dent, 1998], 367). The characters are members of society and family servants, and the novel depicts views of the drawing-room from "back-stage"— that is, from the servants' hall.

SYNOPSIS

Chapter 1: "A Street in Anglebury—A Heath Near It—Inside the "Red Lion" Inn"
Ethelberta, a young widow, and her mother-in-law, Lady PETHERWIN, the widow of Sir Ralph Petherwin, arrive at ANGLEBURY, an old WESSEX town. Ethelberta meets Christopher JULIAN, a former acquaintance. Her untrustworthy maid, Louisa MENLOVE, declares she saw

no one following her, although she herself has spent the afternoon dressed in a fancy hat and jewelry, being courted by a young waiter.

Chapter 2: "Christopher's House—Sandbourne Town—Sandbourne Moor"
Christopher Julian, who lives with his sister, Faith JULIAN, receives an anonymous book of verse, *Metres by E.*, sent by Picotee, a shy girl who is the village teacher. She appears to be a friend of Ethelberta's for whom she does favors. Christopher locates Picotee, but she refuses to tell him the writer's name. They see each other often on the moorland road near SANDBOURNE (Hardy's name for BOURNEMOUTH).

Chapter 3: "Sandbourne Moor (continued)"
Picotee waits in the rain on the chance of seeing Christopher; she is seen by the painter Eustace LADYWELL and his friends, who have been hunting and have taken shelter in a roadside hut.

Chapter 4: "Sandbourne Pier—Road to Wyndway—Ballroom in Wyndway House"
Christopher and Faith Julian are invited to play (Christopher on the piano, Faith on her harp) at an aristocratic evening party at Wyndway House. They are screened from the guests by artificial trees. Christopher sees Ethelberta dancing with many men; he does not know she is a widow, or that she has been instrumental in his invitation to play.

Chapter 5: "At the Window—The Road Home"
It is dawn when the party ends; the Julians are startled to see a beautiful sunrise over the sea when they peep through the curtains after they finish performing. Christopher learns that Ethelberta is a widow.

Chapter 6: "The Shore by Wyndway"
Ethelberta gives Picotee a parcel of gifts for her mother, and a packet of money for her expenses. Picotee is upset to learn that Christopher was once in love with Ethelberta and nearly faints. Ethelberta equivocates about her feelings for him.

Chapter 7: "The Dining-room of a Town House—The Butler's Pantry"
A fashionable London gentleman named John DONCASTLE gives a dinner party; Ladywell attends, along with Alfred NEIGH, Doncastle's nephew. They discuss a recently published volume of verse, *Metres by E.*, which has attracted much critical attention. R. CHICKEREL, the butler, listens avidly; some of the guests note his intelligent look and interest in the verse read. He then writes to Ethelberta, who is his daughter.

Chapter 8: "Christopher's Lodgings—The Grounds about Rookington"
Christopher reads *Metres by E.*, but is unsure whether Ethelberta wrote the book or sent it to him. Faith

thinks the author must be a "nice fast lady," although not a "bad fast lady." Christopher plays his sister Faith an air he has composed to one of the songs in the volume. He then goes to see Rookington Park, where Ethelberta is staying. He sees a man (Ladywell), apparently also waiting to see her. He sees a newspaper article revealing her identity as the author of *Metres by E.*, and sends her the tune he has composed.

Chapter 9: "A Lady's Drawing-rooms—Ethelberta's Dressing-room"
Ethelberta attends an evening party in a house on Hyde Park. Neigh is there, and asks who she is. Mrs. Napper, a middle-aged guest, says she admires her poems. Neigh says he has not read them but knows he must. They discuss poems set to music; Ethelberta says her favorite is one that has reached her that morning, by an "unheard-of man" who lives somewhere in Wessex. Ethelberta sings the song. She writes Christopher and tells him about her father, then throws the letter in the fire and writes another one without mentioning him.

Chapter 10: "Lady Petherwin's House"
Lady Petherwin says Ethelberta has tarnished her son's memory by publishing her book of "ribald verses." She asks Ethelberta to suppress the poems. Ethelberta refuses. She burns her will but repents and sets out for the office of Mr. Chancerly, her attorney.

Chapter 11: "Sandbourne and Its Neighborhood—Some London Streets"
Christopher Julian believes he can earn a living from his music in London and persuades his sister Faith to move there; she observes that "Mediocrity stamped 'London' fetches more than talent marked 'provincial.'" Christopher searches for Ethelberta, but she has gone to France. He then learns of the death of Lady Petherwin in SWITZERLAND and discovers that Ethelberta has moved to Arrowthorne Lodge, Upper Wessex, not far from Sandbourne.

Chapter 12: "Arrowthorne Park and Lodge"
Christopher goes to Arrowthorne Lodge, a small cottage, where he finds Ethelberta living with Picotee, who turns out to be her sister; their bedridden mother, Mrs. CHICKEREL; and a large family of younger siblings.

Chapter 13: "The Lodge (continued)—The Copse Behind"
Christopher discovers Ethelberta in the woods telling the younger children stories she has made up. She informs Christopher that after Lady Petherwin's death she has been left with nothing but the lease of the London house on Exonbury Crescent, although Lady Petherwin had written a letter of intent that she should have £20,000. Her brother, however, had refused to honor it. She has given up poetry and now plans to become a professional storyteller.

They see Mr. Ladywell and Lord MOUNTCLERE going to a party at the principal house on the estate. Christopher learns that Ladywell has sent some of his sketches to Ethelberta.

Chapter 14: "A Turnpike Road"
Christopher is seen off by Ethelberta's brothers Sol CHICKEREL, a carpenter, and Dan CHICKEREL, a house painter.

Chapter 15: "An Inner Room at the Lodge"
Mrs. Chickerel is incapacitated by a "spinal complaint." Her 10 children crowd around her. She has given the seven girls romantic names, and Mr. Chickerel has given the boys traditional names. Ethelberta plans to move them all to London and take in lodgers from the Continent. Her siblings will be her staff. Mr. Chickerel will be glad if they move to London. Picotee, though, will remain in Sandbourne as a teacher.

Chapter 16: "A Large Public Hall"
Ethelberta gives her first performance in London, attended by Ladywell, Neigh, and Christopher and Faith Julian. Ladywell tells Neigh he is in love with Ethelberta. Ethelberta is regarded as a "new sensation," like a "spirit-medium, aëronaut, giant, dwarf, or monarch," and receives newspaper notices. Journalists praise her personal appearance, but say she is conscious of "form and feature" as being "vehicles of persuasion."

Chapter 17: "Ethelberta's House"
The Chickerels are established on Exonbury Crescent. Christopher calls and is shown by Joey CHICKEREL to the drawing room. Ethelberta is there, "the most self-possessed woman in the world." She shows him the house, the walls of which her brothers are decorating with flowers, birds, mice, and spiders. They ask Christopher and Ethelberta not to be seen lingering and talking with them, since they don't want to "bring down" Ethelberta's "gentility"; she has risen to a better class. Her sister Emmeline CHICKEREL is conducting an attic school for the younger children. Christopher tells her that her storytelling has been one of the successes of the London season. Ladywell calls, to Christopher's discomfort. It turns out that Ethelberta is sitting for him for her portrait. Picotee writes, wishing to return to London from Sandbourne, but Ethelberta refuses, saying she has better career opportunities in Sandbourne.

Chapter 18: "Near Sandbourne—London Streets—Ethelberta's
Picotee cries when she receives the letter. She has always obeyed Ethelberta but realizes she is in love with Christopher. She resigns her post and goes to London anyway. She goes downstairs, where Gwendoline CHICKEREL the cook and Cornelia CHICKEREL the housemaid welcome her. Sol and Dan, the "mechanics," have been to their lodgings in Marylebone and "made themselves spruce as bridegrooms." Picotee overhears Ethelberta and Christo-

pher murmuring in the drawing room. After the evening meal Ethelberta comes down to teach Joey and her sisters French. She pretends to welcome Picotee.

Chapter 19: "Ethelberta's Drawing-room"
Ethelberta complains to Picotee that Christopher has not visited her. She does not suspect Picotee's interest in him.

Chapter 20: "The Neighbourhood of the Hall—The Road Home"
Ethelberta comes out from the hall where she has been telling stories and mingles with the crowd; she hopes Christopher has been there, but he has not. Ladywell returns her notebook, which she had dropped. He praises her triumph and tries to express his strong feelings for her, but she repulses him and goes home in her carriage with her "maid" (Picotee). Picotee asks about Ladywell. They arrive home to find Christopher has called, having forgotten Ethelberta is telling stories. She writes him to ask him not to call so often, as the "frequency" has been noticed.

Chapter 21: "A Street—Neigh's Rooms—Christopher's Rooms"
Ladywell and Neigh stroll home from Ethelberta's performance. Ladywell says Ethelberta has refused him. Neigh also loves Ethelberta, but does not tell Ladywell. Christopher Julian returns home to Bloomsbury, to the "little place" he shares with his sister Faith, and complains about Ethelberta's treatment of him. He finds that Faith has attended the storytelling, walking there alone. He confesses that he went to the hall when he thought the performance would be over and saw a man give Ethelberta something. Faith says nothing, but does not admire Ethelberta.

Chapter 22: "Ethelberta's House"
Ethelberta has attended the boat races with Mrs. BEL-MAINE, a society friend. She and a friend have been rowed across the river for a better view, but the boatman could not land them; he returned them to another location. Neigh has been sent by Mrs. Belmaine to rescue them. Picotee gives Ethelberta a letter from Christopher. He is coming that afternoon despite her request; Ethelberta reacts with "glad-displeasure" and resolves to write him not to come, but is irritated that he didn't come the day when he obeys her message; she goes to her room with a headache. Christopher calls on Ethelberta the next day. She sends Picotee to him, instructing her that she will come down only if he says he "must" see her. The drawing-room fire goes out and the room is almost dark when Picotee enters. Christopher kisses her hand, mistaking her for Ethelberta. Picotee bursts out sobbing. He realizes, from her reaction, that she is in love with him. Picotee says Ethelberta loves Ladywell, but then tries to retract her statement and says Ethelberta loves Christopher.

Ethelberta has come down and overheard them; she worries about Picotee.

Chapter 23: "Ethelberta's House (continued)"
Picotee tells Ethelberta she is in love with Christopher; she had met him when she delivered Ethelberta's book of verses to him. Ethelberta tries to talk to her mother and sisters, but is unable to do so. She sees in Picotee her own weaknesses but not her strengths. She assures Picotee she does not really want Christopher and will help her capture him; then, when Picotee leaves, she begins crying and decides to confide in Gwendoline. She has been to see their father, but he seems so unsympathetic that she says nothing. Ethelberta feels disloyalty to her "class and kin." Her mother worries that they will be found out and laughed at. Ethelberta feels they are on the verge of a catastrophe.

Chapter 24: "Ethelberta's House (continued)—The British Museum"
Ethelberta realizes her storytelling is becoming less popular. She is becoming more "impersonator" than a "poetess out of her sphere." She tells Picotee the only way out for the family is to marry; she is entitled to the house for only two more years.

Christopher tells Ethelberta he is going to Melchester (Salisbury) to be assistant organist at the cathedral. He says he cannot become engaged to her without better financial expectations for himself. Ethelberta dismisses him as a prospective husband without intending to do so, and he agrees without meaning to do so. Picotee comes in and invites Christopher to kiss her like a sister. They agree that Picotee and Faith will write and keep each other posted. Ethelberta and Christopher admit, however, that they experience "mutual gravitation" toward each other. He finds Faith in the BRITISH MUSEUM; lost in Assyrian antiquities, she returns to the present long enough for Christopher to tell her his news. She has seen, at the ROYAL ACADEMY OF ARTS, Ladywell's painting of Ethelberta as a lady wooed by a knight—perhaps himself; she is unsure.

Chapter 25: "The Royal Academy—The Farnfield Estate"
Ethelberta takes Sol and Dan to the Royal Academy exhibition. She instructs them in sophisticated behavior. They view Ladywell's painting, which has attracted a crowd of viewers. It is not original but is "happily centred on a middle stratum of taste." She overhears a rumor that Alfred Neigh intends to marry her. That night she hears the younger children, in the attic, conclude that she is a fairy, with silk dresses and other things they don't have. She longs to train their little minds but thinks it impossible without money. She and Picotee go secretly to evaluate Neigh's estate, Farnfield. There is a grand gate and a sweeping road, but instead of a house there are only starving horses, who will be killed to feed the hounds they hear baying from a ken-

nel. They talk to a local man, who tells them Neigh is a "woman-hater" and leases half the property to a brother of Lord Mountclere to use for the kennel. She resolves never to marry him, even if he proposes, which he has not.

Chapter 26: "Ethelberta's Drawing-Room"
Dan and Sol take Picotee, Georgina, and Myrtle CHICKEREL to Kew Gardens for the afternoon. Dan and Sol are acquiring London "airs and manners," but still prefer the companionship of their younger sisters to casual acquaintances.

Mr. Neigh comes to call. He has found out about Ethelberta's visit to Farnfield and proposes to her. She rejects him, but he doesn't give up.

Chapter 27: "Mrs. Belmaine's—Cripplegate Church"
Ethelberta, Neigh, and others go to the church of St. Giles, Cripplegate, to see the tomb of John MILTON. Ethelberta reads passages from *Paradise Lost.*

Ladywell joins the party, not realizing Neigh has been courting Ethelberta. He sees Neigh and notices he has petals of a Harlequin rose; Neigh tells him they are petals from his intended wife. Later, when they see Ethelberta in the churchyard, she has the stem of the rose with missing petals. Ladywell realizes Neigh has been courting Ethelberta and leaves. Neigh is irritated that Ethelberta has not accepted him. Mrs. Doncastle is impressed with Ethelberta and wants to introduce her to a friend of her husband's, Lord Mountclere. Ethelberta accepts, but is very anxious. Her father, Mr. Chickerel, the Mountcleres' butler and her "dearest relative," will be at the dinner; she wonders how her encounter with him can be made "safe and unsuspected."

Chapter 28: "Ethelberta's—Mr. Chickerel's Room"
Ethelberta is puzzled about Neigh and uncertain of her own mind, having become somewhat disillusioned with him. She wants a well-to-do husband who can and will support her large family and leave her free to organize her talent and assist them as well. She still has "plenty of saleable originality" in her. She believes Neigh would never accept her family. She worries also that her father is not better placed. She thinks of several other occupations he might have, such as a country stationer, or a registrar of births or deaths. She only has 18 months before giving up the lease of her house. She learns that Joey, her young brother, is in love with a new maid at the home of the Doncastles.

Ethelberta tells her father she wants him to have a better position. He says he has been in service 37 years and it is an "honourable calling." She says she would like to drop the "Mrs. Petherwin," return to their little cottage, and be "Berta Chickerel" again. She confesses that she is coming to the dinner to meet Lord Mountclere. Mr. Chickerel warns her against him, as he knows his valet. The maid Joey loves turns out to be Louisa Menlove, who is much older than Joey. Menlove rushes in and out, wearing different costumes; Ethelberta tells her Menlove had once been her own maid as well as Lady Petherwin's, and is very flighty. Her father will take Joey in hand.

Chapter 29: "Ethelberta's Dressing-room—Mr Doncastle's House"
Picotee dresses Ethelberta for the dinner and confides that Faith Julian has invited her to visit them in Melchester; she is eager to do so in the future. Ethelberta says the London weather is bad for the children and they should go to Knollsea, a coastal village near Melchester. She wants to get a copy of her aunt's register of baptism (her mother's sister, Aunt Charlotte, Madame Moulin, keeps a hotel in Rouen, the Beau Séjour). Picotee comes to the Doncastles' house; she is met by Jane, one of the maidservants, and smuggled in. Menlove comes to see Picotee and says she knows about her father (but she has not yet connected him with Ethelberta). Picotee gazes down on the people and praises Ethelberta, her "dear mistress." Lord Mountclere is very aged. Menlove shows Picotee around the house and, in one of the drawing rooms, begins dancing with a young footman. Picotee does not join in. Menlove eavesdrops on the men lingering at the table after the ladies have withdrawn. Neigh tells a much embroidered tale of Ethelberta's and Picotee's visit to his "estate." Picotee is hurt on Ethelberta's account. Joey comes for Menlove, but Mr. Chickerel prevents him from seeing her.

Chapter 30: "On the Housetop"
The next morning Ethelberta goes to Picotee's room; they step on to the parapet to watch the sunrise. Ethelberta claims Lord Mountclere is so entertaining that she forgets his age. She tells Neigh they are going to Knollsea, and Lord Mountclere overhears her. He says he will be at Enckworth Court when they are at Knollsea; the Imperial Archaeological Association will be meeting at Corvsgate Castle, near Knollsea. She tells Picotee that Lord Mountclere has proposed; Picotee advises her to choose Ladywell instead. She tells Ethelberta about Neigh's repeating the story of their visit to his estate, and Ethelberta is mortified. She vows she will never marry him.

Chapter 31: "Knollsea—A Lofty Down—A Ruined Castle"
Ethelberta and her family go to Knollsea, where they stay in the house of the boatmen, whose wife looks after all of them. Hiring a donkey from a boy, she rides along a ridge called Nine-Barrow Down to attend the meeting of the Imperial Archaeological Association at Corvsgate Castle. She ties the donkey to a stone protruding from a wall and ascends high up to the inner ward of the castle. There she finds many carriages and ladies and gentlemen looking down at her donkey, who is grazing. Lord Mountclere greets Ethelberta, and introduces her

to the others. She is a "town phenomenon" known for her poetry and her storytelling. They are wondering how the donkey arrived at the castle, but Ethelberta will not explain. She sees Neigh. Dr. Yore begins reading a paper on the history of the castle.

Some of the party plan to go on to Knollsea, but Ethelberta fears they will see the children and declares she is going to Cherbourg by steamer and on to Rouen. Neigh proposes again and says he will come to Rouen for an answer. Lord Mountclere invites them to lunch at Enckworth Court, but Neigh declines, as he is going on to London; Ethelberta declines also, and remains to sketch. A young man climbs to the castle and leaves, without seeing Ethelberta. She remounts her donkey and returns home.

Picotee tells her Christopher Julian has been to Knollsea and accompanied her and her sisters to the beach. It is he she has seen in the distance. Ethelberta says she is going to see their Aunt Charlotte in Rouen and will take Sol and Don so they can see Paris. Picotee doesn't want to go, so Ethelberta decides to take Cornelia as her maid.

Chapter 32: "A Room in Enckworth Court"
At Enckworth Court, Lord Mountclere's valet, Tipman, tells Mountclere that Ethelberta is the daughter of a butler, which he has learned from Menlove. Lord Mountclere plans to sail his yacht to Cherbourg and go on to Rouen and Paris.

Chapter 33: "The English Channel—Normandy"
The steamer *Speedwell* calls at Knollsea for passengers to Cherbourg, including Ethelberta. A schooner-yacht follows the same course; it is identified as Lord Mountclere's *Fawn*. Ethelberta opens a letter she has forgotten from her father. Joey has revealed that the butler is his father. He and Menlove had been in the park when his father tried to talk to him privately. Menlove withdrew, but Joey identified him as his "old man." Ethelberta wonders if it is worth trying to marry again, but decides it probably is, for the sake of her family.

The next morning, as she and Cornelia are getting railway tickets, she sees Lord Mountclere and his valet. Ethelberta detects, by his not altogether respectful manner, that he knows something about her. Ethelberta declares she is going to Paris the next day, but will tour Rouen first. She asks the name of his hotel, which is not her aunt's establishment. Madame Moulin welcomes Ethelberta; her late mother-in-law had once told her she was the only "respectable relative" she seemed to have.

Chapter 34: "The Hôtel Beau Séjour and Spots Near It"
Mrs. Chickerel writes Ethelberta and tells her Menlove has "wormed everything out of poor Joey." She advises her to marry before Menlove exposes her. She has given Ladywell her address in Rouen. Ethelberta tries

to free herself of Lord Mountclere but he finds her at the cathedral and, though out of breath, climbs to the parapet of the tower, which is foggy. He says he had made the climb years ago and found it not worth repeating, but declares he is only "too happy to go to any height" with Ethelberta. She leads him far up in the spire, where it is still foggy, but then it clears, revealing the other spires throughout town and the surrounding valleys. Descending, she recognizes Neigh's voice. She tries to avoid him, but finally tells Lord Mountclere she and Neigh are not engaged. Lord Mountclere asks to call upon her, and she says she will receive him in a month in London. He returns to his hotel, sends her a note, and then drives there.

Chapter 35: "The Hôtel (continued) and the Quay in Front"
At the Beau Séjour, Ethelberta asks M. Moulin whether Mr. Neigh has called for her. He has, and her aunt told him she had gone to the cathedral. Mr. Ladywell also has come. Ethelberta assures him he has not been forgotten. Ladywell refuses to be discouraged. She asks him to wait for a month. Neigh returns to the hotel and is also asked to wait a month. Lord Mountclere comes to the hotel and she sees Neigh in a small drawing room with a window; Neigh and Ladywell both overhear their conversation from the windows of the separate rooms where they are waiting. Each leans from his window; they see each other; they meet in Neigh's room; they both write notes to Ethelberta.

They find a wine shop and sit drinking and "denouncing womankind." Ladywell leaves for Dieppe. Back at the hotel, Sol and Dan have arrived from England with a homemade portmanteau in an accordion style, at which the French guests are amused. Ethelberta appears; Lord Mountclere has proposed, but she has not accepted him, thinking his circle might despise her. She considers marrying Christopher, who will be a middle-class music master. She has no wish to marry Neigh or Ladywell. She sends Sol and Dan off to Paris and resolves to think things over in Knollsea.

Chapter 36: "The House in Town"
Ethelberta returns to London, intending to let utilitarian philosophy help decide her course of action. Leaving Picotee at Knollsea, she goes to Exonbury Crescent and discusses her situation with her parents. Menlove has taken a vow of secrecy which Mr. Chickerel does not understand, but Ethelberta says it makes no difference.

Her plan is to rent the London house to lodgers, managed by her mother and older sisters, while she goes to Knollsea and stays with Picotee. She is planning to become a schoolmistress. She lays out a tedious plan of study for herself and Picotee. Her parents are aghast, and are unable to understand why she does not continue writing poetry or telling stories. She tells them she wants to be free of "the great" and find

Illustration by George du Maurier for The Hand of Ethelberta, *chapter 31 ("So Ethelberta went, after a considerable time pondering how to get there. . ."), published in the* Cornhill Magazine, *January 1876*   (Perkins Library, Duke University)

peace. Mrs. Chickerel wonders if someone has been insulting her. She tells them, obliquely, that she has had an offer of marriage that seems tainted. Her mother protests against her plan, saying it is not necessary to make herself miserable trying to get a high position on their account, but, at the same time, she does not need to rush to "the other extreme and go down in the scale."

Ethelberta retires and thinks things over, deciding to reject Ladywell and Neigh but reconsider Lord Mountclere. She reads a tract on casuistry and decides to tell him the truth.

Chapter 37: "Knollsea—An Ornamental Villa"
Ethelberta goes back to Knollsea. Picotee gives her letter from Lord Mountclere, who wishes to call on Ethelberta. She tells Picotee they must move to a more elegant house. They move in to a villa and she sends word to Lord Mountclere that he may call on her there. They dress and wait for him, but he does not come. They hear the coastguardsmen sending up rockets to practice for shipwrecks. Picotee goes to the launch site, thinking Lord Mountclere might be there. She returns, having seen Christopher Julian. He has told her of a carriage accident in which an old gentleman had a sprained ankle; he has stopped to assist him. Ethelberta is sure it must be Lord Mountclere. He writes a week later to say he had suffered an accident, but would like to invite her to Enckworth Court. She decides to accept.

Chapter 38: "Enckworth Court"
Ethelberta goes to Enckworth Court and tells the story of her own life. She realizes that Lord Mountclere has known of her background, and she decides to accept his offer of marriage.

Illustration by George du Maurier for The Hand of
Ethelberta, *chapter 43 ("Seaward appeared nothing distinct
save a black horizontal band. . ."), in the* Cornhill Magazine,
April 1876   (Perkins Library, Duke University)

Chapter 39: "Knollsea—Melchester"

Ethelberta and Picotee remain in their cottage at
Knollsea. Lord Mountclere calls and sees Christopher's
musical setting of her poem on the piano. He has a
quality of "impishness" and wants to test her. He invites
her to a concert in the cathedral at Melchester. Christopher Julian is to perform. Christopher sees her and
turns pale. Ethelberta turns on Lord Mountclere and
accuses him of being jealous. She goes to Christopher;
Picotee is with him and nearly faints. Lord Mountclere
apologizes but Ethelberta threatens to break the
engagement. When he apologizes she changes her
mind and says she will marry him, but wants to insure a
marriage between Picotee and Christopher. She tells
Picotee the wedding will take place in two days; she will
not tell her parents about it. Picotee has an exalted
vision of Ethelberta's future life, but she plans to live
simply, enjoying the library rather than traveling and
giving dinners. Ethelberta admits she and Lord Mountclere are strangers to each other.

Chapter 40: "Melchester (continued)"

Christopher discovers that Ethelberta is going to marry
Lord Mountclere and decides to stop her. He is now 27.
He sees the viscount buying a ring for Ethelberta. He
realizes he is the man he helped in the carriage accident. Christopher tells Faith the news. He says their
father used to know Mountclere and had told him
shocking news about him that he cannot repeat to
Faith.

Chapter 41: "Workshops—An Inn—The Street"

Lord Mountclere's brother, Edgar, visits Sol in London
and says Ethelberta's family must prevent the marriage.
Sol says he would rather she marry the "poorest man I
know." He has worked near Enckworth and knows
Mountclere is not "respectable." Edgar admits there

are reasons why Ethelberta will not be happy with him.
They decide to go to the cathedral together.

Chapter 42: "The Doncastles' Residence and Outside the Same"

At the Doncastles' home, Menlove has received a love
letter from Lord Mountclere's valet, Tipman, and gives
notice to her mistress. She tells Margaret Doncastle
about the approaching marriage between Ethelberta
and Lord Mountclere. Margaret mentions this to her
dinner guests, and Mr. Chickerel, who is serving dinner, turns pale and announces that Ethelberta is his
daughter. Neigh, who is dining there, is also shocked
but controls himself. Margaret is appalled when she
looks back and realizes Ethelberta was a dinner guest,
served by Mr. Chickerel, and took no notice of him. Mr.
Chickerel determines to stop the wedding.

Chapter 43: "The Railway—The Sea—The Shore Beyond"

Lord Mountclere's brother, Edgar, and Sol are unable
to reach Knollsea from Sandbourne by sea, because of
bad weather. Picotee and Ethelberta wrap themselves
up and go down to the harbor at Knollsea. The *Spruce* is
attempting to land. Captain Flower uses a megaphone
to let the captain know that his wife has had a boy. A
man comes to the Knollsea parsonage and speaks privately to the vicar.

Chapter 44: "Sandbourne—A Lonely Heath—The "Red Lion"—The Highway"

The *Spruce* steams back to Sandbourne with Sol and
Edgar Mountclere on board. They hire a conveyance in
Sandbourne and set out for Knollsea. At Flychett they
stop at an inn, hoping to change horses, but the
innkeeper's wife says the spare horses are away. They
sleep until 6:00, then rush on to Anglebury, change
horses, and depart for Enckworth. After they leave,
Christopher Julian arrives and asks for a conveyance to
go to Knollsea. Ethelberta's father approaches the vehicle before Christopher leaves; he has come by train.
Christopher offers him a ride; they will share the
expense. Ethelberta's face is discernible in her father's,
but Christopher does not notice. Sol and Edgar find
that Lord Mountclere has already departed for
Knollsea; their carriage has a slight collision with the
dogcart carrying Christopher and Mr. Chickerel. Mr.
Chickerel enters the carriage and Christopher follows.
They arrive at the church at 8:40.

Chapter 45: "Knollsea—The Road Thence—Enckworth"

At Knollsea church the signatures of Edgar, Sol,
Christopher, and Mr. Chickerel are already in the marriage register. Picotee is one of the witnesses; the
other is a stranger, possibly the clerk. Edgar pretends
to accept the marriage equably. Mr. Chickerel says the
title is an honor but his "brave girl" will be miserable.
He and Sol go to Enckworth Court. Christopher wanders unhappily about the church and finds Ladywell

in the organ chamber, looking ill. They pretend to be interested in the architectural features of the church and village. Finally they admit their mutual interest in Ethelberta and discuss the wedding. Ladywell departs by steamer. Mr. Chickerel and Sol see the married couple in a carriage; Sol, by his attitude, reveals that Ethelberta is a stranger to him now. Mr. Chickerel can do nothing. Ethelberta tells Picotee she wants to see Sol. He has no wish to enter the house and is hurt that she did not let him and his father know about the marriage ahead of time. He agrees, however, to meet her outside.

Chapter 46: "Enckworth (continued)—The Anglebury Highway"
Sol tells Ethelberta she has "worked to false lines" and is a "deserter" of her "own lot." He is ashamed of her. Sol says Lord Mountclere is a "bad man." Picotee comes to tell Ethelberta her husband wants her to come in. Ethelberta is so upset by her conversation with Sol she decides to wander in the woods of the estate. She discovers an ornamental timber cottage with balconies and a porch. A woman comes to the door and says the cottage belongs to "Miss Gruchette," who attends to the pheasants and poultry but who has two servants herself. The servants actually do all the work connected with the fowls. She invites Ethelberta in to see the cottage. The front room is filled with statuettes, love-birds, French bronzes, and other fancy objects. As Ethelberta leaves she hears two men walk by; one asks whether "lady Mountclere" has gone for good. The woman says they mean Miss Gruchette and whispers the reason why to Ethelberta, who turns pale. She says there is a rumor that Lord Mountclere was married to another woman that morning. The woman says if it's true the "poor thing" (that is, Ethelberta) will suffer, as there will be "murder" between the two women.

When she returns to the main house Lord Mountclere has sent men to search for her. Ethelberta says she had gone out to meet Sol. She frantically sends Picotee to bring Sol to see her. She plans to leave her husband. Christopher gives Picotee a ride and they find Sol. Ethelberta asks him to rescue her and help her get to Rouen, to Aunt Charlotte. Sol refuses and tells her to stick to her husband. He and Picotee leave by train. Christopher pretends to miss the train. He plans to try to help Ethelberta.

Chapter 47: "Enckworth and Its Precincts—Melchester"
A carriage comes for Ethelberta; she believes it to be Sol, but it is Lord Mountclere. He laughs and says he has seen everything. Ethelberta falls down on the leaves. Mountclere has her brought back. Christopher waits in vain. When he returns to Faith, she tells him she has just received a letter saying their cousin Lucy has left them a small income each. Christopher decides they will go to live in Italy to make the inheritance go further.

Sequel: "Anglebury—Enckworth—Sandbourne"
Two and half years after Ethelberta's marriage, Christopher Julian goes to the Red Lion Inn at Anglebury. He hears that Ethelberta is very "sharp" with poor Lord Mountclere and does not offer beer to the servants as he had done; she "holds the reins." She makes him go to church, lets him have only three glasses of wine a day, and makes decisions about who they see; she is "steward, and agent, and everything." She has her own office with ledgers and cash books. He sees her go by in a carriage; she is the driver, but has a boy in livery. He stands thinking, but does not wish Ethelberta were his.

He then takes the steamer from Knollsea to Sandbourne and goes to see the Chickerels. They have a house, Firtop Villa, with a servant girl. They admire Ethelberta's "will of iron" and the fact that she is "mistress now" and the other servants respect her. Mrs. Chickerel says, "it's wonderful what can be done with an old man when you are his darling." Picotee says she is writing an epic poem and employs Emmeline as her reader. She has helped the others, although Sol would

Corfe Castle, between Wareham and Swanage, which figures in The Hand of Ethelberta *and other works*   (Sarah Bird Wright)

Emma Lavinia Gifford (later Emma Hardy) in about 1870, the year in which she and Hardy first met (Dorset County Museum, Dorchester)

only accept money as a loan. Gwendoline and Cornelia have married and gone to Australia.

Christopher praises Picotee for having written Faith so often. He proposes to Picotee and tells her he is now to have the post of chief organist at Melchester cathedral. She is to have £500 when she marries, as arranged by Ethelberta. Picotee is sure Ethelberta will never let them come to want. Christopher says it is "as well to be kin to a coach though you never ride in it." Picotee assures him her father will be very glad, as will Ethelberta.

For further reading: Blishen, "Hardy, *The Hand of Ethelberta,* and Some Persisting English Discomforts"; Boumelha, "'A Complicated Position for a Woman': *The Hand of Ethelberta*"; Davies, "*The Hand of Ethelberta*: De-Mythologising 'Woman'"; Gittings, "*The Hand of Ethelberta*": A Comedy in Chapters; Roberts, "Ethelberta: Portrait of the Artist as a Young Woman: Love and Ambition"; Ward, "*The Hand of Ethelberta*"; Wing, "'Forbear, Hostler, Forbear!': Social Satire in *The Hand of Ethelberta*."

Hankinson, Charles James (1866–1959) Journalist and novelist who wrote a number of books on Hardy, using the pseudonym Clive HOLLAND.

"Hap" A sonnet written in 1866 and published in WESSEX POEMS (1898). The manuscript title was "Chance." The poet wishes that his "love's loss" could be attributed to the deliberate doings of a "vengeful god" more powerful than he. Why, he asks, "unblooms the best hope ever sown?" He perceives that it is all due to "Doomsters," "Crass Casualty" and "dicing Time," all of which are random and not calculated processes. The "purblind Doomsters" might just as well have scattered "blisses" as "pain." In May 1865, a year before the poem was published, Hardy had written, "The world does not despise us; it only neglects us" (*Life*, 48).

The phrases "love's loss" and "the best hope ever sown" have been interpreted as referring to the loss of a woman's affection, but these might instead concern Hardy's disappointment in not finding a publisher for his poems. James O. Bailey attributes the sonnet to the influence of the theory of natural selection put forth by Charles Darwin in *The Origin of Species*. Accident and chance control the universe and determine individual survival (Bailey, *The Poetry of Thomas Hardy*, 51–52).

The poem was set to music by Hubert James Foss in *Seven Poems by Thomas Hardy* (London: Oxford University Press, 1925); *see* Appendix II.

Hardy, Emma Lavinia Gifford (1840–1912) Hardy's first wife, whom he met in 1870 and married in 1874. She was one of five children, the youngest daughter of a solicitor, John Attersoll Gifford, and Emma Farman. The Giffords lived in Plymouth, but later moved to a manor house near Bodmin in CORNWALL. Emma described the home in which she grew up as "a most intellectual one and not only so but one of exquisite home-training and refinement" (Gittings, *Young Thomas Hardy*, 182). Although Emma recalled a home filled with music, family singing, reading, and book discussions, there were problems as well. Her grandmother lived with the family and contributed her own income toward expenses, eventually depleting her capital. She also persuaded Emma's father to give up his small law practice, an act which impoverished the family. In addition, Emma's father was given to drink. Hardy later became convinced there was a strain of insanity in the family, an assessment supported by his second wife, Florence Dugdale HARDY.

In 1868 Emma's elder sister, Helen, married the Reverend Caddell HOLDER, a widower of 65. Emma accompanied them when, immediately after their wedding, they went to ST. JULIOT CHURCH in CORNWALL, where Holder was to be rector. In her "recollections," published in the *Life*, Emma states that her sister "required" her help, as it was a "difficult parish." Emma rode her pony Fanny all along the Cornish cliffs and sometimes visited people in the parish. She also collected sums for her brother-in-law and sold watercolor sketches she had painted so that the "historic old church" might be rebuilt.

Emma and the Holders eagerly awaited the arrival of "the Architect" so that restoration of the church might begin. Hardy first came in March 1870 and was much taken with Emma (*Life*, 67–73). They were married in 1874. Florence Hardy apparently believed, however, on the basis of information from Hardy himself that Emma trapped Hardy into marriage by claiming to be pregnant, and that Helen Holder helped her "scheme." At the time of Hardy's visit to St. Juliot, Emma was 29 and desperate to be married. When Hardy left St. Juliot in August 1870 he considered himself "betrothed" (Millgate, *Thomas Hardy: A Biography,* 130).

At first Emma brought vitality and youth into Hardy's life. She was a talented painter and served as amanuensis to Hardy, helping with his writing. His mother, however, never really accepted Emma. She probably knew, or suspected, that the Giffords looked down on the Hardys because they were not of a professional class and were "countrified." Michael Millgate states that Jemima felt "threatened by Emma's social pretensions" and regarded her as an interloper who lacked "youth, wealth, domestic virtues" and a "Dorset background" (Millgate, *Thomas Hardy,* 145). Later, Emma was afflicted with mental instability, possibly inherited from her father.

The marriage was long delayed, as Hardy could not afford to marry until he began selling his work. Another obstacle to their union may have been the difference in their class. Millgate writes of Emma's father's "class-based contempt for the social pretensions of the Hardys," and his family resented the Giffords for their condescending attitude. None of their parents were present at their wedding at St. Peter's Church, Paddington. They were attended only by the daughter of Hardy's landlady and Emma's brother Walter ("Emma Lavinia Hardy," *The Oxford Reader's Companion to Hardy,* 153). Emma eventually converted the attics at MAX GATE into a flat for herself. She wrote poetry and confided her bitter feelings to her diaries, which were destroyed after her death. She continued to be close to her sister, and was with her in her final illness in the autumn of 1900; Rev. Holder had died in 1882. To assuage his guilt after her unexpected death from heart disease in 1912, Hardy wrote some of his most memorable poetry.

For further reading: Duckworth, "Evoking Emma in 'Poems of 1912–13'"; Gifford, "Thomas Hardy and Emma"; Gittings, "Emma Hardy and the Giffords, Papers Presented at the 1973 Summer School"; Gittings, *Young Thomas Hardy;* Manford, "Emma Hardy's Helping Hand"; Manford, "Who Wrote Thomas Hardy's Novels? A Survey of Emma Hardy's Contribution to the Manuscripts of Her Husband's Novels"; Millgate, ed., *Letters of Emma and Florence Hardy;* Millgate, "'Wives All': Emma and Florence Hardy"; Ramazani, "Hardy and the Poetics of Melancholia: Poems of 1912–13 and Other Elegies for Emma"; Winslow, "Images of Emma Hardy."

Hardy, Florence Emily Dugdale (1879–1937)   Hardy's second wife, the daughter of an Enfield, Middlesex, schoolmaster, Edward Dugdale, and his wife, Emma. She was a journalist and the author of stories for children, and, long before they were married, assisted Hardy with research.

It is uncertain just when and where Florence and Hardy met. She told one of her four sisters they had met in 1904 at a LONDON garden party, and another sister that she had seen Emma HARDY, the author's first wife, at a meeting of the Lyceum Club and asked

Florence Emily Dugdale Hardy, c. 1914, the year she and Hardy were married   (Beinecke Rare Book and Manuscript Library, Yale University)

Florence Dugdale (later Hardy) at the seaside, c. 1911
(Beinecke Rare Book and Manuscript Library, Yale University)

whether she might send Hardy flowers on his birthday. Florence is known to have written Hardy from WEY-MOUTH in August 1905 asking whether she might call on him at MAX GATE, and he agreed, provided she did not publish an account of the visit (Millgate, *Thomas Hardy,* 446). Hardy wrote her on January 2, 1906, thanking her for a box of flowers she had sent him after a visit; it is not clear whether that visit was her first to him (*Letters* III, 193).

By March 1907 she had begun helping him with research for *The DYNASTS* at the BRITISH MUSEUM, where she caught a cold. He wrote on March 21 to chastise her for attempting to search for information if she were not altogether well. The reading room, he continued, "is just the place for you to catch a new influenza of somebody or other," and he would blame himself if she were to become ill (*Letters* III, 249). She apparently had been searching through back issues of the *Times* for a letter he had written the paper. In late April he wrote to thank her and to assure her that her "*not* finding the letter" was as helpful as if she had found it. He then invited her to join him in searching for it at the South Kensington Museum (now the VIC-TORIA AND ALBERT MUSEUM). Richard Michael Purdy and Millgate speculate that the letter in question was one he had written in 1876 about the Waterloo ball (*Letters* III, 253). In September 1907, from the ATHENAEUM CLUB, Hardy wrote a letter to Archibald Marshall, editors of the books supplement of the *Daily Mail,* who had asked him for a poem. He promised to send one when he returned to "the quiet of the country," but that he was writing to "bring under the editorial eye" of the paper a young writer, Miss F. Dugdale,

who had carried out research for him at the British Museum and whose "judgment in literature" would make her very useful to the paper. He suggested that she might review books for young people. He said she had already written "a few things" for the paper, but had not been "sufficiently discovered" by the editors (*Letters* III, 261–62).

In April 1909 Hardy wrote a lengthy letter about English poets occasioned by the death of Algernon Charles SWINBURNE; Florence is believed to be the recipient. By September she had sent him a sketch called "Trafalgar! How Nelson's Death Inspired the Tailor"; he wrote her that it read "remarkably well" and made some suggestions, cautioning her not to feel obligated to accept them. He suggested where she might submit it, including newspapers such as the *Daily Mail.* It was later published in the *Daily Chronicle* (*Letters* IV, 45). In January 1911, for her birthday, he sent her a lamp and a handbook, "Wessex Country" (by Hermann LEA, dealing with real and fictitious places in Hardy's fiction). Later that year, at her home in Enfield, Middlesex, she began typing his prefaces for the new edition of his novels.

Emma Hardy died unexpectedly on November 27, 1912. Florence had been on her way to WEYMOUTH with the intention of attending one or two of the DOR-CHESTER performances of *The TRUMPET-MAJOR.* (Hardy was criticized for allowing them to proceed). She returned briefly to Enfield and then came to Max Gate for several long visits, which led to gossip in Dorchester. Hardy answered many letters of condolence, among them one from Edward and Emma Dugdale, Florence's parents.

On January 29, 1913, he wrote Florence that he was "getting through [Emma's] papers. … It was, of course, sheer hallucination in her, poor thing, & not wilfulness" (a reference to Emma's diaries, which he destroyed, setting out her grievances against him). He added that, if Florence came again to Max Gate, "won't I clutch you tight: you shall stay till spring" (*Letters* IV, 255). In March he went to Boscastle, north CORNWALL, with his brother Henry, to revisit sites he had known long before with Emma. He wrote Florence that the visit had been "very painful." "And now," he continued, "suppose that something shd happen to you, physically, as it did to her mentally!" In an April letter he addressed her as "dearest girl" (*Letters* IV, 270). By January 1914, he wrote Florence that he missed her "every minute." They were married on February 10, 1914; she was 44 and he was 74.

Florence Hardy made an invaluable contribution to Hardy studies in persuading him to write down or to recall, verbally, his early life, which she then transcribed. He was reluctant to record his recollections and, as she writes in her prefatory note to "The Early Life," he would say he "had not sufficient admiration for himself to do so." She argued, however, that it would be the only way to prevent false statements by future biographers. An erroneous "Life," in fact, had already been published as "authoritative," and so "his hand was forced, and he agreed that the facts of his career should be set down for use in the event of its proving necessary to print them" (*Life*, Prefatory Note, vii). She also included his notes for various works, which provide a unique source for the scholarly study of his methods of composition (Evelyn Hardy, *Thomas Hardy: A Critical Biography*, 1–2).

In her diary, Virginia WOOLF described Florence: "She has the large sad lack lustre eyes of a childless woman; great docility & readiness, as if she had learnt her part; not great alacrity, but resignation, in welcoming visitors; wears a sprigged voile dress, black shoes and a necklace" (*The Diary of Virginia Woolf*, III.96; quoted in Millgate, *Thomas Hardy: A Biography*, 564). After they were married, Sir Sydney COCKERELL became Florence's confidante; she had many difficulties in dealing with her husband. After Hardy's death, Cockerell and Sir James BARRIE began, as Millgate puts it, "to assert their male authority" over what Cockerell called "the housefull of women." Believing they could best address "the claims of the world of letters and of the nation," they persuaded the exhausted Florence to consent to the partition of his remains. His heart was removed and buried in the same grave with Emma at STINSFORD CHURCH. His body was cremated; Cockerell and Barrie had arranged for his ashes to be interred in Poets' Corner at WESTMINSTER ABBEY (Millgate, *Thomas Hardy: A Biography*, 573–75). Florence attended the service at Westminster Abbey along with Hardy's sister, Kate. His brother, Henry, was at Stinsford for the burial of his heart. These two services were held simultaneously with a third, at St. Peter's Church, Dorchester.

Florence Hardy inherited considerable wealth from her husband; she became the owner of Max Gate and received a substantial income from his publications. She bought a car, hired a chauffeur, and took an apartment in London. As Hardy's literary executor, however, she had a great deal of work to carry out. In her effort to sustain Hardy's literary reputation, she quarreled with Cockerell. She oversaw publication of the two volumes of the work purporting to be Hardy's autobiography (*see LIFE OF THOMAS HARDY*.) This is now recognized as his pseudonymous autobiography: *The Early Life of Thomas Hardy*, published in 1928, and *The Later Life of Thomas Hardy* (1930). (The two volumes have now been combined, titled *The Life and Work of Thomas Hardy*). They were written by Hardy, except for the final chapter, although Florence honored his memory and wish for secrecy by refusing to reveal this fact. She died of cancer in 1937 (Millgate, *Thomas Hardy: A Biography*, 574–78).

For further reading: Gittings and Manton, *The Second Mrs. Hardy;* Millgate, ed., *Letters of Emma and Florence Hardy;* Millgate, "'Wives All': Emma and Florence Hardy"; Nineham, "The Ancestry of Florence Emily Dugdale: Thomas Hardy's Second Wife"; Roberts; "Florence Hardy and the Max Gate Circle."

Hardy, Henry (1851–1928)   Hardy's younger brother, who succeeded their father in the building business. On September 18, 1874, Hardy wrote Henry from Brighton to tell him that he and Emma Lavinia Gifford (HARDY) had been married the day before and were on their way to Normandy and Paris. They spent the weekend there and then took the boat to FRANCE. None of Hardy's family were present; her uncle performed the ceremony, and her brother and Hardy's landlady's daughter were there. He told Henry they had sent an "advertisement" of the marriage to the *Dorset Chronicle* and hoped Henry might see it (*Letters* I, 31).

After he and Emma moved to LONDON in 1878, Hardy visited DORSET frequently. In 1884 Hardy and Henry traveled to the Channel Islands. Henry built MAX GATE, Hardy's home in Fordington Field, just outside DORCHESTER, which was finished by the end of June 1885. Hardy was able to see more of his family after he and Emma settled there.

Hardy's father owned a farm called "Talbothays" on the road east of West Stafford village (F. B. Pinion, *A Hardy Companion*, 486–87). After the death of both his parents (his father, Thomas HARDY, died in 1892, and his mother, Jemima HARDY, in 1904), Henry Hardy built a home there and named it TALBOTHAYS. Millgate states that he was planning to marry but did not. In 1911 Henry, accompanied by his sisters Mary and Katharine, moved from the family home at HIGHER BOCKHAMPTON to Talbothays, which had more modern conveniences (Millgate, *Thomas Hardy: A Biography*, 346). Hardy named the dairy farm where Tess works, in *TESS OF THE D'URBERVILLES*, for the farm.

In August 1890 he and Henry went to France; Hardy wrote that he went solely on Henry's account. In Paris they went to the Moulin Rouge and saw other sights. Hardy and his brother went cycling through the New Forest to Southampton in July 1899, but the trip had to be shortened because of the heat.

Between 1906 and 1912 Hardy toured English cathedrals with Emma, Henry, and one of his sisters. In 1911 Florence DUGDALE (later Hardy) and her sister Constance went with Hardy and Henry to Lichfield, Worcester, and Hereford Cathedrals. According to Millgate, Hardy tried at this time to interest Henry in marrying Constance, but nothing came of his effort (Millgate, *Thomas Hardy: A Biography*, 473).

After Emma's death in 1912, Florence Dugdale spent a great deal of time at Max Gate, helping Hardy with his correspondence. Emma's niece Lilian GIFFORD, who was mentally unstable, considered Max Gate her second home and herself a substitute for Emma, although she did no work in the house and apparently felt herself to be superior in ancestry to Florence. Hardy and Florence intended to marry but Florence foresaw that she could not coexist with Lilian. Henry and Kate concurred, and helped persuade Hardy to evict Lilian; Henry said it was "the only way to avoid a life of misery" (Millgate, *Thomas Hardy: A Biography*, 492). Hardy did provide an annuity for Lilian, in addition to some stocks.

When Hardy died in 1928, Henry represented the family at the burial of Hardy's heart at STINSFORD CHURCH. Kate, the only surviving sister, made the trip to WESTMINSTER ABBEY and the service there. Henry suffered a slight stroke in 1914, soon after Hardy married Florence Dugdale. Florence wrote Rebekah OWEN that Henry had had a stroke and that she and Hardy had spent a great deal of time at his home. She added that he was "one of the best friends I have ever had—true, strong & generous in every thought & deed" (Millgate, ed., *Letters of Emma and Florence Hardy*, 94). She compared him to Hardy's characters Giles WINTERBORNE or Gabriel OAK. Henry recovered and lived on, dying in early December 1928, in the same year as his elder brother. Kate survived another 12 years, dying in 1940.

Hardy, Jemima Hand (1813–1904)   Hardy's mother. She was the daughter of Elizabeth Swetman Hand, whose father and husband died, leaving her with several children. Elizabeth was reputed to be an omnivorous reader and Jemima was, according to the *Life*, a girl "of unusual ability and judgment, and an energy that might have carried her to incalculable issues" (*Life*, 7–8). She too read every book she could obtain, and also trained herself in cooking and other domestic skills. She married Hardy's father, who owned a building and master-masonry business, when she was 25. He was devoted to church music, as were his father and brother. Their first child, Thomas, who arrived less than five and a half months after they were married, was thought to have been stillborn, but the nurse attending his mother rescued him, saying, "Dead! Stop a minute: he's alive enough, sure!" (*Life*, 14).

When Hardy was about eight, Jemima took him to Hertfordshire to visit Martha Sharpe, one of her sisters. They then went to LONDON, where Hardy remembered seeing Hyde Park without Marble Arch, which was not built on its present site until 1851. They stayed at an old coaching inn, the Cross Keys at Clerkenwell. For years he remembered watching his mother search the large old closets for men hiding there. In Dorset they often set off on expeditions. Hardy recalled that he and his mother were "excellent companions, having each a keen sense of humour and a love of adventure." One time they both pulled cabbage-nets over their faces, and, in disguise, went to Puddletown to see one of Jemima's sisters, who did not recognize them.

Hardy enjoyed playing the fiddle, and was sometimes invited to play at village weddings or parties. Jemima instructed him that under no circumstances was he to accept any money for performing, but on one occasion he collected enough pennies to buy a copy of *The Boys' Own Book*, which he kept in his library his whole life.

In 1875, after Hardy and Emma Gifford HARDY had been married about a year, they invited his mother to meet them at Bournemouth for a holiday. Apparently she had wanted them to come to HIGHER BOCKHAMPTON, where she and his father lived, and sent back a lukewarm reply. Hardy disliked Bournemouth and he and Emma quarreled there (*see* "WE SAT AT THE WINDOW," dated "Bournemouth, 1875"). They went on to Swanage, where Hardy's sisters Mary HARDY and Katharine (Kate) HARDY joined them for two weeks (Millgate, *Thomas Hardy: A Biography*, 176–77).

Hardy's father died in 1892, but Jemima, her son Henry, and two daughters continued to live together. In 1901 the WHITEFRIARS CLUB came to MAX GATE, and were entertained in a tent on the lawn. Jemima Hardy, then 88, was wheeled by her daughters to the end of the private road so that she might see the carriages drive past. She concealed a handkerchief under her lap rug and waved it vigorously, contrary to her daughters' instructions. Long afterward, one of the visitors said to Hardy that, if they had realized who she was, "what cheers there would have been, what waving of handkerchiefs, what a greeting for Thomas Hardy's mother!" (*Life*, 309).

Hardy's mother died on April 3, Easter Sunday, 1904, at the age of 91. She had been afflicted with deafness for a long time, but was mentally "as clear and alert as ever." She was buried in the grave of her husband in the STINSFORD CHURCH graveyard. Hardy wrote that she had been a woman "with an extraordinary store of local memories, reaching back to the days when the ancient ballads were everywhere heard." He praised her taste in literature, shown by the books she chose for her children.

Hardy, Katharine (1856–1940)   Hardy's younger sister, usually called Kate. Hardy was less close to her, who was 16 years his junior, than to Mary HARDY, only a year younger than he.

In 1863, at the age of six or seven, Kate went to Denchworth, a town about 15 miles from Oxford, to attend school and live with her sister Mary, who was teaching at the National School after finishing her teacher training at the Salisbury Training School. Kate and Mary lived together for the rest of Mary's life. They both taught at the National School in Bell Lane, DORCHESTER, for a number of years, and Hardy bought them a small house there in Wollaston Road. In 1911 they moved to TALBOTHAYS, outside Dorchester and a few miles from MAX GATE. Mary died in 1915 and

Henry Hardy and Kate Hardy, brother and sister of Thomas Hardy, c. 1914 (Beinecke Rare Book and Manuscript Library, Yale University)

Henry in 1928; Katharine lived at Talbothays until her death in 1940.

Hardy, Mary (1841–1915)   One of Hardy's two sisters. Born only a year after Hardy, Mary was closer to him than their younger sister Katharine (Kate) HARDY or their brother Henry HARDY. By the time Hardy went to LONDON in 1862 in order to work for the architect Sir Arthur William BLOMFIELD, Mary had attended the Salisbury Training College and qualified as a teacher. In August 1862, Hardy wrote her from Kilburn, London, where he had taken lodgings. His long letter is full of news about his activities, the visit of Horace MOULE, and restaurants where they had dined. He referred to a visit she had made earlier, when they had gone to the theater. Throughout his years in London, Hardy wrote her every few months, sent her books, and took a keen interest in all she was doing.

In 1863, Mary took a post at the National School in Denchworth, 15 miles from Oxford, after finishing her course at the Salisbury Training School. She was forced to take a position as church organist, although she had been instructed only in the piano and the harmonium. She persuaded her mother to let Kate join her at Denchworth and enter school; she was only six. Kate regarded her time at Denchworth as very happy. Eventually both sisters obtained posts at the National School

in DORCHESTER, and Hardy bought them a small villa in Wollaston Road (Millgate, *Thomas Hardy: A Biography*, 82–83) where they lived until moving into TALBOTHAYS. When Hardy received an honorary degree from Cambridge in 1913 Mary wrote him, reminding him of his earlier abandonment of plans to enter the university. She observed that he had "accomplished it all with greater honour than if you had gone along the road you then saw before you" (*Letters* I, 7).

Within a few years after Mary and Kate moved to Talbothays from Wollaston Road, Mary's emphysema worsened, and she died in November 1915, at the age of 74. She left her assets to Kate.

Hardy, Thomas (1840–1928)   Thomas Hardy was born on June 2, 1840, in HIGHER BOCKHAMPTON, near the town of DORCHESTER in Dorset. He was the first child of Jemima HAND, a cook, and Thomas HARDY (the Second), a building contractor and master mason.

Hardy's paternal great-grandparents were John Hardy (1755–1821), of the village now known as Puddletown, who married Jane Knight, and James Head, who married Mary Hopson. The Hardys had four children, including Thomas HARDY (the First). He was the paternal grandfather of Thomas Hardy, and, at age 21, married Mary Head (1772–1857), only child of the Heads. In 1801 his father, John, built the family home at HIGHER BOCKHAMPTON to assist his son. Thomas and Mary were the parents of seven children, including Thomas Hardy (the Second). Thomas Hardy was born in 1840, three years after his grandfather's death. Hardy was the eldest of four children, including Mary HARDY, Henry HARDY, and Katharine HARDY.

Thomas Hardy's maternal great-grandparents were William and Betty Symonds Hand and John and Maria Childs Swetman. The Swetmans' daughter Betty, one of nine children, married George Hand; they had seven children, including Jemima. Betty Swetman Hand, Hardy's grandmother, was an omnivorous reader and was also skilled in cooking and sewing. She lived until 1847, when Hardy was seven, and he remembered her well. Later he called her a woman "of unusual ability and judgement," and believed she had "an energy that might have carried her to incalculable issues" (*Life,* 7–8). The Hands, of yeoman stock, were very poor, and Jemima was forced to earn her living at an early age; she became a cook for the 3rd Earl of Ilchester. The Swetmans had been small landowners in Melbury Osmond, Dorset. Hardy was proud of this branch of his mother's family, who were socially superior to the Hands (Millgate, *Thomas Hardy: A Biography,* 12–13). Jemima Hand and Thomas Hardy (the Second) were married in 1839, a few months before the birth of Thomas. Jemima was always close to her siblings and their families, some of whom had settled at Puddletown. Her children, including

Thomas, walked frequently to Puddletown to see their many cousins.

At birth Thomas Hardy appeared to be so frail that the doctor assumed he had already died. The nurse, however, took another look at him and cried, "Dead! Stop a minute: he's alive enough, sure!" (*Life*, 14). Few of those in the room, however, would have predicted that he would become the most celebrated author of his day.

Hardy was a precocious child; at the age of three he had read a book containing verses of the Cries of London once sung by street vendors as they peddled their wares. He was given a toy concertina at the age of four and, soon afterward, shown how to play and tune a violin; he took a keen interest in music as a child, one that would continue throughout his adult life.

He was fragile physically, however, and would describe himself a half-century later, in the noted poem "IN TENEBRIS III," as "the smallest and feeblest of folk there"; he had heard of a world "wheeling on," but had no wish to grow up, to become a man, to focus on possessions, or to know a great many people (*Life*, 16). He eagerly shared this dream with his mother, who was horrified, and hurt that he was so disillusioned.

Thomas Hardy at age 16   (Dorset County Museum, Dorchester)

When he was eight, his parents decided his health was robust enough that he could attend a small school in the village just established by Julia Augusta Pitney MARTIN, who lived at KINGSTON MAURWARD house. At this time his mother gave him John Dryden's translation of Vergil's *Aeneid*. Hardy greatly admired what Michael Millgate calls her "cultivation and elegance." After a year, however, Jemima Hardy decided to send her son to the British School in Dorchester, founded by Isaac Glandfield LAST. Here his intellect developed rapidly. He studied Latin, French, and advanced mathematics, and read widely.

Hardy finished his formal education at age 16 (Millgate, *Thomas Hardy*, 51–52). About this time he met John HICKS, a Dorchester architect who offered to take him under his wing and teach him the profession of architecture. Hardy's father considered Hicks's proposition an excellent opportunity for his son. For the ensuing few years, Hardy read for several hours each morning, then walked into Dorchester to study with Hicks, whose specialty was Gothic architecture and who was well known as a church restorer. Although Hardy later worked for several well-known London architects, he esteemed Hicks and dedicated a poem to him, "The ABBEY MASON."

During this time in Dorchester Hardy met Horace MOULE, eight years his senior, one of seven sons of the Reverend Henry Moule. They rambled through the fields near Dorchester, discussing literature, and Moule gave him books, such as *Elements of Experiment and Natural Philosophy ... for the use of Youth and Schools,* by Jabez Hogg. Moule helped him study Greek and write poetry. At the time Moule was at Queens' College, Cambridge, and an aspiring author and reviewer. (He later joined the staff of *The SATURDAY REVIEW* and reviewed Hardy's first and second published novels, *DESPERATE REMEDIES* and *UNDER THE GREENWOOD TREE.*

Although Hardy had learned a great deal from John Hicks, he decided he would like to work in LONDON. On Thursday, April 17, 1862, he went to London by train and found lodgings at 3 Clarence Place, Kilburn. He became an assistant architect in the office of Sir Arthur William BLOMFIELD, a son of the Bishop of London. He devoted the next five years to absorbing the culture, architecture, and historic sites of the city. He went to churches, both Anglican and Roman Catholic, saw old friends from Dorset, visited art exhibitions, and attended public events. He was invited to gatherings in the rooms of the Architectural Association which he joined. He was intoxicated with London. He heard Charles Dickens lecture in the spring of 1863, and had his head read at the London School of Phrenology. He also wrote a sketch, "HOW I BUILT MYSELF A HOUSE," for the amusement of his architectural colleagues. It was published in *CHAMBERS'S JOURNAL.*

While he greatly enjoyed the city's cultural life, he was disenchanted with the rigid class structure he found among those who were members of "society"; at the same time he was probably envious. It was at this time that Hardy began searching for a way to enter the field of literary journalism, perhaps by becoming the London correspondent of a country newspaper. He read widely in modern poets and wrote poetry, but it was rejected by publishers. The strain of his work and lack of sleep, combined with dejection over the receding prospect of a successful literary career, began to affect his health. He decided to return to Dorchester in 1867 and assist John Hicks with church restoration work.

At this time he also began his first novel (never published), The POOR MAN AND THE LADY, which has an architect for a hero. In 1868 he completed it, but was unable to find a publisher. In January 1869 he returned to London. He did not work again for Blomfield, although he was invited to return, but visited museums and rewrote the novel. John Hicks died during the winter, and, in April, his successor, George R. CRICKMAY, asked Hardy to finish some of the church restoration projects the firm had taken on. After Hardy worked several weeks in the Dorchester office, Crickmay offered him three months' employment in WEYMOUTH. There he supervised the restoration of several churches. In August or September a new assistant came to Crickmay's office and was represented in Desperate Remedies, the novel on which Hardy was working in Weymouth, as Edward Springrove, the young hero/architect.

In March 1870 Crickmay sent Hardy to CORNWALL to work on the restoration of ST. JULIOT CHURCH. The rector, the Reverend Caddell HOLDER, lived there with his second wife, Helen. Her sister, Emma Lavinia Gifford (HARDY), was living with them at the time. One of five children, Emma was the youngest daughter of a solicitor, John Attersoll Gifford, and Emma Farman. Hardy was immediately attracted to her. He walked beside her as she rode her pony along the Cornish cliffs. They went on picnics and climbed down the rocks and sealcaves. Emma sketched and played the piano, and they discussed literature and poetry.

In May 1870 Hardy left Crickmay and returned to London; he says in his autobiography that he "had left his heart in Cornwall." In London he returned to work for Mr. Blomfield, helping him finish some drawings. He also assisted another architect, Raphael Brandon, the author of a two-volume Analysis of Gothic Architecture and other works. Hardy's second novel, Desperate Remedies, was published anonymously on March 25, 1871, by Tinsley Bros. Hardy assumed some of the risk for the publication. This novel was a tale of mystery and murder with sensational incidents, revealing the influence of Wilkie Collins's novel The Moonstone.

In 1872 Hardy's second novel (or third, counting the never-published The Poor Man and the Lady), was published by Tinsley Bros. This was a tale of rural courtship marked by episodes of rustic humor, titled Under the Greenwood Tree, which was well received. In 1873 Hardy's novel A PAIR OF BLUE EYES was published by TINSLEY BROS. It was the first of his novels with his name on the title page. It was set on the Cornish coast near the location where Hardy first met and courted Emma. In his autobiography Hardy classed it among his "Romances and Fantasies—as if to suggest its visionary nature."

At this time Hardy was invited to write a serial for the prestigious CORNHILL MAGAZINE, edited by Leslie STEPHEN, father of Virginia WOOLF. He was living and working in Higher Bockhampton when he began FAR FROM THE MADDING CROWD, serialized anonymously in the Cornhill Magazine and published in two volumes in November 1874. Hardy observed that it was in this work that he first adopted the word "Wessex," formerly used in the context of early British history, giving it a "fictitious significance as the existing name of the district once included in that extinct kingdom." The novel was very well received, although one critic, Richard Holt Hutton, writing in the SPECTATOR, declared that it must be the work of George ELIOT.

In 1874 Hardy and Emma were married; none of their parents were present. They went to FRANCE on their wedding trip, sending their families postcards announcing the marriage. (Hardy's second wife, Florence Emily HARDY, believed that Emma trapped him into marriage by telling him, falsely, that she was pregnant.) Emma brought vitality and youth into Hardy's life. Although they remained childless, she was a talented painter and helped Hardy with his writing. The Hardys moved to London, Swanage, and Yeovil in the same year.

Hardy was now beginning to sell his novels, which were, as a rule, serialized before publication. In 1876 The HAND OF ETHELBERTA was published, a lighthearted novel set in the social world of London of which Hardy was not a part, but which he partly envied and partly scorned. He and Emma made a second continental tour and moved to Riverside Villa in Sturminster Newton, a period Hardy later described as their "happiest time."

In 1878 The RETURN OF THE NATIVE was published, which some critics consider Hardy's finest novel. The Hardys moved to Tooting, London. He was becoming well known in literary and social circles and joined the SAVILE CLUB, on Savile Row, London. This club was very useful for entertaining and serving as a congenial pied à terre for writing notes and meeting other writers.

Two years later The TRUMPET MAJOR was published, one of the earliest of Hardy's works to manifest his interest in Napoleonic history and traditions. In the

Life he states that when he was only seven or eight he found, in a closet at home, some contemporary numbers of the periodical *A History of the Wars,* which dealt with the Napoleonic wars. His grandfather, who had volunteered in the wars, had subscribed to them. He wrote that their "torn pages," with their "melodramatic prints of serried ranks, crossed bayonets, and dead bodies" actually set in motion "the train of ideas that led to *The Trumpet-Major* and *The Dynasts*" (*Life,* 16–17).

The Hardys then toured Normandy, but, on their return, Hardy fell ill with what doctors believed was an internal hemorrhage or a possible stone in the urinary tract. They recommended immediate surgery. Hardy was terrified, as anesthesia and surgery were primitive at the time, and he chose to avoid both by agreeing to a prolonged stay in bed. He dictated most of *A LAODICEAN* to Emma while lying prone for five months on a board. The novel was published in 1881. It has been called one of Hardy's most intellectual novels, although he himself classified it as a "novel of ingenuity," dealing with a dispute among architects, stolen papers, an historic castle, scheming relatives, and a Continental chase.

At this time the Hardys moved to Wimborne Minster. In 1882 Hardy and his wife visited Paris. His novel *TWO ON A TOWER* was published in 1882, memorable for its depiction of human passions against a cosmic background. The hero is an astronomer, and the heroine the abandoned wife of a nobleman who is sojourning in Africa.

The next year, Hardy decided to build a permanent home in Dorchester but spend part of each year in London. He was able to lease land from the Duchy of Cornwall just outside the town, and construction began in 1883. In 1885 the Hardys moved into the house, called MAX GATE. It was a large, handsome two-story structure; Hardy's father and brother were the builders. The ground floor had a large central hall between a dining room and drawing room; the kitchen and scullery were at the rear. On the second floor there were two bedrooms, a water-closet, a box room, and a study. Several extensions were later made to the house, and, before her death, Emma moved into two attic rooms that had been renovated for her. Hardy's study, which was relocated during later renovations, was on the second floor and deliberately placed far away from household activities and callers. The grounds were well-planned with gardens, lawns, an orchard, and, eventually, a pet cemetery. Hardy tried to include many trees and shrubs of English origin.

The Hardys made a practice of renting furnished flats or houses for part or all of the London season (April through July), bringing their servants or, sometimes, employing servants provided by the owners of the flats. They would entertain their London friends, often at tea, and dine or have tea with other friends.

Among the places they lived were 20 Monmouth Road, Bayswater (1889); 12 Mandeville Place, Manchester Sq. (1891); 70 Hamilton Terrace (1893); 16 Pelham Crescent, South Kensington (1894, 1896); 90 Ashley Gardens, Victoria St. SW (1895); 20 Wynnstay Gardens (1899); 27 Oxford Terrace (1901); 13 Abercorn Place (1904); and 1 Hyde Park Mansions (1905, 1906). In April 1891 Hardy was elected to the ATHENAEUM CLUB, to which he was nominated by Lord CARNARVON. He often wrote letters from that address during the ensuing years.

In 1886 one of the most celebrated of Hardy's novels, *The MAYOR OF CASTERBRIDGE,* set in Dorchester, was published. Hardy asserted that the story was "more particularly a study of one man's deeds and character than, perhaps, any other" of those included in his "exhibition of Wessex life." Michael HENCHARD, the Mayor of Casterbridge, dominates the novel throughout, the first of Hardy's characters to do so. Desmond Hawkins points out that in this respect *The Mayor of Casterbridge* paved the way for *TESS OF THE D'URBERVILLES* and *JUDE THE OBSCURE,* the other two novels in which there is "the subordination of everything else to the one obsessive preoccupation with the display of a single soul in its totality" (Hawkins, *Hardy: Novelist and Poet,* 94).

In 1887 Hardy's novel *The WOODLANDERS* was published. It was praised for its careful representation of rural customs and scenes, and, especially, for its depiction of the two central characters, Grace Melbury FITZPIERS and Giles WINTERBOURNE. The novel has been called Hardy's "closest approach to orthodox realism: to an impression of life as an unselective flow of plausible events" (Guerard, *Thomas Hardy,* 81).

In 1889 the Hardys visited Paris. Hardy's first collection of short stories, *WESSEX TALES: STRANGE, LIVELY, AND COMMONPLACE,* was published by Macmillan. The stories had all been published previously, but the collection still attracted interest. The reviewer for the New York *Critic* declared that the volume offered proof that "rural England, as Shakespeare left it, is rural England as Hardy finds it—with the same broad, bland comfortably obtuse human features."

At this time Hardy began *Tess of the d'Urbervilles.* When it was ready for serial publication, conflicts with editors forced Hardy to bowdlerize the text. It was serialized in *The GRAPHIC* in England and in *HARPER'S BAZAAR* in America. Sections were also published in the *FORTNIGHTLY REVIEW* and in the *National Observer.* It was published in book form in three volumes by OSGOOD, MCILVAINE (London, 1891). This novel was possibly the most admired of Hardy's Wessex novels and outsold, on publication, all of Hardy's previous works.

Another collection of stories, *A GROUP OF NOBLE DAMES,* was also published in 1891. In 1892 Hardy's novel *The WELL-BELOVED* was published serially in the

Illustrated London News, although it was not published in book form until 1897, when it was issued by Osgood, McIlvaine & Co. Hardy wrote his publishers that it was the "story of a face which goes through three generations or more." It is an allegorical fantasy about a sculptor, Jocelyn PIERSTON, who falls in love with a woman, her daughter, and her granddaughter, three manifestations of a single person. The setting is the fictional Isle of Slingers (PORTLAND, near Weymouth).

Hardy's father died on July 20, 1892. Hardy was greatly saddened, as they had always been close. He would later write a poem, "TO MY FATHER'S VIOLIN," evoking his father's playing in the STINSFORD CHURCH choir of instrumentalists and vocalists. In the *Life* he recalled the times when he assisted his father with cider-making, using apples from huge old trees in their garden. This was the year Hardy's marriage began to develop difficulties. It was also the time he began work on *Jude the Obscure*, which would be his final novel.

In 1893 the Hardys were invited to Ireland as guests of Lord Houghton, the Lord-Lieutenant of Ireland, and his wife. They were met at the viceregal lodge by his sister, Florence HENNIKER. Her husband, Major the Hon. Arthur Henry Henniker-Major, fought in the BOER WAR. She was one of the many "society" women Hardy met, whom Emma considered "poison" (Stewart, *Thomas Hardy: A Critical Biography*, 29.). Hardy apparently fell in love with her, but recovered; they remained friends until her death in 1923. Together they wrote a story, "The SPECTRE OF THE REAL."

A volume of nine short stories, *LIFE'S LITTLE IRONIES*, was published in 1894. Most of them were set in the present. One of these stories, "THE SON'S VETO," attacked the rigid class structure of Victorian England, in which such virtues as gentility, sensitivity, and patience were less valued than social rank.

The year 1895 saw the publication of *Jude the Obscure*, which provoked a storm of controversy. It depicted the conflict between spiritual and carnal life and was widely attacked as immoral. The most inflammatory issue in the novel, as Rosemarie Morgan observes, was Sue's rebellion against the institutionalization of marriage by church and state and its unfair treatment of women. Hardy was deeply hurt by the criticism of the novel, and turned to poetry, short fiction, and essays, but did not write another novel. The Hardys also visited Belgium in 1895, where Hardy surveyed the field of Waterloo, south of Brussels. He was already contemplating writing *The DYNASTS*.

In 1897 the Hardys went to SWITZERLAND. Two of Hardy's most memorable poems were written at this time, including "LAUSANNE: IN GIBBON'S OLD GARDEN: 11–12 P.M. *27 June 1897 (The 110th anniversary of the completion of the "Decline and Fall" at the same hour and place).*" The long title suggests Hardy's appreciation of

Portrait of Thomas Hardy, c. 1910   (Beinecke Rare Book and Manuscript Library, Yale University)

the historian Edward Gibbon's monumental work *The Decline and Fall of the Roman Empire*. The Hardys stayed at the Hotel Gibbon, and Hardy sat in the garden at the very hour Gibbon completed his book. He also wrote "ZERMATT: TO THE MATTERHORN," a sonnet begun soon after the Hardys arrived there in June 1897. This poem commemorates the first ascent of the Matterhorn in 1865, in which four of seven climbers were lost.

Hardy's first collection of poems, *WESSEX POEMS AND OTHER VERSES*, was published in 1898. The volume contained a number of important poems, including "The IMPERCIPIENT," "The PEASANT'S CONFESSION," "NEUTRAL TONES," "HAP," and "AMABEL." An anonymous reviewer for the *ATHENAEUM* noted that the poems reflected Hardy's "curiously intense and somewhat dismal view of life." Lionel Johnson, writing in the London *Outlook*, saw mixed sentiments in the collection: "passion, humor, wistfulness, grimness, tenderness, but never joy, the radiant and invincible."

The Boer War began in 1899 and lasted until 1902. It was fought by the South African Republic against Great Britain, which had long been regarded with hostility by the Boers. Hardy found the sight of young

Thomas Hardy at Queen's College, Oxford, June 1923
(Beinecke Rare Book and Manuscript Library, Yale University)

British soldiers departing from Southampton an agonizing sight, and wrote several poems pointing up the heartbreak of the war, including "DRUMMER HODGE," "A CHRISTMAS GHOST-STORY," and "The GOING OF THE BATTERY." Florence Henniker's husband fought in the war, but was not wounded.

Another collection, POEMS OF THE PAST AND THE PRESENT, was published in 1902. In his preface Hardy admitted that the poems represented "a series of feelings and fancies" written in different moods and under varying circumstances and that the collection could be said to lack cohesion. He believed this was justified, however: "Unadjusted impressions have their value."

Hardy's mother, Jemima Hardy, died on April 3, 1904 at the age of 91. Although she had suffered from deafness, her mind had remained clear and she was surrounded by her children throughout her life. Hardy wrote that she had been a woman "with an extraordinary store of local memories, reaching back to the days when the ancient ballads were everywhere heard" (*Life,* 321). This year was also marked by publication of the first of three parts of Hardy's epic drama *The Dynasts.*

In 1905 Hardy received the ORDER OF MERIT as well as the honorary degree of LL.D. from the UNIVERSITY OF ABERDEEN.

Part II of *The Dynasts* appeared in 1906, followed by the third part in 1908. This drama dealt with the era of the Napoleonic wars, with 130 scenes and hundreds of characters. Although little read today, it has been termed a "colossal achievement." Marguerite Roberts calls it a work "without parallel in poetry, at least in the twentieth century" (Roberts, *Hardy's Poetic Drama,* 14). The characters are not the country folk, gentry, and land-owning aristocracy of Hardy's short stories and novels, but members of Parliament, national rulers, and military leaders preoccupied with Napoleon's ambitious attempt to dominate Europe. In compiling this work, Hardy was assisted in research by his secretary and literary assistant, Florence Dugdale, a young woman he had met in 1904 or 1905 through Florence Henniker. She would become his second wife in 1914.

Another volume of poetry, TIME'S LAUGHINGSTOCKS AND OTHER VERSES, was published in 1909. The collection contained more than 90 poems, some of which were among Hardy's most noted, such as "A TRAMP-WOMAN'S TRAGEDY," "A SUNDAY MORNING TRAGEDY," "SHUT OUT THAT MOON," "REMINISCENCES OF A DANCING MAN," "HE ABJURES LOVE," "The BALLAD SINGER," "AFTER THE LAST BREATH," "ONE WE KNEW," AND "A CHURCH ROMANCE." Some critics found many of the poems marked by disillusionment and despair, but Hardy objected to this characterization. In 1909 Hardy also accepted the governorship of the DORCHESTER GRAMMAR SCHOOL and the presidency of the Society of Authors, succeeding George MEREDITH.

In 1910 he was presented with the ORDER OF MERIT, and, in 1912, he received the Gold Medal of the ROYAL SOCIETY OF LITERATURE.

Emma Lavinia Hardy died suddenly on November 27, 1912, at Max Gate. She had become mentally unstable, and at one time claimed to have written Hardy's novels. She did write poetry, and also kept diaries, in which she confided her bitter feelings about her marriage. Hardy destroyed the diaries after her death.

In 1913, Hardy revisited St. Juliot, Cornwall, where he and Emma had met. He began writing the series of poems that would become "The Poems of 1912–13," published in SATIRES OF CIRCUMSTANCE in 1914. Hardy's last collection of short stories, A CHANGED MAN AND OTHER TALES, was published this year. He also received the honorary degree of Litt.D. from CAMBRIDGE UNIVERSITY.

On February 10, 1914, Hardy married Florence Dugdale at St. Andrew's, Enfield. The marriage seems to have been a happy one.

WORLD WAR I began this year. Hardy was deeply affected by the war and pledged allegiance to the Allies, as did a number of writers. Some of his friends' sons were killed. One of his most famous poems, "CHANNEL FIRING," was written about the war. He also published a soldiers' war song called "MEN WHO MARCH AWAY" in the London *Times,* which became enormously popular.

Hardy lost his sister Mary in 1915; she died of emphysema. His brother, Henry, and his other sister, Kate, continued to live together until their deaths, in TALBOTHAYS, a home Henry had built on property originally owned by their father.

In 1917, *MOMENTS OF VISION AND MISCELLANEOUS VERSES,* the largest of his collections of verse, was published by Macmillan. Many war poems were included, as well as many others related to the death of Emma. Hardy found the reaction of many critics "disconcerting," as they seemed to be too concerned with poetic diction than with the message he was attempting to convey. Among the poems in this collection are "AFTERNOON SERVICE AT MELLSTOCK," "WE SAT AT THE WINDOW," "TO SHAKESPEARE," "AT MAYFAIR LODGINGS," "QUID HIC AGIS?", "A JANUARY NIGHT, 1879," "The LAST SIGNAL," "The FIGURE IN THE SCENE," "WHY DID I SKETCH," "ON STURMINSTER FOOT-BRIDGE," "OLD FURNITURE," "DURING WIND AND RAIN," "The FIVE STUDENTS," "HE REVISITS HIS FIRST SCHOOL," and "IT NEVER LOOKS LIKE SUMMER." At this time Hardy began to become reclusive, but started work on the *Life* with Florence. She had persuaded him to write down his recollections to forestall future biographers who would take liberties with his perceptions and convictions.

In 1920 Hardy received the honorary degree of Litt.D. from OXFORD UNIVERSITY. This was followed by the publication of *LATE LYRICS AND EARLIER* in 1922, when Hardy was 82. The volume contains a prose "Apology," regarded by many critics as his most significant and extended utterance on poetry and criticism. He admitted that some "grave, positive, stark, delineations" were mixed among poems of the "passive, lighter, and traditional sort" which would probably appeal to "stereotyped tastes." He commented on the "precarious prospects" of English verse, in view of the "Barbarizing of taste in the younger minds" by World War I.

In 1923 Hardy's drama The *FAMOUS TRAGEDY OF THE QUEEN OF CORNWALL* was published. This was a drama set on the Cornish coast at Tintagel Castle, which Hardy illustrated with a drawing of the castle. He had begun it in 1916 after he visited Cornwall with his second wife, Florence; it was performed locally in 1923. The same year he entertained the Prince of Wales at Max Gate.

Another poetry collection was published in 1925, *HUMAN SHOWS, FAR PHANTASIES, SONGS, AND TRIFLES.* This volume sold better than many of his others, and was soon in its third printing. It contained many of his best-known poems, including "THE ABSOLUTE EXPLAINS," "ON THE ESPLANADE," and "NOBODY COMES."

In 1926 Hardy entertained the novelist Virginia Woolf, daughter of his old friend Sir Leslie Stephen, at Max Gate. Hardy paid a final visit to his birthplace at Higher Bockhampton. This year was also marked by the death of his dog "Wessex" at the age of 13. His grave is at Max Gate.

Hardy made his final public appearance the next year, 1927, with an address at the Dorchester Grammar School stone-laying. This year the *Iphigenia in Aulis* of Euripides was played before Hardy at Max Gate by undergraduates of Balliol College, Oxford. In December 1927 Hardy became ill. He died on January 11, 1928, at Max Gate, of heart disease, at the age of 87.

Florence Hardy agreed to the partition of his body on the advice of Sir Sydney COCKERELL and Edward CLODD, a decision she later bitterly regretted. Cockerell had argued that Hardy belonged to the entire nation. His heart was removed for burial in Stinsford Churchyard, in the grave of his first wife, while his remains were cremated and interred in Poet's Corner, WESTMINSTER ABBEY. The services at Stinsford Church and the Abbey were held simultaneously; at the same time, a memorial service was held at ST. PETER'S CHURCH, Dorchester. Hardy's final volume of poetry, *WINTER WORDS,* was published posthumously in 1928.

The definitive edition of his Hardy's letters has seven volumes. His personal notebooks, which begin in 1867 and include research notes, memoranda, and ideas for various subjects gathered from books and travels, were published in 1979. A collection titled *Thomas Hardy's Personal Writings* includes prefaces to his own writings as well as those of other authors.

Hardy, Thomas (1) (1778–1837) Hardy's paternal grandfather. He married "improvidently" at the age of 21. To assist him, his father, John, built the home at HIGHER BOCKHAMPTON in which, in 1840, Hardy was born. After he married and settled in the parish of STINSFORD, he gathered other instrumentalists and played in the village church, also superintending the choir. Many of the Christmas traditions in Hardy's works, including *UNDER THE GREENWOOD TREE* and "The MELLSTOCK QUIRE," are based on the festivities mounted by Hardy's grandfather and father. For instance, on Christmas Eve the choir would assemble at the Hardys' home before six o'clock, have supper (accompanied by "plenty of liquor"), play outside local houses, and then go to other parts of the parish after midnight, returning at six A.M. They would then manage to perform at morning church services.

Joined by his two sons, Thomas also played at two services every Sunday from 1801 or 1802 until he died in 1837, three years before Hardy's birth. Sometimes he assisted other nearby choirs when he was needed. Hardy depicted him in The *RETURN OF THE NATIVE* as

Thomasin YEOBRIGHT's father, bowing when lending his services to the choir of Kingsbere (*Life*, 8–12, *passim*).

Hardy, Thomas (2) (1811–1892) Hardy's father, he was the son of Thomas HARDY (1). Millgate states that he enjoyed a "superior rank" as a master mason and the "lifehold tenant of a substantial cottage." Hardy himself delineated two "castes" within country villages. The upper one contained "artisans, traders, 'liviers' (owners of freeholds), and the manor-house upper servants," while the lower one consisted of farm laborers. The two groups did not mingle, only rarely going to each other's houses (Millgate, *Thomas Hardy: A Biography,* 26). He and his wife, Jemima Hand HARDY, both had relatives in the lower caste, but were essentially members of the upper one in daily life.

In the *Life*, Hardy states that both his father and grandfather were known as the "best church-players" in the neighborhood. The "Hardy instrumentalists," sometimes as many as four, maintained an "easy superiority" over nearby parishes. After the death of Hardy's grandfather, his father gave up his connection with the choir, needing to devote more time to his building business.

Hardy's sonnet "A CHURCH ROMANCE" describes his parents' first meeting about 1836. From the pew, his mother turned and looked at the "music-men with viol, book, and bow" in the gallery. She imagined that one player was sending her a message, "I claim thee as my own forthright!" Many years later she would remember the "gallery-scene" when she saw him as "minstrel, ardent, young, and trim,/Bowing 'New Sabbath' or 'Mount Ephraim'" (*Life*, 14). Hardy was given a toy concertina at the age of four and, soon afterward, shown how to play and tune a violin; he took a keen interest in music as a child.

Hardy recalls that he often assisted his father with cider-making, using apples from huge old trees in their garden. Hardy's parents did not attend his small wedding to Emma Lavinia Gifford (HARDY), but they did spend Christmas with Hardy and Emma in 1876, two years after they were married.

The Corn Exchange, Dorchester, site of many dramatic performances by the Hardy Players (John Gould, Phillips Academy, Andover)

Hardy Players, the A group of amateur actors in DORCHESTER who, under the name of the DORCHESTER DEBATING AND DRAMATIC SOCIETY, produced adaptations of a number of Hardy's works. The society changed its name to the Hardy Players in June 1916 with a production called *Wessex Scenes from The Dynasts.* Hardy attended the rehearsal, and it was performed two weeks later at the Weymouth Pavilion to good reviews (*Life*, 373).

Hardy does not record another performance by the group until November 13, 1920, when they presented *The RETURN OF THE NATIVE*, dramatized by Alderman T. H. Tilley. At Christmas that year the group came to MAX GATE in costume to present a dramatization of the novel, which contains the mummers' play of "Saint George"(see CHRISTMAS MUMMERS). The small audience consisted of Hardy, Florence HARDY, Hardy's sister Katharine HARDY, his brother Henry HARDY, and several servants. There were carol singers outside, and the occasion, according to Florence, gave Hardy "intense joy" (Millgate, *Thomas Hardy: A Biography,* 534–35).

In June 1921 Hardy attended a production of *The Mellstock Quire* in the castle ruins at STURMINSTER NEWTON. In 1922 the group presented a dramatization of *DESPERATE REMEDIES.* Charles Morgan, the manager of the Oxford University Dramatic Society, attended the performance. In 1929, after Hardy's death and at the request of Florence Hardy, Morgan wrote a memoir of the occasion, when he went to tea afterward at Max Gate. Sitting about the fire after tea, Hardy had told him of his theatergoing in LONDON in his youth; he would attend Shakespearean plays "with the text in his hands and, seated in the front rows, follow the dialogue by the stage light" (*Life*, 402).

In April 1923, when Hardy was 83, he completed a rough draft of his "poetical play" *The FAMOUS TRAGEDY OF THE QUEEN OF CORNWALL*. It was published in November, and, the same month, the Hardy Players produced it in the Corn Exchange, Dorchester.

In February 1924 the group performed *The Famous Tragedy of the Queen of Cornwall* in London. In June Rutland BOUGHTON came to Max Gate to consult Hardy about setting the play to music.

On July 1, 1924, another amateur dramatic group, the BALLIOL PLAYERS from OXFORD UNIVERSITY, visited Max Gate and presented *The Oresteia* as *The Curse of the House of Atreus*. Later that year, Hardy dramatized *TESS OF THE D'URBERVILLES* for the Hardy Players, who were led by Alderman T. H. Tilley. Tilley brought models of the sets for Hardy to inspect. Some of the rehearsals were at Max Gate, and the performance was at the Weymouth Pavilion on December 11. Gertrude BUGLER played Tess. It was such a success that it was "asked for" in London. Gwen Ffrangçon-Davies took the part of Tess in the London production.

For further reading: Purdy, *Thomas Hardy: A Bibliographical Study,* containing a full list of all performances (*see* Appendix VI, 351–53); Wilson, "Thomas Hardy and the Hardy Players: The Evans and Tilley Adaptations."

Harper & Brothers   American book publishing firm that also published periodicals devoted to literature. The firm founded *HARPER'S NEW MONTHLY MAGAZINE* in 1850; in 1900 the title was changed to *HARPER'S MONTHLY MAGAZINE* and in 1925 it became *HARPER'S MAGAZINE*. The firm also published *HARPER'S WEEKLY*.

Harper & Brothers published a number of Hardy's works in America: *A GROUP OF NOBLE DAMES* (1891); *TESS OF THE D'URBERVILLES* (1892); the play *The THREE WAYFARERS* (1893); *LIFE'S LITTLE IRONIES* (1894); *JUDE THE OBSCURE* (1895); *The WELL-BELOVED* (1897); *WESSEX POEMS* (1898; issued 1899); *POEMS OF THE PAST AND THE PRESENT* (1902); and *A CHANGED MAN* (1913). In 1915 they issued the Wessex Edition of Hardy's works as the "Autograph Edition." In 1920 this edition was reissued as the Anniversary Edition.

Harper's Bazar   American magazine in which three of Hardy's novels were serialized. Hardy sometimes singled out *The WOODLANDERS* as his favorite novel; it ran from May 15, 1886, to April 9, 1887. The magazine also published *TESS OF THE D'URBERVILLES* (July–December, 1891) and *The WELL-BELOVED* (October 1–December 17, 1892); the latter was without illustrations.

Harper's Monthly Magazine   Magazine owned by HARPER & BROTHERS, American book publisher. The magazine was known as *HARPER'S NEW MONTHLY MAGAZINE* from 1850 to 1900 and then became *HARPER'S MONTHLY MAGAZINE* from 1900 to 1925. In 1925 the title became *HARPER'S MAGAZINE*.

Several of Hardy's poems were published in *Harper's Monthly Magazine:* "The Satin Shoes" (January 1910). "Beyond the Last Lamp" (December 1911); "The ABBEY MASON" (December 1912); "The Telegram" (December 1913); and *"CIRCUS RIDER TO RINGMASTER"* (June 1925).

Harper's New Monthly Magazine   American literary magazine established in 1850 by HARPER & BROTHERS, book publishers. The title was *Harper's New Monthly Magazine* until 1900, then became *HARPER'S MONTHLY MAGAZINE* after 1900. After 1925 it was *HARPER'S MAGAZINE*. The firm also published *HARPER'S WEEKLY*. Among the British authors published in the magazine were Charles Dickens, Edward Bulwer-Lytton, Anthony Trollope, William SHAKESPEARE, William Makepeace Thackeray, and George ELIOT. From 1869–1919, Henry Mills Alden was the editor. Beginning in 1886, William Dean HOWELLS held an editorial post with the magazine, taking charge of the influential "Editor's Easy Chair" department, offering literary commentary.

From February 1878 to January 1879 *The RETURN OF THE NATIVE* was serialized in America in the magazine, and *A LAODICEAN* was serialized in the European edition of the magazine from December 1880 to December 1881 (*Letters* I, 79). At that time the magazine was under the editorship of RICHARD ROGERS BOWKER. Hardy's last novel, *JUDE THE OBSCURE*, was serialized in the magazine from December 1894 to November 1895.

Among the stories published in *Harper's New Monthly Magazine* were "The FIRST COUNTESS OF WESSEX" (Dec. 1889) and *"Few Crusted Characters, A"* (titled "WESSEX FOLK") March–June, 1891.

The most complete source for Hardy's American publications is Richard Purdy, *Thomas Hardy: A Bibliographical Study,* and the most authoritative source for the sequence of Harper's magazines is Frank Luther Mott, *A History of American Magazines 1885–1905* (Cambridge, Mass.: Harvard University Press, 1957).

Harper's Weekly   American magazine published by HARPER & BROTHERS. Hardy's novel *The MAYOR OF CASTERBRIDGE* was serialized in the magazine from January 2, 1886, to May 15, 1886.

A number of Hardy's short stories were also published in this magazine: "An INDISCRETION IN THE LIFE OF AN HEIRESS" (1878); "The DUCHESS OF HAMPTONSHIRE" (published as "The Impulsive Lady of Croome Castle") (1878); "The DISTRACTED PREACHER" (1879); "FELLOW TOWNSMEN" (1880); "The ROMANTIC ADVENTURES OF A MILKMAID" (1883); "The HONOURABLE LAURA" (published as "Benighted Travellers") (1881); "The THREE STRANGERS" (1883); "The WAITING SUPPER" (December 31 1887–January 7, 1888); and "ON THE WESTERN CIRCUIT" (1891). In addition, four stories from *A GROUP OF NOBLE DAMES* was published in the magazine from November 29 to December 20, 1890. The magazine published several of Hardy's poems, including "The MAN HE KILLED" (1902), "ONE WE KNEW" (under the title "Remembrance," 1903), and "The NOBLE LADY'S TALE" (1905).

The most complete source for Hardy's American publications are Carl Weber, *Hardy in America,* and Richard Purdy, *Thomas Hardy: A Bibliographical Study.*

Harrison, Frederic (1831–1923) English writer and philosopher; he practiced law in London and was regarded as a leader of the Positivist movement. Auguste Comte was considered the principal apostle of this philosophical system of belief, which holds that knowledge is based on the experience of the senses and not on metaphysical intuition.

It is uncertain when Hardy first met Harrison, but he notes in the *Life* that on Bastille Day, July 14, 1890, he heard him lecture at Newton Hall, London, on the French Revolution.

Hardy sent Harrison some of his books, and in July 1901 Harrison wrote Hardy he had found *FAR FROM THE MADDING CROWD* well worth reading. Hardy invited Harrison and his wife to visit MAX GATE on their way back from a vacation they were taking in CORNWALL.

On New Year's Day, 1903, Harrison presented a review of the political and social events of 1902 before the London Positivist Society. Hardy wrote that he had read reports of it and had found pleasure in pondering Harrison's "profound & illuminating views of the times" (*Letters* III, 46).

In 1906 Hardy wrote Edmund GOSSE to ask his assistance in supporting the election of Harrison's son, Austin, who was editor of the *Observer,* to the SAVILE CLUB. Harrison was elected.

After the death of Hardy's first wife, Emma HARDY, in 1912, Harrison wrote a letter of condolence. Hardy replied that he had had no inkling that her health was so precarious. He notes in his autobiography that Harrison paid him a short visit at Max Gate in the fall of 1913. In February 1914, after Hardy married his second wife, Florence Dugdale HARDY, Harrison sent his best wishes.

Harrison was much affected by WORLD WAR I and in 1914 wrote Hardy that he feared for the future and felt as if he were awaiting the verdict while his son was being "tried for murder"; he was then 83 (*Letters* V, 44).

Harrison was the author of several works, including a collection of articles, *Memories and Thoughts. Men—Books—Cities—Art* (1906); he sent a copy to Hardy. He also wrote *National and Social Problems* (London, 1908). At this time he wrote Hardy a letter of appreciation for sending him a copy of *The DYNASTS.* When Hardy wrote to thank him, he said he hoped to "overhaul" it some day; no one, he said, knew better than he "the many too hurried pages it contains" (*Letters* III, 304).

In February 1920 Harrison published an adverse review of Hardy's *MOMENTS OF VISION* (a poetry collection), titled "Novissima Verba," that appeared in the *FORTNIGHTLY REVIEW.* The review argued that because Hardy had "everything that man can wish," including a long life, domestic happiness, friends, and honors, the "monotony of gloom" evinced by his poetry "is not human, not social, not true." Hardy decided their friendship had ended. He drafted a number of replies to the review, but his wife Florence persuaded him not to send them (Millgate, *Thomas Hardy: A Biography,* 529). In October 1921 Hardy did sign an illuminated address to be presented to Harrison on his 90th birthday; there were 100 "representative national names" (*Letters* VI, 102). Harrison died in January 1923, and Hardy wrote a sympathetic letter of condolence to his son Austin, who by then was the editor of the *English Review.*

Hatherell, William (1855–1928) Painter and illustrator. He illustrated each of the 12 installments of *JUDE THE OBSCURE.* The novel ran in America in *HARPER'S NEW MONTHLY MAGAZINE* from December 1894 to November 1895. The first installment was titled *The Simpletons;* the title was then altered to *Hearts Insurgent.* In November 1895 the title became *Jude the Obscure.* Book publication was in 1896. Hardy had the complete set of his illustrations framed and hung in his study (they are now in the DORSET COUNTY MUSEUM). On November 10, 1895, he wrote Hatherell to express his "sincere admiration" for the "Jude at the Milestone," the final illustration. He wrote that the picture was a "tragedy in itself," and that he did not recall ever having an artist "who grasped a situation so thoroughly" (*Letters* II, 94).

"Haunter, The" This poem, published in *SATIRES OF CIRCUMSTANCE* (1914), is in the group "Poems of 1912–13," which were inspired by the death of Hardy's first wife, Emma Gifford HARDY (Purdy, *Thomas Hardy: A Bibliographical Study,* 166).

The poem depicts the imagined reproaches of a deceased wife (Emma) against her husband. She haunts him "nightly" and accompanies him "whither his fancy sets him wandering," but cannot answer his words. While she was living, and could answer, he did not speak his thoughts; when she wished to "join in his journeys / Seldom he wished to go." Now that he wants her with him he never sees her "faithful phantom," although he speaks to her. She does go with him to places "Only dreamers know/…Into old aisles where the past is all to him."

She wishes someone would tell him she is a "good haunter." If he even sighs since she has left him, she goes to his side. She believes that she lends him support in her grave, "doing/All that love can do/Still that his path may be worth pursuing,/And to bring peace thereto."

In her monologue, she regrets that she can no longer "rebuke or console" her husband. Hardy had not, in fact, wanted Emma to accompany him on walks or in exploring old churches (Bailey, *The Poetry of Thomas Hardy*, 298). Now that she is dead, he seems to hear her complaints and recognize her devotion more than he ever did during her lifetime.

Havenpool   Hardy's name for POOLE, a sizable Dorset port. It occurs in "TO PLEASE HIS WIFE," "MASTER JOHN HORSELEIGH, KNIGHT," *The MAYOR OF CASTERBRIDGE* (Richard NEWSON lands there when he returns from Newfoundland), and in other works.

Havill, James   Character in *A LAODICEAN*. An architect in Toneborough (Taunton), he is not as well trained or as knowledgeable as George SOMERSET, who privately regards him as a quack. Havill had begun as a landscape gardener, became a builder, and then a road contractor. It is he who built the badly designed Baptist chapel near Sleeping-Green; he is a deacon there.

Havill and Somerset draft competing plans to restore Castle de Stancy, owned by Paula POWER, who fleetingly imagines building a Greek temple within the castle. Havill is burdened by a large family; his wife dies and he is hounded by creditors. He writes an anonymous letter to a London newspaper called "Restoration or Demolition," pleading that the castle be saved and that a Greek temple not be built within its walls. William DARE discovers the draft of the letter and blackmails him. Havill and Dare illicitly make a tracing of Somerset's plans, including an ingenious solution to an architectural problem. The committee of the ROYAL INSTITUTE OF BRITISH ARCHITECTS, which judges the plans, declares them to be equal in merit. Paula later assigns the restoration job to Havill, as he is in debt, and gives him a retainer of £500 to begin restoration. He listens to a sermon by Mr. WOODWELL at the chapel and resigns his commission. Somerset then resigns, and Havill continues the work, but all of it is lost when Dare sets fire to the castle after removing the most valuable paintings.

Haze, Cunningham   Chief constable of the district in which the Castle de Stancy is located in *A LAODICEAN*. He rightly suspects Captain William DE STANCY's illegitimate son, William DARE, of many offenses, but Dare always manages to evade prosecution.

"He Abjures Love"   Poem written in 1883 and published in *TIME'S LAUGHINGSTOCKS* (1909). Hardy described it in a letter to Alfred NOYES as a "love-poem, and lovers are chartered irresponsibles" (*Life*, 409). In this poem Hardy lays out the consequences for a person who has devoted his life entirely to love, making it the foundation and lodestar of his existence. The dedicated lover looks back over his periods of "heart-

enslavement." Love has beckoned and caused "fatuous fires"; the lover has become "enkindled by his wiles/to new embraces," abandoning "kith and kind" and all else. Hardy presents the stoical viewpoint of a person no longer bewitched by love. His views are more objective and he will no longer fancy that he sees in the wind a "yearning cry" and in the midnight drizzle "dew." A new cynicism and objectivity are born. Yet, he realizes, after love there only come a "few sad vacant hours/And then, the Curtain" [i.e., death].

Evelyn Hardy terms the poem "compact with certitude and decision." She suggests that it embodies Hardy's "mature view of life" at the age of 43, in 1883, when he had "an increasing disillusion with life." She states that it puts forth the "doctrine of resignation and renunciation" Hardy was developing; there is a conflict between his "responsive heart" and the logic of his "fastidious mind" (Evelyn Hardy, *Thomas Hardy: A Critical Biography*, 199). Gilbert Murray wrote Hardy that he delighted in the poem; it was "so like Horace: the thought, the severity and clearness of form, and the fine stinging rhythm" (Bailey, *The Poetry of Thomas Hardy*, 222).

health and illness, Hardy's concern with   When Hardy was born on June 2, 1840, he appeared to be so sickly he was not expected to live, but the nurse took another look at him and exclaimed to the surgeon, "Dead! Stop a minute: he's alive enough, sure!" (*Life*, 14). As a small child he was fragile, and, in a noted poem, described himself as "the smallest and feeblest of folk there" ("IN TENEBRIS III"). Hardy's letters contain many references to colds, coughs, dyspepsia, failing eyesight, headaches, influenza, toothache, lumbago, neuralgia, rheumatism, varicose veins, and other ailments, but most of them seem to have been transient. He suffered, in his last few years, from weakened eyesight, and was unable to read for long periods. In June 1927 he wrote his friend Edward CLODD that his weak eyes prevented his writing anything but short notes (*Letters* VII, 70). Five weeks before he died, his wife Florence HARDY wrote a letter for him in which she said he found letter-writing "very irksome, & trying to his eyes" (*Letters* VII, 87).

His most prolonged illness was in late 1880. In late October Hardy and his first wife, Emma, made a week-long visit to CAMBRIDGE UNIVERSITY, where they were shown much hospitality and escorted through many of the colleges (Hardy had visited the grounds before, but it was new to Emma). When the Hardys returned to London, Hardy felt so unwell they declined an invitation to visit Lord (Richard) Houghton, at Fryston, Yorkshire. Hardy worsened, and a local doctor came at once. He diagnosed an internal hemorrhage and recommended immediate surgery; the problem may have been a stone in the urinary tract. Hardy was terrified, as anesthesia and surgery were primitive at the time, and Emma discussed it with their nearby friends the Alexander Macmillans. The Macmillans sent their own doctor, who agreed with the diagnosis, and said that Hardy might avoid surgery by agreeing to a prolonged stay in bed. Hardy chose this course, and dictated most of *A LAODICEAN* to Emma while lying prone for five months on a board, his body elevated above his head. He described the experience in his poem "A Wasted Illness," in which he visualizes "The door to Death." He made a full recovery and lived on until 1928. Emma did not tell Hardy's parents how ill he was, but kept referring to a "headache."

His final illness began at the end of 1927, with increasing weakness. As described by his wife Florence, he could no longer listen to the reading of prose. On January 10 he rallied slightly and wrote a check to the Pension Fund of the Society of Authors, but his signature was feeble. He asked her to read Robert BROWNING's poem "Rabbi Ben Ezra" to him. He seemed stronger the next day and asked her to repeat a verse from the *Rubaiyat of Omar Khayyam*. In the evening he suffered an acute heart attack. The doctor came, but could do little; Hardy was conscious until "a few minutes before the end. Shortly after nine he died." An hour later Florence went to his bedside and saw, on his face, "a look of radiant triumph such as imagination could never have conceived" (*Life*, 445–46).

Hearts Insurgent One of the early titles of *JUDE THE OBSCURE*. This title was used for some of the early installments of the novel in *HARPER'S NEW MONTHLY MAGAZINE*. The first installment, in December 1894, was under the title *The Simpletons*.

Helmsdale, the Right Reverend Cuthbert The bishop of Melchester, he is the second husband of Lady Viviette CONSTANTINE in *TWO ON A TOWER* and the legal father of her son by Swithin ST. CLEEVE. Their marriage is unhappy, and he dies at the age of 54.

Henchard, Elizabeth-Jane (1) In *The MAYOR OF CASTERBRIDGE*, she is the infant daughter of Michael HENCHARD and Susan HENCHARD. Richard NEWSON, the sailor to whom a drunken Michael Henchard auctions his wife, takes Susan and her daughter to Canada. Elizabeth-Jane dies three months afterward, but Susan has another daughter with Newson (*see* Elizabeth-Jane HENCHARD [2]).

Henchard, Elizabeth-Jane (2) The second Elizabeth-Jane Henchard in *The MAYOR OF CASTERBRIDGE* is the daughter of Susan HENCHARD and Richard NEWSON. She is named for her older half sister, Elizabeth-Jane HENCHARD (1), who died as a baby, the daughter of Susan and Michael HENCHARD. Susan has never told Elizabeth-Jane the true story of her life. Elizabeth-Jane is about 18 when she and Susan arrive in CASTERBRIDGE. Henchard

believes her to be his own daughter, about which Susan had concealed the truth out of embarrassment. When he discovers she is not his daughter, he grows cold to her, although he later comes to love her. Elizabeth-Jane adores Donald FARFRAE but loses him to Lucetta LE SUEUR. After Lucetta's death, she marries Farfrae.

Henchard, Michael As the principal personage in *The MAYOR OF CASTERBRIDGE*, Henchard, "a blundering Titan of a self-made man," is one of the finest of Hardy's creations. The subtitle of the novel, "A Story of a Man of Character," gives little indication of Henchard's depth. He is both primitive and virile, a man of violent passions. Given to drink in his early years, he becomes quarrelsome at the Weydon-Priors country fair and auctions off his wife, Susan HENCHARD, and child, Elizabeth-Jane HENCHARD (1), to a sailor, Richard NEWSON (an "indefensible proceeding"). Henchard goes to CASTERBRIDGE, where he rises to become the rich, respected mayor, but when, years later, his wife and daughter suddenly reappear, his power and reputation are undermined, bringing him to ruin. He thinks for a time that the grown Elizabeth-Jane is his daughter, but eventually learns that his own child died in infancy and the young woman is actually Newson's daughter (*see* HENCHARD, ELIZABETH-JANE [2]). He gives Donald FARFRAE his start, hiring him as manager of his corn business, but then quarrels with him.

Henchard dominates the novel, representing a consciousness divided against itself. In one memorable scene he gazes into the water of Ten Hatches Hole and sees an image of a human body, lying "stiff and stark." He perceives that it is actually himself, floating as if dead.

Henchard is a lone figure within the novel, detaching himself not only from Susan and Elizabeth-Jane, whom he has come to love, but also from Farfrae, Lucetta LE SUEUR, whom he had once courted, and the townspeople. He finally dies alone, on the heath, where he is found by Abel WHITTLE, who informs Elizabeth-Jane and Farfrae. He leaves instructions on a scrap of paper that Elizabeth-Jane not be told of his death and that he be buried in unconsecrated ground with no mourns, flowers, or tolling bells. Elizabeth-Jane follows his instructions but feels guilty for a long time, especially about their last meeting. She wails to Donald that she would not have minded the "bitterness" of Henchard's message so much if it had not been for their final parting. At that time she had chastised Henchard for not telling her Newson was her real father and declared she could no longer love him as she once had.

Henchard, Susan The young wife of Michael HENCHARD in *The MAYOR OF CASTERBRIDGE*. In one of the most noted scenes in all of Hardy's fiction, her drunken husband auctions her at Weydon-Priors Fair. She is purchased by a sailor, Richard NEWSON, who takes her and her baby daughter, Elizabeth-Jane HENCHARD (1) to Canada. She naively assumes that she is Newson's legal wife, since he has purchased her. Her baby dies, but she has another daughter, also called Elizabeth-Jane (*see* HENCHARD, ELIZABETH-JANE [2]). Newson goes to sea and is reported drowned, impelling Susan to bring her daughter back to Falmouth, England, and search for Henchard. She finds him, and he remarries her. She tries to arrange Elizabeth-Jane's marriage to Donald FARFRAE, but Henchard disapproves. She dies about a year after her reunion with Henchard.

"He Never Expected Much" [or] A Consideration [A reflection] on My Eighty-Sixth Birthday   Poem written on the occasion of Hardy's birthday in 1926. It was published in the *Daily Telegraph*, March 19, 1928, and collected in *WINTER WORDS* (1928). The poet addresses the World, stating in the first stanza that the world has "kept faith" with him and has "proved to be/Much as you said you were," he never expected "That life would be all fair."

The World answers that it has received love from many, serenity from others, and contempt from some. In the final stanza, the World declares it does not "promise overmuch," except "neutral-tinted haps and such." The poet responds that he has taken the warning seriously and has been able to avoid, in this way, the "strain and ache" of each year.

In the first and second lines of each stanza a phrase is repeated, almost as a refrain, giving the poem a quality of chant. In the first stanza, the poet addresses the World: "Well, World, you have kept faith with me/Kept faith with me;" The second stanza looks back to his childhood: "'Twas then you said, and since have said,/Times since have said,'" The World responds in the third stanza: "'I do not promise overmuch,/Child; overmuch;'" The stoicism of this poem is similar to the occasional mood of somber reflection that inspired "CHILDHOOD AMONG THE FERNS" (Bailey, *The Poetry of Thomas Hardy*, 602). The poet wishes to see life as it is, a mixture of the agreeable and the unpleasant. It is possible that Hardy was looking back on his less than happy marriage to Emma HARDY, who had died 14 years earlier.

Henniker, Florence (1855–1923)   The daughter of Lord Houghton (*see* Richard Monckton Milnes HOUGHTON) and the sister of the Lord Lieutenant of Ireland Robert Offley Ashburton Crewe-Milnes, Lord HOUGHTON (later the marquess of Crewe); her husband, the Honorable Arthur Henry Henniker, the youngest son of the fourth Lord Henniker, fought in the BOER WAR and rose to the rank of general. Hardy apparently fell in love with her, but had to be content with an intellectual and professional relationship; they remained friends until her death in 1923.

Florence Henniker, c. 1897   (Beinecke Rare Book and Manuscript Library, Yale University)

In 1893 the Hardys were invited to Ireland as guests of Lord Houghton and his wife. They were met by Houghton's sister, Florence Henniker. At that time she was the author of three novels. Compared with Emma, who, at the age of 51, appeared in Dublin in a ridiculously youthful muslin and blue ribbon outfit, Henniker was well-dressed, poised, and highly intelligent (Millgate, *Thomas Hardy: A Biography*, 335). She was one of the many women Hardy met in "London society," which Emma considered "poison" (Stewart, *Thomas Hardy: A Critical Biography*, 29). Hardy wrote in his diary of the "charming, *intuitive* woman" he had met.

In June 1893 he sent her a handbook on architecture and offered to escort her on a tour of Westminster Abbey, which she accepted. He wrote her about the abbey and other churches which "offer excellent features for study," and told her he wanted her "to be able to walk into a church and pronounce upon its date at a glance; and you are apt scholar enough to soon arrive at that degree of knowledge" (*Letters* II, 11). He then embarked on a form of courtship, seeing her when he could and often writing her.

In January 1900 he wrote to congratulate her on her story "Lady Gilian," which had been published in a periodical and would be collected in Contrasts (London, 1903). He said that the story, like her others, "makes one wish there were more of it," and found the opening "beautiful, & tender," although he wished the conclusion had been "worked out at greater length" (*Letters* II, 245).

Eventually, Hardy realized that Florence Henniker's conventional views of marriage would not permit any relationship to exist between them other than a platonic one. She might never have known the true nature and depth of Hardy's feelings (Millgate, *Thomas Hardy: A Biography*, 338, 341). Hardy wrote a sketch of Mrs. Henniker that appeared in the *Illustrated London News* on August 18, 1894; it accompanied her portrait. It was reprinted in July 1896 in her volume *In Scarlet and Grey*. Hardy and Henniker had already begun collaborating on a short story, "The SPECTRE OF THE REAL," which was published in November 1894 in *To-Day*, a magazine owned by the humorist Jerome K. Jerome. At least two of Hardy's poems are thought to be associated with Mrs. Henniker: "A BROKEN APPOINTMENT" and "A Thunderstorm in Town" (F. B. Pinion, *A Hardy Companion*, 363). The latter describes the disappointment of a "time-torn" (aged) man, i.e., Hardy, as he waits for a woman who fails to meet him. Purdy places the scene at the British Museum (Purdy, *Thomas Hardy: A Bibliographical Study*, 113). General Henniker died in February 1912, and Hardy wrote a brief poem in his memory titled "A. H., 1855–1912." It was included in a volume of obituaries and reminiscences Mrs. Henniker published, titled *Arthur Henniker, A Little Book for His Friends* (London: 1912; Purdy, *Thomas Hardy: A Bibliographical Study*, 315). In 1920 Florence Henniker was staying in Weymouth and seemed to have some idea of buying a home in DORSET. Hardy and his second wife, Florence Dugdale HARDY, undertook to show her about the countryside, but she did not settle in the county. She did pay a visit to the Hardys in July 1922, when they went for a drive in Blackmore Vale and to Sherborne, Dorset, scene of *The WOODLANDERS*. She died on April 4, 1923, of heart failure. He mentions the event in the *Life*: "After a friendship of 30 years!" She was buried April 10 at Thornham Magna, Eye, Suffolk (*Life*, 416, 419).

For further reading: Cramer, "'The Spectre of the Real' by Thomas Hardy and Florence Henniker"; Hardy and Pinion, *One Rare Fair Woman: Thomas Hardy's Letters to Florence Henniker, 1893–1922*; Ray, "A Note on Florence Henniker and Solentsea"; Wilson, "Thomas Hardy and Florence Henniker: A Probable Source for Hardy's 'Had You Wept.'"

Herbert, Henry Howard Molyneux   *See* CARNARVON, HENRY HOWARD MOLYNEUX HERBERT, FOURTH EARL OF.

Herbert, Lady Winifred Anne Henrietta Christine (1864–1933),   afterward Lady Burghclere. Hardy met Lady Winifred, the eldest daughter of the earl and countess of CARNARVON, in early 1885, at a house party at Eggesford, Devon, the country home of her uncle and aunt, the earl and countess of PORTSMOUTH. (Lady Portsmouth was Lord Carnarvon's sister.) Emma HARDY was unable to accompany him.

Lady Winifred was apparently much taken with Hardy, and asked her mother to invite him to their London home. He went to evening parties at the town house of Lord and Lady Carnarvon in May and December 1885. Emma remained in DORSET. The Hardys' home, MAX GATE, was nearing completion, but Emma might also have resented Hardy's being taken up by "society."

In December 1885 Hardy went to another evening party at the home of Lord and Lady Carnarvon. He wrote Lady Winifred on January 3, 1886, saying that he had intended to use "Winifred" as the name of his next heroine, but the story was to be a tragic one (*The WOODLANDERS*). He asked her to let him know if she objected. Lady Winifred seemed to have reservations about the "tragic destiny" (*Letters* VII, 102), but she later changed her mind; when Hardy attended a party in December 1886 at the home of Lord and Lady Carnarvon, she said she did want him to call his heroine "Winifred." Hardy replied that it was too late to make the changes. She married Lord Burghclere at the Savoy Chapel on January 10, 1887. He finished *The Woodlanders*, in which the heroine's name is Grace, on February 4, 1887; it was published the following month. (*Life*, 170, 184–185.)

"Heredity"   Poem published in *MOMENTS OF VISION* (1914), arguing that the genetic lineaments of the "family face" are transmitted independent of circumstances of time and geography. The germ of the poem was contained in Hardy's diary entry for February 19, 1889, in which he writes that the "story of a face which goes through three generations or more" would make a "fine novel or poem of the passage of Time" (*Life*, 217). This was, to some extent, the theme of his novel, *The WELL-BELOVED*.

The speaker in the poem is the "family face," which has survived despite the fact that "flesh perishes." The face projects "trait and trace" through time, independent of place. Thus it is empowered to "despite" the "human span of durance," since it is the "eternal thing in man,/That heeds no call to die." Hardy's poem "The Pedigree" (1916) has a similar theme.

"He Revisits His First School"   Poem collected in *MOMENTS OF VISION* (1917). It describes Hardy's visit as an elderly man to the school he had attended for one year, which Mrs. Julia Augusta MARTIN had established in 1848 at Lower Bockhampton (*see* EDUCATION OF HARDY).

He recalls being in the school as a child, but returning to the school is more awkward than he expected. Had he come as a ghost the pupils might have remembered him fondly. Instead, as an old visitor in the afternoon sun, he senses that he is but an interruption; "none wished to see me come there."

The poem refers to Francis Walkingame, the author of an arithmetic textbook, and the "Rule-of-Three," a method of finding a mathematical proportion (Bailey, *The Poetry of Thomas Hardy*, 403). Hardy was eight at the time he attended Mrs. Martin's school.

Herkomer, Sir Hubert von (1849–1914)   Painter, who, with his pupils, drew the serial illustrations for TESS OF THE D'URBERVILLES. In 1892 he sent Hardy the original drawing of Tess's return from the dance, which is now in the DORSET COUNTY MUSEUM (*Letters* I, 255).

In July 1908 Hardy began sitting in London for his portrait by von Herkomer; it also is now in the Dorset County Museum. The painter had so many engagements that he could arrange only two sittings for Hardy per week. Hardy went for a sitting in December 1908 and had to telegraph Emma HARDY to send the clothes he had been wearing when the portrait was begun, a gray-green jacket and a black-and-white knitted waistcoat (*Letters* III, 358).

The Herkomer Company, in which Sir Hubert von Herkomer's son, Siegfried, was active, had purchased the film rights to FAR FROM THE MADDING CROWD from Hardy for £50. Sir Hubert Herkomer died in 1914. In 1915 his son asked Hardy if he could transfer the film rights from MACMILLAN & CO., to Curtis Brown, who took over the responsibility for resolving the matter. This led to complicated negotiations and Hardy's wish "to let the whole thing drop, & return the £50 Herkomer paid as a deposit" (*Letters* V, 103–04). He finally asked Macmillan to convey the film rights directly to the new company, as he had no wish to enter into a new contract (*Letters* V, 106).

Hicks, John (1815–1869)   Dorchester architect who met Hardy in 1856, when Hardy was 16 years old. Hicks offered to take him under his wing and teach him the profession of architecture. Hardy's father considered Hicks's proposition an excellent opportunity for his son. For the ensuing few years, Hardy read for several hours each morning, then walked into DORCHESTER to study with Hicks, whose speciality was Gothic architecture and who was well known as a church restorer. Although Hardy later worked for several well-known London architects, he esteemed Hicks and dedicated a humorous account of the origin of the Perpendicular style, "The ABBEY MASON," to him. This style of architecture has flying buttresses supporting the stone walls, high towers, ribbed vaults, pinnacles, and intricate tracery.

In 1862 Hardy went to London and worked for Sir Arthur William BLOMFIELD. When his health declined, in 1867, he returned again to Dorchester and worked several months for Hicks, returning to London in 1869. Hicks died in the winter of 1869, and his practice was purchased by another architect, G. R. CRICKMAY. It was Crickmay who asked Hardy to assist in his Weymouth office with the completion of some of Hicks's commissions. One of them was the restoration of ST. JULIOT CHURCH in CORNWALL; it was in the course of this work that Hardy met his first wife, Emma Lavinia Gifford HARDY. In time Hardy abandoned the profession of architecture in favor of writing, but he depicted several young architects in his novels, including A LAODICEAN and DESPERATE REMEDIES.

Higher Bockhampton   Hamlet near DORCHESTER where Hardy was born on June 2, 1840. (It is called Upper Mellstock in his novels.)

Hardy's great-grandfather, John Hardy, built the Hardy family home in 1800 for his son, Thomas HARDY (1), who was Hardy's grandfather. Hardy's grandfather died just before Hardy was born, but Hardy's father, Thomas HARDY (2), and his wife, Jemima Hand HARDY, continued to live there with their growing family. An insurance policy of 1829 described the house as "standing alone, mud walls and thatched."

The house is remote enough to have been used by smugglers for storing brandy that had come ashore between Weymouth and Lulworth Cove, a few miles away. It is set in an acre of ground with box, laurustinus bushes, clipped evergreens, and informal plantings of herbaceous plants, bulbs, shrubs, tulips, day lilies, lavender, sweet pea, and other flowers. There are old fruit trees in the garden, in addition to new ones. Hardy used to assist his father in making cider from the fruit of the trees. What was once EGDON HEATH lies to the east, but it has been "afforested" by the Forestry Commission and is no longer wild and untamed.

The cottage itself is made of cob, a material consisting of gravel, sand, chalk, clay, and flint. The original building was smaller than the house today. An extension, thought to be a separate building, at one time, was constructed after his parents were married in 1839, possibly for Hardy's grandmother, Mary Head Hardy. It is believed the two buildings were joined after her death in 1857. The floor of the main room on the ground floor is made of Portland flagstones, and the inglenook fireplace has been restored (it was bricked up at one time). There are window seats and leaded lights. There is also a kitchen with a bread oven.

Upstairs there are three main rooms and a smaller one. Hardy was born in the only bedroom with a window facing east. It has chestnut floorboards and deep window seats.

Thomas Hardy's birthplace, Higher Bockhampton, Dorchester, Dorset   (Sarah Bird Wright)

Hardy returned to his birthplace many times after he moved to MAX GATE, and, later, brought friends by car to show them his family home. He did not like to see it shabby or neglected. When he was no longer able to visit it himself, he talked about it to his second wife, Florence HARDY. It is open to the public on designated days.

For further reading: Hardy's Cottage (National Trust, 1999); Desmond Hawkins, *Thomas Hardy* (National Trust, 1990).

Hill, Vernon (1887–???)   Artist and illustrator who supplied a drawing of Hardy for the frontispiece of the 1923 reissue of Lionel JOHNSON's book *The Art of Thomas Hardy* (London: John Lane, 1923). Hill had hoped to stay at MAX GATE, but Florence HARDY wrote to him saying that Hardy's health prevented their having houseguests. They would, she said, be happy to have him to lunch and tea for the days he was working in the house (*Letters* VI, 140).

Hinton, Adelaide   In *DESPERATE REMEDIES*, the girl to whom Edward SPRINGROVE has long been betrothed.

Cytherea GRAYE loves Edward, but is discouraged to learn of his relationship with Adelaide. Just before Cytherea is forced to marry Aeneas MANSTON to save the health of her brother, Adelaide marries Farmer Bullen, a wealthy man much older than she.

"His Country"   Poem written in 1913 and collected in *MOMENTS OF VISION* (1917). The theme of the poem, which presents a trip abroad taken by an English patriot, is outlined in a marginal chronology contained in glosses attached to each stanza. These glosses, each of which is punctuated at the end, make up a counterpoint to the poem, a summary of each stanza from the point of view of an outside observer. Taken together, with the punctuation retained, they recapitulate the poem and could actually form a sixth stanza.

The first stanza has beside it, in small type, "He travels southward, and looks around;"—in this section the traveler recalls journeying from his "native spot" across the sea; he finds, on the Continent, that people there "laboured and suffered each his lot/Even as I did mine."

The second stanza has beside it the explanation: "and cannot discover the boundary"—The traveler remarks, "It did not seem to me" ... that "my dear country . . . Had ended with the sea." The people "in meads and marts" seem similar to those he has left behind.

The third stanza is beside the phrase "of his native country;" The speaker "further and further went anon," but finds, "all the men I looked upon/Had heart-strings fellow-made." In other words, they are no different from people at home.

The fourth stanza has, beside it, the phrase "or where his duties to his fellow-creatures end;" Going around the globe, the traveler "traced the whole terrestrial round." He tries to find a boundary to his "denizenship." He concludes, "I have found/Its scope to be world-wide."

The fifth and last stanza has the phrase "nor who are his enemies" beside it. In this stanza the speaker asks himself, "Whom have I to fight,/And whom have I to dare,/And whom to weaken, crush, and blight?" His country has been "kept in sight/On my way everywhere."

The poem, ironically, was written before WORLD WAR I was declared. In the *Life,* Hardy states that he felt "common sense had taken the place of bluster in men's minds," a feeling so strong that he wrote the verses based on "the decline of antagonism between peoples" (*Life,* 365). Amiya Chakravarty summarizes the point Hardy is making, that "patriotism of the genuine kind admits the right to similar sentiment in other people, and thus makes for that real international understanding which is based on the recognition of common rights and a unity of aspiration" (*"The Dynasts" and the Post-War Age in Poetry,* quoted in Bailey, 418).

"His Education"   *See* "GOD'S EDUCATION."

"History of the Hardcomes"   *See* "FEW CRUSTED CHARACTERS, A."

Holder, Helen Catherine (c.1838–1900)   The sister of Thomas Hardy's first wife, Emma Lavinia Gifford HARDY, and wife of the Reverend Caddell HOLDER, rector of ST. JULIOT CHURCH, CORNWALL. Helen had married him in 1868, following the death of his first wife in 1867. At the time of their marriage he was 65 and she was 30; Emma was about 28. Helen and Emma were the daughters of John Attersoll Gifford of Bodmin, who had been a solicitor in Plymouth.

Emma attended her sister's wedding and went immediately with her to Cornwall. Her "Recollections," written in 1911, which were discovered after her death, and included in the *Life,* stated that the parish was a "difficult" one and that Helen needed her assistance. It was at St. Juliot that Emma met Hardy in 1870; he was

the long-expected "Architect" who was sent from Weymouth to restore the church. Emma lived with the Holders until her marriage to Hardy in 1874.

In the autumn of 1900 Emma attended her sister in her final illness at Lee-on-Solent in Hampshire. Helen died in early December. Rev. Holder had died in 1882.

For further reading: Gittings, "Emma Hardy and the Giffords, Papers Presented at the 1973 Summer School."

Holder, Rev. Caddell (1803–1882)   Rector of ST. JULIOT CHURCH, CORNWALL, from 1863 to 1882, and brother-in-law of Thomas Hardy's first wife, Emma Lavinia Gifford HARDY. He was the son of a judge in Barbados and had attended Trinity College, Oxford. His first wife had died in 1867, when he was 64. He married Helen Catherine Gifford in 1868. He was apparently well-liked in the parish, which previously had been much neglected.

After Emma's death Hardy found a manuscript dating from 1911, the year before her death, called "Some Recollections," giving details about her sister's wedding and her life at St. Juliot, where she and the Holders lived in the rectory. He included the manuscript in the *Life.* Hardy's verse drama *The FAMOUS TRAGEDY OF THE QUEEN OF CORNWALL* was dedicated to his two wives and to the Holders: E. L. H. (Emma Lavinia Hardy), C. H. (Caddell Holder), H. C. H. (Helen Catherine Holder), and F. E. H. (Florence Emily Hardy).

Holland, Clive (1866–1959)   Pseudonym of Charles James Hankinson. As Clive Holland he wrote a number of books and articles on Hardy. In 1897 he wrote Hardy to ask whether he might be interested in joining him in publishing photographs of the places described in his novels. Hardy declined (*Letters* II, 177).

Holland wrote a three-part article, "Thomas Hardy's Country: Scenes from the Wessex Novels," for *The BOOKMAN* that ran from June to August, 1899, and then sent the photographs used for illustrations to Hardy, who wrote him a letter of thanks.

In June 1901 Holland visited MAX GATE along with other members of the WHITEFRIARS CLUB (a society of London journalists). He then proceeded to give a detailed account of the visit in a November article for *The Bookman,* "Thomas Hardy: The Man, His Books, and the Land of Wessex." Hardy wrote Lady PORTSMOUTH (Eveline, dowager countess of Portsmouth, widow of the fifth earl of Portsmouth) that it had been written against his wishes. The facts, he stated, had been obtained from him "under considerable pressure" (*Letters* II, 302).

Holland frequently approached Hardy about ideas and projects Hardy felt were unsuitable, if not demeaning to him. In 1905 Holland wrote a third article based on Hardy's novels and other writings, "Thomas Hardy and the Land of Wessex," published in *Pall Mall Magazine* in November. He wanted to reproduce a page of one of Hardy's manuscripts as an illustration, but Hardy wrote that there was a "touch of bad taste in an author who allows such a reproduction to be made in his lifetime." He wished to dissociate himself from the article list readers assume he had inspired Holland to write it (*Letters* III, 178).

In 1909 Holland suggested editing an abridged edition of all Hardy's novels, but Hardy reminded him that the press had "derided" a similar scheme for the novels of Sir Walter Scott 20 years earlier, and he refused permission.

Hardy's responses to Holland were polite in tone, but it is obvious he must have been annoyed by Holland's schemes to build a cottage industry, as it were, on the foundation of Wessex. Hardy became so irritated with Holland that he finally refused to allow him to visit Max Gate (Millgate, *Thomas Hardy: A Biography*, 413). Neither *Holland* nor *Hankinson* are indexed in the *Life*.

Holmes, Oliver Wendell (1809–1894)   American man of letters, physician, and professor of anatomy and physiology at Harvard University, and father of the American jurist Oliver Wendell Holmes. When James Russell LOWELL began publishing the ATLANTIC MONTHLY, Holmes not only named the magazine but also contributed the series of essays, fiction, verse, and conversation called "The Autocrat of the Breakfast-Table."

Hardy was introduced to Holmes in 1886 by Edmund GOSSE and his wife. He recorded the meeting in the *Life*, calling him "an aged boy ... a very bright, pleasant, juvenile old man." Holmes told him he did not read novels, but Hardy resisted telling him he had not read Holmes's essays. He saw Holmes at a dinner of the RABELAIS CLUB a few days later, along with Henry JAMES and George MEREDITH.

In 1887 Hardy received a letter from his friend Anne Benson PROCTER that she was displeased by an article Holmes had written. Holmes had said the "most wonderful" thing he had seen in England were "the Old Ladies—they are so active, and tough like Old Macaws." She questioned Hardy: "Now am I like an Old Macaw?—He might have said Parrots" (*Life*, 180–81; 190–91).

Holt, Henry (1840–1926)   American publisher who reprinted UNDER THE GREENWOOD TREE, A PAIR OF BLUE EYES, and DESPERATE REMEDIES without Hardy's knowledge or approval. In March 1874 Hardy wrote his British publisher SMITH, ELDER & CO. that Holt had sent a sum that was "comparatively a trifle"; he hoped that FAR FROM THE MADDING CROWD might be reprinted in America by the publisher most likely "to issue it in the best form, in the best company, and give it most public-

ity" (*Letters* I, 29). Holt published the novel in November 1874; the same month Hardy wrote asking him not to "prejudice [endanger] its issue in the *Atlantic Monthly*" (*Letters* I, 32). Considering the circumstances, Hardy was extremely polite; in February 1875 he wrote requesting a copy of the novel if it would not be "greatly troubling." He permitted Holt to publish the first American edition of The HAND OF ETHELBERTA in May 1876.

In January 1886 Hardy wrote Holt to ask his opinion of several American periodicals, including the *Household Magazine* and *Fireside Companion*. Hardy's story "Our Exploits at West Poley" was published in the former in 1892–93 (*Letters* I, 141).

"Honorable Laura, The"   Short story collected in *A GROUP OF NOBLE DAMES*.

Honorary Fellowships   Hardy was invited to become an Honorary Fellow of MAGDALENE COLLEGE, CAMBRIDGE UNIVERSITY, in 1913, and an Honorary Fellow of QUEEN'S COLLEGE, OXFORD UNIVERSITY, in late 1924. Both invitations were signal honors that Hardy accepted with pleasure. Honorary Fellows are assigned special stalls (tall carved seats) in the college chapel, dine "in hall" (at a special table in the dining room) with the Fellows, and, after dinner, converse with other Fellows in the Common Room.

Hopkins, Arthur (1848–1930)   Artist and younger brother of the poet Gerard Manley Hopkins. Hopkins was a staff illustrator for BELGRAVIA, a periodical edited by the writer Mary Elizabeth Braddon. He had studied at Academy schools and at Heatherley's and would later become a member of the Royal Watercolour Society. He called magazine illustration "fearful work" and "artistic hack work" (Jackson, *Illustration and the Novels of Thomas Hardy*, 40), but was, nevertheless, a mainstay of *Belgravia*.

Hopkins seemed a good choice to illustrate *The RETURN OF THE NATIVE* when it was serialized in *Belgravia* from January to December 1878. In February 1878 Hardy wrote that he liked the first drawing, although he felt Eustacia VYE should have appeared younger (*Letters* I, 52). He then instructed him that Thomasin YEOBRIGHT should be seen as the "good heroine" and Eustacia the "wayward & erring heroine." Hardy said he considered Clym YEOBRIGHT the most important character. He offered to send a rough sketch of any scenes that might be "troublesome" to Hopkins.

On February 20 he sent Hopkins sketches of possible costumes for the May issue, which would contain the Christmas scenes of the mummers' play. He drew three sketches of Eustacia as the Turkish Knight, as well as one of a mummer's staff or spear. He indicated that the pasteboard helmet should be modeled on the "teacosys" currently in use, with a tuft at the top. He would leave Clym's face up to Hopkins; a "thoughtful young man of 25 is all that can be shown" (*Letters* I, 54–55).

The illustrations were not altogether successful, not only because of inferior technical engraving, but also because of Hopkins's limited abilities with perspective and the human figure. The illustrations do, however, convey alienation, a major theme in the novel (Jackson, 88–93).

For further reading: Jackson, *Illustration and the Novels of Thomas Hardy.*

Houghton, Richard Monckton Milnes, first baron (1809–1885)   Politician, man of letters, poet, and father of Florence HENNIKER. In July 1880 Lord Houghton introduced Hardy to the American poet James Russell Lowell; Hardy thought him "charming" and, as a writer, "one of extraordinary talent," but without "instinctive and creative genius" (*Life,* 138). In April 1883 Hardy met Robert BROWNING and the English novelist Rhoda Broughton at a luncheon Lord Houghton gave in London.

In 1884 Hardy attended a dinner given by the lord mayor of London for the INCORPORATED SOCIETY OF AUTHORS, PLAYWRIGHTS, AND COMPOSERS; Lord Houghton was present, as was Walter BESANT. In 1891 Hardy wrote a letter to Lord Houghton's biographer, Thomas Wemyss Reid, thanking him for having mentioned him in *The Life, Letters, and Friendships of Richard Monckton Milnes, First Lord Houghton.* Hardy replied that he had considered the first Lord Houghton "a good friend" up to his death (*Letters* I, 228).

Houghton, Robert Offley Ashburton Crewe-Milnes, second baron (1858–1945)   The son of Richard Monckton Milnes HOUGHTON, the first baron Houghton, he became the second Lord Houghton on his father's death. The brother of Florence HENNIKER, in 1895 he was created earl (of Crewe); he later became marquess of Crewe. In January 1893 Hardy wrote to thank him for a copy of his volume of poetry, *Stray Verses,* saying he liked the "serious" pieces best (*Letters* II, 2). In 1889 Lord Houghton had published, privately, translations of the French poet Pierre Jean de Beranger, titled *Gleanings from Beranger.* He sent Hardy a copy in May 1893, after Hardy and his wife had stayed at the viceregal lodge in Dublin (at the time, Lord Houghton was Lord Lieutenant of Ireland). Hardy wrote at once to thank him. He commented that, "knowing the immense difficulty … of conveying the aroma of verse into another tongue," he was "struck" with his "many felicitous turns of phrase." He believed he must have "long experience" in "the art of translating" (*Letters* VII, 125).

Houghton, Mifflin & Co.   Boston publishing firm. As well as publishing books, the house also published the *ATLANTIC MONTHLY.* Hardy's novel *TWO ON A TOWER* was serialized in the magazine from May to December 1882.

"House of Hospitalities, The"   Poem first published in the *New Quarterly Review* in January, 1909, and collected in *TIME'S LAUGHINGSTOCKS* (1909). It is narrated by a man revisiting his former house. He stands in the principal room, once used for entertaining, and recalls the Christmas festivities once held there.

Now the "worm has bored the viol," the clock is rusty, and there are spiders and moles. At midnight, however, when moonlight falls on the walls and the tree outside, "forms of old time talking" are visible, smiling on him.

Critics have several theories about the house Hardy describes. Hardy once identified the location of the poem as "the house by the well," HIGHER BOCKHAMPTON (Purdy, *Thomas Hardy: A Bibliographical Study,* 140), by which he might have meant his birthplace. The house instead might be one that stood on the northern edge of Lower Bockhampton, where, in December 1919, Hardy opened a "village war memorial" in the form of a village club room where local gatherings were held. He said in his speech that he used to attend a type of Christmas dancing party there called a "Jacob's Join," in which guests contributed toward the expenses of the entertainment. The owner who gave "house-room for the dances" lived, he said, in a cottage that stood on the site of the club room (Bailey, *The Poetry of Thomas Hardy,* 203). A third theory is that Hardy was thinking of a large house on the lane near his birthplace, occupied by Mr. John Cox; it was later subdivided into two cottages. It is thought that the Christmas festivities in *UNDER THE GREENWOOD TREE* were drawn from Hardy's memory of the house as it was before it was divided (Pinion, *A Commentary on the Poems of Thomas Hardy,* 66).

The poem has been set to music in an unsigned manuscript in the DORSET COUNTY MUSEUM (Bailey, *The Poetry of Thomas Hardy,* 203).

Housman, A(lfred) E(dward) (1859–1936)   A. E. Housman, the noted English poet and Latin scholar best known for his collection of poems *A Shropshire Lad* (1896), first met Hardy in June 1899. In August of that year Housman, Edward CLODD, and Frederick Pollock came to MAX GATE and went bicycling.

In April 1903 Florence HENNIKER sent Hardy a copy of *A Shropshire Lad* published by Grant Richards in 1900 and bound in green leather; he replied that he had not known of the edition, but had it in his pocket at that very moment (*Letters* III, 46). In fact, Hardy had received a presentation copy of *A Shropshire Lad* from Richards in October 1898 (*Letters* II, 204), and owned several copies of the volume. Hardy exchanged letters with Housman's brother Laurence HOUSMAN, and contributed a poem to a journal he edited.

Housman was one of six pallbearers representing Literature at the ceremony in which Hardy's ashes were interred in Poets' Corner at WESTMINSTER ABBEY in January 1928.

Housman, Laurence (1865–1959) English novelist, dramatist, and illustrator, the brother of A. E. HOUSMAN. His play *Victoria Regina* (1934), starring Helen Hayes, was a great success in America. He was the coeditor, with Somerset Maugham, of *The Venture: An Annual of Art and Literature,* and in July 1903 wrote Hardy for a contribution. Hardy replied that he had nothing on hand, but might, perhaps, find a "country song or poem of some sort of two or three stanzas," if he knew the deadline. Housman wrote with another request in September 1903, and Hardy sent the manuscript of "The Market Girl (Country Song)" (*Letters* III, 71, 73).

In December 1904 Housman sent him a copy of his newly published novel *Sabrina Warham: The Story of Her Youth.* The opening chapter is set on the Dorset coast near West and East Lulworth. Hardy wrote to thank him, saying he fancied he recognized in the "opening pages the characteristics of some scenery not far from here" (*Letters* III, 134).

"How I Built Myself a House" Sketch published in CHAMBERS'S JOURNAL (March 1865). This was Hardy's first published work, written to amuse his fellow architecture students at the office of Sir Arthur William BLOMFIELD in LONDON. The acceptance of the piece convinced him that writing held more interest for him as a career than architecture.

Timothy Hands observes that, in contrast to Hardy's poem "Heiress and Architect," which emphasizes the importance of practicality in design, the sketch presents the client as focusing on the building's functions and the architect as ignoring his client's individual requirements (Hands, *A Hardy Chronology,* 148). Although this was Hardy's first piece of prose fiction, the subject was a congenial one. His birthplace had been built by his great-grandfather and his father was still engaged in the building business.

The sketch is written from the point of view of a man who lives with his wife, Sophia, and their two children in a suburban house advertised as a "Highly-Desirable Semi-detached Villa." The "villa" has many defects and lacks sufficient room for their guests or their furniture. The owner decides to build a house further out of town.

The sketch is concerned with a series of compromises made among husband, wife, and architect during the design and construction of the new home. The result is that the house is far smaller and more expensive than originally envisioned; there is no much-needed porch once it is finished, the study is filled with smoke from the fire, the nursery has no window bars, and numerous essential components are not included or are ineffective.

Hardy earned £3.15 for the sketch, which was his first published work. In later years he called the piece a "trifle," but Orel deduces that having a work in print possibly turned him toward prose (Orel, *Thomas Hardy's Personal Writings,* 168).

The narrator is prompted to build the house by the prospect of a third baby, perhaps indicating that, even at the age of 25, Hardy envisioned having a family of children at some point. He had not yet met Emma HARDY, but, after they married, it was a source of great distress to him that they remained childless (*see* CHILDLESSNESS).

The sketch is included in Harold Orel, ed., *Thomas Hardy's Personal Writings* (1966).

For further reading: Hands, *A Hardy Chronology;* Smith, "'How I Built Myself a House.'"

Howells, William Dean (1837–1920) American novelist, travel writer, editor, critic, and poet. He was a prolific writer of fiction; *Their Wedding Journey, A Modern Instance,* and *The Rise of Silas Lapham* are among his best-known novels. Before his death, he was considered the dean of American letters; he was president of the American Academy of Arts and Letters, and had substantial influence on the course of American literature during the Gilded Age. This phrase has been used to describe the hectic, materialistic period following the Civil War in America, when substantial fortunes were made and a new industrial society formed. Howells's novel *The Gilded Age* was based on this era.

Howells became editor of the ATLANTIC MONTHLY in 1871, a post he retained until 1881. Apparently he did not read any of Hardy's works during these years, even though A PAIR OF BLUE EYES and The HAND OF ETHELBERTA were favorably reviewed in the magazine. Howells was succeeded by Thomas Bailey Aldrich, who published TWO ON A TOWER serially from May to December 1882. Hardy sent Edmund GOSSE a copy of the novel, which Gosse acknowledged. Gosse added that his friend William Dean Howells, on a recent visit to London, had deeply regretted that he had been unable to meet Hardy, "the man in all England whom he most wanted to see" (Millgate, *Thomas Hardy: A Biography,* 231). Six months later, however, the matter was rectified. On June 25, 1883, Gosse gave a dinner at the SAVILE CLUB and introduced them (Nettels, "Hardy and Howells," 108).

In November 1886 Howells published a positive review of The MAYOR OF CASTERBRIDGE in the "Editor's Study" column he was writing at the time for HARPER'S NEW MONTHLY MAGAZINE. He praised Hardy's power of presenting characters with "living freshness." Hardy wrote immediately to thank him for his "kindly notice," saying that his review was what the book "probably would have deserved" had it been written "as it existed" in his mind, which it had not been (*Letters* I, 156). In 1887 Howells reviewed *The WOODLANDERS* and went so far as to say that Hardy was superior to George ELIOT in his knowledge of nature.

In October 1891, as he was completing the volume form of *TESS OF THE D'URBERVILLES*, Hardy seemed to be pondering the problem of writing fiction. He noted in his journal that Howells and other writers like him forget "that a story *must* be striking enough to be worth telling." The basic requirements for the writer of fiction is an ability to "reconcile the average with ... uncommonness." It is the latter quality that causes "a tale or experience" to "dwell in the memory and induce repetition" (*Life*, 239).

Howells edited *Cosmopolitan* from December 1891 to June 1892. In May 1892 he asked Hardy for a short story; Hardy was unable to supply one at the time, but promised to send one if he could. Hardy also praised Howells's novel *The World of Chance*, saying it was excellent that an American novelist should "exhibit America, where he cannot be gainsaid, rather than alien countries, as so many able American writers insist on doing" (*Letters* I, 267).

In 1895, when *JUDE THE OBSCURE* was published, Howells was one of the few reviewers to defend it. In the "Life and Letters" section of *HARPER'S WEEKLY* (December 7, 1895), he praised Hardy for his "truth" despite the subject matter.

In May 1904, Edward CLODD invited both Hardy and Howells to spend the Whitsunday weekend at his home in Aldeburgh. Hardy went, but Howells did not (*Letters* III, 122).

In July 1910, Howells and his daughter Mildred (his wife had recently died) went to tea at the flat which Hardy and his wife, along with their servants, had taken for the London season at 4 Blomfield Court, Maida Vale (*Letters* IV, 102).

By this time, Howells considered Hardy the most outstanding of contemporary British writers. Elsa Nettels cites an unpublished letter in the collection of the Beinecke Library, Yale University, which he wrote to William Lyon Phelps, declaring, "I should have put Hardy above all the other living English" (Nettels, 109). The two writers continued to see each other when Howells visited England, and to correspond and comment on each other's work until Howells's death in 1920.

For further reading: Nettels, "Howells and Hardy."

Huett, Izz A milkmaid at Talbothays Dairy in *TESS OF THE D'URBERVILLES*. Angel Clare invites her to accompany him to Brazil when he abandons Tess DURBEYFIELD after their marriage. Izz declines his invitation. Talbothays Dairy was based on Talbothays, a farm owned by Hardy's father. His brother Henry HARDY built a home called TALBOTHAYS on the property.

Human Shows, Far Phantasies, Songs, and Trifles Collection of poems published by MACMILLAN & CO., London, in November 1925. On July 29, 1925, Hardy sent a manuscript to George Macmillan provisionally titled "Poems Imaginative & Incidental: with Songs and Trifles." By August 25 he had decided against the title and wrote Sir Frederick MACMILLAN, George Macmillan's cousin, to propose a less "commonplace" one, which was selected (*Letters* VI, 341, 347–48). Macmillan replied that he did prefer *Human Shows* to the first one. Hardy anticipated that the shortened version would be easier for booksellers and readers to remember.

The volume was published on November 20, and by November 25 almost the entire first printing of 5,000 copies had been sold and a second impression, incorporating some of Hardy's corrections, was under way (*Letters* VI, 369). A third impression followed in December; by the beginning of the new year 7,000 copies had been sold. Hardy does not record this success in the *Life*, however, as he was apparently preoccupied at the time with the dramatization of *TESS OF THE D'URBERVILLES* at the Barnes Theatre, Dorchester.

The volume contains many of his best-known poems, including "The ABSOLUTE EXPLAINS," "ON THE ESPLANADE," "NOBODY COMES," "COMPASSION: AN ODE," and "A HURRIED MEETING." In September 1921 Hardy had served as godparent to Caroline Fox Hanbury of KINGSTON MAURWARD House; his christening gift was a parchment manuscript of a poem he had written for the occasion, "To C.F.H., On Her Christening Day," which was included in *Human Shows*. He wished "That your experience may combine Good things with glad ... Yes, Caroline!" Some of the other poems, such as "Louie," "When Oats were Reaped," and "A Leaving," reflect Hardy's memories of his deceased first wife, Emma HARDY; others, such as "Premonitions," reveal a preoccupation with his own death.

Humphrey A furze cutter on the heath in *The RETURN OF THE NATIVE*, a "solemn young fellow." He does not go to church because he doubts that he will be chosen for "up above."

"Hurried Meeting, A" This poem was published in *HUMAN SHOWS, FAR PHANTASIES, SONGS, AND TRIFLES* (1925). It concerns a meeting by August moonlight between a well-born lady and a man of inferior station. Tension is evident from the beginning of the poem. The mansion itself suggests an intractable form of judgment; its "marble front" is "Mute in its woodland wreathing." A bird, the night-jar, "whirrs forlorn" and the "trees seem to withhold their softest breathing." The lady is both chilled and vulnerable in her light muslin.

A man appears from the darkness and they kiss. She confirms that she is pregnant; the baby is due in February. She says they should have "left off meeting"; that "Love is a terrible thing: a sweet allure/That ends in heart-outeating!"

He calls her his "love" and asks what they should do. She will go south (to the Southern Hemisphere) with her mother, who is 41 and bring the baby home as the mother's infant. She admits they have deceived themselves and that she had known such an outcome was possible. She refuses to marry him and is horrified at her plight: "Love is a terrible thing: witching when first begun,/To end in grieving, grieving!"

They kiss and part. The night-jar seems to tell him that he should have "taken warning:/Love is a terrible thing: sweet for a space,/And then all mourning, mourning!"

Hardy might have developed the theme from *The POOR MAN AND THE LADY*, his lost first novel. The poem emphasizes the "social stratification" that makes it impossible for the woman to marry the father of her child (Bailey, *The Poetry of Thomas Hardy*, 572).

Hurst, Mrs.   Bathsheba EVERDENE's aunt in *FAR FROM THE MADDING CROWD*. She has a small farm at Norcombe Hill. Gabriel OAK first meets Bathsheba there when she is visiting her aunt.

"Hussar's Song: 'Budmouth Dears'"   Well-known song from *The DYNASTS*, Part III, Act II, Scene 1. Napoleon has mounted a Spanish campaign, and the English army, along with their Spanish and Portuguese allies, camp on the plain near Vitoria. On the eve of battle, troop-officers discuss their plans. The regiment known as the King's Hussars reminisce about WESSEX, especially Budmouth-Regis (WEYMOUTH) when King GEORGE III was in residence. Sergeant Young sings a song their bandmaster wrote, which he used to conduct in front of Gloucester Lodge at the King's Mess every afternoon. The verses recall the girls who once tempted the troops as they paced up and down Budmouth Beach.

The four-stanza song is regarded as one of the most notable verses in *The Dynasts*. The last line of each stanza is a repetitive rhythmical refrain, which, with slight variations, suggests the military bearing of the young men, torn between the delights of the girls on the beach and their obligations as members of an elite regiment. They march at first "With a smart *Clink! Clink!* up the Esplanade and down"; in the second stanza the girls have "distracted and delayed" them "As we tore *Clink! Clink!* back to camp above the town!" In the third verse they reflect from Spain, sad that they are separated from them. Do the "fair fantastic creatures" miss them now there is" … no more *Clink! Clink!* past the parlours of the town?" They wonder whether they shall, one day, march again and have the girls "archly quiz and con" them, "While our spurs *Clink! Clink!* up the Esplanade and down?"

This song was Hardy's contribution in 1915 to a souvenir program of the Portland Garrison Gala Performance in aid of the Royal Weymouth Hospital (*Letters* V, 131), and was the subject of an article in the *Dorset County Chronicle* on February 27, 1908 (*Letters* III, 299).

"I Found Her Out There"   This poem, dated December 1912, in *Selected Poems,* is in the group "Poems of 1912–13," written after Emma HARDY's death in November 1912, and collected in SATIRES OF CIRCUMSTANCE (1914).

Hardy reviews his courtship of Emma, stating that he "found her out there" on a slope "few see." The location was CORNWALL, but he "brought her here" [to DORSET]. She rests in a "noiseless nest/No sea beats near." It has been his decision that she does not "sleep/By those haunted heights/The Atlantic smites/And the blind gales sweep."

He reminisces about their early excursions together in Cornwall. She would gaze "At Dundagel's famed head" and would "sigh at the tale / Of sunk Lyonnesse." The wind would tug at her hair, which "Flapped her cheek like a flail." He envisions her ghost creeping "underground/Till it catch the sound/Of that western sea/As it swells and sobs." In this poem, Hardy sees Emma as childlike in her enthusiasms, although, when they met in 1870, she was 29. "Dundagel's famed head" is now called Tintagel Head, site of the ruins of the legendary castle of King Arthur.

illustration of Hardy's works   The period in which Hardy was publishing, especially in periodicals, is known for the high quality of its illustrations. The scholar Arlene Jackson has identified three periods of 19th-century English illustration history that are relevant to Hardy's work. The first period in which serial illustrations, including fanciful caricatures, became popular was between 1830 and 1855, when George Cruikshank and "Phiz" illustrated Dickens's novels as they were published in monthly parts. Between 1855 and 1870, magazine illustration attracted excellent artists. John Everett Millais, George DU MAURIER, and others presented the works of Dickens, George MEREDITH, Anthony Trollope, Henry JAMES, and others in a subjective way, with allegorical elements. After 1870 illustrations were more realistic, with contributions by diverse artists (Jackson, 12–16, passim). The Cruikshank-Phiz era (1830–55), when caricatures were popular; the Millais era (1855–70), when representational style was in vogue; and the continuation of the second phase with some modification (1870–95), identified with no particular artist. After 1870 there was an emphasis on realism in both painting and literature that, compounded by the development of photography, led to a definite shift in style and subject matter (Jackson, 12–13).

Among the periodicals founded in the 1850s, 1860s, and 1870s that published the work of Hardy and employed excellent artists and illustrators were the CORNHILL MAGAZINE, GOOD WORDS, the GRAPHIC, the European edition of HARPER'S NEW MONTHLY MAGAZINE, TINSLEY'S MAGAZINE, and BELGRAVIA. Hardy's work was also published in several American periodicals: HARPER'S MONTHLY MAGAZINE, HARPER'S WEEKLY, and the ATLANTIC MONTHLY.

A number of artists illustrated Hardy's serialized novels published between 1873 and 1895, including George DU MAURIER, Helen PATERSON ALLINGHAM, Arthur HOPKINS, John COLLIER, Hubert von HERKOMER, Robert BARNES, Daniel A. WEHRSCHMIDT, and E. Borough JOHNSON. William HATHERELL illustrated the novel JUDE THE OBSCURE, including those installments in which the work was titled HEARTS INSURGENT.

Many of Hardy's short stories were also illustrated, including "A CHANGED MAN" (illustration by A. S. Hartrick) and "A COMMITTEE-MAN OF 'THE TERROR'" (two illustrations by H. Burgess), and "The First Countess Of Wessex" (three illustrations by Alfred Parsons and four by C. S. Reinhart). In addition, Hardy himself illustrated some of his works, including the poem "AMABEL" and the verse drama *The FAMOUS TRAGEDY OF THE QUEEN OF CORNWALL,* for which he supplied drawings of Tintagel Castle, Cornwall.

For further reading: Allingham, "Robert Barnes' Illustrations for Thomas Hardy's *The Mayor of Casterbridge* as Serialised in *The Graphic*"; Allingham, "Six Original Illustrations for Hardy's *Tess of the D'Urbervilles* Drawn by Sir Hubert von Herkomer, R. A., for *The Graphic* (1891)"; Dalziel, "Anxieties of Representation: The Serial Illustrations to Hardy's *The Return of the Native*"; Dalziel, "'She Matched His Violence with Her Own Wild Passion': Illustrating *Far from the Madding Crowd*"; Harvey, Victorian Novelists and Their Illustrators; Jackson, *Illustration and the Novels of Thomas Hardy;* Johnson, "Illustrated Versions of Hardy's Works: A Checklist: 1872–1992"; Page, "Thomas Hardy's Forgotten Illustrators."

"I Looked Up from My Writing" Poem published in *MOMENTS OF VISION* (1917) in which the speaker, a writer, looks up from his work and sees the "full gaze" of the moon fixed on him. He is unnerved, and asks what she is doing there. She says she is scanning the ponds and waterways for the "body of one with a sunken soul" who has committed suicide while in the throes of sorrow for his son, killed in battle. The moon is "curious" to look into the "blinkered mind" of anyone who can write in such a world. The writer feels the moon regards him as one who should drown himself also.

The poem was occasioned by the tragic brutality of WORLD WAR I and its senseless slaughter of millions of young men. Hardy regards it as a futile exercise to write "idealistic poems"; the moon is a "symbol for realistic fact." Only a man whose insight is "blinkered" can find such a world desirable.

"I Look Into My Glass" Short lyric about the problem of aging, possibly written about 1897, and collected in *WESSEX POEMS* (1898). The poet looks into his glass, see his "wasting skin," and wishes his heart had shrunk accordingly, making him immune to "hearts grown cold" and allowing him to await the "endless rest" of death. Instead, however, Time steals only part of him at a time and lets the remainder "abide." As he remembers the "noontide" of his life, he realizes that the feelings he had then are just as strong now that he has aged.

The poem might reflect Hardy's reactions to the storm of criticism over the publication of *JUDE THE OBSCURE*, his matrimonial difficulties with Emma HARDY, and his attachment to Florence HENNIKER. There is an echo of the poem also in *The WELL-BELOVED*, when the hero reflects (Part 2, chapter 12), "'When was it to end—this curse of his heart not ageing while his frame moved naturally onward?'" (Pinion, *A Commentary on the Poems of Thomas Hardy*, 27–28).

"Imaginative Woman, An" Short story dated 1893 and published in *PALL MALL MAGAZINE* in September of that year. It concerns a couple, William and Ella Marchmill, who are about to take lodgings with their children at Solentsea (Southsea), Upper Wessex. William is a gunmaker; Ella is more sensitive, "a votary of the muse," who shrinks from knowing that her husband's business is concerned with the destruction of life.

William has located a terrace house overlooking the English Channel, but there are no free rooms. Mrs. Hooper, the landlady, says that two of them are already occupied by a young poet, Robert Trewe. She tells Trewe of her potential lodgers, and he offers to move, temporarily, to a small cottage on a nearby island.

When Ella looks at Trewe's books, she realizes she knows his work. She herself, daughter of a "struggling man of letters," has been writing poems under the name "John Ivy," which have been published in obscure magazines, in one case on the same page with a poem by Trewe. He is neither "*symboliste* nor *décadent*," but something of a pessimist. Ella had long felt his work was much stronger than "her own feeble lines." When Trewe published a volume of his pieces, Ella had done the same, as "John Ivy." Her book had been extremely expensive to publish, had few reviews, and almost no sales. It had fallen "dead in a fortnight" just as she discovered she was having a third child.

Mrs. Hooper tells Ella that Mr. Trewe is "kindhearted" and "good." She shows her the minute scribblings of his drafts on the wallpaper. Once they move in, Ella is preoccupied with the traces of the scribbling and also with reading more of his poetry. Her husband is happy to go sailing on their yacht and to travel about nearby islands on small steamers without her. She becomes "possessed by an inner flame" and memorizes Trewe's volume of verses. The children discover a raincoat belonging to him, which Ella regards as "The mantle of Elijah." Her fascination with the poet grows; she discovers there is a photograph of Trewe in a frame in her bedroom, under one of a royal couple. Thinking her husband away overnight on a sailing trip, she gazes late one night at his "striking countenance." He has large dark eyes signifying an "unlimited capacity for misery." Her husband discovers the picture and asks if the man is a friend of Ella's, but she makes light of it.

The next day William finds that business summons him home, although the landlady has told Ella that Mr. Trewe might be calling, as he was planning to stay with friends in the neighborhood. Ella pleads to stay a week longer and even goes to Trewe's island house, but leaves the house without seeing him. William says she can stay another week.

She fails to see Trewe, but, back at home, reads another poem of his in a magazine; she recalls a draft of it on her bedroom wall. She writes Trewe a congratulatory note, signing it "John Ivy." A civil response comes and Ella sends him her poems, but he fails to praise them. She cannot think how she might meet him, but then her problem is solved. A friend of her husband's, a newspaper editor, dines with them and says that his brother, a landscape painter, is in Cornwall with his friend Trewe. She invites them to visit and dresses in a robe of "rich material," but only the brother arrives. He says Trewe was "too dusty" and wished to get on home.

Ella is horrified to know Trewe has actually gone past their gates. His friend says Trewe has just been criticized in print for his "erotic and passionate" verse, and that he has been put off by her house, which looks "new and monied." A few days later she reads of Trewe's suicide. The formal newspaper notice of his death praises his recent volume, *Lyrics to a Woman Unknown*. The article includes a letter from Trewe that was read at the inquest, saying that if he had been blessed with a "mother, or a sister, or a female friend of another sort tenderly devoted to me" he would have had a reason to live. His last volume of verse has been inspired by his dream of such an "imaginary woman." Ella collapses, then writes the landlady at Solentsea and asks for a "small portion" of Trewe's hair before the closing of the coffin. It arrives; she puts it in her bodice and sobs over it.

Ella discovers the funeral is to be at Solentsea and sets off to attend it, leaving word for her husband that she has been called away. William has heard of the suicide, and guesses where she has gone. He follows her to the cemetery and finds her crying over Trewe's grave. They return home, almost without speaking. Soon afterward she dies in childbirth, having begun to apologize and explain her strange obsession with Trewe. Two years later William compares the new child, a little boy, with the photograph, and decides he resembles the poet. He tells his son, "Get away, your poor little brat! You are nothing to me!"

For further reading: Ray, "'An Imaginative Woman': From Manuscript to Wessex Edition."

"Impercipient, The" *(At a Cathedral Service)* When published in WESSEX POEMS (1898), this poem was accompanied by one of Hardy's 30 illustrations for the volume. This was a full-page drawing of the nave of Salisbury Cathedral, a favorite of Hardy's. In the *Life* he recalled a visit to Salisbury; the close of the cathedral, "under the full summer moon on a windless midnight, is as beautiful a scene as any I know in England—or for the matter of that elsewhere" (*Life,* 296). He visited the cathedral in August 1897 and underlined a verse in his Bible, from Jeremiah 6: 20: "To what purpose cometh there to me incense from Sheba, and the sweet cane from a far country? your burnt offerings are not acceptable, nor your sacrifices sweet unto me" (Pinion, *A Commentary on the Poems of Thomas Hardy,* 24).

In the manuscript, the poem is titled "The Agnostic." It is narrated by a person who is attending a service in the cathedral, but who feels out of place among "comrades" whose faiths "Seem fantasies" to him. He is unable to find the "joys" of his brethren; their "Shining Land" is no more than "mirage-mists" to him. He regrets "That He who breathes All's Well to these/Breathes no All's-Well to me." At the conclusion he sees himself as a "gazer" whose faith is a mirage. He can only perceive "dark/And windswept pine."

Hardy attended church services throughout his life, but struggled with his faith; *see* RELIGION.

"Incident in the Life of Mr. George Crookhill" *See* FEW CRUSTED CHARACTERS, A.

Incorporated Society of Authors, Playwrights, and Composers   Founded by Walter BESANT, the group was organized in order to defend authors' rights. In 1887 Hardy attended a conference on copyright in London sponsored by the society. When *The* WOODLANDERS was published, the same year, Hardy began to receive royalties instead of payments in cash for his work, a result of the work of the society. In 1891 Hardy wrote his wife Emma that he was acting, at the time, as temporary secretary (*Letters* I, 231).

In May 1909 the president of the society, George MEREDITH, died, and in June Hardy was asked to assume the office; at that time he was widely regarded as the preeminent English writer. He refused at first, responding that he could not be an active president, and, moreover, that his work had been too controversial and that since Algernon Charles SWINBURNE's death there had been "no living English writer who had been so abused by sections of the press as he himself had been in previous years" (*Life,* 346). On June 11 he wrote the essayist and man of letters Maurice Hewlett that there was another reason he felt he should refuse. The society president should be an author "on the tendency of whose writings there is no difference of opinion."

After meeting on July 5, the committee renewed its invitation, and Hardy accepted the presidency, remaining in office until his death (*Letters* IV, 28; VII, 55).

***Independent,* the**   New York periodical owned by Henry Chandler Bowen. His son, John Eliot Bowen, was the assistant editor, and sometimes corresponded with Hardy. Hardy's short story "The DUCHESS OF HAMPTONSHIRE" (*see A* GROUP OF NOBLE DAMES) was published in America in HARPER'S WEEKLY as "the Impulsive Lady of Croome Castle" and as "Emmeline: or Passion versus Principle" in the *Independent* on February 7, 1884.

In 1885 Hardy corresponded with John Bowen about the possibility of serializing *The* HAND OF ETHELBERTA, but arrangements fell through and it eventually appeared in the *New York Times* (*Letters* I, 138). The magazine did, however, publish his story "The DOCTOR'S LEGEND" on March 16, 1891.

In 1895 the magazine published an erroneous account of Hardy's acquisition of the land for MAX GATE, which he found highly offensive. It was written by a society Englishwoman Hardy knew, Rosamund Tomson, under the pseudonym of Graham R. Tomson. Hardy immediately wrote a letter of apology and protest to George Herriot, an official in the London office of the Duchy of Cornwall (which had sold him the land). He made it clear that he had never communicated with the Prince of Wales "through another channel" or found Mr. Herriot to be the "disagreeable person described." Hardy cautioned him, though, that it was best for him to "take no notice" publicly, for it would be "the greatest mistake to write & contradict such reports" (*Letters* II, 66).

"Indiscretion in the Life of an Heiress, An"   Story first printed in the NEW QUARTERLY MAGAZINE and in HARPER'S WEEKLY (in America) from June 29 to July 27, 1878. It is almost a novelette, incorporating some portions of *The POOR MAN AND THE LADY*, Hardy's first novel, rejected by three publishers.

The plot deals with the love of the young schoolmaster at Tollamore, Egbert Mayne, for Geraldine Allenville, the daughter of the local squire, whose seat is Tollamore House. Egbert has saved her life by pulling her away from a threshing machine that had nearly caught her dress. Egbert lives with his grandfather, Farmer Broadford, who is about to lose his house and farm because the squire wants his park extended. At his request, Geraldine speaks to her father, and obtains an indefinite postponement. She then visits Egbert's school and he kisses her. The park extension is again planned.

Farmer Broadford falls from a cornstack and dies, but not until after Egbert confesses his love for Geraldine. She is about to commit a shocking social sin in "loving beneath her, and owning that she so loved." Egbert decides to go to London and try to rise to her level "by sheer exertion."

He begins writing, achieving fame as an author within five years. Geraldine has been abroad with her father, but one day Egbert sees her in a carriage in Piccadilly. He contrives to attend a performance where they will be; he and Geraldine plan to meet at her front door. When he arrives a letter is slipped under the door saying that they must forget each other. The next morning Egbert sees an announcement of her engagement to Lord Bretton. Discouraged, he retires to a nearby village.

He goes to the church to watch the preparations for the wedding. He meets Geraldine, and discovers she does not love Lord Bretton. Deciding to elope, they get married, and go to Melport (Weymouth), where they plan to stay for three days before going on to London. They call on Grace's father at Tollamore House. On meeting him, she faints and ruptures a blood vessel; she has another attack on the third day and dies peacefully.

"In Front of the Landscape"   Poem published in the "Lyrics and Reveries" section of SATIRES OF CIRCUMSTANCE (1914). Hardy projects a double vision of himself: first, as busy passersby see him, a "dull form that perambulates" among "a few tombs," and also as a person "plunging and labouring on in a tide of visions," distraught by memories of his deceased family. His personal associations with landscape have grown sharper and more painful as he matures.

The "customed landscape" spans both DORSET and CORNWALL. The poet is presumably at STINSFORD churchyard, where Emma HARDY was buried, along with Hardy's parents and siblings. In most stanzas the second and sixth lines rhyme; the fourth line rhymes with the second and sixth lines of the next stanza.

Hardy is beset by his memories, which wash over him like eddies of "waste waters." The local landscape he once cherished, with its chalk-pit and other features, are no more substantial than gauze. Faces he has known return to haunt him; his vision is marred by both love and hatred. The graves also evoke "shining sights," including the Cornish "headland of hoary aspect," where he stood with Emma on his first visit to ST. JULIOT CHURCH, "touched by the fringe of an ecstasy/"Scantly descried." The day also unfurls images of "clay cadavers" of those he had "slighted, caring not for their purport." They appear now as "ghosts avenging their slights."

For further reading: Arkans, "Hardy's Poetic Landscapes"; Hawkins, *Thomas Hardy: His Life and Landscape;* Hooker, *Writers in a Landscape;* Miller, "Topography and Tropography in Thomas Hardy's 'In Front of the Landscape.'"

"In Tenebris I"   First poem in the group of three Tenebris poems, written in 1895–96. The three were first titled "De Profundis I, II, and III" but in POEMS OF THE PAST AND THE PRESENT (1902), they were called "In Tenebris I, II, and III" (Purdy, *Thomas Hardy: A Bibliographical Study,* 116).

"In Tenebris" means "In Darkness"; "De Profundis" means "From the Depths." Each poem has a Latin motto from St. Jerome's version of the Psalms; they all reflect Hardy's depression in 1895–96. He had lost his father in 1892, and the hostile reception of TESS OF THE D'URBERVILLES and JUDE THE OBSCURE had been a source of bitter disappointment (Bailey, *The Poetry of Thomas Hardy,* 180).

The motto of "In Tenebris I" (in the Vulgate Scriptures) is, in the King James Version, translated as the fourth verse of Psalm 102: "My heart is smitten, and withered like grass." The poem expresses profound despair, so extreme that the poet takes consolation in the fact that his bereavement and suffering have reached their depths; he is now immune to pain. There are six four-line stanzas; in each the first and last lines rhyme, as do the second and third. Winter "nighs" (comes near) but "twice no one dies." Flower petals "flee," but that "severing scene" cannot "harrow me." Birds "faint in dread," but he cannot lose the "old strength" since his strength has already fled. Leaves "freeze to dun," but friends cannot "turn cold," since he has none. Tempests may "scath" but Love cannot "make smart … his heart/Who no heart hath." The final stanza refers to his eventual death: "Black is night's cope" but "death will not appal/One who, past doubtings all,/Waits in unhope."

For further reading: Green, "Darkness Visible: Defiance, Derision and Despair in Hardy's 'In Tenebris' Poems."

"In Tenebris II" The second of the three "Tenebris" poems, published in POEMS OF THE PAST AND THE PRESENT (1902). The Latin motto of the second poem (in the Vulgate Scriptures) is, in the King James Version, translated as the fourth verse of Psalm 142: "I looked on my right hand, and beheld, but there was no man that would know me: … no man cared for my soul."

Bailey characterizes the second of the three poems as a "defense of pessimism," countering the overly optimistic men who "hailed England's world-wide empire and material progress as utopian perfection (Bailey, *The Poetry of Thomas Hardy,* 181).

There are four stanzas, each consisting of two pairs of rhymed lines. The rhythm is reminiscent of Algernon Charles SWINBURNE's poetry. The first verse addresses the confident "shouts of the many and strong," who are convinced that "things are all as they best may be." Hardy's eyes do not share their optimistic vision; he thinks it would be better if he were not among them.

In the second verse the "stout upstanders" hold that "All's well with us; ruers have nought to rue!" The poet wonders if, since the "potent" say it so often, "can it fail to be somewhat true?" He observes, "Breezily go they, breezily come." Their "dust smokes round their career,/Till I think I am one born out of due time, who has no calling here." Here Hardy refers to I Corinthians 15.8, in which St. Paul refers to himself as "one born out of due time" (Bailey, *The Poetry of Thomas Hardy,* 181).

The third stanza focuses on the optimism and confidence of the the "many and strong" and the "stout uplanders" depicted in the first two verses. Their "dawns bring lusty joys … their evenings all that is sweet." The times are "blessed times" and for every tear there are "many smiles." Then "what is the matter," asks the poet, "Why should such an one be here?"

The poet's point of view is represented by the last line of each of the first three stanzas and by the entire fourth stanza, which has occasioned much critical comment. This section represents the optimists' attack on his position. The poet represents the "low-voiced Best" that is killed by the "clash of the First." His one concession to optimism is that if there is any "way to the Better," it requires "a full look at the Worst." In his view delight exists, but it is a "delicate growth cramped by crookedness, custom, and fear." He is banished for his pessimism; he is "one shaped awry," who "disturbs the order here."

Hardy's insistence that the "only way to the Better" is to take "a full look at the Worst" is apparent in *FAR FROM THE MADDING CROWD* and other novels. Although he pre-

sents himself "as a pariah for holding pessimistic views," he did not find it easy to be "true to his own experience." Publishing JUDE THE OBSCURE despite Emma's objections was an act of courage. As the motto suggests, no one cared for his "soul" (Bailey, *The Poetry of Thomas Hardy,* 181–82).

"In Tenebris III" The third of the three "Tenebris" poems published in POEMS OF THE PAST AND THE PRESENT (1902). The Latin motto of the third poem (in the Vulgate Scriptures) is, in the King James Version, translated as "Woe is me that I sojourn in Mesech, that I dwell in the tents of Kedar. My soul hath long dwelt with him that hateth peace."

This is the most directly autobiographical of the three "Tenebris" poems. There are five stanzas, with the same pattern as "In Tenebris II." The rhyme scheme is *abba.*

The poet recalls his youth, innocent of knowledge that "the world was a welter of futile doing." As a child he knew April was coming as he tended the crocus border, "glowing in gladsome faith that I quickened the year thereby."

In the third stanza he recalls lonely evenings, probably in the fall, on EGDON HEATH with his mother, "She who upheld me … Confident I in her watching … Deeming her matchless in might and with measureless scope endued."

The fourth stanza depicts a "winter-wild night" as he "reclined by the chimney-nook quoin." He became drowsy, being "the smallest and feeblest of folk there,/Weak from my baptism of pain." He heard of a "world wheeling on," but was listless, with "no listing or longing to join." In the final stanza, he almost feels he should have died while young, before learning that "vision could vex or that knowledge could numb," or that "sweets to the mouth in the belly are bitter, and tart, and untoward." His "briefly raised curtain" would have lowered on "some dim-coloured scene." His happy boyhood would not then have ended in the disillusionment of adulthood.

For further reading: Casagrande, "The Fourteenth Line of 'In Tenebris, II'"; Green, "Darkness Visible: Defiance, Derision and Despair in Hardy's 'In Tenebris' Poems"; Larkin, "Irony, Sincerity and In Tenebris II."

"Interlopers at the Knap" Short story first published in WESSEX TALES (1888). Like the others in the collection, it reveals a firm grasp of the genre of the short story. Unlike many of Hardy's tales, which portray shepherds and artisans, "Interlopers" deals with the class of well-to-do tradesmen. The tale, like "FELLOW TOWNSMEN," another Wessex tale, is an account of alienation; in each story the principal male character makes a poor marriage choice.

The story concerns Charles Darton, an unambitious young gentleman farmer, made wealthy by his father's

The Elgin Marbles located in the British Museum, the subject of Hardy's poem "In the British Museum"   (British Museum, London)

enterprising capitalism. He is making a journey by horseback, on a dark night, to his wedding the next day; he is accompanied by his best man and a stableboy. They take the wrong fork in the road, causing his intended bride, Sally Hall, a self-reliant, cheerful girl, and her widowed mother many misgivings. As they wait, Sally's brother Philip, away in Australia for three years, arrives home suddenly, feverish and in ill health, with his wife, Helena, and two small children. He is indigent, having squandered the capital provided by his mother. On the way he has been asked to bring Sally the wedding dress Charles has promised to send, but Phillip has given it to Helena instead, to replace her shabby clothes.

Darton arrives and meets Helena, dressed in the gown, following her into the house "like a man in a dream." As Sally begins to suspect, Darton and Helena are old friends; she had turned him down five years earlier. Within an hour or two Philip dies, making Helena a widow. Mrs. Hall comes downstairs and taps the beehives at the side of the house, following an old belief that when a death occurs in a house the bees, if not awakened, will pine away within a year. The wedding is postponed, and Sally realizes that she will never marry Darton; Helena will. Darton undertakes, several months later, to educate the eldest child, a boy. He marries Helena within a year; they have a baby, and the frail Helena dies. As the story ends, Darton is once again on his way to the Hall residence; Darton intends to propose to Sally, in the "nature of setting in order things long awry, and not a momentary freak of fancy."

The setting of the story is based on the ancestral home of Hardy's mother's family at Townsend, Melbury Osmond.

For further reading: Brady, *The Short Stories of Thomas Hardy: Tales of Past and Present.*

"In the British Museum"   Poem published in SATIRES OF CIRCUMSTANCE (1914). It is set in the BRITISH MUSEUM in the room housing the Elgin marbles brought to England by Thomas Bruce (1766–1841), the seventh earl of Elgin. In 1806 Lord Elgin removed friezes from the Parthenon, a temple dedicated to Athena, built between 447 and 432 B.C. on the Acropolis in Athens, regarded as a masterpiece of Greek architecture, and brought them back to England. He took a section of the continuous band of friezes around the building, which was originally 525 feet in length. Only 335 feet still exist in Athens (this section was damaged in an explosion in the 17th century but is being restored). Lord Elgin also brought back a section of the Erechtheum, another temple on the Acropolis. There is still considerable controversy in Greece about the removal of the marbles to England.

As a young man in LONDON Hardy spent a great deal of time in the Museum. He knew the marbles came from the Acropolis, not the Areopagus, which is a distance of half a mile away. The poem represents a conversation between two speakers. The first is a worldly man who addresses a "laboring man" and displays his knowledge in a rather patronizing way. He inquires why the man is staring at one of the marble sculptures as though he hears something; he is treading quietly like a mouse or a bird. He informs the laborer that "they" (art experts) will tell him it is "the base of a pillar" that came to England from a "far old hill" once called Areopagus. (The Areopagus was a sacred place on a rocky hill where the judicial and legislative council of Athens met).

The laborer responds that he is untutored in art, and views it only as a "stone from a wall"—yet it is a stone which has "echoed/The voice of Paul" [St. Paul]. He envisions Paul preaching beside the marble sculpture, "Facing the crowd," a small figure with "wasted features." St. Paul, he believes, patterned his words after the "marble front." He is very moved to think that the very stone before him "once echoed/The voice of Paul." Bailey points out that the speaker is thinking of St. Paul's preaching in Athens: "And they took him, and brought him unto Areopagus, saying, May we know what this new doctrine, whereof thou speakest, is?" (Acts 17:19–23). He suggests that Hardy may have based the poem on a conversation he overheard (Bailey, *The Poetry of Thomas Hardy*, 318).

The first speaker does not correct him, being as uninformed about Athens as the "labouring man." Hardy knew that the Areopagus was some distance away from the Acropolis, and is making an ironic comment on the stone, which is not an altar but a work actually evincing "ashen blankness." Bailey observes that Hardy satirizes both speakers for their ignorance and for their failure to perceive the magnificence of the Greek sculptures, which are better models for life "than Paulinism" (Bailey, *The Poetry of Thomas Hardy*, 319).

"In the Evening" *In Memoriam Frederici Treves, 1853–1923 (Dorchester Cemetery, 2 Jan. 1924)* This poem was written in memory of Sir Frederick Treves, a DORCHESTER friend of Hardy's, who came from a humble background. His widowed mother kept a stationers' shop in the town. He attended the school run by William BARNES, and then went to the Merchant Tailors' school in London. He qualified as a surgeon, served in the BOER WAR, and became Surgeon Extraordinary to Queen Victoria. In 1902 he operated on King Edward VII. He also wrote several books, including *Highways and Byways in Dorset* (1906) and *The Country of "The Ring and The Book,"* an analysis of the Italian background of Robert BROWNING's dramatic poem. In 1915 Sir Frederick operated on Florence HARDY for nasal catarrh, an inflammation of the nasal membrane.

The poem is a revision of a tribute Hardy paid to Treves in the *Times*. It begins with a visit to his grave the evening of his death, when "the world knew he was dead." Hardy imagines that Treves realizes he has returned to the "chalky bed" of his birthplace and origins, and asks a "spirit attending" why he was called away. The spirit replies that no one knows. The poet suggests, however, that, because of his medical skill he had been summoned into being by Aesculapius (the Greek god of Medicine), Galen (a second-century Greek physician), and Hippocrates of Cos, historically the most celebrated Greek physician. They choose Treves to animate and heal for the span of a lifetime; he has now returned to his origins, "And all is well." The Italianate name "Frederici" recalls Treves's book on Browning.

"In the Garden" (M. H.) Poem dated 1915 and published in *MOMENTS OF VISION* (1917). The initials "M. H." refers to Hardy's sister Mary HARDY, the sibling to whom he was closest. Family members gather about a sundial in the garden at HIGHER BOCKHAMPTON. They watch to see who is first shadowed by the setting sun, as there is a superstition that this is an omen of death (Bailey, *The Poetry of Thomas Hardy*, 413). At the time, they paid little attention when the shadow fell on Mary; but, as it turned out, "her towards whom it made/Soonest had to go." Mary was the first of the four Hardy children to die, 13 years before Hardy, although she was a year younger than he.

"In the Old Theatre (Fiesole)" (April 1887) Poem published in *POEMS OF THE PAST AND THE PRESENT* (1902) and inspired by Hardy's trip to ITALY with his wife, Emma HARDY, in 1887. Wishing to visit the little town of Fiesole, outside Florence, they hired an omnibus to take them up the road to the top. The driver, unfortunately, went to have a drink before driving them up. His horse began running down the hill toward Florence until some workmen stopped it. Hardy and Emma then made the climb on foot. While Hardy was sitting in the stone amphitheater on the summit of the hill, a little girl showed him a coin with an image of Constantine.

The child had evoked, for Hardy, "In swift perspective Europe's history/Through the vast years of Caesar's sceptred line." He thinks of his "distant plot of English loam," where one had only to delve down and find "coins of like impress." The "mute moment" brings home to his "opened mind/The power, the pride, the reach of perished Rome."

Hardy was aware of certain similarities between Fiesole and DORCHESTER, both of which have ancient Roman theaters and many sites that had been excavated, and both of which were once under Roman rule under the Caesars (Bailey, *The Poetry of Thomas Hardy,* 129).

"In Time of 'The Breaking of Nations'" Poem dated 1915, first published in the *SATURDAY REVIEW* for January 29, 1916, and collected in *MOMENTS OF VISION* (1914). Written during WORLD WAR I, the poem focuses on the tragedy of the home front. The country has all but come to a standstill, with a man "harrowing clods" with his old horse that "stumbles and nods" as he walks, and a "maid and her wight," who come "whispering by."

The idea came to Hardy during the Franco-Prussian war of 1870, as he states in the *Life*. He was courting Emma Hardy in CORNWALL, and saw an old horse plowing a field. He had often meditated on the idea that the basic elements in man's life of labor and love continue regardless of whether a society is at war. It was not expressed, however, until George A. B. Dewar, editor of the *SATURDAY REVIEW*, wrote him to ask for a poem.

The poem has been set to music by Gordon Slater (Oxford: Oxford University Press, 1926) and Frederic Austin *(Wessex Songs)*. A manuscript version of a setting by Harper MacKay exists in manuscript in the Colby College Library (Bailey, *The Poetry of Thomas Hardy,* 421–22; *see* Appendix II).

Italy Thomas and Emma Hardy left England on March 14, 1887, for an extensive tour of Italy, via Aix-les-Bains in France. They went on to Turin and Genoa, the first sight of which occasioned Hardy's poem "GENOA AND THE MEDITERRANEAN." At Pisa they visited the cathedral and baptistery and, according to his autobiography, "stood at the top of the leaning tower during a peal of the bells, which shook it under their feet." They saw the sun set from a bridge over the Arno River, and Hardy reflected that Percy Bysshe Shelley had probably seen the sun set from the same bridge many times.

Florence was their next stop, where Lucy Barnes Baxter, the daughter of Hardy's DORCHESTER friend William BARNES, met them. Baxter had found lodgings for them at the Villa Trollope, in the Piazza dell'Indipendenza. Hardy is not specific about their sightseeing, saying only that their experiences were much like "those of other people visiting for the first time the buildings, pictures, and historic sites of that city." When they returned to Florence from Rome, however, he "found the scenery soothing after the gauntness of Rome." He collected his thoughts on the steps of the Lanzi, in the Piazza della Signoria; in a nearby café he noticed the "secondary light" cast by the statue of Neptune. They climbed to Fiesole, an experience Hardy recalled in a sonnet, "IN THE OLD THEATRE," and saw the tomb of Elizabeth Barrett Browning.

Rome was of much interest to Hardy because of its literary associations. He noted in his autobiography that he was more interested in pagan than in Christian Rome. The Hardys stayed in the Via Condotti at the Hôtel d'Allemagne, opposite the Piazza di Spagna, near the house where John KEATS died. Hardy pondered that "no mind could conjecture what had been lost to English literature" by Keats's death (*Life*, 188). The Colosseum had just been cleaned, a process of which Hardy approved as an architect. He could not help wishing, though, that the task had not been done until after his visit. He visited St. Peter's but its "deadly fatiguing size" caused him great weariness, and he almost fell asleep in the Sala delle Muse of the Vatican (*see* "ROME: THE VATICAN—SALA DELLE MUSE"). He also saw the graves of Shelley and Keats. He considered his notes of Rome "very jumbled and confusing," and found many paintings "touched up" so much that only the renovations were visible. He berated himself for not realizing that the church of S. Lorenzo-in-Lucina was the church of Pompilia's marriage in Robert BROWNING's *The Ring and the Book*.

Of all Italian cities Hardy preferred Venice, although he grieved at the decaying marbles, frescoes, and gildings, wishing all of them could be put in a glass case, safe from the rain. In fine weather, though, he felt Venice to be "composed of blue and sunlight." Byron was one of the "phantom poets marshalled through his brain." The Hardys were entertained by Browning's friend Mrs. Bronson, where they met a charming, modest, correct, "modern" countess who was a descendant of one of the powerful Venetian Doge families. An evening party was given for them at the Palazzo Barbarigo.

They returned to England via Milan, where they stayed in the Grand Hotel de Milan and visited the cathedral (later used as a scene in *The DYNASTS*). They also visited Como.

On December 31 he noted in the *Life* that the year had been "a fairly friendly one," showing him "Italy, above all Rome—and it brought me back unharmed and much illuminated" (*Life*, 187–96; 203).

"It Never Looks Like Summer" Poem dated "Boscastle, 8 March 1913" and collected in *MOMENTS OF VISION* (1917). The words in the title were spoken by Emma HARDY when she and Hardy went to Beeny Cliff (in CORNWALL) in the rain on August 22, 1870 (Bailey, *The Poetry of Thomas Hardy*, 400). He had come down in March that year as a young architect to assess the restoration of ST. JULIOT CHURCH, of which her brother-in-law, the Reverend Caddell HOLDER, was rector. Hardy recalls that Emma regarded Boscastle and the Cornish coast as "drear," but he says, "Summer it seemed to me." Now, visiting there in March 1913, after her death (in November 1912), he laments, "It never looks like summer now/Whatever weather's there;/But ah, it cannot anyhow,/On Beeny or elsewhere!" Hardy would marry Florence Dugdale (HARDY) in February 1914.

The poem was set to music by Gerald Finzi in *Till Earth Outwears* (London and New York: Boosey & Hawkes, 1958; *see* Appendix II).

James, Henry (1843–1916) American novelist, short-story writer, and man of letters. James came from a distinguished and moneyed American family, but the fortune had dwindled in time and he had only a modest income. He spent his childhood on the Continent with his parents, three brothers, and a sister, and his French was indistinguishable from that of a native. He entered Harvard Law School in 1862, but withdrew to write, publishing fiction and book reviews in the NORTH AMER-ICAN REVIEW, the ATLANTIC MONTHLY, and other periodicals. He made two trips to Europe as an adult and, in 1875, decided to make his home abroad. He first settled in Paris but in 1876 decided to live in England. He lived in LONDON for two decades, and, from 1898 on, occupied Lamb House, Rye, Sussex. The novels for which he is best known include *The Portrait of a Lady* (1881), *The Wings of the Dove* (1902), *The Ambassadors* (1903), and *The Golden Bowl* (1904). He is noted for his craftsmanship and impeccable technique in the art of fiction. Some of his favorite themes were the confrontation between American and European civilization, the dilemma of the artist in a society inimical to him, and the development of moral perception. He believed the novelist should be "one on whom nothing is lost."

James wrote a "condescending" review of the American edition of FAR FROM THE MADDING CROWD for *The Nation* in 1874, stating that "his superficial novel is a really curious imitation of something better," which angered Hardy ("Contemporary Critical Reception," *Far from the Madding Crowd*, Norton Critical Edition, ed. Robert C. Schweik [New York: W. W. Norton, 1986], 368). Despite his admiration for James as a writer, Hardy never really liked him and did not consider him very manly. He notes in the *Life* that James was not elected to membership in the RABELAIS CLUB because he failed to meet the requirement of producing literature with "virility." In 1880 Hardy's friend Anne PROC-TER, a widow, showed him a photograph of James and declared that James had made her an offer of marriage. Hardy was clearly skeptical, wondering, "can it be so?" Mrs. Procter was 80 at the time.

Hardy spent part of January 1884 in London, and states that he saw Henry James, along with Edmund GOSSE and others. In June 1884 Hardy was back in London, where he attended a dinner at the home of Mrs. Murray Smith and saw Matthew ARNOLD and Henry James, "with his nebulous gaze" (*Life*, 167).

Hardy and James both attended a meeting of the Rabelais Club in the summer of 1886; Hardy noted that James had a "ponderously warm manner of saying nothing in infinite sentences" (*Life*, 181). Hardy read James's 1888 novel *The Reverberator* and declared that, after reading it, he himself was "inclined to be purposely careless in detail." He felt the great novels of the future would not concern themselves with the "minutiae of manners . . . James's subjects are those one could be interested in at moments when there is nothing larger to think of" (*Life*, 211). James was venomous in his remarks to Robert Louis STEVENSON about TESS OF THE D'URBERVILLES, published in 1891, but Hardy was unaware of this at the time. Calling James and Stevenson the "Polonius and Osric" of novelists (Polonius being a garrulous, pompous old man and Osric an affected court fop), he cites James's reference to the novel in the *Life*. He had discovered this in 1892 in the *Letters of Henry James* and jotted it down. James had called the novel "vile," criticizing the language and sexuality. In May 1897 Hardy attended a dinner at the home of Edmund Gosse and his wife at which James was present.

A year before James's death, Hardy conceded that his work had some merit. He noted how remarkable it was that a writer "who has no grain of poetry, or humour, or spontaneity in his productions, can yet be a good novelist" (*Life*, 370). In 1915 James succeeded in persuading Hardy to make a contribution to *The Book of the Homeless*, the book Edith WHARTON was compiling to aid France in WORLD WAR I. He sent a poem, "CRY OF THE HOMELESS."

For further reading: King, *Tragedy in the Victorian Novel: Theory and Practice in the Novels of George Eliot, Thomas Hardy and Henry James;* Laird, "Approaches to Fiction: Hardy and Henry James."

"January Night, A" (1879) Poem published in MOMENTS OF VISION (1917). There are three stanzas, each with the rhyme scheme *abab*. Hardy portrays the ominous implications of a stormy night with startling verbs: the rain "smites," the east wind "snarls and sneezes," and the "tip of each ivy-shoot/Writhes on its neighbour's face." He then suggests that these effects may be supernatural manifestations of a neighbor who has died.

In his autobiography, in a passage dated January 1, 1879, Hardy discusses the poem in the context of a depressing "New Year's thought." He declares that "A perception of the FAILURE of THINGS to be what they are meant to be" lends them a "new and greater interest of an unintended kind." The Hardys were then living at The Larches, 1 Arundel Terrace, Trinity Road, Upper Tooting, London. According to Hardy, they began to feel "there had past away a glory from the earth": it was in this house that "their troubles began" (*Life*, 124).

The poem might refer to the beginning of Emma HARDY's mental illness (Bailey, *The Poetry of Thomas Hardy*, 369). Hardy also might have been discouraged about their continuing CHILDLESSNESS, compounded by his awareness that his parents were getting older and more frail. Hardy's father had written that his mother was unwell and that he had drunk both their healths in "gin and rhubarb wine," but hoped Hardy and Emma would come to DORCHESTER "ere long." Hardy did go down on February 1 (*see* Henry HARDY).

Jarvis, C. W. (fl. 1890) Dramatist and writer who collaborated with Jack Thomas GREIN in several enterprises: they edited the periodical *Weekly Comedy* and founded the Independent Theatre in 1891. They wrote Hardy in 1889 asking permission to dramatize *The WOODLANDERS*. He replied on July 19, 1889, in a joint letter to both of them, stating that he granted his permission with "much pleasure," on condition that "a fair share of profits (if any) be awarded me" (*Letters* I, 195).

Apparently, as time went on and the play was not performed, they appealed to Hardy for advice. In July 1890 Hardy wrote Jarvis, saying that he would let him know if any "idea as to placing the play" reached him. The play was never performed (*Letters* VII, 114).

Jethway, Felix Character in *A PAIR OF BLUE EYES*. A young farmer, he has died of consumption before the novel opens, but we see him through the eyes of his grief-stricken mother, Gertrude JETHWAY. He is buried in Endelstow churchyard; his tomb is a portent of death. His mother blames Elfride SWANCOURT for his death, believing his love for her aggravated his condition, although Elfride had never encouraged him.

Jethway, Gertrude In *A PAIR OF BLUE EYES*, the mother of Felix JETHWAY, a young farmer who has died of consumption. She is convinced he died after being rejected by Elfride SWANCOURT. She haunts Elfride throughout the novel, writing Henry KNIGHT about Elfride's romance with Stephen SMITH. Elfride takes part in two scenes near the tomb of Felix Jethway at Endelstow Church that portend her death. She is killed in the fall of the tower of the West Endelstow church. Gertrude Jethway has been called Elfride's "evil genius."

Jeune, Sir Francis Henry (later, Baron St. Helier) (1843–1905) Jeune was knighted in 1891 and named Baron St. Helier in 1905, just before his death (*Letters* I, 144). A prominent lawyer and divorce court judge, he was the second husband of Mary JEUNE, whose first husband had been Colonel John Constantine Stanley.

In April 1891 Hardy wrote to thank him for his "generous support" in nominating him for membership in the ATHENAEUM CLUB (*Letters* I, 234). The next year Hardy attended an "interesting legal dinner" at the Jeunes's home in London. The other guests, "mostly judges," told stories, "old and boring" to each other, but new to Hardy (*Life*, 251). Having just finished the tales making up *A GROUP OF NOBLE DAMES*, Hardy might have particularly enjoyed the setting of a congenial dinner at which stories and anecdotes were told.

In 1892 *TESS OF THE D'URBERVILLES* was published, and, as it circulated, the novel attracted attention Hardy had "not foreseen," as he put it in his autobiography. One unwelcome result of the novel was the

79 Harley St., London, home of Sir Francis and Lady Jeune. Hardy stayed here in 1894 and 1895 while searching for a flat for the London season.　(Sarah Bird Wright)

arrival of "strange letters" from husbands whose experience resembled that of Angel CLARE and many more from wives "with a past like that of Tess" who had not told their husbands. Some of the writers begged to meet with Hardy privately. He discussed this with Sir Francis, who had had wide experience in presiding over the divorce court. Jeune advised him not to meet the writers alone, "in case they should not be genuine." He himself did not become involved with such letter writers, and Hardy followed suit, but regretted it to some extent, thinking sadly that some of the letters were from "sincere women in trouble" (*Life,* 244–45).

The Jeunes had one child, a son, Christian Francis Seaforth Jeune (1882–1904), who died of enteric fever in August 1904 while serving in India with the Grenadier Guards. At the time of his death Hardy wrote Florence HENNIKER that he had known the young man since childhood and that his father "particularly feels his loss." He had not felt he was "strong enough physically for soldiering, which requires rude health for success" (*Letters* III, 135). Sir Francis never really recovered from the shock, and died in early 1905.

For further reading: Davis, "Happy Days in *Jude the Obscure:* Hardy and the Crawford-Dilke Divorce Case"; Davis, "Sir Francis Jeune and Divorce by 'False Pretences' in *Jude the Obscure.*"

Jeune, Mary Elizabeth (Lady St. Helier) (1845–1931) A longtime friend of Hardy's. Her first husband was Colonel John Constantine Stanley and her second was Francis Henry JEUNE, who was knighted in 1891 and named Baron St. Helier in 1905 (*Letters* VII, 144). She was a well-known and popular London hostess, and "collected" celebrities and undertook philanthropic works with equal enthusiasm. It was at her table that Hardy was introduced to Edith WHARTON. In April 1885 the Hardys were in LONDON and saw Mrs. Jeune at a party given by Lady CARNARVON (*Life,* 171). The next month he went again to her home; Emma had returned home, and he wrote her that he had seen "Mrs. Jeune the irrepressible" (*Letters* I, 133).

Hardy met many people at Lady Jeune's home and became close to the family, especially to Dorothy and Madeleine Stanley, her daughters by her first husband. As children they called him "Uncle Tom" and "displayed an unselfconscious warmth and openness" he found "captivating" (Millgate, *Thomas Hardy: A Biography,* 272; *see* ALLHUSEN, DOROTHY for an account of Hardy's theater trip with the girls when they were young).

In May 1890 the Hardys went to London for the season. In July Emma was summoned to her father's deathbed, but Hardy remained in town. Mrs. Jeune asked him to write an epilogue for a benefit performance of *The Taming of the Shrew* to assist her holiday fund for underprivileged children. Ada Rehan recited the verses. This was the first poem of Hardy's to appear since the publication in 1875 of "The FIRE AT TRANTER SWEATLEY'S."

The Hardys often visited the Jeunes at their country estate, Arlington Manor. Hardy continued to attend functions at the Jeune home in London and, in July 1893, went with Lady Jeune and her daughters to a farewell performance by the noted Shakespearean actor Henry Irving. In April 1895 Hardy stayed with the Jeunes at their town house, 79 Harley Street, while he searched for a place where he and Emma might live for the season.

Lady Jeune was also a journalist, and Hardy seems to have had a high regard for her work. In 1886 he sent her a copy of The MAYOR OF CASTERBRIDGE with a note stating that he knew the novel would not be misunderstood by the writer of the "pathetic & striking articles" she had published in the FORTNIGHTLY REVIEW the previous year. In 1899 he wrote to congratulate her on her article "Children and the State," on underfed children, which had been published in the *Review of the Week* on November 18. He praised her "clear & incisive treatment of the subject" (*Letters* II, 237).

She came to his defense in 1894 when LIFE'S LITTLE IRONIES was criticized by William ARCHER as being immoral, and wrote a letter to the *Daily Chronicle* declaring that not one story in the collection could "offend the most sensitive morality" (*Letters* II, 56).

Lady Jeune also introduced Hardy to the artist Winifred THOMSON, who painted a portrait of him that was exhibited in the fine arts section of the Woman's Exhibition that opened at Earl's Court, London, on May 5, 1900. Lady Jeune was one of the organizers of the exhibition. Her reminiscences, *Memories of Fifty Years,* were published in 1909.

John, Augustus Edwin (1878–1961) British painter and etcher, born in Wales. He was identified with the impressionist school, but also painted a number of portraits of noted people, including Hardy, David Lloyd George, Arthur SYMONS, and George Bernard SHAW.

In 1923 Hardy sat for a portrait by John. The painting was acquired by Sidney COCKERELL for the Fitzwilliam Museum, CAMBRIDGE. Hardy remarked, upon seeing a photograph of it, "Well, if I look like that the sooner I am under ground the better" (Millgate, *Thomas Hardy: A Biography,* 551). In 1924 he signed a reproduction of the portrait; it was to be hung in the Village Club at Iwerne Minster, DORSET. John also signed the portrait (*Letters* VI, 247–48).

Johnson, Ernest Borough (1866–1949) Born in Shropshire, he exhibited at the ROYAL ACADEMY and illustrated the works of Henry Wadsworth Longfellow. He was known as a landscape painter. He was one of three artists who illustrated TESS OF THE D'URBERVILLES for *The* GRAPHIC.

Johnson, Lionel Pigot (1867–1902)   Critic and poet. He sometimes reviewed Hardy's books and was the author of *The Art of Thomas Hardy* (1894; reissued 1923). In June 1896 Hardy wrote Florence HENNIKER from 16 Pelham Crescent, where he and Emma had taken a flat for the London season, to invite her to tea the next week. He mentioned that Johnson and several others were also coming. In November 1898, in another note to Mrs. Henniker, he mentioned the article Johnson had written about himself: "Academy Portraits. Mr. Thomas Hardy," in the *Academy*, November 12, 1898. In 1899 Johnson reviewed Hardy's WESSEX POEMS in the *Outlook*.

Johnson, Matilda   In *The* TRUMPET-MAJOR, an actress who becomes engaged to Robert LOVEDAY. Robert is soon disillusioned (with the help of his brother John) and breaks the engagement. She meets Festus DERRIMAN and plots with him to acquire the wealth of Festus's uncle, Squire Benjamin DERRIMAN. She appears in a play at Budmouth before King GEORGE III. She and Festus, who are well matched in cunning and ambition, marry.

Jopp, Joshua   In *The* MAYOR OF CASTERBRIDGE, a character who has been hired as Michael HENCHARD's manager but who is supplanted by Donald FARFRAE. After Farfrae's downfall, Jopp succeeds him as manager, but loses his job when Henchard is ruined. Henchard goes to live with Jopp. Jopp, without a job, asks Lucetta LE SUEUR to put in a good word for him with Donald Farfrae, but she haughtily refuses. Henchard comes downstairs with a package sealed in brown paper; it contains Lucetta's passionate letters to him, some of which he has already read to Farfrae without revealing the identity of the writer. He asks Jopp to deliver the package to Lucetta. Jopp, still angry with Lucetta for refusing to recommend him for a job, opens the package and discovers the letters. He had been in Jersey and knew of Henchard's affair with her. To take revenge on Lucetta and Henchard, he discloses the contents of the letters to the lower-class inhabitants of CASTERBRIDGE, including Nance MOCKRIDGE.

Jude the Obscure   Hardy's last novel; it appeared serially in *HARPER'S NEW MONTHLY MAGAZINE*, which was published simultaneously in New York and LONDON, from December 1894 to November 1895. The title was *The Simpletons* in the first installment and changed to *HEARTS INSURGENT* for the last 11 installments, before Hardy settled on the final title for both the serial and the book.

The novel depicts the conflict between spiritual and carnal life and exposes the restraints of Victorian tradition. It was widely attacked as immoral, and many critics assumed that its reception caused Hardy to abandon novel writing and return to writing poetry.

Poetry, however, had always been a genre Hardy found more congenial than fiction. The novel was attacked as undermining the institution of marriage and, in addition, for representing a departure from his more pastoral novels. Stewart calls it one of the "most impressively exploratory and intuitive of modern English novels" (*Thomas Hardy: A Critical Biography*, 64). With its focus on man's heroic but unavailing struggle against fate, *Jude*, along with Hardy's other novels, has caused Hardy to be called "the Shakespeare of the English novel."

The genesis of *Jude* was a story Hardy heard about a young man who was suicidal because he had set his heart on going to OXFORD UNIVERSITY, which he was unable to do. The central character is Jude FAWLEY, a poor orphan who hopes to go to Christminster (Oxford) and devotes his youth to studying in order to realize his goal. It is thought that Hardy modeled Jude, in part, on John Antell, who married his maternal aunt, Mary Hand; he was a Puddletown shoemaker (*Letters* I, 94–95; 92). The name *Jude* suggests Judas Iscariot and also Jude, a little-known brother of Jesus and probable author of the Epistle of Jude. In this epistle Jude speaks of those who are "spots in your feasts of charity ... clouds *they are* without water, carried about of winds; trees whose fruit withereth, without fruit, twice dead, plucked up by the roots ... foaming out their own shame ... to whom is reserved the blackness of darkness for ever." They "separate themselves, sensual, having not the Spirit." Martin Seymour-Smith points out that the "idea of betrayal ... of the spirit by the flesh" suggests, on a deeper level, Jude's false sense that he is favored by God.

As Jude delves further into his studies, his hopes expand and he visualizes himself becoming, if not a scholar, at least a "Christian Divine." He becomes an apprentice to a local stonemason as a way of ultimately supporting himself during his studies at Christminster. A local girl, the daughter of a pig breeder, Arabella DONN, spies Jude as he is returning one afternoon from his work as a stonemason, becomes interested in him, and forces him to marry her by falsely declaring she is pregnant. Arabella later leaves Jude and goes to Australia, where she contracts a bigamous marriage.

Jude goes to the town of Christminster, hoping to support himself there by using his skills as a stonemason. There he falls in love with his first cousin, Sue BRIDEHEAD, who works as a religious illuminator. The name *Sue* is from the Hebrew Susanna, or "lily," derived from the tale of Susanna and the Elders in the Apocrypha. The biblical Susanna resisted temptation, as Sue Bridehead ultimately does with Jude; *Bridehead* is a place name in DORSET, but it also represents "bride" and "maidenhead." Seymour-Smith suggests that the name "brilliantly compresses" Sue's ultimate submission to Richard PHILLOTSON, her legal husband but one who repels her, and her profound wish to be a "coquette who shrinks from fulfilling the physical expectations she needs to arouse" (Seymour-Smith, *Hardy,* 513). She thus denies the power of marriage. Jude eventually succeeds in divorcing Arabella.

Jude's passion for Sue brings tragedy to both himself and her, and to Phillotson and Arabella. Sue agrees to live with Jude but not to marry him. They have two children, and she becomes pregnant with a third. Meanwhile, Arabella confesses that she had been pregnant with Jude's child when she went to Australia, and sends the son she had, called "Little Father Time," to live with Jude and Sue. Father Time becomes deranged over the difficulties Jude and Sue are having, in part because they are unmarried. He hangs himself and the other children. Eventually Sue marries Phillotson again, submitting to him sexually, and Jude remarries Arabella, but soon dies. Arabella says he is "a 'andsome corpse."

SYNOPSIS

Part First: "At Marygreen"

The epigraph, from the book of Esdras (in the Apocrypha, lays out the theme of the novel:

> Yea, many there be that have run out of their wits for women, and become servants for their sakes. Many also have perished, have erred, and sinned, for women. ... O ye men, how can it be but women should be strong, seeing they do thus?

Chapter 1

The novel opens in the hamlet of Marygreen, on the edge of the WESSEX downs. The schoolmaster, Richard Phillotson, is packing to leave for Christminster, where he hopes to obtain a university degree, "the necessary hallmark of a man who wishes to do anything in teaching," and be ordained. He has purchased a cottage piano at an auction, and has nowhere to store it temporarily. Jude Fawley, age 11, is among those helping him load the moving cart. Jude's mother committed suicide, and he has now been orphaned by the recent death of his father. He has come to live with his maiden great-aunt, Miss Drusilla FAWLEY. He suggests that Phillotson might leave the piano in her "fuel-house" until he is settled. Miss Fawley is agreeable, and the problem is solved. Phillotson advises Jude to "be kind to animals and birds, and read all you can," and to look him up if he should come to Christminster.

Chapter 2

Jude grows into a tenderhearted adolescent, unable to be cruel to animals. He works making deliveries for his great-aunt, a baker, but develops an interest in knowing more about the university at Christminster.

Chapter 3

Late one afternoon Jude wanders along a road and asks some workmen tiling a weatherbeaten barn where Christminster is. They tell him he can see it far away if the light is right; he begins thinking of it as "the heavenly Jerusalem." After they leave he climbs their ladder and perches on the highest rung. The mist dissolves and he sees the "vanes, windows, wet roof slates, and other shining spots upon the spires, domes, freestonework, and varied outlines" of Christminster. He returns later to see a halo of night lights seeming to be very near. A carter and his helpers stop along the road to rest their horses. Although the carter has never actually been there, he tells Jude "'tis all learning there—nothing but learning, except religion.'" It takes "'five years to turn a lirruping hobble-de-hoy chap into a solemn preaching man with no corrupt passions,'" but the town has beautiful music and the main street is like no other in the world. Jude resolves to visit the "city of light," which he considers "a castle, manned by scholarship and religion."

Chapter 4

Jude is overtaken on the road by Dr. VILBERT, an itinerant quack doctor who sells various remedies to cottagers throughout Wessex. Jude agrees to take orders for Dr. Vilbert's pills in exchange for Greek and Latin grammars, which Dr. Vilbert fails to deliver. Richard Phillotson, meanwhile, has sent for his pianoforte, and Jude slips a letter in the packing case asking him to send the grammars, which he does. Jude is hopelessly discouraged when he comprehends that the grammars are not magic keys to the language through "laws of transmutation" but that the Greek and Latin equivalents for each word must be memorized.

Chapter 5

Over the next few years, Jude applies himself to the classical languages. He teaches his bakery route to the aged horse his great-aunt has acquired, and studies passages from Caesar, Virgil, Horace, and Homer as he delivers bread. He turns to patristic literature and begins deciphering Latin inscriptions on 15th-century church brasses and tombs. Wanting more than ever to go to Christminster, he ponders possible occupations and decides to become a builder. He finds a substitute to take on his bread delivery job and apprentices himself to a stonemason in the nearby town of ALFREDSTON (Wantage, Berkshire). He locates lodgings there and begins restoring the masonry in village churches near Marygreen, returning to his great-aunt's home on weekends.

Chapter 6

One Saturday he walks to his great-aunt's home, feeling particularly encouraged about his prospects of going to Christminster and reciting to himself his program of future classical reading. He is startled when a girl calls to him from the other side of the hedge, "Hoity-toity!" He continues to concentrate, and she throws a pig's pizzle (penis) at him. Hardy remarks in his autobiography that "The throwing of the pizzle, at the supreme moment of his young dream, is to sharply initiate [the] contrast" between the "ideal life a man wished to lead, and the squalid real life he was fated to lead" (*Life*, 171). Jude discovers three young women washing pigs' chitterlings in a brook, and accuses one of them, "a complete and substantial female animal—no more, no less." She lures him onto a small plank bridge with "the unvoiced call of woman to man," and introduces herself as Arabella Donn. ANNY, one of the other girls, tells Arabella that Jude is "simple as a child" and "can be had by any woman who can get him to care for her a bit."

Chapter 7
Arabella constitutes "a new thing, a great hitch … in the gliding and noiseless current" of Jude's life. He abandons his Greek studies and goes to her family's pig farm. A male voice cries out that he has "come coorting" Arabella, and Jude winces. They walk to the Brown House barn, spot a fire in the distance, and begin walking toward it, but it is too far to reach. They return via Alfredston, where they have tea in an inn of the "inferior class." The waitress, who considers Arabella also of an inferior class, is surprised to see Jude with her. Arabella guesses her thoughts and laughs. On the way home Jude kisses her. Her family greets Jude in a congratulatory manner; he is embarrassed, but keeps thinking about Arabella. The next day Jude returns to his work at Alfredston and Arabella tells her friends everything he has said on their walk. They tell Arabella the best way to "catch" Jude is by getting pregnant.

Chapter 8
A few weeks later Jude comes home again and helps Arabella catch some escaping pigs. He tries to kiss her, but she resists. A neighborhood gossip warns her that Jude is determined to go to Christminster. On Sunday afternoon she sends her parents away and she and Jude walk, returning to the cottage for tea. Arabella tells Jude not to touch her, as she is "part eggshell"; she is hatching a rare cochin's egg by carrying it, wrapped in wool and a pig's bladder, in her bosom. It's an old custom, she tells Jude: "I suppose it is natural for a woman to want to bring live things into the world." She plays a game, withdrawing the egg and putting it back, pretending to hide from Jude, until she seduces him upstairs.

Chapter 9
After two months, Arabella meets Dr. Vilbert, in whom she confides. She then tells Jude she is pregnant. The church banns are posted, and they are married, to the consternation of his great-aunt, although she makes him a wedding cake. Arabella wraps up slices for her friends, labeling each one, "*In remembrance of good advice.*"

Jude, now 19, leases a roadside cottage between Brown House and Marygreen so that Arabella might keep a pig and they can raise vegetables. He is shocked to see, when she disrobes, that much of her hair is artificial; she also tells him she was once a barmaid at ALD-BRICKHAM (Reading). Arabella confesses to her friend Anny that she is not pregnant. She is sure Jude will be relieved, but when he discovers the truth he considers himself "caught in a gin" which will "cripple him, if not her also," for a lifetime.

Chapter 10
CHALLOW, the professional pig killer, fails to come to assist Jude and Arabella in killing the pig they have raised, so they must carry out the grueling task themselves, an undertaking very upsetting to Jude.

Chapter 11
Arabella hears rumors that she "trapped" Jude and throws his books on the floor. In trying to control her he loosens her hair and she goes along the road, where people stare at her hair. Jude is convinced the marriage is over. Arabella tells him his father ill-used his mother and his father's sister ill-used her husband and asks if he will treat her the same way. Jude returns home and asks Miss Fawley whether Arabella is right. Miss Fawley says his parents could not get along together and parted when he was a baby; his mother drowned herself and his father took Jude to South Wessex. Similarly, she tells Jude that his father's sister left her husband and took "the little maid" (Sue Bridehead) to London; "the Fawleys were not made for wedlock: it never seemed to sit well upon us."

Arabella leaves Jude a note saying she has gone to her friends; this is followed in several days by a letter stating that she and her parents are emigrating to Australia, since there is little money in the pig business. Jude contributes his household furniture to the Donn family auction. A few days later he discovers a framed photograph of himself a broker has bought at the auction and buys it for a shilling. It demonstrates "the utter death of every tender sentiment in his wife," and he burns it.

After Arabella and her parents leave, Jude returns to the summit from which he has first perceived Christminster. He sees a carving he had chiseled on a milestone soon after he had become an apprentice, with a hand pointing toward Christminster: "THITHER J. F."

Part Second: "At Christminster"

One of the two epigraphs is a line from Swinburne: "Save his own soul he hath no star." The other epigraph, in Latin, is from Ovid's *Metamorphoses*.

Chapter 1
Three years later, Jude has finished his apprenticeship and has seen a photograph of his cousin, Sue Bride-

head, on his great-aunt's mantelpiece. He begins walking toward Christminster, having spent his time reading "almost all that could be read and learnt by one in his position, of the worthies who had spent their youth within these reverend walls, and whose souls had haunted them in their maturer age." In Christminster he wanders among the college quadrangles in the "venerable city" until their gates close, when he imagines in his "mindsight" talking with various scientists, philologists, and authors. Challenged by a policeman, he returns to his lodgings and continues to read and recall the political and religious writings of noted sons of the university, including Matthew ARNOLD.

Chapter 2
The next morning Jude views the colleges differently—as wounded edifices, struggling against weather, time, and man. He sees that there must be work for a stonemason and visits the workyard of a stonemason where the traceries and mullions of Gothic architecture are being repaired (although medievalism is considered "as dead as a fern-leaf in a lump of coal.") Failing to find employment, he asks his great-aunt to send the photograph of Sue, which she does.

As he seeks work he rubs shoulders on the streets with undergraduates, feeling a kinship at times with their conversation, but realizing he is set apart as a workman. He is finally offered a job in the stonemason's yard, which he accepts; he buys a lamp and continues his studies at night. His evangelical great-aunt writes to warn him against seeking Sue, whose father, she believes, has returned to London. She believes Sue is working in an ecclesiastical warehouse, "a perfect seed-bed of idolatry." Eventually he discovers Sue in such a shop; she is engraving, in Gothic letters, "*Alleluya*." He believes her to be very saintly. He obeys his great-aunt's wishes, but, a few weeks later, sees Sue on the street and thinks her very elegant and appealing, with a "pitch of niceness" he attributes to her London upbringing. He resists contacting her because of his own marriage, and his family's unfortunate experiences with marriage. His realization that "a tragic sadness might be intensified to a tragic horror" foreshadows the later catastrophe that befalls Jude and Sue. He decides she will be no more than a "kindly star" to him, while he will be a "kinsman and well-wisher" to her.

Chapter 3
He goes to the morning service in the cathedral church of Cardinal College, hoping in vain to catch a view of Sue. She does not come, but he does see her at the afternoon service.

Some time before the cathedral service, Sue had taken a walk in the country and purchased plaster statues of Venus and Apollo from an itinerant vendor. She had returned with her "heathen load" to the "most

Christian city in the country" and smuggled them into her rented room, pretending to the landlady, Miss FONTOVER, that they were saints. At night she secretly reads the work of the historian Edward Gibbon (author of *The Decline and Fall of the Roman Empire*) and gazes at her treasures. Jude, meanwhile, is reading his Bible in Greek.

Chapter 4
Jude becomes increasingly aware of Sue as he sees her in town, but he is troubled by the fact of his marriage. She learns who he is, asks for him in the stonemason's yard, and sends him a note. She addresses him as "Dear Cousin Jude," and says she has only learned by accident that he is living in Christminster. They meet, and he learns that she knows Richard Phillotson, who is now 45 and a schoolmaster at Lumsdon. They go to call on him. Phillotson remembers, finally, sending grammars to Jude. He has given up the idea of entering the church, unless as a licentiate, but he needs a pupil-teacher in his school. As they return to Christminster, Jude finds Sue "vibrant" and sensitive. She tells Jude that Miss Fontover has broken her statues, but does not tell him they were of Apollo and Venus. Jude persuades Phillotson to hire Sue.

Chapter 5
Sue takes up teaching and is an excellent teacher. The children visit Christminster to see a model of Jerusalem. He discovers she does not appreciate the Christian significance of the city. Jude is also visiting the model. The next day Phillotson discovers that Sue has drawn on her blackboard, in chalk, an excellent perspective view of Jerusalem in her classroom. Sue nearly faints soon afterward at a surprise visit of the school Inspector. Jude sees them walking with Phillotson's arm around her, and realizes they could make a suitable marriage. He is agonized that he belongs to Arabella.

Chapter 6
Jude goes to Marygreen to see his aunt and asks her about Sue. Aunt Drusilla warns him not to become interested in her. She is "townish" and "pert," and was raised to hate the Fawleys. Jude returns to Christminster and writes letters to many heads of colleges asking about his chance of admission. He learns, from talking with people, that his only chance might be to study very hard and win an open scholarship, or save money for 15 years. He receives only one reply to his letters, from Biblioll College, saying his best chance for success in life is to remain in his own sphere as a working man and not try to enter one of the colleges.

He goes to a bar and has several drinks, then goes to Fourways in the middle of the city, an intersection older than any of the colleges. He goes to a public hall and listens to a promenade concert. He writes on the wall of Biblioll college, in chalk, "'*I have understanding as well as you; I am not inferior to you: yea, who knoweth not such things as these?*'—Job xii. 3.'"

Chapter 7

Jude goes at night to a tavern in a court (supposedly based on the Turf Tavern, which still exists in Oxford). He stays there all night drinking, with nothing to eat; he falls in with various customers, including an iron-monger, some clerks, an auctioneer, two ladies of doubtful repute, a travelling actor, and some under-graduates. He roundly criticizes the whole university and says he doesn't "care a damn" for any "Provost, Warden, Principal," or any other official of the univer-sity. The undergraduates cheer him. A mason Jude knows as Uncle Joe asks if Jude can say the Creed in Latin, and he declares he can. An undergraduate chal-lenges him. He stands Jude a whisky, and Jude recites the Creed. He then shouts at them, asking a critical question: "Which one of you knows whether I have said it or not?" The landlord fears a riot, but Jude leaves and goes to Sue's lodging. She puts him in an easy chair and goes up to her flat. Before she returns the next morning he leaves, goes to his flat and finds a letter of dismissal from his job, then goes home to Marygreen. A young curate is praying with his aunt; Jude explains his situation. He says if Jude gives up drinking he might enter the church as a licentiate.

Part Third: "At Melchester"

Chapter 1

Jude is reluctant to enter the church in such a lowly way. He could probably not rise to a higher grade, but could only hope to be a humble curate. He takes various local jobs, such as lettering headstones in the village. Sue writes to say that she is going to a training college at Melchester, and he decides to go there, but, for the moment, continues doing odd jobs in the village.

Sue enters the Melchester Normal School and writes Jude that she is miserable and sorry she went there. He goes to Melchester and lodges at a temper-ance hotel. He stands beneath "the most graceful architectural pile in England" (Salisbury cathedral; *see* "The IMPERCIPIENT"). She tells him she has promised to marry Phillotson in two years. Jude is upset and asks her to sit in the cathedral with him. Sue declares she would rather sit in the railway sta-tion, which is "the centre of the town life now. The Cathedral has had its day!" Jude finds work in doing carving at the cemetery on the hill; he is later engaged in repairing stonework in the cathedral. He lodges near the close gate of the cathedral. He reads Cardinal Newman, the Anglican theologian Edward Bouverie Pusey, and other "modern lights." He also practices chants on a harmonium.

Chapter 2

On Sue's free afternoon they set out for Wardour Cas-tle, which they tour, then decide to get something to eat and walk across the high country to get the train of another railway back to Melchester. They miscalculate the distance, and are forced to ask for shelter in a shep-herd's cottage. They share the dinner provided by the shepherd's mother, and Sue stays in the mother's room; Jude and the shepherd are in the main room. The next morning the shepherd guides them to the train. They reach the training school and ring the bell.

Chapter 3

The previous evening, the 70 young women at the Training School have discussed Sue's absence the night before. Sue returns. The headmistress tells the girls that no one may speak to Sue without permission: she must be in solitary confinement for a week. The girls vote to take her word that she has done nothing wrong. Sue escapes from the back window of the room in which she has been confined, and goes to see Jude. He wraps her in a coat and gives her some brandy; she spends the night in his chair.

Chapter 4

Jude pretends his guest is a young man. Sue tells Jude of an irreligious young journalist she had known in London who broadened her reading. They shared a sit-ting room for 15 months, but she refused to be inti-mate with him. He died, and Sue was his only mourner. He left her some money, which she invested in a "bub-ble scheme" and lost. At that point she returned to Christminster, since her father wouldn't have her back. Jude says he believes she is as "innocent" as she is "unconventional." She shows him a rearranged Bible she has made. Jude thinks she is the dearest woman he has ever met, but they are divided by her "increduli-ties."

Chapter 5

Sue wants to slip out without being seen. She goes to Shaston on the train to stay with the sister of a school friend. Jude is despondent. He gets a letter from Sue saying he can love her. He goes to Shaston to the village schoolhouse and sees her. She says they won't take her back at the training school; she is now a fallen woman. Jude confesses his love for her, but doesn't kiss her. Sue will try to get in another school; Jude thinks she is unreasonable. Sue's perverseness comes close to a desire to inflict pain, not only in the way she treats Jude, but also in the way she treats Phillotson.

Chapter 6

Phillotson has obtained a post at a boys' school at Shas-ton. He wants to make money and marry Sue, who, he imagines, might conduct a nearby girls' school. He is studying Roman-Britannic antiquities as a hobby. He reads historic notes Sue has written, along with her past letters about her experiences at the training school. He considers himself engaged to her, and, in the letters, she has stated that she appreciates his tact in not coming to see her.

Philloston goes to the training school at Melchester and discovers her expulsion two weeks earlier. He visits the cathedral and sees Jude, working on the cathedral renovations. He asks about Sue's escape; Jude says he wants to marry her, but cannot. Phillotson thinks for a moment that Sue was expelled because of intimacy with Jude, but Jude corrects this impression.

Phillotson leaves, and Jude finds Sue. They go into the market house and he tells her about Arabella. Sue is distressed, but observes that her aunt had always said the Fawleys were unfit for marriage.

Chapter 7
Sue writes Jude that she and Phillotson are to be married, and asks Jude to give her away; he accepts. They rehearse in the church of St. Thomas (Doubting Thomas), with Jude as bridegroom, which upsets Phillotson. He hires a small carriage from the Red Lion Inn for the journey to and from the church. After a simple meal at Phillotson's lodging, Jude leaves.

Chapter 8
Jude is miserable; he has a job offer from his old Christminster employer, which he accepts. Then he has word that his aunt Drusilla Fawley is very ill and goes to Marygreen. He writes Sue and offers to meet her at Alfredston and escort her to Marygreen if she wishes to see her. Meanwhile, he meets Tinker Taylor, an ironmonger he has known in Christminster, and agrees to have a drink with him. Arabella is tending bar, but she does not see Jude. He overhears her tell an undergraduate she has left her husband in Australia, which mystifies Jude. When he talks with her, he finds she had returned from Sydney three months earlier; they agree to meet later at night. He realizes he cannot meet Sue at Alfredston, and he and Arabella go to Aldbrickham, staying in a third-rate inn.

Chapter 9
Arabella confesses that she has contracted an illegal marriage in Sydney to Mr. CARTLETT, the gentleman who managed the hotel in which she worked. Jude perceives that it was he to whom she referred when talking to the man in the bar. She says there was one more thing she meant to tell him but it can wait. He meets Sue, by accident, in Christminster. She had gone to Marygreen and found her aunt better. They walk to Alfredston. Jude can see that she is unhappy, and says that "wifedom" has not "squashed up and digested" her. Their aunt, who is a little better, perceives how unhappy Sue is. She returns to Phillotson in Shaston, and Jude stays with his aunt a few days. Arabella writes from London to say her husband has come to England

and they have taken a public house in Lambeth; he will be the landlord and she will tend bar.

Chapter 10
Jude goes to Melchester and "returns with feverish desperation to his study for the priesthood." He hears a hymn he likes and tracks down the composer in Kennetbridge, but when the man discovers Jude's poverty he loses interest in him. He returns to find that Sue had invited him to Sunday dinner, but her note had arrived too late. She invites him for an afternoon visit.

Part Fourth: "At Shaston"

Chapter 1
Jude arrives at Shaston. This is Hardy's name for Shaftsbury, which was originally known as Caer Pallador. He climbs the hill to Sue's school. They have tea at the school, and Sue tells him she is not "really" Mrs. Richard Phillotson, but a "woman tossed about, all alone, with aberrant passions, and unaccountable antipathies." She invites him to come to their house the next week. He wanders about the town before his train and, from outside, sees Sue at their home, Old-Grove Place, looking at a photograph he assumes is his.

Chapter 2
She sends him a note asking him not to come the next week. He returns to find a telegram saying his aunt is sinking. By the time he arrives, she has died. He stays in Marygreen, making arrangements. He notifies Sue of the funeral, and she arrives.

Jude tells Sue she should not have married Richard; she likes him only as a friend, but not as a husband. Jude stays at his aunt's home, and Sue stays with Mrs. Edlin, who had been taking care of Aunt Drusilla. Late at night they talk through the window; Sue confesses her misery, weeps, and kisses him on the top of his head.

Chapter 3
The next morning he escorts her to Alfredston and returns. Jude realizes he cannot become a licentiate (a soldier and servant) of a religion in which sexual love is regarded "as at its best a frailty, and at its worst damnation." He burns all his theological works. Jude's interior monologue, as he disposes of his effects, is one of intense self-analysis, which would have been upsetting to the Victorian conscience, which regarded everything in life to be endured, and nothing to be done or changed.

Meanwhile, Sue returns to Phillotson and tells him she let Jude hold her hand. He is preoccupied with the school committee and the school letterhead. Sue locks herself in a closet and cries. The next morning Phillotson discovers her amid spiderwebs in the closet and muses, "What must a woman's aversion be when it is stronger than her fear of spiders!" Sue tells him she wants to live separately in their house. They exchange notes from their classrooms, and he agrees.

Chapter 4

By mistake Phillotson enters Sue's quarters and she leaps from the window, but is unhurt. The next day Phillotson calls on his friend George GILLINGHAM and consults him. Gillingham says Sue should be "smacked, and brought to her senses." Phillotson cannot coerce Sue, and gives her permission to leave him. He offers her the furniture, which she refuses. Gillingham comes to call, which is a help to Phillotson.

Chapter 5

Sue had written Jude that she was leaving Richard, and he meets her. He suggests they move to Aldbrickham. Arabella has written to ask for a divorce so she can legally marry her Australian "husband." Sue shows Jude a letter from Phillotson, who asks only that Jude be kind to her; he has been a "shadowy third" during their brief life together. They stay at the George, the very inn where Jude had stayed with Arabella. The waiting maid recognizes Jude and mentions his previous stay. Sue has told Jude she wants to be friends only, but is still jealous. Jude tells her of Arabella's new marriage.

Chapter 6

Sue's departure has occasioned gossip in Shaston. Phillotson is asked to resign, and does so; he then becomes ill. Gillingham writes Sue, who goes to see him without Jude's knowledge. Phillotson decides, as a kindness to her, to dissolve their marriage legally.

Part Fifth: "At Aldbrickham and Elsewhere"

Chapter 1

The time is now February of the next year. Sue and Jude are living in a rented house in Aldbrickham. They receive word that Sue's divorce from Phillotson is final. Jude's divorce from Arabella is also final, so they are both free to do as they like. They are living together, but on different landings of the house; they "meet by day." Jude is pleased that they can marry, but Sue is resistant. She has never actually told him she loves him.

Chapter 2

A few weeks later Arabella comes to see Jude, who is out. She has not remarried, after all, and a "sudden responsibility" has been sprung on her from Australia, which prevents her from getting another job as a barmaid. She leaves, and, over Sue's objections, Jude goes out to search for her, but fails. Sue says she will marry him; he plans to post the banns of their marriage. Sue then sets out to the public house and confronts Arabella in her bedroom. Arabella says she can tell Sue is now Jude's (i.e., they have slept together), but she had not been sure the day before. She opens a telegram say-

ing Mr. Cartlett has called her to Lambeth and can't do without her. She says she will write Jude about a "little matter of business."

Chapter 3

Sue and Jude reach the door of the parish clerk, but Sue has second thoughts about marriage. She thinks legal obligations are destructive to relationships. Arabella sends a newspaper clipping stating that she and Mr. Cartlett are married. She also sends a letter saying she and Jude had had a son, born in Australia, and he will soon arrive in England. She asks Jude to take him.

The news comes as a shock to Jude, but he and Sue are willing to take the boy. He arrives on foot from the train, as Arabella's friends had not told Jude when he was coming. He is a small, old-looking child, "Age masquerading as Juvenility." Jude and Sue tell him he would have been met if they had known when he was arriving. Sue sees Jude in him, and also Arabella, which she "can't bear." Sue says she is willing to go through with the marriage ceremony.

Chapter 4

They make a second attempt at marriage. The child is called Father Time because he looks so aged. They invite the Widow EDLIN to the wedding. She comes, and Sue and Jude go to the register office. There they see a woman marrying an ex-convict, and Sue again decides she doesn't like the idea of marrying in a register office any better than in a church. They return home, unmarried, and tell Mrs. Edlin they did not marry after all.

Chapter 5

Time passes, and Sue and Jude take Father Time to the Great Wessex Agricultural Show at Stoke-Barehills. Arabella and her husband appear. Cartlett doesn't know about Arabella's child. Arabella is sure Sue and Jude are not married. They see Dr. Vilbert, who once promised the child Jude he would send him Latin and Greek grammars, but didn't. Jude and Sue have made a model of Christminster University that is on display. The three do not recognize Arabella, who buys a potion from Dr. Vilbert. Father Time is obedient, but disinterested in everything; he seems to have heavy burdens of his own. He asks them not to buy flowers, as they'll soon be withered.

Chapter 6

Little Time, as he is now called, is teased at school. Jude and Sue hire a sitter and go to LONDON; when they come back they let it be known, falsely, that they are married. The townspeople are doubtful and the artisans' wives look past Sue on the pavement. Jude's headstone and epitaph orders decline. He is asked to reletter the Ten Commandments in a nearby church. He accepts, and Sue goes to assist. Soon, however, they hear whispers from the women who clean the church, one of whom has friends on their street. The couple are asked to leave in the middle of the job. They sell Aunt Drusilla's furniture and take lodgings in various towns.

Chapter 7

The family begin a migratory existence, wherever Jude can get work. Three years later, at the Kennetbridge spring fair, they are selling "Christminster" cakes and gingerbreads in the shape of university towers and pinnacles (Jude was brought up by his Aunt Drusilla in the baking business). By this time Sue has two children and is expecting a third. They meet Arabella and learn that Mr. Cartlett has died. She is now living at Alfredston and has become very religious. She has come to attend the laying of the foundation stones of a new chapel.

Chapter 8

Arabella tells her friend Anny she wishes she had Jude back again. She meets Phillotson, who is now teaching once more at Marygreen and she tells him that Sue was innocent at the time of the divorce. After the fair, Arabella and Father Time go to check on Jude, who has been ill. The landlady, Mrs. EDLIN, has been babysitting their other two children. Jude and Sue decide to return to Christminster.

Part Sixth: "At Christminster Again"

Chapter 1

Sue and Jude arrive in Christminster, looking for lodgings. They see an academic procession, and Jude sees Tinker Taylor. Jude is not well, but declaims, before a crowd of the "populace," that a man must be "as coldblooded as a fish and as selfish as a pig" to have a good chance of being "one of his country's worthies." Jude is now in a "state of conflict." He asks, "For who knoweth what is good for man in this life?—and who can tell a man what shall be after him under the sun?" They are caught in the rain, and Jude becomes more ill; they have no lodging. Sue has seen Richard Philloston in the crowd also. They finally find lodgings for Sue and the children in a small back room with a view of one of the colleges, but there is not enough room for Jude. He goes out and finds another place to stay. Sue admits she is not married, and the landlady's husband says she cannot have the room for the week; but may stay overnight. Sue and Father Time put the little ones to bed and search everywhere, but find no place to stay.

Chapter 2

Father Time questions Sue closely about why Jude left; he has deduced that he left to make room for the children. He asks why people have children if they are so much trouble, and says he should never have come

from Australia. He declares that when unwanted children are born they should be killed immediately, before they have souls.

Sue thinks the boy is "too reflective" but tells him there will be another baby in the family soon. The boy jumps up and becomes extremely agitated. He goes into the large closet, in which a bed has been spread on the floor, and Sue hears him say "If we children was gone there'd be no trouble at all!" She tells him not to think that.

Sue goes to breakfast at the tavern where Jude has stayed and they begin searching for lodgings. When they return they discover that Father Time has hanged the other children and himself, and left a sign, "*Done because we are too menny.*" Jude manages to get coffins for the three children and takes them to the cemetery; Sue gives birth prematurely to her third child, which dies.

Chapter 3

Although Sue refuses to marry Jude and informs him she is wicked, she begins going to church at Saint Silas, the Church of Ceremonies. Her father, whom Uncle Joe has mentioned to Jude, before he meet Sue, as "that clever chap Bridehead," had done the wrought ironwork in the church ten years before Jude begins working in Christminster. She comes home with the "fumes" of incense on her clothes, to Jude's astonishment. Sue tells Jude she still considers herself Phillotson's wife.

Arabella comes and apologizes for not having gone to the children's funeral. She has found her son's grave. Although she has shown no feeling for him in life, she wants a headstone erected. She tells Sue and Jude that she is living at Alfredston with her father, who has returned from Australia. Her mother has died of dysentery.

Jude is angry with Sue for feeling so guilty and begs her not to abandon him to his "two Arch Enemies," his "weakness for womankind" and his "impulse to strong liquor." He kisses her weeping face and she leaves.

Chapter 4

Phillotson goes to the Alfredston market and reads the account of the hangings, which distresses him. He meets Arabella in the market, who says Sue does not live with Jude any longer. She tells him the eldest boy was hers. He resolves to write Sue. Sue decides to return to Phillotson, and goes to tell Jude, who is living in Beersheba, a suburb of Christminster.

Chapter 5

Sue finds Phillotson and asks him to take her back. She goes to stay with Mrs. Edlin until their marriage the next day. She burns the pretty nightgown she had bought to please Jude; Mrs. Edlin says Sue is in love with Jude and should not marry Phillotson. Sue insists she is Phillotson's already. Mrs. Edlin tells Phillotson that Sue is forcing herself to marry him. The next morning Sue looks like the lily her name connotes. They are married, but Sue is still timid and Phillotson tells her he won't "intrude" on her privacy.

Chapter 6

Arabella goes to see Jude on the outskirts of Christminster. Her father has turned her out. Jude reluctantly asks the landlord, who agrees to let her stay a day or two. She tells him Sue and Phillotson are remarried, which she has learned from her friend Anny.

Chapter 7

Arbella plots with her father to remarry Jude, who is growing more infirm and confused. She takes him to an upper room in her father's tenement, where he runs a small pork shop. She tells her father she wants to keep Jude upstairs until they are married. They will ply him with brandy and keep him "cheerful." In three days Jude is somewhat better. Arabella invites people to the house to have a continual party with liquor and cards. Eleven hours later the guests are still there. Finally Mr. Donn says that it is a "point of honour" for Jude to marry Arabella, since they have been living under his roof for three days. The clergyman has said "What God hath joined together let no man put asunder."

Chapter 8

After the wedding Jude and Arabella take lodgings in Christminster, but Jude is not well. He asks Arabella to invite Sue to come to see him. Arabella refuses, saying she will not invite "that strumpet" to the house. Jude threatens to kill her, then admits he couldn't really do so, and Arabella agrees to send for Sue but does not. Jude, suspecting the truth, makes a journey to the schoolhouse at MARYGREEN, although he is wretchedly ill. A small boy leads Sue to Jude, who tells her there is nothing in his life more "degrading," "immoral," and "unnatural" than his "meretricious contract" with Arabella. He says Sue is not worth "a man's love" because she has chosen Phillotson over him. She insists her marriage is only a nominal one. Jude tells her their marriages were both made while they were drunk—he was "gin-drunk" and she was "creed-drunk." He returns that night, thoroughly chilled, to Christminster.

Chapter 9

Arabella is waiting for Jude on the platform. He is almost out of his mind and begins talking about all the phantoms who had attended Christminster. It is as though the fog has "death-claws." At Marygreen, Mrs.

Illustration by William Hatherell for Jude the Obscure, *part sixth, chapter 9 ("Jude at the milestone"), published in* Harper's Magazine, *November 1895* (Earl Gregg Swem Library, College of William and Mary)

Edlin tries to talk with Sue, who says she still loves Jude. Sue plans to sleep with Phillotson, and asks Mrs. Edlin to stay overnight. She swears on the New Testament that she will never see Jude again.

Chapter 10
Jude recovers to some extent. Mrs. Edlin tells him Sue and Phillotson are man and wife. Arabella has asked Dr. Vilbert to see Jude; Jude swears at him. She gives Dr. Vilbert some wine and some of his own "love-philter" mixture.

Chapter 11
It is summer, and Jude is still alive. Arabella goes with some of his fellow stoneworkers to see the boat races. She returns to find Jude has died, but goes back out again. Dr. Vilbert is there, during the boat races, and squeezes her. She goes to the home of a woman who does the laying-out of the dead. Two days later Arabella and Mrs. Edlin stand by Jude's coffin in the bedroom. Arabella says she had offered to send for Sue but that Jude had not wanted her to know how ill he was. Arabella declares Sue has "never found peace since she left his arms, and never will again till she's as he is now!"

Jude's lonely death, within hearing of the songs of Remembrance Day at Christminster University, from which he is now forever separated, brings a tragic close to his life. For 20 years he had studied in vain, hoping to perfect his qualifications for admission to one of the colleges. He was scorned by academic Christminster then and relegated to the outer perimeter of the various college walls. The colorful ceremonies he witnessed are but an excruciating barrier to the inner life of the mind he sought. He has suffered, in Dale Kramer's words, "defeats in sex and love" inflicted by two women, Arabella, "sensual and pragmatic," and Sue, "intellectual and intensely seeking" (Kramer, "Hardy and Readers: *Jude the Obscure*," 164)

CRITICAL RECEPTION AND COMMENTARY

When *Jude* was published in book form in November 1895, Hardy thought he was prepared for adverse critical reaction. Many reviewers had attacked TESS OF THE D'URBERVILLES, published four years earlier, especially for its subtitle, "A Pure Woman," which readers considered a cynical comment on the story. *Jude,* however, provoked far more controversy. Hardy had bowdlerized the manuscript for serial publication to make it acceptable to readers, which caused the book itself to incite rabid criticism. Unlike periodical readers, who were believed to be somewhat puritanical, the book-buying public was thought to be more open-minded and able to "judge fairly the consequences of economic and social inequalities" (Kramer, 166). The pig-killing scene provoked severe criticism; Hardy stated

that he hoped it would serve a "humane end in showing people the cruelty that goes on unheeded under the barbarous *régime* we call civilization." It was reprinted in the magazine ANIMALS' FRIEND by the Society for the Protection of Animals in December 1895 (*Letters* II, 94, 97). The themes of the novel were controversial, including the difficulties of Sue's attempt at being an independent woman, her agnosticism, the hypocrisy of the churchgoers who refuse to permit Jude and Sue to work as artisans on the tablet of the Ten Commandments because they are unmarried, and the class-based university admission policies that deny Jude, despite his studies and scholarly ability, a place at any of the colleges.

The most inflammatory issue in the novel, however, as Rosemarie Morgan observes, is Sue's rebellion against the institutionalization of marriage by church and state and its unfair treatment of women. As Morgan explains, Hardy moves, in *Jude,* to the "legal ramifications of the sexual double standard under the prevailing divorce laws." When Sue tries to leave Phillotson, she has no "admissible grounds for divorce"; she must become, herself, the "guilty party" because only the husband can seek divorce. At the time, adultery did not constitute sufficient grounds for a wife to sue her husband for divorce. Moreover, the husband, who owned his wife as "legal property," could seek compensation if she left him ("Marriage," *Oxford Reader's Companion to Hardy,* 256).

In November 1895 Hardy wrote Florence HENNIKER that he was "indifferent" to the public reception of *Jude.* He stated that it was not a "novel with a purpose," but that it turned out to be one that "makes for" humanity, to his surprise. He did not consider the novel a "manifesto" on marriage, except that he wanted to suggest that a "hereditary curse of temperament" can make people unfit for marriage. He believed the novel was addressed to those "into whose souls the iron adversity" had deeply entered, and that it would be "uncongenial" to those who were "self-indulgent" and had lives of "ease & affluence."

The novel was widely reviewed in newspapers and periodicals. An anonymous reviewer for the *Daily Telegraph* regretted the lack of "quaint provincial humour" which had "illumined" Hardy's previous work, but pronounced it a "masterpiece." An anonymous reviewer for the *Morning Post,* termed the chapters describing the "entrapping of Jude" the "most unsatisfactory ever perpetrated by any novelist who could claim a prominent place among contemporary writers." William Dean HOWELLS, writing in HARPER'S WEEKLY, criticized the power of Fate within the novel, in which tragedy is "almost unrelieved by the humorous touch which the poet is master of." He observed that it reflected the "conviction that marriage is the sole solution of the question of sex, while it shows how atrocious and heinous marriage may sometimes be." He praised it, however, as having "the solemn and lofty effect of a great tragedy" (Clarke, *Thomas Hardy: Critical Assessments,* Vol. I, 229, 231 245–47).

The Scottish novelist Margaret Oliphant wrote a lengthy review titled "The Anti-Marriage League," condemning the book for *Blackwood's Magazine.* She called it a "tremendous downfall," an "illustration of what Art can come to when given over to the exposition of the unclean." She saw the entire novel as an attack on the "stronghold of marriage" and a "nauseous tragedy" (Clarkc, *Thomas Hardy: Critical Assessments,* Vol. I, 248–52). Hardy would note bitterly in 1907, "Ever since the days of John Keats, to be bludgeoned by Blackwood has been the hallmark of an author of ideas" (*Letters* III, 256). Jeannette Gilder, writing in the *New York World,* cried, "What has happened to Thomas Hardy? . . . I am shocked, appalled by his story! . . . It is almost the worst book I have ever read. . . . Thank God for Kipling and Stevenson, Barrie and Mrs. Humphry Ward. Here are four great writers who have never trailed their talents in the dirt." Hardy quotes from this review in his autobiography; to his astonishment, Jeannette Gilder then had the temerity to ask him for an interview, as she was coming to England. He declined, writing her, "Those readers who, like yourself, could not see that *Jude . . .* makes for morality more than any other book I have written," were unlikely to be convinced by a newspaper article, "even from your attractive pen" (*Life,* 279–80).

Edmund GOSSE opened his review in *Cosmopolis* by stating that Hardy had become "classical," along with George MEREDITH and Robert Louis STEVENSON. Gosse did not like Hardy's moving the setting out of Wessex to Oxford, but thought his scenes gave a "perfect impression of truth," except that, in all, it was a "ghastly story." He felt the novel "traced the full circle of propriety" from the crude expressions of Henry Fielding and Tobias Smollett to the delicacy of Jane Austen and Sir Walter Scott, to the disregard of mankind's "clamorous passions" by Charles Dickens to the prudery of George ELIOT. He asked, "What has Providence done to Mr. Hardy that he should rise up in the arable land of Wessex and shake his fist at his Creator?" Gosse was not the first critic to wish Hardy would "go back to Egdon Heath and listen to the singing in the heather." He concluded by saying Hardy's "noble" imagination was prone to giving "a shriek of discord" at a moment's notice (Clarke, *Thomas Hardy: Critical Assessments,* Vol. I, 253–59).

For further reading: Benvenuto, "Modes of Perception: The Will to Live in *Jude the Obscure*"; Bloom, *Thomas Hardy's "Jude the Obscure"*; Daleski, "*Jude the Obscure:* The Defective Real"; Davis, "Happy Days in *Jude the Obscure:* Hardy and the Crawford-Dilke Divorce Case"; Davis, "Sir Francis Jeune and Divorce by 'False Pretences' in *Jude the Obscure*"; Doheny, "Characterization in Hardy's *Jude the Obscure:* The Function of Arabella"; Draper, "Hardy's Comic Tragedy: *Jude the Obscure*"; Edwards, Carol, and Duane Edwards, "*Jude the Obscure:* A Psychoanalytic Study"; Edwards, Suzanne, "A Shadow from the Past: Little Father Time in *Jude the Obscure*"; Freeman, "Highways and Cornfields: Space and Time in the Narration of *Jude the Obscure*"; Goetz, "The Felicity and Infelicity of Marriage in *Jude the Obscure*"; Gregor, "Jude the Obscure"; Hagen, "Does Teaching Make a Difference in Ethical Reflection? A Report on Teaching Hardy's *Jude the Obscure* with Attention to Marriage, Divorce, and Remarriage"; Harding, "The Signification of Arabella's Missile: Feminine Sexuality, Masculine Anxiety and Revision in *Jude the Obscure*"; Hellstrom, "Hardy's Use of Setting and *Jude the Obscure*"; Henigan, "Hardy's Emblem of Futility: The Role of Christminster in *Jude the Obscure*"; Kincaid, "Girl-Watching, Child-Beating and Other Exercises for Readers of *Jude the Obscure*"; Kramer, "Hardy and Readers: *Jude the Obscure*"; Langland, "Becoming a Man in *Jude the Obscure*"; LeVay, "Hardy's *Jude the Obscure*"; Melfi, "*Jude the Obscure:* Childhood without Closure"; Morgan, "Marriage"; Morgan, "Women"; Saldivar, "*Jude the Obscure:* Reading and the Spirit of the Law"; Taylor, "The Chronology of *Jude the Obscure.*"

Julian, Christopher Young music teacher in *The HAND OF ETHELBERTA.* He lives with his sister, Faith JULIAN, at Sandbourne (Eastbourne), and has long loved the young widow Ethelberta PETHERWIN. He sets one of her poems to music. He eventually becomes assistant organist at Melchester (Salisbury) Cathedral. He and others try in vain to prevent Ethelberta from marrying the reprehensible Lord MOUNTCLERE. Christopher eventually marries her sister, Picotee CHICKEREL, who is far better suited to him than the ambitious Ethelberta. As the novel ends, he has been promoted to the post of organist at Melchester cathedral.

Julian, Faith The devoted sister of Christopher JULIAN in *The HAND OF ETHELBERTA,* she is small, neat, gentle, and, like her brother, a gifted musician. When her brother persuades her to move to a small flat in Bloomsbury, LONDON, she is reluctant but accompanies him, remarking, "Mediocrity stamped 'London' fetches more than talent marked 'provincial.'" She encourages Christopher's courtship of Picotee CHICKEREL, but does not altogether approve of Picotee's spirited sister Ethelberta PETHERWIN (later, Lady Mountclere).

K

Keats, John (1795–1821) English romantic poet whose works Hardy knew well and admired. Among his most noted poems are "Ode on a Grecian Urn," "Ode to Psyche," "Lamia," "Ode to a Nightingale," La Belle Dame Sans Merci," "The Eve of St. Agnes," "Endymion," "To Autumn," and "On First Looking into Chapman's Homer." Hardy read and assimilated Keat's poetry as a young man and had a lifelong affection for his work.

In March 1880 the Hardys were invited to call on Anne Benson PROCTER in LONDON; it was the first of many times they would attend her "Sunday afternoons" and meet her literary and artistic friends. Mrs. Procter told Hardy that in her youth she had met Leigh Hunt, who was one of the early champions of the poetry of Keats. Hunt had come to see her one day, bringing along "a youth whom nobody noticed much," whom Hunt introduced as "Mr. Keats" (*Life*, 136).

In March 1887, when the Hardys went to ITALY, they stayed in Rome near Keats's house. Hardy wrote, in his autobiography, that "no mind could conjecture what had been lost to English literature" by his death. There they visited the English cemetery to see the graves of Keats and Shelley; Hardy sent Edmund GOSSE two pressed violets he had gathered from Keats's grave (*Letters* I, 163).

In June 1914 Sidney Colvin, an art and literary critic, was working on a biography of Keats. He wrote Hardy to see if he could identify, from the description given by the English painter Joseph Severn, what part of the DORSET coast Keats might have visited in September 1820, when he left England for Rome, seeking a cure for his tuberculosis. Hardy apparently discussed the letter with Florence HARDY, and replied, "we have been weighing probabilities" in order to answer his question. He believed the "splendid caverns & grottoes" meant Durdle Door, near Lulworth Cove. He said it had impressed his wife the same way "when she first saw it as a girl." As late as October 30, before Hardy died in January 1928, Florence Hardy noted that at lunch Hardy talked about Severn, "speaking with admiration of his friendship towards Keats." He stated that at the time Keats had been "comparatively obscure" (*Life*, 442).

Critics have identified several instances in which Keats may have had a direct influence on Hardy's poetry and fiction, and he was certainly sensitive to Keats's connection with Dorset. In September 1920, he wrote the poem

"AT LULWORTH COVE A CENTURY BACK," which evokes the September 1820 landing made by Keats on the Dorset coast as he was setting off for Rome.

In April 1921 the playwright and author St. John Ervine wrote Hardy that a group of young writers wished to present him with a first edition of a volume of Keats's poetry for his forthcoming birthday. Hardy wrote that he felt a first edition would be "of too much value," but they did present him with Keats's *Lamia, Isabella, the Eve of St. Agnes, and Other Poems* on Hardy's 81st birthday, June 2, 1921. The volume was sent by 104 writers, including Virginia WOOLF and Siegfried SASSOON (*Letters* VI, 84–85, 90).

For further reading: Atkinson, "Hardy's *The Woodlanders* and a Stanza by Keats"; Moorhead, "Keats's 'Ode to a Nightingale' and Hardy's 'The Oxen.'"

Kennedy, Hugh Arthur (fl. 1900) Playwright whose unauthorized adaptation of TESS OF THE D'URBERVILLES was first produced at the Coronet Theatre, LONDON, on February 19, 1900. The preceding November Hardy had written to HARPER & BROTHERS that he had arranged to bring Lorimer STODDARD's dramatization, starring Minnie Maddern FISKE, to London from New York. He added that he was not "free to treat with any one for an English version" until he knew whether that arrangement would be carried out (*Letters* II, 239). Kennedy had apparently anticipated having Hardy's permission before the play was performed. Wilson gives a full account of the difficulties Hardy encountered in controlling the various dramatizations of *Tess*.

For further reading: Orel, "Hardy and the Theatre," in Margaret Drabble, ed., *The Genius of Thomas Hardy*; Roberts, *"Tess" in the Theatre*; Wilson, *Thomas Hardy on Stage*.

Kent, Rockwell (1882–1971) American artist. In July 1919 the poet Robert Nichols wrote Hardy that Kent, a friend of his, was quite interested in illustrating some of Hardy's works. Hardy wrote Nichols to say he was very pleased to know of Kent's offer and that he had his full permission to take a "dramatic paragraph or sentence from any novel or poem & make a drawing to it." He suggested "A TRAMPWOMAN'S TRAGEDY." Kent wrote Hardy, thanking him for his encouragement, in September 1919. Kent supplied a two-page headpiece for

Hardy's poem "An ANCIENT TO ANCIENTS" for the CENTURY MAGAZINE in May 1922 (*Letters* V, 319).

"King's Experiment, The"   Poem published in *POEMS OF THE PAST AND THE PRESENT* (1902). It is about the journey of a lover, "Hodge," en route to his beloved, who sees a grim day as beautiful. When he arrives he finds she has died of a poisoned arrow sent by King Doom's messenger. He "clasped her but in death, / And never as his bride." He then perceives a glorious day as one marked by "funereal gloom and cold." The speaker is King Doom, the unfeeling "lord" responsible for Fate.

"King's Soliloquy, A" *On the Night of His Funeral*   Poem written in May 1910 and collected in *SATIRES OF CIRCUMSTANCE* (1914). Hardy recalls in the *Life* that in May 1910 he and Emma HARDY had settled in for a stay at Blomfield Court, Maida Vale, LONDON. At breakfast the first morning they looked out of the window and saw placards announcing the death of King EDWARD VII. Hardy watched from the balcony of the ATHENAEUM CLUB as the body was moved to WESTMINSTER ABBEY, and three days later he saw the procession of the funeral away from the abbey. Two weeks later he celebrated his 70th birthday, and realized he was a year older than the king had been at his death (*Life*, 350).

The poem is written from the point of view of the king the night of May 20, reflecting on the "slow march" and "muffled drum" of his journey to his "final rest." He had reigned for a decade, and, in retrospect, is more grieved that he "by some was loved so much" than that he bored others. He has found that "kingly opportunities" have had "devilries." Although he has enjoyed "what pleasure earth affords to kings," such pleasure eventually "cloyed."

Looking back he would, if he could choose to live again, "prefer the average track / Of average men." The power of "kingship" is limited; "Something binds hard the royal hand," and that "That" (the Immanent Will, as in *The DYNASTS*), has shaped and planned "My acts and me."

Kingston Maurward House   Stately home in DORSET, where Julia Augusta MARTIN, the wife of Francis Pitney Brouncker Martin, lived during Hardy's childhood. She established the first school Hardy attended (*see* EDUCATION, OF THOMAS HARDY). The house was the model for Knapwater House in *DESPERATE REMEDIES*.

Kingsway Theatre   London theater where some scenes from *The DYNASTS*, produced by Harley GRANVILLE-BARKER were presented in 1914. The performance opened on November 14, and ran for 72 performances (*Letters* V, 51).

Hardy wrote the publisher Sir Frederick MACMILLAN on November 10, 1914, that he could not understand how Granville-Barker could get over the "difficulties" of the verse drama. He observed that he himself had stated, in the preface, that the work "*could not* be acted" (*Letters* V, 59). He told him Granville-Barker had some "highly ingenious" plans for the production. Macmillan did see the performance and wrote Hardy to thank him.

Kipling, Rudyard (1865–1936)   English poet, novelist, and short story writer. Hardy apparently first became aware of his works in 1890, when Sir George DOUGLAS was visiting MAX GATE and Emma HARDY read one of his short stories aloud. The consensus, according to Douglas, was, "What is he driving at?" Hardy came to appreciate Kipling, however. As Millgate puts it, Hardy found that Kipling shared his view that "story-tellers were essentially Ancient Mariners." To interest the public, always pressed for time, they must relate "more than the ordinary experience of every average man and woman" (Millgate, *Thomas Hardy: A Biography*, 303).

In May 1890 Hardy met Kipling as well as Miss Caroline Balestier, a young American who would later marry Kipling. Hardy notes in his autobiography that Kipling "talked about the East, and he well said that the East is the world, both in numbers and in experiences." Kipling told them "curious details" of Indian life (*Life*, 226), and later discussed writing with Hardy at the SAVILE CLUB.

Hardy notes in the life that Kipling came down to Max Gate in August 1897 and they went BICYCLING. Kipling had thought he might wish to buy a house near WEYMOUTH, but there were difficulties with the one he liked and he gave up the idea.

At Hardy's funeral on Monday, January 16, 1928, at Westminster Abbey, Kipling was one of six pallbearers representing Literature (the others were Sir James BARRIE, John GALSWORTHY, Sir Edmund GOSSE, A. E. HOUSMAN, and George Bernard SHAW).

Knight, Henry   In *A PAIR OF BLUE EYES*, Henry Knight is one of the suitors of Elfride SWANCOURT. A barrister, essayist, and reviewer, he is more decisive at the game of chess than at the game of courtship. In one of Hardy's most vivid scenes, Elfride ingeniously saves Knight from falling to his death over "the Cliff without a Name" in CORNWALL (actually Beeny Cliff, where Hardy courted his first wife, Emma Gifford HARDY). Knight discovers that Elfride had, before they met, almost eloped with another suitor, his longtime friend and protegé Stephen SMITH. Knight abandons Elfride and goes to the Continent.

Knight and Smith meet by chance at their LONDON hotel. Both realize they have wronged Elfride and compete in pursuing her to Cornwall, only to discover that she has married Lord LUXELLIAN and died of a miscarriage. Her body is in a coffin on the same train, bound for burial in the Luxellian vault at Endelstow.

"Lacking Sense, The" (Scene: *A sad-coloured landscape, Waddon Vale*) Poem published in *POEMS OF THE PAST AND THE PRESENT* (1902). It takes the form of a dialogue between the poet and the "Ancient Mind" of Time, in which, as in a platonic dialogue, the questioner is slowly enlightened. Critics have compared Time in this poem to the Spirit of the Years, one of the observing Phantom Intelligences, in *The DYNASTS*. Waddon Vale is a valley near DORCHESTER with steep, rocky hills, cut off from the sea and in Hardy's time very isolated.

The poet addresses Time, asking why "the Mother" (Mother Nature, as in "The MOTHER MOURNS") looks so moody among her labors, as though she has "wounded where she loves." The answer is that the Mother cannot perceive the effect of her actions. She is not malicious.

The poet inquires how Time can explain Mother Nature's "crimes upon her creatures," when she causes "woundings" and admits decay and "baleful blights."

Time answers that Mother Nature's "orbs are sightless"; she has a "deficience" which prevents her from being omniscient.

The poet observes that Mother Nature "unwittingly" wounds what she loves, although the "seers" marvel at her deft touch.

In the final stanza Time suggests that the poet not scorn Mother Nature as a malicious force, but assist her as much as possible. The poet is her son and is made "of her clay."

Bailey points out that the poem makes a philosophical case for the philosopher J. S. Mills's theory of "evolutionary meliorism": over time generations of men can have a stake in their own improvement (Bailey, *The Poetry of Thomas Hardy*, 144).

Ladywell, Eustace Artist in *The HAND OF ETHELBERTA*. He is one of the many suitors of the young widow Ethelberta PETHERWIN, whom he first sees at a party at Wyndway House. He paints her portrait and is crestfallen when she marries Lord MOUNTCLERE, an elderly reprobate. At her wedding he is present, by accident, "looking as sick and sorry as a lily with a slug in its stalk."

landscape To Hardy, landscape is important not only in terms of topography but also because his narrators project their own ideals and prejudices in their reactions to it. In constructing "WESSEX," his imaginary kingdom that represents two-thirds of southern England, including DORSET, he uses an approach both psychological and allegorical. His rural characters often have a thorough knowledge of the geographical features of the landscape, as well as the legends and folkways associated with it. They also, however, play out inner drives and fears in their interaction with its more ominous aspects: uncontrolled flora, inhospitable terrain, and mutations wrought by violent weather. An example is EGDON HEATH in *The RETURN OF THE NATIVE*, whose mien is at varying times stormy, gloomy, calm, sustaining, ominous, and repressive.

Rosemarie Morgan observes that Hardy's narrators make significant connections between the landscape and the characters that signify intense emotions he otherwise could not delineate without "flouting the obscenity laws." For example, in *TESS OF THE D'URBERVILLES*, the summer field flowers at Talbothays Dairy, bursting with pollen and swelling with sap-milk and moist juices, provide an "external correlative" to the passion experienced by Tess and Angel. In *FAR FROM THE MADDING CROWD* the intense storm allows the narrator to reveal and enhance the "turbulent emotions" of Oak and Bathsheba. The "crushing, rasping, warping" growth of trees at the beginning of *The WOODLANDERS* reflects Mr. Melbury's attempt to mold his daughter Grace for a suitable marriage (personal communication with the author).

Hardy's works are permeated with references to landscape: the Dorset countryside in *Far from the Madding Crowd* and *JUDE THE OBSCURE*; the Salisbury Plain in *Tess of the d'Urbervilles*; the coast of CORNWALL in *The FAMOUS TRAGEDY OF THE QUEEN OF CORNWALL*; the French and German terrain of the many battles and bivouacs in *The DYNASTS*; the Roman remains in *The MAYOR OF CASTERBRIDGE*; the rural roads, forests, farms, and paths of *UNDER THE GREENWOOD TREE*, *The Woodlanders*, and *TWO ON A TOWER*; the coastal scenes at Weymouth in *DESPERATE REMEDIES*—these are only a few of the larger canvases on which his settings are inscribed. There are, in addition, dozens of local landmarks, some of them related to historic events. A few examples are the Monument (a memorial tower to Admiral Hardy) on Black Down, Cross-in-Hand in The LOST PYX; the hill-fortress of Eggar in *The TRUMPET-MAJOR*; Rings-Hill Speer in *Two on a Tower*; and Shadwater Weir in Frome Meadows in *The Return of the Native*. When Hermann LEA first proposed his study of the places depicted by Hardy, Hardy replied that he had no objection "if you print somewhere on the map (or in any text accompanying it) that the places in the novels were only *suggested* by those real ones given— as they are not literally portraits of such" (O'Sullivan, *Thomas Hardy: An Illustrated Biography*, 68–71). His caveat has not prevented scholars and tourists from searching out the sites represented in his work, however, and a number of articles and books have been published dealing with the subject.

As Hardy grew older and lost his parents and first wife, many memories of his favorite landscapes were permeated with visions of joyful times mixed with bitter remorse; *see* "IN FRONT OF THE LANDSCAPE."

For further reading: Arkans, "Hardy's Poetic Landscapes"; Blum and Jesty, "Hermann Lea's Thomas Hardy's Wessex Revisited" [Part 1, 1986; Part 2, 1987; Part 3, 1988]; Brown, *Figures in a Wessex Landscape: Thomas Hardy's Picture of English Country Life;* Drabble, *A Writer's Britain: Landscape in Literature;* Hawkins, *Thomas Hardy: His Life and Landscape;* Hooker, *Writers in a Landscape;* Miller, "Topography and Tropography in Thomas Hardy's 'In Front of the Landscape.'" O'Sullivan, *Thomas Hardy: An Illustrated Biography; Oxford Reader's Companion to Thomas Hardy;* Robinson, "Hermann Lea Reappraised: Followed by Some Corrections to Hardy's Wessex Reappraised."

Lane, John (1854–1925)   Publisher who, after bringing out a bibliography of the works of George MEREDITH, queried Hardy about a similar volume dealing with his writings. Hardy replied on June 30, 1891, that Lane must be the "best judge" of whether the time was "ripe" for a bibliography of his "few productions." Hardy added that if Lane did undertake it, he would "with pleasure give any assistance in the matter of dates, &c." (*Letters* I, 239). Lane did contribute a bibliography of first editions of Hardy's works to Lionel JOHNSON's *The Art of Thomas Hardy* (1894).

In August 1894, on one of his cycling tours, Hardy happened to meet Lane, along with William Watson and Lord Latymer (Francis Coutts) at Glastonbury. They spent "a romantic day or two there among the ruins" (*Life*, 322).

In 1896 Lane published Mrs. Florence HENNIKER's volume *In Scarlet and Grey*, which contained the story she wrote with Hardy, "The SPECTRE OF THE REAL" (Purdy, *Thomas Hardy: A Bibliographical Study*, 304–305).

In 1913 Hardy suggested to Lane that he might undertake a biography of the sculptor Alfred Stevens, who carved the Wellington monument in St. Paul's Cathedral, before it was "too late." Stevens had grown up in Blandford, and he and Lane met there and searched for "facts and scenes" that might be used to illustrate his life (*Life*, 362). The biography apparently was not published, but material Hardy and Lane found was referred to by Kenneth Romney Towndrow in his 1939 biography, *Alfred Stevens . . . a Biography with New Material* (*Letters* IV, 290).

Laodicean, A   Novel serialized in HARPER'S NEW MONTHLY MAGAZINE from December 1880 to December 1881; it was illustrated by George DU MAURIER. The December 1880 issue of the magazine, published in November, was also the first number published in England. Hardy revised the novel for English publication by Sampson Low (3 vols., 1881). Much of the novel was composed while Hardy was convalescing from a serious illness. He had been to France and may have contracted an infection; there was blood in his urine, suggesting internal hemorrhaging and possibly a stone in the urinary tract. Anesthesia was problematic at the time, as was surgery. To avoid it, he lay flat on a board with his feet elevated for several months. He dictated the novel to his wife Emma between November 1880 and May 1881 (*see* HEALTH AND ILLNESS, HARDY'S CONCERN WITH). Much later, in 1917 (after Emma's death), he wrote Edmund GOSSE, "I well remember that illness at Upper Tooting which brought you to my bedside. What a time of it I had—six months!" He called the process of dictating the novel "an awful job" (*Letters* V, 237).

In 1900 Hardy told the American educator William Lyon Phelps that he had put "more of himself" into this novel than into any other. The depiction of architects, the incorporation of architectural terms and theory, the controversy about uninformed and damaging restoration of historic buildings, description of landscapes and towns in FRANCE and elsewhere on the Continent, and the transformation of the British landscape by railway construction are all matters about which Hardy had personal knowledge and strong opinions. In contrast, when *JUDE THE OBSCURE* was published and some critics assumed it revealed Hardy's inner life, he insisted that "no book he had ever written contained less of his own life."

Hardy considered the novel the third in a trilogy of "novels of ingenuity," the first two being *DESPERATE REMEDIES* and *The HAND OF ETHELBERTA*. It is a more intellectual novel than others by Hardy, which may be one reason it has remained a "minor" work. When the novel was published, the writer of an anonymous review in the *ATHENAEUM* (December 31, 1881), praised the "sparing use" of the "rustic element," and suggested that the novel represented an improvement in this respect over *DESPERATE REMEDIES*.

During the period when Hardy worked in the DORCHESTER office of the architect John HICKS, probably about 1857 or 1858, he attended a prayer meeting at the Baptist chapel in Dorchester. The minister, the

Reverend T. Perkins, later became the model for the Baptist minister in *A Laodicean* (*Life*, 30). In July 1879 he attended a garden party at the home of the publisher Frederick MACMILLAN. A terrible thunderstorm interrupted the party; Hardy used this event in writing of the garden party at the Castle de Stancy and the ensuing thunderstorm.

"Laodicean" means "lukewarmness" or "one who is lukewarm." The word is derived from the people of Laodicea who were accused by the author of the book of Revelation. The novel turns on the conflict articulated by Matthew ARNOLD in his famous essay "Culture and Anarchy." In this essay he distinguishes between Hellenism, derived from Greek culture, in which the aim is to "see things as they really are," and Hebraism, which originated in Hebrew culture, emphasizing "conduct and obedience." Hardy embraces the spirit of "new Hellenism" of the latter nineteenth century in England, finding romance in the engineering of railway tunnels. The new industrial millionaires, however, cling to the vestiges of medieval piety and seriousness, buying feudal castles and venerating history. Pinion observes that the heroine, Paula POWER, absorbs both philosophies: she wants to exhibit a modern spirit, but, at the end of the novel, deeply regrets having her castle burn down (F. B. Pinion, *A Hardy Companion*, 57). In the same way, she is equivocal about her emotions. She is at first lukewarm about the young architect George SOMERSET, then develops a passion for him after she believes she has lost him. She considers herself "one of that body to whom lukewarmth is not an accident but a provisional necessity, till they see a little more clearly." She allows herself to be courted by Captain William DE STANCY because she has been told, falsely, that Somerset is addicted to drinking and gambling.

Somerset first sees Paula from the point of view of an onlooker; he watches as she refuses to be baptized by immersion, although her father has raised her as a Baptist. Her friend Charlotte DE STANCY explains that "she could not do it to save her life"; Somerset perceives "a clandestine, stealthy inner life which had very little to do with her outward one," and is intrigued by her.

SYNOPSIS

Book the First: "George Somerset"

Chapter 1

George Somerset, the son of a noted painter (now deceased) who was a member of the Royal Academy of Art, has come from London to sketch an English village church. He hears a clock strike the hour; it is presumably from a nearby mansion. Then, from the valley below, he hears people singing the "New Sabbath," a hymn he has known from childhood.

Chapter 2

He goes to the "edifice" from which the singing comes, which is a chapel, thinking that the historian and architect Augustus Pugin would have thought it a monstrosity." (Pugin was known for his works on medieval architecture and one of the designers of the House of Commons). He discovers a stone on the wall saying it had (within the past decade of Hardy's writing the novel) been erected by John Power; it is a Dissenters' Chapel (that is, a house of worship for a sect other than the established Church of England). It is Baptist, with a pool for the immersion of those who are baptized. He sees strong young men carrying water from a stream into the chapel, perceives that it is for a baptism, and looks on from a distance while an attractive young woman alights from a brougham and comes to the brink of the pool. The minister tries to help her into the pool but she resists and then refuses, despite his plea that it was her father's dying wish. The sermon ends and the young woman and her attendant, another young woman, return to the carriage and leave. Somerset goes to the nearby village of Sleeping-Green to spend the night, but, on the way, sees from afar an imposing castle, a "fossil of feudalism."

Chapter 3

The next morning Somerset goes back to the castle, which he now knows is the Castle de Stancy, and asks if he might visit it. Miss de Stancy is at home, according to the housekeeper. He tours the long gallery of venerable paintings, and notices that one painting is of a young man named Ravensbury. This is the surname of a former school friend, John Ravensbury. He sees a young woman on a distant terrace, but realizes she is not the person who refused to be baptized.

Chapter 4

He descends to the lower story of the castle. The young woman on the terrace comes down and introduces herself; she is Miss de Stancy, and explains that "Paula" would be glad for him to go into the lowest vault of the castle. He remarks that he has seen the pictures, and asks her about the painting of Ravensbury. She explains that he was her cousin, and is dead now. Mr. Wilkins, the former owner of the castle, became blind soon after he became the owner of the castle, and never lived in it. Somerset asks if the paintings are of her ancestors. She affirms that they are, but that the de Stancy family no longer owns the castle; she is there as companion to her friend, Paula Power, daughter of the builder of the chapel—a wealthy railroad contractor. She tells Somerset, regarding the baptism, "she could not do it to save her life." Paula has had a telegraph wire installed in the castle and has made other improvements, such as the new clock in the tower, which Somerset had heard striking. He asks if he may come again to sketch the castle, and she assents. At his inn, Somerset hears from the landlord that the de Stancys are "very low upon the ground and always will be now."

Chapter 5
Somerset returns to the castle. Paula is absent, but Charlotte invites him to lunch at the home of her father, Sir William de Stancy, a baronet. A telegram arrives from Paula directing that "every facility be given to Mr. Somerset to visit any part of the castle he may wish to see. . . . I have two of his father's pictures." It turns out that Charlotte had sent a message to Paula telling her about Somerset.

He is welcomed by Sir William de Stancy, who tells him he is glad to receive a friend of his nephew, John Ravensbury, who had been engaged to Charlotte; Ravensbury's death was a great blow to the family. Sir William is genial, but frugal, and most of his conversation is about money and the "art of doing with little." That evening the inn's landlord tells Somerset that Sir William had been wildly extravagant in his youth, keeping many horses and gambling, and was forced to sell the castle. He was very bitter, and went abroad. He then had an illness that resulted in "softening of the brain" and, since then, has been quite reconciled to his reduced standard of living. He adds that Paula and Miss de Stancy "be more like lovers than maid and maid," and that Paula is "as deep as the North Star." Morgan suggests that this is Hardy's delicate way of dealing with the strong affection Paula has for Charlotte: she is not "Laodicean" or "lukewarm" about her. He could have referred to Sappho, but would have risked a strong protest from censors (personal communication with the author).

Chapter 6
Somerset returns to the castle. A young man sends his card to Miss de Stancy introducing himself as William DARE. He is a "photographic amateur" and wishes to take views of the castle. He had written Paula, but not heard from her. Somerset meets him and dislikes him on sight. His age is indeterminate; he could be 16 or 26 and wears a heavy gold ring in bad taste. He says he has lived much abroad. A man then arrives in a dog cart and asks for Miss Power; he is Mr. James HAVILL. Somerset strolls into the woods and overhears a conversation in the garden pavilion between Miss Power and Mr. WOODWELL, the Baptist minister, who is still trying to persuade her not to withdraw from the congregation. Somerset, had once been a "High-Church infant," meaning that he was raised within a family that embraced Anglo-Catholic liturgy, including incense, sung psalms, ecclesiastical vestments, processions, bells at the elevation of the Sacrament, and other ritualistic observances. He decides to engage in an intellectual tournament with Woodwell.

Chapter 7
Somerset sees Paula in the bower. He argues with the minister for some time; Woodwell then leaves. Somer-

set realizes that Paula assumes he is the new curate. She tells him that Mr. Woodwell is "single-mindedness itself" regarding theology, but gives all he has to the poor, making Somerset ashamed of himself for his attacks on him. He rushes after Mr. Woodwell to return a book he has left; they reconcile and become friendly. Woodwell tells him he loves Paula as his "daughter," despite the "trouble" she gives him. When Somerset returns to the pavilion, she has disappeared.

Chapter 8
The next morning Somerset returns to the castle to retrieve his sketching instruments and sees Paula departing in a carriage. When she sees him she returns and invites him to lunch because of his famous father. At lunch he meets Mr. Havill, who is a Toneborough architect; Mrs. GOODMAN (Paula's aunt) and Mr. Woodwell are also present. Somerset and Havill discuss the architecture of the castle; Somerset, with his superior knowledge and background, easily refutes his assessment of it as Saxon and assures him there is not an arch or wall in the castle "anterior to the year 1100." From the window they see Dare with his photographic apparatus.

Chapter 9
Somerset explores the castle but falls several feet into a turret of the Great Tower and is almost trapped. He spots, on the stonework, a new inscription with the words *De Stancy* and *W. Dare* crossing each other at right angles (this is a bar sinister or baton, a heraldic mark of illegitimacy). He puts his handkerchief through a slit in the window and sees a bone in the corner, which makes him think of Ginevra of Modena, the heroine of "The Mistletoe Bough," a well-known 19th-century ballad by Thomas Hainess Bayly: Ginevra hid herself in a chest during a game on her wedding day; the spring lock shut and she was not discovered for many years. After two hours, Somerset is rescued.

Paula has gone for a drive, but returns before he leaves for the day and sends a message that she wishes to consult him professionally. In her library she inquires about his professional qualifications. He states that he is a Fellow of the Society of Antiquaries and a Member of the Institute of British Architects, though not yet a Fellow. She asks his advice about restoring parts of the castle and says she can spend £100,000, a princely sum. She says she was going to ask Mr. Havill to undertake the work. Somerset suspects he is a "quack," but realizes he needs the money. He then proposes that Paula allow a competition between them, with their plans judged by a committee of the Royal Institute of British Architects. He will walk over the building with her the next day and discuss his architectural ideas.

Chapter 10

Somerset goes around the castle with Paula; she says she is "Greek" and not a medievalist. She thinks of making a Greek colonnade all around the quadrangle. They see Somerset's handkerchief fluttering from a window slit and he confesses that he fell into the turret. In the afternoon Somerset moves to a larger inn at Markton, where he will have more space to lay out his plans.

He then strolls up to the castle and sees his handkerchief suddenly vanish. He sees a "girlish form" standing at the top of the tower looking over the parapet; he suspects that either Paula or Charlotte has gone up to retrieve his handkerchief, but cannot tell which. He then passes beneath the inhabited wing of the castle and hears a piano and a voice singing "The Mistletoe Bough," which he believes was suggested to the singer by her visit to the tower.

Chapter 11

The next day Paula confesses it was she who brought down the handkerchief and sang the ballad. Somerset begins his plans; he has been assigned a studio and he asks for a clerk to do his measuring. Paula is vexed that Somerset insists on the formal competition between himself and Havill. She says she hopes he will not go to London and work on his "other buildings" and forget her castle. He replies that he has no other buildings under way. Paula asks him to promise, as the other architect has, that he will take no other commission until the castle restoration is complete.

She asks about the technical term *undercutting*, and he promises to show her what he means in the chapel. While waiting, he realizes that "a dangerous admiration" for Paula has taken root within him. He takes her hand to show her what he means about the stone undercutting and the shadows. He draws her finger along the arch. Paula says she would adore every stone of the castle, and think feudalism the "only true romance of life," if she were a de Stancy. She tells him her father made "half the railways in Europe." They hear a train in the distance. He remarks that "to design great engineering works" requires a "leading mind," but to "execute them," as Mr. Power did, required only a "following mind." Paula is perturbed by his comment. Somerset realizes he has made a tactical error.

Chapter 12

Somerset sets out to explore the tunnel Mr. Power had built, and finds Paula, Charlotte, and Mrs. Goodman in a carriage, also viewing it. He goes into the tunnel and flattens himself in a recess while a train passes. Paula turns pale and nearly faints, having assumed he had been killed. Somerset reflects on his family stock, "old" though not rich. He is descended from a vice-admiral; his grandfather was a metaphysician; his father is a Royal Academician.

He encounters Mr. Woodwell, who tells him his worst fears are realized: Paula is going out of mourning and will give a dinner party in the name of her aunt, Mrs. Goodman. Somerset says he has heard nothing of it. At his inn, William Dare is waiting. He has found Somerset's advertisement for an assistant in the *Architectural World* and proposes himself. Somerset quizzes him about architecture and accepts him; as Dare walks away he throws away eight other letters of application he has intercepted.

Chapter 13

Somerset is invited to the dinner at the last minute, but declines. He wonders how Paula would look, and what she would wear. When he goes to the castle the next day he sees some of the decorations for the dinner, including an awning and flowering plants in pots. He makes himself miserable thinking about not having gone. In his studio he finds a fragment of swan's down, and is convinced it belongs to Paula. William Dare tells him about the dinner, at which there were 18 guests.

Somerset shows Paula the elevation sketch for the Greek court, but she says she has decided not to build it. He shows her the bit of swan's down and she admits it came from her fan. She reproaches him for not having come, as his not receiving the invitation was an accident. It was supposed to be hand delivered, but was overlooked. She says the guests had been asked to meet him, in particular. He is mortified. She says he can make amends by coming to her garden party.

Chapter 14

Paula sends Somerset an anonymous newspaper letter about the castle entitled "Restoration or Demolition," pleading that the castle be saved and that a Greek temple not be built within its walls. In the afternoon Somerset goes to the village and discovers her coming out of the church with Mrs. Goodman and Charlotte. She is extremely upset and can't imagine who wrote the letter; he tells her not to worry, and agrees to answer it. He begs her to ask Mr. Havill for his plans so they can be independently judged.

He and Paula go in the church and look at the marble effigies of past de Stancy family members. William Dare has been spying on them and not doing his measurements. Somerset warns him he will have to dispense with his services. Dare genially retorts that it is the "true men who get snubbed, while traitors are allowed to thrive," a portent of his role throughout the novel.

Chapter 15

At Paula's garden party, Somerset and Havill confer about their plans. Mrs. Goodman introduces Somerset to some of the guests. He sees the face of Dare looking out of his studio window, smoking and surveying the promenading groups of people. Somerset confronts

Dare in the studio and says he need work no longer that day. He finds Dare has done virtually nothing on the measurements and Dare offers to quit working for him. Somerset tells him goodbye. He dances with Paula and declares it is "the happiest moment I have ever known," but then a terrible thunderstorm strikes the party. He and Paula wait out the storm alone in a small wooden teahouse while the rain forms a "gauze" curtain between them and the dancers. Somerset tells Paula he loves her but she refuses to say she loves him and won't let him kiss her.

Book the Second: "Dare and Havill"

Chapter 1
Dare puts aside his drawing instruments and goes to the garden party. He finds Havill's pocket-book containing a draft of the newspaper letter and realizes Havill wrote it. He seeks out Havill and flatters him as a "well-established professional man" who must be very provoked to have a rival such as Somerset "sprung at him." He says he has removed the notebook leaf with the draft of the letter. Havill is alarmed and says he wrote it when he thought himself supplanted, before he knew of the competition. They eavesdrop at the back of the teahouse and hear Somerset declare his love for Paula. Dare says he has another man in mind for Paula's husband. Dare says Havill should copy Somerset's design and improve on it; Havill is shocked. He declares Dare is proposing "conduct which would be quite against [his] principles as an honest man."

Chapter 2
Dare goes to Havill's office and, while waiting to see him, inspects his drawings. He overhears creditors dunning Havill. Dare goes into his office and congratulates him on receiving the Castle de Stancy commission, for which he will be paid £5,000. The creditor is impressed and leaves. Paula stops in and asks how Havill is getting on, as she is leaving home for several weeks. He offers to show her his designs, but she says it would be unfair to Somerset, as she has not seen his.

Dare and Havill dine together, since Havill's wife and children are away. They then stroll to the castle, meeting Somerset's three London draughtsmen, Bowles, Knowles, and Cockton. Dare leads Havill into the castle through the butler's pantry, using a key he knows about. He takes him into Somerset's studio and shows him the drawings. Havill finds Somerset's designs ingenious and impressive. Havill and Dare trace the work and slip away. They go to the inn at Sleeping-Green, where Dare is staying, and drink several glasses of brandied liquor called "old port." Havill tries unsuccessfully to interrogate Dare on his age and origins. Dare slaps his breast and says "the secret of his birth lies here." Havill decides to spend the night at the inn also,

but it is crowded with farmers and he must share a bed with Dare.

Chapter 3
Havill wakes at 2.30 A.M., sober, and pulls back Dare's nightshirt. He sees a word tattooed "in distinct characters" on his chest. Dare awakes, draws a revolver from beneath his pillow, and holds it at Havill's temple; he has suspected Havill was not asleep. Dare says Havill must keep his secret, for he has the original of the letter Havill wrote the newspaper and a copy of the pilfered tracing from Somerset's studio.

The next morning they hear the rumble of the artillery leaving Toncborough barracks. They go there together the next morning, and Dare inquires when the replacement batteries would arrive. He is told they will arrive at noon, and he offers to help Havill with his designs during the morning. From the window of Havill's house they watch the replacement troops arriving. Dare points out a "fine fellow," a mounted officer with a "sallow, yet interesting face." Havill asks whether he knows him but Dare does not reply. Dare leaves, promising to return later.

Chapter 4
George Somerset finishes his design and leaves the castle, planning to go to London. A man riding a bay horse approaches him and introduces himself as Mr. Cunningham HAZE, chief constable of the district. He tells Somerset that on the preceding Thursday night he had seen two people in his studio. Somerset rightly surmises it was Dare and Havill and decides to make a sketch of Dare; he then remembers the photograph of himself Dare had left on his mantlepiece to show the photographic process he was using.

He encounters Charlotte de Stancy, who presents her brother to him, Captain de Stancy of the Royal Horse Artillery. Captain de Stancy is about 38 (actually, 39), and "ripe, without having declined a digit towards fogeyism." He has a raven black moustache and hair. He is old and experienced enough to "suggest a goodly accumulation of touching amourettes in the chambers of his memory, and not too old for the possibility of increasing the store." He and Somerset discuss Jack Ravensbury, his and Charlotte's cousin. He says he wants to remain a stranger to Paula Power, whom he calls "Miss Steam-Power." They invite Somerset to dine with them, an invitation he accepts. Somerset says he wants to see the chief constable that night; he explains the suspected intrusion into his studio. Captain de Stancy says he will be meeting with him the next morning about furniture in the barracks. Somerset gives him the envelope containing the photograph of Dare and leaves. Suddenly Constable Haze arrives. De Stancy explains the mission he has been asked to execute, and is about to hand over the photograph. He glances at it himself first, and then has a sudden spasm. He hides the envelope in his pocket and pretends it is the wrong one. He goes into the adjoining room and substitutes a photograph from an album. Later he burns Dare's photograph.

Chapter 5
Dare gives up his room at the inn at Sleeping-Green and moves to lodgings in Toneborough that have a view of the lane leading to the barracks. One day he sees de Stancy go into Myrtle Villa; he waits until he comes back and meets him in the street. De Stancy is agitated, though not surprised. Dare asks for money. De Stancy asks why the chief constable has his photograph, but Dare is evasive.

It is revealed that Dare is de Stancy's illegitimate son. He tells de Stancy he has plans for his marriage, but de Stancy says he should have married Dare's mother if he had married anybody. Dare declares the lady he has in mind has "the figure and motions of a sylph, the face of an angel, the eye of love itself." Captain de Stancy says he once vowed never to marry again, in penance for the wrong done Dare's mother. Dare shows him his tattoo, *de Stancy*, which makes his father wince. They see Sir William wandering about the churchyard, but conceal themselves. They begin gambling, and Dare wins; his father must write another check.

They leave and Dare shows his father a view of the Castle de Stancy in the distance. He still insists he is not interested in meeting Paula, although he does care for the "fortress" of his forefathers.

Chapter 6
Dare meets Havill, who tells him that Paula has returned to the castle, Somerset is still in London, and the competition has resulted in a tie. Dare explains his interest in introducing Captain de Stancy to Paula, but he does not explain that he is de Stancy's son.

Dare approaches Milly Birch, Paula's maid, who tells him Paula appears to the best advantage in her own gymnasium, when she wears a boy's costume. Milly won't be bribed, but Dare finds the gymnasium at the castle and plans for his father to see her when she is exercising. He goes to see Havill, who had designed the gym; he says she has had it built "in imitation of those at the new colleges for women."

Chapter 7
Dare takes his father to the gym on a wet morning and induces him to drink from a flask of wine (actually, three-fourths brandy). He removes the wood billet covering the peephole he has found. The captain sees Paula exercising. Mrs. Goodman and Charlotte are watching her. Captain de Stancy is captivated; she is "Grace personified." Dare withdraws and Havill approaches. Dare tells him a "fermentation" is beginning in the captain. Paula then lies in a green silk hammock and swings herself to and fro.

Book the Third: "De Stancy"

Chapter 1
Captain de Stancy is a "changed man," no longer melancholy. Dare sends him a hamper of wine. He apologizes to his sister for having made the remark about "Miss Steam-Power." He says he would like to see her in person and also revisit the interior of the Castle. Charlotte, in answer to his questions, says Somerset does visit the castle. She blushes, and de Stancy realizes Charlotte has an attachment to Somerset. He studies the history of the castle in family documents, in preparation for seeing Paula.

Chapter 2
Charlotte introduces her brother to Paula. They discuss the loss of the castle; de Stancy says that a year or two before he was born his grandfather and father cut off the entail. (This was "a legal limitation on succession of land, usually that it should be held for life only and then pass to the eldest son for life. By the nineteenth century it could be ended by agreement between generations" [Ernest Hardy, notes to New Wessex edition of *A Laodicean*].) Captain de Stancy's father was caught in a "mad bargain" with his visitor as they "sat over wine. My father sat down as host on that occasion, and arose as guest." De Stancy impresses Paula with the breadth and depth of his knowledge of the treasures in the castle. While he is in the castle he is summoned outside by Dare; he is extremely annoyed, but Dare tells him he must find a pretext to return every day, such as copying the pictures or furniture. In the presence of Paula and Charlotte he makes a formal offer to allow the Captain to use his photographic process to copy the ancestral faces in the portraits.

Chapter 3
De Stancy, assisted by Dare, comes every day to copy pictures. He asks to copy a portrait of Paula that had been shown at the Royal Academy exhibition the previous year, but she is affronted and refuses. She tells Charlotte about his request. De Stancy seems to be making no progress. Dare discovers that Havill's creditors have become suspicious and his household is being disassembled and his belongings auctioned off. He asks his father to tell Paula. De Stancy does so, and suggests that since the plans are virtually identical Havill be allowed to go ahead with the first half; the second half will then be turned over to Somerset. Paula hires Havill to begin work to the extent of £20,000, and gives him a £500 retainer. Somerset, as a consequence, has no reason to come to the castle for the next year. Havill's wife dies and he rushes home. Paula gives de Stancy permission to copy her portrait, but is cold toward him.

Somerset, meanwhile, still in London, is hurt that he has not heard from Paula; he cannot understand why the committee of architects pronounced the plans of equal merit, and he seems to be making no progress in winning her affections.

Chapter 4

Following his wife's funeral, Havill has a sense of guilt about the fraud he has perpetrated on Somerset. He writes Paula that he is resigning his commission. Paula is surprised at the letter and tells Charlotte she must telegraph "her architect," Somerset. Charlotte tells de Stancy the news that Somerset will arrive on the 10th; Dare overhears it. He extracts money from his father for dinner and reminds him of their plans for the sixth of the month.

Chapter 5

Somerset goes to see his father to tell him the news. His father reports that he has received an appeal from an old friend to design some theatrical costumes, and asks Somerset to "knock out something" for her before he leaves town. Somerset designs the costumes for a performance of *Love's Labour's Lost,* although he knows no details about where it is to take place. He then gets the key to a box at their bank where his family pedigree is stored. At the bank he sees Paula and overhears her asking for a valuable necklace; she puts it on and leaves. Somerset evades her at the bank, but later follows her carriage and sees her as she emerges from a jeweler's shop.

Chapter 6

Paula tells Somerset she is going to the hunt ball at Toneborough, but is not happy about it. When he gets home he discovers an invitation to the ball and decides to take the train and make a late appearance there. He arrives, and finds Charlotte wearing the necklace. Paula is escorted by Captain de Stancy. Somerset speaks to Paula, but just then Charlotte falls ill (from having seen him); she is taken to a nearby hotel. Paula only stays a little longer and leaves with Mrs. Goodman; they will pick up Charlotte and go back to the castle.

Somerset sees a notice of a play to be performed by officers of the Royal Horse Artillery at the Castle de Stancy to aid the county hospital. Captain de Stancy introduces him to Mrs. Camperton, who has known his father. Mrs. Camperton states that she had asked Mr. Somerset to design the costumes and he has done so (actually they are George Somerset's designs). Mrs. Camperton hopes to secure Miss Power to play the heroine. The whole idea is Captain de Stancy's.

Chapter 7

Somerset goes back to London to make arrangements so that he can return to the castle for a prolonged period. On the 10th he goes to Markton and sees more notices of the theatrical; Paula is playing one of the roles. Captain de Stancy has a leading role. Somerset is incensed at Paula's acting in public. He goes to the castle, meets with Paula, and asks why she is taking part.

She says her father supported the hospital. She says she will not take the part of the princess of France. Somerset feels they have some sort of understanding, but Paula will not say they are engaged.

Chapter 8

Preparations for the play continue. Paula will take the part of the princess, and Captain de Stancy will be Sir Nathaniel. The play is to be presented at the castle and is a tremendous success. Somerset suddenly sees that Captain de Stancy is taking the part of the king of Navarre rather than Mr. Mild, who had originally taken the part. Somerset suspects collusion between them. He regrets taking such pains with the male costumes. De Stancy presents Paula with the necklace she has brought from London. Somerset is shocked, since people who have seen Charlotte wearing the necklace at the ball may now think it symbolizes a de Stancy-Power union. Suddenly de Stancy speaks lines from *Romeo and Juliet* to Paula rather than those in the play itself, and kisses her. Somerset realizes that 500 faces have seen the kiss with no consciousness that it was a "brazen interpolation"; it is a "profanation without parallel, and his face blazed like a coal." He is positive there has been collusion and is sorry he designed the costumes. He wonders if Paula has been keeping him on as a "pet spaniel" until she had an "open engagement" with someone else.

Chapter 9

A stranger slips in the back of the theater and sits near the landlord of the inn at Sleeping-Green. He asks about Paula and Captain de Stancy and sees him kiss her. He gives the landlord two half crowns for clapping loudly and encouraging others to do the same. Somerset talks with Paula after the play and asks whether de Stancy really kissed her. She insists he was an inch away. Somerset tells Paula he loves her "wildly and desperately." She says she will come to him the next day in the Studio, and lets him through a door that opens into a descending turret.

Chapter 10

The next morning Somerset hears the telegraph keys. Paula is summoning an actress to take her part in the play. The answer comes that Barbara Bell can come. Paula goes to the grassy lawn section of the castle enclosure called Pleasance. She tells Somerset that Barbara Bell is on her way down. Somerset goes to his studio, but sees the stranger from the night before conversing with Paula. At that night's performance, however, Mr. Mild plays opposite Barbara Bell. He sees Paula introduce the strange man to Captain de Stancy. He turns out to be her uncle, Abner POWER; he has been lost to her family for 10 years. Mrs. Goodman says Mr. Power has no legal control over Paula, but Somerset worries that he might exert an emotional pull toward de Stancy.

Chapter 11

Somerset sees an item in a two-day-old newspaper that there is likely to be a marriage arranged between Paula Power and Captain de Stancy. He is stunned, but when he reaches the castle Paula shows him a refutation of the item in the morning paper. She tells him that she, her uncle, her aunt, and perhaps Charlotte are going abroad, to Nice and other places, while work is being done on the castle. He is profoundly disappointed, but she tells him he may telegraph her. When the party leaves he goes to see Mr. Woodwell, who says Captain de Stancy saw them off and he believes Paula might marry him. Somerset goes to the local newspaper office and discovers that the rumor of the engagement was instigated by Abner Power.

Book the Fourth: *"Somerset, Dare, and de Stancy"*

Chapter 1

Mentally, Somerset accompanies Paula on her journey, thinking of her constantly. He sends her sketches of the progress made at the castle. She writes from Nice that she finds she does "suffer through separation," but fears, at the same time, he might "weary" of her. She asks him to write a formal business letter, though he could enclose "another sheet." Somerset suspects this is for the benefit of her uncle. He writes a formal letter about an architectural matter a week later, with an ardent personal letter. Paula writes that he has her "very warm affection." He writes that he will always love her.

Chapter 2

Paula writes that her uncle is displeased at her correspondence with him. She will only communicate by telegrams for the present time; vague telegrams ensue. After a period of silence he writes frantically to say that he assumes she means him to write no more.

Chapter 3

Somerset sees Sir William in the garden of Myrtle Villa. He says he misses his son a great deal; that he has taken leave and gone to Nice to see his sister. Somerset is upset. Sir William hints that his son may marry Paula, and Somerset decides to go to Nice. He arrives and engages a room at her hotel, only to find the party has left for Monte Carlo. He follows them to that "beautiful and sinister little spot." He finds that some of the party has left and goes to the gaming-tables at the Casino.

Chapter 4

Somerset succumbs to the "suggestive charm" of the room, though he himself finds the notion of relying on numbers "unreasonable." He sees William Dare at one of the tables; he had assumed he was in Markton. He has never seen him and de Stancy together and wonders if Dare is a traveling artist or courier. He is system-atically losing. Dare tells him the Powers have gone to the Grand Hotel, Genoa. He asks to borrow 200 francs. Somerset refuses to give it to him at the gaming tables; Dare is furious, but controls his feelings and asks that they share a bottle of wine. Somerset refuses. He goes to his hotel in Nice and finds a "saucy" and "cruel" letter from Paula, sent from Genoa. He decides not to follow her there, a "fatal miscalculation." The next morning he sees Dare come from the telegraph office; he has sent a telegram to Paula, purportedly from Somerset, saying he has lost all at Monte Carlo and asking her to send him £100 by Captain de Stancy.

Chapter 5

Captain de Stancy is en route to Nice with a bag of money, tied by Paula's own hands, seen to "tremble." De Stancy had left word at his hotel in Nice that he would be returning, but does not suspect the intervention of Dare. He arrives at Nice after Somerset has gone on an excursion to San Remo. He goes to the Pont-Neuf and discovers Dare there, demanding the money. De Stancy refuses to hand over the money, but gives him £10 to return home. He sends a message to Paula saying Somerset has not appeared.

Book the Fifth: *"De Stancy and Paula"*

Chapter 1

Paula and Charlotte are at Strassburg, as are Mrs. Goodman and Abner Power. She hopes Somerset has come there to study Gothic architecture. Captain de Stancy arrives and tells Paula that Somerset never met him to collect the money. He admits that Dare, acting as his "clerk," had told him he would not come. He does not confess Dare's identity but pretends Somerset had been embarrassed about having sent the telegram. Charlotte sees that Paula's affection for Somerset dwindles. They visit Goethe's house and go to the cathedral to see the famous puppets perform at the striking of the clock. Paula tells de Stancy they are going on to Baden.

Chapter 2

They go to Baden; de Stancy courts Paula, but she is preoccupied and reads Somerset's old letters. They visit the castle and admire the view. Abner Power encourages de Stancy's courtship of Paula. They go on to Carlsruhe.

Chapter 3

Somerset, at San Remo, looks in vain for a letter from Paula, and then goes on to Genoa. He follows their group northward to Strassburg, Baden, and Carlsruhe. There he sees Dare stepping from the same train. He is newly outfitted and apparently has become wealthy. Somerset lingers, unseen. Dare goes to their hotel; de Stancy is mystified about why he has not gone back to England. Dare admits he has had large winnings at the gaming tables. De Stancy tells him "these runs of luck will be your ruin . . . you will be for repeating and repeating your experiments, and will end by blowing your brains out." De Stancy tells him Paula is sending for Somerset. Dare admits concocting the telegram. They see Paula, Charlotte, and Abner Power strolling nearby. Paula recognizes Dare as the young man who was photographing the castle; she has no idea he is de Stancy's son.

Chapter 4
At the hotel de Stancy tells Paula that Dare has been improving his mind, looking at old masters. Paula asks whether he had gone to Nice in company with Somerset, and decides to send for him and ask him about the telegram. Dare enters and says he saw Somerset in the Monte Carlo Casino. Abner Power invites Dare to stay with the group; he is "not fastidious as to company." Dare makes himself agreeable to Power and tries to do the same with Charlotte. Captain de Stancy leaves. Dare pulls out a new silk handkerchief and a card flutters to the floor; it is a distorted photograph of Somerset, looking like a depraved and intoxicated gambler. Charlotte gasps; Paula flings the photograph on the table. Dare apologizes, pretending to be surprised that Somerset would have allowed such a photograph to be made. He steals away like a cat. Neither Charlotte nor Paula suspects the photograph is a fabrication.

Chapter 5
Somerset comes to their hotel and sends up his name to Paula. Dare is alarmed lest Paula discover the false telegram. De Stancy tells him he is sorry he ever acknowledged him as his son; he is "not a lad to my heart" but promises to remember him if his suit should "prosper." When Somerset enters the hotel room Abner Power greets him with "sardonic geniality," but Paula is cold. They look at tracings and he whispers he could not get there earlier. She is still cold toward him. Somerset declines their invitation to dinner. Paula accepts de Stancy "on probation," but is crying as she does so.

Chapter 6
Somerset is hurt by Paula; he has always felt inferior because of her wealth. He leaves for Heidelberg, and discovers Paula, Charlotte, and de Stancy at the table d'hôte. He tells Paula he is leaving for England. She asks whether he is going with a "special photographer," but he does not, of course, comprehend. Paula goes to her room and cries.

Chapter 7
De Stancy pretends great interest in the chivalrous families of Germany; they visit the castle. Paula says she does not feel bound by her statement and he cheerfully offers to release her from it. She decides to walk up to the castle; de Stancy gallantly offers his arm.

Chapter 8
The party go to Mainz and take a steamboat along the Rhine. Mrs. Goodman tells Paula Captain de Stancy is too old for her.

Chapter 9
At Coblenz, Charlotte overhears Abner Power and de Stancy discussing the latter's pursuit of Paula. At Brussels, Abner Power and Paula see a wedding party emerge from the cathedral. Abner says he hopes he will soon see her marry de Stancy, become Lady de Stancy, and live in the castle, thus combining fortune and castle, making a "splendid whole" to them both. Paula is equivocal. She receives a letter from Somerset asking that someone else supervise the restoration work at the castle, since his drawings are complete.

Chapter 10
Abner Power goes to Paris and the others go to Amiens, where Charlotte again becomes ill. She tells de Stancy she is going to the cathedral; he says that even for descendants of Roundheads (Puritans) who knocked down his ancestors' castle there is little else to see in the town. He thus identifies Paula with Protestantism and later calls her a "harsh Puritan." Charlotte grows worse. Paula sits with her and looks up to find her uncle in the doorway. He tells her not to accept de Stancy; he has heard something about a "queer relationship" de Stancy has and is going to England to find out more. She asks him to appoint William Havill as the new architect. De Stancy begs her to marry him.

Captain de Stancy receives a telegram that his father has died, and returns to England; he is now Sir William de Stancy. Before he leaves Paula accepts him for "pity's sake."

Chapter 11
William Dare knocks on the door of Myrtle Villa; Captain de Stancy tells him he and Paula are engaged. He asks William not to come near him on the day of the funeral and says he dreads to think what Paula's reaction will be when she finds out that William is his son. Abner Power has overheard their conversation. The next day Abner Power confronts William Dare. He tells him the marriage is desirable, but that he suspects Dare's motives and is convinced he will haunt the couple with his devious behavior. Power wants to send Dare to Peru as his agent; otherwise, he will tell Paula the truth about Sir William's criminal son. Dare counters with information about Abner's own alliance with certain radical political groups and the invention of an explosive machine, by which he was severely wounded in the face and scarred, his identity concealed. He is wanted by various European governments. The two men gaze at each other and both bring out revolvers. They agree to part, with neither able to use the information he has against the other.

Chapter 12

Three months later Somerset starts on a professional journey and goes to Castle de Stancy. He sees that Havill is working on the castle. He encounters Charlotte and tells her he is going to Normandy via Cherbourg. He asks Charlotte what made Paula alter his behavior, and she tells him it was the telegram. He declares he never sent a telegram. Charlotte informs him the wedding, very small and private, is scheduled for that very week. Somerset begins to suspect Dare. He goes to Toneborough the next morning, meets Havill, and discovers he has hired Dare to help him because de Stancy wishes it. Havill tells him of the night he spent with Dare at the inn. He has deduced that the letters on Dare's chest are evidence of his kinship with de Stancy. They hear church bells and believe the wedding is over. Somerset leaves for France.

Chapter 13

Meanwhile, Charlotte de Stancy puzzles over the telegram and the photograph. She goes to the town photographer, Mr. Ray, and he tells her he has seen the photograph produced by William Dare. She goes to the castle and sees Dare on some scaffolding; she then tells Mrs. Goodman what she has learned. Mrs. Goodman thinks they should not tell Paula until after the wedding.

Chapter 14

Charlotte tells Paula about Somerset's being tricked: he never sent the telegram and never had the photograph made. Paula immediately suspects the hand of William Dare and wants to send for Cunningham Haze. De Stancy arrives and she tells him that Dare, "a boy, or a demon," must be arrested. She tries to ring the bell but he stops her. He finally tells Paula that Dare is his son. She sends de Stancy away. He says he had guessed they would "split on this rock." The boy is his ruin. She will not marry him. De Stancy is not altogether surprised.

Book the Sixth: "Paula"

Chapter 1

Paula and Mrs. Goodman sail to Normandy. She finds Somerset has gone to Lisieux. She searches for him there, even finding where he has been sketching, but he boards an omnibus for Caen. She and her aunt follow.

Chapter 2

The next morning they visit churches; at the Abbaye aux Dames they discover Somerset's father, whom Paula recognizes because of his resemblance to George. She does not explain who she is. After dinner she goes to a nearby church and climbs to the triforium, where she has suspected George might be sketching. It is Mr. Cockton, his draughtsman. He tells her

Mr. Somerset left that day for Étretat. They take a steamboat down the Orne; the elder Mr. Somerset is also on board. After dinner at their inn, Paula sees George Somerset dancing with a young lady and they leave.

Chapter 3

The next day she asks about the Englishman with the sketchbook, and is told he stays at a cottage owned by the inn. The two Somersets come to the inn; George looks tired and ill. George asks his father why Paula's husband is not with her. Mr. Somerset explains that the wedding had been postponed, according to newspapers. After another day he says George is "unwell." He had forced himself to dance with an American lady, from "lethargy," but feels worse. Paula goes herself to the cottage and lets him know she is receptive to a proposal; they become engaged. Paula tells Mrs. Goodman she has "got to like George Somerset as desperately as a woman can care for any man." They plan to marry in France.

Chapter 4

Two months later, at the Lord-Quantock-Arms inn, in Markton, the farmers learn that the Somersets are staying at the inn that night because of the restoration work going on at the castle. Sir William de Stancy and William Dare stand outside the castle; Sir William is selling the furniture in Myrtle Villa and leaving Toneborough. Dare tells him it will be a "light night."

Chapter 5

Dare enters the castle and moves about removing valuable pictures. He brings carpenter's shavings from the site of the restoration work and then sets the Long Gallery on fire.

At the Lord-Quantock-Arms, Somerset and Paula sit talking. Charlotte has written that she is very happy for them and is entering an Anglican convent. Somerset says, "She was genuine, if anybody ever was; and simple as she was true."

Suddenly, from outside, there is the sound of horses and footsteps bringing news of the conflagration, which the whole town gathers to watch. Paula and George realize the castle cannot be saved. Even as they observe the flames, they decide to build an independent mansion next to the ruins, which ivy will cover, and resolve not to attempt the rebuilding of the castle itself. Paula, however, cannot help sighing, "I wish my castle wasn't burnt; and I wish you were a de Stancy!"

For further reading: Austin, "Hardy's Laodicean Narrative"; Beatty, "Colonel Waugh and A Laodicean"; Hardy, B., *"A Laodicean": A Story of To-Day;* Hochstadt, "Hardy's Romantic Diptych: A Reading of *A Laodicean* and *Two on a Tower*"; Ward, "A Laodicean"; Wing, "Middle-Class Outcasts in Hardy's *A Laodicean.*"

This late-18th-century etching by Rowlandson and Pugin, Drawing from Life at the Royal Academy, *depicts the Royal Academy of Arts, of which George Somerset's father was a member in* A Laodicean.   (Victoria and Albert Museum, London/Art Resource, New York)

La Revue Nouvelle   French periodical in which a long article about Hardy, "Hommage à Thomas Hardy," was published after his death, in a double issue of January/February 1928 (*Letters* VII, 65).

Lark, Tabitha   In *TWO ON A TOWER*, a "young and blithe female" when we first meet her at choir practice in the home of "Gammer" MARTIN, grandmother of Swithin ST. CLEEVE. The daughter of a dairyman, she reads to Lady Viviette CONSTANTINE, whose husband is away in Africa. She is also the organist for the village church. She studies music in London and is reputed to have joined the "phalanx of Wonderful women who have resolved to eclipse masculine genius altogether." In time, however, she returns to the village and, at the close of the novel, seems likely to marry Swithin after the sudden death of Lady Constantine, with whom he has had a son.

Last, Isaac Glandfield (1814–1866)   Founder and headmaster of the British School, Greyhound Yard, DORCHESTER, which Hardy entered in 1849, at the age of nine. He had previously attended a small school founded by Julia MARTIN, who lived with her husband at KINGSTON MAURWARD HOUSE, in Bockhampton, near the Hardys. Hardy's parents believed Last's teaching to be superior to that at the DORCHESTER GRAMMAR SCHOOL or at William BARNES's school. In 1853 Last left the British School to establish a "commercial academy" for older students. Hardy went with him to the new school, which he attended from 1853 to 1856. Here he studied, Latin, French and advanced mathematics, and read widely. After the age of 16 he had no further formal schooling (Millgate, *Thomas Hardy,* 51–52).

"Last Chrysanthemum, The"   Published in *POEMS OF THE PAST AND THE PRESENT* (1902). The poem explores the interesting problem of a chrysanthemum that has never opened despite "robin-song" and the "fervid call" of the summer sun. It finally blooms, but its beauty is "too late"; the "season's shine is spent" and it must shiver in "tempests turbulent." The poet wonders whether the flower was "Dreaming in witlessness / that for a bloom so delicately gay Winter would stay its stress?"

The poet then catches himself talking as if the flower were human, but reflects that the flower is "but one mask of many worn By the Great Face behind."

The "Great Face" is probably Hardy's name for the Immanent Will, which figures in *The DYNASTS* (he was working on this drama at the time). Hardy was undoubtedly familiar with the ecological adaptation of various plants, and is not seriously asking a botanical question (Bailey, *The Poetry of Thomas Hardy*, 165–66).

"Last Performance, The" Poem dated 1912 and collected in *MOMENTS OF VISION* (1917). It recounts an incident at MAX GATE before Emma's death in the autumn of 1912. The theme is her foreknowledge of her death. One morning she sits down at the piano and begins playing her "oldest tunes . . . / All the old tunes I know." Hardy goes to town and comes back to find her still playing. Then she closes the piano and states, "It's the very last time . . . / From now I play no more." She dies a few mornings later. The poet reflects that "she had known of what was coming, / And wondered how she knew."

In the *Life*, Hardy recounts what happened. "Strangely enough, she one day suddenly sat down to the piano and played . . . her favourite old tunes, saying at the end she would never play any more" (*Life*, 359).

"Last Signal, The" *(11 Oct. 1886) A Memory of William Barnes (Winterborne-Came Path)* This poem was collected in *MOMENTS OF VISION* (1917). It evokes Hardy's long friendship with the poet William BARNES. Barnes was rector of Winterborne-Came-cum-Whitcombe church. The rectory was very near MAX GATE, and Hardy often visited, especially during Barnes's long final illness. In November 1885 he wrote Edmund GOSSE that Barnes was growing very weak, but Barnes lived on until the next October.

The poem is based on an incident recounted in the *Life*. When he walked across the fields from Max Gate to Winterborne-Came church to attend Barnes's funeral, he took Winterborne-Came path, which descends into a valley and rises to cross a hill; Barnes's rectory was near the path. He suddenly noticed a flash of sunlight coming from the coffin "as with a wave of his hand" (*Life*, 183). Hardy used an internal rhyme scheme, common in Welsh poetry, which Barnes had introduced into English poetry. Hardy wrote an obituary of him, "The Rev. William Barnes, B.D.," published

in the *ATHENAEUM* for October 16 (Bailey, *The Poetry of Thomas Hardy*, 376–77). Many years later Hardy edited a selection of Barnes's poems.

Late Lyrics and Earlier Collection of poems published by MACMILLAN & CO., London, in 1922 when Hardy was 82. The preface, in which Hardy argues that he should not be viewed as a pessimist, is particularly notable. He admits that his later poems do not have the fresh optimism of the earlier ones.

Hardy began writing the preface, called "Apology," in February 1922, after weeks of illness. He asked the advice of Sydney COCKERELL, who approved of his publishing it. The preface expresses Hardy's resentment against those who found his verse awkward and his philosophy bleak. Edmund GOSSE was surprised by his protest and wrote, in the *Sunday Times*, that it was part of Hardy's "genius . . . to be sensitive," but that he was "vexed" to find that "he feels a pea under the seven mattresses of our admiration" (Millgate, *Thomas Hardy: A Biography*, 542–43).

The volume was well received on the whole. It contained several poems about Emma HARDY and one about Helen PATERSON Allingham. The earliest poems date from the 1860s, before Hardy's first marriage: "Dream of the City Shopwoman" (1866) and "A Young Man's Exhortation" (1867). The latest poem included is dated 1921. One poem, "A Two-Years' Idyll," deals with the happiest period of Hardy's first marriage, when he and Emma lived at STURMINSTER NEWTON. Every decade of Hardy's life, except the 1880s, is represented (Purdy, *Thomas Hardy: A Bibliographical Study*, 226).

Latin Hardy had had a grounding in the classics from an early age. At the age of nine, in 1849, he entered the DORCHESTER day school run by Isaac Glandfield LAST, who taught him Latin. During the late 1850s, he read Latin and Greek with his friend Henry BASTOW, his fellow pupil in the Dorchester office of the architect John HICKS. Hardy, at the time, was hoping to obtain entrance to a university (*see* EDUCATION OF HARDY).

In 1903 Hardy and his brother and sisters erected a brass tablet in STINSFORD CHURCH to commemorate the contributions his father, grandfather, and uncle had made to the musical services there. The inscription is in Latin, which Hardy believed would remain "unchanged," whereas English might undergo "great alterations in the future" (*Life*, 318).

"Lausanne: In Gibbon's Old Garden: 11–12 p.m." *27 June 1897 (The 110th anniversary of the completion of the "Decline and Fall" at the same hour and place)* Poem published in *POEMS OF THE PAST AND THE PRESENT* (1902) and occasioned by the Hardys' visit to SWITZERLAND in June 1897. They enjoyed the "charm of a lonely Continent," since England was preoccupied with celebration of Queen Victoria's Diamond Jubilee.

In Lausanne they stayed at the Hotel Gibbon. The hotel was named for the English historian Edward Gibbon (1737–94), author of the monumental history *The Decline and Fall of the Roman Empire*. Published in six volumes between 1776 and 1783, it covers 13 centuries. Some of the information has been supplanted by new discoveries, but it is regarded as a classic even today. Gibbon makes the point that history is essentially a record of "little more than the crimes, follies, and misfortunes of mankind" (*The Reader's Encyclopedia:* New York, Crowell, 1965, 257). The author had often stayed at the hotel.

In a mild rebuke to John Ruskin, Hardy admits that he lacks "that aversion from the historian of the *Decline and Fall* which Ruskin recommended" (*Life*, 292–93). He found that little of the hotel building dated from Gibbon's day, but that "the remoter and sloping part of the garden" was, in all probability, as it had been when Gibbon finished his history. Hardy sat in the garden until midnight on June 27, and imagined Gibbon's finishing his masterpiece. As Gibbon had described it in his autobiography, it had been between eleven P.M. and midnight that "I wrote the last lines of the last page, in a summer house in my garden." He then walked through a covered walk of acacias commanding a "prospect of the country, the lake and the mountains."

In the poem Hardy envisions Gibbon's spirit, "grave withal and grand," in the garden, "a volume in his hand." He closes the book, exclaiming "It is finished!" and "from the Past comes speech—small, muted, yet composed." He thinks wryly that his version of Truth may not endure. In the lines "*Truth like a bastard comes into the world / Never without ill-fame to him who gives her birth,*" Hardy summarizes a passage from John MILTON's *Doctrine and Discipline of Divorce:* "Truth is as impossible to be soiled by any outward touch, as the sunbeam . . . she never comes into the world, but like a bastard, to the ignominy of him that brought her forth; till Time, the midwife rather than the mother of truth, have washed and salted the infant and declared her legitimate" (Bailey, *The Poetry of Thomas Hardy*, 134).

Critics observe that the poem may be related to Hardy's anger at the reception of *JUDE THE OBSCURE*. In the novel, when Sue BRIDEHEAD takes her statues of Venus and Apollo back to her lodging, she begins reading a book her landlady "knew nothing of." It is a volume of Gibbon. In October 1904 Hardy wrote, in an inscription in a first edition of the novel, of the "crass Philistinism" of England and America, and praised the

*The Hotel Gibbon, Lausanne, Switzerland, the setting for "*Lausanne: In Gibbon's Old Garden: 11–12 p.m.*"*   (Musée Historique, Lausanne)

French and Germans for discovering "the author's meaning" even though they were reading the novel in translation (Bailey, *The Poetry of Thomas Hardy*, 135).

Lawrence, T. E. (1888–1935)   Known as Lawrence of Arabia, he was an archaeologist, soldier, and writer. He organized a rebellion of the Arabs against the Turks during WORLD WAR I (recounted in his classic book *The Seven Pillars of Wisdom*), declined both the Victoria Cross and a knighthood, and wrote a prose translation of Homer's *Odyssey*.

In 1923 Lawrence, who was serving pseudonymously at the army camp near Wool in Dorset as Private Shaw, wrote to the poet Robert GRAVES, a friend. Graves then wrote Florence HARDY mentioning his presence, and the Hardys invited Lawrence to tea at MAX GATE in April 1923. In November 1926 Lawrence left for India and came on a motor-bicycle to say good-bye to Hardy. When departing, Lawrence had difficulty starting the machine and Hardy stepped inside to find a shawl; meanwhile, Lawrence was able to start the machine and rode quickly away, fearing that Hardy might take a chill. Hardy wrote in his autobiography of his grief at not seeing the actual departure, for he regarded Lawrence as "one of his most valued friends" (*Life*, 434). He died in January 1928 before seeing Lawrence again.

Lea, Hermann (1869–1952)   A photographer and a friend of Hardy's for many years, Lea was the author of *Thomas Hardy's Wessex* (1913). He was born at Thorpe-le-Soken, Essex. After moving to DORSET, he became an active member of the Dorset Photographic Club, and undertook to capture the WESSEX countryside as portrayed by Hardy. His two guides were issued as a single volume in 1913 and were included in the Wessex edition of Hardy's works.

As early as 1904, Lea proposed his study to Hardy, asking whether the author had any objection. Hardy replied that he had not, "if you print somewhere on the map (or in any text accompanying it) that the places in the novels were only *suggested* by those real ones given—as they are not literally portraits of such" (O'Sullivan, *Thomas Hardy: An Illustrated Biography*, 68–71). Despite this caveat and Hardy's later worry about "trippers with Kodaks," tourists, readers, and scholars still come to Dorset in large numbers and drive or walk across the rural countryside, determined to identify favorite scenes in the novels and short stories with the actual terrain.

Lea's photographs of Dorset scenes can be correlated with features of Hardy's fictional settings, although some features Hardy named do not exist as such. An example is "Rainbarrow" on EDGON HEATH in *The RETURN OF THE NATIVE*. Rosemarie Morgan points out that there is no physical feature called "Rainbarrow." There are, however, three Bronze Age barrows on the actual heath;

Hardy makes them into one and places it centrally on Egdon Heath (personal communication with the author). Blackmoor or Blackmore Vale (Hardy uses both spellings) covers a wider area in the novels than it does in reality. The actual vale is north of STURMINSTER NEWTON (F. B. Pinion, *A Hardy Companion*, 241).

The names of many buildings and sites are changed. Puddletown Church is Weatherbury Church in *FAR FROM THE MADDING CROWD*, and Sherborne Castle is Sherton Castle in "Anna, Lady Baxby," one of the stories in *A GROUP OF NOBLE DAMES*. The region of Wessex includes Dorset as well as Somerset, Gloucestershire, and Wiltshire.

For further reading: Arkans, "Hardy's Poetic Landscapes"; Blum and Jesty, "Hermann Lea's Thomas Hardy's Wessex Revisited" [Part 1, 1986; Part 2, 1987; Part 3, 1988]; Brown, *Figures in a Wessex Landscape: Thomas Hardy's Picture of English Country Life;* Hawkins, *Thomas Hardy: His Life and Landscape;* Hooker, *Writers in a Landscape;* Miller, "Topography and Tropography in Thomas Hardy's. 'In Front of the Landscape.'" O'Sullivan, *Thomas Hardy: An Illustrated Biography;* Robinson, "Hermann Lea Reappraised: Followed by Some Corrections to Hardy's Wessex Reappraised."

Leaf, Thomas   One of the Mellstock singers in *UNDER THE GREENWOOD TREE*. He has a "weak lath-like form" and is described "stumbling along with one shoulder forward and his head inclined to the left." His arms "dangle nervously" as though they are empty sleeves.

lecturing   Hardy was sometimes invited to lecture, but usually refused. In 1886 he was invited by a collector in Cheshire to lecture there. He declined, writing, "lecturing is not in my way," and that it was, in fact, "almost beyond my physical powers" (*Letters* I, 143). In 1893 he was invited to speak by Mary Haweis, a writer on household management, but wrote, "Alas, for my lecturing! It is altogether one of those things which I cannot do" (*Letters* II, 36). In 1904 he turned down an invitation from the Edinburgh Philosophical Institution to deliver one of the lectures in its notable series, saying, "lecturing is beyond my powers & province" (*Letters* VII, 135). In 1906 Hardy's paper "MEMORIES OF CHURCH RESTORATION" was read in his absence at the General Meeting of the Society for the Protection of Ancient Buildings (*Letters* III, 211). In 1919 he was invited by William Lyon Phelps and the governing body of Yale University to deliver the first of a series of lectures established as a memorial to Francis Bergen, an alumnus killed during WORLD WAR I. He declined, writing, "It is however quite out of my power to entertain the notion of such an undertaking" (*Letters* V, 352).

Lee, Vernon (1856–1935)   "Vernon Lee" was the pseudonym of Violet Paget, a scholarly British writer living in ITALY. Her article "Of Hardy and Meredith" appeared in the *WESTMINSTER GAZETTE* on July 20, 1905. When the editor, John Alfred Spender, sent Hardy a copy, he wrote to thank him, saying he might otherwise have missed the article by the "accomplished lady Vernon Lee."

"Leipzig" *(1813)* Scene: *The Master-tradesmen's Parlour at the Old Ship Inn, Casterbridge. Evening.* Collected in *WESSEX POEMS* (1898), this poem is narrated by Old Norbert, a man of German extraction living in WESSEX. His father was a German Hussar and his mother from Leipzig. He recalls his mother's stories of the Battle of Leipzig (October 16–19, 1813), a complex engagement also called the Battle of the Nations. It was a decisive victory by the allies over Napoleon I; there were about 120,000 casualties in the battle. (Napoleon was finally defeated in the Battle of WATERLOO in June 1815.)

After the war, Norbert's father was stationed near DORCHESTER as a member of King GEORGE III's German Legion (the York Hussars); he brought his mother to England from Leipzig. They remained in Wessex and reared their son there. His mother often told him of tapping the tambourine and singing and pirouetting when the "Allies marched in." Norbert retells the story of the Battle of Leipzig and the mistimed blowing-up of the Bridge of Lindenau, which trapped thousands of French troops and played an important part in the allied victory. The story of the Battle of Leipzig is also retold in *The DYNASTS.*

James O. Bailey observes that the poem, with its imaginative use of historical records, is part of Hardy's projected ballad-sequence based on the Napoleonic Wars (Bailey, *The Poetry of Thomas Hardy,* 68).

Le Sueur, Lucetta ("Miss Templeman") In *The MAYOR OF CASTERBRIDGE,* she is the daughter of a military officer who has lost both parents while young. She lives in Jersey and tends Michael HENCHARD when he falls ill. Her conduct causes scandal, but he promises to marry her if she will risk the return of Susan HENCHARD, his legal wife.

Susan returns to CASTERBRIDGE with her daughter, Elizabeth-Jane HENCHARD (2). Lucetta moves to Casterbridge, calling herself "Miss Templeman" to escape her unsavory past. Having inherited a modest fortune from her aunt, Mrs. TEMPLEMAN, she leases High-Place Hall, and engages Elizabeth-Jane as her maid and companion. She then meets Donald FARFRAE and falls in love with him. Both Henchard and Farfrae are now rivals for Lucetta, who marries Farfrae when she learns that Henchard once auctioned off his wife. She has delusions of grandeur and hopes Farfrae will be knighted, but, when her early love letters to Henchard are revealed, she is reviled in Casterbridge, loses her baby, and dies.

"Levelled Churchyard, The" Poem dated 1882 and included in *POEMS OF THE PAST AND THE PRESENT* (1902). The speakers are the souls buried in a neglected churchyard, a "jumble patch" of "wrenched memorial stones." The tombstones have become mixed over the years, eclipsing the identities and locations of the original occupants. Even their names have been obscured by construction of "some path or porch." They cry piteously to be delivered from "zealous Churchmen's pick and plane."

The poem recalls "DURING WIND AND RAIN," about Plymouth, the former home of Hardy's first wife, Emma Gifford HARDY, which he visited after her death. He may have seen some of the Gifford tombstones during a rainstorm. It also recalls "VOICES FROM THINGS GROWING IN A CHURCHYARD," in which those buried identify themselves with the plants growing on their graves. The disturbances of graves in the churchyard at PUDDLETOWN troubled Hardy greatly. In his essay "MEMORIES OF CHURCH RESTORATION" he deplored the practice of leveling churchyards and using the stones to pave churchyard walks, which had caused inscriptions to be "trodden out" within a few years.

Leverre, Henri Husband of Avice III (the third manifestation of Avice CARO in *The WELL-BELOVED.* He is the stepson of the gentleman from Jersey whom Marcia BENCOMB marries after her father does not consent to her marrying Jocelyn PIERSTON. (She later marries Pierston).

Life of Thomas Hardy, The This was Hardy's autobiography, a term he did not use (*see* AUTOBIOGRAPHY AND HARDY). His second wife, Florence HARDY, persuaded him to record memories of his life, which she transcribed. He was reluctant to do so, but she persuaded him that it would be the protection against false statements by future biographers. He finally agreed that the facts of his career should be set down "for use in the event of its proving necessary to print them" (*Life,* vii). The resulting work, purportedly by Florence Hardy, was first published in two volumes: *The Early Life of Thomas Hardy, 1840–1891* and *The Later Years of Thomas Hardy, 1892–1928.* The two volumes were combined in a single edition in 1962 as *The Life of Thomas Hardy* by Florence Emily Hardy. Actually she wrote only the final chapter, Chapter 38, "The Last Scene," covering 1926 through January 1928, when Hardy died. In the present book, all page numbers to the *Life* are to this edition, in which both volumes are combined.

Life's Little Ironies Collection of Hardy's short stories, published in 1894. Some of these tales had previously appeared in periodicals (for example, "The FIDDLER OF THE REELS," *SCRIBNER'S MAGAZINE,* May 1893). Most of them take place in the present, unlike those in *WESSEX TALES* and *A GROUP OF NOBLE DAMES.* The stories in this volume reveal a dissatisfaction on the part of Hardy with the priority on moral conventions that was characteristic of the Victorian era.

Literature Periodical edited by Henry Duff Traill (1842–1900), an author and journalist. Hardy's WESSEX POEMS was reviewed in the periodical on December 31, 1898, and Traill also published his poem "The Dead Drummer" (the title of which was later changed to "DRUMMER HODGE") on November 25, 1899. When Traill died in February 1900 he was succeeded by Frederick Dalton. Hardy wrote Edmund GOSSE that he had liked Traill's "geniality" and was glad he had taken things "too easily to mind what I said to him about his misprints" (*Letters* II, 248).

literature and the writing life, rewards of Hardy was a voracious reader from childhood on. When he was eight his mother gave him John Dryden's *Virgil,* Samuel Johnson's *Rasselas,* and *Paul and Virginia,* the idyllic romance by Bernadin de Saint-Pierre. He read a periodical he discovered in a closet at home called *A History of the Wars,* which dealt with the Napoleonic Wars—a subject about which he would later write in *The* DYNASTS and *The* TRUMPET-MAJOR. At 12 he began studying the Etonian "Introduction to the Latin Tongue" and started readings in Eutropius and Caesar. He went on to Alexander Dumas and Shakespeare's tragedies, and began studying French and German, the latter from John Cassell's *The Popular Educator.* He also read the works of the English historical novelist William Harrison Ainsworth (*Life,* 16–26, *passim*).

Despite his interest in French and Latin, when Hardy was 16, he was expected to think of a suitable profession. His father, a builder, encouraged his interest in ARCHITECTURE. From 1859 to 1861, while working in the DORCHESTER office of the architect John HICKS, he read the *Aeneid,* some Horace and Ovid, and sometimes "caught himself soliloquizing in Latin on his various projects." He studied Greek and read parts of *The Iliad;* he was about to attempt Aeschylus and Sophocles, but his friend Horace MOULE advised him that, if he were going to become an architect, it would "be hardly worth while." He stopped reading Greek and regretted it, but reflected, later, that his "substantial knowledge" of the Greek dramatists was "not small." Later, he seriously thought about applying to CAMBRIDGE UNIVERSITY with a view to entering the church and obtaining a curacy in a country village. His faith was not strong enough, however, to sustain his intention, and he gave up the idea.

In 1862 he went from the office of John Hicks to LONDON, where he worked as an apprentice in the office of the distinguished architect Sir Arthur William BLOMFIELD. In 1863 he moved to 16 Westbourne Park Villas, where his literary career began with the purchase of Samuel Neil's *The Art of Reasoning,* which he believed would be a useful model for the writing of prose. He also purchased a 10-volume edition of the works of Shakespeare and J. R. McCulloch's *Principles of Political Economy* (Millgate, *Thomas Hardy: A Biography,* 85–86).

In 1865 his fictional sketch "HOW I BUILT MYSELF A HOUSE" was published in *CHAMBERS'S JOURNAL,* which he wrote to entertain his fellow architectural apprentices. The same year he studied French under Professor Léonie Stiévenard at King's College. Within two or three years, however, he was "compelled" to try writing prose. He found himself "perilously near coming to the ground between the two stools of architecture and literature." He also wrote a great deal of verse, but kept much of it private, during 1866 and 1867, considering that, as it was concentrated, it formed the "essence of all imaginative and emotional literature" (*Life,* 48).

Hardy's autobiography, in addition to his letters from London to his sister Mary HARDY, give some indication of his prodigious reading despite his daytime position: Horace, Trollope, Thackeray, Cardinal Newman's *Apologia,* Addison, Byron, the poetry of Sir Walter Scott, and Donne. He began converting the book of Ecclesiastes into Spenserian stanzas, but abandoned the effort as he found the original "unmatchable" (*Life,* 47). He attended a series of Shakespeare plays at the Drury Lane theater, seeing Samuel Phelps in *Othello.*

His health suffered, and in 1867 he returned home, working again in the office of John Hicks. He read Browning, Thackeray, Wordsworth, Stuart Mill, Carlyle, Shakespeare, Walpole, Macaulay, Whitman, and Virgil, "of which he never wearied." He also kept literary notebooks in which he outlined possible writing projects and copied passages he liked from various authors, carefully studying their style.

Hardy's first novel, *The POOR MAN AND THE LADY,* was never published and has vanished. His second, *DESPERATE REMEDIES,* was published anonymously in three volumes in 1871, and, for the first time, he began earning money from his writing. By this time he was engaged to Emma Gifford (HARDY), and hoped to marry as soon as it was financially feasible. Long after he became an established writer, however, Hardy was cynical about the monetary rewards of publishing. In 1907 he answered a letter from George Morley, author of novels and books on Warwickshire. He had asked for advice on whether he should continue writing. Hardy replied that, assuming Morley expected "commercial results," it was a problem that no one could solve for him. However, it was his opinion that literature was "a precarious profession at the best of times," and, as a rule, required a "greater expenditure of labour than any other to produce a steady income from—certainly than any trade" (*Letters* III, 259).

After *JUDE THE OBSCURE* was published in 1895 and severely criticized, Hardy abandoned the writing of novels. He continued to receive visits from and correspond with writers, however, and to write poetry throughout his life. In November 1927, two months before he died, he was selecting and editing poems to be included in the collection WINTER WORDS, which he planned to publish on his 90th birthday (it was published posthumously). His second wife, Florence HARDY, read him poetry by Walter de la Mare and Robert BROWNING, among other works, in December. He was eager to absorb literature until the hour of his death at the age of 88. At 8:15 the evening of January 11, 1928, he asked her to read J. B. S. Haldane's *Possible Worlds*, but found it "too deep." His mind began wandering, and he died 45 minutes later (Millgate, *Thomas Hardy: A Biography*, 571–72).

local history and traditions, Hardy's interest in   Hardy had an enduring preoccupation with antiquarian matters, especially as they related to DORSET. Many of his characters, events, and settings have a factual basis. He owned a copy of John Hutchins's volume *The History and Antiquities of the County of Dorset*, which sometimes served to suggest further avenues of research. According to an old catalog description from the Library of Congress, Hutchins (1698–1773) described the book as being complied "from the best and most ancient historians, inquisitiones post mortem, and other valuable records and mss. in the public offices and libraries, and in private hands." Hardy may have owned the third edition. This was in four volumes, published from 1861 to 1874 by J. B. Nichols and Sons, Westminster, London, and included 131 plates, a map, and plans. For example, in 1877, while he and Emma HARDY were living at STURMINSTER NEWTON, he wrote the Reverend Charles Bingham, rector of Melcombe Horsey, Dorset, to ask where he might find copies of the *Sherborne Journal*, mentioned in Hutchins. Parson Tringham, the antiquarian in TESS OF THE D'URBERVILLES who discovered that John DURBEYFIELD was a descendant of the aristocratic d'Urberville family, was based on the Reverend Bingham (*Letters* I, 51).

In 1883 Hardy wrote the barrister and author Walter Pollock about his friend Henry MOULE's new book, *Descriptive Catalogue of the Charters, Minute Books & other Documents of the Borough of Weymouth 1252 and 1800* (*Letters* I, 121). He termed it an interesting contribution to "municipal history." He sometimes found in such volumes of history, as well as in genealogical books, nuggets of history and tradition that were later incorporated in his fiction. For example, the well-known smuggling activities along the Dorset coast provided the foundation of the plot of his short story "The DISTRACTED PREACHER."

He was always keen to preserve the names of earlier structures and streets. About 1893 he wrote the Dorset banker and politician Robert Pearce Edgcumbe about the restoration of the name of "The Bow," the curved wall of St. Peter's Churchyard, "Bull Stake," and "Bowl-ing Alley Walk"; he felt they were "fast sinking into oblivion (*Letters* II, 4). He sometimes wrote letters to the local newspaper, the *Dorset County Chronicle*, to lend his support to such efforts. On the same subject, in 1922 he wrote the journalist William G. Bowman that local names had become "so muddled & neglected by the surveyors of the ordnance maps" as to be fast disappearing; for instance, "Swan-knolls" at the nearby village of Cattistock had become "Sandhills," and "St. Conger's Barrow" had been corrupted to "Conquer Barrow" (*Letters* VI, 131).

He was frequently involved in the effort to distinguish buildings with historic associations. For instance, he advocated that the Gloucester Hotel, WEYMOUTH, where King George III often stayed, be marked in some way. Harry W. CRICKMAY, the current head of the architectural firm for which Hardy had once worked, had designed a commemorative plaque for the hotel. A sketch was sent to Hardy by Edwin Stevens of Dorchester in 1922, and Hardy wrote that he found it "quite suitable for the purpose designed" (*Letters* VI, 171).

He also valued the many traditions of music, dance, entertainment, food, and customs associated with Dorset and preserved them in such works as FAR FROM THE MADDING CROWD, *Tess of the D'Urbervilles*, "The WITHERED ARM," "The MELLSTOCK QUIRE," "The HOUSE OF HOSPITALITIES," "AFTERNOON SERVICE AT MELLSTOCK," UNDER THE GREENWOOD TREE, The WOODLANDERS, "A CHANGED MAN," and dozens of other novels, short stories, and poems.

Locker, Arthur (1828–1893)   Editor of the GRAPHIC from 1870 to 1891. He published one of Hardy's short stories, "The ROMANTIC ADVENTURES OF A MILKMAID," in the summer number, 1883. In 1887 he invited Hardy to write a novel for the periodical, but Hardy replied that he had "quite lately agreed to write two for some other serials" and could not "enter into a further engagement" (*Letters* I, 170).

"Logs on the Hearth" *A Memory of a Sister*   Dated *December 1915* and collected in MOMENTS OF VISION (1917), this poem was written after the death of Mary HARDY, the sister closest to Hardy himself. A year and a half younger than Hardy, she had died on November 24, 1915, of emphysema, at the age of 74. As he watches a log burning on the family hearth, Hardy recalls the life of the apple tree, which had grown in their garden, and had borne "large striped apples by the peck" until its "last hour" of bearing fruit. The felled tree elicits heartbreaking memories of his childhood with Mary. They had climbed through its branches together, "her foot near mine on the bending limb, / Laughing, her young brown hand awave."

London   Hardy began a lifelong attachment to London in late 1848, when, at the age of eight, he traveled with his mother, Jemima Hand HARDY, to Hatfield, outside London, so that she could assist her sister Martha Sharpe in the final stages of her fourth pregnancy. Returning in early 1849, they passed through the city, affording Hardy a glimpse of many noted landmarks (Millgate, *Thomas Hardy: A Biography*, 45).

After finishing his formal education at the age of 16, in 1856, Hardy worked in the DORCHESTER office of the architect John HICKS. On Thursday, April 17, 1862, he went from Dorchester to London by train and found lodgings at 3 Clarence Place, Kilburn. He became an assistant architect in the office of Sir Arthur William BLOMFIELD. He devoted the next five years to absorbing the culture, architecture, and historic sites of the city. He went to churches, both Anglican and Roman Catholic, saw old friends from DORSET, visited art exhibitions, and attended public events such as the procession preceding the wedding of the Prince of Wales and Princess Alexandra of Denmark and the funeral of Lord Palmerston. He tried out the underground railway one day and found it "excellently arranged." He was invited to gatherings in the rooms of the Architectural Association and joined the association himself. Some of his letters to his sister Mary HARDY from that period have survived, enriched with sketches. He heard Charles Dickens lecture in the spring of 1863, and had his head read at the London School of Phrenology. In February 1863 the offices of Blomfield's firm moved from St. Martin's Place to 8 Adelphi Terrace, Kilburn, with a view of the Thames; Hardy wrote Mary it was a "capital place" (Millgate, *Thomas Hardy: A Biography*, 76–79; *Letters* 3–7). In 1863 he moved to 16 Westbourne Park Villas.

During his London years he had an "understanding" with a girl named Eliza Bright Nicholls and, in fact, may have considered himself informally engaged to her. He also began searching for a way to enter the field of literary journalism, perhaps by becoming the London correspondent of a country newspaper, and, at the same time, was writing a great deal of poetry. The relationship with Eliza ended in 1866; she never married but called him almost 50 years later, after the death of his first wife, hoping in vain to resume their relationship. The strain of ending the relationship, combined with discouragement over the prospect of a literary career, in addition to lack of sleep and much reading, all had an adverse affect on Hardy's health. He returned to Dorchester in 1867 to assist John Hicks with church restoration work (Millgate, *Thomas Hardy: A Biography*, 84–85; 100–101).

After Hicks's death, Hardy worked in WEYMOUTH for his successor, George CRICKMAY, who, in 1870, sent him to CORNWALL to work on the restoration of ST. JULIOT CHURCH. Here he met Emma Lavinia Gifford (HARDY), who became his wife in 1874. During the years after their marriage the Hardys did not have a permanent home, but lived in various rented rooms, rental houses, and apartments in Dorset and in London and traveled abroad frequently. From March to July 1875 they lived at 18 Newton Road, Westbourne Grove, London (*Letters* I, 36). They then spent two years in STURMINSTER NEWTON, Dorset, but returned to London and, in March 1878, took a three-year lease on a house at 1 Arundel Terrace, Trinity Road, Upper Tooting, near Wandsworth Common. They stayed there through June 1881, when they moved temporarily to a small house called Llanherne, at The Avenue, Wimborne, Dorset. At this time they decided to "make London a place of sojourn for a few months only in each year, and establish their home in the country" for the remainder of the year. Hardy notes in the *Life* that "residence in or near a city tended to force mechanical and ordinary productions from his pen, concerning ordinary society-life and habits" (*Life,* 149). Hardy had by now joined the SAVILE CLUB (15 Savile Row) and often wrote letters from there during these years. They then moved to a rented house in Shire-Hall Lane, Dorchester, in June 1883 and built MAX GATE (completed in 1885). In 1885 and 1886 Hardy wrote Emma and others from lodgings in London at 29 Montague Street; 23 Montague Street; 56 Great Russell Street (across from the British Museum); 14 Bedford Place, Russell Square; and 28 Upper Bedford Place, Russell Square.

Later he and Emma often took furnished flats or houses for part or all of the London season (April through July), bringing their servants and entertaining London friends. They lived, for example, at 20 Monmouth Road, Bayswater (1889); 12 Mandeville Place, Manchester Square (1891); 70 Hamilton Terrace (1893); 16 Pelham Crescent, South Kensington (1894,

Arundel Terrace, Trinity Road, Upper Tooting, London, home of Thomas and Emma Hardy from March 1878 to 1881
(Beinecke Rare Book and Manuscript Library, Yale University)

The Hardys had a flat at 1 Hyde Park Mansions, London, during parts of April, May, and June, 1905, 1906, and 1907 (Sarah Bird Wright)

1896); 90 Ashley Gardens, Victoria Street (1895); 20 Wynnstay Gardens (1899); 27 Oxford Terrace (1901); 13 Abercorn Place (1904); and 1 Hyde Park Mansions (1905, 1906). In April 1891 Hardy was elected to the ATHENAEUM CLUB, to which he was nominated by Lord CARNARVON. He often wrote letters from that address during the ensuing years.

During his early years in London Hardy came to know such writers as Leslie STEPHEN; Alfred, Lord TENNYSON; Matthew ARNOLD; Henry JAMES; and William Dean HOWELLS, as well as the actor Henry Irving, the painters W. P. FRITH and Edward Burne-Jones, the scientist Thomas Henry Huxley, and other prominent figures. He kept notebooks of his observations of British society and made more use of his knowledge of London social and intellectual circles in his early fiction, such as *The* HAND OF ETHELBERTA, TWO ON A TOWER, and *The* TRUMPET-MAJOR, than in his major masterpieces,

including *The* MAYOR OF CASTERBRIDGE, TESS OF THE D'URBERVILLES, and JUDE THE OBSCURE, all set in rural Dorset (although the latter novel has additional settings, such as Oxford). He joined the London Library in 1906 and kept up his membership for several years (*Letters* III, 186).

The pattern of alternating residences between London and Dorchester continued during the late 1880s, the 1890s, and into the early years of the 20th century. Hardy sought a clear separation between his London and Dorset worlds, a matter that acquired a certain urgency as his fame increased and his readers imagined "WESSEX" as a place to visit. He came to question the value of having, himself, "drifted away" from the way of life his parents knew, though city life had seemed "irresistible" at the time (Millgate, *Thomas Hardy: A Biography,* 268).

***London Mercury,* the**   On October 14, 1919, Hardy had submitted a poem, "Going and Staying" (first two stanzas only), to John Colling SQUIRE, the editor of a new magazine, the *London Mercury.* On returning the corrected proof, however, Hardy decided the poem was "rather grey" for a "new & hopeful" magazine. He sent an alternative one, which he said was "of quite a frivolous kind," called "A Glimpse from a Train" (it was later retitled "FAINTHEART IN A RAILWAY TRAIN"). He thanked Squire for the book of his verses he had sent (*Letters* V, 330). Squire published "Going and Staying" (two stanzas only) in November 1919 and "A Glimpse from a Train" in January 1920.

Squire later published a number of Hardy's poems in the magazine: "THE WOMAN I MET" (April 1921); "VOICES FROM THINGS GROWING IN A CHURCHYARD" (December 1921); a biographical note on his friend Horace M. MOULE to accompany the reprinting of one of Moule's early poems (October 1922); "On the Portrait of a Woman about to be Hanged" (February 1923); "Waiting Both" and "An East-End Curate" (November 1924); and "Epitaph on a Pessimist" (September 1925).

Longman's Magazine   Literary periodical published and edited by Charles James Longman; it was a successor to *Fraser's Magazine* and was first published in November 1882 (*Letters* I, 107). Hardy's story "The THREE STRANGERS" appeared in the magazine in March 1883, and his article "The DORSETSHIRE LABOURER" was published in the magazine in July 1883. In 1887 Longman rejected his story "The WITHERED ARM" as too "grim and unrelieved" for the magazine (*Letters* I, 168). One of the stories included in *A* GROUP OF NOBLE DAMES, "The Lady Penelope," was published in the magazine in January 1890.

Longways, Solomon   Character in *The* MAYOR OF CASTERBRIDGE. He is a small man of about 70, an unsavory associate of Christopher CONEY, employed by Michael

HENCHARD. He often refreshes himself with a drink at the Three Mariners.

"Looking Across" Poem dated December 1915 and published in *MOMENTS OF VISION* (1917). It was occasioned by the death of Hardy's sister Mary HARDY on November 24, 1915; he is "looking across" to the STINSFORD CHURCH cemetery. Each of the five stanzas ends with a reference to a person "out there." The first stanza refers to his father, who died in 1892. The second stanza refers to his mother, who died in 1904: "The dawn is not nigh . . . / And Two are out there." The third stanza evokes Mary's death: it refers to the wind which "drops to die / Like the phantom of Care / Too frail for a cry," and "Three are out there." He then recalls his wife Emma's death in 1912, her life "That once ran rare / And rosy in dye," and finally anticipates his own death: "my wraith asks: Why, / Since these calm lie, / Are not Five out there?"

Hardy noted in his journal, "Buried her under the yew-tree where the rest of us lie. . . . Went to bed at eleven. East wind. No bells heard. Slept in the New Year, as did also those 'out there'" (Bailey, *The Poetry of Thomas Hardy*, 396).

"Lost Pyx, The" *A Medieval Legend* Poem first printed in the *Sphere* on December 22, 1900, and collected in *POEMS OF THE PAST AND THE PRESENT* (1902). A footnote to the poem states that the legend is based on a pillar, called Cross-in-Hand, or Christ-in-Hand, which stands above the Vale of Blackmore. The story given in the poem concerns a medieval priest who once dwelt in a cell at the foot of the dell, at "Cernel Abbey" (Cerne Abbas, midway between Sherborne and Dorchester). He is summoned at night to a lonely cottage to give last rites to a dying man. The priest does not go immediately, but "slept and dreamed; till a Visage seemed / To frown from Heaven at him." He then rises and plods through the dark to the sick man, but finds the Pyx containing the Blessed Sacrament has disappeared. He beats his head, wailing that he has lost "the Body of Christ Himself." Suddenly he sees a ray of light pointing from the sky to a spot on the ground, where he finds the Pyx surrounded by oxen, sheep, doe, hares, badgers, squirrels, rabbits, and many other creatures. The priest thanks the Lord of Love, Blessed Mary, and all the saints. He reaches the dying man "Whose passing sprite had been stayed for the rite" and goes on to serve the abbey. He erects the stone to mark the site of the "midnight miracle."

A variant of the story is given in *TESS OF THE D'URBERVILLES*, in which Tess meets Angel Clare at the spot. Bailey states that the stone column consists of a shaft surmounted by a "mutilated capital" with carving on it. It could be Roman or could date from the 14th century. Hardy wrote Clement SHORTER on December 10, 1900, that the tradition "is a real one" (Bailey, *The Poetry of Thomas Hardy*, 184).

Loveday, John Character in *The TRUMPET-MAJOR*. The son of Miller LOVEDAY, he is 32 when the novel opens. The trumpet-major of the novel's title, he is stationed near Overcombe Mill when the French invasion of 1804 seems imminent. He is in love with Anne GARLAND but defers to his brother Bob (Robert LOVEDAY); he prevents Bob from making a bad marriage to Matilda JOHNSON. He is later killed in Spain.

Loveday, Miller In *The TRUMPET-MAJOR*, he is the cheerful, genial, and devoted father of John LOVEDAY and Robert LOVEDAY and lives at Overcombe Mill. He marries Martha GARLAND, mother of Anne GARLAND. His party at the beginning of the book has been much praised and was one of the scenes dramatized in 1912 by the DORCHESTER DEBATING AND DRAMATIC SOCIETY (known as the HARDY PLAYERS after 1916). (*See* Appendix II, Media Adaptations of the Works of Thomas Hardy.) Miller Loveday gives the party in honor of his son John's regiment, the Dragoons, a horse regiment rather than cavalry. They are stationed in a military camp just outside the mill. The various regiments have been assembled in anticipation of the possible invasion of England by Napoleon. Miller Loveday is the "representative of an ancient family of corn-grinders" whose history is "lost in the mists of antiquity"; that is, they were not prominent, although they performed an essential service.

Loveday, Robert Character in *The TRUMPET-MAJOR*. A son of Miller LOVEDAY, he is a 28-year-old sailor when the novel opens. He is prone to attach himself to women very quickly, without really knowing them; Anne GARLAND is attracted to him. He suddenly becomes engaged to Matilda JOHNSON, a former actress. His brother, John LOVEDAY, who is in love with Anne, saves him from what promises to be a bad marriage. Later, Robert has a fling with a girl called Caroline, a masterbaker's daughter, at Portsmouth, after he returns from the Battle of TRAFALGAR, but comes to his senses and gives her up. He writes the desolate John that his heart has come back to its "old anchorage," Anne. John is killed in Spain. Anne finally agrees to marry Robert if he behaves for six months.

Lowell, Amy (1874–1925) American poet, biographer, critic, and member of a distinguished New England family. She was known for her association with the imagist movement. (This movement, led by Ezra Pound, H. D. [Hilda Doolittle], and other poets, dates from about 1910. It espoused the direct treatment of the object and a mandate for the economical construction of images within brief poems, often no more than a few lines in length, built around a single clear metaphor.) Lowell's eccentric behavior included keeping a troupe of dogs and smoking large cigars.

Amy Lowell and her friend Ada Russell visited MAX GATE on August 1, 1914, at the outset of WORLD WAR I. She had brought her own maroon automobile with her, along with a chauffeur in maroon livery; she then had the car crated and shipped back to America "so that it would not be commandeered" (F. Damon, *Amy Lowell,* quoted by Purdy and Millgate (*Letters* V, 67). Lowell often sought critical commentary from Hardy on her work. On returning to America in 1914 she sent him her volume of poems *Sword Blades and Poppy Seed,* for which he wrote to thank her on December 6, 1914. He apologized for the lateness of his reply, which he blamed on the war. He mentioned several of her poems he particularly liked, including "The Foreigner," "After Hearing a Waltz" (sic; the actual title is "After Hearing a Waltz by Bartok"), and "The Captured Goddess" (*Letters* V, 67).

In 1919 she sent Hardy a copy of her *Can Grande's Castle,* which had been published in 1918. He replied that he was glad to hear from her, not only for "personal reasons" but also because she was so "staunchly zealous in the cause of poetry." He discussed her argument for "polyphonic prose" and said his wife was reading her poetry to him. In taking up her book, he would say, "Let's read some more of 'Cousin Amy,'" referring to the "lady in Locksley Hall." This is a reference to Alfred, Lord Tennyson's poem "Locksley Hall," in which the hero looks back at a seaside mansion called Locksley Hall, where he spent a great deal of time while young. There he fell in love with his cousin Amy (*Letters* V, 292–93).

On Hardy's 80th birthday (June 2, 1920), Amy Lowell was one of the 14 American writers who sent a congratulatory cable. On March 7, 1923, he wrote to thank her for sending him a copy of *American Poetry 1922: A Miscellany,* which included her poem "The Swans." He said he much liked her poem, and that of all the younger American poets she managed free verse "best," although he himself was "too old to do it justice" (*Letters* VI, 186).

In May 1923 Lowell sent Hardy a copy of her dramatic monologue "The Rosebud Wall-paper," which had been published in the *NORTH AMERICAN REVIEW.* He replied that he liked it, and that he hoped her Keats book (her biography of John KEATS) was finished. "Who would have supposed," a century ago, "that that young man's private life and affairs would become so interesting to the world," he remarked. There is evidence, however, that Hardy knew how enduring Keats's legacy would be. In 1887 he and Emma had stayed near Keats's house in Rome; he wrote, in the *Life,* that "no mind could conjecture what had been lost to English literature" by his death (*Life,* 188). He urged her to

"call down and see us" if she were to come to England that year (*Letters* VI, 229–30). When she sent him her biography of Keats in 1925, the year of her death, he thanked her, referring to it as a "valuable book. He remarked that "Not Shakespeare himself . . . has been so meticulously . . . examined" as Keats. He praised her for having "sifted out the legends for & against him" (*Letters* VI, 313).

Luxellian, Lady In *A PAIR OF BLUE EYES* she is the frail wife of Lord LUXELLIAN and the mother of two small daughters, the Honorable Kate and the Honorable Mary. After her death Lord Luxellian marries Elfride SWANCOURT, who also dies young.

Luxellian, Lord Spencer Hugh Character in *A PAIR OF BLUE EYES.* The 15th Baron Luxellian, he lives at Endelstow House. His frail wife, Lady LUXELLIAN, dies, leaving two small daughters, the Honorable Kate and the Honorable Mary. He then marries Elfride SWANCOURT, whom his daughters adore. He is grief-stricken at Eldride's early death after a miscarriage.

Lyceum Club London club for professional women, located at 128 Piccadilly. Florence Emily Dugdale HARDY had been a member before her marriage. On July 13, 1909, Hardy wrote his friend Edward CLODD with detailed instructions about escorting her to the first performance of Baron Frédéric D'ERLANGER'S opera *Tess.* He hoped to "call round" and see them in their seats between the acts and at the end of the performance. If he could then put her in a cab she would go to the London home of her aunt afterward (she actually stayed at the Lyceum Club that night). Clodd took her to the Gaiety Restaurant and then to the theater. The performance ran late, however, and they had to leave early in order for Clodd to catch his train at Victoria Station (*Letters* IV, 32).

For further reading: Desmond Hawkins, "Tess in the Opera House."

Lyceum Theatre London theater at which Thomas Hardy's friend Mary JEUNE (later, Lady St. Helier) arranged a charity performance in aid of a holiday fund for poor city children in July 1890. Hardy was persuaded to write a verse epilogue to be recited by the actress Ada Rehan. The performance was badly attended, with two-thirds of the stalls and pit empty (*Letters* I, 214).

In 1896 Hardy corresponded with Frederick Harrison, the partner of Ian Forbes-Robertson at the Lyceum, about the possibility of a London production of the play of *TESS OF THE D'URBERVILLES* (*Letters* II, 114). In 1901 he attended a performance of Shakespeare's *Coriolanus* at the Lyceum with Sir Henry Irving in the title role (*Letters* II, 285).

Macbeth-Raeburn, Henry Raeburn (1860–1947) Artist and engraver who supplied a frontispiece for each volume of the WESSEX NOVELS edition of Hardy's novels published by OSGOOD, MCILVAINE & CO. in 1895–96. In November 1894 he planned a trip to DORCHESTER to discuss the project with Hardy. Hardy wrote that because MAX GATE was undergoing construction (additions were being made to the back of the house), he could not offer the artist accommodation, but would expect him for dinner. After the visit Hardy wrote and urged him to visit CORNWALL in order to do the illustrations for *A PAIR OF BLUE EYES.* He remarked that it would be a shame for him to prepare them from photographs alone. He recommended a hotel at Boscastle (*Letters* II, 64–65). Macbeth-Raeburn visited the town and depicted the harbor there in the frontispiece to the novel. He came to Max Gate in March 1895, working closely with Hardy on the particular site to be depicted in the frontispiece to each novel (*Letters* II, 69–70).

McCarthy, Lillah (1875–1960) English actress. She was the wife of Harley GRANVILLE-BARKER from 1906 to 1918, and later married Sir Frederick William Keeble. In her memoir, *Myself and My Friends* (1933), she makes no mention of Granville-Barker, but has various recollections of Hardy. About 1908 (her dating is not precise), she was performing in John Masefield's play *The Tragedy of Nan.* Hardy appeared backstage after a performance one night and told her breathlessly, "You must play my Tessy, you *must* play my Tessy. I shall send you the play I have made from my book; and you *will* play my Tessy, won't you? "She did not play Tess, but, in 1914, was in the English scenes from *The DYNASTS* at the KINGSWAY THEATRE, LONDON. She reported that the play was a "splendid failure," because it concerned the heroes of 1814 and "London was too grimly aware of the war of 1914 to come and see us." Hardy, she reported, had fled from the theater before the curtain rose, finding the first night too much of an ordeal.

She described Hardy in her memoir as "slight, neatly dressed, of upright carriage, alert, with something in his eye of the retired sea-captain—direct in speech— utterly objective in speaking of his work. He went on growing all his life." She once asked him whether the scene overlooking Christminster University in *JUDE THE OBSCURE* was drawn from the view of Oxford from Boar's Hill (where she and her second husband had reconstructed a house from an old barn). "'No,' he said, 'it was my own hill and the lights that Jude saw were mine too.'"

She was one of the last people to call on Hardy a few weeks before his death. At that time he told her that, although he had stopped writing novels, "'I now tell the story of a novel in verse of twenty lines'" (Lillah McCarthy, *Myself and My Friends,* 101–03).

MacCarthy, Sir Desmond (1877–1952) English essayist, drama critic, and journalist. His periodical writings have been collected into several volumes, including *Portraits* (1931), *Criticism* (1932), *Experience* (1935), *Memories* (1953), *Humanities* (1953), *Drama* (1940), and *The Court Theatre 1904–1907* (1966). MacCarthy edited the NEW QUARTERLY MAGAZINE from 1907 to 1910 and was later literary editor of the *New Statesman.* After 1929 he served as literary critic of the *Sunday Times.* Many of his essays were never collected, nor were his major book projects, such as studies of Byron and Tolstoy, completed. At the age of 54 he dedicated a collection of his essays and reviews to the young Desmond MacCarthy, acknowledging that his younger self was undoubtedly disappointed with what he had accomplished, reading and writing criticism instead of projecting what he thought about the world "into a work of art—a play, a novel, a biography." He and his wife were intimate friends of the younger generation of the avant-garde writers and artists known as Bloomsbury Group, including Frances and Ralph Partridge.

In 1906 MacCarthy asked Hardy to contribute a poem to the *Speaker,* but Hardy replied that he had just sent the only one he had, "The Spring Call," to the *CORNHILL MAGAZINE* (*Letters* III, 203). In September 1906 Hardy learned that MacCarthy and his new wife, Mary (Molly) Warre-Cornish, would be coming to DORCHESTER, and he arranged to go BICYCLING with them. Afterward he suggested that they come out to MAX GATE (*Letters* III, 228). In September 1907 he wrote MacCarthy to say he had nothing suitable on hand for the new magazine (the *New Quarterly*) MacCarthy was editing but sent kind regards to Mrs. MacCarthy and the new baby (Michael) "so far as he cares to receive them" (*Letters* III, 276).

In 1908 MacCarthy again asked Hardy to contribute a poem to the *New Quarterly*. Hardy replied that it was difficult to select "verse that will bear publication in a periodical, where it stands out of harmony with all around it, & suddenly encounters minds unprepared for its mood." He did contribute "The HOUSE OF HOSPITALITIES," which appeared in January 1909 (*Letters* 353–54).

McIlvaine, Clarence (1865–1912) American-born publisher who, in 1890, formed the firm of OSGOOD, MCILVAINE & CO. with the American publisher James Ripley OSGOOD. When the firm was absorbed by HARPER & BROTHERS he became their London representative (*Letters* II, 47). Osgood died in May 1892, and McIlvaine was one of the two chief mourners at his funeral, which Hardy attended.

In March 1897 McIlvaine and his wife attended the copyright performance (actually a reading) of the play of *TESS OF THE D'URBERVILLES* at the St. James's Theatre. This was intended to establish Hardy's English copyright to the play, and was given simultaneously with the opening of the play in New York at the Fifth Avenue Theatre (*Letters* II, 147).

McIlvaine died on December 12, 1912. Hardy was still in deep mourning for his wife Emma HARDY, who had died on November 27. He wrote the general manager of Harper & Brothers that McIlvaine's death had come as a shock; he had had no idea McIlvaine was not in perfect health (*Letters* IV, 254).

For further reading: R. E. Greenland "Hardy in the Osgood, McIlvaine and Harper (London) Editions."

Macmillan & Co. Publishing house founded by two brothers, Alexander Macmillan (1818–96) and Daniel Macmillan (1813–57). In July 1868 Hardy submitted his first novel, *The POOR MAN AND THE LADY*, to the firm. Hearing nothing from them, by September he wrote an anxious letter remarking that with the passage of time his "production," as he called it, had begun to assume a "small & unimportant shape," and that, as the "time & mood" in which he had written it receded, he almost felt he didn't care "what happens to the book, so long as something happens" (*Letters* I, 8). The firm rejected it, much to his disappointment, as did the second publisher, Chapman, and it was never published. Hardy later became a good friend of Alexander Macmillan.

In 1886 the firm included *The MAYOR OF CASTERBRIDGE* in their Colonial Library edition of books intended for sale in India and the British colonies (*Letters* I, 146). Macmillan published *The WOODLANDERS* in three volumes in 1887 and *WESSEX TALES* in two volumes in 1888. They also published the WESSEX EDITION of Hardy's works in 24 volumes (1912–31). Other editions of Hardy's works published by Macmillan included the *Collected Poems* (1919), the Mellstock Edition of his

works in 37 volumes (1919–20), and *The Short Stories of Thomas Hardy* (1928).

Macmillan & Co. became Hardy's principal publishers when his agreements with OSGOOD, MCILVAINE & CO. and HARPER & BROTHERS expired in 1902. When the New York firm Harper & Brothers took over Osgood, McIlvaine, Hardy transferred the rights to Macmillan as a London-based publisher (Purdy, *Thomas Hardy: A Bibliographical Study,* 285).

For further reading: Morgan, *The House of Macmillan.*

Macmillan, Daniel de Mendi (1886–1965) Elder son of the publisher Maurice Macmillan; he became a publisher also, and later headed MACMILLAN & CO. In 1908 Hardy endorsed him for membership in the SAVILE CLUB. He was the elder brother of Harold Macmillan, publisher and British prime minister from 1957 to 1963.

Macmillan, Sir Frederick Orridge (1851–1936) The son of Daniel Macmillan, cofounder of MACMILLAN & CO. publishers, Sir Frederick was the member of the firm with whom Hardy had the most extensive dealings. In addition to corresponding with Hardy about the one-volume edition of *The DYNASTS*, the WESSEX EDITION and several other editions of his works, he negotiated with Hardy about Spanish, French, and Russian translations of his works. From 1885 through 1925 there was a frequent exchange of letters between them.

For further reading: Morgan, *The House of Macmillan.*

Macmillan's Magazine British periodical, established in 1859, whose pages included fiction, nonfiction, and poetry. Hardy's novel *The WOODLANDERS* appeared serially in the magazine from May 1886 to April 1887. In November 1889 he offered *TESS OF THE D'URBERVILLES* to the editor, Mowbray Morris, for serialization, but Morris refused it (Purdy, *Thomas Hardy: A Bibliographical Study,* 73). Hardy revised it, and it was published in the GRAPHIC.

For further reading: Morgan, *The House of Macmillan.*

Magdalene College, Cambridge
In 1913 Hardy was elected an Honorary Fellow of Magdalene College, CAMBRIDGE, founded in 1428. He was inducted into his stall at Chapel on November 1, 1913 (*Letters* IV, 308–309). Masters, Fellows, and Honorary Fellows of Cambridge colleges are assigned individual stalls, or tall carved seats, in the chapel. Fuller MAITLAND painted an oil portrait of him in October 1913, which hangs in the hall at the college along with those of other Fellows.

"Maid of Keinton Mandeville, The" *(A Tribute to Sir H. Bishop)* Poem dated 1915 or 1916, first published in the *ATHENAEUM* for April 30, 1920, and then collected in

LATE LYRICS AND EARLIER (1922). When it was first published the dedication in parentheses read "A tribute to Sir Henry Bishop on the sixty-fifth anniversary of his death: April 30, 1855"; Bishop (1786–1855) composed operas, cantatas, and other music for the Covent Garden Theatre. Two of the four stanzas end with the refrain "Should he upbraid!," a reference to the song "Should He Upbraid" that Bishop composed, for an 1821 production of Shakespeare's *Two Gentlemen of Verona* at the Convent Garden Theatre (Bailey, *The Poetry of Thomas Hardy*, 431–32).

In the *Life* Hardy recalls a concert he attended at "Stower Town" in 1878, when he heard a girl from Keinton Mandeville sing; he describes her as being of "of matchless scope and skill." Hardy states that he and Emma attended the concert in Sturminster; they were living in STURMINSTER NEWTON in 1878. "Stower Town" is Stourton, about 12 miles north (*Life,* 118; Bailey, *The Poetry of Thomas Hardy*, 433).

In the poem, the singer is able to banish her listeners' troubles with her voice.

Maiden Castle   Originally named "Mai Dun," this is an Iron Age hill fort near DORCHESTER. It figures in Hardy's story "A TRYST AT AN ANCIENT EARTH-WORK" an earlier version of which had appeared as "Ancient Earthworks at Casterbridge" (*English Illustrated Magazine*, December 1893). A photograph of the castle served as the frontispiece to *A CHANGED MAN AND OTHER TALES.* Excavations at Maiden Castle after Hardy's death revealed thousands of Chesil Beach pebbles from PORTLAND (known as the "Isle of Slingers") assembled for sling stones.

In February 1900 exercises were held at the castle for the Yeomanry for South Africa, who were bound for the BOER WAR. Hardy wrote his friend Winifred THOMSON, an artist, that his thoughts were "all Kahki [*sic*] colour" (*Letters* II, 247).

Mail, Michael   The eldest of the Mellstock singers in *UNDER THE GREENWOOD TREE.* He plays the second violin. He is delighted to hear of the cask of port wine being opened for the choir by Reuben DEWY before they make their rounds, serenading each village house on Christmas Eve.

Maitland, R. E. Fuller (unknown)   Figure and portrait painter. After Hardy was elected an Honorary Fellow of MAGDALENE COLLEGE, CAMBRIDGE, in 1913, just after he had received the honorary degree of Litt.D. The master of Magdalene, A. C. BENSON, wrote Hardy that he wanted to arrange for Maitland to paint Hardy's portrait. In October 1913 Hardy wrote Benson that if Magdalene were to honor him "with a wish for a sketch of me" he would sit for it at any convenient time and place. He invited Maitland to stay at MAX GATE while

painting. At the time, Hardy was living there alone; Emma HARDY had died in 1912, and Hardy did not marry Florence Dugdale (HARDY) until February 1914. Benson paid for the portrait himself. Hardy noted in the *Life* that "a good sketch-painting of him" was made by the artist that autumn and would be hung with the other portraits in the hall of Magdalene College.

"Man He Killed, The"   Poem written in 1902 and first printed in *HARPER'S WEEKLY* (New York) and then in the *SPHERE* (London) and collected in *TIME'S LAUGHING-STOCKS AND OTHER VERSES* (1909). This note originally appeared at the head of the poem "Scene: *The settle of the Fox Inn, Stagfood Lane.* Characters: *The speaker (a returned soldier) and his friends, natives of the hamlet*" (Purdy, *Thomas Hardy: A Bibliographical Study,* 147).

The speaker recalls killing another soldier during the BOER WAR, and reflecting, sometime after his return to England, that if they had only met by "some old ancient inn" they would have sat down together to "wet/Right many a nipperkin!" But, face to face, they shot at each other, each believing the other to be his foe. He speculates that the other soldier had enlisted for the same reason he had—"out of work—had sold his traps—/No other reason why." War causes behavior that is completely unnatural, inciting the young soldier to "shoot a fellow down," although, if he met him in peacetime, he would be glad to treat him to a drink in a bar or give him half a crown. Hardy had been very upset by the war, and had seen many DORSET men embark for South Africa.

"Man Was Drawing Near to Me, A"   Poem published in *LATE LYRICS AND EARLIER* (1922). The manuscript has, in parentheses after the title, "Woman's Song." The narrator of the poem is Emma Gifford, Hardy's future wife, who is on the Cornish coast without any thought of Hardy's imminent arrival to work as an architect at St. Juliot Rectory in 1870. The poem is a companion to "The WIND'S PROPHECY," which describes their meeting from Hardy's point of view.

In the *Life,* Hardy quotes from Emma HARDY's volume *SOME RECOLLECTIONS:* "It was on a lovely Monday evening in March . . . that we were on the *qui-vive* for the stranger. . ." They knew that Hardy, the "stranger," would have had a long and tedious journey with many different train connections. In the poem Hardy mentions some of the actual villages along the way, such as Halworthy, Otterham, Tresparret Posts, and Hennett Byre.

In the poem Emma had been thinking of the "trifles—legends, ghosts" that are typical of the folklore of the Cornish coast near TINTAGEL. There was nothing to let her "understand" that "the man was getting nigh and nigher." When he arrives he had a gaze "that bore / My destiny." The poem ends with the visitor's arrival and does not reveal the circumstances that had caused Emma to be thinking of legends and ghosts.

In *Some Recollections,* however, it is clear that Emma apparently had been thinking of writing about CORN-WALL herself. Only 16 miles away, actual witchcraft was secretly practiced, and she had visited a woman in the parish who told her tales and revealed her experiences as a servant. Emma found the "country stories" fascinating (*Some Recollections,* quoted by Bailey in *The Poetry of Thomas Hardy,* 443–44).

Manston, Aeneas   Character in *DESPERATE REMEDIES.* He is the illegitimate son of Cytherea ALDCLYFFE. She follows his career with great interest but does not try to make contact with him until after the death of her father, when she inherits a large estate and makes him her steward. He has secretly married an actress, Eunice, but falls in love with Miss Aldclyffe's companion, Cytherea GRAYE, whom his mother had schemed to introduce to him. Eunice comes to find Manston, but apparently dies in a fire at an inn as she waits for him. Manston persuades Cytherea to marry him, but, before the wedding, Eunice reappears. He strikes and kills her, then stores her body in an old wall oven. A witness, however, claims to have seen Eunice escape from the fire. He produces an impersonator, but loses Cytherea. He is then seen disposing of Eunice's body, but still tries desperately to pursue Cytherea. He is captured and sent to prison, where he writes a confession and then commits suicide.

Manston, Eunice   Character in *DESPERATE REMEDIES.* A Philadelphia-born actress, she marries Aeneas MANSTON in Liverpool. After he becomes steward at Knapwater House he summons her from London to Carriford, the nearby village where he lives. She stays at the Three Tranters Inn, but there is a tragic fire. She escapes and confronts Manston. They quarrel and he strikes her a fatal blow. He stores her body in a wall oven and tries to make it appear that she had died in the fire. A witness, however, has seen Eunice after the fire. Manston secures a woman to impersonate Eunice, but is discovered as he attempts to bury Eunice's body. He is sent to prison, where he kills himself.

"Marchioness of Stonehenge, The"   Short story. *See GROUP OF NOBLE DAMES, A.*

Mark, King   The king of CORNWALL in *The FAMOUS TRAGEDY OF THE QUEEN OF CORNWALL.* King Mark sends his nephew, Tristram, from TINTAGEL CASTLE in Lyonnesse to Ireland to bring back his bride, the dark Iseult, an Irish princess. On the homeward voyage Tristram and Iseult drink a love-potion. King Mark and the dark Iseult marry, although she has fallen in love with Tristram. Tristram, however, has gone abroad and married the fair Iseult of Brittany (Iseult the Whitehanded).

The dark Iseult sails to Brittany to find Tristram but is told he is dead. Tristram is told that the Queen has never come to Brittany. He discovers the falsehood and returns to Cornwall, disguised as a harper; Iseult the Whitehanded follows him. King Mark stabs Tristram and he dies; Queen Iseult stabs King Mark and leaps over the cliff to her death. Iseult the Whitehanded returns to Brittany.

Markton   Fictional name for Dunster in *A LAODICEAN.*

Marlott   Fictional name for Marnhull, in the Vale of Blackmoor, in *TESS OF THE D'URBERVILLES.*

Marston, Edward (1825–1914)   Publisher and partner in the London publishing firm of Sampson Low, Marston, Searle & Rivington. Hardy dealt with both Edward Marston and his son, R. B. Marston. Between 1881 and 1893, a number of Hardy's novels were published in a cheap format by the company (*Letters* I, 171). These included *FAR FROM THE MADDING CROWD, The HAND OF ETHELBERTA, The RETURN OF THE NATIVE, The TRUMPET-MAJOR, A LAODICEAN, TWO ON A TOWER,* and *The MAYOR OF CASTERBRIDGE.*

For further reading: E. Marston, *After Work: Fragments from the Workshop of an Old Publisher.*

Martin, Julia Augusta Pitney (unknown–1893)   The wife of Francis Pitney Brouncker Martin; they lived at KINGSTON MAURWARD, which he had purchased in 1844, near DORCHESTER. This house was the model for Knapwater House in *DESPERATE REMEDIES.* They had no children, and she took a great interest in Hardy. She built a small private school, the Bockhampton School, which he attended for a year when he was eight years old (*see* EDUCATION OF HARDY) She took credit for teaching him to write; he was already a good reader. She was disappointed and even quarreled with Hardy's mother, Jemima HARDY, when she sent him to the British School in Dorchester, founded by Isaac Glandfield LAST. Martin believed Mrs. Hardy had not only deserted her school but also abandoned Anglican precepts (Millgate, *Thomas Hardy: A Biography,* 46). The quarrel led to Hardy's father's losing the estate business (he was a builder).

Hardy had become very attached to Martin, and remained so for many years (see the poem "HE REVISITS HIS FIRST SCHOOL" for a description of his feelings on returning to this school). In the *Life* he states that his "feeling for her was almost that of a lover." In the autumn of 1850, when Hardy was 10, he was taken by one of the local farmer's daughters to a harvest supper in an old barracks on the Kingston Maurward estate. Most of the young people were much older than he and included noncommissioned officers from the barracks (which he recalled when writing *The DYNASTS* and *The TRUMPET-MAJOR*).

According to Hardy, Mrs. Martin arrived and teased him, saying "O Tommy, how is this? I thought you had deserted me!" He assured her tearfully he had not deserted her and never would. She introduced him to a small niece of hers, with whom he danced several times. The manor party then left the gathering. The farmer's daughter who had brought him stayed on, dancing, until three in the morning. Young Tommy was afraid to ask anyone for food or drink, although he knew Mrs. Martin would have certainly given him both, and seen that he was taken home. He notes that this was the only harvest supper he attended until he was an adult, but he recalled years afterward the ballads he had heard (F. E. Hardy, *The Life of Thomas Hardy*, 18–21).

In 1897 he wrote a friend, Mrs. William Mundy, that he had known Martin in his "younger days, & liked her much" (*Letters* II, 179).

Martin, Mrs. ("Gammer")   In *TWO ON A TOWER*, Mrs. Martin is the widow of Giles Martin and the maternal grandmother of Swithin ST. CLEEVE, who lives with her at Welland Bottom. She is an active participant in community affairs.

Marygreen   Small village in the hills south of Wantage, Berkshire. This was the home of Jude FAWLEY of *JUDE THE OBSCURE*, who lived there with his aunt, Drusilla FAWLEY. Hardy modeled it on the village of Fawley, the childhood home of Mary HARDY, his beloved paternal grandmother, who lived with his family when he was a child. Some of his Hardy ancestors are buried there (Pinion, *A Hardy Companion*, 402).

Masefield, John (1878–1967)   English poet, playwright, and fiction writer; he was poet laureate of England from 1930 until his death and received the ORDER OF MERIT in 1935. His works include *Salt Water Ballads, The Tragedy of Nan and Other Plays, A Mainsail Haul*, the verse narrative *The Everlasting Mercy, Ballads and Poems*, and *Basilissa*, a fictional biography of Empress Theodora. His *Gallipoli* is a noted account of that WORLD WAR I campaign.

In November 1911 Masefield sent Hardy a copy of *The Everlasting Mercy*. Hardy wrote to thank him, mentioning that he had bought *Ballads and Poems* and marked several poems he liked, including "The Emigrant" and "The Death Rooms" (*Letters* IV, 189). Hardy sent Masefield a presentation copy (direct from the publisher) of *SATIRES OF CIRCUMSTANCE* when it was published by MACMILLAN in 1914. In September of the same year, shortly after World War I began, Masefield, Hardy, and John GALSWORTHY were among a group of "well-known men of letters" summoned by the chancellor of the Duchy of Lancaster to Wellington House, Buckingham Gate, LONDON, for the purpose of formulating "public statements of the strength of the British case and principles in the war" (*Life*, 366).

In September 1916 Masefield sent him his *Sonnets and Poems*, and Hardy answered that his wife had read some of them to him; he especially praised "Night is on the downland," observing that the scenery was very familiar to him.

In February 1920 Hardy was invited to receive an honorary degree of Doctor of Letters from OXFORD UNIVERSITY, to be presented at the time he was attending a performance of *The DYNASTS* at the theater there. He and Mrs. Hardy went by train, although the members of the Oxford University Debating Society had promised to send a car for him. The degree was presented at the Sheldonian Theatre. In the afternoon they went to see the home of Sir Walter Raleigh and his wife; Masefield was there.

In October 1921 the Masefields went to see Hardy at MAX GATE, taking with them a model of a full-rigged ship made by Masefield called the *Triumph*. In June 1923 the Hardys went to Oxford to stay two nights at QUEEN'S COLLEGE, of which Hardy had been made an Honorary Fellow in 1922. Godfrey Elton escorted them about Oxford. Hardy was tireless and eager to revisit many sites he recalled from his youth. Elton described him as possessing "a bird-like alertness and a rare and charming youthfulness—interested in everything he saw, and cultured, but surely not much occupied with books" (*Life*, 421). They then went to see the Masefields at their house at Boar's Hill, near Oxford.

Masefield built a private theater in the large music room at his home, and in 1924 he asked Hardy whether he might stage *The FAMOUS TRAGEDY OF THE QUEEN OF CORNWALL* there and sent a sketch of its layout. Hardy answered that he was honored by the request, and consented. He did not, however, feel up to coming to see it. The play was performed several times in January 1925 (*Letters* VI, 303).

"Master John Horseleigh, Knight"   Short story published in the Summer Number, 1893, of the *Illustrated London News*, with a headpiece and four illustrations by W. B. Wollen. It was published in America in *McClure's Magazine* in July 1893, with illustrations by Harry C. Edwards. It was later collected in *A CHANGED MAN AND OTHER TALES* (1913).

The story is told by a "thin-faced gentleman" who purports to have taken it from an old volume of the Havenpool (Poole) marriage register. It records the 1539 marriage of Master John Horseleigh to Edith, the widow of John Stocker. The official family pedigree, however, omits this marriage, but mentions his marrying, at an earlier date, another woman, who gave him two daughters and a son.

There is a local tradition that, in 1540 or 1541, a young sailor only known as Roger returned to Havenpool, his home. His sister Edith had married Stocker, who was part owner of the brig in which Roger had sailed. He learns from villagers of Stocker's death and Edith's remarriage to an older stranger from Oozewood who seemed to be untrustworthy and was suspected of already being married. Roger finds his sister in a small house, holding an infant. She says the baby is her husband John's, whom she had married six months after John Stocker's death. Her husband lives in a nearby town and visits her, but the marriage is not supposed to be known. They married quietly in the church at Havenpool, without any of her husband's friends present.

Suddenly master (Sir) John Horseleigh arrives to see Edith. Roger hides until he leaves and follows him through the countryside; he avoids high roads. He enters the gates of a park known as the Vale of Blackmoor and sees a fine manor house, which John enters. Roger spends the night in some hay, and, the next morning, Sunday, sees John enter a chapel on the estate in the company of three children. He asks a servant who they are, and is told he is Master John Horseleigh, knight, and his family. Roger is horrified and worried about the disgrace to his father's name. He goes to CASTERBRIDGE for several days, drinking in taverns, and the next Saturday returns to his sister. He tells her the truth and hides, eavesdropping, while Sir John comes for his weekly visit.

Sir John guesses who has told her, and Roger emerges from hiding. They have a fight and Roger fatally stabs him. Before he dies, Sir John states that Dame Horseleigh is actually the wife of another man. Sir John had thought he had married her as a widow, but then discovered that her husband, Decimus Strong, was still alive in France. Since she had not been a widow, her children were illegitimate. The king had urged Sir John to marry another woman secretly and have legitimate issue.

Soon after Sir John's death his child by Edith also dies. Edith and the clergyman who had married them in the church at Havenpool conceal the facts, and she retires with a nurse companion until her death. Her brother leaves England. Sir John's illegitimate son inherits the estate and honors, and Sir John's only lawful marriage, to Edith in the church at Havenpool, is not disclosed.

"Maumbury Ring"   Article published in the *Times* on October 9, 1908, dealing with the execution of Mary Channing in Maumbury Rings, Dorchester, on March 21, 1705 or 1706, for the crime of poisoning her husband. The exact year is disputed. An ancestor of Hardy's was present at the execution, and the subject had engaged his interest. There is an amphitheater at Maumbury Rings dating from pre-Roman times. At the time Hardy published the article, which had been commissioned by Moberly Bell, manager of the newspaper, there were excavations at the site that had attracted much attention (Purdy, *Thomas Hardy: A Bibliographical Study,* 312).

Max Gate   The home of Hardy in DORCHESTER, completed in 1885. The name derives from the fact that a small cottage once stood on the opposite side of the road belonging to Henry Mack, the tollgate keeper; his gate was known as Mack's Gate.

Hardy's quest for a building site began when he and his wife Emma HARDY were still living at 1 Arundel Terrace, Trinity Road, Upper Tooting, LONDON, near Wandsworth Common, and continued after they moved to The Avenue, Wimborne, DORSET, in the summer of 1881. Hardy was able to lease land from the Duchy of Cornwall. When the house was finished, Hardy paid the price agreed upon, £450, a large sum at the time. The freehold was conveyed in September 1886.

In late 1883 preparatory work on the site had begun; Hardy and his wife were then living at SHIRE-HALL PLACE, Dorchester. Before the house was completed, Hardy planted several thousand trees on his property. Hardy's father and brother were the builders, with very few men working at any one time, and this delayed construction. Romano-British skeletons, urns, and relics were uncovered as the foundations were dug. On May 13, 1884, Hardy read a paper before the members of the DORSET NATURAL HISTORY AND ANTIQUARIAN FIELD CLUB (or "the Field Club," as he usually called it), titled "Some Romano-British Relics Found at Max Gate, Dorchester" (Millgate, *Thomas Hardy,* 245; *Letters* VII, 100). The Hardys were able to occupy the house by June 1885, first sleeping there on June 29.

The red brick house, which Hardy called a villa, had two stories and an attic. The ground floor had a large central hall between a dining room and drawing room; the kitchen and scullery were at the rear. On the second floor there were two bedrooms, a water closet, a storage room, and a study. The house was not connected to municipal water, but had a well. Servants pumped water into a roof tank every morning, which

The Maumbury Rings, south of Dorchester, were built in the Stone Age as a sacred circle; the Romans converted the site into an amphitheater.   (John Gould, Phillips Academy, Andover)

Max Gate   (Beinecke Rare Book and Manuscript Library, Yale University)

provided running cold water in the kitchen and made it possible to have a flushing toilet. The attic had accommodations for servants. Several extensions were later made to the house, and, before her death, Emma moved into two attic rooms that had been renovated for her. Hardy's study, which was relocated during later renovations, was always on the second floor and deliberately placed far away from household activities and callers.

The grounds were well planned, with gardens, lawns, an orchard, and, eventually, a pet cemetery. Hardy tried to include many trees and shrubs of English origin. Visitors had mixed reactions to the house; Arthur Christopher BENSON called it "mean & pretentious," but George GISSING considered it "very nice." Architects have criticized the house because of the asymmetry of windows and turrets on the front and Hardy's failure to follow a particular style such as Gothic, Saxon, or neoclassical. Window sizes were determined by the function of the room and the degree of sunlight at differing times of the year. Although the plumbing seemed antiquated by the 1920s, for the 1880s, it was a "comfortable and well-equipped house" (Millgate, *Thomas Hardy: A Biography,* 256–59).

Hardy lived at Max Gate for more than 40 years. After Emma's death in 1912, he married Florence Dugdale (HARDY) in 1914. He died in his bedroom of heart disease in 1928.

For further reading: Collins, "Talks with Thomas Hardy at Max Gate, 1920–1922"; Jesty, "Max Gate and a Neolithic Causewayed Enclosure"; Jones, "Afternoon Tea—Max Gate, 1913"; Weber, "Two Fires at Max Gate."

Maybold, Parson   Character in *UNDER THE GREENWOOD TREE.* The new parson at MELLSTOCK church, he is "well-intentioned" and can write a sermon, but not "put it into words and speak it." He alienates the Mellstock choir by attempting to replace the instrumentalists with an organist, Fancy DAY, in whom he has a romantic interest. He is vexed when she expects him to officiate at her wedding.

"Mayfair Lodgings, At"   *See* "AT MAYFAIR LODGINGS."

Mayor of Casterbridge, The   This novel was first published serially in England in the *GRAPHIC* from January 2 to May 15, 1886, and in America in *HARPER'S WEEKLY* from January 2 to May 15, 1886. The American installments were, for the most part, set from proofs of the *Graphic*. The text underwent considerable revision before being published in two volumes by SMITH, ELDER & CO. on May 10, 1886. Hardy may have begun the novel in the spring of 1884 and finished in April 1885; it was written at SHIRE-HALL PLACE, DORCHESTER, where he and Emma HARDY lived while MAX GATE was being completed (Purdy, *Thomas Hardy: A Bibliographical Study*, 52–53).

The Mayor of Casterbridge is set in the fictional towns of Weydon-Priors (Weyhill, Hampshire) and CASTER-BRIDGE (Dorchester). In his preface to the 1912 24-volume WESSEX EDITION of his works, Hardy states that the incidents in the novel arise from three events: "the sale of a wife by her husband, the uncertain harvests which immediately preceded the repeal of the Corn Laws, and the visit of a royal personage to the aforesaid part of England." He asserts that the story was "more particularly a study of one man's deeds and character than, perhaps, any other" of those included in his "exhibition of Wessex life."

Hardy apparently found the nucleus of the plot in 1884 while paging through old issues of the *Dorset County Chronicle*. He came across an item about a man who sold his wife for £5. Hardy derived the character of Michael HENCHARD from the autobiography of J. F. Pennie, a debt-ridden writer for the *Chronicle* whose various projects were doomed by his quarrelsome nature. Hardy noted that Pennie was, "seemingly, a man who had chiefly himself to blame for the vicissitudes of his life" (Turner, *The Life of Thomas Hardy*, 92). Henchard is the first of Hardy's major characters to dominate the novel throughout. In this respect *The Mayor of Casterbridge* paves the way for *TESS OF THE D'URBERVILLES* and *JUDE THE OBSCURE*, the other two novels in which Hardy focuses on what Hawkins terms "the display of a single soul in its totality" (Hawkins, *Hardy: Novelist and Poet*, 94).

SYNOPSIS

Chapter 1

In the opening scenes of the novel, Michael Henchard and his wife, Susan HENCHARD, with the infant Elizabeth-Jane HENCHARD (1), wearily approach the small hamlet of Weydon-Priors in the late afternoon, with dwindling funds, searching for work. It is Fair Day in the village but the real business has been concluded for the day, and no work seems to be available. They visit a refreshment tent for "furmity," a warm, nourishing mixture similar to gruel. Henchard perceives that, for a fee, the gypsy-like woman proprietor will lace it with rum—rum that has been illegally smuggled in, as Susan comprehends. As Henchard orders more and more fortified furmity, he becomes, in turn, "serene, . . . jovial, . . . argumentative, . . . over-

bearing, and . . . quarrelsome." The evening ends with his auctioning off Susan to a cheerful passing sailor, Richard NEWSON. She takes the child and disappears with Newson. The scene is one of the most striking in all of Hardy's works, equivalent to Frank TROY's sword exercise in front of Bathsheba EVERDENE in *FAR FROM THE MADDING CROWD* or Arabella DONN's throwing of the pig's pizzle (penis) at Jude FAWLEY in *JUDE THE OBSCURE*. Each of the three incidents has clear sexual implications that are played out in the remainder of the novel.

Chapter 2

The next morning, sober, Henchard searches in vain for Susan. He vows to abstain from drink for 21 years, and goes to Casterbridge in order to find work.

Chapter 3

It is 20 years later. Susan and Elizabeth-Jane, now grown up, visit Weydon-Priors, find the furmity vendor (now without her tent, out in a field), and learn that a year after Henchard sold his wife, he had returned to the village. He asked the woman to tell Susan, if she ever inquired, that he had gone to Casterbridge.

Chapter 4

Susan has never told Elizabeth-Jane the true story of her life. She and Newson had lived in Canada for several years and returned to Falmouth. Her illegal relationship with him had grown increasingly burdensome to her, and she had told him she could not live with him any longer. He left on a ship bound for Bank of Newfoundland; news of his presumed drowning reached Susan. Susan decides to search for Henchard, and she and her daughter go to Casterbridge.

Chapter 5

They make tentative inquires about Henchard, whom Susan has portrayed to Elizabeth-Jane as "our distant relative." Trying to buy bread, they are told it is no good because of "grown wheat." In England the grain called "corn" is actually what Americans know as "wheat." When wheat sprouts before it is reaped, it is called "grown wheat" and makes inferior bread. From the street they observe a grand dinner taking place at the King's Arms Hotel with Henchard facing the window. They learn from bystanders that he is now the mayor of Casterbridge and a prosperous corn merchant. His wine glasses are empty; the townspeople explain that he has taken a vow of temperance and it will not expire for two more years. He is now the "powerfullest member of the Town Council." They blame him, however, for the defective grain.

Chapter 6

A young Scotsman, Donald FARFRAE, comes to town, passes a note to Henchard, and inquires about a moderate hotel. The Three Mariners is recommended.

Susan and Elizabeth-Jane also go to the hotel. After the dinner, Henchard goes to the Three Mariners.

Chapter 7

Finding the hotel expensive, Elizabeth-Jane offers her services as waitress to reduce their lodging fee. She serves Farfrae his dinner in his room, next to theirs. She takes dinner for herself and Susan up to their room, where they overhear Henchard talking with Farfrae. Henchard has mistaken him for an applicant as manager of his corn business. Farfrae has an invention that will improve the bad wheat. He refuses to take payment and turns down the job Henchard offers.

Chapter 8

Farfrae goes downstairs and Elizabeth-Jane removes his supper tray. She hears him singing moving Scottish ballads in the sitting room. The company beg him to stay in Casterbridge but he insists he is bound for the port of Bristol. He and Elizabeth-Jane pass each other on the stairs; she is very attracted to him.

Chapter 9

The next morning Susan and Farfrae both look from their windows at Henchard, who is outside on the street. Farfrae comes out with his carpet bag and he and Henchard continue their conversation. Susan decides to send a note to Henchard, which her daughter takes to his home. It is market day in Casterbridge. Elizabeth-Jane is directed to Henchard's office, where she discovers Farfrae, who has been persuaded to stay in Casterbridge.

Chapter 10

Joshua JOPP, whom Henchard had been expecting as the new manager, arrives; Henchard says he had expected him on Thursday and has now engaged someone else. Jopp says he thought it was either Thursday or Saturday, but Henchard says he is too late. Jopp leaves in anger. Elizabeth-Jane arrives and says a "distant relative," Susan Newson, is in town, and wonders whether Henchard would like to see her. She says she is Susan's daughter. Henchard comprehends that Susan has never told Elizabeth-Jane the full story. He sends Susan a note and five guineas, inviting her to meet him at the Ring on the Budmouth Road that night. He asks her to "keep the girl in ignorance" until then. The money tacitly suggests he has "bought her back again." Susan lets Elizabeth-Jane think the meeting is at Henchard's home.

Chapter 11

Henchard and Susan meet at the Ring (the old Roman amphitheater). He tells her he thought they had died or emigrated; he advertised and took "every possible step" to find them. He dreads Elizabeth-Jane's discovering the truth about the wife sale, and fears it will jeopardize his standing in Casterbridge. He asks that Susan and her daughter take a cottage in town; she will be

known as the "widow Mrs. Newson," and he will meet, court, and marry her as though they had just met. She can think it over in lodgings over the china-shop in High Street, for which he will provide funds.

Chapter 12

Farfrae applies himself to straightening Henchard's books; Henchard invites him for dinner and tells him about the wife sale and Susan's reappearance. Farfrae is stunned; he had heard that Henchard was a widower. Henchard confesses he has been intimate with a young woman from Jersey and become engaged to her. He says he must send a "useful sum of money" to her, and also explains that Elizabeth-Jane does not know who he is.

Chapter 13

Henchard rents a cottage for Susan under the name of Newson and installs her and Elizabeth-Jane there with ornate furniture and a servant. He calls on them several times and asks Susan to name the day for their wedding. The Casterbridge people are surprised by his courtship, as he had hitherto been indifferent to women. Susan has become pale and fragile, but they marry in a crowded church while "idlers," local people of a lower social order, wait outside and exchange gossip.

Chapter 14

Susan and Elizabeth-Jane are installed in Henchard's grand home; Elizabeth-Jane, particularly, appreciates the fine furniture and prosperity, but remains circumspect and modest in her clothing. She has the "field-mouse fear of the coulter of destiny despite fair promise" that is "common among the thoughtful who have suffered early from poverty and oppression." Henchard notices that her hair is light brown and asks Susan whether it had not appeared likely to become black when she was a baby. Susan is discomfited by the question. He offers to change Elizabeth-Jane's family name to Henchard, but she is startled, and nothing is done. Meanwhile, Farfrae manages Henchard's business very successfully. Having been taken into Henchard's confidence, he becomes interested in both mother and daughter.

Elizabeth-Jane receives a note asking her to meet the writer at a granary; she assumes the note is from Henchard and goes there. Farfrae approaches and she climbs in the granary so as not to meet him alone. Farfrae has received a duplicate of her note. Neither can imagine who has summoned them, but they fall into conversation.

Chapter 15

Although Elizabeth-Jane has resolved not to indulge in "gay fancies in the matter of clothes," when Henchard gives her a box of tinted gloves she finds she must have a bonnet to go with the gloves and a dress and sunshade to go with both. Casterbridge decides, falsely, she has been "artful" in her modesty. She feels "unfinished," though; she cannot speak Italian or "use globes" and has no finishing-school accomplishments.

One of Henchard's workers, Abel WHITTLE, invariably oversleeps unless his fellow workers get him up. Henchard goes to his house and calls him at 4 A.M.; Whittle comes to work without his breeches; Farfrae says he can go home and dress; Henchard and Farfrae quarrel over this decision. Another incident occurs, but they make up and renew their friendship. Nevertheless, Henchard regrets having confided in Farfrae.

Chapter 16
Henchard stops inviting Farfrae in for impromptu meals. Farfrae begins planning a public entertainment on a holiday to which he will charge admission. Henchard decides to plan his own free celebration on an upland that is a favorite town gathering place. He plans games, a stage, free tea, and other enticements. Farfrae's own entertainment is on a street beneath with cloths hung from trees. It rains, and Henchard's project fails. The weather clears, but the people have all gone to Farfrae's tent. Henchard finds it is like the nave of a cathedral with Farfrae doing Highland dancing inside; he is much admired by the girls. Henchard is sarcastic to Farfrae, and says he will soon be leaving. Farfrae agrees to resign. Henchard regrets his hasty action immediately.

Chapter 17
Elizabeth-Jane has learned that, as the mayor's stepdaughter, she made a mistake dancing in public. Farfrae escorts her home and tells her he has offended her stepfather and will soon be leaving. He then lets it be known that he will not be leaving town but has joined a rival corn merchant. Henchard, beneath his jovial public face, still has the same "unruly volcanic stuff" beneath the surface as he had years earlier at the wife sale. He resolves to beat Farfrae in business and asks Elizabeth-Jane not to see him again. Henchard writes Farfrae and requests that he not court her, although it would have helped both of them if he were Henchard's son-in-law. Farfrae thinks there is room in town for both of them to do business. He turns down Henchard's customers, but still prospers. His character, Hardy suggests, is responsible for his success. He and Henchard launch a price war.

Chapter 18
After Susan HENCHARD and her daughter come to live with Michael HENCHARD, Susan becomes seriously ill. Henchard receives a letter from Lucetta LE SUEUR, whom he has courted in Jersey even though he was still married to Susan, saying she is going to Bristol to see her only relative, who is wealthy. She will travel via Casterbridge and Budmouth, and hopes she can meet him at the Antelope Hotel, where the coach horses are changed, and return her "letters and other trifles." Hen-

chard meets the coach, but Lucetta does not appear. After Susan's death, Lucetta comes to Casterbridge. She visits Susan Henchard's grave, standing by it a long time. Elizabeth observes her and introduces herself as Susan's daughter. Soon the mysterious lady invites Elizabeth to live with her as companion at High-Place Hall, her new home. She introduces herself as Miss TEMPLEMAN, from Jersey. She writes Henchard that she has come to live in Casterbridge at High-Place Hall. She signs her letter "Lucette [Lucetta] Le Sueur." Henchard assumes at first that Miss Templeman is Lucette's relative, but then deduces that they are the same person. Lucetta writes him again, explaining that she has inherited considerable property from her widowed aunt, Mrs. Templeman, and has taken her name to escape from her own "and its wrongs" (*M.C.*, Chapters 20–22).

Chapter 19
Three weeks after Susan's funeral, Henchard and Elizabeth-Jane converse by the fire. He asks if Newson was a kind father, and whether she could have loved Henchard if he were her father instead of Newson. Feeling estranged from Farfrae and bereft by Susan's death, Henchard then tells Elizabeth-Jane that he is her father, but not about the wife sale. Elizabeth-Jane begins weeping. He asks if she will take his name. She agrees, but is still upset; she feels she is doing a wrong to Newson. Henchard goes upstairs and finds the letter Susan has left. The seal has cracked and it is open. He reads it. Susan says their daughter actually died three months after the wife sale; the present Elizabeth-Jane has the same name, but is Newson's daughter (*see* HENCHARD, ELIZABETH JANE [2]).

Wondering if it is true, he looks at the young woman, sleeping, and can see Newson's features on her face. He goes for a long, depressing walk by the county jail. The next morning Elizabeth-Jane greets him as her father, but he takes no pleasure in it.

Chapter 20
Elizabeth-Jane is bewildered by Henchard's shift in attitude; he has become cold and constrained. He mocks her for using dialect words (she learns in time to avoid them) and for her large handwriting. He scolds her for taking cider and ale to Nance MOCKRIDGE, a woman who makes hay-bonds on their premises. Nance says Elizabeth-Jane has "waited on worse" people than herself, and tells him about Elizabeth-Jane's having assisting at the Three Mariners when she and Susan first arrived. He proceeds to ignore Elizabeth-Jane, who applies herself to her books and studies Latin. She often visits Susan's grave and discovers there, one morning, another woman reading the inscription on her grave.

Henchard discovers that Donald Farfrae is to be elected to the town council and will replace him. He writes Farfrae and encourages his courtship of Elizabeth-Jane.

Meanwhile, Elizabeth-Jane talks with the woman she has seen visiting the grave, who invites her to live with her as a housekeeper and companion. The lady tells her she is moving from Budmouth to Casterbridge and will be living at High-Place Hall. They will discuss the matter in a week.

Chapter 21
Elizabeth-Jane goes to look at the exterior of High-Place Hall, a rather forbidding Palladian mansion overlooking the marketplace, an undesirable location. The front door is open; men are going in and out with packing cases. She goes through the house and out the back door, beneath a keystone which has a forbidding leering mask. Henchard enters the house, but he does not see her. At home, he is indifferent to where she goes, but he offers her a small annuity. Elizabeth meets Miss Templeman in the churchyard. They agree she should come immediately, and she hires a small carriage to convey her luggage, much to the astonishment of Henchard, who had thought she would be leaving "next month, or next year." He begs her not to leave, but she says she must go—but can return. He is stunned when she tells him she is going to High-Place Hall.

Chapter 22
The evening before, Henchard had received a letter from Lucetta announcing that she had come to occupy High-Place Hall. He had known her by the name of Lucette Le Sueur so had not recognized her as Miss Templeman. Lucetta writes that she invited Elizabeth-Jane to live with her to give Henchard an excuse for calling on her. He thinks she is "artful."

Elizabeth-Jane arrives to find Miss Templeman playing cards. She says she has only had a fortune a brief time; she grew up as the daughter of an army officer. She states that she is from Jersey, but her "people" really belong to Bath. The Le Sueurs are an old Jersey family. The next morning the women sit at the window overlooking the market place where "gibbous human shapes" pass back and forth; they represent "ready money." Henchard does not call on Lucetta. Elizabeth-Jane says he doesn't come because he has "taken against" her, his stepdaughter, which causes Miss Templeman to burst into tears.

During the CANDLEMAS Fair, Lucetta sends Elizabeth-Jane out on some errands and asks her to visit the town museum. She then summons Henchard, but it is Donald Farfrae who arrives.

Chapter 23
Farfrae explains that he has been searching for Miss Henchard. Lucetta tells him, falsely, that she will soon arrive. They look at the busy hiring fair in progress outside the windows, and Farfrae explains his business success. She tells him she admires Scotsmen because they are both warm and cold, passionate and frigid, all at the same time. They overhear a dialogue between a farmer and a young man who, if he accepts the job to support his father, must part from the girl he loves. Farfrae decides to hire both the father and son, exciting Lucetta's admiration. Lucetta "longs for some ark" of safety and, though Farfrae is younger, she is appealing to him; he has all but forgotten Elizabeth-Jane. She turns Henchard away and welcomes Elizabeth-Jane on her return.

Chapter 24
Elizabeth-Jane knows nothing of Farfrae's interest in Lucetta, but loves the situation of her house with its constant activity outside. They both watch for him on market day. They see a horse-drill, an enormous and fascinating new farm machine, which Farfrae has been responsible for bringing to town. Elizabeth guesses that Lucetta is interested in Farfrae. She asks Elizabeth-Jane how many "good" years she has before she becomes plain. Elizabeth tells her five, or, with a "quiet life," 10.

Chapter 25
Farfrae calls on Lucetta, and Elizabeth is all but invisible in the room. Henchard proposes to Lucetta, but she does not accept him at once. He and Farfrae vie for her affections.

Chapter 26
Henchard, frustrated by Lucetta's behavior, tries to ascertain whether Farfrae is his rival. They both call on Lucetta. They both accept the same long slice of bread, pulling it in two. Henchard hires Jopp, who had originally thought Farfrae's job was his. Henchard consults a "man of curious repute as a forecaster or weather-prophet" outside of town. He is told the harvest two weeks away will be "rain and tempest." Henchard makes an expensive mistake backing bad weather and buying and storing grain; when the weather turns out to be good, prices go down. He must borrow from the bank. He blames Jopp and dismisses him, making an enemy of him.

Chapter 27
Bad weather sets in just as harvesting begins, but it is too late for Henchard to profit. He feels someone is "roasting a waxen image" of him, bringing him bad luck. Farfrae prospers. Their respective drivers entangle their two wagons. Henchard's man tries to back up but the wagon falls over. Henchard's man describes Farfrae as "a damn young dand—of the sort that he is— . . . one that creeps into a maid's heart like the giddying worm into a sheep's brain—making crooked seem straight." Henchard watches Lucetta's door and sees Farfrae come for her. They go to help in the nearby fields, since the harvest has been delayed by the weather. She and Farfrae talk and seem to reach an agreement about marriage. She leaves and Henchard follows her. He

threatens to let Farfrae know they have been intimate. Lucetta agrees to marry him, in front of Elizabeth, and then faints.

Chapter 28
Henchard, though no longer mayor, is still a magistrate. He goes to the court Petty Sessions the next day to handle the case of a woman charged with being disorderly and a nuisance. She turns out to be the furmity woman from Weydon Fair. She identifies Henchard as the man who sold his wife at the fair. He admits it is true and abdicates his chair as magistrate. Lucetta decides she has to get away from Casterbridge, and goes to Port-Bredy. Elizabeth thinks Lucetta's sadness is because Farfrae is away. She returns, then goes along the road to Port-Bredy again. Henchard asks after her.

Chapter 29
Lucetta walks out of town, hoping in vain to see Farfrae. She turns and finds Elizabeth-Jane coming from town to meet her. A bull rambles down the hillside toward them. They recognize he is a savage older beast; he chases them into a barn. A man grabs the leading-staff, attached to a nose ring. It is Henchard. Elizabeth has climbed, unseen, up a stack of dry clover. Henchard takes Lucetta in his arms. Elizabeth runs back to the barn to retrieve Lucetta's muff and Farfrae approaches in a cart; he gives her a ride to town. Henchard releases Lucetta from her promise of marriage, but asks her to pretend they are engaged in front of Grower, his creditor. She says Grower was a witness of her marriage to Farfrae. They were married at Port-Bredy. Farfrae has his things moved to Lucetta's house.

Chapter 30
Lucetta goes to Elizabeth-Jane in her bedroom and tells her of the marriage. Elizabeth-Jane quotes the Latin poet Ovid, saying that Lucetta was in honor bound to marry the first man (Henchard), whom she had promised to marry. She suddenly thinks that perhaps Lucetta has actually married Henchard, but Lucetta tells her that Farfrae is her husband. Elizabeth-Jane decides to leave Lucetta's house immediately because of her attachment to Farfrae. She takes lodgings across from Henchard's home.

Chapter 31
The town is scandalized by news of Henchard's having sold his wife; it is far worse coming out now than it would have been if it had been known all along. He sinks in social esteem, and has already been ruined financially. Elizabeth-Jane is very sympathetic toward him; he now has a "film of ash" over his face. He takes off his watch. Farmer James EVERDENE (Bathsheba Everdene's uncle in *Far from the Madding Crowd*), one of his creditors, says they don't want his watch, though it is "honourable" in him to offer it. William BOLD-WOOD, a "silent, reserved young man," who is a prominent figure in *Far from the Madding Crowd,* speaks in favor of Henchard's keeping his watch. Henchard is praised by the commissioner for his fair behavior as a debtor.

Henchard avoids Elizabeth. She learns he has gone into Jopp's cottage and goes there. She finds that Donald Farfrae has obliterated his name on Henchard's business and taken it over. Abel Whittle says Farfrae is more easygoing; his corn business is prospering.

Chapter 32
The narrator describes the two bridges at the lower end of High Street, one of brick where people who have never been very successful are prone to gather. Abel Whittle and Christopher CONEY have often stood here. Another one, of stone, attracts people who are "out of situation" from their own fault or because they are out of luck. Henchard comes to this bridge. Jopp arrives and tells him Farfrae and Lucetta have moved into his old house. Henchard is upset. Farfrae has also bid on and purchased Henchard's furniture. Farfrae then drives a gig toward him on the bridge. He invites Henchard to live with them in his old house. Henchard refuses, but Farfrae then invites him to take some of his furniture back.

Elizabeth-Jane has taken lodgings across the street from Farfrae's house. She hears that Henchard is ill and goes to see him. Henchard improves and applies for work at Farfrae's yard; he is hired. It is rumored that Farfrae will be nominated for mayor. Henchard tells SOLOMON LONGWAYS he will be released from his oath not to drink in 12 days.

Chapter 33
On Sunday afternoons after church it is the custom in Casterbridge for churchgoers to go across to the Three Mariners Inn. At the rear is the choir, with bass-viols, fiddles, and flutes. Each man would observe a limit of a half-pint of liquor. Henchard ends his years of abstinence at the Three Mariners just before the choir arrives; he is seated at the huge oak table. Farfrae and Lucetta pass by outside, and Henchard asks the choir to sing Psalm 109, which prophesies doom. Finally they do, and he tells them they have been singing about Farfrae. The choir is shocked. Elizabeth-Jane has heard where Henchard is and comes to accompany him home.

Farfrae enters the hay-trussing yard with Lucetta where Henchard, assisted by Elizabeth-Jane, are working. Lucetta does not realize Henchard is working for her husband. He greets her sarcastically as a "lady." Lucetta, the next day, sends him a note asking him not to speak to her in "biting undertones." Elizabeth-Jane sees Henchard almost knock Farfrae off a ledge, although he restrains himself. She resolves to warn Farfrae.

Chapter 34
Elizabeth-Jane goes out early in the morning to find Farfrae and warn him. He doesn't believe her, and insists that he and Henchard are "quite friendly." She goes away, discouraged. Farfrae goes ahead with a "kindly scheme" on Henchard's account. He plans to rent, for Henchard, a small seedsman's shop. Farfrae would contribute half the amount if the others on the council would subscribe the remainder. The town clerk, through whom Farfrae is trying to make arrangements, tells him bluntly that Henchard hates him. Farfrae drops the idea. The occupier of the shop, disappointed, tells Henchard the council had planned to set him up in a shop but that Farfrae persuaded them not to do it. Henchard is even more bitter.

Henchard and Lucetta have tea and discuss leaving Casterbridge when he receives news that the current mayor has died and Farfrae has been elected mayor. Lucetta asks Henchard again to return any papers that might reveal their intimacy in Jersey. He tells her they are in the dining room safe of his old house, the one she and Farfrae occupy. Henchard becomes more and more bitter as Farfrae's elevation to the mayoralty is celebrated. He asks to collect the papers in the safe. Farfrae puts them on the dining room table. Lucetta has retired early. Henchard reads the letters to Farfrae, but stops short of revealing his past with Lucetta.

Chapter 35
Lucetta has heard the doorbell, crept down, and overheard Henchard reading out her own letters. She realizes he has not told Farfrae her secret, but decides to plead with Henchard himself to keep quiet. She arranges to meet him at the Ring. She dresses plainly, veiling herself, and pleads with Henchard to return the letters. He agrees.

Chapter 36
When Lucetta returns she finds Jopp, who asks her to ask Farfrae for a job for him. She pretends not to know him and refuses, but Jopp says he lived in Jersey for seven years and knew her. Jopp goes home, where Henchard is lodging, and Henchard asks him to deliver a package of letters to Mrs. Farfrae. Jopp resents Lucetta's failure to help him.

On the way Jopp meets two women, Mother CUXSOM and Nance Mockridge, who invite him to go to Mixen Lane, the center of vice in Casterbridge. It is across a brook, but all the cottagers have planks to act as a bridge. At the inn called Peter's Finger, Jopp reads the letters to others. He then delivers the letters, which Lucetta burns in relief.

Chapter 37
A "Royal Personage" is about to pass through Casterbridge en route to the coast, and will stop for a half-hour and receive an address from the corporation of the town. An artist prepares the address on parchment, and the council meets to make final plans. Henchard enters the meeting in his old clothes and asks to walk with the visitor. The council is embarrassed, and Farfrae says it would not be proper, as Henchard is no longer a member. Henchard says he has a particular reason for wanting to assist, but is refused. He determines to welcome his Royal Highness anyway. He drinks a glass of rum that morning, walks down the street, and meets Elizabeth-Jane. He tells her of his "welcome." She is alarmed but can do nothing. She watches while he makes a flag from a Union Jack and a small wand.

As the carriage approaches, Elizabeth-Jane and Lucetta watch, along with Henchard, Lucetta has eyes only for Farfrae. The carriage arrives and a procession is formed. Henchard steps in front of the carriage waving his flag. Farfrae seizes Henchard and drags him away. Observers tell Lucetta that Henchard had been Farfrae's original benefactor, but, out of ignorance, she refuses to believe it. The local people who have heard the reading of the letters would like to "see the trimming pulled off such Christmas candles" and see the lady "toppered." The scandal of the reading of the letters has spread, and a "skimmity-ride," or satirical mummery, is planned. Although they like the mayor, he has lost the charm he had as a "light-hearted penniless young man." Jopp and his friends have already planned the skimmity-ride as a retaliation.

Chapter 38
Lucetta fancies that Farfrae might receive a knighthood. Henchard has overheard her deny that he ever assisted her husband. Jopp asks whether Henchard has had a "snub," and explains that he has had one also. Henchard doesn't listen to him, but resolves to confront Lucetta and Farfrae. That evening he goes to Farfrae's house and asks to meet him at the granaries. He goes to the loft again and waits for Farfrae, who comes in singing the song he had sung at the Three Mariners as a poor young man. Henchard confronts him angrily, saying he has stood his "rivalry" and his "snubbing," but will not stand for his "hustling" him away from the royal carriage.

Henchard challenges Farfrae to a fight; one of them will fall 40 feet from the loft. He has tied one arm behind him so as to take "no advantage" of Farfrae. They have a wrestling match; Henchard brings Farfrae near the precipice. After more struggle Henchard dangles Farfrae's head outside the window. He draws back at the last minute and Farfrae descends safely to the floor. He leaves, and Henchard spends the day in the loft. He climbs down and decides to apologize, but realizes that he has heard that Farfrae has been summoned to Weatherbury and would go there via Mellstock. Henchard walks through the streets and hears a loud commotion; he feels too degraded, however, to pay much attention.

Chapter 39

The anonymous letter has been a contrivance from Farfrae's own men, who have been in on the village plot to get Farfrae out of the way in case the satirical mummery falls flat. They do not protect Lucetta, however, believing there is truth in the scandalous letters. Lucetta, who is pregnant, is waiting for Farfrae's return when she hears a hubbub in the distance and overhears two maidservants talking. One maid describes the scene: two figures are back to back on a donkey, their elbows tied; the woman faces the head and the man the tail. The man is dressed in a blue coat and has a reddish face; the woman is dressed just as "she" was dressed at the play at Town Hall. Lucetta jumps up, and Elizabeth-Jane suddenly enters. Lucetta refuses to let her close the window and they hear more of the description. Lucetta exclaims, "'Tis me! . . . A procession—a scandal—an effigy of me, and him!'" Her face grows wilder and more rigid. She looks out and says "She's me—She's me—even to the parasol—my green parasol!" Then she falls to the floor in an epileptic seizure. She recovers consciousness, but remembers what has happened and has another fit. The doctor comes and says Farfrae must be sent for. He rides off to Budmouth.

Benjamin Grower, a magistrate, tries to stop the procession with constables. When the constables reach the location, though, the parade has dispersed and only bland onlookers remain, who claim to have seen nothing.

Chapter 40

Henchard, meanwhile, has seen the procession; he goes to Farfrae's house. He tells the crowd Farfrae has gone to Mellstock and Weatherbury, not Budmouth, but they don't believe him. Henchard rushes out and chases Farfrae's gig; he recognizes the sound, since it used to be his own vehicle. Farfrae doesn't believe Henchard either and continues to Mellstock. He has left Lucetta in perfect health, and distrusts Henchard. Henchard goes to Farfrae's house and finds that Lucetta is worse. He goes back to his lodgings at Jopp's to find a "sea-captain" has called to see him. When Farfrae does return, Lucetta has had a miscarriage and is nearing death. Henchard stalks the streets all night and, at dawn, learns of Lucetta's death.

Chapter 41

Elizabeth-Jane goes to Henchard's home and tells him about Lucetta, which he knows. He makes her welcome and asks her to rest there while he fixes her breakfast. She goes to sleep on the couch. A knock comes and a stoutly built man stands on the doorstep. Henchard invites him in. He introduces himself as Newson. He says he and Henchard were both "young and thoughtless" at the time of the wife sale. He had deliberately let Susan think he was drowned. Henchard tells Newson that Elizabeth-Jane has also died—he hoping, momentarily, that they can be father and daughter again. Newson leaves, heart-broken. Henchard and Elizabeth-Jane have breakfast and she is affectionate toward him. During the day, however, he is sure she will hear about his deception and grow to hate him. He goes to the weir and almost drowns himself, but then sees a human body float up; he realizes it is a vision of himself. It is his double. He feels a strong sense of the supernatural.

Henchard goes home to find Elizabeth-Jane at his door. They take a walk back to the weir and do see something floating—it is the effigy of Henchard.

Chapter 42

Henchard expects Newson to return, but he does not. Elizabeth-Jane shares Henchard's home. They see Farfrae at rare intervals. Farfrae realizes that Lucetta's history, which he has now learned, would have meant a "looming misery" for him instead of the "simple sorrow" he now has. Her image is in his mind, however. Eventually Henchard's small grain and seed shop prospers. He considers Elizabeth-Jane to be "civil rather than affectionate" toward him, and he feels guilty about Newson. She buys a new muff and he notices the many books in her room. He then sees Farfrae, at the Corn Exchange, looking at Elizabeth-Jane. Perversely, he cannot see that a relationship between Farfrae and Elizabeth would be a good thing, but he forces himself to accept it.

Actually, things are not advancing fast between Farfrae and Elizabeth-Jane. Farfrae gives her books. Henchard restrains himself.

Chapter 43

The town talks about Elizabeth-Jane and Farfrae; he is an eligible bachelor and there are "nineteen superior young ladies of Casterbridge, who had each" considered herself the only one to make Farfrae happy. Henchard pictures himself if they marry: he could be a "fangless lion about the back rooms of the house." Elizabeth goes to the prehistoric fort called Mai Dun, outside Casterbridge. She goes to the meeting place but he does not come; she tells Henchard a trick was played on her earlier. He says for her to go, realizing he cannot remain any longer in Casterbridge. Elizabeth-Jane seems to be engaged to Donald Farfrae. Henchard takes his tool basket and, wearing working clothes, leaves Casterbridge. Elizabeth-Jane meets Farfrae, who has been in touch with Newson; Newson is at that moment in his living room waiting to meet Elizabeth-Jane. She has been separated from him for only six years. They plan that, when she and Farfrae marry, he will provide the drinks. He tells them of Henchard's deception. Elizabeth-Jane is more shocked than Farfrae and Newson.

Chapter 44

Henchard keeps walking away from Casterbridge and arrives at Weydon-Priors on the sixth day. It is the time of the annual fair. He recalls his first arrival in a desperate attempt to socialize himself. He continually looks toward Casterbridge. He asks if Elizabeth-Jane is getting married and learns that she probably is. He decides to go to the wedding. He arrives to find the wedding reception in progress and Mr. and Mrs. Farfrae dancing. He has brought, as a gift, a bird in a cage. He learns about Newson's return. Elizabeth-Jane says she could have loved them both if he had not deceived her. Henchard goes away.

Chapter 45

Newson misses the sea and moves to Budmouth. The bird in the cage has starved to death; Elizabeth-Jane finally realizes Henchard had sent it as a wedding present. She buries the bird and her heart softens toward the "self-alienated man." She and Farfrae search for Henchard and find Whittle out on the heath in a cottage. He tells them Henchard has died, just half an hour earlier. Henchard has left a scrap of paper asking that Elizabeth-Jane not be told of his death and that he have no mourners, not be buried in consecrated ground, have no bell tolled, no "flours" be planted on his grave, and no man remember him. Elizabeth-Jane follows his instructions but feels guilty for a long time, especially about their last meeting. Elizabeth-Jane and Farfrae have a happy marriage, but Elizabeth remains philosophical, believing that "happiness" is but the "occasional episode in a general drama of pain." The narrator calls Henchard a "blundering Titan of a self-made man."

CRITICAL RECEPTION AND COMMENTARY

Hardy remarks in the *Life* that he regarded novel-writing as "mere journeywork," and felt he had damaged *The Mayor of Casterbridge* "more recklessly as an artistic whole" than any of his other novels in his effort to insert an "incident" into each week's part. It was, nevertheless, well received by critics. Robert Louis STEVENSON wrote that he read it with "sincere admiration." He called Henchard a "great fellow" and stated that Dorchester was "touched in with the hand of a master" (*Life*, 179).

Many contemporary reviewers were lukewarm about the novel; R. H. Hutton, writing in the SPECTATOR, criticized Hardy's "pagan" reflections and hints of "fashionable pessimism." He stated that the novel did not lend itself to quotation, although the scenery of Dorset was "admirably given." An anonymous reviewer for the SATURDAY REVIEW pronounced it a "dis-

The King's Arms, Dorchester, which figures in The Mayor of Casterbridge. (Sarah Bird Wright)

appointment" not equal to *Far from the Madding Crowd*, and the wife sale improbable. The reviewer did, however, praise Hardy's depiction of the "average peasant," his grasp of the "workings of the rustic mind," and his sketches of Casterbridge. Another anonymous reviewer, writing in the ATHENAEUM, predicted the novel would not be so popular as *The* TRUMPET-MAJOR and stated that it did not deserve to be because it recounted the adventures of a "self-willed instead of an unselfish hero" (Clarke, *Thomas Hardy: Critical Assessments*, I, 141–47). Other critics, however, assessed the novel in a more positive way. The writer for the *Whitehall Review* pronounced it a "novel of pure character," representing "the novel of the future." Hardy would be one of its "greatest living exponents." The critic for the *Scotsman* called it "one of those dramas of English country life from which Hardy draws an enormous amount of pathos and significance" (Davis and Gerber, *Thomas Hardy: An Annotated Bibliography of Writings about Him*, II, 35–36).

For further reading: Allingham, "Robert Barnes' Illustrations for Thomas Hardy's *The Mayor of Casterbridge* as Serialized in *The Graphic*"; Bloom, *Thomas Hardy's The Mayor of Casterbridge*; Draper, *"The Mayor of Casterbridge"*; Epstein, "Sale and Sacrament: The Wife Auction in *The Mayor of Casterbridge*"; King, *"The Mayor of Casterbridge*: Talking about Character"; Langbaum, "The Minimisation of Sexuality in *The Mayor of Casterbridge*"; Levine, "Thomas Hardy's *The Mayor of Casterbridge*: Reversing the Real"; Menefree, *Wives for Sale: An Ethnographic Study of British Popular Opinions*; Moses, "Agon in the Marketplace: *The Mayor of Casterbridge* as Bourgeois Tragedy"; Pinion, ed., *The Mayor of Casterbridge*, with Introduction and Notes; Raine, "Conscious Artistry in *The Mayor of Casterbridge*"; Schweik, "Character and Fate in Hardy's *The Mayor of Casterbridge*"; Taft, "Hardy's Manipulation of Folklore and Literary Imagination: The Case of the Wife Sale in *The Mayor of Casterbridge.*"

The Dorchester building now housing Barclay's Bank, Corn Street/South Street, is reputed to have been the model for Michael Henchard's house in The Mayor of Casterbridge. (Sarah Bird Wright)

"Melancholy Hussar of the German Legion, The" Short story dated October 1899 and sold that year to TILLOTSON & SON for syndication. It was printed in a number of provincial newspapers in 1890 before being collected in *LIFE'S LITTLE IRONIES* (1894).

The story is set on the south coast, with a view of Portland—"the Isle of Slingers." The narrator recalls a tale told him when he was 15 by Phyllis, a woman then 75. The events had taken place 90 years earlier, in 1804, during the reign of King GEORGE III, at the time of the threatened invasion by Napoleon. The king had often taken the baths at WEYMOUTH.

Phyllis Grove, at the time of the story, is a girl living in the solitary home of her father, Dr. Grove, who has retired and become increasingly withdrawn and irritable. Phyllis is shy and lonely. An admirer, however, has discovered her and proposed marriage. A bachelor of 30, Humphrey Gould is of an old county family who has come to Weymouth as one of many "idlers" claiming to have court connections. Phyllis has accepted his proposal but, when the king leaves Weymouth, Humphrey goes to Bath. He promises to return within a few weeks. Phyllis has a "genuine regard" for Humphrey, although she is not deeply in love with him. He writes regularly, but does not return, saying he cannot leave his elderly father.

Meanwhile, the York Hussars, a regiment of the king's German Legion, have arrived. Since it is summer, they camp on the downs and pastures because the king is in Weymouth, nearby. One day Phyllis, sitting on the garden wall of her father's isolated house, sees a solitary young German hussar walking along the path. He is surprisingly sad. The next day he sees her again, and talks briefly with her. His English is not perfect, but is comprehensible to her. He has been reading and rereading letters from his lonely mother in Germany.

He is Matthäus Tina of Saarbrück, only 22. Phyllis learns that all the young German soldiers are miserably homesick, not gay and carefree, as she had imagined. She and Matthäus talk across the boundary of the wall every day. He does not ask to come inside, but Phyllis grows more and more interested in him.

In time her father hears, from an acquaintance, that Humphrey Gould, who is still in Bath attending his father, believes he is not engaged to Phyllis but has only reached a "half-understanding" with her father. Phyllis feels this information frees her from any attachment to him, but her father disagrees. Having noticed the troops camping on the downs, he forbids her to go out of the garden without his permission. Phyllis continues to meet Matthäus.

One evening she is late coming out, but Matthäus stays past his curfew to talk with her. He is demoted, but proposes to her. She says her father will never permit an engagement and asks him to forget her. He presents a plan whereby he will escape with her and go to the Saar; they will live with his mother. His friend Christoph, an Alsatian, will help. She hesitates, but when she goes home, her father seems to have learned of her conversations with Matthäus and says he is sending her away to her aunt. Phyllis regards her aunt's home as a prison.

The next week Phyllis leaves the house and waits for Matthäus by the road at night. A stagecoach comes along and Humphrey Gould alights with a friend. She overhears Humphrey saying he has treated her badly but has a peace offering for her. When Matthäus arrives she tells him she cannot go with him, which breaks his heart. He determines to flee anyway. She is miserable, but receives Humphrey the next morning.

Humphrey gives her a handsome mirror and tells her of the world of fashion. Then he confesses that he has a problem; he is secretly married and wants her to "praise" his wife. Phyllis goes into a decline. A few days later she goes to the downs and observes the troops gathering around two empty coffins. Matthäus and his friend have been caught; they are shot before her eyes, placed in the coffins, and carried away. Phyllis faints and barely regains consciousness. The two young soldiers are buried in the churchyard of a neighboring village. The narrator says their graves are there still, 90 years later, although they are overgrown and sunken. Phyllis's grave is nearby.

George Cottrell, writing in the *Academy* in 1890, called the story "as melancholy as its title" and said it had a "great deal of unreality" (Gerber and Davis, *Thomas Hardy: An Annotated Bibliography of Writings about Him*, I, 45).

Melbury, George   In *The WOODLANDERS*, Melbury is a prosperous timber merchant who lives with his second wife, Lucy. He had won his first wife unfairly from the father of Giles WINTERBOURNE, and is now the doting but misguided father of Grace MELBURY. He persuades her to reject Giles Winterbourne, who has loved her for many years, and to marry an untrustworthy physician, Edred FITZPIERS, believing that her education has fitted her for an elevated station in life. Fitzpiers's adultery infuriates George; he encourages Grace to divorce her husband and reconcile with Giles but this proves to be impossible. Giles dies, and Grace and Fitzpiers reconcile and move to a distant part of England.

Melbury, Grace   *See* FITZPIERS, GRACE MELBURY.

Melchester   Fictional name for Salisbury in "A COMMITTEE-MAN OF 'THE TERROR,'" "Dame the First—The First Countess of Wessex" and "Dame the Third—The Marchioness of Stonehenge" (both in *A GROUP OF NOBLE DAMES*), *FAR FROM THE MADDING CROWD*, *The HAND OF ETHELBERTA*, "INCIDENT IN THE LIFE OF MR. GEORGE CROOKHILL," *JUDE THE OBSCURE*, *The MAYOR OF CASTER-*

BRIDGE, "ON THE WESTERN CIRCUIT," *TESS OF THE D'URBERVILLES*, and *TWO ON A TOWER*.

Mellstock   Fictional name for three hamlets in STINSFORD and the Bockhamptons (Hardy was born in HIGHER BOCKHAMPTON). It recurs in many of Hardy's works, including *UNDER THE GREENWOOD TREE*, "AT MIDDLE-FIELD GATE IN FEBRUARY," *FAR FROM THE MADDING CROWD*, *JUDE THE OBSCURE*, *TESS OF THE D'URBERVILLES*, *The MAYOR OF CASTERBRIDGE*, "AFTERNOON SERVICE AT MELLSTOCK," "The DEAD QUIRE," "VOICES FROM THINGS GROWING IN A CHURCHYARD," "The NOBLE LADY'S TALE," and others.

"Mellstock Quire, The"   Play based on *UNDER THE GREENWOOD TREE*. It was written by A. H. EVANS, who also dramatized other works of Hardy. The DORCHESTER DEBATING AND DRAMATIC SOCIETY performed the adaptation on November 16, 1910, just after Hardy had been awarded the Honorary Freedom of the Borough of Dorchester. Hardy and his wife were present, as were Henry NEWBOLT and his wife.

The second title of the novel was *The Mellstock Quire* (the Quire, or choir, of the fictional village of MELLSTOCK, which was based on Stinsford). Hardy and his two wives are buried at STINSFORD CHURCH, along with other members of his family.

"Memories of Church Restoration"   An important essay Hardy wrote for the general meeting of the SOCIETY FOR THE PROTECTION OF ANCIENT BUILDINGS in LONDON on June 20, 1906. It was read in his absence by a Scottish architect, Colonel Eustace James Anthony Balfour.

Hardy argues that the late-19th-century mania for preservation of medieval buildings has ruined many of them, and had they been left alone to incur the dilapidations of "time, weather and general neglect" the country would be richer than after the expenditure of millions on preservation. The matter of preserving an old building without hurting its character, according to Hardy, is complicated by the conflicting demands of the incumbent clergyman (who regards the building as a workshop or laboratory), the antiquarian (to whom it is a relic), the parish members (who see it in a utilitarian light), and the outsider (who views it as a luxury).

Hardy explains that much damage has been done by those who replaced structures completely, or destroyed the architectural design by trying to make its structure uniform, or moved memorials and architectural elements from their original places. He cites Milton's monument in Cripplegate church, London, as an example: because it has been moved several times, the location of his "rifled grave" is not known. (A memorable scene in *A LAODICEAN* takes place in this church).

Hardy deplores the practice of replacing "old materials" such as marble tablets and oak carvings, observing that they often lose their value when separated from the original churches and are then destroyed. Hardy also argues that no two "pieces of matter," such as carvings, can be exactly the same when executed by different artisans, and can never be copied successfully. Sometimes, to attain uniformity in the capitals of pillars that might never have existed in the first place, stone carvers chiseled away at old carvings until they were appallingly homogeneous. Fine old oak pews, so skillfully made that not a joint had ever come asunder, have been replaced by cheap wooden benches, made of deal, which have decayed. Hardy says the "fabric of old churches" should be maintained but not regularized; stylistic variations should not be corrected simply in the interest of attaining balance or harmony. Moreover, the "rupture of continuity" has done inestimable damage to the country as a whole; the "protection of an ancient edifice" against the injection of fresh materials is both a social and an aesthetic duty.

In the *Life*, Hardy states that the speakers at the meeting expressed "great satisfaction" because he "laid special emphasis on the value of the human associations of ancient buildings" (*Life*, 331).

The essay was reprinted in the CORNHILL MAGAZINE (August 1906), and is also included in Ernest Brennecke, *The Life and Art of Thomas Hardy* (New York: 1925) and Harold Orel, ed., *Thomas Hardy's Personal Writings* (Lawrence, Kansas: 1996).

"Memory and I"   Published in *POEMS OF THE PAST AND THE PRESENT* (1902), this poem takes the form of a dialogue between the poet, about 60, and his Memory, exploring the inevitable disillusionment that life produces. He asks Memory where the youth is who "used to say that life was truth?" Memory replies that he was seen in a "crumbled cot / Beneath a tottering tree," where he lingers as a phantom. He inquires about his "joy," but is told he wanders in "gaunt gardens lone / Where laughter used to be." His "hope, / Who charged with deeds my skill and scope" (that is, his writing) is only a spectre, buried in a "tomb of tomes, / Where dreams are wont to be." His "faith" is only a ghost in a "ravaged aisle, / Bowed down on bended knee." His "Love" is now a mere phantom, an "ageing shape / Where beauty used to be."

"Men Who March Away" (*Song of the Soldiers*)   Poem dated September 5, 1914, published in the London *Times* on September 9, 1914, and collected in *SATIRES OF CIRCUMSTANCE* (1914). It was later transferred to *MOMENTS OF VISION*, where it is included in the "Poems of War and Patriotism" section. It is one of Hardy's finest patriotic poems, focusing on the "faith and fire" of the young men who are marching away from their rural homes to war, believing their country is worth fighting for and, if necessary, dying for. The poem was set to music by Edgar Lane, who had a school of music in DORCHESTER. Hardy offered it to Harley GRANVILLE-BARKER to use in his production of *The DYNASTS* (Bailey, *The Poetry of Thomas Hardy*, 416–17). The poem has five stanzas, each with a rhyme scheme of *abbbaab*. The soldiers act according to their conviction that "Victory crowns the just, / And that braggarts must / Surely bite the dust."

Menlove, Louisa   Character who is at first a lady's maid to Ethelberta PETHERWIN in *The HAND OF ETHELBERTA* and then works in the same house as Mr. R. CHICKEREL, Ethelberta's father. She attracts the boy Joey, employed in the same house, not realizing he is Chickerel's son and Ethelberta's brother. She is engaged to Tipman, valet to Lord MOUNTCLERE, who marries Ethelberta. She is more quick-witted and devious than most of her employers.

Meredith, George (1828–1909)   English poet, critic, and novelist. His best-known works include *Modern Love*, a tragedy based on his own failed first marriage; *Ballads and Poems of Tragic Life; The Egoist*, a novel based on the theme of selfishness; and *The Ordeal of Richard Feverel*, a novel that examines the consequences of the misapplication of an educational theory. In 1904 Meredith received the ORDER OF MERIT.

In 1869, at the age of 29, Hardy submitted his first novel, *The POOR MAN AND THE LADY*, to MACMILLAN & CO., which rejected it but suggested he try Chapman & Hall. Meredith was the Chapman reader. He told Hardy that the firm would be willing to publish the work if it were subsidized, but recommended that Hardy put the manuscript aside because of its orientation toward social criticism (it was a dramatic satire of the nobility, London society, modern Christianity, and other institutions Hardy wished to reform). Meredith advised that Hardy should, instead, attempt a novel with a purely artistic purpose, Hardy took his advice, abandoned *The Poor Man and the Lady*, and began a new novel, *DESPERATE REMEDIES*.

In the *Life*, Hardy described Meredith's appearance when he met with him in the Chapman office. He did not at first realize who he was, but saw a "handsome man in a frock-coat," with an "ample dark-brown beard, wavy locks, and somewhat dramatic manner" (*Life*, 61–64).

It is probable that Hardy did not meet Meredith again until the summer of 1886, when they both attended a RABELAIS CLUB dinner. In 1894 he called on Meredith at his home at Box Hill.

In May 1909 Hardy was in London and saw an announcement of Meredith's death. Shocked, he went to the ATHENAEUM CLUB and wrote a poem, "George Meredith," which is dated at the end "May 1909." He recalls meeting Meredith 40 years earlier and praises him as one whose "wit can shake / And riddle to the very core / The counterfeits that Time will break. . ." The concluding lines are a paean to Meredith's work: "Through the world's vaporous vitiate air / His words wing on—as live words will." The poem was published in the *Times* and later reprinted in TIME'S LAUGHING-STOCKS. Hardy attended Meredith's memorial service in WESTMINSTER ABBEY.

Hardy was then asked to succeed Meredith as president of the INCORPORATED SOCIETY OF AUTHORS, PLAY-WRIGHTS, AND COMPOSERS. He refused at first, arguing that his work was too controversial and the society needed someone who could bring about literary consensus. There were renewed pleas, however, and in July he accepted the presidency; he remained in office until his own death in 1928.

For further reading: Cook, "Thomas Hardy and George Meredith"; Gatrell, "England, Europe, and Empire: Hardy, Meredith, and Gissing"; Yarker, "Meredith, Hardy, and Gissing."

"Mere Interlude, A"   Short story that appeared in the *Bolton Weekly Journal* October 17 and 24, 1885. It was sold to TILLOTSON & SON, which had a syndication business, and was widely reprinted. It was pirated and published in the United States in Munro's Seaside Library Pocket Edition in December 1885. The story was later collected in *A CHANGED MAN AND OTHER TALES* (1913).

The tale, told by a traveler in (salesman of) school books, concerns Baptista Trewthen, the daughter of a small farmer in St. Maria's, one of the Isles of Lyonesse. They are identified as the Scilly Isles. Her father had sent her to the mainland to be educated as a teacher; at the age of 21 she began teaching at a country school near Tor-upon-Sea. She lodges with a widow, Mrs. Wace.

Mrs. Wace notices that Baptista seems preoccupied and presses her for the reason. Baptista says it has to do with David Heddegan, a middle-aged man from her village who wants to marry her. Her parents are willing, but she is reluctant to marry someone 20 years older. However, she doesn't like teaching. Children to her are "unpleasant, troublesome little things, whom nothing would delight so much as to hear that you had fallen down dead."

Eventually Mrs. Wace comes to agree with Baptista's parents. After her Easter holidays, Baptista returns from home to say she is engaged to Heddegan. His letters are dry and perfunctory, although she only reads stray sentences to Mrs. Wace. She reluctantly leaves her job and lodgings and makes arrangements to return home a few days before her wedding. She arrives at the port of Pen-zephyr (Penzance) on Saturday only to learn that the boat has departed early because of the threat of fog; the next boat is not until Tuesday. She is greatly relieved at not having to see Heddegan earlier.

Securing a room in the town, she wanders about looking at the churches. Suddenly she meets an old beau, Charles Stow, a schoolmaster she had known in the training college she attended. She tells him of her approaching marriage, which he thinks is beneath her.

He makes it clear she should have waited for him. She says she would have waited for him if she had known he wanted to marry her. He begs her to marry him in Trufal and she assents.

They marry there early Monday morning. Returning to Pen-zephyr, they find that the boat does not sail for two hours. They climb up the cliffs and look at St. Michael's Mount. Charles runs down to the beach, goes swimming, and drowns in an unexpected strong current. The local inhabitants cannot find his body. Baptista gathers her things and goes to the pier, where she overhears people discuss the drowning. On the boat she discovers that Heddegan has come to escort her back home. She slips off her wedding ring and tries to be friendly.

At home her parents greet her affectionately; friends drop in for her mother's abundant pies and she has no chance to tell them what has happened. She marries Heddegan, but is shocked to learn that he plans to take her back to Pen-zephyr on a wedding trip, aboard a friend's boat. They find a tavern with vacancies. The best room is occupied, but they persuade the landlady to move the tenant to the next room, which has no view. She recognizes Charles's hat on the back of their door. The maid says it belongs to the corpse now lying in the other room. She asks Heddegan to look for other lodgings, without explaining why. Because the town is full and he has already paid for their room, he refuses. That night, without telling her husband the truth, she lies between the two men she has married, one a corpse next door and one in bed.

The next day Baptista purchases a black bonnet, veil, and gown and, pretending she is going shopping, joins the end of Charles's funeral procession. She and her husband return to Giant's Town, but she encounters a witness of her wedding to Charles. Knowing the truth, he blackmails her and she confesses to David that she had had an earlier marriage. To her astonishment David says he was not a bachelor when he married her, but a widower and the father of four "strapping" daughters who had been illegitimate (he married the mother just before her death). He brings them home. They are plain and not very bright, but unselfish, and, finally, Baptista comes to love them.

Merlin   Character in *The FAMOUS TRAGEDY OF THE QUEEN OF CORNWALL*, a magician who speaks the Prologue and Epilogue.

Mew, Charlotte (Mary) (1869–1928)   A poet whose work Hardy much admired. In June 1919 she contributed a poem, "Love Love Today," to the "POETS' TRIB-UTE," a volume made up by Hardy's poet friends. She sent him the manuscript (now at the University of Virginia library) and he wrote to thank her (*Letters* V, 336).

In 1922 Hardy wrote J. C. SQUIRE, editor of the *New Mercury,* praising *A Book of Women's Verse,* an anthology edited by Squire and published by the Oxford University Press in 1921. Hardy said he was sorry Charlotte Mew had been omitted as he considered her "the greatest poetess I have come across lately" (*CL* VI, 113). In 1924 he helped secure Mew a pension of £75 a year.

Mill, John Stuart (1806–1873)   English philosopher and economist, the author of *On Liberty, Thoughts on Parliamentary Reform, The Subjection of Women,* and other works. He founded the Utilitarian Society, which met for reading and the discussion of essays at the home of the philosopher Jeremy Bentham.

Hardy saw Mill in LONDON while he was working for Sir Arthur William BLOMFIELD; Mill was speaking in front of St. Paul's Church, Covent Garden. Sue BRIDE-HEAD, the heroine of *JUDE THE OBSCURE,* quotes Mill extensively to her husband, Richard PHILLOTSON. Bridehead seems to embrace Mill's utilitarian philosophy calling for all public action to be governed by what effects "the greatest good for the greatest number." This ideology was actually out of date by the 1890s, when Hardy was writing; Bridehead is more attuned to the 1860s.

Milton, John (1608–1674)   English poet and writer of prose, a major figure in English literature. His best-known works are the epic poems *Paradise Lost, Paradise Regained,* and *Samson Agonistes,* as well as his masque *Comus* and his poems "L'Allegro," "Il Penseroso," "Lycidas," "On the Morning of Christ's Nativity," and "When I Consider How My Light Is Spent (On His Blindness)," as well as his prose essay "On Education."

In October 1880 Hardy and his wife went to Cambridge for a week. In the *Life* he recalls attending the five o'clock service at King's College chapel. He comments on "Milton's 'dim religious light'" evidenced there. In December 1887 Hardy noted that Milton, Dante, Homer, Virgil, Aristophanes, Shakespeare's sonnets, and "Lycidas" were among the works he had read that year.

There are elements of *Paradise Lost* in TESS OF THE D'URBERVILLES, with the tempter, Alec D'URBERVILLE, as Satan, and the winter scenes in Flintcombe Ash representing the expulsion from Paradise (Gittings, *Thomas Hardy's Later Years,* 68).

In 1897 the Hardys visited Lausanne, Switzerland, where they stated at the Hotel Gibbon. Hardy wrote a poem, "LAUSANNE: IN GIBBON'S OLD GARDEN," in which he alludes to Milton's *The Doctrine and Discipline of Divorce.*

Mitchell, Mrs. George   *See* RICHARDSON, MAGGIE.

Mockridge, Nance   A woman in *The MAYOR OF CASTER-BRIDGE* who works in Michael HENCHARD's yard and accuses him of selling defective "growed wheat." She tells him about the occasion when Elizabeth-Jane HEN-CHARD (2) served customers at the Three Mariners. This was their first night in CASTERBRIDGE, when she offered to assist the landlady. She is a friend of Mother CUXSOM.

Moments of Love   Published by the DORSET COUNTY MUSEUM in 1997, this is a special limited edition of Hardy's love poems written to his wife Emma HARDY. Only 157 copies were printed. According to the official description issued by the museum, the volume includes 47 pages of high-quality facsimile of Hardy's handwritten poems and 65 printed pages of parallel text. The edition contains an introduction by Dr. James Gibson and a foreword by the earl of Stockton. Every copy includes a genuine signature by Hardy. The autographs were prepared by the author in 1927 for a signed edition of one of his novels, which was never issued.

Moments of Vision and Miscellaneous Verses   Collection of 159 poems published by Hardy in 1917. Published by MACMILLAN & CO., Ltd., the volume is the largest such collection Hardy ever published. Nine of the poems had appeared in *Selected Poems* in 1916, and only six others had been previously published. The most enduring theme in the collection, except for the war poems, is the death of Emma HARDY, his first wife. Hardy only rarely permitted periodical publication of such poems, because of their intimate nature. He inscribed a copy to his second wife, "From Thomas Hardy, this first copy of the first edition, to the first of women Florence Hardy. Nov. 1917" (Purdy, *Thomas Hardy: A Bibliographical Study,* 207–208). The definitive WESSEX EDITION of Hardy's works (Macmillan, 1919) included *Moments of Vision,* combined with SATIRES OF CIRCUMSTANCE.

In February 1918 Hardy wrote Edmund GOSSE to say that he was disappointed in many of the reviews the volume had received. Although it had been kindly received in many quarters, he felt reviewers had not grasped what he had been attempting to say. He believed many critics had been too concerned with the presence or absence of what they considered to be "poetic diction" than with whether the poem had "vision" (CL *Letters,* 253).

See also "AFTERNOON SERVICE AT MELLSTOCK," "AFTER-WARDS," "An APPEAL TO AMERICA ON BEHALF OF THE BEL-GIAN DESTITUTE," "AT A SEASIDE TOWN IN 1869," "AT MIDDLE-FIELD GATE IN FEBRUARY," "A CALL TO NATIONAL SERVICE," "AT THE WORD "FAREWELL," "WE SAT AT THE WINDOW," "TO SHAKESPEARE," "AT MAYFAIR LODGINGS," "QUIC HIC AGIS?", "A JANUARY NIGHT, 1879," "The LAST

SIGNAL," "THE FIGURE IN THE SCENE," "WHY DID I SKETCH?," "ON STURMINSTER FOOT-BRIDGE," "OLD FURNITURE," "DURING WIND AND RAIN," "THE FIVE STUDENTS," "HE REVISITS HIS FIRST SCHOOL," "IT NEVER LOOKS LIKE SUMMER," "LOOKING ACROSS," "THE YOUNG GLASS-STAINER," "I LOOKED UP FROM MY WRITING," "IN THE GARDEN," "LOGS ON THE HEARTH," "THE MUSICAL BOX," "CRY OF THE HOMELESS," AND "IN TIME OF 'THE BREAKING OF NATIONS.'"

For further reading: Lerner, "*Moments of Vision*—and After"; Murfin, "*Moments of Vision*: Hardy's Poems of 1912–13"; Zietlow, *Moments of Vision: The Poetry of Thomas Hardy.*

"Mother Mourns, The" Poem collected in POEMS OF THE PAST AND THE PRESENT (1902). In this poem Nature laments the development of mankind's consciousness. The poet, walking on an autumn night through Yellowham Wood, hears the wind moaning through the fir trees. Nature has permitted evolution, but she has not foreseen the complications of the process in which humans are capable of pain, dreams, and criticism of the works of nature.

Nature has created forests that are now barren and beautiful species that are dwindling. She vows to grow only "mildews and mandrakes, / And slimy distortions" since her children have not preserved the vegetable and animal life they were given. The sublime stars and moon are not appreciated. Mankind has, instead, disdained Nature's "ancient high fame of perfection."

The poem originated in an entry Hardy made in his notebook on November 17, 1883: "Poem. We [human beings] have reached a degree of intelligence which Nature never contemplated when framing her laws." In April he developed his idea further, arguing that "the human race is too extremely developed for its corporeal conditions, the nerves being evolved to an activity abnormal in such an environment" (Bailey, *The Poetry of Thomas Hardy,* 140–41).

Moule, Henry Joseph (1825–1904) Antiquarian and eldest son of the Rev. Henry MOULE. He became curator of the DORSET COUNTY MUSEUM. At the time of his death in 1904 Hardy wrote a long letter to his younger brother the Rev. Arthur MOULE, who had returned to China to resume his missionary work. Hardy observed that his friendship with Henry had reached further back than with anyone else alive, and was "of that staunch, undemonstrative kind which survives all differences of opinion, all contrasting conduct, & all separations."

Hardy described Moule's funeral at FORDINGTON ST. GEORGE CHURCH; the service was conducted by the vicar, the Reverend Sydney Boulter, and the committal by a Mr. Metcalfe. Hardy's mother, Jemima HARDY, then 91, had made a wreath of flowers from the HIGHER BOCKHAMPTON garden and had sent his sister out into the garden after dark with a lantern to collect more greenery lest it should not be finished and sent in time. At the end of the service an old laborer who had known the deceased was heard to exclaim, "That's a good man gone!" It echoed the feelings of all, Hardy told him (*Letters* III, 115).

Moule, Horatio (Horace) Mosley (1832–1873) Fourth son of the Reverend Henry MOULE, vicar of FORDINGTON ST. GEORGE CHURCH, DORSET, and one of Hardy's closest friends as a young man. In 1857 Moule became Hardy's mentor; they rambled through the fields near DORCHESTER, discussing literature, and Moule gave him books, such as *Elements of Experiment and Natural Philosophy . . . for the use of Youth and Schools,* by Jabez Hogg. Moule was, at the time, a student at Queen's College, Cambridge, and an aspiring author and reviewer. He was for many years on the staff of the SATURDAY REVIEW.

Moule was an excellent Greek scholar and willing to tutor Hardy. Hardy was apprenticed to the architect John HICKS of Dorchester. Moule advised Hardy that if he really had to earn a living as an architect he ought to stop reading Greek plays. Hardy did so, but resented it in later years, believing he might have abandoned architecture for a university career. Hardy's poem "An Experience," addressed to "My friend," apparently describes Moule at that time.

Hardy and Moule explored London during the summer of 1870, while Hardy was working in the architectural office of Sir Arthur William BLOMFIELD. Moule, whom Hardy considered "a scholar and critic of perfect taste," believed in Hardy's abilities as a writer and encouraged him to keep writing lest he eventually have visual problems that would keep him from the practice of architecture (*Life,* 87).

Moule reviewed Hardy's first published novel, DESPERATE REMEDIES, in the *Saturday Review* (September 30, 1871), as well as his second, UNDER THE GREENWOOD TREE, also in the *Saturday Review* (September 28, 1872).

In June 1873 Hardy visited Moule at Cambridge. He was profoundly shocked when Moule committed suicide on September 21, 1873, at 41. He attended the funeral at Fordington, Dorchester, and noted in the *Life* that it was a source of "keen regret" that Moule had never met his wife Emma, and that she could never become his friend.

Moule, Rev. Arthur Evans (1836–1918) The sixth son of the Reverend Henry MOULE. He was a missionary and author, and archdeacon of the Missionary Diocese of Mid-China. In 1891 he wrote Hardy to ask him to review his book *New China and Old: Personal Recollections and Observations of Thirty Years.* Hardy replied, thanking him but explaining that he never reviewed books. Hardy suggested that the book would have a good sale because the subject of mission work in China had come to the "front" again (*Letters* I, 243). In 1903 Moule returned to China to carry out missionary work after spending four years as rector of the DORSET parish of Compton Valence. Hardy wrote Moule that his thorough knowledge of Chinese made him unique among English writers, and that if he were not engaged in missionary work his linguistic gift would be of great value in making the Chinese "acquainted with what we westerns think" (*Letters* III, 79).

Hardy was a friend of several of the Moule brothers, including Handley Carr Glynn MOULE, Henry Joseph MOULE, and Horatio (Horace) Mosley MOULE.

Moule, Rev. Handley Carr Glynn (1841–1920)   The youngest son of the Reverend Henry MOULE, vicar of FORDINGTON ST. GEORGE CHURCH. He was a Fellow of Trinity College, CAMBRIDGE, and later bishop of Durham. The bishop was a year younger than Hardy, but Hardy was closer to some of the other brothers, including Arthur, Henry, and Horace. In December 1913 he sent Hardy a copy of his autobiographical account of his childhood, *Memories of a Vicarage.* Hardy thanked him, saying it brought back "all sorts of submerged experiences, dates, & faces of the past" (*Letters* IV, 326). In June 1919 Bishop Handley sent Hardy a volume of his poems; Hardy praised one, "Apollo at Pherae," for its construction (*Letters* V, 315).

Moule, Rev. Henry (1801–1880)   Evangelical vicar of FORDINGTON ST. GEORGE CHURCH and father of eight sons (one died in infancy), most of whom had distinguished careers. Hardy was a close friend of several of them, including Henry Joseph MOULE, Horatio (Horace) MOULE, and the Reverend Handley Carr Glynn Moule. He was the prototype of the Reverend Mr. CLARE in *TESS OF THE D'URBERVILLES* (*Letters* VII, 40).

Rev. Moule achieved national prominence through his writings, and in the cholera epidemics of 1849 and 1854 endangered himself by boiling and burning clothes of the deceased to prevent the spread of infection. He attended to the dying, led the living in prayer, and faulted local officials for their inaction. His courage inspired Hardy's short story "A CHANGED MAN."

On February 11, 1880, Hardy wrote the Reverend Handley Moule to say that he and his brothers had been much in his thoughts. Hardy felt as though he had been Moule's parishioner, although, geographically, he was not. Rev. Handley Moule's sermon, reprinted in the DORSET paper, had brought Handley's father's "life & innermost heart" before all readers with "singular power." Hardy had also discussed his father with Matthew ARNOLD, a friend and admirer of Rev. Moule, who had praised the changes he had brought about in Fordington and used the words "energy is genius" to express Rev. Moule (*Letters* I, 70).

Moulton, Ellen Louise Chandler (1835–1908)   American writer and critic, and the wife of William U. Moulton, a Boston publisher. For many years she spent the summer and fall of each year in London, renting furnished flats, as the Hardys did. She had "at home" afternoons, which Hardy sometimes attended. In July 1893 he offered to conduct Mrs. Florence HENNIKER "through the pestilential vapours of the Underground" to Mrs. Moulton's (*Letters* II, 20).

Her collected verse was published in *The Poems and Sonnets of Louise Chandler Moulton* (1909). In 1889 she sent Hardy a volume of stories, *Miss Gyre from Boston, and Others.* Among her other works were *In the Garden of Dreams: Lyrics and Sonnets,* and *At the Wind's Will: Lyrics and Sonnets.* She sent Hardy a copy of the latter volume (published in 1899), and in August 1900 he wrote to thank her, apologizing for his procrastination in writing but saying that he found some of them "very beautiful." He urged her to spend the autumn or winter at Bournemouth or Torquay so that he and his wife Emma might see her (*Letters* II, 266).

Mountclere, Lord   The husband of Ethelberta PETHERWIN in *The HAND OF ETHELBERTA.* He is a lecherous viscount of about 65 when she marries him, and he keeps a mistress in a cottage on his estate. On their wedding night Ethelberta learns of his dissipation and tries to escape, with the aid of her family, but fails. Although of humble origins, she has a stronger will than he and eventually tames him, dispatches the mistress, and brings some prosperity to her large family of siblings.

mummers, Christmas   *See* CHRISTMAS MUMMERS.

Murray's Magazine   Magazine published by John Murray at 50 Albemarle St., London (*Letters* I, 268). In 1887 Hardy submitted the short story "The WAITING SUPPER" to the magazine; it was accepted and published in January and February 1888 before being collected in *A CHANGED MAN AND OTHER TALES.* In 1891 the editor, Edward Arnold, refused an early version of *TESS OF THE D'URBERVILLES* "virtually because of its improper explicitness" (Purdy, *Thomas Hardy: A Bibliographical Study,* 73). The magazine ceased publication a short time after refusing the novel.

Murry, John Middleton (1889–1957)   English literary critic and journalist, the husband of the writer Katherine Mansfield. His criticism focuses on an author's life and psychology. Among his works are *Fyodor Dostoyevsky, Countries of the Mind, Keats and Shakespeare, Cinnamon and Angelica, The Evolution of an Intellectual,* and *To the Unknown God.* His autobiography, *Between Two Worlds,* reveals much about his stormy relationship with his wife; it was published just after her death.

On February 20, 1919, Murry wrote Hardy to request a poem; he had taken over the editorship of the revived ATHENAEUM and hoped Hardy could supply one for his first issue, scheduled for April 4, 1919. Hardy replied in early March that he had been searching everywhere for one that would be relevant to the periodical's new start. He was glad, he said, that such a famous review was coming to life again, although it had given him some "hard knocks" in its "previous incarnation," 40 or 50 years earlier (*Letters* V, 297–98). A week later he wrote that he had found two verses; he sent two stanzas of "ACCORDING TO THE MIGHTY WORKING," which appeared on April 4, 1919.

In July 1919 Murry sent him his *Poems: 1917–18,* inscribed to Hardy "as a mark of devotion and gratitude." Hardy responded immediately to thank him, and in October wrote that he admired the form of the verses, and would leave it to others to judge the content.

Murry reviewed the one-volume edition of Hardy's *Collected Poems* in the *Athenaeum* on November 7, 1919. When Hardy responded, he praised Murry's remark that there is "no necessary connection between poetic apprehension & poetic method" and urged him to use it as a text for a long article (*Letters* V, 341).

In January 1923 Murry's New Zealand–born wife, Kathleen Beauchamp Murry, who wrote under the name Katherine Mansfield, died of tuberculosis. Hardy wrote a letter of condolence, saying that he and his wife were very familiar with her books. He said he had passed through the same experience Murry was now going through (that is, the loss of his wife), and knew how useless letters were at such a time (*Letters* VI, 184).

Murry began editing a new periodical a few months later—the *Adelphi;* the first issue was dated June 1923. He asked Hardy to contribute to the periodical. Hardy wrote to wish him success, and sent a poem, "A Leader of Fashion," which appeared in November 1925.

museums   Hardy was a lifelong visitor to museums, ranging from the BRITISH MUSEUM to the DORSET COUNTY MUSEUM. As a young man in LONDON, working for Sir Arthur William BLOMFIELD, he frequented the former and wrote the poem "IN THE BRITISH MUSEUM" and "CHRISTMAS IN THE ELGIN ROOM." Later he did research there for such novels as The TRUMPET-MAJOR, assisted by Florence Emily Dugdale (HARDY), the young woman who became his second wife in 1914. The museum owns the manuscripts of TESS OF THE D'URBERVILLES and The DYNASTS, which were donated by Hardy in 1911.

Hardy also often visited what is now the Victoria and Albert Museum, but which was then called the South Kensington Museum. This museum, according to Anthony Burton of the Victoria and Albert Museum, began in 1852 as the Museum of Manufactures or Museum of Ornamental Art, housed in Marlborough House, London. In 1857 this collection of decorative art moved to South Kensington and was augmented by many other collections (machinery, educational equipment, food, animal products, construction materials) to form the South Kensington Museum. Hardy notes in the *Life* that the iron sheds housing the museum were once nicknamed the Brompton Boilers. He frequented their rooms to obtain materials for an essay he submitted to the Royal Institute of British Architects; it won first prize in the spring of 1863 (*Life*, 42). He spent much time there in 1869 studying the pictures.

In April 1894 Hardy was in London searching for flats he and his wife Emma might occupy during the coming season, and wrote her that he liked the one he had found at 16 Pelham Crescent, since it was near the South Kensington Museum. On May 17, 1899, Queen Victoria laid the foundation stone of a new building on the museum site and renamed the South Kensington Museum the Victoria and Albert Museum.

The Dorset County Museum in DORCHESTER has many Hardy artifacts and manuscripts, including the notebooks in which he recorded his early visits to the British Museum. Hardy's close friend Henry Joseph MOULE became curator of the museum in 1883.

Hardy's friend Sidney COCKERELL was director of the Fitzwilliam Museum in Cambridge from 1908 to 1937. It was Cockerell who, in 1911, urged Hardy to distribute his manuscripts to selected libraries in Britain and the United States, which Hardy began doing at that time. Cockerell also had a hand in Hardy's sitting for a portrait by Augustus JOHN in 1923 which he then acquired for the museum.

music   Hardy came from a musical family and was introduced to music at a very early age. His grandfather, Thomas HARDY (1), who died before he was born, had played the violincello in the church at PUDDLETOWN and later played in the village church of STINSFORD, also superintending the choir. Hardy's father, Thomas HARDY (2), was also musical. In the *Life*, Hardy states that both his father and grandfather were known as the "best church-players" in the neighborhood. The "Hardy instrumentalists," sometimes as many as four, maintained an "easy superiority" over nearby parishes. He recalls being able to "tune a violin when of quite tender years," and was moved to tears by some of the "endless jigs, hornpipes, reels, waltzes, and country-dances" that his father played evenings in their home (*Life*, 8–15, *passim*).

When Hardy first lived in London as a young man, he welcomed the chance to hear music. He took his father to the opera *Lurline*, by the Irish composer William Vincent Wallace, at Covent Garden in 1862 (*Letters* I, 2). In 1865 he attended the funeral of the prime minister, Lord Palmerston, at WESTMINSTER ABBEY. He wrote his sister Mary HARDY about the music (the funeral march from Beethoven's *Eroica* Symphony and the dead march from Handel's *Saul; Letters* I, 6). Few of Hardy's letters from this period have survived, but there is little doubt that he attended concerts and operas whenever possible.

Music is an important element in many of Hardy's short stories, novels, and poems. Examples are his sonnet "A CHURCH ROMANCE," "OLD ANDREY'S EXPERIENCE AS A MUSICIAN," "Absentmindedness in a Parish Choir," "MUSIC IN A SNOWY STREET," "The MUSICAL BOX," "The MAID OF KEINTON MANDEVILLE," "A SINGER ASLEEP," "The DEAD QUIRE," *UNDER THE GREENWOOD TREE*, *The HAND OF ETHELBERTA*, *TWO ON A TOWER*, "FOR CONSCIENCE' SAKE," and *FAR FROM THE MADDING CROWD*. He permitted the magazine *Organist and Choirmaster* to reprint excerpts from *Under the Greenwood Tree* in 1905 (*Letters* III, 178).

In 1893 Hardy sent the actor-manager Charles Charrington an amended version of the play *The THREE WAYFARERS*, and noted that he had inserted "tunes & figures as they used to dance them" (*Letters* III, 9).

Some of Hardy's works have been set to music, including "CHANNEL FIRING," "DITTY," "HAP," "IN TIME OF 'THE BREAKING OF NATIONS,'" "IT NEVER LOOKS LIKE SUMMER," "MEN WHO MARCH AWAY," "The HOUSE OF HOSPITALITIES" and portions of *The DYNASTS*. Baron Frederic D'ERLANGER composed an opera, *Tess*, based on *TESS OF THE D'URBERVILLES*, which was performed at the San Carlo Theater, Naples, on April 10, 1906. Hardy attended the opening LONDON performance at the Covent Garden opera in July 1909 and arranged for Florence Dugdale (later HARDY) to see it also, escorted by his friend Edward CLODD. *See* Appendix II, "Media Adaptations of the Works of Thomas Hardy."

For further reading: D'Agnillo, "Music and Metaphor in *Under the Greenwood Tree*"; Pollard, "Thomas Hardy and Folk Music"; Potter, "Poetry and the Fiddler's Foot: Meters in Thomas Hardy's Work."

"Music in a Snowy Street"   Poem written about a scene Hardy witnessed on April 26, 1884; it was collected in *HUMAN SHOWS, FAR PHANTASIES, SONGS, AND TRIFLES* (1925). Hardy described the sight in his journal.

He saw four sisters, itinerant musicians, in the High Street, DORCHESTER. The eldest had a "fixed, old, hard face" and played the violin. The next one had a "coquettish smirk" and also played the violin. The third beat the tambourine, and the youngest, a child, played the triangle and wore a bead necklace. Later in the day he saw them transformed; the first one had "soft solicitous thought" and the second one was "archly tender." The third had the face of an "angel," and the fourth resembled a "cherub." As they played he believed "they were what Nature made them, before the smear of 'civilization' had sullied their existences" (*Life,* 165).

The poem opens in a cemetery in which the graves are covered by snow. The poet imagines that the women buried there were once the mere "damsels" who played the harp and viol and danced during the days of Napoleon Bonaparte or even Marie Antoinette.

"Musical Box, The"   Poem collected in *MOMENTS OF VISION* (1917). In this poem Hardy thinks nostalgically back upon the time he and his first wife, Emma HARDY, spent in a small cottage, Riverside Villa, at STURMINSTER NEWTON. They were, perhaps, happier here than anywhere else they lived.

Hardy recalls assuming their time together was "lifelong to be," as he wanders along, turning the handle of a music box after a walk along the river. He sees Emma waiting for him on the porch. As he approaches the house, he is oblivious of the shadow of a spirit nearby that is gently, unobtrusively, warning him to "value what the nonce outpours—/This best of life—that shines about/Your welcoming!" Emma laughs as she sees him in the twilight with his music box. The spirit sings, "O make the most of what is nigh!" but he does not hear or see the message. Hardy accuses himself of having failed to recognize Emma's loneliness.

The "mindless lyre" he is playing is also a symbol of his lack of interest in Emma. At the time he was preoccupied with the writing of *The RETURN OF THE NATIVE*.

Bailey points out that the poem is a coda to Hardy's poem "Overlooking the River Stour." The music box was probably among the Victorian furniture and other objects the Hardys bought for Riverside Villa (Bailey, *The Poetry of Thomas Hardy,* 382–83).

natural world, the Hardy's outlook was imbued with the significance and vitality of the natural world from childhood. Charles Whibley observes that the first book Hardy was given to read was John Dryden's edition of Virgil's poetry, and infers that his early exposure to Virgil influenced his entire concept of landscape, which is not "bleak and silent" but "the scene of manifold activities and divers superstitions." Virgil was a young man studying philosophy and Greek on his father's farm when Julius Caesar was assassinated in 44 B.C., an event that threw Italy into turmoil and caused many farmers to be dispossessed of their land. Virgil's family had connections that saved them from this fate. He was able to spend his time writing. The *Bucolics,* or poems of farm life, in which he looked on simpler times, influenced Hardy's evocations of rural life in his novels (particularly FAR FROM THE MADDING CROWD, UNDER THE GREEN-WOOD TREE, *The* WOODLANDERS, and TESS OF THE D'URBERVILLES). Many of his poems also reflect his nostalgia for the era when farm laborers had a stable environment and were not subject to the "nomadic exchanges" of the hiring fair (*see* "THE DORSETSHIRE LABOURER"). In his poem "CHILDHOOD AMONG THE FERNS," Hardy recalls taking shelter from a rainstorm within a bank of ferns, which becomes a "spray-roofed house." He ignores the raindrops piercing the "green rafters" and pretends they don't exist; when the sun bursts forth there is a "sweet breath" as the "limp ferns" dry and he thinks, "I could live on here thus till death."

In his poem "DOMICILIUM," he thinks of HIGHER BOCKHAMPTON, his birthplace, as it must have been when his grandparents first settled there. It was wild, surrounded by heath and furze, with heathcroppers their "only friends." Gradually the family planted tall firs and beeches and developed garden plots and orchards, just as Hardy himself would later do at MAX GATE.

Hardy's view of the natural world is not altogether benign, however. In his poem "NATURE'S QUESTIONING," Hardy offers several possible answers to the enigma of the natural world and man's relation to it: perhaps nature operates with complete indifference to man, or conceivably, entropy as a natural force is neither negative nor positive. There might also be high plan that has initiated "Evil stormed by Good, / We the Forlorn Hope." Hardy, when questioned, said his own opinion was irrelevant; he was merely enumerating alternatives.

Hardy discusses the relationship between nature and man in a number of other poems. Examples are "The LACKING SENSE" (in which the "Ancient Mind" of Time explains that the Mother [Mother Nature] has "wounded where she loves") and "The MOTHER MOURNS" (in which the poet observes that Nature has created a beautiful world, but mankind has not properly preserved the vegetable and animal life with which it was endowed). Mother Nature also figures in "DOOM AND SHE" and "AFTERWARDS," in which Hardy hopes that his poetic legacy will include his observations of nature and his concern for all creatures. He imagines the times of day at which he might die and the manifestations of nature that an "onlooker" could assume would have been familiar to him. If it were night, for instance, an observer might see a hedgehog travel furtively over the lawn and recall that Hardy "strove that such innocent creatures should come to no harm."

In "The Dorsetshire Labourer," Hardy clarifies the problems of displaced agricultural workers. He deplored the commercial and industrial development that not only destroyed much of the pastoral character of rural England but also threatened many rustic occupations.

Margaret Drabble argues that Hardy is one of the few novelists, along with Emily Brontë and George ELIOT, to have written extensively about the natural world and to have made the assumption that LANDSCAPE determines character. The dairying scenes in *Tess of the d'Urbervilles,* the sheep shearing and washing scenes in *Far from the Madding Crowd,* the game of dice played by WILDEVE and the reddleman by the light of glowworms, and the bonfires on EGDON HEATH, as well as the rushing waters and Eustacia, VYE's drowning in *The RETURN OF THE NATIVE,* the "white cubes of oolite" on the Isle of Slingers in *The* WELL-BELOVED—these are isolated examples of Hardy's delineation of the natural world in a few of his novels. It may be said that his poetry, novels, and short stories are permeated with the subject. In his poem "The LOST PYX" he mentions the life cycles of "sheep, does, hares, badgers, squirrels, rabbits, and 'many a member seldom seen / Of Nature's family.'" There were few WESSEX insects, animals, species of plants, or geological or geographical features unknown to Hardy. It may be argued that a virtually certain index of an amoral, evil character in Hardy's work is his or her indifference to the natural world or cruelty to living creatures, whether wild or domesticated. *See also* ANIMALS, HARDY'S LOVE OF.

For further reading: Brown, ed., *Figures in a Wessex Landscape*; Drabble, "Hardy and the Natural World"; Mallett, "Noticing Things: Hardy and the Nature of 'Nature'"; Taylor, "Hardy and Wordsworth."

"Nature's Questioning"   Poem collected in WESSEX POEMS (1898). The opening lines depict the poet gazing from the window at dawn and seeing, like "chastened children," such natural elements as "field, flock, and lonely tree." They represent "Earth's old glooms and pains," and exist amid life and death. Dawn often represented a period of depression for Hardy; similar sentiments appear in *The* DYNASTS and *The* WOODLANDERS (Bailey, *The Poetry of Thomas Hardy*, 101–102).

The poem was published with a headpiece showing a broken door-key, an image with particular significance for Hardy. In FAR FROM THE MADDING CROWD Maryann, Bathsheba EVERDENE's maid, tells her of an "unlucky token" that had come to her one morning: "I went to unlock the door and dropped the key, and it fell upon the stone floor and broke into two pieces. Breaking a key is a dreadful bodement" (chapter 33). The headpiece sets the tone of the poem, with its foreboding, anxious speculation about the implications for man of the NATURAL WORLD.

Hardy posits several different meanings of the natural world in the form of questions. The first is whether "some Vast Imbecility" has "Framed us in jest, and left us now to hazardry?"—a deistic view that God sets processes in motion and lets nature take its course. The second question is whether men have been created by an Automaton "unconscious of our pains?" The third question, turning on entropy as a natural force, is whether men are left as unthinking, unseeing shapes, brain and eye now gone? The fourth question is whether there is a high Plan that has initiated "Evil stormed by Good, / We the Forlorn Hope over which Achievement strides?"

The last three lines of the poem suggest that there is no real answer for the poet except an eternal, rather pessimistic conundrum: "Meanwhile the winds, and rains, / And Earth's old glooms and pains / Are still the same, and Life and Death are neighbours nigh."

In 1920 Hardy wrote Alfred NOYES that often it was assumed the words "some Vast Imbecility" represented his principal perception of nature. However, he insisted that the definitions posited in the poem were "merely enumerated . . . as fanciful alternatives to several others, having nothing to do with my own opinion."

"Near Lanivet, 1872"   Poem published in MOMENTS OF VISION (1917), based on an incident that occurred before Hardy and his first wife, Emma HARDY, were married. Lanivet is near Bodmin, CORNWALL, and the handpost (a post with arms pointing in different directions) was on the old St. Austell Road. The speaker, a young man, recalls a walk through the countryside when his companion, a girl, had become tired and leaned against a cruciform handpost, her open palms stretched along the boards and her face turned sideways. From his perspective she looks crucified. He cries, "Don't," but she doesn't seem to hear.

As they resume walking she admits that although she is now rested, something "strange" has come into her mind. She had not realized how she would look, "in the shade, / When I leant there like one nailed." He reassures her, but she says that, although she has not been crucified in body, she might have been in spirit. As they go along, they seem to visualize, "In the running of Time's far glass / Her crucified, as she had wondered if she might be / Some day – Alas, alas!" The final two words are a poignant personal comment on Emma's later mental instability.

Hardy had met Emma in 1870; this event took place during their long engagement on his fourth visit to Cornwall. The scene was an actual one. Emma's father had lived at Kitland, Bodmin; and bitterly opposed their marriage. The signpost no longer exists, but many decades later, the moment lingered in Hardy's mind as symbolizing Emma's future unhappiness with her husband (Pinion, *A Commentary on the Poems of Thomas Hardy*, 124).

Neigh, Alfred   A fashionable man of 35 in *The* HAND OF ETHELBERTA, he is the nephew of John DONCASTLE. He aspires to be in step with the latest trends in the arts although he comes of a family of knackers and tanners. A knacker is someone who would buy old horses and, after they died, sell their meat as dog food. In TESS OF THE D'URBERVILLES, Tess's father refuses to sell the body of the family horse, Prince, to a knacker, but insists on giving it a proper burial because of its long service to the family. Neigh begins courting Ethelberta PETHERWIN, who is shocked to find that his "estate," Fairfield, is not a mansion but instead a park with decrepit horses. Ethelberta, of mediocre lineage, is something of an opportunist herself and refuses Neigh's advances. He later tries in vain to prevent her marriage to Lord MOUNTCLERE.

"Netty Sargent's Copyhold"   See FEW CRUSTED CHARACTERS, A.

"Neutral Tones"   A poem written at 16 Westbourne Park Villas, LONDON, ostensibly in 1867, and collected in WESSEX POEMS (1898). The speaker is a young man addressing a girl whose love he has apparently rejected. They stand on a winter day by a pond beneath a sun so white it seemed to be "chidden of God." The very ground is strewn with gray leaves fallen from an ash tree. Her eyes fix on him, recalling past "riddles," perhaps when she used to try to ascertain his feelings. Her smile is the "deadest thing / Alive enough to have strength to die." Looking back, her feels guilty but not entirely at fault, since he has learned certain lessons; for instance, that "love deceives / And wrings with wrong." Many critics, including Morgan, believe the girl to be pregnant. It has also been suggested that the girl in the poem is Tryphena SPARKS, Hardy's cousin, and that the actual date of composition is later than indicated. Gittings suggests that Hardy courted Tryphena in 1869. (Gittings, *Young Thomas Hardy,* 167).

For further reading: Brown, ed., *Figures in a Wessex Landscape;* Drabble, "Hardy and the Natural World"; Wibley, "Thomas Hardy."

Newbolt, Sir Henry John (1862–1938) English man of letters; he practiced law, edited the *MONTHLY REVIEW,* and wrote novels, poetry, and the official history of the British navy. Among his works were *Drake's Drum and Other Sea Songs, The Book of the Thin Red Line,* and *Studies Green and Gray.*

Newbolt published Hardy's poem "The Dear" in the *Monthly Review* in June 1902. In March 1904 he reviewed *The DYNASTS;* it was an unsigned review, but Hardy correctly detected that Newbolt had written it. Hardy wrote to thank him for his "generous remarks" (*Letters* III, 113).

Newbolt dedicated his *Collected Poems* (1910) to Hardy; Hardy wrote in July 1910 that he felt "touched & honoured" by his doing so (*Letters* IV, 108). In October 1910 Hardy wrote Newbolt to invite him to attend the forthcoming play "The MELLSTOCK QUIRE," the adaptation by A. H. EVANS of Hardy's novel *UNDER THE GREENWOOD TREE.* It was performed in DORCHESTER and also at the Cripplegate Institute, LONDON. Newbolt and his wife attended the first performance, on Wednesday, November 16, and stayed overnight at MAX GATE.

Newbolt and the poet W. B. YEATS paid a visit to Hardy at Max Gate on Sunday, June 2, 1912. Representing the ROYAL SOCIETY OF LITERATURE, they presented Hardy with the society's gold medal on his 72nd birthday. Michael Millgate gives an interesting account of the private presentation ceremony, from which Hardy insisted that Emma HARDY be excluded. The visitors protested, but to no avail; she left the room after lunch. Hardy then read, to the two men, the acceptance speech he had written and had already sent to London reporters. Millgate explains that, conceivably, Hardy was worried that Emma might create a disturbance. She had already made claims that she was the author of much of his fiction and had exhibited marked changes in mood (Millgate, *Thomas Hardy: A Biography,* 477).

In September 1914 Newbolt and Hardy, as well as John GALSWORTHY, were among the group of "well-known men of letters" summoned by the chancellor of the Duchy of Lancaster to Wellington House, Buckingham Gate, for the purpose of formulating a statement setting forth the British reaction to the outbreak of WORLD WAR I *(Life,* 366).

Newbolt spoke to the Royal Society of Literature on October 17, 1917, in a lecture titled "The Poetry of Thomas Hardy." Hardy wrote to thank him, adding that he hoped someday to read the lecture verbatim.

Newson, Richard A jovial passing sailor in *The MAYOR OF CASTERBRIDGE,* he purchases Susan HENCHARD, the wife of Michael HENCHARD for five guineas when Michael offers to auction her off. They move to Canada with the Henchards' daughter, Elizabeth-Jane HENCHARD (1), who dies. They then have a daughter, Elizabeth-Jane HENCHARD (2). Newson returns to sea and is thought lost on a voyage to Newfoundland. In fact, he survives and later returns to England to search for Elizabeth-Jane. He hears from Michael Henchard that she is dead; when he learns she is not he is delighted, and approves of her eventual marriage to Donald FARFRAE. He settles near the sea at BUDMOUTH.

New Quarterly Magazine founded by Desmond MAC-CARTHY, who edited it from 1907 to 1910. (This is not to be confused with the late-19th-century *NEW QUARTERLY MAGAZINE,* in which Hardy published several short stories). MacCarthy asked Hardy for a contribution, but on September 30, 1907, Hardy wrote that he had nothing on hand that would suit a "new magazine." He wished MacCarthy well and assured him he would have no difficulty in attracting other contributors (*Letters* III, 276). Hardy's poem "The HOUSE OF HOSPITALITIES" was published in the magazine in January 1909.

New Quarterly Magazine Magazine published during the late 19th century, not to be confused with the *NEW QUARTERLY* founded by Desmond MACCARTHY in 1907. Several of Hardy's stories appeared in its pages: "An INDISCRETION IN THE LIFE OF AN HEIRESS" (July 1878), "The DISTRACTED PREACHER" (April 1879), and "FELLOW-TOWNSMEN" (April 1880). The only review Hardy ever wrote—of William BARNES's *Poems of Rural Life in the Dorset Dialect*—appeared in the magazine in October 1879. Charles Kegan PAUL was editor at that time and commissioned the biographer and critic Alexandra Sutherland Orr to write a positive appreciation of Hardy's work for the same issue, titled "Mr. Hardy's Novels."

New Review Periodical that, in January 1890, published a symposium Hardy contributed an essay, "CANDOUR IN ENGLISH FICTION." It focused on the problem of requisite prudishness in contemporary novels, an important issue for writers whose work, if sold in public bookstalls or distributed in circulating libraries, had to be "suitable" for young people. The other two essays were written by Sir Walter BESANT and Mrs. Lynn Linton.

Andrew Lang published an adverse review of *TESS OF THE D'URBERVILLES* in the magazine (February 1892), stating that the conclusion was "rather improbable" (*Letters* II, 62).

"New Year's Eve"   Poem first published in the *FORT-NIGHTLY REVIEW* for January 1907, and later collected in *TIME'S LAUGHINGSTOCKS* (1909). The poem takes the form of a colloquy between God and the poet. God announces that he is satisfied with the year he has just finished, with its successive seasons; he has put the processes in place for the cycle to begin again. The poet wonders why God is bothering to speak from an Earth in which man has found little joy. God answers that it may have been illogical that he created creatures who even asked such questions. They actually raise philosophical issues he never anticipated. But God is not affected by these questions, even though they may be legitimate. He continues working as he always has, and the seasons begin again, regardless of whether man is content or not.

Bailey points out that this poem represents the "questioning and answering sides of Hardy's mind." This God is not the omniscient God of Christianity but the "unconscious Will of *The DYNASTS* symbolized as a personality" (Bailey, *The Poetry of Thomas Hardy*, 248). In this poem, God gives no thought to what might be just or unjust from man's point of view.

After the poem was published, Hardy's friend Edward CLODD wrote to him, apparently commenting that people would assume the poem represented Hardy's own belief. Hardy replied, rather ambivalently, that the German philosopher Ludwig Feuerbach had once argued that God was the "product of man," but that he himself concurred with the English philosopher Herbert Spencer that it is "paralyzing" to think that there is no comprehension anywhere in the universe of what seems "so incomprehensible to us" (*Letters* III, 244).

New York Times   Hardy's story "DESTINY AND A BLUE CLOAK" was published in this newspaper on Sunday, October 4, 1874. One of the characters, Farmer Lovill, was the basis for Lord MOUNTCLERE in Hardy's novel *The HAND OF ETHELBERTA*, which ran in the newspaper from June 20, 1875, to April 9, 1876. It was printed from proofs of the *CORNHILL MAGAZINE*. The paper also printed Hardy's poem "Song of the Soldiers" on September 10, 1914, and another war poem, "An APPEAL TO AMERICA," on January 4, 1915.

In 1914 the paper put the question "What Is the Best Short Poem in English?" to 25 well-known poets. Hardy sent a letter to the paper (published July 5, 1914), say-ing, "I fail to see how there can be a 'best' poem, long or short." He deplored such an attempt to "appraise by comparison" and declared it "one of the literary vices of the time" (Purdy, *Thomas Hardy: A Bibliographical Study*, 317).

New York World   New York newspaper. On December 24, 1895, Hardy wrote his American publishers HARPER & BROTHERS, which had published *JUDE THE OBSCURE* in mid-November, to say that he had been distressed by Jeannette Gilder's review of the novel in this newspaper on December 8. Gilder castigated Hardy and suggested that the book was immoral compared with the works of Rudyard KIPLING, Robert Louis STEVENSON, James BARRIE, and Mrs. Humphry WARD. He authorized Harper to withdraw *Jude* in America if they deemed it advisable, saying it was much against his wish "to offend the tastes of the American public, or to thrust any book of mine upon readers there" (*Letters* II, 103). He was astonished to receive a letter from the reviewer in the summer of 1896 asking if she might interview him. He replied that he had declined to be interviewed on the subject of the book, and that a meeting with her would be "painful" to him as well as a disappointment to her. Moreover, he said, those readers who, "like yourself . . . could not see that *Jude* makes for morality more than any other book I have written," are not likely to be "made to do so" by a newspaper article (*Life*, Hardy, 279–80). Hardy's poem "The Dead and the Living One" was published in the paper on January 2, 1916.

"Night of Questionings, A"   Published in *HUMAN SHOWS, FAR PHANTASIES, SONGS, AND TRIFLES* (1925), this poem captures the voices of the dead heard by the poet on the eve of All Souls' Day (November 2), a time when, traditionally, the souls of the dead emerge from their graves. There are five stanzas, each representing a different group of deceased people, all asking the central question, "What of the world now?" In each case they are answered by the wind. The first group consists of those buried outside by the "tottering tower" (possibly that at STINSFORD CHURCH). Those buried beneath the aisles "Of old cathedral piles" and "Walled up in vaulted biers" make up the second group. There are also sailors in the "sunk sea-bed," "troubled skulls that heave / And fust in the flats of France," and convicts who lie "within the pales / Of town and country jails / With the rope-groove on them yet," all posing the same question. The answer given by the wind, in various forms, is always the same: Men have learned little, and will not grow purer; evil will persist in the world.

"Night of the Dance, The"   Poem published in *TIME'S LAUGHINGSTOCKS* (1909). The poem contrasts an indifferent Nature with the preparations in a country home for a dance. References to viols being strung against the contrapuntal "whoo" of owls outside recall Hardy's life-long devotion to music. Old Robert is tending the fire; this might be the Robert Reason of UNDER THE GREEN-WOOD TREE, and his home the setting for the poem (Bailey, *The Poetry of Thomas Hardy*, 219). The speaker hopes for an evening of dancing and love, in contrast with Nature outside, which is impartial and unpredictable. A cold moon gazes down, and the stars seem to "Quiz" the arrangements in a disaffected manner.

For further reading: Phillip Mallett, "Noticing Things: Hardy and the Nature of 'Nature.'"

"Night of Trafalgar, The" *(Boatman's Song)*   Song from *The* DYNASTS (I, V, vii) sung by the "second boatman" at WEYMOUTH at the time of the British victory during the Battle of TRAFALGAR. In the first of three stanzas, the boatmen struggle in a small boat off the Weymouth coast. They listen to the "drub of Deadman's Bay" on a stormy October night, but are unaware of "what the day had done for us at Trafalgar." (The poem is printed with an accent over the final *a* in "Trafalgar," so that the final syllable is emphasized throughout, imitating the rhythmical sound of the oars.) In the second stanza, they pull hard to reach the shore. Finally "snug at home," they sleep. At the same time the British "gallants" have been fighting all day. In the third stanza the scene shifts to Trafalgar, where "victors and the vanquished" are tossed by the storm.

"Noble Lady's Tale, The" *(circa 1790)*   A three-part poem first published as "The Noble Lady's Story" in HARPER'S WEEKLY (New York) on February 18, 1905. It was later collected in TIME'S LAUGHINGSTOCKS (1909). The first two parts represent the noble young lady's recollections, and the third contains the poet's interpretation of her history. According to James O. Bailey, the poem is based on an imaginary incident experienced by Lady Susan Fox-Strangways O'Brien (1743–1827) and her husband, William O'Brien (1738–1815). Lady Susan and her husband are buried in STINSFORD CHURCH in a vault built by Thomas HARDY (1), grandfather of Hardy. The daughter of the first earl of Ilchester, Lady Susan eloped with the Irish comedian William O'Brien when she came of age in 1764. She had met him at private theatrical performances in Holland House, owned by her father. This was a scandalous marriage; Hugh Walpole wrote that "even a footman were preferable." O'Brien was highly accomplished, however, playing a number of well-known Shakespearean characters as well as other parts. Hardy's grandmothers had both seen and admired O'Brien, and he was for many years a member of the Stinsford church congregation. He promised Lady Susan's father he would never again act on a public stage. They lived in Canada for some years. After their father died, Lady Susan's brother, who became Lord Ilchester, gave them

the house next to Stinsford church and found him an appointment as receiver general for Dorset. Stinsford House burned in 1892, a source of great sadness to Hardy (Bailey, *The Poetry of Thomas Hardy*, 33–35, 256).

In part one of the poem, an unnamed noble lady recognizes her husband's unhappiness. He recalls the circumstances of their marriage and the forgiveness of her father on the one condition that he give up performing on the stage. He acknowledges their happiness but says he is called once again to the stage. He longs to return just once before he dies to "tread the boards" he had once trod. The noble lady gives him permission to go despite his pledge to herself and her father, and worries that he will meet some "wild stage-woman" and that his passion will wane.

In part two, he does return but is still sad. He says he failed in his old part; his memory is gone. He seems to feel estranged from his wife. He says he saw her one night at the play, "half-hid," and that her spying on him has made him feel he can never trust her. In vain she pleads that she has never been in the theater. It is, instead, her "wraith" he has seen; it has been projected on him by her "tense brain at home." He dies and is buried in a "little vault with room for one beside."

In the third part, the poet comments that the lady too has died. A memorial tablet has been placed in "Mellstock Quire." (Mellstock is Hardy's fictional name for Stinsford.) The question of whether she did go to see her actor husband perform is left unanswered; however, it is suggested that she should not be blamed if she did go.

"Nobody Comes"   A poem written on October 9, 1924, in which Hardy stands "mute by the gate," waiting for his wife Florence (HARDY) to return after an operation in London. It was published in HUMAN SHOWS, FAR PHANTASIES, SONGS, AND TRIFLES (1925).

Noel, Roden Berkeley Wriothesley (1834–1894)   Poet, fourth son of the first earl of Gainsborough. Hardy apparently met Noel in LONDON in June 1887 at the home of the poet and critic Agnes Mary Frances Robinson. At the time the Hardys had taken lodgings at 5 Campden Hill Road, London (*Letters* I, 165).

In 1892 Noel wrote an article about TESS OF THE D'URBERVILLES, but Richard L. Purdy and Michael Millgate believe it was not published (*Letters* I, 260). It was rejected by the *Edinburgh Review*.

Noel's works include *A Little Child's Monument* and *A Modern Faust*.

Normandy   French province. Hardy knew Normandy well, since Cherbourg was the French port nearest WEYMOUTH, and there were regular shipping and passenger services there. He and Emma HARDY spent their "first continental days" after their marriage in September

1874 at Rouen. He was already planning, at that time, to set some scenes in his novel *The HAND OF ETHELBERTA* (published serially 1875–76; in book form 1876) in Rouen, as he wrote the publisher George Murray Smith in 1875. Smith was head of the publishing firm of SMITH, ELDER.

In July 1880 the Hardys spent several weeks in Normandy, going to Étretât (the site of several scenes in *A LAODICEAN*), where they bathed in the English Channel each day. Hardy later blamed his illness of 1881 on these baths. They went on to Havre and the fashionable resorts of Trouville, Honfleur, Lisieux, and Caen, then returned to DORSET.

North American Review   New York periodical owned and edited by George Brinton McClellan Harvey, a political journalist. The assistant editor was David Munroe. Hardy had encouraged Lady Agnes GROVE to submit some of her work to the *Review* and was sympathetic about her notes of rejection. In July 1903 he wrote Munroe as acting editor, saying that in May he had sent two poems to Colonel Harvey, who was staying at Claridge's Hotel (LONDON), but had heard nothing and assumed that, if they reached their destination, they were "not required" and he would appreciate their return (*Letters* III, 71). One of them, "A TRAMPWOMAN'S TRAGEDY," was published in the *Review* in November 1903. In February 1915 his poem "A Hundred Years Since" was published in the *Review*.

Norton, John (unknown)   Vice president of the Royal Institute of British Architects at the time Hardy first went to LONDON as a young man, in 1862. John HICKS, the DORCHESTER architect in whose office he had worked, was a friend of Norton's, and gave Hardy a letter of introduction to him. Norton invited Hardy to make drawings in his office for a modest payment while he looked for work. When Hardy arrived the following Monday, Norton informed him that he had encountered a friend, Sir Arthur William BLOMFIELD, at the meeting of the Institute of British Architects. Blomfield had asked whether he might know of a "gothic draughtsman" who could do church restoration. Norton had suggested Hardy, and sent him immediately to call on Blomfield. Hardy was hired at once and worked for Blomfield until he returned to Dorchester in the summer of 1867 and eventually began working for George CRICKMAY in WEYMOUTH (*Life*, 36, 63).

Noyes, Alfred (1880–1958)   English poet, essayist, and critic, known for his ballads and narrative verse. His poem "The Highwayman" is perhaps his best-known; he also wrote an epic poem, *Drake,* that was published in *Blackwood's Edinburgh Magazine*. His poem "After Victory" was included in a collection of poems by Hardy's friends that was presented to Hardy in 1919.

In 1920 Noyes gave an address, reported in the *Morning Post* on December 9, stating that Hardy's philosophy held that "the Power behind the Universe was an imbecile jester." Hardy wrote a letter of protest to Noyes, stating that he held no such view. Noyes replied that he had paid a tribute to Hardy as a writer, and cited various passages in Hardy's poems that substantiated his conclusion. Hardy objected in a lengthy letter on December 19, arguing that it was unfair to judge a writer's work as a whole from "picked passages . . . scattered over a period of fifty years." He himself saw some of his poems, written when he was quite young, as "an amusing instance of early cynicism." He then took the poems Noyes cited one by one and defended his position. He insisted that he conceived of a Cause of Things that was neither "moral nor immoral, but *un*moral . . . 'which neither good nor evil knows.'" Hardy later wrote a friend that he actually had no philosophy, "merely what I have often explained to be only a confused heap of impressions, like those of a bewildered child at a conjuring show" (*Life*, 407–10).

Nunsuch, Johnny   In *The RETURN OF THE NATIVE*, Johnny, the son of Susan NUNSUCH, is a boy who helps Captain VYE and becomes much attached to his granddaughter, Eustacia VYE. When Eustacia builds her fire on the hill as a signal to Damon WILDEVE, Johnny feeds it. He is thoroughly familiar with EGDON HEATH, and confides the news of Eustacia's meeting with Wildeve to Diggory VENN. It is Johnny who discovers Mrs. YEOBRIGHT lying on the ground after her fatal snake bite; he hears her last words. When Johnny becomes ill, his mother attributes it to a spell cast by Eustacia. Johnny's role is that of messenger and informant as he roams Egdon Heath; his observations are the catalyst for much of the action in the novel.

Nunsuch, Susan   In *The RETURN OF THE NATIVE*, Susan is the devoted mother of Johnny NUNSUCH. We meet her first on Guy Fawkes Night, when she dances wildly through the bonfire embers. She lives at Mistover, near the home of Captain VYE; she is a "witchlike woman whose stays creaked like shoes whenever she stooped or turned." She believes Eustacia VYE is a witch, but she herself indulges in witchlike ceremonies at times. She stabs Eustacia with a stocking needle at church, convinced she has cast a spell on her son. She also prepares a wax effigy of Eustacia, sticks pins in it, and prays over it; this is the night of Eustacia's death.

O

Oak, Gabriel The hero of *FAR FROM THE MADDING CROWD*, a shepherd of about 28 at the opening of the novel. As he is establishing his own sheep farm at Norcombe Hill, he meets Bathsheba EVERDENE, his neighbor's niece, and is impressed by her beauty, although he also is aware of her vanity. Morgan points out that the narrator does not interpret Bathsheba's gaze as evidence of vanity, and that Oak has a double standard here. When he avoids playing the flute because it makes his mouth pucker in an unpleasant way, he does not consider himself vain (personal communication with the author). He proposes to her, but she rejects him. He loses his flocks when an inept sheepdog drives them over a cliff.

Bathsheba inherits her uncle's farm, and Oak saves her ricks from a fire and begins working for her. He is the hero of the novel's most dramatic scenes, such as the sheep shearing and the terrible storm, in which he saves the farm's cornstacks. By then Bathsheba has married the untrustworthy Sergeant TROY, but Gabriel continues faithfully to rescue her from Troy's blunders. Troy is reported drowned, after which he becomes her bailiff, or overseer, and also the bailiff of William BOLDWOOD, a prosperous but rather wooden bachelor farmer who has also been Bathsheba's suitor. Boldwood makes Bathsheba promise to marry him after seven years, when Troy can be presumed legally dead. Troy reappears, however, and Boldwood shoots him in a mad frenzy. Gabriel then decides to emigrate, which upsets Bathsheba; she induces him to propose again, which he does, having never stopped loving her. They develop a "camaraderie occurring through the similarity of pursuits," which becomes the basis of "the only love which is as strong as death." Throughout the novel, Gabriel matures, becoming increasingly generous, stable, self-reliant, unselfish, and strong, as befits his name.

"Obliterate Tomb, The" Poem published in *SATIRES OF CIRCUMSTANCE* (1914). It was possibly generated from Hardy's search for the family graves of his first wife, Emma Gifford HARDY, at Plymouth, when he was en route to CORNWALL. He has "a traveller's mind" and is "a man of memories." He reflects on people he has known in the past who have wronged him and resolves to forgive them. The next night he takes a lantern and visits the graveyard at the church. He finds the family tomb where they are buried. It has decayed so that the names can scarcely be read. A stranger appears in "foreign" clothes with a tropical sunburn; he is from the Pacific. He is searching for his family tomb also. They realize their ancestors were enemies. The speaker offers to take care of the restoration of the tomb and the stranger leaves. However, he becomes occupied by other things and does not return for a year. The tomb is untouched, but he still refrains from restoring it. He dies.

After many years well-meaning "church-restorers" decide to build a path in the church cemetery but the old tomb lies in the way. They destroy it, since apparently no family member has cared to keep it up. The speaker's impulse has weakened with the passage of time.

"Old Andrey's Experience as a Musician" *See FEW CRUSTED CHARACTERS, A.*

"Old Furniture" Poem published in *MOMENTS OF VISION* (1917) that recalls the cherished furniture and artifacts of Hardy's home at HIGHER BOCKHAMPTON. He envisions the people who have owned and used each familiar object.

The perspective then shifts; he sees receding images of ancestors he has not known himself, but only through family tales: "hands behind hands, growing paler and paler," each becoming frailer. He sees a "foggy finger" setting the minutes of the clock, fingers dancing over the strings of the "old viol," and a face that "kindles to red" as tinder is added to the fire.

He concludes that he must move on, as "the world has no use for one" who sees things in such a nostalgic way.

Bailey observes that Hardy often saw the ghostly life of old houses, as in his description of the Melbury home in chapter 4 of *The WOODLANDERS*.

"Old Mrs. Chundle" Story possibly written about 1888 or 1890. It was first published posthumously in *The Ladies' Home Journal*, Philadelphia, in 1929 by arrangement with Florence Emily HARDY. F. B. Pinion states that the story is true and that the principal character, a landscape artist, may be based on Henry MOULE, brother of Horace MOULE (Pinion, *A Hardy Companion*, 83).

The story is set near the ruins of Corvsgate Castle (CORFE CASTLE). The new curate at Kingscreech has been painting a view of the castle ruins. At lunchtime, he goes to a nearby cottage; the woman living there prepares him a meal. She is Mrs. Chundle, who has never come to church. She tells him she is too deaf to understand the service. He offers to have a speaking-tube installed from the pulpit to her seat.

The next Sunday a vapor rises from the speaking-tube, apparently an odor of onions. The curate drops his handkerchief into the bell-mouth of the tube, but Mrs. Chundle thinks it is an accident and blows through the tube. His handkerchief flies out and floats to the pulpit floor. The curate decides the distracting odor is of peppermint, cider, and pickled cabbage. He puts his thumb into the bell-mouth and abruptly concludes the sermon. Mrs. Chundle tells him she can hear perfectly except when he puts his handkerchief on top of the speaking-tube. The ordeal recurs the next Sunday, and the curate has the speaking tube removed. He then learns that Mrs. Chundle has died; she had overstrained her heart running to church. She had sent for him, but he had not come. She did not send a second message, assuming he was visiting others in need.

She leaves him all she has, in gratitude for his friendship. He is overcome with remorse for not having gone immediately to visit her and feels he has betrayed her. He goes out and kneels down in a lonely part of the road, covering his face.

Oliphant, Margaret (1828–1897) Scottish novelist and historical writer whose books dealt with 19th-century English society. Many critics regard *Salem Chapel*, one of the novels in her series *Chronicles of Carlingford*, as her best work of fiction. She was the wife of the artist Francis Wilson Oliphant. In 1882 she wrote Hardy to suggest that he write some sketches on the problem of the laboring poor of DORSET for *LONGMAN'S MAGAZINE*. He replied that he would like to write such a paper, and also that he welcomed the opportunity "of a direct communication with a writer I have known in spirit so long" (*Letters* I, 107). Her suggestion resulted in his essay "The DORSETSHIRE LABOURER," which was published in the magazine in July 1883.

In May 1886 Hardy was introduced to Oliphant at the home of Lady CARNARVON in London, and wrote Emma HARDY that he did not "care a bit for her. . . . She is propriety & primness incarnate." Oliphant later attacked JUDE THE OBSCURE, saying the novel was a "tremendous downfall" and "an assault on the stronghold of marriage" ("The Anti-Marriage League," *Blackwood's Magazine*, January 1896, 135–49; reprinted in Clarke, *Thomas Hardy: Critical Assessments*, I, 248–52). Her criticism hurt Hardy, who earlier had called on her at Windsor during an illness (Millgate, *Thomas Hardy: A Biography*, 373).

Omar Khayyám Club Club started by Hardy's friend Edward CLODD in 1892. Hardy was elected a founder-member and in July 1895 visited Burford Bridge, Surrey, with the club. The members attended a dinner at the local hotel in honor of the novelist George MEREDITH, who had lived nearby at Box Hill. Both Hardy and Meredith made speeches. In the *Life* Hardy recalls that they were "the first and last ever made by either of them; at any rate it was the first, and last but one or two, by Hardy" (*Life*, 268).

For further reading: Clodd, *Memories*.

"On a Midsummer Eve" Poem first published in *SELECTED POEMS* (MACMILLAN & CO., 1916) and collected in *MOMENTS OF VISION* (1917). The poem reflects the thoughts, possibly of a young man, who cuts a parsley stalk and blows it toward the moon, not thinking "what ghosts would walk" to his tune. In the second stanza he kneels and scoops his hand into a brook; a "faint figure" seems to stand above him. In the third stanza he speaks "rough rhymes of chance, not choice" and hears a voice in his ear that transforms his words into a "tenderer verse."

The two forces in the poem, the young person's actions and the spectral figure, have a parallel motion, closing in on the speaker in narrowing concentric circles. Through his actions he casts a triple spell. In the first stanza, the moon and the ghostly figures are distant; in the second, the "ghosts" condense into a "faint figure" standing above him when he dips his hand into the brook. In the final stanza he speaks rhymes and hears an immediate response in his ear.

Midsummer Eve is traditionally a night associated with magic. In *Folkways in Thomas Hardy*, Ruth Firor states that ghosts of dead lovers appear on Midsummer Eve, and also that the cutting of parsley signifies that the person will be "crossed in love." In The WOODLANDERS the Hintock girls attempt, on this night, to effect a spell that will allow them to see their future husbands. In the poem, the blowing of the parsley toward the moon signifies something sinister. The phantom of the beloved is summoned by the triple actions: the blowing of the parsley, the dipping of his hand in the brook, and the speaking of "rough rhymes of chance" (Bailey, *The Poetry of Thomas Hardy*, 356).

In the second stanza, Hardy reflects that, dwelling in the "ancient lands" of Europe, on which writers and poets have left their mark and which they have "chronicled," he is content to study those chronicles and trace the lives of those who have lived in the past. Hardy did this by writing about "Wessex" in his fiction and poetry. Bailey remarks that instead of visiting a "land of promise" which, underneath, might prove to be crude and immature, he preferred to "pore over the palimpsest of Wessex" (Bailey, *The Poetry of Thomas Hardy*, 140. A palimpsest is a manuscript, usually parchment, from which an earlier text has been erased but is still faintly visible).

"On an Invitation to the United States" Poem collected in *POEMS OF THE PAST AND THE PRESENT* (1902). The poem may owe something to a passage from Henry JAMES's *Hawthorne* that Hardy had copied into the "America" section of his notebook in 1879 (Purdy, *Thomas Hardy: A Bibliographical Study*, 111). It was reprinted in *SELECTED POEMS OF THOMAS HARDY*. Hardy had received many invitations to visit the United States, from Mrs. Pearl Mary Craigie of New York, the Yale University professor and literary critic William Lyon Phelps, the trustees of the Pittsburgh Institute, and others, including, possibly, Rebekah OWEN.

In the first of two stanzas Hardy explains his reasons for declining the invitation to go to the United States. He has lost his "ardours for emprize" (enterprise) now that he is older, and states, "I shrink to seek a modern coast / Whose riper times have yet to be." He sees the "new regions" as free from "that long drip of human tears" left by "peoples old in tragedy."

Hardy had many invitations to visit the United States and refused or ignored them all.

"One We Knew" *(M.H. 1772–1857)* Dated May 20, 1902, this poem was first printed in the *Tatler* and, under the title "Remembrance," in *HARPER'S WEEKLY* (New York) on December 12, 1903. It was later collected in *TIME'S LAUGHINGSTOCKS* (1909). It is a tribute to Hardy's paternal grandmother, Mary Head Hardy, who sat for many hours by the fire during his childhood. He and his siblings would gather at her knees; she would speak to them "not as one who remembers, / But rather as one who sees." The poem has the structure of a ballad, in which Hardy recounts the many events of which she told them: the formations of country dances, such as "The Triumph" or "The New-rigged Ship," the traditions surrounding the planting of the maypole, the day they learned of the Reign of Terror, and of "Bonaparte's unbounded / Ambition and arrogance." Hardy regarded his grandmother as the one person left behind of a "band gone distant." Things in the past were to her "as things existent," in contrast to those in the present, which were "but as a tale."

"On Sturminster Foot-Bridge" *(Onomatopoeic)* Poem published in *MOMENTS OF VISION* (1917). It was first titled, in the manuscript, "On Stourcastle Foot-Bridge (1877)." Hardy has, in his imagination, returned to STURMINSTER NEWTON, where he and his first wife, Emma HARDY had lived at Riverside Villa from 1876 to 1878. These were the happiest years of their married life. He depicts the bridge and the water in dark terms, possibly reflecting his disappointment over their childlessness. Critics of Hardy's time deplored his reproduction of sounds, such as "The current clucks smartly into

each hollow place" or "Reticulations creep upon the slack stream's face," although these sounds were accurate and the meter was intended to be onomatopoeic (Bailey, *The Poetry of Thomas Hardy*, 384).

For further reading: Wightman, "Riverside—Sturminster Newton."

"On the Belgian Expatriation" Sonnet dated October 18, 1914, and first published as "Sonnet on the Belgian Expatriation" in *King Albert's Book* (London, 1914) to benefit the Belgian Fund established by the London *Daily Telegraph*. It was later collected in *MOMENTS OF VISION* (1917).

In the octave, Hardy dreams that Belgian people have come to England from the "Land of Chimes," bringing their bells to hoist in his country. He imagines that they ring them amid markets and, at night, offer solace.

In the sestet he wakes, and discovers, to his horror, the "visioned ones" have come but are "pale and full of fear." They have fled from Bruges, Antwerp, and Ostend. Their enemies have shattered the carillons and bells when they destroyed buildings.

Hardy had heard Belgian chimes before WORLD WAR I in Cattistock, a village about eight miles from DORCHESTER. A Belgian musician had come over from the town of Malines to play the carillon at garden parties (Bailey, *The Poetry of Thomas Hardy*, 418).

"On the Esplanade" *(Midsummer: 10 p.m.)* Poem collected in *HUMAN SHOWS, FAR PHANTASIES, SONGS, AND TRIFLES* (1925). It is reminiscent of "AT A SEASIDE TOWN IN 1869" and presumably is set in WEYMOUTH, where Hardy had worked for G. R. CRICKMAY in 1869. The esplanade, lined with a wide inviting promenade, curves along the seafront for nearly a mile before a row of fine houses and hotels.

Hardy sets the scene along the esplanade with its lamps shining and the moon coming up over the sea. In the third stanza he depicts a young lady playing and singing at an open window. The moon, however, represents Fate; he imagines it creeping upon him from behind even as he watches the young lady. Bailey deduces that Fate represents his 1870 meeting with Emma Gifford, who would become Emma HARDY. They meet after he leaves Weymouth to work on the restoration of ST. JULIOT CHURCH, in CORNWALL (Bailey, *The Poetry of Thomas Hardy*, 510).

"On the Western Circuit" Story published in the *English Illustrated Magazine*, December 1891, with four illustrations by Walter Paget. It was also published in America in *HARPER'S WEEKLY* in November 1891, with one illustration by W. T. Smedley. It was later collected in *LIFE'S LITTLE IRONIES* (1894). (Purdy, *Thomas Hardy: A Bibliographical Study*, 81–82).

The story begins with a young attorney from LONDON, Charles Bradford Raye, standing in MELCHESTER (Salisbury), gazing at the cathedral, "the most homogeneous pile of medieval architecture in England." In the town square, nearby, an evening fair is in progress, with young women riding "steam circuses" (merry-go-rounds) beneath a "smoky glare" that reminds him of Dante's Inferno. He admires one of the women, and converses with her. Her name is Anna; she has come to Melchester to be trained by Mrs. Edith Harnham, the wife of an elderly wine merchant, as a servant. He treats her to another ride. He is traveling the Western Circuit, going from town to town hearing cases on the assizes (court sessions) calendar. Mrs. Harnham comes out to look for Anna and finds her still riding. Charles Raye introduces himself and explains it is his fault. In the confusion, he touches Mrs. Harnham's hand, thinking it is Anna's. When they part, he kisses Anna in the shadows. Mrs. Harnham is perturbed, yet also attracted to him. She sees him next morning when she attends the weekday service in the cathedral, and wishes she had married such a London man.

Raye stays on in Melchester, since the assizes at the forthcoming towns have no business for him. He sees Anna every day, and she pleads for him to return. He has given her only a partial name, however. He returns to London but keeps thinking of her. He writes her, and receives a response in a "neat feminine hand." This was written by Edith Harnham at Anna's request, since she actually is illiterate, there was no school near enough her aunt's house, where she grew up, for her to attend. Edith replies for her, and the correspondence goes on for several weeks. One week Anna is out of town, but Edith answers anyway. Edith becomes obsessed with setting down her own "impassioned and pent-up ideas."

Anna returns, having found she is pregnant. Edith is extremely sympathetic and writes Raye to ask him to come, but he makes excuses. Finally Edith writes the truth but declares that she (writing as Anna) does not want to inconvenience him; he is free to forget what has happened. Anna must eventually leave the house; Hardy hints that Edith's husband is aware of her condition. She returns home and Edith continues writing.

Edith and Anna tell Raye the truth about her condition and he agrees to marry Anna, though he does not know the truth about the letters. Anna begins trying to learn to read and write. Edith helps Anna plan the wedding, although she herself is preoccupied with Raye through a "species of telepathy." She goes to London to be with Anna. During the ceremony Raye is conscious of a "strange and secret gravitation" between himself and Edith.

At the small reception in Raye's lodgings, he and Edith begin conversing; Anna is there but assumes the role of a "domestic animal who humbly heard but understood not." He asks Anna to write a note to his sister before they depart for Knollsea to tell her the wedding is over and she hopes to know her well. This, of course, she is unable to do; she produces a few lines a child might write. She then confesses that Edith has been writing the letters, although she is learning very fast to write herself. Raye is appalled, and asks Edith if she has been Anna's scribe all along. She admits it began that way but insists she continued because it gave her much pleasure. Raye feels betrayed and remarks that he and Edith have been "devoted lovers—by correspondence!" She says yes, in soul and spirit she has married him. He kisses her on the mouth and she begins to cry.

Raye goes to Anna and is kind to her. She does not realize that to him she has become only an "unlettered peasant, chained to his side."

Edith returns to Melchester in a "stupor of grief." Charles and Anna sit at opposite windows in the train to Knollsea; he is reading "the sweet letters" to him signed "Anna."

For further reading: Brady, "Conventionality as Narrative Technique in Hardy's 'On the Western Circuit'"; Plotz, "Motion Sickness: Spectacle and Circulation in Thomas Hardy's 'On the Western Circuit.'"

Oppenheim, Isabelle (unknown)   The eldest of five daughters of the painter W. P. FRITH. In January 1884 Hardy wrote to thank her for her letter about *The TRUMPET-MAJOR*. He said that to hear it had held its own in her imagination "against the realities of Venice" was very gratifying (*Letters* I, 125). In June 1886 she invited the Hardys to dine with her family in London and praised *The MAYOR OF CASTERBRIDGE*, and in early 1904 she wrote Hardy that she had liked the first part of *The DYNASTS* and looked forward to reading the second and third parts (*Letters* III, 106).

Order of Merit   Established in 1902 by King Edward VII, the Order of Merit (or O. M.) is given for military, scientific, artistic, or professional merit. The king awarded it to Hardy in 1910 on the occasion of his 70th birthday: It was announced in the king's Birthday Honours List on July 9, 1910. Portraits of the members are kept at Windsor Castle (*Letters* IV, 108). Hardy received letters of congratulation from many friends, including Edward CLODD, Edmund GOSSE, Alfred PARSONS, Lady Agnes GROVE, Sir George DOUGLAS, and the Dorset novelist Evangeline Smith. He wrote Miss Smith that the chief pleasure in the investiture lay in "discovering how much it has pleased my friends, & would have pleased many more" who were deceased (*Letters* IV, 110).

Later in July 1910, John William Fortescue, librarian of the Royal Library, Windsor Castle, wrote to arrange for Hardy's portrait. Hardy subsequently sat for the painter and etcher William STRANG, who spent the weekend of September 23–24, 1910, at MAX GATE.

Osgood, James Ripley (1836–1892) American-born publisher whose firm, James R. Osgood & Co., was at one time the publisher of the ATLANTIC MONTHLY and also published FAR FROM THE MADDING CROWD. Osgood became the London representative of HARPER & BROTHERS, and in December 1888 Hardy corresponded with him about his story "The First Countess of Wessex," which appeared in HARPER'S NEW MONTHLY MAGAZINE in December 1889. He recommended several illustrators, including Helen PATERSON Allingham (Mrs. William Allingham), Charles GREEN, and Alfred PARSONS, who was the illustrator chosen.

In 1890, Osgood and Clarence MCILVAINE formed the firm of OSGOOD, MCILVAINE & CO. Osgood died in May 1892, and McIlvaine was one of the two chief mourners at his funeral, which Hardy attended.

For further reading: R. E. Greenland, "Hardy in the Osgood, McIlvaine and Harper (London) Editions."

Osgood, McIlvaine & Co. Publishing firm founded in 1890 by James Ripley OSGOOD and the American-born publisher Clarence W. MCILVAINE, with offices at 45 St., London. They became Hardy's publishers with A GROUP OF NOBLE DAMES (1891). When the rights of publishing firm SAMPSON, LOW to the earlier novels expired in June 1894, the firm undertook an important 16-volume edition of Hardy's fiction called The WESSEX NOVELS from 1895–96. It did not include DESPERATE REMEDIES but did include three volumes of short fiction: *Wessex Tales* (1896), *Life's Little Ironies* (1896), and *A Group of Noble Dames* (1896). Purdy terms this edition a very important one because the text of every novel was carefully revised and the names and distances corrected. Hardy wrote a preface for each volume and proofread the entire edition (Purdy, *Thomas Hardy: A Bibliographical Study,* 281).

In 1902 Hardy allowed the seven-year contract he had with the publishing firm to lapse. He felt that he ought to have a publisher in England whose head office was in London and not abroad. He hinted that in the event of his death his widow would not be competent to look after his affairs, particularly if his principal publisher were based in America (*Letters* III, 6–7).

The plates were eventually used by their successors HARPER & BROTHERS (London) and after 1902 by MACMILLAN & CO. for their Uniform Edition (Purdy, *Thomas Hardy: A Bibliographical Study,* 281).

Osgood, McIlvaine & Co. was absorbed by Harper & Brothers. McIlvaine became their London representative (*Letters* II, 47). Osgood died in May 1892; Hardy and McIlvaine attended the funeral.

Ouless, Walter Williams (1848–1933) English portrait painter whose subjects included Charles Darwin and Cardinal Newman. In September 1921 Hardy sat with him for a portrait, which now hangs in the National Portrait Gallery.

"Our Exploits at West Poley" The only story Hardy wrote with the hope of appealing to a youthful audience. It was commissioned by the American magazine YOUTH'S COMPANION in April 1883. Hardy promised to deliver it by the end of the year. He sent it to the magazine November 5, 1883. The magazine announced that "A Story of English Rustic Life" by Hardy would be forthcoming, but the editors seemed dissatisfied with the story and returned it for corrections. It never appeared, and in December 1886 Hardy wrote one of the editors, William H. Rideing, that he hoped they would keep it as long as there was any chance of its appearing in the magazine. He thought it might be too "juvenile" for the children in America. Hardy never heard from the magazine again. At the time the story was acquired, the editor of *Youth's Companion* was Daniel S. Ford. His daughter married a Mr. Hartshorn, for whom Ford purchased another small magazine, the *Household.* Ford allowed Hartshorn to look through his stock of manuscripts from time to time, and he discovered Hardy's story. He did not appreciate Hardy's reputation and merely printed the story in installments between November 1892 and April 1893 (Purdy, "Introduction" to *Our Exploits at West Poley* [London: Oxford University Press, 1952]; *Letters* I, 116).

The story may have mystified most American children at the time, even those nourished on Charles Dickens and Robert Louis STEVENSON. The plot concerns two boys, Steve Draycot and his cousin Leonard, who has been sent to visit Steve and his mother in the village of West Poley. The boys set out to explore the nearby Mendip Caves and, as an experiment, discover that they can shift some of the rocks and clay and change the direction of a stream of water within the cave. When they emerge, they discover that the village of West Poley has been completely deprived of water. The miller has no water for his wheel and is bewailing his fate. He is being consoled by a philosophic man referred to as "the Man Who had Failed." The boys return to the cave and redivert the stream, but after one day it changes course and flows into the village of East Poley. The people there feel blessed and rich. The boys enlist another boy, Job Tray, to help them, and show him how to control the flow of water. They dress as magicians and pronounce themselves "Rhombustas" and "Balcazar."

They are caught when they are seen in East Poley in their magical attire; Steve is recognized. Job finds a third hole and sends water to both villages, but the villagers become suspicious when Steve and his cousin pretend to wave their wands and dramatically turn the water on and off. They realize the boys have somehow found the source of the river. Meanwhile, the water in the cave has become a whirling cauldron, and they can no longer reach the stones to divert the water.

The three boys become trapped in the cave in the rising water. One of them throws a stone at the roof, which opens into a downward slope, above which they hear the miller, who tells the "rascals" to climb up and admit their wrongdoing. The miller falls in, but they rescue him. They discover water is rising about their feet. The Man who had Failed tosses a rope. The water, meanwhile, drains away, and the villagers investigate the caves, sending the boys home.

Steve catches cold from his adventure. He makes a public announcement from his sickbed, which the villagers assemble to hear. He proposes that they close up the gallery by which they first entered.

When they enter, they discover East Poley men trying to close up the outlet of the stream toward West Poley. The situation seems hopeless until Steve thinks of going into the cave and using gunpowder to blast the rocks. He vanishes, but the Man who had Failed and the baker find him and carry him out, unconscious. He is only stunned, however, and apparently the water problem, which is surveyed by engineers, has been solved. Steve's mother lectures him on the virtue of perseverance over "erratic exploits." He asks how the opinions of The Man who had Failed can be of any value. She explains that he has only failed from want of energy, not sense, and is well worth listening to. Steve eventually becomes a gentleman farmer, known for avoiding all "speculative exploits."

As a piece of juvenile fiction, the story is somewhat flawed. It has the ingredients Hardy apparently thought would appeal to children, especially boys, such as the exploration of caves, the conflict over the diversion of the water supply to the villages, the gunpowder explosion, and Steve's nearly fatal accident. Yet the sentences are sometimes convoluted, and the action is hard to follow. The narrator inserts asides that would have puzzled American children (and possibly English ones as well). The Man who had Failed, for example, speaks "in that poetico-philosophic strain which, under more favouring circumstances, might have led him on to the intellectual eminence of a Coleridge or an Emerson." The diction is stilted: "'Zounds take your saucy tongues!'" says the miller, Griffin, to the two boys. The story might have had a disappointing reception, particularly in America.

"Outside the Casement" *(A Reminiscence of the War)* The manuscript of this poem bore the title "After the Battle," which was changed when the work was published in *LATE LYRICS AND EARLIER* (1922). The poem is a poignant evocation of a small gathering during WORLD WAR I. A girl, or woman, is outside the room in the "portico-shade," too far away to hear what the group of people are saying, but smiling, as she guesses they are speaking favorably of her. Suddenly a message is brought in, "fraught / With evil fortune for her out

there." The group inside would gladly have "fenced" her from a "waft of care."

They discuss whether they should "cloak the tidings" or tell her about them at once—should they protect her and "stay the stroke that would blanch and numb?" They decide they will try to soften the blow, which is painful because she keeps looking in and smiling.

Bailey speculates that the message was a telegram announcing the death of Hardy's young cousin on his mother's side, Second Lieutenant Frank William George, who was killed at Gallipoli in August 1915. George had often visited MAX GATE, and Hardy was very fond of him. The woman may have been George's fiancée. Those in the room might have included Hardy and his second wife, Florence HARDY (Bailey, *The Poetry of Thomas Hardy*, 483).

"Overlooking the River Stour" Poem collected in *MOMENTS OF VISION* (1917). The Hardys lived at Riverside Villa, STURMINSTER NEWTON, from 1876 to 1878, and in the manuscript of the poem "(1877)" is added to the title. In June 1916 Hardy revisited the house; the poem probably dates from that time (Purdy, *Thomas Hardy: A Bibliographical Study*, 199).

Hardy describes the river and its wildlife on a rainy day as he gazes from a window of the house. The scene outside is a distraction from his memories of the years in the house, soon after his marriage in 1874, when he and Emma HARDY had been very happy. He expresses remorse and guilt that while they lived there he had not turned away from the view to pay more attention to his wife and the household. The four six-line stanzas have an intricate rhyme pattern: *abbaab*.

Hardy's second wife, Florence HARDY, once explained to a friend that Hardy's happiness with Emma had ended with their years at Sturminster Newton. Emma's brother had paid them a visit and expressed surprise at their living in such a remote backwater. Apparently this awakened in Emma an interest in London and "social snobbishness," which caused them both much unhappiness (Bailey, *The Poetry of Thomas Hardy*, 383).

The poem has been set to music in *Before and After Summer: Ten Songs for Baritone and Piano* (*see* Appendix II).

For further reading: Wightman, "Riverside—Sturminster Newton."

Owen, Rebekah (1858–1939) American woman who became immensely enthusiastic about the works of Hardy. She and her sister Catharine were the daughters of a prosperous New York merchant, Henry Owen, who made a fortune that permitted his daughters, neither of whom married, to live in prosperity, whether in America or Europe. He also began building a large library. Rebekah and Catharine made frequent visits to

England and acquired many works by and about Hardy as well as other books. Many of the books were housed in their home in the Lake District in England. They were acquired by Colby College in Maine early in World War II, and shipped across the Atlantic in small parcels, to avoid loss by submarine attacks, throughout the war. The final volumes did not arrive at Colby until 1950; only two books had been lost. The Owen Collection is one of the most valuable assets of the Colby College Library.

Rebekah and her sister, Catharine ("Tat"), spent the summer of 1886 in Oxford. They returned to England in 1888, and 1890, exploring the Lake District and other regions. They came to DORCHESTER in the summer of 1892. By this time they had read some of Hardy's novels as many as six times, and had organized readings of them in New York. They had a thorough knowledge of his works and geographical locations that even exceeded that of Hermann LEA. Weber observes that there were no guides to "Hardy Country" available at the time, but Rebekah Owen and her sister were able to visit most of the identifiable sites. Rebekah obtained an introduction to Hardy through Canon Baldwin, dean of Northumberland at Berwick-on-Tweed, whom the sisters had met. Canon Baldwin had approached Stuart J. Reid, a director of his publishers, SAMPSON, LOW, MARSTON, SEARLE & RIVINGTON, on her behalf.

Hardy invited the young women to call. Rebekah and Hardy went to the ruins at Winterborne Farringdon, near MAX GATE, the setting of some scenes in *The TRUMPET-MAJOR*. He wrote Florence HENNIKER that Rebekah had a Kodak camera and took "the spots very skilfully" (*Letters* II, 31). Hardy directed Rebekah and Catharine to sites in WEYMOUTH and other places. The sisters and the Hardys also went to Swanage.

Rebekah developed an almost fanatical devotion to Hardy and his works. She thought of writing a biography of him, a plan she never carried out. She did, however, spend half her life studying his writings.

During their four-month stay in Dorchester the sisters also became friends with Margie Moule, the daughter of Hardy's friend Henry J. MOULE, and with many other residents. The sisters returned to England a number of times, renting houses near Dorchester and becoming friends with Hardy himself as well as with Emma HARDY and, later, Florence HARDY.

After his second marriage, however, Hardy came to resent Rebekah Owen's attentions and requests that he autograph his books, which she would mail to him. Gradually Florence Hardy conveyed his lack of interest in her in subtle ways—by saying, for example, that she (without Hardy) would be glad to receive Rebekah "for a few minutes" at Max Gate. Rebekah, though deeply hurt, perceived that she was becoming a nuisance. She tried, thereafter, to attend productions of Hardy's plays in London and Dorchester where she might see him,

but seems to have failed. She spent increasing amounts of time in Italy, especially after Catharine Owen's death.

For further reading: Weber, *Hardy and the Lady from Madison Square.*

"Oxen, The" Published in the *Times* on December 24, 1915, this poem was reprinted as a leaflet four days later for "private circulation" by E. Williams, an antiquarian bookseller in Hove (Brighton). It was collected in *SELECTED POEMS* (Macmillan, 1916) and, a year later, included in *MOMENTS OF VISION* (1917).

The poet recalls the Christmas Eves of his childhood when, sitting in a "flock" by the hearth, he would accept without question the pronouncement of an "elder" at midnight that the oxen were also kneeling down. From his present adult perspective he is, regrettably, more skeptical, but acknowledges that if invited again on Christmas Eve to "see the oxen kneel" he would go, "Hoping it might be so."

Christmas Eve is often associated with the supernatural in Hardy's work, and he had heard this particular legend from his mother (Pinion, *A Commentary on the Poems of Thomas Hardy*, 133). Dated 1915, the poem was written after England had been at war for a year with Germany, and it is possible that Williams's leaflets were intended for servicemen.

Oxford University The city of Oxford and its university held a special fascination for Hardy throughout his life. On December 19, 1863, when he was working as an assistant architect in LONDON, he wrote his sister Mary HARDY that he was glad she had been to Oxford, which "must be a jolly place. I shall try to get down there some time or other" (*Letters* I, 5). She was then teaching in Denchworth, about 15 miles from Oxford. This remark seems dismissive of Oxford. It is unclear why Hardy did not make more of an effort to visit the town. It could be that, since his own formal schooling had ended in 1856, when he was 16, he was envious of the young men who had been sent there as a matter of course. His father was educating his sister Mary to be a teacher, and sending him to Oxford would have been difficult. Hardy was also devoting himself to his chosen profession of architecture. As late as 1865 he was still thinking of taking holy orders, however, and considered applying to CAMBRIDGE UNIVERSITY. In May 1875 Hardy and Austin DOBSON were invited by Francis Stokes to respond to the toast of "Literature" at the Second Annual Shotover Dinner at Oxford. This occasion was an outgrowth of a series of parodies, *The Shotover Papers, or, Echoes of Oxford*, published between February 1874 and February 1875 (*Letters* I, 37). Millgate notes that the *Oxford Undergraduate's Journal* of May 13 mentions that the Shotover staff had entertained "several distinguished Metropolitan and Oxford Literati" at the

Oxford University as Jude Fawley might have seen it in Jude the Obscure, *from the tower of the University Church of St. Mary the Virgin; the dome of the Radcliffe Camera at right is now the reading room of the Bodleian Library*   (Sarah Bird Wright)

dinner at the Mitre Hotel, and speculates that Hardy might have "encountered a certain amount of social condescension" on the part of undergraduates; they might have treated him snobbishly (Millgate, *Thomas Hardy: A Biography*, 176).

As early as April 1888, according to the *Life*, Hardy conceived the nucleus of *JUDE THE OBSCURE*, noting that he might write the story of a young man "who could not go to Oxford," dealing with his struggles, failure, and suicide. Hardy seems to have heard of such a young man, and believed there was something in "the Oxford world" that "ought to be shown, and I am the one to show it to them," though, he reflected, he himself considered going to Cambridge and could easily have gone when he was 25 (*Life*, 207–208). Oxford is the Christminster of the novel.

In June 1893 Hardy went to Oxford during the Encaenia with the apparent purpose of observing the panorama of student life. He recalled seeing "Christ Church and other college balls, garden-parties, and suchlike bright functions, but did not make himself known, his object being to view the proceedings entirely as a stranger. He stayed at the Wilberforce Temperance Hotel" (*Life*, 257).

Hardy noted in his autobiography that *Jude the Obscure* was meant to be "all contrasts . . . Christminster academical, Christminster in the slums. . ." Published in 1895, the novel attracted vitriolic criticism and was the last Hardy wrote.

In 1911 he donated the manuscript of *POEMS OF THE PAST AND THE PRESENT* to the Bodleian Library at Oxford.

In February 1920 Hardy was invited to receive an honorary degree of Doctor of Letters from Oxford University, to be presented at the time he was attending a performance of scenes from *The DYNASTS* at the theater there. The production was mounted by the Oxford University Dramatic Society. He later wrote Florence HENNIKER that he was pleased with the skillfull performance (*Letters* VI, 9). He and Florence HARDY went to

Oxford by train, believing the roads were bad, although the members of the Oxford University Debating Society had offered to send a car for him. The degree was presented at the Sheldonian Theater. In the afternoon they went to the home of Sir Walter Raleigh and his wife; John Masefield was there (*Life,* 397–98).

In 1922 Hardy was made an HONORARY FELLOW of QUEEN'S COLLEGE. He received an invitation to the Gaudies (college feasts), in December 1922, and wrote that he would certainly attend if he were younger (*Letters* VI, 172). In June 1923 the Hardys did spend two nights at Queen's College. Godfrey Elton, a young don, escorted them about Oxford. Elton later wrote several history books and became Godfrey, Lord Elton (first baron Elton; 1892–1973). He later wrote his impressions of Hardy, which apparently pleased him, for he included them in the *Life.* He described Hardy as having "a bird-like alertness and a rare and charming youthfulness—interested in everything he saw, and cultured, but surely not much occupied with books" (*Life,* 421). The Hardys and Elton then went to see John MASEFIELD and his wife at their house at Boar's Hill, near Oxford.

In time, Hardy came to be much admired by Oxford students. In July 1924, when Hardy was 84, the BALLIOL PLAYERS, an undergraduate theater group, visited MAX GATE and performed an English version of Aeschylus' trilogy *The Oresteia,* entitled *The Curse of the House of Atreus,* on the lawn. On June 29, 1926, they performed the *Hippolytus* of Euripides at Max Gate, and, on July 6, 1927, performed *Iphigenia in Aulis* there (Roberts, *Hardy's Poetic Drama,* 6–7).

In April 1926 Hardy donated a sketch of himself by William STRANG to Queen's College, writing the pro-provost, the Reverend Edward Mewburn Walker, that he feared it would seem "a great piece of vanity." At the same time, he hoped Dr. Walker would understand that he was sending it to show in his "feeble way" his sense of the "hospitality mental and corporeal" he and his wife had experienced there (*Letters* VII, 18).

P

Pair of Blue Eyes, A   Novel serialized in *TINSLEYS' MAGAZINE* from September 1872 to July 1873 and published in 1873 by TINSLEY BROTHERS. It was the first of Hardy's novels to have the author's name on the title page. The 11 serial installments were accompanied by illustrations drawn by J. A. Pasquier; at least some of the plates were based on sketches provided by Hardy (Purdy, *Thomas Hardy: A Bibliographical Study*, 9–10).

The setting is the Cornish coast near where Hardy first met Emma Gifford HARDY, his first wife; in many respects Stephen SMITH's courtship of Elfride SWANCOURT parallels Hardy's pursuit of Emma. She was the sister of Helen HOLDER, who had married the Reverend Caddell HOLDER, rector of ST. JULIOT CHURCH, CORNWALL, in 1868, following the death of his first wife in 1867. Emma had gone with them to Cornwall, believing Helen needed her assistance. Hardy was the long-expected architect who was sent from WEYMOUTH to restore the church. In the novel, the rector of the church at Endelstow is a widower, the Reverend Christopher SWANCOURT; his daughter, Elfride, lives with him. Stephen Smith is a rising young architect sent to inspect the church tower.

In the *Life* Hardy classes the novel among his "Romances and Fantasies—as if to suggest its visionary nature." He states in his early preface that he was attempting to show "the influence of character on circumstances." He observes that the story has been "considered to show a picture of his own personality as the architect on this visit," but insists that none of the characters is that of an actual person, because he had always been "shy of putting his personal characteristics into his novels." He states that only the lonely drive across the hills toward the coast and a few "external scenes and incidents" correspond with the facts of his actual visit. The character of Smith, whom many readers had identified with Hardy, is based partly on a mason who had been employed by his father, partly on one who worked near Boscastle. Hardy does admit, however, in a statement unusual for him, that Henry KNIGHT, Elfride's second lover, is more like himself as described in Emma's diary. The church of St. Juliot does have a view of the sea, and he admits that Elfride has some "points in common" with Emma in character and appearance, and that Emma and Elfride were both excellent riders. Otherwise, he insists that he

had thought of the plot and written it down long before he met Emma (*Life*, 73–75). Elfride Swancourt is one of the more intellectual of Hardy's heroines; she plays chess, is well read, and even writes her father's sermons. Like Paula POWER in *A LAODICEAN*, she has definite intellectual beliefs, and, like Cytherea GRAYE in *DESPERATE REMEDIES*, she has been "carefully educated."

SYNOPSIS

Chapters 1–12

The epigraph to the first chapter refers to Elfride Swancourt, age 20, as "A fair vestal, throned in the west." Her emotions "lay very near the surface." Because Parson Swancourt is suffering from a severe attack of gout, Elfride is reluctantly pressed into service as hostess to greet the professional architect from London who is coming to inspect the church tower. Stephen Smith is also 20, with sparkling blue-gray eyes; he soon enjoys an "agreeable repast" served by Elfride. Mr. Swancourt imagines that he is connected with the "ancient county family" of General Sir Stephen Fitzmaurice Smith of Caxbury, which Stephen denies. Downstairs, Elfride plays the pianoforte and sings to him; the image of her singing in a "pale gray silk dress with trimmings of swan's down" is etched in his memory of her.

The next day Stephen inspects the church. Mr. Swancourt, assisted by William WORM, has tried to repair the chancel roof. He asks John Smith, a local mason, to consult with Stephen about the state of the church walls. Elfride waits for Stephen on top of the church tower, but watches in surprise as the two men sit down together and talk, keeping her waiting half an hour. Stephen then vanishes. The next day he tells Elfride he had quite forgotten he was supposed to wave to her, and Elfride confesses that she sometimes writes her father's sermons for him.

Stephen's employer, Mr. Hewby, summons him back to London. Before he returns, however, Mr. Swancourt proposes that they all visit Endelstow House, where he needs to go to find some documents for Lord LUXELLIAN. On the way, Elfride loses some slips of paper, which fly in the wind; the lodge-keeper's little boy retrieves them. Elfride explains that they are notes for a romance she is writing, *The Court of King Arthur's Castle:*

a Romance of Lyonnesse. She often writes while on horse-back. She tells Stephen she does not know what she will do with the manuscript when it is finished.

At Endelstow House, they wander through the rooms and meet the small daughters of Lord and Lady LUXELLIAN, Kate and Mary, who adore Elfride. Elfride sees the shadow of Stephen embracing a lady in one wing of the mansion. She also sees a letter to a lady in the rectory. Stephen is preoccupied, and does not explain himself to Elfride.

He returns to his office, promising to return later in the summer. Both Elfride and her father are very taken with him. He does come back, hoping to make drawings of the ends of some of the church pews that are in danger of being "restored." Stephen and Elfride play chess; Elfride detects a certain awkwardness in his handling of the chess pieces. Mr. Swancourt notices similar flaws in his pronunciation of Latin. Stephen explains that he has learned Latin from an Oxford man, Henry Knight, by corresponding with him. Elfride lets him win at chess, which he realizes; he expresses his love for her. They plan an excursion to Targan Bay, but, because the shaft of the pony cart is damaged, Elfride and Stephen picnic on the cliffs alone. Elfride asks Stephen to keep an eye on her earrings every minute, lest she lose one. She and UNITY, the parlor-maid, reminisce about all the times and places she has lost earrings. During the picnic, Elfride does lose an earring, an echo of an incident that occurred during Hardy's courtship of Emma.

Stephen resolves to explain everything to Elfride, and they walk to Endelstow church. Stephen almost sits down on a new flat tomb, but Elfride stops him, saying she does not wish to sit there. Stephen finally explains that his family is of a lower social class than hers; none of his family are professional people. In fact, his father is a master mason and his mother was a dairy maid before her marriage. It was his mother he was embracing at Endelstow House; she was helping out there. Elfride understands the reason for his "peculiarities in chess-playing" and his odd Latin pronunciation. She explains that the new tomb is that of a former admirer of hers, a young farmer, Felix JETHWAY, who had wanted to marry her; he died of consumption. (His mother, Gertrude JETHWAY, blames Elfride, and will haunt her throughout the novel.)

At the rectory, Stephen learns of an accident his father has had, injuring his hand, and explains to Mr. Swancourt that John Smith is his father. Mr. Swancourt dismisses him as a suitor for the hand of Elfride. Elfride argues that Stephen's position is "what his profession makes him." Her father advises her to get over such "tomfoolery."

Stephen visits his parents, who see no reason for him to marry so young. Elfride, to his mother, is a "nice little thing," but in fact is only a "bankrupt pa'son's daughter." However, she can see that "her people" would consider Stephen "lower."

At the rectory, Stephen and Elfride decide on an immediate secret marriage in Plymouth. He leaves the house. Mr. Swancourt also leaves the rectory the night before Elfride plans to meet Stephen, making a mysterious journey elsewhere. Elfride rides her horse Pansy to St. Launce's, changes her clothes, and takes the train to Plymouth, where she meets Stephen. He has learned that his marriage license is invalid in Plymouth. They go by train to Paddington Station, London, where they can marry. At Paddington, however, Elfride announces that she cannot go through with the wedding, and she returns home on the next train, accompanied by Stephen as far as St. Launce's. There she sees Mrs. Jethway, a woman with "red and scaly eyelids and glistening eyes." Elfride shrinks from the sight of her.

Mr. Swancourt comes home and Elfride prepares to confess the story of her elopement. He announces, however, that he has married a wealthy widow, Charlotte TROYTON, who has inherited a large nearby property and is almost as wealthy as Lord LUXELLIAN. He had not told Elfride about this earlier because she had become involved with the Smiths, "low people," and he did not want her attachment to Stephen to cloud his courtship. Elfride had met Mrs. Troyton two months earlier, but is shocked at the marriage. Her stepmother is friendly toward her, and promises to encourage her pursuits; she will try to see that her romance is published. For the moment, they will take Elfride to Bath while the manor-house is being renovated.

Chapters 13–28
In London, two months later, Stephen Smith talks to his friend Henry Knight in Knight's law chambers. He has an opportunity to go to Bombay to work as an architect; Knight advises him to accept the post. Stephen notices a novelette, *The Court of King Arthur's Castle,* by Ernest Field, which he recognizes as Elfride's work. Knight terms it "reviewable"; he writes reviews for *The Present.*

Nine months later, while Stephen is in India, Elfride and the Swancourts have come to London to stay in Mrs. Swancourt's new Kensington townhouse. As they drive in the park, they speak to Lord and Lady Luxellian, who are in their carriage with their two daughters. Lady Luxellian looks unwell; the little girls climb into Mrs. Swancourt's carriage to be with Elfride. Lord Luxellian mentions an unfavorable review of her novel in *The Present* and says she was unfairly treated. Elfride has never seen it. Mrs. Swancourt recognizes Henry Knight in the park; he is her "kinsman." She invites him to Endelstow at the beginning of August.

At Mrs. Swancourt's home in Endelstow, The Crags, Elfride composes an answer to the writer of the review, signing it with her initials. Knight recognizes her initials and the address and responds, saying they are not really strangers, and that he will be accepting her stepmother's invitation to visit. Elfride and her father both realize that Knight is Stephen's friend.

Knight soon arrives for a visit. He and Elfride discuss fiction; he is much attracted to her. The next morning the Swancourts and Knight climb into the church tower. After her parents leave, Elfride catches her foot and almost falls; Knight saves her. After dinner she and Knight play chess by "club rules"; he outmaneuvers her completely, which she resents. Elfride goes to her room and weeps. The Swancourts are so alarmed that they send for a physician. She repeatedly plays and loses to Knight, at chess and in verbal sparring.

At the evening service, Knight reads the lessons; Elfride is much taken with him in spite of herself, but then sees the "bleak barren countenance" of the widow Jethway in the west gallery. From there Mrs. Jethway has a clear view of the tomb of her son. She gazes bitterly at Elfride. Walking home, Elfride tells Knight of the loss of her earring; Knight observes a star, which, he says, is shining over Bombay, where a young friend is at present.

Knight goes on to Ireland, realizing he has fallen in love with Elfride. In Dublin he buys two pairs of earrings for her, finding it almost impossible to make a choice. He returns to Endelstow; Elfride refuses to accept the earrings, but Knight has a maid take them to her room. Stephen writes that he has deposited £200 in her name with the St. Launce's Bank. A few days later he writes that he is being sent to England to purchase hardware for the houses he is building, and will be going down to Endelstow.

Knight arrives, and he and Elfride climb a cliff. Knight becomes stranded and nearly falls on the rocks far below; Elfride ingeniously devises a plan to rescue him by tearing her petticoats into strips. As he waits for her, he sees an "imbedded fossil, standing forth in low relief from the rock," gazing at him with eyes turned to stone. It is an early Trilobite; he believes he will be equally "small" in significance in his death. The scene is one of the most memorable in Hardy's novels. After the rescue, Elfride hastens home, losing the receipt for the £200 that Stephen had deposited to her account; Knight finds it.

Stephen returns to Cornwall, stepping on the quay at Castle Boterel, the small port near Endelstow. In the distance he sees a small form running, followed by a darker one; they are Elfride and Knight. He goes home with his father and Martin CANNISTER, who had gone to the port to greet him. William Worm and his wife, along with Robert Lickpan, stay for dinner. Elfride sends a note to Stephen saying she will meet him at nine o'clock that night in the church.

Stephen goes to West Endelstow church, but Elfride does not appear. He passes near her new home (The Crags) and hears her laughter, along with the voice of a man. When he returns home he finds that Elfride has deposited his money and written him a check for the same amount. He resolves to go to Birmingham the next morning.

The epigraph to chapter 25 is "Mine own familiar friend." In September, Stephen returns to Castle Boterel and Endelstow, determined to see Elfride. He lingers on the quay so that he can approach her home at night. He sees a man and a woman with a white feather in her bonnet walking toward West Endelstow. He follows them and hears the familiar voice of Elfride in the Belvedere at The Crags; unfortunately, it is mingled with that of Henry Knight, his "friend and preceptor." In a state of shock, he steadies himself by holding a sapling tree; he is shattered as he sees Henry with his arm about Elfride's waist. Gertrude Jethway, known to Stephen as a "crazed forlorn woman," suddenly glides toward him. She has followed Elfride and Henry Knight and wishes the worst for Elfride. Stephen perceives that, to Elfride, Henry Knight is on a pedestal. He associates her fickleness with her father's remarriage to a prosperous woman.

Stephen suddenly hears the East Endelstow church bell tolling and approaches the vault beneath the church. He discovers that Lady Luxellian has died at the age of 31. The laborers are moving coffins around to make room for hers. The men discuss Lady Elfride, Elfride Swancourt's grandmother, who ran away with a singer. Her father had forgiven her and provided a house, garden, and carriage. She died in childbirth, but the baby lived and was brought up by her grandmother. She married Parson Swancourt, and was the mother of the present Elfride.

At the beginning of chapter 27, Elfride analyzes both men. Stephen has ceased to dominate her and this problem, in conjunction with the lower status of his parents, make her lose interest. She had hesitated to meet Stephen and hurt him. Yet, as the days pass, Henry Knight does not avow his love. She realizes he has no idea that Stephen or anyone else had ever wooed her. Her father and his wife regard the match as already accomplished, although her father also has reservations about Knight's accomplishments.

Elfride and Knight pass East Endelstow church and he suggests that they go in and talk to John Smith. They are shocked to discover Stephen in the vault. Knight is rather patronizing toward Stephen, and tells him that he and Elfride are engaged. Knight assists Elfride in mounting her horse, and she and Stephen gaze at each other; Elfride suffers from the reproach she sees in Stephen's eyes. Elfride promises to explain herself to Knight the next morning at eleven o'clock.

The next morning Knight comes, and Elfride tells him her true age which is 20. They go toward the river and Elfride sits on a rustic bench, where Mrs. Jethway overtakes her and accuses her of causing Felix's death because she "proved false" and encouraged Felix. Elfride admits that Felix had tried to kiss her once, but that she had not complained out of respect for him. Mrs. Jethway, however, knows about Elfride and Stephen's failed elopement and plans to tell Knight about it. Elfride denounces her as a "slanderous woman" and she disappears.

Knight gives Elfride the gifts he has bought, and offers to dress her in them. He asks her to set a wedding date. She puts on his earrings, then says, without thinking, that she must be careful, for she has lost another earring "like this." She tries to explain that she means out-of-doors, but he remains perplexed.

Chapter 29–35
The Swancourts have moved on from St. Leonards to London; Knight has gone to the Channel Islands and Normandy, and returned to London also. Knight calls on Elfride and Mrs. Swancourt at their London hotel rooms. He suggests that they go to Cornwall by steamer instead of by train the next day. They agree to do so, but the boat, the *Juliet,* turns out to be a rickety tub; owing to low tide they are unable to set out for many hours. Mr. Swancourt asks to be set ashore at Southampton, to continue by train. Gertrude Jethway is also aboard the boat, to Elfride's horror. Elfride dreams, or possibly hears, a prophetic whisper from Mrs. Jethway in the night: "I shall win, you will find." Elfride wraps herself up and climbs on the deck. She asks Knight whether he has ever been engaged before; he assures her he has not, although he is her senior by 12 years. Elfride is shocked, but vows not to tell him of her flight with Stephen. They reach Plymouth after breakfast; Elfride is reminded of her meeting there with Stephen, when she was his "bride-elect."

At home at The Crags, Knight asks Elfride if she has ever had a lover. She confesses that she once loved someone else, which upsets Knight. As he is leaving, Elfride says she wants to give him something to make him think of her. He asks for a particular potted dwarf myrtle tree which she has raised from a twig belonging to Stephen Smith, who planted it so she would think of him. She cannot part with it and finds another cutting for Knight, which is placed in his room. Knight deduces that the first one was connected with a lover who preceded him. Elfride admits this is true.

Elfride also realizes that Mrs. Jethway is her enemy. She writes a note begging her not to expose her for what she has done, for it would ruin her. She delivers it to Mrs. Jethway's home, but the older woman is out. Meanwhile, Mrs. Swancourt has challenged Knight about an article he published in *The Present* stating that only inexperienced sweethearts can be trusted. He confesses that he is ashamed of it now. He now becomes suspicious about the lost earring. Elfride, however, has been guilty of "docile devotion" to Knight, and he presumes upon it. Had she been more rebellious, it would have been better for her.

They return to the cliffs—not to the site of what Elfride calls their "dreadful adventure," but to Windy Beak, another cliff. There she discovers the lost earring and confesses that she was once engaged to be married. Knight is jealous. On the way home, they see the church tower collapse as a result of the restorers' work. Mr. Swancourt tells Knight they will have a new one, a "splendid tower" designed in the "newest style of Gothic art."

Knight takes Elfride to the church at night, where he realizes that she had sat with her former lover on the tomb of Felix Jethway. Knight thinks "everything" should be cleared up between two people before they marry, but Elfride disagrees. She pretends her lover was Felix, but Knight now realizes two men have pursued Elfride before him. Elfride responds that she has not asked Knight similar questions, but his feelings toward her have changed. Elfride returns home, and Knight goes back to the church with its "ruinous heap of stones." There he discovers the body of Mrs. Jethway. He summons help, and Lord Luxellian comes to assist him. They take her to her cottage; Lord Luxellian rushes to bring the doctor. In the cottage, Knight discovers three early drafts of letters written by Mrs. Jethway; another, apparently, was written, sealed, and mailed, for there is still warm sealing wax on the table. Lord Luxellian returns with the doctor, a coroner, and others, and the inquest is set; Mrs. Jethway has died of suffocation.

The next day Knight receives a letter from Mrs. Jethway with Elfride's letter of appeal enclosed, begging her not to "make a scandal" of her. Knight accuses Elfride of accepting too many kisses; she turns pale and "a rigid and desolate character" shows in her face. He gives her the letter she has written. She admits she had run away with Stephen and that they had planned to marry.

Knight has always perceived Elfride as "more culpable" than she is; he is, himself, extremely rigid and prone to leap to conclusions. Elfride says she did not return home on the same day she left with Stephen, but does not explain the circumstances. Knight declares the engagement is over. He advises her to marry the "other man" and leaves.

Chapter 35–40
Knight returns to his chambers in Bede's Inn; the next day, Elfride follows him. Mr. Swancourt pursues Elfride, accuses Knight of being dishonest in his courtship of Elfride, and takes her away. Knight experiences grave conflict over his behavior, but resolves that his regret shall die. He closes his law chambers and goes to the Continent.

Illustration by J. A. Pasquier for A Pair of Blue Eyes, *chapter 20, published in* Tinsleys' Magazine, *October 1872*   (Perkins Library, Duke University)

Six months later, Stephen Smith has returned to India, and his father has established his own stone and slate yard a mile from St. Launce's. His parents are amazed at their warm reception by the local tradesmen and their wives, which turns out to result from Stephen's noted success in India. He has commissions to design a "large palace," a cathedral, and other structures. His parents decide not to mention Elfride's name.

Knight, meanwhile, has traveled widely, to France, Italy, Greece, and other places. He and Stephen meet in Hyde Park, London; Knight congratulates Stephen on his success. He tells Stephen his engagement was broken off, which surprises Stephen. That evening, Knight comes to Stephen's rooms and realizes that his sketches for medieval saints, to be used in stained glass, all echo Elfride. Stephen admits he was engaged to Elfride and tells Knight the full story of their elopement.

The men decide to breakfast together. They meet again on the first train to St. Launce's. They briefly get off at an intervening station and see a dark carriage or van being shifted about. The train stops again, and the carriage is attached to their train; they recall having seen it at Paddington. Both men are going to propose to Elfride. En route, Stephen dreams that he is in East Endelstow church and Lord Luxellian is at the altar, saying "there is no pride." He realizes that Lady Luxellian has died.

On arrival, there is a crowd at the station, and a hearse. They see Mr. Swancourt also, looking very old. They learn that the deceased is actually Elfride, who has died of a miscarriage in London. Her funeral will be the next day. Both men feel guilty; they argue about which of them Elfride loved best. They meet a man bringing Elfride's coffin-plate to the blacksmith it says,

Elfride,
Wife of Spenser Hugo Luxellian,
Fifteenth Baron Luxellian,
Died February 10, 18 ——

Bewildered, the men enter the Welcome Inn, of which Martin Cannister is now the proprietor. Unity, once the rectory parlor-maid, is now working at the inn, waiting on tables. She had married Martin Cannister the same day Elfride married Lord Luxellian. Elfride had been very good to his two small daughters, but "fell off" after the marriage. Her husband had taken her to the Continent. They were returning home, but she died of a miscarriage in London.

The next day Stephen and Knight visit the Luxellian vault; Lord Luxellian is crying there, and they realize he has more right to be there than they. The novel ends as the two retrace their steps to Castle Boterel.

CRITICAL RECEPTION AND COMMENTARY

Rosemarie Morgan sees *A Pair of Blue Eyes* as a reversal of "Western literary chivalric tradition," since Elfride has certain Knight-like qualities, pursuing Henry Knight and then rescuing him on the cliff; she later demands that he acknowledge her superior mind. Hardy denies Elfride to both Smith and Knight, each of whom renews his efforts to win her. Elfride dies as the wife of a man other than Smith or Knight. The novel is thus an important exploration of relations between the sexes, and, more significantly, a clear defiance of contemporary novelists' practice of "enslaving women by denying them a sexual reality" (*Women and Sexuality in the Novels of Thomas Hardy,* 2).

In Michael Millgate's view, Hardy was forced, under the pressure of serialization, to pad the novel to some extent, producing a "rag-bag" of descriptive passages and information that serve no function within the narrative, but he praises the portrayal of Elfride. She, like many of Hardy's heroines, must "fight her own battles" (*Thomas Hardy: His Career as a Novelist*, 67, 71).

The setting of the novel is closely linked with Hardy's architectural work at St. Juliot. He was not in sympathy with the movement to restore coastal churches. In his 1895 preface to the novel, he writes that it was set at a time when the "craze for church-restoration" had reached the "remotest nooks" of the west coast of England. The "wild and tragic features" of the coastline were in perfect harmony with the "crude Gothic art of the ecclesiastical buildings scattered along it," and the "architectural attempts at newness" were as incongruous as trying to renovate "the adjoining crags themselves." In June 1912 he added a postscript to the preface, stating that the mansion called Endelstow House exists but is located several miles south of the site in the novel.

The novel was well received on the whole. The reviewer for the PALL MALL GAZETTE stated that it showed "a greater power of mental analysis and knowledge of the working of human nature" than UNDER THE GREENWOOD TREE, and called Hardy a "man of genius." According to the reviewer, both novels had "more inborn strength" and "more inborn knowledge" and "fine humor" than any living English novelist except George ELIOT. The London *Times*, however, called it a "fine novel but full of difficult, not to say ridiculous phases." The *Examiner* called Hardy a "masterly analyst of character" (W. Eugene Davis and Helmut E. Gerber, *Thomas Hardy: An Annotated Bibliography of Writings about Him*, vol. 2, *1970–1978* and *Supplement for 1871–1969*, 21–22).

For further reading: Amos, "Accident and Fate: The Possibility for Action in *A Pair of Blue Eyes*"; Blythe, *A Pair of Blue Eyes;* Devereux, "Thomas Hardy's *A Pair of Blue Eyes:* The Heroine as Text"; Halperin, "Leslie Stephen, Thomas Hardy, and *A Pair of Blue Eyes*"; McClure, "A Note on the Cliff Scene in Hardy's *A Pair of Blue Eyes*"; Millgate, *Thomas Hardy: His Career as a Novelist;* Morgan, *Women and Sexuality in the Novels of Thomas Hardy;* Rimmer, "Club Laws: Chess and the Construction of Gender in *A Pair of Blue Eyes*"; Smith, "Natural Settings and Natural Characters in Hardy's *Desperate Remedies* and *A Pair of Blue Eyes*."

Pall Mall Gazette An evening newspaper founded in 1865. Hardy's novel *A PAIR OF BLUE EYES* was reviewed in the *Gazette* on October 25, 1873; the review, which Hardy pasted in his scrapbook of reviews, was possibly written by his close friend Horace MOULE before his death. Portions of the lines Hardy wrote for Lady JEUNE's benefit performance to aid city children, given at the LYCEUM THEATRE in July 1890, were printed in the *Gazette.* In August 1892 the paper published Hardy's essay "WHY I DON'T WRITE PLAYS." This was his response to three questions the editor had put to a number of contemporary novelists on "the present divorce of fiction from the drama" (Purdy, *Thomas Hardy: A Bibliographical Study,* 12, 104, 301). In November 1886 Hardy was hurt to find himself described by the American man of letters James Russell Lowell, who had given an interview to the paper, as "small and unassuming in appearance—does not look like the genius of tradition" (*Letters* I, 157).

"Panthera" A dramatic monologue published in TIME'S LAUGHINGSTOCKS (1909), based on the second-century apocryphal legend of the parentage and crucifixion of Jesus. The speaker, an elderly man, tells of his youthful talks with the Roman centurion Panthera at a time when he was well past middle age, had lost his hand to Barbarians, and was declining. The speaker had told Panthera of his own wish to leave a son, "offspring even of no legitimate claim, / In whose advance I secretly could joy." Panthera had advised against this, for such a son might be a "comfort or a curse" or even a criminal. The speaker had asked if Panthera had a son; Panthera had replied that he had one, but *"the law took him."*

The speaker then tells Panthera's story. At about the age of 50, he had been an acting officer of the garrison charged with maintaining order in Jerusalem under Roman rule (*Pax Romana*). He had ridden out, one spring morning, to keep order while the routine death penalties were carried out. One of the condemned had attracted a large crowd of spectators. Panthera went to the public execution ground, a knoll just outside the city, called "Golgotha, Kranion, or Calvaria." He watched "some three or four . . . stript, transfixed, and nailed," with "no great stir." Then he saw a "weeping woman," the mother of one of those nailed to a cross. This caused him to remember a time at least 30 years earlier, when he was sub-captain of a company that marched from Judaea to Tyre. They had entered a village called Nazareth, where they gathered around a central fountain. He had noticed a young girl who had come to the fountain with her pitcher and had fallen in love with her; they had an affair. He thinks he recognizes the weeping mother on Calvaria as that girl. He guesses that the condemned man on Calvary is his son, although an old man in Nazareth had married the mother out of pity. Panthera learns that the man on the cross had "waked sedition long among the Jews." He signals that a legionary, Longinus, pierce the young man with his lance, since he has refused the drug they offered him. This brings his death. The mother leaves when the young man has died.

Although Panthera has seldom told the story, it has become known. The speaker expresses surprise that the weeping woman did not recognize Panthera as her former lover, and states that he is merely telling Panthera's story, whether or not it is true.

Panthera continued in his career, until his wounding, when "cynic Time proclaimed / His noble spirit broken." The speaker believes this was a great waste of a noble Roman.

In a headnote Hardy refers readers to other forms of the legend, which first became known in the second century. Among those he mentions are *Origen contra Celsem,* the Talmud, Strauss, and Haeckel. "Strauss" refers to David Strauss's *Das Leben Jesu,* or *The Life of Jesus Critically Examined,* which was translated by George Eliot (Mary Ann Evans). "Haeckel" is Ernst Haeckel's *Die Welträtsel,* or *The Riddle of the Universe at the Close of the Nineteenth Century,* translated by Joseph McCabe. Bailey states that these were the chief sources of the story (Bailey, *The Poetry of Thomas Hardy,* 250).

Hardy apparently chose the framework of a narrative monologue within a monologue to keep the reader from immediately recognizing that the central figures, whom Hardy does not name, are Mary and Jesus. Hardy was aware that the story would be offensive to many people. The operation of chance in the initial meeting between Panthera and the girl is not improbable, nor is his departure before the birth of the child, although Bailey considers it unlikely that he would return at the crucifixion too late to save his son (Bailey, *The Poetry of Thomas Hardy,* 252–53).

Paris *See* FRANCE.

Parsons, Alfred William (1847–1920) Painter and graphic artist who contributed three illustrations for "The First Countess of Wessex" (a tale in *A GROUP OF NOBLE DAMES*) when it was published in *HARPER'S NEW MONTHLY MAGAZINE* in December 1889. Four others were the work of C. S. REINHART. In January 1889 Hardy wrote Parsons to arrange for him to come to DORCHESTER and visit Melbury House, owned by the earl of Ilchester, which became the model for "King's-Hintock Court" in the story (Purdy, *Thomas Hardy: A Bibliographical Study,* 63). In July 1910 Parsons wrote to congratulate Hardy on receiving the ORDER OF MERIT from King EDWARD VII. He also wrote a letter of condolence to Hardy when his wife Emma HARDY died in 1912.

Paterson Allingham, Helen (1848–1926) A graphic artist and the illustrator of *FAR FROM THE MADDING CROWD* for the CORNHILL MAGAZINE (1874), Helen Paterson was the only female illustrator of Hardy's novels as they were serialized. Hardy met her in the spring of 1874 before her marriage. She was then 25 and a professional illustrator on the staff of the *GRAPHIC.* At the time, he was engaged to Emma Lavinia Gifford (HARDY). He was extremely attracted to Paterson, and provided sketches of farm equipment for her illustrations. Her friend Annie Thackeray (sister-in-law of Sir Leslie STEPHEN) invited both to dine with her at the Pall Mall Café (Millgate, *Thomas Hardy: A Biography,* 159). That summer, however, she married the Irish poet William Allingham, then 50, and Hardy married Emma on September 17.

In 1888 Hardy wrote the American publisher James R. OSGOOD, the London representative of HARPER & BROTHERS, that Mrs. Allingham was "the best illustrator I ever had" (*CL* I, 181). He repeated this sentiment in 1906 to the critic Edmund GOSSE. Later, Hardy tried to get her to illustrate *A LAODICEAN,* but found that she had given up book illustration (Purdy, *Thomas Hardy: A Bibliographical Study,* 13). He told Gosse he felt "quite romantical" about her, in retrospect and admitted that the two weddings "would have been one but for a stupid blunder of God Almighty" (*Letters* III, 218).

In the poem "The Opportunity (For H.P.)" Hardy writes, "Had we mused a little space / At that critical date in the Maytime, / One life had been ours, one place, perhaps, till our long cold claytime." He regretted that she married in August, just before his September wedding to Emma.

Helen Paterson Allingham was also a noted illustrator of children's books. She had studied at the Birmingham School of Design and at Academy schools in 1867 under the painter John Everett Millais. The illustrators Fred Walker and Frederick Leighton were also among her teachers. Her husband, William Allingham, was a poet and a friend of the poet Alfred, Lord TENNYSON (Jackson, *Illustration and the Novels of Thomas Hardy,* 33).

Patmore, Coventry Kersey Dighton (1823–1896) English poet, best known for *The Angel in the House. The Angel in the House* was a long work celebrating domesticity and married love. It included several shorter poems, including "The Betrothal," "The Espousals," "Faithful for Ever," and "The Victories of Love." He became a Roman Catholic in 1864 and wrote *Rod, Root, and Flower,* a volume of religious prose meditations. In November 1886 Patmore wrote an article for the FORTNIGHTLY REVIEW on Hardy's friend William BARNES and praised Hardy's obituary of him, which had appeared in the ATHENAEUM on October 13, 1886; he also commended Hardy as a novelist. Hardy wrote to thank him, saying his words were what he might have deserved if his novels had been "exact transcripts of their original irradiated conception," before he had attempted to get them down on paper (*Letters* I, 156–57).

In 1890 Patmore sent Hardy his collection of essays, *Principle in Art* (London, 1889). Hardy wrote to thank him, saying he was reading two or three every evening just before bed (*Letters* I, 208). Patmore's favorite among Hardy's novels was *A PAIR OF BLUE EYES,* although he wrote that it "seemed to demand verse for its true rendering" (*Letters* IV, 288).

Paul, Charles Kegan (1828–1902) Author and publisher, editor of the NEW QUARTERLY MAGAZINE and one of Hardy's earliest literary friends. In 1878 he had a hand in Hardy's election to the SAVILE CLUB, for which Hardy thanked him, saying "my acquaintance with you was among my reasons for joining" (*Letters* I, 57). That summer they dined at Paul's home on Kensington Square, London. Among the guests was Alexandra Sutherland Orr, who would later write an essay about Hardy's novels.

In 1879 his firm, Kegan Paul, Trench, Trübner, & Co., published William BARNES's *Poems of Rural Life in the Dorset Dialect,* a collection of his poems, some of which had not been included in the 1844 three-volume edition of his works (*Letters* III, 292). In October of the same year the magazine published Hardy's review of the book, his only known book review. The issue also included an appreciation of Hardy's work, "Mr. Hardy's Novels," by Mrs. Sutherland Orr.

Paul wrote an article praising Hardy's works, "Mr. Hardy's Novels," published anonymously in the *British Quarterly Review* in April 1881.

In 1896 Paul had an accident of some kind on a London street which forced his retirement from publishing. Hardy wrote in sympathy, saying that, although it was a "dear price at which to buy leisure," he hoped it would not hinder him from continuing his literary work. Paul never made a full recovery (*Letters* II, 127).

"Peasant's Confession, The" A ballad-sequence written in 1898 about an incident during the Napoleonic Wars and collected in WESSEX POEMS (1898). It was accompanied by Hardy's own illustration of a night scene of fields in the rain, with distant buildings representing the peasant's hut in a recessed vale (Bailey, *The Poetry of Thomas Hardy,* 72). In the *Life,* Hardy says the idea of writing about such a witness came to him as he was working at the BRITISH MUSEUM doing research for his epic poem *The DYNASTS* (*Life,* 298). The story told may well be Hardy's invention, although the Battle of WATERLOO is treated at length in the final two acts of *The Dynasts.*

The poem is preceded by an epigraph in French from Adolphe Thiers, *Histoire du Consulat et de l'Empire,* vol. 20, book 60, "Waterloo." It takes the form of a confession by a peasant who has witnessed the Napoleonic Wars from his hut in a vale. He speaks as one weary of years of war. He sees the Marshal the Marquis de Grouchy, of an old noble Norman family, commander of Napoleon's Third and Fourth Corps, and his army of 30,000 men pass through the countryside on the way to Wavre. He hopes no army will trouble them again.

Presumably on the night of June 17, the eve of the Battle of Waterloo (June 18), the peasant and his wife and children retire to their hut. There they are accosted by a messenger from Napoleon's army, asking whether they have seen Marshal Grouchy and his army, as they need his assistance in battle. The messenger promises gold and gifts in exchange for the peasant's information. The peasant realizes that, if he tells them the route Grouchy has taken, the battle will take place nearby. His farm will be seized and he will be given worthless "script"; as for gold, the French do not actually have any. On the other hand, if he does not disclose Grouchy's route, the English will win and he will be left in peace with his farm intact.

He leads the messenger away from Grouchy's destination, apparently in a wandering direction. The horseman becomes suspicious and tries to shoot him, but the peasant seizes the messenger's sabre, kills him with it, and hastens home. Grouchy and his forces do not take part in the Battle of Waterloo, in which the French are defeated.

Looking back many years later, the peasant reflects that his farm is safe. Yet, now that he is old, he feels guilt for his lie. He makes his confession to God and asks the Virgin Mary and other saints to "Entreat the Lord for me!"

Bailey states that Adolphe Thiers's account of the incident does not include the murder of the messenger by the peasant, which Hardy seems to have invented. He explains that after defeating the Prussian forces at Ligny, Napoleon ordered Marshal Grouchy to pursue the Prussians and prevent them from joining the English. When Grouchy's forces learned of the Battle of Waterloo, they wished to come to Napoleon's aid, but Grouchy insisted they follow the Prussians. Grouchy's movements have been regarded as "mysterious" by military historians, some of whom believe he had it in his power to save France (Bailey, *The Poetry of Thomas Hardy,* 71).

The legend that Napoleon's defeat turned on the treachery of a peasant has survived in several forms. Hardy chose the form of a dramatic confession by a peasant to a priest. Since the priest could not divulge his secret, the events would not be part of the historical record (Bailey, *The Poetry of Thomas Hardy,* 72).

"Pedigree, The" Dated 1916 and collected in MOMENTS OF VISION (1917), this poem traces the experience of a man who has acquired a pedigree from a "chronicler." He pores over it by the light of the "moon in its old age," seen through moving clouds "Like a drifting dolphin's eye seen through a lapping wave." As he scans his paternal chart, its branches begin to "twist into a seared and cynic face" which "winked and tokened towards the window."

In the third stanza he envisions the chart as a mirror of his "begetters—" that is, many generations of his ancestors. He then deduces that "every heave and coil and move" he makes have been preordained by the "primest fuglemen" of his line. He begins to feel he is but "merest mimicker and counterfeit." He thinks, fleetingly, that he is master of his own thoughts and actions: *"I am I, / And what I do I do myself alone."* He realizes, however, that they have been preordained by his heredity. At this point the "Mage's mirror" disappears and the "stained moon and drift" take their original places.

Hardy had a deep interest in his forebears, although he considered himself to be the end of his branch of the Hardy line. He sketched his pedigree, using old parish registers (Bailey, *The Poetry of Thomas Hardy,* 366).

Penny, Robert   A maker of boots and shoes in UNDER THE GREENWOOD TREE, he has no notable features except for his circular spectacles. He is one of the Mellstock singers who serenade the villagers on Christmas Eve.

Percomb, Mr.   Barber in Sherton Abbas in *The* WOODLANDERS. At first he cuts hair, but then begins shaving the corpses of the well-to-do and making wigs and hairpieces for the local gentry. (He persuades Marty SOUTH to let him cut her hair and makes a hairpiece for Felice CHARMOND.) He then takes down his barber pole and calls himself "Perruquier [hairdresser] to the aristocracy."

Perkins, Rev. Thomas (1842–1907)   Rector of Turnworth, DORSET, author of handbooks on several churches and cathedrals, photographer, and preservationist. In April 1900 he sent Hardy photographs he had taken of some supposed localities in *The* RETURN OF THE NATIVE. Hardy sent him a copy of the novel and explained that his fictional houses, churches, and villages often varied from their prototypes. "Blooms End," for example, was not intended to be an exact description of Bhompston Farm House, and "The Quiet Woman" was actually very different from an earlier time when it was a pub. Perkins published an article, illustrated with his photographs, called "Thomas Hardy's Country" in the *Practical Junior Photographer* for December 1901 (*Letters* II, 254).

Perkins was an active member of the SOCIETY FOR THE PROTECTION OF ANCIENT BUILDINGS and sometimes corresponded with Hardy about preservation and architectural questions. He and H. Pentin edited a book, *Memorials of Old Dorset* (London, 1907), which included a chapter by Hermann LEA, "Some Dorset Superstitions" (*Letters* III, 265).

perpendicular style of architecture   The final Gothic style of architecture from the late 14th to the 16th centuries, characterized by the use of high towers, pointed arches, sculpture, stained glass windows, and intricate lacelike ornament. The perpendicular style gave an effect of soaring height. Hardy admired this style, as he makes clear in the first chapter of *A* LAODICEAN and in *JUDE THE OBSCURE*, in which he refers to Melchester (Salisbury) Cathedral as "the most graceful architectural pile in England" (chapter 3). *See* ARCHITECTURE.

Petherwin, Ethelberta   Heroine of *The* HAND OF ETHELBERTA, one of 10 children of the poor working-class Chickerel family. Her father is a butler and her mother an invalid. Ethelberta is a resourceful young woman who becomes a governess in a noble family and elopes with their son, who soon dies. She publishes a celebrated volume of poetry, alienating her mother-in-law, who nearly disinherits her before she dies. Passionately committed to launching the tribe of young Chickerels, however, Ethelberta parlays the mother-in-law's legacy, a year's lease of a furnished London townhouse, into improvements in their respective situations. She has many suitors but marries an old and dissipated viscount, Lord MONTCLERE. She finally succeeds in dominating him and uniting her family, and begins writing an epic poem.

Petherwin, Lady   Character in *The* HAND OF ETHELBERTA; she is the mother-in-law of the young widow Ethelberta PETHERWIN. She despises Ethelberta for having eloped with her son, but relents when her son and husband both die soon afterward. She grooms Ethelberta as a companion, but is furious when the young woman publishes a celebrated volume of poetry. Lady Petherwin destroys her will, but finally leaves Ethelberta a year's lease of a furnished London townhouse before dying in Switzerland.

"Phantom Horsewoman, The"   Poem dated 1913 and included in SATIRES OF CIRCUMSTANCE (1914). Hardy was shocked at Emma HARDY's death in November 1912 and, despondent, set out on March 6, 1913, for ST. JULIOT CHURCH, 43 years after he first met Emma there. He stayed at Boscastle and revisited Pentargan Bay and Beeny Cliff. The narrator of the poem poses as an objective observer, a witness to Hardy himself, a man standing in a "careworn craze" looking at the sands and sea. When the narrator makes inquires, "they" say Hardy sees the past. Hardy then drops the exterior narrator and admits that he, as both narrator and central figure, sees a certain sight "everywhere / In his brain—day, night." The final stanza explains that he is gazing at a ghostly girl on a horse, impervious to the ravages of time, although he himself continues to decline. As when he first saw her, she "Draws rein and sings to the swing of the tide."

J. I. M. Stewart calls the poem "a splendid taunt hurled at oblivion by the imagination" ("Hardy," in *Eight Modern Writers*, 61).

For further reading: Pinion, "Questions Arising from Hardy's Visits to Cornwall"; Rowse, "Hardy and Cornwall."

"Philosophical Fantasy, A" Poem which Hardy wrote in 1920 and 1926. At the end of the poem, he notes, in italics, *1920 and 1926*, suggesting that he began it in 1920 but did not finish it. He came back to it, apparently, in 1926. It was first published in the *FORT-NIGHTLY REVIEW* in January 1927 and posthumously collected in *WINTER WORDS* (1928). The epigraph is "'Milton . . . made God argue.'—Walter Bagehot." The poem was originally titled "In the Matter of an Intent, A Philosophic Fantasy." The editor of the *Fortnightly Review* did not like the title, and Hardy agreed to change it. He remarked that the poem was "rather of the nature of a dream than a consistent argument" (Purdy, *Thomas Hardy: A Bibliographical Study*, 258).

The poem takes the form of a dialogue between God and the English poet John MILTON. Milton asks why God had not fulfilled all his intentions regarding Earth. It also vexes Milton that he does not know God's sex; he asks if he may address him as "It."

God responds that he may certainly call him "It." He is "sexless" and "in nature vexless." Man can, if he likes, call God "blind force persisting." He says it is folly of man to think that *"Man's shape must needs resemble / Mine."*

God goes on to say that he will pardon Milton's mistake and will meet him in his garden "about the May-time/Of my next, or next, Creation." If he does not meet Milton, he will meet another of man's representatives. Milton might have died and turned to dust, grieved by those he left behind, although God does not know what "grief" is.

At that future time, God will not offer an explanation of the "world's sore situation" with "dramatic stories" (that is, religious beliefs). He regards Earth to be "malleable matter," more suitable for scientific than moral or ethical treatment. God distances himself from the creation of the Earth, which is something "Time" has brought about. He goes on to explain that he is "unconscious" in his "doings." In the final stanza God advises Milton (or those who succeed him) that he is motivated by *"purposeless propension."*

The God of the poem is not Milton's "anthropomorphic God," but actually more akin to the "Immanent Will" of The *DYNASTS*. Bailey observes that when Milton asks why there is injustice and imperfection in the world, the answer is that the God of Hardy's imagination is not "manlike." He exists "outside time" and feels no emotions.

Bailey attributes the ideas in the poem to the German philosopher Arthur Schopenhauer's book *The World as Will and Idea*, Walter Bagehot's essay "John Milton," and other sources (Bailey, *The Poetry of Thomas Hardy*, 607–609).

Phillotson, Richard Character in *JUDE THE OBSCURE*; he is the schoolmaster who first instills in Jude FAWLEY the idea of his someday going to CHRISTMINSTER and studying there, after he departs from MARYGREEN. He also fosters Jude's interest in classical languages by sending him Greek and Latin grammars. When Jude reaches Christminster years later, Phillotson is 45 and in charge of a school at Lumsden. Jude meets and falls in love with his cousin, Sue BRIDEHEAD, who marries Phillotson. When Sue reciprocates Jude's love, Phillotson sets her free to live with Jude. Phillotson is dismissed from his post and returns to his old school at Marygreen. After Sue's children by Jude are killed, Sue feels she has sinned against God and must sacrifice her own happiness. She goes to Marygreen and remarries Phillotson, although she does not love him. Throughout the novel, Phillotson never wavers from his convictions; he is long-suffering, patient, and generous.

Pierston, Jocelyn The leading character in *The WELL-BELOVED*, Pierston is a native of the Isle of Slingers (the Portland peninsula, near WEYMOUTH), who becomes a famous sculptor and a royal academician (an associate of the prestigious ROYAL ACADEMY OF ARTS). He is extremely indecisive and fickle about women; none of them live up to his ideal vision of "the well-beloved." He is enamored of his childhood playmate and neighbor, Avice CARO, but their romance is interrupted by his interest in Marcia BENCOMB; they elope, but do not marry. He returns to the peninsula 20 years later and falls in love with Avice's daughter, Avice II (Ann Avice), but she has secretly married Isaac Pierston and is pregnant. Twenty years after that, he falls in love with Avice II's daughter, Avice III, the granddaughter of Avice Caro. Avice III elopes with Henri LEVERRE. Pierston then meets Marcia Bencomb again. She is now widowed. They marry in old age for convenience, but Pierston falls ill and his sense of beauty becomes warped. He spends his remaining years demolishing the ancient splendors of his native peninsula. His original vision, once powerful, has evaporated.

Pine-Avon, Nichola In *The WELL-BELOVED*, she is one of several women who interest Jocelyn PIERSTON. When he meets her at Lady Channelcliffe's, she is a handsome widow with chestnut hair and "round, inquiring, luminous" grey eyes. She believes, mistakenly, that he has married Marcia BENCOMB, and she loses interest in him; she eventually marries his friend Alfred SOMERS. Once "intellectual" and "emancipated," she has regressed and adopted the "petty and timid mental position" of her mother and grandmother. She carefully guards the literature and art that reaches her "row of daughters."

"Pink Frock, The" Poem collected in MOMENTS OF VISION (1917). The poem was suggested, according to the *Life*, by some words of a countess, Marcia, Lady Yarborough, in May 1894. The Hardys were in London. At the home of an unnamed countess, Hardy was talking with Lady Yarborough, a rich and attractive woman. Her uncle was very ill, and she privately told Hardy that people snubbed her for going out, which he found hard to believe; he assured her it was her imagination.

In the poem the speaker is a lady, a near relation of a man who is dying. The time is most inconvenient for his death, for she has a beautiful pink frock ready for the season. She remarks bitterly, "must I shut myself up, / And go out never?" She wishes her relative had died months earlier so that she would now have the opportunity to wear the frock.

Portraits of women's vanity are common in Hardy's work. In FAR FROM THE MADDING CROWD, for example, we first see Bathsheba EVERDENE as she looks in a mirror.

Robin Milford set "The Pink Frock" to music in *A Book of Songs* (Oxford University Press, 1940; Bailey, *The Poetry of Thomas Hardy*, 375).

Pisa *See* ITALY.

place names The critic Edmund GOSSE once asked, "What has God done to Mr. Hardy, that he should rise up in the arable land of Wessex and shake his fist at his Creator?" (Philip, *Thomas Hardy: Wessex Heights*, 7). Aside from Hardy's often conflicting ideas on the Deity, there was, of course no actual "arable land of Wessex." The name WESSEX came to denote not only DORSET but also parts of Gloucestershire, Somerset, and Wiltshire, eventually expanding to cover more than two-thirds of southern England. Hardy substituted names of his own choosing for many actual villages, towns, cities, structures, and topographical landmarks and formations. There is not always a one-to-one correspondence between the fictional and real places. CASTERBRIDGE, for instance, is not entirely identical with DORCHESTER.

Hardy's position never varied from that expressed in a letter written in 1905 to Hermann LEA. Lea was then trying to compile a touring guide to Dorset. Hardy asked that he state that "the author has never admitted more than that the places named fictitiously were *suggested* by . . . real places." Hardy added that "natural features" sometimes have real names and sometimes invented ones, but were "described in a way that makes identification almost an easy matter" (*Letters* III, 172).

On January 4, 1911, Hardy wrote a scholar, F. O. Saxelby, who was compiling a "Dictionary of the Characters & Places" in Hardy's novels and poems, that he had no wish that such a book be prepared (*Letters* IV, 135).

Despite Hardy's warnings and disclaimers, critics and readers have never ceased trying to correlate the places and natural features of his fiction and poetry with actual ones. Hardy made a table himself in 1896, conceding that Casterbridge was Dorchester; Budmouth Regis, Weymouth; Weatherbury, Puddletown; Sandbourne, Bournemouth; MELCHESTER, Salisbury; Havenpool, Poole; Castle de Stancy, Dunster Castle; Marygreen, Fawley; Shaston, Shaftsbury; Little Hintock, Minterne; and Egdon Heath, a composite of Puddletown Heath, Moreton Heath, Tincleton Heath, Bere-Heath, and other heaths between Dorchester and Bournemouth.

See Appendix V for a list of the fictional and actual places most commonly accepted by commentators and critics today.

"Place on the Map, The" This poem was first published in the *English Review* for September 1913, with the subtitle "A Poor Schoolmaster's Story" (Purdy, *Thomas Hardy: A Bibliographical Study,* 162). It was later collected in SATIRES OF CIRCUMSTANCE (1914). The poem traces the relationship between a a young schoolmaster and the girl he loves. The speaker, many years later, is reminded of the earlier time by a map that hangs near him; it has "shires and towns and rivers" and, particularly, a "jutting height / Coloured purpose, with a margin of blue sea" (Beeny Cliff, in CORNWALL).

The speaker recalls that long ago, on a hot, dry summer day, the two had walked near this spot; there she had "unfolded what would happen by and by." The map evokes the scene "All distinctly to my sight," re-creating their "unforeboded troublous case." The girl has a great deal of tension. They had "loved beneath that blazing blue" for "weeks and weeks." The sky had "lost the art of raining, as her eyes to-day had too." Her news, however, "Shot our firmament with rays of ruddy hue."

Because of the circumstances, the situation is marked by "wormwood" as well as "wonder." "In realms of reason" it would have "joyed our double soul," but instead it "Wore a torrid tragic light / Under order-keeping's rigorous control." He rebels against a system that would force him to marry, although he is too poor to support a family.

Looking at the map revives, for him, "her words, the spot, the time, / And the thing we found we had to face before the next year's prime." The whole "episode comes back in pantomime" as he gazes at the "charted coast."

Carl Weber believes the poem is related to Hardy's relationship with Emma Gifford (HARDY) in 1873. Both knew that Emma's father would not approve of their marriage until Hardy could provide financial security (Bailey, *The Poetry of Thomas Hardy*, 281).

"Play of 'St. George,' The"   In 1920 the HARDY PLAY-ERS were preparing a production of *The RETURN OF THE NATIVE*. Hardy contributed this enlargement of the mummers' play described in book 2, chapters 5 and 6, of the novel. In the novel only fragments of the play are given, mixed with the conversation of the actors. The Hardy Players' version was performed in DORCHESTER on November 17 and 18, 1920, and in LONDON on January 27, 1921. The Players also performed "Saint George" for Hardy at MAX GATE on Christmas night, 1920. His second wife, Florence HARDY, prepared a typescript of the play, which was printed in pamphlet form. In 1928 the play was reprinted, along with a modernized version by Roger S. Loomis, by Samuel French, New York (Purdy, *Thomas Hardy: A Bibliographical Study*, 212). The Max Gate performance is recorded in the *Life* (*Life*, 411).

Poems of the Past and the Present   Poetry collection published by HARPER & BROTHERS, London and New York, in 1902. In his preface, dated August 1901, Hardy acknowledges that the poems in the volume comprise "a series of feelings and fancies" written in different moods and under varying circumstances and that they may be said to lack cohesion. He does not regret this, for "Unadjusted impressions have their value."

The first poem is titled "V.R. 1819–1901." Beneath this title, on a separate line, is the phrase *A Reverie*. The poem was written on the night of Queen Victoria's death, Sunday, January 27, 1901 (Purdy, *Thomas Hardy: A Bibliographical Study*, 107). It was published in the *Times* on January 29, 1901. Hardy refers to the queen's "purposed Life . . . Serene, sagacious, free."

The remainder of the volume is divided into several sections: "War Poems," "Poems of Pilgrimage," "Miscellaneous Poems," "Imitations, etc." (Hardy's translations of Greek, Latin, German, and French works), and "Retrospect" (Purdy, *Thomas Hardy: A Bibliographical Study*, 107–19).

An anonymous reviewer of the volume for the SAT-URDAY REVIEW called it a "grey book," but declared that every poem in the book had "something to say," even though it was sometimes said in a "slow, twisted, sometimes enigmatic manner." The reviewer's final estimate of Hardy was that, although he had no "singing voice," Hardy was a "profoundly interesting" poet. T. H. Warren, president of Magdalen College, OXFORD, writing in *The SPECTATOR*, suggested that poetry was not Hardy's "proper medium," and deplored his "morbid taste for the ghastly and the gruesome." He praised what Hardy termed his "imitations" of Sapho, Catullus, Schiller, Heine, and Victor Hugo, and pronounced him an "accomplished scholar, and that not only in English" (Cox, ed., *Thomas Hardy: The Critical Heritage*, 332–35).

poetry, Hardy's attitude toward   Hardy had a lifelong passion for poetry, considering himself primarily a poet rather than a novelist. He developed strict concepts of form that, toward the end of his life, were at variance with the practices of some of the newer poets, such as Ezra Pound.

At the age of three Hardy read a book containing verses of the Cries of London (the book still exists in the DORSET COUNTY MUSEUM; Gittings, *The Young Thomas Hardy*, 28). The Cries of London were phrases shouted, called, or chanted by peddlers who roamed the streets of LONDON for hundreds of years selling such wares as mackerel, oranges, lemons, cherries, and gingerbread. Their songs have been recorded by the Alfred Deller Consort and other groups. His mother also gave him, in his first year at Julia Augusta MARTIN's school, John Dryden's translation of Virgil's *Aeneid*. From 1859 to 1861, while working in the DORCHESTER office of the architect John HICKS, Hardy read the *Aeneid* in Latin along with some of the poetry of Horace and Ovid. He also studied Greek and read parts of the *Iliad*. In 1865, when he considered applying to CAM-BRIDGE UNIVERSITY, he planned to combine studies in theology and poetry. He was, of course, familiar with the works of SHAKESPEARE. While living in London in 1866 and 1867 he read much poetry, including the works of Lord Byron, Sir Walter Scott, and John Donne. He began converting the Book of Ecclesiastes into Spenserian stanzas, but abandoned the effort. He wrote a great deal of verse, but kept much of it private. He came to believe that poetry formed the "essence of all imaginative and emotional literature" (*Life*, 47–48).

Hardy turned to writing fiction partly because it was more lucrative than poetry. In December 1888, however, he wrote Sir George DOUGLAS that it "is better to fail in poetry than to succeed in prose," because verse offered more "mental satisfaction" (Millgate, ed., *Thomas Hardy: Selected Letters*, 51). In December 1898, after he had given up writing fiction and begun to focus on poetry again, Hardy wrote to Edmund GOSSE, praising his volumes of poetry. He had sent Gosse a copy of *WESSEX POEMS* for Christmas, for which Gosse had thanked him. Hardy remarked that it was difficult to let people who assumed he was making a "fresh start" know that poetry was his "original weakness" (*Letters*, 208).

In 1906 Hardy wrote Arthur SYMONS that he had once shared his view that verse should be reserved for "emotional expression." He had, however, come to the conclusion that even unemotional verse could "be attracted into verse-form by its nearness to emotional verse in the same piece" He explained that the "neutral" lines are "warmed" by the others; even the best lyrical poetry is not "lyrical every moment throughout." Moreover, he observed, this is the justification for the lines of blank verse in Shakespeare's histories, which he transcribed from historic chronicles (*Letters* III, 199). In 1907 Hardy wrote H. W. Massingham, editor of the *Nation,* that he believed there would be a "great reaction in favour of poetry before very long" and that it was absurd of the young critics of the day to conclude that the taste for poetry had died (*Letters* IV, 258). In 1919 he wrote Amy LOWELL that he was very glad to hear from her for personal reasons and also because of her efforts to promote poetry (*Letters* V, 292). Just after his birthday, in June 1919, he was very touched when Siegfried SASSOON presented him with a "POETS' TRIBUTE," a beautifully bound volume of holograph poems from 43 living poets, including Rudyard KIPLING, Robert BRIDGES, William Butler YEATS, Siegfried SASSOON, Robert GRAVES, and D. H. Lawrence.

One of Hardy's more interesting expressions of his concept of poetry is in a letter he wrote Ezra Pound in 1921 in response to Pound's request that he criticize some poems Pound enclosed. Hardy wrote that he could not do so without understanding Pound's aim. He imagined Pound intended his work to be read by a small audience, but he himself was "old-fashioned" and thought "lucidity a virtue in poetry, as in prose." He assumed Pound did not care whether his work was widely understood. He commented on several of Pound's poems, but concluded that it was best for Pound to rely on his own judgment (*Letters* V, 77).

In 1923 Hardy wrote Amy Lowell, who had sent him a copy of an anthology of American poetry, that he liked her verse and thought Edna St. Vincent Millay the most promising of the "younger poets." He felt he was too old to do justice to the free verse in the volume; it often seemed to him "a jumble of notes" containing ideas that were striking or novel or beautiful. Hardy believed that such a jumble could be "transfused into poetry" but was not poetry itself, and so gave him no gratification. Hardy argued that dispensing with traditional poetic forms was only permissible in "ancient poetry, like the English Bible (*Letters* V, 186).

For further reading: Bailey, *The Poetry of Thomas Hardy: A Handbook and Commentary;* Buckler, *The Poetry of Thomas Hardy: A Study in Art and Ideas;* Davie, *Thomas Hardy and English Poetry;* Gibson, "Thomas Hardy's Poetry: Poetic Apprehension and Poetic Method"; Hynes, "The Hardy Tradition in Modern English Poetry"; Johnson, "'Ancestral Voices': Hardy and the English Poetic Tradition"; Langbaum, "The Issue of Hardy's Poetry"; Mitchell, "Passion and Companionship in Hardy's Poetry"; Morgan, "Mr. Thomas Hardy Composing a Lyric"; Morgan, "The Partial Vision: Hardy's Idea of Dramatic Poetry"; Paulin, *The Poetry of Perception;* Pinion, *A Hardy Companion: A Commentary on the Poems of Thomas Hardy;* Taylor, *Hardy's Poetry, 1860–1928;* Taylor, *The Patterns in Hardy's Poetry;* Zietlow, *Moments of Vision: The Poetry of Thomas Hardy.*

"Poets' Tribute" to Hardy Shortly after Hardy's 79th birthday, in June 1919, the poet Siegfried SASSOON presented him with a gift, a beautifully bound volume of holograph poems from 43 living poets. Hardy states that Sassoon arranged the tribute (*Life,* 390). Among the contributors, in addition to Sassoon, were Lascelles Abercrombie, Maurice Baring, Edmund GOSSE, Gilbert Murray, Alfred NOYES, Walter de la Mare, Rudyard KIPLING, Robert BRIDGES, G. K. Chesterton, Sir William Watson, Thomas Sturge Moore, John Middleton MURRY, Charlotte MEW, W. H. Davies, George Russell, William Butler YEATS, Robert GRAVES, Sir Arthur QUILLER-COUCH, and D. H. Lawrence. Hardy was very touched by the gift and wrote in the *Life* that he was determined to answer every contributor personally, believing that if they could take the trouble to write the poems he could "certainly take the trouble to write the letters." He adds that it was his first inkling that an "opinion had silently grown up as it were . . . that he was no mean power in the contemporary world of poetry" (*Life,* 389–90). He was particularly honored to know that his poetry was highly regarded by prominent poets of his day.

politics, Hardy's interest in Hardy wrote little of a purely political nature, although he had strong views on certain issues, especially the treatment of animals. His article "The DORSETSHIRE LABOURER," which appeared in *LONGMAN'S MAGAZINE* in 1883, prompted the editor, Percy Bunting, to ask Hardy for an article about the laborer and his vote. Hardy declined the offer, possibly because he was alarmed by the continuing controversy at the time over the Liberal Party's intention to give the vote to agricultural workers (*Letters* I, 121). Hardy seemed to take little interest in party politics.

In 1906 Hardy wrote Millicent FAWCETT in support of her plan to publish a pamphlet giving the views of eminent men on women's suffrage. He stated that he supported it. He explained that he believed women would vote against certain "pernicious conventions." He cited as a prime example the sport of hunting, as he opposed the idea that "so-called educated men should be encouraged to harass & kill for pleasure feeble creatures by mean stratagems." He was also against slaughterhouses and laws regarding religion, illegitimacy, and other matters (*Letters* III, 238).

Hardy was, nevertheless, frequently asked to comment on social questions with political implications. In 1909 Lady Agnes GROVE sent him a draft of her preface to T. W. Berry's book *Professions for Girls,* apparently expecting him to agree with her arguments in favor of women's having careers. He wrote that he was not convinced, but was unable to answer all her arguments because he never took any active part in politics (*Letters* IV, 3).

In 1914 he wrote Florence HENNIKER that he considered the "Irish question" (the issue of Irish home rule) "perplexing, & gloomy," but feared the Irish temperament would not be "satisfied for long with ANY rule" (*Letters* V, 38). At the time, the Liberal government had proposed an Irish home rule bill that was encountering opposition by the House of Lords; Ulster (northern Ireland) was threatening violence.

In 1921 he wrote John GALSWORTHY, who, with his wife, was visiting California, that neither England nor Europe looked "attractive" politically. He observed that the "extreme party seems to forget that the opposite of error is error still." Purdy and Millgate take this as a general comment on the chaos following WORLD WAR I (*Letters* VI, 70–71).

Poole   Port on the south coast of England, called HAVENPOOL in *The MAYOR OF CASTERBRIDGE*, in two stories contained in *A CHANGED MAN*, and in some of Hardy's poems.

Poor Man and the Lady, The   Hardy's first novel, in which scenes of rural life were blended with satire against the upper classes. He completed it in 1869 and submitted it to MACMILLAN & CO., which rejected it but suggested that he try the publishing firm of Chapman & Hall. The novelist George MEREDITH, the manuscript reader for Chapman, advised Hardy that the firm would be willing to publish the work if it were subsidized, but he recommended putting the manuscript away because of its orientation toward social criticism. He suggested that Hardy "attempt a novel with a purely artistic purpose, giving it a more complicated 'plot'" (*Life*, 82). Hardy took his advice and abandoned *The Poor Man and the Lady,* although he incorporated sections of it in later novels. He destroyed most of the manuscript and began a new novel, *DESPERATE REMEDIES*, which he published anonymously in 1871.

Portland   Peninsula, connected by only a road bridge to Weymouth. It is called the Isle of Slingers in *The WELL-BELOVED* and *The TRUMPET-MAJOR*. Portland is described by Hardy in *The Well-Beloved* as the "ancient Vindillia Island of Roman times and before that the Home of the Slingers." In fact, after Hardy's death, excavations at MAIDEN CASTLE, outside DORCHESTER, revealed thousands of pebbles from Chesil Beach, Portland, assembled for sling stones ("The Country of the Well-Beloved," in *A Walk with Tom Wightman*, The Thomas Hardy Society Guides, Edition 1991–1992).

portraits and busts of Hardy   As Hardy became more famous, painters and sculptors were eager to have him sit for them; in addition, some of his honors, such as his invitation to become an Honorary Fellow of MAGDALENE COLLEGE, CAMBRIDGE, entailed having his portrait painted. Hardy was depicted by John White Alexander (portrait, 1880s); Sir Max BEERBOHM (cartoon, published in *Fifty Caricatures,* 1913); the French artist Jacques-Emile BLANCHE (oil portrait, 1906); H. Furness (cartoon, 1923); Reginald Grenville Eves (oil painting, 1923); Harry Furniss (several pen and ink sketches, c. 1880–1910); Sir Hubert von HERKOMER (oil portrait, 1908); Augustus JOHN (oil portrait, 1923); Fuller MAITLAND (oil portrait, 1913); Walter William OULESS (oil portrait, 1922); Maggie RICHARDSON (bust, 1923); William Rothenstein (sketch, 1915); Theodore Spicer-Simson (bronze medallion, 1921); William STRANG (oil portrait, 1893; pencil sketch, 1919; other likenesses also); Winifred THOMSON (oil portrait, 1895); Sir William Hamo THORNYCROFT (bronze head, 1917); and the Russian sculptor Sergei YOURIÉVITCH (bust, 1924).

Portsmouth   Important coastal port; after the English victory at the battle of TRAFALGAR in October 1805, the HMS *VICTORY* returned here. It is open to visitors today. The battle is described in *The DYNASTS*. Hardy's 1880 novel *The TRUMPET-MAJOR* is set during the time of preparations on the south coast for the French invasion of England, before the naval victory dissolved the threat.

Portsmouth, Earl and Countess of   The earl and countess were Newton Wallop (1825–1891), fifth earl of Portsmouth, and his wife, Eveline, countess of Portsmouth (d. 1906). Hardy first attracted interest from the aristocracy after 1883, when he and Emma HARDY had returned to DORCHESTER and were living at SHIRE-HALL PLACE during the construction of MAX GATE. Hardy had met Lady Portsmouth in London in June 1884. She invited the Hardy's to Eggesford House, her family's country seat in Devon. Hardy went alone in March 1885; Emma was ill and could not make the journey. Lord and Lady Portsmouth made their library available to Hardy, but he actually spent much of his time enjoying the company of the family and their other houseguests and driving about the countryside. He called Lord Portsmouth "a farmer-like man with a broad Devon accent." The Portsmouths had several daughters. Hardy wrote Emma that he was most impressed with Lady Rosamond Christie, the third, who struck him as a "particularly sensible woman" (*Letters* I, 131).

Although in his work Hardy was always sympathetic to lower-class women who were victimized (such as Tess in *Tess of the d'Urbervilles*), he was susceptible to the social, intellectual, and physical charms of upper-class women (Millgate, *Thomas Hardy,* 242–43).

Pouncy, Harry (1870–1925)   Journalist and lecturer. He was on the staff of the *Dorset Country Chronicle* and was assistant secretary of the DORSET NATURAL HISTORY AND ANTIQUARIAN FIELD CLUB for a number of years. He gave recitals of Dorset songs and dialect sketches, but apparently had been having difficulties obtaining old songs. In March 1907 Hardy sent him a list of several that were in print, including "The Spotted Cow," which was in a collection called *Songs of the West* by Baring Gould. He also recommended "Hullah's Song Book," published by MACMILLAN & CO. Hardy advised him not to use blue smockfrocks, because they were modern, but suggested he have some made in DORCHESTER. He offered one of his works for recitation, possibly "A TRAMPWOMAN'S TRAGEDY" (*Letters* III, 247). (The smock-frock was a coarse frock or long shirt worn over other clothes to protect them.)

Pouncy presented "Hours in Hardyland," a lecture illustrated with slides and dramatic scenes from *FAR FROM THE MADDING CROWD*, on October 18, 1907, in the Dorchester Town Hall. Beatrice Hull, a local actress, played Bathsheba. The performance was repeated on Friday, October 25. After the first one, Hardy wrote to say he had enjoyed it, but offered some suggestions: if Pouncy decided to lecture in other towns, he should have an assistant explain a dramatic scene in the beginning, and add a scene that included the four characters together (Bathsheba EVERDENE, Gabriel OAK, Sergeant TROY, and William BOLDWOOD).

Pouncy was showing lantern slides with dissolving views of various locations. For a tour outside of Dorchester, Hardy recommended that he include scenes familiar to those readers. He envisioned a "complete tour of Wessex," encompassing Salisbury, Bath, Winchester, and Shaftesbury. Hardy suggested that, if Pouncy were thinking of an American lecture tour, he find a lecture agent familiar with the United States (*Letters* III, 247, 279–81).

For further reading: Baron, "Hardy and the Dorchester Pouncys."

Power, Abner   Character in *A LAODICEAN*. He is the uncle of Paula POWER. First introduced as a stranger, he has a disfigured face. He reveals himself as the socially ambitious brother of Paula's deceased father. He persuades her to accompany him on a tour of Europe, hoping to promote her marriage to Captain DE STANCY, whose father once owned Castle de Stancy, and deter her from marrying George SOMERSET. He discovers that William DARE is de Stancy's illegitimate son, and prevents Paula's marriage to the Captain. Dare, however, learns that Power's disfigurement is the result of an accident caused by an explosive device he had invented for a revolutionary party in Europe. He had escaped to Peru, but is thinking of settling in England when Dare reveals that he is still wanted by certain governments. Power returns to Peru.

Power, Paula   The heroine of *A LAODICEAN*. Paula is the daughter of a wealthy railroad builder who had pur-

chased Castle de Stancy from Captain William DE STANCY, who was forced to sell it to pay his gambling debts. Her surname links her to the new English industrial aristocracy (Pinion, *A Hardy Companion*, 449). She has strong beliefs and at the beginning of the novel, resisting efforts by Mr. WOODWELL, minister of the chapel her Baptist father had built, to baptize her by immersion before the congregation, although it was her father's dying wish.

She has inherited the castle, portions of which date back several centuries. She is trying to put in modern improvements and extensions, such as a telegraph, even as she does her best to restore the fabric of the building and preserve its splendid furnishings. A young architect, George SOMERSET, undertakes the renovations and falls in love with her. Paula is attracted to him, but she is almost fatally susceptible to what she perceives as the romance and authority of the nobility. As a result, she nearly marries Captain de Stancy, a marriage promoted by de Stancy's unscrupulous illegitimate son, William DARE. Eventually, she rejects the captain, and she and Somerset clear up their misunderstandings, marrying in Normandy. Dare, furious, sets fire to the Castle de Stancy, which burns as Paula and George watch from a nearby village inn. Her original passion for antiquity endures, however; she remarks to George, "I wish my castle wasn't burnt, and I wish you were a de Stancy!"

privacy, Hardy's views of   In 1881, Charles Kegan PAUL wrote an unsigned article about Hardy's novels, published in the *British Quarterly Review*. He stated that Hardy descended from laborers, a source of pride to him. Hardy wrote Paul to thank him for the article, but stated that he believed the "less people know of a writer's antecedents (till he is dead) the better" (*Letters* II, 89). He said he did not object to what Paul had written, but explained "privately" that he was descended from several generations of master masons.

In early February 1901, Hardy was interviewed by the dramatist and critic William ARCHER and apparently spoke freely about his work. In a state of alarm, however, he subsequently wrote Archer on February 15 that he would prefer him to omit "those few words of mine about my writing verse." He stated that he had a "horror" of spreading himself before the public and would like the recorded conversation to be as "*impersonal*" as possible (*Letters* II, 279).

Hardy's aversion to being interviewed, and to distortions by writers and journalists, persisted throughout his life. In April 1922 his second wife, Florence HARDY, wrote Theodore SPICER-SIMSON, who had made some medallions of Hardy, asking that he please let them know when he might be able to visit again. She explained that Hardy found it difficult on the whole to receive people just for a call, because all too often they talked with him and then printed an interview with him (*Letters* IV, 126).

In October of the same year the anthropologist and author John Langdon-Davies, who was then working in the promotion department of the London office of Goldwyn Pictures, which was about to make a film of TESS OF THE D'URBERVILLES, asked permission to come to MAX GATE. He wanted to look at the sites of scenes in the novel and also photograph Hardy for publicity purposes. Florence Hardy wrote that Hardy would give "hints" about actual locations depicted in the novel, but did not want to be filmed in his house or garden. He would not object, however, to a still photograph (*Letters* IV, 163).

The poet and critic Arthur SYMONS proposed a visit in April 1926, two years before Hardy's death. Hardy wrote that he found interviews trying, and hesitated to let Symons make such a journey lest Hardy be confined to bed (*Letters* VII, 20). Later that same year he communicated privately to John Acland, curator of the DORSET COUNTY MUSEUM, to ask that he request the Museum's porter, Albert Kibbey, not to confide any "personal particulars" about him. He had suffered because "gossiping journalists," both in England and America, had printed "all sorts of rubbish, mostly false," which they claimed they had learned from the museum porter. He requested that Acland mention the matter to him "kindly," as he did not object at all to Mr. Kibbey (*Letters* VII, 25).

Procter, Anne Benson (1799–1888)   London hostess and widow of the poet Bryan Waller Procter (who wrote under the pseudonym Barry Cornwall). Hardy first met her about 1874 and delighted in her reminiscences of literary figures, as well as in the celebrities he met at her home, including Robert BROWNING. In 1883 he wrote to thank her for her Christmas card. She had moved to a new home in west London, and he remarked that it was a more suitable location for one "whose house is felt to be a sort of literary rallying-point" than her previous home in Westminster (*Letters* I, 113–14).

"Profitable Reading of Fiction, The"   Essay published in the New York *Forum* in March 1888 and collected in Ernest BRENNECKE's unauthorized book *Life and Art: By Thomas Hardy* (New York: Greenberg, 1925). Brennecke's volume is now quite rare, but the essay has been reprinted in *Thomas Hardy's Personal Writings,* ed. Harold Orel (Lawrence: University of Kansas Press, 1966).

Hardy suggests that the reader of a story or novel experience a "sudden shifting" of his mental perspective, which may include the "material scene" or setting. The narrative must be absorbing, and the writer must encourage the reader not to be unduly critical. To this end, the writer must deal with extraordinary situations that contrast with daily life. Otherwise, if the circumstances resemble the reader's, he begins thinking "serious thoughts" rather than dreaming, which is his proper activity. Hardy defines good fiction as "nearest to the epic, dramatic, or narrative masterpiece" of the past.

Very good novels excel in narrative or portraiture, but novels below the highest level of fiction are the product of "cleverness rather than of intuition." Paradoxically, the didactic novel is less likely to offer "moral profit" to the reader than one written without such a purpose, but one which illustrates the "inevitableness of character and environment in working out destiny." Truths that are "temporary" must be distinguished from those that are "eternal" and those that are "accidental" from those which are "essential." Fidelity to small details is not the same as fidelity to life itself. Trivial and ephemeral details—clothing, tea cups, social minutiae—are far removed from, in the words of a French critic, "the great imaginations which create and transform." The treatment of the subject is more important than the subject itself. Hardy asked that the novelist have the right to treat frankly such controversial topics as sexual relations, religious beliefs, and the position of man in the universe.

Prothero, George Walter (1848–1922)   Historian and editor of the *QUARTERLY REVIEW* from 1899 to 1922. He published a review of TESS OF THE D'URBERVILLES and other literary essays about Hardy.

Puddletown   Town near DORCHESTER, called WEATHERBURY in Hardy's fiction. Hardy's grandfather and great-grandfather both came from Puddletown. St. Mary's Church, Puddletown, was the WEATHERBURY church in FAR FROM THE MADDING CROWD. In 1904 Hardy wrote the Reverend Thomas PERKINS, who was active in the SOCIETY FOR THE PROTECTION OF ANCIENT BUILDINGS and had inquired about work in progress at the church, that he believed the roof was in disrepair and was being strengthened. In 1908 William Gover sent him a copy of his newly published book *A Guide to the Ancient Church of St. Mary, Puddletown.* Hardy's paternal grandfather sometimes played in the church in a "choir" like that depicted in UNDER THE GREENWOOD TREE (*Letters* III, 97, 328–29).

Hardy was close to a number of his relatives who lived at Puddletown, including cousins on both sides of the family. He was particularly close to the children of Maria Sparks, Jemima HARDY's sister.

Purdy, Richard L. (1904–1990)   Noted bibliographer and Hardy scholar; coeditor, with Michael Millgate, of *The Collected Letters of Thomas Hardy* (1978–88) and author of *Thomas Hardy: A Bibliographical Study* (1954).

A native of Middletown, New York, he was Professor of English at Yale. His personal collection of Hardy books, manuscripts, and memorabilia makes up the core collection of the Richard L. Purdy Collection of Thomas Hardy, owned by the Beinecke Rare Book and Manuscript Library, Yale University (accessible to scholars for research).

It was Purdy who revealed that Hardy himself wrote *The Life of Thomas Hardy* (published posthumously in two volumes in 1928 and 1930; republished as one volume in 1962). At Hardy's insistence, it had been attributed to his second wife, Florence Emily HARDY. Her name had been on the title page, and Hardy had rejected the term "autobiography." Purdy revealed this information in a lecture at the Grolier Club, New York, on April 25, 1940. It was repeated in the *New York Times Book Review* of May 12, 1940 (Millgate, *Thomas Hardy*, 516).

Q

Quarterly Review Periodical edited by George PROTHERO from 1899 to 1922. In April 1892 the periodical published an unfavorable review of TESS OF THE D'URBERVILLES by Mowbray Morris. In July 1901 W. H. Matlock wrote an article stating that Hardy and George MEREDITH were the only "genuinely great novelists in England at present" (Gerber and Davis, *Thomas Hardy: An Annotated Bibliography of Writings about Him,* I, 96). Hardy was also the subject of other articles published in the *Review.* His friend Horace MOULE wrote articles for this periodical as well as for the SATURDAY REVIEW and other publications.

Queen of Cornwall, The   See FAMOUS TRAGEDY OF THE QUEEN OF CORNWALL, THE.

Queen's College, Oxford University   In late 1924 Hardy was made an Honorary Fellow of Queen's College; an announcement was made in the *Times* on November 20, 1924. He was unable to visit the college, however, until June 1925. He had been made an Honorary Fellow of MAGDALENE COLLEGE, CAMBRIDGE UNIVERSITY, in 1913.

Queen's College was founded in 1341 by Robert Eglesfield, a chaplain in the household of Queen Philippa. The medieval buildings were rebuilt in the 18th century; at present Queen's is the only college housed in baroque buildings. The Front Quad is particularly noteworthy for its classical architecture.

"Quid Hic Agis?"   Poem collected in MOMENTS OF VISION (1917). The title is from 1 Kings, "What doest thou here?" The poem was printed as a pamphlet under the title "When I Weekly Knew" by Florence Dugdale HARDY in October 1916 (Purdy, *Thomas Hardy: A Bibliographical Study,* 188). At the end of the poem are the italicized words "*The Spectator: 1916: During the War.*" The poem had first been published in the *Spectator* on August 19, 1916, under the title "In Time of Slaughter."

The poem is in three sections, spanning Hardy's boyhood; his time at ST. JULIOT CHURCH, CORNWALL, in the 1870s (where he met Emma HARDY); and his old age, after the deaths of his mother and Emma.

The first stanza depicts Hardy as a boy at STINSFORD CHURCH, listening to, but not understanding, the story of the Hebrew prophet Elijah in 1 Kings. After Elijah

has killed the prophets of Baal, Queen Jezebel threatens to have him killed and he escapes to a cave. The Lord asks, "What doest thou here?" Elijah says his life is in danger, but the Lord sends him to stand upon the mount before the Lord. He survives wind, earthquake, and fire, until a "small voice / Bade him up and be gone." Elijah is carried up to heaven in a whirlwind (2 Kings 2.11). Hardy does not perceive that the poem might apply to his own life, but looks across the aisle and sees his mother smiling in approval.

In the second stanza, whose events take place much later, Hardy is reading the same words at the lectern in St. Juliot church; Hardy apparently filled in when Emma's brother-in-law, the Reverend Caddell HOLDER, was not feeling well. However, he still does not take the words seriously, nor does the congregation. Without his realizing it, time has passed and "Devoured our prime." Bailey dates Hardy's reading of the passage as taking place in August 1870 (Bailey, *The Poetry of Thomas Hardy,* 354–55).

The third stanza is set many years later, after the deaths of his mother and Emma. Hardy describes himself as "spiritless / In the wilderness." He has a sense of doom and hears a voice asking, "What doest thou here?"

The poem also refers to Hardy's seeing the memorial tablet to Emma that he had had placed in the church after her death in 1912. Bailey points out that the memorial window to Hardy in Stinsford church pictures the prophet Elijah in the storm, with the inscription cited in the poem. The same passage recurs in *A PAIR OF BLUE EYES,* when Elfride SWANCOURT's father, Christopher SWANCOURT, reads the same lesson.

Quiller-Couch, Sir Arthur (Thomas) (1863–1944)   English writer and man of letters, born in Bodmin, CORNWALL. He edited the first edition of *The Oxford Book of English Verse* (1900) and several other anthologies. From 1912 until his death he was a professor of English literature at CAMBRIDGE UNIVERSITY, dividing his time between Cambridge and his home in the Cornish port town of Fowey. He also wrote various critical works, as well as poems and a number of successful popular novels under the pseudonym Q.

In 1896, in his *Adventures in Criticism,* Quiller-Couch expressed a preference for George Moore's *Esther*

Waters over *TESS OF THE D'URBERVILLES*. In 1916, however, Hardy wrote that he had not let it disturb him (*Letters* V, 183). In 1903 Quiller-Couch mentioned Hardy's war poetry in his column for the London *Daily News*, stating that Hardy had written "a few drearily memorable lines on the seamy side of war." Hardy wrote him, saying that he had hoped his poems were "true & sad" rather than "dreary," but that, after the Battle of WATERLOO, war had lost its romance (*Letters* III, 51).

In early 1919 Sir Arthur and Lady Quiller-Couch's only son, Beval Quiller-Couch, who had received the Military Cross for his service during WORLD WAR I, died suddenly of pneumonia while awaiting demobilization. Hardy wrote Sir Arthur that he and his wife were "deeply grieved" to hear of their loss, and had thought of them constantly since learning of it (*Letters* V, 295). Later that year Sir Arthur was one of the contributors to the "POETS' TRIBUTE" TO HARDY, for which he thanked him, remarking that he was unworthy of such a tribute (*Letters* V, 328).

Quilter, Harry (1851–1907)   Art critic and journalist. In 1883 he reviewed *TWO ON A TOWER* for the *SPECTATOR*, pronouncing it "a story as unpleasant as it is practically impossible" (Cox, ed., *Thomas Hardy: The Critical Heritage*, 101). Hardy apparently did not hold a grudge against him when, in 1888, Quilter invited him to con-tribute a story to the *UNIVERSAL REVIEW*, which was just beginning publication. Quilter edited the magazine from 1888 to 1890 and published Hardy's short story "A TRAGEDY OF TWO AMBITIONS" in December 1888.

In 1886 Quilter was a candidate for the Slade Professorship of Fine Art at CAMBRIDGE UNIVERSITY and asked for Hardy's support; the post was given to John Henry Middleton. Hardy, was away in Ireland at the time and did not recommend Quilter, but wrote Quilter to say he could not have written on his behalf anyway, because he had no influence at Cambridge and knew nothing of the requirements for the professorship (*Letters* II, 12). Quilter was apparently upset by his response and wrote to apologize for ever having approached him, addressing him as "Dear Mr. Hardy," a colder form of address than his previous "Dear Hardy." Hardy replied at once, assuring him that his reluctance had had nothing to do with Quilter as a candidate, but instead with his own ignorance of the professorship itself (*Letters* II, 15).

In 1890 Hardy wrote Quilter to support his idea of purchasing a "library of fiction" for the People's Palace, which had opened in 1887 in Mile End Road, LONDON, to serve as a recreational and educational center for the poor inhabitants of the East End. The People's Palace eventually became Queen Mary College of the University of London (*Letters* I, 210).

Rabelais Club   Literary club founded by Walter BESANT in 1879, intended as a "a declaration for virility in literature." After Hardy published *The RETURN OF THE NATIVE*, Besant invited him to join; Besant called the novel "the most virile and most humorous of all modern novels" (*Letters* I, 63). In December 1879 Hardy attended the inaugural dinner of the club at the Tavistock Hotel, London, which he described at length in *the Life* as a dismal affair (*Life*, 132). Michael Millgate writes that Hardy's election to the club put Hardy in touch with "a whole series of second-and third-rate metropolitan littérateurs," but observes that in the 1860s this had been exactly the literary life to which he had aspired, because these writers were the counterparts of the worlds once depicted in William Makepeace THACKERAY's *Pendennis* and in Horace MOULE's conversations (Millgate, *Thomas Hardy: A Biography*, 196). George MEREDITH was one of the members whom Hardy liked and respected.

The club had monthly dinners, and Hardy attended as often as he could. Paul Turner observes that Hardy seemed to feel he should justify his membership. He speculates that Hardy modeled the wedding feast in *The TRUMPET-MAJOR*, for which he was doing research in the BRITISH MUSEUM when elected to the club, on a passage in Rabelais describing the "Gastrolaters' sacrifice" (Turner, *The Life of Thomas Hardy: A Critical Biography*, 70). In May 1882 Hardy invited Henry STEVENS, the London representative of the American publisher HOUGHTON, MIFFLIN, & CO., to one of the club dinners. Houghton, Mifflin published the *ATLANTIC MONTHLY*, which at that time was serializing *TWO ON A TOWER* (*Letters* I, 106).

"Rain on a Grave"   Published in *SATIRES OF CIRCUMSTANCE* (1914), this poem is dated January 31, 1913, a little over two months after Emma HARDY's death in November 1912. The manuscript of the poem was titled "Rain on Her Grave." In this poem Hardy mourns Emma's death, particularly the "arrows of rain" falling on her grave. She had been careful to shelter herself from rain at all times, especially from summer thunderstorms. He wishes that he were lying in her grave instead, or else that they were both "folded away there" in one grave. He envisions grass growing from her "mound" and expects that daisies will be "showing / Like stars on the ground" until she forms part of the stars, "Loved beyond measure / With a child's pleasure / All her life round."

Hardy felt guilty after Emma'a death for not having realized the seriousness of her heart condition. He might also have realized that Emma had not, perhaps, felt "loved beyond measure" in her later years. At Hardy's own memorial service at St. Peter's Church, DORCHESTER (there were other services for him at WESTMINSTER ABBEY and STINSFORD CHURCH), the vicar, Mr. Cowley, said that Hardy used to gather "buttercups and daisies and cowslips" and put them on the graves of Emma and other family members (Bailey, *The Poetry of Thomas Hardy*, 296).

"Rash Bride, The" *An Experience of the Mellstock Quire* Poem first printed in *The GRAPHIC* (Christmas number, November 24, 1902) and after much revision, collected, in *TIME'S LAUGHINGSTOCKS* (1909; Purdy, *Thomas Hardy: A Bibliographical Study*, 145).

The 15 stanzas evoke the customary traditional Christmas Eve caroling throughout the village by the Mellstock Quire (reminiscent of the festivities described in *UNDER THE GREENWOOD TREE* and "The DEAD QUIRE"). The speaker recalls the choir as it caroled, greeting the inhabitants of each house, "Good wishes: many Christmas joys to you!"

At the home of a young widow, one youthful member of the choir, John, is joyful and hopes she will "make reply." Then he will speak up and "call her dear / A tenderness will fill her voice, a bashfulness her eyes." She looks out, blushing, and bows her thanks. The choir then sees a man behind her in the room, Giles Swetman, who is from "Woolcomb way," not a native of Mellstock. A small boy says they were married the previous morning, but no one knows about it. John faints. The widow leans out, and asks if anyone has been made ill by "these night labours overtasked." A choir member named Michael accuses her of breaking her promise by "jilting John so true."

Behind her, Giles Swetman says he would not have married her if he had known she was interested in someone else. The widow turns white and cries out, then vanishes; Giles follows but does not know where she has gone. The next morning she cannot be found, until John reports that the well cover is open. She is found deep in the well and is buried the next Sunday. Giles Swetman is the chief mourner, followed by John. They sing Psalm 90, which deals with the brevity of life.

The poem may have been based on a reminiscence handed down by Hardy's father or grandfather, either

Etching of God talking to Thomas Hardy ("But Mr. Hardy, if you only knew all the circumstances. . ."), by Will Dyson (date unknown) (Beinecke Rare Book and Manuscript Library, Yale University)

of whom would have been at an age to consider John "a boy." The vale through which the carolers travel is the valley of the Frome River, and Giles Swetman of "Woolcomb Way" might be modeled on a relative of Hardy's, since Hardy's maternal grandmother was Elizabeth Swetman of Melbury Osmund, not far from Woolcombe (present-day spelling). The "Ninetieth Psalm . . . set to Saint Stephen's tune" is actually "O God, Our Help in Ages Past," a hymn sung at Hardy's funeral and known to be one of his favorites (Bailey, *The Poetry of Thomas Hardy*, 234–35).

"Regret Not Me"   Poem collected in SATIRES OF CIRCUMSTANCE (1914). The speaker, possibly a woman, is dead and addresses a mourner beside her grave. She is slumbering peacefully: she has lived a carefree life, skipping in the morning, running in the evening, making cider, dancing, and singing. She declares, "I grieve not, therefore nothing grieves."

At least one critic has associated this poem with the Stonehenge scene in TESS OF THE D'URBERVILLES, in which the police approach Tess. She says, "I have had enough," and, when they arrive, she says, "I am ready."

The speaker might also be a man, perhaps Hardy himself, who anticipates his own death and argues that his life has been fulfilled by activities he enjoyed.

The poem was set to music by Gerald Finzi (London: Oxford University Press, n.d.)

Reinhart, C. S. (1844–1896)   Artist who supplied four illustrations for Hardy's novelette The ROMANTIC ADVENTURES OF A MILKMAID when it was published in the GRAPHIC in June 1883. Three of his illustrations were used when the same novelette was published in the United States in HARPER'S WEEKLY from June 23 to August 4, 1883 (Purdy, *Thomas Hardy: A Bibliographical Study*, 48). Reinhart also supplied four illustrations for "The First Countess of Wessex" (one of the tales collected in A GROUP OF NOBLE DAMES) when it was published in HARPER'S NEW MONTHLY MAGAZINE in December 1889. Alfred PARSONS contributed a headpiece and three other illustrations (Purdy, *Thomas Hardy: A Bibliographical Study*, 62).

religion   Hardy's writings have often led readers to believe that he discounted all religion. At one time he thought of applying to CAMBRIDGE UNIVERSITY with the idea of taking religious orders and writing poetry. He gave it up because of certain "views" he found incompatible with the idea of becoming a clergyman. In later life he disavowed organized religion and questioned the relevance of the established Church of England and, to some extent, its liturgy.

At the same time, he refuted writers who claimed that he postulated a malicious God, stating that he instead believed in an "indifferent and unconscious force at the back of things," a force that does not know good or evil. The universe is governed not by "Chance" or "Purpose," but by "Necessity" (*Life*, 337). The poem "GOD'S FUNERAL," according to Bailey, suggests that belief is fading in the Christian God who was based on the old Testament deity (Bailey, *The Poetry of Thomas Hardy*, 186). In "CHRISTMAS: 1924," Hardy despairs of peace and reflects ironically that the Christmas greeting "Peace upon earth!" and the celebration of "two thousand years of mass" have only brought civilization as far as "poison gas." Many of his poems present a deity who is not hostile toward man but, instead, indifferent.

Hardy was a Christian, however, and attended church services throughout his life (Pinion, *A Hardy Companion*, 167). He made his own CHRISTMAS CARDS and sent them to his friends and family members. His longtime friend William BARNES was a clergyman, as was the Reverend Henry MOULE, who was vicar of FORDINGTON ST. GEORGE CHURCH from 1829 until his death in 1880. Moule's son Horace MOULE was one of Hardy's closest friends. Emma HARDY's brother-in-law, the Reverend Caddell HOLDER, was rector of ST. JULIOT CHURCH, CORNWALL; Hardy had gone there to restore the church when they met. Hardy's fiction includes several learned and genial clergymen, such as the Reverend Christopher SWANCOURT in A PAIR OF BLUE EYES.

Hardy cared a great deal about church architecture, as is clear from his essay "MEMORIES OF CHURCH RESTORATION" and numerous other works, including *A Pair of Blue Eyes.*

For further reading: Creighton, "Some Thoughts on Hardy and Religion"; Gregor, "Contrary Imaginings: Thomas Hardy and Religion"; Pinion, "Christianity, Scientific Philosophy, and Politics," in *A Hardy Companion;* Tuttleton, "Thomas Hardy and the Christian Religion."

"Reminiscences of a Dancing Man" Poem rejected by the CORNHILL MAGAZINE but published in *Collier's* (New York) on March 27, 1909. It was also published in the *English Review* in April 1909, and later collected in TIME'S LAUGHINGSTOCKS (1909).

While Hardy was still working in DORCHESTER in the office of the architect John HICKS, he learned of the LONDON dance halls from a fellow architectural pupil named Fippard. When he moved to London in 1862, Hardy danced at these halls, particularly Almack's (later Willis's Rooms), which had opened in 1765 in King Street for an "aristocratic clientele." In 1863 the balls were discontinued because of the "plebeian invasion" (Bailey, *The Poetry of Thomas Hardy*, 209).

In the poem, Hardy gives a doubly receding view of the past. He first recalls his own youthful dancing at "Almack's balls," with its upper halls of smooth floors. As he and his friends danced, they had looked back even further, thinking of the ghosts of the Georgian era. He remembers "Jullien's grand quadrilles" where the men whirled about in hats and morning coats, and the "gas-jets winked, and the lustres clinked." He wonders where the damsels who danced then are now. He envisions their ghosts dancing in "The smoky halls of the Prince of Sin."

In 1878, Thomas and Emma Hardy moved to 1 Arundel Terrace, just beyond Wandsworth Common. Emma recalled that one day Hardy suddenly leaped up and ran down the street. He had heard, through the window of his writing room, a barrel organ playing the same tune with which he had become familiar while working for Hicks. The Italian organ-grinder could not speak English, but, when questioned, pointed to the printed index on the instrument and cried, "Quad-ree-ya! quad-ree-ya!" Hardy realized he had probably been playing one of Jullien's quadrilles (*Life*, 274).

Almack's is also mentioned in "The ROMANTIC ADVENTURES OF A MILKMAID."

Return of the Native, The This novel was serialized in *BELGRAVIA* from January to December, 1878, and published in three volumes in November 1878 by the London publishing firm of SMITH, ELDER & CO. It was included in the important OSGOOD, MCILVAINE & CO. edition of the WESSEX NOVELS (1895–1896) and in the definitive WESSEX EDITION of Hardy's works (1912–1931). It has been reprinted many times since, and has long been considered a classic. Samuel Chew has described *The Return of the Native* as Hardy's greatest work of fiction in "balance and control" (Chew, *The Nineteenth Century* and *After (1789–1939)*, 1466).

In his "General Preface to the Novels and Poems" published in the Wessex Edition of his works (I, 1912), Hardy classifies his "fictitious chronicles" in three groups. *The Return of the Native* is in the first, those concerned principally with "Character and Environment" (the other two groups were "Romances and Fantasies" and "Novels of Ingenuity"). Novels in the first group required what Albert J. Guerard calls "realism of character and strangeness of event"; in other words, ordinary people should be subjected to extraordinary and even sinister forces ("Afterword," *The Return of the Native*). EGDON HEATH almost becomes a character in the novel, with its wild transformations of mood and the ceremonies that take place there, such as the dancing around the bonfire on Guy Fawkes night. Diggory VENN is, at first, a mysterious and alien presence on the heath. Eustacia VYE is described as the "raw material of a divinity," with "passions and instincts" that make her a "model goddess" if not an ideal woman. Susan NUNSUCH has witch-like powers. Several benign and sympathetic characters oppose those with attributes suggestive of the supernatural. The widow Mrs. YEOBRIGHT exerts kindly and well-meant strategies on behalf of her son, Clym YEOBRIGHT, and her niece, Thomasin YEOBRIGHT Wildeve, although they often fail, with tragic results. Clym Yeobright turns from the jewelry business to an idealistic calling as an itinerant preacher. His cousin Thomasin YEOBRIGHT (later Wildeve) assists her aunt and forgives her husband for first mismanaging their marriage license and then abandoning her at the altar, although she marries him later. She devotes herself to her small daughter. Guerard suggests that the novel should be read "not as an English *Madame Bovary* nor as a treatise on fatalism, but as a moving and interesting story reflecting universal human longings and frustrations."

SYNOPSIS

Book First: "The Three Women"

Chapters 1–2

Much of the first chapter is devoted to a description of the Heath, which almost becomes a character in the novel. Egdon Heath is slowly turning dark on a Saturday in November. The description of the heath has been likened to the entry of the gods in a Wagner opera (Brooks, *Thomas Hardy: The Poetic Structure*, 302). It is an ancient and immense area open to all, "an obscure, obsolete, superseded country" that figures in the Domesday Book as "Bruaria." It has a "lonely face, suggesting tragical possibilities."

On the white road through the lower levels of the heath (part of the great Western Road of the Romans), a white-haired man walks in clothes of a nautical style; he is Captain VYE. He overtakes a lurid red van, slowly drawn by horses, beside which walks a young driver, Diggory Venn. Venn's cap, clothes, head, boots, face, and hand are all red. He is a "reddleman," dealing in reddle or "redding," which is marketed in the nearby city of Bath and used to mark male sheep to track their tupping (copulating with) the ewes. Venn is not an inhabitant of the heath, but, rather, an itinerant. According to Rosemarie Morgan, the "tinker" quality partly explains his meddlesome ways (personal communication with the author). The narrator remarks that as a class, reddlemen are about to become extinct in WESSEX. The former naval officer and the reddleman exchange greetings. Suddenly there is a cry from a woman within the van—a woman, the reddleman explains, whom he knows slightly and to whom he has given a lift from the nearby town of Anglebury. He explains that her cry comes from her troubled sleep. The men part company.

The reddleman notices that on top of the heath there is a bulky summit. It is Rainbarrow, a Bronze Age burial mound. A figure of a woman rises from the summit "like a spike from a helmet"; she disappears and other figures move in, bearing burdens which they deposit on top of the barrow. No more is seen of the "queen of the solitude."

Chapters 3–5
An observer closer to the barrow would see that the moving figures were men and boys bringing furze-faggots they are laying to form a huge pyramid. They bring matches to make a bonfire, following local custom. From the top of the barrow the bonfires of other parishes and hamlets can be seen for miles around. An elderly man, "Granfer" CANTLE, turns from the fire, begins to do a jig, and sings a song beginning "The king call'd down his nobles all." A middle-aged man, Timothy FAIRWAY, asks Cantle about the "new-married folks" down at the Quiet Woman Inn. They discuss the homecoming of the bride's cousin, Clym Yeobright, who is returning from Paris to see about his mother, who will now be alone in the house she has been sharing with her niece, the bride, Thomasin ("Tamsin") Yeobright. The groom is Damon WILDEVE. The men agree that it is strange the wedding was not held at home, but consider it was more economical. A young woman, Susan Nunsuch, calls it a "mean way" of being married; we learn that Mrs. Yeobright had disapproved of the match. They discuss the fire in the distance in front of Captain Vye's home and his granddaughter, Eustacia. Christian CANTLE, Granfer Cantle's youngest son, is fearful about his masculinity and admits seeing himself as unmarriageable. The heath folk call him a naphrotite—that is, hermaphrodite. He is shy and dominated by superstitions. As the fire dies down, Timothy Fairway, a furze dealer, and Susan Nunsuch dance wildly through the embers.

On Guy Fawkes night, bonfires cover the heath. Hardy notes that some were "large and near, glowing scarlet-red from the shade, like wounds in a black hide." Others were like the "Maenades, with windy faces and blown hair." The occasion is the annual celebration of the deliverance of England from the Gunpowder Plot, a failed conspiracy by English Roman Catholics in 1605 to blow up Parliament. However, as Hardy's biographer J. I. M. Stewart explains, the dance by the rustic inhabitants of Egdon Heath mimics that of their remote ancestors, when "the days shortened and the iron reign of the *Winterkönig* began" (Stewart, *Thomas Hardy: A Critical Biography*, 96.) Guy Fawkes night is still celebrated with bonfires not only in the countryside but also in sizable towns.

Stewart calls Diggory Venn, the reddleman, a "tutelary spirit" of Egdon Heath (97). He interrupts the dance, asking the way to Mrs. Yeobright's house. Mrs. Yeobright herself arrives, looking for Olly Dowden, one of the women in the group; the two women leave for the Quiet Woman Inn, which will be Thomasin's home. Outside the inn, Mrs. Yeobright finds that Diggory Venn is looking for her. He has her niece in his van; she and Wildeve are not yet married. Mrs. Yeobright goes inside the inn to confront Wildeve, who insists he will marry the niece; he explains that there was a mixup in the proper marriage license. The group from Rainbarrow arrives to serenade the newlyweds. Wildeve is irritated that they have come, although he endures their congratulations and offers them some old mead from a stone jar.

Wildeve departs for Mistover Knap, believing the fire on the distant hill in front of Captain Vye's house is a signal from Eustacia Vye.

Chapters 6–7
Eustacia waits for Wildeve; she has persuaded a small boy, Johnny NUNSUCH, son of Susan Nunsuch, to keep feeding the blaze. Wildeve eventually comes, but refuses to say he loves her more than he loves Thomasin (they have been lovers in the past). Eustacia takes vengeance on him by refusing to let Wildeve touch her. Hardy describes Eustacia as almost a goddess, uttering "oracles of Delphian ambiguity" when she chooses not to be direct. (The Greek Delphic oracle spoke in incomprehensible utterances interpreted by priests). In heaven, Hardy states, Eustacia will sit between the "Héloïses and the Cleopatras." (Héloïse was a famous French woman beloved of the poet Pierre Abélard but severely punished for her love; Cleopatra was the Egyptian queen.) As Rosemarie Morgan notes, Eustacia feels trapped, living with her grandfather on the heath. She realizes she is not made for conventional female roles, and struggles with this knowledge. In later chapters she takes the male lead in a play mounted by the CHRISTMAS MUMMERS. She has two lovers at the same time, restlessly walks over the heath at night, builds fires, and, emotionally, stands up to Diggory Venn's bullying (personal communication with the author). She realizes the shortcomings of her relationship with Wildeve and understands, perhaps, that

she is doomed not to have a fulfilling relationship with any man. The fact that she is first seen on Rainbarrow suggests that she is a quasidivinity; she looks at life from afar as an "other," standing apart from others.

Chapters 8–9
Johnny Nunsuch returns home with his tip for having helped Eustacia build her fire, but is frightened by a strange light on the heath and returns to Captain Vye's. He hopes Eustacia will send her servant to accompany him home. He finds that Eustacia and Wildeve are meeting and hesitates to interrupt. Going home, he finds that the pit and the light conceal a van; he wonders if it belongs to gypsies. Spying on the scene, he is startled to see the reddleman darning a red stocking. One of the horses outside disturbs Venn, who comes outside, frightening the boy, although he now recognizes the van of Diggory Venn. In his haste to leave he loses his footing and falls down the hill; Venn surmises that the boy has been watching him. The boy confesses he is going home from Miss Vye's bonfire, and tells him of the conversation he has overheard between Eustacia and Wildeve.

Venn reads to himself an earlier letter from Thomasin. She had rejected an offer of marriage when he was a dairy farmer; this is the reason he had become a reddleman ("rejected suitors take to roaming as naturally as unhived bees"). Venn deduces, wrongly, that Eustacia's signal to Wildeve was the cause of Wildeve's failure to marry Thomasin. Venn keeps up a surveillance on Eustacia and Wildeve, finally eavesdropping on their conversation when they meet at a ditch around Rainbarrow. Wildeve talks of going to America, but Eustacia will not commit herself to going. Venn decides to call on Eustacia.

Chapters 10–11
Venn tells Eustacia he has overheard her talking with Wildeve. He tries to talk her out of her relationship with Wildeve so that Thomasin, who loves Wildeve dearly, might marry him. Eustacia refuses haughtily. Venn offers to help her move to BUDMOUTH (actually WEYMOUTH), the nearby port and watering place where her father had been a military musician. He knows, through his uncle, of an elderly lady who would welcome her as a "companion" (a term Eustacia rightfully interprets as "lady's maid"). Meanwhile, she would meet naval officers of her own rank she might marry. Eustacia is indignant at the idea, telling Venn she would go to such a place only in order to live "as a lady should." Venn asks Mrs. Yeobright for the hand of Thomasin. Mrs. Yeobright tells Wildeve there is another suitor for the hand of Thomasin and he agrees not to interfere if Thomasin accepts the man. Wildeve returns to Eustacia and proposes, but Eustacia turns him down, debating with herself whether she wants a man whom a woman of inferior social rank has

Illustration by Arthur Hopkins for The Return of the Native, *Book First, chapter 9 ("The reddleman rereads an old love letter"), published in* Belgravia, *March 1878* (Perkins Library, Duke University)

rejected. As book I ends, Captain Vye tells Eustacia that Clym Yeobright is coming home to Egdon Heath from Paris for Christmas.

Book Second:"The Arrival"

Chapters 1–3
The furze cutter Humphrey and the turf cutter Sam build a stack of furze-faggots for Captain Vye's use during the winter. Eustacia overhears them discussing Clym Yeobright's future; they think he was better off selling diamonds in Paris than coming back home, but he has become a "real perusing man," a scholar and thinker. They speculate that Clym and Eustacia would make a "very pretty pigeon pair." Eustacia is filled with visions of grandeur. She decides to walk toward Blooms-End, birthplace of Clym.

At Blooms-End, Thomasin and her aunt prepare for Clym's arrival, although these are the "most sorrowful days" of Thomasin's life. She says she will still marry Wildeve but agrees she must wait until asked again. Her aunt hints that Wildeve had an earlier attachment, but stops short of saying it was to Eustacia. Eustacia overhears Clym, his aunt, and his cousin talking as they walk slowly along. Clym sees "friendliness and geniality" in what she sees as "shaggy hills." She experiences a "cycle of visions," but her grandfather tells her she would find the Yeobrights "too countrified" for her taste. That night Eustacia passes through intensely ecstatic phases. In her erotic dreams she dances to "wondrous music" with what seems to be a warrior, although he remains unidentifiable since the visor of his helmet is closed. When he removes his helmet to kiss her, she wakes, but remains "half in love with a vision."

Chapters 4–6
Eustacia realizes that few inhabitants of Egdon Heath attend church; they are more likely to stay at home with relatives and friends. She is at home on December 23, mulling over possible ways to see Clym, when the boy Charley comes to ask whether the mummers (a group of local boys) might borrow Captain Vye's fuel house to practice the traditional English Christmas play, "The PLAY OF 'SAINT GEORGE.'" Eustacia bribes him to let her play the part of the Turkish Knight in exchange for his holding her hand for 15 minutes. Timothy Fairway directs the cast.

On December 24, the mummers wait for the dancing to finish before Father Christmas knocks on the door at Blooms-End, where the Yeobrights are having a party, and asks them to make room: "We've come to show Saint George's play, / Upon this Christmas time." In one of the most memorable scenes in the novel, Eustacia plays the role of the Turkish Knight. At the conclusion of her part she lies on the floor, slain. She discerns Clym at that point. Mrs. Yeobright provides supper for the mummers. Thomasin comes down briefly, having pleaded illness. Eustacia surmises that Clym knows nothing about Wildeve and fears he will fall in love with Thomasin. She goes outside, still in costume. Clym detects that she is a woman and speaks with her, promising not to reveal her identity. She goes home, worrying about Thomasin's "winning ways."

Chapters 7–8
Eustacia confesses her role in the play to her grandfather. Here there is another instance of Eustacia's hermaphroditic, male-oriented quality. Eustacia's grandfather asks why she has been out so late. She replies that she has been "in search of events"; he responds by likening her to "one of the young bucks" he had known in his youth. When she tells him about playing the part of the Turkish Knight, he is astounded and secretly pleased, but says, "no more of it, my girl . . . no figuring in breeches again."

On the heath she encounters Diggory Venn and discovers that he loves Thomasin. She takes refuge in his van to avoid Wildeve's approaching figure. She gives Venn a parcel and a note to give Wildeve; the note says that, since he has not been faithful to her during the two years of their acquaintance, she thinks it best to break off. Wildeve says he has heard Mrs. Yeobright has given Venn permission to marry Thomasin, which Venn denies. Wildeve, knowing nothing of Eustacia's interest in Clym, decides she is playing a part to make him jealous. He goes to Blooms-End and tells Thomasin he wants to be married at once. She agrees, but asks her aunt not to come to the wedding. They meet at church on the appointed morning. Clym is disturbed that he knew nothing of the first plan for their wedding or their present ceremony, and goes out to see them. He is too late, but Diggory Venn is there and says Eustacia gave Thomasin away. Venn vanishes from the heath.

Book Third: "The Fascination"

Chapters 1–3
The local villagers have expected much of Clym and are puzzled when, after his time in Budmouth, London, and Paris, he returns home and makes no plans to leave. But Clym is idealistic; he hopes, by teaching them, "to raise the class at the expense of individuals rather than individuals at the expense of the class." He is ahead of his time, however; the rural world is not ready to put "culture" before "luxury." He shocks his mother by saying he is not returning to Paris but wants to begin a school. She tells him "your fancies will be your ruin." She is agitated because he has no practical plan, no funds, and no experience.

Christian Cantle interrupts with news that, in church, Susan Nunsuch, "a witch," has stabbed Eustacia Vye with a stocking needle so Eustacia would stop "bewitching" the Nunsuch children. The wound was so deep Eustacia screamed and fainted. Sam, the turf cutter, comes to bring the same news, calling Eustacia a "beauty." Clym's interest is piqued, but Mrs. Yeobright says Eustacia is "too idle to be charming." Sam asks Clym to help grapple for the lost water bucket in Captain Vye's well that evening.

Clym goes to Mistover Knap, the Vyes' home, to assist the men. They fail, and plan to try again the next day. Clym sees the circle where Eustacia's bonfire was. He and Eustacia try again to dip water and she gets a rope burn, her second wound that day. She calls the heath a "cruel taskmaster"; he calls it "exhilarating, and strengthening, and soothing." The next night Clym goes back to see Eustacia, which disappoints his mother, who wonders what he sees in her. Her intuition tells her Eustacia will not be a good wife for Clym.

Clym and Eustacia open Rainbarrow and find many pots and charnel bones. Clym gives away his pot of bones to Eustacia. His mother deplores his increasing interest in her. Clym says Eustacia would make a good matron in a boarding school, and he would like to establish a private school for farmers' sons, in which she would help him. His mother calls the plan a "castle in the air" and calls Eustacia a "hussy."

Chapter 4–8
Clym climbs to the top of Rainbarrow. He tells Eustacia he loves her and she says she loves him, but knows his mother will try to dissuade him. He tells her of Paris. She wants him to go back there. Clym calls her "luxurious" but admits he is not. He says he will speak to her grandfather.

Illustration by Arthur Hopkins for The Return of the Native, *Book Fourth, chapter 2 ("Unconscious of her presence, he still went on singing"),* Belgravia, *August 1878*   (Perkins Library, Duke University)

Mrs. Yeobright tells Clym she has heard that he is engaged to Eustacia. He admits they have an understanding but are not planning to be married for a "very long time." Meanwhile, he plans to keep a school in Budmouth. Mrs. Yeobright is horrified; Eustacia's parentage and her grandfather's permitting her to roam the heath augur ill for her upbringing. Also, Mrs. Yeobright knows about Wildeve. She says Eustacia will never make Clym a good wife.

On the heath, Clym tells Eustacia their present existence must end. She realizes his mother is behind it, and says, "I have feared my bliss." Clym says they will be married at once.

Clym packs his belongings. The next day he leases a cottage on the heath near a village five miles away. He says good-bye to his mother, who weeps. Thomasin comes to her aunt to say that Wildeve does not usually give her any money, but Mrs. Yeobright urges her to ask him for some. She says she has some spare guineas left by her uncle that are to be divided between Thomasin and Clym. She then tells Thomasin about her break with Clym.

Wildeve sees the cart taking things to the cottage and learns about the forthcoming marriage. He is jealous.

Clym and Eustacia are married; Mrs. Yeobright does not attend the wedding. She says to herself, "He will rue it some day, and think of me!" Wildeve comes to ask for Thomasin's money. She refuses to entrust the money to him. She decides to send Christian Cantle with the money to Mistover. Christian meets Timothy Fairway, is enticed to go to the Quiet Woman Inn, and confesses he is taking money to Mistover. Wildeve decides to walk with him to Mistover, carrying dice. He persuades Christian to gamble, saying if he is rich he will attract a woman. Wildeve wins all the money. Christian scurries away. Diggory Venn appears from behind a bush; he has heard everything.

Venn wins back all the money and, not realizing half of it is meant for Clym, gives all of it to Thomasin.

Book Fourth: "The Closed Door"

Chapters 1–4
Clym and Eustacia live happily in their little house at Alderworth. Mrs. Yeobright wonders why she has not heard from Clym about the guineas. Christian Cantle confesses miserably that the guineas were won by Wildeve, who, he believes, planned to give half to Clym. Mrs. Yeobright questions Eustacia, who denies knowing anything about the money and deduces that she is suspected of wrongdoing. The women argue over lineage; Eustacia tells Mrs. Yeobright that it is her own fault if her son has turned against her. Mrs. Yeobright says Eustacia is standing on the edge of a precipice.

Eustacia tells Clym of their quarrel; he is distraught. She says he has promised to take her to Paris, and she wants to go, no matter how humbly they live. The next day Thomasin visits Clym and Eustacia and gives them their share of the guineas. Over a period of time Clym develops severe eye trouble from reading too much and has to give up studying. He endures his affliction patiently and takes up furze-cutting as an occupation, which he finds soothing. Eustacia perceives that he will never take her to Paris. He thinks she has lost all tenderness for him.

Eustacia asks Clym for permission to go to a nearby village festival, which he gives, although he is somewhat jealous of her and resentful that she wishes to go. There she meets Wildeve, by chance, and dances with him. He walks her home; they see Clym and Diggory Venn coming toward them. Clym does not recognize Wildeve, who quickly disappears, but Venn does. At the Quiet Woman Inn, Venn tells Thomasin he has seen her husband leading a horse home—"a beauty, with a white face and a mane as black as night." She asks Venn to tell her how she can keep him home in the evenings. When Wildeve arrives, she asks about the "beauty," but Wildeve pretends Venn must have meant someone else. He perceives that Venn's "counter-moves" have begun again.

Venn realizes that Wildeve is neglecting Thomasin and trips Wildeve as he is entering Clym's garden. The next night he signals Eustacia and knocks on the door, but when Clym answers he hides. As he is going home Venn discharges a gun near Wildeve. Venn calls on Mrs. Yeobright and urges her to visit Clym and Thomasin; he says, if she does so, Wildeve would "walk straighter" and she might prevent future unhappiness.

Chapters 5–8
Mrs. Yeobright starts out to Clym's house; it is farther than she imagines. She asks the way of a laborer, who points out Clym; she can hardly believe the furze cutter is her son. She rests as he goes inside the house. Wildeve, meanwhile, has determined to visit Eustacia by day, as though it were a conventional call. He sees Clym asleep on the hearth rug. Eustacia says she married Clym because she loved him, but admits that her love was based partly on a "promise" that it would fulfill her dreams of "music, poetry, passion, war, and all the beating and pulsing that is going on in the great arteries of the world." Wildeve says life means nothing to him without her. They hear a knocking at the door. Eustacia looks out and sees Mrs. Yeobright. She and Wildeve go to the back garden; he leaves; she believes Clym has opened the door. He has not, and when she returns she finds Mrs. Yeobright has left.

Johnny Nunsuch is gathering berries in the hollow and begins following Mrs. Yeobright and talking with her. She says she has seen a terrible sight, "a woman's face looking at me through a window-pane," the face of one who did not let her in. She is exhausted by the

heat. She sends him for water, but it is warm and nauseates her. He says he must go home, and she asks him to tell his mother he has seen "a broken-hearted woman cast off by her son." She continues, exhausted.

Clym awakes and says he has dreamed that they went to his mother's house and couldn't get in, though she was crying for help. He decides to walk to Blooms-End himself. Thomasin is expecting a baby in a month, and can do little for his mother. He discovers the form of his mother on the path; she is moaning and scarcely able to breathe. He begins carrying her and comes to a hut near Timothy Fairway's dwelling; he brings Fairway and other men and Olly Dowden back with a lantern, matches, pillow, and other supplies. They send a boy on Fairway's pony for medical help. Mrs. Yeobright signals that something is wrong with her foot; they find she has been bitten by an adder. They try to cure her by catching other adders, boiling them, and applying their oil.

Eustacia, meanwhile, is lonely. Her grandfather comes to tell her Wildeve has inherited a fortune of £11,000 from an uncle in Canada. Wildeve has not told her, which impresses Eustacia. He comes back and she congratulates him; he says he had not liked to mention it when her "star was not high." He plans to go to Paris, Italy, Greece, Egypt, Palestine, America, and other places. He may take Thomasin if she wants to go. They begin walking down the hill and come across the turf-shed where Mrs. Yeobright is lying. The doctor says she is sinking, in part because of the adder bite, but also because of exhaustion. She dies. Johnny Nunsuch comes in and announces that Mrs. Yeobright had told him to say she was a "broken-hearted woman and cast off by her son." They carry her to Blooms-End.

Book Fifth: "The Discovery"

Chapters 1–3
After Mrs. Yeobright's funeral, Humphrey comes to ask about Clym, who is unwell and feeling terrible guilt about his mother's death, which he feels was his fault. Thomasin has come to visit him, and comes again. Wildeve comes with a horse and gig to take Thomasin home. Eustacia goes outside and tells him she has not told Clym that she did not open the door to Mrs. Yeobright or that Wildeve was in the house at the time.

Clym slowly recovers and walks in the garden. Christian comes to say that Thomasin has had a baby girl; Wildeve is disappointed it isn't a boy. Christian tells Clym that Mrs. Yeobright had been on her way to Clym's house the day she died. He says that Venn knows about it. Clym asks Christian to bring Venn to him. He goes to Blooms-End the next day, to the empty house, and Venn comes. Venn had not known

Illustration by Arthur Hopkins for The Return of the Native, *Book Fifth, chapter 9 ("All that remained of the desperate and unfortunate Eustacia"),* Belgravia, *December 1878* (Perkins Library, Duke University)

of Clym's mother's death. Venn says Mrs. Yeobright had forgiven Clym, but Clym has heard that she thought he had ill-treated her. Clym decides to talk with Johnny. He goes to the boy's home on the heath. Johnny has been ailing, which Susan attributes to Eustacia's being a witch. Johnny tells Clym he first saw Mrs. Yeobright at his house and that she had sat under the trees at the Devil's Bellows. She saw a man go into Clym's house, not Clym but a "gentleman." Johnny had seen Mrs. Yeobright knock and Eustacia look out of the side window at her. When no one came to the door she left. Clym leaves, his eyes "lit by an icy shine."

Chapters 4–6
Clym goes to Alderworth and challenges Eustacia to tell him the truth. He accuses her of shutting the door and of killing his mother. They quarrel and she leaves; just before she goes, they learn from the maid that Thomasin is to name the baby Eustacia Clementine. Eustacia goes to her grandfather's house, but it is locked; he has gone to Weatherbury. Charley builds her a fire and fixes tea for her. She seems so depressed he hides her grandfather's pistols. When her grandfather returns, she asks that her room be made up. He asks no questions.

Charley continues to think devotedly of Eustacia and bring her little presents from the heath. One day she sees a cart in the distance, taking her furnishings from Alderworth to Blooms-End. November 5 (Guy Fawkes Day) comes again, and Charley builds her a bonfire. As it dies down, she hears the splash of a stone in the pond, Wildeve's signal. He thought she was summoning him with the bonfire. She breaks down in front of him and he offers to help her get away and even go with her, but she is indecisive. She says she will signal him at eight o'clock on the night she decides to take the midnight boat.

Clym, meanwhile, at Blooms-End, misses Eustacia. He decides on November 5 to go and see Thomasin. Wildeve is not at home; he is on the way to Eustacia's bonfire. Thomasin does not know that Eustacia has left Clym. Clym realizes Thomasin suspects something between her husband and Eustacia, but she doesn't admit it. Clym writes Eustacia a letter asking her back. When Wildeve returns home, Thomasin says she has feared he had fallen into the river. She admits she followed him to a fork in the road and saw him go toward Eustacia's bonfire. She does not mention Clym's visit.

Chapters 7–9
The next night, November 6, there are dark clouds and a stormy wind. Eustacia signals Wildeve with a flaming bough of furze and lies down to rest. At ten o'clock Timothy Fairway comes to the Vye house with Clym's letter. The captain puts it on the mantelpiece since Eustacia seems to be asleep. He hears her brush past and discovers she has left the house. He cannot hope to overtake her in the dark. At this point the heath is depicted as chaotic, with the moon and stars obliterated and fleshy fungi and twisted furze-roots in all the paths. At Rainbarrow Eustacia realizes she does not have enough money for her journey; everything is "malignant" and the "wings of her soul" are broken by the "cruel obstructiveness of all about her."

She sees the light of a distant house. Within is Susan Nunsuch, fashioning an effigy of Eustacia from beeswax. Susan dresses the shape in a red ribbon and shoes and ties a black thread around the head to resemble a "fillet," or net for confining the hair. She sticks pins in it, utters an incantation, and melts it over the fire.

Meanwhile, Clym Yeobright thinks Eustacia has received his letter and is answering it. He expects she may visit him. Instead, Thomasin comes to say Wildeve is about to leave her and run off with Eustacia. She is carrying the baby, well wrapped up in a huge bundle. Captain Vye comes to Clym's door, searching for Eustacia and fearing she will harm herself. Clym goes to search for Eustacia; the captain goes home, as he doesn't think he can walk far.

Thomasin wraps the baby up and sets out for her home, but becomes disoriented and winds up at Venn's van. Venn thinks the woman is Eustacia, whom he had seen sobbing outside but who left when he opened the door of the van and held out the lantern. He takes the baby and insists on escorting Thomasin home.

Wildeve has seen Eustacia's signal and started out to assist her in her flight and, possibly, to accompany her. He waits for her beside the road until after midnight. He hears the roaring of a ten-hatch weir nearby, where the river approaches the road at the edge of the heath. Clym comes along the road and they both hear a body fall into the adjoining stream, near the weir. They take the lamps from the carriage and, from a plank bridge, see Eustacia's body floating in the weir-pool, borne along by strong backward currents. Wildeve and Clym both jump in and begin struggling. Venn and Thomasin come down from the heath and see the bodies floating. He hands her the baby and she hurries to sound the alarm; Venn jumps in with a weir-hatch or flood-gate, to support him. Men come to help; they pull out Wildeve, then Clym, then Eustacia. Only Clym is still alive. Venn changes his clothes, hurries to the inn, and comforts Thomasin. Clym looks at Eustacia and with a "wild smile" says she is the second woman he has killed this year.

Book Sixth: "Aftercourses"

Chapters 1–4

It is 18 months later. Thomasin has genuinely mourned Wildeve despite his shortcomings as a husband. She has inherited about £10,000 from his estate after his debts are paid. She and little Eustacia move into Blooms-End as tenants, bringing three servants. Clym occupies only two rooms; he has inherited a small income from his mother, sufficient for his needs. Thomasin saves as much as she can for her daughter.

One day Diggory Venn comes to see her. He is no longer red, but white; he has given up dealing in reddle and assumed his father's dairy of 50 cows. He now lives at Stickleford, two miles from Alderworth. Thomasin invites him to tea, but he says he has come only to ask her whether he can put up a maypole outside her door. Clym strolls out that night and sees all the preparations for the maypole, "homage to nature . . . fragments of Teutonic rites to divinities whose names are forgotten." The traditions predate medieval doctrine.

Thomasin sees the maypole the next morning, decorated in flowers and ribbons and hoops. She dresses up in a festive fashion; Clym hopes she is not interested in him, as he has no energy for another love. When a brass band arrives he slips away. On returning, he finds Thomasin on the porch; she has not gone out into the crowd alone. Venn lingers by the maypole. She invites Venn in, but he says he is searching for a glove dropped by one of the maidens. She goes upstairs and watches from the window as he picks up the glove, kisses it, and places it next to his heart.

After a few days Thomasin tells Clym she cannot help being curious about the object of Venn's love. She then discovers that one of her own gloves is missing; her maid confesses she wore them to the maypole and lost one. Mr. Venn gave her money for a new pair, but she has not had a chance to buy them.

The next day Thomasin takes little Eustacia on the heath, to a soft place with green turf, to practice walking. Venn approaches on horseback. Thomasin asks for her glove and he takes it from his breast pocket. He

says he has no thought but making money, but it is harder now, because she is so much richer than she used to be. She says she has made it nearly all over to the baby—that is, she has put it in trust for her, reserving just enough to live on, as it was her duty to do so. Venn is glad, as it makes it easier to be friendly.

Clym, meanwhile, goes every day to his mother's grave and every night to Eustacia's. Otherwise he spends his time studying to be an itinerant preacher. Thomasin says she is thinking of marrying Venn. Clym feels Venn is not "gentleman enough" for her. He thinks she might marry someone of a higher station, professionally, if she went into a town to live. She adamantly refuses, saying she would not be happy away from Egdon.

She tells Clym that Venn is much more respectable now that he is no longer a reddleman, and that her aunt would not have objected to their union. Clym says she must use her own discretion. Humphrey sees Clym on the heath and says Thomasin and Venn have made up, but that Clym and Thomasin should have married. Clym rejects the idea.

On the morning fixed for the wedding the men gather at Timothy Fairway's home to make ticking for a feather mattress as a present for the newlyweds. The open fly drives past with Yeobright, Venn, Thomasin, and a relative of Venn's from Budmouth. Clym says he won't come to the dancing that night, which is taking place downstairs at Bloom's End. Charley comes along and they reminisce about Eustacia; Clym gives him a lock of her hair.

The Sunday after the wedding Clym begins his preaching on Rainbarrow. He is now an open-air preacher and "lecturer on morally unimpeachable subjects." He is "kindly received" everywhere, for all know the story of his life.

CRITICAL RECEPTION AND COMMENTARY

An anonymous reviewer, writing in the ATHENAEUM on November 25, 1878, declared the novel "distinctly inferior" to Hardy's earlier work and "ill-conceived," with unconvincing language on the part of rustics and other characters, who have too "low" a social position. The reviewer compared Eustacia to Flaubert's Madame Bovary, a type that "English opinion will not allow a novelist to depict in its completeness." The reviewer praised Hardy's "keen observation of natural things," however (Clarke, ed., *Thomas Hardy: Critical Assessments*, I, 105–106). W. E. Henley, the reviewer for the *Academy* on November 30, 1878, said the novel was not as good as Hardy's *A PAIR OF BLUE EYES*, but allowed that, as a novel, it "takes high rank among the good romantic work of the generation." According to Henley, the best of the novel is what is "analytic and descriptive," but, overall, it is "well meant rather than happily done." He advised his readers to consult the map provided by Hardy of the locality of the novel (Clarke, ed., *Thomas Hardy: Critical Assessments,* I, 107–108). Another anonymous reviewer declared that Hardy "breaks down" in trying to amuse his readers but praises his depiction of the setting. He believes his invention of characters to be "injudicious" and wishes Hardy would exert his powers in "trying to be more natural and entertaining" (Clarke, ed., *Thomas Hardy: Critical Assessments,* I, 111–12). A third anonymous reviewer, writing in the SPECTATOR on February 8, 1879, praised the novel as "very great in some respects," but insists that Hardy's Wessex peasantry are a "great defect." The reader cannot accept them as "true pictures of rustic life." He argues that his peasant speech is uneven: frequently effective and realistic, but not always. At the same time, the reviewer cites several passages to prove that Hardy is "not only a striking novelist, but in essence at least, a fine poet" (Clarke, ed., *Thomas Hardy: Critical Assessments,* 114–17).

Twentieth-century critics have, as a whole, had a higher estimate of the novel than their 19th-century counterparts. D. H. Lawrence termed it the "first tragic and important novel." He believed both Eustacia and Clym become sidetracked from their true selves. Eustacia thinks she wants Paris and the beau monde, although they would not help her attain her hidden goal of self-realization. Clym wants to serve "the moral system of the community," but in fact he is cowardly. Venn and Thomasin are "genuine people" and as such get "the prize," but Wildeve is unstable. Mrs. Yeobright is one of the "old, rigid pillars" of the system, but the weight is too much for her and it comes "crashing down." The real power of the book lies in its setting, the heath, the "primitive, primal earth, where the instinctive life heaves up." Lawrence sees, in Hardy's novels, "a great background, vital and vivid," which matters more than the characters ("Study of Thomas Hardy: *The Return of the Native*").

Irving Howe does not see it as Hardy's first major novel, but as a flawed effort; he believes the plot is too weak a vehicle for his subject. According to Howe, Hardy fails to convey his ideas about "social restlessness and disorganization" but produces a "romance confined to a triangle of passionate misunderstandings." Howe considers Hardy less a moralist than a recorder of "the recurrent rhythms of life," especially as they are compressed into "small immediate incidents." (Howe, "The Return of the Native").

When Hardy, discouraged by his flawed attempt at social satire in *The HAND OF ETHELBERTA,* decided to write another rural novel along the lines of *FAR FROM THE MADDING CROWD,* he submitted 15 chapters to Leslie STEPHEN, then the editor of CORNHILL MAGAZINE. Stephen had misgivings about its suitability for a "family magazine," and Hardy revised the manuscript. Ian Gregor believes that this process enabled Hardy to

"realize the potential of his imagined world. Clym is a returning native with a "more travelled, more cosmopolitan background" than had been evident in *Far from the Madding Crowd.* He argues that the new conception of Clym led to a recasting of the other characters also: Wildeve, once modeled on Sergeant TROY, is a younger and more sympathetic character; Venn replaces Gabriel OAK in several transformations as "reddleman," "mephistophelean visitant," and "dairy farmer." Eustacia, originally a Bathsheba EVERDENE figure, becomes somewhat "demonic" in contrast to Thomasin, who incorporates the character of Fanny ROBIN but is more resilient.

Morgan points out that, at one time, Hardy thought of the character of Thomasin as Clym's sister and Mrs. Yeobright's daughter. When he changed the relationship to that of cousins, he apparently considered setting up romantic possibilities between Clym and Thomasin (personal communication with the author). Gregor views Clym as the embodiment of Hardy's own dilemma rather than a noble character. Hardy says of Clym, at the end, "Some believed him, and some believed not," but all concurred that it was "well enough for a man to take to preaching who could not see to do anything else." He was, everywhere, "Kindly received" because of the story of his life. Gregor observes that the deaths on the heath and in Shadwater Weir do not "adequately" express a truth about life. However, he finds the true affirmation of the novel to be in the marriage of Venn and Thomasin. He notes that Hardy actually disavowed the final chapter at one time, stating that the ending was chosen for serial publication. Originally Hardy intended to have Venn disappear mysteriously from the heath. Despite his disavowal, however, he never changed the ending in successive editions of the novel (Gregor, "Landscape with Figures").

The Return of the Native is one of the most read of Hardy's novels, and many theatrical and film adaptations of it have been made (*see* Appendix II, "Media Adaptations of Works by Thomas Hardy"). It has been translated into Czech and French, and there is a braille edition.

For further reading: Atkinson, "'The Inevitable Movement Onward'—Some Aspects of *The Return of the Native*"; Bloom (ed.), *Modern Critical Interpretations: Thomas Hardy's "The Return of the Native";* Cox, *Mumming and the Mummers' Play of St. George;* Deen, "Heroism and Pathos in Hardy's *Return of the Native*"; Gregor, "Landscape with Figures"; Howe, "*The Return of the Native*"; Johnson, *The Art of Thomas Hardy;* Lawrence, "Study of Thomas Hardy: *The Return of the Native*"; May, "The Magic of Metaphor in *The Return of the Native*"; Miller, "Topography in *The Return of the Native*"; Southerington, "*The Return of the Native:* Thomas Hardy and the Evolution of Consciousness" (in Pinion,

Thomas Hardy and the Modern World); Temblett-Wood, *The Return of the Native*, with introduction and notes.

Revue des Deux Mondes   Prestigious French periodical in which Leon Boucher published an article about Hardy's novels on December 15, 1875, "Le Roman pastoral en Angleterre." Firmin Roz wrote another article about him, "Thomas Hardy," which appeared in the journal on July 1, 1906 (*Letters* I, 45; III, 225).

Richardson, Maggie (unknown)   Sculptor, born in London; Mrs. George J. Mitchell. She exhibited between 1907 and 1940. In 1923 she executed a bust of Hardy from sittings. It was then exhibited at the British Empire Exhibition, Wembley, and was given to the DOREST COUNTY MUSEUM by the sculptor in 1925. In 1931 Richardson became an Associate of the Royal Society of British Artists and in 1932 she joined the Society of Woman Artists. Her recorded addresses are London (1907), Southport, Lancashire (1915), Montecute, Somerset (1922). Her bust of Hardy may be viewed on the website of The Thomas Hardy Association, URL: http://www.yale.edu/ hardysoc/welcome/welcome.htm.

Richardson, Nelson Moore (1855–1925)   Secretary of the DORSET NATURAL HISTORY AND ARCHAEOLOGICAL FIELD CLUB. In 1900 he invited Hardy to write a paper on Cerne Abbey, but Hardy declined, saying he could not form a "definite opinion" on the abbey without digging, which he could not undertake (*Letters* II, 268). Richardson wrote Hardy in April 1908 that he and the vice presidents of the club had proposed that Hardy be elected an honorary member. Hardy replied that he would be pleased to accept the honor, although he might not be able to attend many of the meetings (*Letters* III, 311).

Rideing, William Henry (1853–1919)   English journalist who lived in the United States and served on the staff of the Boston magazine YOUTH'S COMPANION. In 1886 he had embarked on a book called *The Boyhood of Living Authors* (published in New York, 1887). He asked Hardy for a contribution. Hardy replied that his own early life had been "singularly uneventful & solitary" but, if he thought of anything interesting to communicate, he would do so.

Rideing was apparently, at that time, keeping Hardy's story "OUR EXPLOITS AT WEST POLEY" in the magazine's inventory, which meant that Hardy was unable to place it in England because he had given them exclusive rights to it. Even so, he generously suggested that they hold it as long as there was a chance that they might have room for it; he thought it might be suitable for a Christmas number. It was never published in the magazine. Nine years later it was serialized in another Boston magazine, the *Household* (*Letters* I, 116, 158).

In 1893 Rideing wrote to ask about publishing a map of the scenes in Hardy's novels. Hardy replied that he would not like such a map to be published at that time, but offered to tell him "privately places and points of landscape" he might go for such descriptions (*Letters* II, 21). He would not, in other words, provide an atlas or identify fictional places with real ones.

Hardy turned down some invitations from Rideing and his wife when they visited England. On July 1, 1895, Hardy's last week in London before his return to MAX GATE, he invited the Rideings to call any afternoon at his flat at 90 Ashley Garden (*Letters* II, 80).

Ridgeway, Philip (1891–1954)   Theatrical producer, manager of the Barnes Theatre, LONDON, in a location south of the Thames between Mortlake and Putney. In July 1925 he sent a telegram to Hardy to ask whether the play of TESS OF THE D'URBERVILLES was available for a stage production. Hardy replied that he had some hesitation in endorsing a London production, partly because it would be difficult to find a "satisfactory heroine." Ridgeway mounted a production of the play that opened on September 7, 1925 (*Letters* VI, 334–40, *passim*). Gwen Ffrangçon-Davies played Tess. The play moved to the Garrick Theatre in the West End of London, but Hardy did not go to see it. In December 1925 the cast went down to DORCHESTER and performed the play in the MAX GATE living room (Millgate, *Thomas Hardy,* 558–59).

Ring's-Hill Speer   Fictional site of the tower in TWO ON A TOWER where Swithin ST. CLEEVE mounts his telescope.

Ritchie, Anne Isabella ("Annie") (1837–1919)   The daughter of William Makepeace THACKERAY, she met Hardy in April and May of 1874 when he came to London to talk with her brother-in-law, Sir Leslie STEPHEN, then editor of CORNHILL MAGAZINE. She was unmarried at the time and introduced him to her friend Helen PATERSON, inviting them both to dine with her at the Pall Mall Café (Millgate, *Thomas Hardy: A Biography,* 159). Michael Millgate speculates that Hardy was interested romantically in both women, but Helen Paterson married William Allingham that summer, and Hardy married Emma Gifford (HARDY) in September. Annie Thackeray married Richmond T. W. Ritchie in 1877 (*Letters* I, 177).

In the *Life,* Hardy recalls that at the time he met Annie Thackeray he was worried about becoming a novelist, looking on it as a trade, like architecture, rather than a genre to which he was naturally born. He felt that he did not take enough interests in "manners," which he called "pictures of modern customs and observances." He considered himself interested in the "substance of life only." He confided these doubts to Miss Thackeray, who answered, with surprise, "Certainly: a novelist must necessarily like society!" (*Life,* 104).

Mrs. Ritchie's novel *Mrs. Dymond* appeared in MACMILLAN'S MAGAZINE in 1885 and, in 1913 her novel *Miss Angel* began running in *Cornhill Magazine*.

Robin, Fanny An artless, unassuming servant to Bathsheba EVERDENE in FAR FROM THE MADDING CROWD, she thinks herself beloved of Sergeant Frank TROY. She almost succeeds in marrying him, but on their wedding day she goes to the wrong church. He then betrays her and later marries Bathsheba. Her situation appears, at first, to be the conventional one of Hardy's poem "The RUINED MAID," or of other ballads of the time: she is pregnant, abandoned, and penniless. Her excruciating journey back to the CASTERBRIDGE workhouse, clutching fence posts along the way, her only companion a large dog who pulls her along, is one of Hardy's most memorable passages. She collapses at the workhouse door, where a man stones the dog, her only friend. When Fanny dies the next day, the narrator remarks, "The one feat alone—that of dying—by which a mean condition could be resolved into a grand one, Fanny had achieved" (Chapter 43).

Because her burial falls to the parish of WEATHERBURY, Bathsheba sends one of her workmen to bring the coffin to the church. He and his companions stop for refreshments along the way and arrive too late; the coffin remains overnight in Bathsheba's farmhouse. Bathsheba opens it and discovers a stillborn child beside Fanny. Her husband, Sergeant Troy discovers Bathsheba beside the coffin. He kneels in grief and kisses Fanny, but refuses to kiss Bathsheba. He announces, to Fanny's corpse, that in the sight of heaven she is his "very, very wife." He arranges for Fanny's burial and the erection of a headstone, then disappears.

Fanny Robin, one of the most unforgettable of all of Hardy's heroines, serves as a reminder, as James Wright puts it, that "the most commonplace creatures are not to be approached with condescension" (afterword, New American Library edition of *Far from the Madding Crowd*, 1960).

Rolland, Madeleine (1872–1960) French translator of a number of Hardy's works, including TESS OF THE D'URBERVILLES, The MAYOR OF CASTERBRIDGE, and stories from LIFE'S LITTLE IRONIES. She was the sister of the novelist Romain Rolland. In 1893 Hardy had given Louis Barron permission to translate *Tess*, stipulating that the translation appear before December 6, 1894. Barron did not publish his translation, but in 1896 he approached Hardy again for permission to publish the translation in a French newspaper; Hardy agreed, provided it appear "within a reasonable time." When Mlle. Rolland's translation was announced in 1897, Barron protested, but Hardy wrote a lengthy letter outlining his previous correspondence. Rolland's

translation of *Tess* was published in two volumes by Hachette in 1901 (*Letters* II, 170); a revised edition appeared in 1925. In August 1907 Rolland visited MAX GATE one afternoon; Hardy wrote Lady Agnes GROVE that the translator's excellent English made him wish he were "half as good at French" (*Letters* III, 269). In 1908 Rolland published a translation of "A COMMITTEE-MAN OF THE TERROR" in the *Journal des débats*. In January 1913 she wrote a letter of sympathy to Hardy about the death of Emma HARDY.

In 1921 Hardy gave written permission for Rolland to translate *The Mayor of Casterbridge* and any of his other novels without paying a fee. He pointed out that *The* WOODLANDERS, *The* RETURN OF THE NATIVE, UNDER THE GREENWOOD TREE, and *A* PAIR OF BLUE EYES had never been translated into French. The latter had appeared in Spanish and, he wrote, would "attract French readers more than 'The Mayor' would." He also mentioned that his poems had not been translated into French, but she did not take him up on this suggestion (*Letters* VI, 61). *See* Appendix VI, Translations of Hardy's works.

For further reading: Lawrence, "Fifteen Letters from Madeleine Rolland to Thomas Hardy."

Romantic Adventures of a Milkmaid, The Novelette first published in the GRAPHIC on June 25, 1883, with four full-page illustrations by C. S. REINHART, and collected in *A CHANGED MAN AND OTHER TALES* (1913). (The work is divided into sections by Roman numerals.)

1.
The story opens early one morning at a dairy farm in the foggy valley of the Exe River, just as the cows are being driven into the stalls for milking. Margery Tucker, a young dairymaid, sets out to deliver butter to a remote cottage. On her way home she cuts through the grounds of a manor house and encounters a new tenant, a depressed foreign gentleman with a dark mustache and a white face.

2.
Her conversation saves him from committing suicide. As a gesture of his appreciation, he invites her to suggest something she would like. She learns from the postman that he is a "foreign noble," Baron von Xanten, who is without any true country.

3.
That evening he comes to her home, and she says she would like to go to the Yeomanry Ball at Exonbury. She has never been to a ball. He offers to take her, but she knows only outdated country dances. He returns to say he can easily take her to a ball at Lord Toneborough's home, where neither would be recognized. They practice the latest dances, such as the polka, from Almack's (a London dance hall, mentioned in "REMINISCENCES OF A DANCING MAN"). He invites her to practice the

polka and she crosses the stile ("a Rubicon in more ways than one.") She senses "some power" in him that is "more than human, something magical and compulsory," when he whirls her around. He observes that she should have a ball dress, and she gives him her jacket so that he will know the size.

4.

Margery meets him, without telling her father, at a large elm tree with a rift in its side where he has stored her ball gown, a "heavenly cobweb." There are also many sizes of gloves and shoes, flowers for her hair, and a handkerchief. She emerges from the tree, beautifully dressed, and he wraps her in a long cloak. A coach and horses await them, along with a coachman, a foreigner who "heeds nothing." En route he confides that he has borrowed the invitation from a friend for whom he has done a favor, so they are both there under false pretenses.

5.

They enter as Mr. and Miss Brown. Margery rapidly learns to dance on the polished floor; she is so handsome and dances so well that people notice the couple wondering whether they are sister and brother or father and daughter. The baron shows her through the house; they see the picture galleries and other furnishings. He says their time is up, but she begs for one more dance. He refuses. On her way home she changes her clothes in the tree. He insists on burning all of her finery, which is shattering to Margery. He makes her promise that, any time he summons her, she will come. He carves their initials on a tree as a memorial.

She says she will go to her invalid grandmother's and then go back home, where Jim will come to see her that evening. When the Baron asks about Jim, she says he is the young man she must marry some day. He asks why she has not told him she is engaged, and says she must tell no one about the ball.

6.

Jim Hayward presses Margery to marry him soon as his business has been settled. She says he cannot provide fine ornaments and furnishings such as silver candlesticks and gilded china. He questions her closely.

7.

Jim is far from simple by nature and decides he cannot marry Margery until he can provide the home she wants. The Baron summons Jim and learns about Margery's requirements. Four days later he sends a wagon to Jim's lodgings with all the things Marjorie wanted. She agrees to set the wedding date.

8.

Jim goes to thank the Baron. The Baron meets Margery in the woods, by mistake, and kisses her on the cheek. The wedding is supposed to follow the haymaking process. Several weeks later the Baron summons Margery. He does not realize that he has asked her to come on her wedding day, but she arrives on that day instead of getting married. He gives her a locket. She says since she has come to see him instead of going through with the wedding she cannot accept it.

9.

The Baron drives her furiously to her home but Jim has left. The clerk was waiting, and all was in readiness, but Margery was not there. Since the wedding did not take place, she packs her locket and takes it to the Baron.

10.

The Baron is a mysterious local figure, descended from a noble English mother and a wealthy "foreigner." He is seen fishing and meditating. Jim meets a stranger who had been a musician at the Yeomanry Ball and has seen Margery dancing. He deduces that the Baron took Margery to the ball. He writes "The Baron" on a garden door and watches her startled reaction, which confirms his guess. He resolves to call on the Baron. Margery learns that the Baron is ill; he summons her.

11.

She goes to Mount Lodge, his home. He is surrounded by a parson and a London physician. He asks her to obey him in a final request. She says she will. Jim walks through a door into the bedroom, dressed in his best clothes.

12.

Margery almost screams. The Baron asks if they are willing to marry each other. Jim assents, but Margery says she will only agree if she doesn't have to live with him until she is "in the mind for it." Meanwhile, the gardener, outside, listens to the ceremony from a ladder. He assumes Margery has married the Baron. He tells his daughter about it, even imagining that, if the Baron dies, Margery will be a wealthy widow and take Harriet as a companion. Marjorie returns to her grandmother's home.

13.

The next morning. Jim comes to her grandmother's. She refuses to be called "Mrs. Hayward." Jim tells her the Baron has given them the furniture. He tells her he must break the news to her father, since he is "not friends" with his daughter. Margery's father says sparks from Jim's lime-burner have ignited his hay-rick. Jim announces their marriage but her father is not pleased. Margery returns home.

14.

Margery and Jim live separately. She hears that the Baron has recovered and sailed on a yacht to Algiers. His solicitor meets Margery and asks how her "husband" is. He says she is "Miss Tucker" to the world and "Mrs. Hayward" to him. A new widow in the neighborhood, Mrs. Peach, says she is interested in marrying Jim, the lime-burner, who has now joined the Yeomanry.

15.

Mrs. Peach tells Margery Jim has invited her to the Yeomanry Review; Margery is startled and jealous. Jim and Mrs. Peach conspire to be seen by Margery in the light of the furnace. Mr. Vine, a local man, is in on the plot and has loaned his uniform to Jim.

16.

Mr. Vine drives by for Margery and takes her to the Review. She sees the two together, Jim in his uniform, and is upset. She spies Mrs. Peach in a "forward place," elegantly dressed. Margery slips a note into Mrs. Peach's pocket saying "JIM'S MARRIED." Mrs. Peach pretends to faint. Jim looks for Margery but Mr. Vine says she has gone off with the Baron.

17.

Jim rides after the Baron and talks with him in his carriage. He tells Jim he will not disturb him and Margery any more but will take Margery to Jim's house. Instead, he drives her to the coast where his yacht is at anchor and says she must decide where she is going. She asks to be taken to Jim. Margery's father forgives her, as does Jim. Mrs. Peach goes to Plymouth and finds a sailor. The Baron remains a mysterious, "magical and unearthly" figure; Jim says he has sworn to him that he will never come back, even if Margery should summon him.

In time Margery and Jim are reconciled and have a baby. Margery often thinks of the Baron, but declares that she would not leave Jim and her baby for him.

For further reading: Benazon, "'The Romantic Adventures of a Milkmaid': Hardy's Modern Romance"; Doel, "The Supernatural Background to 'The Romantic Adventures of a Milkmaid'"; Gatrell, "Typography in 'The Romantic Adventures of a Milkmaid'"; Wing, "Tess and the Romantic Milkmaid."

Unsigned reviews: "Recent Novels, 'The Romantic Adventures of a Milkmaid,'" *Nation* (New York), 37 (Sept. 20, 1883), 255; "Romantic Adventures of a Milkmaid," *Literary World* (Boston), 14 (July 28, 1883), 245.

Rome *See* ITALY.

"Rome: At the Pyramid of Cestius near the Graves of Shelley and Keats" (*1887*) Poem dated April 1887, occasioned by the Hardys' visit to the graves of Percy Bysshe Shelley and John KEATS (March 31, 1887) during a journey to ITALY, and collected in *POEMS OF THE PAST AND THE PRESENT* (1902). Cestius was Caius Cestius, a Roman praetor and tribune. His pyramid stands near the gate of St. Paul in Rome. Emma HARDY wrote in her diary that they gathered violets from the graves and that it was a "lovely cemetery very full *Crowded* where Shelley is, his grave up in a place by itself, a quiet corner but not a pretty one, & old door behind." She called the cemetery "hilly & well planted" (Emma Hardy, *Diaries*, 145).

Hardy begins by asking "who was Cestius, / And what is he to me?" Hardy cannot recall anything he did except to leave a pyramid. Beside it, "far down in time," Hardy's two countrymen, "matchless singers," have found their rest. Down through time their "two immortal Shades abide" beside the pyramid, giving Cestius "ample fame."

"Rome: Building a New Street in the Ancient Quarter" (*April 1887*) Poem collected in *POEMS OF THE PAST AND THE PRESENT* (1902). It is set in Rome, "Time's central city." The Hardys had spent several weeks in ITALY in March 1887. In this poem Hardy makes use of his knowledge of Rome and also of his architectural training as he watches the "singing workmen shape and set and join / Their frail new mansion's stuccoed cove and quion." The workmen do not realize that their work, no matter how skillfully it is carried out, will not endure forever. The works of the past were built more skillfully, more powerfully, and more durably, yet there are now "cracking frieze and rotten metope." Hardy asks what impels modern workmen to apply themselves with such energy and cheer, when, as they work, they "invade" past structures, not perceiving their strength and durability, which are far finer and more extensive than the "feeble" modern works superseding them.

"Rome: The Vatican—Sala delle Muse" Poem dated 1887 and collected in *POEMS OF THE PAST AND THE PRESENT* (1902). It was prompted by the Hardy's visit to ITALY in March of that year. In the *Life* Hardy writes that the occasion of the poem was his "nearly falling asleep" in the Muses' Hall of the Vatican Museum. His weariness resulted from "the deadly fatiguing size of St. Peter's" (*Life*, 189). The actual muses represented in the room, the nine daughters of Zeus and Mnemosyne, are Calliope (epic poetry), Terpsichore (dancing), Erato (erotic poetry), Euterpe (music), Melpomene (tragedy), Thalia (comedy), Urania (astronomy), Clio (history), Polyhymnia (higher lyric poetry). They do not correlate exactly with those in Hardy's poem; he mentions Form, Tune, Story, Dance, and Hymn.

Hardy recalls that, as he sat in the room, the figure of "One," a woman, "gleamed forth" beside a marble Carrara column. She inquires whether the Muses make him sad. He responds that his own inconstancy is the problem; he worships one in the morning and another in the evening. She says, "Be not perturbed" and assures him that she and her sisters are all "but phases of one" and she is the collective embodiment of all of them, a projection of his imagination.

The theme "Be not perturbed" was one of Hardy's favorite aphorisms from the Roman emperor-philosopher Marcus Aurelius; he copied the words in his journal on the final day of 1885 and also used them in the final chapter of *TESS OF THE D'URBERVILLES* (Bailey, *The Poetry of Thomas Hardy*, 132).

Rothenstein, Sir William (1872–1945) Painter who did several portrait drawings of Hardy. The first was in 1897 and others were done through 1916. In 1900 Hardy learned that he was planning to visit DORSET with his wife, the actress Alice Mary Rothenstein, and invited them to bicycle over to MAX GATE for lunch (CL II, 266).

Rothenstein wrote several books, including *English Portraits* (1897–1898), *Men and Memories* (1931–1932), *Goya* (1900), and *Six Portraits of Sir Rabindranath Tagore* (1916).

Royal Academy of Arts Founded in 1769 by King GEORGE III, the Royal Academy is housed in Burlington House, Hyde Park Corner, LONDON. There are two yearly exhibitions, one of old masters and one contemporary art. The academy has only 40 members; being an R.A., or Royal Academician, is a prestigious honor. The father of George SOMERSET, hero of *A LAODICEAN*, was an

R.A. In *The HAND OF ETHELBERTA*, Eustace Ladywell's painting of Ethelberta PETHERWIN as a lady wooed by a knight is displayed at the Royal Academy. John COLLIER, the illustrator of *The TRUMPET-MAJOR*, was a member.

Hardy often attended the two annual exhibitions (winter and summer) at the academy, as noted in the *Life* and his letters. The earliest visit may have been May 1870, when he returned to London from CORNWALL and resumed working for Sir Arthur William BLOMFIELD. In 1885 he was invited to attend the private viewing before the public opening; he commented in his autobiography that the great difference was the "loud chatter" prevailing at the former, since everyone knew everyone else (*Life,* 171). Hardy attended the annual academy receptions in 1903 and 1907.

In 1887 he attended the annual dinner of the academy in the company of the duke of Cambridge, Lord Salisbury, Aldous Huxley, and other prominent figures. In January 1889 he attended the exhibition of Old Mas-

The Hall of the Muses in the Vatican Museums, the setting for Hardy's poem "Rome: The Vatican—Sala delle Muse" (Archivio Fotografico)

ters at the academy, and was particularly struck by the watercolors of J. M. W. Turner and the works of George Romney; he did not care for those of Antoine Watteau or Sir Joshua Reynolds. He dined again at the Academy in 1908, 1911, 1914, and in May 1919, in the company of J. M. BARRIE. The latter was the first academy dinner held after the end of WORLD WAR I (*Letters* V, 302).

Royal Institute of British Architects The senior professional association for British architects. In May 1863 Hardy received the Silver medal from the RIBA for an essay he had submitted—"On the Application of Colored Bricks and Terra Cotta to Modern Architecture." His research had been carried out in the Reading Room at the South Kensington Museum, then housed in iron sheds (it later evolved into the Victoria and Albert Museum; *see* MUSEUMS). Hardy considered taking the Voluntary Architectural Examinations of the RIBA, but apparently did not do so. In 1897 he was invited to respond to the toast of "Literature" at a dinner of the RIBA, but refused, as he always did when requested to make a speech (Millgate, *Thomas Hardy*, 389).

Royal Society of Literature In February 1910 Edmund GOSSE wrote Hardy, inviting him to become one of 30 founding members of an English Academy of Letters that was to be modeled on the Académie française. Hardy responded that he was highly honored to accept the invitation, although, he added, he had written some things that were not very "academical" (*Letters* IV, 75). The organization evolved into the RSL. On Hardy's 72nd birthday, in 1912, the RSL presented him with its gold medal; Henry NEWBOLT and William Butler YEATS went to MAX GATE to make the presentation.

In 1916 Hardy's name was placed on the provisional list for the Entente Committee devoted to improving intellectual ties between the United Kingdom and "Allied Countries," although he apparently did not attend any meetings (*Letters* V, 179–80). In 1921 he was elected vice president of the society, and wrote the secretary, William Henry Wagstaff, that circumstances would prevent his "rendering any service to the Society in that honourable position." He had long been a Fellow of the Society (*Letters* VI, 91).

"Ruined Maid, The" Poem written in 1866 at Westbourne Park Villas, LONDON, where Hardy was living at the time, and collected in *POEMS OF THE PAST AND THE PRESENT* (1902). The poem takes the form of a dramatic dialogue between a poor and unfashionable country girl and her former friend "Melia," or Emilia, whom she meets in town. Emilia's appearance is quite startling to her friend, who opens each of the six stanzas with a series of comments and questions. Melia answers her at the conclusion of the stanza. We have a clear picture of Melia's origins; she was poor, her clothes "in tatters," her hands like "paws," her face "blue and bleak." She is now debauched, but has fine clothes and feathers, a "delicate cheek," and tiny gloved hands. Her speech fits her for "high company." Melia is quite complacent about her advancement; being "ruined" is a small price to pay. She calls her former friend a "raw country girl."

One interpretation of the poem is that it represents a dialogue between Melia's former self and her present self. It was written several years before he met Emma. Bailey points out that in Hardy's novel *DESPERATE REMEDIES*, Aeneas MANSTON describes the women he sees in London, "lost women of miserable repute looking as happy as the day is long" (Bailey, *The Poetry of Thomas Hardy*, 173–74).

The poem has been set to music; *see* Appendix II.

S

Sackville-West, Victoria (Vita) (1892–1962) English novelist, poet, biographer, and critic, associated with the Bloomsbury Group of writers and artists; she was a particular friend of Virginia WOOLF. Her most memorable novels are *The Edwardians* and *All Passion Spent;* she also wrote *Knole and the Sackvilles.* She was descended from Thomas Sackville, the first earl of Dorset, and grew up in the Sackville ancestral home, Knole Castle, in Kent.

In 1922 her mother, Lady Sackville, sent her daughter's book *The Heir: A Love Story* to Hardy with a request that he sign it. She also sent several others. A letter written on his behalf, presumably by Florence HARDY, explained that his correspondence was a great burden to him at his age, but that he would sign the books. He requested payment of half a guinea for each autograph, the amount to be given to a charity, the Dorset County Hospital, of which he was a governor. Lady Sackville sent the two guineas immediately (*Letters* VI, 169–70).

On October 13, 1928, Vita Sackville-West published a review of WINTER WORDS titled "Hardy's Poems" in the periodical *Nation and Athenaeum.* She considered his landscape "always wintry" and accused him of "stiff, uncomfortable diction and presentation," but conceded that both matched the winter season and the author (Gerber and Davis, *Thomas Hardy: An Annotated Bibliography of Writings about Him,* 315).

St. Andrews, University of In March 1922 the secretary and registrar of St. Andrews, Andrew Bennett, wrote Hardy that the university wished to confer an honorary degree on him. Hardy wrote that he would not be able to travel to the university, which would probably put the honor out of his reach. The degree was conferred on him *in absentia*. On May 6 Hardy wrote to thank the university authorities for their "considerateness" (*Letters* VI, 123, 127).

For further reading: Coxon, "Recollections of Thomas Hardy in St. Andrews."

St. Cleeve, Swithin The hero of TWO ON A TOWER, he is the orphaned son of a former curate in the village. He lives with his grandmother. He is well educated and an ardent amateur astronomer, hampered by poor equipment. Lady Viviette CONSTANTINE gives him a fine telescope. Through a mysterious alchemy he is transformed from an "abstracted astronomer into an eager lover" despite the existence of Viviette's husband, Sir Blount CONSTANTINE, who has been away in Africa for many years. Swithin loves and secretly marries Lady Constantine, but does not tell her that he forfeits an income of £600 a year by marrying before he is 25. The marriage is declared invalid when they learn that her husband had been falsely declared dead before they had married, so they decide to marry again, publicly—until Lady Constantine discovers what Swithin would sacrifice by doing so, and sends him away. When she finds she is pregnant, she marries the Right Reverend Cuthbert HELMSDALE, the bishop of Melchester, who later dies. Swithin travels abroad; on returning, he meets his son with Lady Constantine and the three climb to the top of the tower, where he proposes. She dies in his arms, of joy.

St. Helier, Lady *See* JEUNE, MARY.

St. James's Theatre In 1880 Hardy dramatized FAR FROM THE MADDING CROWD as *The Mistress of the Farm—A Pastoral Drama* and submitted it to the St. James's Theatre. It was put into rehearsal by the theater management but was then rejected. Hardy and J. Comyns CARR modified the play, but the manager, William Hunter Kendal, rejected it and then produced Arthur Pinero's play *The Squire,* which was similar. Critics believed Hardy had a good case for damages (*Letters* I, 99; 103), but Hardy did not pursue the matter.

On March 2, 1897, a copyright performance, or reading, of the play of TESS OF THE D'URBERVILLES was given at the theater. This reading was intended to establish Hardy's English copyright to the play, and was given simultaneously with the opening of the play in New York at the Fifth Avenue Theatre (*Letters* II, 147).

St. Juliot Church Small parish church near Boscastle, CORNWALL, where Hardy undertook restoration work in 1870. He did so at the request of the architect G. R. CRICKMAY, for whom Hardy had worked in WEYMOUTH in the summer of 1869. The parish was remote, and the journey there from DORSET took more than 12 hours. The rector was the Reverend Caddell HOLDER. His second wife's sister, Emma Gifford, happened to be staying

St. Juliot Church, Boscastle, Cornwall   (Chris Searle, The Old Rectory)

with them in the rectory, assisting with parish matters, when Hardy first arrived. He was much taken with Emma; they married four years later (*see* HARDY, EMMA).

In his autobiography, Hardy quotes Emma's "Recollections," found after her death, in which she describes St. Juliot as "a romantic spot indeed of North Cornwall . . . [with] the wild Atlantic Ocean rolling in with its magnificent waves and spray." She describes the gulls, puffins, cliffs, rocks, and sunsets. After Hardy had completed detailed drawings for the rebuilding of the aisle and tower, Emma laid the foundation stone, and work proceeded.

In the *Life*, Hardy recalls finding the building in a state of "picturesque neglect." Unfortunately a decision had already been made, before he arrived, to raze the historic tower and north aisle of the structure. He deplored this destruction but conceded that it might have been necessary if the church were to remain in use. He did, however, believe that the Norman walls of the former nave could have been saved, as well as a north door "much like a Saxon one," which was destroyed. The old chancel screen was "restored" and,

in the process, ruined by an ignorant but well-meaning builder who told Hardy, to his horror, that he had decided "not to stand on a pound or two" but to give the parish "a new screen instead of that patched-up old

The Old Rectory, St. Juliot Church, where Hardy met Emma Gifford in 1870   (Chris Searle, The Old Rectory)

thing." The original south aisle, at least, was kept intact (*Life*, 65–79, *passim*). Hardy made use of the location, church, and parish in *A PAIR OF BLUE EYES*.

For further reading: Phelps, "Thomas Hardy and St. Juliot Church."

Salisbury   Cathedral city and market center in Wiltshire, southern England, called MELCHESTER in Hardy's fiction. Salisbury cathedral has the highest spire in England (404 feet). Hardy was very fond of Salisbury. In one of his earliest surviving letters, written in 1862 (probably August) from LONDON to his sister Mary HARDY, he stated that he would like to visit "the old Cathedral" within a month or so as autumn was the "proper season" for seeing Salisbury (*Letters* I, 1). In August 1898, on the eve of the BOER WAR, he invited Florence HENNIKER and her husband to come to Salisbury; it was then the center of army movements in the south. In August 1897 he stayed in Salisbury at an inn; he visited the cathedral close by moonlight, as he wrote

Salisbury Cathedral, Salisbury (Hardy's Melchester), Wiltshire, which Hardy mentions in several works, including "On the Western Circuit" and The Hand of Ethelberta   (Visitor Services, Salisbury Cathedral)

his sister Katharine HARDY, and also attended a service in the cathedral. Hardy first met his French translator Madeleine ROLLAND at Salisbury in September 1897 (*Letters* VI, 33). In 1899 Hardy crossed Salisbury Plain in the automobile of Francis and Mary JEUNE and found it quite exhilarating, as he wrote Lady Agnes GROVE (*Letters* II, 230).

In 1923 Hardy attended a meeting in DORCHESTER about cracks in the spire of the cathedral, but was assured that heavy motor traffic had not caused damage (*Letters* VI, 192).

"Melchester" figures in several of Hardy's works, such as his short story "ON THE WESTERN CIRCUIT" and his novels *JUDE THE OBSCURE* and *The HAND OF ETHELBERTA*.

Sampson, Low, Marston, Searle & Rivington   London publishing firm with offices on Fleet Street. Between 1881 and 1893 the firm published eight of Hardy's novels in a cheap format (*Letters* I, 171). These included *FAR FROM THE MADDING CROWD*, *The HAND OF ETHELBERTA*, *The RETURN OF THE NATIVE*, *The TRUMPET-MAJOR*, *A LAODICEAN*, *TWO ON A TOWER*, and *The MAYOR OF CASTERBRIDGE*. In June 1894 their rights to Hardy's earlier novels expired and they passed into the hands of OSGOOD, MCILVAINE & CO., which undertook the first complete edition of Hardy's works (Purdy, *Thomas Hardy: A Bibliographical Study*, 281).

For further reading: E. Marston, *After Work: Fragments from the Workshop of an Old Publisher*.

Sandbourne   Fictional name for Bournemouth in *The HAND OF ETHELBERTA*.

"Sapphic Fragment"   This poem has two epigraphs: "Thou shalt be—Nothing" (a motto from Omar Khayyám) and "Tombless, with no remembrance" (William Shakespeare, from *Henry V*, I, ii). Published in *POEMS OF THE PAST AND THE PRESENT* (1902), the poem consists of one stanza warning that, after death, "nought" will be "told of thee or thought," because the deceased person has "plucked not of the Muses' tree." No "friendly shade" will accompany his or her "shade" even in the halls of Hades.

This is the translation of a Sappho poem given in the classical scholar John Edmonds's edition of the *Lyra Graeca*. Hardy wrote Algernon Charles SWINBURNE on April 1, 1897, that he had tried to find a better equivalent than "Thou, too, shalt die," which most translators had used during the preceding century. He then discovered Swinburne's "Thee, too, the years shall cover" ("Anactoria"), and gave up his effort (Bailey, *The Poetry of Thomas Hardy*, 188).

Sargent, John Singer (1856–1925)   Painter, born in Florence of American parents and educated in Europe.

His first exhibition was in 1878 in Paris. He moved to London in 1884, where he painted celebrity portraits; he is also known for his impressionistic watercolor landscapes, particularly of Venice. In June 1889 Hardy visited the summer exhibition at the ROYAL ACADEMY OF ARTS and saw Sargent's painting of the actress Ellen Terry as Lady Macbeth, which he liked very much (*Letters* I, 191). Hardy's friend Dorothy ALLHUSEN was painted by Sargent in 1908, but she was not happy with the portrait. Hardy wrote that he had feared she would not like it, as many "fair sitters" did not "care to have character" but wished to be depicted "conventionally, like the ladies in fashion-plates." He predicted that she would like it when she grew older (*Letters* III, 302).

In 1918 Sargent went to France as a war artist for the British government. This journey inspired *Gassed,* a large heroic painting of soldiers injured by mustard gas. In 1919 this painting was the "picture of the year" at the Royal Academy's summer exhibition. Hardy wrote his friend Sir George DOUGLAS, whose nephew had been gassed in the war, that he was relieved the nephew had not been seriously hurt. Hardy believed the young man's experience would enable him to appreciate Sargent's painting when he had a chance to see it (*Letters* V, 303).

Sassoon, Siegfried (1886–1967) English poet, well known for his verses delineating the horrors of war. He was the nephew and ward of Hardy's friend Sir Hamo THORNYCROFT. Sassoon's *Counter-Attack and Other Poems* (1918) contains angry poems about trench warfare. He wrote a fictional autobiography, *The Memoirs of George Sherston* (3 vols., 1928–36). His other works include *The Daffodil Murderer, Lingual Exercises for Advanced Vocabularians,* and *The Old Huntsman and Other Poems.* He was wounded twice in WORLD WAR I and received two medals for bravery. He later became a pacifist.

Sassoon visited MAX GATE in November 1918, when he brought the "Little Book," edited by Sir Edward Marsh, and asked Hardy to write a poem in it. A number of Marsh's literary friends were invited to inscribe a sample of their work in the book, which was dedicated to Hardy. Shortly after Hardy's 79th birthday, in June 1919, Sassoon spent a weekend at Max Gate and presented him with a beautifully bound volume of holograph poems from 43 living poets (*see* "POETS' TRIBUTE" TO HARDY). Hardy wrote his friend Sydney COCKERELL that they had gone for a car ride to the top of Blackdon, which offered a view "all down into Devonshire" (*Letters* V, 286, 326). Sassoon introduced Hardy to Robert GRAVES, who spent a weekend at Max Gate with his wife, Nancy Nicholson, in August 1920.

In April 1921 St. John Ervine wrote to Hardy that a group of younger writers wished to honor him on his 81st birthday (June 2, 1921) with a first edition of a work by John Keats. Hardy answered that he felt a first edition would be "of too much value," but they did present him with Keats's *Lamia, Isabella, the Eve of St. Agnes, and Other Poems* The volume was sent by 104 writers, including Virginia WOOLF and Sassoon (*Letters* VI, 84–85, 90). In July 1921, Hardy wrote his friend Florence HENNIKER that a number of poets had stopped in at Max Gate. He called them the "Young Georgians," and mentioned Sassoon, Walter de la Mare, and John MASEFIELD.

Satires of Circumstance Poetry collection published by MACMILLAN & CO., London, in 1914. There are 15 poems in the "Satires of Circumstance" section; many of them had been published in the FORTNIGHTLY REVIEW. Pinion considers these "ironical sketches" to be slighter and more shallow than the others in the volume (Pinion, *A Thomas Hardy Dictionary,* 238). There are additional sections as well: "Lyrics and Reveries," "Poems of 1912–13," and "Miscellaneous Pieces." A postscript contains "MEN WHO MARCH AWAY," a poem transferred in 1919 to MOMENTS OF VISION. In 1915 a revised impression was published; it was later included in Macmillan's 1919 WESSEX EDITION (Purdy, *Thomas Hardy: A Bibliographical Study,* 164–72).

There are a number of poems describing Hardy's courtship of his first wife, Emma Gifford HARDY: "WHEN I SET OUT FOR LYONNESSE," "I FOUND HER OUT THERE," "A DREAM OR NO," "BEENY CLIFF (MARCH 1870–MARCH 1913)," and another, "YOUR LAST DRIVE," describing the last time Emma went out, five days before her death (Purdy, *Thomas Hardy: A Bibliographical Study,* 246–47). Millgate states that the volume brought "profound distress" to Hardy's second wife, Florence Emily HARDY (*Thomas Hardy: A Biography,* 499).

The historian and biographer Lytton Strachey, in a review for the *New Statesman,* argued that Hardy's poems were "modern as no other poems are." He insisted that Hardy brought the "realism and sobriety of prose into the service of his poetry." He argued that in such "contorted" lines as "Dear ghost, in the past did you ever find / Me one whom consequence influenced much?" (from "Your Last Drive"), which some critics might find "flat and undistinguished," Hardy "found out the secret of touching our marrow-bones."

For further reading: Gifford, "Hardy's Revisions: Satires of Circumstance"; Strachey, "Satires of Circumstance" (reprinted in Cox, *Thomas Hardy: The Critical Heritage*).

Saturday Review A British magazine founded in 1855. It was well established by the time Hardy was a young man. In 1862, while living in LONDON, he sent some copies of it to his sister Mary HARDY. In one of the two earliest of his extant letters (March 11, 1862), he wrote her not to return them but to store them so that he might see them when he wanted to do so (*Letters* I, 2).

On September 30, 1871, Hardy's first published novel, DESPERATE REMEDIES, was reviewed in the magazine. Michael Millgate and Richard Purdy believe the review was written by Hardy's friend Horace MOULE, who also reviewed UNDER THE GREENWOOD TREE in the magazine on September 28, 1872 (CL I, 13, 19). On January 4, 1879, after publication of FAR FROM THE MADDING CROWD and The RETURN OF THE NATIVE, an unsigned appraisal of Hardy was published, stating that, if the primary object of a story is "to amuse . . . Mr. Hardy, in our opinion, breaks down." The reviewer praised the characters and the rural scenes in Far from the Madding Crowd, but criticized The Return of the Native: in the "rugged and studied simplicity of its subject" it was "intensely artificial" (Lerner and Holstrom, Thomas Hardy and His Readers, 153–54). On May 29, 1886, The MAYOR OF CASTERBRIDGE was reviewed in its pages. Hardy's friend Edmund GOSSE reviewed The WOODLANDERS for the Saturday Review on April 2, 1887, noting the book's "richness and humanity." The reviewer criticized Hardy, however, for mixing vernacular village speech with "town talk," and found Giles WINTERBORNE too representative of village civilization and "not quite enough of an individual" (Gerber and Davis, 42). Hardy's novel TESS OF THE D'URBERVILLES was reviewed on January 16, 1892, and on February 8, 1896, the magazine published a review of JUDE THE OBSCURE.

The Review also published several of Hardy's short stories and poems, including "The Duke's Reappearance," "A CHURCH ROMANCE," "AH, ARE YOU DIGGING ON MY GRAVE?," and "IN TIME OF 'THE BREAKING OF NATIONS.'"

On April 21, 1928, three months after Hardy's death, the Review published an article about him written by Edward Shanks. Shanks considered that, at the time, Hardy's poems were "more valued than his prose, but insisted that the prose was noteworthy for the "touch of the inevitable."

Savile Club Prestigious London literary club for men, to which Hardy was elected in June 1878. His friend and publisher Charles Kegan PAUL had proposed him for membership. Hardy saw Robert BROWNING, Alfred, Lord TENNYSON, and Matthew ARNOLD at the club, and also met Edmund GOSSE, who became a lifelong close friend. He often stayed there, writing letters and entertaining, or being entertained, at lunch and dinner. In June 1883 he dined at the Savile with Gosse and met William Dean HOWELLS; in June 1887, at another club dinner, he met Lord Goschen (G. J. Goschen, the chancellor of the exchequer), Lord Lytton, and A. J. Balfour. When JUDE THE OBSCURE was published in 1895, however, Hardy was distressed to realize that some of the anonymous reviewers who attacked it as immoral were actually fellow members of the club (Millgate, Thomas Hardy, 373).

Saxelby, F. Outwin (unknown) Compiler of A Thomas Hardy Dictionary (London, 1911). He apparently first wrote to Hardy's publishers on November 25, 1910, having discovered a reference in A GROUP OF NOBLE DAMES (in the WESSEX EDITION) to "the ancient and loyal family of Saxelbye," saying that he was compiling a "Dictionary of the Characters & Places in his novels and poems." The letter was forwarded to Hardy, who replied on January 4, 1911, that he had no wish that such a book be prepared. He did not object to Saxelby's publishing it, but wanted to make it clear that where Saxelby proposed to "identify fictitious place-names with real places" Hardy could "accept no responsibility for such identification" (Letters IV, 135).

Saxelby sent him the proofs of the book, but Hardy declined to give them an "exhaustive examination." He did insist, however, that Saxelby add the following words to the preface: "It is to be clearly understood that Mr. Hardy has not authorized this book, and can accept no responsibility for its production." Saxelby dedicated the book to Hardy, despite Hardy's objection (Letters IV, 172–73).

"Schreckhorn, The" (With thoughts of Leslie Stephen) (June 1897) Sonnet first published, with Hardy's recollections of Leslie STEPHEN, in F. W. Maitland's biography, The Life and Letters of Leslie Stephen (1906). The poem was included in SATIRES OF CIRCUMSTANCE (1914).

Hardy compares Stephen with the alpine mountain (the schreckhorn) itself. In the octet, he describes the mountain, seen from afar, as "a thing of mood and whim," but, when he nears, its "spare and desolate figure" seems less an "Alp-height" than "a depiction of Sir Leslie Stephen. His personality, like the Schreckhorn, had "quaint glooms, keen lights, and rugged trim."

Stephen, about eight years older than Hardy, was an experienced climber and from 1865 to 1868 had served as president of the Alpine Club, which had rooms at 8 St. Martin's Place, where Hardy worked for Sir Arthur William BLOMFIELD in 1862. That year, Stephen had published Peaks, Passes, and Glaciers, which described his 1861 ascent of the Schreckhorn (Bailey, The Poetry of Thomas Hardy, 281).

Virginia WOOLF wrote Hardy that the poem and its reminiscences were "incomparably the truest & most imaginative portrait of him in existence." (Letters V, 76–77).

Scott, Sir Walter (1771–1832) Scottish poet and novelist, much influenced by the medieval French romance and by Scottish history. He was one of the first writers to conceive of history as a source for the novel; Waverley was the first of a series of 32 historical novels centering on Prince Charles Edward Stuart, the Young Pretender, and Captain Edward Waverley, the hero.

Among Scott's best-known books of poetry are *Marmion, A Tale of Flodden Field* (1808), *The Lay of the Last Minstrel* (1805), and *The Lady of the Lake* (1810).

As a young man Hardy preferred Scott's poetry to his novels and considered *Marmion* "the most Homeric poem in the English language" (*Life*, 49). He reiterated these sentiments in 1915 in a letter to Lady Hoare (Alda Hoare, the wife of Sir Henry Hoare) (*Letters* V, 74). In August 1881 Hardy and his first wife, Emma HARDY, went to Scotland. They visited Roslin Castle, the ancient seat of the St. Clair family, celebrated in Scott's "Rosabelle." They also toured Hawthornden, the former home of the Scottish poet William Drummond of Hawthornden, friend of William Shakespeare and Ben Jonson. Their guide, an elderly man, told them he had known Scott.

In March 1902 Hardy wrote his publisher, Sir Frederick MACMILLAN, that a number of books seemed to be coming out about "the Wessex of the novels & poems." He felt he should publish an annotated edition of his works, as Scott had done, to avoid others making "capital" out of his materials (*Letters* III, 16). Hardy did provide revised prefaces and notes to the Macmillan WESSEX EDITION of his works (24 vols.; published 1912–31; Purdy, *Thomas Hardy: A Bibliographical Study*, 282–86).

Scribner's Magazine One of the best American literary periodicals of the period from the late 19th century through the early 20th. In 1881 the publishing firm Scribner & Company sold *Scribner's Monthly*, the original magazine published by the company, to the Century Company. In 1887 the younger Charles Scribner founded *Scribner's Magazine*, which was published until 1939. Hardy's story "The FIDDLER OF THE REELS" was published in the magazine in May 1893 with illustrations by William HATHERELL.

Seaway, Anne Character in *DESPERATE REMEDIES* who poses as the second wife of Aeneas MANSTON.

Selected Poems of Thomas Hardy Poetry collection published by MACMILLAN & CO., London, in 1916. There are 120 poems drawn from *The DYNASTS* and four volumes of poetry up to 1916. Nine were from the unpublished manuscript of *MOMENTS OF VISION*. Hardy hoped the volume would "bring his poetry to a wider public," and he selected them with an eye to the general reader (Purdy, 187).

serialization of Hardy's novels Hardy was always eager to have his novels appear first in serial form, principally for financial reasons. The literary critic Joseph Warren Beach comments on the remarkable compromises Hardy, as an artist, was willing to make with editors who were "indifferent to considerations of artistic integrity"

and "solely concerned not to give offense in the family circle" (foreword, Chase, *Thomas Hardy from Serial to Novel*). He often revised his work, removing sexually suggestive material. His short stories were, as a rule, published serially before being collected.

Of Hardy's 15 novels, 12 originally were published in serial form. In his prefaces, Hardy indicates that only four—*The* MAYOR OF CASTERBRIDGE, TESS OF THE D'URBERVILLES, JUDE THE OBSCURE, and *The* WELL-BELOVED—differed in serial form from the book publication.

In her study of the serial publication of Hardy's novels, Mary Ellen Chase presents the following list of the serialization of the novels:

A Pair of Blue Eyes Tinsleys' *Magazine*, September 1872–July 1873; book publication 1873.
Far from the Madding Crowd Cornhill *Magazine*, January–December 1874; book publication 1874.
The Hand of Ethelberta Cornhill *Magazine*, July 1875–May 1876; book publication 1876.
The Return of the Native Belgravia, January–December 1878; book publication 1878.
The Trumpet-Major Good Words, January–December 1878; book publication 1880.
A Laodicean Harper's New Monthly *Magazine* (European edition), December 1880–December 1881; book publication 1881.
Two on a Tower Atlantic Monthly, 1882, vols. 49 and 50; book publication 1882.
The Mayor of Casterbridge Graphic, January 2–May 15, 1886; book publication 1886.
The Woodlanders Macmillan's *Magazine*, May 1886–April 1887; book publication 1887.
Tess of the d'Urbervilles Graphic, July 4–December 26, 1891; book publication 1891.
The Well-Beloved Illustrated London News, October 1, 1892–December 17, 1892, under the title *The Pursuit of the Well-Beloved*; book publication 1897.
Jude the Obscure Harper's New Monthly *Magazine* (European edition), December 1894, under the title *The Simpletons*, January–November 1895, under the title *Hearts Insurgent*; book publication 1896.

The three novels not published serially were *DESPERATE REMEDIES* (1871), *UNDER THE GREENWOOD TREE* (1872), and *TWO ON A TOWER* (1882).

In *Cancelled Words: Rediscovering Thomas Hardy*, Rosemarie Morgan has made the only detailed study of the progress of *FAR FROM THE MADDING CROWD* from serial to book publication. Her book includes facsimiles of the manuscript as it was submitted for serialization.

For further reading: Allingham, "Robert Barnes's Illustrations for Thomas Hardy's *The Mayor of Casterbridge* as Serialised in *The Graphic*"; Allingham, "Six Original Illustrations for Hardy's *Tess of the D'Urbervilles* Drawn by Sir Hubert von Herkomer, R. A., for *The Graphic*

(1891)"; Dalziel, "Anxieties of Representation: The Serial Illustrations to Hardy's *The Return of the Native*"; Dalziel, "'She Matched His Violence with Her Own Wild Passion': Illustrating *Far from the Madding Crowd*"; Harvey, *Victorian Novelists and Their Illustrators;* Jackson, *Illustration and the Novels of Thomas Hardy;* Johnson, "Illustrated Versions of Hardy's Works: A Checklist 1872–1992"; Morgan, *Cancelled Words: Rediscovering Thomas Hardy;* Page, "Thomas Hardy's Forgotten Illustrators."

Shakespeare, William (1564–1616) English poet and dramatist, generally considered the most widely known author in English literature. Shakespeare exerted a profound influence on Hardy. By the time Hardy was 12 he had read all of Shakespeare's tragedies; he remarks in the *Life* that he had read them "for the plots only," but believed Hamlet's ghost "did not play his part up to the end" as he should have done (*Life*, 24) In his poem "TO SHAKESPEARE" he refers to the poet and playwright as "Bright baffling Soul, least capturable of themes."

In 1866, as a young man in LONDON, Hardy attended the series of Shakespeare's plays at the Drury Lane Theatre starring the actor Samuel Phelps In 1868, while he was waiting for the publisher MACMILLAN & CO. to decide whether to accept his first novel, *The POOR MAN AND THE LADY* (never published), he read various Shakespeare plays. In 1870, after he met Emma Gifford (HARDY) at ST. JULIOT, CORNWALL, he corresponded with her and read Shakespeare, along with the Bible and other works. After *The HAND OF ETHELBERTA* was serialized in the *CORNHILL MAGAZINE* (July 1875–May 1876), the editor, Lesile STEPHEN, advised Hardy not to permit his "perfectly fresh & original vein" to be cramped by "critical canons" but to read Shakespeare, Goethe, Sir Walter SCOTT, and other great writers "who give ideas & dont prescribe rules" (Millgate, *Thomas Hardy*, 180).

Hardy was always fascinated by itinerant actors and theatrical productions. In August 1884 he attended a performance of *Othello* in the market-field, DORCHESTER, by strolling players. He gives an amusing account of it in his autobiography, noting that Emilia was wearing the earrings he saw her wearing that morning while buying the family vegetables. Othello was played by the proprietor of the troupe, whose speeches could be heard "as far as to the town-pump." When the audience laughed after the murder scene, Othello had stopped and chastised them, asking sternly, "Is this the Nineteenth Century?" They were so ashamed of themselves that after the pillow scene they applauded "with tragic vehemence," to show that their hearts were "in the right place after all" (*Life*, 167–68).

In 1887, the year the Hardys went to FRANCE and ITALY, Hardy noted that Shakespeare's sonnets were among the many works he had read that year. In July 1896 the Hardys went to Stratford-upon-Avon and visited various sites associated with Shakespeare's name. They went on to Dover, where Hardy read *King Lear*.

In June 1905 Hardy attended a luncheon at the elite Garrick Club (named for the Shakespearean actor David Garrick) and discussed Shakespeare with the noted actor Sir Henry Irving. That same month he wrote the scholar Israel Gollancz, lecturer in English at Cambridge and honorable secretary of the Shakespeare Memorial Committee, which was proposing a London memorial to the poet, about his view of the matter. He believed that naming an important street or square for him would be "as effectual a means as any" of keeping his name "on the tongues of citizens, & his personality in their minds" (*Letters* III, 174).

In May 1918 Hardy reflected that Shakespeare characters "act as if they were not quite closely thinking of what they were doing." Instead, they seemed to be "great philosophers giving the main of their mind to the general human situation" (*Life*, 386).

Quotations from the following plays appear in Hardy's letters: *Antony and Cleopatra; As You Like It; Coriolanus; Hamlet; Henry IV, Part One; Henry V; King Lear; Macbeth; The Merchant of Venice; A Midsummer Night's Dream; Othello; Pericles; The Tempest; Twelfth Night; and The Winter's Tale.*

For further reading: Hall, "Hawthorne, Shakespeare and Tess: Hardy's Use of Allusion and Reference"; Kim, "Shakespeare and Hardy: Their Tragic Worlds"; Moring, "The Dark Glass: Mirroring and Sacrifice in Shakespeare's *Othello* and Hardy's *Tess of the D'Urbervilles*"; Ray, "Hardy's Borrowing from Shakespeare: Eustacia Vye and Lady Macbeth"; Vandiver, "*The Return of the Native* and Shakespeare."

Shaw, George Bernard (1856–1950) Irish born playwright, critic, and social reformer. Hardy did not know him well, although Shaw was a friend of Sydney COCKERELL, who was in turn a longtime friend of Hardy's. In June 1912, when Cockerell was visiting MAX GATE, Hardy told him of his admiration for Shaw's plays (*Letters* IV, 235). In April 1916 he wrote Cockerell that Shaw and his wife, Charlotte (née Payne-Townsend), had been staying at Weymouth and had come to Max Gate on Friday afternoon for tea. They met the historian John Bagnell Bury and his wife there. John and Jane Bury were both of Irish birth, and Jane Bury and Florence HARDY began arguing about the Irish rising that had begun in Dublin in April 1916 (*Letters* V, 158).

In 1922 Hardy sent a long list of corrections to an American critic, Professor Samuel C. Chew of Bryn Mawr College, Bryn Mawr, Pennsylvania, who had published his book *Thomas Hardy: Poet and Novelist* in 1921. Chew had termed the London scenes in *The HAND OF*

ETHELBERTA weak and dismissed Hardy's attempts to portray the world of London society. Hardy responded that a "well-known society Countess" had asked for an introduction to him because his novel was the only one she had found "which showed people exactly as they were." Moreover, the plot, which many critics had termed "impossible," was used 30 years afterward in a play with "no sense of improbability." The play Hardy had in mind was, according to Richard Purdy and Michael Millgate, Shaw's *You Never Can Tell* (*Letters* VI, 155–57).

Hardy died on January 11, 1928. On Monday, January 16, his heart was buried in the grave of his first wife at STINFORD CHURCH; at the same time, his ashes were interred in POETS' CORNER in WESTMINSTER ABBEY, LONDON, and a service was held at St. Peter's Church, DORCHESTER. Shaw was one of the six pallbearers representing Literature at the Westminster Abbey service; the others were John GALSWORTHY, Edmund GOSSE, A. E. HOUSMAN, James BARRIE, and Rudyard KIPLING.

"She At His Funeral" A poem collected in WESSEX POEMS AND OTHER VERSES (1898), depicting a young woman following the funeral procession of a man she had loved, but whose family does not know her. His kindred wear mourning clothes while she wears a gown of "garish dye," but they appear dry-eyed while her own regret "consumes like fire!"

Hardy supplied a drawing to accompany the poem in *Wessex Poems* showing a young woman peering over the wall of Stinsford churchyard. Her shadow is visible on the wall, cast by the afternoon sun, which Bailey believes recalls the "fire" of the poem. The word "regret" may suggest that she has some responsibility for his death (Bailey, *The Poetry of Thomas Hardy*, 56–57).

"She Hears the Storm" Poem published in TIME'S LAUGHINGSTOCKS (1909) in which the speaker, apparently a widow, is listening to a bad storm outside her house. She reflects on a time when she would have worried about her aging husband, who might have been coming home on the road without cover. But now she does not fret, because her husband has died. In the manuscript the poem was titled "The Widow's Thought."

The imagery in the poem suggests Hardy's birthplace, and the poem may be an imaginary meditation by Hardy's grandmother, Mary Head Hardy, whose husband, Thomas HARDY (1), died in 1837, or by Hardy's mother after his father died in 1892 (Bailey, *The Poetry of Thomas Hardy*, 247).

"She, to Him" A group of four sonnets—"She to Him, I," "She to Him, II," "She to Him, III," and "She to Him, IV"—all dated 1866. They were published in WESSEX POEMS (1898).

In "She to Him, I" A woman is speaking to her beloved, asking that, when he sees her as an elder withered woman, he will realize that in her soul she is the "very same." She would die to spare him "touch of ill," and asks if he will at least, remember their former love and, at the very least, venture into their declining years as long-time friends.

In "She to Him, II," the woman imagines that, after her death, "another woman, will remind him of her and that he will think, "Poor jade!" She hopes he will sigh and recall her as completely devoted to him. He, of course, will never realize that his brief recollection of her was not a fleeting phantom-thought" to her. It was her "Whole Life," even though she was only a passing thought in his life. This poem has a note, "prosed in Desperate Remedies.'" In his preface to the volume Hardy had stated that in a few cases "the verses were turned into prose and printed as such, it having been unanticipated at that time that they might see the light" (Purdy, *Thomas Hardy: A Bibliographical Study*, 98). Bailey states that the reference seems to be to Miss Aldclyffe's statement to Cytherea that men are fickle in love: "You . . . will fade and fade—bright eyes will fade—and you will perhaps then die early. . . . Whilst he, in some gay and busy spot far away, . . . will long have ceased to regret you" (chapter 6, 1; Bailey, *The Poetry of Thomas Hardy*, 59).

In "She to Him, III," she tells him she will always be faithful to him, even though she is surprised still to be alive, since she has belonged to Death ever since "that last Good-bye!" She cares nothing for her friends or relatives but is now numb. Her "old dexterities in witchery" are gone.

In "She to Him, IV," the woman focuses her grief on her rival: "I can but maledict her, pray her dead, / For giving love and getting love of thee—/Feeding a heart that else mine own had fed!" She hopes he does not hate her as an "envier," because "Love is lovelier / The more it shapes its moan in selfish-wise."

Lois Deacon identifies the woman as Tryphena SPARKS, and the fourth sonnet as her reaction to his courtship of Emma Gifford (later HARDY), but James O. Bailey observes that such an inference would require the reader to assume that Hardy predated the sonnets 1866 to conceal later events (he did not meet Emma until 1870). Hardy supplied a drawing in *Wessex Poems* showing "the eastern slope of a darkening hill" with a monument on top; the sun is sinking behind the hill and two figures are descending a downward path (Bailey, *The Poetry of Thomas Hardy*, 58). It is uncertain whether Hardy is writing to an actual woman or whether he is simply elaborating on the universal situation of the rejected woman.

"Shelley's Skylark" (***The neighbourhood of Leghorn: March 1887***) Poem published in POEMS OF THE PAST

AND THE PRESENT (1902), in which Hardy philosophizes about the imaginary remains of the actual skylark that occasioned Percy Bysshe Shelley's poem "To a Skylark." He conjectures that they lie somewhere near Leghorn, Italy, in a field. The speaker envisions the end of its "meek life," when it falls from the sky, "A little ball of feather and bone," piping "farewell." He enjoins the "faeries" to go and find its remains, now "priceless dust," and "consecrate it to endless time," because it inspired Shelley to reach "Ecstatic heights in thought and rhyme." Hardy often expressed the idea that deceased birds and animals became part of the organic life of a given place, as in "VOICES FROM THINGS GROWING IN A CHURCHYARD."

The Hardys had traveled to ITALY in March 1887 and had visited Pisa. Bailey suggests that they might have made a side trip to Leghorn, where Shelley stayed (at Casa Ricci) in 1820. Hardy regarded their journey as a pilgrimage, and saw Shelley's grave in Rome (Bailey, *The Poetry of Thomas Hardy*, 127–28).

For further reading: Bartlett, "Hardy's Shelley"; Runcie, "On Figurative Language: A Reading of Shelley's, Hardy's and Hughes's Skylark Poems"; Tillman-Hill, "Hardy's Skylark and Shelley's."

Sherborne   A market town in DORSET, approximately 20 miles north of DORCHESTER. The Norman cathedral there no longer stands but Sherborne Abbey, rebuilt in the Gothic perpendicular style in the 15th century, was a notable landmark in Hardy's time and remains one of the finest buildings in Dorset. Sherborne figures as Sherton Abbas in *The WOODLANDERS*.

Sherton Abbas   Fictional name for SHERBORNE in *The WOODLANDERS*.

Shinar, Frederic   Character in *UNDER THE GREENWOOD TREE*. He is a farmer and MELLSTOCK churchwarden, wealthy but rude, deserting his dance partner for Fancy DAY. He is "composed of watchchain, with a mouth always hanging on a smile, but never smiling." He persuades Parson MAYBOLD to supplant the Mellstock choir of skilled singers and instrumentalists with an organist (Fancy Day).

Shire-Hall Place   Historic house in Shire-Hall Lane, DORCHESTER, which Hardy and his wife rented between June 1883 and the completion of MAX GATE in 1885. It was here that Hardy wrote *The MAYOR OF CASTERBRIDGE* (Purdy, 53). Within a few years of creating a Mayor of "Casterbridge" Hardy himself was appointed magistrate of its real-life counterpart, Dorchester (Rosemarie Morgan, personal communication with the author).

Shorter, Clement King (1857–1926)   Journalist and editor. Under his editorship the *Illustrated London News* published Hardy's *The Pursuit of the Well-Beloved* (serial title of *The WELL-BELOVED*); he also edited the *English Illustrated Magazine*. Subsequently he was founder and editor of the *Sketch* and the *SPHERE*, and also editor of the *Tatler*. He frequently published Hardy's fiction and poetry, including "ON THE WESTERN CIRCUIT" and "Ancient Earthworks at Casterbridge" (*see* "A TRYST AT AN ANCIENT EARTHWORK") in the *English Illustrated Magazine;* and, in the *Sphere*, "A CHANGED MAN," "The DEAD AND THE LIVING ONE," and "The LOST PYX." In 1894 Hardy prompted Shorter to review the novel *Outlines*, written by his friend Florence HENNIKER (Millgate, *Thomas Hardy*, 358).

Shorter and Clive HOLLAND (Charles J. Hankinson) led the WHITEFRIARS CLUB, a group of London journalists, on "A Pilgrimage to Wessex" in June 1901, and brought them all to MAX GATE for tea. Millgate calls it a "visitation," and observes that Hardy had by then learned to "distrust and dislike" Shorter, although his editorships made him useful (Millgate, *Thomas Hardy*, 413).

In late 1912, when Hardy was courting his second wife, Florence Dugdale (later HARDY), she remained for long periods of time at Max Gate, assisting him with his papers and letters. She and Hardy were always "chaperoned" by his sisters or Emma Hardy's niece, Lilian GIFFORD. However, Florence shared many details of life at Max Gate with Hardy's close friend Edward CLODD; she perhaps did not realize that he passed them along to Shorter. Hardy was aware of Shorter's curiosity about Max Gate, and invited him and Clodd down for a long weekend in July 1913 (Millgate, *Thomas Hardy*, 490–91).

Florence Hardy was inclined to like Shorter, as he had commissioned her as a reviewer for the *Sphere* and had provided literary work for her before she and Hardy were married in 1914. After WORLD WAR I, however, Shorter irritated Hardy by privately reprinting some of his poems. Shorter also arrived, uninvited, at Max Gate for tea on the occasion of Hardy's 78th birthday in 1918 (Millgate, *Thomas Hardy*, 525).

In 1920, at Shorter's request, Hardy wrote a preface to *A Dull Day in London,* a posthumous collection of sketches by Shorter's first wife, Dora Sigerson Shorter, who had died in 1918.

For further reading: Purdy, "A Note on the Privately Printed Pamphlets of Clement Shorter and Mrs. Hardy."

"Shut Out That Moon"   Poem dated 1904 and published in *TIME'S LAUGHINGSTOCKS* (1909). In the first stanza, Hardy turns away from the moon, which reminds him of a time in his youth when he played the lute and before family names were carved on a white stone. This may be a reference to the music Hardy and his father made before his father's death in 1892. In the second stanza he seems to refer to his mother, once fair, now faded (she died in 1904), with whom he had gazed at the constellations Lady's Chair, Orion, and the Less and Greater Bear. The third stanza mentions the "sweet sentiments" breathed to "you and me" by the "midnight scents" of a bough, possibly outside the window. This may refer to Hardy's courtship of Emma Gifford (later HARDY). In the last stanza, the moon and the trees evolve into the prison of the "common lamp-lit room," a reminder that "Life's early bloom" brought only "tart" fruit. The voice of the poet becomes that of a stoic (Bailey, *The Poetry of Thomas Hardy,* 208).

The symbolism of the moon is complex. At first "she" represents filial love and then romance, but both are terminated by death and disillusionment. In the folklore of DORSET, seeing the moon through glass is a bad omen (Bailey, 208); therefore, the poet enjoins the reader to close the window and shut out the moon. The poem has been set to music in a manuscript signed "AM," which is in the DORSET COUNTY MUSEUM (Bailey, 208).

"Sick Battle-God, The" Collected in *POEMS OF THE PAST AND THE PRESENT* (1902), this is the last in a series of war poems occasioned by the BOER WAR. Hardy recalls the days when men found glory and joy in war. Even corpses once wore the war-god's "glory-gleam," which was attractive to General Wolfe (the English general who died during the English capture of Quebec in 1759), Marshal Ney (who led Napoleon's troops in attacks on the British at WATERLOO) and Admiral Nelson (whose naval finery made him fatally visible at TRAFALGAR). Now, however, there is only a ghost of the battle-god; his crimes were so dire he can never be exalted. He has few champions and is "bepatched with paint and lath." In the final stanza Hardy declares "The Battle-god is god no more." *See* WAR, HARDY'S ATTITUDE TOWARD.

"Singer Asleep, A" *(Algernon Charles Swinburne, 1837–1909)* Poem written after Hardy visited the grave of Algernon Charles SWINBURNE at Bonchurch, Isle of Wight, in March 1910. It was published in the *English Review* in April 1910 and collected in *SATIRES OF CIRCUMSTANCE* (1914). Hardy had met Swinburne several times and regarded him as one of England's finest poets. He recalls reading Swinburne's poetry with unusual dedication when he was a young architect working in London.

In the poem he describes Sappho, a Greek poetess of passion, "the Lesbian, she the music-mother" of the "tribe that feel in melodies." She drowned herself for unrequited love of Phaon by leaping from the Leucadian promontory into the sea (Bailey, *The Poetry of Thomas Hardy,* 283). His ghost may go to the edge, the water and meet hers and ask where her songs are, she might reply to her "Disciple true and warm" that his

own songs are now sufficient. Hardy sadly leaves Swinburne in his grave; he had been the peer of the waves in sad improvisations.

In its alliteration and rhythm the poem has echoes of Swinburne: "The Fates have fitly bidden," "In fulth of numbers freaked," "His leaves of rhythm and rhyme," "passionate pages," "fitful fire," "heaving hydrosphere," "daylight gleam declines," "capes and chines."

For further reading: McGhee, "Swinburne Planteth, Hardy Watereth': Victorian Views of Pain and Pleasure in Human Sexuality"; Murfin, *Swinburne, Hardy, Lawrence and the Burden of Belief.*

"Sleeping-Green" Imaginary village near Castle de Stancy in *A LAODICEAN,* where James HAVILL and William DARE are forced to share a room; Havill discovers the secret of Dare's illegitimate birth.

"Sleep-Worker, The" Sonnet collected in *POEMS OF THE PAST AND THE PRESENT.* The poet addresses "Mother," presumably Mother Nature, inquiring when she will awake and realize that her labors, often carried out by "vacant rote and prepossession strong," have actually produced mixed results. Although there are "fair growths" there are also "foul cankers" and "curious blends of ache and ecstasy." He asks three questions. If "thou" (Mother Nature) were to awaken and, somehow, realize "All that Life's palpitating tissues feel," what would be the outcome? Would "thou" then "destroy, in one wild shock of shame," the entire "high heaving firmamental frame"? Or, perhaps, "patiently adjust, amend, and heal?"

Bailey points out that Hardy "blurs" the identity of the being he addresses. She could be "a fusion of Mother Nature as a 'subaltern'" (or subordinate), but could also represent the "unconscious Will operating through nature." If Hardy intends the latter interpretation, it is possible that he is reflecting Von Hartmann's *Philosophy of the Unconscious,* which he had read. The Spirits sing, in the final chorus of *The DYNASTS,* "Consciousness the Will informing, till It fashion all things fair!" The poem was set to music by Hubert James Foss in *Seven Pieces by Hardy Set to Music* (Bailey, *The Poetry of Thomas Hardy,* 147–48).

Smallbury, Liddy The daughter of William SMALLBURY and great-granddaughter of the maltster Warren SMALLBURY in *FAR FROM THE MADDING CROWD,* she works as Bathsheba EVERDENE's maid at Weatherbury Farm. At her suggestion, Bathsheba sends the ill-fated valentine to William BOLDWOOD.

Smallbury, Warren Father of Jacob SMALLBURY in *FAR FROM THE MADDING CROWD.* He is the proprietor of Warren's Malthouse, where most of the conversations among Hardy's rural characters take place and where news is reported and events are discussed. Fanny ROBIN's disappearance is reported here, and the men go out to search for her. Fanny's letter to Gabriel OAK, announcing her engagement to Sergeant Frank TROY, is delivered here. At the end of the novel, the village men gather at the Malthouse and see Frank Troy, thought to have drowned, looking in. Soon afterward Troy is shot and killed by William BOLDWOOD at his Christmas party.

Smallbury, William The son of Jacob SMALLBURY and grandson of Warren SMALLBURY in FAR FROM THE MADDING CROWD, he is a "child of forty" who is the father of Liddy SMALLBURY. He works on Bathsheba EVERDENE's farm and tries to help Fanny ROBIN by searching for Sergeant Francis TROY at Casterbridge Barracks. Troy's regiment, however, has moved to MELCHESTER.

Smith, Elder & Co. London publishing house that rejected Hardy's first novel, The POOR MAN AND THE LADY, in 1869. The firm later published FAR FROM THE MADDING CROWD (two volumes, 1874); The HAND OF ETHELBERTA (two volumes, 1876); The RETURN OF THE NATIVE (three volumes, 1878); The TRUMPET-MAJOR (three volumes, 1880); A PAIR OF BLUE EYES (two volumes, 1886), and The MAYOR OF CASTERBRIDGE (two volumes, 1886). The firm also published CORNHILL MAGAZINE.

George Murray Smith, elder son of the founder of Cornhill, was with Smith, Elder from 1881 to 1890 (Letters I, 127). In May 1885, Hardy went to a gathering at the London home of Lady CARNARVON and wrote Emma HARDY that Murray Smith had been among those present and was "very warm" (Letters I, 133).

Smith, Jane The mother of Stephen SMITH in A PAIR OF BLUE EYES and the wife of John SMITH, she is a "matron whose countenance addressed itself to the mind rather than to the eye" and exhibits a "sound common sense." She is an excellent cook and has a good relationship with her husband and son.

Smith, John Master mason for Lord LUXELLIAN in A PAIR OF BLUE EYES, the husband of Jane SMITH, and the father of Stephen SMITH, he has "too much individuality" to be "a typical working-man'"; he is capable of handling bricks, gardening, and felling and sawing trees. Well-linked in the village, he encourages Stephen, who is courting Elfride SWANCOURT, to tell her father the truth about his background.

Smith, Stephen Fitzmaurice A young architect in A PAIR OF BLUE EYES. As Hardy himself had done, he comes to CORNWALL to prepare plans for the restoration of a church. At Endelstow Rectory he falls in love with Elfride SWANCOURT. Neither she nor her father, the Reverend Christopher SWANCOURT, realizes that he is a native of the village, the son of John SMITH, the master mason of Lord LUXELLIAN, who lives nearby. Stephen has learned Latin and Greek by corresponding with a friend, Henry KNIGHT. When Rev. Swancourt learns of Stephen's origins he withholds his consent to the marriage. Elfride and Stephen elope, but she has doubts about a clandestine marriage ceremony and returns home. Stephen leaves for India, where he achieves success and fame. He comes back to Endelstow at the height of Henry Knight's courtship of Elfride; disheartened, he returns to India. Henry and Stephen later meet in London, discuss Elfride, and set off separately to seek her hand. En route they discover that their train is carrying a coffin with her body; she married Lord Luxellian but died after a miscarriage.

"Snow in the Suburbs" Poem collected in HUMAN SHOWS, FAR PHANTASIES, SONGS, AND TRIFLES (1925). Hardy watches a snowstorm in progress, presumably from a window, seeing that every branch of a tree is "big with it" and every branching fork is "like a white web-foot." A sparrow is overturned by a "snow-lump thrice his own slight size"; he flies to a "nether twig," setting off "a volley of other lodging lumps with a rush." In the last four-line stanza, he recalls the "blanched slope" of the steps, up which "with feeble hope, / A black cat comes." He is "wide-eyed and thin," but the poem ends on a note of hope: "And we take him in."

The manuscript has an erased title, "Snow at Upper Tooting" (Purdy, Thomas Hardy: A Bibliographical Study, 237). The Hardys lived at The Larches, No. 1 Arundel Terrace, Trinity Road, Upper Tooting, LONDON, from 1878 to 1881.

Society for the Protection of Ancient Buildings Trained as an architect, Hardy was a member of this Society for 48 years. He was always in great sympathy with its work and was often consulted about the restoration and preservation of early churches.

In October 1881 Charles George Vinall, then secretary of the society, wrote Hardy about a problem connected with Wimborne minster. This was the subject of Hardy's poem "Copying Architecture in an Old Minster." He replied that he was only a temporary resident of Wimborne, but would be glad to assist the society in any way he could (Letters I, 95).

In December 1889 Hardy wrote Hugh Thackeray TURNER, then secretary of the society, reporting a rumor that the church of the village of Stratton (within two or three miles of DORCHESTER) was to be pulled down. He told Turner that "judicious repair" was all that was necessary (Letters I, 205).

In October 1902 Hardy wrote the Reverend Edward Filleul, rector of All Saints' Church, Dorchester, where some restoration was contemplated. Hardy was concerned that no elevations of the church had been made, but suggested that an early sketch of the building might be among the "musty records" of the original building firm (*Letters* III, 35).

On June 20, 1906, Hardy's important essay, "MEMORIES OF CHURCH RESTORATION," was delivered before the General Meeting of the Society for the Protection of Ancient Buildings in London. It was read in his absence by an architect, Colonel Eustace James Anthony Balfour. The essay was reprinted in *CORNHILL MAGAZINE* (August 1906), as well as in Ernest Brennecke, ed., *The Life and Art of Thomas Hardy* (New York: 1925).

Hardy was particularly concerned with the protection of FORDINGTON ST. GEORGE CHURCH in Dorchester. In November 1906 he wrote the secretary of the society to protest plans to destroy the chancel of the church (*Letters* III, 236). Between 1906 and 1927, the church was subjected to renovations that greatly increased its size and dismayed Hardy (Millgate, *Thomas Hardy*, 423).

For further reading: The Architectural Notebook of Thomas Hardy; Beatty, "Hardy the Architect"; Betjeman, "Hardy and Architecture"; Cox, "The Poet and the Architect"; Moore,"The Poet within the Architect's Ring."

"Society of Dorset Men in London" Organization founded in 1904 by William Watkins; he invited Hardy to a meeting in July of that year. Hardy declined, but wished it every success and hoped such an association might change DORSET's reputation as one of "the most narrow-minded of English counties" (*Letters* III, 129). The society is still in existence.

The inaugural dinner, to which Hardy was invited by Sir Frederick TREVES, a DORCHESTER friend, was held in 1905. He was unable to attend, but took much interest in the group, serving first as vice president and then, from 1907 to 1909, as president.

In 1906 Hardy wrote to apologize for being away from MAX GATE when members of the society planned to tour Dorset. He said that he had, in a sense, already welcomed them to the neighborhood "in a rather lengthy speech of some twenty volumes" [of his writings]. He hoped they would consider them as "delivered on the occasion" (Millgate, *Thomas Hardy*, 421).

In December 1907 Hardy wrote A. M. Broadley to see whether he might help locate some Dorset psalm tunes the society had asked him to find. They had to be related to Dorset: "composed by Dorset men, much sung in Dorset, or bearing names of Dorset places." Hardy knew of "Wareham," but was seeking additional ones (*Letters* III, 285).

In April 1908 Hardy was invited to give the presidential address at the annual dinner on May 11. As usual, he refused to deliver it himself, pleading an attack of influenza, but sent a copy to London. He was irritated to discover it was not read at the dinner, nor was it read at the annual meeting on November 13, 1908, as William Watkins feared other speeches might take all the time available (*Letters* III, 312). Watkins called it a "marvellous piece of writing" (*Letters* VII, 146).

Stage versions of several of Hardy's works were performed before the society or presented by them: *FAR FROM THE MADDING CROWD* on November 24, 1909 (*Letters* IV, 46), "The MELLSTOCK QUIRE on December 1, 1910 (*Letters* IV, 129), *The WOODLANDERS* on December 8, 1913 (*Letters* IV, 325), and *The RETURN OF THE NATIVE* on January 27, 1921 (*Letters* VI, 57).

Solentsea Fictional name for Southsea, near Bournemouth, in *The HAND OF ETHELBERTA*.

Some Recollections Volume of reminiscences written by Hardy's first wife, Emma Gifford HARDY, over several years before her death in November 1912. The manuscript, which Hardy found after her death, was dated January 4, 1911. The book consists of 74 brief sketches of memories of her childhood in Plymouth; dramatic productions mounted by her siblings and neighboring children; their schools; her various relatives; the family's move to Bodmin, CORNWALL; her sister Helen's marriage to the Reverend Caddell HOLDER, rector of ST. JULIOT CHURCH, Cornwall; and the appearance there of "The Architect" (Hardy), who had been sent to restore the church. The memoir ends with Hardy's courtship of Emma and their marriage.

Emma writes that her parents, three brothers, and sister, continually talked of books at home and with friends at teas. They had access to the public library at the Mechanics; Institute in Plymouth. They read Charles Dickens, William Makepeace THACKERAY, Anthony Trollope, Edward Bulwer-Lytton, Walter SCOTT, and Harriet Beecher Stowe. Mr. Gifford, an attorney, loved SHAKESPEARE and frequently quoted his works. Her mother read the Bible with "exceeding diligence." Emma's piety later became a source of difficulty with Hardy, whose religious views as expressed in his fiction and poetry were unorthodox and sometimes incomprehensible to Emma.

The volume is illustrated with sketches by Emma and Hardy, as well as with photographs. As published in 1961, the volume, edited with notes by Evelyn Hardy and Robert Gittings, includes several poems relevant to Emma by Hardy.

Somers, Alfred Character in *The WELL-BELOVED*. He is a longtime friend of Jocelyn PIERSTON, and a painter with a studio in Mellstock Gardens, London. He marries the widow who had once interested Pierston, Mrs. Nichola PINE-AVON. Once as "youthful" and "picturesque" as his paintings, he becomes a "middle-aged family man with spectacles, "observing his "row of daughters" on the Budmouth esplanade.

Somerset, George   The hero of *A LAODICEAN*, a novel set mainly in the county of Somerset. As a young architect, he reflects many of Hardy's own experiences as an architect in DORCHESTER, LONDON, and WEYMOUTH. Pinion remarks that George Somerset, like Hardy, attaches more importance to "poetry, theology, and the reorganization of society" than to the profession of architecture (Pinion, *A Thomas Hardy Dictionary*, 252). He is stalwart and persistent in his ultimately successful pursuit of Paula POWER.

"Son's Veto, The"   Story published in the *Illustrated London News*, December 1, 1891, with two illustrations by A. Forestier. It was later collected in *LIFE'S LITTLE IRONIES* (1894; Purdy, *Thomas Hardy: A Bibliographical Study*, 81).

The story begins in a LONDON park at a bandstand, where a young woman with an elaborately braided coiffure, in a wheeled chair, attends a concert. She is accompanied by a boy of about 13, who wears a public school uniform and calls her "mother." He wheels her home, correcting her grammar. The narrator then flashes back to her history.

As a girl of 19, from the village of Gaymead, near ALDBRICKHAM, Sophy works as a parlor maid in the home of a Mr. Twycott, a parson. His wife dies and she sets out to notify her parents, who live in the same village. Sam Hobson, the vicar's young gardener, escorts her home and tells her he will soon be able to offer her her own home. She tells the vicar she wishes to leave and marry Sam, who will provide a home for her. The vicar realizes he cannot do without her; she is a "kitten-like, flexuous, tender creature." She stays in the household, although another girl leaves. Carrying a tray to the vicar one day when he is ill, she slips on the stairs and twists her foot. She is told she must not strain it by standing long on her feet. She tries to resign, but the vicar, upset by the prospect of her departure, proposes to her. She assents. Mr. Twycott knows he has committed "social suicide" by marrying her. He finds a church in the south of London and they move. Her language fails to equal his, despite years of tutoring. She gives birth to a son, Randolph, on whose education the vicar spares no expense. Randolph comes to perceive and be embarrassed by her deficiencies. Sophy walks little and braids her hair a great deal.

Mr. Twycott dies, and Sophy lives in a little villa he has provided for her, on a busy road. The son is to finish school, go on to Oxford, and be ordained. Randolph becomes increasingly snobbish. Early one

morning Sophy sees a procession of wagons filled with produce going toward Covent Garden. Walking beside one of them is Sam Hobson, from Gaymead. She calls to him; he is now manager at a market-gardener's in South London. He has learned of her widowhood and managed to secure his present job, hoping to see her. She admits she is very unhappy and tells him about her son. She says she will never be a "lady" but that her son is a "gentleman."

One day Sam invites her to ride to Covent Garden and lifts her into his wagon. He tells her he wishes to become a greengrocer in Aldbrickham, and proposes to her. She says that she will lose everything she has if she remarries. She would also have to tell her son. Sam says she is the adult, not her son. She decides to tell Randolph at a public school cricket match, but she can't manage to do so. When she does tell him she is considering remarrying, he says he hopes she will choose a gentleman. She explains who Sam is, and Randolph bursts into tears, claiming it would ruin him and "degrade" him "in the eyes of all the gentlemen of England." Meanwhile, Sam has secured his shop. He implores Sophy to marry him, but Randolph finally asks her to kneel before a little altar in his room and swear that she will not marry Sam.

By the time Randolph is ordained, his education has "sufficiently ousted his humanity to keep him quite firm." Sophy becomes more and more withdrawn. About four years later, her funeral procession goes through Aldbrickham. Sam, a prosperous greengrocer, watches with wet eyes.

Shigeru Fujita, a Japanese scholar, considers that Randolph represents urban sophistication, Sam is aligned with ruralism, and Sophy is "a child of nature at the mercy of these two sets of values" (Gerber and Davis, *Thomas Hardy: An Annotated Bibliography of Writings about Him*, 684). This interpretation does not, however, take into account the rigid English class structure of which Randolph is clearly a contemptible product, despite his ordination, and which neither Sophy nor her husband can contest. The move to South London does not transform Sophy but only forces her to repress her roots, much to the detriment of her son's character. Only Sam represents the virtues of true gentility, sensitivity, steadfastness, and patience—qualities he shares with Gabriel OAK of *FAR FROM THE MADDING CROWD*. The story is also a commentary on the lack of Christianity in the church itself, a theme Hardy would explore more fully in *JUDE THE OBSCURE*.

A. E. Coppard, writing in 1931, argues that the story makes it clear that Hardy's "real mission was to write stories, not poetry" (Gerber and Davis, *Thomas Hardy: An Annotated Bibliography of Writings about Him*, 351).

For further reading: Coppard, "On First Getting into Print"; Fujita, "Symbolism in 'The Son's Veto'"; Ray, "Thomas Hardy's 'The Son's Veto': A Textual History."

Sophocles (496–406 B.C.) Greek tragic dramatist. Of more than 100 plays he wrote, only seven tragedies and part of another play survive. His influence may be seen in Hardy's novels and especially in Hardy's underlying thesis of the amorality of nature, incomprehensible to humans, and his insistence on the search for truth and understanding in relation to the existing moral order. Hardy admired the survival of Sophocles' intellectual powers, writing Hall CAINE that Sophocles had produced some of his best tragedies when nearly 90 (*Letters* V, 246). As a young man Hardy began reading his plays in Greek, but his friend Horace MOULE persuaded him not to continue if he were planning to earn his living as an architect. Hardy "secretly wished" Moule had advised him to continue (*Life*, 33). In January 1912 Hardy attended Max Reinhardt's production of *Oedipus Rex* at Covent Garden (*Letters* V, 198).

"Souls of the Slain, The" Poem written in December 1899, first published in *CORNHILL MAGAZINE* in April 1900, and later collected in *POEMS OF THE PAST AND THE PRESENT* (1902). Hardy added a note when it was published in *Cornhill:* "The spot indicated in the following poem is the Bill of Portland, which stands, roughly, on a line drawn from South Africa to the middle of the United Kingdom." He explained that, if a bird made a flight along a "great circle" of the earth, from South Africa through the British Isles, he might land at Portland Bill.

The poem has 16 six-line stanzas. The speaker begins from the vantage point of the Bill of Portland, where he is alone at night. He feels he must "brood and be still." Beside him there is "the Race," a turbulent area of churning tides off the Bill of Portland. Suddenly many night-moths whirr past, and deposit, on the bluff, the spirits or souls of soldiers slain while at war.

From the north there approaches a "senior soul-flame, " the leader of the slain men. They tell him they are going homeward to "feast on our fame." He tells them he has already flown there, and has learned that their kin have forgotten their glorious deeds. Mothers think of them as active boys or babies with "quaint ways." Their fathers wish they had set their sons to "some humble trade" so they would not have had any "passionate martial desire" to go to war. The men ask the general to reassure them that their sweethearts have been loyal. He tells them some have found new loves. Those who are married ask whether their wives dwell on their deeds. Their leader says they think of their glory less than their old "homely acts."

Some of the spirits regret raising the tomb door, others insist that they once prized fame but now prize love. The spirits then disband in two groups: those whose "record was lovely and true" went northward toward home (i.e., England). Others left the land and flew seaward. They bent over the tides of the Race, "That

engulphing, ghast, sinister place—Whither headlong they plunged, to the fathomless regions / Of myriads forgot." The first group went homeward "Like the Pentecost Wind; / And the whirr of their wayfaring thinned / And surceased on the sky, and but left in the gloaming / Sea-mutterings and me."

South, John The father of Marty SOUTH in *The WOODLANDERS.* As he lies ill, he fancies that a tall elm outside his window will blow down and kill him. Giles WINTERBORNE cuts down the tree, but the sight of the vacant space is too great a shock and South dies. His death signals the end of his family's lease on their land, which passes into the hands of Felice CHARMOND. Hardy deplored this system of landholding, which caused great anxiety to farm tenants, in his article "The DORSETSHIRE LABOURER."

South, Marty Country girl in *The WOODLANDERS.* She sells her long hair to obtain medical treatment for her father, and meekly loves Giles WINTERBORNE, who has long loved Grace Melbury. Grace finally realizes, after Giles dies, that Marty, more than she herself, "approximated to Winterborne's level of intelligent intercourse with Nature." It was Marty who knew, intuitively, everything about the crops, animals, and woodland. Marty toils to continue making cider, using Giles's cider press, assisted by the faithful Creedle.

Sparks, Tryphena (1851–1890) Hardy's cousin, with whom, according to some critics, he was in love when he was a young man. The daughter of his mother's sister, Maria Hand Sparks, she was 11 years younger than he. Robert Gittings states that they took walks on the heath between Hardy's home at HIGHER BOCKHAMPTON and hers at Puddletown. Hardy might have given her a ring, which she returned when she met and became engaged to Charles Gale (appendix, *Young Thomas Hardy,* 315–16).

According to Gittings, in 1966 two scholars, Lois Deacon and Terry Coleman, published a book called *Providence and Mr. Hardy* which argued that Hardy and Tryphena had been engaged. In 1971 F. R. Southerington published *Hardy's Vision of Man,* which contained a photograph of a boy said to be the illegitimate son of Hardy and Tryphena.

In December 1877, Tryphena married Charles Frederick Gale of Topsham, Devon; they had four children. One of their daughters, Eleanor Tryphena Bromell, told Lois Deacon in 1959 of an "understanding" between Hardy and Tryphena. Mrs. Bromell was then 80. Tryphena's own daughter considered it a formal engagement. Gittings considers the story this far to be accurate and a valuable "adjunct" to a large-scale biography of Hardy. Deacon, however, then arrived at the idea of an illegitimate son. She selected at random a photograph of an unidentified boy from the Gale family album; Mrs. Bromell then identified it as a "little boy who used to come and see Tryphena at Plymouth." Gittings considers this remark "baffling." Lois Deacon kept showing Mrs. Bromell the photograph for several years, receiving the same answer. Just before her death, when her mind was confused, Mrs. Bromell told Deacon he was "Hardy's boy" and a "cousin." She called him "Randy," short for Randolph or Randal, and also "Henery." Gittings observes that Emma HARDY had a nephew named Randolph and Hardy an uncle named Henery. Mrs. Bromell said the boy had been raised by Tryphena's sister, Rebecca, and then by her brother, Nathaniel. She never stated unequivocally that he was the illegitimate son of Hardy and Tryphena, and few scholars today believe they had such a child. There is no mention of him in the voluminous Sparks family letters, and he is generally considered a myth. Gittings attributes the entire story to Deacon's "preconceived theories" (Appendix, *The Young Thomas Hardy*).

Most scholars believe Hardy's poem "THOUGHTS OF PHENA AT NEWS OF HER DEATH" is an account of Tryphena. In his diary for March 5, 1890, he states that he wrote the first four to six lines in a train going to London. The woman he was thinking of, "a cousin," was dying at the time; her actual death occurred "six days later," although he did not realize it. The actual death of Tryphena Sparks was on March 17, more than six days after Hardy began writing the poem. He finished it after her death (Bailey, *The Poetry of Thomas Hardy*, 93–95).

For further reading: Bartle, "Some Fresh Information about Tryphena Sparks: Thomas Hardy's Cousin"; Cox, "Tryphena Sparks and 'Young Thomas Hardy'"; Gittings, "Hardy and Tryphena Sparks" (appendix, *Young Thomas Hardy*).

Spasskaia, Vera Mikhailovna (1855–1938)   Translator. A Russian, she translated into Russian from several languages. On July 31, 1892, she wrote Hardy, saying she was a "translatress" employed by the periodical *Russian Thought*. She asked permission to translate TESS OF THE D'URBERVILLES into Russian. She asked a number of questions about the novel, which she had read in the Tauchnitz edition (published in Leipzig: Bernard TAUCHNITZ's Collection of British Authors).

Hardy replied on August 26, 1892, that she had his full permission to make such a translation; he requested only that she send him a copy of it when it was finished. However, she became ill after completing 29 chapters, writing Hardy to this effect in May 1893. The translation was to be completed by another translator. Some of the novel appeared in monthly numbers of the Russian periodical *Russkaia mysl* (March–August 1893). It is unclear in which periodi-

cal the remainder of the translation, finished by someone else, was published (Purdy, *Thomas Hardy: A Bibliographical Study*, I, 283).

***Spectator*, the**   British weekly periodical, founded in 1828. From 1861 to 1897 it was under the joint editorship of Richard Holt Hutton and his brother John Hutton, and from 1898 to 1925 it was edited by John St. Loe Strachey, cousin of the biographer Lytton Strachey.

The reviewers were sometimes harsh in their criticism of Hardy's novels. In 1871 the *Spectator* published an unfavorable review of DESPERATE REMEDIES; Hardy characterized the periodical as bringing down "its heaviest-leaded pastoral staff" on volumes that had been praised in the *Athenaeum* and other publications (*Life*, 84–85). Purdy states that the review was so savage "Hardy never forgot his bitterness and discouragement on first reading it" (Purdy, *Thomas Hardy: A Bibliographical Study*, 5). Their reception of A PAIR OF BLUE EYES in 1873 was more favorable; it was called a "really powerful story, well proportioned in its parts" (*Letters* I, 22). Hardy's novel FAR FROM THE MADDING CROWD was published anonymously in the CORNHILL MAGAZINE (Jan.–Dec. 1874). A writer for the *Spectator* imagined that it might have been written by George ELIOT but declared that if it were not, "then there is a new light among novelists." Hardy's identity was revealed in a review the following month, February 1874 (Purdy, *Thomas Hardy: A Bibliographical Study*, 16–18).

In 1906 the periodical published "The Ejected Member's Wife" (in the WESSEX EDITION the title became "The Rejected One's Wife.") The poem "AFTER THE VISIT" was published in its pages in August 1910. The poem "In Time of Slaughter" was printed there in August 1916; the title later became "When I Weekly Knew" and it was collected in MOMENTS OF VISION (1917) as "QUID HIC AGIS?" (Purdy, *Thomas Hardy: A Bibliographical Study*, 188).

"Spectre of the Real, The"   A story Hardy wrote with Florence HENNIKER, published in *To-Day* in November 1894, with five illustrations by H. R. Millar. They had written the story in October 1893. In the *Life*, Hardy notes that at the end of 1893, he had finished his LONDON engagements, "which included the final revision with Mrs. Henniker of a weird story in which they had collaborated" (*Life*, 261).

The story, Hardy's only acknowledged collaboration, is reprinted in *Thomas Hardy: The Excluded and Collaborative Stories*, edited with introduction, explanatory notes, and textual notes by Pamela Dalziel. Dalziel observes that Hardy was attracted to Henniker and wished to establish an "intimate friendship." Mrs. Henniker, however, had no thought of a "romantic liaison," and she believes that their collaboration, although of no professional benefit to him, was Hardy's way of ensuring that they would correspond and meet from time to time. Rosemarie Morgan believes, however, that Florence Henniker was more interested in Hardy than she admitted. She points out that Florence wrote him frequently, sometimes several times in one day, for nearly 20 years. They met regularly in London for plays and dinners, and, when apart, wrote frequent notes to each other (personal communication with the author).

Dalziel has made a close examination of the text and refutes Richard Purdy's theory (to which Michael Millgate, Simon Gatrell, and Jeffrey S. Cramer also subscribe) that Hardy provided the outline for the story and Henniker filled it in. Dalziel argues that "Desire," the initial "sketch" Hardy sent Henniker, was far more than an outline. There were problems from the beginning, however, because Hardy and Henniker had conflicting views of fiction. He suggested putting it aside in favor of a "still better story," but she declined to do so. Dalziel traces the course of their collaboration and concludes that the plot was the work of Hardy and the "detailed working out of events" was Henniker's contribution. She notes that Hardy's collaboration with Henniker must have seemed "inexplicable" to critics, and marked a "turning point" in their "literary relationship." Henniker's status was elevated publicly, but there was no subsequent effort to collaborate. Shorter wished at one point to represent Hardy as the coauthor of Henniker's stories, which would have increased sales of his magazine. Hardy adamantly refused, but did assist in placing her fiction from time to time (Dalziel, "Introduction" to "The Spectre of the Real").

The story begins with a girl, Rosalys Ambrose, leaving a country manor house at ten o'clock one night to join a young officer, Jim Durrant. She says she must break off with him, as her family will not allow such an alliance. He argues that her family turned his out of their freehold, and that his lineage is older. She and her mother are to go to London; she begs Jim to come also. He consents on the condition that she secretly marry him there. Their marriage could not be known for a time, as he will not be able to support her and could not take her abroad.

Part two is set in fashionable Eaton Place, in London. Rosalys emerges from a town house, on the way to her wedding. She encounters Jim's father, Mr. Durrant, a busy land agent, who is temporarily in London for his employer, Lord Parkhurst. He invites her to tea with him and his wife and Jim, whom he calls a "lazy young beggar," also in town. She meets Jim at the church, where she learns he has lied about having lived in London for 15 days (a prerequisite for marriage). They marry, adjourn for luncheon, then separate.

In part three, Mr. Durrant has returned to the country; Jim is staying in town and sees Rosalys when he can, at hotel luncheons and teas. His passion begins to wane, however, and she begins to hate their deceit. They quarrel: he feels he has lost his freedom; she feels he is humiliating her. She hates him for forcing her to behave surreptitiously; he says "most girls" with her upbringing would not have come out to secret meetings with him. Both know their romance has died.

Part four begins with Rosalys and Jim meeting in August in the country. Rosalys's mother is not well, and Jim is about to leave for "years." They stroll to an old summerhouse, but quarrel. Jim argues that no one would ever know they had married in the church in East London. They decide to pretend it never happened. Coming out of the summerhouse, they meet Jim's parents and Rosalys's mother.

Part Five opens seven years later. Mrs. Ambrose has died. Rosalys has not heard from Jim, and is engaged to marry Lord Oswald Parkhurst. They are to dine with his uncle, Colonel Lacy.

In Part six, Rosalys and Lord Parkhurst enter Colonel Lacy's drawing room and find Jim Durrant there. He has learned of Rosalys's forthcoming marriage and returned to talk with her. He says he will not stop her from marrying Parkhurst, but then persuades her to sleep with him.

In Part seven Jim confesses he has a "Mrs. Durrant" at a London hotel. Rosalys frantically writes a letter to Lord Parkhurst. In the morning a maid informs her Mr. Durrant has drowned in the meads near the river. Rosalys puts the letter in her pocket and marries Lord Parkhurst. They leave for Dover and the Continent. The morning papers inform Colonel Lacy that Lord Parkhurst has shot himself early in the morning in the Dove hotel. "No reason can be assigned for the rash act." It is implied that he had been told about Rosalys' marriage to Durrant.

It is probable that the ending was Hardy's, as, according to Dalziel, Henniker wrote Coulson Kernahan that the story "is not really a *sympathetic*, or pleasant story. For, before the tragedy of the close, *some* of it might have been more agreeable" (Dalziel, introduction, to her edition of the story, 286).

For further reading: Cramer, "'The Spectre of the Real' by Thomas Hardy and Florence Henniker"; Dalziel, "Hardy as Collaborator: The Composition of 'The Spectre of the Real'"; Dalziel, ed., *Thomas Hardy: The Excluded and Collaborative Stories* (includes "The Spectre of the Real"); Evelyn Hardy and Pinion, eds., *One Rare Fair Woman: Thomas Hardy's Letters to Florence Henniker 1893–1922.*

Sphere, the Periodical founded and edited by Clement King SHORTER. Several of Hardy's works were published in the *Sphere,* including the poems "At the War Office After a Bloody Battle," "The LOST PYX," "The MAN HE KILLED," "The DEAD AND THE LIVING ONE," and "TO MEET, OR OTHERWISE." The short stories "A

CHANGED MAN" and "BENIGHTED TRAVELLERS" were also first published in the magazine.

A portrait of Hardy's mother was reproduced in the issue of April 23, 1904 (she had died on April 3, 1904).

Hardy's second wife, Florence Dugdale HARDY, was a reviewer for the magazine. On February 21, 1914, Shorter published a photograph of her, along with one of her with Hardy and Edward CLODD at Aldeburgh. In June 1916 Hardy wrote his friend Florence HENNIKER that his wife had just sent six reviews of other books to Shorter (*Letters* V, 166). In May 1917 he wrote Henniker that Florence was still keeping up her reviewing, but was planning to drop it, not having "sufficient spare time with the household to look after, & the garden also," which she had taken on, much to his relief (*Letters* V, 215).

Spicer-Simson, Theodore (1871–1959)   American sculptor and portrait medalist. He sculpted portrait medallions from life of many world and literary figures during the first half of the 20th century, including a bronze medallion of Hardy in 1921. His writings and works are held in an archive at the University of Miami, Miami, Florida. *See* PORTRAITS AND BUSTS OF THOMAS HARDY.

For further reading: Men of Letters of the British Isles: Portrait Medallions from the Life by Theodore Spicer-Simson (New York: W. E. Rudge, 1924).

Springrove, Edward   A young architect and the principal male character in *DESPERATE REMEDIES* (1871). At the time Hardy wrote the novel, his first after the unpublished *The POOR MAN AND THE LADY*, Hardy was a trained architect and had experience with church restoration, especially at ST. JULIOT CHURCH in CORNWALL. Springrove is, like Hardy, of unpretentious origins, being the son of a local farmer, but he is also a poet who knows SHAKESPEARE "to the very dregs of the footnotes." He is an ardent, often frustrated, but ultimately successful, suitor of Cytherea GRAYE.

"Squire Petrick's Lady"   *See GROUP OF NOBLE DAMES, A.*

Squire, J(ohn) C(ollings) (1884–1958)   Poet, man of letters, and editor of the *LONDON MERCURY*. The first number of this literary monthly was in November 1919. Squire published Hardy's poem "A Glimpse from the Train" in the January 1920 issue (it was later retitled "FAINTHEART IN A RAILWAY TRAIN" and collected in *LATE LYRICS AND EARLIER*). In June 1919 Squire contributed a poem to the "POETS' TRIBUTE" TO HARDY.

Squire gave a radio broadcast in honor of Hardy's 84th birthday, June 2, 1923, called "An Appreciation of the Life and Work of Thomas Hardy." It was broadcast over the London and Bournemouth stations of the BBC. Apparently Florence HARDY was in on the plan, because on June 3 Hardy wrote Squire a letter saying he

had been "inveigled into setting up (i.e., persuaded to set up) Wireless." He declared that he had not known what was going to happen. The preceding evening they had heard his lecture, "every word, beautifully delivered we thought." He thanked Squire for taking the trouble to give it, and added, "Our dog listened attentively" (*Letters* VI, 251–53).

The same year, Squire dedicated his poetry collection *American Poems and Others* to Hardy, who wrote a gracious letter of appreciation. He mentioned several poems by name, including one called "The Stockyard" that he said had a "paralyzing attraction" (*Letters* VI, 199). Squire compiled and edited several poetry anthologies, including *A Book of Women's Verse* (1921) and *Poems in One Volume* (1926).

Stephen, Sir Leslie (1832–1904)   Writer, philosopher, editor, alpine climber, and man of letters; father of Virginia WOOLF and the artist Vanessa Bell. He was the editor of the *Dictionary of National Biography* and highly respected in intellectual circles in England at the end of the 19th century. He was also editor of *CORNHILL MAGAZINE*, and, having read *UNDER THE GREENWOOD TREE*, wrote Hardy to ask for a serial story for the *Cornhill*. Hardy replied that the novel he had just finished was "arranged for" (*A PAIR OF BLUE EYES*), but he was about to embark on another one, in which the main characters would probably be "a young woman-farmer, a shepherd, and a sergeant of cavalry." Stephen replied with interest and Hardy sent him part of *FAR FROM THE MADDING CROWD* in September 1873. The first installment, illustrated by Helen PATERSON, appeared on newsstands in December 1873, to Hardy's surprise and delight (*Life*, 95–98). Stephen's acceptance of the novel and the friendship that ensued were events of paramount importance in Hardy's literary career.

Stephen later solicited *The HAND OF ETHELBERTA* but declined *The TRUMPET-MAJOR* for the *Cornhill*. His daughter Virginia Woolf and her husband, Leonard WOOLF, published Stephen's book *Some Early Impressions* in 1924; they owned and operated the Hogarth Press in London.

In June 1897 Hardy wrote a sonnet about Stephen, "The SCHRECKHORN." He compared the "spare and desolate" Schreckhorn with Stephen's personality, which, like the mountain, had "quaint glooms, keen lights, and rugged trim." Virginia Woolf called it "incomparably the truest & most imaginative portrait of him in existence" (*Letters* 76–77).

Stevens, Henry (1819–1886)   American bookseller who lived in London and was the agent for several collectors and libraries, in addition to being the business representative of the Boston publishing firm HOUGHTON, MIFFLIN & CO. This firm published the *ATLANTIC MONTHLY*, which serialized TWO ON A TOWER from May to December 1882. In May 1882 Hardy invited Stevens to one of the monthly dinners at the RABELAIS CLUB (*Letters* I, 95).

Stevenson, Robert Louis (1850–1894)   Scottish writer and man of letters, the author of *Treasure Island, Kidnapped, The Strange Case of Dr. Jekyll and Mr. Hyde, The Body Snatcher and Other Stories,* and many other works.

In 1896 Hardy was invited to attend a meeting in Edinburgh to plan a memorial to Stevenson. He replied that distance would prevent his going, but that he was in "cordial agreement" with the proposal of the committee, and believed "no more fitting place could be found for the inception of their design" than Edinburgh, the city Stevenson "knew and loved so well" (*Letters* VII, 129–30).

In 1922 Hardy contributed a sketch, "Robert Louis Stevenson," to a collection of personal reminiscences of the writer, *I Can Remember Robert Louis Stevenson,* compiled by Rosaline Masson. He recalled meeting Stevenson only a few times, once at a dinner given by Sir Sidney Colvin, Keeper of Prints and Drawings at the BRITISH MUSEUM. He remembered more vividly Stevenson's unexpected visit to MAX GATE in August 1885. Stevenson, his wife, her son, and her cousin had been staying in DORCHESTER at the King's Arms Hotel on their way to Dartmoor. Stevenson was eager to see the room in which Hardy wrote, but, because the Hardys had just moved into the house, he was able to show him only a "temporary corner."

After *The* MAYOR OF CASTERBRIDGE was published in May of 1886 Stevenson wrote Hardy for permission to dramatize it. Hardy replied that the idea made him feel "several inches taller," and gave him permission, but the dramatization was never completed. Hardy was hurt about Stevenson's ensuing silence, writing in his essay that "to my vision he dropped into utter darkness from that date: I recall no further sight of or communication from him." When TESS OF THE D'URBERVILLES was published in 1891 Stevenson gave an interview stating that he disapproved of the morals in the novel. Hardy knew that he hated it and deduced that his reaction to the novel "probably had led to his silence" ("Robert Louis Stevenson," 214–16).

For further reading: Thomas Hardy, "Robert Louis Stevenson."

Stinsford   One of three hamlets outside DORCHESTER making up an entity Hardy calls MELLSTOCK. The other two are HIGHER BOCKHAMPTON, where Hardy was born, and Lower Bockhampton. Stinsford is two miles east of Dorchester. STINSFORD CHURCH, where Hardy's heart is buried in the grave of his two wives, is in this hamlet.

Stinsford Church   Hardy described this small stone church as "an interesting old church of various styles

Stinsford Church, outside Dorchester, to which the family of Thomas Hardy belonged for several generations   (Sarah Bird Wright)

from Transition-Norman to late Perpendicular" (*Life,* 9). It played an important role in his life. His mother first saw his father there; he described this scene in the sonnet "A CHURCH ROMANCE." His discussion in the *Life* includes his detailed drawing of the west gallery as it was in 1835, showing the placement of the singers and instrumentalists. His father and grandfather sang and played in the choir. Hardy's grandfather is listed as "T.H sen.," sitting in the front of the gallery, playing the violoncello and singing bass; (he eventually became superintendent of the choir); his father, "T.H. jun.," is positioned behind him, playing the violin and singing tenor. The church had no organ. The choir figures in Hardy's novel UNDER THE GREENWOOD TREE and also in the poem "The DEAD QUIRE." MELLSTOCK is Hardy's fictional name for three hamlets in Stinsford and the Bockhamptons (Hardy was born in HIGHER BOCKHAMPTON). The gallery is being restored.

Hardy had a lifelong interest in the church and, as an architect knowledgeable about construction, was often consulted about various problems. In 1914 he was asked for advice about the restoration of the historic font, which had been found in seven pieces, buried beneath rubbish in the churchyard. He believed it to be very early Norman or "even Saxon." It was restored and supplied with a new base according to his design (*Letters* V, 3–4). In 1926 he was consulted about the recasting of the historic Stinsford church bells and made a contribution to the cost. The 15th-century treble bell was recast and rehung with the other two bells, which date from the 17th century (*Letters* VII, 8).

Hardy's father died in 1892; Hardy prepared leaflets for a memorial service, including Psalm 90, to be held in the church on July 31, 1892. His mother, Jemima HARDY, was buried in the churchyard in the same tomb after her death in 1904. Hardy sent the local stonemason drawings for this and other family tombs. Hardy's first wife, Emma, was also buried in the churchyard after her death in November 1912. Hardy designed her tomb, which was inscribed "This For Remembrance." Hardy's oldest sister, Mary, was buried in the graveyard at Stinsford church in December 1915.

On November 4, 1927, Hardy and his second wife, Florence, went to Stinsford to put flowers on the family graves and then called on his brother Henry and surviving sister, Katharine, at the home of his brother, TAL-BOTHAYS. Florence, to whom the final chapter is attributed, writes, "Thus ended a series of visits paid regularly to his family extending over forty years." She notes that to Hardy the churchyard was "the most hallowed spot on earth" (*Life*, 442–43).

Hardy died on January 11, 1928. On Monday, January 16, his heart was buried in the grave of his first wife, among the Hardy tombs, in the graveyard at Stinsford church; at the same hour his ashes were interred in Poet's Corner, WESTMINSTER ABBEY, LONDON. Simulta-

Grave in Stinsford churchyard where the heart of Thomas Hardy is buried in the grave of his two wives (Sarah Bird Wright)

neously a memorial service was held at St. Peter's Church, DORCHESTER.

Stoddard, Lorimer (1864–1901) American playwright whom Hardy authorized to dramatize *TESS OF THE D'URBERVILLES* for the New York stage, with Minnie Maddern FISKE in the title role. Hardy himself had made a dramatization of the novel in five acts, "in the old English manner." Mrs. Patrick CAMPBELL wanted to play Tess in the London production, which she and Hardy discussed, but Hardy was dissatisfied with the terms and decided to arrange, through HARPER & BROTHERS, for the play to be given in New York. He wrote the publishing firm that his play had been approved by "one of our most eminent dramatic critics, & two eminent actors," and believed any stage manager would be "ill advised in making more than trifling alterations" (*Letters* II, 111–12). Stoddard made revisions in Hardy's play, which amounted, according to Richard Purdy, to a "new dramatization." It opened at the Fifth Avenue Theatre in New York on March 2, 1897, and was a great success. A reading of this play was held simultaneously at St. James's Theatre, LONDON, for copyright purposes (Purdy, *Thomas Hardy: A Bibliographical Study*, 78. *See* Appendix II, "Media Adaptations of the Works of Thomas Hardy"). Marguerite Roberts gives the texts of these dramatizations in her book *Tess in the Theatre*.

For further reading: Roberts, *Tess in the Theatre.*

Stonehenge The prehistoric (Neolithic or early Bronze Age) monument on Salisbury Plain, Wiltshire. It may have been built as early as 1680 B.C. and could have been a Bronze Age burial ground. The formation consists of standing stones in the midst of a large circular ditch 300 feet in diameter. There are two concentric circles of large upright stones enclosing two rows of smaller stones and a block of blue marble called the Altar Stone. Hardy refers to Stonehenge in several of his works: the poem "CHANNEL FIRING," the short story "Dame the Third—The Marchioness of Stonehenge" (the story is part of *A GROUP OF NOBLE DAMES*); and, most notably, in the novel *TESS OF THE D'URBERVILLES*. In Chapter 58 Tess is arrested at Stonehenge for the murder of Alec d'Urberville. Here the monument is characterized as a "forest of monoliths." Angel CLARE cries out that it is "older than the centuries; older than the d'Urbervilles!" and Tess falls asleep on the blue marble altar. As dawn breaks Angel holds her hand and the band of 16 men who have come to arrest her stand in the pre-dawn light, watching her, until she is awakened by the sun. *Tess* was published in 1891, creating a furor.

In 1899 Hardy was purportedly interviewed by a "Special Correspondent" for the *Daily Chronicle* (London), which resulted in an article or essay titled "Shall Stonehenge Go?" Orel, Purdy, and other critics believe it was written by Hardy himself. There seems to have been some discussion in the press about England's selling the "relic." Apparently at one time Stonehenge was considered to be privately owned and about to be partitioned and sold.

In this essay Hardy makes the point that Stonehenge is a "national possession" and England ought to have the "final guardianship over any monument or relic which is of value to it as a page of history," even if the history cannot be completely deciphered. He argues that Stonehenge must remain the "wonder" and "sacred possession" of Salisbury Plain and of England. The owner of property on which there is a national relic becomes, automatically, the "custodian for the nation of that relic." Hardy suggests that England should buy at least the 2,000 acres that contain Stonehenge and a surrounding tract of land.

He also discusses the effects of weather, particularly rain, on the exposed ruins and urges tree plantings outside the circles to strengthen the soil and offer some protection. He states that on a day of threatening weather the monument's "charm is indescribable" and in a gale of wind it emits a "strange musical hum." In these conditions, he says, Stonehenge is far more impressive than in brilliant sun when it is visited by people on bicycles with "sandwich papers."

For further reading: Hardy, "Shall Stonehenge Go?" In *Thomas Hardy's Personal Writings,* ed. Orel, 196–201.

Strang, William (1859–1921)   Painter and etcher who made a portrait etching of Hardy in 1893, in preparation for which he visited MAX GATE in September 1892. He made a pencil sketch of Hardy in 1919 and a number of other likenesses after that. *See* PORTRAITS AND BUSTS OF HARDY.

In 1926, Hardy wrote the Reverend Edward Mewburn Walker, Pro-Provost of QUEEN'S COLLEGE, OXFORD UNIVERSITY, of which Hardy had been an honorary fellow since 1922, to say that he had sent the sketch to the college on the chance of its being exhibited there. He said he felt ashamed at what seemed to be vanity, but said he had nothing valuable to present to express his gratitude and fondness for the hospitality he had experienced at Queen's. The portrait was hung in the Common Room Gallery (*Letters* VII, 18).

"Strange House, The" *(Max Gate, A.D. 2000)*   Poem collected in *LATE LYRICS AND EARLIER* (1922) in which Hardy imagines future residents of MAX GATE, in the year 2000, fancying that the spirits of Hardy and his first wife, Emma, are cohabiting the house. The poem is a dialogue between one who is psychic, imagining various sounds and sights, and one who sees and hears nothing except what is literally present.

The psychic speaker hears the piano (played by Emma), but learns the old one was "sold and broken";

Stonehenge, a Bronze Age sanctuary in Wiltshire that dates from 1250 B.C. and figures in Tess of the d'Urbervilles   (Steve Day for Salisbury District Council)

then seems to hear the parlor door, but "no soul's in range." He or she senses "a figure on the stair," but the other speaker sees nothing except a bough waving outside, its shade visible in moonlight. This speaker acknowledges that the other has apparently had a sense or vision of what had once happened in the house. He or she has heard tales that the house once held "two love-thralls" who perhaps "imprinted / Their dreams" on the walls. They were "Queer in their works and ways." Although some folk could not "abide" in the house, he or she insists that "we" [the present occupants] "do not care / Who loved, laughed, wept, or died here, / Knew joy or despair." Bailey points out that Hardy often "fancied old houses to emanate the presence of people who lived in them" (Bailey, *The Poetry of Thomas Hardy,* 445).

Sturminster Newton   A small town in DORSET about 15 miles from Hardy's birthplace, HIGHER BOCKHAMPTON. Thomas and Emma Hardy lived in Riverside Villa (or Rivercliff Villa), Sturminster Newton, from July 1876 to March 1878. It was here that Hardy wrote *The RETURN OF THE NATIVE* in 1877. The house is situated on a bluff overlooking the River Stour, about which Hardy wrote in his poem "OVERLOOKING THE RIVER STOUR." Another poem, "The MUSICAL BOX," also recalls the period at Riverside Villa, which Hardy remembers nostalgically as one of the happiest times of their married life. In "ON STURMINSTER FOOT-BRIDGE" Hardy returns, in a visionary way, to Sturminster Newton; Hardy depicts the bridge and the water in dark terms.

Sturminster Newton was, at the time, a market town with about 1,500 inhabitants, and the Hardys were on "calling and dining terms" with the town's leading families by the autumn of 1876. Hardy records, in his notebooks, his enjoyment of local life; he made a point of going to fairs and sideshows. Emma's brothers visited them at Sturminster and Hardy took Emma to HIGHER BOCKHAMPTON for Christmas (Millgate, *Thomas Hardy,* 180–86).

By early 1878 the Hardys had decided to move nearer London: Hardy felt this was important for his professional contacts, and Emma had decided the river was unhealthy. By this time Sturminster had recognized Hardy's importance as a writer, and when they attended a Sturminster Literary Institute concert in March 1878, two newspapers took notice (Millgate, *Thomas Hardy,* 193). Despite this local recognition, they moved to 1 Arundel Terrace, Trinity Road, Tooting, near Wandsworth Common.

"Subalterns, The"   Poem collected in POEMS OF THE PAST AND THE PRESENT (1902), in which four "subalterns" speak. Hardy was writing *The* DYNASTS at this time, and, according to James O. Bailey, the subalterns represent two forces of "outer nature" (dull weather and freezing temperatures) and two forces of "human decay" (sickness and death). The voices of dull weather are the dark leaden sky and the north wind. Sickness and death also speak. Bailey terms them four "malicious forces" that are subject to an impersonal, exterior will. The earth, although she is a spirit friendly to man, is controlled by this outside will. The will, as Bailey explains it, is a "mysterious, unconscious force" that establishes natural laws which are amoral and indifferent to man's feelings or needs (Bailey, *The Poetry of Thomas Hardy,* 146–147).

"Sunday Morning Tragedy, A" *(circa 186–)*   A ballad dated 1904, first printed in the *English Review* in December 1908, and collected in TIME'S LAUGHING-STOCKS (1909). Ford Madox Ford, the founder and editor of the *Review,* sometimes said that he had founded the magazine in order to publish this poem, which had been rejected elsewhere as being immoral. Hardy wrote John GALSWORTHY that he had wanted to produce the poem as a "tragic play" before publishing it as a ballad (Purdy, *Thomas Hardy: A Bibliographical Study,* 139).

Rivercliff Villa, Sturminster Newton, Dorset, home of Thomas and Emma Hardy from July 1876 to March 1878   (courtesy of Christine O'Connor)

The speaker, a mother, mourns a daughter she bore in "Pydel Vale." As the girl grows she is attractive to men, and one seduces her; she becomes pregnant. The mother goes to the sweetheart's door and begs him to marry her daughter, but he refuses: he plans to become a sailor and "sail the main." The mother seeks out a shepherd and asks for an "herb" for her daughter, presumably to end the pregnancy. He brings the herb the next day, saying he uses it to "balk ill-motherings" in his flock. She stirs the potion all night, and, the next morning, gives it to the girl. It makes her ill.

When the villagers come from church, the mother learns that the young man has arranged to marry her daughter and the banns have been announced in church, as a surprise. He comes to the house, but he and the mother find the girl dead.

The action takes place in the first three lines of each of the 32 stanzas, while the final line of each stanza is reserved for the mother's most profound forebodings. She blames herself and is bitterly remorseful, but begs not to be pitied. Her daughter has been wronged and is "sinless"; the fault lies with the irresponsible young man.

Swancourt, Christopher The father of Elfride SWANCOURT in A PAIR OF BLUE EYES. A widower, he is the rector of Endelstow church on the Cornish coast. He is a learned man and an excellent chess player who has taught his daughter to play as well. He is socially snobbish, and initially encourages Stephen SMITH in his courtship of Elfride. Learning that Smith is the son of a local mason, however, Swancourt turns against him. Swancourt then marries a rich widow, Charlotte TROYTON, the aunt of Henry KNIGHT. (Knight, by chance, is the tutor of Stephen). Swancourt is related to the aristocratic Luxellian family through marriage to Elfride's mother.

Swancourt, Elfride The heroine of A PAIR OF BLUE EYES. She is the daughter of Christopher SWANCOURT and the granddaughter of Lady Elfride LUXELLIAN, who eloped with the singer Arthur Kingsmore. Elfride's mother, long deceased when the events of the novel take place, had eloped with Mr. Swancourt. Sensitive and intelligent, Elfride often composes her father's sermons, is a very good chess player, and writes a novel, *The Court of King Arthur's Castle*. She falls in love with Stephen SMITH, a young architect, but her father does not consider his family to be good enough. She then falls in love with Smith's close friend Henry KNIGHT and saves his life, but he deserts her. She marries Lord LUXELLIAN, whose delicate wife has died, leaving two young daughters, but Elfride then dies young.

Swinburne, Algernon Charles (1837–1909) English poet and man of letters who rebelled against Victorian religion and social conventions. An admirer of Victor Hugo and Percy Bysshe Shelley, he sympathized with various revolutionary political movements and was influenced by the Pre-Christian pagan spirit of Greece, Elizabethan drama, and medieval romance. As a young man he was eccentric and dissipated. His behavior shocked "respectable" people, and his friends feared for his health, which was threatened by alcoholism. The critic Theodore Watts-Dunton took Swinburne into his home at Putney in 1879, acting as friend and guardian for the remaining 30 years of his life.

Swinburne's major works include the poetic drama *Atalanta in Calydon, Tristram of Lyonesse, Astrophel, Essays and Studies, Hymn to Artemis, Hymn to Proserpine,* and *The Triumph of Time.* He also wrote *A Song of Italy* and *Songs before Sunrise,* dealing with the question of Italian union and independence. For centuries ITALY was made up of a number of rival states, such as Naples, Genoa, and Milan, which were not unified as a single country. FRANCE and Spain, as well as Napoleon BONAPARTE, tried to conquer them but failed. There was a nationalist movement for unification in the nineteenth century (the Risorgimento). Italy was united by 1861, except for Venetia (Venice) and ROME; Venetia was acquired in 1866 and Rome in 1870.

In 1887 Hardy wrote Swinburne from MAX GATE, sending a copy of *The WOODLANDERS.* He said he had hoped they might meet, but it seemed unlikely. Hardy had, in the 1860s, lived within a half mile of Swinburne (*Letters* I, 165). He first met Swinburne about 1887, after which they corresponded. In 1897 Hardy sent Swinburne a copy of *The WELL-BELOVED,* for which Swinburne thanked him. Hardy wrote Swinburne that if it had "any faint claim to imaginative feeling" it would owe "something of such feeling to you." He had, he said, thought of many of Swinburne's lines as he was writing (*Letters* II, 158). He quoted *Atalanta in Calydon* in TESS OF THE D'URBERVILLES. In 1899 he wrote to Theodore Watts-Dunton, Swinburne's guardian, who had written praising WESSEX POEMS (lent by Swinburne). On June 20, 1899, he visited Swinburne at Putney and liked his "engaging, fresh, frank, almost childlike manner." He went again in 1905, noting at the time, "Swinburne's grey eyes are extraordinarily bright still—the brightness of stars that do not twinkle—planets namely." Swinburne mentioned a quotation in a Scottish newspaper: "Swinburne planteth, Hardy watereth, and Satan giveth the increase" (Bailey, *The Poetry of Thomas Hardy,* 282–83; see the McGhee article cited in *For Further Reading,* below).

Hardy had been a tremendous admirer of Swinburne's poetry since 1866, when he purchased his *Poems and Ballads* and read it while wandering along the London streets, at risk of "being knocked down" (Millgate, *Thomas Hardy: A Biography,* 88). His poetry was clearly influenced by Swinburne, although he was never to see much of him. His infrequent visits in Swinburne's later years were not because Watts-Duncan discouraged visitors but, probably, because Hardy had become busier with his writing, and it was more difficult for him to make the journey to Putney. In 1905 Hardy lent his support to the nomination of Swinburne for the Nobel Prize in literature, although it was not awarded to him (Millgate, *Thomas Hardy: A Biography*, 88, 438).

In April 1909 Hardy wrote a lengthy letter about English poets occasioned by Swinburne's death. Florence Dugdale (later HARDY) is believed to have been the recipient. He recalled the way the reception of Swinburne's works by the press in 1866 had made "the blood of some of us young men boil." He asked whether any other country in Europe would have had such an attitude toward a "deceased poet of his rank" as England. He stated that he was so late in getting "his poetical barge under way" and Swinburne was so "early with his flotilla" that, although he read his works, he did not personally know him until long after the *Poems and Ballads* were published (*Letters* IV, 15–16). In this remark Hardy is deprecating his own work as a mere "barge" compared with Swinburne's body of poetry, representing a "flotilla."

Swinburne is buried at Bonchurch, on the Isle of Wight, near the sea. Although Hardy did not attend the funeral, he visited the grave in March 1910 (Bailey, *The Poetry of Thomas Hardy*, 282) and, after his journey, wrote a poem about Swinburne, "A SINGER ASLEEP."

For further reading: McGhee, "'Swinburne Planteth, Hardy Watereth': Victorian Views of Pain and Pleasure in Human Sexuality"; Murfin, *Swinburne, Hardy, Lawrence and the Burden of Belief.*

Switzerland Thomas and Emma Hardy went to Switzerland in June 1897, crossing the English Channel from Southampton and continuing on to Le Havre, Paris, and Dijon. From the frontier town of Pontarlier they went to Neuchâtel, where, he wrote his sister Katharine HARDY, they were staying in a hotel that faced "the whole Alpine chain" (*Letters* II, 166). He said they were "almost the first English to arrive" and were "warmly received at the best hotels." After a few days they went to Berne, where they stayed at the Hôtel Belle Vue.

In less than a week they were at the Hôtel Gibbon, Lausanne, where Hardy wrote a poem dedicated to Edward Gibbon, author of *The History of the Decline and Fall of the Roman Empire* (1776–1788): "LAUSANNE: IN GIBBON'S OLD GARDEN: 11–12 P.M." *"27 JUNE 1897 (THE 110TH ANNIVERSARY OF THE COMPLETION OF THE "DECLINE AND FALL" AT THE SAME HOUR AND PLACE)."* The Hardys' next destination was ZERMATT, which they reached on June 28. Here Hardy thought of Edward Whymper's

successful ascent of the Matterhorn in 1865 and the catastrophe that ensued during Whymper's descent. Soon after their arrival he began a sonnet, "ZERMATT: TO THE MATTERHORN (JUNE–JULY 1897)," commemorating the loss of four climbers (out of seven) who had attained the summit, in itself "a tragic feat of manly might." He had heard the story from Edward Whymper, the sole survivor of the four English members of the climbing team. The poem was finished later and collected in *POEMS OF THE PAST AND THE PRESENT* (1902).

The Hardys' last stop was Geneva, where they stayed at the Grand Hôtel de la Paix Genève. Hardy wrote Florence HENNIKER about their sightseeing excursions to the top of the Wengern Alp facing the Jungfrau, as well as to Interlaken and Thun. They returned to England in early July (*Letters* II, 168–69).

Symonds, John Addington (1840–1893) Poet, man of letters, and essayist. In April 1889 he wrote Hardy, praising *The RETURN OF THE NATIVE*. Hardy replied that he had greatly enjoyed reading Symonds's essays years before they met; he considered them "correctives to those of M. Arnold" (Matthew ARNOLD). When Hardy wrote anything Symonds liked, he considered it a "great delight" (*Letters* I, 190).

Hardy wrote of his difficulty in keeping the "tragical conditions of life" that marked *The Return of the Native* out of his work. He would begin a work intending to make it "brighter & gayer than usual" but would be defeated by "the question of conscience." He had come to believe that, although his stories were sad, only by studying tragedy in fiction could one expect to "escape the worst forms of it, at least, in real life" (*Letters* I, 190).

Symons, Arthur William (1865–1945) Poet, critic, and editor. In September 1900 Symons asked Hardy to supply information for an article about him forthcoming in the *Encyclopaedia Britannica*. Hardy was clearly flattered. He wrote enclosing information, assuring Symons that he would find any other details that Symons needed. He admitted that he had inserted "a good bit of detail under ancestry," but explained that it was because of "absurdities" that had been published about him.

In 1908 Symons suffered a nervous breakdown and was certified as insane, although he recovered two years later. When Hardy first learned of Symons's condition, he wrote his wife, Rhoda, offering consolation and questioning whether his condition were really hopeless, since Symons was not old; Hardy also wrote that the sudden onset of the disease augured well for Symons's recovery. He advised her to take comfort that her husband was in a "proper place, & well taken care of" (possibly in Italy). He reminded her that Symons had come to MAX GATE once and stayed several days.

Talbothays Substantial home built by Henry HARDY, brother of Thomas Hardy, on the farm owned by his father, located on the road east of West Stafford village (F. B. Pinion, *A Hardy Companion*, 486–87). He designed it in 1893, apparently contemplating marriage, but the engagement was broken off. He then rented it until 1911. At that time he moved in with his sisters Mary and Katharine ("Kate") and their cousin Mary ("Polly") Antell, the daughter of Jemima's sister Mary (Millgate, *Thomas Hardy*, 264).

Lower Lewell Farm, the model for the dairy farm in Tess of the d'Urbervilles; *Hardy's father owned a dairy farm here.* (Sarah Bird Wright)

The name "Talbothays" is derived from the family of Talbots who had owned the property in the reign of Henry VIII (*Life*, 6). The name figures in *TESS OF THE D'URBERVILLES* as the dairy farm Talbothays, where Tess works until she marries Angel CLARE.

Tall, Laban Employed by Bathsheba EVERDENE on her farm in *FAR FROM THE MADDING CROWD*, Laban is also the local parish clerk. He loves music, but his new wife, Susan, is cold toward him in public and refuses to let him listen to Gabriel OAK play the flute at Warren's Malthouse. He is known as "Susan Tall's husband" because he has "no individuality worth mentioning."

Tangs, Timothy In *The WOODLANDERS*, the jealous husband of Suke DAMSON, who sets a trap for Dr. Edred FITZPIERS. He and his wife emigrate to New Zealand.

"Templeman, Miss" Assumed name of Lucetta LE SUEUR when she first comes to CASTERBRIDGE in *The MAYOR OF CASTERBRIDGE*. She takes the name of a wealthy aunt in Bristol, Mrs. TEMPLEMAN, in order to escape her unsavory past in Jersey.

Templeman, Mrs. The wealthy Bristol aunt of Lucetta LE SUEUR in *THE MAYOR OF CASTERBRIDGE*. She does not appear in the novel, but leaves Lucetta a modest fortune, which enables her to move to CASTERBRIDGE.

Tauchnitz, Christian Bernhard (Baron von Tauchnitz) (1816–1895) German baron whose Leipzig publishing firm specialized in publishing English books for the mainland European market. The Tauchnitz Collection of British Authors eventually included almost all of Hardy's fiction. In 1881 Tauchnitz sent Hardy, as a Christmas present, Henry Morley's *Of English Literature in the Reign of Victoria, with a Glance at the Past*, in which Hardy is mentioned. Hardy thanked him for his "very charming" present and said it was "the most interesting book of the kind" with which he was acquainted (*Letters* I, 102).

Tennyson, Alfred, Lord (1809–1892) Appointed poet laureate of England in 1850, Tennyson was a noted Victorian poet, widely read and admired. He was influenced by the romantic poets, especially John KEATS. Among his most celebrated works are *Poems, Chiefly Lyrical; Locksley Hall; The Princess; In Memoriam; Maud; Idylls of the King; Lord of Burleigh; The Charge of the Light Brigade;* and *Enoch Arden.*

In March 1880 Hardy and his friend Mrs. Anne Benson PROCTER were invited to lunch in London with the Tennysons at the house they had temporarily taken on Belgrave Street. Mrs. Tennyson presided at the table. Hardy remarked that he was "surprised to find such an expression of humour in the Poet-Laureate's face," contrary to that shown in his portraits. Tennyson told Hardy he liked *A PAIR OF BLUE EYES* the best of his novels. The Tennysons invited Hardy to visit them at Freshwater, on the Isle of Wight, and Hardy later regretted that he never did so (*Life, Hardy,* 136–37). He was familiar with Tennyson's works and sometimes quoted from "In Memoriam" and "Locksley Hall," among others (*see* Amy LOWELL).

When Tennyson died in 1892, Hardy received a card of admission to attend his funeral in WESTMINSTER ABBEY. He called the music at the service "sweet and impressive." Afterward he lunched at the National Club with Edmund GOSSE and several other writers.

In 1917 he jotted down, in the *Life,* his idea that the mission of poetry is to "record impressions, not convictions." He wrote that both Tennyson and William WORDSWORTH fell into the error of "recording the latter" when they grew old (*Life,* 177–78).

For further reading: Campbell, "Tennyson and Hardy's Ghostly Metres"; Schur, *Victorian Pastoral: Tennyson, Hardy, and the Subversion of Forms;* Taylor, "Hardy's Copy of Tennyson's *In Memoriam*"; Taylor, "Hardy's Use of Tennyson's *In Memoriam.*"

Terry, Ellen (1847–1928)   Noted English actress. She played Shakespearean roles with Henry Irving and was a friend of George Bernard SHAW. She was made a Dame Grand Cross, Order of the British Empire, in 1925.

In June 1889, after visiting the summer exhibition of pictures at the ROYAL ACADEMY OF ARTS in LONDON, Hardy wrote his friend Mary Sheridan that the paintings were "not very great" on the whole, but praised John Singer SARGENT's portrait of Ellen Terry as Lady Macbeth (*Letters* I, 191).

Hardy was in London in January 1891, staying with Mary and Francis JEUNE. On Saturday, January 24, he wrote his wife Emma that they had pressed him to stay on until Monday because they were having Sir Henry Irving and Ellen Terry for dinner on Sunday. He noted in the *Life* that Miss Terry was "diaphanous—a sort of balsam or sea-anemone, without shadow" and "like a machine in which, if you press a spring, all the works fly open" (*Life,* 232).

In March 1897 he wrote Mrs. Jeune (by then Lady Jeune) that there was to be a copyright performance of the play of *TESS OF THE D'URBERVILLES* and that Terry might give advice, since she had said she wished to play Tess. (This was a reading, not an actual performance, to establish that Hardy held the English copyright to the play. It took place on March 2, 1897, at St. James's Theatre.) Ellen Terry did not take part; it was delivered by the theater's actor-manager, George Alexander (*Letters* II, 147, 149).

Tess of the d'Urbervilles: A Pure Woman Faithfully Presented   One of Hardy's best-known novels, it was serialized in the GRAPHIC in England, July to December 1891, and in HARPER'S BAZAAR in the United States. Sections were also published in the FORTNIGHTLY REVIEW and in the *National Observer.* It was then published in book form in three volumes by OSGOOD, MCILVAINE & CO. (London, 1891) and included in the WESSEX EDITION of Hardy's works (1912–31). The publishing history of *Tess* is extremely complicated: portions of the novel were excised or published separately for serial publication.

The novel had an unfortunate beginning. It was refused by two publishers, and Hardy was then forced to edit it radically during serial publication to make it palatable to family readers. Once it was published in its intended form, in 1891, it was denounced by the press and by many readers for its polemical attack on social prejudice. Tess is actually more admirable than either of the two men in her life, both of whom presumably are higher in the social scale than she. Each, however, has a false concept of human relationships, derived from his particular background.

Rosemarie Morgan observes that the greatest outrage provoked by the novel was about the sexuality of Tess DURBEYFIELD, the central character. She is openly sexual and openly bears an illegitimate child; moreover, she is openly loved by a middle-class clergyman's son and is openly defended by Hardy as a "pure woman." In Victorian fiction it was acceptable to have the fallen woman suffer poverty, illness, misery, isolation, destitution, and death, but not to evoke sympathy on the part of the author and, even more shocking, on the part of the reader. Tess's purity is the point of the book; she remains uncorrupted throughout. Even as she kills Alec she is in a state of emotional shock. She does not apologize, but simply says, "I am ready." As she gives herself up, she still seems to manifest innocence (personal communication with the author).

SYNOPSIS

Phase the First: "The Maiden"

Chapters 1–3
As John Durbeyfield, a peddler and father of seven, returns to his village of Marlott after a day in a nearby

town, he is startled when the aged Parson Tringham addresses him as "Sir John." The parson explains that he has been doing antiquarian research, and has found that the Durbeyfields are descended from Sir Pagan d'Urberville, a Norman knight who came to England with William the Conqueror. The family is mentioned in the Pipe Rolls, which are annual rolls containing the pipes, or statements of the King's revenue and accounts; they date from the 12th century. As a county family the d'Urbervilles no longer exist, and they have lost their ancient lands and fortune. However, their crypts remain in the church in the town of Kingsbere. John Durbeyfield begins to feel highly distinguished and orders a carriage from the village inn, equipped with a tot of rum, in which to ride home. As he passes through the village he sees his eldest child, Tess, a girl of 16, who is participating in the traditional "CLUB-WALKING," or May Day procession, in which all the girls and women of the village take part. Her father's appearance embarrasses her, but she continues to participate in the festivities. After the procession the young men of the village dance with the girls on the village green. Angel CLARE, on a walking tour of rural England with his brothers, takes part, but does not notice Tess until he is leaving. Tess also notices Angel.

She returns home to find her father has not arrived. Her mother tells her about the news her father has brought, and also says he has been told that afternoon that he has a grave heart condition. Tess offers to go to Rolliver's Inn, where her father has gone to drink and boast of his lineage, to bring him home. Her mother asks her to watch the six younger children so that she can go herself. Tess realizes her mother hopes to enjoy an hour or two at Rolliver's Inn, and agrees to keep the children. Her parents do not return; Tess sends her brother after them, but finally must bring them back herself.

Chapter 4–7
At the tavern, Joan DURBEYFIELD remembers that there is a wealthy lady outside the town of Trantridge named d'Urberville, and wonders whether the Durbeyfields might be distantly related to her. She tells John that she will send Tess to "claim kin" with her, which might lead to a good marriage. Abraham DURBEYFIELD, sent to fetch his parents, overhears this conversation. Tess appears, and her parents return home with her. John's ill health and drink make him unable to take the family beehives to market the next day; Tess and Abraham set out with the beehives in their cart. They fall asleep on the way and have an accident in which the mailcart kills their old horse, Prince. Tess feels tremendous guilt and blames herself more than her parents do. Her father digs a grave for Prince.

The remorseful Tess agrees to visit Mrs. d'Urberville. She arrives at a new pleasure mansion, not an ancient family seat. She is not aware that Simon Stoke, a wealthy merchant, had built the house before his death; he had

no association with the d'Urberville family, but took on the name because it was more prestigious than Stoke and suggested an association with the old family. (Rosemarie Morgan points out that at this time there was a black market trade in the unlawful selling of ancient titles and coats of arms. This practice had followed the rise of a new and wealthy class of industrialists and manufacturers [personal communication with the author]). Tess meets young Alec d'Urberville, who says his mother is an invalid. He is impressed by Tess, and tells her he will do something for her. On returning home, Tess finds a letter offering her a position tending Mrs. d'Urberville's fowls at Trantridge. She hopes, with her earnings, to buy a new horse for her family. Alec arrives in a fancy gig to bring Tess to Trantridge; Joan has serious reservations about the young man. The younger children cry as Tess disappears into the distance.

Chapter 8–9
Alec is a reckless driver, and Tess is frightened. He says he will be careful if he can kiss her; he does, and she wipes her cheek. This angers Alec. Tess's hat blows off; she retrieves it, but refuses to return to the gig. They continue on with Tess walking and Alec riding. The next morning Tess meets Mrs. d'Urberville, who is blind. She asks Tess to whistle to her bullfinches each morning, which she does. Tess wants to return home, but also wants to help her family. Mrs. d'Urberville has not been told of their supposed family link (which Tess does not realize), and is indifferent in her manner toward her. Tess considers this proper, however. She gets used to Alec's presence and goes about her work peacefully.

Chapters 10–11
On a Saturday in September, Tess attends the weekly market at Chaseborough and discovers a fair in progress. Alec offers her a ride home that night, but she prefers to wait for the work-folk and walk home. She has had nothing to eat or drink and must wait three hours for them. Her companions are intoxicated, however, and on the way home a quarrel arises between Tess and some of the other girls to whom Alec has paid attention. Alec appears and again offers Tess a ride home; this time she accepts. He asks her to also accept his attentions, which she refuses to do. He purposely allows them to get lost and tells her he has bought her father a new horse, along with toys for the Durbeyfield children. By the end of chapter 11, it is clear that Tess has been seduced by the sinister Alec.

Phase the Second: "Maiden No More"

Chapters 12–14
On a Sunday morning Tess, "another girl than the simple one she had been at home," is leaving Tantridge with her bundles. Alec gives her a ride; she says she loathes herself for her weakness and was "dazed" by him for a short

Illustration by Daniel A. Wehrschmidt for Tess of the d'Urbervilles, *chapter 4 ("Prince lay alongside still and stark. . ."), published in the* Graphic, *July 18, 1891*   (Perkins Library, Duke University)

while. He infuriates her by replying, "That's what every woman says." She lets him kiss her, but remains stony; she tells him she can never love him. When she arrives home at Marlott, she confesses the tale of her seduction to her mother, who is upset because Tess will not marry Alec.

Tess's spirits are momentarily lifted when her friends, laughing girls, come to visit, but she becomes melancholy again. She eventually goes to church, sitting in an obscure place. She is terrified by a "cloud of moral hobgoblins," but they are "out of harmony with the actual world, not she."

Chapter 14–15

One August day a young man watches the reaping machine in a cornfield near Marlott village. Field-men and field-women bind the corn left by the machine. Tess, one of the girls, stops at lunch and begins suckling the child one of her sisters brings her. She returns home later to find that the baby, who is small and puny, has

been taken ill. Her father refuses to send for the parson; Tess baptizes the child herself, calling him Sorrow. The vicar, who had heard of the baby's illness and had been to the house, says her baptism is valid, but he cannot give the child a Christian burial. Tess buries him in a box that says "Keelwell's Marmalade" on the outside, makes a little cross, and places a jar of flowers by the grave.

Tess decides she can never be comfortable again in her family home and goes as a milkmaid to Talbothays, not far from the d'Urbervilles' stately home.

Phase the Third: "The Rally"

Chapters 16–19

Tess leaves Marlott for the second time and goes to the "Valley of the Great Dairies," an area with dairy farms much larger than she has known. She accepts a ride part of the way, but walks the remainder, reciting the canticle "O All Ye Works of the Lord, Bless Ye the

Lord," from the service for Morning Prayer. After three "silent reconstructive years" at home her spirits have recovered, to some extent, from her ordeal.

She meets the dairyman, Richard CRICK, who says he has heard of her family from an aged woman, now deceased, who had told him they were an "old ancient race that had all but perished off the earth." Tess seems to discount this report of her genealogy and begins milking with a practiced hand. The large farm employs nearly 100 men and maids as milkers. Mr. Crick mentions William DEWY, an elderly man from MELLSTOCK, who was once chased by a bull and escaped by turning toward him and playing his fiddle (he figures in UNDER THE GREENWOOD TREE). She then realizes that one of the milkers is Angel Clare, whom she last saw at the Marlott dance and has never forgotten. That night one of the other girls tells her his name, and that he is a "gentleman-born" and the son of the Reverend Mr. Clare at Emminster, "the earnestest man in all Wessex."

We learn that Angel's father had been horrified to see that his son had ordered a book on philosophy and confronted him. Angel had said he did not wish to take holy orders. His father decided it was pointless to send him to Cambridge if he were not going to enter the church. Angel, now 26, is working at the dairy and boarding at the dairyman's. He has delighted in the companionship of the other workers and enjoys the outdoor life. For several days he is reading at meals and doesn't notice Tess; once he does, he remembers seeing her before, but does not recall where.

The dairy maids and men try to milk the same cows; Mr. Crick tries to make them switch around, in case a milkmaid or milking-man leaves. Angel Clare surreptitiously tries to send Tess the cows she likes. She has heard him playing a secondhand stringed harp in the attic, and tells him, in the garden, he can "raise up dreams" with his music and drive away "horrid fancies." She is puzzled about why he is at the farm, coming from a clerical family and having a good education. He is surprised to hear her express anxiety about what Rosemarie Morgan terms the "deracination of the modern individual, uprooted from the ancestral village." Tess also recognizes the problems accompanying the "growth of industrialism and subsequent separation from the rhythms of nature," since "in the natural world there are no clocks or timetables dictating the measure of one's existence" (personal communication with the author). Her philosophy that goes beyond her "Sixth Standard training."

Angel offers to teach Tess more about history or other subjects, but she only wants to know why "the sun do shine on the just and the unjust alike." She wonders whether he would think more of her if he knew that the "knightly d'Urbervilles" in the Kingsbere church were her own forefathers. Mr. Crick, however, insists that Angel cannot "stomach old families."

Chapters 20–24

Tess is happier than she has ever been, and Angel Clare is becoming preoccupied with her. She becomes, in the dawn, when they milk the cows before breakfast, the "visionary essence of woman," and he calls her, secretly, "Artemis" and "Demeter."

Sometimes, after breakfast, their churning does not bring butter. Mrs. Crick says it may be because someone is in love. Tess, feeling faint, goes to the door. That night the three other girls who room with Tess—Retty Priddle, Marian, and Izz HUETT—see Angel from their bedroom window and discuss him; they agree he likes Tess best. Tess pretends to be asleep, but feels she cannot allow any man to marry her in view of her history; if she were to leave Talbothays he would settle on another girl.

The milking-men find there is garlic in the meadow, which has affected the cows' butter, and the dairy workers go out to cut it down. Tess praises the other girls to Angel. He behaves honorably toward all of them.

One Sunday morning Angel, who prefers "sermons in stones" to "sermons in churches," comes along and sees the four girls on their way to church. He carries each one, in turn, over the flooded road. The other three all love him but are not jealous of Tess, as they have been raised in families where "fatalism is a strong sentiment." Tess hears them say his family has chosen a doctor of divinity's daughter for Angel, a lady "of his own rank," so Tess tries to think no more of him.

One morning Angel watches Tess milk Old Pretty, thinking of her lips and teeth as "roses filled with snow" (an Elizabethan simile). He embraces her and tells her he loves her.

Phase the Fourth: "The Consequence"

Chapters 25–30

Angel has come to the dairy thinking it will be merely an episode in his life before he returns to the "world without." But his love for Tess and, in addition, his "subjective experiences," have unexpectedly become of great importance to him. He realizes he must not trifle with Tess. He decides to visit his family, which upsets the four girls immeasurably. Mr. Crick says cheerfully he will probably not stay at the dairy farm longer than four more months when he returns.

Angel rides toward his home, worried about whether he dares marry Tess. He is carrying presents of black puddings and mead from the Cricks. As he nears his home he sees Mercy CHANT, the girl rumored to be intended for him. She is about to hold a Bible class. He slips past without speaking to her, hoping she has not seen him. His father, Parson Clare, is a spiritual descendant of Wycliff, Luther, and Calvin, and "Evangelical of the Evangelicals." He has a kindly heart, however, and he and his wife welcome Angel. To their son, however, the vicarage life seems alien. His parents see his growing likeness to a farmer, in contrast to his brothers. Felix and Cuthbert, who are educated, correct, and conventional; they adhere to the latest fashions in spectacles, writers, and art. Angel finds them mentally limited; they find him socially inept. The midday meal is sparse and frugal, served late, after his parents' visits to the sick and elderly. They have given away the black puddings to a parishioner and found the mead so alcoholic that they have put it in their medicine cabinet. Angel tells his father he might like to become a farmer; his father says he has saved money for him toward the purchase or lease of land. He says that Angel, at 26, might like to marry. His father suggests a "truly Christian woman" such as Mercy Chant. Angel describes Tess, but cannot say she comes of as good a family as Mercy, since he does not know about the d'Urberville tombs at the Kingsbere church. His parents say they would like to see her. Mr. Clare never asks whether Tess is well-to-do, and Angel feels he is closer to his father in many ways than either of his brothers is.

Angel returns to Talbothays and in the mid-afternoon, Tess comes down, having been taking a nap. She regards him as "Eve at her second waking" might have regarded Adam. Angel helps her with the skimming. He proposes to her; she says she cannot be his wife and begins to cry. She pretends it is because his family is better than hers. He says his father told her he went on a missionary visit to Tantridge and met a "lax young cynic" (Alec d'Urberville) there, prompting a "disturbance." Tess resolves not to marry him.

Angel is not discouraged. Tess promises to tell him everything, but can't bring herself to tell him about herself. She goes with him to drive the cans of milk to the train station; they pass the d'Urberville manor house. She tells him she is a d'Urberville. She accepts Angel's proposal without telling him about Alec. Angel then recalls seeing her at Marlott.

Chapters 31–34

Tess writes her mother; Joan replies that under no circumstances must she ever tell Angel the truth. Tess remains silent for the moment. Angel presses her to set a date for the wedding. They set it soon after Christmas.

They go to an inn at Trantridge; a man recognizes Tess and tells her story. Clare strikes the man, who apologizes and says it was someone else. He later tells his companion it was Tess in fact, but he had not wanted to "hurt the gentleman's feelings." Tess asks to put off the wedding a bit.

Tess writes Angel a four-page narrative of her history, including her seduction and pregnancy and the death of the baby. She seals it in an envelope and slips it under Angel's door. When he acts the same toward her afterward, she assumes he has forgiven her. In her

hurry, however, she has actually placed the letter under the carpet as well as under the door, so he has not seen it. They marry before Angel learns the truth; only a few people are in the church. As they leave Talbothays a cock crows in the afternoon, a bad omen they try to forget.

They go to Wellbridge (Wool, or Woolbridge), pass over the five arches of the Elizabethan bridge, and take lodgings in an inn, part of a building once owned by the d'Urbervilles. Their luggage does not arrive, but a letter from Angel's father is delivered in which his godmother's jewels, bequeathed to Angel's wife, are enclosed. Tess puts them on and looks beautiful. Jonathan Kail, the man bringing the luggage, is late; he has been at the dairy and learned that Retty Priddle had tried to drown herself that afternoon. They all know about the cock's crowing. Marian, moreover, was found "dead drunk" and Izz is "low in mind." Kail takes in the luggage and Angel gives him a tip and some ale.

Tess determines to tell Angel the truth; she needs to "pay," since the other girls, innocent though they are, have been so unhappy. But first Angel tells her he has a confession; he had once fallen into 48 hours of "dissipation" with a strange woman. This releases her inhibitions, and she tells him about Alec and the results. Ominously, "each diamond on her neck" gives "a sinister wink like a toad's" as she leans forward to tell him.

Phase the Fifth: "The Woman Pays"

Chapter 35–44

Angel's face has withered at Tess's disclosure. He cannot believe her, and cannot understand why she has not told him earlier. He is "paralyzed" to his depths. She asks him to forgive her as she has forgiven him. He says she is now "another person," and breaks into "horrible laughter." Tess is stricken and says she only wants to make him happy. He says she is no longer the woman he has been loving; he has been loving "another woman in your shape." She perceives that her apprehensions had been correct; to him she is a "guilty woman" posing as an innocent one. She becomes abject, saying he can leave her, never speak to her again, anything, and she will never complain. He says there is a contrast between her past mood of "self-sacrifice" and her present one of "self-preservation." She sits silent while he is "smothering" his affection for her. He leaves to take a walk.

She follows him. He walks over the five "yawning arches" of the Elizabethan bridge; he says nothing, and she catches up and walks beside him. He says she is not deceitful, just not the same. He will not reproach her. He forgives her, but "forgiveness is not all." He will not say he loves her. She says she knows other girls in worse straits and their husbands have not minded. Angel merely says "Different societies, different manners," and remarks that perhaps she had never been "initiated into the proportions of social things." He associates her family's decline with her "want of firmness." She is the "belated offspring of an effete aristocracy." They return to the inn separately; Angel sleeps in the sitting room.

The next morning, Angel fixes breakfast and calls Tess. He begs her to say what she has told him is not true, but she cannot. She tells him that, although the baby died, the man is alive. She tells him he can divorce her; otherwise she would not have told him. He says he cannot. She says she almost committed suicide, but he makes her promise not to end her life.

After breakfast he leaves to go to the miller's, having planned to learn that business. At the midday meal they manage to converse about what he has learned. That night he says she is his wife, not his servant, but she begins crying and says that that is not true. Her tears do not melt Angel: "within the remote depths of his constitution . . . there lay hidden a hard, logical deposit, like a vein of metal in a soft loam." This has "blocked his acceptance of the Church" and has the same effect on his acceptance of Tess.

He says he cannot live with her in the "ordinary sense." If they had children they would be taunted and scorn her. She decides she should go home; they pack separately.

In the night Angel, sleepwalking, picks her up and walks around with her, intoning, "My wife—dead, dead!" He carries her downstairs toward the river. She realizes he is thinking of the Sunday morning when he carried her through the water with the other dairymaids. He stands on the river bank, but does not drown her. He carries her across the river to the ruined choir of the abbey church. He kisses her and puts her in an empty stone coffin and lies down on the ground. Tess steps out but cannot rouse him. She speaks to him gently, persuading him to return with her. She puts him on his sofa bed and lights a fire to dry him. The next morning he remembers nothing. They leave by coach, stopping at Talbothays. Tess bids her favorite cows good-bye.

They continue on in a carriage. Near her mother's house, Angel gets out. He tells her not to write him unless she is ill; if he can "bring himself" to come to her, he will let her know. She is too proud to plead with him or become hysterical. He takes the jewels to put back in the bank. He sees the carriage off, wishing she would look at him from the window for a minute. She cannot do so; she is lying inside in a "half-dead faint."

She reaches her home and tells her mother everything. Her mother scolds her for telling Angel the truth; she then takes the news as she would have taken a crop failure, as something to be endured. Tess overhears her mother telling her father, who is mortified. He can't believe such a fate has come to "Sir John," the descendant of the d'Urbervilles. He even wonders if Tess has been married.

Angel Clare writes that he has gone to the North of England to look at a farm. Pretending to join him, Tess leaves, giving her family £25 of the £50 Clare has given her.

Angel goes to his home at Emminster. He pretends Tess is with her parents "temporarily" since he is going to Brazil. They cannot understand what has happened but infer that she is simple, virtuous, and beautiful. His father reads the chapter in Proverbs in praise of a virtuous wife. His mother questions Clare; he admits that he and Tess have had a difference. She guesses that Tess's "history" will not bear investigation, but Angel becomes agitated and declares she is "spotless." Angel realizes he has wrecked his career with his marriage, and he resents Tess for making him deceive his parents.

The narrator declares that Tess is "as deserving of the praise of King Lemuel as any other woman endowed with the same dislike of evil," and that she is "moral" by "tendency."

At breakfast Angel and his parents discuss Brazil. He goes into town and, coming back, meets Mercy Chant. She glories in her Protestantism, and he begins arguing with her about the virtues of Roman Catholicism.

Angel leaves, stopping at Wellbridge to collect a few things. At the inn he meets Izz Huett, who has called to see him and his wife. He gives her a ride to her destination and tells her he is going to Brazil. He suddenly invites Izz to go to Brazil with him. She tells him she loves him, but not more than Tess, who would have laid down her life for him. Angel suddenly tells her he has changed his mind and orders her to get out, which she does, in racking sobs. He almost drives to see Tess but embarks for Brazil instead.

Eight months later, Tess is working at another dairy. Her mother begs for money for a new roof, which she sends. She thinks of getting the jewels back and selling them. Angel, meanwhile, is lying ill with a fever in Brazil.

On her way to another dairy, Tess is overtaken by the man Clare had knocked down at the inn. She runs away and hides; when she wakes she is surrounded by dying pheasants from a recent shoot, which she tenderly puts out of their misery.

Tess puts on an old gown, shaves off her eyebrows, and ties a handkerchief around her face as though she has a toothache. She arrives at Flintcomb-Ash, a "starve-acre farm" where Marian is also working. Tess signs an agreement as a field worker. Izz comes also. The work in the fields is hard. Her employer turns out to be the Trantridge man from whom Tess fled; he is a brutal man angry at her rejection. Izz and Marian cover for her. Marian, after drinking, tells her Angel had nearly taken Izz to Brazil with him.

Early one Sunday morning, Tess sets out for Emminster. She tries to find Angel's parents, overtakes his brothers but can't bring herself to speak to them, and ultimately discovers Alec d'Urberville, now an evangelical, preaching in a barn.

Phase the Sixth: "The Convert"

Chapters 45–52

Tess stares at Alec, horrified at the incongruity of his preaching and his actions four years earlier. He has undergone a "transfiguration," the sensuous curves of his mouth now modulated to express "supplication." He recognizes Tess and follows her. She is cold toward him, but he says he has repented and changed. He says he was much influenced by Angel's father, Rev. Clare, and by the death of his mother. She tells him about the baby, which stuns him, and asks him not to come near her. At Flintcomb-Ash she sees Izz Huett and a young man, a dairy worker from Talbothays, and learns that he has come to court her.

Alec tracks Tess down in the field. He has a marriage license and proposes, but she says she is already married. Farmer Groby sees them talking and blames Tess; he still holds a grudge against her. In February nearly all the workers except Tess attend the CANDLEMAS fair at which laborers are hired for the next year. Alec comes to the cottage where Tess is lodging and says it has been announced that he will speak at the Casterbridge fair but that, because of his love for her, he will not go.

In March, Alec comes again, having put aside his clerical garb. He tells Tess he has given up preaching, and that Angel is neglecting her. He declares he will be her "master" again. The girls' work, among huge farm machines, is grueling, and Tess is exhausted. Alec says he can make her little brothers and sisters comfortable if she will yield. She refuses, goes to her lodging, and writes Angel a long letter begging him to come to her.

Illustration by Hubert Herkomer for Tess of the d'Urbervilles, *chapter 50 ("The fire flared up, and she beheld the face of d'Urberville"), in the* Graphic, *December 5, 1891* (Perkins Library, Duke University)

Her letter is sent on to Angel by his parents. His father bitterly regrets not having sent Angel, though he was an unbeliever, to Cambridge with his brothers.

At this time, Angel is on a mule headed for the coast. He sees that the English farm workers lured to Brazil by the "Brazil movement" among English agriculturalists has failed; the workers are ill and their babies die of fever. He has also become ill. An Englishman traveling with Angel tells him he was very wrong to leave Tess; the man then dies of fever.

Meanwhile, 'Liza-Lu, Tess's sister, comes to fetch her; their mother is dying. Tess tells Marian and Izz, and leaves for home. The mother improves. Alec d'Urberville appears at the Durbeyfield home. Suddenly, John Durbeyfield dies of heart trouble; his lease on their house ends with his life, and the family will be turned out. The tenant-farmer will regain the house for his own laborers.

At Old Lady-Day, in April, the agricultural community is in flux, workers moving from farm to farm. Tess's parents, the Durbeyfields, belonged to a class above agricultural laborers—cottagers who are life-holders (carpenters, smiths, shoemakers, and the like). This class is gradually being forced out in favor of agricultural laborers who needed their houses. Tess's mother and siblings must leave. Tess blames her own reputation for their being turned out and not kept on as weekly tenants. Alec appears to offer them a house at Trantridge, which Tess refuses.

The next day the Durbeyfield family is packed up and on their way to rooms at Kingsbere. They pass Izz and Marian, also changing jobs. When they arrive at Kingsbere, their rooms have been taken. They camp in the church by the d'Urberville tombs. Alec finds Tess but she sends him away. Marian and Izz write Clare that Alec is pursuing Tess.

Phase the Seventh: "Fulfilment"

Chapter 53–59

Angel arrives home; he is ill. His family gives him Tess's last letter, which says she can never forgive him for his treatment of her. His parents learn the reason for their separation and have great sympathy for Tess. Angel sets out to find Tess. He finds the grave of John Durbeyfield; the caretaker says Durbeyfield had wanted to be buried at Kingsbere with his noble ancestors, but the family could not afford it.

Angel finds Mrs. Durbeyfield, who reluctantly tells him Tess is at Sandbourne (Eastbourne). He finds Tess at a seaside villa, The Herons, staying with Alec. The landlady overhears Tess berating Alec in their room for keeping her from "her own true husband," and then Tess goes out, nicely dressed and wearing a black veil. A large red spot appears on the ceiling below Tess and Alec's room. Angel and the landlady discover that Alec

has been stabbed in his bed and has died; word spreads throughout the town.

Angel receives a telegram saying his brother Cuthbert is engaged to Mercy Chant. He walks along the street; Tess catches up with him. She tells him she has killed Alec. He had called Clare a "foul name." She is content, unable to realize the "gravity of her conduct." At last Clare is tender toward her and promises not to desert her. They walk past the train station under fir trees, on fir needles. Clare fetches wine and food from an inn, and they picnic; they are like children in a dream. They go through the New Forest. They find a deserted house, Bramshurst Court, where a woman caretaker comes at intervals, and go in through a window. They hide while the caretaker is there; she leaves and they have another meal.

She tells him of his laying her in the Froom coffin when they were at Wellbridge; he has no recollection of it. They stay five days in the house; Angel goes out and brings in tea, bread, and butter. They never speak of the immediate past. On the sixth day the caretaker comes to open the house. She cracks the bedroom door and sees them asleep. They awake with a sense that something is wrong, and slip away. They cross the countryside, going through Melchester (Salisbury) and arrive, at night, at STONEHENGE. Angel promises to marry 'Liza-Lu if Tess dies.

Tess asks Angel whether they will meet again after death; he cannot answer. She falls asleep on a prehistoric pagan altar at Stonehenge. They are soon surrounded by men who have come for her. She tells Angel their happiness could not have lasted and that she will not live for him to despise her; she then surrenders to the police.

Angel and 'Liza-Lu ascend a long hill toward Wintonchester (Winchester). The clocks in the town strike eight. A black flag is raised from an octagonal tower, signifying that Tess has been executed. Angel and 'Liza-Lu go on, hand in hand.

CRITICAL RECEPTION AND COMMENTARY

This novel had germinated in Hardy's mind for at least 10 years, with a working title of "Too Late Beloved." The subtitle, *A Pure Woman*, comes from the voluntary work a friend of the Hardys, Mary JEUNE, had done with "fallen women" in a London settlement house. She saw many girls who, like Tess, were veritable "saints," with "fine and noble dispositions." Nevertheless, the novel was seen as a "frontal attack" on certain Victorian mores and the subtitle attracted a storm of protest. Hardy thought it unconscionable to blame the innocent victim of a seducer rather than the seducer himself. From a Victorian point of view, Tess has twice fallen: she has given birth to an illegitimate child, married, been deserted by her husband, and then lived with her seducer. Hardy also pilloried the notion that the "better" classes were actually "better" than simple country folk.

Hardy also explores what Richard C. Carpenter terms "the effect on ordinary people of economic instability and social climbing" (Carpenter, *Thomas Hardy,* 127). Much of the action, for example, is initiated by John Durbeyfield's fancy that he is important because of his noble Norman ancestry. Hardy was also well aware of the plight of life-holder cottagers, who would often be forced to move on the death of the last life-holder, even if he had a large family, as in the case of John Durbeyfield. The transient life of agricultural workers, moving from farm to farm each year on Old Lady-Day, undermines their stability and security.

The essential theme of *Tess of the d'Urbervilles* is that of the destruction of a good and natural character by the forces of circumstance and of society itself; it is a reenactment of the scapegoat myth. Tess battles poverty and social prejudice, her belated true love blighted by her seduction and abandonment. Tess is the most admirable character in the novel, and finer than the two men in her life who have false ideas of their worth stemming from their respective backgrounds.

The settings evoke the reader's empathy—the Durbeyfields' humble cottage, Rolliver's Inn, and the serene, nourishing Talbothays Dairy. One of Hardy's favorite themes is the invasion of the pastoral world by alien forces, in this case the threshing machine on which Tess struggles. The choice of the neolithic monument of Stonehenge for the final flight of Angel and Tess suggests the primeval days of ritual sacrifice, magic, and the intolerance of society for those who stray outside its rigid mores.

The idea of chance operates in this novel, as in some of Hardy's other works. Such coincidences as Angel's letter sliding under the carpet, where it is invisible, and the mail-cart's shaft piercing Prince's heart are examples of what one critic has called Hardy's use of chance as his weapon "to strike through surface reality to areas where the poetry of man offers resistance to the drab starkness of a malevolent universe" (Carpenter, *Thomas Hardy,* 138).

The archetypal myth of death and rebirth works symbolically in the novel. At Talbothays Tess is "born" into a full natural existence; she "dies" at Flintcomb-Ash. The color red is an early symbol: Tess is the only one of the girls in the "club-walking" procession to wear a red ribbon in her hair above her white dress, linking her with passion, guilt, sacrifice, and purity. Both Angel and Alec feed Tess fruit, the emblem of the human fall from grace. Both men are associated with fire: Alec in its murky, red aspect; Angel with the fire of hell and heaven.

The novel was not universally condemned, however. Many 19th-century critics found much to praise despite their reservations. Andrew Lang applauded its "moral passages of great beauty," such as the club-walking scene, but criticized Hardy for using overly elaborate language at times. For instance, instead of saying people are drinking beer, he says they "seek vinous bliss" (Clarke, ed., *Thomas Hardy: Critical Assessments,* I, 188). The "Baron de Book-Worms," an anonymous reviewer for *Punch,* declared the novel melodramatic in places, especially in the character of Alec d'Urberville, a "stage-scoundrel."

Margaret OLIPHANT, writing in BLACKWOOD'S EDIN-BURGH MAGAZINE, found it equally inconceivable that Tess was a "Pure Woman" or that she would have stabbed Alec, although she believed the book as a whole to be "far finer" than anything Hardy had done previously (Clarke, ed., *Thomas Hardy: Critical Assessments,* I, 211). Mowbray Morris, on the other hand, declared in the QUARTERLY REVIEW that calling Tess "A pure woman faithfully presented" entails "a strain upon the English language." He declares Tess "rises through seduction to adultery, murder, and the gallows," but a girl actually "raised by the mixture of gentle blood in her veins to a higher level of thought and feeling" would not have acted as Tess does (Clarke, ed., *Thomas Hardy: Critical Assessments,* I, 216–18). Francis Adams, reviewer for the *Fortnightly Review,* considered the novel a failure despite Hardy's authentic depiction of many of the rural villages and farms. Sandbourne, Bramshurst Court, and the "weird journey to Stonehenge," however, are all highly improbable; the book should have been a masterpiece but has "missed its aim" (Clarke, ed., *Thomas Hardy: Critical Assessments,* I, 220).

In *The English Novel: Form and Function* (1953), Dorothy van Ghent applies what might be considered a 20th-century point of view. She observes that the "really great crises" of the book are psychologically motivated, such as Alec's seduction of Tess, her rejection by Angel, and her murder of Alec. She believes Hardy's universe has "aesthetic integrity," relying more than his other works on the accidental, such as Prince's death, the undelivered letter, and the absence of the Clares from their home when Tess finally arrives. She does not find the scene at Stonehenge melodramatic; it is inevitable and a fitting place. The dignity of Tess's "last gesture" is recognized by the ritual sacrifices that have occurred on the monoliths (Clarke, ed., *Thomas Hardy: Critical Assessments,* IV, 118–24).

P. N. Furbank, in his introduction to the New Wessex edition by Macmillan in 1974, states that the novel expresses Hardy's aestheticism, which is rooted in his view of England as a "tomb" for which his "fictional creation" compensates. He cites his poem "On AN INVITATION TO THE UNITED STATES," in which he declares he "shrinks" to see a "modern coast" whose "riper times have yet to be." He also suggests that Hardy expresses "his heart more completely in this novel than in any other," and that in the characters of Angel and Tess he is "dramatising the life- denying and life-affirming elements in his own temperament." Furbank links the theme of the decline of the d'Urbervilles to his own worries about the decline of the Hardy family in marrying beneath themselves. He wrote in his diary in September 1888 about a distant relative who had many children and was poor: "So we go down, down, down" (P. N. Furbank, Introduction to *Tess of the d'Urbervilles*, 11–23). Hardy was also greatly disappointed in his own CHILDLESSNESS.

For further reading: Carpenter, *Thomas Hardy;* Chew, *Thomas Hardy: Poet and Novelist;* Craik, "Hardy's *Tess of the d'Urbervilles*," *Explicator*, 53.1 (fall 1994), 41–43; Davis, "The Rape of Tess: Hardy, English Law, and the Case for Sexual Assault"; Gibson, "*Tess of the d'Urbervilles*, 1891–1991"; Herbert, "Hardy's Views in *Tess of the d'Urbervilles*"; Langbaum, *Thomas Hardy in Our Time;* LaValley, ed., *Twentieth Century Interpretations of Tess of the d'Urbervilles;* Padian, "'Daughter of the Soil': Themes of Deep Time and Evolution in Thomas Hardy's *Tess of the d'Urbervilles*"; Parker, "'Pure Woman' and Tragic Heroine? Conflicting Myths in Hardy's *Tess of the d'Urbervilles*"; Pettit, *Reading Thomas Hardy;* Pettit, ed., *New Perspectives on Thomas Hardy;* Shumaker, "Breaking with the Conventions: Victorian Confession Novels and *Tess of the d'Urbervilles*."

Thackeray, William Makepeace (1811–1863) English novelist and essayist, known for his satirical depiction of the English middle and upper classes. His best known novel is *Vanity Fair;* others include *Pendennis, Henry Esmond,* and *The Virginians.* He also wrote many number of essays, was on the staff of *Punch,* and edited CORNHILL MAGAZINE from 1860 to 1862. He lectured in the United States as well as Great Britain.

In 1863 Hardy wrote his sister Mary HARDY from London, where he was working for the architect Sir Arthur William BLOMFIELD, about his critical opinion of Thackeray. He said that, if one viewed novel writing as a "truthful representation of ordinary life," Thackeray was the "greatest novelist of the day."

In 1908 Hardy was given an autograph letter of Thackeray's, which he kept in his library until it was auctioned as part of his library in 1938 (*Letters* VII, 145).

theater   Hardy had a lifelong devotion to the theater, ranging from classic SHAKESPEARE plays to productions put on at country fairs. When he went to live in LONDON as a young man he thought of writing plays in blank verse and even of trying the stage as a profession, but nothing came of either venture. Later he wrote the noted verse drama *The* DYNASTS as well as *The* FAMOUS TRAGEDY OF THE QUEEN OF CORNWALL.

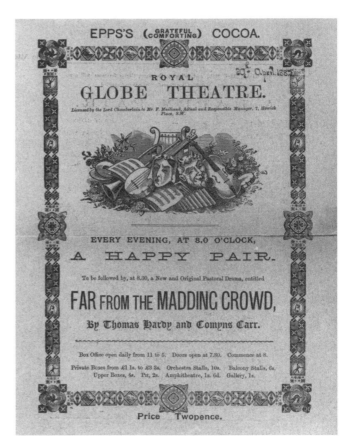

Program of performance of Far from the Madding Crowd, *the Royal Globe Theatre, London, written by Thomas Hardy and J. W. Comyns Carr, April 1882, starring Marion Terry* (Beinecke Rare Book and Manuscript Library, Yale University)

Ruth Firor, in her noted study *Folkways in Thomas Hardy*, lists "Folk-Drama" as one of the important elements in Hardy's work. He was thoroughly conversant with Shakespeare's plays and in 1866, as a young man in London, attended the series of Shakespeare's plays at the Drury Lane Theatre starring the actor Samuel Phelps. He admired the plays of SOPHOCLES, and had studied Greek as a young man. Although he gave it up because he planned to become an architect, he wrote in the *Life* that he had a "substantial knowledge" of the Greek dramatists (*Life*, 33).

Plays figure in several of Hardy's novels, including *A* LAODICEAN and *The* RETURN OF THE NATIVE. Many have been dramatized.

Hardy knew many modern dramatists and producers, and admired the stage productions of Harley GRANVILLE-BARKER and his first wife, Lillah MCCARTHY. Harry POUNCY of Dorchester produced dramatic scenes from *FAR FROM THE MADDING CROWD.* Thomas Henry TILLEY, the Dorchester mayor and an amateur actor, dramatized *The Return of the Native* and also produced *TESS OF THE D'URBERVILLES.* A. H. EVANS, a Dorchester chemist and father of the Shakespearean actor Maurice Evans, dramatized *The TRUMPET-MAJOR* in Dorchester, as well as *Far from the Madding Crowd*, UNDER THE GREENWOOD TREE, *The MAYOR OF CASTERBRIDGE*, and *The WOODLANDERS*. These performances led to the formation of the group known as the HARDY PLAYERS, who sometimes gave private performances at MAX GATE. One member of the company was the Dorset actress Gertrude BUGLER, who played Eustacia VYE, Marty SOUTH, and Tess DURBEYFIELD in various productions. Hardy thought she was extremely talented. During a December 1924 performance in WEYMOUTH as Tess, she reduced a friend of Hardy's to tears, causing her to flee from the theater before he could introduce them. Hardy wrote her, "That was your doing, young lady!" (*Letters* VI, 297).

In February 1920 Hardy went to OXFORD UNIVERSITY to receive the honorary degree of Doctor of Letters; during the same visit, he attended a performance of scenes from *The Dynasts* at the theater there. The production was mounted by the Oxford University Dramatic Society; there were 110 characters with speaking parts.

Another undergraduate theatrical group at Oxford devoted to the works of Hardy were the BALLIOL PLAYERS. In July 1924, when Hardy was 84, they visited Max Gate and performed an English version of Aeschylus' trilogy *The Oresteia,* titled *The Curse of the House of Atreus,* on the lawn. Because it was daytime, they carried spikes of a giant flowering spiraea in lieu of lighted torches. On June 29, 1926, they gave another performance at Max Gate, *Hippolytus of Euripides;* on July 6, 1927, they performed *Iphigenia in Aulis* there (Roberts, *Hardy's Poetic Drama,* 6–7).

On September 7, 1925, a dramatization of *Tess of the d'Urbervilles* opened at the BARNES THEATRE, Surrey, produced by Philip RIDGEWAY. Hardy was unable to attend because of ill health. The 100th performance took place in London at the Garrick Theatre, which was named for the famous Shakespearean actor. On September 8, 1926, the Barnes Theatre mounted a production of *The Mayor of Casterbridge*, dramatized by John Drinkwater. See Appendix II, Media Adaptations of the Works of Thomas Hardy.

"Then and Now" Poem written in 1915 and published in the *Times* of London on July 11, 1917; it was later collected in *MOMENTS OF VISION* (1917). In the first two stanzas, Hardy describes the "chivalrous sense of Should and Ought" in earlier wars: soldiers, whether they lived or died, believed honor would be their reward. They were "Gentlemen of the Guard" who wished to "fight fair"; according to the rules, no man dared practice "perfidy."

The third stanza evokes the horrors of WORLD WAR I, in which "honour is not." Hardy compares this war with the biblical account (Matthew 2: 16–18) of Herod's slaying of the children in Bethlehem: "Rama laments / Its dead innocents; / Herod breathes: 'Sly slaughter / Shall rule!'" Modern warfare is compared with Matthew's account of the event: "In Rama was there a voice heard, lamentation, and weeping, and great mourning, Rachel weeping for her children" (Matthew 2:16–18; cited by Purdy, *Thomas Hardy: A Bibliographical Study,* 424).

According to the New Testament scholar Reginald H. Fuller, the story given in Matthew derives from Jeremiah 31:15: "Thus saith the Lord; A voice was heard in Ramah, lamentation *and* bitter weeping; Rahel [Rachel] weeping for her children refused to be comforted for her children, because they *were* not." He observes that there are two traditions regarding the burial of Rachel. The first is that she was buried outside Jerusalem and the second that she was buried five miles north of Jerusalem. "Ramah" means "height" (personal communication with Dr. Fuller).

Thomas Hardy Association, The The TTHA was founded in 1997 to promote the study and appreciation of Thomas Hardy's writings in every corner of the world. Both its organizing principle and its membership reflect this global character. Based in the United States, The Thomas Hardy Association is governed by an international team of scholars, unpaid, who are members of its Council of Honorary Vice Presidents and Board of Directors. Together they maintain a site on the World Wide Web with a dozen departments focusing on Hardy's life and work and more than 300 links to other sites of interest to Hardy lovers. TTHA membership dues includes a subscription to *The Hardy Review,* an annual journal currently published at Yale University and edited by Rosemarie Morgan. The association makes available to members a comprehensive "Bibliographical Checklist" of recent works on Hardy, a fully edited compilation of Hardy's "Collected Poems," and a full poetry concordance on a compact disk, provided by Martin Ray. The website also offers the full archives of TTHA's Poetry Page (POTM, or Poem of the Month), posted and monitored by William W. Morgan. The active worldwide on-line Thomas Hardy list welcomes participants from many countries.

The mailing address is The Thomas Hardy Association, 124 Bishop St., New Haven, Conn. 06511. The website address is http://www.yale.edu/hardysoc/Welcome/welcomet.htm

Thomas Hardy Society, The The Society began its life in 1968 when, under the name "The Thomas Hardy Festival Society," it was set up to organize the festival marking the 40th anniversary of Thomas Hardy's death. So successful was that event that the society continued its existence as an organization dedicated to advancing "for the benefit of the public; education in these works of Thomas Hardy by promoting in every part of the world appreciation of study of these works." Based in England, it is a nonprofit cultural organization and its officers are unpaid, receiving no more than small honoraria. It is governed by a Council of Management of between 10 and 18 managers, plus representatives from Dorchester, Dorset, and West Dorset.

The society welcomes anyone interested in Hardy's writings, his life, and his times. It takes pride in the way in which nonacademics and academics mix at its meetings and conferences, which would have delighted Hardy himself. Among its members are many distinguished literary and academic figures and many more who love and enjoy Hardy's work sufficiently to meet fellow enthusiasts and share their enthusiasm and appreciation.

Every other year the Society organizes a conference that attracts lectures and students from all over the world. It also arranges Hardy events not only in Wessex but also in London, and, it is hoped, in other centers in the future.

Members receive *The Thomas Hardy Journal;* it is published three times a year. Applications may be made to Thomas Hardy Society, P.O. Box 1438, Dorchester, Dorset, DTI IYH, United Kingdom.

The Thomas Hardy Society website address is http://www.webuser.com/hardy/default.asp

Thomson, Winifred (unknown) Artist who painted a portrait of Hardy in 1895. Hardy's friend Lady Mary JEUNE had introduced him to the portrait painter during the London season of 1894. She told Hardy the artist was "a *very* nice girl," but "*not* pretty." The next spring Hardy and his wife Emma took a flat at Ashley Gardens, Westminster, for the London season, and Thomson began his portrait, completing it there in 1896. Apparently Hardy did find Thomson pretty and wrote her several times in the ensuing years in the "slightly arch, mildly flirtatious style" he used when writing women he "liked but did not deeply care for" (Millgate, *Thomas Hardy,* 358).

Thomson was the stepdaughter of John Fletcher Moulton, the liberal M. P. for South Hackney. Her sister, Elspeth, was married to Kenneth Grahame, author of *The Wind in the Willows* (Millgate, *Thomas Hardy,* 396).

Thornycroft, Sir William Hamo (1850–1925) Sculptor, whom Hardy met as early as 1884; in the *Life* he mentions seeing him in London in January of that year. On the evening of July 2, 1889, Hardy was placed next to Sir Hamo's wife, Agatha Thornycroft, at a dinner at the home of his friend Sir Edmund GOSSE; her husband was in France. Hardy later told Gosse that he thought she was the most beautiful woman in England and had

been (unconsciously) his model for Tess in *TESS OF THE D'URBERVILLES* (Millgate, *Thomas Hardy,* 298). In July 1900 he bicycled to WEYMOUTH with Sir Hamo and Lady Agatha. At that time Sir Hamo was carving a statue of William Gladstone, who had been prime minister of England four separate times, for the Strand in London, and another of King Alfred, which would be placed in Winchester.

In 1915 Sir Hamo proposed that he carve a white marble bust of Hardy. Hardy wrote to say it would give him the "greatest pleasure" to have his name associated with his in such a way, and asked him to propose a time that would be convenient. The marble bust is now in the DORSET COUNTY MUSEUM and a bronze copy is in the National Portrait Gallery, London.

"Thoughts of Phena" At News of Her Death Poem dated March 1890, and published in *WESSEX POEMS;* (1898). In his diary for March 5, 1890, Hardy writes that he composed the first four to six lines in a train going to LONDON. He calls the act "a curious instance of sympathetic telepathy," since the woman he was thinking of was dying at the time; her actual death occurred "six days later," although he did not realize it. The actual death of his cousin Tryphena SPARKS, whom scholars assume was the subject of the poem, was on March 17, more than six days after Hardy began writing it. He finished the poem after her death (Bailey, *The Poetry of Thomas Hardy,* 93–95).

The speaker laments having nothing by which to remember her. He wonders what scenes surrounded her in her last days—"Sad, shining, or dim?" He can only retain in his mind the "phantom" of the "maiden of yore." The last three lines echo the first three. In this flashback he is once again a young suitor; he has only the "phantom" of the girl he knew —no writing, no lock of her hair; nothing substantial to mark her time on earth.

The entire question of Hardy's relationship to Tryphena Sparks remains unsettled. Some scholars, especially Lois Deacon, argue that they were lovers and that she had a son whom her family accepted as Hardy's; others find this theory implausible.

Richard Purdy writes that, when the poem was collected in *Selected Poems,* there was an illustration depicting the shrouded body of a woman laid out on a sofa that resembles one that had been in the MAX GATE dining room (Purdy, *Thomas Hardy: A Bibliographical Study,* 101–102).

"Three Strangers, The" Short story published in *LONGMAN'S MAGAZINE* in March 1883 and, in the United States, in *HARPER'S WEEKLY* in two installments (March 3 and 10, 1883). It was one of five stories collected as *WESSEX TALES* in 1888. The others were "The WITHERED ARM," "FELLOW-TOWNSMEN," "INTERLOPERS AT THE KNAP," and "The DIS-

TRACTED PREACHER." In Macmillan's definitive WESSEX EDITION of Hardy's works (1912), two other tales were transferred to the volume of tales: "The MELANCHOLY HUSSAR OF THE GERMAN LEGION" and "A TRADITION OF EIGHTEEN HUNDRED AND FOUR."

The story opens on a cold March night during the 1820s at a lonely hut called Higher Crowstairs, on the downs at the intersection of two footpaths. Shepherd Fennel and his family are the tenants. There is a celebration going on inside the hut in honor of the christening of his second daughter. Nineteen people are at the gathering, which includes musicians; they begin dancing.

Outside a lonely figure, a man of about 40, climbs the hill. It is raining, and vessels have been set out to catch the water; he drinks from one of them. He knocks on the door of the hut and is invited in. He is told that a birth and a christening are the occasion for the celebration. The Fennels provide him with a pipe and he settles in the chimney-corner. Soon there is another knock at the door, and a second stranger, older than the first, is admitted, asking for shelter. The first stranger hands the second the large family mug of strong mead and he drinks generously, shocking Mrs. Fennel. The second man says he must leave for CASTER-BRIDGE, but will accept some more mead. Mrs. Fennel privately makes strong objections, for the family knows nothing about the man. The first stranger says he is a wheelwright by occupation. The second one begins leading them in song, singing verses that suggest he is actually a hangman. Those present realize he is going to Casterbridge to execute a poor clockmaker, Timothy Summers, who stole a sheep because his family was starving.

The two strangers clink their cups together. There is a third knock at the door and another stranger is admitted: a short, small man of fair complexion, dressed in "a decent suit of dark clothes." The second stranger continues singing; he says the next day is a "working day" for him and "the lad who did it" has been "ta'en." The third stranger stands with trembling knees and shaking hands, then flees. The second stranger leaps up and declares that the trembling man must be the prisoner who stole the sheep, escaped from jail.

They hear the alarm gun being fired at Caster-bridge. One of the guests is actually a constable and volunteers to look for the escapee. The men all find lanterns and prepare to chase the escapee. They rush out. The child who had been christened begins to cry. The first stranger, who had been in the chimney-corner, returns from outside and begins drinking more mead and eating. The older stranger returns and joins him. They agree they don't want to break their limbs running over the countryside. They finish eating and drinking and depart.

The pursuers fall down treacherous flint slopes, climb out, and go into the moist briery vale. They discover the escapee, Johnny Pitcher. He surrenders and they return to the shepherd's living room. There are two jail officers there along with a magistrate, who say John Pitcher is not the condemned man at all. It turns out to be, in fact, the man in the chimney-corner, the first stranger. Johnny Pitcher confesses that the first stranger is actually his brother. Johnny had intended to go to the jail to bid him farewell and was stunned to find, in the shepherd's cottage, both the prisoner and the executioner. The second man had not heard about the escape of the prisoner. The prisoner had thrown "a glance of agony" at his brother, who had not identified him.

Johnny is released. The next day they search for the fugitive, who is nowhere to be found. Many people, in fact, sympathize with him as his crime was not too great, and admired him for hobnobbing with the supposed executioner.

It is many years later. The narrator says that the man in the chimney-corner was never captured. The shepherd and his wife have died; the baby is a "matron herself." The story of the three strangers is still well known in the country near Higher Crowstairs.

The story is particularly memorable for its depiction of rural justice, for the image of the shepherd's hut with its christening celebration, and for the cold night landscape with its treacherous flint slopes and vale full of briers.

The story was dramatized as "*The THREE WAYFARERS.*"

For further reading: Wilson, "Hardy and the Hangman: The Dramatic Appeal of 'The Three Strangers,'"; Marroni, "'The Three Strangers' and the Verbal Representation of Wessex."

"Three Wayfarers, The"   Hardy's dramatization of his short story "The THREE STRANGERS." It was performed in London at Terry's Theatre on June 3, 1893, and again in London in the fall of 1900 by the Incorporated Stage Society (founded in London in 1899). In November 1911 it was produced in DORCHESTER; Thomas Henry TILLEY was one of the performers. It also was performed by the Scottish Repertory Theatre at the Royalty Theatre, Glasgow, in February–March 1911 (*Letters* IV, 12) and at Keble College, Oxford, on June 21 and 25, 1925. *See* Appendix II, Media Adaptations of the Works of Thomas Hardy.

Tilley,   Thomas   Henry (1864–1944)   Dorchester mayor and amateur actor who dramatized *The RETURN OF THE NATIVE* and also produced *TESS OF THE D'URBERVILLES*. He was a leading member of the DORCHESTER DEBATING AND DRAMATIC SOCIETY. In October 1911 the society produced "The THREE WAYFARERS," adapted from Hardy's short story "The THREE STRANGERS." The play begins with a hornpipe dance;

Hardy's sent Tilley the music and dance instruction, on October 16, noting that he was going away for a few days and Tilley might need them. Hardy wanted to make sure that the playbill specified that the piece was "dramatized from the story called 'The Three Strangers' in the volume entitled 'Wessex Tales'" (*Letters* IV, 180, 183).

Tillotson & Son Bolton, Lancashire, newspaper syndicate for which TESS OF THE D'URBERVILLES was initially written. The firm had been founded by W. F. Tillotson, a Congregationalist and Sunday school worker who wanted materials suitable for family reading. He had died six months before the firm arranged for *Tess*, but had been succeeded by William Brimelow, who held the same views.

As the installments of the novel arrived (it was then titled *Too Late Beloved*) they were given to the printer, and it was not until the firm had received half of the manuscript, including the scenes in which Tess is seduced and baptizes her baby at midnight, that they decided they could not send it out to family newspapers. They asked Hardy to rewrite much of it and delete certain scenes. Hardy refused, and Tillotson's returned it along with the illustrations already commissioned. They also paid Hardy for his work as promised. *Tess* was refused by several other periodicals and was bowdlerized to make it acceptable to the GRAPHIC, where it appeared before book publication.

Tillotson's also purchased and distributed *The Pursuit of the Well-Beloved* (first title of *The WELL-BELOVED,*) "A MERE INTERLUDE," "ALICIA'S DIARY," "BENIGHTED TRAVELLERS" ("The HONOURABLE LAURA"), and "The MELANCHOLY HUSSAR OF THE GERMAN LEGION." See Purdy, *Thomas Hardy: A Bibliographical Study*, 340–41, which has an explanatory appendix: Appendix III, A Note on Tillotson & Son and Their Newspaper Fiction Bureau.

Time, Father Child in JUDE THE OBSCURE, also known as Little Father Time. Born in Australia, he is the son of Arabella DONN Fawley and Jude FAWLEY. Arabella sends him to live with Jude and Sue BRIDEHEAD after she contracts a bigamous marriage to Mr. CARTLETT. Jude had known nothing of her pregnancy.

Time's Laughingstocks and Other Verses Collection of poems published by MACMILLAN & CO. in 1909. The poems included were written over a range of 40 years; 10 were written during the 1860s. Hardy inscribed copies to his sister Mary HARDY, Florence Dugdale, later HARDY, Edward CLODD, Edmund GOSSE, Henry NEWBOLT, and Dr. T. H. Warren, vice chancellor of OXFORD UNIVERSITY.

The collection contained more than 90 poems, some of which were among Hardy's most noted. It included "A TRAMPWOMAN'S TRAGEDY," "A SUNDAY MORNING TRAGEDY," "SHUT OUT THAT MOON," "REMINISCENCES OF A DANCING MAN," "The DAWN AFTER THE DANCE," "HE ABJURES LOVE," "The BALLAD-SINGER," "AFTER THE LAST BREATH," "The MAN HE KILLED," "ONE WE KNEW," "A CHURCH ROMANCE," "The DARK-EYED GENTLEMAN," "SHE HEARS THE STORM," "GOD'S EDUCATION," "PANTHERA," and "The RASH BRIDE."

A reviewer for the *Daily News* complained that, throughout the volume, "the outlook [is] that of disillusion and despair." Hardy wrote a letter to the newspaper retorting that more than half the 90-odd poems in the volume "do not answer to the description at all" (Purdy, *Thomas Hardy: A Bibliographical Study*, 313).

Tinsley, William (1831–1902) Hardy's first publisher. Tinsley and his brother, Edward, founded the firm of TINSLEY BROTHERS. (Edward died in 1866, before Hardy first approached the firm about publishing his fiction.) William Tinsley accepted DESPERATE REMEDIES, with the proviso that Hardy underwrite a portion of the cost. It was not serialized. The firm published TINSLEYS' MAGAZINE, in which A PAIR OF BLUE EYES, was serialized before publication. Hardy's second novel, UNDER THE GREENWOOD TREE, was not serialized.

Tinsley Brothers Publishing firm established by Edward and William TINSLEY; the firm was located at 18 (later 8) Catherine Street, Strand, London. Edward died in 1866; therefore, Hardy's correspondence with the firm was handled by William Tinslye. Hardy submitted his first novel, unpublished, THE POOR MAN AND THE LADY, to the firm in 1869, but it was rejected. In 1870 he submitted the manuscript of his first published novel, DESPERATE REMEDIES, which, after some negotiations in which Hardy assumed part of the publication cost, was published on March 25, 1871. In 1872 the firm published UNDER THE GREENWOOD TREE, and, in 1873, A PAIR OF BLUE EYES. The latter was the first novel with Hardy's name on the title page.

The firm also published TINSLEYS' MAGAZINE. The business records of the firm have been dispersed and destroyed, although the extant correspondence from Tinsley to Hardy, now in the Bliss Collection, sheds light on a relatively obscure time in Hardy's life (Purdy, *Thomas Hardy: A Bibliographical Study*, 329).

Tinsleys' Magazine Literary magazine published by the firm of TINSLEY BROTHERS. Edward Tinsley died in 1866; his brother William TINSLEY was Hardy's first publisher. Hardy's novel A PAIR OF BLUE EYES was serialized in the magazine from September 1872 to July 1873.

Tintagel A small village on the north coast of CORNWALL, about a half mile from the sea, in the heart of the region consecrated to Arthurian legends. The remains of the actual castle said to be that of King

Tintagel Castle, Cornwall, setting for The Famous Tragedy of the Queen of Cornwall   (Sarah Bird Wright)

Arthur are on Tintagel Head, reached by a long ascent up and around a rocky promontory. The deep cove is extremely scenic. Hardy set his drama *The FAMOUS TRAGEDY OF THE QUEEN OF CORNWALL* (1916) on the Cornish coast at Tintagel Castle, illustrating it with his own drawings. His novel *A PAIR OF BLUE EYES* is also set in this vicinity.

Hardy courted his first wife, Emma Gifford HARDY, at nearby ST. JULIOT CHURCH, where he was carrying out restoration; they often walked, rode, and picnicked along the adjacent coast. In September 1916 he wrote Sidney COCKERELL that he and his second wife, Florence Dugdale HARDY, had gone to Cornwall and had visited the church at St. Juliot and seen the memorial tablet to Emma. Cockerell had asked him to write a poem on Iseult (the English or British "Helen"). Hardy answered that Cockerell's hopes for a poem would be disappointed: "I visited the place 44 years ago with an Iseult of my own, & of course she was mixed in the vision of the other" (Letters V, 179).

"To C.F.H." *On Her Christening Day* Poem published in *HUMAN SHOWS, FAR PHANTASIES, SONGS, AND TRIFLES* (1925). In September 1921 Hardy had served as god-

parent to Caroline Fox Hanbury of KINGSTON MAURWARD HOUSE; his christening gift was a parchment manuscript of this poem, written for the occasion. He wished "That your experience may combine Good things with glad . . . Yes, Caroline!"

"To Lizbie Browne" Poem possibly written about 1888 and collected in *POEMS OF THE PAST AND THE PRESENT* (1902). In Hardy's boyhood Lizbie Browne was the daughter of the gamekeeper and a noted village beauty. He mentions her in his diary on March 1, 1888, which may be a clue to the date of the poem (Purdy, *Thomas Hardy: A Bibliographical Study*, 112).

In the poem, comprising nine six-line stanzas, he wonders where Lizbie Browne is now—is she still alive or "past joy, past pain"? He wonders who else had hair as red as hers. She married before he could express his feelings; he regrets that he never kissed her. He visualizes a day in the future, if Lizbie is still alive, when men will speak of him, and she will say, "And who was he?"

"To Meet, or Otherwise" Poem written to Florence Dugdale HARDY a few weeks before she and Hardy were married. It was first printed in the *SPHERE* on December

20, 1913, and then collected in SATIRES OF CIRCUMSTANCE (1914).

Hardy is contemplating whether or not to "sally forth" and meet her, "girl of my dreams." He visualizes the distant day when they will be dead and buried and it will not matter. Then he decides to make the most of the present, when they can meet and consider "some path or plan." The meeting will at least lead to a moment of "human tenderness" in a universe marked by pain.

Hardy believed himself to be revealing his feelings for Florence in this poem. It meant a great deal to him emotionally (Bailey, *The Poetry of Thomas Hardy*, 268).

"To My Father's Violin" Poem written in 1916. Hardy's father had died in 1902. The poem was collected in MOMENTS OF VISION (1917). In the manuscript the poem is titled "To My Father's Fiddle" and does not have the third stanza. When the poem was collected the title was changed and the stanza added. The violin hung in the MAX GATE study. After Hardy's death the violin was inherited by his sister Kate HARDY. It is now in the DORSET COUNTY MUSEUM along with two others; it is uncertain which was Hardy's father's instrument (Bailey, *The Poetry of Thomas Hardy*, 361).

Hardy addresses the violin in the first stanza, wondering whether his father would like it to be with him in death, when time may pass slowly.

In the second stanza he reminds the violin of STINSFORD CHURCH, where the violin, played by him, guided the choir's "homely harmony" for many years.

The third stanza recalls the other times when his father "the instrument speak his heart / As in dream, / Without book or music-chart" for pleasure.

In the fourth stanza he tells the violin it "cannot, alas, / The barrier overpass / That screens him in those Mournful Meads hereunder." No fiddling can be heard there; no bird "Thrills the shades" and no viol is "touched for songs or serenades."

The fifth stanza evokes the present, when the strings are a "tangled wreck" and there are "ten worm-wounds" in the neck of the violin. He sadly contemplates its "present dumbness" and reads its "olden story."

In the *Life* Hardy speaks of receiving a letter from a reader objecting to his use of a pagan "Virgilian reminiscence . . . of Acheron and the Shades" (a reference to Hardy's mention of the "Nether Glooms"). He marveled that Hardy was not in a "madhouse." Hardy wrote Alfred Noyes citing the letter, remarking, "Such is English criticism, and, I repeat, why did I ever write a line!" (*Life*, 410).

Toneborough Fictional name for Taunton in *A LAODICEAN*.

"Tony Kytes, the Arch Deceiver" *See* "FEW CRUSTED CHARACTERS, A."

"To Outer Nature" Poem collected in WESSEX POEMS (1898); it was called "To External Nature" in the manuscript. In *Wessex Poems* it is illustrated with a headpiece picturing a vase holding wilted, dangling flowers, symbolizing decay. Hardy wishes he could see nature as he had viewed it as a boy: he had then assumed nature had been created entirely for his pleasure. Time, however, has made him see things "Cease to be things" that had existed in the "morning" of his life.

Bailey observes that in the beginning of the poem Hardy views nature in a Wordsworthian way, as made for human pleasure. In maturity, however, he substitutes the Darwinian view of nature as evolutionary. He sees nature as a complex process rather than an isolated landscape.

"To Please His Wife" Story published in the London periodical *Black and White* in June 1891, with a small portrait of Hardy and two illustrations by W. Hennessey (Purdy, *Thomas Hardy: A Bibliographical Study*, 82). It was later collected in LIFE'S LITTLE IRONIES.

The story opens in St. James's Church, HAVENPOOL. A sailor appears at the church door just as the Sunday service is ending. He tells the parson he wants to offer thanks for his escape from a shipwreck. Before the congregation leaves, the parson reads the prayer of thanksgiving for "After a Storm at Sea" from the Book of Common Prayer.

The townspeople recognize the young sailor as Shadrach Jolliffe, a local man whose parents had died; he had gone to sea when quite young. He tells the townsmen he is now captain of his own small boat, which survived the storm. He sees two girls he once knew, Emily Hanning and Joanna Phippard. He has tea with Emily Hanning and her father, and an "understanding" develops—although they are not engaged. Joanna, however, wins Shadrach away, although she is not in love with him.

Joanna enters the shop Emily and her father keep and hides in back when Shadrach comes in. Emily comes in from an outside errand, and he tells her that when a sailor comes home from the sea he is "blind as a bat" and can't evaluate women. He loves her, he says, not Joanna. Joanna determines that she must have him. When Shadrach calls at Joanna's house, she says he promised to marry her.

After their wedding, Joanna's mother dies, and Joanna decides she cannot permit Shadrach to go to sea. They manage her family's grocery business and have two sons, who come to love all the "nautical arts and enterprises."

Emily, meanwhile, has married an older widower. They have two children and live in a grand house. She hires a governess for them.

Shadrach is not suited for retail business. Joanna is envious of Emily and her children. Shadrach points out that Joanna did Emily a good turn by taking him away from her, which enrages Joanna. She tells Shadrach to go to sea again and become successful. He buys an interest in a brig and prospers. He brings home a bag of money to Joanna, but she says Emily and her family are much wealthier. He says he will make more if he can take their sons to sea.

She agrees, reluctantly, and the brig *Joanna* sails in the spring. It does not return by autumn, although Joanna continually searches the horizon. For the next six years she keeps hearing footsteps in the street and imagining she sees her husband and sons at the door, but they never return. The townspeople treat her kindly; they are convinced the brig *Joanna* is at the bottom of the sea.

Torkingham, Parson   In *TWO ON A TOWER*, he is the vicar at Welland. He has hopes of establishing a close relationship between the parsonage and the manor house, occupied by Lady Viviette CONSTANTINE. He helps bring Bishop Cuthbert HELMSDALE and Lady Constantine together.

"To Shakespeare" *(After Three Hundred Years)*   Poem written as a contribution to the tercentenary celebration of Shakespeare's death and first printed in *A Book of Homage to Shakespeare,* ed. Israel Gollancz (London, 1916). It was published in *MOMENTS OF VISION AND MISCELLANEOUS VERSES.*

There are four parts. The first consists of two stanzas offering a tribute to Shakespeare's "Bright baffling Soul." Despite his artistry, Shakespeare will remain "at heart unread," that is, he will always be baffling to some degree.

The third stanza is about Shakespeare's death. Even though the town clocks chimed and the Avon River flowed as usual at his death, his life had been the most significant of his time. His entire "age was published" when the bells tolled for his passing.

The fourth and fifth stanzas give a view of Shakespeare as his neighbors and fellow townsmen knew him. As the bells toll his death, one townsman might have said to a woman coming in to shop, "Yes, a worthy man and well-to-do" but in fact he had only nodded to him in a neighborly way. Someone else might have remarked that Shakespeare had led his "busier life" elsewhere [i.e., in London]. Another person might have said, "Witty, I've heard . . . but Death comes to all." In other words, his contemporaries might have failed entirely to recognize and appreciate his genius.

The final stanza offers brilliant homage to Shakespeare, who has been, in life, like a "strange bright bird" at the barn door, mingling with the ordinary "barn-door brood." His strange mind flies briefly into man's "ordinary existence," lodges there as a "radiant guest," and then flies away.

"Tradition of Eighteen Hundred and Four, A"   A short story first published in 1882, and collected in *LIFE'S LITTLE IRONIES* (OSGOOD, MCILVAINE & CO., 1894); later it was removed to *WESSEX TALES.* In June 1919 Hardy added a note to the earlier preface stating that the "incident of Napoleon's visit to the English coast by night, with a view to discovering a convenient spot" for the invasion, was his own invention. He had some doubts about it "because of its improbability." He was greatly surprised several years later "to be told that it was a real tradition. How far this is true he is unaware" (*Collected Short Stories,* New Wessex Edition [London: Macmillan, 1988], 5.)

The tale had already been published as "A Legend of the Year Eighteen Hundred and Four" in *Harper's Christmas* in December 1882. It was called "Napoleon's Invasion" in advertisements for that issue.

The narrator of the tale recalls listening to a story told by Solomon Selby at an inn on a rainy night. He is the son of a former shepherd, and remembers the years 1803, 1804, and 1805 clearly. It was a time after the "first peace" when "Bonaparte was scheming his descent upon England." He had collected more than 2,000 flat-bottomed boats to use as ferries; some had a stable for horses to haul cannon. The speaker's father had driven his sheep up on the high downs of Sussex and could see the drilling going on across the English Channel on the French coast. There was much speculation about where he would land.

The speaker's father is often up at night with lambing. When the speaker is a young boy, he takes his father's place out on the downs so his father can rest. One night his uncle is visiting, and goes out with him. They fall asleep at the sheep fold, waking up to see two men in "boat-cloaks, cocked hats, and swords" speaking French and consulting maps; they are only 20 yards away. Light falls on one of them and the uncle gasps; he is positive it is "Bonaparty. . . . The Corsican ogre." The boy also recognizes him. They watch as a boat picks up the men in the cove.

The narrator admits that Napoleon's army never actually landed but suggests that Selby's tale is a compelling evocation of such as invasion.

For further reading: King, "Hardy's 'A Tradition of Eighteen Hundred and Four' and the Anxiety of Invention."

Trafalgar, Battle of   On October 21, 1805, the British fleet, under the command of Lord Nelson (Viscount Horatio Nelson), defeated the combined French and Spanish fleets off Cape Trafalgar. His flagship, the HMS *VICTORY,* signaled the message, "England expects that every man will do his duty." He was killed during the battle, which is one of the central events in Hardy's dramatic epic *The DYNASTS.*

"Tragedy of Two Ambitions, A"   Short story published in the *Universal Review* in December 1888 with six illustrations by George Lambert. It was collected in *LIFE'S LITTLE IRONIES* (1894).

As the story opens, two studious brothers, Joshua and Cornelius Halborough, are reading the New Testament in Greek inside their house while the village boys shout and play outside. Their father, a millwright, reels up to the side of the house, his promised work not done. One of the brothers puts him in the shed to hide him from their sister Rosa, 14. Their mother had saved £900 for them, enough money to send them to a university, but after her death their father squandered their legacy. The brothers have no hope of earning a degree. If they work very hard they might become schoolmasters, attend a theological college, and become ordained as "despised licentiates." After a few months, the brothers leave for a training college; Rosa is placed in a school at Sandbourne (Eastbourne), a "fashionable watering-place."

In the second part, Joshua Halborough arrives in a provincial town. He is now at a theological college in a cathedral town and will soon be ordained. Cornelius is the town schoolmaster and hopes to go to a theological college, but Joshua believes Cornelius is not working hard enough. Joshua has borrowed money to give Rosa a second year in Brussels, where she now is living. Both brothers regret the blighting of their ecclesiastical ambitions by their father, who is still asking them for money.

The next morning, a Sunday, Joshua sees his father on the lawn of the cathedral, accompanied by a gypsy woman. To Joshua's horror, His father tells the subdean that he has married the woman, Selinar. They ask him to the Cock-and-Bottle but he declines. Joshua writes his brother suggesting that he and Cornelius try to raise money to send the couple to Canada. He says having such people as parents is "fatal" to a clergyman. He hates for them to bring Rosa down to "the level of a gipsy's step-daughter."

Joshua Halborough, now a curate, preaches in the parish of Narrobourne one day and is a tremendous success. The owner of the estate, Albert Fellmer, a young widower, is particularly impressed. He and his mother invite Joshua to dine with them, but he says he must be with his sister, who has just returned from Brussels; they invite her to come also. She is now "fair, tall, and sylph-like" and has a proper evening dress with satin shoes. Mrs. Fellmer is shocked, as she expected a plain "Martha" to be the curate's sister. Albert is fascinated by Rosa. Joshua writes Cornelius about the evening; Cornelius answers that Selinar has left their father, who does not like Canada and is coming home.

Albert tells his mother he must have Rosa, but his mother says Rosa will not be content living simply and caring for his child, when they have one. Cornelius and Rosa arrive the next day. When Joshua comes, Cornelius tells him their father has been imprisoned for a week for breaking windows in a nearby town, Fountall. The visit goes well and Albert seems about to propose to Rosa. However, the final night of her visit the brothers cannot dine with the Fellmers; they must try to remove their father from the area on his release. They go to fetch him at the Castle Inn, but he has already left, looking disreputable. They intercept him just before he reaches the manor house gate.

Their father declares that if Rosa is going to marry the squire he will, as her father, give her away. He declares the gypsy woman was more his "lawful wife" than his children's mother had been until after Joshua was born. It is crushing news to Joshua that he was born out of wedlock. The millwright waves his stick and continues on the way to Narrobourne House. The brothers watch him fall in a weir. Joshua persuades Cornelius not to try too hard to rescue him, although their father calls out to them. Mr. Halborough drifts into a barrel arch, or culvert, where the current is stronger, and they are unable to rescue him.

They change their clothes and go to the manor-house. Rosa says Fellmer wants to speak to Cornelius about marrying her. Six months later Rosa and Albert have married. Rosa wonders why her father has not written from Canada. His body is finally found and a funeral service, conducted by Joshua, is held.

Rosa, who still believes her father to be in Canada, tells them she had heard a cry from the distant meadow the night she was at Albert's home and was sure she heard her own name shouted. Albert ran to get his hat, and by the time he returned they decided it was not a cry for help but a "drunken shout."

Cornelius tells Joshua, privately, that Rosa will find out the truth sooner or later. After they attend the christening of Rosa and Albert's son, they walk together in the fields. Each one is haunted by guilt. They see a white poplar growing near the weir and realize it is their father's rough-cut walking stick, which has taken root. Both brothers admit to each other that they see his ghost every night, and both have contemplated committing suicide in the same spot where he drowned.

In 1889 Edmund GOSSE wrote Hardy that "A Tragedy of Two Ambitions" was "one of the most thrilling and most complete stories Hardy had written." He added that he "walked under the moral burden of it for the remainder of the day. . . I am truly happy—being an old faded leaf and disembowelled bloater and wet rag myself—to find your genius ever so fresh and springing" (*Life,* 215).

"Trampwoman's Tragedy, A"   Ballad written in April 1902 and first published in the *NORTH AMERICAN REVIEW* in November 1903 and collected in *TIME'S LAUGHING-*

STOCKS (1909). The editor of *CORNHILL MAGAZINE* had rejected it as unsuitable for a family periodical. The poem, which Hardy considered his most successful, was based on a local story of an event that took place between 1820 and 1830 (*Life*, 311–12).

Hardy wrote Edmund GOSSE that the poem was written after a bicycle journey to Poldon Hill and on to Glastonbury, Somerset, and that the woman's name was Mary Ann Taylor, who had then been dead for half a century (Purdy, *Thomas Hardy: A Bibliographical Study*, 139).

The ballad has 13 stanzas, followed by a half page of notes about places and persons to which the poem refers.

The speaker, a woman, describes a journey with her "fancy-man" (whom she loves), "Mother Lee," and another man known as "jeering John." They struggle under the hot summer sun from Wynyard's Gap northward. Their shoulders stick to their packs; their backs are burning from the blaze of the sun. They avoid "sad Sedge-Moor" (Sedgemoor, a tract of moorland in central Somerset). At sunset they climb "toilsome Poldon crest" and see an inn "that beamed thereby."

They have traveled for months through the Great Forest, (the Vale of) Blackmore, and over the Mendip ridge. She and her "fancy-man" have loved "lone inns"; she recalls inns where they have celebrated together, probably drinking ale. Among them are the "King's Stag," "'Windwhistle' high and dry," "'The Horse' on Hintock Green," and "many another wayside tap / Where folk might sit unseen."

As they go she teases her fancy-man by walking beside "jeering John"; she ignores her lover's "dark distress." At the top of Poldon Hill they see the inn "Marshal's Elm" and all four settle down in a row. She sits next to John, who takes her on his knee and says it's his turn to be her "favoured mate."

Her lover asks, in a voice she has never heard before, "Whose is the child you are like to bear? / *His?* After all my months o' care?" Still teasing, she nods. He springs up and, with his knife, kills John.

Her lover is then taken to jail and is hanged, although before this incident he had done no misdeed except taking a horse "in time o' need." The woman bears a stillborn child. Mother Lee has died by this time, so no one tends her.

As she lies weak in the night her lover's ghost returns and asks if the child was his or John's. She tells the ghost that he was her only lover. The ghost smiles and disappears; she remains alone, walking on the moors.

Hardy wrote Hermann LEA that the poem was set at Marshall's Elm, an inn near Glastonbury (*Letters* III, 138). In his note he says the "highness and dryness of Windwhistle Inn" was impressed on him several years before, when he called there for tea. There was no water; however, there were full barrels that "testified to a wetness of a certain sort" (presumably holding ale), but it was not "at that time desired." He states that Marshal's Elm is no longer an inn, although the house remains. "Blue Jimmy," the woman's true love, was a "notorious horse-stealer of Wessex" in those days and was hanged at Ilchester (or Ivelchester) jail. He observes that "Its site is now an innocent-looking green meadow."

For further reading: Cox, "A Trampwoman's Tragedy, Blue Jimmy and Ilchester Jail."

translations of Hardy's works   *See* Appendix VI, Translations of Thomas Hardy's Works.

Troy, Sergeant Francis   Character in *FAR FROM THE MADDING CROWD*. His mother was a French governess, and his presumed father was Lord Severn. Before his birth his mother had married a "poor medical man." Troy had been a law clerk for a time, but then enlisted in the 11th Dragoon Guards. He is arrogant and proud of his conquests of women. He nearly marries Fanny ROBIN, a servant to Bathsheba EVERDENE, but is prevented by coincidence from doing so. He abandons Fanny and marries Bathsheba; Fanny dies; he leaves Bathsheba and is thought drowned, but is actually picked up by a ship and taken to the United States. On his return he works for a traveling circus. He appears uninvited at a Christmas party given by William BOLDWOOD, who hopes to announce his engagement to Bathsheba. Boldwood, unhinged, shoots him.

Troyton, Charlotte   Wealthy widow in *A PAIR OF BLUE EYES*, whom Christopher SWANCOURT, the father of Elfride SWANCOURT, marries. Charlotte is the aunt of Henry KNIGHT.

Trumpet-Major, The   Novel issued serially in *GOOD WORDS* from January to December 1880 with illustrations by John COLLIER. It was published serially in the United States, without illustrations, in *Demorest's Monthly Magazine* (New York) from January 1880 to January 1881. It was then published in three volumes in 1880 by SMITH, ELDER & CO., London. Purdy believes it was written at UPPER TOOTING from 1879 to 1880. Hardy took special pains with the historical background, as shown in a notebook about the novel now in the DORSET COUNTY MUSEUM. It has passages from contemporary newspapers, sketches of costumes, and other materials such as caricatures.

This novel is one of the earliest of Hardy's works to show his interest in Napoleonic traditions. In the *Life* he writes that when he was only seven or eight he found, in a closet at home, some contemporary issues of the periodical *A History of the Wars*, which dealt with the Napoleonic Wars. Hardy's grandfather, who had volunteered in the wars, had subscribed to them. Hardy says their "torn pages," with their "melodramatic prints of serried ranks, crossed bayonets, and dead bodies" actually set in motion "the train of ideas that led to *The Trumpet-Major* and *The Dynasts*" (*Life,* 16–17).

The novel was well received on publication. George Saintsbury, writing in the *Academy,* praised Hardy for leaving aside "much of his extravagant phraseology," but said the "true merit" of the novel cannot be appreciated until "the last page is read." He considered the main characters well drawn. The critic for the SPECTATOR called Hardy a novelist "born, not made," and considered the novel "conceived and put together with capital ingenuity." The reviewer for the ATHENAEUM declared that Hardy was second to none "in the art of making one see his scenes and know his characters" (Gerber and Davis, *Thomas Hardy: An Annotated Bibliography of Writings about Him,* 31–32).

Pinion considers the novel a "by-product" of Hardy's research for *The* DYNASTS. While living at STURMINSTER NEWTON, Hardy had been reading about the Napoleonic Wars at the BRITISH MUSEUM. He then came down to WEYMOUTH to make notes on the royal watering place scenes in the novel. The novel is set in period from 1804 to 1805, between the time the French were thought to be planning to land on the south coast and the English victory at TRAFALGAR in October 1805, after which the chance of invasion was considered remote. He believes that, had the novel appeared anonymously, and had it not contained WESSEX place names, "few would have suspected that it was written by the author of *The Return of the Native*" (F. B. Pinion, *A Hardy Companion,* 36).

SYNOPSIS

Chapter 1–8

Anne GARLAND and her mother, Martha GARLAND, have come to live in one wing of the Overcombe Mill after the death of Anne's father, an artist, which has left them in reduced circumstances. They observe extensive military preparations in the fields near their home in one wing of the Overcombe Mill. Miller LOVEDAY, a man of about 55, explains that his son John LOVEDAY is the trumpet-major of one of the regiments setting up camp. His other son, Robert LOVEDAY, is at sea. Anne dimly remembers Johnny Loveday as a child, when he studied painting with her father.

Miller Loveday invites the Garlands to a party he is giving in John's honor; he is also entertaining some of the German, Hungarian, and Swedish noncommissioned officers, all of whom speak some English, along with some villagers. After some hesitation the women agree to attend, although they will be the only female guests. The party is a rollicking affair with songs. The overbearing Festus DERRIMAN appears and calls Anne a "fair angel"; she shrinks from him.

The next day Anne takes a copy of the community newspaper to the querulous farmer, Squire Benjamin DERRIMAN at Oxwell Hall. He thinks little of the soldiers, who, he expects, will be breaking his hedges and stealing eggs from his hens' nests. Anne is patient with him. His nephew Festus, about 23, arrives; Benjamin detests him, but pretends to be delighted. Anne leaves, but Benjamin tells Festus with veiled irony that he hopes his bravery in "these warlike times" will not carry him away. When they leave he springs up to the attic and watches Festus approach Anne on the path home. Anne gets the better of Festus in an argument. She encounters Granny Seamore, a local woman who informs her that Festus will inherit everything from his uncle.

The following week, Anne meets Festus again as she goes to his uncle's. She goes home by a circuitous route to avoid him; her mother assumes she has been trying to avoid John Loveday and encourages her to think seriously about Festus, the "heir-presumptive" to Oxwell Hall. Anne is secretly horrified.

Chapters 9–16

It becomes known that Benjamin Derriman has gone for a week's holiday to the royal watering place nearby (probably BUDMOUTH). Anne goes to a christening party in the adjoining parish; it rains and she accepts her hosts' invitation to spend the night. John Loveday comes to see if she is safe, and asks if he may escort her home. He says her father taught him to draw horses. As they pass Oxwell Hall there is a commotion; Festus has brought a dozen young men to dine at his uncle's house. The farmer returns unexpectedly; he peers in the window and can hardly believe the scene, with his "best silver tankards" in use and many candles blazing. He overhears Festus inviting all of the guests to spend the night. The farmer begins shouting "Man a-lost!," imitating the call of a distressed traveler, and the guests all run out to help search. He then flies inside and bolts the door. They bang on it and he appears in a tasselled nightcap at the window. He assures them his nephew is "miles away" and "sound asleep."

John Loveday calls on Anne; her mother prefers Festus because of his supposed wealth, but does not interfere. Meanwhile, Miller Loveday is becoming very interested in Mrs. Garland. She tells Anne she approves of John. Miller Loveday proposes to the widow.

John Loveday sees Anne in the garden and tells her the king is coming to Gloucester Lodge; John's regiment will go to see him pass by at three o'clock in the morning. Miller Loveday and Mrs. Garland also plan to go, so Anne, initially reluctant, joins them. John asks Anne if he may court her; his position as trumpet-major is a good one, but, after his enlistment, he plans to live in the mill. She gently discourages his advances. The king and queen come by in an old carriage drawn by four horses, followed by two others with their daughters and attendants, but do not look out of the window. One spectator says the sight of the "dusty old leather coaches" is not worth waiting for. When the royal family reaches Weymouth the town bells begin ringing.

The Garlands and Miller Loveday gather, with many others, on the downs to watch the royal family. Miller Loveday learns he has a letter at Budmouth, an unusual event. Anne, John, and the miller go there to fetch it. John reads it, at his father's request, and learns that Robert (Bob) Loveday is coming home to be married.

The squire asks Miller Loveday to take charge of his papers in case something happens to him and says he will bring him a box for safe keeping while he is away on a trip. John and his father and the Garlands go to Budmouth to welcome Bob, who arrives at home to find them absent. When they return, they find that he has brought many gifts. He gives Anne cap-ribbons because he says Matilda JOHNSON, his fiancée, has enough finery. Mrs. Garland is surprised to know that Anne knows Bob; she confesses that she had never thought the Loveday family "high enough" for them.

The miller finds that Bob has known Matilda only two weeks and has not met any of her family. They prepare for her wedding; Mrs. Garland cleans Overcombe Mill thoroughly. Matilda does not take the Royal Mail coach, for which Bob has paid, but the road-wagon several hours later. She claims she has come that way to save money; in reality she has spent Bob's money on clothes. She only has a tiny trunk, however; she claims she has left most of her clothes at her rich aunt's. Matilda's eyes are described as "eel-colour," suggesting that she is deceptive and unscrupulous. Bob describes Budmouth as small and undistinguished except for the presence of the Royal Family, and the "actors and actresses." Matilda inquires whether Elliston (a play producer) is paying good salaries this summer, suggesting that she has a connection with the theater, which startles Bob. She covers up her admission by pretending she has read about the theater in the newspaper. Bob naively offers to take her to a theater one night; she declares she has never been into one.

Chapters 17–26

Matilda admires the miller's house and mill, but is frightened by Crumpler, one of the miller's cows, and startled by the sound of John's trumpet. At tea John meets Matilda; he is startled to see her and she nearly faints. In the garden he is solicitous of Bob; privately he is extremely agitated. Farmer Derriman delivers his box of papers to Miller Loveday. John goes along the passage to Matilda's bedroom and asks to speak to her; she pretends she has never met him. He lets her know he is aware of her bad reputation as a loose woman among the troops John has known. He descends and joins the family in singing psalms. He has asked for two days'

leave, but keeps it to himself, planning to meet Matilda in the garden. Farmer Derriman decides that a rivalry for Anne exists between Festus and John, and he takes his box of papers back.

The next morning the miller and Bob discuss the mill and wait for Anne to join them before having breakfast. David, the man who assists the miller, announces that Matilda has departed. Bob asks Anne to help him search for her. He kisses Anne's fingers as they descend into a quarry, which upsets her. He explains that after he has been at sea "women-folks seem so new and nice that you can't help liking them, one and all in a body." Bob thinks his father or David must have appeared uncouth.

John and Bob meet in the field, and John admits he encouraged Matilda to leave and gave her all his money. Bob resents his interference and leaves to search for Matilda. Anne sits in the garden, pondering the mystery of Matilda's sudden departure. Festus Derriman, on horseback, peers over the wall. He says his uncle heard John and Anne in the garden the previous night; Anne realizes it was John and Matilda he heard, and that he knows what happened to Matilda. Bob gives up on his search and returns to the mill. He explains to his father that Matilda has left and the engagement has been broken. The miller asks if it would hurt Bob's feelings if he and Mrs. Garland married. Bob is happy for his father, but hopes the wedding will not be too festive.

Bob helps with the preparations; the couple marry in the morning and have the reception that evening. The neighbors are so preoccupied with the military preparations they say little about the wedding. The cottagers' daughters are each invited to bring a young man from camp; the excess food and drink are given to the poor and needy.

John arrives and announces that his regiment is going to Exonbury. After he leaves, he sits near the brink of the millpond and watches Anne shut her bedroom window. The next morning Anne and her mother and the miller go to see John off. Festus appears and says now there's a chance for him, with John's departure. Anne denies this indignantly.

Bob pores over his nullified marriage license. He realizes that he has little appetite and is missing much in life he might otherwise enjoy. He becomes more at ease with Anne and makes her an Aeolian harp that makes music when attached to the millhead. Later he confesses that John designed the harp and asked him to make it. Anne likes the instrument, and Bob tells her he has always been interested in her, but was easily distracted by "new faces." She is chilly to him because of Matilda, but he puts up with it; "his patience testified strongly to his good-humour."

Anne's mother, now Mrs. Loveday, believes she has married beneath her and wonders if Anne should not reconsider Festus. On a rainy afternoon she invites Festus in. Anne hides by joining Bob in the mill, and asks Bob to walk with her to church on Sunday.

On the way to church they read a notice posted on a tree, "Address to All Ranks and Descriptions of Englishmen." (In the preface, Hardy states that he copied the actual document in a local museum, probably the DORSET COUNTY MUSEUM.) The notice states that the French are "assembling the largest force that was ever prepared to invade this Kingdom." The notice calls for men to enter their names on parish lists to volunteer as soldiers, laborers, or wagon drivers.

Bob promptly decides to join. The sergeant who nailed up the notice tries to shape up the local volunteers. Anne and Bob enter the church, where the religion of the country seems to have shifted from "love of God to hatred of Napoleon Buonaparte." Bob worries that John, as a trumpeter, will be "picked off" and die in battle.

Bob wants to clear John's name, explaining his reasons for evicting Matilda. He does not explain to Anne, who thinks John wanted to marry Matilda and had known her before. Bob does tell the story to Mr. Loveday, hoping he will tell Mrs. Loveday, who will tell Anne.

Old Mr. Derriman sends a gig for Anne and shows her where his papers are. He fears the French will cause his estate to go to Festus. He gives Anne a cryptic clue to the location of the papers, and she tucks the paper in her bosom.

Festus goes to ask his uncle for money for the summer. On the way he meets a fashionably dressed lady out for a walk. She is Matilda Johnson, who is joining the Budmouth theater company when they arrive for the season. Festus also spots Anne going home and runs after her, pretending to be ill and leaping up again. She dislodges a little plank crossing the river, which causes Festus to fall in the water. Bob comes to meet her. While struggling with Festus, Anne has lost the paper Benjamin gave her with the clue to the location of his papers, but she makes a copy from memory. Matilda has found the paper but cannot understand it.

They all hear the boom of a large distant gun. The French have supposedly landed in West Bay. Festus learns it was a false report, but does not tell Anthony CRIPPLESTRAW, his servant. He urges him to go to Budmouth and be prepared to fight. Squire Benjamin, meanwhile, sings to himself from a window, *"Twen-ty-three and half from N.W. Six-teen and three-quar-ters from N.E."* (the location of his papers in the cellar). Festus meets some soldiers who discover he had already known of the false report; they resent his not informing them.

Chapters 27–35

Festus fails to tell Miller Loveday and other householders, who have struggled out armed with flint-boxes and pickets, that the French have not landed. Anne and her mother have ridden ahead with Molly, the servant. Festus misdirects Bob. When the wheel comes off Anne and her mother's carriage, Anne is injured and is left in a shepherd's empty house. Festus traps Anne in the locked cottage, but, speaking from the window, she rejects him. She escapes, flings herself on Champion sideways, and rides along until John Loveday, startled at the sight of a "military horse with a bundle of drapery across his back," stops him and rescues Anne. She is incoherent but revives.

John sets out to find Festus, who is in a tavern asleep in the bar, and pummels him. Festus, inebriated, believes Bob is his assailant. Later he quizzes his uncle on the meaning of the cryptic code he has seen him scratching on the ground.

John has changed and become gray and sad, but tries to be cheerful in accepting Bob's courtship of Anne. He pretends he does not care for her. Anne falsely deduces that John is interested in an actress at Budmouth. Anne, Bob, and John decide to go to a play; John buys tickets but pretends the actress has given them to him.

At the Theatre Royal in Budmouth they see Matilda Johnson appear in the play, to Anne's astonishment. When they leave the theater they see a slim boat in the harbor, but Bob does not recognize it. The boat is the *Black Diamond,* whose officers are empowered to organize press-gangs—that is, to recruit reluctant men for military service. Festus Derriman is at the harbor, and begins talking with Matilda Johnson, whom he has seen once or twice before and recognizes. The officers from the ship talk with him about possible recruits, and Festus points out Bob Loveday, then walking along with Anne, telling them where he lives. Matilda is upset.

The landlord at the inn where Bob's horse has been stabled mentions the *Black Diamond* and the men ready to find recruits. Bob turns pale, hoping to continue life as a miller, having already served aboard the brig *Perwil.* He realizes he cannot marry Anne if he is sent to sea, although he misses shipboard life somewhat. The men come to the mill, but Bob escapes. In doing so, he sustains a mild head injury and loses consciousness. Anne and Matilda find him hours later, conceal him under a bridge, and manage to take him home. He recovers, but fluctuates between wanting to go to sea and to stay at home with Anne. He takes a lock of Matilda's hair to John, believing, somehow, that John is interested in her. It becomes clear to Bob that John has sacrificed his own love for Anne so that Bob can have her.

In Weymouth, Bob learns that Captain Thomas Hardy (an ancestor of Hardy's; he was Lord Nelson's captain aboard the *Victory* and figures in *The Dynasts*) has come to see the king. Bob goes to see Captain Hardy at the family home, where his sisters live, a "small manorhouse" at Pos'ham (Portisham, a village six miles north of Weymouth). Captain Hardy is a bachelor of 35. Bob tells Captain Hardy he realizes he should be aboard a man-of-war but has been hampered by his attachment to a young woman, the daughter of the painter Garland. Captain Hardy shows him a painting by Garland, a view of the village, hanging on the wall.

Bob asks if he might serve aboard the *Victory.* The captain says Bob will not be allowed to choose his ship, but says he will ask on Bob's behalf. Bob returns home and announces the news to his family. He thinks his enlistment is necessary in order to remove the danger of the French invasion from Britain. Anne begins crying but recovers quickly. Before she wakes the next day, Bob has gone to Budmouth and boarded the ship as a volunteer.

Bob has told John to take Anne if she seemed interested in him. Festus Derriman is satisfied to see Bob go. John brings newspapers stating that Captain Hardy wished Bob to sail with him aboard the *Victory.* Anne goes to Budmouth to see the ship and climbs Portland Bill, or Beal, a "wild, herbless, weather-worn promontory." An old sailor who has a son aboard the ship joins her; he has a spyglass, but his vision is very poor. Anne looks through the spyglass and describes the ship offshore as large, with "three masts, three rows of guns along the side, and all her sails set." She sees the jack, the ensign, Admiral Nelson's flag, and the figurehead, a "coat-of-arms, supported on this side by a sailor." The man tells her more about the ship and says the admiral will not return alive. She watches until the *Victory* disappears. She begins reciting the prayer in the church of England litany, "those that go down to the sea in ships, that do business in great waters. . ." A man's voice finishes it for her, and she turns to see John Loveday. He says Admiral Nelson took his own coffin on board the ship.

John offers to take Anne to a cove and send her across the bay with a man he knows; he turns out to be the sailor, who has two sons. She goes into a little lane and begins crying near a sulphurous spring. Two strangers walk past; one, wearing a blue coat with gilt buttons, asks her why she is crying. To her astonishment, it is King GEORGE III. She tells him a friend has gone to sea aboard the *Victory,* and he asks his name, which she tells him. She curtseys and the king smiles.

No news reaches Overcombe of the blockade off Cadiz, but in time John arrives with news of the Battle of TRAFALGAR and the death of Nelson. Captain Hardy has survived, but they know nothing of Bob until Jim Cornick, the son of the old sailor, James Cornick, finally comes with the news that Bob is alive and well. Cornick says they have not heard from Bob because he is courting a young woman at Portsmouth. Anne sends him her best wishes, goes upstairs, and faints. She moans to herself, "If he had been dead I could have borne it, but this I cannot bear!"

Chapters 36–41

Festus Derriman inquires about Bob. When he learns that Bob is to be married to someone from Portsmouth he is delighted, thinks the danger of a duel with Bob is past, and hastens to the mill. He finds Mrs. Loveday alone, and asks for Anne's hand. She replies that Anne is ill, but that she will ask her when she is better. Festus declares that Bob gave up Anne in John's favor, but Mrs. Loveday declares John is in love with "that actresswoman." John enters, hears this from Mrs. Loveday, and follows Festus. He tells Festus to mind his own business; Festus decides to court Matilda to spite John. He finds Matilda in Budmouth and says he has come to displace John in her affections. She pretends John is constantly wooing her. She returns the paper she found, the cryptic note his uncle had given to Anne. Festus is positive it marks the spot where Benjamin has hidden something away. He promises to give Matilda half.

Bob finally writes to say he had walked in Admiral Nelson's funeral procession, and that he might go to Portsmouth to see a "valued friend." The miller urges John to marry Anne. She almost accepts him, but Bob writes him to say he will be faithful to Anne after all. John is acutely depressed.

John and Anne climb up to see the image of King George carved in a chalk hill. Things go badly for them, however; John tries to persuade himself to turn her over to Bob, by praising him; Anne strives to see John's good qualities. News comes that Matilda and Festus are engaged.

John hears that Bob has become a lieutenant on a sloop. He writes Bob that if he wants Anne he must come immediately. He does come, but Anne is cold to him. He has a scar on his cheek from a grenade thrown from the *Redoutable.* One night Bob and Anne watch fireworks from an attic window, shot from Budmouth in honor of the king. Bob begs her again to forgive him, but she refuses. He angrily leaves, saying whatever she hears has happened to him is her doing.

Benjamin Derriman appears again with his tin box and gives it to Anne. Festus and Matilda have been digging for it in the next cellar. Anne and Bob become friends again; Benjamin Derriman slips in and snatches up his box just as Festus tries to grab it. Benjamin disappears with it, but dies on the way home. They discover it months later behind the chimney board of Anne's bedroom. Apparently he had fled from the front door with the box, then doubled back and entered from the rear, depositing the box in Anne's room.

Benjamin's will is inside; he has named Anne the executrix of the will and the heir of all he has except five small freehold houses in a back street in Budmouth. Anne inherits Oxwell Hall.

John's regiment of the Dragoons are ordered to join Sir Arthur Wellesley in the Iberian Peninsula. He has walked past a church on the way home to make his final call and has seen Festus and Matilda emerge from a church as bride and groom. John leaves for Spain; Bob tells him, just before he leaves, that Anne has agreed to marry him. We are told that he blows his trumpet until he is "silenced forever upon one of the bloody battlefields of Spain." Anne promises to marry Bob in six months if he behaves.

For further reading: Cox, "Thomas Hardy's *Trumpet-Major* Notebook"; Johnson, "In Defence of *The Trumpet-Major:* Papers Presented at the 1975 Summer School"; LaBelle, "Hardy's *The Trumpet-Major*"; Mistichelli, "The Trumpet-Major's Signal: Kinship and Sexual Rivalry in the Novels of Thomas Hardy"; Nemesvari, "The Anti-Comedy of *The Trumpet-Major*"; Spurr, "'Splendid Words': Hardy's *Trumpet-Major* and 'Church Verse.'"

"Tryst at an Ancient Earthwork, A" Short story first published as "Ancient Earthworks and What Two Enthusiastic Scientists Found Therein" in the *Detroit Post* on March 15, 1885, then as "Ancient Earthworks at Casterbridge" in the *English Illustrated Magazine,* December 1893, with four photographs by W. Pouncy of DORCHESTER. In 1913 it was collected as "A Tryst at an Ancient Earthwork" in *A CHANGED MAN AND OTHER TALES.*

When the story was published in the *English Illustrated Magazine,* the location was only given as CASTERBRIDGE, but the editor identified Casterbridge as Dorchester. As soon as it appeared, Hardy wrote his friend Florence HENNIKER that he regretted the editor's mentioning Dorchester, because he feared that one of the characters might be identified with "a local man, still living," although it had really been meant "for nobody in particular" (*Letters* II, 43). Michael Millgate and Richard Purdy, however, state that Edward Cunnington of Dorchester was actually the model for the antiquary (*Letters* IV, 203).

The story opens outside MAIDEN CASTLE ("the fort"), the "largest Ancient-British work in the kingdom." It is likened to a "cephalopod in shape," covered in a green mantle of vegetation. It is prehistoric, predating the Roman occupation of Britain. The narrator has a midnight appointment at the fort. The night is cold and windy as he ascends to the second acclivity (on the opposite side from the actual entrance); suddenly there is a heavy hailstorm. The main entrance gate is some way ahead. The narrator reflects that men must have gone out through the gates "to battle with the Roman legions under Vespasian."

The narrator then ascends the third and last escarpment. The interior is so enormous as to be an "upland plateau," but the stones and architraves have long since been carried away to use in building neighboring villages. From the central mound, by day, there would be a view "of almost limitless extent." Suddenly a voice pronounces the name of the narrator. It is his friend, a well-known antiquary, who is standing with lantern, spade, and pickaxe. He is dressed in black and "bespattered with mud" from his feet to his hat. The narrator asks why he did not plan their stroll through the earthworks for daytime; the antiquary says, ominously, that his purpose is to dig and that he could not have obtained permission for his enterprise. There are many signs posted announcing penalties for digging.

The narrator believes that his friend has lost the "moral sense" that would inhibit him from his illegal activity. After a time the friend's pickaxe strikes a Roman mosaic pavement in an area of the fortress thought to be exclusively Celtic. The Romans have been guided by a Celtic framework and produced a work with exquisite tesserae (tiny bits of marble or glass) in many colors and intricate patterns. He digs further and finds a bottle, a piece of weapon, and a perfect skeleton; he believes the man must have been a warrior who had fallen fighting on the spot. There is also a bronze-gilt (or possibly gold) figure of Mercury. The narrator observes that they might as well be standing in the Roman Forum and not on a hill in WESSEX.

The antiquary says he has proved his point and begins replacing the objects. However, the skeleton disintegrates in the air; they must bury the fragments only. The narrator thinks he sees him slip something into his coat pocket, but the antiquary denies it. They finish just before dawn. The narrator suspects his friend neglected to rebury the small statuette, however. After he dies a gilt statuette representing Mercury, labeled "Debased Roman," is found among his effects. There is no explanation of how he came to acquire it. He bequeathed it to the Casterbridge Museum.

Turner, Hugh Thackeray (1853–1937) Architect and secretary for 29 years to the SOCIETY FOR THE PROTECTION OF ANCIENT BUILDINGS (SPAB). Hardy frequently corresponded with Turner about the threatened destruction of various buildings, such as the village church in Stratton in 1889 (*Letters* I, 205). In January 1895 Turner asked whether Hardy knew anything about the proposed restoration of the church at Toller Porcorum, west of Maiden Newton, DORSET (*Letters* II, 67), and in January 1904 he wrote of his concern about faulty renovations at St. Mary's, Puddletown (*Letters* III, 97). They were still concerned about St. Mary's and exchanged letters regarding its preservation in 1910. In February, Hardy wrote that it was the only one in the county that "has not been tampered with, & I agree with you in deploring the contemplated enlargement." He had made inquires about the usual size of the congregation and found it was "never full, & seldom half-full" (*Letters* IV, 73–74). By August of that year, he reported that officials in Puddletown had pulled down the medieval house in the village in order to use the stones in the new channel, which was to be constructed. On October 5, 1910, he sent a despairing one-line letter to Turner: "Have you seen what has happened to Puddletown Church?" Three days later Hardy wrote again to say that the channel had been pulled down, along with a wall and an adjoining arch, and the gravestones had been removed from the churchyard. The site had been cleared and foundations dug. Hardy's letter appeared in its entirety in the SPAB's annual report for 1911, with an expression of regret that despite their endeavors the work had gone forward (*Letters* IV, 122).

Puddletown was very near Hardy's birthplace, HIGHER BOCKHAMPTON, and he had many aunts, uncles, and cousins there on both sides of the family, whom he visited frequently. He was always horrified by the failure to preserve historic buildings, but the destruction of the medieval house and the violation of the Puddletown Church must have been particularly painful to him.

Two on a Tower   Novel serialized in the ATLANTIC MONTHLY (1882, vols. 49 and 50) and published by SAMPSON LOW, MARSTON, SEARLE, & RIVINGTON, London, in 1882. It was memorable for its depiction of human passions against a cosmic background. It was actually, in the words of one critic, an indication of the incipient "rumblings of British prudery" (Samuel S. Chew, *The Nineteenth Century and After*).

The novel, although not so thoroughly pessimistic as JUDE THE OBSCURE or *The* RETURN OF THE NATIVE, or TESS OF THE D'URBERVILLES, is a tragedy, or as F. B. Pinion expresses it, a "tragi-comedy" (preface to *Two on a Tower* [New Wessex Edition, London: Macmillan, 1975]). The novel embodies Hardy's serious interest in astronomy and science. In the preface to the New Wessex Edition, written in July 1895, Hardy states that the novel grew out of a wish to "set the emotional history of two infinitesimal lives against the stupendous background of the stellar universe, and to impart to readers the sentiment that of these contrasting magnitudes the smaller might be the greater to them as men." He was not altogether satisfied with it, and wished he had been able to rewrite it. The style in the early chapters is "compact and disciplined," as Pinion puts it, but it declines in later chapters. J. I. M. Stewart suggests that Hardy's theme of the "rival attractions of study and love" come from his reading of SHAKESPEARE's *Love's Labour's Lost*. Hardy's friend Edmund GOSSE recommended the title page quotation from Richard Crashaw's "Love's Horoscope" (Pinion, *A Hardy Companion*, 38–40). Pinion suggests that Hardy's interest in astronomy began when he was about 15; he read a periodical titled *The Popular Educator* and viewed the stars through a telescope with Handley MOULE of nearby Fordington.

The setting is near WIMBORNE, where the Hardys lived from June 1881 until June 1883.

SYNOPSIS

Chapters 1–9

Lady Viviette CONSTANTINE, of Welland House, is beautiful and has "Romance blood in her veins." She is bored; her husband, Sir Blount CONSTANTINE, has left her to shoot lions in Africa. She has the idea of visiting a tower on her property, but her coachman says there is no road. She must wait until the weather is dry and will allow a coach to cross over land.

Several months later she walks to the pillar herself, opens the door, and climbs the stairs. She meets a youth, Swithin ST. CLEEVE, who has a complexion like that "with which Raffaelle enriches the countenance of the youthful son of Zacharias." He is watching, through his telescope, a cyclone in the sun. He tells her he has taken possession of her column, which was erected in memory of one of the Constantines in 1782. A key was given to his great-grandfather to show visitors in; no one has ever come. Swithin tells her he aspires to be Astronomer Royal.

Lady Constantine meets Amos FRY ("Haymoss"), a laborer at Welland, her estate, who explains that Swithin was educated at Warborne and that his father had been high-born (Parson St. Cleeve); he had married Farmer Giles Martin's daughter. His grandfather and both parents died and Swithin was sent to grammar school. He has "two stations of life in his blood" so he's "good for nothing."

Swithin goes home to his grandmother, Mrs. MARTIN ("Gammer"). The locals come to choir practice and comment on Sir Blount in Africa; they realize how bored Lady Constantive is. Haymoss arrives and they talk about ailments. Parson TORKINGHAM comes also. He is summoned to see Lady Constantine and the meeting ends. She admits she joins Swithin at night to take him up on his offer to show her the stars. She confesses she has received a letter, but cannot speak of it at the time.

Swithin goes to his tower. Lady Constantine visits him and reads to him. He quizzes her on the stars. She decides to send him to London to investigate rumors she has heard about Sir Blount. He says he will go if she will go to the tower in his absence and write down everything she sees.

Swithin writes from London that he is coming back; when he returns he finds that she has not watched the stars every night. He brings an expensive lens he needs, but it breaks; she orders another one. She delivers it to the tower but finds him asleep; she cuts off some of his hair.

Swithin receives the new lens joyfully and says if he makes any discoveries he will give her credit. She writes that she had never realized the grandeur of astronomy until he revealed them. She takes the letter to the tower but changes her mind and tries in vain to retrieve it. She doesn't hear from Swithin, and finds at church that his telescope "won't work." He needs an equatorial, a special and expensive piece of equipment. Tabitha LARK comes to read to Lady Constantine but finds her reading obsolete astronomy volumes. Lady Constantine writes Swithin and invites him to call. She realizes his chance of becoming Astronomer Royal is remote. She summons him to Welland House and says she wishes to buy him an equatorial; he will be *her* "Astronomer Royal." He informs her that the "secret of productive study is to avoid well," and he seldom reads books on any subject except astronomy.

A wagon loaded with packing cases comes to the Great House. Lady Constantine goes to the tower to see the equatorial assembled. Swithin says he will never marry: "a beloved science is enough wife for me." He tells her about the stars, and she says she will return to the tower when his theory is published.

Swithin makes a discovery regarding variable stars and writes a paper about it, "A New Astronomical Discovery." He then disappears from view, to Lady Constantine's consternation. Hearing that he is dying, she hastens to his grandmother's house. Swithin has gone into a decline at the discovery that someone else had just published a pamphlet on the very same subject. The doctor tells Lady Constantine there is a change for the worse; she flings herself on the bed and kisses him.

Chapters 10–20

Swithin recovers. Old Hannah, who assists Swithin's grandmother, declares there is a comet getting brighter each night. Swithin is enthralled at the prospect of a new comet, which saves his life. The wonders of the sky "resumed their old power over his imagination." He attaches an old telescope to his bedpost and views the comet while he convalesces, hoping to revive enough to see it through the equatorial in the tower. He sees Lady Constantine approach the house and turn back; she longs to see him but cannot quite bring herself to visit him. Her feelings are so strong she believes it would lead to disaster.

She wanders into the church and hears Tabitha Lark playing the organ. Being "as impressionable as a turtle-dove," Lady Constantine sees the Ten Commandments on two tablets and believes she is about to break one of them on the right side ("Thou shalt not commit adultery"). She decides to provide Swithin with the "ideal maiden" since she is technically still married.

Mr. Torkingham comes to the church and tells Lady Constantine that she has been a widow for more than 18 months: he says Sir Blount became ill with dysentery and malaria in South Africa and died on the banks of the Zouga on October 24, 18—.

Sir Blount's death has left his widow impoverished; he had debts and annuities committed to distant relatives. Lady Constantine sells her horses and other property and moves to one room in her manor house. The comet vanishes. Swithin returns to the tower; while he is gone, Lady Constantine calls to ask if he might leave the tower door open so she can observe the skies. He sends a key to Welland House. When he arrives at the tower, she is already there. She says she doesn't mind poverty and has developed a love of astronomy. Swithin supposes she will "fall a prey to some man, some uninteresting country squire" and be "lost to the scientific world." She denies it. Some of the work-folk approach, having been invited to view the comet.

Swithin locks the door, but hears the workers talking about the comet, the death of Sir Blount, and the possibility of Swithin's marriage to Lady Constantine: "she's rather meaning to commit flat matrimony wi' somebody or other, and one young gentleman in particular." They describe Swithin as "planned, cut out, and finished for the delight of 'ooman." Their speculation is "an awakening" to him. He tells them he has another engagement, and they respond that they will come the next night. Meanwhile, Lady Constantine's house servant and maid arrive at the tower, searching for her. Swithin smuggles her out while the servants take shelter from the rain in a hut.

Lady Constantine is not sorry about her "reverses" but finds them comforting. Although she is nearly 10 years older than Swithin, a certain alchemy has changed him from an astronomer "into an eager lover and . . . spoilt a promising young physicist." Swithin does not present himself at his door right away, and she does not put herself in his way.

Finally, from the tower, he sees Lady Constantine seated in a donkey carriage instead of her former landau, attended by a single boy in a coat with buttons, who is both coachman and footman. Swithin goes to the turnpike road and meets her walking along; in her absence he "has become a man." She has sent the boy with a book Swithin needed.

Swithin declares his love for her, saying her eyes will be his "stars for the future." She worries about their age difference, however, and calls their attachment an "interlude." They take a different road to avoid Mr. Torkingham, whom they have seen from afar leaning over a gate, but Lady Constantine's page sees them from an apple tree. She decides she and Swithin must not meet for some time.

They do not meet for three months. Then Swithin writes to say he can do nothing with astronomy; he is too miserable. She comes to the tower and he proposes a private marriage. He says the only alternative is for him to go away. She agrees to marry him; he plans to get a marriage license in London. Before he can do so, a terrible storm destroys the dome of the tower and part of the house he shares with his grandmother. Because he must assist with the repair of the roof and the house, he sends Lady Constantine to stay in the parish the required amount of time to obtain the license. In London she reads a letter from her brother, Louis GLANVILLE, saying he has returned from Rio Janeiro and is coming to visit; he does not offer condolences on Sir Blount's death, but wants her to marry a "genial squire."

Alarmed to know her brother is in London, she takes her maid, who is not told her purpose, and goes to Bath. After 13 days she goes to the abbey and obtains a marriage license from the surrogate. She frantically writes Swithin to come. The maid receives a letter saying her child is ill, and goes home.

As Swithin leaves for Bath, he receives a letter from a solicitor informing him that his paternal great-uncle, a physician, has died and left him a bequest of £600 a year if he does not marry before he is 25. He pays no attention and hastens to Bath, where Lady Constantine meets him at the station. They are married at the church, spend the night, and board the train to Warborne. At the junction for the branch line, as they are waiting outside the station, a phaeton speeds by; the driver whips the horse, and a corner of the whip cuts Lady Constantine's cheek. The driver climbs out of the phaeton and asks to apologize to the lady, who has fled to the waiting room. Swithin goes to summon her, but learns the driver is her evil brother Louis. She realizes he is going to Warborne. The couple decide to go to Warborne in separate carriages and stay in the cabin until the cut disappears. Swithin catches some birds for dinner, and the next morning brings breakfast food from his grandmother's home.

He tells Lady Constantine that when he arrived at his grandmother's she was so open and kindly he had longed to tell her of the marriage. Lady Constantine begs him to say nothing. They observe the stars at night, but the next morning Lady Constantine believes she must return to Welland House. Swithin learns that Louis has gone to BUDMOUTH for several weeks, but will return. They walk to Warborne, take the train to the junction, claim her luggage, and return by train to Warborne as though from Bath; she orders a carriage and goes to Welland House. He goes to the cabin by the tower.

Chapters 21–30
Now that they are married, Swithin calmly resumes his astronomical studies and Lady Constantine returns to her old life in a wing of Welland House. They pretend to be strangers when they meet in Welland, but she tells him her brother has gone to Paris. She will be on the lawn that evening. When he comes, she shows him through her small section of the house; the remainder

is filled with cobwebs and mice. The house is hers for life, but because of the annuities to Sir Blount's distant relatives she has very little to live on except her private income.

There is an old church organ in one of the rooms, which reminds her that Swithin has never been confirmed. She asks that he be confirmed in the spring; he agrees. Suddenly Louis Glanville returns. Lady Constantine tells Swithin he can stay, but he decides it is better to return to his cabin. It has begun to rain; he throws an old greatcoat around him. Lady Constantine comes to the door and shrieks when she sees the greatcoat in the shadows. Louis runs up; she pretends she has seen the ghost of Sir Blount.

On his way home, Swithin encounters the rustic laborers but does not speak to them. They whisper to each other and ride on ahead. At his grandmother's home he leaves the greatcoat in the outhouse. Hannah tells him the work-folk are in the kitchen; he pretends he has just come from upstairs and listens to their tale of seeing the ghost of Sir Blount. They speak of Swithin's confirmation; his grandmother says it was a "piece of neglect."

Swithin realizes how much dread the thought of Sir Blount evokes in his wife. He writes a note asking her to meet him at Rings-Hill column; she finally comes, after her brother has gone out. She says her brother tells her every day that she must remarry for money and position.

Swithin thinks more about his uncle's will; he was to receive payments beginning at age 21. He does not want Lady Constantine to know he has given up his legacy for her. In May he learns that the bishop is coming to stay at the vicarage and will attend a grand luncheon at Welland House. Lady Constantine does not mention it to Swithin, although he strolls near the house and observes the preparations, for which Louis is paying. Swithin will be confirmed but is not invited to the luncheon. He says he is sorry Lady Constantine is less interested in astronomy than she used to be.

On the morning of the confirmation service Swithin arrives at church and sees Lady Constantine and her brother. She is the handsomest woman in church, yet Swithin thinks the casual spectator would have assumed one of the "muslin-clad maidens" in the confirmation class to be Swithin's "natural mate." Louis Glanville stares at Swithin; Swithin tries to look at Viviette, but his view is obscured and he looks at Tabitha Lark at the organ. Tabitha pulls out her handkerchief to alert the boy blowing the bellows, and spills her personal articles out at Swithin's feet. She is mortified; he collects them and hands them back. He offers to take her out into the air, but she declines. After the service he watches Lady Constantine and the others go into Welland House for luncheon. Swithin realizes, however, that on entering the marriage he had agreed to keep their outward lives the same.

In Welland House the luncheon proceeds. Lady Constantine is indifferent to the bishop and thus fascinates him. Bishop Helmsdale asks about Swithin; Viviette pretends she knows little about him. The bishop finds him very handsome and realizes he had known his father, St. Cleeve of All Angels (a college name suggested by All Souls, Oxford). Mr. Torkingham explains that he himself "rashly contracted a marriage" with the daughter of a farmer and must now live on a small income. Bishop Helmsdale remarks that half-incomes do men "little good" unless they happen to be geniuses. Viviette stops herself from crying out that Swithin is a genius. Mr. Torkingham explains that he is a scientist; she adds, "an astronomer." Louis says Swithin is as interested in "one of his fellow-creatures as in the science of astronomy," but he means Tabitha Lark. Viviette remembers that Tabitha used to come and read to her.

That night Mr. Torkingham invites Viviette and her brother to dinner at the vicarage with the Bishop; she pleads a headache and does not go, which the Bishop finds disappointing. Viviette slips out of the house and goes to see Swithin in the tower to see if he has flirted with Tabitha. He says he resents her shutting her gates against him while entertaining "big-wigs." All is resolved when they hear a tapping at the door. It is Mr. Torkingham, Louis, and Bishop Helmsdale. Viviette hides between the divan and the wall. Swithin takes them up the spiral stairs to the roof and embarks on a long explanation; Viviette flees while they are upstairs. When they come down again the Bishop asks Swithin to meet him in the churchyard the next morning.

When Swithin arrives at the church he hears laughter and voices in the enclosure. Climbing to the belfry, he sees the Bishop, Viviette, and Louis bowling on the lawn. They continue for more than an hour; Swithin becomes incensed at the delay. He turns to see Tabitha behind him; she has come to practice on the organ. The Bishop finally looks at his watch and goes into the churchyard; Swithin joins him. Louis Glanville is suspicious and eavesdrops. The Bishop tells Swithin he has known his father, but would not have confirmed Swithin himself if he had known then what he discovered later—he found a coral bracelet on the divan in Swithin's cabin. The Bishop flings it down on a tombstone and leaves. His countenance brightens as he sees Viviette with a basket, going to see poor cottagers.

Louis Glanville finds the bracelet. He assumes it belongs to Tabitha, who is coming out of the church, and gives it to her. She thinks it is a present, not recognizing that it is one of a pair Swithin gave Viviette on their wedding day. Soon she remembers seeing Viviette wearing it. She plans to return it that evening.

The Bishop leaves, and Viviette and Louis dine alone. Louis tells her she has "done well" but might have been "warmer." She declares she has no more thought of the bishop than of the pope and is sorry he came to lunch. Louis says she could be the "spiritual queen of Melchester." Her hair will soon be grey and young men won't look at her or, if they do, they will soon "despise" her as an "antiquated party." She says she could not accept the bishop; she does not love him. Louis vows to stay on until she accepts the bishop. He goes out to smoke a cigar, but returns for his case; he discovers Swithin outside the window talking with Viviette. Swithin leaves, and Viviette says he is merely an acquaintance. Louis declares he is a "regular young sinner," and that the Bishop had discovered the previous night that he was "not alone in his seclusion." Viviette says she has lost her bracelet; Louis realizes where the bracelet had been found.

Swithin retreats as far as the churchyard; Viviette runs out to him as soon as Louis goes upstairs. Swithin says the bishop found the bracelet and put it on a tombstone, where Louis found it. When Lady Constantine returns home, Tabitha Lark is waiting for her with the coral bracelet. She tells Tabitha to keep the bracelet and divide it into two separate small bracelets but not to explain anything to Louis. Louis sees Tabitha wearing the bracelets the next morning. Then he tells Viviette he knows who has her bracelet, but she has divided the remaining one into two and holds out both wrists. He is mystified but not convinced and plans to set a trap.

Louis calls on Swithin in his tower and invites him to dinner to see some old scientific volumes. He then invites Swithin to spend the night. When they retire, Louis takes a cobweb and puts it across Swithin's door. When he checks the door later, he finds the cobweb missing and hears Viviette's voice murmuring. He goes to Viviette's room and declares that their guest has vanished. Viviette says she was saying her prayers. Louis browbeats her until she admits she loves Swithin, who was never in Viviette's room. Swithin comes tiptoeing in from his observatory, carrying his boots.

Chapters 31–41

At breakfast Viviette opens a letter from Bishop Helmsdale proposing to her. If she accepts his proposal, he will show her a few "plain, practical rules" he has drawn up for their future guidance. Even if she has a "deficiency of warmth," he writes, she will have an "immense power" to do good. She tells Louis she will decline. Her brother cannot comprehend why she will not accept the opportunity to leap into such a "leading position," and says her answer must be yes. "And yet it will be no," she responds. She is sure Louis does not know of her actual marriage to Swithin. He leaves Welland House.

She answers the bishop that she esteems him but must give him a negative reply. She hopes for a "life-long friendship" with him. She puts the letter aside;

Swithin enters. She tells him she thinks it best to be honest about their marriage. Swithin is about to leave for Greenwich. Lady Constantine works on a new letter to the bishop explaining everything, but is interrupted by a visit from the clerk representing her solicitor in Warborne. He brings a newspaper dispatch quoting the companion of Sir Blount, saying that he had not died when they thought, but lived on until the previous December; it was a companion who had actually died earlier. In the interim, Sir Blount married a native princess, drank heavily, and shot himself in a fit of depression. Viviette realizes that, at the time of her marriage to Swithin, Sir Blount was still alive and still would have been alive at least six weeks after her marriage. Therefore, Swithin was not her husband "in the eyes of the law."

The next day Mr. Cecil arrives, and Viviette asks how they could have proven Sir Blount's will without absolute evidence of his death. He answers that his death had been "presumptive." She frantically writes to Swithin at Greenwich saying they are not legally married. Her letter crosses his; he had seen the dispatch at Greenwich. He writes that he plans to come back Saturday night and that they should arrange their remarriage promptly. She receives a newspaper with a cartoon of the suicide of Sir Blount, showing the native princess.

Before Swithin can return, he receives a letter from his solicitors about his uncle's annuity. He plans to tell his solicitors that he is not eligible for the annuity. He explains his uncles' bequest to Viviette. She cries, and says she has ruined him by making him ineligible for the annuity. Swithin wants to plan their public wedding. He talks about Greenwich Observatory and the details of an expedition he hopes to join that will observe the transit of Venus at a remote southern station.

Viviette reads the letter from Dr. St. Cleeve in which he states that he had attached such conditions in order to save his nephew from "a woman" (i.e. Viviette), of whom he had heard. He believes her too old for his nephew, and thinks she should have realized it. "She is old enough to know that a *liaison* with her may, and almost certainly would, be your ruin . . . unless she is a complete goose." Viviette, though terribly hurt, realizes that, even if Swithin does not agree, "such thoughts of her had been implanted in him" and would germinate. She determines to sacrifice her happiness so that he can accept the annuity and travel.

Lady Constantine tells Louis that Swithin is not her lawful husband; then writes to Swithin, releasing him from marriage and freeing him to travel and make his fortune, although she loves him even more than she once did. Swithin wishes he had never told her about the bequest. At first she refuses to see him, and she sends Louis to tell him it is to his advantage to leave on his travels and make his mark as an astronomer. She

then yields and goes to his cabin again, but tells him he must leave on his travels; she agrees to marry him as soon as he returns and is 25.

Bishop Helmsdale writes to sympathize with her about the recent news of her husband's death, and to renew his proposal. She goes about demolishing Swithin's cabin (at Swithin's request) and has the equatorial packed. She has a vision of a golden-haired, toddling child in the woods and, that night, realizes she is pregnant. She thinks she must "die outright." She rushes to Southampton, but finds that Swithin's ship has just sailed. She then takes the train back to Warborne and goes to Swithin's grandmother, but she and Hannah only have a vague idea of where Swithin is going. She writes letters to observatories and telegraphs him in various places.

She then considers whether Swithin would not be better off without a wife and child. She finally tells Louis the news about her pregnancy, and explains about her invalid marriage to Swithin.

Louis arises the next morning and goes to Melchester to meet the bishop. He tells him Viviette truly loves him and, if she could be married in a month or so, it would save her from melancholia and, possibly, death. The bishop agrees to think it over. Louis goes back to Viviette and says he has been unable to find Swithin's address. He lets her suffer another night and day; then the bishop's carriage comes to the door. Louis tells her the bishop has come for an immediate answer of yes or no. He takes the bishop to her apartment. When the bishop comes out, he says Viviette has accepted him and they will be married the first week in September. He believes he has offered a "true shelter from sadness," not realizing it is actually a shelter from scandal.

Swithin, meanwhile, is not aboard the *Occidental* at all, but has gone straight to the Cape of Good Hope. He then goes to Melbourne and Cambridge, and joins the transit expedition. By February the transit of Venus is over and Swithin has returned to the Cape. There he finds a newspaper announcement of Viviette's marriage to the Bishop, sent by his grandmother. Viviette has also written, telling him about the baby, whose life she could not "blight." While he is at the Cape, he receives an announcement of the birth in April of a son to the wife of the Bishop of Melchester.

Three years later Swithin is still at the Cape. His grandmother sends a newspaper with an announcement of the death of the Bishop of Melchester, age 54. His grandmother writes later to say that Lady Constantine is coming back to Welland House, bring her little boy, between three and four years of age. By another autumn, Swithin's work is done, and he tells his grandmother he is coming home. She mentions that she frequently sees Lady Constantine, and that Lady Constantine had shown great interest in his return.

On his way from Warborne, Swithin sees Mr. Tork-ingham, who has come to meet him. He imparts all the local news. Torkingham tells Swithin that Viviette was not very happy with the Bishop. He is worried about her; there is a "nameless something on her mind—a trouble—a rooted melancholy" no one can reach. They pass a crying child who has fallen and stop to help him—"a lovely little fellow with flaxen hair." Mr. Tork-ingham gives him some sweets and tells Swithin he is Lady Constantine's boy, a "seven-months baby" but remarkably healthy. (He was, of course, full term, since Swithin was the father).

On reaching his grandmother's house Swithin sees Tabitha Lark telling her good-bye. Hannah, his grandmother's servant, has died and his grandmother has aged. Tabitha has studied music with great success in London and plays at concerts and oratorios. Tabitha says she will be his amanuensis for his notes.

The next morning Swithin sees someone on top of Rings-Hill tower, goes over, and ascends the staircase. He finds Viviette, dressed in black, with the little boy. Viviette is worn and faded; her hair has a "faint grey haze." To perceptive eyes she has "more promising material beneath" her features than she had had in her youth, but Swithin believes the "silly period" in a woman's life is her "only period of beauty." Viviette can read his thoughts and realizes he no longer loves her. He descends halfway down the steps, turns back, and takes her in his arms, saying he wants to marry her. She utters a shriek of "amazed joy" and falls in his arms. He looks down to see that she has died; "sudden joy after despair" has been too much of a strain on her heart. The child cries; Swithin says, "Hush, my child, I'll take care of you." On the horizon he sees Tabitha Lark bounding in the fields, a harbinger of his future. "The Bishop was avenged." He had acted as the father to Swithin's child, but always suspected his parentage.

CRITICAL RECEPTION AND COMMENTARY

Contemporary reviews of the novel were lukewarm, unlike those of The MAYOR OF CASTERBRIDGE. The *Daily News* commentator declared that the "humor, insight, and psychological analysis of human motive are unsurpassed by anything Hardy has done." The reviewer for the *St. James Gazette* criticized Hardy for the "plot, incidents, and the "bluntness and irreverence of the language." He or she wondered "whether Hardy intended an insult to the Church by having a Bishop marry a fallen woman, Lady Constantine?" Hardy replied he meant no insult whatsoever (Gerber and Davis, *Thomas Hardy: An Annotated Bibliography of Writings about Him*, 32–34).

For further reading: Barloon, "Star-Crossed Love: The Gravity of Science in Hardy's *Two on a Tower*"; Bawer,

"*Two on a Tower:* Hardy and Yeats"; Bayley, "The Love Story in *Two on a Tower*"; Grundy, "*Two on a Tower* and *The Duchess of Malfi*"; Hochstadt, "Hardy's Romantic Diptych: A Reading of *A Laodicean* and *Two on a Tower*"; Irvin, "High Passion and High Church in Hardy's *Two on a Tower*"; Maxwell, "Mrs. Grundy and *Two on a Tower*"; Plotz, "The Pinnacled Tower"; Sumner, "The Experimental and the Absurd in *Two on a Tower*"; Ward, "*Two on a Tower:* A Critical Revaluation"; Wing, "Hardy's Star-Cross'd Lovers in *Two on a Tower.*"

"Two Rosalinds, The"   Poem first printed in *Collier's* (New York) on March 20, 1909. It was followed by "REMINISCENCES OF A DANCING MAN" under the collective title "London Nights" in the *English Review*, April 1909. It was later collected in *TIME'S LAUGHINGSTOCKS*.

The poem juxtaposes two LONDON evenings. The first is in the 1860s, when, as a young man, Hardy had gone to a performance of SHAKESPEARE's *As You Like It*, enticed by the marquee announcing the actress playing Rosalind, the heroine. He had entered the theater and, for a brief time, was in the enchanted forest of Arden. Forty years later, again in London, he sees the "self-same portal" announcing the same play. He enters but the actress is "a mammet," not the one "in memories nurst." *Mammet* is a variation of *maumet*, meaning a "person of grotesque appearance or costume"; in other words, an actress who was a doll, a fake, in the role, and not a convincing actress such as the one he remembered and "nursed" in his memories. He immediately leaves; as he goes out he sees an old woman, a "hag," who is hawking the play. "So, you don't like her, sir?" she says. "Ah—*I* was once that Rosalind!—I acted her—none better— / Yes—in eighteen sixty-three." He realizes that "his" Rosalind is still present within the body of the old woman: "Thereon the band withinside lightly / Beat up a merry tune." (He can hear within—in his memory—her long-ago performance).

In an 1890 entry in the *Life*, Hardy recalls being in London with his wife Emma and meeting the actress Ada Rehan. Two days later they went to the Lyceum to see Rehan as Rosalind in *As You Like It*. He notes, "It is possible that the dramatic poem entitled 'The Two Rosalinds' was suggested by this performance combined with some other" (*Life*, 228).

Evidence suggests that the famous actress Mrs. Scott-Siddons made her debut as Rosalind not at the Lyceum, but instead at the Haymarket Theatre in 1867. She was acting as late as 1881, but was treated unkindly by critics. She might have been the "hag" of the poem, reduced to "hawking" or selling copies of the text outside the theater (Bailey, *The Poetry of Thomas Hardy*, 199–200).

U

"Unborn, The" Poem dated 1905 and first printed under the title "Life's Opportunity" in *Wayfarer's Love* (1904). This volume, edited by the duchess of Sutherland, was sold to aid the Potteries and Newcastle Cripples' Guild, London. The poem was later collected in *TIME'S LAUGHINGSTOCKS* (1909).

Hardy imagines visiting the "Cave of the Unborn" one night; the inhabitants can hardly wait to be born. They imagine earth to be a "pure delight, a beauty-spot / where all is gentle, true and just" and there is no darkness.

The poet admits that his heart is "anguished for their sake." The unborn seem to sense, from his face, what awaits them. He silently retires as they "come helter-skelter out / Driven forward like a rabble rout" into the world they had "so desired, / By the all-immanent Will."

Here Hardy again relics on the "immanent Will" to support his contention that being born is actually a disaster. However, whatever deity exists is neither benign nor malevolent toward human beings as a whole. They must accept what comes and not build up unrealistic expectations.

Hardy once asked Clive HOLLAND whether he would have chosen to be born if he had had a choice. Holland replied with a question, "Would you?" Hardy replied, "No, surely not." He also observes that there is a parallel passage in chapter 3 of *TESS OF THE D'URBERVILLES*, when he considers the Durbeyfield children a disaster, on the whole, "passengers in the Durbyfield ship." The "six little helpless creatures had never been asked if they wished for life" (Bailey, *The Poetry of Thomas Hardy*, 254).

Under the Greenwood Tree Hardy's second published novel, which followed *DESPERATE REMEDIES* (1871) and was published by TINSLEY BROTHERS in early June 1872; it was not serialized. Hardy had begun writing it at WEYMOUTH and HIGHER BOCKHAMPTON in the summer of 1871. In October 1871 he wrote William TINSLEY that, early in the summer, he had begun "and nearly finished, a little rural story," and inquired whether Tinsley might be interested in publishing it, as he had already published *Desperate Remedies*. Tinsley did accept the manuscript and published it anonymously, with a print run of 500 copies. Despite good reviews, the novel did not sell very well and was later remaindered (Purdy, *Thomas Hardy: A Bibliographical Study*, 6–8).

Leslie STEPHEN, the editor of *CORNHILL MAGAZINE*, liked it enough to inquire about the identity of the author. He wrote Hardy that he had read it with "very great pleasure indeed" and thought the "descriptions of country life admirable." He invited him to submit any further work for consideration in the magazine. Purdy remarks that Leslie Stephen was "much the finest critic Hardy encountered in his career as a novelist," and believes his philosophy influenced Hardy "more than that of any other contemporary" (Purdy, *Thomas Hardy: A Bibliographical Study*, 336).

Stephen had a clear philosophical influence on Hardy. According to Rosemarie Morgan, within a few weeks of meeting Hardy, Stephen invited him to his rooms late at night. There he asked him to serve as a witness as he abjured Thirty-Nine Articles of the Christian faith. This declaration of agnosticism was remarkable for Stephen, who came from a family of devout members of the Church of England. Morgan suggests that, even on short acquaintance, Stephen saw in Hardy a sympathetic soul and one of similar persuasion (personal communication with the author).

SYNOPSIS

I. Winter

In the opening section of the book we meet the choir of the rural parish of MELLSTOCK, about to make their Christmas round of carol singing. Dick DEWY, Michael MAIL, Robert PENNY, Elias Spinks, Joseph Bowman, and Thomas LEAF are on the way to Dick's home, where they will be joined by his father, the tranter (or carrier) Reuben DEWY, and his father, William DEWY. As they partake of fortified cider and prepare to go caroling, they discuss Geoffrey DAY and his daughter, Fancy DAY, the schoolmistress. They spend several hours playing and singing before every house in East Mellstock, West Mellstock, and Lewgate. Fancy Day appears at her window, wrapped in a white robe with her rich hair tumbling about her shoulders. They are praised and thanked everywhere except at the home of farmer Frederic SHINAR, a bachelor of about 35 and a churchwarden, who complains of their noise.

On Christmas Day the villagers attend Mellstock church. Hardy recalls, in his description of the musicians in the gallery, the days when his own father and grandfather were among the players at STINSFORD CHURCH. Arthur MAYBOLD, the new young vicar, is very much aware of Fancy's presence.

There is a jovial party at the Dewy home on Christmas night; country dancing begins just after midnight. Mr. Shinar is there and manages to dance with Fancy. As the first part of the novel ends, Dick Dewy finds himself "accidentally" passing Fancy Day's school as often as possible.

II. Spring

The romance between Dick and Fancy slowly develops. Meanwhile, the Mellstock choir is unnerved by the frequency of Mr. Maybold's calls on parish members, and by the rumor that he wishes to replace them with an organist, Fancy Day. They decide to call on him.

To Mr. Maybold's alarm, the choir members all arrive in his parlor. He admits that Shinar has suggested that Fancy play the organ in church. He compromises with the choir, and says they can play in church until Michaelmas (in October). The choir speculates that both Maybold and Shinar are in love with Fancy Day.

The week after Easter, Dick cheerfully drives his mare Smart to Yalbury Wood, where Geoffrey Day, Fancy's father, is a gamekeeper, to bring more of Fancy's possessions to her dwelling at Mellstock. Her late mother, a governess in a county family, had collected two of everything, from clocks to dumbwaiters and warming pans, to furnish Fancy's eventual home. Dick stays for the midday meal. He realizes that her father much prefers Shinar to himself as a suitor for Fancy. Mr. Day tells him that wives are a "provoking class of society," because "though they be never right, they be never more than half wrong."

As soon as Dick takes Fancy home and helps move her things in, Mr. Maybold arrives; Dick flees, so as not to be seen, but is upset to see that Maybold is helping her with books and pictures.

Reuben Dewy, a tranter, a carrier of goods, tells Dick he is spending too much time worrying about Fancy. He advises him that, when he makes up his mind to marry, to "take the first respectable body that comes to hand—she's as good as any other." Eventually Dick writes Fancy a letter asking whether she means anything by her "bearing toward him."

III. Summer

Several months later, Dick is in Budmouth (Weymouth) and sees Fancy. He offers to drive her home. She admits she loves him "a little." A new stylish gig overtakes them; it is driven by a handsome man, and Shinar is his companion. Dick proposes to Fancy, who accepts him.

Three months later, Fancy and Susan Dewy, Dick's sister, are picking apples. Dick has gone to a gypsy-party or gypsy celebration, alone, which worries Fancy. She tells Dick she has let Mr. Shinar become fond of her. He has taught her how to catch bullfinches in the river, and proposed to her. Although she has refused him,

her father has encouraged him. In fact Geoffrey has known nothing of Fancy's attachment to Dick. Fancy says she is going home to help with the honey-taking, and Dick promises to come and see her, so her father will realize they have an understanding.

IV. Autumn

Before they go to Fancy's home, Dick and Fancy each have a half-day's holiday and plan to go gather nuts. Fancy, however, says she must alter her dress, which takes all afternoon. Dick becomes impatient; they quarrel, take separate walks in the woods, and reconcile.

Some time later Fancy, Dick, Shinar, and Geoffrey Day are taking honey at Fancy's family home. A bee stings Fancy on the inside of her mouth, and both men try to help her. Dick asks for Fancy's hand, but her father tells him he is not good enough; she has had a fine education, and he wants her to marry a "gentleman" with "polish."

A month later, Fancy leaves her father's house in the rain and walks toward Mellstock. She consults Mrs. Elizabeth Endorfield, a woman who is thought by some to be a witch. She promises to tell Fancy how to "bewitch" her father into letting her marry Dick. She whispers lengthy instructions to Fancy.

Fancy lets it be known in the village that she does not feel well and has no appetite; soon people are asking her father how she is. Geoffrey Day comes to tea and she eats only a fragment of bread. Enoch, Geoffrey's helper, tells Fancy's father he hopes she will be able to keep on teaching; the tradesmen say she is ordering only a fraction of her usual bread and butter. Fancy asks her father not to send her the young rabbits he usually supplies; he tries to pay her butcher's bill but she has scarcely ordered anything for a month. He goes to see her, but she is in bed and her charwoman says she has not been asked to carry her dinner. He yields, but she says she doesn't want permission to marry Dick against his will. He says they may marry the next Midsummer. He calls on William Dewy, who says his grandson has not been well and doesn't speak.

The couple visit Geoffrey and things appear to be settled; they have several happy days. At the time of the harvest Thanksgiving, however, Dick must be away at a funeral and Fancy is about to play the organ in church. Mr. Maybold calls on Fancy, who emerges, radiant and beautifully dressed. He is very conscious of her beauty. The choir is now scattered in the congregation; they feel "out of place, abashed, and inconvenienced by their hands." They disapprove of Fancy's "crowded chords and interludes."

Dick comes to Fancy's home in the rain, dishevelled and untidy. She sends him home and Mr. Maybold appears, trembling, and proposes to her. He says he has loved her for six months. She says yes, but immediately regrets it. The vicar goes home and writes a long letter about his engagement to a friend in Yorkshire.

The next day the vicar meets Dick, who tells him he and Fancy are engaged. Maybold has a "cold and sickly thrill throughout him." He tears up the letter to his friend and throws the fragments in the river. He writes Fancy to ask why she has misled him. His letter crosses one she has written him explaining that she cannot marry him because his love would "blight the happiness" of the man she really loves.

V. Conclusion

At the home of Geoffrey Day, just before Dick and Fancy's wedding, Mrs. Dewy and Mrs. Penny are dressing Fancy. Jane DAY, her strange stepmother, has shut herself up in an inner bedroom. Dick's father and Mr. Penny call up to say they have never seen such "sorrowful envy" as was on the other maidens' faces when the banns were called in church the previous Sunday. The older women tell Fancy she will feel very brave during the ceremony but she must drop her face and look "modest"; she must say to herself, "'Tis to be, and here goes!" The bridesmaids arrive to do their duty as "obedient ministers of the will of that apotheosized being—the Bride."

After the ceremony there is dancing under the trees. Fancy contrives to look privately at the ring on her left hand, although it is continually open to view as she hands out cups, glasses, knives, and forks. Dick cannot feel himself a married man. They prepare for the journey to Dick's new cottage. Meanwhile, Mrs. Day is cleaning out drawers and cupboards rather than joining in the festivities. Fancy and Dick drive off to his cottage and vow to have no secrets from each other; Fancy vows to herself she will never tell him of her flirtation with Farmer Shinar.

CRITICAL RECEPTION AND COMMENTARY

Under the Greenwood Tree is one of Hardy's finest pastoral novels. The first four parts, "Winter," "Spring," "Summer," and "Autumn," suggest the importance of the rhythm of the seasons in a rural community. There is the tapping of the fine oak cask of hard cider before the Mellstock Choir of instrumentalists and singers sets out on Christmas Eve to serenade the outlying homes, followed by the fine spring evening when the choir assembles outside Robert Penny's workshop to discuss the supplanting of the instrumentalists by a new church organ. Summer brings festivity in Budmouth as Fancy DAY waits for the carrier to Mellstock on the seafront, before the green and opal ocean; this is followed by autumn with its annual honey-taking. These scenes and others recapitulate the seasons; taken together they impart the flavor of the uncorrupted country patterns of life Hardy embraced and whose passing he deplored in his essay "THE DORSETSHIRE LABOURER." The characters speak in what he termed the "unwritten, dying, Wessex English that they had learnt of their parents." Their style of life and their agricultural work had not been subjected to the devastating plethora of "reforms"

he deplores in the essay, particularly the eviction of life-holders from their cottages.

Hardy knew the rural world was changing in irreversible ways. In this novel, however, he manages to fix an indelible impression of it at its finest and most charming, exemplified in the final scene of the fifth part, the "Conclusion." The wedding of Fancy Day and Dick DEWY is celebrated in Yalbury Wood, a paradise that, in Hardy's universe, embraces not only birds, rabbits, chickens, and pheasants, but also moles and earthworms. There is country dancing, a lavish supper, storytelling, and, finally, the gratifying departure of the young couple beneath a full moon along a lane between two copses.

Hardy's friend Horace MOULE reviewed the novel for the *SATURDAY REVIEW* on September 28, 1872. He described it as "a series of rural pictures full of life and genuine coloring" and praised its "humour and general observation." An anonymous reviewer in the *ATHENAEUM* believed the "excellent descriptions of rustic life" were "even more vital and vibrant" than those in *Desperate Remedies*. Another anonymous reviewer, writing in the *PALL MALL GAZETTE*, was more critical, holding that the "humble heroes and heroines" of the tale were "much too shrewd" and said "too many good things" to be "truthful representatives of their prototypes in real life." In July 1873, the American reviewer for *The Nation* called it a "charming little tale" and announced that those who were going away for the summer could not "do better than slip this volume into their trunks" (Gerber and Davis, *Thomas Hardy: An Annotated Bibliography of Writings about Him*, 20–21).

Barbara Hardy, writing in 1985, remarks that Hardy blends "the comic and the serious in one medium . . . [which is] a steady and consistent one, sustained throughout the short novel, to report and register a range of comic and serious feelings" ("Passion in Context," in *Forms of Feeling in Victorian Fiction*, rpt. Kramer, ed., *Critical Essays on Thomas Hardy: The Novels*, 84).

For further reading: Beatty, "The Tranter's Cottage in *Under the Greenwood Tree*"; D'Agnillo, "Music and Metaphor in *Under the Greenwood Tree*"; Edwards, "The Ending of *Under the Greenwood Tree*"; Grigson, "*Under the Greenwood Tree*, or, The Mellstock Quire: A Rural Painting of the Dutch School"; Hardy, "*Under the Greenwood Tree*: A Novel about the Imagination"; Irvin, "Hardy's Comic Archetype: *Under the Greenwood Tree*"; Kossick, "*Under the Greenwood Tree*"; Spector, "Flight of Fancy: Characterization in Hardy's *Under the Greenwood Tree*"; Page, "Hardy's Dutch Painting: *Under the Greenwood Tree*."

"Under the Waterfall" Poem collected in *SATIRES OF CIRCUMSTANCE* (1914). It is based on an incident at ST. JULIOT CHURCH, CORNWALL, when Hardy first met his future wife, Emma Gifford (later HARDY). In her manuscript *SOME RECOLLECTIONS*, found after her death and edited and published by Hardy, she recalls Hardy's visit in August 1870 to Cornwall. They explored the cliffs and "sketched and talked of books"; she would ride her mare, Fanny, as he walked by her side. One hot day they took a picnic to Boscastle harbor and went down the Valency Valley. They had to "jump over stones" or "get through a narrow pathway" from time to time. They lost a "tiny picnic-tumbler, and there it is to this day no doubt between two of the boulders." When Hardy edited the manuscript, he verified this incident in a footnote.

In the poem, Emma speaks years later, explaining that whenever she plunges her arm in a basin of water she recalls the "sweet sharp sense of a fugitive day / Fetched back from its thickening shroud of gray."

Hardy intervenes as questioner, asking why this act brings "throbs to your soul?" She then explains how "My lover and I" had walked under the hot August sky and had a picnic; they shared a glass of wine and afterward she had rinsed the glass in the waterfall, where it was lost despite their search for it, "With long bared arms." Ever since, when she thrusts her arm in a basin, it becomes the pool and its edge the "hard smooth face of the brook-side ledge." The "leafy pattern of china-ware" evokes "The hanging plants that were bathing there." She thinks of their "chalice" still there, intact: "No lip has touched it since his and mine / In turns therefrom sipped lovers' wine."

In the manuscript the poem was titled "The Glass in the Stream." At the time, Hardy drew a pencil-sketch of Emma as she knelt and searched for the glass; he inscribed it "F. L. G. by T. H. Aug. 19, 1870. Searching for the glass (water colour sketching in Valency valley)." The sketch is reproduced by Evelyn Hardy and Robert Gittings in *Some Recollections by Emma Hardy* (Bailey, *The Poetry of Thomas Hardy*, 292). Bailey notes that Hardy misspells the place name *Vallency*.

Unity In A *PAIR OF BLUE EYES*, the parlor-maid at Endelstow Rectory, residence of Christopher SWANCOURT and his daughter Elfride SWANCOURT. Although she is a servant, she knows Elfride well. She is also her friend, just as Liddy SMALLBURY is not only the servant, but also the companion/friend, of Bathsheba EVERDENE in *FAR FROM THE MADDING CROWD*. Morgan points out that the relationship between Unity and Elfride is "the first of many woman-woman relationships that have a warmth, trust and closeness in Hardy's world of hyper-critical men" (Rosemarie Morgan, personal communication with the author).

Unity marries Martin CANNISTER, sexton of the church at Endelstow. They open the Welcome Home inn in Endelstow, where she relates the final events of Elfride's life to Henry KNIGHT and Stephen SMITH.

Universal Review, **the** Periodical edited by the art critic and journalist Harry QUILTER from 1888 to 1890. He published Hardy's short story "A TRAGEDY OF TWO AMBITIONS" in December 1888 with six illustrations by George Lambert.

University of Aberdeen Scottish university that conferred an honorary Doctorate of Laws degree on Hardy in 1905. According to Michael Millgate, this honor meant a great deal to Hardy as a "gesture from that world of formal education" which he had not been privileged to know as a young man. He decided to accept the degree in person and, in early April 1905, traveled to Aberdeen. His welcome from the university was a cordial one. He ordered the doctoral gown from a local outfitter and "delighted in the ceremonials and accoutrements associated with the degree ceremony itself" (Millgate, *Thomas Hardy*, 438).

"Unkindly May, An" Poem written, or revised, November 27, 1927, and first printed in the *Daily Telegraph*, April 23, 1928. It was later collected in *WINTER WORDS* (1928).

As the poem opens, a shepherd is standing by a gate, holding it ajar as he counts his flock. There is a "sour spring wind" and buds are failing to open. The sun frowns through "passing cloud-holes." The speaker thinks, "Nature, you're not commendable to-day!" Nature seems to respond, "Better to-morrow!" The shepherd is not cognizant of the weather at all; he still stands in his "white smock-frock," "Unnoting all things save the counting his flock." He endures the winter weather stoically, worrying only that one of his sheep will stray.

Unwin, William Cawthorne (1838–1933) Engineer; in 1881 he was Professor of Hydraulics and Mechanical Engineering at the Royal Indian Engineering College at Runnymede, near London. When Hardy was working on *TWO ON A TOWER* he apparently wrote Unwin to order a book on lens grinding. The book was sent along with a catalog from the factory of the gunmaker and inventor Charles William Lancaster. Hardy wrote Unwin to thank him, stating that the book contained all he would need to know on the subject. If he read it "too thoroughly," he observed, he might be tempted to air his knowledge of lenses "at the expense of narrative interest." He added that he would also find the telescope making in the catalog useful (*Letters* I, 97–98).

Upper Tooting On March 22, 1878, Hardy and his wife Emma Gifford HARDY moved from STURMINSTER NEWTON, DORSET to 1, Arundel Terrace, Trinity Road, Upper Tooting, within greater London, where they lived until June 22, 1881, when they moved to WIMBORNE, Dorset. Their three-year lease had run out on Lady Day (April 6), but Hardy was still suffering from the illness contracted on the Continent that had made writing *A LAODICEAN* so difficult for him. The Hardys were able to get a three-month extension and began searching for another residence in late May.

V

Vaughan Williams, Ralph (1872–1958) English composer whose music is derived from both English folk and classical traditions. In addition to nine symphonies and other orchestral works, he also composed numerous choral and song settings of poems by such poets as George Herbert, Walt Whitman, and others. In 1908 he queried Macmillan about the possibility of setting one of the songs from *The DYNASTS* to music. Hardy replied, through his publisher, that Vaughan Williams was such a "good & well-known composer" that he would not charge him for permission, provided he would state, on the title page of the song, that it was from his drama *The Dynasts*. Hardy preferred that he set to music the Soldier's Song entitled "Budmouth Dears" or the "Woman's Song," both from Part Third.

Vaughan Williams chose a Soldiers' Song from Part First. On November 29, 1908, Hardy wrote Vaughan Williams directly, giving permission for him to call it "Buonaparty," if he stated where it came from. It was published as a song for voice and piano in 1909; the words are from *The Dynasts*, Part First, Act First, Scene I (*Letters* III, 355, 358). *See* Appendix II, Media Adaptations of the Works of Thomas Hardy.

Venice This was the Italian city Hardy preferred over all others; he visited there in March 1887 with his wife Emma HARDY. *See* ITALY.

Venn, Diggory In *The RETURN OF THE NATIVE*, Venn is a former dairy farmer who is now a reddleman, supplying farmers with special red dye, called "redding," with which to mark their sheep. He inhabits a van on EGDON HEATH and has a pivotal role in events there. He brings Thomasin YEOBRIGHT home from Anglebury in his van after her wedding to Damon WILDEVE fails to take place; he loves her, but she has rejected his offer of marriage because her aunt, Mrs. YEOBRIGHT, considers a reddleman beneath her. Thomasin and Wildeve are eventually married, but Wildeve is in love with Eustacia VYE. After Wildeve and Eustacia drown, Venn returns to dairy farming at Stickleford and marries Thomasin.

verse drama Hardy had a lifelong attachment to many forms of theater. Ruth Firor, in her noted study

Folkways in Thomas Hardy, lists "Folk-Drama" as one of the important elements in Hardy's work. He had read the plays of SHAKESPEARE when very young, and in 1866, while working in London, attended a series of Shakespeare's plays at the Drury Lane Theatre starring the actor Samuel Phelps. Hardy had studied Greek as a young man and wrote in the *Life* that he had a "substantial knowledge" of the Greek dramatists. He was also fascinated by itinerant actors and theatrical productions. He had, moreover, a profound love of the natural world, being passionate about the landscape of his native DORSET and, later, about the rocky north coast of CORNWALL. English history, moreover, held a special fascination for Hardy. It is not surprising that, in time, Hardy would combine these obsessions and explore the genre of verse drama. He finished *The DYNASTS* in 1912 and began *The FAMOUS TRAGEDY OF THE QUEEN OF CORNWALL* in 1916, finishing it in 1923.

Hardy declared of *The Dynasts* that it was intended only for "mental performance, and not for the stage." Portions were, however, dramatized by the noted playwright and producer Harley GRANVILLE-BARKER. The play opened at the Kingsway Theatre, London, on November 25, 1914, and ran for 72 performances before closing in 1915 (Orel, *Thomas Hardy's Epic-Drama*, 102).

Hardy began *The Famous Tragedy of the Queen of Cornwall* in 1916, after visiting Cornwall with his second wife, Florence HARDY. He wrote Sydney COCKERELL that he was sorry his hopes for a poem on Iseult were to be disappointed, but that he had visited the place 44 years earlier with "an Iseult of my own" (*Letters* V, 179). His play was published seven years later. It was performed in Dorchester locally in 1923 and set to music by Rutland Boughton in 1924. Hardy told Florence that he finished it to please the "Dorchester Amateurs, who want something new."

Both works are based on historical events, actual or legendary. *The Dynasts* recapitulates the Napoleonic Wars and *The Famous Tragedy of the Queen of Cornwall*, the tale of Tristan and Iseult.

For further reading: Collier, "Thomas Hardy's *The Famous Tragedy of the Queen of Cornwall:* Its Artistry and Relation to His Life, Thought, and Works"; Dean, *Hardy's Poetic Vision in The Dynasts: The Diorama of a Dream;* Deane, "The Sources of *The Famous Tragedy of the*

Queen of Cornwall"; Gittings, "Note on a Production of *The Famous Tragedy of the Queen of Cornwall*"; Orel, *The Dynasts;* Orel, "The Dynasts on the English Stage, 1908–1919"; Orel, *Thomas Hardy's Epic-Drama: A Study of "The Dynasts";* Roberts, *Hardy's Poetic Drama and the Theatre: "The Dynasts" and "The Famous Tragedy of the Queen of Cornwall";* Wain, ed., *The Dynasts;* Wickens, "Hardy's Inconsistent Spirits and the Philosophic Form of *The Dynasts";* Wilson, "'Flower of Man's Intelligence': World and Overworld in *The Dynasts";* Wright, *The Shaping of The Dynasts: A Study in Thomas Hardy.*

Victory HMS   Admiral Nelson's flagship during the Battle of TRAFALGAR, one of the central events of Hardy's verse drama *The DYNASTS.* She was designed by Thomas Slade, Senior Surveyor of the Navy, and was commissioned in 1778. She is docked at the naval base in the coastal city of Portsmouth and is open to visitors.

Vilbert, Dr.   Quack physician in *JUDE THE OBSCURE.* Jude promises to advertise his pills if Vilbert will send him Greek and Latin grammar books to study. Jude carries out his promise, but Vilbert never sends the books. Later, at the agricultural show, the doctor sells Arabella DONN a love philtre to win back Jude. At the end of the novel he tends Jude in his final illness but is more interested in Arabella. After Jude's death, there are indications that she will succeed in marrying him.

"Voice, The"   This poem is dated "December 1912," the month after the death of Hardy's first wife, Emma HARDY, on November 27, 1912. It was later collected in *SATIRES OF CIRCUMSTANCE* (1914), appearing in the "Poems of 1912–13" section of that book. Although Emma had been mentally unstable in her later years, her death was a tremendous shock to Hardy, as well as a source of guilt because of his treatment of her. In the years following he wrote some of his most memorable poetry.

In this poem he addresses Emma and imagines that her spirit is asking him to remember her not as she was in later life but as she was when they first met.

He views her as she was when he first "drew near to the town / Where you would wait for me: yes, as I knew you then, / Even to the original air-blue gown!" Then he asks himself whether it is "only the breeze" listlessly "Travelling across the wet mead to me here," and whether she might be "ever dissolved to wan wistlessness" and "heard no more gain far or near." The poet depicts himself as "faltering forward" . . . / In the north wind "And the woman calling." The woman is calling him to join her in death.

In this poem Hardy contrasts the bleak emptiness of the present with his early introduction to Emma in August 1870, at St. Juliot (*see* ST. JULIOT CHURCH). As Bailey observes, however, he denies himself the comfort of belief in a reunion of their spirits in the afterlife (Bailey, *The Poetry of Thomas Hardy*, 298).

"Voices from Things Growing in a Churchyard"   This poem, first titled "Voices from Things Growing," was written about June 1921 and published in the *LONDON MERCURY* in December 1921. When it was collected in *LATE LYRICS AND EARLIER* (1922), the title was expanded to its present form; at this time Hardy added the note on "Eve Greensleeves" (Purdy, *Thomas Hardy: A Bibliographical Study*, 213).

The poet is wandering among the graves in a churchyard, and imagines the flowers and plants speaking. Each of the seven stanzas ends with the refrain "All day cheerily, / All night eerily!" The first six stanzas each describe one of the persons buried, with the plants now growing from their graves. The first voice is that of little Fanny Hurd, who once "flit-fluttered like a bird / Above the grass, as now I wave / In daisy shapes above my grave." Bachelor Bowring, "Gent," was once encased in a coffin of "shingled oak," but now he has become a "dancer in green as leaves on a wall." Thomas Voss has "burrowed away from the moss" that covers the sod of his grave and entered a yew tree, where he now has merged into "berries of juice and gloss." The Lady Gertrude, once "proud, high-bred," is a laurel whose leaves shine as once did her "satins superfine." The fifth voice is that of Eve Greensleeves, the original of whom is identified in a note as Eve Trevillian or Trevelyan, whom Hardy identifies in a footnote as "the handsome mother of two or three illegitimate children, *circa* 1784–1795." She now climbs as "innocent withwind" (a variant of "withywind," probably the European virgin's bower, a variety of clematis, or the bittersweet *solarnum dulcamara*). The sixth voice is that of Old Squire Audeley Grey, who was "aweary of life, and in scorn withdrew"; he now clambers up as "ivy-green."

In the final stanza, all the people buried there speak to visitors and have "much to teach," since their "murmurous accents seem to come/Thence hitheraround in a radiant hum."

On June 17, 1921, Hardy walked with Walter de la Mare through the graveyard at STINSFORD CHURCH and explained that "Fanny Hurd" was actually Fanny Hurden, a "delicate child" with whom he had gone to school. Benjamin Bowring is commemorated on a tablet in the church. Thomas Voss is actually a character in *UNDER THE GREENWOOD TREE;* he brings refreshments to the Mellstock "Quire" after midnight as they go on their caroling rounds. The prototype of Lady Gertrude has not been identified, but there is a marble monument to Squire Audeley Grey in the church (Bailey, *The Poetry of Thomas Hardy*, 463–64). The poem has been set to music; *see* Appendix II, Media Adaptations of the Works of Thomas Hardy.

Vye, Captain In *The RETURN OF THE NATIVE*, he is a retired naval officer and the grandfather of Eustacia VYE. He lives with Eustacia at Mistover Knap on EGDON HEATH. He opposes Eustacia's marriage to Clym YEO-BRIGHT and foresees, correctly, that it will fail. Although he cares for his granddaughter a great deal, he is unable to tame her restless longing for a stylish life in Paris, or to comfort her when Damon WILDEVE makes her miserable. He takes her in when she leaves Clym. He enjoys visiting the Quiet Woman Inn, drinking grog, and telling stories of his days at sea.

Vye, Eustacia Heroine of *The RETURN OF THE NATIVE*. She is first seen from a distance, presiding over the construction of a bonfire on Rainbarrow, at the top of EGDON HEATH, on November 5, Guy Fawkes Night. (This was a scheme to blow up the English houses of Parliament on November 5, 1605; Fawkes, one of the conspirators, was arrested and has been burned in effigy on November 5 ever since). Eustacia's form, as she glides about at dusk, is like an "organic part" of the barrow. She is 19 at the beginning of the novel. A beautiful, well-educated young woman, she is the daughter of a deceased Corfiote (from Corfu) regimental bandmaster at BUDMOUTH (Weymouth) whose father had taken her mother's maiden name. She lives with her devoted grandfather, Captain VYE, at Mistover Knap on Egdon Heath. Hardy calls her the "raw material of a divinity." A voluptuous creature with an "utter absence of fear," noted for her "extraordinary fixity, her conspicuous loneliness, her heedlessness of night," she has visions of a larger world than she knows in her grandfather's house and longs to escape from the heath. Her heroes are William the Conqueror and Napoleon Bonaparte. She desires love "as one in a desert would be thankful for brackish water."

Eustacia signals Damon WILDEVE with her bonfire. She has loved him in the past and hopes to bewitch him. Hardy alludes to her as the Fates, the Sphinx, and Cleopatra. She has not realized her greatest desire, "to be loved to madness," for which she blames Destiny.

Eustacia marries Clym YEOBRIGHT after becoming enthralled with his stories of Paris, where he has been working, but he has no desire to return to France. A studious man who takes up furze cutting when his eyesight grows dim, he is unable to make Eustacia happy and the marriage withers. Clym's mother comes to see them, but Wildeve is in the cottage and Eustacia does not open the door at first. She hears Clym say, "Mother," and assumes Mrs. Yeobright has come in, and shows Wildeve out from the back. Actually Clym has been talking in his sleep, and no one has admitted his mother. She dies on the way home of exhaustion and a snake bite.

After his mother's death, Clym begins to imagine that Eustacia has killed her and has committed adultery, neither of which is true. Eustacia endures his false accusations and leaves him, accepting Wildeve's invitation to accompany him to Paris. Attempting to meet Wildeve on a stormy night, she falls into Shadwater Weir; Wildeve tries to rescue her, and both drown.

W

Wagner, Richard (1813–1883) German composer. A major figure in 19th-century musical romanticism, Wagner conceived of opera as a fusion of music and drama on an epic scale. He wrote his own librettos, drawing on German mythology. Among his most important works are *Tristan and Isolde, Parsifal,* and the four operas comprising *The Ring of the Niebelung.* Hardy liked Wagner's music, explaining to the composer Edvard Grieg once that it was "*weather* and *ghost* music—whistling of wind and storm, the strumming of a gale on iron railings . . . low screams of entreaty and agony through key-holes." He explained that such music could express "emotions" but not their "subject or reason" (*Life,* 181).

"Wagtail and Baby" Poem first titled "An Incident of Civilization" and published in the *Albany Review,* April 1907. It was collected in *TIME'S LAUGHINGSTOCKS* (1909). A wagtail, a migrant bird, is drinking in a ford, watched by a human baby onshore. The wagtail "showed no shrinking" when a "blaring bull" went wading through the water and "held his own unblinking" when a stallion "splashed his way across." The baby then sees a mongrel cur "slowly slinking." The wagtail "does not falter." Then a "man comes near," and the wagtail "With terror rose and disappeared." The baby "fell a-thinking." Animals exhibit instinctive reactions to events while humans draw thoughtful conclusions.

The poem was set to music by Benjamin Britten in *Winter Words* (London and New York: Boosey & Hawkes, 1954).

"Waiting Both" Poem first printed, together with "An East-End Curate," in the *LONDON MERCURY* in November 1924. It was later collected in *HUMAN SHOWS, FAR PHANTASIES, SONGS, AND TRIFLES* (1925).

The poem takes the form of a dialogue between a star and a person. The star remarks, "Here I and you / Stand, each in our degree: What do you mean to do, / Mean to do?" The other speaker says he will wait, "and let Time go by, / Till my change come." "So mean I:— / So mean I," the star replies.

Here Hardy's pessimism is evident; there will be no future for either the star or the person, only a grim mortality that the star and the person must both accept.

In the *Life,* Hardy explains that the poem is based on a verse in Job: "All the days of my appointed time will I wait, till my change come."

The poem has been set to music by Gerald Finzi in *Earth and Air and Song* (London: Boosey & Hawkes, 1936; Bailey, *The Poetry of Thomas Hardy,* 503).

"Waiting Supper, The" Short story published in *MURRAY'S MAGAZINE* in January and February 1888, and, in America, in *HARPER'S WEEKLY,* December 31 and January 7, 1887–88. Purdy gives details of its earlier existence as "The Intruder, A Legend of the 'Chronicle' Office" (Purdy, *Thomas Hardy: A Bibliographical Study,* 152). It was collected in *A CHANGED MAN AND OTHER TALES* (1913).

The tale is concerned with the long romance between Christine Everard, the daughter of a squire, and a local farmer, Nicholas Long. Their early romance, which has been in progress three years at the time we meet them, is thwarted by the local vicar, who refuses to marry them without her father's permission. An embarrassing but false story that they have already married travels about the parish. To avert gossip Christine marries her father's choice, James Bellston, a well-traveled but tactless and insensitive young man whose uncle lives nearby; Bellston is abusive and makes her miserable. Nicholas, dispirited, leaves for many years of travel.

He returns after 15 years to find that Squire Everard has died and Bellston has left Christine, who is almost destitute. Bellston has not been heard of for eight or nine years and is thought to have died. Nicholas and Christine decide to marry; the evening before a wedding supper is laid, just before Nicholas arrives, the tall clock crashes to the floor, a portent of a violent death in the family. As Christine waits for Nicholas a messenger arrives with Bellston's overcoat and announces that he has arrived at Casterbridge and is on his way to Christine. When Nicholas arrives Christine faints. Nicholas learns of Bellston's imminent arrival and leaves. Christine waits for Bellston's arrival all evening and into the next day. After a week he has not come, but she is still afraid to marry Nicholas for fear of Bellston. Years of companionship ensue, until she is 50 and Nicholas 53. At that point a skeleton is discovered in a nearby weed-choked stream with the remains of Bellston's gold watch.

"You might have married me on the day we had fixed," Nicholas says sadly, and they would have had "tall sons and daughters." He asks if it is too late to marry. Christine says perhaps they are happier as they are, with the "weight" gone from their lives and no further shadow. She asks him to let them "be joyful together . . . in the days of our vanity; and 'With mirth and laughter let old wrinkles come.'" Nicholas yields. From time to time he still asks her to reconsider, "but not with the fervour of his earlier years."

This story, like many of Hardy's others, including "THE SON'S VETO," "A TRAGEDY OF TWO AMBITIONS," "A MERE INTERLUDE," and "An INDISCRETION IN THE LIFE OF AN HEIRESS," points up the unhappiness that ensues from the rigid acceptance of class values. In many of Hardy's stories rank takes priority over genuine love in marital alliances, resulting in lifelong despair for the major parties.

For further reading: Ray," "'The Waiting Supper': A Textual History."

"Walk, The"   Poem written after the death of Emma HARDY and published in the "Poems of 1912–13" section of *SATIRES OF CIRCUMSTANCE* (1914). Hardy recounts the times before her death when, "weak and lame," she did not walk with him to the "hill-top tree/By the gated ways." He would go alone and "not mind," because she would be waiting at home for his return.

At the time of writing, however, he has walked to the familiar spot but is devastated by her absence.

The tree may be Culliford Tree, nearly three miles from MAX GATE (Bailey, *The Poetry of Thomas Hardy*, 295).

Wallop, Lady Eveline Camilla (?– 1894)   One of the daughters of the fifth earl and countess of PORTSMOUTH. In the *Life* Hardy recounts a visit to their country home, Eggesford House, in Devon. Lady Camilla had told him that a woman was "never so near being in love with a man she does not love" as immediately after he has left her because she refused him (*Life*, 170).

Wallop, Lady Margaret (?– 1943)   The fifth daughter of the fifth earl and countess of PORTSMOUTH. In 1887 Hardy gave her a leatherbound copy of *A PAIR OF BLUE EYES* for her birthday and wrote that he wished it were more worthy of the occasion (*Letters* I, 161).

war, Hardy's attitude toward   Hardy deplored the concept of war; his horror is expressed in some of his most memorable poems. In 1899 he wrote his friend Florence HENNIKER, whose husband was to be involved in the BOER WAR, "It seems a justification of the extremest pessimism that at the end of the 19th Century we settle an argument by the Sword." He remarked that it was

the same as they would have done in the 19th century B.C. (*Letters* II, 229). His poems about the Boer War include "A CHRISTMAS GHOST-STORY," "DRUMMER HODGE," "EMBARCATION," and "The GOING OF THE BATTERY." Those related to WORLD WAR I include "CHANNEL FIRING," "CRY OF THE HOMELESS," "CHRISTMAS: 1924," "An APPEAL TO AMERICA ON BEHALF OF THE BELGIAN DESTITUTE," "AT THE ENTERING OF THE NEW YEAR," "ENGLAND TO GERMANY IN 1914," "I LOOKED UP FROM MY WRITING," "ON THE BELGIAN EXPATRIATION," and "THEN AND NOW."

Although he disapproved of the wars he witnessed, he was also fascinated by the Napoleonic Wars, in which some of his ancestors had fought. One was Sir Thomas Masterman Hardy, a baronet and Nelson's flag-captain during the Battle of TRAFALGAR. To some extent he romanticized this conflict, although he recognized its horrors also. He treated it in the verse drama *The DYNASTS*, the novel *The TRUMPET-MAJOR*, the short story "A TRADITION OF EIGHTEEN HUNDRED AND FOUR," the poem "The ALARM and other works." The latter has an epigraph: "In Memory of one of the Writer's Family who was a Volunteer during the War with Napoleon."

In 1899 Hardy was asked by W. T. Stead to comment on "A Crusade of Peace," in a periodical he was about to publish called *War against War*. Hardy responded by suggesting, as a preliminary, that all civilized nations ban the use of horses in warfare except for transport. "Soldiers, at worst, know what they are doing, but these animals are denied even the poor possibilities of glory and reward as a compensation for their sufferings" (*Life*, 303). After the beginning of World War I, he was asked to respond to a circular letter announcing that the horrors of the war would eventually be eclipsed by future wars, with "hundreds of thousands of submarines" and more advanced munitions-making. He replied that if that were true, he did not think "a world in which such fiendishness is possible to be worth the saving." He felt it was better to let Western "civilization" perish, and give "the black and yellow races" a chance. He declared, however, that he was really a meliorist and hopeful about the world (*Life*, 387).

For further reading: Dean, *Hardy's Poetic Vision in "The Dynasts:" The Diorama of a Dream;* King and Morgan, "Hardy and the Boer War: The Public Poet in Spite of Himself"; King, "Hardy's 'A Tradition of Eighteen Hundred and Four' and the Anxiety of Invention"; Orel, *Thomas Hardy's Epic-Drama: A Study of "The Dynasts,"* Wright, *The Shaping of "The Dynasts": A Study in Thomas Hardy.*

Ward, Mary Augusta Arnold (*Mrs. Humphry Ward*) (1851–1920)   English novelist and social worker. Her husband, Thomas Humphry WARD, was an Oxford don and the editor of *Men of the Reign* and other works. Mrs.

Ward was a niece of Matthew ARNOLD and the granddaughter of Thomas Arnold. Her novels, which were somewhat religious and polemical, were extremely popular, particularly the spiritual romance *Robert Elsmere* (1888).

Hardy regarded the Wards as his friends although he had written disparagingly of the "New Christians" or the "'Robert Elsmere' school" to Frederic Harrison in 1888. He remarked that they believed "everything is both true & false at the same time" (*Letters* I, 178). Robert Elsmere is a disaffected nineteenth-century clergyman whose doubts cause him to leave the Anglican church. Ward argues that Christianity should focus on social questions and not divine mysteries.

Unlike many reviewers, Mrs. Ward praised TESS OF THE D'URBERVILLES (Millgate, *Thomas Hardy*, 321). In April 1892 she asked Hardy to inscribe a quotation and his signature on parchment to be preserved by the city of Milan in commemoration of the 400th anniversary of the discovery of America by Columbus. He replied that seeing her handwriting was the next best thing to seeing her, and said he would be glad to sign the parchment.

In 1905 she sent Hardy her novel *The Marriage of William Ashe*, which he received very favorably, although he also offered suggestions about improving its structure. He said reading it was "a treat" and that she had exhibited "unexpected dramatic powers" (*Letters* III, 163).

In 1906 Hardy sided with Mrs. Ward in a dispute with the *Times* Book Club, which wished to sell books at a discount and evade an earlier arrangement called the Net Book Agreement of 1899 (*Letters* III, 234).

This agreement, formed on January 1, 1899, among the Booksellers of Great Britain and Ireland, the Society of Authors, and the Publishers' Association, gave publishers the right, but not the obligation, to fix a price for every book published. The bookseller was obliged to sell the book at not less than that price in return for their discount from the publisher.

When she sent Hardy *The Coryston Family* in 1913, he wrote her that the people were "remarkably distinct & living, all through" and that she had "never written a finer one." He suggested that she read Frederic Harrison's *The Evolution of Religion*.

She was very concerned about the devastation caused by WORLD WAR I and made at least three visits to the French battlefields, an experience she wrote about in *Fields of Victory* (London, 1913; *Letters* V, 299).

Ward, Thomas Humphry (1845–1926) Oxford don, journalist, and writer. He was the husband of Mary Augusta WARD and the editor of *The English Poets: Selections with Critical Introductions by Various Writers,* to which Hardy contributed the article on William BARNES, which appeared in volume five in 1918.

Hardy's letters mention Ward as a fellow member of the ATHENAEUM CLUB (*Letters* III, 90). He considered the Wards to be his friends, although he did not altogether approve of Mary Ward's polemical religious novels.

Waterloo, Battle of The last action of the Napoleonic Wars, fought in southern Belgium in June 1815. Under the command of Napoleon I, the marquis Emmanuel de Grouchy defeated a detachment of the Prussian army commanded by Field Marshal Gebhard Leberecht von Blücher at Ligny. Blücher's main force, however, eluded the French and joined the English duke of Wellington. Wellington withdrew to a position south of Waterloo, where Napoleon attacked. The French were routed. Grouchy did not aid Napoleon at Waterloo; he was later created marshall of France. Napoleon abdicated on June 22.

Hardy treated the Battle of Waterloo in depth in his verse drama *The DYNASTS*; it also figures in the novels *The RETURN OF THE NATIVE* and *The TRUMPET-MAJOR* and in the ballad "The PEASANT'S CONFESSION."

Weatherbury Fictional name for PUDDLETOWN in FAR FROM THE MADDING CROWD. Waterston Manor, in nearby Lower Waterston, is called Weatherbury Farm in the novel.

Weatherbury Church Fictional name for St. Mary's Church, PUDDLETOWN. Sergeant Francis TROY spends the night in the porch of the church in FAR FROM THE MADDING CROWD. The west gallery of the church also figures in UNDER THE GREENWOOD TREE as the home of the traditional musicians Hardy celebrated.

Wehrschmidt, Daniel A. (1861–1932) According to Philip V. Allingham, Wehrschmidt was a portrait painter and lithographer. He was a native of Cleveland, Ohio. His portrait of the Arctic explorer Robert Falcon Scott hangs in the National Portrait Gallery, LONDON.

He was a pupil of Sir Hubert HERKOMER, who shared the commission to illustrate TESS OF THE D'URBERVILLES with three students. Wehrschmidt contributed eight illustrations (Jackson, *Illustration and the Novels of Thomas Hardy,* 57).

Well-Beloved, The Novel serialized as *The Pursuit of the Well-Beloved* in the *Illustrated London News* from October 1 to December 17, 1892, and published in book form under the title *The Well-Beloved* in 1897. The full title is *The Well-Beloved: A Sketch of a Temperament.*

Hardy wrote the novel after the turmoil caused by TESS OF THE D'URBERVILLES (1891), in order to "offend no one." In September 1889 Hardy and the publisher TILLOTSON & SON cancelled their agreement for the publication of a proposed novel by Hardy called *Too*

Late Beloved (which became *Tess of the d'Urbervilles*). Tillotson's asked him for another serial, and he proposed something "light," half the length of *Tess*. Hardy sent a prospectus saying that the novel was "entirely modern in date and subject" and embraced many extremes of society, from "peers, peeresses, and other persons of rank and culture, to villagers." He noted that some of the settings would be London studios and drawing rooms of fashion, cottages and cliffs of a remote island in the English Channel, and a little town on the island. He added an ironical assurance to his publishers that there would not be a word or scene which could "offend the most fastidious taste." After the novel ran in the *Illustrated London News,* however, Hardy abandoned it for four years, then revised it in 1896; it was published March 16, 1897 (*JUDE THE OBSCURE* had been published in the interim in 1895). It became the 17th volume in OSGOOD, MCILVAINE's edition of the WESSEX NOVELS. It was published in America by HARPER & BROTHERS (Purdy, *Thomas Hardy: A Bibliographical Study,* 92–96).

When the novel was revised for book publication in 1897, Hardy made some major changes. The closing chapter was completely rewritten and a new conclusion added. In the 1892 version in the *Illustrated London News* the book was divided into three parts. The earlier ending is often appended to the 1897 standard edition of the novel.

The novel is a semiallegorical platonic fantasy, based loosely on Plato's idea that "all men are pursuing a shadow, the Unattainable." The main character is Jocelyn PIERSTON, a sculptor obsessed by the concept of ideal beauty. The name of Avice, the heroine (who appears in three manifestations, as Avice I, her daughter, Avice II, and her granddaughter, Avice III; *see* CARO, Avice), is taken from a daughter of the Talbots family (the family that once owned TALBOTHAYS farm, one of the settings of *Tess of the d'Urbervilles*). Hardy remarks in the *Life* that the kernel of the novel is his wish to trace "the story of a face which goes through three generations or more." After the novel was published he wrote the poet Algernon SWINBURNE that it was "a fanciful exhibition of the artistic nature, and has, I think, some little foundation in fact." He noted that if the work made "any faint claim to imaginative feeling" it would owe "something of such feeling" to Swinburne (*Life,* 6, 217, 287). Hardy's premise is that beauty is subjective, existing only in the mind of the beholder, a creation of the imagination.

SYNOPSIS

Part I, Chapters 1–9   The first part is titled "A Young Man of Twenty."
As a young man, Jocelyn Pierston, a successful sculptor, returns to his native home on the Isle of Slingers (PORT-LAND, near WEYMOUTH). He is extremely indecisive and fickle about women, as none of them live up to his ideal vision of "the well-beloved." He believes that a relationship with a woman who can be considered the "well-beloved" is, in essence, fleeting and migratory; at any one time her spirit is likely to change and his feelings will undergo a necessary metamorphosis.

He has long been enamored of his childhood playmate and neighbor, Avice Caro, and imagines that the "elusive idealization" he calls his "Love" has come to live in her body. They become engaged, although he finds her wanting. Before they can leave the island he becomes interested in another native daughter, Marcia BENCOMB; they elope, but do not marry. He goes to live in London and is made an R.A., or Royal Academician, a fellow of the ROYAL ACADEMY OF ARTS, which is a signal honor at his age. He continues his "professional beauty-chase" in LONDON, fancying actresses, society women, blondes, brunettes, and others.

Part II, Chapters 1–13   The second part is titled "A Young Man of Forty."
In this section Jocelyn has returned to the Isle of Slingers to settle his late father's estate. To his surprise he finds that while he has been pursuing a career as a sculptor, "modelling and chipping his ephemeral fancies into perennial shapes," his father, proprietor of a large stone-cutting business, had been "persistently chiselling for half a century at the crude original matter of those shapes" (II, Chapter 1). Jocelyn has been left relatively wealthy.

He returns to London, where, at a party, he sees a woman he had admired earlier without knowing her name; she is Nichola PINE-AVON, recently widowed. He enjoys talking with her and later calls on her at her London home. He receives a letter from the wife of one of his father's former workmen telling him of the death of Avice Caro. She had married her cousin Jim Caro but had been widowed. He cannot stop thinking of her and the Caro family, whom, he believes, have a Roman lineage "grafted on the stock of the Slingers." He gazes at an old photograph of her and returns to the island for her funeral.

At the funeral he discovers that Ann Avice (Avice the Second), Avice I's daughter, is now employed as a laundress at Sylvania Castle (actually Pennsylvania Castle, which still exists today). He thinks of her as the "double" of Avice the First, and falls in love with her. He returns to London, and, one day, sees her near the wharf. She is about to take a boat to the Isle of Slingers.

He rents Sylvania Castle, from which he has a view of the home of the "resuscitated Avice" (that is, the reincarnation of Avice Caro, his first love). He considers that the spirit of the "well-beloved," once lost, has been found again and resides in Ann Avice. Her teeth are like her mother's were, although her speech is not polished. He follows her to church and sees Mrs. Pine-Avon there.

He overhears a man speaking to a woman he believes might be Ann Avice. Nichola Pine-Avon comes down and makes more advances, but Jocelyn is interested only in Avice. He induces her to come to London as his housekeeper. He proposes to her, but she says she is already married to a man who has left her and gone to Guernsey in the Channel Islands. Meanwhile, she has become enamored of a soldier.

Jocelyn takes her back to her cottage at Portland, although she is sobbing. He goes to the church and checks the marriage register, finding that she is indeed married. Her husband, Isaac Pierston, called Ike, eventually comes home in an apologetic frame of mind. Ann Avice, who had been pregnant the whole time, has a baby girl, christened Avice. Jocelyn Pierston returns to London, sighing, "'Here endeth that dream!'"

Part III, Chapters 1–8   The third part is titled "A Young Man of Sixty."

Jocelyn has lived abroad for many years. In Rome one evening he overhears two Americans discussing a Mrs. Leverre they had known as a young woman, when her father had retired from his business of being a stone-merchant in the Isle of Slingers. He instantly deduces that they are discussing Marcia Bencomb, and wants to see her.

Meanwhile, he receives a letter from Ann Avice saying that Ike has been killed in a quarry accident. Jocelyn returns to the Isle of Slingers and calls on her; she is now in bad health and living in his old house. He sees Avice III, an elegant "ladylike creature," outside the house, but she doesn't come in. She is a governess at the castle and was educated at Sandbourne.

Jocelyn rescues Avice III from a crevice in the rocks. She does not know who he is, but he tells her mother he feels he has known her for years because of her heritage and would like to marry her. Ann Avice says she will help him win her daughter.

Jocelyn's friend Alfred somers comes to the Isle of Slingers with his wife, the former Nichola Pine-Avon. Avice, meanwhile, agrees reluctantly to marry Jocelyn. He takes a fine house and invites Ann Avice and Avice to spend a week with him. They go back to the Isle of Slingers to wait for Pierston's return. When he goes there on the eve of the wedding, he sees a young stranger struggling up the hill; he says he is a "Jersey man."

Early the morning of the wedding, Ann Avice tells her nurse that she worries about Avice's going through with the wedding. She had fancied another young man of 25, Henri leverre of Sandbourne. She learns that he is the stepson of Marcia Bencomb.

Jocelyn comes to collect his bride, only to find that Avice has departed. She had gone to see Henri Leverre,

the young man Jocelyn had seen struggling up the hill, to return his books, and found him ill. He improved with some brandy. Henri writes to say they "love each other beyond expression."

Jocelyn and the servants go up to tell Ann Avice, only to find she has died of the shock added to a feeble heart.

Meanwhile, Avice and Henri, who have not managed to marry, are walking down to the harbor. Henri is not well. They commandeer a boat but have no oars and nearly drown before being rescued.

Jocelyn sits by Ann Avice's corpse, thinking of his family and hers. He hears voices below and discovers Henri Leverre's stepmother has arrived; she is actually Marcia Bencomb. News comes of the flight of Henri and Avice; Marcia thinks they will be married the next morning. Ann Avice's funeral is held, which Jocelyn attends. No one has known how to reach Avice, but they arrive in a hired vehicle. Jocelyn returns to London but develops a chill and fever. Marcia helps nurse him. When he recovers she says Henri and Avice have married; Avice was brokenhearted over her mother's death. Jocelyn realizes that his and Avice's marriage would have been a terrible idea. As Marcia nurses him and he gets better, she sees the "sensuous side" of Jocelyn's nature. Jocelyn says he can no longer love, but he admires her. Marcia is the "image and superscription of Age . . . pale and shrivelled . . . her hair white as snow." He tells her she has put back the clock of Time 30 years.

He continues to see Marcia and, finally, decides to marry her. Marcia has an attack of rheumatism and must be wheeled to the church in a chair. They hear from Avice, who is living with Henri at Sandbourne in a house Jocelyn bought for them. She comes to London, having left Henri, just as her mother had left Ike. Marcia and Jocelyn send her back to her husband.

Jocelyn spends his old age demolishing the ancient splendors of his native peninsula. His original Vision, once powerful, has evaporated. He is considered "a man not without genius, whose powers were insufficiently recognized in his lifetime."

CRITICAL COMMENTARY

J. Hillis Miller argues that Pierston's "evasive well-beloved" is actually his own self-image, his "wraith" or double "in a changed sex." The novel's epigraph, "One shape of many names," is from Percy Bysshe Shelley's *The Revolt of Islam.* The reference is to the three-in-one Avices. He considers the novel one of the "most important nineteenth-century novels about art," and compares Hardy's exploration of the association of "love, repetition and artistic creativity" with that of Marcel Proust in *À la recherche du temps perdu.* He believes Hardy's reiteration of the themes of betrayal and dissat-

Avice's Cottage, now part of the Portland Museum; in The Well-Beloved, *Portland is the "Isle of Slingers"*   (Sarah Bird Wright)

isfaction in love are his final attempt to pose the question of why human beings repeat the same mistakes, "inflicting on themselves and on others the same suffering, again and again?" He sees the novel as a parody of Hardy's earlier novels in proving that, ultimately, despite the "psychological and social verisimilitude" of some of them, they are all a form of "artifice," because life as represented by "the great Victorian realists" is actually irrelevant. At the end, Jocelyn is "fully demystified" and bitter. He says, "Thank heaven I am old at last. The curse is removed"(introduction to the Macmillan edition, London, 1975).

Michael Ryan also finds bitterness in the novel and considers it the result of Tillotson's rejection of *Tess of the d'Urbervilles* on moral grounds. He regards it not only as a "fable of the artistic temperament" but, more significantly, as a "mockery of aestheticism." When Pierston loses his creativity at the end of the novel, he also loses his ability to appreciate art; he is no longer moved, in the National Gallery, by the works of Perugino, Titian, or Sebastiano. Ryan observes that Hardy mocks "the continuities . . . of Temperament, of art, of genealogy, of geography, of the Beloved." Pierston's aesthetic temperament is lost, as is his interest in art. His marriage to Marcia represents the breaking of genealogical tradition, as she is a "kimberlin," or newcomer. Pierston destroys geographical continuity as he pulls down Elizabethan cottages because they are damp. Marcia's appearance at her second wedding in a wheelchair because of rheumatism mocks the conventional novel. In the final paragraph of the novel Pierston is sometimes mentioned as "the late Mr. Pierston" by "gourd-like young art-critics and journalists" (Wilde and Pater), and, as Ryan points out, Hardy identifies himself with Pierston when he says Pierston's produc-

tions are "alluded to as those of a man not without genius, whose powers were insufficiently recognized in his lifetime."

Tom Wightman identifies a number of sites in the novel that may still be visited today: Weymouth (Budmouth), Portland (the Isle of Slingers), Chesil Beach ("precarious bridge" in the novel), Fortune's Well (The Street of Wells), Easton (East Quarriers), the Portland Museum (containing Avice's Cottage), Pennsylvania Castle (Sylvania Castle), Church Hope Cove (near the ruined St. Andrew's Church), Sandsfoot Castle (the Tudor castle of Henry VIII), and the two lighthouses at Portland Bill.

For further reading: Bulaila, "'The Clay but Not the Potter: Love and Marriage in *The Well-Beloved*"; Davidson, "On Reading *The Well-Beloved* as a Parable of Art"; Elliott, "The Infatuated Artist: Thomas Hardy and *The Well-Beloved*"; Miller, introduction to the Macmillan edition of *The Well-Beloved* (1975); also *"The Well-Beloved": A Sketch of Temperament;* O'Toole, "Genealogy and Narrative Jamming in Hardy's *The Well-Beloved*"; Page, "*The Well-Beloved* and Other Hardyan Fantasies"; Ryan, "One Name of Many Shapes: *The Well-Beloved*"; Wightman, "A Walk with Tom Wightman: The Country of *The Well-Beloved*" (pamphlet 12, *Thomas Hardy Society Guides*).

Wells, H(erbert) G(eorge) (1866–1946)   H. G. Wells was an English novelist and journalist, known for his science fiction, satirical novels, and accounts of science and history written for the popular market. He was the author of *The Time Machine, The War of the Worlds, Tono-Bungay, Love and Mr. Lewisham, Kipps, Mr. Britling Sees It Through,* and many other works. The son of a tradesman, he managed to study at the Royal College of Science under Thomas Huxley, and became a teacher and a Fabian. He was attacked by Virginia WOOLF for his naturalistic novels and by the conservative English Catholic author G. K. Chesterton for his ideas, which Chesterton considered too radical.

In 1896 he wrote a favorable (but unsigned) review of JUDE THE OBSCURE, calling it a "great novel." He praised Jude's final lament, calling it "the voice of the educated proletarian, speaking more distinctly than it has ever spoken before in English literature" (Gerber and Davis, *Thomas Hardy: An Annotated Bibliography of Writings about Him,* 81).

In 1918 Wells sent Hardy a copy of his novel *Joan and Peter: The Story of an Education.* Hardy thanked him, saying he had a "preternatural knowledge of what people do!" He believed Wells could "go down a street a mile long & see through the house-fronts & describe the movements of every inhabitant" (*Letters* V, 280). On January 26, 1919, Wells wrote from the Royal Hotel, WEYMOUTH, and asked if he might call at MAX GATE and bring Cicily Isabel Andrews (Rebecca West, the novelist). Hardy responded on January 27, inviting them to come about four o'clock on Wednesday, which they did (January 29, 1919; *Letters* V, 293). Wells sent Hardy copies of several other novels, including *The Undying Fire: A Contemporary Novel* (London, 1919) and *The World of William Clissold* (three volumes, London, 1926). The latter was a set of the limited signed issue. In his letter thanking him Hardy said it was a "depressing business" to "advance thought ever so little along the road to rationality," because, although one's arguments may be listened to with "respect," they may also be forgotten in 20 years (*Letters* VII, 40–41).

"We Sat at the Window" *(Bournemouth, 1875)* Poem published in *MOMENTS OF VISION* (1917) recounting a visit Hardy and his wife Emma HARDY made to Bournemouth in July 1875, not quite a year after they were married (September 1874). The rain comes down "like silken strings." It is St. Swithin's Day (July 15). They have "nothing to read, nothing to see" and are "irked by the scene." Hardy feels their time was tragically wasted. Although their two souls were "in their prime," that prime was wasted by their immaturity, their dearth of feeling, and their insensitivity to each other.

Bournemouth (as Sandbourne) figures in *The HAND OF ETHELBERTA* and also in the final section of *TESS OF THE D'URBERVILLES*. In the latter novel, Tess DURBEYFIELD Clare and Alec D'URBERVILLE flee to Bournemouth; she stabs him in a seaside villa called The Herons, where Angel CLARE finds her.

Wessex During most of the 19th century, *Wessex* was simply a term designating the southwestern region of Britain that had, in the Middle Ages, been ruled by the West Saxons. As Simon Gatrell observes, the term has now come to mean not only the region populated with imaginary characters, but "the whole culture—predominantly rural and pre-industrial—found in Hardy's novels and poems" ("Wessex," *The Cambridge Companion to Thomas Hardy*). Hardy's regionalism has been eagerly noted by readers and well documented by critics since his earliest novels were published. J. I. M. Stewart considers it Hardy's good fortune to have established himself early as a regional writer. He was "the natural historian and the social historian of Wessex . . . spreading powers of observation and humour and memory, as well as of pathos and tragedy, over a field very reasonably full of a diversity of folk." His poems, Stewart believes, deepen our knowledge of Wessex, transforming it into a "country of the mind" (Stewart, *Thomas Hardy: A Critical Biography*, 219.)

What, exactly, is Wessex, and what geographical reality does it have? During the Anglo-Saxon period, England was divided into seven kingdoms (the Heptarchy). Wessex was the area lying south of the River Thames, bounded by Cornwall to the west and Sussex to the East. Hardy was aware of the early name

for this geographical territory, but did not think of adopting it as a fictitious regional setting until his first three novels had been published.

Rosemarie Morgan explains the later evolution of "Wessex." In *FAR FROM THE MADDING CROWD* Hardy refers to the fair taking place in South Wessex almost as though he had come to the name accidentally. As he continued writing his novels, however, the concept of "Wessex" began to emerge and take on more substance. By 1912, when he was making his revisions to his novels, he changed names and mileages to fit the idea of Wessex as coherently as he could. It is possible that he made hundreds of small changes to the novels as he worked (personal communication with the author).

Wessex came to suggest a realistic domain that, in time, acquired a legendary power of its own (as in the case of Anthony Trollope's Barsetshire chronicles or C. S. Lewis's Narnia tales). As the concept evolved, Hardy used specific dialects long associated with the region, along with distinctive accents and pronunciation. He carefully reproduced this diction in his rustic characters.

Hardy's conception of Wessex began as a representation of his native county, DORSET, but slowly expanded to cover over two-thirds of the southern part of England, eventually including parts of CORNWALL, Devon, Gloucestershire, Somerset, and Wiltshire. Readers were fascinated by the topography of the novels, which acquired something of a cult status, and began coming to Hardy's door. To satisfy them, he drew a map, which was later supplemented by individual maps for the various novels, such as *The RETURN OF THE NATIVE* and *TESS OF THE D'URBERVILLES*. He also tried to standardize the correlation between fictional and actual places. As early as 1904 a study of his Wessex was proposed and eventually published (Hermann Lea, *Thomas Hardy's Wessex*, 1913). When he began the undertaking, Lea asked Hardy whether he had any objection. Hardy replied that he had not, "if you print somewhere on the map (or in any text accompanying it) that the places in the novels were only *suggested* by those real ones given—as they are not literally portraits of such" (O'Sullivan, *Thomas Hardy: An Illustrated Biography*, 68–71). Despite this caveat and Hardy's later worry about "trippers with Kodaks," tourists, readers, and scholars still come to Dorset in large numbers and drive or walk across the rural countryside, determined to correlate favorite scenes in the novels and short stories with the actual terrain.

Gatrell observes that Hardy first used the term *Wessex* in *Far from the Madding Crowd* (1874), but did not at that time conceive of its ultimate extent. In 1895, however, he wrote prefaces to the Osgood, McIlvaine editions of *Tess of the d'Urbervilles* and *Far from the Madding Crowd*. He declared in the first preface that the descriptions of "landscape, prehistoric antiquities, and especially old English architecture" had been "done from the real." In the second one he was even more explicit, stating that his projected series of novels was "mainly of the kind called local." He believed they required a "territorial definition" for the purpose of unity. Since he had found that a single county was insufficient for his purpose, he "disinterred the old one."

It is not dry geography that defines Wessex so much as the familiar scenes he preserved in his writings: the Wessex horned breeds of sheep arriving at the Greenhill agricultural fair, with "vermiculated horns lopping gracefully on each side of their cheeks in geometrically perfect spirals, a small pink and white ear nestling under each horn," and Warren's Malthouse in *Far from the Madding Crowd;* the Quiet Woman Inn and the CHRISTMAS MUMMERS in *The Return of the Native;* the MELLSTOCK choir on its round of carol singing in *UNDER THE GREENWOOD TREE;* the "battalion" of men and maids milking in the dawn light at the Talbothays dairy farm in *Tess of the d'Urbervilles,* the pub in "The TRAMP-WOMAN'S TRAGEDY," the Highland dancing under FAR-FRAE's tent in *The MAYOR OF CASTERBRIDGE,* the

Kennetbridge spring fair in *JUDE THE OBSCURE,* the furze bush shelter on the downs, the flock of several hundred lambing ewes, and the distant castle in the story "WHAT THE SHEPHERD SAW"—these scenes and dozens of others would have dwindled and faded had Hardy not imported them into his work, preserving the now vanished Wessex.

For further reading: Brown, ed., *Figures in a Wessex Landscape: Thomas Hardy's Picture of English Country Life;* Margaret Drabble, *A Writer's Britain;* Gatrell, "Wessex"; Lea, *Thomas Hardy's Wessex* (1913; included in the definitive Wessex Edition of Thomas Hardy's works and reissued in two volumes as Hermann Lea, *The Hardy Guides,* ed. James and Gregory Stevens Cox, 1986). See also *Thomas Hardy Society Guides* to the novels of Hardy: 1. J. P. Skilling and M. R. Skilling, "The Country of *The Woodlanders*"; 2. J. P. Skilling and M. R. Skilling, Tour No. 1, "The Country of *Tess of the D'Urbervilles*"; 3. J. P. Skilling and M. R. Skilling, Tour No. 2, "The Country of *Tess of the D'Urbervilles*"; 4. J. P. Skilling and M. R. Skilling, "The Country of *The Return of the Native*";

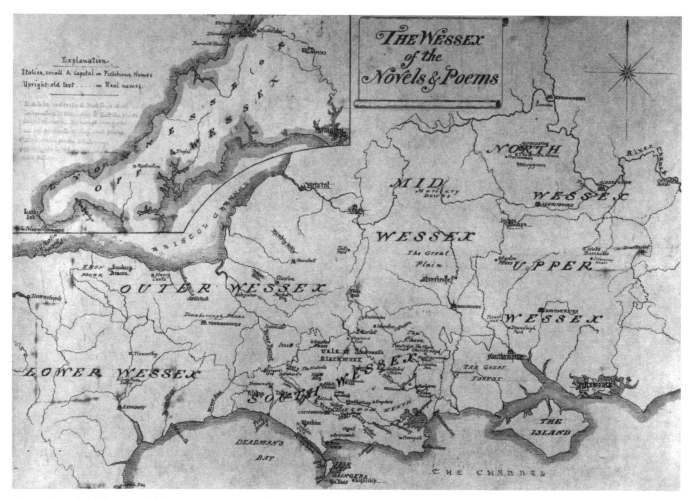

Thomas Hardy's Wessex. Fictitious names are in italics   (Dorset County Museum, Dorchester)

5. K. N. Fowler (based on original guide by A. D. Winchcombe), "The Country of *Under the Greenwood Tree*"; 6. J. P. Skilling and M. R. Skilling, "The Country of *Far from the Madding Crowd*"; 7. N. J. Atkins, K. N. Fowler, and E. P. Fowler, "The Country of *The Mayor of Casterbridge*"; 8. J. P. Skilling and M. R. Skilling, "The Country of *The Trumpet-Major*"; 9. A. D. Winchcombe and M. A. Winchcombe, "The Country of *A Pair of Blue Eyes*"; 10. T. R. Wrightman and Charles P. C. Pettit, "The Country of *Jude the Obscure*"; 11. J. P. Skilling, "The Country of *The Hand of Ethelberta*"; 12. Tom Wightman, "A Walk with Tom Wightman: The Country of *The Well-Beloved*"; 13. A. D. Winchcombe and M. A. Winchcombe, "The Country of *Desperate Remedies*."

Wessex (Wessie) Wessex, or Wessie, Hardy's dog at MAX GATE from 1913 to 1926, was a wire-haired terrier apparently possessed of great intelligence. One evening in the spring of 1925 Mr. William Watkins of the SOCIETY OF DORSET MEN IN LONDON arrived at Max Gate and was greeted by Wessex, according to the *Life*, with "vociferous barks." Suddenly these "gave way to a piteous whine." Wessex continued to be ill at ease, and frequently went up to Watkins and touched his coat with his paw, withdrawing it with a "sharp cry of distress." Watkins left at about ten o'clock. The next morning Watkins's son telephoned to say that his father had died an hour after returning to his hotel. Wessex usually barked when the telephone rang, but on this occasion, according to Hardy, "remained silent, his nose between his paws." Wessex died at the age of 13 on December 27, 1926. He was buried in a small grave in the shrubbery on the west side of Max Gate with several cats and one other dog, Moss. His headstone reads:

THE
FAMOUS DOG
WESSEX
August 1913–27 Dec. 1926
Faithful. Unflinching

Wessex had been with Hardy throughout the years he had been married to Florence HARDY, taking walks with them to Frome Hill, where the dog would sit and appreciate the view. Hardy wrote a poem about him, "DEAD 'WESSEX' THE DOG TO THE HOUSEHOLD."

Wessex Edition The 24-volume definitive edition of Hardy's works published between 1912 and 1931 by MACMILLAN & CO., London. Purdy gives a complete listing of the contents of each volume in his bibliography. The first 18 volumes contained Hardy's novels and short stories and the last six were devoted to his volumes of poetry, the verse drama The DYNASTS, and The FAMOUS TRAGEDY OF THE QUEEN OF CORNWALL. The volumes were bound in maroon cloth gilt; each had a frontispiece and a "Map of the Wessex of the Novels and Poems." Hermann LEA's *Thomas Hardy's Wessex* (Macmillan, 1913) was issued in a matching format.

"Wessex Folk" Title of the manuscript of some of the sketches later published as "A FEW CRUSTED CHARACTERS." Purdy states that the manuscript is a "very rough hurried first draft" of a kind "Hardy almost invariably destroyed." In July 1913 Hardy gave the manuscript, bound in red morocco, to Edmund GOSSE (Purdy, *Thomas Hardy: A Bibliographical Study*, 84). "A Few Crusted Characters," dated March 1891, a group of nine sketches with an introduction, was included in LIFE'S LITTLE IRONIES, which also contains eight other stories.

"Wessex Heights" Poem written in December 1896, the year which Bailey calls the "year of Hardy's deepest despair." The poem was written, but not published, after JUDE THE OBSCURE had been published and savagely criticized; it was later collected in SATIRES OF CIRCUMSTANCE (1914). The speaker begins by mentioning "some heights in Wessex," such as Ingpen Beacon eastward or Wales-Neck westward, where he experiences "crises." He is "tracked by phantoms" everywhere he goes.

Four women are described in the poem. Critics have speculated that one was dead and three alive in 1896, but that only one was alive in 1914 when the poem was published. It is possible that the woman in the second stanza, "who suffereth long and is kind," may be Emma HARDY, from whom he has been sadly distanced. There is also a "great grey Plain" and a "figure against the moon" no one else can see. The "great grey Plain" may well signify EGDON HEATH. The figure may represent Jemima Hand HARDY, Hardy's mother. Haunted by the ghosts of those he knew, the poet is unable to go the "tall-spired town" (possibly DORCHESTER).

Hardy then mentions the "ghost at Yell'ham Bottom chiding loud at the fall of the night" and also a "ghost in Froomside Vale"; both may represent Tryphena SPARKS, the lost love of his youth. The final woman, "one rare fair woman," has long be assumed to be Florence HENNIKER, for whom Hardy might well have left Emma, except that Henniker had no desire to leave her husband.

In the final stanza, Hardy visualizes himself walking alone, on Ingpen Beacon, or Wylls-Neck to the west, or homely Bulbarrow, or Pilsdon Crest, places "where men have never cared to haunt, nor women have walked with me." It is only in such places, where "ghosts keep their distance," that he "knows some liberty."

For further reading: Bailey and Page, "'Wessex Heights' Visited and Revisited"; Ford, "The View from Wessex Heights: Thomas Hardy's Poetry of Isolation"; Giordano, "Hardy's Farewell to Fiction: The Structure of 'Wessex Heights'"; E. Hardy and F. B. Pinion, eds., *One Rare Fair Woman: Thomas Hardy's Letters to Florence*

Henniker, 1893–1922; Miller, "'Wessex Heights': The Persistence of the Past in Hardy's Poetry."

Wessex Novels   A 16-volume edition of Hardy's WES-SEX novels, subtitled "First Uniform and Complete Edition," published by OSGOOD, MCILVAINE & CO., London, 1895–96. They were bound in dark green cloth; each volume contained an etched frontispiece by H. MAC-BETH-RAEBURN, a scene from the novel drawn at the site, and a map titled "The Wessex of the Novels" drawn by Hardy. The text of each novel was carefully revised, topographical names and distances corrected, chapters retitled, and much rewriting done (Purdy, *Thomas Hardy: A Bibliographical Study,* 279–81).

Wessex Poems and Other Verses   Collection of poems published in 1898 by HARPER & BROTHERS with 30 illustrations by the author. The volume contained a number of important poems, including "The IMPERCIPIENT," "THOUGHTS OF PH[EN]A," "The PEASANT'S CONFESSION," "NEUTRAL TONES," "HAP," AND "AMABEL." The volume received mixed reviews. Writing in the London *Outlook,* Lionel JOHNSON stated that in the 50 poems there were "passion, humor, wistfulness, grimness, tenderness, but never joy, the radiant and invincible." An anonymous reviewer for the ATHENAEUM believed the most successful poems were those that concentrated on Hardy's "curiously intense and somewhat dismal view of life." W. M. Payne, writing in the *Dial,* declared that the poems displayed "much rugged strength and an occasional flash of beauty." He believed there were several that almost persuaded him "a true poet was lost when Mr. Hardy became a novelist." The reviewer for the *Academy* believed his "lyrical and personal" poems were superior to the ballads in the volume (Gerber and Davis, *Thomas Hardy: An Annotated Bibliography of Writings about Him,* 88–90).

Wessex Scenes from The Dynasts   Dramatization of selected scenes from *The DYNASTS* by the HARDY PLAYERS. *See* Appendix II, Media Adaptations of the Works of Thomas Hardy.

Wessex Tales: Strange, Lively, and Commonplace   Two-volume edition of Hardy's short stories published by MACMILLAN & CO., London and New York, in 1888. It contained five stories, all of which had been published in serial form earlier: "The THREE STRANGERS" (*LONG-MAN'S MAGAZINE,* March 1883 and, in America, *HARPER'S WEEKLY,* March 1883); "The WITHERED ARM" (*BLACKWOOD'S EDINBURGH MAGAZINE,* January 1888); "FELLOW-TOWNSMEN" (*NEW QUARTERLY MAGAZINE,* April 1880 and, in America, *Harper's Weekly,* April–May 1880); "INTERLOPERS AT THE KNAP" (*English Illustrated Magazine,* May 1884); and "The DISTRACTED PREACHER" (as "The Distracted Young Preacher" in *New Quarterly Magazine,* April 1879, and, in America, *Harper's Weekly,* April–May, 1879).

The reviewer for the London periodical *Literary World* called the stories "remarkable for their genuine local colouring, painted with all the charm of Mr. Hardy's best style." The writer for the New York *Critic* declared that the volumes offered proof that "rural England, as Shakespeare left it, is rural England as Hardy finds it—with the same broad, bland comfortably obtuse human features." The GRAPHIC reviewer observed that some of the stories were "strikingly and delightfully strange," but refused to guess how much Mr. Hardy had "drawn upon local legend and romance."

Westminster Abbey   Located in London to the south of Parliament Square and opposite the Houses of Parliament, the Abbey is said to have been founded in the seventh century, rebuilt by Edward the Confessor, and to date in its present form from the latter half of the 13th century. There have been many important additions since that time.

Westminster Abbey, London   (Sarah Bird Wright)

Poets' Corner, Westminster Abbey, where Hardy's ashes are buried (Dean and Chapter of Westminster)

In 1865, while a young man, Hardy went to the morning service in the Abbey and, as he noted in the *Life*, "stayed to the Sacrament." He found it a very "odd experience, amid a crowd of strangers" (*Life*, 50). The same year he attended the funeral of the prime minister, Lord Palmerston, in the Abbey. He wrote his sister Mary HARDY that he and a friend obtained tickets through friends and were admitted to the triforium, or monks' walk, of the Abbey. He wrote his sister Mary about the music (the Funeral March from Beethoven's *Eroica* Symphony and the Dead March from Handel's *Saul*) (*Letter* I, 6).

When the poet Alfred, Lord TENNYSON died in 1892, Hardy received a card of admission to attend his funeral in Westminster Abbey. He called the music "sweet and impressive." In June 1899 Hardy and some friends were admitted to the Abbey at midnight by Miss Bradley through the deanery; they rambled through the Abbey "by the light of a lantern" (*Life*, 304).

Hardy attended a memorial service for George MEREDITH in the Abbey in May 1909. In May 1910, after the death of King EDWARD VII, he watched from the window of his club, the ATHENAEUM, the procession as his body was taken to the Abbey, and the procession of the funeral from the Abbey three days later. This experience occasioned a poem, "A KING'S SOLILOQUY." He was invited to attend the coronation of King George V in the Abbey in June 1911, but declined in order to tour the Lake District with his brother, Henry HARDY (*Life*, 346, 350, 355).

Hardy died on January 11, 1928; On January 16, his ashes were interred in POETS' CORNER at the Abbey. Simultaneously a memorial service was held at St. Peter's Church, DORCHESTER, and his heart was buried in the grave of his first wife, among the Hardy tombs, in the graveyard at STINSFORD CHURCH. The six pallbearers representing Literature at the Abbey service were John GALSWORTHY, Edmund GOSSE, George Bernard SHAW, Sir James BARRIE, A. E. HOUSMAN, and Rudyard KIPLING. Other pallbearers were Stanley Baldwin, the prime minister and Ramsay MacDonald, the leader of the Opposition (representing the government and Parliament), as well as the master of Magdalene College, Cambridge (Mr. A. S. Ramsey) and the pro-provost of Queen's College, Oxford (Dr. E. M. Walker), who represented the colleges of which Hardy was an Honorary Fellow. A spadeful of Dorset earth was sprinkled on the casket (*Life*, 446).

Westminster Gazette, The Newspaper in which Hardy's short story "A CHRISTMAS GHOST-STORY," depicting the phantom of a young British soldier killed during the BOER WAR, was published on December 23, 1899.

Weymouth Holiday seaside town about seven miles from DORCHESTER. It originally consisted of two independent and competitive towns, Weymouth, whose charter dates from the 13th century, and Melcombe Regis. The two towns were joined by a bridge in 1593, although their rivalry remained. Today Melcombe Regis is a part of Weymouth.

It became a holiday resort in the late 18th century, when King GEORGE III began spending holidays there. The crescent-shaped harbor has many handsome Georgian buildings. One of the town's most notable landmarks is the large memorial statue to the king, which is situated near the beach. The town is close to the Isle of Portland, which Hardy called the "Isle of Slingers" in *The WELL-BELOVED*.

Hardy worked for the architect George CRICKMAY at Weymouth in 1869; he directed the rebuilding of Turnworth Church, west of Blandford Forum. He also supervised the restoration of several other churches. In February 1870 Crickmay asked him to go to CORNWALL to look at ST. JULIOT CHURCH, which was the last of the churches his original employer in Dorchester, John HICKS, had begun restoring before his death in 1869. It was at St. Juliot that he met Emma Lavinia Gifford (later HARDY). He resumed working for Crickmay in March 1871, and remained there until 1872, when he returned to LONDON.

Weymouth figures as BUDMOUTH in several of Hardy's works, including *The TRUMPET-MAJOR*, *The RETURN OF THE NATIVE*, *UNDER THE GREENWOOD TREE*, *FAR FROM THE MADDING CROWD* and many short stories. In *The MAYOR OF CASTERBRIDGE* Lucetta LE SUEUR writes Michael HENCHARD that she will be traveling from Bristol via CASTERBRIDGE to BUDMOUTH, where she will take a packet boat to Jersey. Today there is still boat service to the Channel Isles from Weymouth.

Wharton, Edith (1862–1937) American novelist, poet, travel writer, and short-story writer. She was born in New York City, but lived the last 20 years of her life in France, often traveling to England. She was the author of *The House of Mirth, The Age of Innocence, The Custom of the Country, A Motor-Flight Through France, Italian Backgrounds,* and other works. Soon after her first volume of short stories, *The Greater Inclination,* was published in 1899, Wharton and her husband met the popular London hostess Lady St. Helier (Hardy's friend Mary JEUNE). They became friends, and several times Jeune invited the Whartons to dinner parties at which Hardy was present. Wharton recalls in her autobiography, *A Backward Glance,* that Hardy was "as remote and uncommunicative as our most unsocial American men of letters," but attributed this attitude to his inborn shyness. In 1902, when TESS OF THE D'URBERVILLES was dramatized by Lorimer STODDARD, Wharton reviewed the performance of Mrs. (Minnie Maddern) FISKE.

During WORLD WAR I Hardy contributed a poem, "CRY OF THE HOMELESS," to Wharton's fund-raising anthology *The Book of the Homeless.* In the chapter on telling a short story in *The Writing of Fiction* (1925), Wharton singles out Hardy, for praise, along with Henry JAMES and Joseph Conrad.

"What the Shepherd Saw" Short story published in the Christmas number of the *Illustrated London News* on December 5, 1881. It was then pirated and reprinted in the United Stated in Munro's Seaside Library. It was collected in A CHANGED MAN AND OTHER TALES (1913).

The story takes place over four nights on the Marlbury Downs as an elderly shepherd and his young boy assistant, Bill Mills, care for a flock of 800 ewes during lambing season. The scene is near a Druidical trilithon or dolmen called the Devil's Door. The shepherd goes home to sleep on the first night, and the boy watches from a furze bush shelter as a man and woman meet on the downs. He listens to them. He is Captain Fred Ogbourne, and the woman is Harriet, a duchess, whose husband does not treat her well. Captain Ogbourne has come 2,000 miles to see her and has written, begging her to meet him. She confesses that she did love him once and that her husband is unkind to her. She agrees to meet him the next night and leaves. A third figure, a stout man in boots, whom Bill recognizes as the duke, who lives in Shakeforest Towers, appears; Bill deduces that he saw the couple but could not hear what they said.

The second night, Bill is wide awake. The figure of the duke approaches; he walks around the trilithon toward the concealed hut. Bill closes the stove and conceals himself in straw; the duke enters the hut and watches until Captain Ogbourne arrives. He accosts him, saying he has dishonored his wife and must die. The boy discerns a shadow in "quick muscular movement" and watches as he drags an inert body into an old ruin. He then waits for his wife, but she does not come. Bill, terrified, overtakes the duke and watches as the door of his mansion opens and the duchess runs out. She says he has come a day early and she had ordered a surprise bonfire to be ready on the night of his arrival. She tells him the truth about her cousin, Fred Ogbourne—that he had been fond of her, but that she had always discouraged his attentions. She suggests that they go together the next night and "read him a lesson on his foolishness." The duke asks, moodily, why they should do such a thing, but she says he is miserable and needs kind treatment.

On the third night, Bill sees the duke and duchess strolling toward his hut. Captain Ogbourne is not there, but she suggests they look in the hollow behind the Devil's Door. They see the shepherd's boy standing by the trilithon. He admits he is there "off and on" but is silent when asked whether he has seen anyone. They leave, but the duke returns and interrogates the boy, who declares he has never seen him walking or dragging a heavy load. The duke states that, if he will keep a secret all his life, he will make sure his clothes are more comfortable and he will be sent to school and "be made a man of." He will have a carriage eventually, but must never admit he has been a shepherd. He will also provide for his widowed mother. He makes the boy swear by the trilithon, "once a holy place," that he will never speak of what he has seen done on "this Marlbury Down." The next night Bill sleeps in Shakeforest Towers and is sent away to a remote village for tuition, then to a preparatory establishment, and eventually to a public school.

The fourth night takes place many years later. Bill has risen to the post of steward with a well-furnished office in Shakeforest Towers. He seeks out the duke in his library and warns him that the village bell is tolling for the old shepherd, who has died at 94. He has learned that the old shepherd was actually on the hill himself all three nights, and that he made a deathbed confession about what he saw to the vicar. The duke apparently discounts this information. That night, however, Bill goes out on the downs and sees the white nightshirt of the duke as he goes into the hollow and begins scratching the earth like a badger; then he leaves. Next day the porter tells Bill the duke is dead; he had gone out during the night and, on returning, lost his balance and fell downstairs.

The steward then tells the tale of the events that took place on the down. He dies some years later. The high furze bushes have been removed and Lambing Corner is no longer used for lambing. Present shepherds say that during the nights of Christmas week "flitting shapes are seen in the open space around the trilithon, together with the gleam of a weapon, and the shadow of a man dragging a burden into the hollow."

"When I Set Out for Lyonnesse" *(1870)*   A lyric with three stanzas, published in *SATIRES OF CIRCUMSTANCE* (1914), celebrating Hardy's journey to ST. JULIOT CHURCH in CORNWALL on March 7, 1870, when he first met Emma Gifford (HARDY), who would become his first wife.

In the first stanza he recalls that "the rime was on the spray" and "starlight lit my lonesomeness" as he set out for Lyonnesse, "A hundred miles away" (the name is derived from Arthurian tradition). In the second stanza he reflects that no prophet "durst declare, / Nor did the wisest wizard guess" what would "bechance at Lyonnesse / While I should sojourn there." He refers to meeting Emma. The third and final stanza exalts his return "With magic in my eyes. . . / My radiance rare and fathomless."

The journey from DORCHESTER of about a hundred miles entailed a series of trains, a horse-drawn wagonette, and a long walk as well. He stayed three days. Hardy was attracted to the vital Emma, who had been galloping over the hills on her mare, Fanny, and who was well read and interested in writing and painting. She had sold some of her sketches to help restore the church. When Hardy returned to HIGHER BOCKHAMPTON, his "mother noticed that something had happened but said nothing" (Bailey, *The Poetry of Thomas Hardy*, 269–70).

On December 23, 1914, Hardy wrote his friend Florence HENNIKER, who had praised the volume of poems, saying he was so glad she liked it, as it was "exactly what happened 44 years ago" (*Letters*, V, 70).

For further reading: Fairhall, "Hardy's 'When I Set Out for Lyonnesse.'"

"When I Weekly Knew"   *See* "QUID HIC AGIS?"

"Where the Picnic Was"   Poem published in *SATIRES OF CIRCUMSTANCE* (1914), recalling Hardy's visit to the site of a past summer picnic. It was placed in the "Poems of 1912–13" section of the book.

Hardy climbs through "winter mire" and is able to "scan and trace / The forsaken place / Quite readily." He himself is the "last relic of the band / Who came that day!" There had been four people; since then two have moved to the city, and one has died.

Critics have disagreed about the subject of the poem. Carl Weber believes the picnic was at Beeny Cliff, CORNWALL, in August 1870; but, in that case, the final two lines cannot refer to Emma HARDY, who died in 1912. James O. Bailey believes Hermann LEA's interpretation is more plausible. He argues that the picnic was the weekend of June 1, 1912. Hardy notes in the *Life* that Henry NEWBOLT and William Butler YEATS had

come to MAX GATE that weekend to present him with a gold medal from the ROYAL SOCIETY OF LITERATURE. Lea speculates that they might have gone on a sightseeing tour that included a picnic, and suggests, as the site, Ridgeway, a place south of DORCHESTER overlooking Weymouth Bay and the sea. Emma died five months later, in November 1912.

The poem has been set to music by Gerald Finzi. *See* Appendix II, Media Adaptations of the Works of Thomas Hardy.

Whistler, James (Abbott) McNeil (1834–1903)   American painter and etcher who, except for short periods, lived in England and France most of his life. Hardy met Whistler during the London season of 1886, along with the American writer Bret Harte and the British Shakespearean actor Charles Keene. He saw Whistler's *Study in Red* at the National Gallery one morning and, that evening, called on Mary JEUNE, who was wearing a "rich pink-red gown" very similar to the one he had seen in Whistler's painting (*Life*, 181, 184).

In January 1907 Hardy corresponded with the American etcher Joseph Pennell, who had written a biography of Whistler, saying that he would try to join those proposing memorials to him in London, Paris, and New York.

Whitefriars Club   A society of writers and journalists whose members included Edward CLODD, Clive HOLLAND, Richard GARNETT, and Arthur Spurgeon. On June 29, 1901, members of the club visited MAX GATE.

For further reading: Holland, *Thomas Hardy, O. M.: The Man, His Works, and the Land of Wessex.*

Whittle, Abel   In *The MAYOR OF CASTERBRIDGE* he is a young man who works for Michael HENCHARD. He is sorry when Donald FARFRAE topples Henchard, for Henchard had always been good to Abel's mother. Abel is one of the few people who help Henchard at the end of the book, attending him at his death on the heath.

"Why Did I Sketch"   This poem was published in *MOMENTS OF VISION* (1917), and recalls Hardy's courtship, in CORNWALL, of Emma Gifford (HARDY). He has returned to the site of the restoration of ST. JULIOT CHURCH, and is now wondering why he placed Emma in all his sketches at the time. He was enchanted by her as she rode her mare around the hills and cliffs and spoke of art and literature. However, she is no longer alive (she died in November 1912), and seeing her figure in his own sketches makes him despondent. Since one person in the picture has "ceased to be seen" it "waxes akin / To a wordless irony."

In the second stanza he advises all would-be artists to show the escarpments of downs or cliffs "stark and stiff / As in utter solitude" so they will not remind him of a happier time.

The final stanza brings bitter remorse that he permitted himself, on a "thoughtless day," to sketch, laugh, sing, and "rhyme." He then paints her in "for love," After the end of the poem, Hardy appends the words "From an old note."

"Why I Don't Write Plays" Article published in the PALL MALL GAZETTE on August 31, 1892. It is Hardy's reply to three questions that were put to a number of contemporary novelists in a symposium on "the present divorce of fiction from the drama," inviting them to justify their preference for only one medium. It was reprinted in *Life and Art* (New York, 1925).

The questions were:

(1) Whether you regard the present divorce of fiction from the drama as beneficial or inimical to the best interests of literature and the stage;
(2) Whether you yourself have at any time had, or now have, any desire to exercise your gifts in the production of plays as well as of novels; and if not,
(3) Why you consider the novel the better or more convenient means for bringing your ideas before the public you address.

Hardy answered the first question by saying that it was inimical to the best interest of the stage, but not injurious to literature.

His response to the second was that he did occasionally have a desire to produce a play and had written "skeletons of several," but he had no such desire "just now."

Regarding the third question, he asserted that he believed the novel afforded more scope than the play for "getting nearer to the heart and meaning of things." He felt at present parts had to be "moulded to actors" rather than the reverse, and that managers would not risk a "truly original play." Moreover, scenes had to be arranged in a "constrained and arbitrary" way to suit the requirements of scene-building even though spectators were indifferent to "order and succession" if they could have set before them "a developing thread of interest." Such an arbitrary arrangement in fact subordinated "the presentation of human passions" to the presentation of "mountains, cities, clothes, furniture, plate, jewels and other real and sham-real appurtenances." This caused neglect of emphasis on "the high-relief of the action and emotions." In fact, "accessories" should merely suggest place and time, and the stage should be no more than a "figurative arena" ("Why I Don't Write Plays," *Life and Art by Thomas Hardy*, 116–17).

Wildeve, Damon In *The RETURN OF THE NATIVE*, Wildeve is an engineer who had worked in BUDMOUTH (Weymouth) before becoming landlord of the Quiet Woman Inn. Hardy says he is "one in whom no man would have seen anything to admire, and in whom no woman would have seen anything to dislike." Mrs. YEOBRIGHT, the mother of Clym YEOBRIGHT, is an exception; she disapproves of him and does not wish her niece, Thomasin YEOBRIGHT, to marry him in church. As a result he takes Thomasin to Anglebury, but the marriage license is not valid there. Diggory VENN brings Thomasin home, unmarried. Venn's interest in Thomasin prompts Wildeve to marry her; they have a baby, but he is relatively indifferent to his wife and child. Hardy describes him: "To be yearning for the difficult, to be weary of that offered; to care for the remote, to dislike the near; it was Wildeve's nature always. . ."

After Eustacia leaves Clym, she agrees to go with Wildeve to Paris. As she tries to meet him on the heath on a dark, stormy night, she falls into Shadwater Weir and drowns; he drowns also, trying to rescue her.

Wildeve, Thomasin (Tamsin) Yeobright *See* YEOBRIGHT, THOMASIN.

Wimborne On June 22, 1881, Thomas and Emma Hardy moved from UPPER TOOTING to a house called Lanherne, at The Avenue, Wimborne, DORSET; they slept there for the first time on June 25. They were delighted with the garden, which had "old-fashioned flowers in full bloom," such as Canterbury bells and sweet williams. There were also currants, gooseberries, apples, and unripe peaches. This was after the serious illness Hardy suffered before and during the writing of *A LAODICEAN*. In the *Life* he says that he and his wife had decided to establish their principal residence in the country "for reasons of health and for mental inspiration." Life in or near LONDON "tended to force mechanical and ordinary productions from his pen, concerning ordinary society-life and habits" (*Life*, 149). They stayed here until late June 1883, when they moved to SHIRE-HALL PLACE, DORCHESTER, where they lived during construction of MAX GATE.

While at Wimborne, Hardy was asked by the building surveyor Charles George Vinall, an early secretary of the SOCIETY FOR THE PROTECTION OF ANCIENT BUILDINGS, to assist in the preservation of Wimborne Minster. Hardy replied that he had only taken a cottage there for a brief time because of his health, but would be glad to assist. The minster is the scene of his poem "Copying Architecture in an Old Minster" (*Letters* I, 95).

Windle, Bertram Coghill Alan (1858–1929) Anthropologist and writer on science, medicine, history, and topography. While staying at the Hôtel de la Poste in Brussels in September 1896, Hardy answered a letter from Bertram Windle, an English correspondent who proposed to write a handbook giving a key to Hardy's place names and their corresponding actual places (*see*

PLACE NAMES). Hardy compiled a list, which he termed "rudimentary notes," covering several pages, and prefaced it with a warning, underlined twice: "For *private reference only—not to be printed in this form*." His list is still one of the principal starting points for the accurate correlation of fictional and actual place names (*Letters* II, 130–31).

Windle was not alone in attempting to make such identifications, however. Others were Hermann LEA, who prepared a handbook to Wessex (1905), and the scholar F. O. SAXELBY, who in 1911 wrote Hardy that he was compiling a "Dictionary of the Characters & Places" in his novels and poems.

See Appendix V for a list of the fictional and actual places most commonly accepted by commentators and critics today.

"Wind's Prophecy, The"   Poem collected in *MOMENTS OF VISION* (1917) that describes Hardy's first journey into CORNWALL and the drive from Launceston to ST. JULIOT CHURCH, where he met his future wife, Emma, on March 7, 1870. It should be read as a companion poem to "A MAN WAS DRAWING NEAR TO ME."

Hardy, traveling to the rectory at St. Juliot, in Cornwall past "barren farms . . . / Against a cloud that speaks of wrecks," says he has left "my lady's arms . . . those arms I love the best." The wind replies, "'Nay, toward her arms thou journeyest.'"

In the second stanza, he sees a gray "distant verge" and "clots of flying foam / Break from its muddy monochrome." He sighs that his eyes now, as all day, "behold her ebon loops of hair!" The wind responds, "Nay; wait for tresses flashing fair!"

He hears the tides, screened by coastlands, as they cause "smitings like the slam of doors." The swell "cleaves through caves unseen." He says to himself, "Her city home is matched of none!" The wind answers, "Thou shouldst have said her sea-bord one."

In the fourth stanza he glimpses the "one quick timorous transient star" and cries, "there reigns the star for me!" But the wind outshrieks him: "Here, westward, where it downs, mean ye!" In the final stanza, he sees the headland and tells himself, "I roam, but one is safely mine." The wind replies, "Thy Love is one thou'st not yet known."

As the weather worsens, the warnings become more incensed and furious.

The girl with the "ebon loops of hair" is assumed by most critics to be Tryphena SPARKS, then a student at Stockwell Training College in London. She might have been engaged to Hardy at the time he went to Cornwall. She married Charles Frederick Gale of Topsham, Devon, in December 1877 (Bailey, *The Poetry of Thomas Hardy*, 393).

At the bottom of the poem is Hardy's notation "Rewritten from an old copy."

Winterborne, Giles   Principal character in *The WOODLANDERS*. A woodsman and cider maker, he spends his life in devotion to Grace MELBURY. Too late she realizes the "purity of his nature, his freedom from the grosser passions, his scrupulous delicacy." His true soulmate, in many ways, is the humble Marty SOUTH, who had reached his level of "intelligent intercourse with Nature" and, like Giles, could read the "heiroglyphs" of the Hintock woods as "ordinary writing," but, as she herself admits, he has never spoken to her of love. One of the most heroic of Hardy's male characters, he suffers a premature death from illness and exposure.

"Winters and the Palmleys, The"   *See* a "FEW CRUSTED CHARACTERS, A."

Winter Words in Various Moods and Metres   Poetry collection published posthumously, in 1928, by MACMILLAN & CO., London. It is a collection of 105 poems which Hardy had been assembling at the time of his death in January 1928. He apparently had planned to bring out the volume on his 88th birthday, June 2, 1928, but had realized it would be "probably my last appearance on the literary stage." The last poem is "He Resolves to Say No More." He had come to believe that, after the "madness" of WORLD WAR I and the excesses of the 1920s, leading to widespread "selfishness in all classes," he believed the world was threatened with a "new Dark Age." The portal to this new dark age had been World War I.

Hardy might well have deleted some poems and added others. However, the volume includes poems written over 60 years; every decade except the 1870s is represented; in this respect, the collection is in Purdy's words, "highly characteristic of the author." The collection covers Hardy's youthful years as an architect in DORCHESTER, his period in LONDON when he roamed about the city attending plays and visiting museums, and his return to Dorchester. These years were followed by his courtship of Emma Gifford HARDY and their period of early married life, apparently happy except for their CHILDLESSNESS. After the Hardys settled at MAX GATE he entered his final productive years in the writing of fiction, producing such major novels as *TESS OF THE D'URBERVILLES* and *JUDE THE OBSCURE*. The collection also has poems from the later years, after Hardy ceased writing novels. This was a period when Emma was increasingly afflicted with mental illness, but also a time when Hardy wrote some of his finest poetry. It was included in Macmillan's definitive WESSEX EDITION in 1931, combined with *HUMAN SHOWS, FAR PHANTASIES, SONGS, AND TRIFLES* (Purdy, *Thomas Hardy: A Bibliographical Study*, 261–62).

Among the poems it contains are "DEAD 'WESSEX', THE DOG TO THE HOUSEHOLD," "HE NEVER EXPECTED MUCH," "CHILDHOOD AMONG THE FERNS," "An UNKINDLY MAY," "CHRISTMAS 1924" "CHRISTMAS IN THE ELGIN

ROOM," "CONCERNING AGNES," and "A PHILOSOPHICAL FANTASY."

Southworth suggests that the volume "adds little to his artistic stature," despite the insights it offers into his character "both as man and poet" (*The Poetry of Thomas Hardy*, 195).

For further reading: Pritchard, "Hardy's Winter Words."

"Withered Arm, The"   Short story published in BLACK-WOOD'S EDINBURGH MAGAZINE in January 1888 and collected later the same year in WESSEX TALES.

SYNOPSIS

I. "A Lorn Milkmaid"

The story is set in an 80-cow dairy. The milkers are discussing the age of Farmer Lodge's new bride, whom he is bringing from Anglebury. The dairyman, who must pay Lodge nine pounds a year for each milker, asks them to stop speculating and get on with their work. Rhoda Brook, a "thin, fading woman of thirty," evokes secret sympathy from the women milkers.

After the milking is done, Rhoda takes her son, about 12, up to their small cottage in a high field. She tells him his father, Lodge, will be bringing home his young wife the next day. She asks him to tell her whether the new wife is "dark or fair," whether she has ever done housework or whether she "shows marks of the lady on her."

II. "The Young Wife"

The next evening, at sunset, a new gig driven by a "yeoman in the prime of life" comes up the hill toward Holmstoke. Beside him is Gertrude, the young wife, almost a girl. They pass a boy carrying a heavy bundle, who turns and looks at the farmer's wife "as though he would read her through and through." The farmer seems annoyed at the boy, but does not order him to get out of the way. Gertrude has noticed the boy and asked about him, wondering whether he might have hoped they would relieve him of his load. The farmer says he believes the boy lives with his mother a mile or two away, and that "these country lads" think nothing of carrying "a hundredweight."

The boy reports to his mother that the new wife is plain and ladylike, and has blue eyes and white teeth when she smiles. The next day Rhoda sends him to Holmstoke church in a clean shirt. He reports to his mother that Gertrude is rather short but "lovely." He describes her dress. At the daily milking, the dairyman always keeps the conversation from gossip that would annoy Rhoda.

III. "A Vision"

Rhoda dreams that Gertrude Lodge, in a white dress but much aged, is sitting on her chest, an incubus. With great effort she seizes the left arm of the specter with her right hand and casts it to the floor. As she milks at dawn she looks haggard. She comes home to breakfast; her son asks what the noise was in the night, but she cannot explain. Between 11 and 12 o'clock she sees the woman of her vision standing at the garden gate. The boy sees her too, and is pleased she has come. She has talked with him in the lane and promised to bring him better boots. She is kind and sweet, which makes Rhoda feel guilty. She comes again, bringing other useful articles. One day she tells Rhoda she does have one "little ailment" she cannot understand. Her left hand and arm are discolored; she tells Rhoda she was dreaming that night when a pain shot through her arm. Rhoda sees that there are "faint marks of an unhealthy colour, as if produced by a rough grasp." She wonders whether she has inflicted the stigma on Gertrude; she has been called a "witch" since giving birth to her son.

IV. "A Suggestion"

As the summer draws on, Rhoda develops an affection for Gertrude. One day, in the fields, she meets her and learns that her arm is much worse. Gertrude has seen a doctor, but he is mystified also. When Rhoda looks at it she sees the outline of the four fingers even more distinctly. She tells Rhoda her husband has noticed the disfigurement and wondered whether "some witch, or the devil himself," had taken hold of her and "blasted the flesh." Rhoda tells her to keep her arm covered, but Gertrude says he knows the mark is there.

Gertrude says she is about to consult a clever man on EGDON HEATH that she has been told Rhoda would know about. "Not Conjurer Trendle!" Rhoda replies. Gertrude loses interest when she discovers his name, and says she will only consult a medical man. Rhoda realizes she has the reputation of a sorceress, one who would know about Conjurer Trendle. She fears that she will be blamed as a "malignant influence" leading to Gertrude's injured arm.

Two days later, Gertrude returns to Rhoda and says she will visit Conjurer Trendle. Rhoda says he is "in the heart of Egdon," five miles away. She says she will meet Gertrude and go with her.

V. "Conjurer Trendle"

When Rhoda and Gertrude meet, Gertrude is wearing her arm in a sling. They climb up the slopes of the heath, possibly the same heath that had "witnessed the agony of the Wessex King Ina." King Ina of Wessex (688–728) succeeded King Ceadwall and bravely fought King Ceolred and defeated the South Saxons. They find Trendle's house by a cart track. He is a dealer in furze, turf, and other local products. He pretends to have no powers and to disclaim his part in the disappearance of warts and other ailments.

Trendle looks at Gertrude's arm and pronounces it "the work of an enemy." "What enemy?" she asks, as Rhoda draws back. He takes Gertrude into his dwelling, while Rhoda waits outside. He breaks an egg into a tumbler of water and asks if she recognizes any face or figure as it sinks down. Gertrude murmurs a low reply; when she comes out she is pale and will not speak of what he has said. That winter it is whispered that her affliction is because she has been "overlooked" by Rhoda. Rhoda does not mention the incubus, but in the spring she and her son disappear from the neighborhood.

VI. "A Second Attempt"
After six years the Lodges' marriage is in decline. Gertrude's arm is disfigured and she has not had a child. Although she is only 25 she has become irritable and superstitious. Lodge tells her she needs "someone to cheer her" and that he once thought of adopting a boy, but he was too old now. She guesses who he means, and has heard the story of the son he has had with Rhoda.

She returns to Trendle. He tells her she must touch the limb to the neck of a man who has been hanged, before he is cut down from the gallows. She must go to the jail when there is a hanging.

VII. "A Ride"
CASTERBRIDGE, more than a dozen miles away, often has hangings, but Gertrude cannot gather her courage to go to one. Then she hears there will be assizes, a circuit court session, held in March, but it is too soon for her to make arrangements to attend. She goes to the July assizes on a cart horse, reaching the White Hart Inn. People are not surprised to see her, as farmers' wives often ride on horseback. The innkeeper does not know the Lodges, and supposes her to be a "harums-karum young woman" who had come to see the hangings.

VIII. "A Water-Side Hermit"
Gertrude sets out to locate the Casterbridge hangman, who is named Davies. He tells her the execution will not take place until noon, in case the London mail coach brings a reprieve. The accused is being hanged for arson, but Davies thinks he was not at fault. He tells her to come to a little wicket in the wall at one o'clock and he will give her a piece of the corpse.

IX. "A Rencounter"
The next day, Gertrude goes to the wicket and the hangman holds her arm across the dead man's neck. There is a shriek from behind her; it is Rhoda, accompanied by Farmer Lodge. The hanged man was their son. Rhoda calls Gertrude a hussy, "to come between us and our child now!" She says this outcome was the meaning of what Satan had showed her in the vision.

Gertrude faints. Lodge has come to claim the body with Rhoda; they have a wagon and a sheet waiting. Gertrude is taken into town, but dies after three days of the double shock that follows the strain to which she has subjected herself. Her husband is never seen in Casterbridge again. He becomes a chastened and thoughtful man. He gives up his farms in Holmstoke and his livestock, and goes to live in Port-Bredy (Bridport). When he dies he has bequeathed his estate to a reformatory for boys, except for a small annuity to Rhoda Brook, if she can be found.

The story points up the survival of belief in witchcraft among country people. This subject was explored in depth by Ruth Firor in *Folkways in Thomas Hardy*. It is also manifested in a number of Hardy's poems, such "SIGNS AND TOKENS," with its "red-cloaked crone," and "AT THE PIANO," with its "cowled Apparition."

Rhoda eventually returns to her old parish, but refuses the annuity. She resumes milking at the dairy and her dark hair becomes white. Those watching "wonder what sombre thoughts were beating inside that impassive, wrinkled brow, to the rhythm of the alternating milk-streams."

For further reading: Ebbatson, "'The Withered Arm' and History"; Keys, "Hardy's Uncanny Narrative: A Reading of 'The Withered Arm.'"

women's suffrage, Hardy's views on   Hardy came to approve of women's suffrage, on the whole, but with reservations. He took the position that, when legalized, it might bring dire consequences for women that they had not anticipated, such as less protection for them within marriage. In November 1895, the month *JUDE THE OBSCURE* was published, Lady Agnes GROVE asked him to review a response she had written to an article, "Why Women Do Not Want the Ballot," by the bishop of Albany, New York, that had appeared in the *North American Review* (*Letters* II, 92). In 1899 she sent him another article containing her refutation of objections to women's suffrage, and he responded with praise for her forceful rhetoric (*Letters* II, 226).

In 1908 Lady Grove sent Hardy her book *The Human Woman*. He replied that the whole was "really a series of brilliant & able essays, which all who favour woman suffrage should be grateful for." He added that he had long held that "in justice" women should have votes, but that some of her "ingenious arguments" had not occurred to him (*Letters* III, 354).

That year he specified his concerns in a letter to Miss Helen Ward, a member of the Magazine Sub-Committee of the National Union of Women's Suffrage Societies. He cautioned that women's suffrage might result in "the probable break-up of the present marriage-system, the present social rules of other sorts, religious codes, legal arrangements on property, &c. (through men's self protective countermoves)." He did not necessarily believe such results would be "a bad thing," he stated, or he would not have written *Jude the Obscure* (*Letters* III, 360).

Emma HARDY was an active member of the National Union of Suffrage Societies, which held a banquet on April 28, 1909, in honor of delegates to the annual conference of the International Woman Suffrage Alliance. Clement SHORTER apparently wrote to ask whether Hardy was going to attend the banquet. He answered that he knew nothing about it, but that he did not object to the "coming of woman-suffrage" because men might be able to "strike out honestly right & left." In 1906 he had written Millicent Garrett FAWCETT expressing his support of "woman-suffrage" because he believed the woman's vote would "break up" many conventions related to "manners, customs, religion, illegitimacy . . . and other matters." Also, he hoped that women would join in putting down "blood-sport, slaughter-house inhumanities, the present blackguard treatment of animals generally, &c." (*Letters* IV, 21). In August of that year Hardy wrote the essayist and journalist Henry W. Nevinson that he believed the position of women one of "ninetynine things in a hundred that are wrong in this so-called civilized time, & that the vote is theirs by right (though whether it will be for their benefit at first I have some doubt). He worried that the tactics women had used which had once been a help had lost their novelty and were now harming their cause (*Letters* IV, 39).

Woodlanders, The   Novel serialized in *MACMILLAN'S MAGAZINE* from May 1886 to April 1887 and published in 1887. It was praised for its careful representation of rural customs and scenes, and especially for its depiction of the two central characters, Grace Melbury FITZPIERS and Giles WINTERBORNE. The novel has been called Hardy's "closest approach to orthodox realism: to an impression of life as an unselective flow of plausible events" (Guerard, *Thomas Hardy,* 81).

The setting of the novel is a hamlet called Little Hintock, in a rural setting that, according to Hardy, "cannot be regarded as inferior to any inland scenery of the sort in the west of England, or perhaps anywhere in the kingdom" (September 1895 preface to *The Woodlanders*). He declares he cannot himself give the specific location of Little Hintock, even though he had spent several hours on a bicycle searching for it.

The novel has all the pastoral charm of *UNDER THE GREENWOOD TREE*, but with a tragic outcome. The beauty of the rural landscape contrasts sharply with Edred FITZPIERS's corruption and infidelity. Ideal love is represented not by Grace Melbury Fitzpiers, but by the humble Marty SOUTH, who knows she cannot win Giles Winterborne, but whose devotion to him is unwavering.

SYNOPSIS

Chapters 1–12
As the novel opens, Mr. PERCOMB, a barber, has called on Marty South in the small cottage she shares with her father, John SOUTH; she is secretly doing his work in the fields, making spars for thatchers. Percomb asks Marty to sell him her hair to make a wig for a wealthy widow, Felice CHARMOND, the owner of the Hintock estate. Marty is horrified and refuses, but must eventually give in. Her father is the last leaseholder of their cottage, which puts both of them in a precarious position. Giles Winterborne holds the South cottage and several belonging to other villagers; all will be lost to Marty and to Giles through John South's death, reverting to the estate of Mrs. Charmond. In order to have dilapidated houses rebuilt, their ancestors had been persuaded to exchange their old copyholds, or right of indefinite occupation by the tenant and his decedents, for life-leases extending only for three lifetimes. Mrs. Charmond gives Marty a ride in her carriage one day; her head is shorn; Mrs. Charmond is "gratified at her denuded appearance."

Giles works for George MELBURY, who had won his late first wife by tricking his father out of winning her. Melbury feels guilty about it. Giles is now courting his only child, Grace Melbury. George hopes to right this wrong by approving the match. He has sent Grace away to a boarding school for a fine education. On her return he sends Giles to meet her at the market town of SHERTON ABBAS (SHERBORNE) when she comes from school. Giles notices that she has forgotten some of her country interests and knowledge, which dismays him. She tells him about places she has visited, such as Brighton, Cheltenham, and cities on the Continent.

Mrs. Charmond decides she needs a companion for her trip abroad, and interviews Grace. She shows her a collection of cruel man-traps on the wall, collected by her late husband. These were used to catch poachers. Mrs. Charmond mentions Edred Fitzpiers, whom Grace has not met. As she leaves, Mrs. Charmond sees a reflection of both of them in a mirror, and realizes Grace makes her appear far older. This mirror image also startles her into a deep attraction to Grace. Grace is excited about traveling with Mrs. Charmond on the Continent. Giles decides to move toward winning Grace by having a Christmas high tea, with supper a few hours later. He is vague about the time, which causes Mr. Melbury, his wife, Lucy, and Grace to arrive much too early, to his embarrassment. The ancient Albert CREEDLE, his helper, struggles in the kitchen with the aid of a kitchen boy. Grace finds a well-boiled slug on her plate, which causes Giles to murmur, "O yes—'tis all over!"

Mrs. Charmond fails to invite Grace on her journey.

Chapters 12–24
Charmond's coachman has a confrontation with Giles on a narrow road; Giles wins, but at a high cost. John South dies because of Edred Fitzpiers's treatment. He advises him to have the tree cut down outside his bed-

room window. He had thought he wanted it done, but the shock kills him. Giles loses his houses after South's death, since he had forgotten to renew his lease, Mrs. Charmond's agent will not consent to his belated renewal of the lease. Marty stays alone in the house with her father's corpse until his burial, "the repose of a guileless soul that had nothing more left on earth to lose, except a life which she did not over-value." Mr. Melbury then convinces Giles he has nothing to offer Grace, although Grace is more than willing at this point to marry him.

Grammer Oliver, the Melburys' servant, has promised her own brain to Fitzpiers after death, for scientific experimentation. She begs Grace to dissuade him from taking it. Grace calls on Fitzpiers and is impressed by his intellectual interests and scientific investigations. He has a piece of John South's brain under his microscope, which repels Grace yet also impresses her.

The process of barking the Melbury trees begins; Fitzpiers watches and sees more of Grace, who convinces herself she has lost interest in Giles. He helps her find the purse Giles had given her years earlier. Fitzpiers watches as the village girls attempt to cast a spell on Midsummer Eve. Grammer Oliver predicts Fitzpiers will capture Grace, but tries to encourage Winterborne. Fitzpiers, thanks to Grace's stepmother, captures and holds Grace when the girls run down the slope from the woods after sowing hempseed. He later seduces Suke DAMSON.

Giles meets an "Italianized American," born in South Carolina but living on the Continent, who is searching for Hintock House. The traveller is sure Mrs. Charmond is there, but, on finding she is still in London, leaves. Mr. Melbury asks Fitzpiers to look at Grace, who caught a cold on Midsummer Eve. Fitzpiers asks if he may court Grace, and Melbury assents with enthusiasm. Grace receives this news listlessly. Fitzpiers takes her to talk on a nearby hill and points out the former village of Oakbury Fitzpiers; Grace is impressed despite herself and, one day, visits the ruins of Sherton Castle, the home of Fitzpiers's maternal ancestors. He continues courting her. When she agrees to marry him, he scorns the idea of being married at the "horrid little church" in the village with the "yokels staring round," but wants to marry at a registry office.

One night a month before the wedding Grace sees, from a window of her home, Suke Damson emerge from Fitzpiers's house and go to her own dwelling. Grace tells her father she does not want to marry Fitzpiers, but will marry Giles instead. Her father admits he has not kept their engagement a secret but told all his acquaintances. Grace confronts Fitzpiers about the girl on the porch, but he assures her a young woman whose name he does not know had come to him with a toothache and he had pulled the tooth. Grace believes him, but demands that, if they marry, it must be in church. Giles withdraws and ceases to court Grace, who marries Fitzpiers.

Chapters 25–36
After traveling for eight weeks, Fitzpiers and Grace are in the Earl of Wessex Hotel at Sherton Abbas. Grace, beautifully dressed with rings on her hands, fancying she has married well, sees Giles, busy making cider at the inn's apple press; Robert Creedle is working with him. She calls to Giles, but he bitterly accuses her of opening old wounds. Edred looks down on Giles; she reminds him her family is not better than that of Giles. Edred is depressed as they continue back to Hintock.

Workmen have set up Edred's office in one wing of the Melbury house, and he has given up his residence in the home of Mrs. Cox. Mrs. Cox, disgruntled, tells Fitzpiers he has married beneath himself and that Mrs. Charmond has come home.

The Melburys have invited all the neighbors in for a homecoming supper. Fitzpiers tries to enjoy himself, but he tells Grace they must have no more to do with the Hintock woodlanders. The local people, for their part, consider him no longer one of the "old Oakbury Fitzpierses" but "one of themselves," and are less deferential. He considers going to BUDMOUTH (Weymouth).

Giles has given up his house and sleeps in a hut in the woods. His old home is being torn down, and, one night, Mrs. Charmond drives a phaeton into the ruins, thinking it is the road. She summons Fitzpiers to attend to her, although she is not really injured. She is lying on a couch, smoking, and tells him she has only been shaken up. She tells him they met years earlier in Heidelberg when he was a medical student and she was there with her family. He assures her he will call the next day.

Felice Charmond is a "woman of perversities, delighting in piquant contrasts." She is fond of mystery—"in her life, in her love, in her history." She learns from her maid that Grace and Giles did not marry because of her agent's refusal to renew the leases on the houses. She resolves to help Giles, and goes to stay at Middleton Abbey.

Edred abuses Grace's horse, Darling, given to her by Giles, by riding it too far and not caring for it properly in the stable on their return. Grace suspects that Edred has gone to Middleton Abbey. She sees Giles, who admits he has seen Edred and Felice there. She sees Suke Damson eating nuts and discovers she has had no teeth pulled. Grace is disillusioned about Fitzpiers, but not jealous. Fitzpiers stays out all night one night; the farm workers find Darling in her stall with him on her back, asleep. Another horse would probably have thrown him. Grace's father realizes, with astonishment, that Fitzpiers has allowed himself to look on someone other than Grace. Lucy Melbury, Grace's stepmother, assures Mr. Melbury that Mrs. Charmond would not have encouraged Fitzpiers.

Melbury sees Fitzpiers embracing Mrs. Charmond. He asks Grace to confront her, but she refuses. Grace tells her father she despises "genteel life" and wishes she had married Giles.

The affair between Fitzpiers and Mrs. Charmond becomes generally known. Mr. Melbury goes to Giles and tells him he wishes he were his son-in-law. Melbury confides the story of his having won Grace's mother away from his father and says Grace still loves Giles. Giles tells him Felice Charmond was once an actress.

Mr. Melbury goes to Hintock House and pleads with Mrs. Charmond to give up Fitzpiers. She pretends not to know what he is talking about, but he points out that scandal will touch her as well as Fitzpiers. He goes on to Sherton Abbas on business, but Grace, worrying about him, finds Giles in the woods. Felice Charmond then arrives; Grace realizes Felice loves Fitzpiers. Felice denies it. Grace says Felice will suffer far more from Fitzpiers than she herself has done. They part coldly, but each gets lost in the woods, and they find each other again. They clasp passionately; Grace buries her face in Mrs. Charmond's muff. Mrs. Charmond then admits that Fitzpiers is her lover. Poor Marty South writes Fitzpiers to let him know that Mrs. Charmond's hair is actually Marty's own.

Fitzpiers's practice is dwindling. He goes to see Felice on the horse Blossom, followed by Mr. Melbury, riding the mate Darling. Blossom throws Fitzpiers. Melbury rescues him, manages to get him on Darling, and fortifies him with rum. Fitzpiers, not recognizing Melbury, rambles on about being tied to Grace. Melbury pulls Fitzpiers off Darling, finds Blossom, and leads both horses home. Suke and Felice both come to the Melbury home, worried about Fitzpiers after hearing of the accident. Mr. Melbury says Fitzpiers is fine; he has walked away from being thrown from the horse. Actually, however, Fitzpiers is still in the woods.

Fitzpiers makes his way to Hintock House, where Felice hides and nurses him.

Chapters 37–48

It becomes known that Mrs. Charmond has taken Fitzpiers to the Continent. In Sherton Abbas for market day, Mr. Melbury asks a local dandy and lawyer's clerk, Fred Beaucock, about a divorce for Grace. Beaucock assures him Grace can be freed of Fitzpiers. Mr. Melbury tells Giles about it on the way home, before he sees Grace. Grace is ill, and made worse by the discovery of Fitzpiers's hat, which seems to portend his coming home. Mr. Melbury goes to London and believes he has set in motion legal redress for Grace.

Giles is delighted to know Grace might be freed, although he is skeptical. Mrs. Melbury and Grace go to Sherton Abbas on errands, where Grace sees Giles. Like "Arcadian innocents" they discuss Grace's freedom, without understanding the almost insurmountable difficulties. Giles orders dinner for Grace in a simple tavern, frequented by butchers and dairymen, which embarrasses her (she does not realize that Fitzpiers has never paid for their lodging at the Earl of Wessex Hotel, where they stayed at the end of their wedding trip).

The next day, Melbury writes Giles to say he has failed to secure Grace's divorce: Fitzpiers has not been sufficiently cruel to Grace to allow her to divorce him. Grace is hopeful, and invites Giles to kiss her, which he does; he cannot bring himself to tell her about the letter denying her divorce. Mr. Melbury arrives, and tells them the truth; Giles does not admit that he had received a letter from Beaucock telling him the news.

Rosemarie Morgan points out that the entire divorce issue was of much interest at the time in England. She observes that, in the novel, it is unclear whether Melbury is pursuing the 1870s amendment to the Matrimonial Causes Act (which gave more opportunity for wives to divorce) or whether Fred Beaucock, the quack lawyer he consults, is completely unreliable. At the time there was tremendous confusion about the divorce laws, including the "New Law" that the quack lawyer mentions. He declares a new statute has been enacted making "unmarrying" as easy as "marrying" without an Act of Parliament. Hardy terms Beaucock's information "exaggerated," but does not say whether it was caused by "ignorance" or "dupery" (personal communication to the author).

Grace stays inside, miserable, and Giles goes to his hut, feverishly ill. Fitzpiers writes Grace that he is living alone and sailing to Budmouth, then coming to Hintock. He asks her to meet his steamer. She does not do so, but he sends word he is arriving in Hintock anyway. She gathers her things and escapes, leaving a note that she has gone to visit a school friend. She finds Winterborne in his little hut and asks him to help her get to Ivell and on to Exonbury. Winterbourne is ill, but says nothing about it. He is roasting a rabbit, but insists that she take his little hut; he will go to a shelter outside. She fixes his dinner and breakfast and puts it on the window ledge, believing he is working somewhere. A hard rain sets in, and he stops eating; Grace calls to beg him to come in, but he does not answer. She finally goes and searches for him, finding him feverish, wild-eyed, and incoherent in his little shelter. She has underrated his chivalry, the "purity of his nature, his freedom from the grosser passions, his scrupulous delicacy." Grace nurses him tenderly, but realizes he needs medical help. Disguising her voice, she summons Fitzpiers, who follows her. He cannot help Giles. After Giles dies, Grace becomes hysterical. Fitzpiers tells her Felice Charmond has also died; it emerges that she was shot by the South Carolina gentleman who had followed her to the Continent. Fitzpiers and Felice had quarreled when Marty South's letter about her hair reached Fitzpiers. Fitzpiers had left Felice and she was following him when she was shot.

Grace returns home with her father and stepmother, but becomes ill with Giles's fever, since she has kissed him before and after death. She drinks some medicine Fitzpiers had left at the hut, and slowly recovers.

Grace and Marty South go to Giles's grave. Grace realizes that Marty alone had really understood Giles; she had "approximated to Winterborne's level of intelligent intercourse with Nature." They had been able to read the "heiroglyphs" of the Hintock woods as "ordinary writing." Grace feels Giles should have married Marty, because they could speak "the tongue of the trees and fruits and flowers themselves." Marty says Giles had never loved her. Grace can only hope he would have died even if she had not let him put her in the little shelter.

Fitzpiers has gone to a town in the Midlands (that is, in the industrial region of central England), where he is miserable. He wonders if Grace was really unfaithful to him with Giles. He returns to Hintock and goes to Marty's cottage. She is polishing Giles's tools; he promises to buy his apple mill and press for her. She tells him Giles gave up his hut to Grace, thus, probably, sacrificing his life.

Fitzpiers writes Grace that he is living in the Midlands and dreams of her and hopes she will join him. She agrees to meet him if Marty can accompany her. On the way to meet Grace, Fitzpiers sees Suke Damson's wedding procession. She is like a "giantess" beside her small husband, Tim TANG. They are leaving for New Zealand; she begins crying because she will not be able to find such a clever doctor in New Zealand if she should be wanting one in a few months. (Suke is apparently pregnant.)

When Fitzpiers sees Grace, he begs her to return to him. She refuses, but he insists on coming to meet her every two weeks. Tim Tang, however, sees him as he saunters along and wonders whether he is still seeking Suke, who has admitted her "past levities." Tim does not want to go to New Zealand and leave his father, but Suke's reputation will be ruined if they stay. He keeps seeing Fitzpiers pass by, and recalls a man-trap he has seen in the former dwelling of a gamekeeper. He retrieves it from beneath the roof eaves; it is three feet long and half as wide. He sets it and hastens to bed. He and Suke hear a loud cry.

Grace, meanwhile, has come out to meet Fitzpiers; her skirts are caught in the man-trap, and she screams. Fitzpiers begins rocking in distress over her skirt, but she appears, above him, unhurt. He sobs in delight and relief, which touches her. He tells her he has bought a partnership in the Midlands and will leave in a week. She goes with him to the Earl of Wessex Hotel.

Grace's father, alarmed, searches for her with Creedle and two other laborers; they go all the way to Sherton Abbas, and go to the hotel. They learn of the arrival of Grace and Fitzpiers; Grace tells her father of his purchase of the practice. They stay at the hotel, and the men, after having some rum in the same tavern where Giles provided lunch for Grace, go back to Little Hintock. Marty South has faithfully waited for Grace to visit Giles's grave. She finally goes alone, and replaces the wilted flowers with fresh ones. She possesses Giles at last.

CRITICAL RECEPTION AND COMMENTARY

The London *SATURDAY REVIEW* called the novel "rich and human, but objected to the intrusion of "two persons from the world of fashion," whose romance throws the "primitive society into discord." The Boston *Literary World* reviewer praised the character of Marty South but declared that the novel leaves the reader "baffled, stupified, cast down" because of its pessimism. The poet Coventry Patmore, writing in *St. James's Gazette,* declared the novel "not up to H's usual standard" because the reformation of Fitzpiers is unbelievable. He declared that Hardy's love of nature was "so passionate and observant" that he was wasting his powers "by expending them upon prose." R. H. Hutton, writing in the *SPECTATOR,* called the novel "powerful and disagreeable"; he considered Grace Melbury's father the "best study in the book" and Hardy's study of the woodlands its best feature. The reviewer for the *ATHENAEUM* criticized Hardy for making his "peasants sound like Greek philosophers."

In 1913, A. H. EVANS dramatized the novel for the HARDY PLAYERS. They performed it in DORCHESTER, LONDON, and Weymouth. The *Dorset Yearbook* pronounced the London production "the most successful of the Hardy plays imported from the Mother County" (Gerber and Davis, *Thomas Hardy: An Annotated Bibliography of Writings about Him,* 41–43, 161; *see* Appendix II, Media Adaptations of the Works of Thomas Hardy.

For further reading: Ball, "Tragic Contradiction in Hardy's *The Woodlanders*"; Glance, "The Problem of the Man-Trap in Hardy's *The Woodlanders*"; Hubbart, "Thomas Hardy's Use of Folk Culture in *The Woodlanders*"; Kiely, "The Menace of Solitude: The Politics and Aesthetics of Exclusion in *The Woodlanders*"; Lodge, introduction to *The Woodlanders;* Morrison, "Love and Evolution in Thomas Hardy's *The Woodlanders*"; Pinion, "The Country and Period of *The Woodlanders*"; Saunders, "The Significance of the Man-Trap in *The Woodlanders*"; Skilling, "Investigations into the Country of *The Woodlanders*"; Stewart, "Hardy's Woodlanders."

Woodwell, Mr.   In *A LAODICEAN,* a fiery Baptist minister who attempts, in vain, to dissuade the heiress Paula POWER from her resistance to baptism by immersion. He is "single-mindedness itself" regarding theology, but gives all he has to the poor. He is a portrait of an actual person, one of the few in Hardy's works, based on the Reverend Thomas Perkins, the rector of Turnworth, Dorset. Hardy approved of Perkins's support of justice for animals.

Woolf, Leonard (1880–1969)   English political writer and novelist, literary editor of the *Nation and Athenaeum* from 1923 to 1930, and husband of Virginia WOOLF. In 1917, he and his wife founded the Hogarth Press, which became a successful publishing house.

In April 1921 the playwright and author St. John Ervine wrote Hardy that a group of young writers wished to present him with a first edition of a volume of Keats's poetry for his forthcoming birthday. Hardy wrote that he felt a first edition would be "of too much value," but they did present him with Keats's *Lamia, Isabella, The Eve of St. Agnes, and Other Poems* on his 81st birthday, June 2, 1921. The volume was sent by 104 writers, including Leonard and Virginia Woolf (*Letters* VI, 84–85, 90).

Woolf, Virginia (1882–1941)   English novelist, essayist, and critic, and member of the Bloomsbury Group; she was one of the daughters of Sir Leslie STEPHEN. In his home she was reared in an atmosphere that valued literature and learning, and she met many of the leading authors of the day. She was also related to several noted literary families, including those of Charles Darwin and John Addington SYMONDS. She was a friend of Desmond MACCARTHY, Lytton Strachey, and Victoria ("Vita") SACKVILLE-WEST. She and her husband, the novelist, critic, and editor Leonard WOOLF, founded the Hogarth Press, a successful publishing house.

Woolf's novels are poetic and symbolic, using the technique of the interior monologue, in the stream of consciousness vein of writing. Among her more famous novels are *To the Lighthouse, Mrs. Dalloway,* and *The Waves.* She was an astute critic, writing "Mr. Bennett and Mrs. Brown" and two series of literary essays titled *The Common Reader* (1925, 1932).

In 1897 Hardy wrote a sonnet called "The SCHRECK-HORN," in which he compared the Schreckhorn (a mountain in the Alps) with Woolf's father, Sir Leslie Stephen. The poem was collected in *SATIRES OF CIRCUM-STANCE* (1914), and in January 1915 Woolf wrote Hardy that the poem and its reminiscences were "incomparably the truest & most imaginative portrait of [Stephen] in existence" (*Letters* V, 76).

In 1923 Woolf asked Hardy for a contribution to the *Nation and Athenaeum,* of which her husband had become the literary editor, but Hardy regretfully refused because of his advanced age. He wrote that there were "plenty of young pens available" and he would take much interest in the paper (*Letters* VI. 196).

In June 1926 the Woolfs called on Hardy at MAX GATE. In her diary Woolf recalled him as "a little puffy cheeked cheerful old man, with an atmosphere cheerful & businesslike." She was impressed by his "freedom, ease & vitality," very 'Great Victorian' doing the whole thing with a sweep of his hand . . . & setting no great stock by literature; but immensely interested in facts; incidents; & somehow, one could imagine, naturally swept off into imagining & creating without a thought of its being difficult or remarkable; becoming obsessed; & living in imagination" (*The Diary of Virginia Woolf, III: 1925–1930,* 96, 100).

In 1932, after Hardy's death, Woolf wrote an essay, "The Novels of Thomas Hardy," for *The Second Common Reader* (London: 1932). She stated that his death had left English fiction "without a leader," although the "unworldly and simple old man" would have been embarrassed by the rhetoric of her praise. The essay traces Hardy's career as a novelist, beginning with *DESPERATE REMEDIES,* in which he could "create characters but not control them." His second novel, *UNDER THE GREENWOOD TREE,* is, she says, "accomplished, charming, idyllic," but lacks the "stubborn originality" of the first. She regrets that, in the early books, there is a sense of waste: "first one gift would have its way with him and then another." He was both poet and realist, "a faithful son of field and down" who was also "tormented by the doubts and despondencies bred of book-learning." She classes him with a group of writers who are "unconscious of many things," unlike Henry JAMES or Gustave Flaubert, who are "aware of all the possibilities of every situation, and are never taken by surprise." Hardy is more like Charles Dickens or Sir Walter SCOTT, suddenly lifted on a wave, which then sinks.

She believes his "moments of vision" describes the passages of "astonishing beauty and force" found in each of his books, in which a single scene "breaks from the rest," as in the scene in *FAR FROM THE MADDING CROWD* when the wagon with Fanny's dead body inside travels beneath the dripping trees. But there are also stretches of "plain daylight" that make the novels unequal. She praises *Far from the Madding Crowd* as a novel holding first place among English novels. Others meriting the term "greatness" are *The RETURN OF THE NATIVE, The WOODLANDERS,* and *The MAYOR OF CASTERBRIDGE*—but not *JUDE THE OBSCURE,* which she finds pessimistic and painful. It is also flawed, she believes, because "argument is allowed to dominate impression."

According to Woolf, the WESSEX NOVELS, as a whole, are not "one book but many" that, in the aggregate, produce an effect "commanding and satisfactory." What they provide is not so much a "transcript of life at a certain time and place" as a "vision of the world and of man's lot as they revealed themselves to a powerful imagination, a profound and poetic genius, a gentle and humane soul."

Woolf attended Hardy's funeral in WESTMINSTER ABBEY, occupying one of the reserved seats.

For further reading: Woolf, "The Novels of Thomas Hardy."

Wordsworth, William (1770–1850)   Leading English poet identified with the Romantic movement. During the late 18th century, the British attachment to the classical and intellectual mode of writing, in which emotion was suppressed, gave way to Romanticism, which was marked by a more imaginative approach to the representation of life. Humor, pathos, and passion replaced the former emphasis on the impersonal and detached. Wordsworth is known for his worship of nature and his sympathy with liberal principles and the lives of ordinary people. He hoped poetic diction would employ, as he proposes in his preface to *Lyrical Ballads,* "a selection of language really used by men." This was a principle put fully into practice by Hardy in such poems as "A TRAMPWOMAN'S TRAGEDY" and "The RUINED MAID" and in his novels and short stories. Wordsworth was named poet laureate of England in 1843. One of his principal works is the long didactic poem *The Excursion,* which forms part of *The Recluse* (1814). Among his better known short poetic works are "Ode: Intimations of Immortality," "Daffodils," and "Lines Composed a Few Miles Above Tintern Abbey."

Hardy refers ironically to Wordsworth's "Lines Written in Early Spring" in TESS OF THE D'URBERVILLES when he deplores the situation of the Durbeyfield family to a ship with its "half-dozen little captives" sailing into "difficulty, disaster, starvation, disease, degradation, death." He asks "whence the poet whose philosophy is in these days deemed as profound and trustworthy as his song is breezy and pure, gets his authority for speaking of 'Nature's holy plan'" (chapter 3, "The Maiden"). In other words, Hardy does not believe life is governed by a benign God.

There is no doubt, however, that Hardy revered Wordsworth in many ways. In 1916 he wrote J. S. Udal that he had "motored past" the farmhouse of Racedown Lodge, near Pilsdon, where he had lived for a time.

In February 1918 he wrote his friend Edmund GOSSE that he had thought of his poem "The Widow Betrothed" about 1867 and wrote it after he had read Wordsworth's famous preface to *Lyrical Ballads,* "which influenced me much, & influences the style of the poem, as you can see for yourself."

For further reading: Davies, "Order and Chance: The Worlds of Wordsworth and Hardy"; Gatrell, "Hardy's *Under the Greenwood Tree* and Wordsworth's 'Phantom of Delight'"; Taylor, "Hardy and Wordsworth."

World War I (1914–1918)   Hardy deplored the outbreak of World War I, which was precipitated by the assassination, by a Serbian, of Archduke Francis Ferdinand of Austria-Hungary in Sarajevo on June 28, 1914.

Hardy made a note in his diary on August 4, 1914, at 11 P.M.: "War declared with Germany." He had written a prophetic poem, "CHANNEL FIRING," in April 1914, on the theme of "All nations striving strong to make / Red war yet redder." The British Expeditionary Force crossed the Channel between August 9 and August 15 to assist FRANCE and BELGIUM, which Hardy noted in his journal. In late August 1914, Hardy wrote Sidney COCKERELL to ask that Cockerell act as one of Hardy's literary executors. He remarked that the "recognition that we are living in a more brutal age than that, say, of Elizabeth . . . does not inspire one to write hopeful poetry, or even conjectural prose" (*Letters* V, 45). Hardy was deeply affected by the war, which had an immediate effect on the lives of many of his friends as their sons were drafted.

On September 2 Hardy was summoned to London by Mr. Masterman, chancellor of the Duchy of Lancaster, for the purpose of organizing public statements "of the strength of the British case and principles in the war by well-known men of letters." He recalled the "yellow September sun" as the group sat around a large blue table, "full of misgivings yet unforeseeing in all their completeness the tremendous events that were to follow" (*Life,* 366). Among the others who were summoned were John GALSWORTHY, Sir James BARRIE, John MASEFIELD, H. G. WELLS, and Arnold Bennett.

In September he published a poem in the form of soldiers' war-song called "MEN WHO MARCH AWAY" in the London *Times,* which, he recalls in the *Life,* "won an enormous popularity." It was collected in MOMENTS OF VISION (1917).

In October he wrote "ENGLAND TO GERMANY IN 1914." First published in a pamphlet in February 1917 for his second wife, Florence HARDY, this poem also was collected in *Moments of Vision.* It is dated autumn 1914, when the horror of the war was beginning to register in England. He also wrote a sonnet, "ON THE BELGIAN EXPATRIATION," for *King Albert's Book.*

Hardy also wrote two letters on the German bombardment of Rheims cathedral that appeared in the *Manchester Guardian:* "Rheims Cathedral" (October 7, 1914) and "A Reply to Critics" (October 13, 1914). These were bound together in a pamphlet published in 1914, *Letters on the War.* Both are reprinted in *Life and Art.* In the first letter, he mourned the "mutilation of a noble building . . . almost the finest specimen of mediaeval architecture in France." He recalled, as a young architect in training, copying the "traceries and mouldings" from Rheims and other French cathedrals, and found it tragic that "the curves we used to draw with such care should have been broken as ruthlessly as if they were a cast-iron railing replaceable from a mould." He would not, three months earlier, have imagined any "inhabitants of Europe" capable of such willful destruction, and blamed the bombastic writings of the German philosopher Friedrich Nietzsche for the demoralization of Germany. When the newspaper received letters complaining about his attack on Nietzsche, he remarked, in the second letter, that he seemed to him to be "an incoherent rhapsodist who jumps from Machiavelli to Isaiah as the mood seizes him" and that few men who had lived long enough to see the "real color of life" could believe in him as a thinker (*Life and Art*, 137–39).

On October 28, 1914, Hardy wrote Lady Alda Weston Hoare, the wife of Sir Henry Hugh Arthur Hoare, of his sorrow that their only child, Henry Colt Arthur Hoare, had been sent to war. (The younger Hoare was killed in 1917.)

The ravages of war were especially severe in Belgium. Hardy's poem "AN APPEAL TO AMERICA ON BEHALF OF THE BELGIAN DESTITUTE," dated December 14, 1914, was first published in the *New York Times* on January 4, 1915, and later reprinted in *Moments of Vision*.

In 1915 the American writer Edith WHARTON edited *The Book of the Homeless,* a project for which she solicited literary and artistic contributions from well-known writers and artists. It was published in early 1916, earning about $10,000 for war relief, and is now a valuable collectors' item. Hardy contributed a poem, "CRY OF THE HOMELESS (After the Prussian Invasion of Belgium)," written in August 1915.

Hardy deplored the impact of the war on the home front. In 1915 he also wrote "IN TIME OF 'THE BREAKING OF NATIONS,'" lamenting that England had almost come to a standstill. In "I LOOKED UP FROM MY WRITING," Hardy grieved over the senseless slaughter of many hundreds of young men.

Hardy wrote other letters about the German air raids, the blackout regulations, gasoline (petrol) restrictions, and the submarine menace. In January 1916 he published "The DEAD AND THE LIVING ONE," which he called "a war ballad of some weirdness," in the *SPHERE* and the *New York World*. Later that year he and his wife Florence visited the POW camp in DORCHESTER, which housed about 5,000 German prisoners of war. He remarked that the prisoners seemed to think England was "fighting to exterminate Germany," whereas he believed the country, was fighting to "save what is best in Germany" (*Life*, 372–74). In September 1916 he wrote Florence HENNIKER of his excitement that a German zeppelin had been brought down in London, but added that he thought the papers were "rather too sanguine" as England had "not beaten the Germans by any means yet" (*Letters* V, 177).

When the armistice finally came on November 11, 1918, Hardy did not comment on it in his journals. He wrote J. S. Udal that "European events are bigger than can be realized" (*Letters* V, 285). In May 1919 he wrote Sir George DOUGLAS that the end of the war had been unexpected, and that he did not "pretend to understand" how it could be prevented from beginning again in the future (*Letters* V, 303). In June 1919 he expressed misgivings about the Treaty of Versailles in a letter to Colonel J. H. Morgan (*Letters* V, 311). The same month he wrote his friend Edward CLODD that the peace "seems to me far from satisfactory, & I have visions ahead of ignorance overruling intelligence, & reducing us to another Dark Age" (*Letters* V, 315).

See also "ACCORDING TO THE MIGHTY WORKING" and "AT THE ENTERING OF THE NEW YEAR."

Worm, William   In *A PAIR OF BLUE EYES*, he is servant to the Reverend Christopher SWANCOURT at Endelstow. He calls himself a "weak wambling man," and he hears continuous noises in his head, but accepts them philosophically. He leaves Rev. Swancourt to manage a turnpike gate.

X

"Xenophanes, the Monist of Colophon" *Ann: aet: suae XCII.–A: C: CCCCLXXX* The Latin note may be read as "In the ninety-second year of his age, at about the year 480, B.C." (James O. Bailey, *The Poetry of Thomas Hardy*, 518). Poem written in 1921 and first published in *Nineteenth Century* in March 1924; it was later collected in *HUMAN SHOWS, FAR PHANTASIES, SONGS, AND TRIFLES* (1925).

Bailey considers Xenophanes a dramatic spokesman for Hardy's "concepts of the Immanent Will as set forth in *The Dynasts*," but observes that the term "All" used by Xenophanes is not found in the epic drama. Hardy, he asserts, was a "monist," not a "pantheist" (Bailey, *The Poetry of Thomas Hardy*, 518–19). Xenophanes, a poet and religious reformer, is thought to have been born about 570 B.C. at Colophon in Ionia. He probably lived in Sicily and then moved to Elea in southern Italy, where he lived until he was about 92. His works survive only in fragments, but he is regarded as the founder of the Eleatic school of philosophy. The Eleatic school of philosophers, which included Parmenides and Zeno, postulated that the real universe is a single, indivisible, unchangeable whole. Xenophanes contributed to the founding of this philosophic system, setting forth the monistic theory that God is One. Plato, in the *Sophist*, states that "the Eleatic school, beginning with Xenophanes and even earlier, starts from the principle of the unity of all things" (*Encyclopaedia Britannica*, 1960 edition).

In the poem, Xenophanes speaks to the "Mover" or the impersonal First Cause, or "It," which he also addresses as "O Great Dumb!" and "close Thing," asking whether it causes events "unknowing" or as a quest. If he were to receive an answer, he would "write it again / With a still stronger pen / To my once neighbour-men!" (that is, those in Colophon). The "listening Years," which Bailey equates with the "Spirit of the Years" in *The DYNASTS*, inform him that he may muse at Elea "unseen," but he had best not send his ideas back to Colophon, because he was banned for his ideas. Even three thousand years later, men who try to guess the riddle and "treat it as new, / Will be scowled at, like you, O Xenophanes!" "It" says, *"Some day I may tell, / When I've broken My spell."* The Years concede that, eventually, "Its doings may mend," but it will be when Xenophanes has been forgotten.

Y

Yeats, William Butler (1865–1939) Irish poet and dramatist, considered one of the leading poets of the 20th century. A leader of the Irish renaissance and one of the founders of the Abbey Theatre in Dublin, he received the Nobel Prize in literature in 1923.

In June 1912, on Hardy's 72nd birthday, Yeats and Henry NEWBOLT came to MAX GATE to present Hardy with a gold medal from the ROYAL SOCIETY OF LITERATURE. Emma HARDY was excluded from the ceremony, over the protests of the visitors; Millgate believes Hardy thought she might create a disturbance, as she had been acting in a paranoid way, claiming she had written much of his fiction (Millgate, *Thomas Hardy: A Biography*, 477). In the *Life* Hardy does not state that Emma was absent, but says that "everything was done as methodically as if there had been a large audience. . . . Newbolt wasted on the nearly empty room the best speech he ever made in his life, and Yeats wasted a very good one: mine in returning thanks was as usual a bad one, and the audience was quite properly limited" (*Life*, 358).

It is possible that this visit included a picnic that became the subject of "WHERE THE PICNIC WAS," in which Hardy revisits the site of a picnic a year later and recalls that there had been four present; two have now wandered into "urban roar" and one has "shut her eyes / For evermore." Emma died in November 1912.

Hardy apparently first met Yeats at a dinner at the home of Edmund GOSSE in July 1896. The Gosses also gave a dinner on May 8, 1904, at which the guests included Hardy, Yeats, and Max BEERBOHM. In June 1904 Hardy attended the first performance of Yeats's play *Where There Is Nothing* at the Royal Court Theatre, London; he was invited by Yeats's great friend and patron Lady Augusta Gregory to sit in her box. In July 1909 he wrote Lady Gregory, who had sent him a letter praising *The DYNASTS*, that he could not understand why Mr. Yeats did not "give us some more verse about those misty people he is personally acquainted with & nobody else in the world" (*Letters* III, 124; *Letters* IV, 37). Hardy may be referring to Yeats's early interest in Irish lore and legends, when his poetry was mystical, slow-paced, and lyrical. In later years, Yeats was also fascinated by the dichotomy between the physical and the spiritual, the real and the imagined, an interest manifested in such poems as "The Second Coming" and "Sailing to Byzantium."

For further reading: Alexander, "Fin de siècle; fin du globe: Yeats and Hardy in the Nineties"; Bawer, "*Two on a Tower*: Hardy and Yeats"; Hynes, "How to Be an Old Poet: The Examples of Hardy and Yeats."

Yeobright, Clym (Clement) In *The RETURN OF THE NATIVE*, he is the calm, studious, nature-loving son of Mrs. YEOBRIGHT. He is also idealistic and impractical. He returns to EGDON HEATH from Paris, where he has worked as the manager of a diamond business, to become "a schoolmaster to the poor and ignorant." He has been compared to John the Baptist and St. Paul, believing in "plain living" and "high thinking." Though "gentle as a child," he can be "hard as steel." He marries Eustacia VYE, but they are incompatible; she mistakenly assumed they would return to the glamour of Paris. His eyesight becomes impaired, and he takes up work as a furze cutter. When, in error, he believes Eustacia to have forbidden his mother to enter their house, they quarrel, and she leaves him. His mother dies of a snake bite and of bitter sorrow toward him. Clym is all but inconsolable, wracked with guilt. He returns to life as an itinerant preacher. While he is not altogether successful, he is "kindly received" everywhere, for his story has become "generally known."

Yeobright, Mrs. In *The RETURN OF THE NATIVE*, she is the widowed mother of Clym YEOBRIGHT. She lives with her niece Thomasin YEOBRIGHT at Blooms-End while Clym is in Paris working for a diamond merchant. Mrs. Yeobright is frustrated when Clym gives up his lucrative career and returns home hoping to enlighten the "poor and ignorant" as a schoolteacher. Although her husband was a farmer, she was a curate's daughter and is, therefore, socially superior to many villagers. She hopes Clym will marry Thomasin and is greatly disappointed when he falls in love with Eustacia VYE. Mrs. Yeobright dies of exhaustion and a snakebite after trying unsuccessfully to effect a reconciliation with her son; she erroneously believes herself to have been turned away from his house.

Yeobright, Thomasin (Tamsin) The niece of Mrs. YEOBRIGHT in *The RETURN OF THE NATIVE*, she lives with her aunt at Blooms-End. She rejects the reddleman Diggory VENN, her first suitor, because her aunt hopes she will marry a professional man. She falls in love with the landlord of the Quiet Woman Inn, Damon WILDEVE, but the marriage license he obtains in BUDMOUTH is invalid in Anglebury, where she has chosen to be married. Venn rescues her and prevents a scandal; she eventually marries Wildeve and has a daughter, but Wildeve has fallen in love with Clym YEOBRIGHT's wife, Eustacia VYE. After Wildeve's death Thomasin marries Venn, who has given up selling reddle to farms and become a dairyman.

"Young Glass-Stainer, The" Poem collected in *MOMENTS OF VISION* (1917). Hardy originally called it "The Glass-stainer." The poem is written from the point of view of a young glass-stainer working in a Gothic church. He is frustrated by the complicated process: "With cusp and foil, and nothing straight or square / And fitting in Peter here, and Matthew there!"

The speaker much prefers the "Hellenic norm." When he paints Martha he dreams of "Hera's brow," and, while painting Mary, thinks "of Aphrodite's form." At the time of writing, Hardy was working on *JUDE THE OBSCURE*, and Purdy calls the poem "a little reminiscent" of that novel (Purdy, *Thomas Hardy: A Bibliographical Study*, 205).

"Young Man's Epigram on Existence, A" *(16 W. P. V., 1866)* A witty and cynical poem dated 1866 and collected in *TIME'S LAUGHINGSTOCKS* (1909). Hardy was 26 at the time, working in LONDON in the architectural office of Sir Arthur William BLOMFIELD. The poem views existence as a "senseless school" but a necessary one in order that "we may learn to live." Only a "dolt" memorizes, by rote, "Lessons that leave no time for prizes" and fails to live life to its fullest. When he wrote this poem, Hardy was living at 16 Westbourne Park Villas, LONDON, where he had moved in 1863.

"Your Last Drive" Poem dated December 1912, the month after Emma HARDY died. It was collected in *SATIRES OF CIRCUMSTANCE* (1914). Hardy addresses Emma, recalling that she had returned from a drive eight days before her death, oblivious of having passed the spot (the graveyard at STINSFORD CHURCH) where she would lie eight days later and "be spoken of as one who was not."

Hardy had not accompanied his wife on her drive, but even if he had, he would not have seen that Emma would soon die. He would not have read, on her face, any intuition of mortality or sense of relief from his criticism: "Should you censure me I shall take no heed, / And even your praises no more shall need." He addresses her directly: "Dear ghost, in the past did you ever find / The thought 'What profit,' move me much?" He realizes that, finally, "you are past love, praise, indifference, blame."

When Lytton Strachey reviewed *Satires of Circumstance* in the *New Statesman* in December 1914, he argued that, despite the "cacophony" in this poem, Hardy had "found out the secret of touching our marrow-bones" (Strachey, "On *Satires of Circumstance*," reprinted in Clarke, *Thomas Hardy: Critical Assessments*, III, 157–60). One of the lines Strachey disliked, "Me one whom consequence influenced much?" was later replaced by "The thought '"What profit,' move me much?"

Martin Ray, who has completed a study of Hardy's poetry reviews, states that "Strachey's is the most important one in that it prompted Hardy to make more revisions to his poems than any other single review. The version of 'Your Last Drive' which Strachey quotes is an early one which was later altered" (personal communication with the author, April 2001).

Youriévitch, Serge (1876–1969) Sculptor, born in France of Russian parents. His work was influenced by the French sculptor Auguste Rodin. He wrote Hardy in July 1924 asking permission to execute a portrait-bust of him. Hardy replied that he was sure it would be an excellent one, but that he would not be able to buy a portrait-bust of himself at that time. However, if he were in the neighborhood, he would not mind "giving a few sittings" (*Letters* VI, 266). Hardy did sit for the bust from August 25 to August 30, 1924. It was made in Hardy's study at MAX GATE; he notes in the *Life* that he enjoyed conversation with the sculptor but found the sittings tiring on account of his age and announced that he would no longer agree to do them.

Millgate and Purdy state that Florence HARDY told Sidney COCKERELL that she went out to the Max Gate stable and helped Youriévitch cast the bust in plaster. That bust is now in the DORSET COUNTY MUSEUM. A bronze miniature, six and a half inches high, is at the University of Texas, but the location of other versions of the sculpture is not known (*Letters* VI, 266).

In December 1924 Hardy wrote Sir James BARRIE that the sculptor had been down to make a bust of him. The sculptor had asked that Hardy give him an introduction to Barrie in order than he might ask Barrie to sit for a bust also, but apparently no bust of Barrie was executed. Barrie told Hardy that the bust, of which he had seen a photograph, was "the best thing of you that has been done" (*Letters* VI, 298).

Youth's Companion American magazine, published in Boston, which commissioned a children's story from Hardy in April 1883. Hardy delivered "OUR EXPLOITS AT WEST POLEY," which was never published in the magazine. Apparently the editor did not believe it would appeal to children. The editor had acquired, for his son-in-law, the magazine *The Household*, which finally serialized the story from November 1892 to April 1893.

"Yuletide in a Younger World" Poem that Hardy wrote in 1927 at the request of Richard de la Mare, son of the poet Walter de la Mare, who had requested it for the purpose of launching a series of gift booklets. It was collected in WINTER WORDS (1928; Purdy, *Thomas Hardy: A Bibliographical Study,* 249–50).

The poem focuses on the cynicism and disillusionment that have afflicted him during the Christmas season. He looks back on his youth, when he and his friends or siblings would glimpse "Imminent oncomings of radiant revel—Doings of delight." Now there is no such sight.

Long ago he and his friends had vivid imaginations; they enjoyed "divination," and were able to see and hear phantoms of the dead. Now he marvels at his youthful simplicity and gullibility, and asks, "Can such have ever been?"

In 1927 the anthologist Louis Untermeyer was preparing a new edition of *Modern British Poetry* and asked to include the poem. Hardy answered that he had promised his publishers not to reprint it for some time. He added that it was "not a poem I value" and suggested substituting another one, such as "WAITING BOTH."

Zangwill, Israel (1864–1926) Writer, philanthropist, and Zionist. Hardy read his novel *Merely Mary Ann,* published in 1893, and wrote Florence HENNIKER that he thought it "very good" but only up to "the point at which she comes into the dollars" (*Letters* II, 13). Hardy and his wife Emma were invited to his wedding in November 1903, but were unable to attend (*Letters* III, 84).

In 1905 Zangwill sent Hardy a pamphlet about the Zionist movement to establish an autonomous Jewish state. Hardy replied that he believed such a state might be formed in a country such as East Africa, a "stepping-stone to Palestine," for which they might make a bid "100 years hence." He added that "nobody outside Jewry" could take a deeper interest than he in a people of such "extraordinary character and history"; a people, moreover, who brought forth a "young reformer" who, "though only in the humblest walk of life, became the most famous personage the world has ever known" (*Life,* 328).

In 1909 Zangwill wrote Hardy to congratulate him on the publication of *The DYNASTS,* which he called a "magnificent work" (*Letters* IV, 44).

Zermatt Resort and mountaineering center in southern SWITZERLAND in Valais canton near the Matterhorn. In July 1897, while Hardy and his wife Emma HARDY were staying in Geneva at the Hôtel de la Paix, they made an excursion to Zermatt, Interlaken, Thun, and the Wengern Alp. Hardy wrote Florence HENNIKER that he saw the "exact place where the tragedy occurred" on the Matterhorn, referring to the loss of four climbers there in 1865 (*see* "ZERMATT: TO THE MATTERHORN").

While the Hardys were in Switzerland, James Robert Cooper, an Englishman, disappeared at Zermatt four days before the Hardys arrived there. Hardy recalls, in the *Life,* that while he was walking with a Russian gentleman to the Riffel-Alp Hotel, he was informed that Cooper had disappeared along the path Hardy and the gentleman were following. He and Emma lunched at the hotel and he sent her on with a guide, riding a pony. He then went down the track on foot "looking for a clue to the missing man." He wrote a letter to the *Times* afterward saying there was "no sign visible of foul play anywhere on the road." The walk down the mountain and back up in the hot sun exhausted him; on their return to Geneva he was confined to bed in their

hotel (*Life,* 294). His letter on the subject, "The Disappearance of an Englishman at Zermatt," was published on July 8, 1897 (Purdy, *Thomas Hardy: A Bibliographical Study,* 305–306). *See:* "Zermatt: To the Matterhorn."

"Zermatt: To the Matterhorn" *(June–July 1897)* Sonnet commemorating the loss of four climbers (out of seven) who ascended the Matterhorn in 1865, which Hardy calls "a tragic feat of manly might." Hardy heard the story of their successful ascent of the mountain, and the catastrophe that ensued during their descent, from Edward Whymper, the sole survivor of the four

The Matterhorn, Zermatt; the first ascent in 1865 by seven climbers is the subject of Hardy's poem "Zermatt: To the Matterhorn." (Zermatt Tourist Bureau)

English members of the climbing team. Hardy and his wife Emma HARDY went to SWITZERLAND in June 1897, reaching ZERMATT on June 28. Soon after their arrival he reflected on "the terrible accident" on whose summit, 32 years before this date, had so impressed him at the time of its occurrence (*Life,* 294), and began the sonnet. The poem was finished later and collected in *POEMS OF THE PAST AND THE PRESENT* (1902).

Zola, Emile (1840–1902)   One of the leading novelists of the French school of naturalism. Hardy mentions Zola in his essay "The Science of Fiction"; he considers him a "scientific realist," with an interest in heredity, opposing him to the English novelist Mrs. Radcliffe and other writers of romance.

Hardy was invited to attend an Authors' Club dinner in honor of Zola on September 28, 1893, and wrote his friend Florence HENNIKER that he was planning to be there. However, for some reason he did not go to the dinner. His absence was noted by a writer for the *World* on October 4, 1893, who regretted Hardy's failure to appear and declared that he "thus deprived his fellow-writers of a fine opportunity of mentally comparing the author of *Tess* with the author of *Nana.*" *Nana* is a novel about a prostitute. (*Letters* II, 34–36).

Hardy did not admire Zola as a novelist. Florence Henniker had assumed he did, but he wrote on March 31, 1897, that she was mistaken (*Letters* II, 157).

When Zola died of carbon monoxide poisoning during the night of September 28–29, 1902, Hardy wrote Clive HOLLAND that it was a "tragic death" and he was "deeply sorry." He called him "a real moralist, reformer, & truth-seeker, though perhaps not an artist—indeed, certainly not" (*Letters* III, 34).

For further reading: Ebbatson, "Hardy and Zola Revisited"; Mason, "Hardy and Zola: A Comparative Study of Tess and Abbé Mouret."

Zurbarán, Francisco de (1598–1664)   Spanish painter, known for monastic portraiture and religious paintings. In January 1905, Hardy noted in his journal his interest in Zurbarán's paintings. He stated that he preferred them to "all others of the old Spanish School," and even thought that eventually they would be regarded more highly than those of Velásquez (Millgate, *The Life and Work of Thomas Hardy*, 347).

APPENDICES

Appendix I   **Topical List of Entries**

Appendix II   **Media Adaptations of Thomas Hardy's Works**

Appendix III   **Chronology of Thomas Hardy's Life and Works**

Appendix IV   **Family Trees**

Appendix V   **Glossary of Place-Names in Thomas Hardy's Works**

Appendix VI   **Translations of Thomas Hardy's Works**

Appendix VII   **Bibliography**

APPENDIX I

Topical List of Entries

1. Family, Friends, Acquaintances, Employers, Nobility

Lawrence, T. E.
Lea, Hermann
Martin, Julia Augusta Pitney
Moule, Henry Joseph
Moule, Horatio (Horace) Mosley
Moule, Rev. Arthur Evans
Moule, Rev. Handley Carr Glyn
Moule, Rev. Henry
Norton, John
Oppenheim, Isabelle
Owen, Rebekah
Procter, Anne Benson
Richardson, Nelson Moore
Sparks, Tryphena
Turner, Hugh Thackeray
Wallop, Lady Eveline Camilla
Wallop, Lady Margaret
Ward, Mary Augusta Arnold (Mrs. Humphry)
Ward, Thomas Humphry
Wessex (Wessie), Max Gate dog
Windle, Bertram

2. Novels

Desperate Remedies
Far from the Madding Crowd
Hand of Ethelberta, The
Jude the Obscure
Laodicean, A
Mayor of Casterbridge, The
Pair of Blue Eyes, A
Poor Man and the Lady, The (unpublished)
Return of the Native, The
Tess of the d'Urbervilles
Trumpet-Major, The
Two on a Tower
Under the Greenwood Tree
Well-Beloved, The
Woodlanders, The

3. Short Fiction

"Absent-mindedness in a Parish Choir" (*see* "Few Crusted Characters, A")
"Alicia's Diary"
"Andrey Satchel and the Parson and Clerk" (*see* "Few Crusted Characters, A")
"Benighted Travellers"
"Changed Man, A"
"Committee-Man of 'the Terror,' A"
"Dame the First—The First Countess of Wessex" (*see Group of Noble Dames, A*)
"Dame the Second—Barbara of the House of Grebe" (*see Group of Noble Dames, A*)
"Dame the Third—The Marchioness of Stonehenge" (*see Group of Noble Dames, A*)

"Dame the Fourth—Lady Mottisfont" (*see Group of Noble Dames, A*)
"Dame the Fifth—The Lady Icenway" (*see Group of Noble Dames, A*)
"Dame the Sixth—Squire Petrick's Lady" (*see Group of Noble Dames, A*)
"Dame the Seventh—Anna, Lady Baxby" (*see Group of Noble Dames, A*)
"Dame the Eighth—The Lady Penelope" (*see Group of Noble Dames, A*)
"Dame the Ninth—The Duchess of Hamptonshire" (*see Group of Noble Dames, A*)
"Dame the Tenth—The Honourable Laura" (*see Group of Noble Dames, A*)
"Destiny and a Blue Cloak"
"Distracted Preacher, The"
"Doctor's Legend, The"
"Duke's Reappearance, The" (*see Changed Man and Other Tales, A*)
"Enter a Dragoon"
"Fellow-Townsmen"
"Few Crusted Characters, A" (contains Introduction and nine stories; published in *Life's Little Ironies*)
"Fiddler of the Reels, The"
"For Conscience' Sake"
"Grave by the Handpost, The"
"History of the Hardcomes, The" (*see* "Few Crusted Characters, A")
"Imaginative Woman, An"
"Incident in the Life of Mr. George Crookhill" (*see* "Few Crusted Characters, A")
"Interlopers at the Knap"
"Master John Horseleigh, Knight"
"Melancholy Hussar of the German Legion, The"
"Mere Interlude, A"
"Netty Sargent's Copyhold" (*see* "Few Crusted Characters, A")
"Old Andrey's Experience as a Musician" (*see* "Few Crusted Characters, A")
"Old Mrs. Chundle"
"On the Western Circuit"
"Our Exploits at West Poley"
"Romantic Adventures of a Milkmaid, The"
"Son's Veto, The"
"Spectre of the Real, The"
"Superstitious Man's Story, The" (*see* "Few Crusted Characters, A")
"Three Strangers, The"
"To Please His Wife"
"Tony Kytes, the Arch-Deceiver" (*see* "Few Crusted Characters, A")
"Tradition of Eighteen Hundred and Four, A"
"Tragedy of Two Ambitions, A"
"Tryst at an Ancient Earthwork, A"
"Waiting Supper, The"
"What the Shepherd Saw"

"Winters and the Palmleys, The" (*see* "Few Crusted Characters, A")
"Withered Arm, The"

Collections
Changed Man and Other Tales, A
Group of Noble Dames, A
Life's Little Ironies
"Wessex Folk" (manuscript only)
Wessex Tales

4. Poetry

"Abbey Mason, The"
"Absolute Explains, The"
"According to the Mighty Working"
"After a Journey"
"After a Romantic Day"
"Afternoon Service at Mellstock"
"After the Last Breath"
"After the Visit"
"Afterwards"
"Ageing House, The"
"Ah, Are You Digging on My Grave?"
"Alarm, The"
"Amabel"
"Ancient to Ancients, An"
"And There Was a Great Calm"
"Apostrophe to an Old Psalm Tune"
"Appeal to America on Behalf of the Belgian Destitute, An"
"Aquae Sulis"
"At a Bridal"
"At Casterbridge Fair"
"At Castle Boterel"
"At a Country Fair"
"At a Lunar Eclipse"
"At a Seaside Town in 1869"
"At Lulworth Cove a Century Back"
"At Mayfair Lodgings"
"At Middle-Field Gate in February"
"At the Entering of the New Year"
"At the Piano"
"At the Railway Station, Upway"
"At Rushy-Pond"
"At the Word 'Farewell'"
"August Midnight, An"
"Barthélémon at Vauxhall"
"Beeny Cliff"
"Before and After Summer"
"Before Life and After"
"Bereft"
"Beyond the Last Lamp"
"Bride-Night Fire, The"
"Broken Appointment, A"
"By the Earth's Corpse"

"By the Runic Stone"
"Call to National Service, A"
"Channel Firing"
"Childhood Among the Ferns"
"Christmas: 1924"
"Christmas Ghost-Story, A"
"Christmas in the Elgin Room"
"Church Romance, A"
"Circus-Rider to Ringmaster"
"Collector Cleans His Picture, The"
"Colonel's Soliloquy, The"
"Comet at Yell'ham, The"
"Compassion"
"Concerning Agnes"
"Convergence of the Twain, The"
"Could I But Will"
"Cry of the Homeless"
"Curate's Kindness, The"
"Dance at the Phoenix"
"Dark-Eyed Gentleman, The"
"Darkling Thrush, The"
"Dawn after the Dance, The"
"Dead and the Living One, The"
"Dead Quire, The"
"Dead 'Wessex,' the Dog to the Household"
"Ditty"
"Domicilium"
"Doom and She"
"Dream or No, A"
"Drummer Hodge"
"During Wind and Rain"
"Embarcation"
"England to Germany in 1914"
"Eve of Waterloo, The"
"Everything Comes"
"Face at the Casement, The"
"Faintheart in a Railway Train"
"Figure in the Scene, The"
"Fire at Tranter Sweatley's, The" *see* "Bride-Night Fire, The"
"Five Students, The"
"Garden Seat, The"
"Genoa and the Mediterranean"
"God-Forgotten"
"God's Education"
"God's Funeral"
"Going, The"
"Going of the Battery, The"
"Great Things"
"Had You Wept"
"Hap"
"Haunter, The"
"He Abjures Love"
"He Never Expected Much"
"He Revisits His First School"
"Heredity"
"His Country" (see "God's Education")

"House of Hospitalities, The"
"Hurried Meeting, A"
"Hussar's Song: 'Budmouth Dears'"
"I Found Her Out There"
"I Look Into My Glass"
"I Looked Up from My Writing"
"Impercipient, The"
"In Front of the Landscape"
"In Tenebris I"
"In Tenebris II"
"In Tenebris III"
"In the British Museum"
"In the Evening"
"In the Garden"
"In the Old Theatre" (Fiesole)
"It Never Looks Like Summer"
"January Night, 1879, A"
"King's Experiment, The"
"King's Soliloquy, A"
"Lacking Sense, The"
"Last Chyrsanthemum, The"
"Last Performance, The"
"Last Signal, The"
"Lausanne: In Gibbon's Old Garden: 11–12 p.m."
"Leipzig"
"Levelled Churchyard, The"
"Logs on the Hearth"
"Looking Across"
"Lost Pyx, The"
"Maid of Keinton Mandeville, The"
"Man He Killed, The"
"Man Was Drawing Near to Me, A"
"Memory and I"
"Men Who March Away"
"Mother Mourns, The"
"Music in a Snowy Street"
"Musical Box, The"
"Nature's Questioning"
"Near Lanivet, 1872"
"Neutral Tones"
"New Year's Eve"
"Night of the Dance, The"
"Night of Questionings, A"
"Night of Trafalgar, The" *(Boat Man's Song)*
"Noble Lady's Tale, The"
"Nobody Comes"
"Obliterate Tomb, The"
"Old Furniture"
"On a Midsummer Eve"
"On an Invitation to the United States"
"On Sturminster Foot-Bridge"
"On the Belgian Expatriation"
"On the Esplanade"
"One We Knew"
"Outside the Casement"
"Overlooking the River Stour"

"Oxen, The"
"Panthera"
"Peasant's Confession, The"
"Pedigree"
"Phantom Horsewoman, The"
"Philosophical Fantasy, A"
"Pink Frock, The"
"Place on the Map, The"
"Quid Hic Agis?"
"Rain on a Grave"
"Rash Bride, The"
"Regret Not Me"
"Reminiscences of a Dancing Man"
"Rome: At the Pyramid of Cestius near the Graves of Shelley and Keats"
"Rome: Building a New Street in the Ancient Quarter (April 1887)"
"Rome: The Vatican—Sala delle Muse"
"Ruined Maid, The"
"Sapphic Fragment"
"Schreckhorn, The"
"She—At His Funeral"
"She Hears the Storm"
"She, to Him"
"Shelley's Skylark"
"Shut Out That Moon"
"Sick Battle-God, The"
"Singer Asleep, A"
"Sleep-worker, The"
"Snow in the Suburbs"
"Souls of the Slain, The"
"Strange House, The"
"Subalterns, The"
"Sunday Morning Tragedy, A"
"Then and Now"
"Thoughts of Phena at News of Her Death"
"To C.F.H."
"To Lizbie Brown"
"To Meet, or Otherwise"
"To My Father's Violin"
"To Outer Nature"
"To Shakespeare"
"Trampwoman's Tragedy, A"
"Two Rosalinds, The"
"Unborn, The"
"Under the Waterfall"
"Unkindly May, An"
"Voice, The"
"Voices from Things Growing in a Churchyard"
"Wagtail and Baby"
"Waiting Both"
"Walk, The"
"We Sat at the Window"
"Wessex Heights"
"When I Set Out for Lyonesse"
"Where the Picnic Was"

"Why Did I Sketch?"
"Wind's Prophecy, The"
"Xenophanes, the Monist of Colophon"
"Young Glass-Stainer, The"
"Young Man's Epigram on Existence, A"
"Your Last Drive"
"Yuletide in a Younger World"
"Zermatt: To the Matterhorn"

Collections
Human Shows, Far Phantasies, Songs, and Trifles
Late Lyrics and Earlier
Moments of Love
Moments of Vision and Miscellaneous Verses
Poems of the Past and the Present
Satires of Circumstance
Time's Laughingstocks and Other Verses
Wessex Poems and Other Verses
Winter Words in Various Moods and Metres

5. Dramatic Works and Dramatizations

Dynasts, The
Famous Tragedy of the Queen of Cornwall, The
Characters in *The Dynasts: A Drama of the Napoleonic Wars* and *The Famous Tragedy of the Queen of Cornwall* are treated within the entries for these works. For dramatizations and media adaptations of Hardy's novels and short stories, *see* Appendix II.
Mellstock Quire, The (play based on *Under the Greenwood Tree*)
"Play of 'St. George,' The"
"Three Wayfarers, The"
Wessex Scenes from The Dynasts

6. Principal Characters in the Novels of Thomas Hardy

Desperate Remedies
Aldclyffe, Captain Gerald Fellcourt
Aldclyffe, Cytherea
Gradfield, Mr.
Graye, Ambrose
Graye, Cytherea
Graye, Owen
Hinton, Adelaide
Manston, Aeneas
Manston, Eunice
Seaway, Anne
Springrove, Edward

Far from the Madding Crowd
Aldritch, Dr.
Ball, Cain
Boldwood, William
Clark, Mark
Coggan, Bob

Coggan, Jan
Coggan, Mrs.
Everdene, Bathsheba
Everdene, Farmer James
Hurst, Mrs.
Moon, Matthew
Oak, Gabriel
Robin, Fanny
Smallbury, Jacob
Smallbury, Liddy
Smallbury, Warren
Smallbury, William
Tall, Laban
Troy, Sergeant Francis

Hand of Ethelberta, The
Belmaine, Mrs.
Chickerel, Cornelia
Chickerel, Dan
Chickerel, Emmeline
Chickerel, Georgina
Chickerel, Gwendoline
Chickerel, Joseph
Chickerel, Mr. R.
Chickerel, Mrs.
Chickerel, Myrtle
Chickerel, Picotee
Chickerel, Sol
Doncastle, John
Doncastle, Margaret
Gruchette, Miss
Julian, Christopher
Julian, Faith
Ladywell, Eustace
Menlove, Louisa
Mountclere, Lord
Neigh, Alfred
Petherwin, Ethelberta
Petherwin, Lady

Jude the Obscure
Anny
Bridehead, Sue
Cartlett, Mr.
Challow
Donn, Arabella
Donn, Mr.
Donn, Mrs.
Edlin, Mrs.
Fawley, Drusilla
Fawley, Jude
Fontover, Miss
Gillingham, George
Phillotson, Richard
Time, Father
Vilbert, Dr.

Laodicean, A
Dare, William
de Stancy, Captain William
de Stancy, Charlotte
de Stancy, Sir William
Goodman, Mrs.
Havill, James
Haze, Cunningham
Power, Abner
Power, Paula
Somerset, George
Woodwell, Mr.

Mayor of Casterbridge, The
Cuxsom, Mother
Farfrae, Donald
Henchard, Elizabeth-Jane
Henchard, Michael
Henchard, Susan
Jopp, Joshua
Le Sueur, Lucetta
Longways, Solomon
Mockridge, Nance
Newson, Richard
Whittel, Abel

Pair of Blue Eyes, A
Cannister, Martin
Jethway, Felix
Jethway, Gertrude
Knight, Henry
Luxellian, Lady Helen
Luxellian, Lord Spenser Hugo
Smith, Stephen
Swancourt, Christopher
Swancourt, Elfride
Troyton, Charlotte
Unity
Worm, William

Return of the Native, The
Cantle, Christian
Cantle, Granfer
Charley
Nunsuch, Johnny
Nunsuch, Susan
Venn, Diggory
Vye, Captain
Vye, Eustacia
Wildeve, Damon
Yeobright, Clym
Yeobright, Mrs.
Yeobright, Thomasin (Tamsin)

Tess of the d'Urbervilles
Clare, Angel
Clare, Cuthbert

Clare, Felix
Clare, Mrs.
Clare, Rev. James
Crick, Richard
d'Urberville, Alec
d'Urberville, Mrs.
Durbeyfield, Abraham
Durbeyfield, Eliza Louise ("Liza-Lu")
Durbeyfield, Joan
Durbeyfield, John
Durbeyfield, Teresa ("Tess")
Huett, Izz

Trumpet-Major, The
Cripplestraw, Anthony
Derriman, Squire Benjamin
Derriman, Festus
Garland, Anne
Garland, Martha
George III, King
Johnson, Matilda
Loveday, John
Loveday, Miller
Loveday, Robert

Two on a Tower
Constantine, Lady Viviette
Constantine, Sir Blount
Fry, Amos ("Haymoss")
Glanville, Louis
Helmsdale, The Right Reverend Cuthbert
Lark, Tabitha
Martin, Mrs. ("Gammer")
St. Cleeve, Swithin
Torkington, Parson

Under the Greenwood Tree
Day, Fancy
Day, Geoffrey
Day, Jane
Dewy, Ann
Dewy, Dick
Dewy, Reuben
Dewy, William
Endorfield, Elizabeth
Leaf, Thomas
Mail, Michael
Maybold, Parson
Penny, Robert
Shinar, Frederic

Well-Beloved, The
Bencomb, Marcia
Caro, Avice
Caro, Mrs.
Leverre, Henri

Pierston, Jocelyn
Pine-Avon, Nichola
Somers, Alfred

Woodlanders, The
Charmond, Felice
Damson, Suke
Fitzpiers, Edred
Fitzpiers, Grace Melbury
Melbury, George
South, John
South, Marty
Tangs, Timothy
Winterbourne, Giles

7. Miscellaneous Nonfiction by Thomas Hardy (Articles, Essays, Memoirs, Notebooks)

Architectural Notebook of Thomas Hardy, The
"Candour in English Fiction"
"Dorsetshire Labourer, The"
"How I Built Myself a House"
"Maumbury Ring"
"Memories of Church Restoration"
"Profitable Reading of Fiction, The"
"Why I Don't Write Plays"

8. Literature (Writers and Poets Known to Hardy, or Whose Works Were Important to Him)

Arnold, Matthew
Austin, Sir Alfred
Barnes, Rev. William
Barrie, Sir James Matthew
Beerbohm, Sir Max
Benson, A(rthur), C(hristopher)
Besant, Sir Walter
Blackmore, Richard Doddridge
Bridges, Robert
Browning, Robert
Caine, Hall
Clairmonte, Mary Chavelita
Dobson, Henry Austin
Eliot, George
Ellis, Henry Havelock
Fawcett, Millicent Garrett
Galsworthy, John
Garnett, Richard
Gissing, George
Grove, Lady Agnes Geraldine
Hankinson, Charles James (*see* Holland, Clive)
Harrison, Frederic
Holland, Clive
Holmes, Oliver Wendell
Housman, Alfred Edward
Housman, Laurence
Howells, William Dean

James, Henry
Johnson, Lionel Pigot
Keats, John
Kipling, Rudyard
Lawrence, T. E.
Lea, Hermann
Lee, Vernon (Violet Paget)
Lowell, Amy
Masefield, John
Meredith, George
Mew, Charlotte (Mary)
Mill, John Stuart
Milton, John
Moulton, Ellen Louise Chandler
Newbolt, Sir Henry John
Noel, Roden Berkeley Wriothesley
Noyes, Alfred
Oliphant, Margaret
Perkins, Rev. Thomas
Sackville-West, Victoria (Vita)
Sassoon, Siegfried
Scott, Sir Walter
Shakespeare, William
Sophocles
Stevenson, Robert Louis
Swinburne, Algernon Charles
Symonds, John Addington
Symons, Arthur William
Tennyson, Alfred Lord
Thackeray, William Makepeace
Wells, H(erbert) G(eorge)
Wharton, Edith
Woolf, Leonard
Woolf, Virginia
Wordsworth, William
Yeats, William Butler
Zangwill, Israel
Zola, Emile

9. Fine Arts (Busts and Portraits of Thomas Hardy, Painters, Sculptors, Exhibitions, Dramatists, Actors, Actresses, Theaters and Theater Groups, Music)

Abbey, Edwin Austin
architecture
Balliol Players
Barnes Theatre
Bernhardt, Sarah
Blanche, Jacques-Emile
Bugler, Gertrude Adelia
Campbell, Mrs. Patrick
Carr, J. W. Comyns
d'Erlanger, Baron Frédéric
Du Maurier, George Louis Palmella Busson
Evans, Alfred Herbert

Fiske, Minnie Maddern
Frith, William Powell
Granville-Barker, Harley
Green, Charles
Grein, Jack Thomas
Hardy Players, The
Herkomer, Sir Hubert von
Hill, Vernon
Hopkins, Arthur
Jarvis, C. W.
John, Augustus (Edwin)
Kennedy, Hugh Arthur
Kent, Rockwell
Kingsway Theatre
Lea, Hermann
Lyceum Theatre
Macbeth-Raeburn, Henry Raeburn
Maitland, R. E. Fuller
McCarthy, Lillah
Oppenheim, Isabelle
Ouless, Walter Williams
Parsons, Alfred William
Pouncy, Harry
Richardson, Maggie
Rothenstein, Sir William
St. James's Theater
Sargent, John Singer
Spicer-Simson, Theodore
Stoddard, Lorimer
Strang, William
Terry, Ellen
theater and Thomas Hardy
Thomson, Winifred
Thornycroft, Sir William Hamo
Tilley, Thomas Henry
Vaughn Williams, Ralph
verse dramas
Wagner, Richard
Whistler, James Abbott McNeil
Youriévitch, Serge
Zubarán, Francisco de

10. Special Interests and Concerns of Thomas Hardy

animals, Hardy's love of
Animals' Friend
Bible, the
bicycling
childlessness of Thomas and Emma Hardy
dialect
drawings
education of Hardy
fiction and Hardy
health and illness, Hardy's concern with
landscape

Latin
lecturing
literature, and the writing life, rewards of
museums
music
mythology
natural world
poetry, Hardy's attitude toward
politics, Hardy's interest in
privacy, Hardy's views of and concern for
religion
Stonehenge
war, Hardy's attitude toward
women's suffrage, Hardy's views on

11. Travels, Places of Residence, and Houses

Belgium
Corfe Castle (Dorset)
Cornwall
Dorchester
Dorset
France
Higher Bockhampton (Dorset)
Italy
London
Maiden Castle
Max Gate
St. Juliot Church
Portsmouth
Salisbury
Stinsford
Stonehenge
Sturminster Newton
Switzerland
Talbothays
Tintagel
Upper Tooting
Weymouth
Wimborne

12. Publishers and Publishing (Editors, Critics, Journalists, Translators, Illustrators, Periodicals)

Archer, William
Athenaeum, The
Atlantic Monthly, The
Barnes, Robert
Barron, Louis
Belgravia
Blackwood, John
Blackwood's Edinburgh Magazine
Bookman, The
Bowen, John
Bowker, Richard Rogers
Caine, Hall
Century Magazine, The

13. Clubs, Institutions, Libraries, Museums, Societies, Organizations, Schools, Universities

Society for the Protection of Ancient Buildings
South Kensington Museum (*see* museums)
University of Aberdeen
Whitefriars Club

14. Religious Architecture, Celebrations, Traditions, Feasts, Holidays, Churches

Bible, the
Christmas mummers
Fordington St. George Church, Dorset
religion and Thomas Hardy
Stinsford Church, Dorset
St. Juliot Church
Wimborne
Westminster Abbey

15. Secular Architecture, Folklore, Fables, Dialects, Superstitions, Oral Traditions, Mythology

Candlemas
club-walking
folklore
local history and traditions, Hardy's interest in
Maiden Castle

16. Historic Events and Personages (Wars, Ships, Treaties, Rulers, Political Figures)

Asquith, Herbert Henry
Boer War
Edward VII (Albert Edward, Prince of Wales)
Edward VIII (Edward, Prince of Wales)
George III, King
Trafalgar, Battle of
Victory, H.M.S.
Waterloo, Battle of
World War I

17. Honors and Prizes

Authors' Club of New York
Cambridge University
Freedom of Dorchester
Honorary Fellowships
Magdalene College, Cambridge University
Order of Merit
Oxford University
"Poets' Tribute" to Thomas Hardy
Queen's College, Oxford University
Royal Society of Literature
St. Andrews, University of
University of Aberdeen

APPENDIX II

Media Adaptations of Thomas Hardy's Works

I. The Hardy Players Productions: A Checklist

The following information was provided by Keith G. Wilson, University of Ottawa, who has generously granted permission to make use of his research, posted on the following website: Thomas Hardy Drama Page, URL: http://aix1.uottawa.ca/~kgwilson/hplayers.htm. Wilson gives the following commentary about the origin of the Hardy Players and the nature of their productions.

Between 1908 and 1924, the Dorchester Debating and Dramatic Society performed a series of stage adaptations of Hardy's work. The core group of actors, all enthusiastic amateurs drawn primarily from the local middle-class business and professional community, became known as the Hardy Players, their annual productions as the Hardy Plays, a somewhat ambiguous designation that generated considerable journalistic confusion about actual authorship. The plays received the active support and patronage of Hardy himself, with differing degrees of involvement from production to production depending on his own varying interests and circumstances.

The adaptations were of three kinds. The first and largest group *(The Trumpet-Major, Far from the Madding Crowd, The Mellstock Quire, The Distracted Preacher, and The Woodlanders)* comprised those made by Alfred Herbert Evans, a Dorchester chemist and initial producer of the plays. The second group (comprising only *The Return of the Native* and *A Desperate Remedy*) was prepared by Evans' successor as producer, Thomas Henry Tilley, a builder and monumental mason who, like his father before him, became Mayor of Dorchester, thereby providing the Players with inevitable publicity about their association not only with Hardy himself but with a real-life "Mayor of Casterbridge." The third and most important group *(The Three Wayfarers, Wessex Scenes from "The Dynasts," The Famous Tragedy of the Queen of Cornwall, and Tess)* comprised those made by Hardy himself.

The production of *Tess* received, and has continued to receive, most attention, for reasons more biographical than critical. It was Hardy's own adaptation of his most famous novel, which starred the beautiful Gertrude Bugler, with whom he became somewhat unwisely infatuated, and led to a professional London production with Gwen Ffrangçon-Davies in the title role. But *The Famous Tragedy of the Queen of Cornwall* was perhaps Hardy's most surprising, and complimentary, gift to the Hardy Players. It was not an adaptation but an original verse play, written specifically for stage performance by these local enthusiasts. Because of the direct Hardy connection, the degree of attention that the plays, particularly the later ones, received in the national and international press was out of all proportion to both their qualities as drama and, it has to be said, the amateur performers' abilities as actors. It was primarily occasioned by the rumours, which by the time of *The Queen of Cornwall* and *Tess* had become incontrovertible fact, of Hardy's direct involvement and his public appearances at certain performances. But whatever their ultimate status, these productions allowed Hardy a regular and locally accessible indulgence of his theatrical interests, even as he advanced into frail old age. Well on into the 1920s they played a very significant part in both popular and more serious press fascination with England's most enduring and eminent Victorian writer."

The following is a checklist of the Hardy Players productions, with performance dates and full cast details. Unless otherwise indicated, Dorchester performances were staged at the Corn Exchange, London performances (before the Society of Dorset Men) at the Cripplegate Institute, and Weymouth performances at the Pavilion Theatre. A parenthetical (2) after a date indicates both matinée and evening performances. The main repositories for scripts of these plays, as well as allied materials relating to them (including stage plans, sketches, cast photographs, and programs), are the Dorset County Museum, the Dorset County Library, and the Library of the University of California at Riverside.

1908

The Trumpet-Major, adapted by Alfred H. Evans. November 18 and 19 (2), 1908 (Dorchester); December 31, 1908 (Herrison [Dorset County Asylum], Dorchester); February 8, 1910 (Weymouth).

Cast: John Loveday, H. O. Lock; Bob Loveday, H. A. Martin; Miller Loveday, Walter R. Bawler; Squire Derriman, Edwin J. Stevens; Festus Derriman, A. H. Evans; David (Miller's servant), Reginald C. Barrow; Cripplestraw, Thomas H. Tilley; Corporal Tullidge, Thomas Pouncy; Sergeant Stanner, W. J. Fare; Cornick, R. N. Dawes; Press Gang Officer, W. B. Fussell; Sergeant of Hussars, A. S. Hill; Widow Garland, Miss Rowston; Anne Garland, Eveline Lock; Matilda Johnson, Miss A. Tilley. (At the matinée, the part of Anne Garland was taken by Mrs. A. H. Evans).

1909

Far from the Madding Crowd, adapted by A. H. Evans. November 17 and 18 (2), 1909 (Dorchester); November 24, 1909 (London); 20 December 1909 (Herrison, Dorchester); February 7, 1910 (Weymouth).

Cast: Gabriel Oak, A. H. Evans; Sergeant Troy, E. J. Stevens; Mr. Boldwood, H. A. Martin; Jan Coggan, W. R. Bawler; Joseph Poorgrass, T. Pouncy; Billy Smallbury, R. C. Barrow; Laban Tall, William H. Jameson; Cain Ball, Dick Dawes; Maltster, R. N. Dawes; Bathsheba Everdene, Mrs. A. H. Evans; Liddy Smallbury, Miss Witham; Mary Ann Money, Myfanwy Hill.

1911

The Mellstock Quire, adapted by A. H. Evans from *Under the Greenwood Tree.* November 16, 17 (2), and 18, 1910 (Dorchester); December 1, 1910 (London); February 9, 1911 (Weymouth).

Cast: Reuben Dewy, W. R. Bawler; Dick Dewy, E. J. Stevens; Parson Maybold, H. O. Lock; Farmer Shinar, H. A. Martin; Geoffrey Day, W. H. Jameson; Robert Penny, R. C. Barrow; Michael Mail, W. H. Vine; Joseph Bowman, L. L. Renwick; Thomas Leaf, T. H. Tilley; Granfer William, T. Pouncy; Elias Spinks, Dick Dawes; Enoch, C. R. Selley; Other Quiremen, A. Russell, T. Perham; Charlie Dewy, Master Arthur Bugler; Jimmy Dewy, Master Stovey; Fancy Day, Ethel Hawker; Mrs. Dewy, Mrs. T. H. Tilley; Mrs. Penny, Ethel Major; Mrs. Day, Mrs. A. S. Hill; Susie Dewy, Molly Dawes; Elizabeth, Myfanwy Hill; Schoolchildren, Vera Stevens, Doris Walne, Arthur Henry Bugler, William Ewart, Master Stovey, Rex Fare, Eileen Smith, Vera Walne, Leslie Bailey, Gwennie Evans, Muriel Evans, Kenneth Hyde, Sybil Smith, Frank Thornton, Leslie Bawler.

The Three Wayfarers, adapted by Thomas Hardy from his short story "The Three Strangers," and *The Distracted Preacher,* adapted by A. H. Evans. November 15, 16 (2), and 17, 1911 (Dorchester); November 27, 1911 (London); December 15, 1911 (Weymouth).

Cast for The Three Wayfarers: Shepherd Fennel, W. R. Bawler; Parish Constable: T. Pouncy; Timothy Sommers, T. H. Tilley; Joseph Sommers, E. J. Stevens; Hangman, W. H. Jameson; Elijah New, D. Dawes; Magistrate,

H. A. Martin; Turnkey, R. N. Dawes; Mrs. Fennel, Mrs. A. S. Hill; Damsel, Miss Franklin.

Cast for The Distracted Preacher: Richard Stockdale, H. O. Lock; Jim Owlett, H. A. Martin; Joseph Hardman, W. R. Bawler; Matt Gray, R. C. Barrow; Thomas Ballam, A. Russell; Jim Clarke, T. Pouncy; Landlord, W. H. Jameson; Will Latimer, E. J. Stevens; Preventive Guardsmen, D. Dawes, O. G. Campfield, A. D. Wright, J. C. Jackson; Lizzie Newberry, Ethel Hawker; Mrs. Simpkins, Ethel Major; Martha-Sarah, Myfanwy Hill; Mrs. Hardman, Molly Dawes; Mrs. Gray, Mrs. T. H. Tilley; Mrs. Clarke, Miss Franklin; Miss Owlett, M. Wells.

1912

The Trumpet-Major (revised), adapted by A. H. Evans. November 27 and 28 (2), 1912 (Dorchester); December 5, 1912 (London).

Cast: The same as for the 1908 production, with the following modifications: Sergeant of the Line, E. J. Stevens; Festus Derriman, W. H. Jameson; Cornick, H. W. Perham; Press Gang Officer, A. G. Stone; Members of the Press Gang, A. D. Wright and Dick Dawes; Anne Garland, Ethel Hawker; Matilda Johnson, Ethel Major.

1913

The Woodlanders, adapted by A. H. Evans. November 19 and 20 (2), 1913 (Dorchester); December 8, 1913 (London); January 22, 1914 (Weymouth).

Cast: Giles Winterborne, H. A. Martin; Dr. Edred Fitzpiers, S. A. Dunn; George Melbury, E. J. Stevens; John Upjohn, W. R. Bawler; Robert Creedle, T. Pouncy; Percomb, T. H. Tilley; Beaucock, R. M. Dawes; Cawtree, A. D. Wright; Timothy Tangs, R. C. Barrow; Mrs. Melbury, Ethel Major; Grace Melbury, Myfanwy Hill; Mrs. Charmond, Miss M. C. Hodges; Marty South, Gertrude Bugler; Grammer Oliver, Mrs. T. H. Tilley; Ellis, Miss M. F. Rogers; Mrs. Cawtree: Mrs. E. J. Stevens.

1916

Wessex Scenes From "The Dynasts," adapted by Thomas Hardy. June 22, 1916 (Weymouth); December 6 and 7 (2), 1916 (Dorchester).

Cast: Speaker of Prologue and Epilogue, Ethel Hawker; Traveller and Second Sailor, Albert C. Cox; Londoner and First Coach Passenger, A. E. Robson; Messenger and Official, Rex Fare; Schoolmaster, T. H. Rogers; First Beacon Keeper, T. Pouncy; Second Beacon Keeper and Rustic, R. C. Barrow; Recruiting Sergeant, H. A. Martin; Townsman, Ivor Creech; Boatman and Second Coach Passenger, W. R. Bawler; First Sailor, H. W. Perham; Private Cantle and Shepherd, T. H. Tilley; Young Soldier and Shepherd's Son, Miss N. Jones; Mail Guard, W. J. Fare; Vicar of Durnover, R. N. Dawes; Town Boy, Master Kenneth Holland; Apple-Woman, Ethel Major; Waiting-Maid (Soldier's Sweetheart), Gertrude Bugler; Mrs. Cantle, Miss M. F. Rogers.

1918

The Mellstock Quire (revised), adapted by A. H. Evans. January 31 (2) and February 1, 1918 (Dorchester).

Cast: the same as for the 1910 production, with the following modifications: Parson Maybold, Graham Poock; Geoffrey Day, A. C. Cox; Michael Mail, H. W. Perham; Joseph Bowman, Arthur H. Bugler; Elias Spinks, Archie K. Holland; Enoch, A. H. Davey; Charlie Dewy, K. Holland; Jimmy Dewy, Kenneth Major; Counterpoint Boys, Leonard Parsons, Ralph Pomeroy; Fancy Day, Gertrude Bugler; Mrs. Penny, Eileen Bugler; Mrs. Day, Molly Dawes; Susie Dewy, Gwendolen Evans; Lizzie, M. F. Rogers; Elizabeth and Mrs. Crumpler, Ethel Major.

1920

The Return of the Native, adapted by T. H. Tilley. November 17, 18 (2), 19, and 20, 1920 (Dorchester); January 27, 1921 (London).

Cast: Clym Yeobright, E. W. Smerdon; Damon Wildeve, E. J. Stevens; Diggory Venn, H. A. Martin; Timothy Fairway, W. R. Bawler; Humphry, A. C. Cox; Sam, A. H. Davey; Grandfer Cantle, T. Pouncy; Christian Cantle, T. H. Tilley; Charley, J. Keniston; Susan Nonsuch, Molly Dawes; Olly Dowden, Eileen Bugler; Johnny Nonsuch, Sheila Major; Eustacia Vye, Gertrude Bugler; Mrs. Yeobright, Ethel Major; Heath Folk, Guests, A. D. Wright, H. W. Perham, Dorothy H. Paulley, Gwendolen Evans, Mrs. T. H. Tilley; Egdon Mummers: Father Christmas, E. J. Stevens; Valiant Soldier, J. Keniston; Turkish Knight, Gertrude Bugler; St. George, H. A. Martin; Saracen, A. H. Davey; Doctor, H. W. Perham.

1922

A Desperate Remedy, adapted by T. H. Tilley from Hardy's novel *Desperate Remedies.* November 15, 16 (2), and 17, 1922 (Dorchester); November 21, 1922 (King's Hall, Covent Garden, London).

Cast: Edward Springrove, R. Fare; Farmer Springrove, W. R. Bawler; Owen Graye, P. H. Morton; Aeneas Manston, E. W. Smerdon; Rev. Raunham, H. A. Martin; Clerk Crickett, E. J. Stevens; Gad Weedy, A. C. Cox; Robert Reason, R. C. Barrow; Andrew Vatcher, A. H. Davey; Sam Clarke, J. Keniston; Man in Black, T. H. Tilley; Miss Aldclyffe, Mrs. Wacher; Cytherea Graye, Ethel Fare; Mrs. Crickett, Ethel Major; Elizabeth Leat, Molly Dawes.

1923

The Famous Tragedy of the Queen of Cornwall, "O Jan! O Jan! O Jan!," and *the Play of "Saint George,"* by Thomas Hardy. November 28, 29 (2), and 30 and December 1, 1923 (Dorchester); February 21 (2), 1924 (King George's Hall, Tottenham Court Road, London: for London performance the "Old-Time Rustic Wedding Scene" from The Mellstock Quire replaced The Play of "Saint George").

Cast: for The Queen of Cornwall: King Mark, E. J. Stevens; Sir Tristram, E. W. Smerdon; Sir Andret, R. Fare; Messenger, J. Wacher; Watchman, T. Pouncy; Iseult the Fair, Queen of Cornwall, Kathleen Hirst; Iseult the Whitehanded, Ethel Fare; Dame Brangwain, Mrs. Wacher; Damsel, Augusta Bugler; Knights, Squires, Attendants, Norman J. Atkins, J. Wacher, Molly Dawes, Sheila Major; Chanters, R. C. Barrow, A. C. Cox, H. A. Martin, Ethel Major, Miss G. M. Lock, Miss J. V. Stevens; Merlin, T. H. Tilley.

Cast for "O Jan! O Jan! O Jan!": Fashionable Gentleman, P. H. Morton; Fashionable Lady, Miss J. V. Stevens; Jan, W. R. Bawler.

Cast for The Play of "Saint George": St. George, H. A. Martin; St. Andrew, T. Pouncy; St. Patrick, N. J. Atkins; St. David, R. C. Barrow; Father Christmas, E. J. Stevens; Dragon, T. H. Tilley; Princess Sabra, Molly Dawes; Black Prince, R. Fare; Slasher, J. Keniston; Turkish Knight, A. C. Cox; Saracen, A. H. Davey; Doctor, H. W. Perham.

1924

Tess, adapted by Thomas Hardy from *Tess of the d'Urbervilles.* November 26, 27 (2), 28, and 29, 1924 (Dorchester); December 11 (2), 1924 (Weymouth).

Cast: Angel Clare, E. W. Smerdon; Alec d'Urberville, N. J. Atkins; John Durbeyfield, T. Pouncy; Felix Clare, R. Fare; Jonathan Kail, A. C. Cox; Labourer, R. C. Barrow; Tess, Gertrude Bugler; Joan Durbeyfield, Ethel Major; 'Liza-Lu, Landlady's Servant, Augusta Bugler; Sarah, a club girl and Labourer's Wife, G. Lock; Marian, Molly Dawes; Izz, Ethel Fare; Landlady, Mrs. Wacher.

II. Major Professional Productions Staged in Hardy's Lifetime: A Checklist

The following information, was provided by Keith G. Wilson, University of Ottawa, who has generously granted permission to make use of his research. **Source:** Thomas Hardy Drama Page, URL: http://aix1.uottawa.ca/~kgwilson/profprod.htm. Downloaded March 12, 2002.

The following is a checklist of professional productions, staged during Hardy's lifetime, of adaptations based upon his works and of which he was aware (even if, as occasionally happened, the only interest he took in them was fuelled by the vigorous hope of their discontinuance). The only exception to the list's restriction to performances occurring during Hardy's life is the inclusion of the posthumous (1929) revival of the Philip Ridgeway production of Hardy's own *Tess,* which gave Gertrude Bugler the opportunity at last to play the title role on a professional stage.

1882

Far from the Madding Crowd, by J. Comyns Carr and Thomas Hardy. Opened at the Prince of Wales Theatre, Liverpool, 27 February 1882, with Marion Terry as Bathsheba and Charles Cartwright as Troy. After a provincial tour that included Bradford, Glasgow, Edinburgh and Newcastle, it opened at the Globe Theatre, London, April 29, 1882.

Cast: (London): Gabriel Oak, Charles Kelley; Frank Troy, John H. Barnes; Joseph Poorgrass, A. Wood; Jan Coggan, H. E. Russell; Matthew Moon, C. Medwin; Will Robin, Mr. Carleton; Fanny Robin, Maggie Hunt; Lydia Smallbury, Alexis Leighton; Bathsheba Everdene, Mrs. Bernard-Beere.

1893

The Three Wayfarers, adapted by Thomas Hardy from his short story "The Three Strangers." Opened on a bill with four other one-act plays (*Becky Sharp,* by James Barrie; *Bud and Blossom,* by Lady Colin Campbell; *Foreign Policy,* by Arthur Conan Doyle; *An Interlude,* by Walter H. Pollock and Mrs. W. K. Clifford), Terry's Theatre, London, June 3, 1893. These plays ran for six performances. It was performed again by the same cast with five other plays (*Puppets,* by J. F. McArdle; *The Burglar and the Judge,* by Charles Brookfield and F. C. Phillips; *A Visit to a Music Hall,* performed by Bruce Smith; *Mrs Hilary Regrets,* by. S. Theyre Smith; *A Pair of Lunatics,* by W. R. Walkes) in a matinée at the Criterion Theatre, London, July 20, 1893.

1897

Tess of the d'Urbervilles, adapted by Lorimer Stoddard. Opened at the Fifth Avenue Theatre, New York, March 2, 1897. With changes in the cast, Minnie Maddern Fiske then toured with the play, including presentations in Boston, Philadelphia, and Chicago. It was back at the Fifth Avenue Theatre in March 1898, and remained in her touring repertoire for many years.

Cast: Angel Clare, Edward M. Bell; Alec d'Urberville, Charles Coghlan; John Durbeyfield, John Jack; Abraham Durbeyfield, Alice Pierce; Farmer Crick and Sheriff, W. L. Branscombe; Jonathan, Wilfred North; James, W. E. Butterfield; Tim, Alfred Hickman; Joan Durbeyfield, Mary E. Baker; Tess, Minnie Maddern Fiske; Liza Loo, Edith Wright; Marian, Annie Irish; Izz, Nellie Lingard; Retty, Bijou Fernandez.

1900

Tess, adapted, without Hardy's authority, by Hugh Arthur Kennedy. Opened at the Coronet Theatre, Notting Hill Gate, February 19, 1900. Somewhat revised, it transferred to the Comedy Theatre, April 14, 1900. Hardy wrote to the *Times* (February 21, 1900) to disavow all connection with this play, which was eventually closed by an injunction from Minnie Maddern Fiske.

Cast: Angel Clare, William Kittredge; Alec Trantridge, Whitworth Jones; Rev. Cuthbert Clare, Bangley Imeson; John Durbeyfield, James Craig; Dairyman Crick, Leonard Hubert; Abraham, Garnet Vayne; Mrs. Durbeyfield, Lillian Hingston; Marian, Annie Webster; Retty, Rosalind Ivan; Izz, Gertrude Lovel; 'Liza-Lu, Miss Vayne; Tess, Mrs. Lewis Waller. There were some cast modifications on transferral to the Comedy, the most significant of which saw Oswald Yorke cast as Angel and Fred Terry as Alec.

1913

The Three Wayfarers. Opened, on a double bill with G. K. Chesterton's *Magic,* at the Little Theatre, London, November 21, 1913.

1914

The Dynasts, adapted by H. Granville-Barker and Thomas Hardy. Opened at the Kingsway Theatre, London, November 25, 1914.

Cast: Reader, Henry Ainley; Strophe, Esmé Beringer; Antistrophe, Carrie Haase.

Part I—Trafalgar:
First Passenger, Cecil Bevan; Second Passenger, Clifford Marquand; Third Passenger, C. Croker-King; Pedestrian, Allan Wade; First Spectator, F. B. J. Sharp; Second Spectator, John Sargent; Third Spectator, Charles Koop; First Old Man, Charles Daly; Second Old Man, W. O. Billington; Mrs. Cantle, Esmé Hubbard; Private Cantle, Norman Page; Admiral Villeneuve, Clarence Derwent; Flag Captain Magendie, Nicholson Tucker; Lieutenant Daudignon, John Astley; Petty Officer, Gerard Clifton; Nelson, Nicholas Hannen; Dr. Scott, Frank Darch; Captain Hardy, Frederick Ross; Officer, Henry Hargreaves; Lieutenant, William Muir; Pollard, Franklin Bellamy; Dr. Magrath, Charles Maunsell; Dr. Beatty, A. Harding Steerman; First Citizen, A. G. Poulton; Second King, Charles King; Boy, Arthur Burrell; Third Citizen, Charles Stone; Boatman, Rutland Barrington.

Part II—The Peninsula:
First Deserter, Charles Koop; Second Deserter, Franklyn Bellamy; Third Deserter, Sam Wilkinson; Fourth Deserter, Charles King; Fifth Deserter, Reginald Tippett; Sergeant, John Sargent; Officer, John Astley; Napoleon, Sydney Valentine; French Officer, Gerrard Clifton; Marshal Soult, A. Harding Steerman; Straggler, Clifford Marquand; Colonel Graham, Cecil Bevan; Captain Hardinge, Charles Maunsell; Sir John Moore, H. R. Hignett; Sir John Hope, Bert Thomas; Major Colborne, William Muir; Surgeon, F. B. J. Sharp; Chaplain, V. Tarver Penna; Sentinel, A. G. Poulton; Mrs. Dalbiac, Beatrice Smith; Mrs. Prescott, Pauline Strauss; Lord Fitzroy Somerset, Henry Hargreaves; Lord Wellington,

Murray Carrington; Sergeant Young, Albert Chapman; Second Hussar, Allan Wade; Marshal Ney, Edward Irwin; Marshal Caulaincourt, E. H. Brooke; Marshal Macdonald, Frank Darch; Roustan, Clarence Derwent; Constant, A. Lubimoff.

Part III—Waterloo:
Rustic, Charles Daly; Yeoman, W. O. Billington; Girl, Dorothy Warren; Woman, Hilda Francks; Longways, Reginald Tippett; Vicar, F. B. J. Sharp; Private Cantle, Norman Page; Coach Guard, John Sargent; Young Officer, Franklyn Bellamy; His Partner, Vera Cunningham; Her Mother, Florence Haydon; General Sir Thomas Picton; Cecil Bevan; Duke of Richmond, H. G. Hignett; Duchess of Richmond, Mary Fenner; Duke of Wellington, Murray Carrington; Muffling, Allan Wade; Prince of Orange, Frank Darch; Duke of Brunswick, C. Croker-King; Gentleman next door, Charles Stone; Napoleon, Sydney Valentine; Marshal Soult, A. Harding Steerman; Another Marshal, E. H. Brooke; Third Marshal, V. Tarver Penna; Aide, Eric H. Messiter; Another Aide, Clifford Marquand; Colonel Marbot, Gerard Clifton; Prussian Prisoner, Charles Koop; Bridgeman, Charles Maunsell; Earl of Uxbridge, Nicholson Tucker; Lord Fitzroy Somerset, Henry Hargreaves; Aide, Albert Chapman; Colonel Heymès, Bert Thomas; Aide, H. Brough Robertson; Another Aide, Charles King; Lord Hill, Edward Irwin; Colonel Colborne, William Muir; Lord Saltoun, William Moore.

1925
Tess, adapted by Thomas Hardy. Philip Ridgeway production. Opened at the Barnes Theatre, London, September 7, 1925. Transferred to Garrick Theatre, November 2, 1925. With Christine Silver in the title role, this production went on tour in 1926, with performances at the King's Theatre, Hammersmith, and in Bournemouth, Glasgow, Liverpool, Harrogate, Sheffield, and Manchester.

Cast: Angel Clare, Ion Swinley; Alec d'Urberville, Austin Trevor; John Durbeyfield, Stanley Lathbury; Mr. Tringham, C. Leveson Lane; Felix Clare, Arthur J. Mayne; Jonathan Kail, H. Saxon-Snell; Labourer, John Le Hay; Boy, Baron Salomons; Tess, Gwen Ffrangçon-Davies; Joan Durbeyfield, Margaret Carter; 'Liza-Lu, Gabrielle Casartelli; Sarah, Natalie Moya; Labourer's Wife, Drusilla Wills; Landlady, Elizabeth Webster; Izz, Phyllis de Lange; Marian, Betty Belloc; Maidservant, Tita Casartelli.

1926
The Mayor of Casterbridge, adapted by John Drinkwater. Philip Ridgeway production. Opened at the Barnes Theatre, London, September 8, 1926.

Cast: Furmity Woman and Pauline, Lilian M. Revell; First Rustic and Alderman Tupper, Arthur Ewart; Sec-ond Rustic, S. D. I. Rector; Third Rustic, A. M. Stone; Fourth Rustic, George S. Field; Young Man, Donald King; Girl, Elizabeth Wills; Woman, Mary Desmond; Susan Henchard, Christine Silver; Michael Henchard, Lyn Harding; Newson and Solomon Longways, Milton Rosmer; Elizabeth Jane, Moyna MacGill; Nance Mockridge, Cathleen Orford; Christopher Coney, Basil Dyne; Donald Farfrae, Colin Keith-Johnston; Polly, Queenie Russell; Mrs. Stannidge, Mary Desmond; Mrs. Cuxsom, Annie Hill; Abel Whittle, Dan F. Roe; Girl, Monica Stracey; Carter, Peter Baxter; Townsman, Edward Sinclair; Lucetta, Louise Prussing.

1927
Tess, adapted by Thomas Hardy. Hugh Bernard production. Pavilion Theatre, Weymouth, September 8, 9, and 10, 1927.

Cast: Mr. Tringham, Labourer, Eric Westwood; John Durbeyfield, Arthur Knight; Joan Durbeyfield, Edith Griffith; Sarah, Marion, Landlady, Clare de la Grange; Tess, Hilda Moss; Alec d'Urberbville, T. Edward-Martin; 'Liza-Lu, Izz, Labourer's Wife, Audrey Beresford; Felix Clare, Wilfred Granville; Angel Clare, Norman Mathews; Jonathan Kail, W. Nelson; Maidservant, B. Ford.

1929
Tess, adapted by Thomas Hardy. The year after Hardy's death, the Philip Ridgeway production of Hardy's own *Tess* was revived, with Gertrude Bugler in the starring role. It opened at the Duke of York's Theatre, London on July 23, 1929.

Cast: Angel Clare, Lawrence Anderson; Mr. Tringham, Drelincourt Odlum; John Durbeyfield, A. S. Homewood; Boy, Leonard Hayes; Joan Durbeyfield, Barbara Gott; Sarah and Izz, Irene Barnett; Tess, Gertrude Bugler; Alec d'Urberville, Martin Lewis; 'Liza-Lu, Joyce Moore; Felix Clare, Arthur Mayne; Jonathan Kail, Harold Young; Marian, Sonia Bellamy; Labourer's Wife, Drusilla Wills; Labourer, H. Saxon-Snell; Landlady, Marjorie Caldicott; Maidservant, Tita Casartelli.

III. Film Productions

The following information was contributed by Keith G. Wilson, David Herrick, and Lisa Cacicia to The Thomas Hardy Association online list, 2001, and condensed from the Internet Movie Database at http://us.imdb.com/Name?Hardy,+Thomas.

A. Films Produced in Hardy's Lifetime

1911 [Silent]
Far from the Madding Crowd 12-minute film made by Thomas Edison.

1913 [Silent]
Tess (USA) Film made by the Famous Players Film Co., directed by J. Searle Dawley.

Cast: Tess Durbeyfield, Minnie Maddern Fiske; Mrs. Durbeyfield, Mary Barker; Angel Clare, Raymond Bond; Mrs. Clare, Camille Dalberg; Izz, Caroline Darling; Crick, James Gordon; Mrs. d'Urberville, Katherine Griffith; Parson Clare, Franklin Hall; 'Liza-Lu, Justina Huff; Marian, Irma La Pierre; Parson Tringham, J. Liston; John Durbeyfield, John Steppling; Alec d'Urberville, David Torrence; Jonathan, John Troughton; Reta, Boots Wal; Mrs. Crick, Maggie Weston.

1915 [Silent]
Far from the Madding Crowd (UK) Film produced by Larry Trimble.

Cast: Bathsheba, Florence Turner; Troy, Campbell Gullan [from the Royalty Theatre]; Boldwood, Malcolm Cherry [from the Royalty Theatre]; Fanny Robin, Marion Grey; Lyddie, Dorothy Rowan; Gabriel Oak, Henry Edwards.

Wilson notes that the Dorset County Museum collection contains a souvenir booklet distributed at the first showing of the film with a plot summary and list of characters, including Gabriel Oak's dog, called "Jean" in the cast list.

1921 [Silent]
The Mayor of Casterbridge (UK?) Film produced by Sidney Morgan.

1924 [Silent]
Tess of the d'Urbervilles (USA) Film made by MGM, directed by Marshall Neilan; adapted by Dorothy Farnum.

Cast: Tess Durbeyfield, Blanche Sweet; Angel Clare, Conrad Nagel; Alex d'Urberville, Stuart Holmes; John Durbeyfield, George Fawcett; Joan Durbeyfield, Victory Bateman; Dick, Courtney Foote; The Priest, Joseph J. Dowling.

According to Keith G. Wilson, Hardy often negotiated for film rights, and a number of film possibilities were discussed that never resulted in films. Wilson observes that there was "ongoing interest in filming Hardy's work, and while this did not result in a very large number of actual films (seemingly five in all in TH's lifetime), Hardy always showed willingness in principle to considering possibilities, arranged for film rights to be sold, and maintained a rather puzzled interest in the oddities of the new medium."

B. Films Produced Since Hardy's Death

1929
Under the Greenwood Tree (UK) Directed by Harry Lachman; written by Sidney Gilliat and Monckton Hoffe.

Cast: Fancy Day, Marguerite Allan; Frederic Shinar, Nigel Barrie; Dick Dewey, John Batten; Maid, Antonia Brough; Tranter Dewey, Tom Coventry; Old Maid, Maud Gill; Thomas Leaf, Bill Shine; Parson Maybold, Wilfred Shine. (Also known as *The Greenwood Tree*, 1930, USA).

Herrick notes that this film is one of the earliest surviving British "talkies."

1944
Man Ki Jeet (*Tess of the d'Urbervilles*) (India; in Hindi) Directed by Wahid-ud-din Zia-ud-din-Ahmed. Also known as *Tan Ki Haar; The Victory of the Mind.*

1953
The Secret Cave (UK) Based on "Our Exploits at West Poley." Directed by John Durst; written by Joe Mendoza.

Cast: Steve Draycott, David Coote; Leonard Hawkins, Nicholas Edmett; Margaret Merriman, Susan Ford; Miller Griffin, Lewis Gedge; Job Tary, Trevor Hill; Charlie Bassett, Johnny Morris.

1967
Far from the Madding Crowd (UK) Directed by John Schlesinger; written by Frederic Raphael.

Cast: Bathsheba Everdene, Julie Christie; Sergeant Troy, Terence Stamp; William Boldwood, Peter Finch; Gabriel Oak, Alan Bates; Liddy, Fiona Walker; Fanny Robin, Prunella Ransome; Mrs. Hurst, Alison Leggatt; Henery Fray, Paul Dawkins; Jan Coggan, Julian Somers; Joseph Poorgrass, John Barrett; Cainy Ball, Freddie Jones; Andrew Randle, Andrew Robertson; Matthew Moon, Brian Rawlinson; Mark Clark, Vincent Harding; Billy Smallbury, Victor Stone.

1971
Jude the Obscure (UK) (BBC television miniseries, Six episodes, 50 mins. each). Directed by Hugh David; written by Harry Green.

Cast: Jude Fawley, Robert Powell; Sue Bridehead, Fiona Walker; Richard Phillotson, John Franklyn-Robbins; Aunt Drusilla Fawley, Daphne Heard; Arabella Fawley, Alex Marshall.

1973
A Tragedy of Two Ambitions (UK, television film) Directed by Michael Tuchner; written by Dennis Potter.

Cast: Mr. Harlborough, Paul Rogers; Cornelius Harlborough, David Troughton; Countryman, Dan Meaden; Farm Laborer, Andrew McCulloch; Clergyman, John Rainer; Principal, Peter Bennett; Selimar, Heather Canning; Mrs. Fellmer, Betty Cooper; Rosa Harlborough, Lynne Frederick; Joshua Harlborough, John Hurt; Squire Fellmer, Edward Petherbridge.

1978

The Mayor of Casterbridge (UK) Directed by David Giles; written by Dennis Potter.

Cast: Michael Henchard, Alan Bates; Companion, Alec Bregonzi; Mrs. Goodenough, Avis Bunnage; Hoer, Anthony Douse; Donald Farfrae, Jack Galloway; Lucetta, Anna Massey; Elizabeth Jane Henchard, Janet Maw; Susan, Anne Stallybrass.

1979

Tess of the d'Urbervilles (France/UK) Directed by Roman Polanski; written by Gérard Brach and John Brownjohn.

Cast: Mr. Durbeyfield, John Collin; Parson Tringham, Tony Church; Tess Durbeyfield, Nastassja Kinski; Angel Clare, Peter Firth; Felix Clare, John Bett; Cuthbert Clare, Tom Chadbon; Mrs. Durbeyfield, Rosemary Martin; Alec d'Urberville, Leigh Lawson.

1985

Exploits at West Poley (Our Exploits at West Poley) Directed by Diarmuid Lawrence; written by James Andrew Hall.

Cast: The Man Who Has Failed, Anthony Bale; Aunt Draycott, Brenda Fricker; Leonard Hawkins, Charlie Condou; Miller Griffin, Jonathan Adams; Job Tray, Noel O'Connell; Farmer Will Gant, Thomas Heathcote; Millhand, James Coyle; Washerwoman, Jelena Budimir; Old Woman, Diana King; Susan, Kelita Groom; Branded Man, Brian Coburn; Scarred Man, Sean Bean; Shepherd, George Malpas; Fiddler, Barry Dransfield; Young Boy, Jacob Thomas.

1994

The Return of the Native (UK; television film) Directed by Jack Gold; written by Robert Lenski.

Cast: Eustacia Vye, Catherine Zeta-Jones; Damon Wildeve, Clive Owen; Clym Yeobright, Ray Stevenson; Diggory Venn, Steven Mackintosh; Thomasin Wildeve, Claire Skinner; Captain Vye, Paul Rogers; Mrs. Yeobright, Joan Plowright; Susan Nunsuch, Celia Imrie; Humphrey, Richard Avery; Timothy, Peter Wight; Sam, Jeremy Peters; Charley, Gregg Saunders; Granfer Cantle, John Boswall; Christian Cantle, William Waghorn; Johnny Nunsuch, Matthew Owens.

1996

Jude the Obscure (UK) Directed by Michael Winterbottom; written by Hossein Amini.

Cast: Jude Fawley, Christopher Eccleston; Sue Bridehead, Kate Winslet; Richard Phillotson, Liam Cunningham; Arabella Fawley, Rachel Griffiths; Aunt Drusilla Fawley, June Whitfield; Little Jude, Ross Colvin Turnbull; Boy Jude, James Daley; Anny, Caitlin Bossley; Uncle Joe, James Nesbitt; Tinker Taylor, Mark Lambert.

1998

Far from the Madding Crowd (Granada Television, UK) Directed by Nicholas Renton; written by Thomas Hardy (novel), Philomena McDonagh.

Cast: Bathsheba Everdene, Paloma Baeza; William Boldwood, Nigel Terry; Gabriel Oak, Nathaniel Parker; Sergeant Frank Troy, Jonathan Firth; Parson Thirdly, Will Coggan; Cain Ball, Luke Redbond; Mark Clark, Andy Robb; Mrs. Hurst, Linda Spurrier; Liddy, Tracy Keating; Fanny Robin; Jan Coggan, Phillip Joseph.

The Scarlet Tunic (UK) Based on "The Melancholy Hussar of the German Legion." Directed by Stuart St. Paul; written by Colin Clements and Mark Jenkins.

Cast: Matthaus Singer, Jean-Marc Barr; Frances Groves, Emma Fielding; Captain Fairfax, Simon Callow; Dr. Edward Grove, Jack Shepherd; Humphrey Gould, John Sessions; Emily Marlowe, Lynda Bellingham; Christoph Singer, Thomas Lockyer; Muller, Andrew Tiernam; William Parsons, Gareth Hale; Amy Parsons, Lisa Faulkner; Fridon, Roger May; Dotty Marlowe, Laura Aikman; Strasser, Erich Redman; Lizzie, Landlady, Jean Heard; Officer Hubbard, Tom McCabe.

Tess of the d'Urbervilles (UK) Directed by Ian Sharp; written by Ted Whitehead.

Cast: Tess Durbeyfield, Justine Waddell; Alec d'Urberville, Jason Flemyng; Angel Clare, Oliver Milburn; Jack Durbeyfield, John McEnery; Joan Durbeyfield, Lesley Dunlop; Mrs. d'Urberville, Rosalind Knight; Crick, Anthony O'Donnell; Mrs. Crick, Christine Moore; Kail, Bryan Pringle; Marian, Debbie Chazen; Izzy, Candida Rundle; Retty, Amanda Brewster.

The Woodlanders (UK) Directed by Phil Agland; written by David Rudkin.

Cast: Grace Melbury, Emily Woof; Giles Winterbourne, Rufus Sewell; Dr. Edred Fitzpiers, Cal Macaninch; Mr. Melbury, Tony Haygarth; Marty South, Jodhi May; Felice Charmond, Polly Walker; Old Creedle, Walter Sparrow; Grandma Oliver, Sheila Burrell.

2000

The Claim (UK) Loosely based on *The Mayor of Casterbridge*. Directed by Michael Winterbottom; written by Frank Cottrell Boyce.

Cast: Daniel Dillon, Peter Mullan; Lucia, Milla Jovovich; Dalglish, Wes Bentley; Elena Dillon, Nastassja Kinski; Hope Dillon, Sarah Polley; Annie, Shirley Henderson; Bellanger, Julian Richings; Sweetley, Sean McGinley; Priest, Randy Birch.

2001

The Mayor of Casterbridge (UK; television film) Directed by David Thacker; written by Ted Whitehead.

Cast: Michael Henchard, Ciarán Hinds; Donald Farfrae, James Purefoy; Elizabeth-Jane, Jodhi May; Susan
Henchard, Juliet Aubrey; Lucetta, Polly Walker.

IV. Musical Adaptations of Hardy's Works

1906

Tess, an opera by Baron Frédéric d'Erlanger based on
Tess of the d'Urbervilles, was performed at the San Carlo
Theater, Naples, on April 10, 1906. The first London
performance, attended by Hardy, took place at the
Covent Garden opera house on July 14, 1909.

1909

"A Soldiers' Song" (one of several such songs) from *The
Dynasts,* Part First, Act First, Scene I, set to music by
Ralph Vaughan Williams. He called it "Buonaparty"; it
was published as a song for voice and piano in 1909.

1914

"Men Who March Away" (poem) was set to music by
Edgar Lane, who had a school of music in Dorchester;
Hardy offered it to Harley Granville-Barker to use in
The Dynasts (Bailey, *The Poetry of Thomas Hardy,* 416–17).

1919

"The Oxen" (poem) was set to music by Edward Dent
in 1919; a copy is in the Dorset County Museum.

Other settings are by Graham Peel, *The Oxen* (London: Chappell & Co., 1919); Gerald Finzi, *By Footpath
and Stile* (London: J. Curwen & Sons, 1925); Leslie
Cochran, *The Oxen* (London: Augener, 1927); Robert
Fleming, *The Oxen* (London: Oxford University Press,
1945); C. Armstrong Gibbs, *The Oxen* (London: Boosey
& Hawkes, 1953); and Harper MacKay, *Five Songs* (1957;
manuscript in Colby College Library). Source: Bailey,
The Poetry of Thomas Hardy, 371.

1923

An opera, *The Queen of Cornwall,* by Rutland Boughton,
based on *The Famous Tragedy of the Queen of Cornwall,* was
performed at Glastonbury, Malvern, Bournemouth, and
Bath. It was published in 1923 (London: Joseph
Williams). Source: Bailey, *The Poetry of Thomas Hardy,* 655.

1925

The poems "Hap" and "The Sleep-Worker" were set to
music by Hubert James Foss (*Seven Poems by Thomas
Hardy;* London: Oxford University Press, 1925).

1925

"Where the Picnic Was" (poem) was set to music by
Gerald Finzi (*By Footpath and Stile,* London: J. Curwen
& Sons, 1925). Source: Bailey, *The Poetry of Thomas
Hardy,* 308.

1933

"Ditty" (poem) was set to music by Gerald Finzi (*A
Young Man's Exhortation,* Oxford University Press, 1933.
Source: Bailey, *The Poetry of Thomas Hardy,* 60.

1940

"The Pink Frock" (poem) was set to music by Robin
Milford (*A Book of Songs,* Oxford University Press,
1940). Source: Bailey, *The Poetry of Thomas Hardy,* 375.

1949

"Channel Firing" (poem) and "He Abjures Love"
(poem) were set to music and published in *Before and
After Summer: Ten Songs for Baritone and Piano* (London:
Boosey & Hawkes, 1949). Source: Bailey, *The Poetry of
Thomas Hardy,* 222, 264.

1958

"It Never Looks Like Summer" (poem) was set to music
by Gerald Finzi and published in *Till Earth Outwears*
(London and New York: Boosey & Hawkes, 1958).
Source: Bailey, *The Poetry of Thomas Hardy,* 400.

1963

Wessex Tune Book (London: Schott, 1963). Contains folk
dances from a manuscript book belonging to the family
of Thomas Hardy; arranged by Elna Sherman for des-
cant recorder (or oboe or violin) and piano.

Date uncertain:

"The House of Hospitalities:" A musical setting of the
poem exists in an unsigned manuscript in the Dorset
County Museum. Source: Bailey, *The Poetry of Thomas
Hardy,* 203.

"Regret Not Me" was set to music by Gerald Finzi (London: Oxford University Press; not dated).

"Shut Out That Moon": A musical setting of the poem
signed *AM* exists in a manuscript in the Dorset County
Museum. Source: Bailey, *The Poetry of Thomas Hardy,*
208.

APPENDIX III

Chronology of Thomas Hardy's Life and Works

Publishers are only given for Great Britain, with the exception of *The Three Wayfarers* in 1893; for names of American publishers, see individual entries.

1840
Thomas Hardy is born to Thomas and Jemima (Hand) Hardy on June 2 at Higher Bockhampton, Dorset. His father and grandfather are master stonemasons and excellent musicians who play instruments in the "quire" of the local parish church.

1848
Hardy attends the Bockhampton School, founded by Julia Augusta Pitney Martin, in Lower Bockhampton, for one year. His mother gives him Dryden's *Virgil* and other books.

1849
Jemima Hardy decides to send Hardy to the British School in Dorchester, founded by Isaac Glandfield Last. He learns Latin, plays fiddle for dances and weddings.

1853
Isaac Last leaves the British School to establish a "commercial academy" for older students. Hardy attends this school until 1856, studying Latin, French, and advanced mathematics.

1856–61
Hardy is articled to John Hicks, a Dorchester architect. He studies Greek and Latin and writes verse, and meets Horace Moule, a friend who influences his thought and studies. He witnesses a woman's public execution, an episode that later figures in the ending of *Tess of the d'Urbervilles*.

1862–67
Hardy moves to London, where he works in the office of Sir Arthur William Blomfield, a restorer and designer of churches. While in London he becomes involved with the city's cultural life, but is disenchanted with society and rigid class structure. He also studies paintings in the National Gallery, reads widely in modern poets, and writes poetry, but his work is rejected by publishers.

1865
Hardy's article "How I Built Myself a House" appears in *Chambers's Journal;* this is his first published work.

1867
Hardy's health declines in London; he returns to Dorset to work for Hicks on church restoration. He begins *The Poor Man and the Lady*, but the novel is rejected by publishers.

1869
John Hicks dies and Hardy goes to Weymouth, a nearby seaside town, to work for the architect G. R. Crickmay.

1870
Crickmay sends Hardy to work on restoration of the church at St. Juliot, a hamlet in Cornwall. There he meets his future wife, Emma Gifford. He visits Boscastle, Tintagel, and Beeny Cliff. He writes his first published novel, *Desperate Remedies*.

1871
Desperate Remedies is published anonymously by Tinsley Brothers.

1872
Under the Greenwood Tree is published anonymously by Tinsley Brothers and is well received.

1873
A Pair of Blue Eyes is serialized in *Tinsleys' Magazine* (September 1872–July 1873) and published by Tinsley Brothers. It is the first of his novels to have his name on the title page. Hardy is invited to write a serial for *Cornhill Magazine*. While working in Higher Bockhampton, he begins *Far from the Madding Crowd*. His friend Horace Moule commits suicide.

1874

Hardy marries Emma Gifford on September 17. They go to the Continent on their wedding trip; on their return they take lodgings in St. David's Villa, Hook Road, Surbiton (a suburb of London). Hardy's novel *Far from the Madding Crowd* is serialized anonymously in the *Cornhill Magazine* (January–December 1874), then published by Smith, Elder & Co.

1875

The Hardys move to Newton Road, off Westbourne Grove. In July they rent rooms in West End Cottage, Swanage, Dorset. *The Hand of Ethelberta* begins running in July in the *Cornhill Magazine*.

1876

In March the Hardys take rooms at 7 Peter St., Yeovil, Somerset. In December they rent Riverside Villa, Sturminster Newton, Dorset. The final installment of *The Hand of Ethelberta* runs in *Cornhill Magazine* in May; it is then published by Smith, Elder & Co. The Hardys make a second continental tour.

1878

The Return of the Native is serialized in *Belgravia* (January–December 1878) and published by Smith, Elder & Co. The Hardys move to 1 Arundel Terrace, Trinity Road, Upper Tooting, London. He begins his study of the Napoleonic Wars and becomes known in literary and social circles; he joins the Savile Club.

1880

The Trumpet Major is serialized in *Good Words* (January–December 1880) and published by Smith, Elder & Co. The Hardys tour Normandy. Hardy falls seriously ill on their return, forcing him to dictate *A Laodicean* to his wife while lying prone in bed with his feet elevated. *A Laodicean* is serialized in *Harper's Monthly Magazine* (European edition; December 1880–December 1881).

1881

A Laodicean is published by Sampson Low, Marston, Searle & Rivington. The Hardys move to Lanherne, The Avenue, Wimborne Minster, Dorset, in June.

1882

The Hardys visit Paris. *Two on a Tower* is serialized in the *Atlantic Monthly* (May–December 1882) and published by Sampson Low, Marston, Searle & Rivington.

1883

Hardy realizes he is distracted by London social life and decides to live in Dorset the better part of each year with protracted stays in London. He designs a house, Max Gate, to be built outside Dorchester. He and Emma rent Shire-Hall Place while their home is being constructed.

1884

Hardy works on *The Mayor of Casterbridge* at Shire-Hall Place. He meets Lady Portsmouth (the countess of Portsmouth) in London in June 1884. Hardy and his brother Henry visit the Channel Islands.

1885

Hardy may have finished *The Mayor of Casterbridge* in April. The Hardys move into Max Gate, but make extended annual visits to London. Hardy is introduced to Mary Jeune (Mrs. Francis, later Lady Jeune) in London.

1886

The Mayor of Casterbridge is serialized in the *Graphic* (January 2–May 15, 1886) and published in book form by Smith, Elder & Co. in May. *The Woodlanders* is serialized in *Macmillan's Magazine*, May 1886–April 1887.

1887

The Woodlanders is published by Macmillan & Co. The Hardys tour Italy, visiting the graves of Shelley and Keats. They spend some months in London.

1888

The Hardys visit Paris. Hardy writes many short stories between 1888 and 1891. His first collection of short stories, *Wessex Tales*, is published (2 vols., Macmillan). He begins *Tess of the d'Urbervilles* with the title *Too Late Beloved*.

1889

Conflicts with editors force Hardy to bowdlerize the text of *Tess*.

1890

In August Hardy and his brother Henry go to Paris. They see many sights and visit the Moulin Rouge.

1891

Tess of the d'Urbervilles is serialized in the *Graphic* (July 4–December 26, 1891) and published in book form by Osgood, McIlvaine & Co. The novel is well received but also heavily criticized. *A Group of Noble Dames* is published.

1892

The Well-Beloved, a novella written prior to *Jude the Obscure*, is serialized in the *Illustrated London News* under the title *The Pursuit of the Well-Beloved* (October

1, 1892–December 17, 1892). Hardy's father dies on July 20. Hardy's marriage becomes increasingly difficult. He begins work on *Jude the Obscure.*

1893

Hardy meets Florence Henniker in Dublin; she invites them to visit the Viceregal Lodge in Dublin. Hardy may have formed an attachment to her. Emma Hardy grows more and more eccentric. *The Three Wayfarers,* a dramatization of Hardy's story "The Three Strangers," is published by Harper & Brothers, New York, for copyright purposes only.

1894

Hardy works on *Jude the Obscure. Life's Little Ironies,* a collection of short stories, is published by Osgood, McIlvaine & Co. *Jude the Obscure* is serialized under the titles of *The Simpletons* (first installment only) and *Hearts Insurgent* in *Harper's Monthly Magazine* (December 1894–November 1895).

1895

Jude the Obscure is published by Osgood, McIlvaine, causing a furor. By February 15, 1896, 20,000 copies had been published. The novel receives harsh criticism, prompting Hardy to give up novel writing. The Hardys visit Belgium, where Hardy surveys the field of Waterloo, south of Brussels.

1897

The Well-Beloved is published in book form by Osgood, McIlvaine & Co. The Hardys visit Switzerland and the West Country.

1898

Hardy's volume of poetry *Wessex Poems and Other Verses* is published by Harper & Brothers. He makes many cycling trips, sometimes with Emma and sometimes with his brother Henry. The Hardys take a flat in Wynnstay Gardens, London.

1899

The Hardys take another flat in Wynnstay Gardens. Hardy meets A. E. Housman for the first time and visits Algernon Charles Swinburne at Putney. In October he witnesses the departure of troops for the Boer War from Southampton. His poem on the century's end, "The Darkling Thrush," is published in the *Graphic* in December 1900 under the title "By the Century's Deathbed."

1902

Poems of the Past and Present is published by Harper & Brothers (the Preface is dated 1901). He begins writing *The Dynasts.*

1904

Hardy's mother dies on April 3. The first part of his epic, *The Dynasts,* is published by Macmillan & Co., Ltd. The preface is dated 1903.

1905

Hardy receives the honorary degree of LL.D. from the University of Aberdeen.

1906

The Dynasts, Part II, is published by Macmillan & Co., Ltd. Hardy and his brother Henry make a tour to some English cathedrals, including Lincoln, Ely, the Cambridge colleges, and Canterbury. Later in the summer they bicycle in Dorset and Somerset.

1907

Hardy works with his secretary and literary assistant, Florence Dugdale, a young woman he had met in 1904 through Florence Henniker; she looks up references for *The Dynasts.*

1908

Hardy completes *The Dynasts;* Part III is published by Macmillan & Co., Ltd., London.

1909

Time's Laughingstocks and Other Verses is published by Macmillan & Co. Hardy accepts the governorship of the Dorchester Grammar School and the presidency of the Society of Authors, succeeding George Meredith.

1910

Hardy is presented with the Order of Merit.

1911

Hardy and his brother Henry continue their plan of visiting or revisiting all the English cathedrals. They also make a tour of the Lake District. Hardy takes his sister Katharine to north Somerset. Sydney Cockerell, of the Fitzwilliam Museum, Cambridge, asks Hardy to give him his old manuscripts so that he can distribute them to museums.

1912

Hardy receives the Gold Medal of the Royal Society of Literature. Emma Lavinia Hardy dies suddenly on November 27 at Max Gate, Dorchester.

1913

Hardy revisits St. Juliot, Cornwall, and begins writing the series of poems that would become *The Poems of 1912–13. A Changed Man and Other Tales* is published by Macmillan & Co. He receives the honorary degree of Litt.D. from the University of Cambridge in June and in November is elected an Honorary Fellow of Magdalene College, Cambridge.

1914

Hardy marries Florence Dugdale on February 10 at St. Andrew's, Enfield. World War I begins; Hardy pledges allegiance to the Allies, as do a number of writers. *Satires of Circumstance* (including "Poems of 1912–1913") is published by Macmillan & Co.

1915

Hardy's sister Mary dies of emphysema.

1916

Selected Poems of Thomas Hardy is published by Macmillan & Co. Hardy, Florence, and Hardy's sister Katharine make a journey to Riverside Villa, Sturminster Newton, where he had lived with Emma. They also go by train to Cornwall, visiting the church at St. Juliot to view the tablet Hardy had designed in Emma's memory.

1917

Moments of Vision and Miscellaneous Verses is published by Macmillan & Co. Hardy begins to become reclusive, but starts work on his autobiography (posthumously published) with Florence. He and Florence go to Plymouth.

1919

On his birthday (June 2) Hardy, Florence, and his sister Katharine travel to Salisbury by the old route Hardy's forefathers had once used in their journeys to London, via Blandford, Woodyates Inn, and Harnham Hill. In October Hardy is much moved by the "Poets' Tribute," a bound volume of about 50 holograph poems by contemporary poets, each one signed.

1920

Hardy receives the honorary degree of Litt.D. from the University of Oxford. He accepts an honorary fellowship from Queen's College, Oxford.

1922

Late Lyrics and Earlier is published by Macmillan & Co. Hardy visits Stinsford. He accepts an honorary fellowship from Queen's College, Oxford.

1923

The Famous Tragedy of the Queen of Cornwall is published by Macmillan and Co. Hardy entertains the Prince of Wales at Max Gate.

1924

Hardy sits for the Russian sculptor Serge Youriévitch for a bust-portrait. He and Florence visit the barn behind Kingston Maurward house where, as a child, he had listened to the singing of village girls.

1925

Human Shows, Far Phantasies, Songs, and Trifles is published by Macmillan & Co. In December actors from the Garrick Theatre, London, perform scenes from *Tess* in the drawing room at Max Gate.

1926

Hardy entertains Virginia Woolf at Max Gate. His dog Wessex dies. Hardy pays a final visit to his birthplace at Higher Bockhampton. He resigns the governorship of the Dorchester Grammar School.

1927

Hardy makes his final public appearance with an address at the Dorchester Grammar School stone-laying. The *Iphigenia in Aulis* of Euripides is played before Hardy at Max Gate by undergraduates of Balliol College, Oxford. He becomes ill in December.

1928

Hardy dies at Max Gate, at the age of 87, on January 11. His heart is buried in his first wife's grave in Stinsford churchyard; his ashes are buried in Poets' Corner, Westminster Abbey. His final volume of poetry, *Winter Words,* is published posthumously by Macmillan & Co.

APPENDIX IV

Family Trees

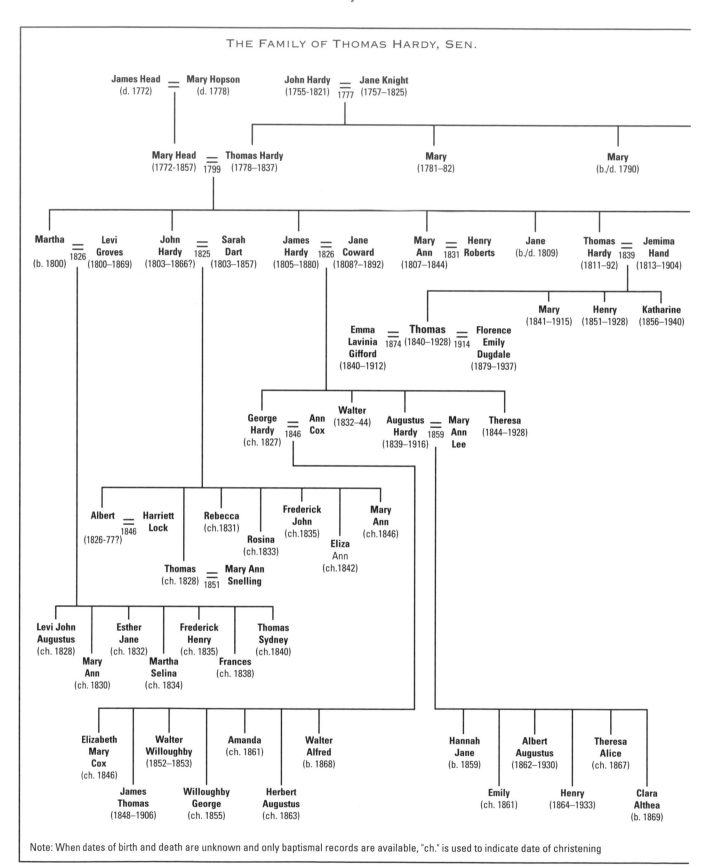

The Family of Thomas Hardy, Sen.

Note: When dates of birth and death are unknown and only baptismal records are available, "ch." is used to indicate date of christening

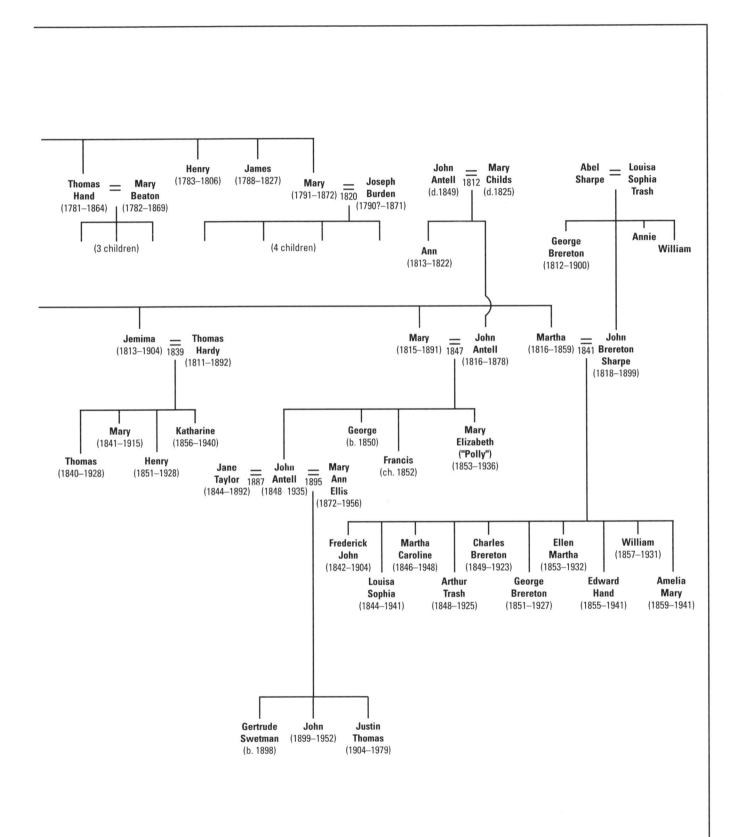

Compiled by Michael Millgate and Vera Jesty; from *Thomas Hardy: A Biography* (New York: Random House, 1982); reproduced courtesy of Michael Millgate

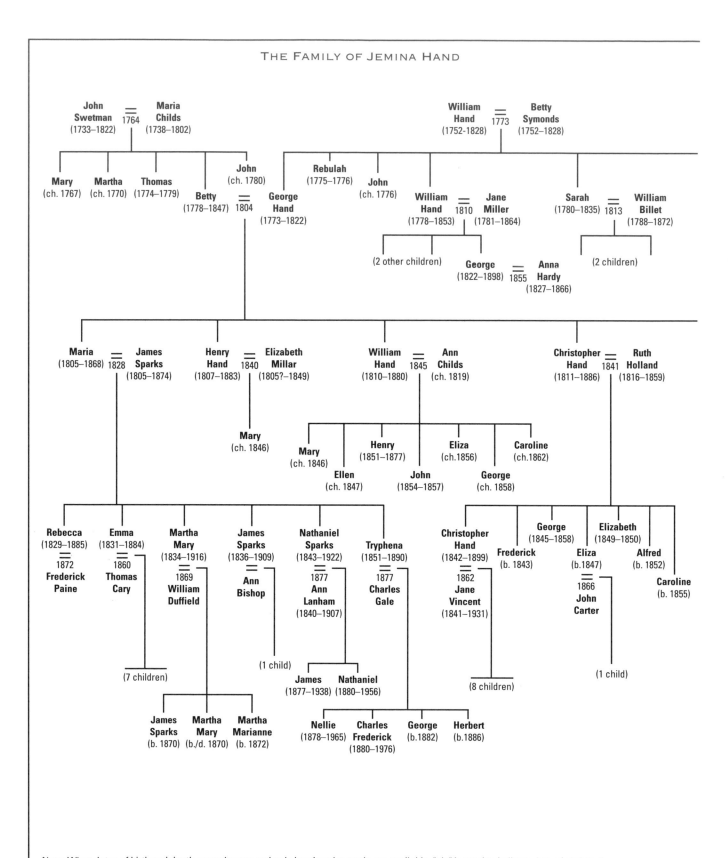

THE FAMILY OF JEMINA HAND

Note: When dates of birth and death are unknown and only baptismal records are available, "ch." is used to indicate date of christening

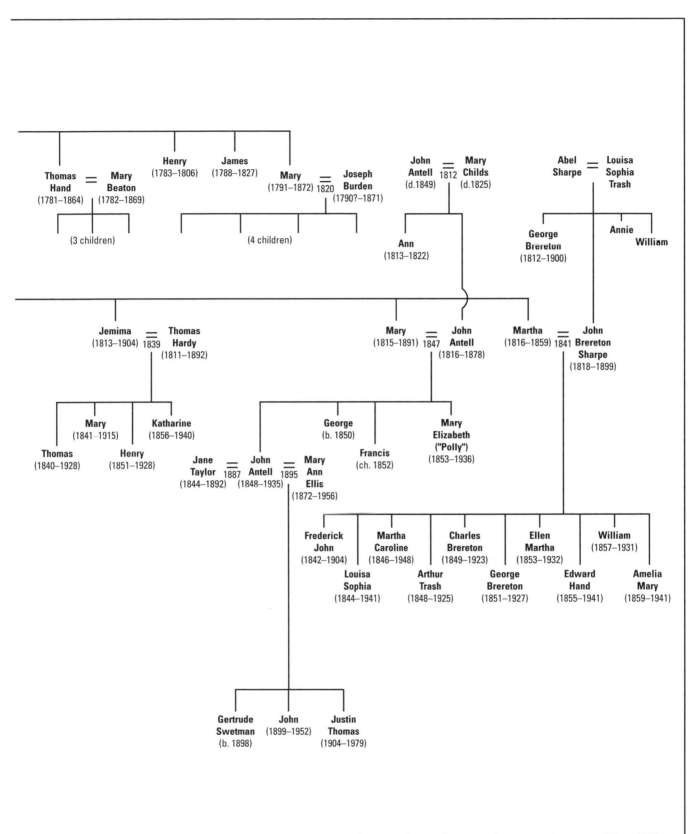

Compiled by Michael Millgate and Vera Jesty; from *Thomas Hardy: A Biography* (New York: Random House, 1982); reproduced courtesy of Michael Millgate

APPENDIX V

Glossary of Place-Names in Thomas Hardy's Works

As early as 1896 journalists and authors of tour guides appealed to Hardy for permission to publish keys to the correlation of fictitious place names in his works with actual ones. Invariably, he tried to discourage them. Bertram Windle (1896), Hermann Lea (1905), and F. O. Saxelby (1911), as well as Hardy himself, all prepared such lists. Hardy was reluctant to concede their accuracy, asking Lea to state that "the author has never admitted more than that the places named fictitiously were *suggested* by … real places." He continued, however, to admit that, if one assumed that the places mentioned in fiction and in verse were "idealizations," then the "majority" of them could be recognized in "substance" (*Letters* III, 172). Hardy wished to make it clear to readers that where Saxelby proposed to "identify fictitious place-names with real places" he could "accept no responsibility for such identification" (*Letters* IV, 135); he refused to review the proofs.

The list of place names Hardy gave to Bertram Windle in 1896, marked "For private reference only—not to be printed in this form," is published in the *Collected Letters*, volume II, 131–33. Although it serves as a useful starting point, it is incomplete and has been superseded by later compilations. The following glossary is an amalgamation of three lists: the one compiled by Saxelby and published in F. B. Pinion, *A Thomas Hardy Dictionary* (New York: New York University Press, 1989, xxiii–xxv), one made by J. Stevens Cox and published as Appendix 2, D. F. Barber, *Concerning Thomas Hardy* (London: Charles Skilton, Ltd. 1968; 172–79), and a third, given by F. B. Pinion in the notes to the New Wessex Edition of Thomas Hardy, *Collected Short Stories* (Macmillan London, 1988; 932–34).

Note: Locations of small places are given in mileage and direction from well-known places. Places in italics are fictional.

Hardy's Name	Identification
I. General Regions	
Lower Wessex	Devon
Mid Wessex	Wiltshire
North Wessex	Berkshire
Outer Wessex	Somerset
South Wessex	Dorset
Upper Wessex	Hampshire
II. Places	
Abbot's-Cernel	Cerne Abbas, 7 miles N of Dorchester
Aldbric\ham	Reading
Alfredston	Wantage
Anglebury	Wareham
Arrowthorne Lodge	House on north side of the New Forest between Romsey and Fordingbridge
Athelhall	Athelhampton, near *Weatherbury*
Aquae Sulis	Bath
Barwith Strand	Trebarwith Strand, Cornwall
Blooms-End	Farmhouse called Bhompston, off the heath in the direction of Lower Bockhampton to south of road from Stinsford to Tincleton
Bramshurst Manor-House	Moyle's Court, near Ringwood
Broad Sidlinch	Sydling St. Nicholas, 3 miles SW of *Abbot's-Cernel*
Buckbury Fitzpiers	Okeford Fitzpaine
Budmouth (Regis)	Weymouth
Camelton	Camelford, Cornwall
Carriford (Carriford Village, the Three Tranters Inn)	Parts of West Stafford, Puddletown
Casterbridge	Dorchester
Castle Boterel	Boscastle

Castle Royal	Windsor Castle	**Endelstow**	St. Juliot, Cornwall
Chalk-Newton	Maiden Newton, 7 ½ miles NW of Dorchester	**Endelstow House**	Between Lesnewth and St. Juliot Church, Cornwall
Chasetown or Chaseborough	Cranborne	**Enkworth**	Encombe, near Swanage
		Enkworth Court	Encombe House, near Swanage
Chene Manor	Canford Manor	**Evershead**	Evershot, 6 miles WNW of *Abbot's Cernel*
Christminster	Oxford		
Clammers Gate	Gate of Melbury Park opening into Melbury Osmund (former spelling)	**Exonbury**	Exeter
		Falcon Hotel	White Hart Hotel, Launceston, Cornwall
Cliff-Martin	Combe Martin, North Devon	**Falls Park**	Mells Park, Somerset
Climmerston	Higher Waterston, 4 ½ miles NNE of Dorchester	**Farnfield**	Farnborough
		Fernell Hall	Embley House, near Romsey, Hants.
Corvsgate	Corfe		
Corvsgate Castle	Corfe Castle	**Flintcomb Ash**	Dole's Ash, near Puddletrenthide (Saxelby); site of Iron Age village, Barcombe Down, near Altan Pancras (Barber)
Cresscombe	Letcome Bassett		
Creston	Preston, 3 miles NE of Weymouth		
Crimmercrock Lane	Cromlech Crock Lane (Maiden Newton to Crewkerne)	**Flychett**	Lytchett Minster, near Poole
		Forest of the White Hart	Blackmoor Vale
Cross-in-Hand	Crossy Hand on Batcombe Down	**Forum (Shottsford)**	Blandford Forum
Dagger's Grave	Dagger's Gate, 1 mile NW of Lulworth Cove	**Fountall**	Wells, Somerset
		Froom-Everard	West Stafford House, 4 miles ESE of Dorchester
Dairies, The Valley of Great	Vale of the Frome or Var		
		Froom-side Vale	Frome Valley
Dairies, The Valley of Little	Blackmoor Vale	**Gaymead**	Shinfield (near Reading)
		Giant's Town	Hugh Town, St. Mary's, Isles of Scilly
Deansleigh Park	Broadlands near Romsey		
Devil's Kitchen	Real name of dell between Dogbury Hill and High-Stag	**Glaston**	Glastonbury
		Great Forest	New Forest, Hants.
Downstaple	Barnstaple, North Devon	**Great Grey Plain**	Salisbury Plain? [Cox's question mark]
Dundagel	Tintagel, Cornwall		
Durnover	Fordington (southeast side of Dorchester)	**Great Hintock**	Minterne Magna
		Great Plain, The	Salisbury Plain
Durnover Green	Fordington Green	**Great Pool (Shadwater Weir)**	The Weir, Woodsford Meadows, 4 miles E of Dorchester on the River Frome
East Egdon	Affpuddle		
East Endelstow	Lesnewth, Cornwall		
East Quarriers	Easton, Isle of Portland	**Greenhill**	Woodbury Hill, ½ mile E of Bere Regis, 10 miles ENE of Dorchester
Eggar	Eggardon Hill		
Egdon (Heath)	The heaths between Dorchester and Wareham (Saxelby); Puddle-town Heath and eastward, north of the Frome valley (Pinion)		
		Haggardon Hill	Eggardon Hill
		Havenpool	Poole
		Henry the Eighth's Castle	Sandsfoot Castle, Portland Harbor, Weymouth
Elm-Cranlynch	Montacute House, Somerset		
Elsenford	Islington, 1½ miles from Weatherbury	**Higher Crowstairs**	Solitary hill on Long Ashley Lane (Dorchester to Ilchester Roman road) near Grimstone Down
Emminster	Beaminster		

Higher Jirton	Higher Forston, 4 miles N of Dorchester	**Markton**	Dunster
Holloway Lane	Long Ash Lane	**Marlbury Downs**	Marlborough Downs
Holmstoke	In the region of West Holme, Stokeford, and East Stoke, 2–4 miles W of Wareham	**Marlott**	Marnhull, 6 miles WSW of Shaftesbury
		Marshwood	Middlemarsh
Hope Church	Church Hope, Portland	**Marygreen**	Fawley Magna, Berks.
Icenway House	3 miles S of Basingstoke	**Melchester**	Salisbury
Idmouth	Sidmouth	**Melchester, Old**	Old Sarum, 2 miles N of Salisbury
Isle of Slingers	Portland	**Mellstock**	Stinsford (1 mile ENE of Dorchester) and the Bockhamptons
Ivelchester	Ilchester		
Ivell	Yeovil	**Mellstock Cross**	Stinsford Cross
Jordon Grove	Preston Vale	**Mellstock, East**	Lower Bockhampton
Kennetbridge	Newbury	**Mellstock Lane**	Road leading N from Mellstock Cross
King's Bere	Bere Regis		
King's Hintock	Melbury Osmond, 7 miles NW of *Abbot's-Cernel*	**Mellstock Rise**	Stinsford Hill
		Mellstock, West	Stinsford
King's Hintock Court	Melbury House, 1 mile S of *King's Hintock*	**Mellstock, Lower**	Lower Bockhampton, 1 mile S of *Lewgate*
Knapwater House	Kingston Maurward House	**Middleton Abbey**	Milton Abbey
Knollingwood Hall	Wimborne St. Giles House (near Cranborne)	**Millpond St. Jude's**	Milbourne St. Andrew's
		Millpool	Milborne Port, 3 miles NE of Sherborne
Knollsea	Swanage		
Lane of Shire	Slyer's Lane, near Dorchester	**Mistover**	Cob-built cottages on Egdon Heath near Rainbarrow; they have disappeared
Leddenton	Gillingham		
Lewgate	Lewstock [Pinion gives Higher Bockhampton, 2 miles ENE of Dorchester; not used in Hardy's lifetime].	**Mistover Knap**	House near Rainbarrow; has disappeared
		Mixen Lane	Mill Street, Fordington, Dorchester
Little Enkworth	Kingston, 2 miles S of Corfe Castle	**Monksbury**	Probably Abbotsbury, 7 miles NW of Weymouth
Little Hintock	Melbury Osmond		
Little Weatherbury Farm	Druce Farmhouse, 1 mile NW of Puddletown	**Montislope**	Montacute, 4 miles W of Yeovil
		Moreford	Moreton, 7 miles E of Dorchester
Little Welland	Winterborne Zelstone	**Narrowbourne**	East or West Coker, 2–3 miles SW of Yeovil
Longpuddle	Piddlehinton, 3 miles NW of *Weatherbury,* and Piddletrenthide, 2 miles NNW of Piddlehinton		
		Nether-Moynton	Owermoigne, 65 miles SE of Dorchester
Lorton	Horton, 5 miles NNE of Wimborne	**Norcombe Hill**	Toller Down
		Nuzzlebury	Hazelbury Bryan
Lulstead Cove	Lulworth Cove	**Oakbury Fitzpiers**	Okeford Fitzpaine
Lower Mellstock	Lower Bockhampton	**Old Melchester**	Old Sarum
Lulwind Cove (Lulstead)	Lulworth Cove	**Oozewood**	Ringwood, Hampshire
Lumsdon	Cumnor	**Overcombe**	Sutton Poyntz
Lyonesse, Isles of	Scilly Isles	**Oxwell**	Poxwell
Maidun Castle	Maiden Castle	**Pen-zephyr**	Penzance

Port-Bredy	Bridport
Pos'ham	Portisham
Pummery	Poundbury, Dorchester
Pure Drop Inn	The Crown, Marnhull
Quartershot	Aldershot
Red King's Castle	Rufus Castle, or Bow-and-Arrow Castle, Portland
Redrutin	Redruth, Cornwall
Reveller's Inn	Revels Farm, near Middlemarsh and Minterne Magna
Ringsworth	Ringstead Bay, 5 ½ miles ENE of Weymouth
Rookington Park	Hern Court, near Christchurch, Hants.
Roy-Town	Troy Town, 3 ½ miles NE of Dorchester
Sandbourne	Bournemouth
Scrimpton	Frampton
Shadwater Weir (also Great Pool, Shadwater Weir)	The Weir, Woodsford Meadows, 4 miles E of Dorchester, on the River Frome
Shaston	Shaftesbury
Sherton Abbas	Sherborne
Shottsford Forum	Blandford Forum
Sleeping Green	Carhampton or Withycombe, Somerset
Solentsea	Southsea
Springham	Warmwell, 4 miles SE of Dorchester
Stagfoot Lane	Hartford Lane, near Marnhull
St. Aldhem's Head	St. Alban's Head
St. Launce's	Launceston
St. Maria's	St. Mary's (Scilly Isles)
Stancy Castle	Dunster Castle
Stapleford	Stalbridge
Stickleford	Tincleton, 1 ½ miles SSE of *Weatherbury*
Stoke-Barehills	Basingstoke
Stourcastle	Sturminster Newton
Street of Wells	Fortune's Well, Portland
Sylvania Castle	Pennsylvania Castle, Portland
Talbothays Farm	Norris Hill Farm, by Dorchester (Lea, however, stated that the dairy house was "drawn from no particular building"; Cox, quoted in Barber, 178)
Targan Bay	Pentargen Bay, Cornwall
Tivworthy	Tiverton, Devon
Tolchurch	Tolpuddle
Toneborough	Taunton
Tor-upon-Sea	Torquay
Trantridge	Pentridge
Trufal, Trufoe	Truro
Upper Longpuddle	Piddletrenthide
Upper Mellstock	Higher Bockhampton
Vindilia	Portland
Warborne	Wimborne
Warm'ell Cross	Warmwell Cross
Weatherbury	Puddletown, 4½ miles NE of Dorchester
Weatherbury Farm	Waterson House, ½ miles W of Puddletown
Welland House	Charborough House, near Wimborne Minster
Wellbridge Abbey	Bindon Abbey
Wellbridge House	Woolbridge House, near Wool
Wellbridge Abbey and Mill	Woolbridge Abbey and Mill
West Endelstow	St. Juliot Church, Cornwall
Weydon Priors	Weyhill, near Andover
Windy Beak	Cambeak, a cliff near Boscastle, Cornwall
Wintoncester	Winchester
Yalbury Hill	Yellowham Hill, near Dorchester
Yalbury Wood	Yellowhampton Wood, 3 miles NE of Dorchester
Yewsholt Lodge	Farrs House, 1½ miles W of Wimborne Minster

APPENDIX VI

Translations of Thomas Hardy's Works

Source: The following information comes from World Cat database, accessed online through the Online Computer Library Center.

Novels

Desperate Remedies (1871)

Russian:
Otchaiannye sredstva. Trans. I. Trenevoi. Moscow: Khudozhestvennaia lit-ra, 1969.

Far from the Madding Crowd (1874)

Basque:
Zoritxarreko amodioak. Trans. Iñaki Mendiguren. Donostia: ELKAR, 1988.

Chinese:
Yuan li chen xiao. Trans. Clare West and Jiaolan Wang. Beijing: Wai yu jiao xue yu yan jiu chu ban she, Niu jin da xue chu ban she, 1999.

Czech:
Daleko od hlucícího davu. Trans. Jarmila Rosíková. Prague: Svoboda (Rudé Právo), 1981.

German:
Am Grünen Rand der Welt. Translator not given. Munich: Deutscher Taschenbuch Verlag, 1984.

Korean:
Kwanglan ui Mulilul Meolli Hako. Trans. Hoe-jin Kim. Seoul: Yongpung Munko, 1997.

The Hand of Ethelberta (1876)

Japanese:
Eserubata no Te. Trans. Tomoko Tachibana. Tokyo: Senjo, 1991.

Jude the Obscure (1895)

Chinese:
Wu ming ti Ch'iu-te. Trans. Ku-jo Chang. Beijing: Jen min wen hsüeh ch'u pan she, 1958. *Wu ming ti Ch'iu-te.* Trans. Ku-jo Chang. Tienjin: Pai hua wen i ch'u pan she, 1981.
Wu ming di Qiude. Trans. (Yingguo) Hadai zhu, Zhang Guruo yi. Beijing: Ren min wen xue chu ban she, 1995.

Croatian:
Neslavni Jude. Zagreb, Yugoslavia: Zora, 1964.

Czech:
Neblahý Juda. Translator not given. Prague: Státní nakladatelství krásné literatury, hudby a umení, 1956.
Neblahý Juda. Trans. Marta Stanková; [? Kveta Marysková]. Prague: SNKLU (Svoboda 1), 1963.

French:
Jude l'obscur. Trans. Firmin Roz. Paris: Ollendorff, 1901.
Jude l'obscur. Trans. F. W. Laparra; preface by Edmond Jaloux. Paris: Albin Michel, 1996.
Jude l'obscur. Trans. Firmin Roz and Hélène Seyrès. Paris: L'Archipel, 1996.

German:
Juda, der unberuhmte. Trans. A. Berger. Stuttgart, 1901.

Japanese:
Judo:ningen'ai no shukumei higeki. Trans. Yutaro Ito. Tokyo: Daidokan Shoten, 1927.
Hikagemono Judo. Trans. Mamoru Osawa. Tokyo: Iwanami Shoten, 1970.
Hikagemono Judo. Trans. Seiichi Kobayashi. Tokyo: Senjo, 1988.
Hikagemono Judo. Trans. Shizuko Kawamoto. Tokyo: Kokusho Kankokai, 1988.

Korean:
Piwhun ui Jude. Trans. Hoe-jin Kim. Seoul: Yongpung Munko, 1997.

Polish:
Juda nieznany. Trans. Ewa Kolaczkowska. Warsaw: Panstwowy Instytut Wydawniczy, 1997.

Portuguese:
Judas, o obscura. Trans. Maria Franco e Cabral do Nascimento. Lisbon: Portugália Editora, 1965.
Judas, o obscuro. Trans. Octavio de Faria. São Paulo: Abril Cultural, 1971.

Spanish:
Jude, l'obscur. Trans. Quim Monzó. Barcelona: Edicions 62, 1997.

The Mayor of Casterbridge (1886)

Chinese:

Kasiteqiao shi zhang. Trans. L. H. Mei-yüeh kai hsieh; Xiaobao yi. Shanghai: Shanghai yi wen chu ban she, 1989.

K'a-ssu-t'e-ch'iao shih chang. Trans. Shih-heng. Shanghai: Shang-hai ch'u pan kung ssu, 1955.

Czech:

Starosta casterbridgeský. Trans. Jarmila Emmerová. Prague: Tok, 1999.

French:

Le Maire de Casterbridge: Histoire d'un homme de caractère. Trans. Philippe Neel. Paris: Gallimard, 1957.

German:

Der Bürgermeister von Casterbridge: Leben u. Tod e. Mannes von Charakter. Trans. Eva-Maria König. Stuttgart: Reclam, 1985.

Meistererzhlungen. Trans. Rainer Zerbst. Zurich: Manesse-Verl., 1988.

Japanese:

Kasutaburiji no Shicho. Trans. Kazuo Ueda, Tokyo: Ushio Shuppansha, 1971.

Polish:

Burmistrz Casterbridge. Trans. Ewa Kolaczkowska. Warsaw: Panstwowy Instytut Wydawn., 1959.

Spanish:

El alcalde de Casterbridge. Trans. Ramón Echeverría. Buenos Aires: Sudamericana, 1941.

A Pair of Blue Eyes (1873)

French:

Les yeux bleus. Trans. Georges Goldfayn. Paris: J. Losfeld, 1997.

The Return of the Native (1878)

Chinese:

Huan xiang. Trans. Guruo Zhang. Beijing: Ren min wen xue chu ban she, 1958.

Ku li jen kuei. Trans. Ch'ing-chih Liang. Taipei: Cheng chung shu chü, 1960.

Huan hsiang chi. Trans. Hsüeh-men Ch'en. Taipei: Cheng wen shu chü, 1972.

Huan hsiang. Trans. Ku-jo Chang. Beijing. Jen min wen hsüeh ch'u pan she, 1980.

Xiao shuo./Yi zi. Trans. Shouren Wang. Nanjing Yi lin chu ban she, 1997.

Gui xiang ji. David Oliphant. Abridged edition in cartoon format. Taipei: Lu qiao wen hua shi ye you xian gong si, 1998.

French:

Le Retour au pays natal. Trans. Marie Canavaggia. Paris: Nouvelles éd., 1980.

Italian:

La brughiera. Trans. Ada Prospero. Milan: Garzanti, 1981.

Japanese:

Kikyo. Trans. Mamoru Osawa. Tokyo: Kawade Shobo, 1955.

Korean:

Kuehyang. Trans. Pyung-jo Chong. Seoul: Ulyou Muhwasa, 1998.

Punjabi:

Pa watanam wala phera. Trans. Pritama Singha. Lahore: Pañjaba Kitaba Ghara, 1944.

Persian:

Bazgasht i bumy. Trans. tarjumah'i sirvan Azad. Tehran: Nashr-i Nuw, 1990.

Tess of the d'Urbervilles (1891)

Chinese:

T'ai-ssu. Trans. Ku-jo Chang. Shanghai: Wen hua kung tso she, 1953.

Te-po-chia ti T'ai-ssu. Trans. Ku-jo Chang. Shanghai: Hsiang-Kay, 1960. Republished Beijing: Jen min wen hsüeh ch'u pan she, 1980.

Tai-ssu ku niang. Trans. Pi-yün Sung. Taipei: Yüan ching ch'u pan shih yeh kung ssu, 1980.

Debo jia di Taisi. Trans. Dimu Huo'er gai xie; Zhou Lingyi yi. Shanghai: Shanghai yi wen chu ban she, 1983.

Debo jia di Taisi. Trans. Guruo Zhang. Beijing: Ren min wen xue chu ban she, 1984.

Daisi gu niang. Trans. Wu Zhengyi, Lü Yuqin. Tainani: Da qian wen hua chu ban shi ye gong si, 1992.

Te-po chia ti T'ai-ssu. Trans. Ch'ing-pang Liu. Beijing: Hua-hsia ch'u pan she, 1994.

Daisi gu niang. Trans. Hadai zhu. Tainani: Xiang yi chu ban she, 1996.

Dai-si gu niang. Trans. Sun Zhili and Tang Huixin yi. Taipei: Lin yu wen hua shi ye you xian gong si, 1997.

Czech:

Tess z d'Urbervillu. Trans. Josef J. David. Prague: Aventinum, 1927.

Finnish:

Tessin Tarina. Trans. Uuno Aleksanteri Varis. Helsinki: Kustannusosakeyhtiö otava, 1909.

French:

Tess d'Urberville. Trans. Madeleine Rolland. Paris: Hachette, 1901.

Tess d'Urberville. Trans. Madeleine Rolland 1901. Reprint, Paris: Je sers, 1951.

Tess d'Urberville. Trans. Madeleine Rolland 1901. Reprint, Paris: Le livre de poche, 1974.

Japanese:

Tesu. Trans. Tokuboku Hirata. 2 vols. Tokyo: Kokuminbunko Kankokai, 1925, 1926.

Tesu. Trans. Shinzaburo Miyajima. Tokyo: Shinchosha, 1933.

Tesu. Trans. Michinosuke Takeuchi. Tokyo: Mikasa Shobo, 1951.

Tesu. Trans. Yoshio Yamauchi. 2 vols. Tokyo: Kadokawa Shoten, 1957.

Tesu [and "Alicia's Diary"]. Trans. Kin'ichi Ishikawa, Ichiro Kono. Tokyo: Kawade Shobo, 1967.

Tesu. Trans. Sakiko Nakamura. Tokyo: Obunsha, 1972.

Tesu. Trans. Soji Inoue and Eiji Ishida. Tokyo: Iwanami Shoten, 1960; rpt. 1981.

Dababiruke no Tesu. Trans. Seiichi Kobayashi. Tokyo: Senjo, 1989.

Korean:

Tess. Trans. Tae-yong yok Yi. Seoul: Chubu Saenghwalsa, 1971.

Tess. Trans. Pyong-jo Chong. Seoul: Tonghwa Ch'ulp'an Kongsa, 1973.

Tess. Trans. In-sop Chong. Seoul: Tongso Munhwasa, 1974.

Tess oe. Trans. Chang-hwan Yi. Seoul: Chongumsa, 1979.

Nat'asya K'insuk'i ui T'esu. Trans. Kwang-je An. Seoul: Kaesonun Ch'ulp'ansa, 1981.

Tess. Trans. Hoe-jin Kim. Seoul: Pomusa, 1981.

Tess. Trans. Hyok Chong. Seoul: Kumsong Ch'ulp'ansa, 1984.

Tess. Trans. Man-p'yong Kim. Seoul: Ch'ongmoksa, 1985.

Tess. Trans. Sin-gwon Cho. Seoul: Samsongdang, 1988.

Tess. Trans. Un-bin Maeng. Seoul: Ilsin Sojok Kongsa, 1988.

Tess. Trans. Jin-sok Lee. Seoul: Chongmoksa, 1989.

Tess. Trans. Yong-chul Kim. Seoul: Ulyou Munhwasa, 1989.

Tess. Trans. Hye-sook Kang. Seoul: Haseo Ch'ulp'ansa. 1990.

Tess. Trans. Un-bin Haeng. Seoul: Ilsin Sojok Kongsa, 1990.

Tess. Trans. Ka-hyong Yi. Seoul: Umungak, 1990.

Tess. Trans. Ho-kyu Lee. Seoul: Hyewon Ch'ulp'ansa, 1991.

Tess. Trans. Sung-ho Chong. Seoul: Onul, 1991.

Tess. Trans. Dae-Hyun Sin. Seoul: Hongsin Munhwasa, 1992.

Tess. Trans. Dal-sik Choi. Seoul: Kyoyuk Munhwa Yeonkuhoe, 1994.

Tess. Trans. Dong-in Lee. Seoul: Sodam Ch'ulp'ansa, 1994.

Tess. Trans. Ka-hyong Yi. Seoul: Hagwonsa, 1994.

Tess. Trans. Hoe-jin Kim. Seoul: Pomusa, 1994.

Tess. Trans. O-sok Kwon. Seoul: Taeil Ch'ulp'ansa, 1995.

Tess. Trans. O-sok Kwon. Seoul: Taeil Ch'ulp'ansa, 1997.

Tess. Trans. Hyun-sun Pong. Seoul: Hyewon Ch'ulp'ansa, 1998.

Tess. Trans. Po-won Kim. Seoul: Daehakkyo Ch'ulp'anbu, 2000.

Tess. Trans. Jung-hwan Kim. Seoul: Yukmunsa, 2000.

Persian:

Tiss. Trans. Mina Sarabi. Tehran: Nashr-i Dunya-yi Naw, 1997.

Romanian:

Tess d'Urberville. Chisinau: Eus, 1993.

Russian:

Tess iz roda d'Erbervillei. Trans. A. Krivtsovoi. Kaliningrad: Kaliningradskoe Knizhnoe Izdatel'stvo, 1994.

Spanish:

Tess d'Uberville. Trans. Javier Franco Aixelá. Madrid: Ediciones Temas de Hoy, 1994.

The Trumpet-Major (1880)

French:

Le Trompette-Major. Trans. Yorik Bernard-Derosne. Paris: Hachette: 1885.

Two on a Tower (1882)

French:

A la lumière des étoiles. Trans. Marie Cresciani. Paris: Nouvelles éditions Oswald, 1981.

Japanese:

Tojo no Futari. Trans. Shigeshi Fujii, Tokyo: Senjo, 1987.

Romanian:

Idila pe un turn. Trans. Antoaneta Ralian. Bucharest: Editura Eminescu, 1988.

Under the Greenwood Tree (1872)

Japanese:

Midori no Kokage: Oranda-ha den'enga. Trans. Tomoji Abe. Tokyo: Iwanami Shoten, 1936. Reprinted, 1951.

Polish:

Pod drzewem, pod zielonym. Trans. Ewa Kolaczkowska. Warszw: Panstwowy Instytut Wydawn, 1957.

The Well-Beloved (1892)

French:

La bien-aimée. Trans. Eve Paul-Margueritte. Paris: Plon, 1909.

Japanese:

Koitama. Trans. Sueno Takiyama, Tomoko Tachibana. Tokyo: Senjo, 1988.

The Woodlanders (1887)

French:

Les Forestiers. Trans. Antoinette Six. Paris: Nouvelles éditions Oswald, 1980.
Les Forestiers. Trans. Antoinette Six and Robert Sctrick. Paris: Phebux, 1996.

Japanese:

Mori ni Sumu hitobito. Trans. Masanobu Oda. Tokyo: Kawade Shobo, 1940.

Poetry

The Dynasts (Verse Drama) (1904, 1906, 1908)

Chinese:

T'ung chih che. Trans Heng Tu. Shanghai: Shang wu yin shu kuan, 1936.

Japanese:

Sho'o no Fu. Trans Yasuo Nagatani. Tokyo: Seibido, 1979.

Collected Poems

French:

Poésies. Trans. Marie-Hélène Gourlaouen, Bernard Géniès. Paris: Les Formes du secret, 1980.

Japanese:

Tomasu Hadi Zenshishu. Trans. Kensuke Morimatsu. 2 vols. Tokyo: Chuo University Press, 1995.

Human Shows

Japanese:

Ningen no Kyoen. Trans. Sueno Takiyama, Tomoko Tachibana, Tokyo: Senjo, 1992.

Satires of Circumstance

Japanese:

Kyogu no Fuushi. Trans. Sueno Takiyama, Tomoko Tachibana. Tokyo: Senjo, 1989.

Moments of Vision

Italian:

Momenti di visione: identità poetica e forme della poesia in Thomas Hardy: ottanta liriche con testo a fronte. Trans. Maria Stella. Milano: FrancoAngeli, 1992.

Short Fiction

"A Changed Man"

Japanese:

"Kawarihateta Otoko to hokano monogatari." Trans. Shigeyuki Oenoki, Yoshitsugu Uchida. Osaka: Osaka Kyoiku Tosho, 2000.

"A Group of Noble Dames"

French:

"Nobles dames, nobles amours." Trans. Françoise Dottin. Befort: Circé, 1997.

Japanese:

Kifujin no Mure. Trans. Yasushi Kamiyama, Yoshitsugu Uchida. Tokyo: Senjo, 1983.

"Alicia's Diary" (with Tess of the d'Urbervilles)

Japanese:

"Arishia no nikki hoka." Trans. Kin'ichi Ishikawa, Ichiro Kono. Tokyo: Kawade Shobo, 1967.
Wesekusu Monogatari. Trans. Shigeru Fujita, Yoshitsugu Uchida and others. Osaka: Osaka Kyoiku Tosho, 2001.

Korean:

"Alisa ui ilgi." Trans. Soul T'ukpyolsi: Tongso Munhwasa, 1974.

"An Imaginative Woman"

Korean:

"Hwansang ul tchotnun yoin." Trans. Tongso Munhwasa. Seoul: 1974.

"Life's Little Ironies"

Jinsei no Chiisana Hiniku. Trans. Seiichi Kobayashi. Osaka: Sogensha, 1984.

"The Melancholy Hussar of the German Legion"

Korean:

"Uulhan kyonggibyong." Trans. Tongso Munhwasa. Seoul: 1974.

"Old Mrs. Chundle"

Japanese:

Chandoru Baasan. Trans. Seiichi Kobayashi, kenji tachiya, Yoshitsugu Uchida. Tokyo: Senjo, 1985.
Chandoru Baasan to hokano monogatari [with *The Famous Tragedy of Queen of Cornwall*]. Trans. Shigeyuki Oenoki, Yoshitsugu Uchida. Osaka: Osaka Kyoiku Tosho, 2001.

"Our Exploits at West Poley"

Spanish:

"Nuestras hazañas en la cueva." Trans. Juan M. San Miguel. Madrid: Editorial Escuela Espanõla, 1987.

The Short Stories of Thomas Hardy

Chinese:
Ha-tai tuan p'ien hsiao shuo chi. Trans. Li-fu Wu. Shanghai: Shang-hai i wen ch'u pan she, 1985.

"The Three Strangers"

Scottish Gaelic:
"An triuir choigreach." Trans. John G. MacKinnon. Edinburgh: T. agus A. Constable, 1944.

"To Please His Wife"

Korean:
"Anae rul wihayo." Trans. Tongso Munhwasa. Seoul: 1974.

Wessex Tales

French:
Contes du Wessex. Trans. Pierre Leyris. Paris: Imprimerie nationale, 1995.

Japanese:
Wesekusu Monogatari. Trans. Seiichi Kobayashi, Katsuya Taki, Kenji Tachiya, Yoshitsugu Uchida. Tokyo: Senjo, 1987 Wessekusu.

"The Withered Arm"

Chinese:
"Hadai xiang tu xiao shuo." Trans. Lin Zhang. Shanghai: Shanghai wen yi chu ban she, 1997.

Korean:
"Choju padun p'al." Trans. In-sop Chong. Seoul: Tongso Munhwasa, 1974.

Short Stories (Selected stories)

French:
Sous le regard du berger: Recueil de nouvelles. Trans. Pierre Coustillas et al. Lille: Presses universitaires de Lille, 1984.

Japanese:
Hadi Kessaku Tanpenshu. Trans. Seiichi Kobayashi. Osaka: Sogensha, 1984.
Hadi Tanpenshu. Trans. Hiroyuki Ide. Tokyo: Iwanami Shoten, 2000.

APPENDIX VII

Bibliography

I. Works by Thomas Hardy

Only first editions are listed.

A. Novels

Desperate Remedies. London: Tinsley Brothers, 1871.
Far from the Madding Crowd. London: Smith, Elder, 1874.
The Hand of Ethelberta. London: Smith, Elder, 1876.
Jude the Obscure. London: Osgood, Mcilvaine, 1895.
A Laodicean. London: Sampson Low, Marston, Searle & Rivington, 1881.
The Mayor of Casterbridge. London: Smith, Elder, 1886.
A Pair of Blue Eyes. London: Tinsley Brothers, 1873.
The Return of the Native. London: Smith, Elder, 1878.
The Trumpet-Major. London: Smith, Elder, 1880.
Tess of the d'Urbervilles. London: Osgood, McIlvaine, 1891.
Two on a Tower. London: Sampson Low, Marston, Searle & Rivington, 1883.
Under the Greenwood Tree. London: Tinsley Brothers, 1872.
The Well-Beloved. London: Osgood, McIlvaine, 1897.
The Woodlanders. London: Macmillan, 1887.

B. Short Fiction

A Changed Man and Other Tales. London: Macmillan, 1913.
A Group of Noble Dames. London: Osgood, McIlvaine, 1891.
Life's Little Ironies. London: Osgood, McIlvaine, 1894.
Wessex Tales. London: Macmillan, 1888.
Our Exploits at West Poley. Oxford, U.K.: Oxford University Press, 1952. *The Household,* Boston, Nov. 1892–Apr. 1893. (Although book length at more than 20,000 words, this work was not published in book form during Hardy's lifetime.)

C. Poetry

Human Shows, Far Phantasies, Songs, and Trifles. London: Macmillan, 1925.
Late Lyrics and Earlier. London: Macmillan, 1922.
Moments of Vision and Miscellaneous Verses. London: Macmillan, 1917.
Poems of the Past and Present. London: Harper & Brothers, 1902.
Satires of Circumstance (including *Poems of 1912–1913*). London: Macmillan, 1914.
Selected Poems of Thomas Hardy. London: Macmillan, 1916.

Time's Laughingstocks and Other Verses. London: Macmillan, 1909.
Wessex Poems and Other Verses. London: Harper & Brothers, 1898.
Winter Words. Published posthumously. London: Macmillan, 1928.

D. Dramatic Works

The Dynasts: a Drama of the Napoleonic Wars, in three parts, nineteen acts, & one hundred and thirty scenes. London: Macmillan, Ltd.: Part I, 1904; Part II, 1906; Part III, 1908).
The Famous Tragedy of the Queen of Cornwall. London: Macmillan, 1923.
The Three Wayfarers (a dramatization of Hardy's short story "The Three Strangers"). New York: Harper & Brothers, 1893.

E. Collected Editions

Only collected editions published during the lifetime of Thomas Hardy are listed here.

For miscellaneous uncollected contributions to books, periodicals, and newspapers, including obituaries, prefaces to the works of others, addresses, biographical notes, symposia, and sketches, *see* Richard Purdy, *Thomas Hardy: A Bibliographical Study* (Oxford, U.K.: Oxford University Press, 1954), 289–325.
Collected Poems. London: Macmillan, Ltd., 1919.
Mellstock Edition. (37 vols.) London: Macmillan, 1919–1920.
The Short Stories of Thomas Hardy. London: Macmillan, 1928, a reprinting of four earlier collections published posthumously on March 23, 1928.
Wessex Edition (24 vols.) London: Macmillan, 1912–1931.
The Wessex Novels (16 vols.) London: Osgood, McIlvaine, 1895–1896.

F. Other Works

The Architectural Notebook of Thomas Hardy. Foreword by Sir John Summerson; introduction by C. J. P. Beatty. Dorchester: Dorset Natural History & Archaeological Society, 1966.
The Collected Letters of Thomas Hardy. Edited by Richard Little Purdy and Michael Millgate. 7 vols. Oxford: Clarendon Press, 1978–1988.
The Early Life of Thomas Hardy, 1840–1891. London: Macmillan, 1928. (Compiled by Florence Hardy; now recognized

as the work of Thomas Hardy, along with *The Later Years of Thomas Hardy, 1892–1928*. Published as one volume in 1962.)

"General Preface to the Novels and Poems," Wessex Edition, I, 1912. Reprinted in *Thomas Hardy's Personal Writings*. Edited by Harold Orel. Lawrence: University of Kansas Press, 1966.

The Later Years of Thomas Hardy, 1892–1928. London: Macmillan, 1930. (*See The Early Life of Thomas Hardy, 1840–1891*; both volumes now recognized as the work of Thomas Hardy.)

Life and Art by Thomas Hardy. Essays, Notes, and Letters collected for the first time with introduction by Ernest Brennecke Jr. New York: Greenberg, 1925.

The Life and Work of Thomas Hardy. Edited by Michael Millgate. Athens: University of Georgia Press, 1985.

The Literary Notebooks of Thomas Hardy. Edited by Lennart A. Björk. New York: New York University Press, 1985. (Originally published as *The Literary Notes of Thomas Hardy*. Göteborg, Sweden: Acta Universitatis Gothoburgensis, 1974).

The Personal Notebooks of Thomas Hardy. Edited by Richard H. Taylor. New York: Columbia University Press, 1979.

Select Poems of William Barnes: Chosen and Edited, with a preface and glossarial notes, by Thomas Hardy. London: Henry Frowde, 1908.

Thomas Hardy: Selected Letters. Edited by Michael Millgate. Oxford: Clarendon Press, 1990.

II. Secondary sources

Adey, Lionel. "Styles of Love in *Far from the Madding Crowd*." *Thomas Hardy Annual* 5 (1987): 47–62.

Ahmad, Suleiman. Far from the Madding Crowd *in the British Provincial Theatre. Thomas Hardy Journal* 16, no. 1 (Feb. 2000).

Alexander, Edward. "Fin de siècle; fin du globe: Yeats and Hardy in the Nineties." *Bucknell Review* 23, no. 2 (1977): 142–63.

Allingham, Philip V. "Robert Barnes' Illustrations for Thomas Hardy's *The Mayor of Casterbridge* as Serialised in *The Graphic*." *Victorian Periodicals Review* 28, no. 1 (spring 1995): 27–39.

———. "The Significance of 'Darkling' in Hardy's 'The Darkling Thrush.'" *Thomas Hardy Journal* 7, no. 1 (Feb. 1991): 45–49.

———. "Six Original Illustrations for Hardy's *Tess of the D'Urbervilles* Drawn by Sir Hubert Von Herkomer, R. A., for *The Graphic* (1891)." *Thomas Hardy Journal* 10, no. 1 (Feb. 1994): 52–70.

Amos, Arthur K. "Accident and Fate: The Possibility for Action in *A Pair of Blue Eyes*." *English Literature in Transition (1880–1920)* 15 (1972): 158–67.

Arkans, Norman. "Hardy's Poetic Landscapes." *Colby Library Quarterly* 15 (1979): 19–35.

Armstrong, Tim. "Hardy, Thaxter, and History as Coincidence in 'The Convergence of the Twain.'" *Victorian Poetry* 30 no. 1 (spring 1992): 29–42.

Asker, D. B. D. "'The Birds Shall Have Some Dinner': Animals in Hardy's Fiction." *Dutch Quarterly Review of Anglo-American Letters* (Amsterdam, Netherlands) 10 (1980): 215–29.

Atkinson, F. G. "'The Inevitable Movement Onward'—Some Aspects of *The Return of the Native*." *Thomas Hardy Yearbook* (Guernsey, Channel Islands, U.K.) 3 (1972–73): 10–17.

Austin, Linda M. "Hardy's Laodicean Narrative," *Modern Fiction Studies* 35, no. 2 (summer 1989): 211–22.

Babb, Howard. "Setting and Theme in *Far from the Madding Crowd*." *English Literary History* 30 (1963): 147–61.

Bailey, James O. *The Poetry of Thomas Hardy: A Handbook and Commentary*. Chapel Hill: University of North Carolina Press, 1970.

Bailey, James O., and Norman Page. "'Wessex Heights' Visited and Revisited," *English Literature in Transition* 15 (1972): 57–62.

Ball, David. "Tragic Contradiction in Hardy's *The Woodlanders*." *Ariel: A Review of International English Literature* (Calgary, Alberta, Canada) 18, no. 1 (Jan. 1987): 17–25.

Barber, D. F., ed. *Concerning Thomas Hardy: A Composite Portrait from Memory*. London: Charles Skilton Ltd., 1968. (Contains glossary of place-names compiled by J. Stevens Cox.)

Barloon, Jim. "Star-Crossed Love: The Gravity of Science in Hardy's *Two on a Tower*." *Victorian Newsletter* 94 (fall 1998), 27–32.

Baron, David. "Hardy and the Dorchester Pouncys." *Somerset and Dorset Notes & Queries* (March 1981).

Bartle, G. F. "Some Fresh Information about Tryphena Sparks: Thomas Hardy's Cousin." *Notes and Queries* 30 (Aug. 1983): 320–22.

Bartlett, Phyllis. "Hardy's Shelley." *Keats-Shelley Journal* 4 (winter 1955): 15–29.

Baugner, Ulla. *A Study on the Use of Dialects in Thomas Hardy's Novels and Short Stories with Special Reference to Phonology & Vocabulary*. Stockholm: Stockholm University Press, 1972.

Bawer, Bruce. "*Two on a Tower*: Hardy and Yeats." *Yeats-Eliot Review* 7, nos. 1–2 (June 1982): 91–108.

Bayley, John. "The Love Story in *Two on a Tower*." In *Thomas Hardy Annual*. Edited by Norman Page. 1 (1982): 60–70.

Beatty, C. J. P. "Colonel Waugh and *A Laodicean*." *Thomas Hardy Yearbook* 1 (1970): 19–21.

———. "The Tranter's Cottage in *Under the Greenwood Tree*," *Notes and Queries* 10 (1963): 26.

Beebe, Maurice, Bonnie Culotta, and Erin Marcus. "Criticism of Thomas Hardy: A Selected Check-List." *Modern Fiction Studies* 5 (autumn 1960): 258–79.

Beegel, Susan. "Bathsheba's Lovers: Male Sexuality in *Far from the Madding Crowd*." *Tennessee Studies in Literature* 27 (1984): 108–27.

Benazon, Michael. "Dark and Fair: Character Contrast in Hardy's 'Fiddler of the Reels.'" *Ariel: A Review of International English Literature* 9, no. 2 (1978): 75–82.

———. "'The Romantic Adventures of a Milkmaid': Hardy's Modern Romance." *English Studies in Canada* 5 (1979): 56–65.

Benvenuto, Richard. "Modes of Perception: The Will to Live in *Jude the Obscure*." *Studies in the Novel* 2, no. 1 (1970): 31–41.

Benzing, Rosemary. "In Defence of 'Tess.'" *Contemporary Review* (London) 218 (1971): 202–204.

Betjeman, John. "Hardy and Architecture." In *The Genius of Thomas Hardy*. Edited by Margaret Drabble. New York: Alfred A. Knopf, 1976.

Blishen, Edward. "Hardy, *The Hand of Ethelberta*, and Some Persisting English Discomforts." In *Celebrating Thomas Hardy: Insights and Appreciations*. Edited by Charles Pettit. New York: St. Martin's Press, 1996.

Bloom, Harold, ed. *Modern Critical Interpretations: Thomas Hardy's "Jude the Obscure."* New York: Chelsea House, 1987.

———. *Modern Critical Interpretations: Thomas Hardy's "The Mayor of Casterbridge."* New York: Chelsea House, 1988.

———. *Modern Critical Interpretations: Thomas Hardy's "The Return of the Native."* New York: Chelsea House, 1987.

Blythe, Ronald. *A Pair of Blue Eyes*. London: Macmillan, 1975.

Boumelha, Penny. "'A Complicated Position for a Woman': *The Hand of Ethelberta*." In *The Sense of Sex: Feminist Perspectives on Hardy*. Edited by Margaret R. Higgonet. Urbana: University of Illinois Press, 1993.

———. "The Patriarchy of Class: *Under the Greenwood Tree, Far from the Madding Crowd, The Woodlanders*." In *The Cambridge Companion to Thomas Hardy*. Edited by Dale Kramer. Cambridge: Cambridge University Press, 1999.

———. "*Tess of the d'Urbervilles*': Sexual Ideology and Narrative Form." In *Tess of the d'Urbervilles/Thomas Hardy*. Edited by Peter Widdowson. New York: St. Martin's Press, 1993.

———. *Thomas Hardy and Women: Sexual Ideology and Narrative Form*. Totowa, N.J.: Barnes & Noble, 1982.

Brady, Kristin. *The Short Stories of Thomas Hardy: Tales of Past and Present*. London: Macmillan, 1982.

———. "Thomas Hardy and Matters of Gender." In *The Cambridge Companion to Thomas Hardy*. Edited by Dale Kramer. Cambridge: Cambridge University Press, 1999.

Brennecke, Ernest. *The Life of Thomas Hardy*. New York: Greenberg, 1925.

———. *Thomas Hardy's Universe: A Study of a Poet's Mind*. New York: Haskell House, 1996.

———, ed. *Life and Art: By Thomas Hardy*. New York: Greenberg, 1925.

Brooks, Jean. *Thomas Hardy: The Poetic Structure*. Ithaca, N.Y.: Cornell University Press, 1971.

Brown, Joanna Cullen, ed. *Figures in a Wessex Landscape: Thomas Hardy's Picture of English Country Life*. London: W. H. Allen, 1987.

Buckler, William E. *The Poetry of Thomas Hardy: A Study in Art and Ideas*. New York: New York University Press, 1983.

Bulaila, Abdul Aziz M. "'The Clay but Not the Potter': Love and Marriage in *The Well-Beloved*." *Thomas Hardy Journal*, 9, no. 2 (May 1993): 61–71.

Burns, R. A. "Imagery in Hardy's 'The Darkling Thrush.'" *Concerning Poetry* (Bellingham, Wash.), 10, no. 1 (1977): 87–89.

Butler, Lance St. John. *Thomas Hardy*. Cambridge, U.K.: Cambridge University Press, 1978.

Campbell, Matthew. "Tennyson and Hardy's Ghostly Metres." *Essays in Criticism: A Quarterly Journal of Literary Criticism* 42, no. 4 (Oct. 1992): 279–98.

Campbell, Michael L. "Thomas Hardy's Attitude toward Animals." *Victorians Institute Journal* (Norfolk, Va.; now at Greenville, N.C.) 2 (1973): 61–71.

Carpenter, Richard C. "Hardy's 'Gurgoyles.'" *Modern Fiction Studies*, 6, no. 3 (autumn 1960): 223–32.

———. "How to Read A Few Crusted Characters." In *Critical Approaches to the Fiction of Thomas Hardy*. Edited by Dale Kramer. London: Macmillan, 1979.

———. "The Mirror and the Sword: Imagery in *Far from the Madding Crowd*." *Nineteenth Century Literature* 18 (1964): 331–45.

———. *Thomas Hardy*. New York: Twayne, 1964.

Carter, Kenneth, and June M. Whetherly. *Thomas Hardy Catalogue: A List of the Books by and about Thomas Hardy, O.M. (1840–1928) in Dorset County Library*. 2nd ed. Dorset, England: Dorset County Council, 1973.

Casagrande, Peter J. "The Fourteenth Line of 'In Tenebris, II.'" *Thomas Hardy Annual* 2 (1984): 110–30.

———. "'Something More to Be Said': Hardy's Creative Process and the Case of Tess and Jude" In *New Perspectives on Thomas Hardy*. Edited by Charles Pettit. New York: St. Martin's Press, 1994.

Cecil, Lord David. *Hardy, the Novelist: An Essay in Criticism*. London: Constable, 1943.

Chase, Mary Ellen. *Thomas Hardy from Serial to Novel*. New York: Russell & Russell, 1927.

Chew, Samuel C. *Thomas Hardy, Poet and Novelist*. New York: Alfred A. Knopf, 1928.

———. *The Nineteenth Century and After (1789–1939)*, vol. IV of *A Literary History of England*. Edited by Albert C. Baugh. New York: Appleton-Century-Crofts, 1948.

Clarke, Graham, ed. *Thomas Hardy: Critical Assessments of Writers in English*. Vol. 1: *The Contemporary Response;* Vol. 2: *Writer and Poet;* Vol. 3: *Writers, Writing, and Wessex;* Vol. 4: *Twentieth Century Overview*. Mountfield, East Sussex: Helm Information, 1993.

Clements, Patricia, and Juliet Grindle, *The Poetry of Thomas Hardy*. Totowa, N.J.: Barnes & Noble, 1980.

Clodd, Edward. *Memories*. New York: G. P. Putnam, 1916.

Collier, James G. "Thomas Hardy's *The Famous Tragedy of the Queen of Cornwall*: Its Artistry and Relation to His Life, Thought, and Works." In *Dissertation Abstracts International* (Chapel Hill, N.C.) 31 (1971): 6005A–06A.

Collins, Philip. "Hardy and Education." In *Thomas Hardy: The Writer and His Background*. Edited by Norman Page. New York: St. Martin's Press, 1980.

Collins, Vere. *Talks with Thomas Hardy at Max Gate, 1920–1922*. Garden City, N.Y.: Doubleday, Doran 1928. Reprinted, St. Peter Port, Guernsey, Channel Islands, U.K.: Toucan, 1971.

Combs, John R. "Cleaving in Hardy's 'The Convergence of the Twain.'" *Critic* 37, no. 1 (1974): 22–23.

Cook, Cornelia. "Thomas Hardy and George Meredith." *The Poetry of Thomas Hardy*. Edited by Patricia Clements and Juliet Grindle. Totowa, N.J.: Barnes & Noble, 1980.

Coppard, A. E. "On First Getting into Print." *Colophon* 6 (May 1931): unpaged.

Cox, D. Drew. "The Poet and the Architect." *Agenda* (London) 10, nos. 2–3 (1972): 50–65.

Cox, Gregory Stevens. "Thomas Hardy's *Trumpet-Major* Notebook." *Thomas Hardy Yearbook* 2 (1971): 7–28; 84–90; 84–96.

———. "A Trampwoman's Tragedy, Blue Jimmy and Ilchester Jail." *Thomas Hardy Yearbook* 1 (1970): 82–85.

———. "Tryphena Sparks and 'Young Thomas Hardy.'" *Thomas Hardy Yearbook* 5 (1975): 28–30.

Cox, James S., ed. *Mumming and the Mummers' Play of St. George*. Guernsey Channel Islands, U.K.: Toucan, 1970.

Cox, James, and Gregory Stevens Cox, eds. *The Hardy Guides* (2-vol. reprint of Hermann Lea's *Thomas Hardy's Wessex*, 1913). New York: Viking Penguin, 1986.

Cox, R. G., ed. *Thomas Hardy: The Critical Heritage*. New York: Barnes & Noble, 1970.

Coxon, Peter W. "Recollections of Thomas Hardy in St. Andrews." *Thomas Hardy Yearbook* 8 (1978): 10–11.

Craik, Roger. "Hardy's Tess of the d'Urbervilles." *Explicator* 53, no. 1 (fall 1994): 41–43.

Cramer, Jeffrey S., ed. "'The Spectre of the Real' by Thomas Hardy and Florence Henniker." *Thomas Hardy Yearbook* 13 (1986): 6–34.

Creighton, T. R. M. "Some Thoughts on Hardy and Religion." *Thomas Hardy after Fifty Years*. Edited by Lance St. John Butler. Totowa, N.J.: Rowman & Littlefield, 1977.

Cunningham, Andrew David. "Three Faces of 'Hodge': The Agricultural Labourer in Hardy's Work." In *Dissertation Abstracts International* 51 (Sept. 1990): 860A.

D'Agnillo, Renzo. "Music and Metaphor in *Under the Greenwood Tree*." *Thomas Hardy Journal* 9 no. 2 (May 1993): 39–50.

Daleski, H. M. *Thomas Hardy and Paradoxes of Love*. Columbia: University of Missouri Press, 1997.

Dalziel, Pamela. "Anxieties of Representation: The Serial Illustrations to Hardy's *The Return of the Native*." *Nineteenth Century Literature* 51, no. 1 (June 1996): 84–110.

———. "Exploiting the Poor Man: The Genesis of Hardy's *Desperate Remedies*." *Journal of English and Germanic Philology* 94, no. 2 (April 1995): 220–32.

———. "Illustrations." In *The Oxford Reader's Companion to Hardy*. Edited by Norman Page. Oxford, U.K.: Oxford University Press, 2000.

———. "A Pair of Blue Eyes." In *The Oxford Reader's Companion to Hardy*. Edited by Norman Page. Oxford: Oxford University Press, 2000.

———. "The Return of the Native." In *The Oxford Reader's Companion to Hardy*. Edited by Norman Page. Oxford: Oxford University Press, 2000.

———. "'She Matched His Violence with Her Own Wild Passion': Illustrating *Far from the Madding Crowd*." In *Reading Thomas Hardy*. Edited by Charles Pettit. New York: St. Martin's, 1998.

———, ed. *Thomas Hardy: The Excluded and Collaborative Stories*. New York: Oxford University Press, 1992.

Davidson, Arnold E. "On Reading *The Well-Beloved* as a Parable of Art." *Thomas Hardy Yearbook* 14 (1987): 14–17.

Davie, Donald. *Thomas Hardy and English Poetry*. New York: Oxford University Press, 1972.

———. *With the Grain: Essays on Thomas Hardy and Modern British Poetry*. Edited and introduced by Clive Wilmer. Manchester, England: Carcanet, 1998.

Davies, Cecil W. "Order and Chance: The Worlds of Wordsworth and Hardy." *Thomas Hardy Yearbook* 8 (1978): 40–50.

Davies, Sarah. "*The Hand of Ethelberta*: De-Mythologising 'Woman,'" *Critical Survey* 5, no. 2 (1993): 123–30.

Davis, W. Eugene, and Helmut E. Gerber, eds. *Thomas Hardy: An Annotated Bibliography of Writings About Him*, vol. 2. De Kalb: Northern Illinois University Press, 1983. (2 vols.; for vol. 1, see Gerber, Helmut E. and Eugene W. Davis).

Davis, William A., Jr. "Happy Days in *Jude the Obscure*: Hardy and the Crawford-Dilke Divorce Case." *The Thomas Hardy Journal* 13, no. 1 (Feb. 1997): 64–74.

———. "Hardy, Sir Francis Jeune and Divorce by 'False Pretences' in *Jude the Obscure*." *Thomas Hardy Journal* 9, no. 1 (Feb. 1993): 62–74.

———. "The Rape of Tess: Hardy, English Law, and the Case for Sexual Assault." *Nineteenth Century Literature* 52, no. 2 (Sept. 1997): 221–31.

Dean, Susan. *Hardy's Poetic Vision in* The Dynasts: *The Diorama of a Dream*. Princeton, N.J.: Princeton University Press, 1977.

Deane, Andrew R. "The Sources of *The Famous Tragedy of the Queen of Cornwall*." *Thomas Hardy Journal* 9, no. 1 (Feb. 1993): 76–89.

Deen, Leonard. "Heroism and Pathos in Hardy's *Return of the Native*." *Nineteenth-Century Fiction* 15 (Dec. 1960): 207–19.

Devereux, Jo. "Thomas Hardy's *A Pair of Blue Eyes*: The Heroine as Text." *Victorian Newsletter* 81 (spring 1992): 20–23.

Doel, Geoffrey. "The Supernatural Background to 'The Romantic Adventures of a Milkmaid.'" *Somerset & Dorset Notes & Queries* 30 (March 1978): 324–35.

Doheny, John R. "Characterization in Hardy's *Jude the Obscure*: The Function of Arabella." In *Reading Thomas Hardy*. Edited by Charles Pettit. New York: St. Martin's Press, 1998.

Drabble, Margaret. "Hardy and the Natural World." In *The Genius of Thomas Hardy*. New York: Alfred A. Knopf, 1976.

———. *A Writer's Britain*. London: Thames and Hudson, 1987.

———, ed. *The Genius of Thomas Hardy*. New York: Alfred A. Knopf, 1976.

Draper, Ronald P., and Martin Ray. *An Annotated Critical Bibliography of Thomas Hardy*. Ann Arbor: University of Michigan Press, 1989.

———. "Hardy's Comic Tragedy: *Jude the Obscure*." In *Critical Essays on Thomas Hardy: The Novels*. Edited by Dale Kramer and Nancy Marck. Boston: G. K. Hall, 1990.

———. "*The Mayor of Casterbridge*." *Critical Quarterly* 25, no. 1 (spring 1983): 57–70.

Duckworth, William C., Jr. "Evoking Emma in '*Poems of 1912–13*.'" *University of Mississippi Studies in English* 10 (1992): 134–43.

Ebbatson, Roger. "Hardy and Zola Revisited." *Thomas Hardy Journal* 13, no. 1 (1997): 83.

———. "'The Withered Arm' And History." *Critical Survey* (Oxford, U.K.) 5, no. 2 (1993), 131–35.

Edwards, Carol, and Duane Edwards. "*Jude the Obscure:* A Psychoanalytic Study." *University of Hartford Studies in Literature: A Journal of Interdisciplinary Criticism* 13, no. 1 (1981): 78–90.

Edwards, Duane. "The Ending of *Under the Greenwood Tree.*" *Thomas Hardy Yearbook* 8 (1978): 21–22.

Edwards, Suzanne. "A Shadow from the Past: Little Father Time in *Jude the Obscure.*" *Colby Library Quarterly* 23, no. 1 (Mar. 1987): 32–38.

Ellegard, Alvar. *The Readership of the Periodical Press in Mid-Victorian Britain.* Göteburg, Sweden: Göteburg University Press, 1957.

Elliott, Ralph W. V. "The Infatuated Artist: Thomas Hardy and *The Well-Beloved.*" *Thomas Hardy Journal* 3 no. 2 (May 1987): 20–33.

Ellis, Havelock. "The Ancestry of Genius." *Atlantic Monthly,* March 1893, 386–87.

———. "Thomas Hardy's Novels." *Westminster Review,* April 1883.

Epstein, Leonara. "Sale and Sacrament: The Wife Auction in *The Mayor of Casterbridge.*" *English Language Notes,* 24, no. 4 (June 1987), 50–56.

Fain, John Tyree. "Hardy's 'The Convergence of the Twain.'" *Explicator* 41, no. 3 (spring 1983): 34–36.

Fairhall, James. "Hardy's 'When I Set Out for Lyonnesse.'" *Explicator* 45, no. 1 (1986): 25–27.

Fayen, George S., Jr. "Thomas Hardy." In *Victorian Fiction: A Guide to Research.* Edited by Lionel Stevenson. Cambridge, Mass.: Harvard University Press, 1964.

Firor, Ruth. *Folkways in Thomas Hardy.* Philadelphia: University of Pennsylvania Press, 1931; reprinted, New York: Russell & Russell, 1968.

Ford, Mary. "The View from Wessex Heights: Thomas Hardy's Poetry of Isolation." *Dalhousie Review* 59, no. 4 (Dalhousie, Halifax, N.S.: Dalhousie University Press (winter 1979–1980): 705–16.

Freeman, Janet H. "Highways and Cornfields: Space and Time in the Narration of *Jude the Obscure.*" *Colby Library Quarterly,* 27, no. 3 (Sept. 1991): 161–73.

Fujita, Shigeru. "Symbolism in 'The Son's Veto.'" *Bulletin of the Hardy Society of Japan* I (Nov. 1966): 15–21.

Furbank, P. N. "Introduction," The New Wessex Edition, *Tess of the d'Urbervilles.* London: Macmillan, 1974.

Gatrell, Simon. "England, Europe, and Empire: Hardy, Meredith, and Gissing." In *The Ends of the Earth: 1876–1918.* London: Ashfield, 1992.

———. "*Far from the Madding Crowd* Revisited." *Thomas Hardy Journal* 10, no. 2 (May 1994): 38–50.

———. "Hardy the Creator: *Far from the Madding Crowd.*" In *Critical Approaches to the Fiction of Thomas Hardy.* Edited by Dale Kramer. London: Macmillan, 1979.

———. "Hardy's *Under the Greenwood Tree* and Wordsworth's 'Phantom of Delight.'" *Thomas Hardy Yearbook* 6 (1976): 26–27.

———. *Hardy the Creator: A Textual Biography.* New York: Oxford University Press, 1988.

———. "Typography in 'The Romantic Adventures of a Milkmaid.'" *Thomas Hardy Journal* 3, no. 3 (Oct. 1987): 38–45.

———. "Wessex." In *The Cambridge Companion to Thomas Hardy.* Edited by Dale Kramer. Cambridge: Cambridge University Press, 1999.

Gerber, Helmut E., and W. Eugene Davis, eds. *Thomas Hardy: An Annotated Bibliography of Writings about Him,* Vol. I. De Kalb, IL: Northern Illinois University Press, 1973. (2 vols.; for vol. 2, see Davis, W. Eugene and Helmut E. Gerber.)

Gibson, James. "Tess of the d'Urbervilles, 1891–1991." *The Thomas Hardy Journal.* 7, no. 3 (Oct. 1991): 34–47.

———. "Thomas Hardy's Poetry: Poetic Apprehension and Poetic Method." In *Celebrating Thomas Hardy: Insights and Appreciations.* Edited by Charles Pettit. New York: St. Martin's, 1996.

———. *Thomas Hardy: A Literary Life.* New York: Macmillan, 1996.

Gifford, Henry. "Hardy's Revisions: Satires of Circumstance." *Agenda* 10, nos. 2–3 (1972): 126–37.

Giordano, Frank R., Jr. "Characterization and Conflict in Hardy's 'The Fiddler of the Reels.'" *Texas Studies in Literature and Language: A Journal of the Humanities* 17 (1975): 617–33.

———. "Hardy's Farewell to Fiction: The Structure of 'Wessex Heights,'" *Thomas Hardy Yearbook* 5 (1975): 58–66.

Gittings, Robert. "Emma Hardy and the Giffords." In *Thomas Hardy and the Modern World.* Edited by F. B. Pinion. Dorchester, England: Thomas Hardy Society, 1974.

———. *"The Hand of Ethelberta" A Comedy in Chapters.* London: Macmillan, 1975.

———. "The Improving Hand: Hardy the Poet." *Encounter* (London) (July 1976): 47–60.

———. "Note on a Production of *The Famous Tragedy of the Queen of Cornwall.*" *A Festschrift for Professor Marguerite Roberts, on the Occasion of Her Retirement from Westhampton College, University of Richmond, Virginia.* Edited by Frieda Elaine Penninger and George M. Modlin. Richmond, Va.: University of Richmond Press, 1976.

Gittings, Robert, and Jo Manton. *The Second Mrs. Hardy.* Seattle: University of Washington Press, 1979.

———. *Thomas Hardy's Later Years.* Boston: Little, Brown, 1978.

———. *Young Thomas Hardy.* Harmondsworth, Middlesex, England: Penguin, 1978.

Glance, Jonathan C. "The Problem of the Man-Trap in Hardy's *The Woodlanders.*" *Victorian Newsletter* 78 (fall 1990): 26–29.

Goetz, William R. "The Felicity and Infelicity of Marriage in *Jude the Obscure.*" *Nineteenth Century Literature* 38, no. 2 (Sept. 1983): 189–213.

Graves, Roy Neil. "Pomp and Circumstance—Hardy's 'The Convergence of the Twain.'" *Explicator* 53, no. 2 (winter 1995): 96–99.

Green, Brian. "Darkness Visible: Defiance, Derision and Despair in Hardy's 'In Tenebris' Poems," *Thomas Hardy Journal* 6, no. 2 (June 2, 1990): 126–46.

Greenland, R. E. "Hardy in the Osgood, McIlvaine and Harper (London) Editions." *Thomas Hardy Journal* 4, no. 3 (Oct. 1988): 57–60.

Gregor, Ian. "Contrary Imaginings: Thomas Hardy and Religion." In *The Interpretation of Belief: Coleridge, Schleiermacher and Romanticism*. Edited by David Jasper. London: Macmillan, 1986.

———. "Landscape with Figures." In *Modern Critical Interpretations: Thomas Hardy's* The Return of the Native. Edited by Harold Bloom. New York: Chelsea House, 1987.

Gregor, Ian, and David Lodge, "Thomas Hardy." In *The English Novel*. Edited by Cedric Watts. London: Sussex, 1976.

Grigson, Geoffrey. *"Under the Greenwood Tree," or, The Mellstock Quire: A Rural Painting of the Dutch School*. London: Macmillan, 1974.

Grundy, Joan. *Hardy and the Sister Arts*. London: Macmillan, 1979.

———. *"Two on a Tower* and *The Duchess of Malfi."* Thomas Hardy Journal, 5, no. 2 (May 1989): 55–60.

Guerard, Albert. "Afterword," *The Return of the Native*. New York: Washington Square, 1967.

———. *Thomas Hardy*. Cambridge, Mass.: Harvard University Press, 1949. Reprint, New York: New Directions, 1964.

Guerard, Albert, ed. *Hardy: A Collection of Critical Essays*. Englewood Cliffs, N.J.: Prentice Hall, 1963.

Haarder, Andreas. "Fatalism and Symbolism in Hardy: An Analysis of 'The Grave by the Handpost.'" *Orbis Litterarum: International Review of Literary Studies* (Odense, Denmark) 34 (1979): 227–37.

Hagen, June Steffensen. "Does Teaching Make a Difference in Ethical Reflection? A Report on Teaching Hardy's *Jude the Obscure* with Attention to Marriage, Divorce, and Remarriage," *Christianity and Literature*, 33, no. 3 (spring 1984): 23–35.

Hall, William F. "Hawthorne, Shakespeare and Tess: Hardy's Use of Allusion and Reference," *English Studies: A Journal of English Language and Literature* (Nijmegen, Netherlands) 52 (1971): 533–42.

Halperin, John. "Leslie Stephen, Thomas Hardy, and *A Pair of Blue Eyes." Modern Language Review* 75 (1980): 738–45.

Hands, Timothy. *A Hardy Chronology*. Basingstoke: Macmillan, 1992.

Harding, James M. "The Signification of Arabella's Missile: Feminine Sexuality, Masculine Anxiety and Revision in *Jude the Obscure." Journal of Narrative Technique* 26, no. 1 (winter 1996): 85–111.

Hardy, Barbara. *Forms of Feeling in Victorian Fiction*. Athens: Ohio University Press, 1985.

———. *Thomas Hardy: Imagining Imagination: Hardy's Poetry and Fiction*. New Brunswick, N.J.: Athlone Press, 2000.

———. *"Under the Greenwood Tree: A Novel about the Imagination."* In *The Novels of Thomas Hardy*. Edited by Anne Smith. New York: Barnes & Noble, 1979.

Hardy, Emma. *Emma Hardy Diaries*. Edited with an introduction by Richard H. Taylor. Manchester: Mid-Northumberland Arts Group and Carcanet, 1985.

———. *Some Recollections, Together with Some Relevant Poems by Thomas Hardy*. Edited with notes by Evelyn Hardy and Robert Gittings. London: Oxford University Press, 1961.

Hardy, Evelyn. *Thomas Hardy: A Critical Biography*. London: Hogarth, 1954; New York: Russell & Russell, 1970.

———. "Some Unpublished Poems by Thomas Hardy." *London Magazine*, 3 (1956).

Hardy, Evelyn, and F. B. Pinion, eds. *One Rare Fair Woman, Thomas Hardy's Letters to Florence Henniker, 1893–1922*. Coral Gables, Fla.: University of Miami Press, 1972.

Hardy, Florence. *The Life of Thomas Hardy, 1840–1928*. London: Macmillan, 1962. (Recognized as Hardy's own work, edited by his second wife. *The Life* contains both *The Early Life of Thomas Hardy: 1840–1891* and *The Later Years of Thomas Hardy 1892–1928*.)

Harper, Marcia Mitchell. "The Literary Influence of Sir Edmund Gosse upon the Victorian Age." *Dissertation Abstracts International* 49, no. 8 (Feb. 1989): 2229A.

Harvey, J. R. *Victorian Novelists and Their Illustrators*. New York: New York University Press, 1971.

Hawkins, Desmond. "Concerning Agnes." *Encounter*, Feb. 1977.

———. *Hardy at Home: The People and Places of His Wessex*. London: Barrie & Jenkins, 1989.

———. *Hardy: Novelist and Poet*. New York: Harper & Row, 1976.

———. "Hardy's Wessex." *Essays by Divers Hands* 43 (1984): 75–89.

———. "Introduction," *The New Wessex Edition of The Complete Short Stories of Thomas Hardy* (single volume edition). London: Macmillan, 1988.

———. "Tess in the Opera House." *Contemporary Review* 225 (1974): 26–31.

———. *Thomas Hardy: His Life and Landscape*. London: National Trust, 1990.

———. "Thomas Hardy and the Ruined Maid." *Hatcher Review* 3, no. 29 (spring 1990): 418–23, 458.

Healey, Frank G. "Proust and Hardy: An Update." *Thomas Hardy Journal* (Dorchester, Dorset, U.K.) 10, no. 2 (May 1994): 51–57.

Hellstrom, Ward. *"Jude the Obscure* as Pagan Self-Assertion." *Victorian Newsletter* 29 (1966): 26–27.

Henderson, Jeff. "Symbolic Meaning in Hardy's 'The Convergence of the Twain.'" *Language of Poems* (Columbia, S.C.), 6 (1977), 13–17.

Henigan, Julie. "Hardy's Emblem of Futility: The Role of Christminster in *Jude the Obscure." Thomas Hardy Yearbook* 14 (1987): 12–14.

Henry, Nat. "Hardy's 'The Convergence of the Twain,'" *Explicator* 31, Item 4 (1972).

Herbert, Lucille. "Hardy's Views in *Tess of the d'Urbervilles." English Literary History* 37 (1970): 77–94.

Herzog, Toby. "Hardy's 'Fellow-Townsmen': A Primer for the Novels." *Colby Library Quarterly* 18, no. 4 (Dec. 1982) 231–40.

Higonnet, Margaret R., ed. *The Sense of Sex: Feminist Perspectives on Hardy*. Urbana: University of Illinois Press, 1993.

Hochstadt, Pearl R. "Hardy's Romantic Diptych: A Reading of *A Laodicean and Two on a Tower." English Literature in Transition (1880–1920)* 26, no. 1 (1983): 23–34.

Holland, Clive. *Thomas Hardy, O.M.: The Man, His Works, and the Land of Wessex*. 1933. Reprint, New York: Haskell House, 1966.

Hooker, Jeremy. *Writers in a Landscape*. Cardiff: University of Wales Press, 1996.

Howe, Irving. *"The Return of the Native."* In *Modern Critical Interpretations: Thomas Hardy's "The Return of the Native."* Edited by Harold Bloom. New York: Chelsea House, 1987.

———. *Thomas Hardy.* New York: Macmillan, 1967.

Hubbart, Marilyn Stall. "Thomas Hardy's Use of Folk Culture in *The Woodlanders,*" *Kentucky Folklore Record* 23 (1977): 17–24.

Hyde, W. J. "Thomas Hardy: The Poor Man and the Deterioration of His Ladies." *Victorian Newsletter,* 36 (1969): 14–18.

Hynes, Samuel. "The Hardy Tradition in Modern English Poetry." *Thomas Hardy Journal* 2, no. 3 (Oct. 1986): 32–49.

———. "How to Be an Old Poet: The Examples of Hardy and Yeats." Papers Presented at the Thomas Hardy Society's Twelfth International Conference, held in Dorchester, Dorset, 1996. In *Reading Thomas Hardy.* Edited by Charles Pettit. New York: St. Martin's Press, 1998.

Irvin, Glenn. "Hardy's Comic Archetype: *Under the Greenwood Tree. Thomas Hardy Journal* 6, no. 3 (Oct. 1990): 54–58.

———. "High Passion and High Church in Hardy's *Two on a Tower.*" *English Literature in Transition* 3 (1985): 121–29.

Jackson, Arlene. *Illustration and the Novels of Thomas Hardy.* Totowa, N.J.: Rowman & Littlefield, 1981.

Jesty, Vera. "Max Gate and a Neolithic Causewayed Enclosure." *Thomas Hardy Journal* 3, no. 3 (Oct. 1987): 9–30.

Johnson, H. A. T. "In Defence of *The Trumpet-Major;* Papers Presented at the 1975 Summer School." In *Budmouth Essays on Thomas Hardy.* Edited by F. B. Pinion. Dorchester, U.K.: Thomas Hardy Society, 1976.

Johnson, Lionel. *The Art of Thomas Hardy.* New York: Dodd, Mead, 1923.

Johnson, Trevor. "'Ancestral Voices': Hardy and the English Poetic Tradition." *Victorian Poetry* 29, no. 1 (spring 1991): 47–62.

———. "Illustrated Versions of Hardy's Works: A Checklist 1872–1992." *Thomas Hardy Journal* 9, no. 3 (Oct. 1993): 32–46.

Jones, Bernard. "Afternoon Tea—Max Gate, 1913." *Thomas Hardy Journal* 9, no. 3 (Oct. 1993): 47–54.

Jones, Lawrence O. "'A Good Hand at a Serial': Thomas Hardy and the Serialization of *Far from the Madding Crowd.*" *Studies in the Novel* 10 (1978): 320–34.

———. "Imitation and Expression in Thomas Hardy's Theory of Fiction." *Studies in the Novel* 7 (1975): 507–25.

Kay-Robinson, Denys. "Hardy's Wessex." In *The Genius of Thomas Hardy.* Edited by Margaret Drabble. New York: Alfred A. Knopf, 1976.

———. *The Landscape of Thomas Hardy.* London: Webb and Bower, 1984.

Keith, W. J. "Thomas Hardy's Edition of William Barnes." *Victorian Poetry* (summer 1977).

Keys, Romey T. "Hardy's Uncanny Narrative: A Reading of 'The Withered Arm,'" *Texas Studies in Literature and Language* 27, no. 1 (spring 1985): 106–23.

Kiely, Robert. "The Menace of Solitude: The Politics and Aesthetics of Exclusion in *The Woodlanders.*" In *The Sense of Sex: Feminist Perspectives on Hardy.* Edited by Margaret R. Higonnet. Urbana: University of Illinois Press, 1993.

Kim, Yong-chol. "Shakespeare and Hardy: Their Tragic Worlds." *The English Language and Literature* (English Literature Society of Korea) 14 (1963): 106–24.

Kincaid, James R. "Girl-Watching, Child-Beating and Other Exercises for Readers of *Jude the Obscure.*" In *The Sense of Sex: Feminist Perspectives on Hardy.* Edited by Margaret R. Higonnet. Urbana: University of Illinois Press, 1993.

King, Jeannette. *"The Mayor of Casterbridge:* Talking about Character." *Thomas Hardy Journal* 8, no. 3 (Oct. 1992): 42–46.

———. *Tragedy in the Victorian Novel: Theory and Practice in the Novels of George Eliot, Thomas Hardy and Henry James.* Cambridge: Cambridge University Press, 1978.

King, Kathryn R. "Hardy's 'A Tradition of Eighteen Hundred and Four' and the Anxiety of Invention." *Thomas Hardy Journal* 8, no. 2 (May 1992): 20–26.

King, Kathryn R., and William W. Morgan. "Hardy and the Boer War: The Public Poet in Spite of Himself." *Victorian Poetry* 17 (1979): 66–83.

Kossick, S. G. *"Under the Greenwood Tree."* *Essays in Literature* 1, no. 1 (1973): 30–34.

Kramer, Dale, ed. *The Cambridge Companion to Thomas Hardy.* Cambridge: Cambridge University Press, 1999.

———, ed. *Critical Approaches to the Fiction of Thomas Hardy.* London: Macmillan, 1979.

———. "Hardy and Readers: *Jude the Obscure.*" In *The Cambridge Companion to Thomas Hardy.* Edited by Dale Kramer. Cambridge: Cambridge University Press, 1999.

Kramer, Dale, and Nancy Marck. *Critical Essays on Thomas Hardy: The Novels.* Boston: G. K. Hall, 1990.

Laird, J. T. "Approaches to Fiction: Hardy and Henry James." *Thomas Hardy Annual* 2 (1984): 41–60.

Langbaum, Robert. "The Issue of Hardy's Poetry." *Victorian Poetry* 30, no. 2 (summer 1992): 151–63.

———. "The Minimization of Sexuality in *The Mayor of Casterbridge.*" *Thomas Hardy Journal* 8, no. 1 (Feb. 1992): 20–32.

———. *Thomas Hardy in Our Time.* New York: St. Martin's, 1997.

Langland, Elizabeth. "Becoming a Man in *Jude the Obscure.*" In *The Sense of Sex: Feminist Perspectives on Hardy.* Edited by Margaret R. Higonnet. Urbana: University of Illinois Press, 1993.

Larkin, Peter. "Irony, Sincerity and 'In Tenebris, II.'" *Thomas Hardy Yearbook* 14 (1987): 6–9.

LaValley, Albert J., ed. *Twentieth Century Interpretations of "Tess of the d'Urbervilles"* Englewood Cliffs, N.J.: Prentice Hall, 1969.

Lawrence, Berta. "Fifteen Letters from Madeleine Rolland to Thomas Hardy." *Thomas Hardy Journal* 5, no. 1 (Jan. 1989): 72–77.

Lawrence, D. H. "Study of Thomas Hardy: *The Return of the Native.*" In *Modern Critical Interpretations: Thomas Hardy's "The Return of the Native."* Edited by Harold Bloom. New York: Chelsea House, 1987.

Lea, Hermann. *Thomas Hardy's Wessex, illustrated from photographs by the author.* Published in the definitive Wessex edition of Hardy's works, 1913. Reprinted St. Peter Port, Channel Islands, Toucan Press, 1969. Reprinted in 2 volumes, titled *The Hardy Guides,* ed. James Cox and Gregory Stevens Cox. Harmondsworth, Middlesex, U.K.: Penguin; New York: Viking Penguin, 1986.

———. *A Handbook to the Wessex Country of Thomas Hardy's Novels and Poems.* London, 1905.

———. "Wessex Witches, Witchery, and Witchcraft." *Nineteenth Century,* June 1903.

Leavis, L. R. "The Late Nineteenth-Century Novel and the Change towards the Sexual: Gissing, Hardy and Lawrence." *English Studies: A Journal of English Language and Literature* (Lisse, Netherlands) 66, no. 1 (Feb. 1985): 36–47.

Lerner, Laurence. "Moments of Vision—and After." In *Celebrating Thomas Hardy: Insights and Appreciations.* Edited by Charles Pettit. New York: St. Martin's Press, 1996.

Lerner, Laurence, and John Holmstrom. *Thomas Hardy and His Readers.* London: Bodley Head, 1968.

LeVay, John. "Hardy's *Jude the Obscure.*" *Explicator* 49, no. 4 (summer 1991): 219–22.

Levine, George. "Thomas Hardy's *The Mayor of Casterbridge:* Reversing the Real." In *Critical Essays on Thomas Hardy: The Novels.* Edited by Dale Kramer and Nancy Marck. Boston: G. K. Hall, 1990.

Lloyd, Richard. "Hopkins's 'The Wreck of the *Deutschland*' and Hardy's 'The Convergence of the Twain.'" *Explicator* 50, no. 1 (fall 1991): 23–25.

Lock, Charles. "'The Darkling Thrush' and the Habit of Singing.'" *Essays in Criticism* 36, no. 2 (Apr. 1986): 120–41.

Lodge, David. The Woodlanders *by Thomas Hardy.* London: Macmillan, 1974.

Lombardi, Betty Ritch. "Thomas Hardy's Collecting Techniques and Sources for the Folklore in His Wessex Novels." *Midwestern Journal of Language and Folklore* 2 (1976): 20–30.

Lothe, Jakob. "Variants on Genre: *The Return of the Native, The Mayor of Casterbridge, The Hand of Ethelberta.*" In *The Cambridge Companion to Thomas Hardy.* Edited by Dale Kramer. Cambridge: Cambridge University Press, 1999.

Mallett, Phillip. "Hardy and Time." Comprises Papers Presented at the Thomas Hardy Society's Twelfth International Conference, Held in Dorchester, Dorset, 1996. In *Reading Thomas Hardy.* Edited by Charles Pettit. New York: St. Martin's Press, 1998.

———. "Poems of the Past and Present." In *The Oxford Reader's Companion to Hardy.* Edited by Norman Page. Oxford: Oxford University Press, 2000.

———. "Sexual Ideology and Narrative Form in *Jude the Obscure.*" *Journal of the English Association* 38, no. 162 (autumn 1989): 211–24.

———. "Thomas Hardy and Sincerity." *Thomas Hardy Journal* 8, no. 1 (Feb. 1992): 45–54.

Marroni, Francesco. "The Negation of Eros in 'Barbara of the House of Grebe.'" *Thomas Hardy Journal* 10, no. 1 (Feb. 1995): 33–41.

———. "'The Three Strangers' and the Verbal Representation of Wessex." *Thomas Hardy Journal* 8, no. 2 (May 1992): 26–39.

Maxwell, J. C. "Mrs. Grundy and *Two on a Tower.*" *Thomas Hardy Yearbook* 2 (1971): 45–46.

Maynard, Katherine Kearney. *Thomas Hardy's Tragic Poetry: The Lyrics and The Dynasts.* Iowa City: University of Iowa Press, 1991.

MacCarthy, Desmond. *Desmond MacCarthy: The Man and His Writings.* Introduction by David Cecil. London: Constable, 1984.

McCarthy, Lillah (Lady Keeble). *Myself and My Friends.* London: Thornton Butterworth, 1933.

McClure, Paul. "A Note on the Cliff Scene in Hardy's *A Pair of Blue Eyes.*" *Durham University Journal* (New Elvet, Durham, England) 52, no. 1 (Jan. 1991): 53.

McGhee, Richard D. "'Swinburne Planteth, Hardy Watereth': Victorian Views of Pain and Pleasure in Human Sexuality." *Tennessee Studies in Literature* 27 (1984): 83–107.

Manford, Alan. "Emma Hardy's Helping Hand." In *Critical Essays on Thomas Hardy: The Novels.* Edited by Dale Kramer and Nancy Marck. Boston: G. K. Hall, 1990.

———. "Who Wrote Thomas Hardy's Novels? A Survey of Emma Hardy's Contribution to the Manuscripts of Her Husband's Novels." *Thomas Hardy Journal* 6, no. 2 (June 2, 1990): 84–97.

Manning, F. "Novels of Character and Environment." *Spectator,* Sept. 7, 1912, 335. Reprinted in *Thomas Hardy: Critical Assessments of Writers in English,* Vol. 3: *Writers, Writing, and Wessex,* 132–35. Edited by Graham Clark. Mountfield, East Sussex: Helm Information, 1993.

Marston, Edward. *After Work: Fragments from the Workshop of an Old Publisher.* New York: Charles Scribner's Sons, 1904.

Mason, D. G. "Hardy and Zola: A Comparative Study of Tess and Abbe Mouret." *Thomas Hardy Journal* 7, no. 3 (Oct. 1991): 88–102.

May, Charles E. "The Magic of Metaphor in *The Return of the Native.*" *Colby Library Quarterly* 22, no. 2 (June 1986): 111–18.

Melfi, Mary Ann. "*Jude the Obscure:* Childhood without Closure." *Durham University Journal* (New Elvet, Durham, England) 87, no. 2 (July 1995): 315–20.

Menefree, Samuel Pyeatt. *Wives for Sale: An Ethnographic Study of British Popular Opinions.* Oxford: Blackwell Publishers, 1981.

Meyers, Terry L. "An Allusion to Donne in Hardy's 'Drawing Details in an Old Church.'" *Thomas Hardy Journal* 13, no. 3 (Oct. 1997): 94–95.

Meynell, Viola, ed. *Friends of a Lifetime: Letters to Sydney Carlyle Cockerell.* London: Jonathan Cape, 1940.

Miller, J. Hillis. *Thomas Hardy, Distance and Desire.* Cambridge, Mass.: Harvard University Press, 1970.

———. "Topography and Tropography in Thomas Hardy's 'In Front of the Landscape.'" In *Post-Structuralist Readings of English Poetry.* Edited by Richard Machin and Christopher Norris. Cambridge: Cambridge University Press, 1987.

———. "Topography in *The Return of the Native.*" *Essays in Literature* 8, no. 2 (fall 1981): 119–34.

———. "Introduction" to Thomas Hardy, *The Well-Beloved, A Sketch of a Temperament* (London: Macmillan, 1975).

Miller, J. Hillis. "'Wessex Heights': The Persistence of the Past in Hardy's Poetry." *Critical Quarterly* 10 (1968): 339–59.

Millgate, Michael. "Distracted Preacher: Thomas Hardy's Public Utterances." In *Reading Thomas Hardy*. Edited by Charles Pettit. New York: St. Martin's, 1998.

———, ed. *Letters of Emma and Florence Hardy*. Oxford: Clarendon Press, 1996.

———. "Thomas Hardy: The Biographical Sources." In *The Cambridge Companion to Thomas Hardy*. Edited by Dale Kramer. Cambridge: Cambridge University Press, 1999.

———. *Thomas Hardy: A Biography*. London: Oxford University Press, 1982.

———. *Thomas Hardy: His Career as a Novelist*. London: Bodley Head, 1971.

———. "'Wives All': Emma and Florence Hardy." In Charles Pettit, ed. *Celebrating Thomas Hardy: Insights and Appreciations*. New York: St. Martin's, 1996.

Mistichelli, William J. "The Trumpet-Major's Signal: Kinship and Sexual Rivalry in the Novels of Thomas Hardy." *CEA Critic* 56, no. 3 (spring–summer 1994): 43–61.

Mitchell, P. E. "Passion and Companionship in Hardy's Poetry." *Victorian Poetry*, 27, no. 1 (spring 1989): 77–93.

Moore, Kevin. "The Poet within the Architect's Ring: *Desperate Remedies*, Hardy's Hybrid Detective-Gothic Narrative." *Studies in the Novel* 14, no. 1 (spring 1982): 31–42.

Morgan, Charles. *The House of Macmillan*. New York: Macmillan, 1944.

Morgan, Rosemarie. "Bodily Transactions: Toni Morrison and Thomas Hardy in Literary Discourse." In *Celebrating Thomas Hardy: Insights and Appreciations*. Edited by Charles Pettit. New York: St. Martin's, 1996.

———. *Cancelled Words: Rediscovering Thomas Hardy*. London, New York: Routledge, 1992.

———. *Editing Hardy: Thomas Hardy Association Occasional Series*, Vol. I (1999).

———. "Inscriptions of the Self: Thomas Hardy and Autobiography." *Thomas Hardy Annual*, 5 (1987): 137–56.

———. "Marriage." In *The Oxford Reader's Companion to Hardy*. Edited by Norman Page. Oxford: Oxford University Press, 2000.

———. "Passive Victim? *Tess of the d'Urbervilles*." *Thomas Hardy Journal*, 5:1 (Jan. 1989): 31–54.

———. "Women." In *The Oxford Reader's Companion to Hardy*. Edited by Norman Page. Oxford: Oxford University Press, 2000.

Morgan, Rosemarie, ed. *The Hardy Review*. New Haven, Conn.: Hardy Association Press, 1998.

Morgan, Rosemarie, and William W. Morgan, eds. *Thomas Hardy's Emma Poems*. New Haven, Conn.: Hardy Association Press, 2001.

Morgan, Rosemarie, and Richard Nemesvari. *Human Shows: Essays in Honour of Michael Millgate*. New Haven, Conn.: Hardy Association Press, 2000.

Morgan, William W. "Form, Tradition, and Consolation in Hardy's 'Poems of 1912–13.'" *Publications of the Modern Language Association of America* 89 (1974): 496–505.

———. "Guide to the Year's Work in Victorian Poetry: 1995: Thomas Hardy," *Victorian Poetry*, 33, nos. 3–4 (autumn 1995): 534–40.

———. "Mr. Thomas Hardy Composing a Lyric." *Journal of English and Germanic Philology* 92, no. 3 (July 1993): 342–58.

———. "The Partial Vision: Hardy's Idea of Dramatic Poetry." *Tennessee Studies in Literature* 20 (1975): 100–108.

———. "Syntax in Hardy's 'Neutral Tones,' Lines Seven and Eight." *Victorian Poetry* 11 (1973): 167–68.

———. "Thomas Hardy." *Victorian Poetry* 29, no. 3 (autumn 1991): 278–82.

———. "Thomas Hardy." *Victorian Poetry* 31, no. 3 (fall 1993): 303–10.

———. "Thomas Hardy." *Victorian Poetry* 32, nos. 3–4 (autumn–winter 1994): 469–77.

———. "Thomas Hardy." *Victorian Poetry*, 34:4 (winter 1996): 591–94.

———. "Thomas Hardy's Apprenticeship to the Craft of English Verse." *Victorians Institute Journal* (Greenville, N.C.) 13 (1985): 1–10.

Moring, Meg M. "The Dark Glass: Mirroring and Sacrifice in Shakespeare's *Othello* and Hardy's *Tess of the d'Urbervilles*." *Conference of College Teachers of English Studies* (Denton, Tex.) 56 (Sept. 1991): 12–18.

Morrison, Ronald D. "Love and Evolution in Thomas Hardy's *The Woodlanders*." *Kentucky Philological Review* 6 (1991): 32–37.

Moses, Michael Valdez. "Agon in the Marketplace: *The Mayor of Casterbridge* as Bourgeois Tragedy." *South Atlantic Quarterly* 87, no. 2 (spring 1988): 219–51.

Moss, Mary. "The Novels of Thomas Hardy." *The Atlantic Monthly* (September 1906), 354–67.

Murfin, Ross. "Moments of Vision: Hardy's Poems of 1912–13." *Victorian Poetry* 20, no. 1 (spring 1982): 73–84.

———. *Swinburne, Hardy, Lawrence and the Burden of Belief*. Chicago: University of Chicago Press, 1978.

Nakano, Tomoko. "Hardy's New Conception of Nature in *Far from the Madding Crowd*." *Sophia English Studies* (Tokyo) 7 (1982): 47–61.

Neale, Catherine. "*Desperate Remedies*: The Merits and Demerits of Popular Fiction." *Critical Survey* 5, no. 2 (1993): 117–22.

Nemesvari, Richard. "The Anti-Comedy of *The Trumpet-Major*." *Victorian Newsletter* 77 (spring 1990): 8–13.

Nettels, Elsa. "Howells and Hardy." *Colby Library Quarterly* 20, no. 2 (June 1984): 107–22.

Nineham, A. W. "The Ancestry of Florence Emily Dugdale: Thomas Hardy's Second Wife." *Thomas Hardy Journal* 12, no. 3 (Oct. 1996): 83–96.

Orel, Harold. "Annotated Critical Bibliography of Hardy." *English Literature in Transition* 33, no. 2 (1990): 221–23. (Review of Ronald P. Draper and Martin Ray, *An Annotated Critical Bibliography of Thomas Hardy*. Ann Arbor: University of Michigan Press, 1989).

———, ed. *Critical Essays on Thomas Hardy's Poetry*. New York: Macmillan, 1995.

———. *The Dynasts*. London: Macmillan, 1978.

———. "*The Dynasts* on the English Stage, 1908–1919." *Thomas Hardy Journal*, 8, no. 1 (Feb. 1992): 63–70.

———. "Hardy and Textual Biography." *English Literature in Transition,* 33, no. 1 (1990): 98–103. (Review of Simon Gatrell, *Hardy the Creator: A Textual Biography.* Oxford: Clarendon, 1988.)

———. "Hardy and the Theatre." In *The Genius of Thomas Hardy.* Edited by Margaret Drabble. New York: Alfred A. Knopf, 1976.

———. "The Literary Friendships of Thomas Hardy." *English Literature in Transition (1880–1920)* 24, no. 3 (1981): 131–45.

———. *Thomas Hardy's Epic-Drama: A Study of "The Dynasts."* Lawrence: University of Kansas Press, 1963.

———, ed. *Thomas Hardy's Personal Writings.* Lawrence: University of Kansas Press, 1966.

O'Rourke, May. "Young Mr. Thomas Hardy." *Monographs on the Life, Times and Works of Thomas Hardy.* Guernsey, Channel Islands, U.K.: Toucan, 1966, no. 9, 7–19.

O'Sullivan, Timothy. *Thomas Hardy: An Illustrated Biography.* London: Macmillan, 1975.

O'Toole, Tess. "Genealogy and Narrative Jamming in Hardy's *The Well-Beloved.*" *Narrative* 1, no. 2 (Oct. 1993): 207–22.

Ownby, E. S. "A Reading of Thomas Hardy's 'The Darkling Thrush.'" In Howard Creed, *Essays in Honor of Richebourg Gaillard McWilliams.* Edited by Howard Creed. Birmingham, Ala: Birmingham-Southern College, 1970, 29–32.

Padian, Kevin. "'Daughter of the Soil': Themes of Deep Time and Evolution in Thomas Hardy's *Tess of the d'Urbervilles.*" *Thomas Hardy Journal* 13, no. 3 (Oct. 1997): 65–81.

Page, Norman. "Art and Aesthetics." In *The Cambridge Companion to Thomas Hardy.* Edited by Dale Kramer. Cambridge: Cambridge University Press, 1999.

———. "Hardy's Dutch Painting: *Under the Greenwood Tree.*" *Thomas Hardy Yearbook* 5 (1975): 39–42.

———, ed. *The Oxford Reader's Companion to Hardy.* Oxford: Oxford University Press, 2000.

———. *Thomas Hardy.* London: Routledge & Kegan Paul, 1977.

———. "Thomas Hardy's Forgotten Illustrators." *Bulletin of the New York Public Library* 77 (1974): 454–64.

———. "*The Well-Beloved* and Other Hardyan Fantasies." *Thomas Hardy Journal* 8, no. 3 (Oct. 1992): 75–83.

Parker, Lynn. "'Pure Woman' and Tragic Heroine? Conflicting Myths in Hardy's *Tess of the d'Urbervilles.*" *Studies in the Novel* 24, no. 3 (fall 1992): 273–81.

"Paternal Query." Unsigned review in the *Times Literary Supplement,* July 25, 1968, of F. R. Southerington, *Hardy's Child: Fact or Fiction?* Mount Durand, Guernsey, Channel Islands, U.K.: Toucan, 1968.

Paulin, Tom. *The Poetry of Perception.* London: Macmillan, 1975.

Peck, John. "Hardy and the Figure in the Scene." *Agenda* (London, England) 10, nos. 2–3 (1972): 117–25.

Pettit, Charles P. C., ed. *Celebrating Thomas Hardy: Insights and Appreciations.* New York: St. Martin's, 1996.

———. *New Perspectives on Thomas Hardy.* New York: St. Martin's, 1994.

———. *Reading Thomas Hardy.* New York: St. Martin's, 1998.

Phelps, Kenneth. "Thomas Hardy and St. Juliot Church." *Thomas Hardy Yearbook* 5 (1975): 31–34.

Philip, Neil. *Wessex Heights, An Illustrated Selection/Thomas Hardy.* London: Bloomsbury Publishing, 1988.

Pinion, F. B. "The Country and Period of *The Woodlanders.*" *Thomas Hardy Yearbook* 2 (1971): 46–55.

———. *A Hardy Companion. A Commentary on the Poems of Thomas Hardy.* London: Macmillan, 1976.

———. *A Hardy Companion. A Guide to the Works of Thomas Hardy and Their Background.* New York: St. Martin's, 1968.

———. "Hardy's House in Dorchester and Two Important Houses in Casterbridge." *Thomas Hardy Yearbook* 3 (1972–73): 17–24.

———, ed. *The Mayor of Casterbridge,* with introduction and notes. London: Macmillan, 1975.

———. "Questions Arising from Hardy's Visits to Cornwall." In *New Perspectives on Thomas Hardy.* Edited by Charles Pettit. New York: St. Martin's, 1994.

———. *A Thomas Hardy Dictionary: With Maps and Chronology.* New York: New York University Press, 1989.

———, ed. *Thomas Hardy and the Modern World.* Dorchester, U.K.: Thomas Hardy Society, 1974.

———, ed. *Budmouth Essays on Thomas Hardy.* Dorchester, England: Hardy Society, 1976.

———, ed. *Two on a Tower.* London: Macmillan, 1975.

Pitts, Arthur W., Jr. "Hardy's 'Channel Firing'" *Explicator* 26, Item 24 (1967).

Plotz, Helen. *The Pinnacled Tower.* New York: Macmillan, 1975.

Potter, Vilma Raskin. "Poetry and the Fiddler's Foot: Meters in Thomas Hardy's Work." *Musical Quarterly* 65 (1979): 48–71.

Pritchard, William H. "Hardy's Winter Words," *Hudson Review* 32 (1979): 369–97.

Purdy, Richard Little. *Thomas Hardy: A Bibliographical Study.* Oxford: Clarendon, 1954.

Purdy, Richard Little, and Michael Millgate. *The Collected Letters of Thomas Hardy.* 7 vols. Oxford: Clarendon, 1978–1988.

Raine, Craig. "Conscious Artistry in *The Mayor of Casterbridge.*" In Charles Pettit, ed., *New Perspectives on Thomas Hardy.* Edited by Charles Pettit. New York: St. Martin's, 1994.

Ramazani, Jahan. "Hardy and the Poetics of Melancholia: Poems of 1912–13 and Other Elegies for Emma." ELH 58, no. 4 (winter 1991): 957–77.

Ray, Martin. "'An Imaginative Woman': From Manuscript to Wessex Edition." *Thomas Hardy Journal* 9, no. 3 (Oct. 1993): 76–83.

———. "'The Fiddler of the Reels': A Textual Study." *Thomas Hardy Journal,* 9, no. 2 (May 1993): 55–60.

———. "Hardy's Borrowing from Shakespeare: Eustacia Vye and Lady Macbeth." *Thomas Hardy Yearbook* (St. Sampson, Guernsey, Channel Islands, U.K.) 14 (1987): 64.

———. "Hardy's 'The First Countess of Wessex': A Textual Anomaly." *Notes and Queries* 42 (June 1995): 2, 205.

———. "A Note on Florence Henniker and Solentsea." *Thomas Hardy Journal.* 10, no. 2 (May 1994): 70–71.

———. "Thomas Hardy's 'The Duke's Reappearance.'" *Notes and Queries* 43 (Dec. 1996): 435–36.

————. "Thomas Hardy's 'The Son's Veto': A Textual History." *Review of English Studies* 47, no. 188 (Nov. 1996), 542–57.

————. "'The Waiting Supper': A Textual History." *Thomas Hardy Journal* 10, no. 2 (May 1994): 58–65.

Renner, Stanley. "William Acton, the Truth about Prostitution, and Hardy's Not-So-Ruined Maid." *Victorian Poetry* 30, no. 1 (spring 1992) 19–28.

Rimmer, Mary. "Club Laws: Chess and the Construction of Gender in *A Pair of Blue Eyes*." In *The Sense of Sex: Feminist Perspectives on Hardy*. Edited by Margaret Higonnet. Urbana: University of Illinois Press, 1993.

Riquelme, John Paul. "The Modernity of Thomas Hardy's Poetry." In *The Cambridge Companion to Thomas Hardy*. Edited by Dale Kramer. Cambridge: Cambridge University Press, 1999.

Roberts, Marguerite. *Hardy's Poetic Drama and the Theatre: "The Dynasts" and "The Famous Tragedy of the Queen of Cornwall."* New York: Pageant, 1965.

————. "Florence Hardy and the Max Gate Circle." *The Thomas Hardy Yearbook* 9 (1979): 3–96.

————, ed. *"Tess" in the Theatre: Two Dramatizations of "Tess of the d'Urbervilles" by Thomas Hardy; One by Lorimer Stoddard*. Toronto: University of Toronto Press, 1950.

Roberts, Patrick. "Ethelberta: Portrait of the Artist as a Young Woman: Love and Ambition." *Thomas Hardy Journal* 10, no. 1 (Feb. 1994): 87–99.

————. "Patterns of Relationship in *Desperate Remedies*." *Thomas Hardy Journal* 8, no. 2 (May 1992): 50–57.

"Romantic Adventures of a Milkmaid, The": Unsigned Reviews: "Recent Novels, "The Romantic Adventures of a Milkmaid,' *The Nation* (New York) 37 (Sept. 20, 1883): 255.

"Romantic Adventures of a Milkmaid," *Literary World* (Boston) 14 (July 28, 1883): 245.

Roti, Grant C. "Hardy's 'The Convergence of the Twain.'" *Explicator* 51, no. 1 (fall 1992): 25–28.

Rowse, A. L. "Hardy and Cornwall." In Margaret Drabble, ed., *The Genius of Thomas Hardy*. Edited by Margaret Drabble. New York: Alfred A. Knopf, 1976.

Runcie, Catherine. "On Figurative Language: A Reading of Shelley's, Hardy's and Hughes's Skylark Poems." AUMLA: *Journal of the Australasian Universities Language and Literature Association* (Christchurch, New Zealand) 66 (Nov. 1986): 205–17.

Ryan, Michael. "One Name of Many Shapes: *The Well-Beloved*." In *Critical Approaches to the Fiction of Thomas Hardy*. Edited by Dale Kramer. London: Macmillan, 1979.

Saldivar, Ramon. "*Jude the Obscure*: Reading and the Spirit of the Law." ELH 50.3 (fall 1983): 607–25.

Saunders, Mary M. "The Significance of the Man-Trap in *The Woodlanders*." *Modern Fiction Studies*, 20 (1974–75): 529–31.

Sasaki, Toru. "On Boldwood's Retina: A 'Moment of Vision' in *Far from the Madding Crowd* and Its Possible Relation to *Middlemarch*." *Thomas Hardy Journal* 8, no. 3 (Oct. 1992): 57–60.

————. "Viewer and Victim in *Desperate Remedies*: Links between Hardy's Life and His Fiction." *The Thomas Hardy Journal* 10, no. 1 (Feb. 1994): 77–86.

Scannell, Vernon. "Some Hardy Poems Considered—No. 4: 'During Wind and Rain' and 'Channel Firing,'" *Thomas Hardy Journal* 5, no. 2 (May 1989): 69–75.

Schur, Owen. *Victorian Pastoral: Tennyson, Hardy, and the Subversion of Forms*. Columbus: Ohio State University Press, 1989.

Schweik, Robert C. "Character and Fate in Hardy's *The Mayor of Casterbridge*." *Nineteenth Century Fiction* 21 (1966): 249–62.

————. "The Influence of Religion, Science and Philosophy on Hardy's Writings." In *The Cambridge Companion to Thomas Hardy*. Edited by Dale Kramer. Cambridge: Cambridge University Press, 1999.

————. "The Narrative Structure of *Far from the Madding Crowd*." In *Budmouth Essays on Thomas Hardy*. Edited by F. B. Pinion. Dorchester, England: Hardy Society, 1976.

Seymour-Smith, Martin. *Hardy*. New York: St. Martin's, 1994.

Sherrick, Julie. *Thomas Hardy's Major Novels: An Annotated Bibliography*. Lanham, Md.: Scarecrow, 1998.

Shires, Linda M. "Narrative, Gender, and Power in *Far from the Madding Crowd*." In *The Sense of Sex: Feminist Perspectives on Hardy*. Edited by Margaret R. Higonnet. Urbana: University of Illinois Press, 1993.

————. "The Radical Aesthetic of *Tess of the d'Urbervilles*." In *The Cambridge Companion to Thomas Hardy*. Edited by Dale Kramer. Cambridge: Cambridge University Press, 1999.

Showalter, Elaine. "The Unmanning of the *Mayor of Casterbridge*." In *Critical Approaches to the Fiction of Thomas Hardy*. Edited by Dale Kramer. London: Macmillan, 1979.

Shumaker, Jeanette Roberts. "Abjection and Degeneration in Thomas Hardy's "Barbara of the House of Grebe." *College Literature* 26, no. 2 (spring 1999): 1–17.

————. "Breaking with the Conventions: Victorian Confession Novels and *Tess of the d'Urbervilles*." *English Literature in Transition* (1880–1920) 37, no. 4 (1994): 445–62.

Simpson, Matt. "Pomp and Circumstance—Hardy's 'The Convergence of the Twain,'" *Critical Survey* (Oxford, England) 5, no. 2 (1993), 167–73.

Singh, V. D. "The Superstitious in Hardy's Tess." *Rajasthan University Studies in English* (Jaipur, India) 6 (1972): 45–53.

Skilling, Margaret R. "Investigations into the Country of *The Woodlanders*." *Thomas Hardy Journal* 8, no. 3 (Oct. 1992): 62–67.

————. "Walk Round Dorchester (Casterbridge) with Hardy." Crewkerne, Somerset: Hardy Society, 1975.

Smith, Curtis. "Natural Settings and Natural Characters in Hardy's *Desperate Remedies* and *A Pair of Blue Eyes*." *Syracuse University Graduate Studies in English* 8 (1967): 84–97.

Smith, Leonard. "'How I Built Myself a House,'" *Thomas Hardy Journal*, 6, no. 2 (June 1990): 149–57.

Southerington, F. R. *The Early Hardys*. St. Peter Port, Guernsey, Channel Islands, U.K.: Toucan Press, 1968.

————. *Hardy's Child: Fact or Fiction?* Mount Durand, Guernsey, Channel Islands, U.K.: Toucan, 1968. (*See* "Paternal Query," unsigned review.)

————, "*The Return of the Native*: Thomas Hardy and the Evolution of Consciousness." In *Thomas Hardy and the Modern*

World. Edited by F. B. Pinion. Dorchester, England: Thomas Hardy Society, 1974.

Southworth, James. *The Poetry of Thomas Hardy.* New York: Columbia University Press, 1947; Reprinted, Russell & Russell, 1966.

Spector, Stephen J. "Flight of Fancy: Characterization in Hardy's *Under the Greenwood Tree.*" *English Literary History* 55, no. 2 (summer 1988): 469–85.

Springer, Marlene. "Invention and Tradition: Allusions in *Desperate Remedies.*" *Colby Library Quarterly* 109 (1974): 475–85.

Spurr, Barry. "'Splendid Words': Hardy's *Trumpet-Major* and 'Church Verse.'" *Thomas Hardy Journal* 13, no. 1 (Feb. 1997): 77–82.

Squillace, Robert. "Hardy's Mummers." *Nineteenth Century Literature* 41, no. 2 (Sept. 1986): 172–89.

Steel, Gaylor R. *Sexual Tyranny in Wessex: Hardy's Witches and Demons of Folklore.* New York: Peter Lang, 1993.

Stevenson, Lionel. "Thomas Hardy." *Darwin among the Poets.* Chicago: University of Chicago Press, 1932.

———. *Victorian Fiction: A Guide to Research.* Cambridge, Mass.: Harvard University Press, 1964.

Stewart, J. I. M. "Hardy," in *Eight Modern Writers.* Vol. 12 of *The Oxford History of English Literature.* Edited by F. P. Wilson and Bonamy Dobrée. Oxford: Clarendon Press, 1963.

———. *Thomas Hardy: A Critical Biography.* New York: Dodd, Mead, 1971.

Stewart, Ralph. "Hardy's Woodlanders." *Explicator* 48, no. 3 (1990): 195–96.

Strachey, Lytton. "Mr. Hardy's New Poems." In *Literary Essays.* New York: Harcourt Brace, 1949.

———. "On *Satires of Circumstance.*" *New Statesman,* Dec. 19, 1914 (Reprinted in Clarke, ed., *Thomas Hardy: Critical Assessments of Writers in English,* 3, 157–60). Edited by Graham Clark. Mountfield, East Sussex: Helm Information, 1993.

Sumner, Rosemary. "The Experimental and the Absurd in *Two on a Tower.*" In *Thomas Hardy Annual* 1 (1982). Edited by Norman Page.

———. "Hardy Ahead of His Time: 'Barbara of the House of Grebe.'" *Notes and Queries* 27 (1980): 230–31.

Sutton, Max Keith. "Hardy's Fiddler and the Bull: A Debt to Baring-Gould?" *English Language Notes* 32, no. 2 (Dec. 1994): 45–53.

Taft, Michael. "Hardy's Manipulation of Folklore and Literary Imagination: The Case of the Wife Sale in *The Mayor of Casterbridge.*" *Studies in the Novel* 13, no. 4 (winter 1991): 399–407.

Tarr, Rodger L. "Hardy's 'Channel Firing.'" *Explicator,* 36, no. 4 (1978): 17–18

Taylor, Dennis. "The Chronology of *Jude the Obscure.*" *Thomas Hardy Journal* 12, no. 3 (Oct. 1996): 65–68.

———. "Hardy and Wordsworth." *Victorian Poetry* 24, no. 4 (winter 1986): 441–54.

———. "Hardy's Copy of Tennyson's *In Memoriam.*" *Thomas Hardy Journal* 13, no. 1 (Feb. 1997): 43–63.

———. "Hardy's Use of Tennyson's *In Memoriam.*" *Tennyson Research Bulletin,* 7, no. 1 (1997): 32–41.

———. *Hardy's Poetry, 1860–1928.* New York: Columbia University Press, 1981.

———. "The Patterns in Hardy's Poetry." *English Literary History* 42 (1975): 258–75.

Thatcher, David S. "Hardy's 'The Convergence of the Twain,'" *Explicator,* 29 Item 34 (1970): 13–33.

Thomas Hardy Society Guides: 1. "The Country of *The Woodlanders*" (J. P. Skilling, map drawn by M. R. Skilling, 1978; rpt. 1998); 2. "The Country of *Tess of the d'Urbervilles,*" covering "Egdon Heath" and the "Vale of the Great Dairies" (J. P. Skilling, map drawn by M. R. Skilling, 1972; rev. 1994); 3. "The Country of *Tess of the d'Urbervilles,*" covering Tess's Journeys and the "Vale of the Little Dairies" (J. P. Skilling, map drawn by H. J. C. Mann, 1972; rev. M. R. Skilling, map drawn by M. R. Skilling and E. P. Fowler, 1998); 4. "The Country of *The Return of the Native*" (J. P. Skilling, map drawn by M. R. Skilling, 1972; rev. 1995); 5. "The Country of *Under the Greenwood Tree*" (A. D. Winchcombe, 1972; rev. K. N. Fowler, map drawn by E. P. Fowler, 1998); 6. "The Country of *Far from the Madding Crowd*" (J. P. Skilling, map drawn by M. R. Skilling, 1973; rev. M. R. Skilling, map rev. by M. R. Skilling and E. P. Fowler, 1995); 7. "The Country of *The Mayor of Casterbridge*" (N. J. Atkins, 1974; rev. K. N. Fowler, map drawn by E. P. Fowler, 1996); 8. "The Country of *The Trumpet-Major*" (J. P. Skilling, map drawn by M. R. Skilling, 1974; rev. M. R. Skilling, 1989); 9. "The Country of *A Pair of Blue Eyes*" (A. D. Winchcombe, map drawn by M. A. Winchcombe, 1975; rev. 1990); 10. "The Country of *Jude the Obscure*" (T. R. Wightman, 1975; rev. Charles P. C. Pettit, 1995); 11. "The Country of *The Hand of Ethelberta*" (J. P. Skilling, map drawn by M. R. Skilling, 1976); 12. "The Country of *The Well-Beloved:* A Walk with Tom Wightman" (1991–1992); 13. "The Country of *Desperate Remedies*" (A. D. Winchcombe, map drawn by M. A. Winchcombe, 1977). These guides—some of which are now out of print—may be obtained from The Thomas Hardy Society, Box 1438, Dorchester, Dorset DT1 1YH, U.K.

Tillman-Hill, Iris. "Hardy's Skylark and Shelley's." *Victorian Poetry* 10 (1972): 79–83.

Turner, Paul. *The Life of Thomas Hardy: A Critical Biography.* Oxford: Blackwell, 1998.

Tuttleton, June Martin. "Thomas Hardy and the Christian Religion." *Dissertation Abstracts International* 26 (1965): 1637.

Vance, Norman. "Hardy's 'The Darkling Thrush' and G. F. Watts's Hope." *Victorian Poetry* 33, no. 2 (summer 1995): 295–98.

Vandiver, Edward P., Jr. "*The Return of the Native* and Shakespeare." *Furman Studies* 12, no. 1 (1964): 11–15.

Wain, John, ed. *The Dynasts.* London: Macmillan, 1965.

———. *The New Wessex Selection of Thomas Hardy's Poetry.* Chosen by John and Eirian Wain. Introduction by John Wain. London: Macmillan, 1978.

———. *Selected Shorter Poems of Thomas Hardy,* rev. ed. London: Macmillan, 1975.

Wanchu, D. P. "Thomas Hardy's 'Enter a Dragoon: A Note." *Rajasthan University Studies in English* (Jaipur, India) 11 (1978): 43–48.

Ward, Paul. "*Desperate Remedies* and the Victorian Thriller." *Thomas Hardy Yearbook* 4 (1973–74): 72–76.

———. "*The Hand of Ethelberta.*" *Thomas Hardy Yearbook* 2 (1971): 38–45.

———. "*A Laodicean.*" *Thomas Hardy Yearbook* 11 (1984): 28–30.

———. "*Two on a Tower:* A Critical Revaluation." *Thomas Hardy Yearbook* 8 (1978): 29–34.

Watts, Cedric, ed. *The English Novel.* London: Sussex Books, 1976.

Weber, Carl J. *Hardy in America: A Study of Thomas Hardy and His American Readers.* Waterville, Me.: Colby College Press, 1946. Reprinted New York: Russell & Russell, 1966.

———. *Hardy and the Lady from Madison Square.* Port Washington, N. Y.: Kennikat Press, 1973.

———. *Hardy of Wessex: His Life and Literary Career.* New York: Columbia University Press, 1940; rpt. 1966.

———. "Two Fires at Max Gate." In *Essays in American and English Literature Presented to Bruce Robert McElderry, Jr.* Edited by Max F. Schultz, William D. Templeman, and Charles R. Metzger. Athens: Ohio University Press, 1968.

———, ed. *The First Hundred Years of Thomas Hardy 1840–1940.* New York: Burt Franklin, 1942.

Whibley, Charles. "Thomas Hardy." *Blackwood's Magazine,* June 1913, 823–31. Reprinted in *Thomas Hardy: Critical Assessments of Writers in English,* Vol. 3: 136–44. Edited by Graham Clarke. Mountfield, East Sussex: Helm Information, 1993.

Whitehead, James. "Puzzled Phantoms" [on "A Christmas Ghost Story"]. *Times Literary Supplement,* Dec. 24, 1999, i5047, p. 12.

Wickens, C. Glen. "Hardy's *Desperate Remedies.*" *Explicator,* 39, no. 1 (1980): 12–14.

———. "Hardy's Inconsistent Spirits and the Philosophic Form of *The Dynasts.*" In *The Poetry of Thomas Hardy.* Edited by Patricia Clements and Juliet Grindle. Totowa, N.J.: Barnes & Noble, 1980.

———. "Romantic Myth and Victorian Nature in *Desperate Remedies.*" *English Studies in Canada* 8, no. 2 (June 1982): 154–73.

———. *Thomas Hardy, Monism, and the Carnival Tradition: The One and the Many in* The Dynasts. Toronto: University of Toronto Press, 2002.

Widdowson, Peter. "Hardy and Critical Theory." In *The Cambridge Companion to Thomas Hardy.* Edited by Dale Kramer. Cambridge: Cambridge University Press, 1999.

———, ed. *Tess of the d'Urbervilles* New York: St. Martin's, 1993.

Wightman, T. R. "Riverside—Sturminster Newton," *Thomas Hardy Journal,* 6, no. 1 (Feb. 1990): 47–49.

Wike, Jonathan. "Hintock by Bicycle: Wessex as Critical Orientation." *Thomas Hardy Journal* 8, no. 1 (Feb. 1992): 55–62.

Williams, Harold. "The Wessex Novels of Thomas Hardy," *North America Review* (Jan. 1914): 120–34. In Graham Clarke, ed. *Thomas Hardy: Critical Assessments of Writers in English,* Vol. 3: *Writers, Writing, and Wessex,* 145–56.

Williams, Merryn. *A Preface to Hardy.* New York: Longman, 1976.

Wilson, Keith G. "Aldous Huxley and Max Beerbohm's Hardy." *Notes and Queries* 31 (December 1984): 515.

———. "'Flower of Man's Intelligence': World and Overworld in *The Dynasts.*" In *The Poetry of Thomas Hardy: A Commemorative Issue.* Edited by Frank Giordano, Jr. *Victorian Poetry* 17, no. 1 (spring–summer, 1979): 124–33.

———. "Gertrude Bugler," "Dramatizations," "The Hardy Players," "The Theatre." In *The Oxford Reader's Companion to Hardy.* Edited by Norman Page. Oxford: Oxford University Press, 2000.

———. "Hardy and the Hangman: The Dramatic Appeal of 'The Three Strangers,'" *English Literature in Transition (1880–1920)* 24, no. 3 (1981): 155–60.

———. "Hardy's *The Dynasts:* Some Problems of Interpretation." *Colby Library Quarterly* 12, no. 4 (Dec. 1976): 181–90. Reprinted in *Thomas Hardy: Critical Assessments.* Vol. 2 Edited by Graham Clarke. London: Helm, 1993.

———. "Hardy's 'In a London Flat.'" *Notes and Queries* 20 (March 1973): 98.

———, ed. *The Mayor of Casterbridge.* With an introduction, full notes, note on the text, two appendices, and glossary. Harmondsworth: Penguin Modern Classics, 1997.

———. "Revisiting Hardy's Verse Dramas." *English Literature in Transition* 39 (1996): 333–44.

———. "Thomas Hardy and the Hardy Players: The Evans and Tilley Adaptations." *English Literature in Transition (1880–1920)* 31, no. 1 (1988): 7–26.

———. "Thomas Hardy and Florence Henniker: A Probable Source for Hardy's 'Had You Wept.'" *Thomas Hardy Yearbook* 6 (1976): 62–66.

———. *Thomas Hardy on Stage.* New York: St. Martin's, 1995.

———. "Thomas Hardy's 'The Ruined Maid,' Elsa Lanchester's Music Hall, and the Fall into Fashion." *Thomas Hardy Journal* 15, no. 2 (May 1999): 41–48.

Wing, George. "'Forbear, Hostler, Forbear!': Social Satire in *The Hand of Ethelberta.*" *Studies in the Novel* 4 (1972): 568–79.

———. "Hardy's Star-Cross'd Lovers in *Two on a Tower.*" *Thomas Hardy Yearbook* 14 (1987): 35–44; *Victorian Newsletter* 94 (fall 1998): 27–32.

———. "Tess and the Romantic Milkmaid." *Review of English Literature* 3 (Jan. 1962): 22–30.

———. *Thomas Hardy.* New York: Grove 1963.

———. "Middle-Class Outcasts in Hardy's *A Laodicean.*" *The Humanities Association* Review La Revue de l'Association des Humanités, (Kingston, Ontario, Canada) 27 (1976): 229–38.

Winslow, Donald J. "Images of Emma Hardy." *Thomas Hardy Yearbook* 10 (1980): 55–59.

Woolf, Virginia. "The Novels of Thomas Hardy." *The Common Reader,* Second Series. Reprinted in *Thomas Hardy: Critical Assessments of Writers in English,* Vol. 3, 230–38. Edited by Graham Clarke. Mountfield, East Sussex: Helm Information, 1993.

Wright, Terence. "Space, Time, and Paradox: The Sense of History in Hardy's Last Novels." *Essays and Studies* (Leicester, England) 44 (1991): 41–52.

Wright, Walter F. *The Shaping of "The Dynasts": A Study in Thomas Hardy.* Lincoln: University of Nebraska Press, 1967.

Yarker, Patrick. "Meredith, Hardy, and Gissing." In *The Victorians (The Sphere History of Literature in the English Language).* Edited by Arthur Pollard. New York: Bantam, 1969.

Zietlow, Paul. *Moments of Vision: The Poetry of Thomas Hardy.* Cambridge, Mass.: Harvard University Press, 1974.

INDEX

Note: **Boldface** numbers indicate primary discussions of a topic. *Italic* numbers indicate illustrations.